# CONTENTS ★ ★ ★ ★ ★ ★ ★

# UNIT 6   EXPANSION AND CIVIL WAR
## *1840–1877*

**xiii**

# UNIT 10  WORLD LEADERSHIP
## *1945–Present*

## ★ MAPS

## ★ CHARTS AND GRAPHS

## ★ GAINING SKILL

## ★ PRIMARY SOURCES

## ★ LINKING PAST AND PRESENT

## ★ AMERICAN HIGHLIGHTS

## ★ CAUSE AND EFFECT FLOW CHARTS

## ★ OUR PRESIDENTS

★ ★ ★ ★ ★ ★ ★ ★ ★ ★ ★ ★

# HANDBOOK OF BASIC REVIEW

*America's Story* takes you on a journey through the history of your country, from the very beginnings to the present day. The following Handbook pages will help make that journey easier and more interesting.

## 1 HOW TO READ THIS BOOK

All books, including school textbooks, are valuable possessions, and they should be treated as such. Your teacher will tell you how to handle and care for this book.

### Units and Chapters

*America's Story* is organized into 10 units and 32 chapters. Each unit covers a specific period of time and deals with an important development in America's story.

Each unit is made up of two or more chapters. At the beginning of each chapter there is a picture that previews the part of America's story told in the chapter. Directly below the chapter title there is a time line showing the chapter's major events.

At the right you see part of a chapter time line from this book. The red bar contains the names of American Presidents. The tan boxes contain important events. Each tan box is connected to a ruler that begins with a year. In the example the beginning year is 1800. Each line on the ruler equals one year. Therefore the time line shows that in 1803 the Supreme Court case *Marbury* v. *Madison* was decided and the Louisiana Purchase was made. In 1804 the Lewis and Clark expedition began. You can also see that Jefferson was President during those years.

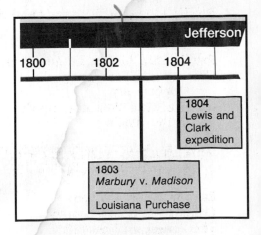

## Chapters and Sections

Each chapter begins with a "Preparing to Read" paragraph that gives a brief idea of the chapter content. The numbered questions given there will help you focus on the main ideas of the chapter.

Each chapter is divided into sections, with a title like this:

## 1   What led people to settle the West?

Notice that the section title is a question. In fact, it is one of the questions from "Preparing to Read." If you can answer the question fully, you have learned the main idea of the section.

While you are reading, you will notice that some words are set off in different type. **Vocabulary words** appear in **boldface** type with a blue highlight. A brief definition follows immediately. **Key terms** are set in boldface type with no highlight. Key terms include the names of places, things, or events that are important to know in American history.

Every section ends with a **Section Review.** In the Section Review, you will be asked to remember and think about what you have read. At the end of every chapter there is a **Chapter Summary** that briefly sums up the main events of the chapter. Vocabulary words, key terms, and important people are underlined. To help you remember facts and think about ideas from the chapter, there is a two-page **Chapter Review.** At the end of each unit there is also a two-page **Unit Review.** This includes a summary, helpful activities, and a bibliography. Your teacher will tell you more about the Chapter Reviews and Unit Reviews and how to use them.

You can see from what you have just read that the basic structure of this book includes the following parts: Unit, Chapter, Section, Section Review, Chapter Summary, Chapter Review, and Unit Review. The **Contents** pages at the front of the book provide a more detailed outline of the book.

## Pictures and Charts

There are many paintings, photographs, and other pictures in this book. Next to each picture is a **caption,** with a red line separating the caption from the rest of the page. The

This photograph is typical of the pictures you will find in *America's Story.* It shows Dr. Martin Luther King, Jr., leading a group of marchers in a voting rights demonstration in Alabama.

caption tells about the picture. Sometimes the caption asks a question. Usually you can answer the question by looking at the picture or by remembering what you have read on the same page.

Charts, graphs, and diagrams squeeze a lot of information into a small space. In this book, special **Gaining Skill** pages include activities on reading and comparing such graphic aids. Graph skills can help you organize and understand information. They can also help you on standardized tests. These tests usually contain questions about graphs, especially **bar graphs,** like the one at the right.

## Maps

Maps are important in history, because maps always answer the question *Where?* Maps have certain basic parts. Look at the following map. The parts of the map have been numbered so you can find them easily.

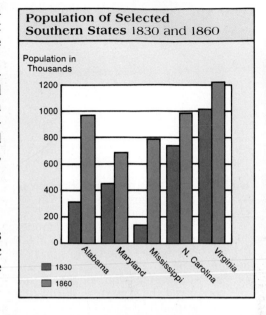

1. The white box contains the map's **title,** which tells you what the map is about.
2. Black dots locate **towns** or **cities.**
3. The actual town or city **name** can be found near the dot.
4. The **scale** shows distance.
5. The **compass rose** shows the map's directions—north, east, south, and west.
6. In this book's maps, **boundaries** or **borders** are usually shown by white lines. The lines on this map show the shapes of states as they are today.
7. **Rivers** are usually shown as wiggly blue lines, because rivers are rarely straight.
8. Sometimes a river forms a boundary. When that happens, the boundary becomes wiggly too. As a general rule, a wiggly boundary means that a river is involved.
9. The **legend,** or **key,** explains something special about the map. On this map, yellow areas show where gold is mined. Green shows where silver is mined.
10. In general, light blue means a **body of water,** such as an ocean or a lake.
11. This shading, or **relief,** shows that here the earth's surface is not flat. If you looked down from an airplane, you would see hills or mountains below you.
12. The names of **mountain ranges** and oceans often appear in capital letters, using slanted, or italic, type.

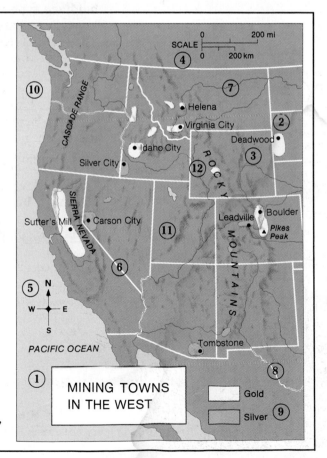

Under most maps in this book, you will find this green heading: **Map Study.** The Map Study tells about the map and asks questions about it.

You will find out more about maps in some of the **Gaining Skill** activities. Being able to understand maps is an important skill in the study of history. This skill may also help you on standardized tests, which often contain questions about map reading and geography.

## The Reference Section

The reference section at the back of the book contains several different parts, including a **Time Chart** of history and an **Atlas,** or collection of full-page maps. The **Glossary** includes all vocabulary and key terms in the book, arranged alphabetically, as in a dictionary. At the left are a few examples from the Glossary.

The **Index** will help you find many kinds of information in *America's Story,* including maps (*m*) and pictures (*p*). Entries are in alphabetical order, as in the example at the left. Notice that within longer entries, however, the information is not arranged alphabetically. Look at the entry **voting,** for example. This entry shows that you can find out about voting in the New England Colonies on page 82. On pages 345–346 you can find out about voting reforms in the 1800's. Still later in the book comes information about voting rights guaranteed to blacks, Native Americans, and women. You see that these Index entries, just like history and like the book as a whole, are organized **chronologically**—by the movement of time.

## 2 CAUSE AND EFFECT

History as we know it today began when historians started explaining events by finding their causes. The first to use this approach were Greek historians, writing more than 2,500 years ago. These historians did more than just list events. They tried to provide full, accurate reports of what happened. Then they tried to explain why these events happened, using their knowledge of the events, of human nature, of geography, and of life in general. Historians have followed this example ever since, applying cause-and-effect reasoning to their subjects.

In *America's Story* you will learn how to organize your thinking about the causes and effects of important historical events. Then you, too, will be able to follow the example of the Greek historians by applying cause-and-effect reasoning as you study history.

## Asking Questions to Find Causes

Cause-and-effect thinking is not easy. It is hard to teach, and it is hard to learn about. Even so, we do this kind of thinking all the time. Consider everyday questions like these: Why is the bus late? Why is my friend so happy? What was the reason for that accident? What made that scary sound in the night? Why did our team win? Within each of these questions there is an **effect**—an event, or something that happened. Each question seeks to find the **cause** of that event.

Historians ask the same kinds of questions. They do not, however, ask these questions about just one moment or just one year. Instead, historians look at hundreds of events, over hundreds of years.

Imagine, for example, your favorite sport, perhaps baseball, football, soccer, or field hockey. Imagine this game spread over a gigantic field, as big as a country or even the world. Imagine it never ending, just stretching on, 24 hours a day for years and years. The players change, the coaches change, even the rules slowly change. *That* is something like history.

People need a way of thinking about something so large and complicated. Historians use causes and effects to help organize their thinking about history.

## Cause-and-Effect Flow Charts

You will find charts in this book that help you think about why big events in history happen. They are called cause-and-effect flow charts. There is one chart in every unit. You read these charts from top to bottom. At the top is the "beginning." At the bottom is the "end"—a point later in time. Look at the next page to see an example of how these flow charts work. The flow chart shows some causes and effects of an imaginary event: a team's winning of the league championship.

Read the cause-and-effect flow chart, starting with the contributing causes. Notice that there is an explanation of each section of the flow chart at the far left. Think about how the contributing causes listed are different from the main causes and how the effects listed are different from the long-term effects.

As you can see, this chart covers only a few years and just one event. As you can also see, cause-and-effect relationships are not simple, but they do help make sense out of why things happen.

**The Confederate attack on Fort Sumter was one cause of the Civil War.**

# CAUSES and EFFECTS

## League Championship ★ ★ ★

**Contributing causes** are background causes; they existed earlier in time, before the event.

Team is noted for strong defense

Winning record for five straight seasons gives team self-confidence

Off-season trades bring key players to team

### CONTRIBUTING CAUSES

**Main causes** are causes that led directly to the event.

Team has no serious injuries

Several players have their finest season

Team wins all the "big" games—everybody helps

### MAIN CAUSES

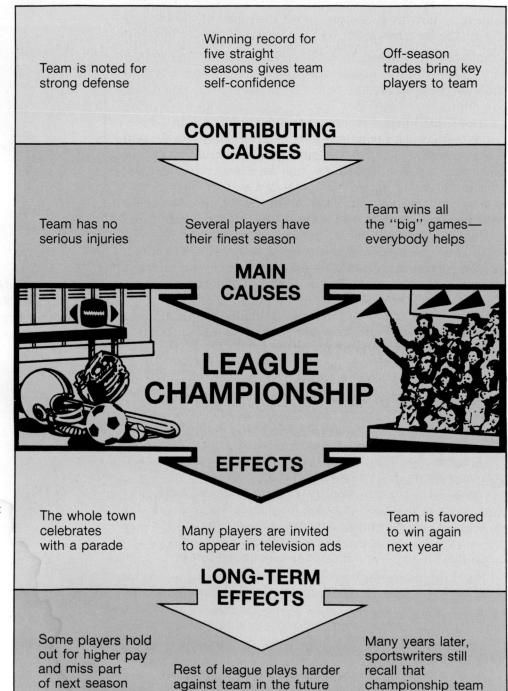

This is the **event** that happened as a result of the contributing and main causes.

### LEAGUE CHAMPIONSHIP

### EFFECTS

**Effects** are things that happened a short time after the event and were directly caused by the event.

The whole town celebrates with a parade

Many players are invited to appear in television ads

Team is favored to win again next year

### LONG-TERM EFFECTS

**Long-term effects** are things that happened later, often indirectly caused by the event.

Some players hold out for higher pay and miss part of next season

Rest of league plays harder against team in the future

Many years later, sportswriters still recall that championship team

# 3 AMERICAN GEOGRAPHY

The study of American history often demands a knowledge of American geography. From the Battle of Bunker Hill during the Revolutionary War to the recent population shift to the Sunbelt, geography has played an important role.

## America's Size

The United States is a huge country on the North American continent. Not counting Alaska and Hawaii, the United States measures about 2,500 miles (4,000 kilometers) east to west and 1,500 miles (2,400 kilometers) north to south. These 48 contiguous states—the states that touch each other—are bordered on the north by Canada, on the south by Mexico, on the east by the Atlantic Ocean, and on the west by the Pacific Ocean.

In size, the United States is the fourth largest nation in the world. Compare the United States with the other countries shown at the right. The total area of all these countries is less than the area of the United States. About 240 million Americans live on the more than 3.6 million square miles (9.2 million square kilometers) that our country covers.

America's size has had many effects on our history. For example, Americans are famous for inventing machines that allow fewer workers to do more work. One such invention was the mechanical reaper. The reaper made it possible for farmers to take full advantage of the vast areas in America available for planting. Also, the great distances of America led to many inventions for speedy, cheap transportation. The steamboat, faster trains, mass-produced cars, and jumbo jets are just a few examples.

America's size also partly explains our heritage as a country that has become home for people from all over the world. People have always wanted to come here, and there has always been plenty of room for them. Even today Americans live on only a small fraction (about one-fortieth) of the land.

## America's Land and Water

Almost every **landform** is to be found somewhere in the United States. A landform is a feature of the earth's surface such as a mountain, plain, or canyon. Another common geographical feature is water. Our rivers, lakes, and other bodies of water are essential parts of our country. They supply water for drinking and farming and, in some cases,

**THE UNITED STATES**

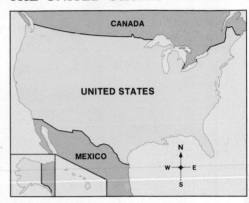

**SIZE COMPARISONS OF SELECTED COUNTRIES**

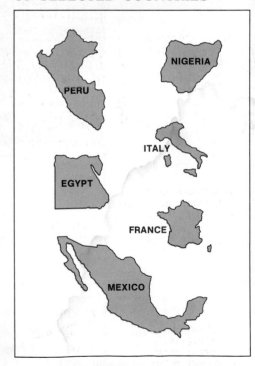

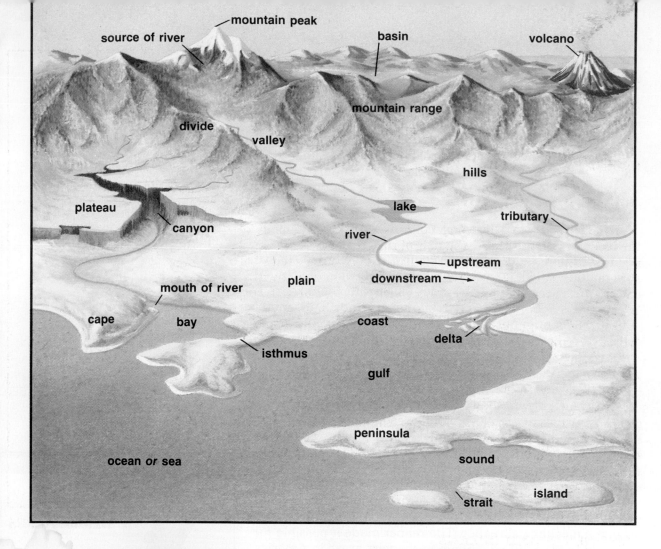

Labels in illustration: mountain peak, source of river, basin, volcano, mountain range, divide, valley, hills, plateau, lake, tributary, canyon, river, upstream, downstream, mouth of river, plain, cape, bay, coast, delta, isthmus, gulf, peninsula, sound, ocean *or* sea, island, strait

# A GEOGRAPHICAL DICTIONARY

**basin**  A bowl-shaped area that is surrounded by higher land.

**bay**  Part of a body of water that extends into the land.

**canyon**  A very narrow valley with steep sides.

**cape**  A piece of land that juts out into a body of water.

**coast**  Land next to a sea or ocean.

**delta**  The land area formed from soil deposited at a river's mouth.

**divide**  A stretch of high ground that separates streams flowing in one direction from those flowing in the opposite direction.

**downstream**  The direction in which a river flows; toward a river's mouth.

**gulf**  Part of a body of water that extends into the land; usually larger than a bay.

**hill**  A raised area of land; not as high as a mountain.

**island**  An area of land completely surrounded by water; smaller than a continent.

**isthmus**  A narrow strip of land connecting two larger land areas.

**lake**  A large body of water surrounded by land.

**mountain**  An area of land that rises to a peak high above its surroundings; higher than a hill.

**mountain range**  A long series of mountains or mountain ridges alike in form and direction.

**mouth**  (of a river) The place at which a river empties into a larger body of water.

**ocean**  One of the large bodies of salt water that cover much of the earth's surface.

**peninsula**  A piece of land almost surrounded by water.

**plain**  A large area of nearly level land.

**plateau**  A large area of high, flat land.

**river**  A large body of flowing water that empties into a lake, an ocean, or another river.

**sound**  A long, wide passage of water connecting two larger bodies of water.

**source**  (of a river)  The spring or lake at which a river begins.

**strait**  A narrow passage of water connecting two larger bodies of water.

**tributary**  A stream or river that flows into a larger river.

**upstream**  The direction from which a river flows; toward a river's source.

**valley**  A long, low area between two ranges of hills or mountains.

**volcano**  A mountain formed by melted rock thrust out of an opening in the earth.

for running power plants. They are also natural highways upon which enormous amounts of goods are moved every year. The Geographical Dictionary on the opposite page includes examples of both landforms and bodies of water. Examine the map and read the definitions.

## America's Location

The United States, like most countries in the world, is in the **Northern Hemisphere,** the half of the earth north of the equator. The United States is also in the **Western Hemisphere,** the half of the earth west of Europe and Africa. Until about 500 years ago, mapmakers did not know that the Western Hemisphere existed.

For thousands of years, the Atlantic Ocean separated the Western Hemisphere from the ancient civilizations of Egypt, Greece, Rome, and Western Europe. The even wider Pacific Ocean cut off the Western Hemisphere from ancient civilizations in China, Japan, and India.

Today, of course, ships and planes crisscross the oceans in a matter of days or hours, and the United States "faces" both east and west. It faces east toward Europe and west toward Asia. Indeed, our fiftieth state, Hawaii, sits more than 2,000 miles (3,200 kilometers) out in the Pacific, about one third of the way to Asia.

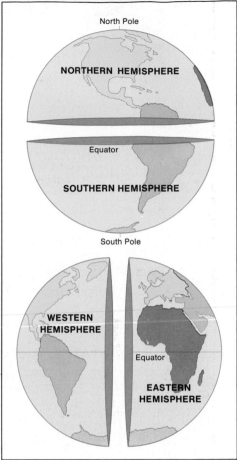

**THE HEMISPHERES**

**CONTINENTS AND OCEANS**

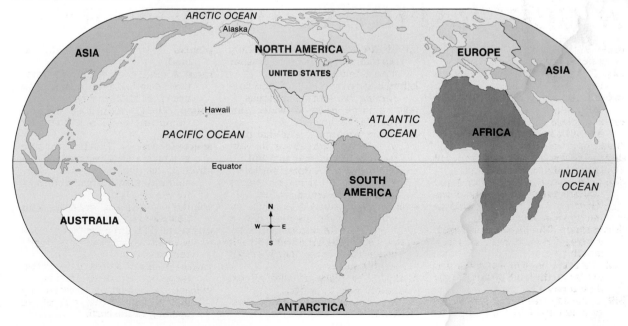

H9

For much of their recorded history, however, the North and South American continents have faced east toward Europe. From about A.D. 1500 to A.D. 1800 the European countries of France, England, Spain, and Portugal controlled much of the Western Hemisphere. Their effect on this hemisphere is still felt today.

The United States began as a few small villages on the Atlantic Coast, settled by English-speaking people. For the next 360 years or so, our country generally grew in a westerly direction—toward the Pacific Ocean, toward the setting sun, and toward Asia. That helps explain why our national capital, Washington, D.C., is closer to Great Britain than it is to Hawaii or the western shores of Alaska. In fact, Alaska and Hawaii are so far away from the rest of the country that they usually must be presented as **insets** on maps of the United States. This is the case with the **political map** that appears below.

## THE UNITED STATES: A POLITICAL MAP

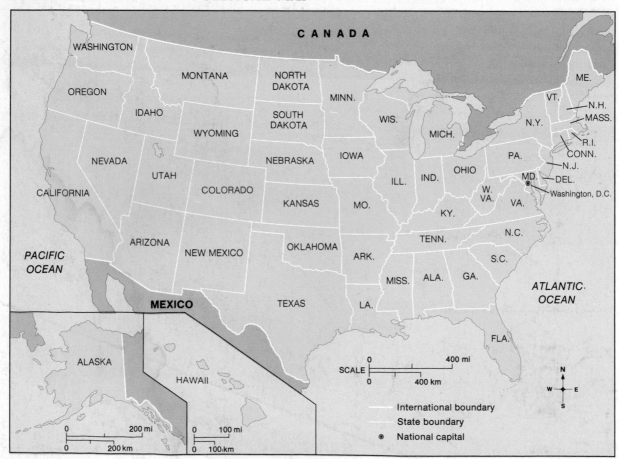

## Sections of Our Country

The map on this page shows how the Bureau of the Census divides the United States into sections. Of course, there are different ways to divide the country and other possible names for the sections. However, nobody will be confused if you refer to different parts of the country as shown. In what section of the country is your state?

## Land Regions of Our Country

Our country has seven main land regions. They are the **Coastal Plains,** the **Appalachian Highlands,** the **Central Plains,** the **Ozark Highlands,** the **Rocky Mountains,** the **High Plateaus and Basins,** and the **Pacific Coast.** As you can tell from the map on the next page, these regions generally run in a north-south direction. This means that settlers

### SECTIONS OF THE UNITED STATES

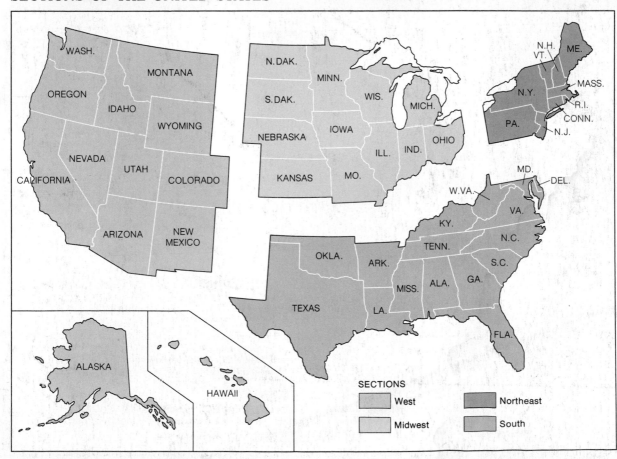

SECTIONS

West

Midwest

Northeast

South

usually had to cross these regions when moving from east to west. The key to the map lists some of the things that make each region special.

The farther south you go in most regions of the United States, the warmer it gets. Also, the closer you go toward a coast, the higher are the rainfall levels. The central regions of the country are relatively dry. These regions also tend to be cold in winter and hot in summer.

## LAND REGIONS OF THE UNITED STATES

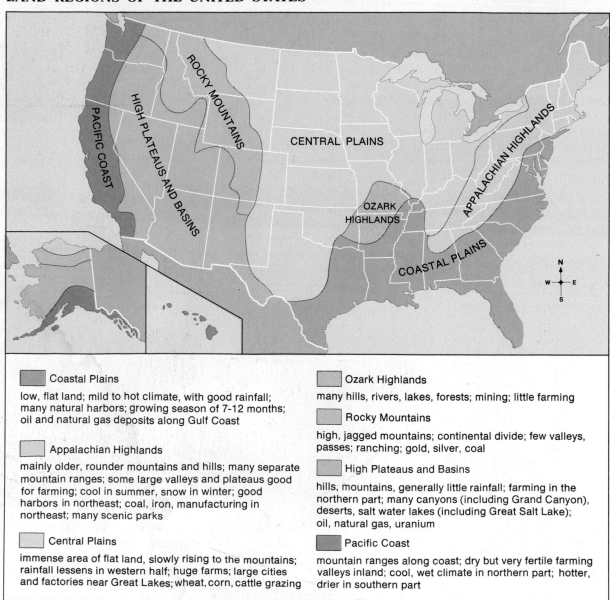

**Coastal Plains**

low, flat land; mild to hot climate, with good rainfall; many natural harbors; growing season of 7-12 months; oil and natural gas deposits along Gulf Coast

**Appalachian Highlands**

mainly older, rounder mountains and hills; many separate mountain ranges; some large valleys and plateaus good for farming; cool in summer, snow in winter; good harbors in northeast; coal, iron, manufacturing in northeast; many scenic parks

**Central Plains**

immense area of flat land, slowly rising to the mountains; rainfall lessens in western half; huge farms; large cities and factories near Great Lakes; wheat, corn, cattle grazing

**Ozark Highlands**

many hills, rivers, lakes, forests; mining; little farming

**Rocky Mountains**

high, jagged mountains; continental divide; few valleys, passes; ranching; gold, silver, coal

**High Plateaus and Basins**

hills, mountains, generally little rainfall; farming in the northern part; many canyons (including Grand Canyon), deserts, salt water lakes (including Great Salt Lake); oil, natural gas, uranium

**Pacific Coast**

mountain ranges along coast; dry but very fertile farming valleys inland; cool, wet climate in northern part; hotter, drier in southern part

★ ★ ★ ★ ★ ★ ★ ★ ★ ★ ★

# Thinking Geographically

You have perhaps already figured out that geography is mainly about places, just as history is mainly about events in time. When people think about geography, they ask three basic questions.

One question is this: *What is the place like?* In order to answer this question, you first need a general description of the place. Is it a field, a town, a whole river valley? Is it a country or a continent? Next you are ready to consider features and climate. Is it hilly or flat? Is there a source of water? Is it hot or cold, wet or dry? Then you might determine the forms of life. Are there trees, shrubs, or grasses? What kinds of animals live there? Are there any people?

Actually, you know more about geography than you might think. For example, imagine this scene: The landscape is dry and sandy. There are low shrubs, some grasses and other plants, and one small tree standing alone in the harsh sun. A lizard sits in the shadow of a large rock. What geographical area does this scene describe? You probably recognize this as a desert. Given just a few details, you could probably recognize other geographical areas as well.

Another basic question is this: *Where is it?* This question is not always so easy to answer. Consider the desert described above. Where do you think it is? Most of the world's continents have deserts. It would be difficult to guess even the continent on which this desert lies. You would need a lot more information to determine its exact location. Trying to answer this *where* question suggests how complicated geography can sometimes be.

A grassland in Nebraska.

Bald cypresses growing in a North Carolina swamp.

**California's Mojave Desert in bloom.**

The third basic geographical question is this: *Why is it there and not in some other place?* This is the hardest question of all. Why is a desert there and not a forest? Why did a lake form in that spot? Why was a town built there and not farther down the river? The answers to these questions are complex, and they all involve geography.

You might apply this third basic question to a local geographical formation: the path. A path may be very old. People may have used it for years as a safe and quick shortcut from one place to another. Why does this path run through the woods and fields in a certain way? Curves in the path may go around trees or hills or wet ground. The actual land, in a sense, "told" people where the best path should be. Suppose, however, the path curves for no reason you can see. What might be the reason for that? Was there once a big tree in that spot? Once you ask questions like these, you have made an important connection. You have begun to explore the link between geography and the past.

## THE UNITED STATES: A PHYSICAL MAP

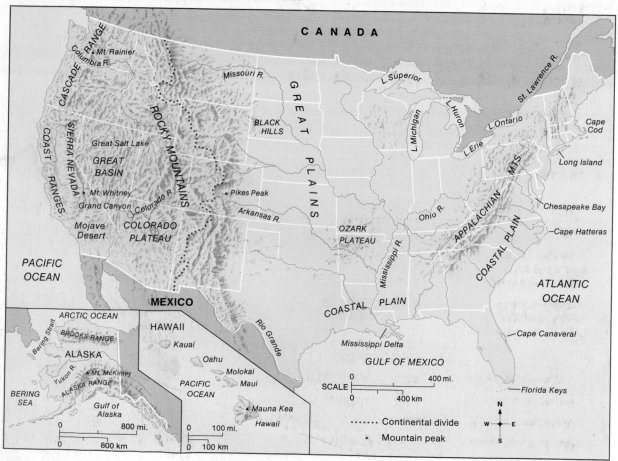

H14

# Some Facts About the United States

| | | |
|---|---|---|
| **Longest Rivers** | 1. Mississippi River<br>2. Missouri River<br>3. Rio Grande | 2,348 miles<br>2,315 miles<br>1,885 miles |
| **Largest Lakes** | 1. Lake Superior<br>2. Lake Huron<br>3. Lake Michigan<br>4. Lake Erie<br>5. Lake Ontario | 31,820 square miles<br>23,010 square miles<br>22,400 square miles<br>9,930 square miles<br>7,520 square miles |
| **Largest Deserts** | 1. Mojave Desert (California)<br>2. Painted Desert (Arizona)<br>3. Great Salt Lake Desert (Utah) | 25,000 square miles<br>7,500 square miles<br>4,000 square miles |
| **Highest Elevation** | 1. Mount McKinley (Alaska)<br>2. Mount Saint Elias (Alaska)<br>3. Mount Foraker (Alaska) | 20,320 feet<br>18,008 feet<br>17,400 feet |
| **Lowest Elevation** | Death Valley (California) | 282 feet below sea level |
| **Greatest Yearly Average Rainfall** | Mount Waialeale (Hawaii) | 460 inches |
| **Lowest Yearly Average Rainfall** | Death Valley (California) | 1.63 inches |
| **Highest Recorded Temperature** | Death Valley (California) | 134°F on July 10, 1913 |
| **Lowest Recorded Temperature** | Prospect Creek (Alaska) | −80°F on January 23, 1971 |
| **Strongest Recorded Surface Wind** | Mount Washington (New Hampshire) | 231 miles per hour on April 12, 1934 |
| **Largest States by Area** | 1. Alaska<br>2. Texas<br>3. California | 570,833 square miles<br>262,017 square miles<br>156,299 square miles |
| **Smallest States by Area** | 1. Rhode Island<br>2. Delaware<br>3. Connecticut | 1,055 square miles<br>1,932 square miles<br>4,872 square miles |
| **Largest States by Population (1986 estimate)** | 1. California<br>2. New York<br>3. Texas | 26,981,000<br>17,772,000<br>16,682,000 |
| **Smallest States by Population (1986 estimate)** | 1. Wyoming<br>2. Alaska<br>3. Vermont | 507,000<br>534,000<br>541,000 |
| **Largest Cities by Population (1984 estimate)** | 1. New York City<br>2. Los Angeles<br>3. Chicago<br>4. Houston<br>5. Philadelphia | 7,164,742<br>3,096,721<br>2,992,472<br>1,705,697<br>1,646,713 |
| **Northernmost Point** | Point Barrow (Alaska) | 71°N, 156°W |
| **Southernmost Point** | Ka Lae (Hawaii) | 19°N, 156°W |
| **Easternmost Point** | West Quoddy Head (Maine) | 45°N, 67°W |
| **Westernmost Point** | Cape Wrangell (Alaska) | 53°N, 172°E |

# UNIT 1

# AMERICA'S BEGINNINGS
# Prehistory—1610

40,000 B.C. – A.D. 1610

40,000 B.C.    A.D. 1000    1100    1200    1300    1400

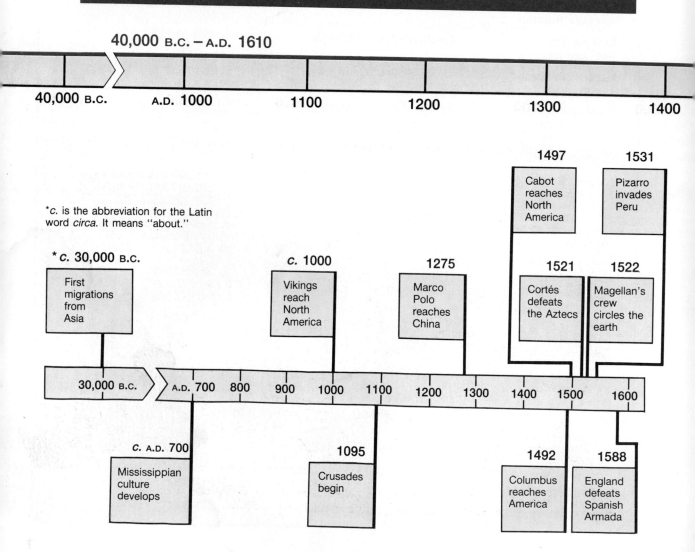

*c. is the abbreviation for the Latin word *circa*. It means "about."

**1497** Cabot reaches North America

**1531** Pizarro invades Peru

\* *c.* 30,000 B.C. First migrations from Asia

*c.* 1000 Vikings reach North America

**1275** Marco Polo reaches China

**1521** Cortés defeats the Aztecs

**1522** Magellan's crew circles the earth

30,000 B.C.    A.D. 700    800    900    1000    1100    1200    1300    1400    1500    1600

*c.* A.D. 700 Mississippian culture develops

**1095** Crusades begin

**1492** Columbus reaches America

**1588** England defeats Spanish Armada

## CHAPTERS IN THIS UNIT

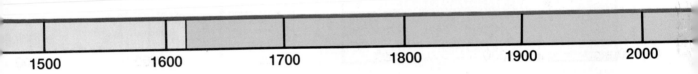

1500  1600  1700  1800  1900  2000

**Queen Isabella and King Ferdinand of Spain bid Christopher Columbus
farewell as he prepares to leave Palos, Spain, on August 3, 1492.**

1

# 1 Explorers Reach the Americas

## 40,000 B.C.—A.D. 1500

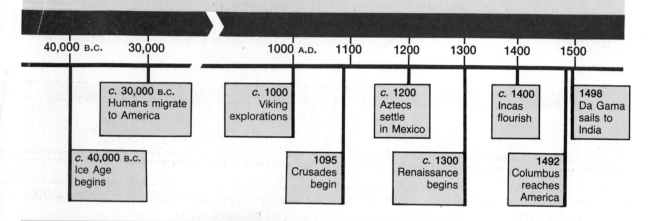

| 40,000 B.C. | 30,000 | 1000 A.D. | 1100 | 1200 | 1300 | 1400 | 1500 |

*c.* 30,000 B.C.
Humans migrate
to America

*c.* 1000
Viking
explorations

*c.* 1200
Aztecs
settle
in Mexico

*c.* 1400
Incas
flourish

1498
Da Gama
sails to
India

*c.* 40,000 B.C.
Ice Age
begins

1095
Crusades
begin

*c.* 1300
Renaissance
begins

1492
Columbus
reaches
America

A Plains Indians' camp, showing the Native Americans' way of life during the hunting season, is the subject of John M. Stanley's painting.

## Preparing to Read

The beginning of American history is sometimes traced to the late 1400's, the time when European explorers began steadily voyaging to the Americas. Yet America's story really begins much, much earlier. The first Americans came to North America from Asia between 20,000 and 40,000 years ago. By the time Europeans reached the continent, these Native Americans had already developed rich and varied ways of life. As you read this chapter, try to answer the following questions:

1. Who were the first Americans, and how did they live?
2. What changes in Europe led to an age of discovery?
3. Why did Europeans seek new sea routes to Asia?
4. What led Columbus west, and what did he achieve?

# 1 Who were the first Americans, and how did they live?

## Vocabulary

| | |
|---|---|
| glacier | prehistory |
| nomad | irrigate |
| migration | adobe |
| culture | pueblo |
| artifact | tepee |
| archeologist | civilization |
| | empire |

For thousands of years the Americas were a vast wilderness. Plants grew in abundance and many kinds of animals roamed the land, but the Americas were empty of human life. Then, over a period of many thousands of years, human beings spread throughout the Americas and developed many different ways of life.

## The First Americans

Sometime between 20,000 and 40,000 years ago, the first people began arriving in the Western Hemisphere from Asia. Others followed in waves over several thousand years. Thus, by about 10,000 years ago, these people and their descendants had spread throughout the Americas.

**Hunters cross a land bridge to the Americas.** Most scientists believe that the earliest people to settle in the Americas came from Asia during the last **Ice Age.** This was a period when temperatures on earth grew very cold. Much of North America became covered by huge **glaciers** —slow-moving sheets of ice. So much of the earth's water was frozen in these glaciers that the level of the oceans fell 300 feet (90 meters) or more. Areas of land that had once been under water were uncovered and dry.

Scientists believe that at this time, part of the sea floor under the Bering Strait became dry ground. (See map on page 5.) A bridge of land stretched from Asia to North America. Groups of people wandered across this land bridge and entered the Western Hemisphere. These people were **nomads** —people who do not live in one place but move about searching for food. They followed wandering herds of animals that they hunted for food and clothing. These people knew how to make stone tools, and they used fire for cooking and keeping warm.

The first Americans reached the northernmost regions of present-day Canada and Alaska. New generations, seeking better hunting grounds, pushed farther and farther into the continent. These **migrations** — movements from one region to another— happened over thousands of years. As the earliest people slowly migrated south and east, other groups came from Asia to settle in the north. Finally there were people living throughout North, Central, and South America. The descendants of these early people are known today as Native Americans or American Indians.

**The first Americans adjust to new environments.** The Ice Age came to an end about 10,000 years ago. The earth's climate grew warmer, and the huge glaciers melted. Water flowed back into the oceans and cut off the land bridge from Asia. Water also filled basins in the land, creating new lakes and rivers. New kinds of plant life appeared as well. Forests began to grow in eastern

North America, while other lands became dry deserts. In addition, many of the huge animals hunted by the early Americans began to die out.

Native Americans had to change their ways of living in order to survive under these new conditions. They developed new kinds of food, clothing, and shelter that were suited to the areas where they lived. In time, each group of early Americans developed a special **culture** —way of life.

These ancient Indian cultures left no written records. People today learn about the lives of early Americans by examining ancient campsites, bones, and **artifacts.** Artifacts are tools, ornaments, and other objects made by people. Scientists who search for and study such remains from the past are called **archeologists** (ahr-kee-AHL-uh-jists). By piecing together the evidence they find, archeologists can describe the cultures of people who lived during **prehistory** —the time before written records were kept.

## Early Farming Cultures

After the large Ice Age animals disappeared, hunting continued to be important for many Native Americans. Deer, antelope, buffalo, bears, and rabbits provided food and skins for making clothes. Gradually, however, many Native Americans began to live by farming.

**Food crops develop.** Native American hunters added variety to their diets by gathering wild plants, roots, seeds, and berries. Then, about 9,500 years ago, Native Americans began planting seeds. The first crops grown were probably pumpkins, peppers, and beans. About 7,500 years ago, Indians in present-day Mexico began to develop corn and other crops, including squash and cotton. These crops produced a steady supply of food, and made people less dependent on hunting. Throughout much of the Americas, farming took hold. Some groups relied almost entirely on the food crops they grew. Others practiced a mixture of farming, hunting, and gathering.

**Settled farming communities arise.** The demands of farming led to a more settled

---

## LINKING PAST AND PRESENT

## ★ ★ ★ *Indian Words*

The Europeans who came to the Americas in the 1500's had never seen a skunk, tasted squash, or paddled a kayak. Because they had no words for unfamiliar things, Europeans naturally borrowed Native American terms. The leather slippers we call moccasins and the nuts we know as pecans got their names from Indian words. Native Americans also gave us the words for such animals as the moose, opossum, and raccoon.

The strongest traces of Native American languages, however, remain in the names of places throughout the United States. Thousands of our cities, including Chicago, Seattle, Omaha, and Tampa, bear Indian names. More than half our states, too, have Native American names—Utah, Texas, and Kentucky, to name just a few.

4

WHERE NATIVE AMERICANS LIVED

ARCTIC OCEAN

Bering Strait

INUIT

INUIT

FAR NORTH
Hudson Bay
INUIT

ALEUT

TLINGIT
BLACKFEET
CREE

NORTHWEST COAST

KWAKIUTL

MOHAWK
SENECA
ONONDAGA
ONEIDA
CAYUGA

CHINOOK

PLATEAU
NEZ PERCE
CAYUSE

MANDAN
SIOUX
CROW
CHIPPEWA

ALGONQUIN
OTTAWA
HURON

GREAT PLAINS

SAUK
FOX

IROQUOIS

WAMPANOAG
PEQUOT

MODOC
SHOSHONE
CHEYENNE

MIAMI
ILLINOIS
EASTERN WOODLANDS
DELAWARE

GREAT BASIN

ARAPAHO

POWHATAN

POMO
PAIUTE

SHAWNEE

CALIFORNIA

NAVAJO
HOPI
ZUNI

CHEROKEE
TUSCARORA

MOHAVE

WICHITA
CHICKASAW
CREEK

SOUTHWEST

COMANCHE
SOUTHEAST
CHOCTAW

APACHE

SEMINOLE

MEXICO AND MIDDLE AMERICA

Gulf of Mexico

AZTEC EMPIRE

MAYA EMPIRE

TAINO

ATLANTIC OCEAN

CARIBBEAN
Caribbean Sea

PACIFIC OCEAN

N
W E
S

CARIB

ARAWAK

SCALE

0        1,000 mi
0    1,000 km

AMAZON

INCA EMPIRE

ANDES

## Map Study

Native American tribes and nations can be grouped according to the environments that helped to shape their ways of life. These groupings are called culture areas. In what culture area did the Creek and Cherokee live? Name the Native American groups who lived in the Plateau area.

way of life. People needed to stay in one place in order to plant seeds, tend the fields, and gather the harvest. Villages grew as Indians built permanent homes from materials such as grasses, wood, earth, or stone. In their villages, the Indians developed new tools for digging, sewing, and other tasks. They wove cloth from the cotton they grew, and made pots, bowls, and baskets for cooking and storing food. Eventually, Indians in different areas began trading with each other for such goods.

**The Mound Builders prosper in North America.** One of the most active trading groups was the Hopewell culture located in the present-day Ohio River valley. The Hopewell people are often called **Mound Builders** because they made huge earthen mounds where they buried their dead or held religious ceremonies. In the remains of such mounds, archeologists have found objects from distant parts of North America. These objects include shells from coastal beaches, grizzly bear teeth from the Rocky Mountains, and copper goods from the Great Lakes region.

The Hopewell people influenced the development of other Mound Builder cultures in eastern North America. The greatest was the Mississippian culture, which arose in the Mississippi River valley and lasted from about A.D. 700 to the 1500's. The Mississippians created large ceremonial centers throughout the Southeast. Their largest settlement was Cahokia (kah-HO-kee-uh) near present-day East St. Louis, Illinois. At one time, Cahokia's population reached about 20,000. Its largest temple mound covered about 15 acres (6 hectares).

**Farming groups inhabit the American Southwest.** Several important farming cultures developed in the American Southwest. Among them were the Anasazi (ahn-uh-SAHZ-ee) and the Hohokam (ho-HO-kuhm). Both groups learned to **irrigate** —bring water to—their crops. They dug canals or built dikes and dams to channel the water to their fields from nearby streams.

Both peoples also built their homes from sun-dried clay bricks called **adobe** (uh-DOH-bee). Clay was plentiful in the Southwest, and clay homes stayed cool in the desert heat. The Anasazi built villages several stories high and with hundreds of rooms. These villages, called **pueblos** (PWEB-loz), had no windows or doorways at ground level. The Indians entered their homes by climbing ladders to upper-level openings. The ladders could then be drawn inside to keep enemies out. Some Anasazi pueblos were built on ledges in the sides of steep cliffs.

The Anasazi culture came to an end in the late 1200's. Scientists believe that a long period of very dry weather forced the Anasazi to leave their pueblos. Many Anasazi customs, however, were carried on by other Indians who came to the area later.

In the Southwest, Native Americans built adobe villages called pueblos, like this one in present-day Taos, New Mexico. Families lived in apartments built to a height of five stories or more. Pottery and bread were baked in domed clay ovens. How did people reach the upper-level apartments?

# Culture Areas of North America

By the 1500's, when Europeans reached the Americas, hundreds of different Indian groups were living in North America. (See map on page 5.) Each group had its own customs, language, and government. Indians who lived near each other and in similar environments often had similar cultures. Several of these large culture areas developed in North America.

**Southwest Indians thrive in a hot, dry climate.** The peoples in the Southwest in the 1500's were descendants of the ancient Hohokam and Anasazi. They included the Zuñi (ZOO-nyee), the Hopi (HO-pee), and other groups. Most of these groups lived in pueblos and are sometimes called Pueblo Indians. Over the centuries, these peoples had found ways to farm despite the heat and dryness of their region. They planted their fields so the crops could catch the morning dew, and they carefully collected any rain that fell. They also developed great skill in weaving and pottery-making.

On the ground floor of each pueblo was a large ceremonial room. Here the religious leaders met to conduct ceremonies that sometimes lasted for days. The Indians performed these ceremonies to please the spirits that, they believed, ruled people and nature. Most Pueblo Indians were peaceful people who believed in sharing work and cooperating. Their policies were made to benefit the whole community rather than individual members.

Later groups to come to the Southwest were the Apaches and Navajos. These peoples were chiefly hunters and gatherers. They were also strong warriors and often raided neighboring Pueblo villages.

**People on the Great Plains combine hunting and farming.** The grasslands that stretch from the Mississippi River to the Rocky Mountains make up the Great Plains. Native American groups in this region, such as the Cheyenne (shy-AN) and the Sioux (SOO), met their needs by hunting and farming. During much of the year they lived in villages of dome-shaped earth lodges made from logs covered with dirt and brush.

In the summer small groups of hunters gathered to track wandering herds of buffalo. Before the Native Americans had horses, they followed the buffalo on foot. When a hunting party drew near a herd of buffalo, the men killed the animals with knives and spears or stampeded them over a cliff. They used the buffalo meat for food, the bones for making tools, and the hides for clothing. Buffalo skins also provided material for the **tepees** —cone-shaped tents— that the hunters carried with them.

Like other Native Americans, the Indians of the plains placed great importance on religion. Each summer most of the groups in this region held a ceremony called the Sun Dance. For several days the people danced, sang, and prayed for success in farming, hunting, and fighting. During the Sun Dance they hoped to receive visions from the Great Spirit.

**Groups in the Eastern Woodlands have rich resources.** Many groups of Native Americans, including the Iroquois (EER-uh-kwoy), the Algonquin (al-GAHNG-kwin), and the Hurons (HYUR-uhns) lived in the eastern part of North America. Amid dense forests, rushing rivers, and sparkling lakes, they built large villages. Their homes were bark-covered "long houses" with space for as many as 10 families. The long houses also contained large rooms for meetings and religious ceremonies. To protect the villages, the Indians built high fences of logs driven upright into the ground.

In the surrounding fields the Indians grew corn, beans, and squash. They also gathered fruit and nuts in the forests and used hooks, spears, and nets to catch fish. To vary their diet and to get furs and skins for clothing, they hunted deer, bears, and other animals.

Because warfare was common, many of the Eastern Woodland tribes banded together for protection. In present-day New York, five tribes formed the League of the Iroquois. Women held an important place in the Iroquois culture. They were viewed as the heads of the families, and they chose the tribal chiefs. Some women became priests and shared in supervising religious activities.

7

Eastern Woodland Indians lived in villages of several families. They grew corn and vegetables, hunted, and fished. This 1585 painting by an English artist shows an Algonquin village. How does the picture suggest a thriving community?

**Native Americans in the Southeast build strong communities.** The southeastern part of North America was home to many Indian groups. These included the Cherokees, the Seminoles, and the Natchez. To the north, in present-day Alabama and Georgia, about 50 villages joined together to form an organized group. The Creek villages were divided into White Towns and Red Towns. From the White Towns came most of the chiefs and peacetime leaders, while the Red Towns trained warriors.

Native American villages in the Southeast were clusters of 100 or more grass and mud homes. The men and women worked together to raise corn, beans, melons, and other crops. The people also hunted and fished, gathered nuts and berries, and grew sunflowers for their tasty seeds. Each year after the harvest a ceremony was held to celebrate the renewal of life. The Indians broke old pottery, mended quarrels, and cleaned their villages.

## Indians of Central and South America

In Central and South America, Native American culture reached its highest level of development. Powerful **civilizations** — advanced cultures—arose in these regions. These great civilizations were built by the Mayas, the Aztecs, and the Incas. (See map on page 5.)

**Mayan culture advances learning and art.** The Mayas controlled a large region that stretched across parts of present-day Mexico, Guatemala, Belize, El Salvador, and Honduras. In the forests of these lands, the Mayas built great religious centers. Richly decorated temples sat atop stone pyramids hundreds of feet high. Other public buildings, terraces, palaces, and even courts for ball games surrounded the pyramids. These Mayan centers were also homes for the powerful priests and warriors who led Mayan life. Most Mayas, however, lived outside the great centers in small villages.

The Mayas valued religion, art, and learning. The most respected members of Mayan society were the priests. They were scholars as well as religious leaders. They invented a system of mathematics and a way of writing with picture symbols. The Mayas also studied the stars and developed a calendar that was more accurate than any European calendar at the time. Mayan artists created stone carvings, jewelry, and masks.

Mayan civilization reached its peak between the years A.D. 200 and 800. Trade with other Native American groups flourished for many years. Then, sometime after the year A.D. 800, the Mayas began leaving many of their cities. Other peoples moved into the Mayan territory, gradually absorbing much of the culture.

**The Aztecs rule in Mexico.** Several centuries later, the Aztecs developed another great civilization in the central valley of Mexico. The Aztecs were wandering hunters who settled in present-day Mexico in the 1200's. They built a great capital, Tenochtitlán (teh-nawch-teet-LAHN), where Mexico City now stands. By the year 1500, Tenochtitlán was one of the world's largest cities, with a population of about 300,000 people. Pyramids and temples, beautiful parks, and busy marketplaces stood among the houses and courtyards of the people. Built on an island in a shallow lake, Tenochtitlán was connected to the mainland by raised roadways.

The Aztecs were powerful and warlike, and their well-trained armies conquered the neighboring Indian groups. By 1500 the Aztecs controlled an **empire** —many lands ruled by a single leader—of about 5 million people. The government demanded regular payments of cloth, hides, and jewels from these conquered peoples. In this way, the Aztecs collected great wealth, but they also came to be hated by their subjects.

The Aztecs worshipped many gods. The most important was the god of the sun and war. To honor these gods, Aztec priests made daily human sacrifices. The sacrificial victims were most often captives taken from the other Indian groups that the Aztecs had conquered.

**The Incas rule the largest empire in the Americas.** Far to the south of the Aztecs

The Native Americans of Central and South America built grand cities with canals, schools, temples, and paved streets. A modern drawing based on Spanish accounts shows what the Aztec city of Tenochtitlán probably looked like. How does Tenochtitlán resemble a modern city?

lived another powerful group of Native Americans. These were the Incas, whose territory stretched more than 2,000 miles (3,200 kilometers) over the Andes Mountains in South America. Like the Aztecs, the Incas built a huge empire by conquering neighboring Indians. When Inca civilization reached its height, between 1438 and 1532, the empire included about 7 million people.

A great strength of the Incas was their highly organized government. Their ruler, who was thought to be a descendant of the sun god, had unlimited power. He required most of his subjects to spend part of their time performing public service. Many people helped build and maintain a vast network of roads and bridges connecting distant parts of the Inca empire. Other subjects served as messengers, carrying important news along these roads. In return for their labor, the Inca people received government help when they grew old, became sick, or found themselves without food.

Most Incas were farmers who made skillful use of their mountainous land. They cut terraces into the steep mountainsides to create flat fields, and they developed irrigation systems to water their crops. The Incas were also expert builders. Many Inca stoneworks still stand, centuries later.

## Lasting Contributions of Native Americans

After the coming of Europeans to the Americas, Indians were forced to change their way of life. Yet the influence of Native American culture is still felt throughout the United States.

**Indian peoples leave their mark on American culture.** Many of the foods commonly eaten in the United States today were first grown by American Indians. Among these foods are corn, white and sweet potatoes, peanuts, pumpkins, squash, tomatoes, and certain beans and berries. Native Americans also discovered ways to use herbs and other plants as medicines.

Native American inventions, such as canoes, ponchos and parkas, hammocks, and snowshoes, are still in use today. Other traces of Indian culture linger in American place names. The state of Alaska, for example, takes it name from a Native American word meaning "great land."

**Indian art and ideas enrich American life.** Today nearly 1.5 million Native Americans live in the United States. Some still preserve the ways of their ancestors, speaking Indian languages and keeping alive their legends, art forms, and customs. Other Native Americans retain few of the old ways, but remain proud of their people's contributions to American history.

Americans have come to appreciate the beauty of Indian crafts. Many artists find inspiration in traditional Indian designs. Many Indian values, too, have become widely held. Americans today believe that the land, air, and water are precious resources that must be carefully protected. As one government official wrote recently:

We have slowly come back to some of the truths that the Indians knew from the beginning. . . . [People] need to learn from nature, to keep an ear to the earth, and to replenish their spirits in frequent contacts with animals and wild land.

## SECTION REVIEW

1. **Vocabulary** glacier, nomad, migration, culture, artifact, archeologist, prehistory, irrigate, adobe, pueblo, tepee, civilization, empire
2. **People and Places** Bering Strait, Mound Builders, Cahokia, Anasazi, Pueblo, Iroquois, Creek, Mayas, Aztecs, Tenochtitlán, Incas
3. **Comprehension** Why did Native Americans develop settled communities?
4. **Comprehension** What different kinds of housing did Indians build in the Southwest and on the Great Plains?
5. **Critical Thinking** In what ways were the Native Americans of Central and South America more advanced than those of North America?

# CRITICAL THINKING: Using Historical Evidence

Historians try to build a true understanding of what happened and how people lived in the past. To do this, they examine many kinds of historical materials. Historians then evaluate each piece of evidence to decide whether it provides accurate information.

There are two types of historical information. **Primary sources** are materials written or made at the time of the events they tell about. **Secondary sources** are descriptions or interpretations of the past, made by people not directly involved in the events described.

Primary sources can take a number of forms. *Written materials* include first-hand accounts of events by participants and witnesses. Government records, church records, bills of sale, and ships' cargo lists can also provide valuable information. *Oral accounts* are spoken eyewitness reports of historical incidents. *Pictures*—paintings, drawings, and photographs—can show how places looked and how people lived. Finally,

*physical remains* provide important clues to the past. Physical remains include ancient buildings, artifacts, and even the remains of human skeletons.

The picture below was painted by a Mayan artist about 1,000 years ago. It shows life in a Mayan seacoast village of that time. Study the picture and then answer the questions on a separate sheet of paper.

1. Why would this painting be considered a primary source?
2. Do you think the picture provides accurate information about how the Mayan people lived?
3. What kinds of sea animals were the Mayas familiar with?
4. What can you tell about Mayan houses from the picture?
5. What method of cooking is shown?
6. What Mayan methods of transportation are shown in the picture?

# 2 What changes in Europe led to an age of discovery?

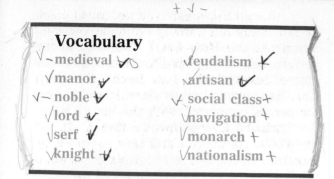

## Vocabulary

- medieval
- manor
- noble
- lord
- serf
- knight
- feudalism
- artisan
- social class
- navigation
- monarch
- nationalism

For thousands of years Europeans remained unaware of the Americas and the Native Americans. Then, sometime around A.D. 1000, a group of seafarers from northern Europe visited North America for the first time. It was not until the late 1400's, however, that Europeans began a wave of exploration to these unmapped lands.

## Viking Voyages

In the 800's, seafarers called **Vikings** lived in Scandinavia—present-day Denmark, Sweden, and Norway. These fierce adventurers roamed the coasts of Europe in wooden boats powered by sails and oars. The Vikings traveled great distances, reaching Russia to the east and settling in Iceland and Greenland to the west.

**The Vikings journey to North America.** About the year A.D. 1000, groups of Vikings came to North America. Almost 180 men and women are known to have been on one voyage. The Vikings told legends about the fertile, grape-growing land they found, which they called **Vinland.** They made at least one settlement, in present-day Newfoundland, Canada.

**The Viking voyages are forgotten.** The Vikings stayed in Vinland for several years. Eventually, for unknown reasons, they lost interest and left their settlements. Few other Europeans even heard about the Vikings'

voyages to North America. At the time, most people lived in isolated communities and received no news of far-off events.

## Europe in the Middle Ages

Historians give the name **Middle Ages** to the years between about 500 and 1400. They use the term **medieval** to refer to this period. Life in medieval times was unsettled and full of hardship. Kings and queens had little power and could not maintain law and order in their lands. Poor roads made long journeys difficult, and travelers risked attacks by robbers. As a result, most Europeans spent all their lives in the community where they were born.

**Most Europeans live on manors.** During the Middle Ages, the nations of Europe that exist today had not yet taken shape. Instead, the kings and queens of Europe divided their lands into **manors.** A manor was a large estate that usually included a castle, a church, and a small village surrounded by farmland and forests. Each manor was given to a **noble** —someone born to a high position in society. This owner, called the **lord,** lived in the castle and ruled over everyone who lived on his land. The lord promised to be loyal to the king or queen, and less powerful nobles in turn promised loyalty to the lord. In this way, medieval nobles built up a complicated system of loyalties called **feudalism.**

Nobles often failed to keep their promises of loyalty, and fighting was almost constant. Many lords relied on **knights** to defend their manors. Knights were less wealthy nobles trained to fight on horseback. In return for promising loyalty to a lord, a knight was usually granted some of the lord's land.

Each manor was a self-contained community, able to fight and survive without using many products from the outside world. The work on the manor was done by serfs —peasants who were born on the lord's land and did not have the freedom to leave. The serfs farmed the lord's fields, repaired his roads and bridges, and cared for his animals. They also grew crops, wove cloth, and made tools and weapons. In exchange for their labor, serfs received small cottages, farmland for their own use, and the lord's protection against outsiders' attacks.

**Medieval society centers on the Church.** Almost all medieval Europeans were Christians who belonged to the **Roman Catholic Church.** The Church was a powerful force in Europe. It not only controlled religious matters, but also influenced politics, education, and the arts. By persuading lords not to make war against each other, the Church was able to help maintain peace.

The Church was also the focus of daily life. Most people devoted large parts of their lives to worship, the celebration of holy days, and other religious activities. People also believed that religion was the most important business of life. If they followed the teachings of the Church faithfully, they believed, they would someday reach heaven.

## The Crusades

Although Europeans did not travel much in their daily lives, many did make the long journey to the **Holy Land.** This area at the eastern end of the Mediterranean Sea was where Jesus Christ had lived. European Christians went there to worship and to visit the places connected with the life of Jesus.

**Christian Europe faces a threat.** In the mid-600's, the Holy Land was captured by **Muslims.** Muslims are followers of **Islam,** a religion based on the teachings of the Arab religious leader Mohammed. After seizing the Holy Land, the Muslims conquered all of North Africa and much of Spain. For years the Muslims pushed hard against the Christians in Europe, always trying to gain more land and spread Islam. After about 1070 the Muslims also began to interfere with Christian travelers to the Holy Land.

European Crusaders often took months to prepare for the long trip to the Holy Land. The different flags and crests on this ship showed that several noble families sponsored this voyage. How was the vessel powered? What shows that the Crusaders planned for war?

European Christians were determined to fight back. In 1095 the Pope, the head of the Roman Catholic Church, held a great meeting. He persuaded the Christians to declare war on the Muslims to recover the Holy Land. Filled with enthusiasm, thousands of knights set off for the Holy Land to battle the Muslims.

For nearly 200 years, waves of Christians traveled east to fight for the Holy Land. This series of wars was called the **Crusades,** and the Europeans who took part in them were called **Crusaders.** In the end the Crusaders failed, and the Holy Land remained in the hands of the Muslims. As a result of the Crusades, however, life in Europe changed greatly.

**The Crusades help to increase trade.** The Crusades drew thousands of Europeans to the lands east of the Mediterranean Sea. There they became familiar with many useful articles and luxuries unknown in Europe. The Crusaders tasted sugar and flavorful spices such as pepper, nutmeg, cloves, cinnamon, and ginger. They discovered new medicines, dyes to color cloth, and fragrant perfumes. For the first time they admired glassware, china, and silks that were more beautiful than any in Europe.

When they returned to Europe, the Crusaders wanted to continue using these luxuries. They began buying these goods from Italian merchants, who had been trading in the East for some time. Large Italian ships were soon making frequent trips to Mediterranean ports. There they exchanged European leather, tin, and woolen cloth for spices, silks, and jewels. The Italian merchant ships also sailed into the Atlantic Ocean, taking goods to seaports along the west coast of Europe. Other traders then carried these goods by river and by land far into the interior of the continent.

**Tales of foreign lands spread.** Some Europeans wanted to see for themselves the unfamiliar lands of Asia. Adventurous travelers visited Persia (present-day Iran), the Spice Islands (present-day Indonesia), India, and China. (See map on page 15.) The most famous of these travelers was Marco Polo, an Italian from the city of Venice. When he was only 17, Marco Polo set out with his father and his uncle on an overland journey to Asia. Marco Polo was gone for 24 years, from 1271 to 1295. During that time he traveled over a great part of Asia.

After Marco Polo returned to Europe, a book was written about his adventures. It told about the treasures Marco Polo had seen: fine carpets, splendid woods, precious stones, and good weapons. Europeans marveled at Marco Polo's story of a black stone that burned, for they had never seen coal. As such reports spread, the demand for Eastern goods rose steadily.

**The middle class develops.** The increase in trade encouraged the growth of marketplaces and towns. Life in a medieval town was very different from manor life. Unlike serfs, townspeople had their freedom and made their own laws. Instead of serving a lord, people in towns worked as merchants, moneychangers, and **artisans** —skilled workers. Artisans practiced a variety of trades, from shoemaking and weaving to baking and goldcrafting. The artisans and other townspeople were not peasants or nobles. They made up a new **social class** —a group holding a particular position in society. These merchants and tradespeople became the "middle class."

## A New Age

The increase in travel, the boost in trade, and the rise of the middle class caused great changes in European life. They also caused great changes in the way Europeans thought about the world. Europeans began to question the religious views held in the Middle Ages. They began to explore new ideas and to make important scientific discoveries about the world.

**Europe enters a new period of learning.** The changes in European thinking marked the beginning of the **Renaissance** (ren-uh-SAHNS), a period lasting from about 1400 to 1600. *Renaissance* means rebirth. During this period there was a new birth of interest in art, literature, and scientific learning. Painters and sculptors created masterpieces of art. Scholars eagerly sought knowledge

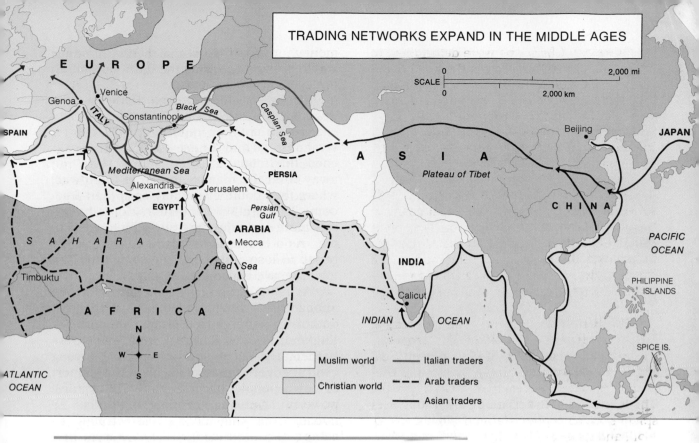

## Map Study

By the 1400's the Italian trading cities controlled trade in the Mediterranean Sea. Merchants from Venice and Genoa traded with Arab and Asian merchants for the riches of Africa and Asia. What Asian countries supplied the new trade goods that Europeans wanted?

about medicine, chemistry, and mathematics. Observations of the stars and planets led to new discoveries about the earth.

In addition, new developments occurred in **navigation** —the science of sailing ships. Since the 1100's, sailors had been using compasses. Compasses could tell them in which direction they were heading, but sailors also needed to be able to tell their location at sea. For this purpose, instruments called the cross-staff and the astrolabe (AS-truh-layb) were invented. With these new tools to guide them, captains dared to sail into unknown waters.

**The desire for knowledge leads to advances in printing.** The knowledge explosion that took place during the Renaissance awakened interest in reading. People wanted to read the books of ancient Greece and Rome and the new books being written by scholars and travelers. In the Middle Ages, each page of a book had to be copied by hand, letter by letter. This process could take as long as a year. Then, in the 1440's, Johann Gutenberg, a German, invented a new method of printing. He molded separate letters of the alphabet onto small pieces of metal. By rearranging these pieces of type, he could quickly prepare to print any book. Using his invention of movable type, Gutenberg was soon copying about 300 pages in a single day. By 1456, Gutenberg had completed printing the first book from his press— the Bible.

The inventions of the printing press and movable type transformed European life. For the first time, books and maps could be copied quickly, inexpensively, and in large numbers. Printing contributed to the spread of knowledge that brought Europe into a new age of discovery and exploration.

As a result of printing advances, stories of new lands spread far and wide. Europeans who journeyed to unknown places could now write accounts of their trips and make maps showing their routes. Then these maps and reports could be printed for the use of all travelers. In this way, the invention of printing encouraged world travel and exploration.

**The power of the Church is questioned.** The development of printing also meant that, for the first time, ordinary people could afford to own a copy of the Bible. Some Europeans began to think that the teachings of the Roman Catholic Church did not agree with what they read in the Bible. The Bible, they believed, described a simple religious faith, but the Church had become rich and powerful. These people believed that the Church owned too much land and required too much money for support. In time, many Christians would break away from the Catholic Church to develop other churches.

**Strong nations arise.** Between the years 1200 and 1500, European society changed in another important way. The revival of trade and the growth of towns weakened the feudal system. Many serfs ran away from the manors to live in the towns, where they could eventually earn their freedom. To maintain the manors, lords had to rely more and more on trade with townspeople. As a result, the lords of feudal society began to lose power. At the same time, the townspeople became more important.

As feudal lords lost their power, strong **monarchs** —kings and queens with great authority—emerged in Europe. The rulers of England, France, Portugal, and Spain were particularly successful in building strong central governments. They won the support of townspeople because they could raise powerful armies to keep law and order. As countries became more unified, travel became safer and trade flourished. For the first time, Europeans developed a new feeling of **nationalism** —love for and loyalty to one's country. European monarchs, supported now by their subjects, began seeking ways to strengthen their countries by reaching out to other parts of the world.

## SECTION REVIEW

1. **Vocabulary** medieval, manor, noble, lord, knight, feudalism, serf, artisan, social class, navigation, monarch, nationalism
2. **People and Places** Vikings, Vinland, Holy Land, Muslims, Crusaders, Marco Polo, Johann Gutenberg
3. **Comprehension** Why did Europeans begin trading with the East during the Middle Ages?
4. **Comprehension** What scientific advances were made during the Renaissance?
5. **Critical Thinking** In what ways was the Renaissance an age of discovery?

# Why did Europeans seek new sea routes to Asia?

## Vocabulary

| | |
|---|---|
| caravan | profit |
| monopoly | ambassador |
| | equator |

The thirst for knowledge during the Renaissance was matched by the thirst of the new European nations for wealth and power. Italian traders had become rich by buying Asian goods and selling them to Europeans. Before long, other European nations were looking for ways to share in this valuable trade.

## Rivalry Over Trade Routes

The Italian merchants controlled the routes used to bring Asian goods to Europe. Other Europeans were prevented from using these routes, and began to look for other ways to get to Asia. The Portuguese led the way in this search.

**Italian cities dominate Asian trade.** Since the 1300's Italian cities, especially Venice, Genoa, and Florence, had been trading with Asian lands. Italian merchants did not actually go to Asia themselves. Instead they bought goods from Muslim traders who traveled to China, India, and other distant lands.

Goods moved westward along three main routes. (See map on page 15.) Some Muslim merchants traveled overland across Asia to seaports on the Black Sea. Other traders first crossed the Indian Ocean and the Red Sea before journeying overland to seaports in Egypt. A third route was through the Indian Ocean and the Persian Gulf. At this point merchant **caravans** —groups traveling together—took the goods overland to the seaports of the eastern Mediterranean.

At the ends of all these routes, Italian merchants waited to buy Eastern goods from the Muslims. The Italians had persuaded Muslim traders to do business only with them. This gave the Italians a **monopoly** on the Asian trade. A monopoly is complete control over a product or service.

**Other Europeans compete.** The other seafaring countries of Europe envied the Italian cities. The Italians sold goods for more than they paid. As a result they were making huge **profits** —money left after expenses are paid. Merchants in other parts of Europe had no chance to share in the trade routes controlled by the Italians and the Muslims. If, however, they could discover another way to reach Asia, they too could become wealthy and powerful.

In Portugal, Spain, France, Holland, and England, many bold seafarers dreamed of discovering new trade routes. They were full of nationalist spirit, and wanted to help their homelands gain power and riches. With the new maps and navigation tools now available, they hoped to find sailing routes to Asia that bypassed the Mediterranean lands.

## Portuguese Discoveries

The small country of Portugal led the search for an all-water route to Asia. Prince Henry, the brother of the Portuguese king, supported many explorations that greatly expanded European knowledge of the world. Eventually, Portuguese sailors found a new route to India.

**Portuguese sailors explore the African coast.** Prince Henry hoped that by sailing steadily farther along the African coast, the Portuguese might discover an all-water route to Asia. To help prepare his sailors, he built a navigation school in southwestern Portugal. There he gathered the most expert ship captains, mapmakers, and scholars of the time. Soon the sailors and ships of Portugal became the finest anywhere, and Prince Henry came to be known as "the Navigator."

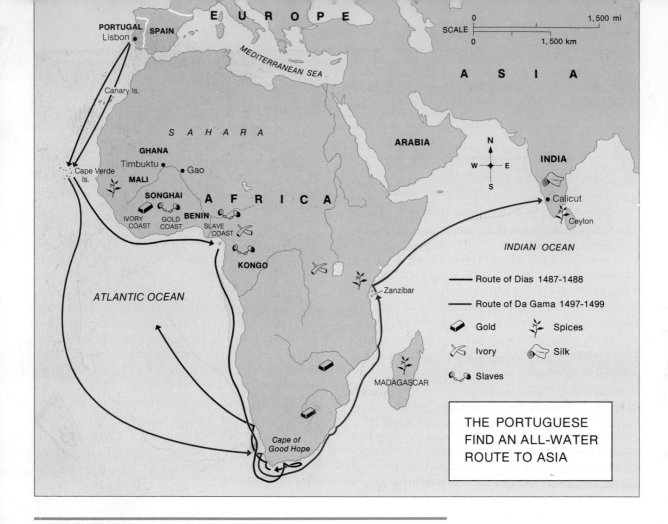

**THE PORTUGUESE FIND AN ALL-WATER ROUTE TO ASIA**

Route of Dias 1487–1488
Route of Da Gama 1497–1499

Gold    Spices
Ivory    Silk
Slaves

## Map Study

**The Portuguese hoped that by sailing around Africa to Asia they could bypass the Arab and Italian trading networks. In this way they could make greater profits. What resources did the West African kingdoms offer? In what year did the Portuguese reach India?**

Prince Henry sent ship after ship to explore the west coast of Africa. By the time of his death in 1460, the Portuguese had sailed as far as present-day Sierra Leone. In Africa Portuguese sailors learned about vast and rich kingdoms ruled by powerful emperors. These kingdoms included Songhai (SONG-hy), Benin (beh-NEEN), Kongo, Ghana, and Mali. (See map on this page.)

For centuries these West African kingdoms had been trading with Muslims in North Africa. The center of trade was Timbuktu (tim-buhk-TOO), a city in the interior of Africa near the southern edge of the Sahara. From Timbuktu camel caravans traveled north across the desert carrying gold and cotton. They returned with cloth, copper, and salt. Timbuktu was also the site of a great university where African scholars studied mathematics and religion.

By the mid-1400's Portugal had built up a rich trade in gold and ivory along this coast. Portugal also sent **ambassadors** to live in Benin and Kongo. An ambassador is a government's official spokesperson in a foreign country.

18

**The Portuguese establish the slave trade.** When Portugal first started trading with the African kingdoms, the Portuguese were seeking mostly gold. They soon began to trade for slaves also. Certain African groups practiced slavery among themselves and with Arab traders. When slaves were offered to the Portuguese in exchange for weapons, cloth, and other goods, the Portuguese accepted.

The Portuguese believed that the sale of slaves in Europe would help pay for their voyages of exploration. They also wanted slaves to provide cheap labor on Portuguese farms. By the time of Prince Henry's death, almost 1,000 slaves were brought to Portugal each year. Soon other European nations also began to take part in this tragic business.

**Portuguese sailors reach Asia.** Portuguese captains continued to explore the African coast, and by 1473 they had crossed the **equator.** The equator is the imaginary line that divides the Northern Hemisphere from the Southern Hemisphere. In 1487 Bartholomew Dias (DEE-ahs) sailed around the tip of Africa. The king of Portugal hoped that Dias had found a route to India and named the tip of Africa the **Cape of Good Hope.**

In 1498 another Portuguese explorer, Vasco da Gama (duh GAM-uh), fulfilled the king's hope. Da Gama followed Dias's route around the Cape of Good Hope and then continued north along the eastern coast of Africa. Then, turning east, he sailed across the Indian Ocean until he reached India. Finally, the Portuguese had found an all-water route to Asia! Da Gama sailed home with a shipload of spices, silks, and jewels. The cargo was worth 60 times what the voyage had cost.

Because it cost less to transport goods by water than by land, Portuguese merchants could sell Eastern goods more cheaply than the Italians could. Portugal quickly became the leader in the rich Eastern trade. In the early 1500's, Lisbon, the capital of Portugal, became the richest and most important port in Europe. Soon, however, Spain and other European nations would challenge Portugal's lead.

Trade between Portugal and the kingdom of Benin began in the late 1400's. Benin artists were noted for their ivory carvings.

## SECTION REVIEW

1. **Vocabulary** caravan, monopoly, profit, ambassador, equator
2. **People and Places** Portugal, Prince Henry the Navigator, Benin, Kongo, Timbuktu, Bartholomew Dias, Cape of Good Hope, Vasco da Gama, Lisbon
3. **Comprehension** Why did Europeans want to find new trade routes to Asia?
4. **Comprehension** What made Portugal the leader in trade with Asia?
5. **Critical Thinking** How might Portugal's location have contributed to its discovery of the all-water route to the East?

# 4 What led Columbus west, and what did he achieve?

## Vocabulary
sponsor
*terra incognita*

Even before Da Gama reached India, the voyages of earlier Portuguese explorers had set other Europeans thinking. They realized that a water route controlled by Portugal would be no better for them than the old routes controlled by the Italian cities. Brave explorers from other nations would soon seek out new routes to the East.

## A Daring Idea

Some Europeans had a daring new idea— to try to find a water route to Asia by sailing *west*. At one time, many people had believed that the earth was flat. By the 1400's, however, most educated Europeans knew that the earth was round. It made sense that by heading west, a ship would eventually circle the globe and arrive in the East.

**Columbus plans a voyage to Asia.** Christopher Columbus, an Italian sailor, was certain that Asia could be reached by traveling west. Columbus had grown up in the

## ★ ★ AMERICAN HIGHLIGHTS

### PROFILE • Christopher Columbus and His Crew

When Columbus set sail from Palos, Spain, on August 3, 1492, he had with him about 90 sailors. Almost all were from Palos or nearby villages. On board the ships, the crew faced many hardships. Cooking was done on the ship's decks. Only a few officers had bunks. The pay for ordinary sailors was 1,000 *maravedis*—about $10—per month.

As the voyage lengthened, the sailors grew nervous. Many began to fear they would never return to Spain. Columbus began to keep a false record, showing the ships' daily progress to be less than it really was. Columbus kept the true distance from Spain to himself. Even this trick was not enough to ease the sailors' worries. On October 10, after 10 weeks at sea, the crew requested that Columbus turn back for Spain. Columbus persuaded them to sail west for 3 more days. Shortly after midnight on October 12, the lookout on the *Pinta*, Rodrigo de Triana, sighted land. The long voyage was over!

**Christopher Columbus**

port of Genoa, where he had sailed since childhood. As a young man, he studied ocean maps and charts and carefully read the reports of new voyages. Slowly his dream of sailing westward to Asia became a definite plan.

Columbus thought that reaching Asia would be easier than it really was. He believed the earth to be much *smaller* than it is, and Asia to be much *larger* than it is. Although many scholars of the time disagreed, Columbus estimated that Asia was about 3,000 miles (4,800 kilometers) west of Portugal. The true distance, however, was more than three times as far. In addition, Columbus had no idea that two continents would block his way to the East.

**Columbus sails from Spain.** To carry out his plan, Columbus needed a sponsor. A sponsor is someone who supports and helps pay for a project. Columbus first approached King John II of Portugal for help. The king's advisers mistrusted Columbus's calculations. They convinced King John not to support the expedition. Columbus then traveled to Spain. There he tried to persuade King Ferdinand and Queen Isabella to sponsor his voyage of discovery.

At first the Spanish rulers paid little attention to Columbus's idea. They were busy fighting a war and had no money to spare for exploration. Columbus waited six years for a decision. Finally, in 1492, advisers to Queen Isabella convinced her that Columbus had a good idea. Isabella thought such a voyage might bring Spain fame, wealth, and the chance to overtake Portugal's control of the seas. Isabella was also a devout Roman Catholic. She believed it was the duty of the Spanish to spread Christianity to other parts of the world. As a result, she agreed to sponsor Columbus's trip.

On the morning of August 3, 1492, Columbus prepared to set sail. He stood on the deck of a small ship, the *Santa María,* and gave orders to the crew of 40 sailors. The *Santa María* slowly put out to sea from the Spanish village of Palos. Two other ships, the *Niña* (NEE-nyah) and the *Pinta,* each with a crew of 25 on board, also sailed under Columbus's command.

The American illustrator N.C. Wyeth showed Columbus and his crew as they might have appeared when they first landed in 1492.

## Columbus's Discovery

Columbus and his crew had a long and difficult voyage. Every day the sailors grew more fearful as the ships slid farther into unknown waters. Columbus restlessly walked the deck, keeping watch. Finally, on October 12, a full 10 weeks after leaving Palos, the voyagers saw signs of land.

**Columbus finds another world.** Columbus and his crew landed on one of the Bahama Islands, located southeast of present-day Florida. Columbus gave the island the name *San Salvador,* Spanish for "Holy Savior." Here, instead of finding golden palaces and people wearing fine silks and jewels, Columbus saw simple grass houses and people with few clothes. Columbus thought he was just off the Asian coast,

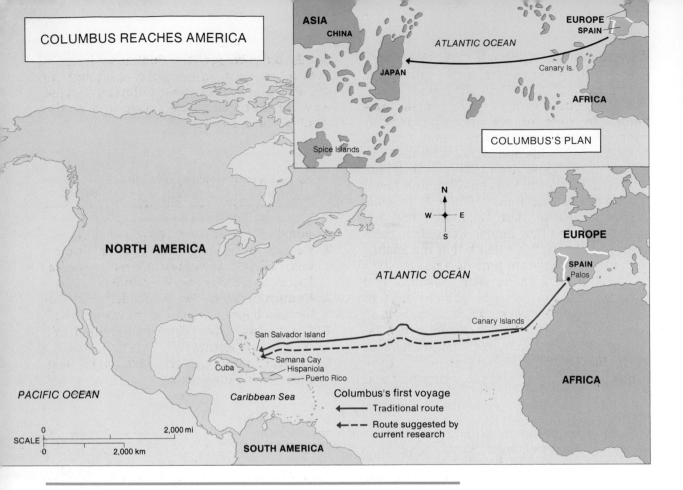

COLUMBUS REACHES AMERICA

COLUMBUS'S PLAN

Columbus's first voyage
Traditional route
Route suggested by current research

## Map study

Until 1986 most historians believed Columbus landed on the island now known as San Salvador. New research in 1986 suggested that he landed instead on the island now known as Samana Cay. The suggested route to Samana Cay takes into account newly discovered facts about the strength of ocean currents and winds. Study the inset map. Where did Columbus expect to land?

in the East Indies. As a result he called the Native Americans who lived on the island *Indians*. The term is still used today, and the islands of this region are sometimes called the West Indies.

From San Salvador Columbus sailed to Cuba and then to Hispaniola (his-puhn-YO-luh), the island of the present-day countries of Haiti and the Dominican Republic. Believing that he had reached Asia, Columbus returned to Spain in the spring of 1493. He did not realize that he had landed at the edge of North America and South America.

**Columbus continues to explore.** Many Spaniards had looked on Columbus as foolish in 1492. When he returned from "the Indies," the next year, he received a hero's welcome. King Ferdinand and Queen Isabella gave him the grand title of Admiral of the Ocean Sea. Yet Columbus still wished to claim Asia's riches for Spain.

Columbus persuaded Ferdinand and Isabella to sponsor another voyage late in 1493. Twice more, in later years, Columbus led fleets across the Atlantic Ocean for Spain. On these journeys he landed at islands in the

Caribbean Sea. Although Columbus never saw North America, he sailed along the coasts of South and Central America.

**Columbus's discovery opens up new lands.** In spite of his efforts, Columbus never reached Asia, and he never brought back the riches his sponsors had hoped for. His sponsors grew tired of supporting him, and after his fourth voyage Columbus could not obtain further funds. Other Europeans began to realize that Columbus had not found Asia, but new lands. Columbus, however, insisted until his death that the islands he had explored were part of Asia.

In 1506 Columbus died, disappointed that he had not brought great riches to Spain. Today, however, he is remembered for an even greater achievement—the discovery of the Americas. If Columbus had not made his voyages, Europeans might have continued for many years to write the Latin words *terra incognita* —"unknown land"— over a large part of the globe. Although he did not know it at the time, Columbus led the way for European exploration and settlement of the Americas.

## SECTION REVIEW

1. **Vocabulary**   sponsor, *terra incognita*
2. **People and Places**   Christopher Columbus, King Ferdinand, Queen Isabella, Palos, San Salvador, West Indies
3. **Comprehension**   On what ideas did Columbus base his plans for reaching Asia?
4. **Comprehension**   Why were Columbus's voyages important?
5. **Critical Thinking**   In what way was Columbus's idea risky?

# Chapter 1 Summary

The first Americans migrated from Asia to the Western Hemisphere between 20,000 and 40,000 years ago. Their descendants gradually settled throughout North, Central, and South America. There they learned to farm and developed varied cultures. Three of the most advanced Native American groups were the Mayas, Aztecs, and Incas. They created vast empires and developed rich civilizations in Central and South America.

Most Europeans remained unaware of the Americas until the 1400's. Although the Scandinavian Vikings visited North America in about A.D. 1000, news of their voyages did not spread. The Middle Ages were a time of isolation and hardship for most Europeans. Poor serfs labored on the manors of powerful feudal lords. Most people in Europe belonged to the Roman Catholic Church.

In the 1100's and 1200's, Catholic Crusaders fought the Muslims for control of the Holy Land. Although Europeans failed to gain this land, they did learn about Eastern luxuries. Europeans began buying such goods from Italian merchants, who had a monopoly on Eastern trade.

In the 1300's Europe entered the Renaissance, a great period of new interest in learning and the arts. New scientific advances in navigation made travel safer, while new printing methods spread interest in exploring the world. At the same time, Europe changed politically as powerful monarchs built strong countries.

By the mid-1400's, European monarchs were searching for new trade routes to the East. Portugal profited from trade with African kingdoms and from Vasco da Gama's discovery of an all-water route to India in 1498. King Ferdinand and Queen Isabella of Spain sponsored the voyages of Christopher Columbus. By sailing west, Columbus hoped to reach Asia. Instead he landed in 1492 in the Americas.

# Chapter 1 REVIEW

## Vocabulary and Key Terms

Match each of the following terms with its correct definition. Write your answers on a separate sheet of paper.

artisan    nationalism
prehistory   civilization
monarch    monopoly
empire     feudalism
migration   Middle Ages

1. ruler with great authority
2. love for and loyalty to one's country
3. advanced culture
4. complete control over the supply of a product or service
5. the time before events were written down
6. a political system based on loyalties among nobles
7. many lands controlled by a single ruler
8. skilled worker
9. movement from one region to another
10. the years A.D. 500 to 1400 in Europe

## Recalling the Facts

1. By what route did the first Americans migrate to the Western Hemisphere?
2. How did settled communities first arise in the Americas?
3. What are three examples of the importance of religion in Native American life?
4. In what ways were the cultures of the Mayas, Aztecs, and Incas more advanced than those of North American Indians?
5. Which European group came to North America around A.D. 1000?
6. What new ways of thinking arose during the Renaissance?
7. How did scientific advances help to promote exploration in the 1400's?
8. Why did Europeans seek new trade routes to Asia?

9. What did the Portuguese learn about Africa in the 1400's? What types of trade did Portuguese merchants establish with Africa?
10. For what reasons did Queen Isabella decide to sponsor Christopher Columbus's voyage?
11. Why did Columbus call the Native Americans *Indians*?

## Places to Locate

Match the letters on the map with the places listed below. Write your answers on a separate sheet of paper.

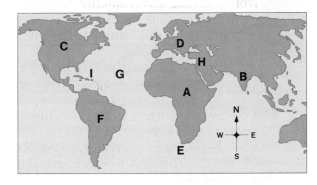

1. North America
2. South America
3. Europe
4. Holy Land
5. Africa
6. Cape of Good Hope
7. India
8. Atlantic Ocean
9. West Indies

## Critical Thinking

1. How successful were the Native Americans in adapting their cultures to their environments? Consider the following topics in your answer:
   a. farming techniques developed by the Pueblo Indians and Incas
   b. Indian housing in the Southwest, the Great Plains, and the Eastern Woodlands

2. In what ways did the desire for wealth spur European exploration of the world between 1100 and 1500? Consider the following topics in your answer:
   a. new knowledge gained from the Crusades
   b. the role of Italian cities in Asian trade
   c. the reasons for Portuguese sea exploration
   d. Columbus's motives for his voyages
3. Who do you think deserves the credit for discovering America? Explain.

## Understanding History

1. Reread the section "The Incas rule the largest empire in the Americas" on page 9. Then answer these questions.
   a. **Culture.** How were religion and government connected in Inca life?
   b. **Citizenship.** How did Incas benefit from a strong government?
2. Reread the section "Medieval Society centers on the Church" on page 13. Then answer these questions.
   a. **Religion.** How did the Roman Catholic Church affect people's lives in medieval times?
   b. **Citizenship.** How was the Church important in keeping order?
3. Reread the section "Portuguese sailors reach Asia" on page 19. Then answer these questions:
   a. **Geography.** In which directions did the Portuguese sail to reach India?
   b. **Economics.** Why did the Portuguese quickly send more ships to Asia after Da Gama returned?

## Projects and Activities

1. **Creating Art.** Find pictures or examples of traditional Native American artwork. Use these as a guide to create your own pottery, beadwork, masks, or drawings showing Indian themes.
2. **Organizing Information.** Make a table listing all the important people mentioned in the chapter. Note the time that each person lived and the contributions he or she made.

3. **Giving an Oral Report.** Find out more about a famous Renaissance figure and share your information with the class. Possible subjects include the artists Michelangelo and Leonardo da Vinci, the scientists Galileo and Copernicus, and the writer Petrarch.
4. **Labeling Information on a Map.** On an outline map of the world, label all the areas that were known to the Europeans in 1500. Then list some of the trading goods for which each area was known.
5. **Presenting an Argument.** Reenact a meeting between Christopher Columbus, Queen Isabella, and King Ferdinand in the early 1490's. Columbus must convince the monarchs to sponsor his voyage to Asia. The rest of the class can serve as members of the royal court, asking questions and offering advice.

## Practicing Your Skill

The Great Serpent Mound in present-day Ohio, shown in the picture below, was built by the prehistoric Mound Builders. It is more than 1,300 feet (400 meters) long. Like many other Indian mounds, the Great Serpent Mound was used as a ceremonial site. If you were an archeologist, which of the following kinds of evidence would you expect to find in the mound?

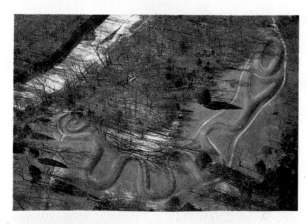

1. artifacts such as jewelry and tools
2. diaries kept by the Mound Builders
3. artifacts such as ceremonial vases
4. newspaper photographs
5. artifacts such as clocks and compasses

# 2 Europeans Explore the New Lands
## 1492–1610

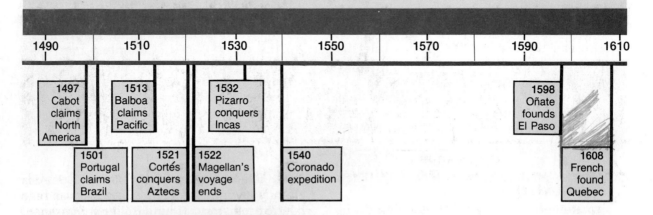

| 1490 | 1510 | 1530 | 1550 | 1570 | 1590 | 1610 |

**1497** Cabot claims North America

**1513** Balboa claims Pacific

**1532** Pizarro conquers Incas

**1598** Oñate founds El Paso

**1501** Portugal claims Brazil

**1521** Cortés conquers Aztecs

**1522** Magellan's voyage ends

**1540** Coronado expedition

**1608** French found Quebec

**This mural by Jay Datus, illustrating Spanish contributions in the history of the American Southwest, hangs in the Arizona state capitol.**

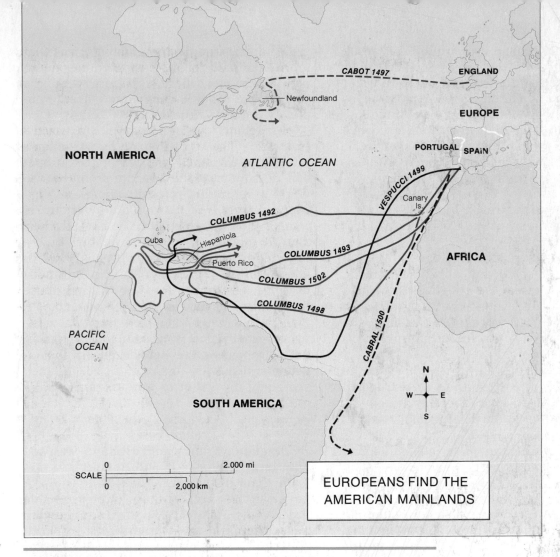

CABOT 1497    ENGLAND

Newfoundland

EUROPE

NORTH AMERICA    ATLANTIC OCEAN    PORTUGAL SPAIN

VESPUCCI 1499

COLUMBUS 1492    Canary Is.

Cuba    Hispaniola

Puerto Rico    COLUMBUS 1493    AFRICA

COLUMBUS 1502

COLUMBUS 1498

PACIFIC OCEAN    CABRAL 1500

SOUTH AMERICA    N
W   E
S

SCALE    0          2,000 mi
         0      2,000 km

**EUROPEANS FIND THE
AMERICAN MAINLANDS**

## Map Study

**The voyages of Columbus inspired others to sail west. Spain,
Portugal, and England were the first to compete for land in the
Americas. Who sailed for England and discovered the coast of North
America? Within how many years did all the voyages shown on this
map take place?**

Spaniards, Africans, and Native Americans,
set out on foot across the Isthmus of Panama. The explorers had to cut their way
through a thick tropical forest filled with
stinging insects and poisonous snakes. At
last they reached the high mountains said to
overlook the "other sea" to the south. Balboa insisted on climbing the last steep distance alone. There before him, as far as he
could see, stretched great waters. Balboa

became the first European to look on the Pacific Ocean from the shores of America.

Four days later, the explorers reached
the edge of the Pacific. Balboa stepped into
the gentle waves, claiming the ocean and the
lands it touched for the Spanish **Crown** —
monarch. Balboa named his discovery the
South Sea because he had reached it by
marching south. (See map on page 37.) The
ocean was later renamed the Pacific.

29

**• Magellan finds a way around the world.**
News of Balboa's discovery convinced other Europeans to continue searching for a water route to Asia. Among these explorers was Ferdinand Magellan, a fearless Portuguese sea captain. Magellan undertook a voyage that was to prove Columbus had been right: Asia *could* be reached by sailing west. Unpopular in his own country, Magellan obtained the king of Spain's support for his plan. He hoped to reach India by finding a passage through the land Columbus had discovered.

In September 1519 Magellan set out from Spain with 5 ships and about 240 sailors. The ships crossed the rough Atlantic and then turned south along the coast of South America. As they continued south, the weather grew steadily colder and more bitter. The explorers then came to a **strait** —a narrow passage of water—near the tip of the continent. For 38 days the ships struggled through stormy weather in this waterway, now called the Strait of Magellan. At last Magellan and his crew reached Balboa's South Sea. The ocean was so calm and quiet that they renamed it the Pacific, meaning "peaceful."

For the next four and a half months, Magellan and his crew sailed across the Pacific Ocean. Hunger, thirst, and disease tortured the sailors. Finally they reached the islands they named the Philippines, in honor of Philip, the prince who later became king of Spain. In the Philippines the seafarers rested and recovered their strength. Magellan befriended the chief of the island people and converted him to Catholicism. Unfortunately, Magellan also became involved in a local war and was killed. The remainder of his group, however, continued the voyage.

From the Philippines, Magellan's crew headed south to the Spice Islands, where they picked up a load of cloves. Then, in a long sweep across the Indian and Atlantic oceans, they sailed around southern Africa. By the time they reached Spain in 1522, all but 1 ship and its crew of 18 had perished. The ship's captain, Juan Sebastián del Cano (CAH-no) was handsomely rewarded and honored by the king of Spain. Cano and his crew had returned with valuable spices that more than paid for the cost of their expedition. Moreover, these explorers were the first people to **circumnavigate** —sail completely around—the earth.

**Magellan's voyage reveals the world's true size.** The voyage made by Magellan's crew was extremely important to Europeans. First, it provided absolute proof that the world was round. Magellan's sailors had traveled west from Europe and, without retracing their course, had come back to their starting point. Even more important, the voyage led to new knowledge about world geography. Not only was Asia an enormous distance west of Europe, but between these two continents lay another great land. Finally, Magellan had indeed found a westward route to Asia. It was too long for trade, but Europeans were not discouraged. Magellan's discovery inspired them to keep searching for a shorter way to Asia.

## Exploring North America

England, France, and Holland watched with envy as Portugal and Spain grew rich from their discoveries. These other European nations wanted a share in the profitable Asian trade. While the Spanish continued to make claims in the southern part of North America, other Europeans explored farther north. As a result of these early explorations, England, France, and Holland established their own claims to North America.

**Cabot voyages for England.** One of the earliest explorers of the North American coast was John Cabot. In 1497, more than 20 years before Magellan's historic voyage, Cabot set out from England with a crew of 18. Like Columbus, Cabot believed he could reach Asia by heading west.

Setting a more northerly course than Columbus had, Cabot crossed the Atlantic Ocean in two months. When he came to the northeastern shores of North America, he sighted plentiful forests and great quantities of fish. Although disappointed to find no rich cities, Cabot felt sure he had reached Asia. He claimed this land for England, and then returned to Europe.

## GEOGRAPHY • The Northwest Passage

Many a storm, and rock and mist, and wind, and tide, and sea, and mount of ice, have I in this discovery encountered.... Many a despair and death had, almost, overwhelmed me.

With these words, Thomas James, an English sailor in the 1600's, described the dangerous search for a Northwest Passage. By the time of James's voyage, many explorers were trying to find a route north of the continent rather than a waterway through North America. Most of those who undertook this voyage never returned. Choppy waters and huge icebergs caused ships to splinter and sink. Many sailors froze to death in the severe Arctic cold or lost their lives because of disease.

In 1906, however, a Norwegian vessel safely passed through the Arctic seas. The ship's captain, Roald Amundsen, had succeeded where other explorers had failed for 400 years. At last a Northwest Passage had been found!

**A sailing ship in Arctic waters**

In 1498 Cabot tried again to reach Asia. Cabot had explored a new part of North America, but his achievement attracted little notice. Europeans were so eager to gain Asia's wealth that they ignored Cabot's discovery at the time. A century later, however, the English would begin founding settlements in the region Cabot claimed.

**European explorers search for a shortcut to Asia.** Magellan, in searching for a route to Asia, had discovered a strait through the southern tip of South America. In the 1520's Europeans began to hope there might also be a waterway through the continent of North America.

For more than 100 years England, France, and Holland sent daring explorers to search for a **Northwest Passage.** Such a waterway would provide a direct route between Europe and Asia. Merchant ships would be able to reach the East in far less time.

**France begins the quest for a Northwest Passage.** One of the first explorers to seek a Northwest Passage was Giovanni da Verrazano (ver-uh-ZAH-no). Although Verrazano was an Italian, his most important voyage was made for France. This voyage took place in 1524, just two years after Ferdinand Magellan's sailors made their trip around the world.

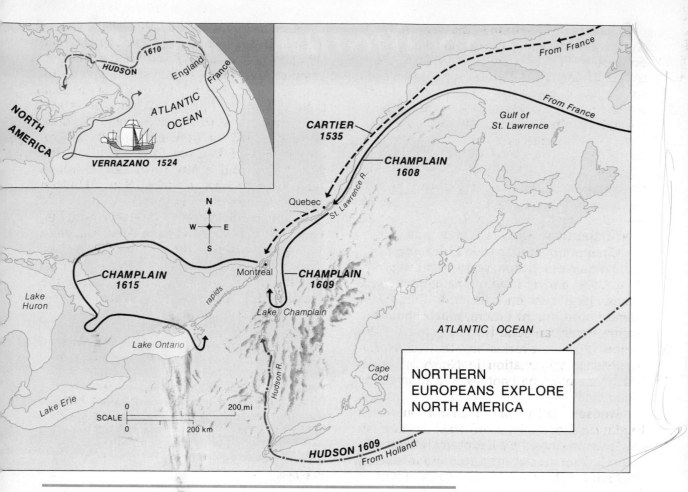

**NORTHERN EUROPEANS EXPLORE NORTH AMERICA**

## Map Study

France and Holland sent expeditions to North America. What French explorer first sailed up the St. Lawrence River? In what direction did Champlain travel in 1615 to reach Lake Huron? Which of Hudson's discoveries was claimed for the Dutch?

Verrazano sailed westward from France to look for a Northwest Passage to Asia. He followed the coast of North America from present-day North Carolina as far north as Newfoundland, Canada. (See map on this page.) Verrazano realized that the land he explored was not the same region that Columbus had discovered. Verrazano, however, found no passage through the land, and he returned disappointed to France.

About 10 years later, Jacques Cartier (kahr-TYAY), another explorer for France, followed Verrazano to America. In 1535 Cartier discovered the **St. Lawrence River** in present-day Canada. Hoping this waterway might cut through the continent, Cartier followed the St. Lawrence for hundreds of miles. Finally he came to a large Indian village where the city of Montreal now stands. Rapids prevented his ships from going farther inland, and Cartier realized that the St. Lawrence was only a river.

Cartier discovered no new trade routes to Asia, but he paved the way for fur trading in North America. Soon the French were exchanging knives, combs, and other small items for beaver furs, bear skins, and fish caught by the Indians.

**Champlain continues the search for a Northwest Passage.** Europeans did not give up hope of finding a shortcut to Asia. Samuel de Champlain (sham-PLAYN), a French sea captain, made his first trip to North America in 1603. He explored the Atlantic coast from the mouth of the St. Lawrence River to the southern part of present-day Massachusetts. In 1608, at a site on the St. Lawrence River, Champlain founded a fur-trading post that he named Quebec. The first permanent French settlement in North America, Quebec is today one of Canada's most important seaports.

Champlain later traveled farther inland, discovering Lake Champlain in present-day New York and exploring the upper Great Lakes. (See map on page 32.) Champlain learned, and taught others, much about the Native Americans and the geography of the region. His discoveries laid the foundation for French colonization in North America. Still, Champlain had not found a short-cut to Asia.

**Hudson sails for Holland and for England.** Henry Hudson was an English explorer employed by Dutch merchants. In 1609 Hudson set out from Holland in a small ship named the *Half Moon*. His goal was to find a route to China. Hudson followed a westward course across the Atlantic until he reached North America. Then he turned south, sailing along the coast as far as present-day North Carolina. Hudson soon realized that he could not reach China by this route. Turning back north, he came upon the river that now bears his name, the Hudson. He followed this river inland into present-day New York, opening the way for Dutch colonists to settle the region later.

Disappointed that the Hudson River was not a Northwest Passage, Hudson returned to Europe. In 1610, however, he made another trip to North America. This time he was sailing under the banner of his own country, England. In the small ship *Discovery*, Hudson and his crew headed to the northeast coast of present-day Canada. After fighting their way through an ice-blocked strait, they discovered a great body of clear water, today called Hudson Bay.

All summer, Hudson sailed these waters in search of a Northwest Passage to Asia. When winter came, he and his crew had to camp on the frozen shores of the bay. Cold, hunger, and physical hardship soon took their toll on the group. When springtime drew near, most of the sailors with Hudson decided to give up their exploration and return to England. They forced Hudson, his young son, and a few loyal sailors into a small boat and set it adrift. Henry Hudson was never heard from again.

**Exploration brings long-term benefits.** The early expeditions to the Americas were not as successful as Europeans had hoped. Explorers did not discover a Northwest Passage to Asia, nor did they find in America the silks and spices they sought. Yet these new

Henry Hudson brought his son with him on his voyages to North America. In 1610, on the fourth voyage, the crew rebelled after a bitter, icebound winter. They set their captain adrift in Hudson Bay, where Hudson and his son perished. The crew returned to England, claiming they had found the Northwest Passage.

lands offered other precious resources: abundant forests, rich fishing grounds, valuable furs.

In addition to providing new sources of wealth, the European voyages greatly expanded knowledge of world geography. The explorers who followed Columbus placed two unknown continents—North and South America—on the map. Gradually, Europeans learned more about the rivers, lakes, and other features of the land.

Finally, the explorations sponsored by European nations gave them the right to claim new territory. By custom land belonged to the country whose explorers first saw it. At first the European nations established fisheries and fur-trading posts. In time, these same nations would also found **colonies** —settlements ruled by a distant parent country.

## SECTION REVIEW

1. **Vocabulary**    treaty, Crown, strait, circumnavigate, colony
2. **People and Places**    Amerigo Vespucci, Pedro Cabral, Vasco Núñez de Balboa, Pacific Ocean, Ferdinand Magellan, Strait of Magellan, John Cabot, Giovanni da Verrazano, Jacques Cartier, St. Lawrence River, Samuel de Champlain, Quebec, Henry Hudson, Hudson Bay
3. **Comprehension**    Why was Magellan's voyage important?
4. **Comprehension**    Why did explorers for England, France, and Holland search for a northern route to Asia?
5. **Critical Thinking**    How did the Treaty of Tordesillas affect exploration of North and South America?

# 2  How did Spain create an empire in Central and South America?

**Vocabulary**

conquistador
missionary

convert
ally
technology

Spain led the other nations of Europe in establishing American colonies. As early as 1493, Spanish colonists sailed to the islands Columbus had discovered in the Caribbean Sea. The settlers included bold adventurers and penniless soldiers who flocked to Cuba and Hispaniola to make their fortunes. A number of priests came as well.

Although some of the early settlements failed, others were prosperous. Sugar cane, cotton, and cattle were raised successfully. The Spaniards did not, however, find much gold on these islands. Adventurers in search of greater riches soon set out to explore the mainland.

## Spanish Conquests in Central America

In an amazingly short period of time, the Spanish built a huge empire in the Americas. The starting point for their conquests was Central America. As explorers and settlers marched through this region, they found the gold and other treasures they dreamed of. They also encountered Native Americans with cultures very different from their own.

**The Spanish pursue several goals in the Americas.** In the 1500's many Spaniards wanted careers as soldiers. The Americas, an unknown and unexplored wilderness for Europeans, promised them adventure. These young Spaniards were excited by the idea of risking their lives for fame and fortune. They became the **conquistadors** (kahn-KEE-stuh-dawrs)—conquerers—who led the exploration and conquest of the

34

**In 1519 Cortés landed at Veracruz in present-day Mexico. Within two years the empire of the Aztecs fell to Spanish rule. What items in the picture suggest the power of the conquistadors?**

Americas during the 1500's. Members of the Spanish ruling class followed the conquistadors to establish and govern the colonies.

In addition to the desire for gold and glory, Spaniards had another reason for coming to the Americas. The Spanish were followers of Catholicism, the religion of the Roman Catholic Church. They were not only deeply committed to their faith, but eager to share it with nonbelievers. Thus many people came to America as **missionaries** — people sent to spread religion in another land. The missionaries hoped to teach the Native Americans about the church and **convert** them to Christianity. To convert is to bring about a change in beliefs, especially religious beliefs.

**Cortés leads an expedition to Mexico.** Spanish explorers who visited the American mainland west of Cuba heard of a treasure-filled land to the northwest. This land, in present-day Mexico, was ruled by the powerful Aztecs. The governor of Cuba ordered an ambitious soldier, Hernando Cortés (kor-TEZ), to explore the region and seize its riches. The daring Cortés, about 33 years old, was eager for adventure. He gladly accepted his task.

Cortés left Cuba in 1519 with 11 ships and a crew of 600. He was accompanied by priests, Native Americans, and a group of Africans. The Spanish fleet landed in Mexico where the city of Veracruz now stands, and Cortés claimed the land for Spain. From

## LINKING PAST AND PRESENT

## ★ ★ ★ *Sources of Wealth*

Gold and silver were the riches that first lured Spaniards to North and South America. Europeans had long prized these metals for making coins, jewelry, dishes, and religious objects. In the 1500's, many explorers risked their lives to obtain the gold and silver of Mexico and Peru.

Today new sources of wealth have become important in the world. One of the most precious natural resources now is petroleum—the oil found underground and in the ocean floor. Thousands of products are made from petroleum: gasoline, asphalt, fabrics, medicines, cosmetics, and phonograph records. Petroleum is so valuable it is sometimes called "black gold."

the inhabitants of that region he heard more about the Aztecs and their emperor, Moctezuma (mahk-tay-ZOO-mah).*

In the meantime, swift runners carried to Moctezuma news of Cortés's approach. The messengers told of white, bearded strangers who rode on great beasts and carried weapons that made sounds like thunder. The Aztecs did not have horses or guns of their own, nor had they ever seen such things.

Listening to the runners' reports, Moctezuma recalled an old Aztec legend about a fair-skinned god who once ruled the land. Hundreds of years before, the legend said, the god had departed in a great canoe, promising to return one day. Moctezuma thought that perhaps the leader of the pale strangers was the ancient Aztec god. He sent messengers to Cortés with greetings and gifts. Among the gifts were two plates as large as wagon wheels, one of gold and one of silver.

---

* Although this ruler's name is often spelled "Montezuma," the spelling "Moctezuma" is more accurate.

**Cortés makes a daring plan.** Cortés was now more eager than ever to meet the Aztec ruler. He made a bold decision to overpower Moctezuma and capture the Indians' wealth. In place of the Aztec empire, he would establish a new Spanish colony.

Cortés was an inspiring leader, and his crew gladly agreed to his plan. To make sure that no one had second thoughts, Cortés burned all his ships! Then, in August 1519, he and his followers set out for Tenochtitlán, the capital city of the Aztecs. They were joined by a large number of Native Americans who hated Aztec rule.

**Cortés meets Moctezuma.** Two months later, the Spaniards and their allies — partners in a common cause—stood outside the magnificent Aztec capital. Although Moctezuma feared the strangers, he welcomed them into the city. The Spaniards were given houses and treated as honored guests. For several months they lived peacefully in Tenochtitlán, storing up gold and treasure through trade. The Aztecs did not appear to be hostile, but Cortés realized that his small group was greatly outnumbered.

Eventually fighting did break out. As part of a religious celebration, the Aztecs made preparations for many human sacrifices. The Spaniards, horrified by this practice and fearful of being attacked, decided to strike first. Bitter fighting went on for several days. Then Cortés and his soldiers decided to flee the city. Even their superior weapons were no match for thousands of Aztec warriors. Loaded down with gold and jewels, the Spaniards tried to steal away in the night. Their flight was discovered, however, and a fierce battle followed. Hundreds of Spaniards were killed on what became known as *La Noche Triste* (lah NO-cheh TREES-teh), or "The Night of Sorrow."

**Cortés conquers Mexico.** Cortés and his soldiers had suffered a terrible defeat, but Cortés did not give up. He assembled a large army, which included thousands of Native Americans who were enemies of the Aztecs. Part of Cortés's forces built boats and attacked Tenochtitlán from the lake surrounding the city. Other soldiers fought on horseback or on foot. In August 1521 Cortés

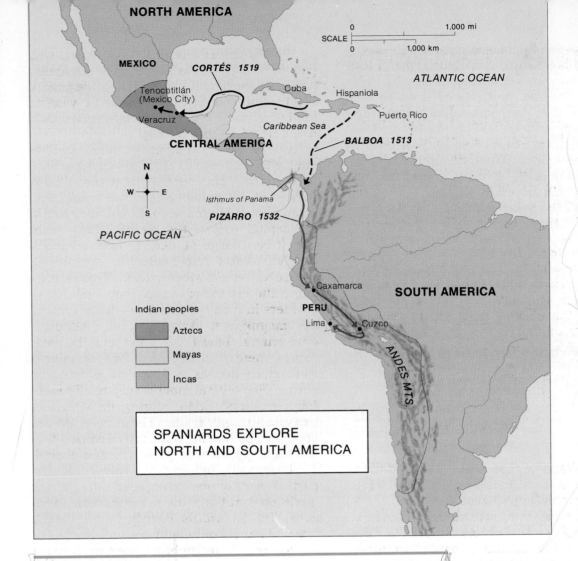

NORTH AMERICA

MEXICO

*CORTÉS 1519*

Tenochtitlán
(Mexico City)

Veracruz

CENTRAL AMERICA

Cuba

Hispaniola

Puerto Rico

ATLANTIC OCEAN

*Caribbean Sea*

*BALBOA 1513*

SCALE

0 — 1,000 mi

0 — 1,000 km

N
W + E
S

*Isthmus of Panama*

*PIZARRO 1532*

PACIFIC OCEAN

Caxamarca

SOUTH AMERICA

PERU

Lima

Cuzco

ANDES MTS.

Indian peoples

Aztecs

Mayas

Incas

SPANIARDS EXPLORE
NORTH AND SOUTH AMERICA

## Map Study

The Spanish conquistadors invaded Mexico, Central America, and South America. Study the routes of Balboa, Cortés, and Pizarro. From what island did Balboa sail? What body of water did he cross? Whose empire did Cortés invade? In what direction did Pizarro travel to reach Cuzco?

finally defeated the Aztecs. The conquerers then began to rebuild the ruined capital. Catholic churches soon replaced the Aztec temples, and a new Spanish city, Mexico City, arose.

**Several factors contribute to Spanish success.** The conquest of the Aztecs was a remarkable feat. With just 600 Spaniards, Cortés won control of a vast empire with millions of people. Such a victory would have

been impossible without the aid of Native Americans who opposed the Aztecs. Cortés had other important advantages, too.

First, the Aztec legend about a fair-skinned god led Moctezuma to welcome the Spaniards. Another factor in Cortés's favor was superior **technology** —scientific knowledge put to practical use. The European guns and cannon were far more powerful than the knives and arrows of the Aztecs.

**37**

Finally, the Spaniards received aid from an unexpected source, smallpox. One of the conquistadors in Tenochtitlán, ill with this European disease, had passed it on to the Aztecs. Native Americans had never suffered from smallpox, and the Aztecs had no natural resistance to it. Hundreds of people fell sick and died. Thus smallpox reduced the number of Aztecs who could fight against Cortés and his forces.

**Spaniards take control of Central America.** Cortés did not stop with the conquest of the Aztecs. As commander of the Spanish forces in Mexico, he sent expeditions throughout the Aztec empire and into Central America. Cortés seized the gold and silver mines that he found and forced the Native Americans to work for the Spaniards. Soon shiploads of gold, silver, and jewels were being sent back to Spain.

## Spanish Conquests in South America

The conquest of the Aztec empire brought Spain great riches. Conquistadors heard stories, however, of an even richer kingdom far to the south of the Aztec lands. The mighty Inca empire, in present-day Peru, was said to be immensely wealthy. Francisco Pizarro (pih-ZAHR-o), who had crossed the Isthmus of Panama with Balboa, decided to find the rich Inca kingdom.

**Pizarro sets out to conquer the Incas.** Pizarro knew that invading the Inca empire would be difficult. The Incas lived high in the Andes Mountains, and their kingdom could be reached only by weeks of climbing. Pizarro spent nearly two years gathering an army and supplies for his great venture. In 1530 he sailed from Panama to Peru, where he took over an Inca town on the coast.

Two years later, with a band of about 180 Spaniards and Africans, Pizarro set out for the Inca cities inland. Pizarro was counting on firearms and horses to overcome the Incas, who greatly outnumbered his small group. He and his soldiers struggled up the steep mountainsides, leading their horses after them. They came at last to the city where the Inca ruler awaited them.

**Pizarro launches a surprise attack.** The Inca ruler, Atahualpa (ah-tah-WAHL-pah), was carried into the great square on a gold throne. Surrounded by thousands of his subjects, Atahualpa listened politely as Pizarro's priest spoke to him through an interpreter. The priest handed Atahualpa a prayer book and tried to persuade him to become a Christian. Atahualpa, however, was not interested. The Incas believed in a sun god and considered their ruler to be the sun god's child. When Atahualpa let the prayer book drop, the Spaniards grew angry. Pizarro ordered his foot soldiers to fire. Soon thousands of Incas lay dead. Pizarro then took Atahualpa prisoner.

**Pizarro conquers Peru.** When the royal prisoner realized how eager the Spaniards were for gold, he made a bargain for his freedom. Atahualpa went to the wall of a small room and touched a spot high above his head. He promised to fill the room that high with gold if his captors would release him. Pizarro agreed. During the next two months, the Incas filled the room with gold objects from palaces and temples. Atahualpa had carried out his side of the bargain, but Pizarro had the Inca leader killed.

Pizarro went on to conquer other Inca cities, and soon he controlled the whole empire. (See map on page 37.) In 1535 he founded a new Spanish city, **Lima** (LEE-muh), in Peru. Lima soon grew to be one of the most important cities in South America.

## SECTION REVIEW

1. **Vocabulary**  conquistador, missionary, convert, ally, technology
2. **People and Places**  Hernando Cortés, Moctezuma, Tenochtitlán, Mexico City, Francisco Pizarro, Atahualpa, Lima
3. **Comprehension**  What were the goals of the conquistadors and the missionaries?
4. **Comprehension**  What made Cortés successful in conquering the Aztecs?
5. **Critical Thinking**  How did religious differences spark fighting between the Spaniards and the Incas?

# CRITICAL THINKING: Cause and Effect

In building their pictures of the past, historians constantly ask the question *Why?* For example, when studying the European exploration of the Americas, historians might ask *Why did some Europeans want to undertake such dangerous voyages?*, or *Why did Spain lead in the colonization of the Americas?* By asking such questions, historians are using **cause-and-effect reasoning.** This skill is vital to the study of history.

A cause is an action that produces an event. An effect is the event produced by an action. For example, because Spain and Portugal each claimed newly discovered land, the Pope established the Line of Demarcation. This cause-and-effect relationship can be shown in the following diagram:

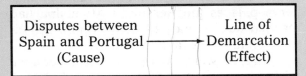

Disputes between Spain and Portugal (Cause) ⟶ Line of Demarcation (Effect)

When reading history books, look for language clues that indicate cause-and-effect relationships. The list below gives some examples of these words and phrases.

| | |
|---|---|
| as a result | for this reason |
| because | led to |
| brought about | produced |
| caused | therefore |
| followed from | thus |

Sometimes an effect produced by a cause may itself become the cause of another effect. This kind of cause-and-effect relationship is shown below:

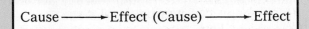

Cause ⟶ Effect (Cause) ⟶ Effect

Such relationships may become clear only after many years have passed. So historians interested in causes and effects may have to study the periods long before and long after an event. Often they discover that **multiple**—many—causes combine to produce a single effect. Similarly, a single cause may produce more than one effect. Multiple cause-and-effect relationships are shown in the following diagrams:

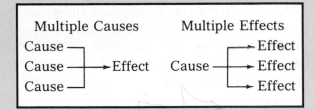

Multiple Causes

Cause —
Cause — ⟶ Effect
Cause —

Multiple Effects

Cause — ⟶ Effect
⟶ Effect
⟶ Effect

Each statement below contains a cause and an effect. On a separate sheet of paper, make each statement into a cause-and-effect diagram by writing the cause on the left and the effect on the right, with an arrow connecting them. Remember, the cause may not be stated first in the sentence.

1. Because the Spaniards hoped to spread the Catholic faith, missionaries came to the Americas.
2. Moctezuma's friendliness to Cortés helped bring about the downfall of the Aztecs.
3. Cortés was able to conquer the Aztecs in part because the Spaniards had horses and more powerful weapons.
4. The Spaniards' desire for gold led them to decide to conquer Peru.
5. The Incas lived high in the Andes Mountains. As a result, Pizarro spent two years preparing for his attack.
6. Atahualpa filled a room with gold in order to buy his freedom.

# What led to Spanish settlements in North America?

## Vocabulary
peninsula
presidio

By the mid-1500's, Spanish colonies were scattered throughout Central and South America. In addition to conquering Mexico and Peru, bold adventurers had explored present-day Venezuela, Guatemala, Ecuador, Colombia, Chile, and Argentina. Settlements were established, and Spain was becoming wealthy from the gold and silver found in its empire. Yet the Spanish believed that even greater riches could be found north of Mexico.

## The Lure of North America

Encouraged by their successes in Central and South America, the Spanish soon eyed North America as well. There they hoped to find new lands to conquer, great wealth to acquire, and many more people to convert to Christianity.

**A fanciful story leads to the discovery of Florida.** One of the earliest Spanish explorers of North America was Juan Ponce de León (POHNS duh LEE-uhn). Ponce de León became the governor of Puerto Rico after conquering the island in 1509. Native Americans there told tales of a northern land with a "fountain of youth." This fountain, they said, was a natural spring with magical powers. Old people could become young again by drinking from the fountain or bathing in its waters.

Ponce de León set out to look for this land in 1513. He never found the legendary fountain, but he discovered a flower-covered **peninsula** —a long finger of land nearly surrounded by water. Ponce de León gave the land a Spanish name, *Florida*, meaning

"flower-covered." Although the explorer considered his expedition unsuccessful, he claimed Florida for Spain. Thus Spaniards were later able to settle in the area. Florida also became a base for exploring other parts of North America.

**The search for gold leads Spaniards to the Gulf Coast.** In 1527 Pánfilo de Narváez (nahr-VAH-es) set out from Spain with a crew of 600. The expedition arrived at Tampa Bay, on Florida's west coast, in April 1528. Narváez divided his group in two, sending some of the crew to sail along the coast while about 200 others proceeded by land. Those who explored on foot, led by Narváez, wandered for months without finding any riches. Their companions, meanwhile, had also grown discouraged and had sailed back to Spain.

Left with no ships for an Atlantic crossing, Narváez and his followers decided to head for Mexico. They cut down trees to build boats and made sails from their shirts. The small boats, however, were no match for the storms in the Gulf of Mexico. Most of the group, including Narváez, were lost at sea. About 80 crew members washed ashore in November 1528 near present-day Galveston, Texas. By the following spring, only 15 were still alive. These survivors spent the next few years as captives of different Indian groups. Finally only four remained to plan an escape.

**Cabeza de Vaca makes an incredible journey.** The four survivors included Alvar Núñez Cabeza de Vaca (kah-BEH-sah duh VAH-kah) and Estevanico (ays-tay-vah-NEE-ko), a servant of African and Arab descent. In 1535 Cabeza de Vaca and his companions began an 18-month journey across the continent. Walking west from the Gulf of Mexico to the Pacific Ocean, they then turned south. During their travels they gained the trust of many Native Americans by posing as healers. They convinced the Indians they could cure illnesses with prayers and herb treatments.

In 1536 Cabeza de Vaca and his group met Spanish soldiers who took them to Mexico City. There they were greeted as heroes. Their accounts of the great journey became an important source of information about present-day Texas and Mexico.

## Exploration of the Interior

In Mexico City, Cabeza de Vaca and Estevanico described all they had seen. They also repeated Native American reports of golden cities north of Mexico. Many Spaniards believed these might be the Seven Cities of Cíbola (SEE-bo-luh), made famous in a European legend.

**Spaniards search for the golden cities.** In 1539 the priest Marcos de Niza (duh NEE-zuh) led a group from Mexico to find Cíbola. Ahead of the explorers went Estevanico, acting as their guide. In present-day New Mexico, Estevanico came to the outskirts of a Zuñi Indian community. The Indians' multi-storied pueblos glistened in the sun, making them look like golden cities. Estevanico sent word to De Niza that he had found Cíbola. Shortly afterward, more news came: Estevanico had been killed by the Zuñis.

De Niza was too frightened to continue all the way to Cíbola, but he viewed the pueblos from afar. When he returned to Mexico, he falsely reported that Cíbola was larger than Mexico City. De Niza's stories grew more exaggerated as they spread throughout Mexico.

**Coronado leads an expedition to New Mexico.** While De Niza and Estevanico searched for Cíbola, Francisco Vásquez de Coronado (kawr-uh-NAHD-o) was preparing an army in Mexico. He assembled hundreds of Spaniards, Native Americans, and Africans. He also gathered horses, oxen, sheep, cows, pigs, and mules to carry supplies.

In 1540 Coronado led this huge force north to find and conquer Cíbola. The explorers followed the Rio Grande and then turned east onto the Great Plains. There Coronado sent scouting parties in different

Juan Ponce de León explored Florida's shores in 1513. Ponce de León and his followers searched for the Fountain of Youth, an imaginary spring whose waters could make old people young again.

directions to search for the cities of gold. One group discovered the Grand Canyon in present-day Arizona. Other members of Coronado's expedition explored parts of present-day New Mexico, Oklahoma, and Kansas. Coronado reported reaching a region that

is the best I have ever seen for producing all the products of Spain, for besides the land itself being very fat and black and being very well watered by rivulets and springs and rivers, I found prunes like those of Spain and nuts and very good sweet grapes and mulberries.

41

During the two-year expedition, Coronado and his soldiers reached the Zuñi pueblos thought to be Cíbola. They realized that the reports had been wrong and that there was no gold to be found. Coronado continued north in search of Quivira (kee-VEER-uh), another imaginary kingdom of gold. Quivira turned out to be a Wichita Indian village in Kansas. In 1542 Coronado returned to Mexico empty-handed.

**De Soto explores inland from Florida.** While Coronado was exploring the Southwest, Hernando de Soto led an expedition to Florida. In 1539 he sailed into Tampa Bay with a crew of 700. From Florida De Soto led his expedition through parts of present-day Georgia, Alabama, Mississippi, Arkansas, and Oklahoma. In 1541 De Soto and his followers became the first Europeans to cross the wide Mississippi River. After De Soto died of a fever in 1542, the rest of the expedition returned to Mexico. De Soto and his followers had failed to find any riches, but their journey increased Spanish knowledge about the geography of the North American interior. Meanwhile, other Spaniards were exploring the Pacific coast far to the north of Mexico.

**Cabrillo lays claim to California.** In 1542 Juan Rodríguez Cabrillo (kuh-BREE-yo) sailed along the Pacific coast of present-day California. Cabrillo reached San Diego Bay and claimed the area around it for Spain. Although Cabrillo died in 1543, his crew continued the voyage north. They sailed as far as present-day Oregon, claiming the entire Pacific coast of North America for Spain.

**Searching for gold, Coronado led his party through the present-day southwestern United States. Frederic Remington's painting shows missionary priests traveling with Coronado. What was the priests' main purpose?**

Hernando De Soto was the governor of Cuba when he decided to search for gold on the North American mainland. In 1539 he landed with 600 soldiers near Tampa Bay, Florida. The area traveled by De Soto's party included parts of 10 present-day states.

## Spanish Settlement of the Southwest

The Spanish explorers who pushed northward from Mexico were followed by missionaries, ranchers, and settlers. As towns were established, the Spanish empire grew in size and strength.

**Oñate guides colonists to the Southwest.** In 1598 Juan de Oñate (aw-NYAH-teh) led a group of soldiers and settlers north from Mexico City. Oñate hoped to find not only riches but also suitable places to establish colonies. He brought along African and Native American slaves, several thousand horses and cattle, and more than 80 wagons to carry supplies.

Oñate and his followers did not find any treasures, but they started the settlement of El Paso, Texas, on the Rio Grande. They also took over an Indian town in present-day New Mexico, which they renamed San Juan

(san WAHN). Using San Juan as a base, the Spanish made expeditions to present-day Kansas and the Gulf of California. In 1609 the San Juan settlers founded a new town at Santa Fe (san-tuh FAY). Today Santa Fe, New Mexico, is the oldest capital city in the United States.

**Colonization of the Southwest continues.** Many Spaniards continued to believe in the cities of gold. From time to time, colonists from Santa Fe explored present-day Texas in hopes of discovering great wealth. During these years, the Spanish founded San Antonio and a number of smaller outposts.

Although little treasure was found, Spain tried to encourage steady colonization in North America. Settlements would help secure and protect Spanish claims. Over the years, churches were founded, **presidios** — forts—were built, and colonies grew up in the lands claimed by Spain.

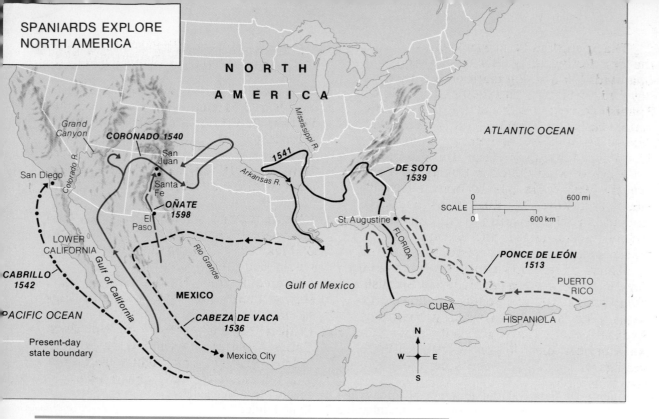

NORTH AMERICA

ATLANTIC OCEAN

Grand Canyon

CORONADO 1540

San Juan

1541

DE SOTO 1539

Mississippi R.

San Diego

Colorado R.

Santa Fe

OÑATE 1598

El Paso

Arkansas R.

St. Augustine

FLORIDA

0        600 mi
SCALE
0        600 km

LOWER CALIFORNIA

Rio Grande

PONCE DE LEÓN 1513

CABRILLO 1542

Gulf of California

MEXICO

Gulf of Mexico

PUERTO RICO

PACIFIC OCEAN

CUBA

HISPANIOLA

Present-day state boundary

CABEZA DE VACA 1536

N
W · E
S

Mexico City

## Map Study

**Coronado traveled as far north as present-day Kansas. Use the Atlas in the back of the book to name the present-day states De Soto explored. In what general direction did Cabrillo sail to reach the place he named San Diego?**

## Lasting Spanish Influences

In a very short span of time, the Spaniards dramatically altered life in North America. Their arrival had an immediate and powerful effect on the Native Americans who had occupied the land for generations. Even today the Spanish influence remains strong in the United States.

**The Spanish change Native American ways of life.** Spain's conquest of North America had devastating results for the Indians. They lost their lands, their wealth, and much of their culture. Although they often tried to resist the Spanish, their weapons were no defense against European cannon, guns, and swords. As a result, the conquistadors swiftly crushed most Indian uprisings. Sometimes the Spanish treated peace-loving Native Americans harshly. Yet the conquistadors, who were greatly outnumbered by the Indians, had to be alert to enemy attacks. Demonstrating their own force was the best way to protect themselves.

The Spanish acted not only for their own survival but also for the glory of God. As devout Christians, the Spanish believed their religion was superior to all others. They felt they had a duty to convert Native Americans to their faith.

The Spanish, however, brought more than Christianity to the Native American people. They introduced useful technology and European animals. Horses soon became widely used by the buffalo-hunting Indians of the Great Plains. Cattle were raised for beef, and sheep supplied wool that Indian weavers turned into blankets and cloth.

**The Spanish influence still remains.** As the first European settlers in America, the Spaniards left a strong mark on the present-day United States. Thousands of people of Spanish descent now live in the states of Arizona, California, Florida, New Mexico, and Texas. Throughout the country, more than 15 million Americans claim Spanish roots.

Much of what the early Spanish settlers brought with them has become a part of American culture. The English language, for example, is rich in Spanish words. Examples include *corral, siesta,* and *tornado.* Many places, too, bear Spanish names.

American ranchers also owe a debt to the Spanish. The western saddle was a Spanish invention, and the practice of branding cattle began with the Spanish. Finally, the early Spaniards made important contributions to the American diet. Wheat, olives, oranges, and figs were first planted in America by settlers from Spain.

## SECTION REVIEW

1. **Vocabulary**    peninsula, presidio
2. **People and Places**    Juan Ponce de León, Florida, Pánfilo de Narváez, Alvar Núñez Cabeza de Vaca, Estevanico, Marcos de Niza, Francisco Vásquez de Coronado, Hernando de Soto, Mississippi River, Juan Rodríguez Cabrillo, Juan de Oñate, Santa Fe
3. **Comprehension**    What legendary places did Spanish explorers hope to find north of Mexico? What did they believe they would find there?
4. **Comprehension**    How did the Spanish secure their claims to the lands they found?
5. **Critical Thinking**    How do you think Native Americans reacted to the conquistadors' arrival? Why might some groups have reacted differently than others?

# Chapter 2 Summary

After Columbus reached the Americas, named for Amerigo Vespucci, many more explorers sailed west. In 1500 Cabral claimed present-day Brazil for Portugal. Thirteen years later, Balboa claimed the Pacific Ocean for Spain. Magellan's voyage for Spain from 1519 to 1522 proved that it was possible to circumnavigate the earth.

England, France, and Holland also sent explorers to North America. Verrazano, Cartier, Champlain, and Hudson all looked in vain for a Northwest Passage to Asia. Their voyages resulted in important discoveries about North American geography and resources.

Meanwhile Spain was starting to establish colonies in the Americas. The longing for adventure, wealth, and glory, as well as the desire to spread Christianity, led many Spaniards west. Cortés conquered Moctezuma and the Aztecs in Mexico. Pizarro conquered the Inca empire in Peru, bringing even greater wealth to Spain.

Other Spanish explorers turned to the lands north of Mexico. Ponce de León claimed Florida in 1513. Cabeza de Vaca, Estevanico, and two other survivors of the Narváez expedition walked hundreds of miles through present-day Texas. Their stories of Cíbola led De Niza and Coronado to explore the American Southwest. De Soto, meanwhile, traveled from Florida to the Mississippi River. Cabrillo explored the coast of present-day California, and Oñate established settlements in Texas and New Mexico. As the Spaniards built their vast colonial empire, they changed the Indian ways of life forever.

## Vocabulary and Key Terms

Choose one term from the following list to replace each blank in the paragraph below. Write your answers on a separate sheet of paper.

colonies
conquistadors
converting
Crown

missionaries
Northwest Passage
presidios

    Magellan's voyage inspired other explorers to search for a __1__ through America. Soon Spain grew interested in America itself. Bold __2__ came to seek wealth, fame, and glory for the Spanish __3__. Christian __4__ hoped to spread their religion by __5__ the Native Americans to Catholicism. In time, __6__ were founded and __7__ were built.

## Recalling the Facts

1. Why did the Pope establish the Line of Demarcation?
2. How did America get its name?
3. What facts about the world did Magellan's voyage prove?
4. Which explorers searched for a Northwest Passage? What resulted from their voyages?
5. For what reasons did Spaniards come to the Americas?
6. What did Cortés and Pizarro achieve?
7. How did Florida become part of the Spanish empire?
8. How did the Spanish change Native Americans' lives?

## Places to Locate

Match the letters on the map with the regions listed below the map. Write your answers on a separate sheet of paper.

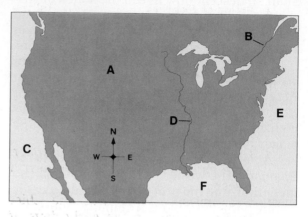

1. Atlantic Ocean
2. Pacific Ocean
3. North America
4. St. Lawrence River
5. Gulf of Mexico
6. Mississippi River

## Critical Thinking

1. What ideas led to the creation of the Line of Demarcation and the Treaty of Tordesillas? Consider the following questions in your answer:
   a. What ideas were held about the power of the Church?
   b. What attitude did Europeans have toward people who lived in the lands being claimed?
   c. How much was known about the size and shape of the earth in 1494?
2. Magellan, Balboa, Hudson, Narváez, and De Soto did not complete their expeditions. What do their deaths suggest about the problems early explorers faced? Do people still "explore" the world today? Are there still dangers in doing so? Explain.
3. Compare the Spanish conquest of Central and South America with Spanish exploration in North America. Address the following topics in your comparison:
   a. encounters with Native Americans
   b. the riches found in each region
   c. the role of legends

## Understanding History

1. Reread the section "Balboa seeks riches and adventure" on page 28. Then answer these questions.
   a. **Primary Sources.** How did Balboa know there were riches in Peru?
   b. **Primary Sources.** According to Balboa, why was the Spanish king the "lord" of Peru?
2. Reread the section "Champlain continues the search for a Northwest Passage" on page 33. Then answer these questions.
   a. **Geography.** Why might Champlain have chosen to found Quebec near a river?
   b. **Economics.** What was the chief trading activity in the early days of Quebec?
3. Reread the section "Pizarro launches a surprise attack" on page 38. Then answer these questions.
   a. **Religion.** Why might Atahualpa have shown little interest in becoming a Christian?
   b. **Science and Technology.** What technology did the Spaniards use to overpower the Incas?

## Projects and Activities

1. **Writing a Report.** Find out about more recent explorers who succeeded in finding a Northwest Passage. Look for information about Roald Amundsen's trip in 1903–1906, the route found by the United States Navy in 1957, and the 1958 trip by the American submarine *Nautilus*. Write a report using the information you find.
2. **Making a Chart.** Prepare a chart listing all the explorers discussed in this chapter. Fill in information under the headings "Explorer," "Country," "Dates of Voyage," "Area Explored," and "Importance."
3. **Interviewing.** Stage a talk show with some of the early explorers as your guests. Interview them about their experiences and invite classmates in the audience to ask questions.

4. **Researching Place Names.** The Strait of Magellan, the Hudson River, Hudson Bay, and Lake Champlain are all named for their discoverers. Find out the history and meaning of other place names in this chapter, such as Montreal, Quebec, Puerto Rico, Galveston, San Diego, El Paso, and Santa Fe.

## Practicing Your Skill

Copy the chart below onto a separate sheet of paper. Then complete the chart by filling in the missing causes and effects.

**Cause:** A storm blows Cabral west of his course.

**Effect:** Cabral reaches Brazil and claims the land for Portugal.

**Cause:** _____

**Effect:** The Dutch settle the New York region.

**Cause:** _____

**Effect:** Many Native Americans become Cortés's allies.

**Cause:** Coronado searches for Cíbola.

**Effect:** _____

**Cause:** Cabrillo's crew sails north from Mexico to present-day Oregon.

**Effect:** _____

# CHAPTER
# 3 Europeans Compete for Colonial Empires
## 1492–1610

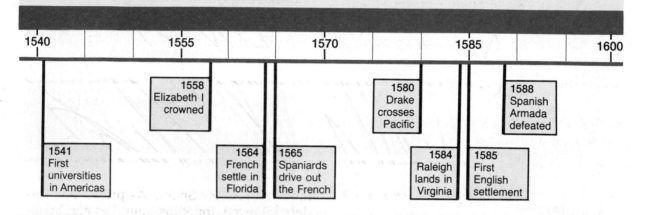

| 1540 | 1555 | 1570 | 1585 | 1600 |

**1558** Elizabeth I crowned

**1580** Drake crosses Pacific

**1588** Spanish Armada defeated

**1541** First universities in Americas

**1564** French settle in Florida

**1565** Spaniards drive out the French

**1584** Raleigh lands in Virginia

**1585** First English settlement

John White founded Roanoke, Virginia, in 1587. By the time he returned in 1590, all the colonists had vanished, leaving behind only a puzzling message.

## Preparing to Read

In the years following Christopher Columbus's voyages, Spain took the lead in exploring and settling the Americas. Other nations watched enviously as Spain carved out a powerful and prosperous colonial empire. England and France had also claimed North American lands. They, too, wanted to profit from colonies in the Americas. In the late 1500's, England emerged as a strong rival to Spain. While Spain's power slowly weakened, the English sought a firm foothold along the eastern coast of North America. As you read this chapter, try to answer the following questions:

1. What was it like to live in Spain's American colonies?
2. How did other nations challenge Spain's power?
3. What came of England's first settlement attempts?

# 1 What was it like to live in Spain's American colonies?

### Vocabulary

| | |
|---|---|
| viceroy | encomienda |
| peninsulares | mission |
| Creole | rancho |
| mestizo | plaza |
| hacienda | mercantilism |
| economy | raw materials |

As early as Columbus's second westward voyage in 1493, Spain began sending colonists to the Americas. By 1600, between 200,000 and 300,000 Spaniards were living in the Americas as permanent settlers. They brought a new way of life to the land and to the Native Americans already living there.

### Spain's American Empire

Spanish exploration flourished during the 50 years after Columbus reached the West Indies. As the time list on page 50 shows, Hernando Cortés and other conquistadors had claimed a huge amount of land in the Americas for Spain. As priests and settlers followed, founding churches and building communities, the Spanish created a vast empire.

**Spanish America covers an immense territory.** By the mid-1500's the lands controlled by Spain stretched for thousands of miles. These lands included most of South America (except Brazil, which Portugal claimed), all of Central America, the islands of the West Indies, and Mexico. Spain's empire also extended north into the present-day United States. Florida, the coast around the Gulf of Mexico, and the Southwest were all included in the Spanish empire. (See map on page 51.)

This enormous area was divided into two parts. One part, called **New Spain,** included Venezuela and all the land and islands north of the Isthmus of Panama. The capital of New Spain was Mexico City. The other part of the empire, **Peru,** included the Spanish possessions in South America, except Venezuela. Peru's capital was Lima.

**The empire is ruled by the king of Spain.** At the head of the empire the monarch of Spain reigned supreme. It was the king who made the rule allowing only Catholics born in Spain to settle in the Americas. The king also decided which Spaniards would be given grants of land.

The American colonies, however, were a great distance from Spain. The journey across the Atlantic Ocean took two months or more. The king realized that it was necessary to set up a system of local government in the Americas. The king appointed two **viceroys** (VYS-royz)—colonial governors—to rule New Spain and Peru in the name of the Crown.

The viceroys and their advisory councils held enormous power. These royal officials made rules regulating almost every detail of colonial life. They established laws about the important matter of taxation, for example, and about property inheritance. The viceroys even set dress codes. In Lima only certain women were allowed to wear silk dresses. Those who broke the law might be whipped or forced to leave the city.

**Work is linked to social class.** The people living in Spanish America were divided into several different social classes. Their rights and privileges depended on the class to which they belonged. The most privileged group was the *peninsulares* (pen-in-soo-LAH-rays)—Spaniards born in Spain. The *peninsulares* occupied the most important positions in the Church and the government. They held almost all the political power and ruled the life of the colonies.

The second group, below the *peninsulares,* was the **Creoles** (KREE-ols)—people of Spanish ancestry who were born in New Spain. Many of the landowners and merchants were Creoles. Although they were often very wealthy, Creoles were looked down upon by the *peninsulares.*

The third social class was made up of **mestizos** (mes-TEE-soz)—people of mixed Spanish and Indian ancestry. Mestizos worked as artisans in the cities or as laborers on farms and ranches. The least privileged members of the society were Native Americans and black slaves from Africa. These people did the hardest work in the fields and mines. They often lived in poverty and near-starvation.

**Women's and men's roles differ.** By Spanish custom, the social position of married women depended on their husbands' class. Like their husbands, mestizo and slave women worked at trades, on the land, or in the households of wealthy Spaniards. In addition, women had most of the responsibility for taking care of their families.

For most well-to-do Spanish women, tending to their families was a full-time activity. Running a busy household with many servants required good supervisory skills. Some women also handled business affairs when their husbands were away from home. Hernando de Soto's wife, for example, governed Cuba while her husband explored North America. Another Spanish woman, María de Escobar, grew rich by running a large farm.

## Spanish Communities

The Spanish empire in the Americas was many times the size of Spain. This huge territory included farmlands, grassy plains, vast stretches of desert, high mountains, and

## TIME LIST

### Spanish Exploration   1492–1542

| | |
|---|---|
| 1492 | Columbus lands in West Indies |
| 1499 | Vespucci explores South American coast |
| 1508 | Ponce de León conquers Puerto Rico |
| 1513 | Ponce de León claims Florida; Balboa sights Pacific Ocean |
| 1519 | Cortés conquers Mexico |
| 1520 | Magellan discovers Strait of Magellan |
| 1528 | Narvaez explores Florida's Gulf coast |
| 1532 | Pizarro conquers Peru |
| 1536 | Cabeza de Vaca reaches Mexico City |
| 1539 | De Niza explores New Mexico |
| 1540 | Coronado explores Southwest |
| 1541 | De Soto crosses Mississippi River |
| 1542 | Cabrillo explores California coast |

humid rain forests. In these widely different geographic conditions, a variety of communities grew up.

**Landholders manage large estates.** To encourage colonization, the king of Spain granted large estates, called **haciendas** (hah-see-EN-duhz), to Spanish nobles. The haciendas, spread throughout the countryside, were the center of farming activity. In addition, they formed a vital part of the **economy** —system of producing goods and services. On the haciendas of New Spain and Peru, farmers raised a variety of crops. They grew corn and beans, as Native Americans had done for years. The Spanish also planted crops that were new to the Americas but long known to Europeans. These included olives, oranges, wheat, and sugar cane.

Many hacienda owners received not only land but an *encomienda* (en-ko-mee-EN-dah) as well. An *encomienda* was the right of a property owner to demand labor from the Indians on the land. According to Spanish law, the Native Americans were supposed to receive wages and fair treatment. Many landowners, however, ignored the law. Often they lived so far from the centers of government that they could not be forced to obey it.

Under Spanish rule, most Native Americans were no better off than European serfs during the Middle Ages. The Indians were not allowed to leave the land. Those who tried to escape and who were recaptured became slaves. Often they were overworked and poorly fed.

The owners of the haciendas, however, led more comfortable lives. They directed the workers, deciding what crops to plant and how to farm. In their free time, they often practiced horseback riding or entertained visitors.

**The mission system develops.** Another kind of community important in Spanish America was the **mission.** Missions were religious settlements founded by priests for the purpose of spreading the Catholic faith. Missions were often located far from other Spanish settlements. They usually included a church, a village, a fort, and farmland.

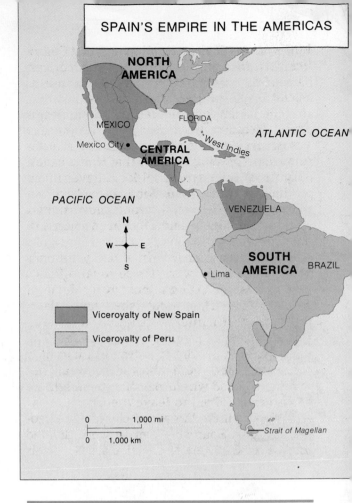

SPAIN'S EMPIRE IN THE AMERICAS

NORTH AMERICA
MEXICO
FLORIDA
Mexico City
CENTRAL AMERICA
West Indies
ATLANTIC OCEAN
PACIFIC OCEAN
VENEZUELA
SOUTH AMERICA
BRAZIL
Lima
Strait of Magellan

■ Viceroyalty of New Spain

▢ Viceroyalty of Peru

0   1,000 mi
0   1,000 km

## Map Study
**Spain's American empire spanned parts of two continents. Name the two continents. What areas were part of New Spain? What part of Spain's empire had its capital at Lima?**

The priests not only converted the Indians to Catholicism, but also introduced them to the Spanish language and Spanish customs. Often hundreds of Indians lived and worked around a mission. Under the direction of the priests, the Indians raised crops, cared for the animals, and did other work such as cooking and cleaning. They also built houses, workshops, and churches.

Over the years, missions spread throughout the Spanish empire. Two dedicated priests who founded missions were Eusebio Kino (oo-SEH-bee-o KEE-no) and Junípero Serra (hoo-NEE-peh-ro SER-uh). In the

**51**

1600's Kino and his companions built more than 20 missions in northern Mexico and present-day Arizona. Later, Serra established missions along California's coast that stretched from San Diego north to San Francisco. (See map on page 53.)

**Silver and gold pour out of the Americas.** Next to farming, mining was the most profitable activity in the colonies. The productive mines of Mexico and Peru were a source of great wealth for Spain. Indian workers climbed in and out of deep mountain pits carrying heavy loads of silver and gold ore. The ore was then turned into solid bars of silver and gold and taken by mule train to colonial mints. There the precious bars were turned into Spanish coins.

Ships bound for Spain carried one fifth of this wealth back to the Crown. The rest of the silver and gold belonged to the mine owners. For hundreds of years, Spanish coins called doubloons and dollars were the most common form of money throughout the Americas. People in North America used these coins even as late as the 1850's.

**Various other economic activities develop.** Spanish colonists made profits in other kinds of work besides mining and

In about 1584 a Spaniard painted this scene of silver mining in present-day Bolivia. Native Americans mined the silver ore and used mules and llamas to carry the ore down the mountain. The ore was then melted to separate the pure silver from the rock. Workers poured the liquid silver into molds to make bars or coins.

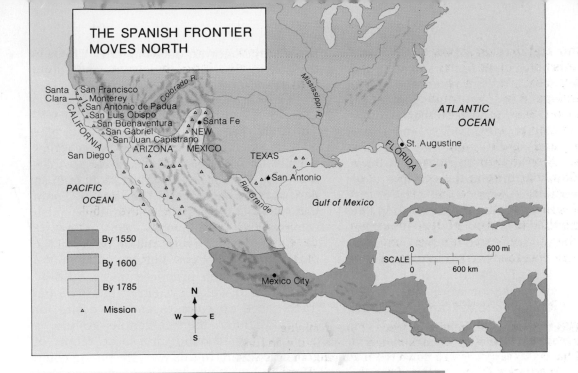

**THE SPANISH FRONTIER MOVES NORTH**

Santa Clara
San Francisco
Monterey
San Antonio de Padua
San Luis Obispo
San Buenaventura
San Gabriel
San Juan Capistrano
San Diego

CALIFORNIA

ARIZONA

NEW MEXICO

Santa Fe

Colorado R.

Mississippi R.

ATLANTIC OCEAN

St. Augustine

FLORIDA

TEXAS

San Antonio

Rio Grande

PACIFIC OCEAN

Gulf of Mexico

Mexico City

By 1550
By 1600
By 1785
Mission

N
W E
S

SCALE
0          600 mi
0          600 km

## Map Study

**As Spanish missionaries moved northward to spread their faith, Spanish settlers followed. What symbol represents a mission? Name the northernmost Spanish mission established by 1785. On what coast of North America was St. Augustine founded?**

farming. Raising livestock was a big success. The Spaniards who settled in the Americas brought with them cattle, pigs, sheep, goats, and horses. On **ranchos** — cattle ranches—tough, longhorn steer were bred. In the Andes Mountains, many people raised sheep and llamas.

Some Native Americans in Spanish America worked as artisans. Talented weavers created products of great beauty. Other Native Americans made pottery or fashioned goods out of leather or metal. These Indian handicrafts were highly prized by the Spaniards. They were often of better quality than goods available in Spain.

**Black slavery develops.** Throughout New Spain and Peru, many Indians were overworked. They also suffered from disease and poor food. Some priests tried to protect the Indians from mistreatment. Bartolomé de Las Casas worked for years to persuade the Spanish king to do away with the

*encomienda* system. The king eventually agreed and the law was changed. However, many landowners continued to ignore the law, and life for most Indians remained harsh.

In time, so many Native Americans died that the Spanish began bringing black slaves from Africa. Spaniards believed that Africans were hard workers and used to a hot climate. The labor of the slaves proved especially important on the large sugar-growing farms in present-day Cuba, Haiti, and Puerto Rico. Black slaves also did much of the most difficult work in the bustling ports of South America.

In the late 1500's the Spanish government began to limit the number of slaves that could be brought to the Americas each year. Some traders, however, brought in more slaves than were allowed. By 1600 about 75,000 Africans were living in New Spain and Peru.

**City life flowers in Mexico City and Lima.** Most blacks and Indians lived in the countryside where they worked, but many Spaniards resided in large towns and cities. Government and trade were centered in the two great capitals, Mexico City and Lima. Like most Spanish cities, Mexico City and Lima were built around a **plaza** —a large public square. In the plaza stood the viceroy's palace and a great cathedral. The cathedral was the church of the archbishop, the highest Catholic official in the province. Mexico City and Lima also housed two great universities. Founded in 1551, these are the oldest universities in the Americas.

Luxury and splendor were part of city life. Wide, well-paved roads ran through the heart of Mexico City and Lima. Down these avenues parades marched to welcome a new viceroy or honor an outgoing one. The rich dressed in fine silks and jewels and often held grand parties.

## Trade as a Tool of Empire

The wealthy *peninsulares* and Creoles who lived in the cities enjoyed great prosperity. They did not have total freedom in business matters, however. The king of Spain had set strict trade policies that the Spanish colonists had to follow.

**Colonies play a vital role in trade.** Like most other European countries in the 1500's and 1600's, Spain practiced **mercantilism.** Mercantilism was a system of international trade based on colonies and the desire for wealth. Under the mercantile system, a country tried to build up a large supply of gold and silver. In this way, the nation could afford to buy items that it did not produce.

A country also tried to sell more goods than it bought. Colonies were an important way to meet this goal. Colonies were supposed to provide **raw materials** —natural resources used to make other goods. Also, the colonists were supposed to buy finished goods made in the parent country. In this way, makers of finished goods in the parent country avoided competition from colonists.

**Spain enforces strict mercantilism.** Spain built up a valuable trade with its colonial empire. The regions of New Spain and Peru provided wheat, barley, rye, rice, beans, peas, sugar cane, bananas, oranges, hides, and wool. From the mines and storehouses of the Americas flowed great quantities of gold and silver.

Twice each year Spanish merchants sailed from Seville, Spain, to the colonies. The ships stopped at all major ports in the Americas, including Havana in Cuba and Veracruz in Mexico. There the merchants bought low-priced raw materials. At the same time, they sold high-priced finished goods from Spain, such as shoes, clothing, and tools.

Under the system of mercantilism, a nation's colonies existed only to benefit the parent country. The Spanish colonists were not to trade with foreign nations, for example.

---

**LINKING PAST AND PRESENT**

## ★ ★ ★ *Spanish Words*

The Spanish left their imprint on America in many ways. One of the most important is their rich contribution to our everyday language.

From the tip of Florida to the California coast, thousands of places across the nation bear Spanish names. Examples include the state of Colorado and the cities of Los Angeles, San Francisco, Las Vegas, El Paso, and San Antonio. Spanish words are also used for many landforms. *Canyon* and *mesa* are Spanish terms. *Sierra Nevada* means "snow-capped mountains," and *Rio Grande* is Spanish for "big river."

Many words associated with ranching— *lasso*, *rodeo*, and *lariat*, for example— are Spanish. *Barbecue*, *patio*, and *fiesta* are other terms that early American settlers borrowed from the Spanish. Some well-known animals, including the alligator, mosquito, bronco, and burro, also have Spanish names.

## CULTURE • Spanish Influences on Architecture

On the northeast coast of Florida, in the city of St. Augustine, stands the oldest stone fortress in the United States. Built between 1672 and 1696, the Castillo de San Marcos, or Castle of Saint Marcos, once helped guard Spain's American empire. Today the fortress is a national monument that thousands of people visit each year.

Many of the Spanish missions in California, Texas, Arizona, and New Mexico also attract crowds of visitors. The lovely mission churches still showcase delicate wood carvings and religious paintings created more than 200 years ago.

The Spanish imprint can be seen, too, in more modern buildings. Spanish-style houses are especially popular in California and the Southwest. Such homes usually have thick, white adobe walls, beautiful tile work, and gently curving arches. Sometimes they are built around an open courtyard filled with flowers.

**The mission of San Antonio de Padua**

They could sell their products only to Spain, at prices set by Spain. The colonists were also restricted in the raw materials they could produce. For example, they were not allowed to raise chives or hemp. Those crops were already being grown in Spain, and Spanish farmers wanted no competition from the colonists. The aim of Spain's strict rules was to gain the greatest possible wealth for the royal treasury.

**Spain guards its empire with military might.** To protect its rich colonies, the Spanish government built a large fleet of warships. These ships escorted merchant vessels taking gold and other cargoes to and from the colonies. These ships, and the troops they carried, were also needed to protect Spain's valuable colonies from attack by other nations. During the mid-1500's Spain was at war in Holland. The French and the English, who often sided with the Dutch, were another threat. France and England envied Spain's prosperous empire. They did not dare attack Spain, but they might strike at the American colonies.

## SECTION REVIEW

1. **Vocabulary** viceroy, *peninsulares*, Creole, mestizo, hacienda, economy, *encomienda*, mission, rancho, plaza, mercantilism, raw materials
2. **People and Places** New Spain, Mexico City, Peru, Lima, Eusebio Kino, Junípero Serra, Bartolomé de Las Casas
3. **Comprehension** How were social class and work connected in Spanish America?
4. **Comprehension** What were the major economic activities in Spanish America?
5. **Critical Thinking** Do you think the Spanish colonists liked or disliked the mercantile system? Explain.

## 2 How did other countries challenge Spain's power?

By the early 1500's, Spain was Europe's richest and most powerful country. The other nations of Europe, jealous of Spain's empire, were soon competing for colonial wealth. Challenges from England and France eventually weakened Spanish power.

### Spain's Power and Its Rivals

By the late 1500's King Philip II of Spain ruled over a far-reaching empire in Europe and the Americas. Other European countries resented and feared the power of Spain. They were also envious of Spain's many wealthy colonies, and wished to develop American colonies of their own. England and France had already explored and claimed territory in the Americas. These countries began to look for ways to strike at Spain without fighting a direct war.

**European nations seek to weaken Spain.** One way for other nations to defy Spain was to carry on secret trade with its American colonies. Even though Spanish laws forbade such activities, traders from other countries delivered goods to Spanish colonial seaports. The foreign merchants anchored off the coast and brought their cargo ashore at night. Spanish colonists were quite willing to deal with these traders, for the illegal goods arrived more often and were priced lower than Spanish products. As a result of this illegal trade, the Spanish Crown lost much wealth.

Another way to weaken Spain was by **piracy** —robbery at sea. In the mid-1500's, armed pirate ships from France, Holland, and England began roaming the seas. Their crews often captured Spanish ships and **plundered** —robbed—rich towns along the coasts of Spanish America. The treasure and other **booty** —stolen goods—snatched by these pirates was worth millions of dollars. No government openly approved of piracy, because it violated laws important to all nations. England and France, however, did little to stop their pirates, as long as they stole only from Spain.

Later on, daring sea rovers even made settlements on Spanish territory. French pirates took over the western end of Hispaniola and attacked Spanish trade in the Caribbean. English pirates based themselves on the coast of Central America. Dutch pirates held the island of Aruba, off the coast of present-day Venezuela.

**Spain crushes rival colonies.** The governments of England, France, and Holland could not risk direct challenges to Spain. As the dominant power in Europe as well as the Americas, Spain was too dangerous an enemy. France, however, did attempt to establish colonies in the Americas.

Since the early 1500's, the French had been fishing off the coast of Newfoundland, Canada. In June 1542 a group of 200 French men and women arrived to settle there. During the winter, however, disease, hunger, and cold weather killed half the colonists. The rest abandoned their settlement the following September. France then turned its attention to Florida. In 1564 a group of about 300 French settlers established Fort Caroline near present-day Jacksonville. Another expedition the following year brought more men, women, and children to the colony.

For King Philip of Spain, a French settlement in Florida was far too close to Mexico. Therefore, in the summer of 1565 Philip sent 5 ships and 800 soldiers to put a stop to French colonization. The Spaniards set up a base at St. Augustine, near Fort Caroline.

After clashing with the French at sea, the Spaniards mounted a land attack. They killed almost all the French settlers, and destroyed Fort Caroline. St. Augustine continued as an outpost of the Spanish empire. Today it is the oldest city founded by Europeans in the United States.

## England's Challenge and Victory

Although the Spanish had to be on guard against the French, they were more alarmed by the English. Elizabeth I had become queen of England in 1558. Under her capable leadership, England rapidly grew stronger.

**English sailors provoke Spain.** England was the most successful of all the European countries in striking at Spain. Centuries of living on an island had helped the English become good sailors and skillful shipbuilders. They also became able pirates. In a flash, heavily armed English pirate vessels swooped down on big, slow Spanish treasure ships. The captains of these English pirates were called **sea dogs.**

Queen Elizabeth did not authorize the sea dogs' attacks, but she was pleased by the damage they caused Spain. Writing to one of the sea dogs in 1587, the queen made her feelings clear. She wanted to avoid actions that could be considered acts of war, and yet still gain Spanish treasure. In one part of the letter, she prohibited certain attacks:

> [You are not to] enter forcibly into any of the [King of Spain's] ports or havens, or to offer violence to any of his towns or shipping within harbouring, or to do any act of hostility upon the land.

Later in the letter, however, Elizabeth encouraged the sea dogs to plunder Spanish ships at sea:

> You should do your best . . . to get into your possession such shipping of the said King or his subjects as you shall find at sea.

**Francis Drake angers the king of Spain.** The most famous of all the sea dogs was Francis Drake. Brought up in a town on the

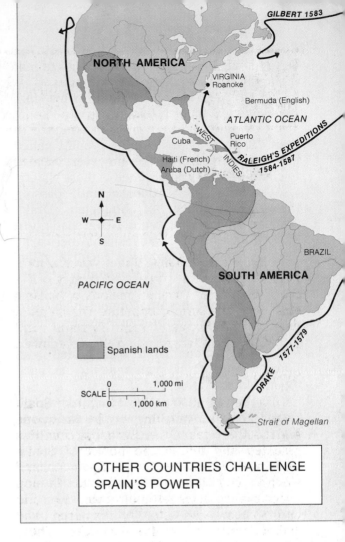

OTHER COUNTRIES CHALLENGE SPAIN'S POWER

## Map Study

**The English, French, and Dutch attacked Spanish shipping and claimed land in the Americas. Study the routes of Drake and Raleigh. In what general direction did Drake sail to return to England? Name the territory granted to Raleigh and the settlement he founded.**

English coast, he had learned the ways of the sea before he was 10 years old. Drake felt a bitter hatred for the Spaniards. In 1567 his ship had been attacked and many of his companions killed by Spanish sailors pretending to be friendly. For many years afterward, Drake sought revenge by capturing Spanish vessels and raiding Spanish towns. The

Spaniards feared him and called him "The Dragon." King Philip offered a huge sum of money to anyone who could kill him.

In 1577 Drake left England in his ship, the *Golden Hind*, on a dangerous expedition. The Spaniards had never been attacked in their "Spanish lake," as they proudly called the Pacific Ocean. Drake, however, decided to challenge their dominance of these waters.

Crossing the Atlantic and passing through the Strait of Magellan, Drake reached the Pacific Ocean. As he sped north along the western coast of South America, he raided towns and captured Spanish ships. His greatest prize was the Spanish treasure ship nicknamed the "Glory of the South Sea." Taking the ship completely by surprise, Drake seized precious stones, chests full of gold pieces, and tons of pure silver. When the *Golden Hind* was loaded with booty, Francis Drake was ready to sail back to England.

Drake knew that the Spaniards would expect him to return the way he had come. Ship captains would be watching for him, hoping to capture "The Dragon" and recover Spanish treasure. Drake did not give them a chance. Instead he boldly turned north and sailed along the coast of California. He landed briefly at a magnificent bay, now called Drake's Bay, just north of present-day San Francisco. From there he crossed the Pacific Ocean to the Philippine Islands, where he stopped for supplies. Then he continued across the Indian Ocean, around the Cape of Good Hope, and north along the west coast of Africa. At last, in 1580, he reached England. Drake and his crew became the second group of voyagers to circumnavigate the world.

Drake returned to England with Spanish treasure worth millions of dollars. In addition, he had proved that the Pacific Ocean was no longer a "Spanish lake." When he arrived home, he was welcomed as a great hero. Queen Elizabeth herself visited the *Golden Hind* when it docked. She was so pleased that she made Drake a knight right on the ship. He was now Sir Francis Drake.

**Spain prepares to attack England.** King Philip II of Spain was furious over the sea dogs' attacks. Philip sent word to Queen Elizabeth that Drake was nothing but a pirate and ought to be hanged. However, Philip had a deeper reason for being angry at England. Several European countries, England among them, had broken away from the Roman Catholic Church earlier in the 1500's. Most English people had thus become **Protestants**—members of Christian churches founded in *protest* against Catholic teachings. Europe was bitterly divided between Protestants, who did not recognize the Pope's authority, and Catholics, who did.

King Philip, the most powerful Catholic ruler in Europe, decided that the time had come to crush England. Philip gathered a fleet of 130 warships, put on board 19,000 soldiers and 8,000 sailors, and sent them to invade England. This huge force was thought to be **invincible** —incapable of being beaten. It was called the **Invincible Armada**—the unconquerable fleet. When Sir Francis Drake heard about the Armada, he wrote a letter advising Queen Elizabeth to be prepared:

> God increase your most excellent Majesty's forces both by sea and land daily; for thus I surely think: there was never any force so strong as there is now ready or making ready against your Majesty.

**The Spanish Armada is defeated.** The Armada sailed from the Portuguese city of Lisbon, which was then under Spanish rule, in May 1588. When the fleet reached the English Channel—the narrow strait between England and France—it was met by at least 170 English vessels. The commanders of the English fleet included Drake and other daring sea dogs such as Sir Humphrey Gilbert. The English ships were smaller, faster, and easier to handle than most of the Spanish ships. The English also had cannon that could shoot more accurately. Darting back and forth around the ships of the Armada, the English fired and quickly sailed away before the heavy enemy vessels could shoot back. The English also set some of their old, unmanned ships on fire and let them drift among the Spanish vessels. These fire ships caused great confusion and destruction.

In 1580 Queen Elizabeth I of England made Francis Drake a knight for his daring campaigns against the Spanish. Drake had plundered silver and gold from the Spanish colonies. He also circumnavigated the world in his ship, the *Golden Hind.* Where did the ceremony making Drake a knight take place?

For more than a week the battle raged. The English were able to sink or damage a number of Spanish ships without losing a single vessel themselves. Finally the Spaniards fled up the English Channel. The English followed at first, but lack of food and ammunition forced them to turn back. Then nature came to England's aid. A fierce gale blew up, and high winds battered the Spanish ships. Many were driven ashore or swamped off the coast of Scotland. The ships that survived were hopelessly scattered. Proud Spain had suffered a terrible defeat. It lost more than 40 ships and 10,000 of its troops, while the English lost no ships and about 100 sailors.

The defeat of the Armada in 1588 was costly to Spain in another way. For almost a century Spain had been the strongest nation in Europe. Now England had proved to the world that Spain could be beaten. No longer would the Spanish dominate the oceans—or the American continents.

## SECTION REVIEW

1. **Vocabulary**   piracy, plunder, booty, invincible
2. **People and Places**   Philip II, Elizabeth I, Francis Drake, English Channel
3. **Comprehension**   In what ways did European nations challenge Spain?
4. **Comprehension**   How was the Spanish Armada defeated?
5. **Critical Thinking**   When Spain was the richest country in Europe it also was the most powerful. Why did wealth bring Spain power?

# 3. What came of England's first settlement attempts?

While English and Spanish sea rivalry was growing, England was also pursuing its claims to land in the Americas. In 1497 John Cabot had explored the northeastern coast of North America. The region, as yet unsettled, seemed a safe distance from Spanish strongholds in Florida. It was here that England decided to launch its first colony.

## First Attempts at English Settlement

The nationalist spirit was strong in England in the late 1500's. Adventurers wanted to explore and conquer for the glory and honor of their country. They also hoped to gain wealth and fame for themselves.

**Gilbert and Raleigh try to plant colonies.** In 1578 Queen Elizabeth gave Sir Humphrey Gilbert permission to found a settlement in North America. On his first voyage, Gilbert failed to reach America. He set out again in 1583 and landed in Newfoundland, but he lacked the funds to build an outpost. As he was sailing back to England, Gilbert and his crew were shipwrecked and lost at sea.

Gilbert's half-brother, Walter Raleigh (RAW-lee), then got the queen's permission to establish a colony in North America. Raleigh raised the funds to send two ships on an expedition in 1584. After more than two months at sea, the party reached **Roanoke Island** (RO-uh-nok), off the coast of present-day North Carolina. There the English explorers found friendly Indians and land

"most beautiful and pleasant to behold." They enthusiastically described the abundance of deer, fish, fowl, grapes, and sweet-smelling cedar trees.

Queen Elizabeth was so encouraged by these reports that she rewarded Raleigh by making him a knight. She also granted him the rights to the entire seacoast north of Spanish Florida. Sir Walter Raleigh, as he was now called, named this territory Virginia. He soon began preparations for a second expedition to Roanoke.

**An outpost is built on Roanoke.** In April 1585 Raleigh sent 7 ships and about 600 soldiers to establish the first English settlement in America. It was late July before the English reached Roanoke. Supplies were running low by then, and most of the group stayed only a few weeks on the island. They sailed back to England in August, leaving behind 107 men to establish the colony.

These settlers lived on Roanoke for nearly a year. They built a small fort with cottages outside its walls. From this base they explored the coast of present-day North Carolina. Eventually, however, they returned to England because of food shortages and trouble with the Native Americans and the Spanish.

**John White leads another colonization attempt.** The original settlement on Roanoke had been little more than a military post. When it failed, John White, a talented artist, convinced Sir Walter Raleigh to try a different approach. White's idea was to attract settlers who would bring their families with them and invest some of their own money in the colony. Each settler would receive 500 acres (200 hectares) of land and some voice in the government.

In spring 1587 White set sail with his daughter, his son-in-law, and about 120 other men, women, and children. When the group reached Roanoke, they quickly started

# CAUSES and EFFECTS

# European Exploration ★ ★ ★

Renaissance encourages new ideas

Crusades increase trade with Asia

Strong nations emerge

Merchant class develops

## CONTRIBUTING CAUSES

Europeans seek gold, glory, and land

Nations compete for new trade routes

Inventions make sailing safer

Catholic Church wants to spread beliefs

## MAIN CAUSES

## EXPLORATION

## EFFECTS

Two continents are discovered

Colonies are established

A water route to Asia is found

Colonial trade enriches Europe

Spain becomes most powerful nation

## LONG-TERM EFFECTS

New tools and techniques come to Americas

Slave trade increases

England develops powerful navy

Indians lose lands, and wealth

repairing the cottages left by the earlier settlers. It was clear, however, that more supplies would be needed to maintain the colony through the winter.

White was reluctant to leave the newly founded community. He now had a newborn granddaughter as well—Virginia Dare, the first English child born in America. The other Roanoke colonists, however, believed that White should make the trip back to England. He finally agreed and departed late in the summer of 1587.

**Roanoke becomes the "Lost Colony."** White was not able to return to Roanoke until 1590. Conflict between the English fleet and the Spanish Armada in 1588 put a stop to all other sea travel. When White finally did reach Roanoke again, he was shocked to discover that all the colonists had completely vanished. The only clues White found were the letters *CRO* carved on a tree and the word *CROATOAN* on a doorpost. White assumed that the settlers had gone to a neighboring island where friendly Croatoan Indians lived. Storms, however, kept him from reaching the Croatoans and forced his return to England. To this day there is no firm evidence of what really happened to the "Lost Colonists" of Roanoke Island.

## Learning from Early Experiments

John White lacked the funds to make another voyage to North America. Sir Walter Raleigh, meanwhile, lacked interest. The Roanoke colony had been a great financial loss for Raleigh rather than a source of profit. Yet in a broader sense the English did gain from the experience. Their failure to make a success of Roanoke taught them some useful lessons about founding colonies.

**England recognizes its mistakes.** Roanoke Island was chosen as the site of the first English colony largely for geographic reasons. The island was far enough south to have a relatively warm climate. Thus the Roanoke settlers would not have to face the bitter cold that had driven French settlers out of Newfoundland in the 1540's. It was hoped, too, that the climate would prove suitable for crops that could not be grown in England.

Though the weather was indeed mild, the colonists had overlooked a serious drawback to the island. Roanoke lacked a protected harbor where ships could safely anchor. The shallow coastal waters and shifting tides put ships in danger of running aground.

Choosing a poor location for their colony was not the only mistake the English made. Perhaps the most important reason for Roanoke's failure was the lack of enough people, funds, and supplies. Raleigh and his backers had underestimated the risks and hardships of building a settlement thousands of miles from Europe. Each time England sent colonists to Roanoke, first in 1585 and then in 1587, only about 100 people stayed. With limited food and tools, they were ill-prepared to face dangers: enemy attacks, violent storms, food shortages. The English soon realized that if American colonies were to thrive, better planning was necessary.

**Interest in America remains strong.** In spite of Roanoke's failure, many people in England continued to support the idea of founding colonies. English merchants who had profited from whaling, fur trading, and other businesses were seeking new ways to make money. Many of them had gained a favorable impression about economic opportunities in America from reading the works of Richard Hakluyt (HAK-loot).

Hakluyt had written a long article in 1584 explaining how England could benefit from American colonies. He also published several huge volumes containing the letters and records of explorers from all over Europe. As Hakluyt reported, these early explorers found the Americas bursting with resources:

> They found there gold, silver, copper, lead, and pearls in abundance; precious stones, as turquoises and emeralds; spices . . . as pepper, cinnamon, cloves; . . . silk worms, fairer than ours of Europe; white and red cotton; . . . all kinds of beasts; . . . all kinds of fowls for food and feathers; . . . excellent vines in many places for wines; the soil apt to bear olives for oil; all kinds of fruits, as oranges, almonds, . . . figs, plums; . . . all kind of [fragrant] trees and date trees, cypresses, cedars . . . and exceeding quantity of all kind of precious furs . . . oil to make soap, and . . . fish.

Lacking funds from the royal treasury, English merchants and shipbuilders formed joint-stock companies to pay for voyages to North America. Investors in the company shared the costs and the profits of trading with the English colonies.

**Merchant interest in North America builds.** Merchants who read Hakluyt's reports believed that America offered valuable trade opportunities. Of course the settlers who had gone to Roanoke had not discovered precious jewels or spices. They had not succeeded in growing some of the crops they desired, such as bananas, pineapples, and sugar cane. However, grapes flourished, and hemp, rice, and cotton seemed promising. In addition, the forests of America were clearly valuable. Fine woods could be shipped to England and made into furniture. The sap from trees could also be sold profitably for use in making ink and medicines.

English merchants became a powerful force in encouraging settlement of America. In Spain most of the enthusiasm and funding for colonies had come from the Crown. In England, too, the monarchs were interested in planting colonies. However, they usually lacked the money to do so. They could not persuade **Parliament,** England's law-making body, to support such risky projects with government funds.

**The English find a way to pay for colonies.** Voyages of exploration and colonization cost a great deal. Ships had to be fitted out with sails, navigation tools, supplies for the voyage, and other items the colonists would need to build settlements. If these ships sank or were captured, the losses would be great. Rarely could any one person afford such risks. As a result, English people looked for a way to share the costs of establishing colonies.

The solution that business owners and merchants found was to start **joint-stock companies.** These were trading companies backed by **investors** —people who put money into a project in order to earn profits. Each investor received **shares of stock** in the company—equal parts in owning it. Thus the investors jointly accepted the risks of starting a colony. They would split any profits they made and divide any losses they suffered.

**The monarch grants charters.** To encourage colonization further, the English Crown decided to grant **charters.** A charter is a paper giving certain rights to a person or group. Charters for colonization meant that the English government officially recognized the colony as legal. Such charters were often granted to joint-stock companies. Some charters were also given to rich nobles who were friends of the monarch. These nobles, who used their own money to start colonies, were called **proprietors.**

**The colonies attract settlers.** Both proprietors and trading companies needed men and women willing to make the dangerous and long voyage to America. They posted advertisements for settlers in public places. Many English men and women responded to these advertisements.

Colonists were expected to pay for their passage to America and their supplies. However, this did not mean that only the rich could make the trip. Merchants and proprietors developed a system to help ordinary people settle in America even if they had little money. Such men and women could become **indentured servants.** Indentured servants were workers who sold their labor in exchange for passage to the colonies in America.

Indentured servants agreed to work for a colonist for a certain length of time, usually four to seven years. Although they received no wages during this period, indentured servants were not slaves. When they had served the agreed-upon time, they could leave their employer to take up land or a trade of their own. For thousands of people, becoming an indentured servant was the only way to get to the Americas.

Beginning in the early 1600's, England successfully planted colonies in Virginia, New England, Bermuda, and the British West Indies. As these early English colonies prospered, it became easier for the joint-stock companies and proprietors to attract more settlers.

## SECTION REVIEW

1. **Vocabulary**  joint-stock company, investor, shares of stock, charter, proprietor, indentured servant
2. **People and Places**  Humphrey Gilbert, Walter Raleigh, Roanoke Island, Virginia, John White, Virginia Dare, the "Lost Colony," Richard Hakluyt
3. **Comprehension**  What factors contributed to Gilbert's and Raleigh's failure to establish colonies?
4. **Comprehension**  Did poor people have an opportunity to settle in America? Explain your answer.
5. **Critical Thinking**  Do you think English monarchs appreciated or resented merchant involvement in colonization? Explain your answer.

# Chapter 3 Summary

In the 1500's Spain ruled a huge empire in the Americas. The Spaniards who came to these lands, called New Spain and Peru, established a new way of life. Priests built missions where they taught Indians the Catholic faith. Spaniards in the upper classes owned haciendas, ranchos, and mines. The Native Americans and blacks were laborers and slaves who often suffered mistreatment.

Spain profited greatly from the rich resources of the Americas. To support its empire, Spain built a huge fleet of warships and strictly controlled colonial trade according to the principles of mercantilism. Other European nations resented Spain's power and envied its wealth. Thus England, France, and Holland began illegally trading with Spanish America, raiding Spanish treasure ships, and taking over land in the Americas. England's defeat of the Invincible Armada in 1588 greatly weakened Spain.

England failed in its early attempts to found colonies in Newfoundland and on Roanoke Island. To pay for new colonizing expeditions, investors pooled their money and formed joint-stock companies. Rich proprietors also founded colonies with their personal funds. The English Crown supported settlement efforts by granting charters that legally recognized colonies. Finally, ordinary people were given the opportunity to go to America as indentured servants.

## CRITICAL THINKING: Understanding Chronology

To understand the events of the past, it is necessary to understand **chronology**—the arrangement of events in time. Sometimes a history book will tell you the exact day or year that an event took place. At other times, certain "clue words" help you understand when things happened. Words such as *before*, *after*, and *meanwhile* indicate the order of events. The words *decade* and *century* describe a period of time.

A decade is a period of 10 years. For example, the years 1540 through 1549 make up the decade of the 1540's (read as "fifteen-forties"). A century is a period of 100 years. Most of the events described in this chapter took place in one century, the 1500's. The 1500's are sometimes called the sixteenth century. (See the table below.)

| Years | Century |
|-------|---------|
| 1–100 | First century |
| 101–200 | Second century |
| 201–300 | Third century |
| 1801–1900 | Nineteenth century |
| 1901–2000 | Twentieth century |

One way to show the chronology of events is to place them on a time line. In this book, time lines appear at the beginning of each unit and chapter. The time line below includes some important events in England's exploration of the Americas. Study the time line carefully, and then answer the following questions on a separate sheet of paper.

1. In what century did the events on the time line take place?
2. What event took place in 1588?
3. Who set sail first—Gilbert or Drake?
4. How many years passed between John White's two trips to Roanoke?
5. Did settlement on Roanoke begin before or after the defeat of the Armada?
6. Copy the time line onto your paper. Then indicate the appropriate place for each event listed below.
   a. Drake completes his voyage around the world in 1580.
   b. Sir Walter Raleigh sponsors the first expedition to Roanoke in 1584.
   c. Virginia Dare is born in 1587.

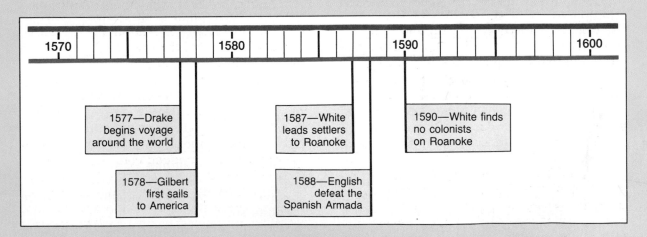

1570    1580    1590    1600

1577—Drake begins voyage around the world

1578—Gilbert first sails to America

1587—White leads settlers to Roanoke

1588—English defeat the Spanish Armada

1590—White finds no colonists on Roanoke

# Chapter 3 REVIEW

## Vocabulary and Key Terms

Use one of the following terms to replace each underlined phrase in the sentences below. Write your answers on a separate sheet of paper.

haciendas
Invincible Armada
joint-stock companies
missions
Parliament

*peninsulares*
raw materials
sea dogs
shares of stock
viceroys

1. The colonial governors of New Spain and Peru were Spaniards born in Spain.
2. Many Native Americans worked on large farming estates or at Catholic religious settlements.
3. Spain's colonies provided resources that could be used to make other goods.
4. English pirate captains helped defeat Spain's unbeatable fleet.
5. England's law-making body would not grant funds to start colonies.
6. English merchants bought equal parts of ownership in trading organizations.

## Recalling the Facts

1. What areas made up New Spain and Peru?
2. What role did priests play in Spanish America?
3. What controls did mercantilism place on the Spanish colonies?
4. How did Francis Drake anger the king of Spain?
5. What resulted from the battle between the Spanish Armada and the English fleet?
6. What did the English learn from their failures to build a colony at Roanoke?
7. How did joint-stock companies reduce the risk of starting colonies?
8. Why did some people come to America as indentured servants?

## Places to Locate

Match the letters on the map with the places listed below. Write your answers on a separate sheet of paper.

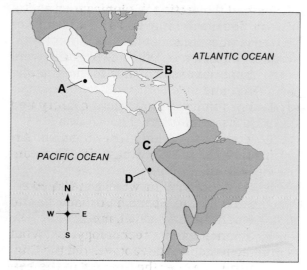

1. New Spain
2. Peru
3. Mexico City
4. Lima

## Critical Thinking

1. How successful was Spain in building and maintaining a large empire? Consider the following points in your answer:
   a. Spain's success in meeting its economic goals
   b. Spain's success in meeting its religious goals
   c. Spain's success in defending its empire against rivals
2. Give three examples of ways in which Spanish American colonists ignored Spanish laws. Why might they have done so?
3. Do you think Queen Elizabeth I of England was right to encourage the sea dogs' activities? Explain.

## Understanding History

1. Reread the section "Work is linked to social class" on page 50. Then answer these questions.
   a. **Culture.** In general, what factors determined the classes of people in Spanish America?
   b. **Culture.** Do you think people could move easily from one class to another? Why or why not?
2. Reread the section "Colonies play a vital role in trade" on page 54. Then answer these questions.
   a. **Economics.** What two goals were most important under the mercantile system?
   b. **Economics.** How was a country tied to its colonies by mercantilism?
3. Reread the section "The Spanish Armada is defeated" on page 58. Then answer these questions.
   a. **Geography.** In what general direction did the Spanish Armada sail to reach the English Channel?
   b. **Science and Technology.** What technological advantages did the English have over the Spanish in the battle with the Spanish Armada?
4. Reread the section "Interest in America remains strong" on page 62. Then answer these questions.
   a. **Economics.** Why were English merchants interested in colonies in North America?
   b. **Primary Sources.** What sources of food did Hakluyt say were available in the Americas?

## Projects and Activities

1. **Reviewing Information.** Make flash cards to quiz classmates on the vocabulary words and key terms in the chapter.
2. **Identifying Cause and Effect.** Imagine that you are an English or a Spanish sailor during the battle with the Spanish Armada in 1588. Explain the reasons that you are fighting and describe what might happen if you win and if you lose.

3. **Making a Map.** Use an outline map of the world to show Sir Francis Drake's route between 1577 and 1580. Find out where he stopped and label these places on the map, giving the dates of his visits.
4. **Writing a Report.** Find out more about the Spanish missions in America in the 1600's. Write a report that describes daily life at a mission. Illustrate your report with a diagram of the mission.
5. **Creating an Advertisement.** Imagine that you are an English proprietor trying to found an American colony in the early 1600's. Write and illustrate an advertisement to convince people to come to your colony.

## Practicing Your Skill

The time line below shows some important events during the height of the Spanish American empire. Use the time line to answer the questions that follow. Write your answers on a separate sheet of paper.

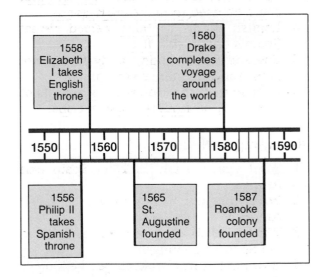

1. How many complete decades are included in the time line?
2. In what year did Drake's voyage end? What decade? What century?
3. Which monarch came to power first—Elizabeth I or Philip II?
4. How many years passed between the founding of St. Augustine and the founding of the Roanoke colony?

# UNIT 1 REVIEW

## Unit Summary

★ **Europeans, seeking new routes to Asia, found the Americas.**

- Native Americans developed many cultures, including Aztec and Inca civilizations.
- The Crusades led to European demand for trade with Asia.
- Many Europeans, blocked by the Italian monopoly of Asian trade, looked for new routes to the East.
- Portuguese sailors found a water route around Africa to India.
- Columbus, trying to reach Asia by traveling west, landed in the Americas in 1492.

★ **Following Columbus, other Europeans explored new lands.**

- Magellan sailed around South America and circled the globe.
- The French and English explored North America for a route to Asia.
- Cortés and Pizarro conquered the Aztec and Inca empires, bringing great wealth to Spain.
- In North America, Spaniards explored lands from Florida to California.

★ **Other European nations challenged Spain's empire.**

- English, French, and Dutch pirates raided Spanish ships and violated trade laws.
- Spain's sea power was broken by England's defeat of the Armada.
- The first English attempts to colonize North America failed.
- Joint-stock companies set the stage for new English colonies.

## Understanding Chronology

Study the Unit 1 time line on the page opposite page 1. Then answer the following questions on a separate sheet of paper.

1. How many centuries are included between A.D. 700 and A.D. 1600?
2. In which centuries did most exploration occur?
3. In which centuries were the Americas explored?
4. For about how many years did Spain lead Europe in exploration?
5. What event before 1492 would you add to the time line? Why?

## Writing About History

1. **Comparing Ideas.** Write two paragraphs comparing European and Native American beliefs about nature and land ownership. Then explain how their different ideas led to conflict between the two groups.
2. **Creating a Journal.** Imagine you are a member of Magellan's crew. Write entries for a journal and describe your voyage that circled the globe. Include your feelings about the experience.
3. **Writing a Newspaper Article.** Write a newspaper account of the Spanish Armada's defeat. Explain the Armada's fame and then describe the battle and its background. Include an appropriate headline.
4. **Developing a Story.** Write a story about a young colonist who leaves England and settles in North America. Describe the differences between life in England and life in the colony. Include a description of the geography.
5. **Preparing a Speech.** Write a speech that Henry Hudson might have given when he and his son were forced off their ship. Try to persuade the crew to spare you.

SOME DAY, SON...
NONE OF THIS
WILL BE YOURS.

**6. Interpreting a Cartoon.** Write a paragraph describing the point of view of the cartoon above. Then write a paragraph describing the opposite view.

## Projects

**1. Organizing Information.** Make a chart comparing Native American lifestyles in different cultures. Give the geographic area for each culture and include information about how each group acquired its food, clothing, and shelter.

**2. Making Models.** Work in small groups to make models of different kinds of shelters used by Native Americans. Use materials that show how each kind of shelter reflected its environment.

**3. Preparing a Report.** Do research on advances and discoveries made during the Renaissance. Explain how the compass and astrolabe aided navigation and describe how the invention of printing led to the Age of Discovery.

**4. Organizing a Class Project.** Hold a fiesta to honor Hispanic influences in our country. Include Hispanic foods and music. Prepare posters or presentations that show Hispanic influence on our language, place names, and architecture. Invite others to share in the celebration.

**5. Researching Facts.** Find information on Sir Francis Drake and the sea dogs. Explain Drake's background and how he became a pirate. Describe the ships used by the sea dogs and how they defeated the Spanish Armada.

**6. Presenting a Play.** Prepare a class play about the lost colony of Roanoke. Base the play on the historical facts of the story. Write dialogue for the characters. Prepare scenery and costumes. Present the play for other classes.

## Finding Out More

Amon, Aline. *The Earth Is Sore: Native Americans on Nature.* Atheneum, 1981. Indian songs and poetry have been adapted to depict the Native Americans' love of nature.

Beck, Barbara L. *The Incas.* Watts, 1983. Using archeological and historical resources, the author traces the rise and fall of the Incas from prehistory through the Spanish conquest.

Goodnough, David. *Christopher Columbus.* Troll, 1979. This book traces the life of Columbus from boyhood until he became the Admiral of the Ocean Seas.

Hogan, Paula Z. *The Compass.* Walker, 1982. This story of an invention that changed history also includes directions on constructing and testing homemade instruments.

Irwin, Constance. *Strange Footprints on the Land.* Harper, 1980. An investigation presents evidence that the Vikings preceded Columbus to America.

Karen, Ruth. *Feathered Serpent: The Rise and Fall of the Aztecs.* Four Winds, 1979. This survey of the Aztec civilization includes quotes from primary sources.

Le Sueur, Meridel. *Conquistadores.* Watts, 1973. This easy-to-read book covers the explorations of the Spaniards Columbus, Cortés, Pizarro, Cabeza de Vaca, and Coronado.

O'Dell, Scott. *The Captive.* Houghton Mifflin, 1979. A young missionary travels to Central America as part of a Spanish expedition where he poses as the reincarnation of a Mayan deity.

Tunis, Edwin. *Indians.* Crowell, 1979. Native American creativity in meeting basic needs is explored as the author studies nine North American groups before their first encounter with white settlers.

# UNIT 2 COLONIAL SETTLEMENT 1607–1763

40,000 B.C.     A.D. 1000     1100     1200     1300     1400

The Pilgrims of Plymouth Colony make their way to church through the wilderness. George Henry Boughton painted this scene in the mid-1800's.

1607 – 1763

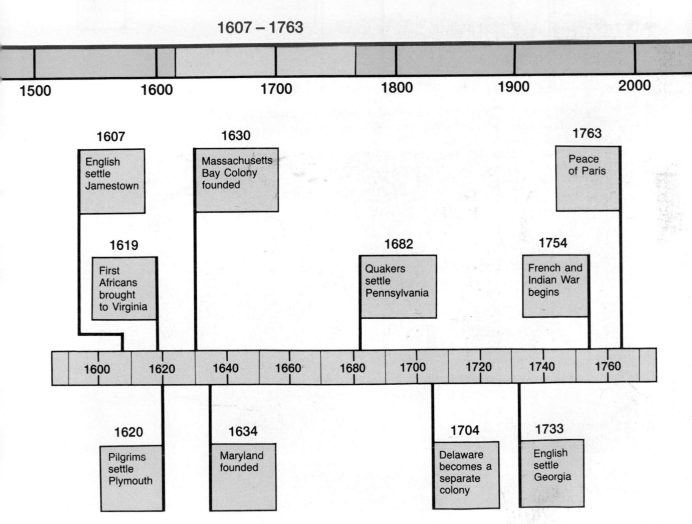

1500    1600    1700    1800    1900    2000

**1607** English settle Jamestown

**1630** Massachusetts Bay Colony founded

**1763** Peace of Paris

**1619** First Africans brought to Virginia

**1682** Quakers settle Pennsylvania

**1754** French and Indian War begins

1600   1620   1640   1660   1680   1700   1720   1740   1760

**1620** Pilgrims settle Plymouth

**1634** Maryland founded

**1704** Delaware becomes a separate colony

**1733** English settle Georgia

# 4 English Colonies Thrive in North America 1607–1763

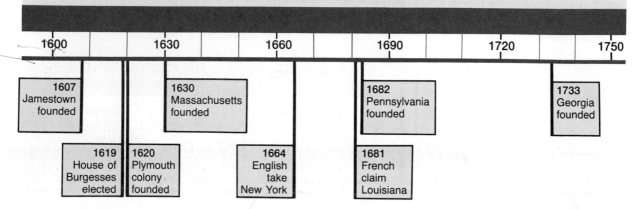

| 1600 | 1630 | 1660 | 1690 | 1720 | 1750 |

1607
Jamestown
founded

1630
Massachusetts
founded

1682
Pennsylvania
founded

1733
Georgia
founded

1619
House of
Burgesses
elected

1620
Plymouth
colony
founded

1664
English
take
New York

1681
French
claim
Louisiana

In 1620 the *Mayflower,* covered with ice in W.F. Halsall's 1882 painting, brought the Pilgrims to the shore of North America.

## Preparing to Read

In 1607 England launched its first successful colony in North America. In the next 125 years, 12 more English colonies took root along the Atlantic coastal plain. These settlements proved to be highly successful. The colonial population grew rapidly as each year ships brought thousands of new people from Europe and Africa. As the English colonies expanded, they took over smaller Dutch and Swedish settlements. In time the colonies pushed westward, away from the Atlantic toward lands that were claimed by Native Americans, the French, and the Spanish. The conflicting claims often led to war. As you read this chapter, try to answer the following questions:

1. Why did people come to live in the English colonies?
2. Why did the Jamestown and Plymouth settlements succeed?
3. How were other English colonies founded?
4. What challenges did the English face on their frontiers?

# 1 Why did people come to live in the English colonies?

## Vocabulary
game
dissent
persecute
confiscate
divine right

The English settlers who came to America in the 1600's took great risks. First they had to make a dangerous ocean crossing in small, uncomfortable ships. When they arrived in America, they faced hunger, cold, and the dangers of life in an unknown wilderness. In spite of these risks, thousands of English men and women left England to settle in America. They were willing to take the chance because America offered them the opportunity for a better life.

## Opportunities in America

Most English colonists came to America seeking new opportunities. They hoped to own their own land, to earn a better living, and to escape the crowded cities of England.

**Many English people lack the chance to own land.** In the early 1600's many men and women in England had no chance to own land. Most property belonged to nobles, who handed it down to their oldest sons. The ordinary farmers rented their homes and fields from the noble landowners.

In the late 1500's the demand for woolen cloth rose sharply. Many nobles discovered they could make more money raising sheep and selling the wool. The nobles fenced off much of their property and turned it into pastures for herds of sheep. This was known as the **enclosure movement.**

Only a few workers were needed to tend the large flocks that grazed where many farmers had once lived and worked. As a result, thousands of farmers lost their homes and jobs. Some found work in towns. Many landless families were forced to wander about looking for work. The English government treated such wanderers harshly.

**City life is unpleasant.** Many landless farmers moved to English cities hoping to find work and better living conditions. So

73

many people poured into London, the English capital, that the city's population grew from nearly 150,000 in 1595 to more than 330,000 about 40 years later. The cities were crowded, dirty, and unhealthy. Disease and hunger caused many people to die at an early age. Jobs and houses were scarce.

City dwellers heard the news of vast lands in America from explorers returning from their voyages. These exciting stories described rich forests, plentiful fish, and game —wild animals hunted for food. In the cities English merchants often put up posters advertising wonderful opportunities in America. To homeless people who had little chance of finding a job, the dangerous trip to America seemed worth the risk. America offered the hope of owning land and of enjoying a better life than in England.

## Desire for Religious Freedom

English people in the 1600's had many disagreements about religion. According to English law, all the people were to belong to the Church of England, sometimes called the **Anglican Church.** This church had broken away from the Roman Catholic Church in 1535. All English people were required to believe in the Church of England's teachings, to accept the English monarch as its head, and to give money for its support.

**Many people resist the Church of England.** Some English people wanted to remain members of the Roman Catholic Church. Catholics believed the Pope was the Church's true leader and that it was wrong to accept the English monarch as the head of the Church. They also disagreed with many of the teachings of the Anglican Church.

Other English people thought the Church of England was too much like the Catholic Church. They **dissented** from—disagreed with—the Church of England because they thought it was too elaborate and rich. These dissenters believed that religious services should be simplified.

Some dissenters remained in the Church of England. They tried to purify it by eliminating music, elaborate ceremonies, and the elegant dress of the priests. These people came to be called **Puritans.** The Puritans, however, did not agree among themselves. Some small groups broke away from the Puritans and from the Church of England. These groups, called **Separatists,** established new churches that were separate from the Church of England.

**English dissenters suffer mistreatment.** The English monarchs insisted that all their subjects belong to the Church of England. The Crown feared that religious disagreements, no matter how small, would cause disorder. As a result, the English rulers

In the early 1600's many Protestants left England because of religious persecution. This 1918 painting by Charles Shimmin shows a group of Separatists departing for Holland in 1608. In 1620 this same group sailed to America. (See page 79.)

## ECONOMICS • The Land

Throughout most of European history, owning land was considered a great source of wealth. As late as the 1500's, however, few people in Europe owned the land on which they lived and worked. Most land belonged to nobles or monarchs.

In the Americas, Europeans discovered millions of acres of unspoiled land. Ordinary men and women suddenly—perhaps for the first time in history—had the chance to own land. This opportunity became a key factor in the settlement of the English colonies. During the 1600's millions of people chose to cross the Atlantic to settle on property of their own. The private ownership of land by ordinary people, rather than by wealthy nobles, quickly became common.

**Unspoiled land**

**persecuted** —mistreated—people who refused to belong to the Church of England.

The Crown persecuted Catholics, Puritans, Separatists, and others during the late 1500's and 1600's. Dissenters who held their own religious services risked jail. The government sometimes **confiscated** —took away—dissenters' belongings. In some cases, the English courts sentenced dissenters to death. Thus many English dissenters looked to America as a place where they could worship freely.

People in other European countries also suffered for their religious beliefs. French Protestants, or **Huguenots** (HYOO-guh-nots), suffered in Catholic France. Protestants and Jews could not live safely in Catholic Spain and Portugal. In other Protestant countries, Catholics were persecuted. Many European dissenters hoped to find religious freedom in America.

### A Greater Voice in Government

English citizens in the 1600's had more voice in government than people in most European countries. Some English men and women, however, were dissatisfied with their government and felt their rights were threatened.

**English monarchs claim great powers.** England was ruled by monarchs, but these monarchs did not have power to do whatever they wished. They were expected to share power with Parliament. James I, who became king in 1603, claimed that he ruled by **divine right** —authority given to monarchs by God. James I, and later his son Charles I, believed that subjects should obey without question. These monarchs ignored Parliament, collected harsh taxes, and limited religious freedom.

Many English citizens resented the monarchs' highhanded ways. These people looked to America as a place to live with little interference from the monarch.

**Africans come to America against their will.** Most people who moved to America chose to come because they hoped for better lives. Africans were the only group of people forced to come to the colonies. Dutch vessels brought the first blacks to the English colonies in the early 1600's. These blacks became indentured servants and were able to

In 1619 the Dutch brought 20 Africans to Virginia and sold them to the English colonists as indentured servants. By 1640, however, colonists often denied blacks their freedom. In 1662 Virginia passed a law recognizing slavery.

gain their freedom. Before long, however, white colonists treated Africans as slaves and forced them to work for life.

As the English colonies grew in the 1600's and 1700's, settlers began to buy more slaves. The cruel slave trade brought thousands of Africans to the colonies. The Africans suffered terribly during the **Middle Passage,** the long voyage across the Atlantic. To carry more slaves, ship captains crowded the men and women into tiny spaces. The Africans were chained together so they could not rebel or jump ship. Poor food and filthy conditions caused as many as half the slaves to die during the voyage.

Slaves helped the colonies grow. They worked the fields, tended farm animals, and did household chores. Cut off from their way of life in Africa, the slaves quickly learned to survive in a new environment. Yet they did not willingly accept their lot. They longed for the freedom and opportunities that America offered others.

## SECTION REVIEW

1. **Vocabulary** game, dissent, persecute, confiscate, divine right
2. **People and Places** Puritans, Separatists, Huguenots
3. **Comprehension** What happened to English farmers when landowners fenced off land for pastures?
4. **Comprehension** In what ways were Puritans and Separatists alike and different?
5. **Critical Thinking** What factors did an English settler have to consider before deciding to come to America?

# 2 Why did the Jamestown and Plymouth settlements succeed?

## Vocabulary
representative
representative government

In the early 1600's English people established two successful colonies in North America. At first, life in these colonies was bitterly hard. Hundreds of settlers died from disease, hunger, and cold. Eventually the colonies survived and prospered as the settlers learned how to manage life in their new surroundings.

### Jamestown

In April 1607 about 100 men aboard 3 small ships, the *Discovery,* the *Susan Constant,* and the *Godspeed,* sighted the coast of North America. Reaching Chesapeake Bay, between present-day Virginia and Maryland, they found the mouth of a wide river. After a few days of exploring, they chose a spot to build a village. The settlers had reached Virginia, a huge land grant given to the **London Company.** The London Company was a joint-stock company formed to develop trade in America.

King James I of England had granted the company a charter to settle Virginia and search for gold and silver. In honor of the king, the colonists named the river the James and their village Jamestown. (See map on page 86.)

**The colonists face many problems.** From the start the Jamestown settlers endured hardships. The site of the settlement was swampy and filled with mosquitoes. Many colonists fell sick from drinking the bad river water. The settlers also feared the nearby Indians, who were well-organized and powerful.

About 36 of the settlers considered themselves too good to work with their hands. They spent their time searching for gold instead of raising food and building shelter.

Problems in the settlement grew as the food supply ran out. By autumn of the first year, two thirds of the Jamestown settlers had died. The struggling settlement would have failed without the leadership of Captain John Smith. Smith directed the building of defenses to make sure the colony could protect itself. He solved the food shortage by

Captain John Smith guided the Jamestown settlement through its first difficult years. How does this portrait suggest that Smith was a strong leader?

persuading the Indians to trade corn to the colonists. To ensure that all the settlers would work for the colony's survival, he set a rule of "no work, no food." Unfortunately, after being badly burned in a gunpowder explosion, Smith returned to England in 1609. He never came back to Virginia.

Conditions worsened in Jamestown after Smith's departure. There was so little food during the winter of 1609 to 1610 that the colonists later called it the "starving time." When spring came, the weak survivors planned to return to England. Just as they reached the mouth of the James River, they met ships bringing supplies and more colonists. Greatly encouraged, the colonists returned to the settlement.

**Jamestown grows stronger.** After the "starving time" Jamestown began to prosper. The new settlers who came were skilled in carpentry and trades and helped the colony grow. In 1619 a shipload of women arrived, and many of the men of the colony married and started homes and families.

One of the settlers, John Rolfe, married an Indian woman named Pocahontas. She was the daughter of a chief, and the marriage led to peace with the Indians.

In 1607 Jamestown was settled as England's first permanent colony in North America. With its three walls, James Fort was easier for the small group of colonists to defend than a fort with four walls. What provisions did the colonists have for defense?

An important step toward Jamestown's success came when the colonists began to grow tobacco. John Rolfe had learned how to produce good-quality tobacco that quickly became popular in England. King James I disliked tobacco and called it a "scurvy weed." Despite the king's objections, great amounts of tobacco were sent to England—more than 2,200 pounds (1,000 kilograms) annually by 1620. The profits from tobacco sales led to rapid growth. Jamestown thus became the first successful settlement in the colony of Virginia.

Tobacco farming created a demand for more workers in Jamestown. Many indentured servants came from England to labor in the tobacco fields, but still more help was needed. When the settlers tried to use Native Americans as workers, the Indians ran off into the forests. In 1619 a Dutch ship brought about 20 Africans to Jamestown, where they became indentured servants. They were the first blacks to settle in the English colonies. Before long, many more Africans were brought to Jamestown to provide labor for tobacco growers.

**The colonists gain a voice in their government.** As a settlement of the London Company, Jamestown was first ruled by officials of the company. In 1619, however, the company allowed the Virginia settlers to choose **representatives.** Representatives are people selected to speak for others in matters of government. The Virginia representatives met in a group called the **House of Burgesses.** By 1625 the House of Burgesses made most of the governmental decisions in Virginia. The creation of the House of Burgesses marked the beginning in America of **representative government** —government in which people choose those who make laws and decisions. In just a few years after the English colonists first landed in America, they had begun to govern themselves.

## Plymouth Colony

In 1607, the same year the first settlers landed at Jamestown, another group of English people moved to the city of Leiden in Holland. These people were called **Pilgrims.**

Pocahontas, a Powhatan princess, married James Rolfe, a Jamestown settler. In 1616 she and Rolfe sailed to England.

A pilgrim is a person who goes on a journey for a religious purpose. These Pilgrims were Separatists, and they hoped to worship freely in Holland.

The Pilgrims lived and worshipped in Leiden for several years, but they were not happy in their new home. They had trouble finding work and their children began to speak Dutch instead of English. They decided to make a new start in America, working the land and keeping alive their English traditions.

**The Pilgrims sail to America.** The Pilgrims' leaders returned to England to make plans for the voyage to America. They received a charter from the London Company, which agreed to furnish a ship and supplies. In return the Pilgrims became indentured servants, agreeing to work for the company for 7 years. In September 1620 about 35 Pilgrims and 66 other colonists set sail for Virginia aboard a small ship, the *Mayflower*.

# ★ ★ ★ *Corporations*

In 1629 wealthy English Puritans formed the Massachusetts Bay Company. The Company obtained a charter from King Charles I to start a colony in America. The company then sold shares of stock to raise money for ships and supplies. By 1630 the company had settled in Massachusetts Bay and was in business. The Puritans brought their charter with them, so their company became the first American **corporation.**

Today corporations are a common form of business organization in America. They operate in almost the same way the Massachusetts Bay Company did more than 350 years ago.

A corporation obtains a charter, or license to operate, from a state government. A corporation sells shares of stock to raise money. It uses the money to buy supplies and hire workers, and it shares its profits with the people who bought stock.

---

A winter storm blew the *Mayflower* far north of its destination. In November the *Mayflower* landed at Cape Cod, in present-day Massachusetts. Rather than attempt to sail south in the rough Atlantic, the Pilgrims decided to stay where they were. This area was not part of the London Company's land grant, however, so the Pilgrims' charter did not apply. As a result, the Pilgrims created a plan for managing their affairs.

**The Pilgrims plan their government.** Before going ashore the leaders met in the cabin of the *Mayflower.* They drew up the **Mayflower Compact,** an agreement to make laws for the benefit of the whole settlement. The Mayflower Compact was the start of self-government by the Pilgrims.

**Native Americans help the Pilgrims survive.** The Pilgrims named their new settlement **Plymouth,** after the town from which they set sail. It was December when the Pilgrims finally went ashore and too late to plant crops. As a result, they had to survive on the supplies left from the voyage and the game they hunted. Supplies quickly ran low. During their first terrible winter at Plymouth, more than half of the settlers died.

The Pilgrims refused to give up, and in the spring conditions improved. Samoset, an Indian who had learned some English, befriended the Pilgrims. He taught the settlers how to plant corn and how to trap animals for furs. Samoset brought Squanto, a Wampanoag (wahm-puh-NO-ahg) who also spoke English, to meet the Pilgrims. Squanto gave the Pilgrims good advice about catching fish and planting corn and vegetables. With the help of these Native Americans, the Pilgrims learned to hunt wild turkeys and deer. They also learned to harvest lobsters and clams from the sea.

**The Pilgrims celebrate the first Thanksgiving.** After their first harvest the Pilgrims set aside a day to celebrate their survival. They invited their Indian friends to share in a great feast that included food, games, and especially, prayers of thanks to God. This was the beginning of the Thanksgiving feast that Americans still celebrate.

The Plymouth settlement was guided by strong and fair leaders. Plymouth never grew large, but it was strong and successful. Plymouth's success encouraged other English people to settle new colonies.

## SECTION REVIEW

1. **Vocabulary**  representative, representative government
2. **People and Places**  Jamestown, John Smith, Pocahontas, John Rolfe, Pilgrims, Plymouth
3. **Comprehension**  How did John Smith help the Jamestown settlers survive?
4. **Comprehension**  What events led to the first Thanksgiving?
5. **Critical Thinking**  Why is the Mayflower Compact an important document in American history?

# 3 How were other English colonies founded?

Following the success of Jamestown and Plymouth, other colonies sprang up along the Atlantic coast of North America. Men and women from several countries and of many faiths settled in these new colonies.

## New England Colonies

Within a few decades after the settlement of Plymouth in 1620, several other colonies took root in New England. These settlements, like Plymouth, developed because people sought religious freedom.

**The Puritans found Massachusetts Bay Colony.** After Plymouth, the next New England settlement was the Massachusetts Bay Colony, founded by English Puritans in 1630. Like the Pilgrims, the Puritans came to America in search of religious freedom. They believed that they could build a new life and a better church in the North American wilderness.

Most of the Puritans were educated, middle-class people. Many Puritans belonged to a joint-stock company, called the Massachusetts Bay Company, that had been granted land and a charter by the Crown. The charter made the colony largely self-governing from the very start. Led by John Winthrop, the Puritans arrived in Massachusetts Bay in the spring of 1630 with a fleet of 17 ships. They started the village of Boston. More settlers followed, and by the end of the first summer, more than 1,000 Puritans had settled in Boston or nearby.

The Puritans' first year in the Massachusetts Bay Colony was difficult, but they quickly learned to farm the rocky soil of New England. In time many Massachusetts colonists turned to trade and industry for their livelihood. By 1640 more than 20,000 settlers had joined the Puritan settlement. Massachusetts Bay Colony became much larger and wealthier than the neighboring colony of Plymouth. In 1691 Massachusetts Bay received a new charter, which joined the two colonies under the name of Massachusetts.

Religion governed the Puritans' lives in many ways. The Puritans had strict rules of behavior, and the Puritan ministers had great power in the colony's government. The Puritans had come to America to worship in their own way, but they were unwilling to allow others the same right. Settlers who were not Puritans could live in the colony only if they obeyed Puritan rules and paid taxes to support the Puritan church.

**Rhode Island is founded.** Soon after Massachusetts Bay Colony was started, a young minister named Roger Williams began to preach ideas that displeased the Puritan leaders. Williams said that the English Crown had no right to give land to the Puritans. The land, he said, should be bought from the Indians. Williams also insisted that people should be able to worship God in their own way.

The Puritan leaders, angered by these ideas, decided to send Roger Williams back to England. Williams learned of their plans, and in 1636 he fled from Massachusetts Bay Colony. Helped by friendly Indians, Williams moved south until he reached the shores of Narragansett Bay. There he settled on the site of present-day Providence, Rhode Island. Soon other settlers fled Massachusetts and made their homes nearby. In 1644 Williams obtained a charter, and the area became the separate colony of Rhode Island.

Among the settlers who fled from Massachusetts Bay was Anne Hutchinson. She challenged the Puritan ministers by saying

# A MODEL OF CHRISTIAN CHARITY 1630

John Winthrop, a deeply religious man, led the Puritans to New England where they started the Massachusetts Bay Colony. As their ships sailed toward New England, Winthrop delivered a lecture reminding the Puritans of their religious ideals. He wanted the colony to be an example of Christian life for England and the rest of the world. Winthrop later became the first governor of the colony.

## Read to Find Out

1. What phrase does Winthrop use to show that the Puritans' colony would be an example for the rest of the world?
2. According to Winthrop, what will happen if the Puritans fail to do God's work in their colony?

---

. . .The Lord shall make us a praise and glory, so that men shall say of succeeding plantations: "The Lord make it like that of New England." For we must consider that we shall be like a City upon a Hill; the eyes of all people are on us.

If we deal falsely with our God in this work we have undertaken and so cause Him to withdraw His present help from us, we shall be made a story and a byword throughout the world; we shall open the mouths of enemies to speak evil of the ways of God and all believers in God; we shall shame the faces of many of God's worthy servants and cause their prayers to be turned into curses upon us, till we are driven out of the new land where we are going.

### John Winthrop

that personal religious experience was more important than formal religion and church attendance. Hutchinson was tried for her beliefs and forced to leave Massachusetts Bay in 1637. Anne Hutchinson, her family, and some of her followers fled to Rhode Island, where she founded the settlement of Portsmouth.

The Rhode Island settlers agreed that all people should have the right to worship in their own way. After Rhode Island became a separate colony, this right was made part of its charter. It was the first colony to guarantee religious freedom to all its people.

**Connecticut and New Hampshire are founded.** Other New England colonies were started by people who left Massachusetts

Bay Colony. Thomas Hooker, a minister, disagreed with the Puritan rule that only male church members could vote. He left Massachusetts in 1636 with a number of followers and founded the town of Hartford, Connecticut. Other Puritans had already moved into the area hoping to find better farmland. Soon the settlers built villages at Windsor, Wethersfield, and New Haven.

In 1639 the settlers from these towns joined together and wrote the **Fundamental Orders of Connecticut.** The Fundamental Orders established a government similar to that of Massachusetts. A chief difference, however, was that all adult men could vote. In 1662 Connecticut received a charter from the king and became a separate colony.

Several small settlements had been started north of Massachusetts Bay Colony by people from England. Adventurous colonists from Massachusetts Bay joined these settlements. These settlers had many disagreements about religious beliefs, however, and lacked unity. Finally in 1679 the English Crown made these settlements into the separate colony of New Hampshire.

Other northern settlements were made in Maine by people from the Massachusetts Bay Colony. Massachusetts's 1691 charter officially made Maine part of Massachusetts, and it remained so until 1820. (See map on page 86.)

## The Southern Colonies

While the New England colonies were growing, other settlements took root near the first southern colony of Virginia. These other colonies included Maryland, the Carolinas, and Georgia. Unlike the New England Colonies, however, they were started by proprietors who had been given grants of land by the English monarchs.

**English Catholics settle Maryland.** In the 1600's English Catholics were severely persecuted. Sir George Calvert, whose title was Lord Baltimore, was a devout Catholic and a friend of King Charles I. Lord Baltimore, who wished to provide a **refuge** — safe place—for Catholics, asked Charles I for land in America. Charles granted Baltimore 10 million acres (4 million hectares) north of Virginia. Lord Baltimore became the proprietor of the colony, but he died before it got started. His son, Cecilius Calvert, the second Lord Baltimore, continued his father's plans.

In 1634 two ships carrying English colonists landed near the mouth of the Potomac River. They founded a settlement called St. Marys on the rich land. The colony was named Maryland, in honor of Queen Henrietta Maria, the wife of Charles I. Maryland was open to people of all religious beliefs.

Maryland grew quickly as wealthy settlers established large estates with many workers. People with less money bought small farms. In a short time tobacco became the Maryland settlers' most important crop.

Anne Hutchinson was put on trial in Massachusetts because she disagreed with Puritan teachings. After the Puritans forced her to leave Massachusetts, she founded a settlement in Rhode Island dedicated to religious freedom.

Protestants in the colony soon outnumbered Catholics. In 1649, with the encouragement of Lord Baltimore, Maryland enacted the **Act of Toleration.** This law said that no Christian could be persecuted because of his or her beliefs. Although Jews and other non-Christians were not included, the Act of Toleration was an important step toward religious freedom in the colonies.

**North and South Carolina are established.** In 1663 King Charles II gave a huge stretch of land south of Virginia to eight nobles. The proprietors named their colony Carolina, a Latin form of *Charles*, in honor of the king. In 1670 the proprietors sent out colonists who founded Charles Town, present-day Charleston, South Carolina. Meanwhile, tobacco farmers from Virginia had moved south into present-day North Carolina. The settlements were far apart and the people had little contact with each other. As a result, in 1712 the English Crown divided the colony into two parts, North Carolina and South Carolina.

North Carolina, which included the Virginians' settlements, was made up of small farms. Tobacco became its most important crop. South Carolina included Charleston and other nearby settlements. South Carolina grew slowly at first, but expanded rapidly after many French Huguenots settled there in 1685. The rich soil and warm climate were ideal for growing rice. The fine harbor at Charleston became a center of trade with England and the West Indies.

**Social reformers found Georgia.** In 1732 King George II gave land south of the Carolinas to James Oglethorpe. The king hoped that a new colony in this region would prevent the Spanish from expanding north from Florida. Oglethorpe was a member of Parliament who wanted to **reform** — improve—living conditions for the poor people of England. In England, people were sent to prison for not paying their debts. Oglethorpe wanted a place where such people could start a new life. Oglethorpe set strict rules for the colony. Farms were limited to 50 acres (20 hectares), slavery was outlawed, and the sale of rum was forbidden.

In 1733 Oglethorpe brought about 100 settlers from England. They founded a village called Savannah, and named their colony Georgia, in honor of King George II. Other settlers came to Georgia from Ireland, Scotland, Italy, and Austria. A group of Portuguese Jews also settled there.

At first the colony grew slowly. Many settlers resented the strict rules. Later, after

In 1734 Pierre Fourdrinier made this sketch of Savannah for the planners of the Georgia colony. The planners used the sketch to attract settlers and investors. What features might encourage people to settle or to invest in the colony?

Governor Oglethorpe changed the rules and permitted large farms and slavery, the colony grew rapidly.

## The Middle Colonies

Between the New England Colonies and the Southern Colonies another group of settlements took shape. These settlements became known as the Middle Colonies. Not all these colonies were started by English people. New York and the Hudson River region were first settled by the Dutch. Delaware was first settled by Swedes.

**New Netherland becomes New York and New Jersey.** In the early 1620's, the Dutch started a settlement called New Amsterdam on the island of Manhattan, in present-day New York City. From there Dutch settlements spread up the Hudson River to Fort Orange. (See map on this page.) Later, Dutch control spread south to the Delaware River. The whole colony, called New Netherland, soon developed a brisk fur trade with the Indians. Other Dutch settlers became successful farmers.

In the 1660's New Amsterdam was ruled by Peter Stuyvesant (STY-vuh-suhnt), a hot-tempered governor who had lost a leg in a fight in the West Indies. Stuyvesant believed strict rule was necessary to ensure the colony's survival. He often punished law-breakers with heavy fines or whippings.

The English saw the prosperous Dutch colony as a problem. It separated New England from the southern English settlements. The English were also envious of New Amsterdam's fine harbor. Finally, rivalry between the English and the Dutch led to war in Europe. In 1664 English warships sailed into the harbor to take over the colony. Stuyvesant wanted to fight the English, but the people of New Amsterdam refused to support the strict governor. The colony surrendered without a fight.

King Charles II made his brother, the Duke of York, proprietor, and the colony was renamed New York in the duke's honor. The duke later divided the colony, giving the land east of the Delaware River to two English nobles, who named their colony New Jersey.

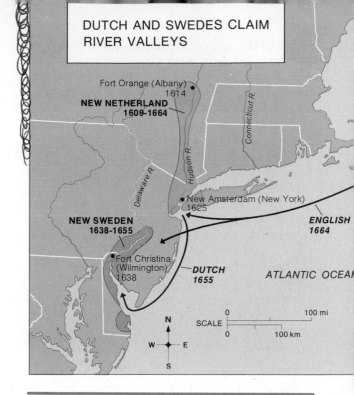

DUTCH AND SWEDES CLAIM RIVER VALLEYS

NEW NETHERLAND 1609-1664
Fort Orange (Albany) 1614
New Amsterdam (New York) 1625
NEW SWEDEN 1638-1655
ENGLISH 1664
Fort Christina (Wilmington) 1638
DUTCH 1655
ATLANTIC OCEAN
Delaware R.
Hudson R.
Connecticut R.
SCALE 0 100 mi / 0 100 km
N S E W

## Map Study
**The Dutch and Swedes first settled areas that later became English colonies. In what river valleys did the Swedes and the Dutch settle? In what year did the English seize all the Dutch lands? What name did the English give to the Dutch settlement of New Amsterdam?**

New Jersey was settled by people from many nations. English Puritans, French Protestants, Dutch, Swedes, Irish and Scots all prospered in the colony. The king granted New Jersey a charter that allowed religious freedom.

**Pennsylvania is a "Holy Experiment."** Pennsylvania was founded by William Penn, an English **Quaker.** Penn was the son of a wealthy admiral, but while at Oxford University, Penn became a Quaker. The Quakers believed that ministers and fancy church ceremonies were unnecessary. They refused to pay taxes to support the Church of England. They also believed that war was wrong, and they refused to take part in it.

The Quakers were one of the most bitterly persecuted religious groups in England. For a time, Penn was put in jail for his

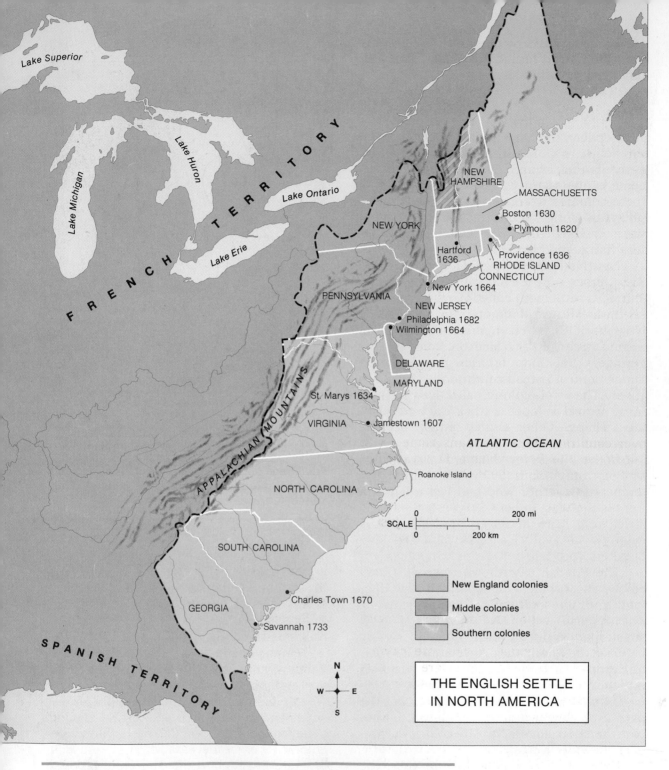

The English colonies extended along the coast of North America. The map shows colonial settlements and territories.

Lake Superior
Lake Michigan
Lake Huron
Lake Ontario
Lake Erie

FRENCH TERRITORY

NEW HAMPSHIRE
MASSACHUSETTS
Boston 1630
Plymouth 1620
NEW YORK
Hartford 1636
Providence 1636
RHODE ISLAND
CONNECTICUT
New York 1664
PENNSYLVANIA
NEW JERSEY
Philadelphia 1682
Wilmington 1664
DELAWARE
MARYLAND
St. Marys 1634
VIRGINIA
Jamestown 1607

ATLANTIC OCEAN

Roanoke Island

APPALACHIAN MOUNTAINS

NORTH CAROLINA

SCALE
0       200 mi
0       200 km

SOUTH CAROLINA

GEORGIA
Charles Town 1670
Savannah 1733

SPANISH TERRITORY

New England colonies
Middle colonies
Southern colonies

N
W   E
S

THE ENGLISH SETTLE
IN NORTH AMERICA

## Map Study

**The English colonies extended along the coast of North America.
What natural feature formed the the western boundary of the
colonies? What countries claimed land west of the English colonies?**

beliefs. After Penn was released, he planned to create a refuge where Quakers could live and worship peacefully.

Penn's father had loaned a large sum of money to King Charles II. After his father died, Penn asked the king to grant him land in America to cancel the debt. Charles II agreed, but insisted that the colony be named Pennsylvania, meaning Penn's woodlands, in honor of the admiral.

Penn's land grant was located west of the Delaware River between the present-day states of New York and Maryland. Penn's colony was to become a "Holy Experiment" in Christian living. In 1682 Penn arrived with a group of settlers to oversee the start of Philadelphia—the "City of Brotherly Love." Penn, like Roger Williams, paid the Native Americans for the land and insisted they be treated fairly. As a result, the colonists enjoyed peace with the Indians.

Penn welcomed people of all faiths to his colony. He wrote glowing pamphlets advertising for settlers. Many settlers were Germans who had been treated harshly in their own country. These Germans came to be known as the Pennsylvania Dutch. Other settlers came from Ireland, Scotland, France, and Holland.

Penn was a wise and fair proprietor, and his colony grew rapidly. By 1685, just 3 years after the colony's founding, the population had grown to about 9,000. Pennsylvania's farmers grew wheat, corn, and rye. Soon merchants were carrying on a busy trade with other colonies. By the late 1700's Philadelphia was the largest and busiest city in the English colonies.

**Delaware becomes a separate colony.** The area of present-day Delaware was first settled in 1638 by Swedes, who called it New Sweden. The Dutch of New Netherland took over New Sweden in 1655. Finally, after New Netherland became an English possession, the land belonged to the Duke of York.

Because Pennsylvania had no coastline, William Penn in 1682 obtained the coastal land of Delaware from the Duke of York. However, the people of Delaware did not want to be a part of Pennsylvania. In 1704, Delaware became a separate colony.

**William Penn believed in the teachings of the Society of Friends, a religious group whose members became known as Quakers. Penn founded Pennsylvania in 1682 as a haven for Quakers and others seeking religious freedom.**

## SECTION REVIEW

1. **Vocabulary**   refuge, reform
2. **People and Places**   New England Colonies, John Winthrop, Roger Williams, Anne Hutchinson, Thomas Hooker, Southern Colonies, Lord Baltimore, James Oglethorpe, Middle Colonies, New Amsterdam, William Penn, Quakers
3. **Comprehension**   What religious groups came to the English colonies seeking freedom of worship?
4. **Comprehension**   Why did the English want to take over the Dutch colony of New Netherland?
5. **Critical Thinking**   How successful were the English colonies in providing religious freedom for settlers?

# CRITICAL THINKING: Researching a Hypothesis

No history book can tell you everything about the events of the past. In your reading you will most likely find topics that you would like to **research**—gather more information about. To guide your research, it helps to have a **hypothesis** (hy-PAHTH-uh-sis). A hypothesis is a guess about what you think is probably true about your particular topic. As you learn more about your topic, you may find that this new information shows your hypothesis was correct. In other cases the new information may show that your hypothesis was mistaken. In that case, you may need to make another hypothesis based on your new findings.

## Making Your Hypothesis

On page 81 of this book, you learned that Roger Williams angered the Puritans by saying the colonists had no right to the land unless they paid the Indians for it. You might want to learn more about Puritan ideas about the rights of Indians to the land. This would be your research topic. To make a hypothesis, reread the first paragraph under "Rhode Island is founded" on page 81. What do you think the Puritans probably believed about Indians' rights to the land? On a separate sheet of paper, complete this sentence to form your hypothesis:

*The Puritans thought _____.*

## Researching Your Hypothesis

The library has several resources to help you find information about your topic. The **card catalog** provides three different cards for each factual, or **nonfiction,** book. One card is filed by the author's last name, one is filed by the book's title, and one is filed by

the book's subject. You may also find information in **encyclopedias** in the library's reference section. More information may be found in magazines, or **periodicals.** Magazine articles are listed in the *Reader's Guide to Periodical Literature.*

In researching your topic, you might find the paragraphs below in a book called *Old South Leaflets,* by the Puritan leader, John Winthrop. These paragraphs explain Winthrop's ideas about land rights in America. Read these paragraphs and then answer the questions that follow.

> ...There is a natural right and a civil right. The first right was natural, when men held the earth in common, every man sowing and feeding where he pleased. And then, as men and cattle increased, they took certain pieces of land by enclosing and occupying them. And this in time gave them a civil right. . . .
>
> The natives in New England enclose no land. They have no settled areas, and no tame cattle to improve the land by, and so have just a natural right to the land. If we leave them enough for their use, we may lawfully take the rest, there being more than enough for them and us.

1. What two kinds of rights does Winthrop say people can have to the land?
2. According to Winthrop, what gives people a civil right to the land?
3. What kind of right does Winthrop say the Indians have to the land?
4. Why, according to Winthrop, can the Puritans lawfully take the land from the Indians?
5. Was your hypothesis correct about what the Puritans thought about land rights? If not, write a new hypothesis based on the paragraphs you have just read.

# What challenges did the English face on their frontiers?

At first the English colonies were small villages along the Atlantic coast of North America. The colonists knew very little about the huge continent beyond their settlements. They did know, however, that Native Americans and European countries had claims to land in America. At times, the English colonists came into conflict with these other groups.

## Conflict with Native Americans

Most Native Americans had been friendly to the first English settlers and had helped them learn how to survive in the wilderness. The Indians, however, soon realized that the English settlers' way of life clashed sharply with their own. The Indians began to fight to protect their land, traditions, and customs.

**English settlements expand.** As the English colonies grew and prospered, the settlers spread out from the established communities to the **frontier** —the unsettled area at the edge of the wilderness. The men and women who venture to a frontier are sometimes called **pioneers** .

Pioneers moved to the frontier for a variety of reasons. Some were attracted by adventure and wanted to live without the rules of a settled community. Others were trappers who came seeking furs. Still other pioneers moved to the frontier because the land was cheap. Many indentured servants, for example, bought land on the frontier after they had worked off their debt.

**The Indians resist the spread of settlements.** The Native Americans depended on the game they hunted for food and clothing. They saw the pioneers taking over land for farms, cutting down the forests, and destroying game. As more and more pioneers moved to the frontier, Native Americans began to fight back. The colonists, determined to spread westward, continued to take the Native Americans' lands. Agreements between the Indians and the settlers were often broken. The settlers were suspicious of the Indians and viewed them as savages or **heathens** —unbelievers—because they did not accept Christianity or European customs and ideas.

Indian attacks posed an ever-present threat to frontier settlers. In the 1630's a series of battles occurred between the New England colonists and the Pequots. A group of Puritans, seeking revenge against the Indians, attacked a Pequot village in 1637. The colonists blocked the entrances to the village and burned it to the ground. Several hundred Pequot men, women, and children burned to death. In 1675 several New England Indian groups joined together to attack the English colonists. The Indians were led by the Wampanoag Chief Metacomet, known to the colonists as King Philip. In a series of attacks known as King Philip's War, the Indians destroyed about 25 settlements in Massachusetts Bay Colony, New Hampshire, and Maine. The colonists fought back savagely and eventually killed or drove west most of the New England Indians. The fighting continued for many years, and the bloodshed moved westward with the frontier.

## New France and New Spain

While English colonists were settling along the Atlantic coast of North America, French adventurers were exploring the interior west of the Appalachian Mountains. As a result the French claimed a huge territory

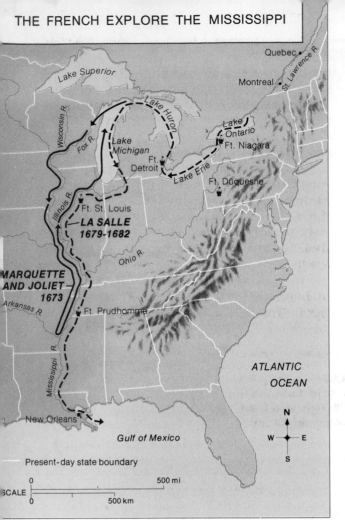

## Map Study

The French, looking for a water route to the Pacific Ocean, explored the interior of North America. In what body of water did La Salle's journey begin? In what body of water did it end? How did the French mark their claims to the Mississippi and Ohio valleys?

in North America, called New France. To the south of the English colonies lay part of the huge Spanish empire. In time the claims of both the French and the Spanish came to conflict with the rapid growth of the English colonies.

**The French develop friendships with the Native Americans.** The early French explorers had been friendly with the Indians and traded freely with them. French trap-

pers learned to live in the forest as the Indians did, and French missionaries converted some of the Indians to Christianity.

The population of New France grew slowly, in part because the French king strictly ruled the colony. The king allowed only Catholics to move to New France. In addition, the French Crown refused to allow any self-government and granted land only to nobles. These nobles were expected to bring settlers to the colony. Because ordinary settlers could not own land, however, few chose to move to New France. Thus farming never became widespread or profitable. Most French colonists preferred to earn their living by trapping and trading.

Many Native American groups were friendly with the French because the French traded with them and did not try to take away their land. Some Indians, especially the Hurons and Algonquins, became allies of the French. The Indians also helped the French explore the interior of the North American continent.

**The French explore the Ohio and Mississippi valleys.** Father Jacques Marquette (mahr-KET), a missionary priest, and the French explorer Louis Joliet (JO-lee-et) heard Indian tales of a "great water" that emptied into an even larger one. Marquette thought this might be the Northwest Passage that so many people had been seeking. In 1673 Joliet and Father Marquette set out to look for the Northwest Passage.

Marquette, Joliet, and five companions left Lake Michigan and paddled up the Fox River. They carried their canoes a short distance to the Wisconsin River and then floated down the Mississippi. At first they believed this might be the fabled Northwest Passage. They soon realized, however, that the river flowed southward and emptied into the Gulf of Mexico. Disappointed, Marquette and Joliet returned to Lake Michigan. (See map on this page.)

**La Salle reaches the mouth of the Mississippi.** Robert de La Salle was a noble who left France to explore the wilds of North America. After hearing the story of Marquette and Joliet's exploration, La Salle decided to find the mouth of the Mississippi.

In December 1681 La Salle set out with 23 French followers and 31 Indians. Traveling slowly by canoe across Lakes Erie, Huron, and Michigan, the explorers then dragged their canoes across the snow on sleds to the Illinois River. They then paddled the canoes down the Illinois and the Mississippi rivers and reached the Gulf of Mexico in April. La Salle claimed

> this country of Louisiana ... in the name of the most high, mighty ... and victorious Louis the Great, by Grace of God King of France....

La Salle defined Louisiana as the Mississippi River valley from the Great Lakes to the Gulf of Mexico.

**New France borders the English colonies.** The vast area claimed by France lay to the north and west of the English colonies. It included much of present-day Canada and stretched down the Mississippi to the Gulf of Mexico. Throughout the 1600's Quebec and Montreal were the only towns of any size in New France.

Quebec, built upon rocky bluffs high above the St. Lawrence River, was the first French town in New France. Settled about the same time as Jamestown, Quebec had only about 100 colonists in the 1630's. Montreal began as a fur-trading post in an Indian town.

In 1718 the French founded New Orleans in Louisiana near the mouth of the Mississippi. The French, however, were slow to

This 1869 painting by the German artist Wilhelm Lamprecht features Father Marquette, who explored the Mississippi Valley in search of a passage to Asia. Marquette is shown with Natchez Indians who lived in the present-day state of Mississippi. What information might the Native Americans be providing?

develop the area of Louisiana. By 1745 only 3,200 Europeans and 2,000 black slaves lived in a thin line of settlements along the lower Mississippi and the Gulf of Mexico.

**The French fear the growth of the English colonies.** Throughout the 1600's and early 1700's an important French goal was to keep the English settlements from spreading west. The French did not want to lose their land and the valuable fur trade to the English. To achieve their goal, the French gave their Indian allies guns and other weapons. The French also encouraged Indian attacks against the English settlers.

To protect their lands, the French built a chain of forts to the west of the English colonies. These forts stretched from New Orleans along the Mississippi River to Canada.

With the English frontier pushing westward, war between the English and French was only a matter of time.

**English and Spanish colonists come into conflict.** The English founded Georgia partly to prevent the Spanish from expanding north from Florida. The Spanish, however, claimed the region and were angered by the English settlement there. Disagreement led to war between the colonists in 1739. James Oglethorpe, the governor of Georgia, had become friendly with the Creek and the Cherokee who lived in the area. These Indian groups joined the English colonists in the fighting against the Spanish. Conflict with the Spanish continued for several years until a peace treaty was signed in 1748.

The American artist George Catlin painted this scene in the 1830's. The scene portrays a 1682 meeting in northern Louisiana between La Salle and the chief of the Taesna Indians. Catlin became famous for his portraits of Native Americans and their ways of life.

**The English colonies develop an independent spirit.** The English settlers, separated from their homeland by thousands of miles, quickly learned to solve problems themselves. After years of struggling to survive, the English colonies grew and prospered. Yet threats from various enemies remained. In time the English settlers developed **self-reliance** —confidence in their own abilities. This self-reliance helped the colonists thrive in the wilderness and hold off their enemies.

Self-reliance was a key reason why the 13 English colonies became more successful than the French and Spanish colonies. Because of this independent spirit, the English settlers boldly faced challenges. Instead of being weakened by their separation from England, the colonies grew stronger.

1. **Vocabulary**   frontier, pioneers, heathen, self-reliance
2. **People and Places**   Chief Metacomet, Father Marquette, Louis Joliet, Lake Michigan, Robert de La Salle, Louisiana, New Orleans
3. **Comprehension**   What groups were threatened by the growth of the English colonies?
4. **Comprehension**   What methods did the colonists in New France use to try to prevent the westward spread of English settlement?
5. **Critical Thinking**   Why might settlers in the English colonies have felt threatened? Explain your answer.

# Chapter 4 Summary

In the 1600's thousands of settlers came to live in the English colonies. Some came because the enclosure movement forced them from their land. Other settlers were religious dissenters who came to escape persecution. Still others believed America offered a chance for self-government. Africans were brought to America against their will as slaves.

Jamestown in Virginia was founded in 1607. John Smith helped the settlement survive its first difficult years. A brisk tobacco trade with England helped the settlement prosper. In 1619 self-government took root in America when the Virginia colonists elected representatives to the House of Burgesses. The Pilgrims who founded Plymouth Colony in 1620 agreed in the Mayflower Compact that they would pass laws for the benefit of the whole colony.

Puritans founded Massachusetts Bay Colony in 1630. Roger Williams, denied religious freedom by the Puritans, founded a new colony in Rhode Island. Other people from Massachusetts Bay helped start colonies in Connecticut and New Hampshire. In the south, Maryland was founded by Lord Baltimore as a refuge for Catholics. Religious freedom was guaranteed there by the Act of Toleration. The Carolinas were divided into South Carolina and North Carolina. Georgia was founded by James Oglethorpe, a social reformer. New Netherland was taken over by the English and became New York and New Jersey. William Penn, an English Quaker, founded Pennsylvania where he welcomed people of all faiths. Delaware became a separate colony in 1704.

The colonists faced many challenges on their frontiers. Indians fiercely resisted the spread of English settlements. The French explorers Marquette, Joliet, and La Salle claimed much of the interior of North America. The French and their Indian allies tried to prevent the growth of English colonies. In Georgia English settlers came into conflict with colonists from Spanish Florida.

# Chapter 4 REVIEW

## Vocabulary and Key Terms

Use the following terms to complete the sentences below. Write your answers on a separate sheet of paper.

dissented        frontier
reform           persecuted
Puritans        self-reliant
representatives  Mayflower Compact
Pilgrims        Act of Toleration

1. The English rulers _____ people who _____ from the Church of England.
2. Dissenters who wanted to purify the Church of England were called _____.
3. The Jamestown settlers chose _____ to speak for them in making laws.
4. Before landing at Plymouth, the _____ made an agreement known as the _____.
5. A law called the _____ permitted religious freedom in Maryland.
6. James Oglethorpe wanted to _____, or improve, living conditions for poor English people.
7. Many English colonists went to live on the _____, or the edge of the settled area.
8. As the English colonies grew and prospered, the settlers became more _____.

## Recalling the Facts

1. What was the enclosure movement?
2. How was tobacco important to the success of the Jamestown colony?
3. Why did some Puritans leave Massachusetts Bay and start a new colony in Rhode Island?
4. Why was the colony of Georgia founded?
5. How did New York become an English colony?
6. What area did France claim in North America?
7. Why did the French and some Native Americans become allies?

## Places to Locate

Match the letters on the map with the colonies listed below. Write your answers on a separate sheet of paper.

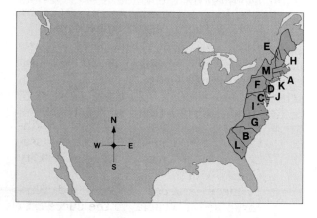

1. New Hampshire
2. Massachusetts
3. Connecticut
4. Rhode Island
5. New York
6. Pennsylvania
7. New Jersey
8. Delaware
9. Maryland
10. Virginia
11. North Carolina
12. South Carolina
13. Georgia

## Critical Thinking

1. Why was religious freedom an important issue in the early days of the English colonies? Consider these questions in your answer:
   a. How did religious disagreements in Europe affect the American colonies?
   b. What policies did the colonies have about religious freedom?
2. Compare Jamestown and Plymouth—the first two successful English settlements in North America. Consider the following questions in your comparison:
   a. In what ways were the two colonies alike? How were they different?
   b. What factors helped make each colony successful?

3. What groups other than the English colonists claimed land in North America? Was conflict over the claims unavoidable? Why or why not?

## Understanding History

1. Reread the section "Native Americans help the Pilgrims survive" on page 80. Then answer these questions.
   a. **Geography.** Why were the Pilgrims unable to plant crops soon after they landed at Plymouth?
   b. **Geography.** What natural resources helped the Pilgrims survive their first year in America?
2. Reread the excerpt by John Winthrop on page 82. Then answer these questions.
   a. **Primary Sources.** What did Winthrop mean when he said the Massachusetts Bay Colony should be a "City upon a Hill"?
   b. **Primary Sources.** What did Winthrop see as crucial to the success of the colony?
   c. **Primary Sources.** How does the excerpt show the importance of religion in the Massachusetts Bay Colony? Explain your answer.
3. Reread the section "English Catholics settle Maryland" on page 83. Then answer these questions.
   a. **Religion.** Did the Act of Toleration protect all religious groups? Explain.
   b. **Religion.** Why was the Act of Toleration important for Catholics in Maryland?

## Projects and Activities

1. **Developing a Plan.** Imagine that you and a group of colonists are about to begin a settlement in North America in the 1600's. Make up a plan of government to guide your colony. Include the rights and responsibilities of the colonists. Decide how work will be done and what laws will be needed. Share your plan with the rest of the class.
2. **Defending Opinions.** With several other students, present a panel discussion about religious freedom in New England in the 1600's. Some students should take the parts of Puritan ministers. Others should take the parts of challengers such as Roger Williams and Anne Hutchinson. The class can represent townspeople and ask questions of the panel.
3. **Organizing Information in a Chart.** Make a chart showing the religious groups that came to the English colonies. Include the following headings in the chart: "Religious Group," "Colony They Settled," "Date They Came," "Where They Came From," and "Other Information." Include at least five groups on your chart.
4. **Making a map.** Draw a map to illustrate the explorations of Marquette, Joliet, and La Salle in North America. Use reference sources to find out more about their explorations. On your map, use arrows to show the journeys. Explain the arrows in a map key. Use dates to show the progress of each exploration. Label all other necessary information on the map and give the map a title.

## Practicing Your Skill

Reread "Pennsylvania is a 'Holy Experiment'" on page 85. Make a hypothesis about how Penn would probably treat settlers who came to his colony by completing this sentence on a separate sheet of paper:

*Penn would probably treat settlers* _____.

Now read the words below that Penn wrote to Europeans who might come to his colony. Then answer the questions that follow.

You shall be governed by laws of your own making, and live as a free, and if you will, as an industrious people. I shall not take away the right of any.

1. Who does Penn say will make the laws?
2. What does Penn say about people's rights?
3. How do you think Penn would treat people who might settle in his colony?
4. Was your hypothesis accurate? Why or why not?

# 5 Colonial Life Varies from Region to Region
## 1607–1763

| 1670 | | | 1690 | | | 1710 | | | 1730 | | | 1750 | | | 1770 |
|---|---|---|---|---|---|---|---|---|---|---|---|---|---|---|---|

**1688**
Quakers
protest
slavery

**1691**
Salem
Witch Trials
begin

**1693**
William and
Mary College
founded

**1747**
Settlers
form
Ohio Company

**1754**
French and
Indian War
begins

**1759**
Battle
of
Quebec

**1763**
Treaty
of Paris
ends war

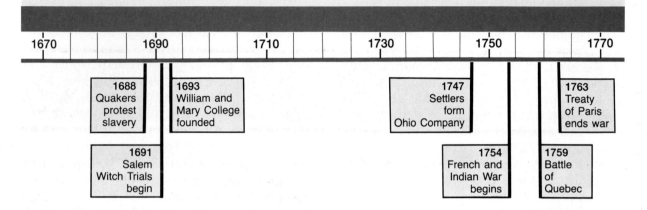

**Farming was essential to the colonies' development. This 1757 painting shows the prosperous farms of Bethlehem, Pennsylvania.**

## Preparing to Read

The early colonists had come to America for many different reasons. These different reasons, combined with the geography of the new land, strongly shaped the colonists' lives. The settlers adapted their farms and trades to fit the soil, climate, harbors, and resources of their region. As the English settlers continued to spread west, the long-standing struggle with the French erupted into a decisive war. As you read this chapter, try to answer the following questions:

1. How did the colonists live in New England?
2. What was life like in the Southern Colonies?
3. What was life like in the Middle Colonies?
4. How did Great Britain drive France from North America?

# 1 How did the colonists live in New England?

## Vocabulary

surplus                commerce
common                 hornbook
apprentice             grammar school

Most of the first New England colonists were farmers and Puritans. Religion was central to Puritan life, and New Englanders lived by strict rules. As the colonies grew and prospered, many colonists turned to fishing or trade for their livelihood. Rich merchants became important leaders in New England society, and the Puritans' strict control faded away.

## New England Society

Most New Englanders lived and worked on small farms. The soil and climate made farming difficult, however, and in time many New Englanders became tradespeople or merchants. Seaport towns grew into important centers of trade.

**Geographic conditions make farming difficult.** The first settlers found that New England was not well suited for farming. Thick forests covered the hilly land, and boulders dotted the rocky, thin soil. The settlers also faced a harsh climate. New England winters were cold and long. The short, mild summers allowed only a brief growing season and limited the kinds of crops farmers could raise.

In spite of these poor conditions, the first settlers of the region were farmers. The settlers had to grow their own food to survive in the wilderness. Starting a farm in New England was hard work. The land had to be cleared of trees, and then the boulders had to be hauled away. At first New England farmers could grow only enough grain and vegetables to support themselves and their families. Later, the farmers grew more than they could use. They were then able to sell or trade the **surplus** —extra amount.

For most New Englanders land was easy to obtain. Most settlers became landowners, and as a result workers were hard to find. Because most farmers did all the work themselves, farms tended to be small. Most New England farmers made their own tools, clothes, shoes, and furniture.

**New England towns develop.** New Englanders lived close together for two important reasons. First, good roads did not

97

exist. Second, the settlers wanted to stay close together for protection against Indian attacks. As the population of the New England Colonies grew, the countryside became dotted with towns.

New England towns were built around an area called the **common** —an open field where cattle grazed. Around the common, the townspeople built their church, school, and town hall. Each family's house and garden were located around the common. New England farmers lived in the towns and went out each day to work in the fields. At night they returned to the security of the towns.

**Fishing grows in importance.** Although New England was not especially good for farming, it had other geographic advantages. The jagged coast held many protected natural harbors. Not far off the coast lay some of the world's richest fishing grounds, with huge numbers of codfish, halibut, and many other kinds of fish.

Many New Englanders soon turned to fishing for their livelihood. The natural harbors of the coast provided safety for their fishing boats. After the boats returned, the huge catches were dried in the sun. The surplus fish were traded to other colonies or to the West Indies. In the 1600's New Englanders also began to hunt for whales, which provided oil for lamps. By the late 1600's whaling had grown into a very profitable business.

**Trade grows in New England.** The brisk fishing industry that quickly developed in New England gave rise to other trades. Shipbuilding, lumbering, and barrel making all flourished to fulfill the needs of the fishing industry. To fill the need for ships, for example, New Englanders became expert shipbuilders. Skilled workers also began to make furniture and household goods for sale.

Many New England workers learned their trades by serving as **apprentices.** An

In 1945 members of a historical society in Plymouth, Massachusetts, decided to build a copy of the Pilgrims' first settlement. The builders used records from the 1620's to recreate the Plymouth Colony, now a popular tourist attraction.

The kitchen was the most important room in a New England colonial home. Families ate their meals, spent their evenings, and did many chores in the kitchen. Women tended the hearth, cooked meals, and made cheese, bread, butter, and herbal medicines. Women also spun and dyed flax and wool to make the family's clothing.

apprentice was a young person who learned a skill or trade from a master worker—a sailmaker, a carpenter, or a blacksmith, for example. Apprentices lived with the master's family and usually received no wages for several years while they learned their trade. They were then given a little money and were free to work for themselves.

With the growth of business and the expanding number of skilled workers, New England became a trading center. By the 1700's commerce —the buying and selling of goods—had become an important part of the New England colonists' lives. Seaport towns bustled with activity along the docks and in the offices of merchants and shipowners. As the merchants and shipowners prospered, they built large and elegant homes. By the late 1700's many merchants' homes had expensive furnishings that rivaled those of England.

✐ **Women play a vital role in New England life.** Women worked hard on colonial New England farms. Their tasks included taking care of the livestock, tending the vegetable garden, and salting and smoking meat. They made cheese and butter and produced the family's cloth, soap, and candles.

Women also took care of the children. Families were often large. In the early colonial years, the average family had 9 children, and it was not unusual for a child to have 12 or even 15 brothers and sisters. The colonists lacked modern health care, however, and many children died of disease before reaching adulthood.

Women took an active part in church life and often spoke out on religious matters, as Anne Hutchinson did. (See Chapter 4.) Some, such as the Quaker Mary Dyer of Boston, protested against Puritan intolerance. Others, however, such as the poet Anne Bradstreet, expressed satisfaction with life in Puritan New England. Bradstreet wrote the first book of poems in America.

As the New England colonies grew, women found jobs in the towns and cities. Some worked as servants, weaving or sewing for wealthy families. Others ran schools, shops, inns, or lighthouses. For the most part, however, colonial women married and worked at home.

**Blacks in New England have limited freedom.** Slavery remained legal in New England until the time of the American Revolution. Not many New Englanders owned slaves, however. By 1700 fewer than 1,000 slaves lived in New England. Puritan slaveowners did not force their slaves to work on Sunday. They gave their slaves religious instruction and sometimes taught them to read and write. Phillis Wheatley, a slave in the household of a Boston tailor, gained fame as a poet. A book of her poems was published in London in 1773.

More free blacks lived in New England than in any of the other colonies. Free black men became merchants, soldiers, sailors, printers, and carpenters. Blacks were allowed to own land in New England, and many black families ran farms.

## Puritan Values

The New England Puritans placed great importance on religion and education. Their communities were strict, serious places that emphasized worship and hard work. Later, as the colonies grew in size and wealth, the focus of New England life broadened, and the Puritans lost influence.

**Religion is important in colonial New England.** The early Puritans wanted their colony to be "a city upon a hill" that would serve as an example to all other Christians. They hoped to build not just a better society but a perfect one. The Puritans believed that God wanted people to lead serious, purposeful lives. They worked hard, and they disapproved of amusements such as dancing and playing games.

The church was the center of Puritan social life, and before or after services on Sunday everyone met friends and heard the news. The law required everyone to attend church services, where the ministers gave long sermons both morning and afternoon. Prayers alone often lasted three quarters of an hour. The churches had no heat, and the hard benches were uncomfortable. The men sat in one part of the church, and the women sat in one part of the church, and the women

and girls in another. The boys usually sat together in the balcony, and if there was any noise, the offenders were punished in front of the whole congregation. The Puritans disapproved of work or travel on Sundays. They believed Sundays should be spent worshiping and reading the Bible.

Not all New Englanders were Puritans. Roger Williams and Anne Hutchinson started settlements in Rhode Island, a colony that welcomed settlers of varying beliefs. (See Chapter 4.) In the mid-1600's, Quakers began to speak out against Puritan intolerance in Massachusetts. Many of them were forced to go to Rhode Island. Some, however, stayed to face punishment and even hanging at the hands of the Puritans.

**Punishments are severe in colonial New England.** The Puritan laws were strict, and lawbreakers were punished in ways considered very cruel today. About 15 crimes carried the penalty of death. One of these crimes was witchcraft, and in 1691 and 1692 a number of men and women were hanged as witches during the **Salem Witchcraft Trials** in Salem, Massachusetts.

Less serious crimes also received severe punishments. People who lied might be forced to sit with their hands and legs fastened in a board called the stocks. Other offenders might be required to stand on a platform with their head and hands locked in a wooden frame called a pillory. For some crimes people were given a certain number of lashes on the back with a whip. Of course, such punishments were also common in England in the 1600's.

**New England Puritans believe in education.** The Puritans wanted everyone to be able to read the Bible. For this reason, more children in New England attended school than in the other groups of colonies. As early as 1647, Massachusetts passed a law requiring all villages with a certain number of families to establish schools. Books were expensive and scarce, and children usually learned from a **hornbook.** A hornbook was a single printed page pasted to a board and protected by a thin covering. A hornbook usually contained the alphabet and a Christian prayer.

In larger communities of New England, **grammar schools** —advanced schools— prepared older boys for college. Girls could not attend grammar schools or college. Harvard, the first college in the colonies, was established in 1636, only six years after Massachusetts Bay Colony was founded.

**Puritan influence declines.** The Puritans believed in hard work, and by the 1700's their work had made the New England colonies large and prosperous. As the colonies grew, however, the power of the Puritans began to fade. New generations of colonists did not share the strict religious views of their elders. They were often more interested in the growing opportunities for trade and business. The Puritan ministers began to complain that their "city upon a hill" was full of merchants.

More and more colonists moved west, away from the strict control of the Puritan leaders. England began to exert more control over the colonies, too. In 1691 England pressed Massachusetts to allow non-Puritans to vote. Without political control of the colony, the Puritans soon found their influence slipping away.

**The Great Awakening revives religion.** Between 1720 and 1750 there was a new wave of religious interest in New England and throughout the colonies. Ministers traveled from town to town, holding meetings at which they urged people to turn back to their religious faith. This movement was known as the **Great Awakening.** It was started in New England by Jonathan Edwards, a fiery preacher from Northampton, Massachusetts. Similar movements also sprang up in the Middle and Southern Colonies. These religious movements were joined together when George Whitefield (WIT-feeld), a well-known English preacher, traveled throughout the colonies.

Whitefield and the other preachers of the Great Awakening said it was important for all people to have personal religious experience, rather than to simply follow the rules set by a church or its ministers. The Great Awakening aroused much excitement among the colonists. It set a pattern for later religious movements in America.

George Whitefield, a preacher from England, became a leader of the Great Awakening, the American religious revival movement of the 1700's. Whitefield often preached outdoors.

## SECTION REVIEW

1. **Vocabulary**  surplus, common, apprentice, commerce, hornbook, grammar school
2. **People and Places**  Mary Dyer, Anne Bradstreet, Phillis Wheatley, Salem, Jonathan Edwards, George Whitefield
3. **Comprehension**  What were some of the main ways of making a living in the New England Colonies?
4. **Comprehension**  How did life in New England change as the colonies grew?
5. **Critical Thinking**  In your opinion, what were the advantages and disadvantages of living in Puritan society?

# 2 What was life like in the Southern Colonies?

## Vocabulary

| | |
|---|---|
| plantation | tenant farmer |
| indigo | overseer |
| planter | self-sufficient |

Geographical conditions in the south favored farming, and most people in the Southern Colonies depended on the soil for their livelihood. Southern society included wealthy landowners, small farmers, and many African slaves. There were fewer merchants or tradespeople than in New England. Social life was dominated by the wealthy landowners.

## Social Groups in the South

Among white colonists in the south there were three main groups—wealthy landowners, small farmers, and those who owned no land. In addition to these groups were African slaves, who did much of the labor on southern farms.

**The geography of the South favors farming.** Unlike New England, the south had rich soil and a warm climate. Settlers in the south found a broad coastal plain that stretched several hundred miles inland from the Atlantic. This region of flat, rich land was called the **Tidewater,** because the ocean tides swept far up the rivers from the sea. By the mid-1600's **plantations** —large farms— had spread throughout the Tidewater.

Tobacco was the south's first and most important product. Rice and **indigo** —a plant used in making blue dye—were later grown in South Carolina and Georgia. These crops brought high prices, and farmers raised them in large amounts. Because these crops also wore out the soil, successful farmers had to buy more and more land. In this way large plantations were established.

**Plantation owners dominate life in the Southern Colonies.** The leading people in southern society were the **planters** — plantation owners. The rich planters sought to live in the style of the wealthy landowners of England. Their homes, filled with fine furniture, paintings, and silverware brought from Europe, resembled English manor houses. The planters adopted the sports of the English upper class, such as horse racing and fox hunting.

Only a small percentage of southern colonists owned large plantations, however. Small landowners made up a large middle group in southern society. Some of these people owned one or more slaves, but most did not. Many small landowners lived much like the farmers of New England.

Settlers who owned no land made up the lowest group in white southern society. Most of these people were **tenant farmers** — people who worked on land owned by others. The tenant farmers in the Tidewater usually had little chance to get an education or to better their lives.

To claim land for themselves, many tenant farmers moved inland to the hilly frontier region known as the **Backcountry.** This area remained sparsely settled until the mid-1700's. The people who settled the Backcountry were fiercely independent and often rough-mannered. At first the Backcountry settlers cleared small patches of land and built rough log cabins. In time, wider areas were cleared, and the settlers grew larger crops of grains, potatoes, and fruit. The Backcountry gradually developed into a land of farming villages and orchards.

**Plantation farming depends on slaves.** Small farmers in the Tidewater and the Backcountry did most of the work on their farms themselves. Planters, however, could not farm their huge plantations without the work of many people. To solve their need for labor, planters bought African slaves. Africans were usually transported first to the West Indies and then sent on to the Southern Colonies for sale to planters or other buyers. Those Africans who survived the terrible conditions of the slave ships faced a life of hard, forced labor. Most of the slaves were field hands, who received orders from an **overseer** —supervisor of slaves. For any violation of the owner's rules, overseers punished the slaves, usually by whipping them.

On some large plantations, the slaves learned skilled trades. The following description of such a plantation was written by the daughter of the owner:

My father had among his slaves carpenters, [barrel makers], sawyers, blacksmiths, [leather workers], shoemakers, spinners, weavers and knitters.... His carpenters and sawyers built and kept in repair all the dwelling houses, barns, stables, plows, harrows, gates, etc., on the plantations.... His [barrel makers ] made the [barrels] the tobacco was [packed] in.... The [leather workers]...tanned and dressed the skins...

and the shoemakers made them into shoes for the [slaves].... The blacksmith did all the iron work required by the establishment, as making and repairing plows, harrows, teeth chains, bolts, etc., etc. The spinners,... made all the coarse cloths and stockings used by the [slaves], and some of finer texture worn by the white family....

Few plantations were as large as the one described above, however, and most slaves did not have the chance to learn a trade.

**Southern planters trade with England.** Southern planters profited by raising huge crops of tobacco and other products and selling them to English merchants. With their profits they bought many English goods such as fine furniture and clothing. A thriving trade grew up between the planters and the English merchants. Such seaports as Charleston, South Carolina, and Savannah, Georgia, became important trading centers. The Southern Colonies kept up a lively trade with England into the 1770's. They did not trade much with each other or with the other colonies, however. Because most of the

Plantation work was done almost entirely by slaves. On this tobacco plantation in Virginia, overseers supervise slaves preparing dried tobacco leaves for shipment to England. What tasks are being done in the picture?

Rice Hope was the name of this 20,000-acre plantation near Charleston, South Carolina. Jonathan Lucas, who invented machines for milling rice, received the plantation in a royal grant. In colonial times, rice was South Carolina's most important export.

trade with England was carried in English ships, shipbuilding and other industries did not develop in the south.

## Plantation Life

Plantations formed the basis of life in the south. Each plantation formed a separate community controlled by the planter. The planter's wife performed many essential tasks, and slaves labored from dawn until dusk in the fields or in the planter's home.

**Plantations form separate communities.** Because plantations were so large, most southern planters lived far apart. The best location for a plantation was near a river, so that crops could be loaded onto a ship from the planter's own wharf. This often meant that plantations were located far from towns or cities. As a result, plantations sought to be self-sufficient —able to produce all the

goods that were needed. On a typical plantation, the largest building was the Great House—home to the planter and his family. The Great House had a parlor for visitors, a library, and many bedrooms. To keep the Great House cool, the kitchen was often a separate building.

The slaves lived in rough cabins not far from the Great House. Near the slaves' cabins were the blacksmith shop, the stables, and other buildings. Thus the plantation had many characteristics of a small town. The planter ruled this small community with great authority.

**Education takes place on the plantation.** Because plantations were so far apart, children had to be taught at home. In some cases, teachers from England taught the children of several planters. The children of slaves and small farmers, however, had little chance to learn to read and write.

The sons of some rich planters attended college in England. Others went to the College of William and Mary in Virginia. This college, founded in 1693, was the second in the English colonies. Young women in the south were not allowed to go to college.

While religion was important in southern life, it was not as strict nor were ministers as powerful as in New England. Many southerners belonged to the Church of England rather than to the Puritan church. Furthermore, most southerners had come to America for economic reasons, rather than to establish religious communities.

**Southern women play an important role.** Wealthy southern women helped manage the affairs of the family plantation. Planters' wives supervised the slaves in the house, garden, dairy, and poultry yard. They took care of sick family members and slaves and prepared medicines themselves. Planters' wives sometimes led prayers on the plantation and supervised the schooling of the children. Women also ran farms or plantations when their husbands or fathers were absent. Most slave women worked in the fields. Others worked as cooks, maids, and household servants.

**Slaves cope with harsh conditions.** The life of all slaves was difficult. Some planters treated their slaves considerately and provided adequate food and clothing. Slaves, however, were denied all legal rights and had no protection from careless or cruel owners.

An owner could punish slaves, sell them, or take away their children. According to the law of the time, the planter owned a slave's children. The children became workers who might be sold for a profit. Slaves were not allowed legal marriages and the slaveowner had the power to sell husbands and wives away from each other. Many families were broken up in this cruel way.

Black men and women resisted the conditions of slavery in a number of ways. From time to time they rose in open revolt. These slaves received severe punishment. Slaves more often resisted by slowing down work, allowing goods to be damaged, or carrying out orders incorrectly. Slaves risked punishment to slip off and visit family members on

## LINKING PAST AND PRESENT

### ★ ★ ★ *Plantations*

From Virginia south to Georgia, southern colonists set up huge plantations to grow tobacco, rice, and indigo. Many of these estates covered hundreds and sometimes thousands of acres, and their wealthy owners lived in stylish elegance.

Today these colonial plantations are an important part of the heritage of the south. The restoration of colonial plantations began as early as the mid-1800's and continues to the present day. Thousands of Americans visit restored plantations each year for a brief glimpse of life in the colonial South.

nearby plantations. Some ran away and tried to pass as free blacks in other colonies. Because the northern colonies did not ban slavery until after the Revolution, runaway slaves were not safe anywhere. They were usually caught and returned to their owners.

By 1765, almost 350,000 blacks lived in the Southern Colonies. Of these, the vast majority were slaves. Slaves were seldom freed in the later colonial years. The few free blacks in the south lived in towns, earning a living as servants or skilled workers.

## SECTION REVIEW

1. **Vocabulary** plantation, indigo, planter, tenant farmer, overseer, self-sufficient
2. **People and Places** Tidewater, Backcountry
3. **Comprehension** How did plantations and slavery become established in the south?
4. **Comprehension** How did life in the Backcountry differ from plantation life?
5. **Critical Thinking** Do you think the southern plantations could have survived without slavery? Why or why not?

# CRITICAL THINKING: Using a Picture as a Primary Source

Historians depend heavily on primary sources as they study the past. Written records are one very important primary source. Pictures—drawings, paintings, and photographs—can also be useful as historical evidence, because they show how people lived.

Careful study of pictures can provide a great deal of information. To get the greatest amount of information from drawings, paintings, and photographs, you should ask the following questions:

1. What is the subject of the picture? A quick way to answer this question is to give the picture a title.
2. What does the picture tell about people's lives? Describing the houses, clothes, tools, and other everyday materials shown in the picture will help you answer this question.
3. Is the picture a dependable source of information? In other words, has the person who made the picture told the "true story" of the event shown?

In answering these questions you will be drawing conclusions suggested by the information in a single picture. If you were a professional historian, you might examine a whole series of pictures in this way, in order to make sure that your information was as complete and accurate as possible.

The picture below shows Baltimore, Maryland, as it looked in 1752. Study the picture and then answer the following questions on a separate sheet of paper.

1. What title would you give this picture?
2. List three ways in which people are making a living.
3. Describe the landscape beyond the edge of the town. Suppose that new residents wanted to build more houses to enlarge the town. What would they have to do first?
4. Judging by the way the houses are arranged in the settlement, do you think that the people were fearful of Indian attacks? Why or why not?

# 3 What was life like in the Middle Colonies?

## Vocabulary

cash crop     import

export     manufacturing

The Middle Colonies, located between New England and the Southern Colonies, showed characteristics of both regions. Like the south, the Middle Colonies had a broad coastal plain and rich soil. The swifter and longer rivers in the Middle Colonies served as highways into the land away from the coast. The climate in the Middle Colonies, warmer than New England but cooler than the Southern Colonies, made this an excellent region for farming.

## Farming and Trade

The first settlers of the Middle Colonies made their living by farming the rich soil. Later, some colonists became merchants, trading with the other colonies and with England. Many skilled workers also settled in the Middle Colonies.

**Farming thrives in the Middle Colonies.** As in New England and the South, the first settlers were farmers. The farmers of the Middle Colonies, however, did not live in small villages or on grand plantations. Instead, the settlers lived on large farms that extended inland from the seacoast. Such large farms were possible because the land was fertile, long rivers made fine highways, and relations with the Indians were fairly good.

Farmers in the Middle Colonies gathered rich harvests of wheat, barley, rye, and other grains. Fruit and livestock flourished in New York, Pennsylvania, and New Jersey. Farmers in the Middle Colonies soon produced surplus grains. These grains were called **cash crops** —crops grown to be sold. The farmers sold their surplus and used the money to buy other things they needed, including food they could have grown themselves. By 1760 New York farmers were **exporting** —selling outside the colony— more than 80,000 barrels of wheat flour a year. Because the Middle Colonies exported so much wheat and other grain, they became known as the **breadbasket colonies.**

**Trade develops in seacoast cities.** As the Middle Colonies prospered, the farmers had larger surpluses to trade. Other settlers had timber and fur for sale. Two seaports, New York at the mouth of the Hudson River and Philadelphia near the mouth of the Delaware River, quickly grew into trading centers. Goods from the Middle Colonies were exported to other colonies, to the West Indies, and to Europe.

Because roads were poor, shipping a load of goods across the Atlantic was cheaper than sending the same items 100 miles (161 kilometers) within the colony. As a result, a brisk European trade developed. Colonial merchants took wheat and other items to Europe and returned to the colonies with **imports** —goods brought from other countries. Many merchants in the Middle Colonies grew rich from this trade. By 1768, Philadelphia was the largest seaport in the colonies.

The first settlers of the Middle Colonies made the items they needed in their homes. As the colonies prospered, however, widespread **manufacturing** —making of goods— developed. Women and men toiled in workshops that produced clocks, watches, guns, locks, cloth, hats, and glassware. The iron industry in Pennsylvania and New Jersey grew quickly after many skilled German workers settled there. Iron ore, mined in the Middle Colonies, was heated in forges and turned into pig iron. From pig iron workers made nails and iron tools.

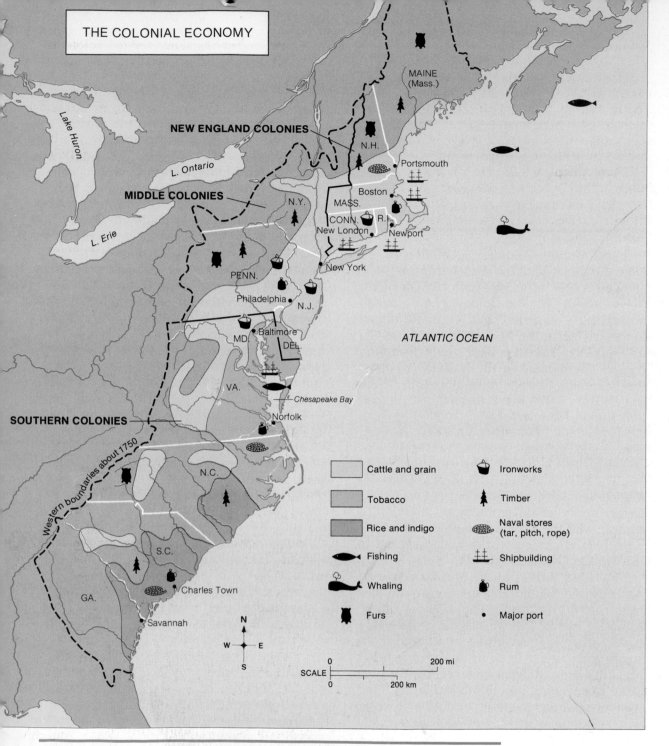

THE COLONIAL ECONOMY

MAINE
(Mass.)

NEW ENGLAND COLONIES

L. Ontario

N.H.

Portsmouth

MIDDLE COLONIES

N.Y.

Boston

MASS.

CONN.  R.I.

L. Erie

New London

Newport

New York

PENN.

Philadelphia

N.J.

ATLANTIC OCEAN

MD.  Baltimore

DEL.

VA.

Chesapeake Bay

SOUTHERN COLONIES

Norfolk

Lake Huron

N.C.

Western boundaries about 1750

S.C.

GA.

Charles Town

Savannah

| | Cattle and grain | | Ironworks |
| | Tobacco | | Timber |
| | Rice and indigo | | Naval stores (tar, pitch, rope) |
| | Fishing | | Shipbuilding |
| | Whaling | | Rum |
| | Furs | | Major port |

N
W  E
S

SCALE
0                    200 mi
0        200 km

## Map Study

The English colonies produced goods for sale in America and for export to England. The key indicates the economic activities and chief products of each region. In what group of colonies were shipbuilding, fishing, and whaling most important? What were the chief products of the Middle Colonies? What were South Carolina's main crops?

## Society in the Middle Colonies

The Middle Colonies attracted a greater variety of settlers than New England or the South, and the Middle Colonies tended to be tolerant of the differences between people. Most colonists believed in religious freedom, and a few wanted to end slavery.

**Many peoples make the Middle Colonies home.** The Dutch and the Swedes first settled the areas that became New York, New Jersey, and Delaware. English Quakers later founded Pennsylvania, but German and Scotch-Irish people also settled there. Welsh, Irish, Scottish, French, and Jewish colonists added to the variety of people in the Middle Colonies.

The Middle Colonies are sometimes called a **melting pot** because of the different groups who settled and mingled there. Each of these groups contributed aspects of their native culture to their new homeland. For example, the Swedes built log cabins in America, as they had done in Sweden. The Dutch constructed brick homes with a wooden porch called a stoop. The Germans developed an efficient woodburning stove that other colonists copied. The variety of people helped the colonies prosper.

As in the South, many rugged colonists settled in the frontier regions of the Middle Colonies. At first these people worked small plots of land. Later, large prosperous farms grew up, and their owners developed a brisk trade with the colonists along the coast.

**The Middle Colonies welcome people of many religions.** Unlike the New England Colonies, the Middle Colonies became home for a variety of religious groups. In some areas a single group was strong. These groups did not, however, try to make every colonist join them.

Both the Dutch and the Quakers believed in religious toleration. The Quakers welcomed German Protestants to Pennsylvania. The Dutch allowed Catholics and Jews to settle in New York. Some prejudice still existed, however. It was not until the 1750's that Jews in New York were allowed to build a synagogue for their religious services.

**Religious groups found schools and colleges.** The Middle Colonies had fewer schools and colleges than did New England. Religious groups ran most of the early schools. The Dutch Reformed Church opened the first school in the New York area. Quakers in Pennsylvania and Jesuit priests in Maryland also started schools.

Metalworking was an important colonial industry. This eighteenth-century engraving shows a shop in which tin objects were manufactured and sold. A saleswoman shows goods to a customer. Tinsmiths heated tin in a forge, hammered the metal into sheets, and fashioned the sheets into finished products.

Several colleges grew up in the Middle Colonies in the mid-1700's. Religious groups founded the College of New Jersey (now Princeton University) to train ministers. Colonial authorities founded King's College (now Columbia University) and accepted white men of any faith. As in the other colonies, however, women and blacks could not attend college.

**A few colonists oppose slavery.** As in the other colonies, slavery continued to be legal in the Middle Colonies until the time of the Revolutionary War. Fewer slaves lived in the Middle Colonies than in the South, however, partly because the Quakers opposed slavery. In addition, the wheat and other crops grown in Middle Colonies required fewer workers than did the tobacco and rice of the South.

The movement to free the slaves began in the Middle Colonies. In 1688 the Quakers in Germantown, Pennsylvania, drew up the earliest American protest against slavery. Soon Quakers throughout the colonies opposed slavery.

## SECTION REVIEW

1. **Vocabulary**   cash crop, export, import, manufacturing
2. **People and Places**   New York, Philadelphia
3. **Comprehension**   Why may the term *breadbasket* be used to describe the Middle Colonies?
4. **Comprehension**   Why can the Middle Colonies be called a melting pot?
5. **Critical Thinking**   How did the lack of cheap inland transportation influence trade in the Middle Colonies?

# 4 How did Great Britain drive France from North America?

## Vocabulary
stockade
prime minister

In North America, as well as in other parts of the world, Great Britain and France fought for superiority. The struggle lasted for years, with neither side winning a clear advantage. Finally, in the mid-1700's, the two rival nations fought a decisive war.

## English-French Rivalry

England and France had long been rivals in Europe, and their competition spread to America. Throughout the 1600's and 1700's wars erupted between the two nations. The final contest between these rivals began as a small clash in the Ohio Valley.

**The English and the French fight a series of wars.** Beginning in the late 1600's the English and the French engaged in a great struggle. They fought for dominance in Europe and for control of North America and other parts of the world. Naturally, when England and France were at war, each nation's colonists also fought.

Three times between 1689 and 1743 Great Britain* and France went to war. In America these wars were named for the monarch who ruled Great Britain at the time. These three wars were called King William's War, Queen Anne's War, and King George's War.

---

\*   In 1707 the countries of England, Wales, and Scotland were joined in a single kingdom called Great Britain. The names *Great Britain* or *Britain* are commonly used for the kingdom after that date.

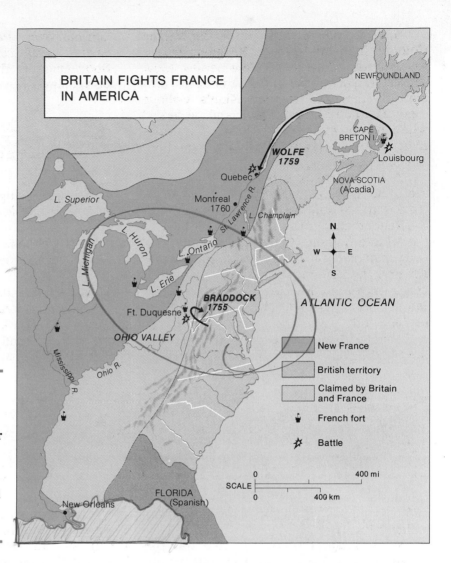

BRITAIN FIGHTS FRANCE IN AMERICA

NEWFOUNDLAND

WOLFE 1759

CAPE BRETON I.

Louisbourg

Quebec

NOVA SCOTIA (Acadia)

L. Superior

Montreal 1760

St. Lawrence R.

L. Champlain

L. Michigan

L. Huron

L. Ontario

L. Erie

N
W    E
S

BRADDOCK 1755

ATLANTIC OCEAN

Ft. Duquesne

OHIO VALLEY

Mississippi R.

Ohio R.

New France

British territory

Claimed by Britain and France

French fort

Battle

SCALE
0          400 mi
0          400 km

New Orleans

FLORIDA (Spanish)

## Map Study

During the French and Indian War, Britain and France fought to extend their claims in Canada and the Ohio Valley. What key waterways did French forts defend? What British general was defeated by the French at Fort Duquesne?

In North America these wars accomplished little. The French and their Indian allies attacked English settlements. The English struck back by attacking the chief settlements in New France—Quebec and Louisbourg. Each war ended with an uneasy peace. As a result of these wars, there were few changes in the American possessions of either nation. France, however, did recognize England's claims to Acadia (present-day Nova Scotia) and Newfoundland.

**The British and the French claim the Ohio River valley.** Because of the discoveries of Robert de La Salle, the French claimed the rich lands along the Ohio River. (See Chapter 4.) The French planned to build a

line of forts and trading posts in this region. These outposts would connect the French settlements on the lower Mississippi River with the rest of New France.

On the other hand, the English also claimed the Ohio River valley. Some English colonists were eager to trade with the Native Americans. Others wanted to settle and farm the rich lands west of the Appalachian Mountains. In 1747 a group of Virginia colonists formed the Ohio Company to settle the area. King George II granted about 200,000 acres (81,000 hectares) of land to the Ohio Company. When the governor of New France learned of the English plans, he speeded up the building of French forts. Fort

## GEOGRAPHY • Routes of the Pioneers

From the moment the first Europeans set foot in North America, the geography of the continent determined how they traveled and where they settled. The settlers soon discovered that they could travel quickly and easily by following the rivers of North America.

The Indians showed the settlers natural water routes into the interior of the continent. These rivers became the highways of colonial times. As more settlers arrived from Europe, daring men and women followed the rivers and established farms and villages away from the coast. River valleys also showed colonists the best routes across the Appalachian Mountains to the west. Settlers followed these routes in a steady stream, and by the 1760's new settlements dotted the lands west of the Appalachians.

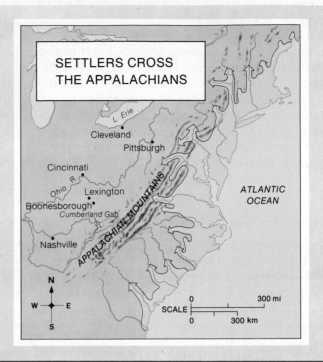

SETTLERS CROSS THE APPALACHIANS

Duquesne (doo-KANE) and other French outposts quickly sprang up in the Ohio River valley.

**The British attempt to drive out the French.** In 1753 the British sent young George Washington to the Ohio River valley to warn the French to abandon their forts. The French ignored the warning. In 1754 Washington returned to the Ohio country, leading a small group of Virginia militia, with orders to seize Fort Duquesne. (See map on page 111.)

Greatly outnumbered, Washington and his troops were chased by a French force from Fort Duquesne. The Virginians quickly put up a **stockade** —a high fence—for protection, calling it Fort Necessity. The French surrounded the fort and forced the Virginians to surrender. Washington and his troops returned home to Virginia. This brief clash in the wilderness marked the beginning of the **French and Indian War.** Two

years later, in 1756, France and Great Britain went to war in Europe. The fighting in Europe was known as the Seven Years' War.

## The French and Indian War

At first France won victory after victory against the British troops in North America. A change in British leadership then led to a key British victory. Eventually, Great Britain emerged victorious—with vast lands in North America and an empire spread across the globe.

**France and Great Britain each have advantages.** France had four major advantages in the struggle against Britain. First, France controlled more land in North America than did Britain. Next, New France had a single colonial government that could act quickly. The British, on the other hand, had to ask for help from the 13 separate colonial governments. Also, France sent ships and professional soldiers to America, rather than depending on military help from its colonists. Lastly, the French could count on help from such loyal Indian allies as the Hurons and the Algonquins.

Great Britain had four advantages of its own. First, many more settlers lived in the British colonies than lived in New France. Next, the British colonies, concentrated along the Atlantic coast, were easier to defend. In addition, most of the English colonists had settled down for good. They were willing to fight hard to save their land, homes, and families. Finally, the British could count on help from the Iroquois, warriors of great skill.

**The French win a series of victories.** In 1755 General Edward Braddock, the British commander, led his troops through the wilderness to capture Fort Duquesne. Braddock ignored the advice of colonial soldiers about frontier warfare. As his troops marched in formation through the wilderness, the French and the Indians launched a surprise attack. The British, in bright red uniforms, made easy targets for enemy sharpshooters. Braddock was killed in the fighting. George Washington, who accompanied Braddock, took command and ordered a retreat. As a

British troops led by General James Wolfe stormed the steep cliffs of Quebec, surprised the French defenders, and won a great victory. This painting by an eyewitness shows the daring British assault. Why might the French have been surprised by the British attack?

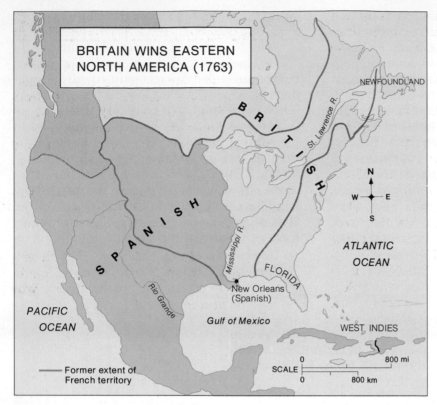

**BRITAIN WINS EASTERN NORTH AMERICA (1763)**

NEWFOUNDLAND

BRITISH

St. Lawrence R.

SPANISH

Mississippi R.

Rio Grande

FLORIDA

New Orleans (Spanish)

Gulf of Mexico

WEST INDIES

PACIFIC OCEAN

ATLANTIC OCEAN

N W E S

Former extent of French territory

SCALE
0 — 800 mi
0 — 800 km

**Map Study**

The Treaty of Paris ended the French and Indian War and gave Great Britain control of eastern North America. What river formed the western boundary of British territory? Who controlled the Great Lakes region and St. Lawrence River valley? What peninsula did the British acquire from France's ally, Spain?

result of this British defeat, the French won control of the Ohio Valley.

In the two years following Braddock's crushing defeat, the French and their Indian allies won a string of victories against the British. Then, in 1757, the fortunes of war began to change.

**British victories turn the tide of the war.** In 1757 a new British prime minister —head of government—William Pitt, came to power. Pitt was a bold, confident leader. He poured vast amounts of money into the conflict, putting Britain deeply into debt. He persuaded the colonies to furnish more troops and money. Pitt also sent young, vigorous generals to America. These commanders led Britain to victory after victory.

In 1758 the British captured the strategic French fort at Louisbourg. The British also captured several forts in the Ohio Valley, including Fort Duquesne. The British renamed it Fort Pitt in honor of William Pitt. From that small fort has grown the modern city of Pittsburgh.

**The Battle of Quebec decides the war.** The city of Quebec served as a supply center for French forts farther up the St. Lawrence River. The British planned to capture Quebec, cut off supplies, and thus win the war. Quebec, however, was well defended. Located on a high cliff, Quebec was protected by strong walls and many cannon.

In 1759 General James Wolfe led a British fleet up the St. Lawrence River and anchored it below Quebec. One night he decided on a daring move. He led his soldiers up the cliff at a point left undefended by the French. The next morning, General Louis Montcalm, the French commander, ordered his troops to attack. A fierce battle followed. Montcalm and Wolfe were both killed in the fighting, but the British won a smashing victory.

The **Battle of Quebec** was a turning point in history. After Quebec the British captured Montreal, putting an end to the fighting in North America. The British now controlled the huge French empire in North America.

The war continued in other parts of the world, with the British winning victory after victory. Finally, the war ended with the **Treaty of Paris of 1763.**

**France gives up all claims in North America.** The Treaty of Paris was a humiliating blow to France. Great Britain took from France all of its territory east of the Mississippi River except New Orleans. This vast territory included settlements in present-day Canada and the region south of the Great Lakes. (See map on page 114.) Spain, which had sided with France in the war, gave Florida to Britain. To make up for this loss, France gave Spain New Orleans and the French claims west of the Mississippi. Except for two small islands near Newfoundland and some islands in the Caribbean Sea, France lost all of its North American lands.

(See map on page 114.)

## SECTION REVIEW

1. **Vocabulary**   stockade, prime minister
2. **People and Places**   Ohio River valley, Fort Duquesne, General Edward Braddock, William Pitt, General James Wolfe, General Louis Montcalm, Quebec
3. **Comprehension**   Why did France and Britain come to conflict over the Ohio River valley?
4. **Comprehension**   How did European claims in North America change as a result of the British victory in the French and Indian War?
5. **Critical Thinking**   If more French settlers had lived in North America, might the results of the French and Indian War have been different? Explain.

# Chapter 5 Summary

The first settlers of New England were farmers. In time towns and villages, each built around a common, dotted New England. Because the colonies had poor soil but good harbors, commerce became important. Fishing and whaling thrived, and fishers traded their surplus with other colonies or the West Indies. New England Puritans were strictly religious and favored education. In the early 1700's, however, the influence of the Puritans declined. Beginning about 1720, a religious movement known as the Great Awakening sprang up in New England and spread throughout the colonies.

The rich soil of the Southern Colonies favored the development of plantations. The planters employed overseers to manage the slaves who worked the plantations. Among the plantations' chief crops were tobacco, rice, and indigo. Slaves toiled endlessly on the plantations and were deprived of all rights.

Farmers in the Middle Colonies ran large farms, raised cash crops, and exported the surplus. Seacoast cities like New York and Philadelphia flourished as centers of trade. Manufacturing developed in the Middle Colonies. The Middle Colonies had many different religious groups and settlers from many countries.

Britain and France waged a series of wars over land claims in North America. The French and Indian War was a struggle for the rich lands along the Ohio River. The British suffered an early defeat at Fort Duquesne in 1755, but in 1759 they captured Quebec. The Battle of Quebec turned the tide of the war. The British defeated France, and in the Treaty of Paris of 1763 the French agreed to give up their claims in America. Britain won French lands east of the Mississippi, except New Orleans. Spain gave Florida to Britain, but received New Orleans and French lands west of the Mississippi.

# Chapter 5 REVIEW

## Vocabulary and Key Terms

Choose the italicized term in parentheses that best completes each sentence. Write your answers on a separate sheet of paper.

1. Workers known as (*apprentices/overseers*) supervised slaves on plantations.
2. (*Common/Surplus*) crops were often shipped to other colonies or to Europe.
3. The fourth war of the English-French struggle for control of North America was called (*the French and Indian War/ the Battle of Quebec*).
4. A (*stockade/plantation*) was a high fence, put up for protection.
5. (*Grammar schools/Hornbooks*) prepared older boys for college.
6. People who worked on land owned by other settlers were called (*planters/ tenant farmers*).

## Recalling the Facts

1. Why did shipbuilding become important in New England?
2. What tasks did New England women perform?
3. Who led the Great Awakening in New England?
4. Why did plantation owners dominate life in the Southern Colonies?
5. Why did many plantations become self-sufficient?
6. What kind of work did most slaves do?
7. How did farming in the Middle Colonies differ from farming in New England?
8. What factors made trade important in the Middle Colonies?
9. What were some of the contributions of the different groups who settled in the Middle Colonies?
10. How did the French and Indian War begin? Where did it begin?
11. What was the result of the British victory in the Battle of Quebec?

## Places to Locate

Match the letters on the map with the places listed below. Write your answers on a separate sheet of paper.

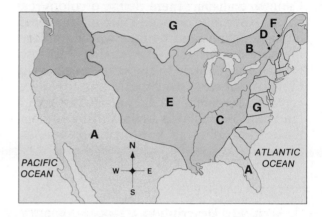

1. New France
2. British territory
3. Spanish territory
4. St. Lawrence River
5. Quebec
6. Montreal
7. Ohio River

## Critical Thinking

1. Why did Puritanism decline in New England? Consider the following issues in your answer:
   a. the economy of New England
   b. the movement of settlers westward
   c. the influence of England on the colony
2. Why did plantations become a profitable method of farming in the South?
3. What do you think was the most decisive factor in the British victory over the French in North America?

## Understanding History

1. Reread the section "Religion is important in colonial New England" on page 100. Then answer these questions.
   a. **Religion.** Why did the Puritans have strict rules for trying to regulate people's behavior?

b. **Religion.** What role did the church play in Puritan life?

2. Reread the section "Trade develops in seacoast cities" on page 107. Then answer these questions.
   a. **Economics.** To what places were the products of the Middle Colonies exported?
   b. **Economics.** Why was it often cheaper to ship goods overseas than to transport them within a colony?

3. Reread the section "The Battle of Quebec decides the war" on page 114. Then answer these questions.
   a. **Geography.** Why was Quebec easy to defend?
   b. **Geography.** What did the victory in the Battle of Quebec mean to Great Britain?

## Projects and Activities

1. **Writing a Description.** Suppose you are a member of a group of English colonists in North America in the 1600's. Decide where you live and write about what a typical day is like. Include details about what kind of tasks you do, and remember that you have no modern conveniences to help you.

2. **Researching Information.** Find out more about the life of Phillis Wheatley, the colonial poet. Write a report about her experiences in America and her opinion of slavery.

3. **Presenting a Skit.** Find out more about the Salem, Massachusetts, witchcraft trials of the 1690's. Determine the circumstances and the key people involved in the trials. Use your information to write a brief skit. Present your skit to the class.

4. **Making a Chart.** Make a chart about life in the New England, Middle, and Southern Colonies. Include a column heading for each group of colonies. Then list the following information in rows under each column: major cities; major resources; ways of making a living; other information.

5. **Condensing Information.** Create a pamphlet explaining the French and Indian War. Imagine that the pamphlet is one of a series entitled *Events in American History* and use a question-style format to present your information. For example, you might use questions such as these: What was the French and Indian War? When and where was the war fought? Who were the important military leaders on each side? What were the terms of the treaty that ended the war? Illustrate the pamphlet with maps.

## Practicing Your Skill

Study the picture below, which shows William Penn buying land from Indians. Then answer the following questions on a separate sheet of paper.

1. Where was the deal made—in the Indians' village or the colonists' settlement? How can you tell?
2. What were the English offering the Indians as payment?
3. What evidence suggests that the sale was not simply a handshake agreement? Explain your answer.

# CHAPTER

# 6 Self-Government Develops in the Thirteen Colonies

## 1607–1763

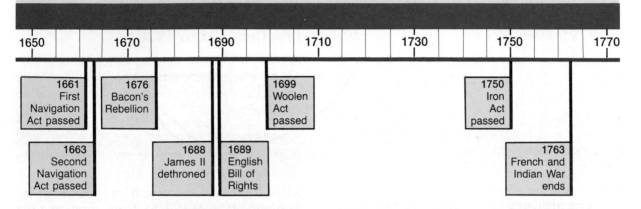

| 1650 | | 1670 | | 1690 | | 1710 | | 1730 | | 1750 | | 1770 |

**1661** First Navigation Act passed

**1676** Bacon's Rebellion

**1699** Woolen Act passed

**1750** Iron Act passed

**1663** Second Navigation Act passed

**1688** James II dethroned

**1689** English Bill of Rights

**1763** French and Indian War ends

**The first meeting of elected representatives in colonial Virginia marked the beginning of self-government in America.**

## Preparing to Read

All of England's American colonies shared a common heritage. An especially important part of the English peoples' heritage was their system of government. Under this system, citizens hold certain rights, including the right to be represented in their government. The English system of government helped the colonies grow from small outposts in the wilderness to important parts of the British Empire. In time, the colonists began to strongly disagree with some of the strict laws and policies of English rule. As you read this chapter, try to answer the following questions:

1. What rights did the English colonists bring to America?
2. What kinds of government grew up in the English colonies?
3. What disagreements developed between England and the colonists?

# 1 What rights did the English colonists bring to America?

## Vocabulary

document
freemen
jury
limited monarchy
legislature

The colonists of New France and New Spain had few rights and little voice in their government. English colonists, on the other hand, believed that they had certain rights that could not be taken away. Because of these rights, English colonists had much more control over their own lives and government than did the colonists from other European countries.

## The English Heritage

The rights that English colonists enjoyed stemmed from the freedoms won by their ancestors in England. The English colonists brought this heritage of freedom to their new home in America.

**The English people limit royal power.** When the Americas were being settled, monarchs ruled England, France, and Spain. The monarchs of France and Spain had become all-powerful in their countries. The people of England, however, had from time to time acted to limit the power of their rulers.

*The Magna Charta.* In the early 1200's England was ruled by King John, a harsh monarch who wished to govern as he pleased. King John taxed the people unfairly and ruled cruelly. In 1215 a group of nobles, upset by King John's highhanded ways, forced him to accept a **document** —an official paper—called the **Magna Charta** (MAG-na KAR-tuh). *Magna Charta* is a Latin term that means "Great Charter."

The Magna Charta limited the king's power. In it King John agreed that nobles and **freemen** —landholders—should not be punished at the whim of the king. Instead, they must be tried by a **jury** —a group of citizens who listen to a trial and give judgment. The jury followed the laws of the land. The king also agreed to consult the Great Council of nobles and church officials about taxes and other important matters. At first, the benefits of the Magna Charta applied only to nobles and freemen. In time, the rights promised in the Magna Charta were extended to all English people.

119

*The Petition of Right.* Charles I ruled England when the Puritans set sail for America. Like King John, Charles was determined to rule as he saw fit. He rarely consulted Parliament. King Charles taxed the people without Parliament's consent. Charles did so despite the long-standing tradition that the monarch must consult Parliament to raise taxes. In 1628 the protests against the king's actions became so great that Charles was forced to accept an important document called the **Petition of Right.** This document stated that the people could not be taxed without the consent of Parliament.

*The English Bill of Rights.* Another English king, James II, ignored Parliament and abused the rights of the people. In 1688 the English people forced James II to leave the

country. In 1689 the new monarchs, William and Mary, accepted a document called the **English Bill of Rights.** The English Bill of Rights declares that elections for Parliament are to be held often. It permits citizens to bear arms, forbids cruel and unusual punishment, and asserts the right to a jury trial.

By accepting these three important documents—the Magna Charta, the Petition of Right, and the English Bill of Rights—the English monarchs admitted that their subjects possessed important rights. As a result, by the late 1600's the English government was a **limited monarchy** —a monarchy in which the ruler does not have complete power. The English people were proud of their success in limiting the power of the Crown, and they were proud of the liberty

**The right to a trial by jury is part of the American system of justice. As practiced today, this right continues a tradition that began in England in the Middle Ages and thrived in England's American colonies.**

they enjoyed. They were determined to maintain their rights against anyone who tried to deny them.

## American Colonial Rights

The English colonists who settled in America claimed the same rights as the people who lived in England. Indeed, many colonists came to America because they wanted greater rights, or because they thought their rights were not completely respected in their homeland.

**English rights are brought to America.** The colonial charters granted by the English Crown supported the colonists' claims. The charters often declared that the English colonists in America were to have the same "liberties ... as if born within this our realm of England."

The charters thus guaranteed that English colonists would have the right to a jury trial and the right to bring complaints to the attention of the Crown. Settlers in the colonies also had a voice in their colonial government. Men who owned a certain amount of property usually could vote for representatives to serve in the legislature —a group of people chosen to pass laws and govern the colony. Colonial legislatures usually decided important questions. Among these questions were how much tax each colonist would pay and who could vote.

**Colonists lack certain rights.** English colonists did not have all the rights that belong to Americans today. Many colonists, including women, slaves, and indentured servants, could not vote or own property. In many colonies certain religious groups were denied their rights because of their faith. In addition, the rights of American Indians were generally ignored.

Nevertheless, by 1750 the English colonists had greater freedom than the people elsewhere in the Americas or in most parts of Europe. Most important, the settlers in the English colonies believed that their rights could not be taken away from them. The colonists had learned to insist that their rights and freedoms be respected by their government leaders.

## LINKING PAST AND PRESENT

## ★★★ Common Law

English settlers brought English legal customs, or **common law,** to the colonies. Common law is a group of legal customs that arose over the years in England. Today Americans still keep many traditions from common law. One of the most important is the right to a trial by jury. In addition, American judges make decisions based on **precedent**—court rulings made in the past.

American laws governing land rights often come from common law. In the United States today, for example, landowners must have written proof called titles and deeds to show that they own a piece of land. Still another American law stems from English tradition. Under English law the Crown owned all land. Today in the United States, the government has the right to all land. This right is called **eminent domain.** If the government wants to build a highway through your yard, you must give up your land. The government, however, must pay you a fair price for it.

## SECTION REVIEW

1. **Vocabulary**   document, freemen, jury, limited monarchy, legislature
2. **People and Places**   King John, Charles I, James II, William and Mary
3. **Comprehension**   What rights did the English colonists have?
4. **Comprehension**   Why did English colonists have greater freedom than colonists in New France and New Spain?
5. **Critical Thinking**   If England's government had not been a limited monarchy, how might American colonial rights have been different?

# 2  What kinds of government grew up in the English colonies?

## Vocabulary
legislator
town meeting
justice of the peace

In the early days of the American colonies, the English rulers usually left the colonists to govern themselves. As the colonies grew in wealth and population, England began to take a greater interest in their affairs. By the mid-1700's, the British government had worked out a plan for governing its far-off colonies. Under this system, the British government gave overall direction to colonial policies. The colonial leaders then worked out the details necessary for effective government in the colonies. For a time, this arrangement proved beneficial for the English people on both sides of the ocean.

## Colonial Government

American colonial governments all had structures based on the government of Great Britain. The colonial governments differed in some details, such as how governors were chosen. In general, however, the colonial governments were much alike.

**Colonial governments are modeled on the government of Great Britain.** At the head of the British government was the monarch. In each colony, the monarch's role was mirrored by the governor, who was the head of the colonial government. Each colony also had a legislature that was modeled on the British Parliament. Colonial legislatures made laws for the colonies and approved taxes. Each colony also had a system of courts similar to those of Great Britain.

The colonial governments usually held a great deal of power over the local affairs of the colonies. The English government, however, always had the last word in colonial affairs. For example, Parliament could overrule laws passed by a colonial legislature, but laws passed by Parliament had to be obeyed in the colonies.

**Colonial governors are chosen in various ways.** The way the governor was chosen depended on the colony. In Rhode Island and Connecticut, **legislators** —members of the legislature—elected the governors. Because these two colonies were governed by the terms of their charters, they were called **charter colonies.** Only these two colonies gave the people an indirect voice in choosing their governors.

In Maryland, Pennsylvania, and Delaware, the proprietor chose the governor. For this reason, these three colonies were called **proprietary colonies.** In these colonies, the governor selected by the proprietor had to be approved by the Crown.

The eight remaining English colonies—Massachusetts, New Hampshire, New York, New Jersey, Virginia, North Carolina, South Carolina, and Georgia—had been founded by trading companies or proprietors. At first the founders had the power to appoint governors. In time, however, the Crown took control of these colonies and thus gained the power to appoint their governors. These eight colonies were known as **royal colonies.** The citizens of the royal colonies did not have any voice in choosing their governors.

**The voters choose the lawmakers.** Colonial governors shared the work of governing with the legislatures. Most legislatures had two branches or houses—an upper house and a lower house. The governor appointed the members of the upper house. The upper house was smaller and less powerful than the lower house. The lower house, often called the assembly, was made up of representatives elected by the

The tradition of the New England town meeting has continued to the present day. This reenactment of an early 1800's town meeting was staged in Sturbridge Village, Massachusetts. Why would the town meeting be an impractical form of government for large cities?

voters. Each town or county in the colony was allowed to send at least one representative to this lower house. In this way, the people had a voice in the passing of laws.

Not everybody had the right to vote for representatives. Throughout the colonies, women were denied the right to vote. Slaves and most free blacks were also denied the vote. In general, only white men at least 21 years of age who owned a certain amount of property were given this right. In some places, property owners also had to belong to a particular church to vote.

## Local Affairs

The British government made important decisions on matters that affected all the colonies. In local affairs, however, each colonial government had almost complete control. The people held the governor and the colonial legislature responsible for what happened in their colony. At times the people rebelled against unpopular decisions made by their colonial governments.

**The colonists manage their local governments.** In the New England Colonies, each town took care of its own affairs. Each town held **town meetings.** A town meeting is a form of local government in which people speak for themselves directly instead of electing representatives. Town meetings were useful in New England, where communities were small and farms were close together. The voters voiced their opinions. They then voted for town or county officers and made decisions about local affairs. The town meeting allowed for a great deal of self-government.

In the Southern Colonies the town meeting was not practical. Because the plantations covered many acres, the people lived great distances apart and there were few towns. As a result, counties formed the basis of local government in the Southern Colonies. Each county covered a large area. The local affairs of each county were handled by a sheriff and several **justices of the peace.** A justice of the peace is an official with many duties, including judging court cases, collecting taxes, and providing for roads. Oftentimes, the planters served as justices of the peace and were appointed by the governor. Colonial citizens did not elect these officials.

In the Middle Colonies, a mixture of town and county government developed. In New York, for example, the town became the common form of local government. In Pennsylvania the county type of government was used more often.

**Conflicts often arise in colonial government.** As might be expected, disputes often arose between the governors and the colonists. Sometimes a royal governor acted against the wishes of the people. At other times, governors objected to the colonial legislature's handling of money. The legislature voted on tax laws and determined the governor's salary. Thus, the legislature of each colony was able to strictly limit the governor's power.

Sometimes, too, the colonists did not agree among themselves. The people on the frontier and those in seacoast towns often had very different interests. Some farmers and frontier settlers complained that the rich merchants in the cities had too much political power. These disagreements sometimes led to conflict.

**Problems lead to Bacon's Rebellion.** In the 1670's, the frontier farmers of Virginia grew angry about increased taxes and poor representation in the Virginia Assembly. The farmers' main complaint was that Governor William Berkeley did not act to protect frontier settlements from Indian attacks. In 1676 the farmers asked Governor Berkeley in Jamestown to send English soldiers to the frontier, but he refused.

Nathaniel Bacon, a wealthy landowner, sympathized with the farmers. He led a group of farmers, including some free blacks, in an attack against the Indians. Instead of fighting enemy Indians, Bacon and his followers slaughtered the Occaneechees, who had harmed no one. Nevertheless, Bacon was hailed as a hero by many settlers on the frontier.

Frontier settlers practiced local self-government by electing representatives to make laws. Interested citizens attended the representatives' meetings, which were often held outdoors. This meeting of delegates was held at Boonesborough, Kentucky, in 1775.

## CITIZENSHIP • Freedom and Responsibility

Americans today believe strongly in freedom of the press—the right of newspaper and magazine publishers to print what they want. In colonial times, however, the royal governors held power over the press. Anyone who dared write critically about government officials might be charged with **libel**—printing statements that unfairly harm a person's reputation.

In 1735 John Peter Zenger, printer of *The New York Weekly Journal,* was arrested for libeling the governor. After spending almost 12 months in jail, Zenger finally came to trial. Zenger's lawyer made a brilliant defense. Libel, he said, was not a matter of simply criticizing someone in print, but writing *false* criticism. He convinced the jury that Zenger's charges against the governor were true. The jury thus found Zenger innocent.

Thanks to this landmark court case, people began to accept the idea that a newspaper could print whatever it wished, as long as what it printed was true. A great victory for a free, but responsible, press had been won.

**The royal governor ordered the burning of Zenger's newspaper.**

Governor Berkeley became alarmed when he heard that Bacon had organized the farmers. The governor quickly allowed the election of a new assembly giving better representation to the farmers. The frontier, however, remained unprotected. Bacon and his followers marched to Jamestown, where they forced the governor to flee and then burned the town. This attack on Jamestown became known as **Bacon's Rebellion.** Soon after the attack, Bacon became ill and died. English soldiers put down the rebellion, and Governor Berkeley returned to power. He then ordered that 23 of Bacon's followers be hanged.

The news of Bacon's Rebellion and Governor Berkeley's actions angered the English government. King Charles II quickly appointed a new governor. Bacon's Rebellion was an early sign that the colonists would insist that their governments listen to the people's wishes.

## SECTION REVIEW

1. **Vocabulary**   legislator, town meeting, justice of the peace
2. **People and Places**   Governor Berkeley, Nathaniel Bacon
3. **Comprehension**   How were all the colonial governments similar?
4. **Comprehension**   What was Bacon's Rebellion?
5. **Critical Thinking**   Were some colonial governments more representative than others? Why or why not?

# MAPS AND GRAPHS: Reading a Diagram

As you read through this book, you will notice that historical information is often presented in **graphic**—visual—form for quicker and easier understanding. One graphic form that historians often use is the **diagram.** A diagram shows how something is organized and how its parts work together.

Diagrams A and B below show two different kinds of English colonial government. Each diagram shows the parts of government (monarch, Parliament, governor, upper and lower houses of the legislature, and colonists) and the laws these parts of government create. The connecting arrows show the flow of power from one part to another. The color of each arrow represents a kind of power: to appoint, to elect, and to pass or reject laws. The direction of the arrow shows who the power affects. In other diagrams, arrows may not represent power. The meaning of the arrows will depend upon the content and purpose of each diagram.

Using the diagrams on this page and the information in Section 2 of this chapter, answer the following questions on a separate sheet of paper.

1. In the type of government shown in Diagram A, how is the governor chosen?
2. In both diagrams, which part of the government do the colonists have the power to elect?
3. In both diagrams, how are members of the upper house chosen?
4. How is the governor chosen in the system shown in Diagram B?
5. Based on your reading, name two colonies that had governments similar to the one shown in Diagram B.
6. What powers do the monarch and the Parliament exercise in both systems of government?
7. Under which system—A or B—do the colonists have greater power? Why?

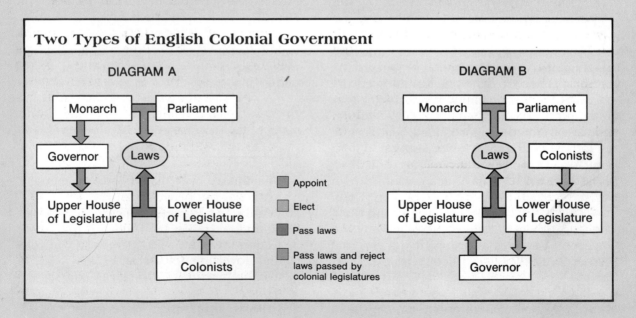

Two Types of English Colonial Government

# 3 What disagreements developed between England and the colonists?

England's policies governing colonial trade and manufacturing were designed to benefit England first and the colonies second. The colonists, however, developed profitable foreign trade routes and often ignored the English trade laws. In many cases, the English laws were not strictly enforced.

## English Colonial Policy

Trade with the American colonies became a source of great wealth for England. To protect this wealth, Parliament passed laws restricting colonial trade and manufacturing. Nevertheless, many colonial merchants grew rich under England's trade laws.

**Mercantilism greatly benefits England.** Throughout the 1600's and 1700's the English government followed the policy of mercantilism. Under this policy, the colonies existed so that England would become wealthy. The colonies provided England with a plentiful supply of crops the English could not grow at home. The crops included tobacco, indigo, and rice. The colonies also sold raw materials such as cotton, wood, and iron to English factories. These raw materials were used in English manufacturing.

In return for American raw materials, England supplied the colonists with the manufactured products they needed. Such manufactured goods as clothes, hats, kettles, dishes, weapons, and tools were in great demand in the colonies. The manufacturing of goods for the colonies provided many jobs for people in England. Manufacturing also brought great profits to English business leaders. English merchants made money transporting goods to and from the colonies. English shipbuilders and shipowners also profited from the busy colonial trade.

**England passes laws to control colonial trade.** In order to protect England's trade with its colonies, Parliament passed laws known as **Navigation Acts.** Two of the most important of these acts were passed by Parliament in the 1660's. The Navigation Acts included three important regulations.

First, the colonists were required to sell certain products only to England or to other English colonies. At the start only a few products, such as sugar, tobacco, and indigo, were restricted. As time went on, however, more articles made in the colonies were added to the list.

Next, all goods coming to the colonies from other countries first had to pass through England. For example, if a cargo of tea were being sent from China to New York, it had to be taken to England first. There the English government taxed the tea before it was shipped to New York.

Finally, all goods going to or coming from the colonies had to be carried by ships built in England or in the colonies. Three fourths of each ship's crew had to be English.

In many ways the Navigation Acts restricted colonial trade. On the other hand, some of the laws benefited the colonies. For example, shipbuilding increased in the colonies because the laws prevented goods from being shipped in foreign vessels.

**The triangular trade grows profitable.** In spite of English restrictions, the colonies played an active part in foreign trade. Colonial merchants developed a series of trade routes known as the **triangular trade.** These routes followed triangular patterns from the colonies to ports in England or other parts of the world, especially Africa or the West Indies. On one triangular trade route, rum from New England was sent to Africa and exchanged for slaves and gold. The slaves and gold were shipped to the West Indies and traded for molasses and sugar. Finally, the molasses and sugar were brought to New England and made into rum.

On another triangular trade route colonial grain, lumber, and other goods were shipped to the West Indies and exchanged for sugar, molasses, and fruit. These goods were brought to England where they were traded for manufactured items. On the last leg of this route, the manufactured items were shipped to New England.

Colonial merchants earned great profits from the triangular trade. To increase their profits, merchants often disobeyed English trade laws. For example, one law required traders to buy sugar and molasses only from English colonies in the West Indies. The

demand for these goods was so high, however, that colonial merchants illegally bought sugar and molasses from the French, Dutch, and Spanish.

**England controls most colonial manufacturing.** In the early days of settlement, the colonists had little time to manufacture goods. As the colonies became more prosperous, people began to make goods in their homes. In time colonial manufacturing became a threat to the sale of English-made goods. As a result, Parliament passed laws restricting manufacturing in the colonies.

Under these laws colonists could make certain goods for their own use, but not for sale in other colonies or countries. In 1699, for example, Parliament passed the Woolen Act. This law prohibited the colonies from sending wool to England or from one colony

New England colonists harpoon a whale in this 1835 painting by William Page. Lamp oil and fats for making candles and ointments were important products of the colonial whaling business. How does the picture suggest the dangers of whaling?

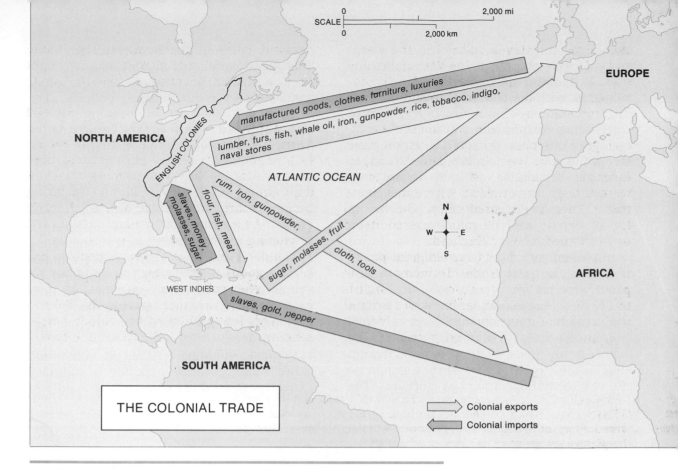

SCALE

0 — 2,000 mi
0 — 2,000 km

EUROPE

NORTH AMERICA

ENGLISH COLONIES

ATLANTIC OCEAN

manufactured goods, clothes, furniture, luxuries

lumber, furs, fish, whale oil, iron, gunpowder, rice, tobacco, indigo, naval stores

rum, iron, gunpowder,

flour, fish, meat

slaves, money, molasses, sugar

sugar, molasses, fruit

cloth, tools

N
W ◆ E
S

AFRICA

WEST INDIES

slaves, gold, pepper

SOUTH AMERICA

THE COLONIAL TRADE

Colonial exports
Colonial imports

## Map Study

**Triangular trade routes developed among England, the colonies, and Africa. What did the colonies export to England? Note the triangle formed by the routes between the colonies, Africa, and the West Indies. Colonists used sugar from the West Indies to make rum, which they traded in Africa for slaves. By what route did slaves reach the English colonies?**

to another. The Iron Act of 1750 allowed iron from the colonies to be shipped to England. This law stopped the colonists from setting up iron mills to manufacture hardware from iron. The colonial iron, however, could be made into hardware in English factories and returned to the colonies to be sold.

## Colonial Disagreement

At first, the laws controlling trade, shipping, and manufacturing did not seriously hurt the colonial economy. Because certain colonial goods had to be sold to England, the colonists were sure of a steady market. Furthermore, the Navigation Acts were not enforced carefully. Until the mid-1700's, the British practiced **salutary neglect** —a policy of allowing the colonies to develop their own economy with little interference from the British government. The colonies were growing rapidly, and England was profiting from the colonial trade. As a result, the British chose not to interfere very much in colonial economic matters.

**The colonists ignore many of the trade laws.** The British policy of salutary neglect allowed the colonists to ignore many of the

laws regulating trade. The British government in turn ignored the breaking of its trade laws. Britain did not want to upset the profitable trade with the colonies. In addition, the British were busy fighting wars with France and dealing with business at home.

Many officials appointed to enforce the Navigation Acts never crossed the Atlantic to carry out their duties. Officials did not keep the colonists from trading with other countries. Therefore, **smuggling** —shipping goods secretly and illegally—was common and very profitable. Colonial merchants, for example, smuggled tea from Holland instead of buying it from English traders whose prices were higher.

**The colonists disagree with Britain about colonial government.** Most colonists did not feel that it was wrong to violate the British trade laws. The colonists, though loyal to the Crown, believed they should be allowed to manage their own affairs. The colonists believed that British leaders knew little about conditions in America.

The British government, on the other hand, held to its mercantilist policies. The British overlooked colonial smuggling, but they continued to believe they could rule the American colonies as they wished.

## SECTION REVIEW

1. **Vocabulary**   salutary neglect, smuggling
2. **People and Places**   Africa, West Indies
3. **Comprehension**   Why did England require foreign goods to pass through England before reaching the colonies?
4. **Comprehension**   What was the triangular trade?
5. **Critical Thinking**   Why, do you think, did England allow a policy of salutary neglect toward the colonies?

# Chapter 6 Summary

English colonists had important rights that were part of their English heritage. Three great documents—the Magna Charta in 1215, the Petition of Right in 1628, and the English Bill of Rights in 1689—limited the power of English monarchs and increased the rights of English people. English rights included the right to a trial by jury, the right of freemen to elect a legislature, and the right of the legislature to approve taxes.

In all colonial governments the highest-ranking official was the governor. In the charter colonies of Rhode Island and Connecticut, the governor was chosen by the legislators. In the proprietary colonies of Maryland, Delaware, and Pennsylvania, the governor was chosen by the proprietor and approved by the Crown. The remaining eight colonies were royal colonies, in which the governor was chosen by the Crown. Local government was carried on either in town meetings or by county officials. During Bacon's Rebellion in 1676, Virginia farmers unhappy with their colonial government burned Jamestown and tried to oust Governor William Berkeley.

In the 1600's and 1700's England followed a policy of mercantilism. Parliament passed restrictive trade laws known as the Navigation Acts to make sure England profited from colonial trade. England also passed laws limiting colonial manufacturing. In time triangular trade routes developed. One route went from New England to Africa and then to the West Indies. Another route went from New England to the West Indies and then to England. Many colonial merchants grew wealthy from the triangular trade, and some merchants became smugglers. Under a policy of salutary neglect, however, English trade laws were not strictly enforced. Until 1763, loose enforcement of British laws suited both Great Britain and the colonists.

# CAUSES and EFFECTS

## Colonial Self-Government ★ ★ ★

England has a Parliament and a Bill of Rights

England is a limited monarchy

Many colonists seek religious freedom

English colonies begin as joint-stock companies

### CONTRIBUTING CAUSES

Britain ignores most colonial affairs

Colonists develop self-reliance

Colonial governments grow strong

English rights are extended to new colonies

### MAIN CAUSES

### SELF-GOVERNMENT

### EFFECTS

Town and county government develops

Colonial leaders emerge

Colonists protest harsh trade laws

Colonists fight to expand westward

### LONG-TERM EFFECTS

Spirit of independence grows strong

Colonies resist British rule

Colonies fight for independence

# Chapter 6 REVIEW

## Vocabulary and Key Terms

Use the following terms to complete the sentences below. Write your answers on a separate sheet of paper.

jury
limited monarchy
Magna Charta
town meeting

salutary neglect
triangular trade
legislature

1. The _____ was the common form of local government in New England.
2. King John was forced to sign the _____, which guaranteed certain rights to nobles and freemen.
3. By the late 1600's, the English government was a _____.
4. A _____ is a group of citizens who listen to a trial and give judgment.
5. Many colonial merchants grew very wealthy by shipping goods on the _____ routes.
6. A _____ is a group of people chosen to pass laws and help govern.
7. The policy of _____ allowed England's American colonies to develop with little interference.

## Recalling the Facts

1. How did the Magna Charta limit royal power?
2. Why did the English people force King Charles I to accept the Petition of Right?
3. What were the requirements for voting in the colonies?
4. How were colonial governments organized?
5. How were local governments in the colonies run?
6. In what ways did the colonies produce wealth for England?
7. In what ways did the Navigation Acts restrict colonial trade?

## Places to Locate

Match the letters on the map with the places listed below. Write your answers on a separate sheet of paper.

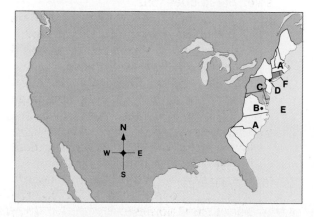

1. proprietary colonies
2. royal colonies
3. charter colonies
4. Atlantic Ocean
5. New York
6. Jamestown

## Critical Thinking

1. Was England's tradition of limited royal power important for representative government in our country? Consider these questions in your answer:
   a. How did England limit royal power over the years?
   b. In what way was colonial government representative?
   c. How has American government today gone beyond English and colonial ideas of representative government?
2. In what ways was the organization of colonial governments similar to the organization of state governments today?
3. What kinds of problems in colonial government were shown by Bacon's Rebellion? Consider these issues in your answer:
   a. the government's duty to different groups in society

b. law and order

c. the colonial government's relationship with England

4. If you were a colonial manufacturer in the 1700's, what might your attitude be toward the English government?

## Understanding History

1. Reread the section "The voters choose the lawmakers" on page 122. Then answer these questions.

   a. **Citizenship.** How were the members of the colonial legislatures chosen?

   b. **Citizenship.** Which colonists could not vote for representatives?

2. Reread the section "The colonists manage their local governments" on page 123. Then answer these questions.

   a. **Geography.** Why were town meetings a good form of local government for New England?

   b. **Geography.** Why was the county form of government used in the Southern Colonies?

3. Reread the section "Mercantilism greatly benefits England" on page 127. Then answer these questions.

   a. **Economics.** Why were colonial raw materials important to English trade?

   b. **Economics.** How did mercantilism help the colonial economy? How did it hurt the colonial economy?

## Projects and Activities

1. **Writing a Report.** Find out more about the Magna Charta, the Petition of Right, or the English Bill of Rights. Use reference books to help you determine what events led to the signing of the document you chose. Write a two-page report on your findings.

2. **Performing a Skit.** Consider what would happen if Nathaniel Bacon stood trial in Virginia after his uprising was put down by English soldiers. With two or three other students, prepare to act out part of Bacon's imaginary trial in class. You may wish to include the parts of Bacon, the judge, a lawyer, the colonial governor, or ordinary citizens.

3. **Interpreting Information.** Make a list of the issues a New England town meeting might have considered in the early 1700's. Be prepared to discuss the issues in class and to decide which of them would still be relevant today.

4. **Organizing Information.** Review the information on mercantilism found in this chapter. List reasons why mercantilism was a good policy from the British point of view. Then list reasons why the colonists opposed mercantilism.

## Practicing Your Skill

Use the diagram of colonial government below to answer the following questions.

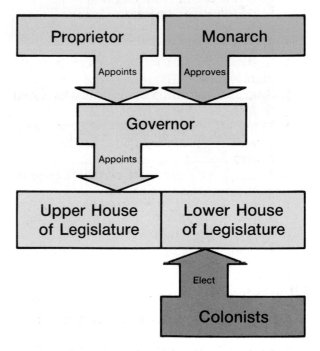

1. How is the governor chosen in the colony in this diagram?

2. What role does the monarch play in the organization of this colonial government?

3. How is the upper house of the legislature chosen?

4. How is the lower house of the legislature chosen?

5. What type of colonial government does this diagram represent?

# UNIT 2 REVIEW

## Unit Summary

★ **England began to colonize North America in the 1600's.**

- English settlers wanted the freedom and land unavailable in their homeland.
- The London Company established the first permanent English colony at Jamestown in 1607.
- Groups seeking religious freedom started other colonies.
- English colonists threatened the Native Americans' way of life.

★ **Ways of life differed in the English colonies.**

- The New England Colonies made religion and education an important part of life.
- The Southern Colonies, aided by a warm climate and good soil, developed the plantation system.
- The Middle Colonies became centers of farming and trade.
- France gave up all claims to North America after the French and Indian War.

★ **Self-government developed in England's American colonies.**

- Colonists brought their rights as British citizens to America.
- Great Britain allowed local self-rule but retained final authority over colonial affairs.
- Parliament passed several laws to protect colonial trade and to restrict manufacturing.
- The colonists and the British disagreed about how the colonies should be governed.

## Understanding Chronology

Study the Unit 2 time line on page 71. Then complete the following activity on a separate sheet of paper.

Several significant events occurred during the 1630's. Make a time line for that decade showing the dates that colonies and settlements were established. Include on your time line other events that make the 1630's an important decade.

## Writing About History

1. **Identifying Important People.** Write entries for a book titled *Who's Who in the English Colonies.* Choose several people and write two or three sentences about the accomplishments or contributions of each one. Include the years of each person's birth and death, as well as his or her birthplace.

2. **Writing an Essay.** Write an essay explaining where you would prefer to have lived—in the New England Colonies, the Southern Colonies, or the Middle Colonies. Base your choice on the different lifestyles found in each colonial region. Include the reasons for your choice.

3. **Researching an Event.** Find more information about the first Thanksgiving celebration. Write a report describing what kinds of food were served, who attended, and what activities the day included. Then compare the first Thanksgiving celebration with how we observe it today.

4. **Comparing Ways of Life.** Write a report comparing the English settlers with the French settlers in North America. Explain how their differing attitudes and ways of life made them rivals. Imagine the ways that life would be different today if the French had won the French and Indian War.

JOIN, or DIE.

5. **Interpreting a Cartoon.** Study the political cartoon above. Benjamin Franklin drew this cartoon to promote colonial unity during the French and Indian War. The drawing is based on the eighteenth-century belief that a snake cut in pieces would live again if the pieces were joined. The letters along the drawing represent the colonies. Write a newspaper editorial expressing the idea Franklin portrayed in the cartoon.

## Projects

1. **Identifying Cause and Effect.** List the conditions in seventeenth-century England that caused people to move to North America. Explain how each condition led people to settle the American colonies in search of new opportunities.
2. **Organizing Information.** Make a chart of the English colonies. List the following information for each colony: its founder, the date founded, reasons for its establishment, and important settlements. Add other facts that distinguish one colony from another.
3. **Demonstrating Crafts.** Work in small groups to research colonial crafts such as shipbuilding, printing, barrel making, soap making, silversmithing, spinning and weaving, or flour milling. Demonstrate these crafts for the class by actually doing them or by presenting diagrams and illustrations to show how they were done.

4. **Presenting Points of View.** List several issues that caused disagreements between England and the colonies. For example, you might list mercantilism, trade laws, manufacturing, and self-government. Work in teams to present both sides of each issue in a class discussion.
5. **Making Models.** Prepare a three-dimensional model that depicts life in one of the English colonial regions. For example, you might create a model of a southern plantation that shows the owner's house, the fields, and the slave quarters. Or, you might make a New England seaport and model the ships used by the fishing industry. Present your project to the entire class.
6. **Comparing Ideas.** Make a poster for each of the following English documents: Magna Charta, Petition of Right, and English Bill of Rights. On each poster list the rights and freedoms guaranteed by the document, and then summarize the ways that the American colonists were allowed to exercise those rights.

## Finding Out More

Avi. *Encounter at Easton.* Pantheon, 1980. This story tells of two runaway indentured servants in eighteenth-century America.

Clapp, Patricia. *Witches' Children: A Story of Salem.* Lathrop, 1982. Salem, Massachusetts, in 1692 is the setting for this story about the effects of the witchcraft trials on 10 girls.

Cousins, Margaret. *Ben Franklin of Old Philadelphia.* Random, 1981. The author presents a well-rounded portrait of an outstanding American.

Fritz, Jean. *The Double Life of Pocahontas.* Putnam, 1983. This is the biography of a Native American woman and her friendship with Captain John Smith.

Tunis, Edwin. *Colonial Living.* Crowell, 1976. Life in colonial America is portrayed here with drawings and explanations of the food, clothing, tools, and customs of American settlers.

40,000 B.C.    A.D. 1000    1100    1200    1300    1400

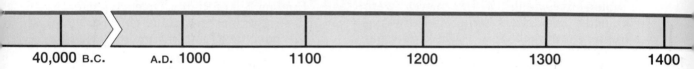

Crossing the Delaware River, General George Washington and his troops
attacked the British at Trenton, New Jersey, on Christmas night, 1776.

136

1763 – 1783

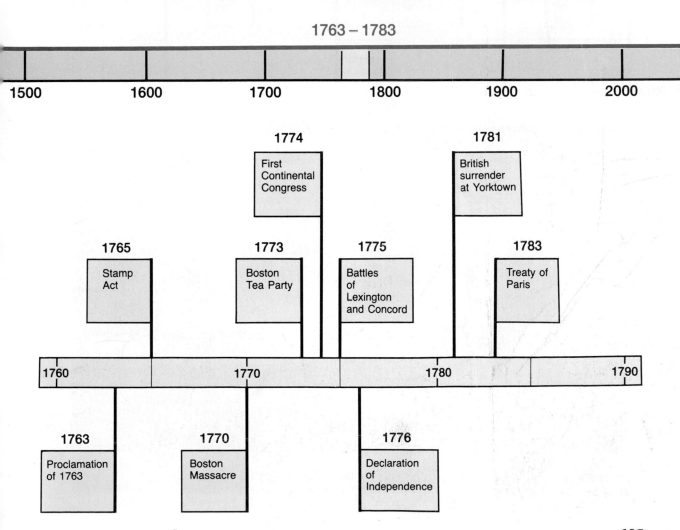

# 7 The Colonists Seek Greater Freedom
## 1763–1775

| 1763 | 1765 | 1767 | 1769 | 1771 | 1773 | 1775 |
|------|------|------|------|------|------|------|

1765
Stamp
Act
passed

1767
Townshend
Acts passed

1773
Boston
Tea
Party

1775
Revolutionary
War begins

1763
Pontiac's War
———————
Proclamation of 1763

1766
Stamp
Act
repealed

1770
Boston
Massacre

1774
First
Continental
Congress

**Disagreements between the colonists and the British gave way to warfare at Concord, Massachusetts, in April 1775.**

## Preparing to Read

For years the 13 colonies had been allowed to govern themselves with little British interference. The colonists still felt loyalty to Great Britain, but they had become used to making their own decisions about government, taxes, and land. After the French and Indian War, however, the British began to exert more control over the colonies. The colonists then saw the new policies of Great Britain as a threat to their own rights and freedoms. As you read this chapter, try to answer the following questions:

1. Why did Britain tighten its control over the American colonies?
2. How did the Americans react to strict control by Britain?
3. What happened when Britain punished the colonists?

# 1 Why did Britain tighten its control over the American colonies?

## Vocabulary

| | |
|---|---|
| militia | revenue |
| proclamation | currency |

The American colonists had helped the British win the French and Indian War. After the victory, however, disagreement arose between the colonists and British officials. The colonists grew angry when the British tried to prevent them from settling in western lands. They were also shocked to find that the British expected them to help pay war debts through new taxes.

## Strife on the Frontier

After the defeat of the French, American colonists poured into the new British lands in the west. Angry Native Americans attacked the settlers, and Britain decided to bar colonists from the western lands.

**The new territory draws attention.** In the Treaty of Paris of 1763, France gave Britain a vast tract of land beyond the Appalachian Mountains. American colonists quickly began moving into the new British lands.

The colonists felt they had a right to settle there. Not only were they British colonists, but their colonial **militias** (muh-LISH-uhz)— groups of citizens trained as soldiers—had helped Britain win the lands from the French. The colonists refused to admit that the western lands belonged to the Native Americans already living there.

**Pontiac's War interferes with western settlement.** In 1763 several Indian groups banded together to stop the settlers. These Native Americans lived west of the Appalachian Mountains. (See map on page 140.) During the last 150 years, these groups had been pushed westward by white settlers. This time they were determined to keep their land.

An extraordinary Ottawa chief named Pontiac united the Shawnee, Delaware, Chippewa, Ottawa, and other tribes. In spring 1763, Pontiac led attacks on forts and settlements in the Ohio region. He and his warriors burned cabins, killed settlers, and captured many British forts. After the British sent additional forces to the frontier, Pontiac was finally defeated.

**Pontiac's War** raised doubts about western settlement. The British government realized that Native Americans and colonists

139

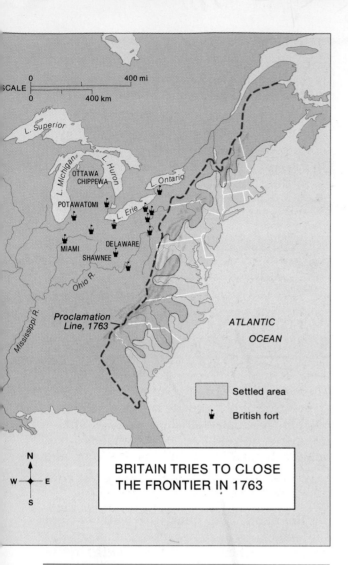

**BRITAIN TRIES TO CLOSE THE FRONTIER IN 1763**

## Map Study

**After Pontiac's War, Britain ordered colonial settlers to stay out of the Ohio Valley. What line marked the western limit of the lands colonists were permitted to occupy?**

could not peacefully share western lands. The British decided to bar colonists from the Ohio region.

**The Proclamation of 1763 closes the frontier.** In fall 1763 King George III issued a **proclamation** —an official announcement. The **Proclamation of 1763** forbade settlement west of the Appalachian Mountains. It ordered settlers already in the region "to

remove themselves." It also stated that the British government would control trade with the Indians. To enforce the Proclamation, the British sent about 10,000 additional British soldiers to the colonies.

## Grenville's New Program

Sending more troops to America was expensive, and Britain was already worried about the high cost of protecting the colonies. To raise more money, the British government decided to end the policy of salutary neglect. The British began enforcing old trade laws and imposing new taxes on the colonies.

**Britain needs money to pay war debts.** The British government did not have enough money to pay its debts from the French and Indian War. In 1763 the British prime minister, George Grenville, decided that American colonists should help pay the war debts. After all, the French and Indian War had been fought partly to protect their lands. Grenville also wanted the colonists to pay half the cost of keeping the British army in North America.

Prime Minister Grenville planned to get more **revenue** —government income—by changing British colonial policies. As he carefully studied colonial tax reports, Grenville discovered that Great Britain was actually losing money in the colonies. Britain was paying its idle customs officials four times the money it was getting back in revenue. Grenville decided to end the policy of salutary neglect. He then began to strictly enforce the existing tax and trade laws. He also planned to set up new taxes.

**Britain tries to enforce the Navigation Acts.** Parliament passed the Navigation Acts during the 1660's. The Navigation Acts had been designed to give England a large share of the profits from colonial trade. (See Chapter 6.) Most colonists ignored the laws, and for years the British did not enforce them. In 1763, however, Grenville sent new officers to the colonies to enforce the Navigation Acts. British warships then began keeping a close lookout for smugglers in American waters.

**140**

**Parliament approves two new taxes.** In 1764 George Grenville pushed the **Sugar Act** and the **Currency Act** through Parliament. The Sugar Act put taxes on sugar, coffee, indigo, and molasses. It produced revenue for Britain and discouraged the Dutch, French, and Spanish West Indies from selling goods to the colonists. Some colonial merchants lost business because of the Sugar Act. Others managed to smuggle goods into the colonies.

Before 1764 most of the American colonies had issued their own currency —paper money. The Currency Act, however, prohibited the colonies from doing so. The Currency Act also required the colonists to pay all debts in gold or silver. It was difficult for the colonists to obey the Currency Act because they were already short of gold and silver. If they used the gold and silver they had to pay British taxes, there would soon be no gold or silver left in the colonies.

**Parliament passes the Stamp Act.** In 1765 Parliament passed another tax proposed by Grenville. The **Stamp Act** placed taxes on legal papers, advertisements, newspapers, almanacs, calendars, and playing cards. All such materials had to bear a stamp showing that the tax had been paid. Even newspaper owners had to purchase the stamps for their publications.

The purpose of the Stamp Act was to raise money to pay the British soldiers stationed in America. Some of the stamps cost only a few cents, but others were more expensive. For example, the tax on a deck of playing cards was one shilling, but the tax on a pamphlet might range from one-half penny to 20 shillings. A colonial document appointing a person to public office might carry a tax as expensive as 4 pounds. Not surprisingly, the Stamp Act was unpopular and angered the American colonists.

The British government felt that the new tax laws were fair. In Britain, citizens already paid a stamp tax and other taxes. It seemed reasonable, therefore, to ask the colonists in America to do the same thing. The British did not realize what a storm of protest these new taxes and their policies would raise in the colonies.

Angry colonists read about the Stamp Act. This law made it illegal to print newspapers or documents on paper lacking a government seal showing that a tax had been paid.

## SECTION REVIEW

1. **Vocabulary** militia, proclamation, revenue, currency
2. **People and Places** Appalachian Mountains, Allegheny Mountains, Pontiac, George III, George Grenville
3. **Comprehension** What effect did Pontiac's War have on British colonial policy?
4. **Comprehension** Why did the British government need to find new sources of revenue in 1763?
5. **Critical Thinking** Was Great Britain justified in thinking that the colonies should pay for part of their own defense? Why or why not?

141

# 2 How did the American colonists react to strict control by Britain?

## Vocabulary

barter          repeal
delegate        writ of assistance
boycott         duty

The new British taxes met great protests in the American colonies. The colonists believed that the British had no right to tax them without their consent. Colonial protests prompted the British government to remove some taxes, but the British maintained the right to make laws for the colonies in America. In time, colonial protests grew louder.

## Anger in the Colonies

The colonists disliked Grenville's new policies. They objected most of all to the Stamp Act, and they carried on lively protests against it.

**Grenville's new policies anger the colonists.** The Proclamation of 1763 stirred up opposition in the colonies. Colonists grew angry because the proclamation ignored the "sea to sea" land grants made in some colonial charters. It also denied the rights of British colonists to British lands. Many colonists disobeyed the proclamation and settled in the Ohio valley.

Colonial merchants and shipowners opposed stricter enforcement of the Navigation Acts. If smuggling were stopped, they could not make as great a profit. They criticized the British government for denying smugglers the right to a jury trial.

The Currency Act came as a blow to colonists who were in debt. These colonists seldom had the gold and silver required to pay back lenders. In addition, paper money had

In 1766 Benjamin Franklin traveled to Britain to protest the Stamp Act to George Grenville (standing, right) and other members of Parliament. Parliament repealed the Stamp Act but soon passed other laws restricting colonial freedoms.

been useful to all the colonists. Gold and silver were so scarce that without paper money, people might be forced to **barter** —trade—goods and services.

**The colonists oppose taxation without representation.** The Stamp Act aroused the greatest protests among the colonists. Almost everyone was affected by this law. Even a marriage license required a government stamp. The colonists' main objection to the tax was that it had been passed by Parliament in which they had no representatives. According to the colonists, "taxation without representation" was a violation of their rights as British citizens.

In the past the colonists had accepted British taxes. They had paid **external taxes**—taxes on trade outside the colonies. Now, however, they were being required to pay **internal taxes**—taxes on trade within the colonies. After all, the Stamp Act taxed such items as newspapers, which were written, printed, and sold within the colonies. This was strictly colonial business, and most colonists believed that only the colonial legislatures should have the power to pass such a tax.

The colonists knew that if they let Britain pass one internal tax, then more would follow. Samuel Adams, a colonial leader from Boston, spoke for many colonists when he asked:

> Why not our lands? Why not the produce of our lands, and everything we possess or make use of? . . . If taxes are laid upon us in any shape without our having a legal representative where they are laid, are we not reduced from . . . free subjects to slaves?

In the Virginia House of Burgesses, young Patrick Henry, a member from the frontier region, denounced "taxation without representation." Inspired by Patrick Henry's speech, the House of Burgesses condemned the Stamp Act. Its members declared that they alone had the power to tax the people of Virginia. News of this bold action spread to other colonies and sparked heated debates.

**The colonists take action against the Stamp Act.** In October 1765 **delegates** —

representatives—from nine colonies took part in the **Stamp Act Congress** in New York. They drew up a formal protest and sent it to Great Britain. The delegates began this protest by promising their loyalty to Britain. They then declared that the right to tax the colonists belonged not to Parliament but to the colonial assemblies.

Some colonists were not happy with a formal protest. The colonists organized groups called **Sons of Liberty** and **Daughters of Liberty** to protect their rights. Feelings ran high against the officials appointed to sell the hated stamps. In Boston a mob wrecked the office of the local stamp agent and then attacked the home of the royal lieutenant governor. Stamp agents in other colonies quit their jobs after being threatened by angry crowds.

**Parliament repeals the hated Stamp Act.** The colonists also protested the Stamp Act by refusing to buy British goods. This **boycott** —refusal to buy goods—proved effective. The British government might ignore the Stamp Act Congress and the colonial mobs. It could not, however, ignore the loud complaints of British business leaders. When trade with the American colonies dropped off sharply, British merchants and manufacturers demanded a change in colonial policy.

In March 1766 Parliament **repealed** —withdrew—the Stamp Act. At the same time, it passed the **Declaratory Act.** This law stated that Parliament had "full power" to pass laws governing the colonies "in all cases whatsoever." In other words, Parliament still claimed the right to tax the colonies if it saw fit. At the time, the colonists paid little attention to the Declaratory Act. All that mattered to them was the repeal of the Stamp Act. Throughout the colonies there was great rejoicing. Bells rang, crowds shouted, and people proclaimed their loyalty to Britain.

## New Laws and New Protests

Colonial resentment of British taxes increased with the passage of a series of strict new trade laws. The colonial protests did not stop after Parliament repealed all but one of these new laws. The outraged colonists had become determined to avoid paying even one tax to Great Britain.

**Parliament passes the Townshend Acts.** In 1767 Parliament passed new laws to control the colonies. The British finance minister, Charles Townshend (TOWN-zend), proposed laws known as the **Townshend Acts.** Economic times were hard in Britain, and the British were more determined than ever to raise money in the colonies.

The Townshend Acts included four important provisions. First, the Navigation Acts were once again to be strictly enforced. The British officers were now allowed to use **writs of assistance** —general search warrants—to look for smuggled goods. Search warrants usually gave officers the right to search a single building for a specific reason. Writs of assistance gave officers the right to search any building for any reason.

Next, the Townshend Acts placed **duties** —taxes—on imported goods such as lead, paper, paint, glass, and tea. British officers collected these duties at the port where the goods entered the colonies.

Third, the money raised under the Townshend Acts was to be used to pay the salaries of British officials in America, including the governors of royal colonies.

Finally, the Townshend Acts forbade meetings of the New York Assembly. Townshend wanted to punish the Assembly because it had not provided supplies for British troops stationed in the colony.

**The Townshend Acts outrage the colonists.** The Townshend Acts started a new wave of protest in the colonies. The writs of assistance angered merchants who thought that homes and warehouses should be safe from government officials. The colonists also objected to paying officials' salaries from tax moneys. This practice meant that colonial legislatures no longer had to approve the officials' salaries. As a result, the colonists had less influence over how the British officials carried out their duties. Finally, many colonists feared that what had happened to the New York Assembly might happen in other colonies.

The colonists were most angry about taxes on imports. Unlike the Stamp Act, the Townshend Acts did not set up internal taxes. Colonists now argued, however, that Britain did not always have the right to collect external taxes. They said that Britain could set up external taxes to regulate trade, but not just to raise revenue. The colonists said they would only accept taxes to raise revenue if the colonial legislatures gave their approval.

**The colonists resist the Townshend Acts.** As the wave of protest gained strength, colonists gathered in the streets and in meetinghouses to speak out against the Townshend Acts. Led by Samuel Adams, the Massachusetts legislature sent the other colonies a letter urging them to oppose the new taxes. The Virginia House of Burgesses condemned the Townshend Acts because they ignored the colony's right to vote on its own taxes. As in the case of the Stamp Act, Americans boycotted British goods. Trade between Britain and the colonies once again dropped sharply.

**The Boston Massacre strengthens opposition.** Anti-British feeling ran especially high in Boston. British soldiers were sent to Boston to maintain order, but their presence only made matters worse. The British wore bright scarlet uniforms, and many Bostonians taunted them with names such as "redcoats" and "lobsterbacks."

On a snowy night in March 1770, a crowd of boys began throwing snowballs at a British sentry, who called other soldiers to his aid. Soon a threatening crowd gathered. Some of the soldiers fired into the crowd, killing several citizens. Among those who fell was Crispus Attucks, a black sailor and one of the leaders of the crowd. This incident became known as the **Boston Massacre.** The people of the city were so outraged after the shooting that the British troops had to withdraw to a fort in Boston Harbor.

At the time of the Boston Massacre, the British government already had plans to repeal the Townshend Acts. The colonial boycott was hurting British trade, and British business leaders were once again complaining. In April 1770 Parliament repealed the

Crispus Attucks, a black sailor, was one of the victims of the Boston Massacre. The event shocked both the colonists and the British. What suggests that the artist who drew this picture was American rather than British?

Townshend Acts, except for the tax on tea. Parliament kept the tea tax to show that it still had the right to tax the colonists.

**The Tea Act stirs up trouble.** The colonists celebrated the repeal of the Townshend Acts, but they were not willing to overlook the tea tax. They saw the tax as a sign of British authority. Many colonists protested the tax by boycotting tea imported from England. Chests of tea began to pile up unsold in the warehouses of London.

In 1773 Parliament passed the **Tea Act,** which gave the British East India Company the right to ship tea directly from Asia to America. Because the ships would not stop in England and pay taxes there, the tea would be cheaper than usual. The tea would still be taxed, of course, in America.

The Tea Act sharply lowered the price of tea in the colonies. In spite of this, many colonists opposed the new law. They saw the Tea Act as a British trick to stop the colonial boycott, and they still refused to pay the tea tax. Colonial merchants were especially alarmed. They feared that the low prices of the British East India Company would drive American tea importers out of business.

**Boston holds a tea party.** The colonists refused to let the British East India Company sell its tea in the colonies. In Charleston colonists unloaded the tea and stored it in damp cellars so it would rot. In New York and Philadelphia the ships were turned away from the harbors. In Boston, late in 1773, a group of colonists dressed as Indians boarded East India Company ships by night and heaved 342 chests of tea into the water. One of the men who took part in the **Boston Tea Party** gave the following account of it:

It was now evening, and I immediately dressed myself in the costume of an Indian, equipped with a small hatchet ... and a club.... [After painting] my face and hands with coal dust in the shop of a blacksmith, I [went] to Griffins Wharf, where the ships lay that contained the tea. When I first appeared in the street, after being thus disguised, I fell in with many who were dressed, equipped, and painted as I was, and [we] marched in order to the place of our destination [and boarded the ships]....

We then were ordered by our commander to open the hatches, and take out all the chests of tea and throw them overboard, and

145

Patriots, disguised as Native Americans, protested the Tea Act by dumping British tea into Boston Harbor. Some colonists approved of the Boston Tea Party, but others disapproved of destroying property— even for a just cause. Which view does this picture express?

we immediately proceeded to execute his orders; first cutting and splitting the chests with our tomahawks, so as thoroughly to expose them to the effects of the water.

In about three hours from the time we went on board, we had thus broken and thrown overboard every tea chest to be found in the ship, while those in the other ships were disposing of the tea in the same way, at the same time. We were surrounded by British armed ships, but no attempt was made to resist us. We then quietly returned to our several [homes], without having any conversation with each other, or taking any measures to discover who were our associates. . . .

Many colonists rejoiced when they heard about the Boston Tea Party. They believed it would show how strongly they objected to taxation without representation. Other colonists were shocked to hear what the Bostonians had done. They did not think that destroying property was the best way to solve the debate over taxes. Even Benjamin Franklin suggested that the colonists pay the British East India Company for the ruined tea. The debate over the best response to strict British laws would continue almost three more years.

## SECTION REVIEW

1. **Vocabulary**   barter, delegate, boycott, repeal, writ of assistance, duty
2. **People and Places**   Samuel Adams, Patrick Henry, Charles Townshend, Crispus Attucks
3. **Comprehension**   Why did colonists call the Stamp Act "taxation without representation"?
4. **Comprehension**   Why did colonists object to the Tea Act?
5. **Critical Thinking**   In what ways were colonial protests against the Stamp Act and the Townshend Acts similar? Explain your answer.

## CRITICAL THINKING: Analyzing Primary Sources

Earlier you read that historians depend on primary sources—most often written documents—to study the past. Such documents as treaties, letters, diaries, cargo lists, and tax records written at the same time as the events they describe are all primary sources.

When primary sources are printed in a book, two special kinds of punctuation are often used to save space or to make the meaning clearer. A set of dots like this ... is called an **ellipsis** (ih-LIP-sus). It shows that some words have been left out. Brackets like these [ ] sometimes enclose a word. Brackets show that the word is not part of the primary source. It either replaces an unfamiliar word or gives the reader extra information.

The four steps below will help you analyze primary sources. First, identify the author of the document. Then, note when and where the document was written. Third, skim the document to get an idea of its content. Finally, read the document carefully and try to recognize the author's feelings and opinions. Sometimes, the author's views of an event can indicate how others were feeling at the time.

Below is an excerpt from a letter to John Adams, a Patriot leader, from his wife Abigail. Use the four steps just described to read this primary source. Then answer the questions that follow on a separate sheet of paper.

1. When and where was this letter written?
2. What event did the author witness?
3. Were the people who took the gunpowder Patriots or Tories? What evidence for this is in the letter?
4. Do you think the author is a Patriot or a Tory? Why do you think so?
5. What is the mood of the people as reflected in this letter?
6. What events did Abigail Adams report although she did not actually see them? What phrase gives you a clue that she did not see the events?
7. How do you think the author felt about the events reported in this letter? Cite examples to support your answer.

---

Braintree [Massachusetts]
14 September, 1774

... About eight o'clock Sunday evening there passed by here about two hundred men, preceded by a horsecart, and marched down to the powder-house, from whence they took the [gun] powder, and carried it into the other parish and there [hid] it. I opened the window upon their return. They passed without any noise, not a word among them till they came against this house, when some of them, [seeing] me, asked me if I wanted any powder. I replied, No, since it was in so good hands. The reason they gave for taking it was that we had so many Tories [people loyal to Britain] here, they dared not trust us with it. ... This town appears as [excited] as you can well imagine, and, if necessary, would soon be in arms. Not a Tory but hides his head. The church parson [a Tory] thought they were coming after him and ran up [to his attic]; they say another jumped out of his window and hid among the corn, whilst a third crept under his board fence.

[Abigail Adams]

# What happened when Britain punished the colonists?

## Vocabulary

intolerable

quarter

The harsh British laws were stretching colonial loyalty to the breaking point. The 13 colonies began working together to protest the laws. When these protests failed, the colonies began training soldiers who could stand up to the British on the battlefield.

## British Restrictions

The Boston Tea Party prompted the British government to pass harsh laws punishing Massachusetts. In response, the colonists organized protests against the new laws. The colonists soon joined together to assert their rights.

**Parliament passes laws to punish Massachusetts.** When news of the Boston Tea Party reached London, the British government decided to punish the colonists of Massachusetts. In 1774 Parliament passed four harsh laws called the Coercive Acts. The colonists found the laws **intolerable** —unbearable—and called them the **Intolerable Acts.** One law closed the port of Boston until colonists paid for the destroyed tea. A second law increased the power of the Massachusetts royal governor and weakened the state legislature. A third law called for the colonists to **quarter** —provide food and housing for—British soldiers. A fourth law stated that certain British officials accused of crimes could be tried in other colonies or in England.

To enforce the Intolerable Acts, King George III sent more British troops to Boston. He appointed the commander of the troops, General Thomas Gage, as the new governor of Massachusetts.

**Patriots organize resistance to the Intolerable Acts.** The Intolerable Acts outraged the **Patriots**—colonists who opposed strict British control. They viewed the new laws as an attack on the right of self-government. The Massachusetts colonists grew especially angry, because the laws directly affected them. Throughout the colonies Patriots spoke out against the British and defended Massachusetts.

The Patriots began to organize their protests through groups known as **Committees of Correspondence.** The Patriot leader Samuel Adams had formed the first of these groups in Boston in 1772. Its members promised to spread information by corresponding with, or writing to, other colonists. Similar groups to protect colonial rights soon sprang up in other colonies.

The Committees of Correspondence circulated pamphlets against the Intolerable Acts. Committee members organized protests against the laws, such as the day of prayer and fasting declared by the Virginia House of Burgesses. The committees arranged to send supplies to the citizens of Boston because the Intolerable Acts had closed the port. Supplies poured into Boston from as far away as the Carolinas, and the Bostonians soon had more food and supplies than they needed.

**The First Continental Congress meets.** The Patriot leaders could send messages through the Committees of Correspondence, but they wanted to meet in person to discuss their rights. In September 1774, delegates from all the colonies except Georgia assembled in Philadelphia at a meeting called the **First Continental Congress.**

The delegates to the First Continental Congress demanded a change in British policy. They did not want independence from Britain, but they wanted recognition of their rights as British subjects. The delegates took

# Conflict Widens Between Britain and America

| Year | Actions of the British Parliament | Colonists' Reactions |
|------|-----------------------------------|----------------------|
| 1763 | Issues Proclamation of 1763 to close the frontier | Ignore Proclamation |
| 1764 | Passes the Sugar Act to raise money from colonial imports | Protest taxation without representation in Parliament |
| 1765 | Passes the Stamp Act to pay for British troops in the colonies | Establish the Stamp Act Congress; boycott British goods |
| 1766 | Repeals the Stamp Act; passes the Declaratory Act to assert its authority | End the boycott |
| 1767 | Passes the Townshend Acts to raise more money from colonial imports | Organize new boycotts; clash with British troops (Boston Massacre) |
| 1770 | Repeals the Townshend Acts, except for a tax on tea | Welcome repeal of the Townshend Acts |
| 1773 | Passes the Tea Act to give a monopoly on tea trade to the East India Company | Protest the Tea Act by staging the Boston Tea Party |
| 1774 | Passes the "Intolerable Acts" (Boston port closed; Massachusetts charter suspended; troops stationed in colonial homes; western settlements outlawed) | Establish the First Continental Congress; boycott British goods |
| 1775 | Declares Massachusetts in a state of rebellion; sends troops to Lexington and Concord, Massachusetts | Establish the Second Continental Congress and a Continental Army |

## Chart Study

**British actions and colonial reactions established a cycle of conflict that led to the outbreak of war. Britain tried to control its colonies by making strict laws. What were the two main ways in which the colonists rebelled?**

four important steps at the Congress. First, they asserted that the colonial legislatures had the right to make all colonial laws. They called for the repeal of the Intolerable Acts, which violated this right. Next, they threatened to halt exports to Britain and the British West Indies if the Intolerable Acts were not repealed within a year. Third, they organized a boycott of British goods. They resolved to form local committees to make sure that citizens took part in the boycott. Finally, the delegates promised to meet again in May 1775 if relations with Great Britain had not improved by then.

## Taking Up Arms

Angry at the British failure to repeal the Intolerable Acts, the Patriots organized an army. When the British marched from Boston to capture Patriot leaders and weapons, the colonial militia openly resisted. This clash began the **Revolutionary War.**

**The colonists prepare to fight.** The Patriots expected the colonial boycott of British goods to make Parliament repeal the Intolerable Acts. After all, past boycotts had led to the repeal of the Stamp Act and the Townshend Acts. This time, however, Parliament

## PROFILE • Benjamin Franklin

At the age of 17 Benjamin Franklin ran away from his job as a Boston printer's apprentice and traveled to Philadelphia. A hard worker with a passion for self-education, Franklin soon bought his own printing shop and a newspaper called the *Pennsylvania Gazette*. He became clerk of the Pennsylvania Assembly and used his newspaper to propose ideas for colonial reform.

Franklin became known for his clever writing, his scientific experiments, and his good works in the city of Philadelphia. In 1751 he was elected to the Pennsylvania Assembly, where he defended the power of the common people.

Franklin later spent several years in England as a representative of Pennsylvania. He wrote essays protesting British taxes on the colonies, and finally traveled home to take part in the Continental Congress. After helping to draft the Declaration of Independence in 1776, Franklin sailed for Paris. There he used his influence in French society to get crucial French aid for the Patriots.

**Benjamin Franklin**

would not back down. Instead, Parliament added new restrictions on colonial trade and sent more British soldiers to America. By the end of 1774, some colonists began preparing to fight the British. In many towns and villages, militias met for military drill. The colony of Massachusetts defied its royal governor, General Gage, and started to organize an army.

Most Patriot leaders thought that the fighting would be short. They believed a show of force by the colonists would make the British repeal the Intolerable Acts. The Americans would then continue to be loyal British subjects. Few Patriots expected a war of independence. One who did, however, was Patrick Henry, the fiery Virginia Patriot. In a stirring speech before the Virginia Convention of Delegates in March 1775, Patrick Henry declared:

Gentlemen may cry, peace, peace—but there is not peace. The war is actually begun! The next gale that sweeps from the north will bring to our ears the clash of resounding arms! Our brethren are already in the field! Why stand we here idle? What is it that gentlemen wish? What would they have? Is life so dear, or peace so sweet, as to be purchased at the price of chains and slavery? Forbid it, Almighty God! I know not what course others may take; but as for me, give me liberty, or give me death!

**The British move on Lexington and Concord.** General Gage soon learned that the Massachusetts colonists had formed an army

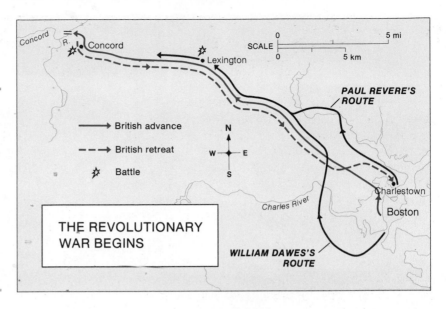

THE REVOLUTIONARY WAR BEGINS

- → British advance
- --→ British retreat
- ✳ Battle

PAUL REVERE'S ROUTE

WILLIAM DAWES'S ROUTE

Concord R.   Concord   Lexington   SCALE   0   5 mi   0   5 km   N   W   E   S   Charles River   Charlestown   Boston

**The British planned to arrest Revolutionary leaders in Lexington, Massachusetts, and to capture the colonial weapon supply in Concord. Paul Revere, William Dawes, and others raised the alarm. Which rider took a southern route from Boston? From what town were the British forced to retreat?**

in defiance of his orders. Gage discovered that the Patriots had stored arms and ammunition in **Concord,** a town northwest of Boston. On the night of April 18, 1775, Gage ordered troops to march on Concord and seize the weapons. He also ordered them to capture two Patriot leaders, Samuel Adams and John Hancock, at the nearby town of **Lexington.**

The Patriots had planned for a sudden British move. The Patriot soldiers, called **minutemen,** stood ready to assemble at a minute's notice. A few Patriots were keeping watch on the British troops at Boston. When they learned of Gage's plans, three Patriot riders galloped out of Boston to alert the minutemen. (See map on this page.) In a nighttime ride that has become a famous American legend, Paul Revere reached Lexington and warned Adams and Hancock, who were able to escape. The poet Henry Wadsworth Longfellow later wrote these verses about Paul Revere:

> He said to his friend, "If the British march
> By land or sea from the town tonight,
> Hang a lantern aloft in the belfry arch
> Of the North Church tower as a signal
>   light,
> One, if by land, and two, if by sea;
> And I on the opposite shore will be,
> Ready to ride and spread the alarm

> Through every Middlesex village and
>   farm,
> For the country folk to be up and to arm.

The friend kept watch in Boston and learned that the redcoats were preparing to march. The poet continued his description:

## LINKING PAST AND PRESENT

# ★★★ *Revisiting Battles*

Every year on April 19, the townspeople of Lexington, Massachusetts, get up before sunrise and meet on the village green. Smoke drifts from the barrels of old-fashioned muskets as minutemen seem to exchange shots with British redcoats. Six miles away, citizens of Concord gather on the bridge across the Concord River. They hold their ground as the redcoats march toward them. After several pretended volleys of shots, the British turn back in defeat.

Each year Americans reenact these and other battles against the British. These reenactments are one way of honoring the Patriots who made today's America a reality.

Paul Revere's ride became a legend in a poem by Henry Wadsworth Longfellow. The poem describes how Revere watched for signal lights to flash from a church tower, alerting him that the British were coming. When he got the signal, he rode through the night warning others.

Meanwhile, impatient to mount and ride,
Booted and spurred, with a heavy stride
On the opposite shore walked Paul
    Revere.
And lo! as he looks, on the belfry's height
A glimmer, and then a gleam of light!
He springs to the saddle, the bridle he
    turns,
But lingers and gazes, till full on his sight
A second lamp in the belfry burns!

So through the night rode Paul Revere;
And so through the night went his cry of
    alarm
To every Middlesex village and farm.

The British troops halted Revere and another rider, William Dawes, before they reached Concord. Dr. Samuel Prescott, the third rider, made it to Concord and warned the townspeople to take up arms.

**A shot is "heard round the world."** The British reached Lexington in the early morning of April 19, 1775. The minutemen had gathered in the center of town. The British officers urged them to throw down their weapons, but the minutemen held their ground. Shots rang out, and 8 Patriots were killed and 10 more wounded.

The British then marched six miles to Concord, where they burned the courthouse and destroyed Patriot military supplies. At a bridge on the edge of town, they met another group of determined minutemen. The two forces exchanged shots, and the minutemen forced the British to retreat. As the redcoats made their way along the road to Boston, the Patriots fired on them from behind trees and stone walls. By the time the British force reached safety, nearly 300 British soldiers were dead, wounded, or missing.

The Patriots had taken a bold stand against the British. They did not realize it, but the battles at Lexington and Concord were the opening shots of the Revolutionary War. The bravery of the minutemen was to become the inspiration for people struggling for freedom around the world. For this reason, the scholar and poet Ralph Waldo Emerson wrote of the events at Concord:

> By the rude bridge that arched the flood,
> Their flag to April's breeze unfurled,
> Here once the embattled farmers stood,
> And fired the shot heard round the world.

## SECTION REVIEW

1. **Vocabulary**   intolerable, quarter
2. **People and Places**   Thomas Gage, Patriots, Concord, Lexington, John Hancock, Paul Revere, William Dawes, Dr. Samuel Prescott
3. **Comprehension**   Why did Parliament pass the Intolerable Acts?
4. **Comprehension**   What led to fighting at Lexington and Concord?
5. **Critical Thinking**   Why, do you think, did the colonial boycott fail to make Parliament repeal the Intolerable Acts?

# Chapter 7 Summary

Colonial settlers poured into western lands won by the British during the French and Indian War. In Pontiac's War Native Americans tried to force new settlers out. British prime minister George Grenville closed these western lands to settlement in the Proclamation of 1763. Faced with war debts, Grenville also authored new policies, such as the Stamp Act of 1765, to raise more revenue from the colonies.

The colonists carried on a boycott of British goods until the Stamp Act was repealed in 1766. Parliament angered the colonists again in 1767 by passing the Townshend Acts, which authorized writs of assistance and set new duties on imported goods. The colonists again protested. In 1770 several colonists were shot by British soldiers in a protest known as the Boston Massacre. That same year Parliament repealed the Townshend Acts, leaving only one tea tax in place. When the British enforced that tax by passing the Tea Act in 1773, the citizens of Boston staged the Boston Tea Party.

Parliament punished Massachusetts for the Boston Tea Party by passing the Intolerable Acts in 1774. These new laws attacked the colonial right of self-government. They prompted Patriots to organize protests and to form the First Continental Congress. Parliament ignored the demands of the Congress for a change in policy, and the colonists began to form an army. When the British tried to seize colonial arms in April 1775, American minutemen fought them at Lexington and Concord.

# Chapter 7 REVIEW

## Vocabulary and Key Terms

Match each of the following terms with its correct definition. Write your answers on a separate sheet of paper.

**boycott**
**Patriots**
**First Continental Congress**
**Proclamation of 1763**
**delegate**
**Coercive Acts**
**militia**

1. a group of citizens trained as soldiers
2. a representative at a meeting or convention
3. laws passed by Parliament to punish Boston after the Boston Tea Party
4. the name given to colonists who resisted strict control by the British
5. a 1774 meeting of colonists to discuss settling differences with Great Britain
6. a refusal to buy goods
7. King George's announcement that colonists could not settle west of the Allegheny Mountains

## Recalling the Facts

1. How did the end of the French and Indian War change British policies toward the colonies?
2. What was Pontiac's War?
3. Why did Parliament pass the Sugar, Currency, and Stamp Acts?
4. What does the slogan "no taxation without representation" mean?
5. What were the Townshend Acts, and how did the colonists react to them?
6. What was the Boston Tea Party?
7. What was the main goal of the Coercive Acts?
8. Why were British soldiers sent to Concord, Massachusetts, in 1775?

## Places to Locate

Match the letters on the map with the places listed below. Write your answers on a separate sheet of paper.

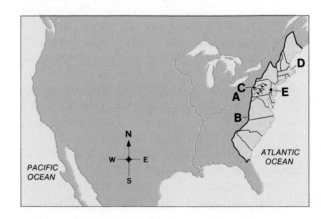

1. Allegheny Mountains
2. Ohio region
3. Philadelphia
4. Proclamation Line of 1763
5. Boston Harbor

## Critical Thinking

1. Do you think it was wise of Great Britain to repeal the Stamp Act? Consider these points in your answer:
   a. Why did Great Britain repeal the law?
   b. Why was the repeal of the Stamp Act a victory for the colonists?
   c. What example was set by repealing the act?
2. Great Britain strengthened its rule over the colonies after many years of salutary neglect. Why did the colonists have trouble accepting stricter rule after so many years? Might the colonists have protested as strongly if they had always experienced tight control by Great Britain?
3. Were colonial protests of British policies well organized? Consider these questions in your answer:

a. How well did the colonists communicate with one another?

b. What part did mob violence play in protest, and how effective was it?

c. What was the end result of the colonists' protest? Do you think it was planned this way? Why or why not?

## Understanding History

1. Reread the section "Pontiac's War interferes with western settlement" on page 139. Then answer these questions.
   a. **Geography.** Could the land west of the Allegheny Mountains be called the frontier of the 1760's? Why?
   b. **Geography.** Why, do you think, did the British government not want the Indians and the colonists to clash in the Ohio region?
2. Reread the section "The Tea Act stirs up trouble" on page 145. Then answer these questions.
   a. **Economics.** Why did the colonists refuse to buy the East India Tea Company's tea, even though its price was low?
   b. **Economics.** Why were colonial merchants unhappy about the low cost of the East India Tea Company's tea?
3. Reread the section "The First Continental Congress meets" on page 148. Then answer these questions.
   a. **Citizenship.** On what basis did the Continental Congress call for repeal of the Intolerable Acts?
   b. **Citizenship.** How was the First Continental Congress an example of representative decision making?

## Projects and Activities

1. **Interpreting Information.** Imagine that you are an American colonist in the early 1770's. List all the items you would put in a time capsule to give later generations a picture of the struggles of the time.
2. **Summarizing Information.** Choose five people who are mentioned in this chapter. For each one, write a statement such as the following description of Pontiac: "I am an Ottawa chief who tried to keep the settlers out of the western lands." Read your descriptions to a classmate and have him or her try to identify each person described.
3. **Illustrating an Event.** Draw an editorial cartoon that illustrates Britain's reaction to the Boston Tea Party. Have the cartoon show either a sympathetic or an unsympathetic bias toward the colonists.
4. **Writing a Report.** Write a news account of the events at Lexington and Concord, Massachusetts, in April 1775. Consult reference sources to find details for your account. Invent comments of people who might have been there.

## Practicing Your Skill

The excerpt below is from a letter written in 1775 by C.S., an American woman living in Philadelphia. Read the excerpt and answer the questions that follow.

I will tell you what I have done. My only brother I have sent to the camp with my prayers and blessings. . . . I am confident he will behave with honor, and emulate the great example he has before him; and had I twenty sons and brothers they should go. I have retrenched every superfluous expense in my table and family; tea I have not drank since last Christmas, nor bought a new cap or gown since your defeat at Lexington, and what I never did before, have learnt to knit, and am now making stockings of American wool for my servants, and this way do I throw in my mite to the public good. I know this, that as free I can die but once, but as a slave I shall not be worthy of life. I have the pleasure to assure you that these are the sentiments of all my sister Americans. They have sacrificed both assemblies, parties of pleasure, tea drinking, and finery to that great spirit of patriotism. . . .

1. What specific things has C.S. done to help the American cause?
2. According to C.S., do other American women share her feelings? How can you tell?
3. Based on the excerpt, is C.S. a Patriot or a Loyalist? Why?

# 8 The Thirteen Colonies Win Independence 1775–1783

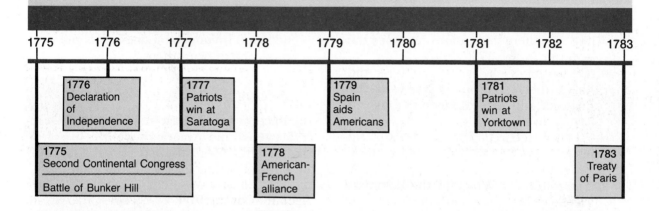

1775     1776     1777     1778     1779     1780     1781     1782     1783

**1776**
Declaration
of
Independence

**1777**
Patriots
win at
Saratoga

**1779**
Spain
aids
Americans

**1781**
Patriots
win at
Yorktown

**1775**
Second Continental Congress

Battle of Bunker Hill

**1778**
American-
French
alliance

**1783**
Treaty
of Paris

**American colonists raise a liberty pole to celebrate declaring their independence from Great Britain.**

## Preparing to Read

Even after the battles at Lexington and Concord, many colonists did not want to break with Great Britain. Their hopes for a peaceful agreement faded, however, when the British government made its colonial trade policies even stricter. In 1776 the Patriots declared the independence of the United States. After a long and costly war with Great Britain, the United States finally emerged as a new, independent nation. As you read this chapter, try to answer the following questions:

1. Why did the 13 colonies decide to declare their independence?
2. What strengths and weaknesses did Americans have in the Revolution?
3. How did the 13 colonies win their independence?

# 1 Why did the 13 colonies decide to declare their independence?

### Vocabulary
petition
mercenary
resolution

In the early battles of the Revolution—before independence was declared—the Patriots proved to be skillful fighters. Many colonists hoped that the strong Patriot stand would convince Great Britain to make compromises. When Great Britain refused, the colonists decided to declare independence.

## Drifting Toward Independence

News of the fighting at Lexington and Concord quickly spread through the colonies. In Philadelphia Patriot leaders met to discuss their plans. Meanwhile, new battles broke out.

**The Second Continental Congress meets.** When the First Continental Congress broke up in 1774, the delegates agreed to meet again if relations with Great Britain did not improve. On May 10, 1775, soon after the battles at Lexington and Concord, the **Second Continental Congress** gathered in Philadelphia.

The Congress set up the **Continental Army** and named George Washington as its commander-in-chief. The delegates made plans to defend the colonies and drive the British out of Boston.

Meanwhile, the delegates made one final effort to avoid war. On July 5, 1775, Congress voted to send a petition, known as the **Olive Branch Petition,** to King George III. A **petition** is a written request for a right. Signed "your faithful colonists," the plea urged the Crown to protect the colonists from the unfair policies of Parliament. George III refused to read the petition.

**The Patriots fight a series of early battles.** Colonial militias began fighting the British forces even while the Congress was still hoping for peace. In June 1775, after learning that British troops in Boston were planning to occupy the hills outside the city, the New England militia fortified Breed's Hill overlooking Boston. (They had been given orders to fortify nearby Bunker Hill, but chose Breed's Hill instead.) On June 17, 1775, the British commander, General Gage,

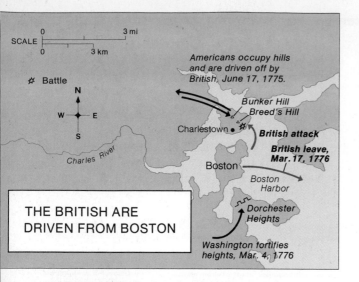

THE BRITISH ARE
DRIVEN FROM BOSTON

SCALE
0 — 3 mi
0 — 3 km

★ Battle

Americans occupy hills
and are driven off by
British, June 17, 1775.

Bunker Hill
Breed's Hill

Charlestown •

British attack

British leave,
Mar. 17, 1776

Boston

Boston
Harbor

Dorchester
Heights

Charles River

Washington fortifies
heights, Mar. 4, 1776

## Map Study

**To drive out the British, the Patriots surrounded Boston and fortified Dorchester Heights with 59 captured cannon. By what route did the British retreat?**

ordered an attack on Breed's Hill. The British soldiers were thrown back twice before the Patriots, short of ammunition, were forced to retreat. This battle became known as the **Battle of Bunker Hill.** The British had won the battle, but they had lost more than 1,000 troops out of a force of 2,200. The Battle of Bunker Hill warned the British that the Patriots would fight valiantly for their cause.

Patriots from present-day Vermont, led by Ethan Allen, delivered another early blow to the British in northeastern New York. Known as the Green Mountain Boys, these Patriots attacked and captured Fort Ticonderoga (ty-kahn-duh-RO-guh) in New York on May 10, 1775. Two days later, they captured a second British fort at Crown Point, New York. These unexpected victories prompted two Patriot expeditions to invade Canada in the fall and winter of 1775. The Patriots captured Montreal, but failed to take Quebec. By spring 1776 the Patriots withdrew from Canada.

**Colonial troops force the British to leave Boston.** In July 1775 George Washington took command of Patriot forces near Boston.

For months General Washington and his soldiers tried but failed to drive the British out of the city. Then in early 1776 the Patriots received 59 cannon that had been dragged overland from the captured Fort Ticonderoga. In a surprise move, Washington's soldiers set up the cannon on Dorchester Heights overlooking Boston. General Howe, the new British commander, decided that he could not hold Boston under the constant threat of cannon fire. The British troops sailed to Halifax, Nova Scotia, leaving Boston to the Patriots.

**Southern Patriots take up arms.** The British hoped to defeat the Patriots with the help of **Loyalists.** The Loyalists, sometimes called **Tories,** were Americans who wanted to remain British subjects. The royal governor of North Carolina recruited a troop of Loyalists to fight for the Crown. In February 1776, however, North Carolina Patriots defeated the Loyalists at Moore's Creek. In June, South Carolina Patriots built a makeshift fort on the shore at Charleston. From the fort they bombarded a British fleet that

## LINKING PAST AND PRESENT

### ★ ★ ★ "Yankee Doodle"

Yankee Doodle came to town
Riding on a pony,
Stuck a feather in his hat
And called it macaroni.

When foreigners called Americans "Yankees" in the 1750's, they meant it as an insult. By the start of the Revolutionary War, however, Americans were proud to be called Yankees.

The British troops considered the Americans to be ignorant country people. They sang the song "Yankee Doodle" to make fun of colonial soldiers.

The colonists, however, soon came to be proud of "Yankee Doodle." After the Battle of Bunker Hill, they began to sing and whistle the song themselves. It became a famous American tune.

had been sent to attack the city. The British ships, suffering heavy damage, returned to New York. (See map on this page.)

## Colonial Independence

During the first year of fighting, between spring 1775 and spring 1776, many Americans still hoped to come to an agreement with Great Britain. As a result of the fighting, however, British policies grew even stricter. Finally, in 1776 the Patriots declared the colonies independent of Great Britain.

**The British government takes a firm stand.** The Patriots at first hoped that by fighting they would show the king and his ministers how bitterly they opposed British policies. They hoped that the king would loosen controls. The king refused. After rejecting the Olive Branch Petition, George III issued the **Proclamation of Rebellion** on August 23, 1775. The Proclamation stated that the American colonies were in open revolt against Great Britain. The British government punished the colonists by passing even stricter trade laws. In addition, the British hired **mercenaries** —soldiers who are paid to fight for a foreign army—to serve in the British army in America. The mercenaries were Hessians, from the German state of Hesse. The colonists saw the Hessians as unwelcome outsiders in the quarrel.

**Thomas Paine stirs public opinion.** Thomas Paine was an English writer who came to America on the recommendation of Benjamin Franklin. In January 1776 Paine published a pamphlet called _Common Sense_, in which he called on Americans to break away from Great Britain. Paine argued that such a vast continent as America should not be ruled by a small island thousands of miles away. He told colonists that they should not obey laws that hurt their trade and industry. The colonists, Paine declared, were foolish to pledge loyalty to a king who sent armies to oppress them. Paine wrote, "Everything that is right or reasonable pleads for separation."

_Common Sense_ was a great success in the colonies, selling 100,000 copies in 3 months. By their firesides and in public places, Americans read and discussed

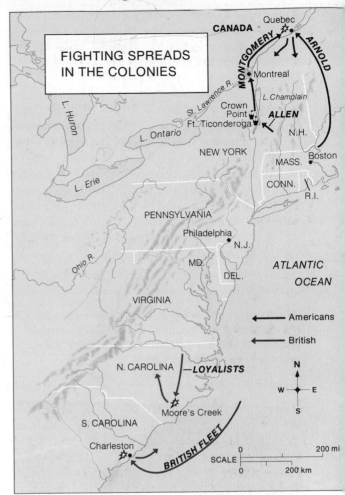

**FIGHTING SPREADS IN THE COLONIES**

## Map Study

After seizing Fort Ticonderoga, Americans invaded Canada but were turned back at Quebec. In the south, Patriots won victories in two early battles. What southern city was successfully defended against a British sea attack?

Paine's pamphlet. As they considered Paine's ideas, many colonists began to favor American independence.

**The Second Continental Congress moves toward independence.** By spring 1776, many of the delegates to the Second Continental Congress supported complete independence from Great Britain. Then, on June 7, 1776, Richard Henry Lee of Virginia

159

presented Congress with a **resolution** —a formal suggestion to be voted on by the delegates. The resolution stated "that these United Colonies are, and of right ought to be, free and independent states."

Lee's resolution caused great excitement among the delegates. The Congress appointed a committee of five delegates to draw up the **Declaration of Independence.** The committee was made up of Thomas Jefferson, John Adams, Benjamin Franklin, Roger Sherman, and Robert Livingston. Its ideas were put into words by Jefferson, the 33-year-old delegate from Virginia. Jefferson wrote a clear and elegant draft of the Declaration, which the committee agreed to accept

**"The Spirit of '76" by A.M. Willard hangs in the town hall at Marblehead, Massachusetts. The music of fifes and drums was a call to arms in Revolutionary times.**

with some changes. The committee then put the complete Declaration of Independence before Congress.

**The Declaration of Independence is adopted.** The Declaration of Independence had two important purposes. First, it expressed a bold new idea about the rights of the people. In the past, many people thought that the government had the authority to decide what rights to give its citizens. Jefferson believed, however, that all people were born with "unalienable rights" that could not be taken away by any government. Jefferson took this idea from the writings of John Locke, an English scholar who lived during the 1600's. In the Declaration of Independence Jefferson put this idea into the following words:

> We hold these truths to be self-evident, that all men are created equal, that they are endowed by their Creator with certain unalienable Rights, that among these are Life, Liberty and the pursuit of Happiness.

Jefferson added that the purpose of a government is to protect the rights of the people. No government can rule without the "consent of the governed." In other words, it must have the approval of the people that it governs. If the government tries to take away the people's rights, then "it is the Right of the People to alter or to abolish it."

Second, the Declaration of Independence broke all ties with Great Britain. Jefferson listed 27 "Tyrannical Acts of the British King" against the American colonies. He explained that harsh and unfair treatment had forced the colonists to seek independence from Britain. Jefferson ended the Declaration with a promise that the colonists would fight to defend their freedom. He wrote:

> And for the support of this Declaration, with a firm reliance on the protection of divine Providence, we ... pledge to each other our Lives, our Fortunes and our sacred Honor.

Thus the Declaration ended with a firm commitment to freedom.

The Second Continental Congress approved the Declaration of Independence. This painting, begun in 1784 by Robert Pine, shows the signers of the Declaration, including John Adams (standing left) and Benjamin Franklin (seated, center).

The Declaration of Independence was signed in bold handwriting by John Hancock, President of the Congress, so that, as he said, "George III might read it without his spectacles." Later the other delegates added their signatures. (The complete text of the Declaration of Independence is on pages 180–183.)

**A new nation is born.** Congress adopted the Declaration of Independence on July 4, 1776. After months of uncertainty, the delegates had taken the decisive step toward independence. The Americans were no longer fighting for their rights as British subjects. Now they were fighting as the citizens of a new nation. They no longer spoke of themselves as the United Colonies. Instead they spoke proudly of the United States of America.

## SECTION REVIEW

1. **Vocabulary**   petition, mercenary, resolution
2. **People and Places**   Breed's Hill, Ethan Allen, Fort Ticonderoga, General Howe, Moore's Creek, Thomas Paine, Richard Henry Lee, Thomas Jefferson, John Hancock
3. **Comprehension**   What new British policies pushed the colonists to break with Britain in 1776?
4. **Comprehension**   What major ideas did Thomas Jefferson express in the Declaration of Independence?
5. **Critical Thinking**   Why was the Declaration of Independence also a declaration of war?

## MAPS AND GRAPHS: Reading a Flow Chart

One way to present historical information clearly is on a **flow chart.** A flow chart may show a sequence of events or decisions, or it may show how power, information, or supplies flow from place to place.

The flow chart below shows how information flowed between the Continental Congress and ordinary soldiers. The solid green lines show pathways for orders or commands. They appear as arrows, because orders only flow one way—from the person who gives orders to the one who receives them. The broken lines show pathways for administrative information—information needed to carry out commands. For example, the commander-in-chief might want to know when supplies will arrive. This administrative information would help the commander decide what commands to give.

Study the flow chart carefully. Then answer the following questions on a separate sheet of paper.

1. Who could give commands to the commander-in-chief of the Army?
2. According to the flow chart, from what sources can the Continental Congress get administrative information?
3. What group shown on the chart neither received nor gave commands?
4. How many levels of command separated the commander-in-chief from ordinary soldiers serving in companies?
5. Who had the larger command in the Continental Army—the leader of a brigade or the leader of a regiment?
6. Why, do you think, is it important for an army to have a clear command structure?

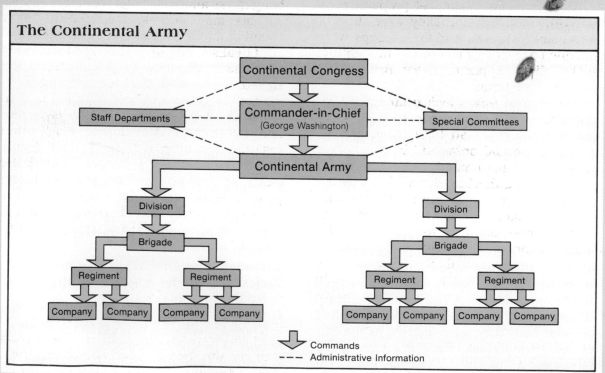

The Continental Army

Commands
--- Administrative Information

# 2 What strengths and weaknesses did Americans have in the Revolution?

## Vocabulary

enlistment

specie

alliance

As news of the Declaration of Independence spread through the states, Americans considered their chances in a war against Great Britain. It was one thing for the Congress to declare the United States independent from British rule. It was another thing for Americans to win a war against the most powerful nation in the world.

## Weaknesses of the United States

The Patriots were not well prepared for a war with Great Britain. They were short of money and supplies, and their troops were untrained and poorly equipped. In addition, the Loyalists supported Great Britain and opposed the Patriots.

**The Patriot forces lack training and organization.** The officers and soldiers of the Continental Army had little experience in fighting large and organized battles. Their training had been limited mostly to frontier warfare during the French and Indian War. Another weakness was that the Continental Army was made up of volunteers. Many of the volunteers felt free to return to their homes whenever their short **enlistments** — terms of service—ended. For this reason the leaders of the Continental Army often could not tell from day to day how many troops were under their command. Finally, the colonies had no real navy. The British Navy was the strongest in the world. The Americans, on the other hand, did not have a single first-class fighting ship. Thus, the Americans had to begin building a navy.

**The Patriots lack equipment and money.** It was difficult for the Second Continental Congress to raise money because it did not have the power to tax the people. To carry on the war, however, the Patriots needed muskets, cannon, ammunition, uniforms, and food. Congress could only ask the states to give money, and the sums received were disappointingly small.

Congress tried to buy supplies with paper money that it printed in large quantities. Most people did not like to take this money in payment for goods. Paper money is not worth much unless it is issued by a stable government or can be exchanged for **specie** (SPEE-shee)—gold and silver coins. The Continental Congress was an unstable government with little specie. As the war dragged on, Continental paper money bought less and less. "Not worth a continental" became a popular saying of the times, meaning that something was worthless.

**Loyalists oppose the Patriots.** Even after the Declaration of Independence was signed, about one third of Americans remained Loyalists. About 60,000 Loyalists joined the British forces. Others gave food and shelter to British soldiers. The Patriots regarded Loyalists as traitors to the American cause. Patriots sometimes tarred and feathered well-known Loyalists and forced them to leave town. Patriots also attacked Loyalists' homes and destroyed or seized their property. As a result, many Loyalists fled to Canada.

## Strengths of the United States

The Patriots had the advantage of fighting on home ground under a commander-in-chief they trusted. In addition, the Patriots received the help of other countries. These factors helped the Patriots defeat the British army.

The first colonial "coins" were cut from pine trees in Massachusetts. Of course, no one would accept these wooden coins outside the colony. The early colonists also bartered or traded their goods.

As the colonies grew, the lack of money became a problem. Parliament would not allow the export of English coins to the colonies. At the same time, Parliament forbade the colonies to mint their own coins. Colonists had to use such foreign coins as the Spanish "piece of eight."

The Continental Congress issued a great deal of paper money, but few coins, to finance the Revolution. The value of the paper money fell rapidly, and the government neared financial collapse. In 1781 France helped save the Revolution by sending $200,000 in gold to the United States.

**A rare Continental Dollar**

**The Patriots fight in their own country.** Many of the Continental soldiers, used to outdoor life, knew the countryside in which they fought. This knowledge helped them to win battles and make the most of scarce supplies. In addition, the Continental soldiers had more at stake than the British troops. They were fighting for their homes, their families, and their freedom. The Patriots knew that they would be considered guilty of treason if the British won the war.

The British army, on the other hand, was filled with soldiers who had been forced into service. Far from their homes across the ocean, the British and Hessian soldiers had less reason to fight hard in the colonies.

**The Patriots profit from British mistakes.** The British generals sent to serve in the colonies were rarely topnotch commanders. They were often appointed because they had powerful friends in the British government. Trained in Europe, they were not used to the vast spaces, wilderness, and winter fighting of the colonies. They underestimated the bravery of the colonial soldiers.

Sure of victory, the British generals moved slowly. A few, like General Howe, still hoped to make peace with the rebels. Finally, all of the British generals counted too heavily on military support from the Loyalists in the colonies.

**The Patriots receive foreign aid.** The Patriots were helped by freedom-loving Europeans who came to America to serve as officers in the Continental Army. The 19-year-old Marquis de Lafayette (mahr-KEE duh lah-fee-ET) was among these volunteers. A French noble, Lafayette defied the French king's orders in coming to aid the American colonists. Lafayette asked to serve without pay under George Washington and soon became one of the Patriots' bravest commanders. The Baron Friedrich von Steuben (STOO-buhn) was another volunteer who helped the Patriots win. A Prussian officer, he drilled the Continental soldiers until they became an effective fighting force.

The Baron Johann de Kalb, a German soldier who became a general in the Continental Army, was killed in battle about a year before the end of the Revolution. From Poland came Casimir Pulaski (poo-LAS-kee) and Thaddeus Kosciusko (kahs-ee-UHS-ko). These leaders helped plan American defenses at two places in present-day New York State—West Point, and Bemis Heights near Saratoga.

**Benjamin Franklin helps win French support.** As the war progressed, foreign governments began to help the Patriots. France, an old enemy of Britain, wanted to strike a blow at the British by aiding the United States. The French did not, however, want to get involved in a hopeless cause. The Continental Congress sent Benjamin Franklin to France to argue for the Patriots. The French had great respect for Franklin's intelligence and scientific ability. Impressed by Franklin and by the Patriots' military victories, France entered an **alliance** with the United States in 1778. An alliance is an agreement by two or more nations to act together in a cause. Without French aid, the Patriots probably would not have won the Revolutionary War.

The news of the American-French alliance prompted Great Britain to declare war on France. Soon other European nations were drawn into the struggle. Britain declared war on Holland when Dutch bankers lent money to the American colonists. France persuaded its ally, Spain, to enter the war on the American side. In the later years of the war, Spanish ships attacked the British navy, and Spanish soldiers fought in America. In 1779 and 1780 General Bernardo de Gálvez, the Spanish commander of Louisiana, captured the British outposts to the southwest of the United States. (See map on page 171.)

**George Washington proves an excellent leader.** Another important reason for the American victory was George Washington's leadership. Washington was a brave and resourceful general who won the respect and confidence of his troops. He mixed new recruits with experienced soldiers to create an effective fighting force. When British generals made careless mistakes, Washington quickly took the advantage. Furthermore, at key points during the Revolutionary War,

he led successful surprise attacks. When money and supplies ran low, he fought steadily on. A former delegate to the Continental Congress, Washington worked well with government officials. In the darkest days of the war, Washington's patience and strength often kept the Patriots from giving up.

**Blacks support the cause of independence.** Black Patriots fought in every major battle of the Revolutionary War. Black minutemen faced the British at Lexington and Concord. The Reverend Lemuel Haynes, Primas Black, and Epheram Blackman were black Patriots who joined Ethan Allen's Green Mountain Boys and helped take Fort Ticonderoga from the British. Peter Salem,

Peter Salem, a free black, became a hero at the Battle of Bunker Hill. James Earl Taylor drew this picture in the 1840's.

Abigail Adams, wife of Boston Patriot John Adams, stayed in Boston during the Revolution. There she managed her family's property, cared for refugees, and encouraged prominent men and women to support the war effort.

**Women aid the Patriot cause.** Many American women played important parts in the Patriot victory. Before the fighting broke out, colonial women took part in boycotts of British goods. They formed groups called the Daughters of Liberty to protest British taxes. (See Chapter 7.) Mercy Otis Warren of Massachusetts wrote pamphlets calling on the colonists to resist British policies.

During the war years, women collected lead and helped manufacture bullets. They held sewing bees to make uniforms for the soldiers, and they distributed medical supplies. Many women ran farms or businesses while their husbands or brothers were at war. Some served with the troops as doctors, nurses, cooks, guides, or spies.

A few Patriot women became soldiers. A former indentured servant from Massachusetts, Deborah Sampson, disguised herself as a man and joined the Continental Army. Sampson fought until she was wounded in a battle outside Philadelphia. Another woman, Margaret Corbin, took over her husband's cannon after he was killed in a battle in New York in 1776. Mary Ludwig Hays, known as "Molly Pitcher," carried pitchers of water to the soldiers during a battle at Monmouth, New Jersey. After her husband suffered heatstroke, she took over his cannon and joined in the fighting. General Washington later honored her by making her a sergeant in the Continental Army.

who also fought at Concord, was hailed as a hero for his part in the Battle of Bunker Hill. Later, at the Battle of Yorktown, a French military officer wrote that "three-quarters of the Rhode Island regiment consists of [black men], and that regiment is the . . . best under arms, and the most precise in its maneuvers."

In the early years of the fighting, American slaveholders had tried to keep blacks out of the Continental Army. When the British offered freedom to any slaves willing to fight on their side, however, the American army began to accept black soldiers. In all, nearly 5,000 black Patriots, both free and slave, fought in the Revolutionary War.

## SECTION REVIEW

1. **Vocabulary**   enlistment, specie, alliance
2. **People and Places**   Marquis de Lafayette, Friedrich von Steuben, Johann de Kalb, Bernardo de Gálvez, Lemuel Haynes, Peter Salem, Deborah Sampson, Mary Ludwig Hays
3. **Comprehension**   What were the Patriots' disadvantages in the Revolutionary War?
4. **Comprehension**   What were the Patriots' advantages in the Revolutionary War?
5. **Critical Thinking**   How did the Patriots' leadership compare with British leadership? Explain.

# How did the 13 colonies win their independence?

## Vocabulary

privateer

man-of-war

negotiate

Patriot troops fought the British in every section of the United States, on the frontier, and at sea. The fighting in the southern states finally gave the United States victory in the Revolutionary War.

## The War in the Middle States

After the British gave up Boston in spring 1776, the focus of the Revolutionary War shifted to the middle states. The British took New York City, but the Patriots recovered with a series of hard-won victories in New Jersey and New York.

**The British take New York City.** The British sought to capture New York City for two reasons. First, they wanted to use the city's fine harbor for their supply ships. Second, by holding New York City and the Hudson River, the British could cut New England off from the rest of the states. The states would be easier to defeat if they were divided into two sections.

General Washington realized that the British hoped to capture New York City. In spring 1776, he moved the Continental Army from Boston to Long Island. (See map on page 168.) The army remained on Long Island until August 1776, when the British forces under General Howe attacked and forced the Patriots to retreat. Under cover of darkness and fog, Washington and his troops escaped to the north of New York City. The British marched into the city, where they were welcomed by wealthy Loyalists. The British controlled New York City until the end of the war.

**Nathan Hale gives his life for his country.** Eager to uncover the plans of British generals, Washington asked for volunteers to enter New York City. Captain Nathan Hale, a 21-year-old schoolteacher from Connecticut, entered the city in disguise. Hale was captured by the British, convicted of spying, and hanged. As he faced execution, Hale's last words were: "I only regret that I have but one life to lose for my country."

**Washington retreats into New Jersey.** Washington and his troops did not stay in New York for long. A few weeks after the loss of New York City, Washington suffered another defeat. The British captured two American forts on the Hudson River and took 2,600 prisoners.

Washington needed to get away from the British forces and to regroup his battered troops. In October 1776 he led the Continental Army in a retreat across New Jersey. The British pursued the Patriots until they escaped over the Delaware River into Pennsylvania. (See map on page 168.)

By this time the American Revolution looked like a lost cause. Many soldiers had deserted the Continental Army, and Washington had only 6,000 troops left. He had hoped to find recruits in New Jersey, but fewer than 100 soldiers joined the army. General Howe was sure that Washington would surrender during the winter. Howe and his army spent Christmas in New York. He sent only a few thousand troops to New Jersey to keep watch on the Continental Army.

**Victories at Trenton and Princeton cheer the Patriots.** Washington refused to be discouraged by the problems facing his army. He decided to attack the British troops in New Jersey. On Christmas night 1776 Washington and his soldiers rowed back across the icy Delaware River. At Trenton, New

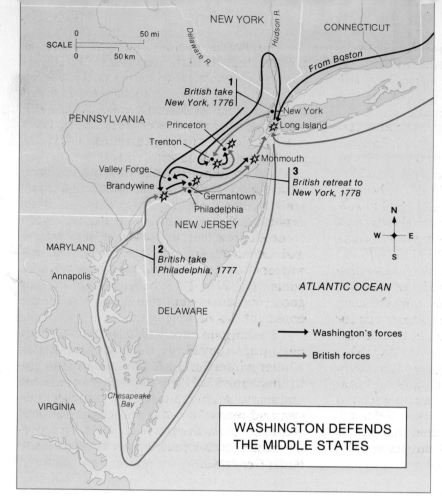

WASHINGTON DEFENDS
THE MIDDLE STATES

Jersey, they surprised 1,400 Hessians who were sleeping soundly after their Christmas celebration. The Continental Army captured weapons, supplies, and 1,000 prisoners.

British troops under General Cornwallis rushed toward Trenton. They arrived on the night of January 2, 1777, and prepared to attack in the morning. Washington and his troops slipped away in the darkness, however, leaving their campfires burning so that the British would not realize they had gone. The Continental troops did heavy damage to three British regiments at nearby Princeton and then withdrew to the hills in northern New Jersey. Faced with these unexpected losses, the British pulled out of New Jersey and returned to New York.

**The British plan to crush the Patriots.** In 1777 the king ordered the British generals to take control of the Hudson River valley. The plan called for three British armies to meet at Albany, New York. If they succeeded, they would cut New England off from the rest of the states. The first army was stationed at Fort Oswego on Lake Ontario. It was to march east across New York to reach Albany. General Howe commanded the second army, which was to march north to Albany from New York City. The third army, led by General John Burgoyne, was to march south to Albany from Canada.

From the start the British plan was unsuccessful. The army from Fort Oswego fought one bloody skirmish with the American troops at Oriskany (or-ISS-kuh-nee), New York. The British troops then heard rumors that another large force of American soldiers was approaching. The British panicked at the news and retreated to Canada. In New York City, General Howe ignored his orders to march to Albany. Instead, Howe and his troops sailed south to Chesapeake

Bay. After landing in Maryland, Howe's army marched north in an attack on Philadelphia. (See map on page 171.) This left General Burgoyne on his own as he led the third army south towards Albany.

**Patriots win a victory at Saratoga.** General Burgoyne's march from Canada began well. His troops captured Fort Ticonderoga from the Patriots on July 5, 1777. Burgoyne was overconfident, however. Nicknamed "Gentleman Johnny" by his soldiers, Burgoyne liked to travel slowly and throw lavish parties between battles. His slow pace gave the Patriots the chance to cut down trees across the road. They also burned crops and drove off cattle, leaving the countryside bare of supplies. When Burgoyne sent 700 German soldiers to search for supplies, Patriots surrounded and defeated them at Bennington, in present-day Vermont. Burgoyne's troops met the main American forces near Saratoga, New York. (See map on page 171.) Outnumbered and low on supplies, the British were defeated. General Burgoyne surrendered his entire force of almost 6,000 troops on October 17, 1777.

The **Battle of Saratoga** was a turning point in the Revolutionary War. By defeating Burgoyne, the Patriots won new support for their cause. France decided to enter the Revolution on the Patriots' side. After signing a treaty of alliance on February 6, 1778, the French sent troops, money, and supplies to help the Patriots win the war.

**Washington struggles through the winter at Valley Forge.** To the south, Washington's troops tried to prevent Howe from capturing Philadelphia. The Patriots were defeated, however, in battles at Brandywine and Germantown. General Howe and his soldiers took over Philadelphia and spent the winter of 1777 to 1778 there. The British had good food and comfortable quarters in the houses of the occupied city.

Washington and his troops set up camp nearby at Valley Forge, Pennsylvania. It was a bitter winter for the Patriot troops. Rough log huts provided the only shelter from wind and snow. All of the men suffered from hunger, and many lacked warm clothes to protect them from the bitter cold. Washington described conditions at Valley Forge in a letter to Congress.

After the British took Philadelphia, Washington and the Continental Army camped 20 miles away in Valley Forge during the bitter winter of 1777 to 1778. William Trego portrayed the march to Valley Forge in this 1883 painting. How does the picture show that the Americans were not equipped for winter weather?

Washington wrote that:

The soap, vinegar, and other articles allowed by Congress, we see none of.... The first, indeed, we have now little occasion for; few men having more than one shirt ... and some none at all. In addition ... as a further proof of the inability of [the] army ... to perform the common duties of soldiers, ... no less than two thousand eight hundred and ninety-eight men now in camp [are] unfit for duty, because they are barefoot and otherwise [unclothed].

In spite of these hardships, the Continental soldiers did not give up hope. All winter long the Prussian officer Baron von Steuben drilled the troops. When spring came the Continental Army was better trained than ever before.

**Fighting ends in the middle states.** In June 1778 the British abandoned Philadelphia and began a march across New Jersey to New York City. Washington pursued the British and nearly defeated them in a battle at Monmouth, New Jersey. The British managed to reach New York City, where Washington kept them bottled up until the end of the war. Monmouth was the last important battle in the middle states.

**Benedict Arnold betrays his country.** A disloyal Patriot, Benedict Arnold, later tried to help the British. Arnold was a brilliant general who had helped lead the Patriots to victory at Saratoga. He wrote secretly to the British in 1779, offering to join their side. Arnold planned to turn the fort at West Point, New York, over to the British in exchange for money and a post in the British army.

Benedict Arnold's plot was discovered in 1780 with the capture of Major André (AHN-dray), the English officer with whom Arnold was dealing. André was executed as a spy, but Arnold managed to reach the British lines in safety. He fought for the British during the rest of the Revolutionary War.

## War on the Frontier and at Sea

As early as 1778, Patriot forces began to fight the British on the frontier and at sea. Patriots attacked British forts in the West, and the small American navy attacked British warships patrolling the Atlantic coast.

**George Rogers Clark attacks forts in the West.** British troops held forts in the 13 states and in the frontier region as well. In 1778 the Virginia Patriot George Rogers Clark led a force of 200 soldiers down the Ohio River and up the Mississippi. A brave leader, Clark won Indian aid and captured the British forts at Kaskaskia and Cahokia in present-day Illinois. He also captured Vincennes (vin-SENZ) in present-day Indiana. (See map on page 171.)

Clark suffered a setback in December 1778, when the British retook Fort Vincennes from the handful of Americans that he had left there. The British expected that Clark would wait until spring to attack Vincennes again. In February 1779, however, Clark led his soldiers on a 170-mile (275-kilometer) march through the frozen woods to Vincennes. They surprised the British and recaptured the fort. Clark's victories gave Americans a hold on the vast Ohio region.

**American privateers capture enemy supply ships.** While Patriot soldiers fought the British on land, American sailors were waging war against the British at sea. Many British supply ships were captured by American privateers. Privateers were ships privately owned but authorized by the government to attack and capture enemy ships. The Americans who sailed on privateers were fighting partly for their own profit. When they captured a British merchant ship, they were allowed to sell the cargo and divide the money among themselves. In the later years of the war, British men-of-war —heavily armed warships—kept a close watch along the coast for privateers, and fewer American ships dared to venture out.

**The Patriots build a navy.** As British colonists, the Americans had depended on the British naval fleet for protection. When the Revolutionary War broke out, the Patriots had no military vessels to send against the British. With the help of France, the Patriots organized a navy of about 50 ships. This small Continental Navy could not defeat the huge British fleet, but it did score vital victories over the British. A key victory of

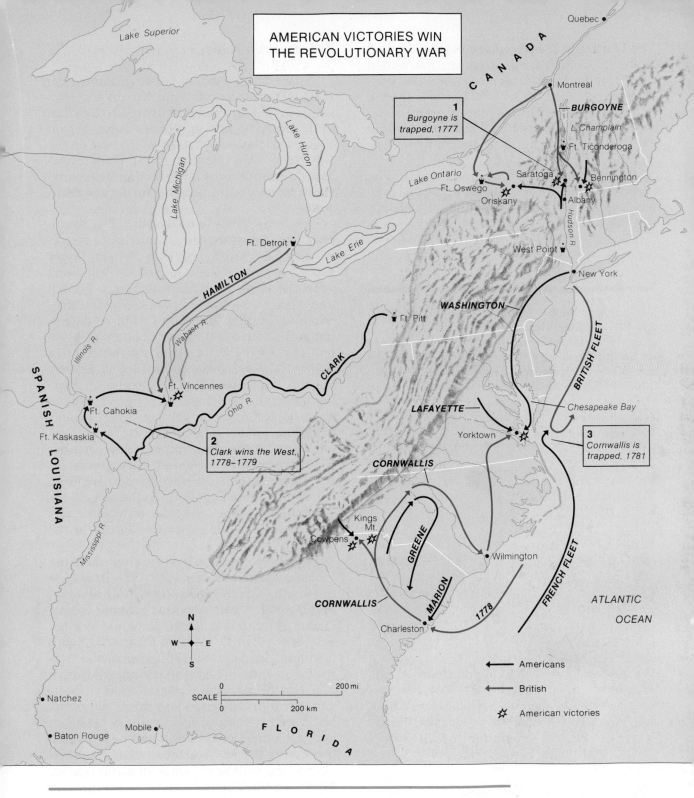

AMERICAN VICTORIES WIN THE REVOLUTIONARY WAR

1
Burgoyne is trapped, 1777

2
Clark wins the West, 1778–1779

3
Cornwallis is trapped, 1781

CANADA

Quebec

Montreal

BURGOYNE

L. Champlain

Ft. Ticonderoga

Lake Superior

Lake Huron

Lake Michigan

Lake Ontario

Lake Erie

Ft. Oswego

Saratoga

Bennington

Oriskany

Albany

Hudson R.

West Point

New York

Ft. Detroit

HAMILTON

Wabash R.

CLARK

Ft. Pitt

WASHINGTON

BRITISH FLEET

Illinois R.

Ft. Vincennes

Ohio R.

LAFAYETTE

Chesapeake Bay

Ft. Cahokia

SPANISH LOUISIANA

Ft. Kaskaskia

Mississippi R.

Yorktown

CORNWALLIS

Kings Mt.

Cowpens

GREENE

Wilmington

CORNWALLIS

MARION

1778

FRENCH FLEET

ATLANTIC OCEAN

Charleston

N
W    E
S

0          200 mi
SCALE
0          200 km

Natchez

Baton Rouge

Mobile

FLORIDA

← Americans

← British

✯ American victories

## Map Study

Americans won victories at Saratoga, Vincennes, and Yorktown. What was
the role of the French fleet in the Battle of Yorktown?

the Continental Navy was won by John Paul Jones, a Scottish sea captain who had settled in Virginia. In 1779 Jones's ship, the *Bonhomme Richard* (buh-NAWM ree-SHAHR), attacked a larger British man-of-war, the *Serapis*, off the coast of England. Jones's ship was badly damaged early in the fight. Unwilling to give up, Jones sailed the *Bonhomme Richard* next to the *Serapis*. The British commander shouted, "Have you lowered your flag?" Jones replied, "I have not yet begun to fight!" After three more hours of fighting, the British ship surrendered.

**Modern-day militia, using copies of eighteenth-century clothing and weapons, celebrate American independence by restaging the events of the Revolutionary War. The 1981 restaging of the Battle of Yorktown commemorated the two-hundredth anniversary of the victory.**

## American Victory

After three years of fighting, the British realized that they could not win an easy victory. The Americans had proved to be stubborn fighters. British worries increased in 1778 when the French entered the war on the American side. Hoping to gain additional help from southern Loyalists, the British decided to move the fighting to the southern states.

**Fighting shifts to the south.** The southern campaign started with a series of victories for the British. In 1778 British forces gained control of Georgia, and the following year they held Savannah against a French and American attack. In May 1780 the British took Charleston, South Carolina, defeating more than 5,000 Patriot soldiers. Only a few scattered Patriots kept up the fight in South Carolina. One of these was Francis Marion, nicknamed "the Swamp Fox." Marion hid in the woods with his troops and led successful surprise attacks on small groups of British forces.

The Patriots' luck improved in October 1780, when they defeated Tory troops at Kings Mountain, on the border between North and South Carolina. At the same time, Washington sent the daring Nathanael Greene to lead the American forces in the south.

Under General Greene's command the Patriots did heavy damage to the British in the south. Greene took the risk of dividing up his small forces, sending Virginia Patriot Daniel Morgan into South Carolina. Morgan defeated a British force at Cowpens, South Carolina, in January 1781. General Cornwallis and his British force chased Morgan into North Carolina. Greene rejoined Morgan at Guilford Court House, North Carolina, and together their troops dealt Cornwallis a heavy blow. Cornwallis was not defeated, but his losses were so great that he abandoned the campaign and withdrew to the safety of the Atlantic coast. (See map on page 171.)

**Cornwallis is caught in a trap.** In summer 1781, General Cornwallis led his troops north into Virginia. They set up camp at

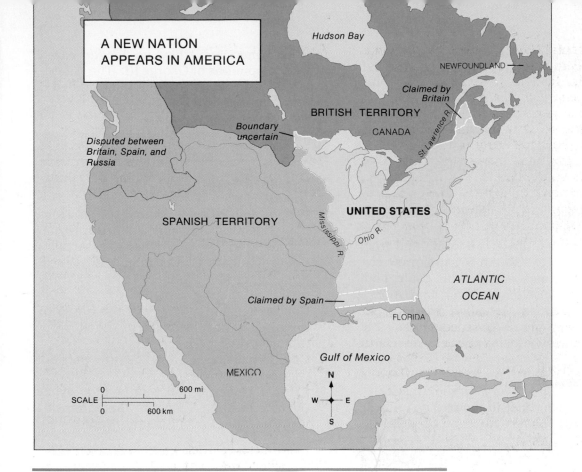

A NEW NATION APPEARS IN AMERICA

Hudson Bay

NEWFOUNDLAND —

Claimed by Britain

BRITISH TERRITORY

Boundary uncertain

CANADA

St. Lawrence R.

Disputed between Britain, Spain, and Russia

UNITED STATES

Mississippi R.

Ohio R.

SPANISH TERRITORY

ATLANTIC OCEAN

Claimed by Spain —

FLORIDA

Gulf of Mexico

MEXICO

SCALE
0 ────── 600 mi
0 ────── 600 km

N
W ◆ E
S

## Map Study

**By signing the Treaty of Paris of 1783, Great Britain recognized American independence. What natural feature formed the western boundary of the United States? What nation disputed the southern boundary? What made the northern boundary uncertain?**

Yorktown, located on a peninsula in Chesapeake Bay. The overconfident Cornwallis ignored warnings that Yorktown was open to attack. He thought that even if the Americans attacked by land, the British fleet would supply him by sea.

It was at this moment that the French fleet arrived from the West Indies. Washington sent the French ships to block the mouth of Chesapeake Bay, cutting Cornwallis off from his supply ships. Washington then led his troops from New York to Yorktown. The Patriots were joined by 6,000 French troops under Comte de Rochambeau (ro-sham-BO) and by the American soldiers already in the south. The 17,000 American and French troops trapped Cornwallis in Yorktown.

**Cornwallis surrenders.** On October 19, 1781, Cornwallis and his 6,000 soldiers surrendered to the Americans and the French. The British troops marched out between the victorious American and French armies. They gave up their weapons while the British band played "The World Turned Upside Down." Angry and ashamed at his defeat, Cornwallis refused to meet Washington and the French generals. Cornwallis sent one of his soldiers to surrender his sword.

**Great Britain recognizes American independence.** The **Battle of Yorktown** ended the Revolutionary War. At the time, however, no one was sure that peace would be declared. The United States sent Benjamin Franklin, John Jay, John Adams, and Henry

173

Laurens to Paris to **negotiate** —discuss arrangements for—a peace agreement.

The British wanted a quick end to the war. They also wanted to weaken the American-French alliance. For both these reasons, the British offered generous terms to the American delegates.

The **Treaty of Paris of 1783,** signed on September 3, recognized the United States as an independent nation. Under the terms of the treaty Britain gave Florida to Spain. The United States received the territory that stretched from Canada to Florida and from the Atlantic Ocean to the Mississippi River. The United States and Britain could both trade on the Mississippi River, and Americans could fish in Canadian waters. The Americans promised to recommend that states pay their war debts and return Loyalist property.

King George III remarked sourly that considering the "knavery" of the Americans, perhaps it might "not in the end be an evil" for the British Empire to be rid of them. As for the Americans, they no longer cared about the opinions of George III. The Americans had won their freedom and founded a new nation.

## SECTION REVIEW

1. **Vocabulary**   privateer, man-of-war, negotiate
2. **People and Places**   Nathan Hale, Trenton, General Cornwallis, John Burgoyne, Saratoga, Valley Forge, Benedict Arnold, George Rogers Clark, John Paul Jones, Francis Marion, Nathanael Greene, Yorktown
3. **Comprehension**   Why was the Battle of Saratoga a turning point in the Revolutionary War?
4. **Comprehension**   How did the Patriots capture Yorktown?
5. **Critical Thinking**   In your opinion, what factor contributed most to the American victory in the Revolutionary War?

# Chapter 8 Summary

The Second Continental Congress met in Philadelphia in May 1775. The Congress set up the Continental Army and named George Washington as its commander-in-chief. Congress also drew up the Olive Branch Petition asking King George III to protect the colonies from the policies of Parliament. In June 1775 British and Patriot troops clashed near Boston in the Battle of Bunker Hill. The British government declared the colonies in rebellion and sent British troops and German mercenaries to the colonies. On July 4, 1776, the Congress adopted the Declaration of Independence, which explained the rights of the people and broke all ties with Britain.

The Continental Army lacked soldiers, supplies, and money. Continental paper money had little value because the government lacked specie. The Patriots faced the opposition of Loyalists as well as British troops. The Patriots had the advantage, however, of fighting on home ground. Washington proved to be a strong leader.

The Patriots lost New York City to the British in August 1776, but gained victories over the British in New Jersey. In October 1777 the Patriot victory in the Battle of Saratoga gained French support for the United States. The following year the war shifted from the middle states to the south. In October 1781 American and French forces trapped General Cornwallis and his troops at Yorktown, Virginia, and forced them to surrender. The Treaty of Paris of 1783 recognized American independence and gave the United States the territory from Canada in the north to New Spain in the south and from the Atlantic west to the Mississippi River.

# CAUSES and EFFECTS

# The American Revolution ★ ★ ★

Britain wants to raise money and control colonies

Britain faces economic problems

Britain imposes harsh taxes

Britain outlaws western expansion

## CONTRIBUTING CAUSES

Boston Tea Party arouses Britain's anger

Colonists protest British taxes

Colonists form militias

Intolerable Acts attack colonial self-government

## MAIN CAUSES

## AMERICAN REVOLUTION

## EFFECTS

Washington becomes a national leader

Independence is declared

Colonies achieve a common goal

Continental army and navy are formed

## LONG-TERM EFFECTS

United States gains large territory

A democratic nation is born

America inspires revolutions in other countries

# Chapter 8 REVIEW

## Vocabulary and Key Terms

Match each of the following terms with its correct definition. Write your answers on a separate sheet of paper.

**Loyalists**
**Declaration of Independence**
**mercenary**
**resolution**
**specie**
**enlistment**
**Olive Branch Petition**
**privateer**

1. paid soldier in a foreign army
2. term of military service
3. petition asking for changes in Great Britain's policies
4. formal suggestion to be voted on
5. gold and silver coins
6. Americans who wanted to remain British subjects
7. private ship authorized to attack enemy ships
8. statement breaking all ties with Great Britain

## Recalling the Facts

1. What actions did the Second Continental Congress take in 1776?
2. What was the subject of Thomas Paine's pamphlet *Common Sense*?
3. According to the Declaration of Independence, what are unalienable rights?
4. How did the Patriot troops compare with the British forces?
5. What countries were United States allies during the Revolution?
6. In what ways did American women aid the Patriot cause during the Revolutionary War?
7. What prompted the Continental Army to accept black soldiers?

8. How did the Battle of Saratoga change the course of the war?
9. What victory ended the Revolutionary War?
10. What borders did the Treaty of Paris give the United States?

## Places to Locate

Match the letters on the map to the battles of the Revolution listed below. Write your answers on a separate sheet of paper.

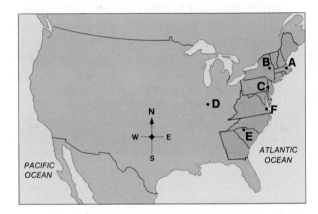

1. Trenton
2. Vincennes
3. Kings Mountain
4. Bunker Hill
5. Saratoga
6. Yorktown

## Critical Thinking

1. In your own words, explain Thomas Jefferson's theory of the "consent of the governed." Do you think it means that a government should be overthrown whenever the people disagree with it? Why or why not?
2. Explain why the Americans were able to win the Revolution. Consider the following factors:
   a. foreign aid
   b. British overconfidence
   c. Washington's leadership
   d. military strategy

3. Explain why Great Britain offered generous terms to the United States in the Treaty of Paris. What did the United States gain? How much did the United States have to give up in return?

## Understanding History

1. Reread the section "The Declaration of Independence is adopted" on page 160. Then answer these questions.
   a. **Citizenship.** According to Jefferson, what is the purpose of government?
   b. **Citizenship.** How did Jefferson make it clear that the colonists would fight to defend their freedom?
2. Reread the section "The Patriots lack equipment and money" on page 163. Then answer these questions.
   a. **Economics.** What power did the Second Continental Congress need to raise more money?
   b. **Economics.** How is the value of paper money determined?
3. Reread the section of the Declaration of Independence titled "Tyrannical Acts of the British King" on pages 181-182. Then answer these questions.
   a. **Primary Sources.** Who is the "he" referred to repeatedly?
   b. **Primary Sources.** According to the Declaration, how have the colonial legislatures been interfered with?
   c. **Primary Sources.** Do you think the Declaration exaggerated British offenses? Explain.

## Projects and Activities

1. **Debating Issues.** Stage a debate in the Continental Congress over whether or not the colonies should declare independence. Have one group of students favor independence and another group oppose it. Have the class discuss which view was most convincing.
2. **Making a Chart.** Make a chart showing the battles of the Revolution. List the date, location, and winner of each battle.

3. **Analyzing Information.** Obtain a copy of Thomas Paine's *Common Sense*. Study the arguments and discuss them in class. Why do you think Paine's arguments were so persuasive?
4. **Making a Time Line.** List the important events of the Revolution and make a time line that shows them in order.

## Practicing Your Skill

Use this flow chart about the Second Continental Congress to answer the following questions.

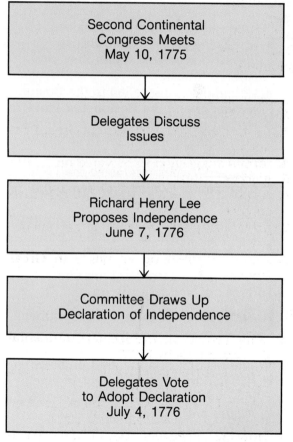

Second Continental
Congress Meets
May 10, 1775

↓

Delegates Discuss
Issues

↓

Richard Henry Lee
Proposes Independence
June 7, 1776

↓

Committee Draws Up
Declaration of Independence

↓

Delegates Vote
to Adopt Declaration
July 4, 1776

1. What did the delegates do first?
2. How long after the delegates' first meeting was independence from Great Britain proposed?
3. Who proposed that the United States become independent?
4. When was the Declaration of Independence adopted?

# UNIT 3 REVIEW

## Unit Summary

★ **The American colonists resisted strict British control.**

- Great Britain wanted the colonies to help pay war debts and to support the British army in America.
- Parliament enacted tax laws to increase revenue and to strengthen its hold on the American colonies.
- The colonists boycotted British goods to protest taxation they considered unjust.
- Colonial resistance led to the Boston Massacre and the Boston Tea Party.
- Britain passed the Coercive Acts to punish the colonists for their violent protests.
- The Americans organized the First Continental Congress to demand a change in British policy.
- Fighting between the British and the colonists began at Lexington and Concord on April 19, 1775.

★ **The English colonies won their independence from Britain.**

- Patriot leaders formed the Continental Army and made George Washington its commander-in-chief.
- The Second Continental Congress adopted the Declaration of Independence on July 4, 1776, thus breaking all ties with Great Britain.
- Many European volunteers and governments helped the Patriots in the Revolutionary War.
- On October 19, 1781, Britain's General Cornwallis surrendered to the Americans.
- In 1783 the Treaty of Paris recognized American independence.

## Understanding Chronology

Study the Unit 3 time line on page 137. Then complete the following activity on a separate sheet of paper.

Copy the Unit 3 time line and then add the following events to it: Intolerable Acts, Pontiac's War, Battle of Saratoga, publication of *Common Sense*, and French alliance with the American revolutionaries. Consult your textbook for the dates.

## Writing About History

1. **Writing a Dialogue.** Write a dialogue that might have occurred between a Patriot and a Loyalist during the American Revolution. Have each defend his or her position regarding independence from Britain.
2. **Preparing a Diary.** Write a diary that an American Patriot woman might have kept during the Revolution. Explain what the woman did to aid the Patriot cause, and describe her feelings about the war.
3. **Creating Newspaper Headlines.** Write a series of newspaper headlines announcing important events of the Revolution. Then choose one of the headlines and write an article to explain it.
4. **Composing a Letter.** Imagine you were a soldier at Valley Forge during the winter of 1777. Write a letter to your family describing the weather, the living quarters, the food and clothing, troop morale, and your feelings about the experience.
5. **Developing a Story.** Write a story about the Ottawa chief, Pontiac, and his attacks on British settlements. Tell the story from Pontiac's point of view, explaining why he organized other Indian groups, why he chose certain targets, and what he hoped to achieve by fighting.

**6. Interpreting a Cartoon.** The political cartoon above expresses the colonists' dissatisfaction with British taxes. The colonists in the drawing are forcing a tarred and feathered tax collector to drink tea. Explain the meaning of the cartoon and describe how the artist shows emotions.

## Projects

**1. Identifying Cause and Effect.** Make a list of the British laws imposed on the American colonies. Begin your list with the Proclamation of 1763 and end it with the Intolerable Acts of 1774. Briefly describe how each law affected the colonists and the colonists' reactions to the laws.

**2. Organizing Information.** Make a chart of the hardships that the Continental Army faced during the Revolutionary War. Include those caused by the British, by the geography and climate, and by the weaknesses of the army itself. Then explain how the Continental Army overcame the hardships to defeat the British.

**3. Conducting an Interview.** Work with a partner to present an interview with a famous person from the American Revolution. The interview should be about a major issue or event. For example, interview Baron von Steuben about the winter at Valley Forge, or Mary Ludwig Hays about her role as a soldier in the Continental Army.

**4. Presenting Living Biographies.** Choose one person from the Revolution and prepare a biography of him or her. Then present a first-person account of the biographical information to the class. Add to the presentation by wearing a costume or by using props.

**5. Demonstrating Point of View.** Draw a political cartoon showing how a British soldier might have described the Boston Massacre. Then draw another cartoon that represents a Patriot's view of the same event.

**6. Paraphrasing a Document.** Reread the preamble to the Declaration of Independence on page 180. Rewrite the paragraph in your own words.

## Finding Out More

Avi. *The Fighting Ground.* Harper, 1984. The problems of the Continental Army come to life as thirteen-year-old Jonathan marches off to fight the British.

Collier, James Lincoln, and Christopher Collier. *The Bloody Country.* Four Winds, 1976. A young man tells the hardships endured by his family in Pennsylvania at the time of the Revolution.

Fritz, Jean. *Traitor: The Case of Benedict Arnold.* Putnam, 1981. The story of this fascinating military hero-turned-traitor is told in a straightforward manner.

Steele, William O. *The Man with the Silver Eyes.* Harcourt Brace Jovanovich, 1976. A young Native American develops respect for a peace-loving settler in Tennessee during the Revolution.

Stein, R. Conrad. *The Story of Lexington and Concord.* Children's Press, 1983. This is an easy-to-read account of the first battles of the Revolution.

# THE DECLARATION OF INDEPENDENCE
## 1776

The first paragraph, known as the Preamble, explains why the American colonists felt it necessary to make a political break with Great Britain.

When in the Course of human events, it becomes necessary for one people to dissolve the political bands which have connected them with another, and to assume among the powers of the earth, the separate and equal station to which the Laws of Nature and of Nature's God entitle them, a decent respect to the opinions of mankind requires that they should declare the causes which impel them to the separation.*

### [The Right of the People to Control Their Government]

This paragraph states that all people are born with certain God-given rights which are "unalienable." In other words, these rights cannot be given away or taken away by any government. Governments get their authority from the "consent" or approval of the people they govern. If a government lacks the consent of the people, then the people have a right to change or dissolve it. The people should, however, only resort to such change when the existing government has abused its powers.

**endowed**  provided
**usurpations**  wrongful uses of authority
**Despotism**  unlimited power
**Tyranny**  unjust use of power
**candid**  fair

We hold these truths to be self-evident, that all men are created equal, that they are endowed by their Creator with certain unalienable Rights, that among these are Life, Liberty and the pursuit of Happiness. That to secure these rights, Governments are instituted among Men, deriving their just powers from the consent of the governed, That whenever any Form of Government becomes destructive of these ends, it is the Right of the People to alter or to abolish it, and to institute new Government, laying its foundation on such principles and organizing its powers in such form, as to them shall seem most likely to effect their Safety and Happiness. Prudence, indeed, will dictate that Governments long established should not be changed for light and transient causes; and accordingly all experience hath shown, that mankind are more disposed to suffer, while evils are sufferable, than to right themselves by abolishing the forms to which they are accustomed. But when a long train of abuses and usurpations, pursuing invariably the same Object evinces a design to reduce them under absolute Despotism, it is their right, it is their duty, to throw off such Government, and to provide new Guards for their future security. Such has been the patient sufferance of these Colonies; and such is now the necessity which constrains them to alter their former Systems of Government. The history of the present King of Great Britain is a history of repeated injuries and usurpations, all having in direct object the establishment of an absolute Tyranny over these States. To prove this, let Facts be submitted to a candid world.

---

* In punctuation and capitalization the text of the Declaration follows accepted sources.

## [Tyrannical Acts of the British King]

He has refused his Assent to Laws, the most wholesome and necessary for the public good.

He has forbidden his Governors to pass Laws of immediate and pressing importance, unless suspended in their operation till his Assent should be obtained; and when so suspended, he has utterly neglected to attend to them.

He has refused to pass other Laws for the accommodation of large districts of people, unless those people would relinquish the right of Representation in the Legislature, a right inestimable to them and formidable to tyrants only.

He has called together legislative bodies at places unusual, uncomfortable, and distant from the depository of their Public Records, for the sole purpose of fatiguing them into compliance with his measures.

He has dissolved Representative Houses repeatedly, for opposing with manly firmness his invasions on the rights of the people.

He has refused for a long time, after such dissolutions, to cause others to be elected; whereby the Legislative powers, incapable of Annihilation, have returned to the People at large for their exercise; the State remaining in the mean time exposed to all the dangers of invasion from without, and convulsions within.

He has endeavoured to prevent the population of these States; for that purpose obstructing the Laws for Naturalization of Foreigners; refusing to pass others to encourage their migrations hither, and raising the conditions of new Appropriations of Lands.

He has obstructed the Administration of Justice, by refusing his Assent to Laws for establishing Judiciary powers.

He has made Judges dependent on his Will alone, for the tenure of their offices, and the amount and payment of their salaries.

He has erected a multitude of New Offices, and sent hither swarms of Officers to harass our People, and eat out their substance.

He has kept among us, in times of peace, Standing Armies without the Consent of our legislatures.

He has affected to render the military independent of and superior to the Civil power.

He has combined with others to subject us to a jurisdiction foreign to our constitution, and unacknowledged by our laws; giving his Assent to their Acts of pretended Legislation:

For quartering large bodies of armed troops among us:

For protecting them, by a mock Trial, from Punishment for any Murders which they should commit on the Inhabitants of these States:

For cutting off our Trade with all parts of the world:

For imposing Taxes on us without our Consent:

This section lists the colonial grievances against George III and his government. Each of these 27 British offenses occurred between 1763 and 1776. The language of this section is often very emotional. Words such as *despotism, annihilation, ravaged,* and *perfidy* express the seriousness of the King's offenses against the colonies. The list of grievances makes it clear that King George no longer has "the consent of the governed," and so should not continue to rule the colonies.

**Assent** approval
**relinquish** give up
**inestimable** too valuable to be measured
**formidable** causing fear
**fatiguing** tiring
**Annihilation** destruction
**convulsions** violent disturbances
**Naturalization** the process of becoming a citizen
**tenure** term

**Arbitrary** tyrannical
**abdicated** given up
**ravaged** destroyed
**perfidy** treachery
**constrained** forced
**insurrections** rebellions

For depriving us in many cases, of the benefits of Trial by Jury:

For transporting us beyond Seas to be tried for pretended offences:

For abolishing the free System of English Laws in a neighboring Province, establishing therein an Arbitrary government, and enlarging its Boundaries so as to render it at once an example and fit instrument for introducing the same absolute rule into these Colonies:

For taking away our Charters, abolishing our most valuable Laws, and altering fundamentally the Forms of our Governments:

For suspending our own Legislatures, and declaring themselves invested with power to legislate for us in all cases whatsoever.

He has abdicated Government here, by declaring us out of his Protection and waging War against us.

He has plundered our seas, ravaged our Coasts, burnt our towns, and destroyed the lives of our people.

He is at this time transporting large Armies of foreign Mercenaries to compleat the works of death, desolation and tyranny, already begun with circumstances of Cruelty & perfidy scarcely paralleled in the most barbarous ages, and totally unworthy the Head of a civilized nation.

He has constrained our fellow Citizens taken Captive on the high Seas to bear Arms against their Country, to become the executioners of their friends and Brethren, or to fall themselves by their Hands.

He has excited domestic insurrections amongst us, and has endeavoured to bring on the inhabitants of our frontiers, the merciless Indian Savages, whose known rule of warfare, is an undistinguished destruction of all ages, sexes and conditions.

## [Efforts of the Colonies to Avoid Separation]

In every stage of these Oppressions We have Petitioned for Redress in the most humble terms: Our repeated Petitions have been answered only by repeated injury. A Prince, whose character is thus marked by every act which may define a Tyrant, is unfit to be the ruler of a free people.

Nor have We been wanting in attentions to our British brethren. We have warned them from time to time of attempts by their legislature to extend an unwarrantable jurisdiction over us. We have reminded them of the circumstances of our emigration and settlement here. We have appealed to their native justice and magnanimity, and we have conjured them by the ties of our common kindred to disavow these usurpations, which, would inevitably interrupt our connections and

This section states that the colonists tried, without success, to settle their grievances with the king. George III ignored the colonists' repeated petitions for change. The British people, too, failed to listen to the colonists' pleas. The colonists must now look on them as enemies in war and friends in peace.

**Oppressions** unjust uses of power
**Petitioned for Redress** asked for the correction of wrongs
**unwarrantable jurisdiction** unjust control
**magnanimity** generous nature

correspondence. They too have been deaf to the voice of justice and of consanguinity. We must, therefore, acquiesce in the necessity, which denounces our Separation, and hold them, as we hold the rest of mankind, Enemies in War, in Peace Friends.

consanguinity   blood relationship
acquiesce   accept

## [The Colonies Are Declared Free and Independent]

We, therefore, the Representatives of the United States of America, in General Congress, Assembled, appealing to the Supreme Judge of the world for the rectitude of our intentions, do, in the Name, and by Authority of the good People of these Colonies, solemnly publish and declare, That these United Colonies are, and of Right ought to be Free and Independent States; that they are Absolved from all Allegiance to the British Crown, and that all political connection between them and the State of Great Britain, is and ought to be totally dissolved; and that as Free and Independent States, they have full Power to Levy War, conclude Peace, contract Alliances, establish Commerce, and to do all other Acts and Things which Independent States may of right do. And for the support of this Declaration, with a firm reliance on the protection of divine Providence, we mutually pledge to each other our Lives, our Fortunes and our sacred Honor.

The final paragraph states that the colonies are now free and independent states. All political ties between the United States of America and Great Britain are broken. The United States now has the power to declare war, make peace treaties, form political alliances, and establish trade. In the last sentence, the delegates (signers) pledge their support to the Declaration of Independence. They express their reliance on the protection of God.

rectitude   honesty
Absolved   free
divine Providence   God's
   guidance

**[NEW HAMPSHIRE]**
Josiah Bartlett
William Whipple
Matthew Thornton

**[MASSACHUSETTS]**
John Hancock
Samuel Adams
John Adams
Robert Treat Paine
Elbridge Gerry

**[RHODE ISLAND]**
Stephen Hopkins
William Ellery

**[CONNECTICUT]**
Roger Sherman
Samuel Huntington
William Williams
Oliver Wolcott

**[NEW YORK]**
William Floyd
Philip Livingston
Francis Lewis
Lewis Morris

**[NEW JERSEY]**
Richard Stockton
John Witherspoon
Francis Hopkinson
John Hart
Abraham Clark

**[PENNSYLVANIA]**
Robert Morris
Benjamin Rush
Benjamin Franklin
John Morton
George Clymer
James Smith
George Taylor
James Wilson
George Ross

**[DELAWARE]**
Caesar Rodney
George Read
Thomas McKean

**[MARYLAND]**
Samuel Chase
William Paca
Thomas Stone
Charles Carroll
   of Carrollton

**[VIRGINIA]**
George Wythe
Richard Henry Lee
Thomas Jefferson
Benjamin Harrison
Thomas Nelson, Jr.
Francis Lightfoot Lee
Carter Braxton

**[NORTH CAROLINA]**
William Hooper
Joseph Hewes
John Penn

**[SOUTH CAROLINA]**
Edward Rutledge
Thomas Heyward, Jr.
Thomas Lynch, Jr.
Arthur Middleton

**[GEORGIA]**
Button Gwinnett
Lyman Hall
George Walton

Turn to page 190

# UNIT 4

# A FIRM FOUNDATION

## 1781–1815

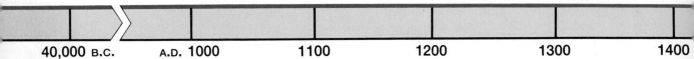

40,000 B.C.　　A.D. 1000　　1100　　1200　　1300　　1400

On April 30, 1789, George Washington was sworn in as the first President of the United States at Federal Hall in New York City.

1781 – 1815

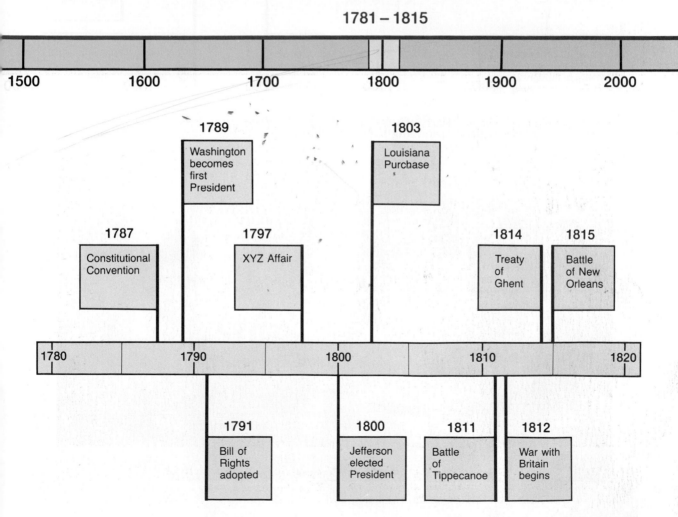

# 9 The Thirteen States Create a Constitution

## 1781–1789

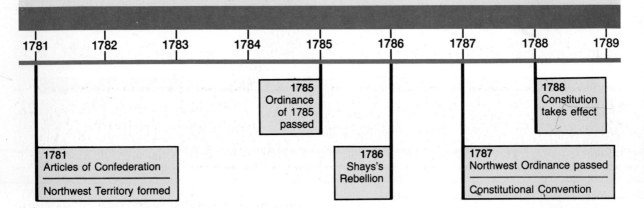

1781 | 1782 | 1783 | 1784 | 1785 | 1786 | 1787 | 1788 | 1789

**1785**
Ordinance
of 1785
passed

**1788**
Constitution
takes effect

**1781**
Articles of Confederation

Northwest Territory formed

**1786**
Shays's
Rebellion

**1787**
Northwest Ordinance passed

Constitutional Convention

**The Constitution of the United States was signed on September 17, 1787. George Washington is shown standing behind the desk.**

## Preparing to Read

After gaining independence from Britain, Americans faced a new problem. The 13 states needed to work together as a single nation. The country's first system of government gave great power to the individual states. Within a few years, however, Americans realized that the central government needed more authority in order to steer the nation steadily. Representatives from the states decided to draw up a plan for a new government. This plan, the Constitution, strengthened the central government while it protected personal liberties. The Constitution proved to be a wise framework that has lasted, with few changes, to the present day. As you read this chapter, try to answer the following questions:

1. How was the United States first governed?
2. Why did the first central government fail?
3. How did the Constitution become the foundation of American government?

# 1 How was the United States first governed?

## Vocabulary

| | |
|---|---|
| constitution | unicameral |
| bill of rights | ratify |
| | confederation |

Even while Americans celebrated their victory in the Revolutionary War, they worried about the future. The 13 states no longer faced a common enemy. Americans in different parts of the young nation had different interests and different problems. Yet the states clearly needed to work together if the United States was to survive as an independent nation. Even before the Revolution ended, colonial leaders saw the need for a national government that could deal with the concerns of all the states.

## Early Attempts at Unity

In the Declaration of Independence, Thomas Jefferson had proclaimed the colonies to be the "United States of America." All 13 states were indeed united in their desire for freedom. Yet organizing a national government was no easy task. Each state wanted to preserve its independence, and few people felt ready to give up state powers to a more remote government.

**Americans have limited experience in working together.** By the time they declared war against Britain, some of the colonies were more than 150 years old. They had grown used to acting on their own, without

### TIME LIST

### Early Steps in Unity   1765–1776

| | |
|---|---|
| 1765 | 9 colonies send delegates to the Stamp Act Congress |
| 1772 | Colonists begin forming Committees of Correspondence |
| 1774 | 12 colonies send delegates to the First Continental Congress |
| 1775 | Delegates from all colonies meet at the Second Continental Congress |
| 1776 | All colonies support the Declaration of Independence |

help from their neighbors. People in each colony had different ways of earning a living and different systems of government. Poor roads and slow methods of transportation were another barrier to unity. Colonists did little traveling, and news spread slowly from one region to the next. The colonies had weak economic ties as well. They traded more with the West Indies and Europe than with each other.

In the past, even common dangers had failed to bring Americans together. When the French and Indian War broke out, for example, colonists talked about jointly fighting the French. In 1754, representatives from most of the colonies met in Albany, New York. There they created a plan for their common defense. An elected council would have the power to make treaties with the Indians, build forts, and raise armies to protect all the colonies. The **Albany Plan of Union,** as it was called, offered clear military advantages. Yet Americans rejected it. Each colony wanted complete freedom to handle its own affairs.

**The fight for independence builds colonial unity.** Only when Britain tightened its hold over the colonies did Americans begin working together. In the 1770's, as the time list on page 187 shows, people throughout

**By the end of the Revolution, most of the new state constitutions guaranteed freedom of religion. This painted tray portrays Reverend Lemuel Haynes, who fought at Concord and Ticonderoga, preaching to a New England congregation.**

the colonies joined forces against the British. Even after winning independence, however, people felt stronger loyalties to their home states than to the new nation. They continued to think of themselves as, say, Virginians or New Yorkers rather than as American citizens.

**Each state forms a new government.** After signing the Declaration of Independence, the citizens of each state drew up a written **constitution** —plan of government. Connecticut and Rhode Island revised their existing charters. Other states wrote brand new documents.

The constitutions in all 13 states had much in common. Each state provided for a government with three branches. A legislature made laws, a governor or executive council enforced the laws, and courts judged violations of the laws. The legislative branch generally held the most power, including control over taxation.

Most state constitutions also included a **bill of rights** —a list of essential freedoms guaranteed to citizens. These rights included freedom of speech, freedom of the press, religious freedom, freedom of assembly, and the right to a fair trial. Citizens in each state wanted to make sure that no future government would again take away their rights and liberties.

## The First National Government

While each state wrote its own constitution, other American leaders worked to set up a central government for all the states. During the Revolutionary War, the Second Continental Congress governed the country. It declared independence, directed the war effort, and made the alliance with France. The Congress, however, acted only as an emergency government. It had no written authority from the states to use governmental powers.

**The states plan for a national government.** The members of the Second Continental Congress knew that the United States needed a permanent government. In 1777, after a year of discussion, they agreed on a plan. They proposed that the states join together in a **confederation** —a loose union of independent states. The document outlining this union was called the **Articles of Confederation.**

Before the Articles of Confederation could take effect, each state had to **ratify** —approve—them. Twelve states quickly did so. Maryland, however, refused to ratify the Articles until a land dispute was settled. At the time, about half the states claimed large areas of land west of the Appalachian Mountains. (See map on page 190.) As a small state, Maryland feared the growth of its neighbors. If these states gained more land and became more powerful, they could threaten Maryland and other small states. As a result, Maryland insisted that the western lands be turned over to the new national government.

For some time Virginia, New York, and the other states claiming western lands objected. Finally, however, they decided that the need for a central government outweighed their desire for more territory. They gave up their claims, and the Articles were adopted in 1781. By then, the War of Independence was almost over.

**The Articles of Confederation set up a national government.** The central government established under the Articles of Confederation took a different form from the state governments. Instead of a three-part structure, with legislative, executive, and judicial branches, the Confederation had a single governing body, Congress. Congress did not have an upper and a lower house. It was a **unicameral** —one-house—legislature made up of delegates from all the states. Each state sent between two and seven delegates to Congress. Regardless of the number of delegates, however, each state received only a single vote. As a result, small states such as Rhode Island had as much say in the government as large states such as Pennsylvania or Virginia.

Under the Articles of Confederation, more power lay with the individual states than with the central government. Each state kept control of important matters such as taxes and law enforcement. Congress's main powers were waging war and making

# THE STATES YIELD THEIR WESTERN CLAIMS

Claimed by Britain

Claimed by N.Y. and N.H.
Adjusted 1791

BRITISH TERRITORY

Lake Superior

Lake Huron

Lake Michigan

Claimed by Virginia

MASS. 1785

CONN. 1786

1784

1800

Lake Ontario

Lake Erie

VT.

N.H.

MASSACHUSETTS

NEW YORK

CONN.

R.I.

PENNSYLVANIA

NEW JERSEY

MARYLAND

DELAWARE

VIRGINIA

Ohio R.

Admitted as state
of Kentucky, 1792

1790

1787

Mississippi R.

SPANISH TERRITORY

NORTH CAROLINA

SOUTH CAROLINA

Claimed by Georgia
1802

GEORGIA

Disputed with Spain

SPANISH TERRITORY

ATLANTIC OCEAN

N
W E
S

SCALE

0 — 200 mi
0 — 200 km

## WHY CLAIMS OVERLAPPED

NW

Colonies such as Massachusetts
were granted all land due west
from the coast.

W

Area of overlap

MASS.

VIRGINIA

But Virginia was granted
land west _and northwest_
from the coast.

## Map Study

The creation of a national government required that states give up their
claims to western lands. The dates on the map tell when states dropped their
claims. Which state's claims overlapped with those of Connecticut and
Massachusetts? What state was created in 1792 from Virginia's claim?

## CITIZENSHIP • Freedom and Cooperation

When the Articles of Confederation were proposed in 1777, Maryland refused to sign them. Maryland said that Virginia, New York, and other states claiming western lands would first have to turn over this property to the federal government. Maryland's demands angered many Americans. As one Virginian asked, "[If we give in] to her on this, may she not play the same game to gain any future point of interest?"

In time, however, the land-rich states accepted Maryland's terms. They saw that cooperation was essential to forming a government, and that government was essential "to our very existence as a free ... and independent people." New York gave up its western land claims in 1780. Virginia, too, declared itself willing to "make great sacrifices to the common interests of America." One by one, the other states followed suit.

By turning over western lands to Congress, the states put an end to boundary disputes. They also gave the national government a way to raise money. Instead of taxing citizens, they thought, Congress could meet its expenses by selling land to settlers. Congress did just that. Adventurous pioneers began moving west at once, and thousands soon settled in this area.

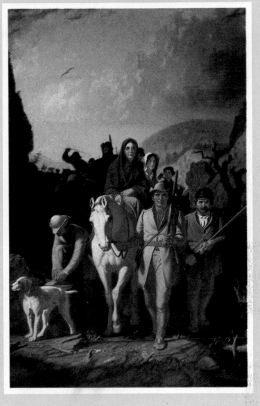

**Settlers heading west**

peace, and handling foreign affairs. Congress also had authority to regulate trade with the Indians, arrange for mail service, and borrow and issue money. The government, however, could take no action unless 9 of the 13 states agreed to do so. Furthermore, any change in the Articles of Confederation, no matter how small, required approval by all 13 states.

The writers of the Articles of Confederation purposely created a weak government. Because of their experience with the British monarch and Parliament, they feared a powerful central government. Soon, however, many Americans would see the need for a stronger national government.

## SECTION REVIEW

1. **Vocabulary**   constitution, bill of rights, confederation, ratify, unicameral
2. **People and Places**   Albany, Maryland
3. **Comprehension**   What obstacles did Americans face in forming a national government?
4. **Comprehension**   What form did the government have under the Articles of Confederation?
5. **Critical Thinking**   What do you consider the most important of the powers Congress had under the Articles of Confederation? Why?

# 2 Why did the first central government fail?

## Vocabulary

| | |
|---|---|
| ordinance | arsenal |
| survey | convention |

The government under the Articles of Confederation left many Americans unhappy. Although successful in some ways, it lacked the power to cope with many of the country's problems. In time, dissatisfaction with the Confederation caused Americans to call for a new government.

## Weaknesses of the Confederation

Some of the problems the Confederation faced would have challenged any government. Farming and business had slowed during the war years. Prices were high and goods were scarce. The country had a more serious trouble, however. Under the Articles of Confederation, the central government did not have the powers it needed.

**The government fails to bring unity to the nation.** After the Revolution, the threat of a common enemy no longer held the states together. The states often acted more like 13 separate nations than a single country. Each state, eager to prosper, made its own trade laws. Merchants in New York, for example, persuaded their state government to place heavy taxes on products from other states. Such protective taxes sharply reduced trade between the states. Congress could not solve the problem because it lacked the power to regulate commerce among states.

Indeed, Congress found it almost impossible to make any laws. The Articles of Confederation required that nine states agree to any proposed law. Yet just gathering enough delegates for a vote was hard. Getting them to agree was harder still.

Even when Congress did pass laws, the government had no power to enforce them. Under the Articles, Congress was only a legislative body. No executive branch existed to carry out the laws. Nor were there United States courts to settle arguments between states. The Confederation thus had no satisfactory way of settling such quarrels. When Pennsylvania and Connecticut both claimed the same piece of land, their dispute nearly led to a battle.

**The Confederation suffers economic troubles.** Money problems had plagued the new nation since the start of the Revolution. While Congress could issue new money, the states could do the same. As a result, Congress had no control over the money supply. Americans used many different kinds of money. They used paper money printed by the Continental Congress during the war, bills printed by the states, Spanish gold pieces, and other foreign coins. The variety of currencies in use created great confusion. Many merchants refused to accept money from other states because they could not be sure of its value. This situation kept the nation's economy from growing.

More economic troubles arose because the Second Continental Congress had printed so much paper money during the Revolution. By the war's end, Americans had lost faith in the value of government bills. It took about 40 paper dollars to equal the value of a one-dollar coin.

In addition to these problems, the government could not raise enough money to pay its bills. Congress had no power to tax American citizens. It depended entirely on the states to provide the money it needed. The states, however, had expenses of their own and rarely sent funds to Congress. As a result, the Confederation sank deeply into debt. The government could not even pay all the soldiers who had served in the War.

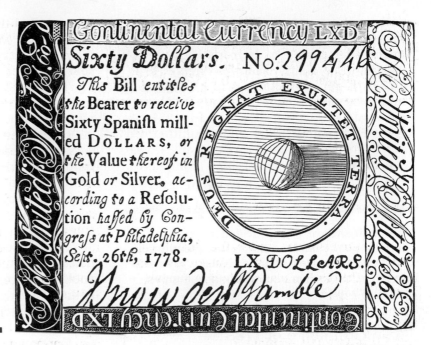

Under the Articles of Confederation the national government had no control over the supply of money. Each state issued its own coins and bills. The use of many types of money of different values threatened the new nation's prosperity.

**The Confederation proves weak in foreign affairs.** The government also failed to deal firmly with other countries. Some states, ignoring the Treaty of Paris, refused to return Loyalist property they had seized. Others did not repay their debts to British merchants. Great Britain in turn broke its promise to withdraw from all forts and trading posts on American soil. Congress made no attempt to drive out the British. While the Confederation had the power to raise an army and navy, it did not have the means.

Britain dealt the United States another blow by closing its ports in the West Indies and Canada to American ships. Other countries, too, took advantage of the Confederation's weakness. North African pirates seized hundreds of American merchant ships and imprisoned their crews. Spain prevented American traders from using the port of New Orleans.

## Achievements Under the Articles of Confederation

Although it had many failures, the Confederation did have some success. Its greatest achievement was its plan for the lands west of the Appalachian Mountains.

**The Confederation organizes western lands.** New York had been the first state, in 1780, to give up its land claims on the western frontier. Connecticut, Virginia, and other states soon followed. The land turned over to the national government became known as the **Northwest Territory.** This vast region extended north from the Ohio River to the Great Lakes and west to the Mississippi River.

Many people from the East had already started moving into the Northwest Territory. The government had to decide quickly how this new land should be settled and governed. Congress resolved these matters by passing the **Ordinance of 1785** and the **Northwest Ordinance.** An ordinance is a government regulation.

**The Ordinance of 1785 arranges for the sale of land.** The Ordinance of 1785 was Congress's master plan for dividing the Northwest Territory. Congress decided to survey —measure—the land into squares 6 miles (9.6 kilometers) long on every side. These townships, as they were called, were then divided into 36 smaller sections of 640 acres (259 hectares) each. The national government kept four sections for its own use. Another section was given to the people of

193

the township to support education. By renting or selling this land, the townspeople could raise money to help pay for public schools. (See diagram on this page.)

The other 31 sections of each township were to be sold to the highest bidder. No section could be sold for less than $640 ($1 per acre). Few people in the 1780's could afford to buy a section of land. As a result, investors in the East formed land companies.

**The Ordinance of 1785 provided a plan for dividing public lands in the western territories into townships. How much area did a township cover? What section was reserved to support public schools?**

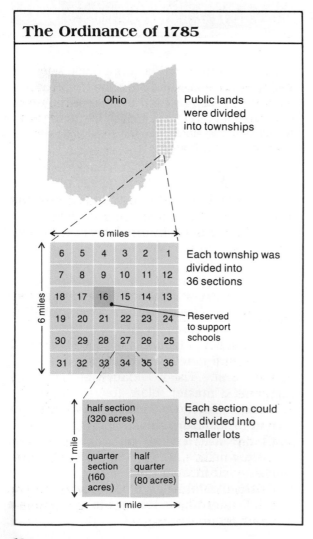

## The Ordinance of 1785

Ohio

Public lands were divided into townships

6 miles

| 6 | 5 | 4 | 3 | 2 | 1 |
| 7 | 8 | 9 | 10 | 11 | 12 |
| 18 | 17 | 16 | 15 | 14 | 13 |
| 19 | 20 | 21 | 22 | 23 | 24 |
| 30 | 29 | 28 | 27 | 26 | 25 |
| 31 | 32 | 33 | 34 | 35 | 36 |

6 miles

Each township was divided into 36 sections

Reserved to support schools

half section (320 acres)

quarter section (160 acres)

half quarter (80 acres)

1 mile

Each section could be divided into smaller lots

1 mile

They pooled their money and jointly bought land in the Northwest. Then they divided their holdings into smaller lots, which they sold to settlers at a profit.

**The Northwest Ordinance sets up a territorial government.** The Northwest Ordinance, passed in 1787, created a policy for governing settlements in the Northwest Territory. At first Congress would choose a governor and three judges to manage the affairs of the Territory. When the population grew large enough, the Territory would become self-governing. This was to happen in two stages.

First, when at least 5,000 adult free men had settled in the Northwest Territory, they could elect an assembly. This assembly, together with a governor and judges named by Congress, would control all territorial affairs. The settlers could also send a delegate to Congress to suggest laws and make speeches. This representative, however, could not vote.

Second, when a region's population climbed to 60,000 free citizens, that region could take steps to become a state. The residents could prepare a constitution and then ask permission to enter the Union as a state. If Congress agreed, the region would become a state "on equal footing with the original states in all respects whatsoever." Over the next 60 years five states—Ohio, Indiana, Illinois, Michigan, and Wisconsin—were carved out of the Northwest Territory.

The Northwest Ordinance set three other important conditions for Americans in the Northwest Territory. First, the ordinance outlawed slavery. Second, it promised residents freedom of worship, freedom of speech, the right to trial by jury, and protection from harsh punishments. Third, the ordinance said that Indians in the Territory were to be treated with good faith.

The Northwest Ordinance proved to be a workable plan that outlasted the Confederation. It protected settlers' freedom and allowed the government to change as the population changed. Later, as the United States grew larger, the plan for governing the Northwest Territory became a model for developing other new lands into states.

## The Need for Change

While settlement of western lands went smoothly, Congress still faced state quarrels, economic disorder, and trouble from foreign countries. These problems seemed so grave that Americans began to fear the collapse of the United States. As John Jay, a leader in the government, wrote, "Our affairs seem to lead to some crisis.... I am uneasy and apprehensive; more so than during the war."

**Shays's Rebellion signals flaws in the Articles of Confederation.** In 1786 an event occurred that alarmed many Americans. Daniel Shays, a Revolutionary War veteran and farmer in western Massachusetts, led a band of armed farmers to the state capital in Springfield. The unstable economy had forced many Massachusetts farmers into debt. Before the war, they had profited by selling their products in the West Indies. Now that the British had cut off these markets, farmers struggled to make a living. They had to barter their crops for goods. They also had to borrow money to pay the heavy state taxes on their land. Many farmers, unable to pay their debts, had already been imprisoned.

To keep any more debtors from going to prison, Shays and his supporters seized a number of courts in Massachusetts. Then the farmers tried to take over the United States **arsenal** —weapons storehouse—in Springfield. The national government, having no army, was powerless to protect its property. The governor of Massachusetts, however, quickly sent the state militia to crush the rebellion.

**The states agree to change the Articles of Confederation.** Shays's Rebellion convinced many Americans that the country needed a new government. In 1786 representatives from five states came together in Annapolis, Maryland, to talk about trade regulations. Soon the leaders decided to make a recommendation to Congress. They suggested that all the states send representatives to a **convention** —meeting of delegates—in Philadelphia the following year. Here they could review the Articles and make changes to strengthen the central government.

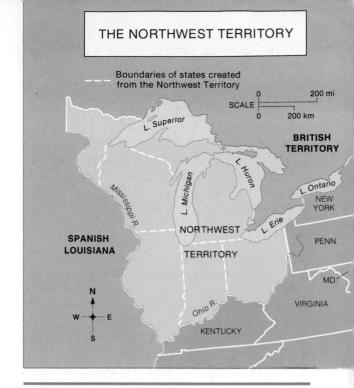

### THE NORTHWEST TERRITORY

Boundaries of states created from the Northwest Territory

SCALE
0 — 200 mi
0 — 200 km

BRITISH TERRITORY

L. Superior

L. Michigan

L. Huron

L. Ontario

NEW YORK

L. Erie

PENN.

Mississippi R.

SPANISH LOUISIANA

NORTHWEST

TERRITORY

MD.

VIRGINIA

N
W—E
S

Ohio R.

KENTUCKY

## Map Study

The Northwest Ordinance laid the foundation for government in the Northwest Territory. The ordinance also determined how the territories would become states. What natural features defined the Northwest Territory?

Congress agreed to call such a meeting, and 12 states accepted the invitation to attend. Only Rhode Island chose not to send delegates.

## SECTION REVIEW

1. **Vocabulary**    ordinance, survey, arsenal, convention
2. **People and Places**    Northwest Territory, Daniel Shays
3. **Comprehension**    In what ways did the nation suffer under the Articles?
4. **Comprehension**    What was the government's main achievement under the Articles of Confederation?
5. **Critical Thinking**    What powers do you think might have helped the government work more effectively?

195

# CRITICAL THINKING: Writing an Outline

Many people begin the task of writing by developing an **outline.** An outline is a collection of notes arranged into three categories: main ideas, subtopics that support the main ideas, and details that add more information. A good outline provides a framework for the writer to follow. It summarizes essential information and shows how ideas and facts are related.

Outlining is useful for readers, too. Outlining what you read will give you clear notes about the main ideas, subtopics, and supporting details.

To outline Section 2 of this chapter, begin by writing the title, "Why did the first central government fail?" on your paper. Then look for the main ideas—the broad answers to this question. Check the three main headings in the section to see if they express the main ideas. If you use the section headings as the source for main ideas and label them with Roman numerals, your outline will look something like this:

---

**Why Did the First
Central Government Fail?**

I. Weaknesses of the Confederation
II. Achievements Under the Articles of Confederation
III. The Need for Change

---

Now identify the subtopics under main topic I. One possibility is to use shortened forms of the paragraph headings printed in dark type. Label subtopics with capital letters and list them below the main topic.

Then read the paragraphs discussing each subtopic to find supporting details. Briefly list details under the subtopic, numbering each detail with an Arabic numeral.

Now the outline should look something like this:

---

**Why Did the First
Central Government Fail?**

I. **Weaknesses of the Confederation**
  A. **Failure to unify**
    1. **No control over interstate commerce**
    2. **Hard to pass or enforce laws**
    3. **No United States courts**
  B. **Economic troubles**
    1. **Many kinds of money**
    2. **Paper money loses value**
    3. **No power to tax**
    4. **Could not pay debts**
  C. **Problems with foreign countries**
    1. **British refuse to leave forts**
    2. **No United States army or navy**
    3. **Interference with American shipping**

---

Reread the parts of Section 2 in this chapter that relate to main ideas II and III. Then answer these questions on a separate sheet of paper.

1. Which of the following would not be included as a subtopic under main idea II, "Achievements Under the Articles of Confederation"?
   a. The Ordinance of 1785
   b. The Northwest Ordinance
   c. Shays's Rebellion
2. Which details support the subtopic "The Northwest Ordinance?"
   a. a governor and three judges rule territory in early days
   b. land sold to highest bidder
   c. statehood for regions with 60,000 inhabitants
   d. Shays's Rebellion

Early in May 1787, the delegates to the Convention in Philadelphia began to arrive. Over the next three and a half months, these leaders discussed the failings of the Confederation and their ideas for change. Out of these debates came a new plan for governing, the **Constitution** of the United States.

## A Distinguished Gathering

The 55 delegates to the Convention gathered in a first-floor room of Philadelphia's State House, now called Independence Hall. Loose dirt had been shoveled onto the street outside so that the noise of passing carriages and wagons would not disturb the meeting. Inside, the delegates kept the doors and windows closed, in spite of the summer heat. They were concerned not only about noise but also about privacy. They wanted to keep secret what went on in their meetings until they had agreed on a course of action.

**George Washington leads the delegates.** The first formal session of the Convention began on May 25, 1787. The Convention delegates **unanimously** —with no disagreement—chose George Washington to chair the meeting. Fifty-five years old at the time, Washington was serious, thoughtful, and widely respected for his role in the Revolution. As the leader at the Convention, Washington tried not to take sides in the heated debates. He spoke only to head off arguments or to urge the delegates to be patient.

**Able leaders attend the Convention.** Washington found himself in the company of many talented men. Of the 55 delegates at the Convention, 34 practiced law. Others were successful manufacturers, shippers, planters, bankers, and merchants. Most of these leaders came from the older villages and cities near the Atlantic coast. They had taken part in the Revolution and become well known in their states. A number had gained valuable experience in politics by serving as governors, state legislators, and judges. Almost half had graduated from college—a rare achievement for the times—and many were under 40 years old.

One of the most outstanding delegates was James Madison, a 35-year-old Virginian. Madison attended every session of the Convention and made detailed notes about what went on. He spoke quietly and modestly, but the delegates listened to him carefully. Madison knew a great deal about government, having studied the political systems of many countries. He had also won election to the legislatures of Virginia and the United States, both during and after the Revolution. Madison contributed so much during the Convention that he is often called the "Father of the Constitution."

Benjamin Franklin, a long-time citizen of Philadelphia, also lent his wisdom and experience to the Convention. At 81 he was the oldest delegate there. Like Washington, Franklin had a calming influence on the delegates. He often cooled hot tempers by making a joke at the right moment.

Another influential speaker, Gouverneur Morris, was also part of the Pennsylvania delegation. Morris had a wooden leg and a paralyzed arm, but his mind was keen and alert. Blessed with a gift for language, he expressed his thoughts clearly and directly. Morris wrote most of the words of the Constitution, although all the delegates contributed their ideas.

Among the youngest delegates was Alexander Hamilton of New York. Hamilton had served bravely in the War for Independence.

He later gained wealth as a lawyer. As a supporter of strong government, Hamilton had encouraged Congress to call the Convention.

## Proposals for a New Government

The states had been invited to send delegates to Philadelphia for one purpose—to improve the Articles of Confederation. Yet the meeting had hardly begun when the delegates agreed on a bold step. They decided to abandon the unsatisfactory Articles. Instead they would draw up an entirely new plan of government. Because this meeting gave birth to the Constitution, it has been called the **Constitutional Convention.** The delegates hoped to create a government strong enough to succeed, yet not so strong that it would overpower the states.

**Virginia presents a plan for a strong government.** On May 29, just four days after the meetings began, the delegates from Virginia suggested a plan to the Convention. The **Virginia Plan,** devised chiefly by James Madison, proposed a federal system of government. Under federalism, the individual states keep certain powers of government but give final authority to the central, or federal, government.

According to the Virginia Plan, the government of the United States was to be made up of three parts: (1) a congress to make the laws; (2) an executive branch, headed by a president, to carry out the laws; and (3) United States courts to see that justice was done under the laws. Congress now would be bicameral —made up of two houses. The voters would directly elect representatives to the lower house. These representatives in turn would choose the members of the upper house. The number of people in each state would determine the number of representatives it sent to Congress. Thus a state such as Delaware might have only one representative because of its small population. A state with many people, such as Virginia, might have 10 or more representatives.

**New Jersey offers an alternative plan to benefit small states.** A number of the Convention delegates opposed the Virginia Plan. Some believed that ordinary people could not be trusted to elect capable representatives to the congress. These delegates thought that the state governments, not the people, should choose the representatives. Other members of the Convention complained that the Virginia Plan gave too much power to the national government and left the states too weak. The delegates from less populous states had another objection. They worried that small states would have little voice in the congress, because the representatives from the large states would always outnumber them.

William Paterson of New Jersey offered another plan to the Convention. The **New Jersey Plan,** like the Virginia Plan, called for a stronger central government with three branches. The legislature, however, would be unicameral. In addition, each state, regardless of its population, would send the same number of representatives to the congress. This way the small states would have just as many votes as the large states.

A number of delegates objected to the New Jersey Plan for two reasons. First, the representatives would be chosen by the state governments, not by the people. Second, citizens in the large states would not be represented fairly. Pennsylvania, for example, would have no more say in the congress than Delaware, although Pennsylvania's population was 11 times greater.

## Reaching Agreement

For many days the delegates discussed the two proposals for a new government. The large states naturally supported the Virginia Plan. The small states favored the New Jersey Plan. This conflict caused such strong feelings that it threatened to break up the Convention. Finally the delegates decided to compromise —reach an agreement by having each side give up something.

**The states vote for a bicameral legislature.** On July 16, the members accepted the **Great Compromise.** This plan, suggested by Roger Sherman of Connecticut, provided for a bicameral **Congress.** In the lower house, the **House of Representatives,** each of the states would be represented according to its population. This meant that the large states would have more representatives than the small states. However, in the upper house, called the **Senate,** the states would be equal. Each would have two senators and two votes. Equal representation in the Senate would protect the small states, because every law needed the approval of both houses.

The Great Compromise also settled disagreement over the election of representatives. Members of the House of Representatives were to be elected directly by the people. Members of the Senate were to be chosen by the state legislatures.

**The delegates make other compromises.** After agreeing on the Great Compromise, the delegates found solutions to three other problems.

*Counting Population.* By the terms of the Great Compromise, the number of representatives that each state sent to the House of Representatives depended on how many people lived in the state. The southern states had many more slaves than the northern states. Northerners argued that because slaves could not vote, they should not be included in the population count. Southerners, however, wanted to include slaves in the population figures. In this way, the southern states could gain more votes in the House. The delegates eventually worked out the **Three-Fifths Compromise** to settle this matter. They decided that five slaves would count as three persons for the purposes of representation. (See the Constitution, Article I, Section 2, Clause 3.)

*Regulating Trade.* The Convention members also debated how much power Congress should have over trade. All the delegates agreed that the national government should control interstate trade. The northern states wanted Congress to control foreign trade as well. Because many northerners made a living by shipping, they wanted the same trade laws in force everywhere. Southerners, however, preferred to let each state set its own policy. Southerners exported large amounts of rice, tobacco, and indigo. They worried about losing foreign customers if Congress taxed these goods.

The South also feared that Congress might stop the slave trade. Many northerners opposed slavery and believed it should be against the law everywhere. Once more, both sides compromised. The delegates gave Congress the power to control trade with other countries and to tax imports but not exports. The delegates also said that Congress could not interfere in the slave trade for the next 20 years.

*Electing the President.* Another question arose over selection of the **President.** As head of the executive branch, the President would have a great deal of power. If Congress chose the President, it would be able to control that official. On the other hand, some delegates did not trust the judgment of the people to choose a President. The Framers of the Constitution reached another compromise on this issue. They decided to let each state choose as many **electors** — qualified voters—as it had senators and representatives. These electors would form the **Electoral College,** the group that elected the

## LINKING PAST AND PRESENT

# ★★★ *The Constitution*

The Constitution of the United States celebrated its Bicentennial—200th birthday—in 1987. It is the world's oldest written constitution, yet it still remains fresh and vital today. The Framers of the Constitution deserve the credit for the document's lasting success. Gouverneur Morris, with a committee of four other men, wrote the actual words of the Constitution. They put the ideas of all the Framers into clear, graceful English, creating a forceful yet flexible document.

The Constitution still guides lawmakers and judges every day. It has also provided a model for many other countries. From Latin America to Europe, from Africa to Asia, dozens of countries have borrowed parts of the Constitution for their own plans of government.

## Federal Powers Increase Under the Constitution

(✓ = powers granted)

| Powers | Articles of Confederation | United States Constitution |
|---|:---:|:---:|
| Declare war; make peace | ✓ | ✓ |
| Organize and direct an army and navy | ✓ | ✓ |
| Regulate trade with the Indians; manage Indian affairs | ✓ | ✓ |
| Set standards of weights and measures | ✓ | ✓ |
| Establish postal services | ✓ | ✓ |
| Borrow money to pay expenses | ✓ | ✓ |
| Manage foreign affairs | ✓ | ✓ |
| Prevent the states from issuing money | | ✓ |
| Impose taxes | | ✓ |
| Call out state militia | | ✓ |
| Regulate trade between the states and with foreign nations | | ✓ |
| Organize a system of courts | | ✓ |
| Protect copyrights and patents | | ✓ |
| Govern the capital city and territories of the United States | | ✓ |
| Take other action, as needed, to carry out the above powers | | ✓ |

**Chart Study**
The Constitutional Convention corrected the weaknesses of the Articles of Confederation by granting the federal government more power under the Constitution. How is the last item on the chart an example of the Constitution's flexibility?

President and the **Vice President.** If no presidential candidate won the votes of more than half the electors, the House of Representatives would decide among the three candidates with the most votes. (See the Constitution, Article II, Section 1, Clause 2.)

**The Convention completes its work.** The delegates worked all summer to hammer out their differences. At last they finished writing the Constitution and prepared to go home. Although nobody felt totally satisfied, the Framers believed they had written the best Constitution possible. The new federal government would have important powers not given to the Confederation government. These powers included the rights to tax citizens and to control trade among the states. At the same time the states kept enough powers to control their local affairs. (See chart on this page.)

With its work finished, the Constitutional Convention ended on September 17, 1787. Before the delegates parted, however, Benjamin Franklin rose to speak. Pointing to

George Washington's chair, which had a half-sun carved into the high wooden back-rest, he noted:

I have often and often in the course of this session looked at that [sun] without being able to tell whether it was rising or setting. But now at length I have the happiness to know that it is a rising and not a setting sun.

## Ratifying the Constitution

The delegates at the Constitutional Convention had spoken for the interests of their states. They did not, however, have the power to ratify the Constitution on behalf of their states. In the fall, each state called its own special convention to decide whether or not to accept the new federal government. If 9 of the 13 states gave their approval, the Constitution would become "the supreme law of the land."

**Americans take different stands on the Constitution.** The decision to accept or reject the Constitution depended not on the state legislatures but on the American people. Voters in each state would choose new representatives to speak for them at the state convention. All over the country—in homes, in meeting places, and on street corners—Americans talked about the Constitution.

Some people, known as **Federalists,** strongly favored the new plan of government. Others, called **Antifederalists,** opposed the Constitution because they feared it would create too strong a central government. Antifederalists also argued that there was nothing to prevent this government from taking away their rights.

**Jefferson has praise and criticism for the Constitution.** Thomas Jefferson did not attend the Constitutional Convention. His duties as ambassador to France kept him in Europe at the time. When Jefferson received a copy of the Constitution, he approved much of it. He also saw important weaknesses. In a letter to James Madison he expressed his views:

I like the organization of the government into legislative, judiciary, and executive [branches]. I like the power given the [Congress] to levy taxes, and . . . I approve of the greater House being chosen by the people directly. . . . I will now tell you what I do not like. First, [there is no] bill of rights, providing clearly . . . for freedom of religion, freedom of the press, protection against standing armies, . . . and trials by jury in all matters [that may be tried] by the laws of the land. . . . Let me add that a bill of rights is what the people are entitled to against every government on earth. . . .

## Chart Study

The Federalists believed that the United States needed a strong central government. Antifederalists feared that a strong central government might oppress the people. How did the Federalists and Antifederalists disagree on the issue of foreign policy?

### Federalists and Antifederalists Hold Opposing Views

| Policies Favored by the Federalists | Policies Favored by the Antifederalists |
|---|---|
| Strong national government | Limited national government |
| Government controlled by wealthy and educated citizens | Government controlled by ordinary citizens |
| Policies favorable to trade, business, and finance | Policies favorable to farmers, artisans, and skilled workers |
| A national bank | State banks |
| Protective tariffs | Free trade |
| Strong ties with Britain, but not with France | Strong ties with France, but not with Britain |

The Federalists held a parade to celebrate the ratification of the Constitution in New York. The Constitution had won approval by a margin of only three votes. Why might the float name Alexander Hamilton?

**Friends of the Constitution work for its adoption.** In answer to objections such as Jefferson's, Federalists insisted that citizens' rights were perfectly safe. After all, each state constitution already contained a bill of rights. Furthermore, Congress could pass no laws unless the people's representatives in the House agreed. Thus the central government could not take away the people's rights.

Those who favored the Constitution spoke at meetings in the 13 states. The new federal government, they said, would have the strength to provide sound leadership. It would be able to improve the country's economy, keep law and order among the states, and gain respect abroad.

The Federalists argued their views in newspapers and pamphlets as well. The best known writings were a group of 85 essays collected under the title *The Federalist*. These essays were the work of James Madison, Alexander Hamilton, and John Jay—all supporters of a strong central government. They clearly explained the Constitution and presented strong reasons for its ratification.

**The Constitution wins approval.** Slowly the Federalist cause gained favor. Delaware ratified the Constitution first, on December 7, 1787. Soon Pennsylvania, New Jersey, Georgia, Connecticut, Massachusetts, Maryland, and South Carolina added their votes of approval. When a ninth state, New Hampshire, ratified in June 1788, the Constitution officially took effect. (See the Constitution, Article VII.)

Four other states, however, had not yet ratified the Constitution. Federalists worked hard to win the votes of Virginia and New York. Without Virginia the new government would not have the support of the most populous state. Without New York the country would be separated into two parts.

In Virginia, Patrick Henry, the fiery speaker of Revolutionary days, argued against the Constitution. Like other Antifederalists, Henry feared giving the federal government too much power. James Madison, however, solidly defended the Constitution. At last Virginia accepted the document by the close vote of 89 to 79.

202

In New York the margin of victory was even narrower. The Constitution won acceptance by only three votes. The remaining two states, North Carolina and Rhode Island, did not ratify the Constitution until more than a year later. North Carolina approved in 1789 and Rhode Island finally ratified the Constitution in 1790.

**Americans prepare for the new government.** In September 1788 the Congress of the Confederation arranged for the new Congress to meet in New York City the following spring. Meanwhile the states scheduled elections to choose their senators, representatives, and members of the Electoral College. These electors would vote for the first President on February 4, 1789. Soon afterward, the new government would begin its work.

Americans had high hopes for their new union. The Framers of the Constitution had worked hard to shape a plan for a strong and stable government. They succeeded brilliantly. For more than 200 years, the United States Constitution has united all the states under a strong federal government. (The complete text of the Constitution is on pages 206–235, along with notes that explain it.)

(The complete text of the Constitution is on pages 206–235, along with notes that explain it.)

## SECTION REVIEW

1. **Vocabulary**   unanimous, federal, bicameral, compromise, elector
2. **People and Places**   Philadelphia, George Washington, James Madison, Benjamin Franklin, Gouverneur Morris, Patrick Henry
3. **Comprehension**   What disagreement did the Great Compromise settle?
4. **Comprehension**   On what other matters did the Framers of the Constitution compromise?
5. **Critical Thinking**   If Washington, Madison, and Franklin had been Antifederalists, do you think Americans would still have ratified the Constitution?

# Chapter 9 Summary

After declaring their independence from Britain, the colonists set up state governments. The Second Continental Congress acted as a national government for the states until 1781, when the states ratified the Articles of Confederation. This plan united the states under a weak central government with no president and no federal court system.

The Confederation passed laws organizing the lands west of the Appalachian Mountains. The Ordinance of 1785 provided for the division and sale of western lands. The Northwest Ordinance, passed in 1787, provided for territorial government. The Confederation was not strong enough to govern the states and to deal with foreign nations. It lacked the power to enforce laws, to tax the states, to regulate the money supply, to control trade, and to build an army or navy. The economic troubles of the Confederation led to Shays's Rebellion, a farmers' uprising, in 1786.

Americans soon realized that the nation needed a change in government. In 1787, delegates from 12 of the 13 states met in Philadelphia for the Constitutional Convention. The delegates included George Washington, Benjamin Franklin, James Madison, and other important leaders. Through a series of compromises they produced the Constitution of the United States. The Constitution provided for a strong central government, with a President, a federal court system, and a bicameral Congress. After much debate between Federalists and Antifederalists, the states ratified the Constitution. In the spring of 1789, the new government was ready to begin.

## Vocabulary and Key Terms

Use the following terms to complete the sentences below. Write your answers on a separate sheet of paper.

| | |
|---|---|
| compromise | House of Representatives |
| confederation | Northwest Ordinance |
| Constitution | ratify |
| convention | Senate |
| federal | unanimous |

1. A weak union of independent states is a _____.
2. Congress passed the _____ in 1787 to set up a plan for governing western lands.
3. At a _____ in Philadelphia in 1787, American leaders wrote the _____.
4. Congress includes an upper house called the _____ and a lower house called the _____.
5. People with opposing views sometimes _____ to reach an agreement.
6. The Constitution did not have _____ approval from the states until North Carolina and Rhode Island agreed to _____ it.
7. In a _____ system of government, independent states are united under a strong central government.

## Recalling the Facts

1. What was the Albany Plan of Union?
2. Why did it take nearly four years to ratify the Articles of Confederation?
3. What decisions did Congress make concerning the Northwest Territory?
4. What was Shays's Rebellion?
5. Why did the Constitutional Convention meet?
6. How did the Virginia Plan and the New Jersey Plan differ?
7. What was the Three-Fifths Compromise?
8. Why did many Americans oppose ratification of the Constitution?

## Places to Locate

Match the letters on the map with the places listed below. Write your answers on a separate sheet of paper.

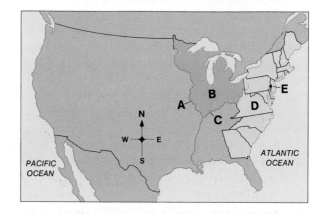

1. 13 original states
2. Mississippi River
3. Ohio River
4. Northwest Territory
5. Philadelphia

## Critical Thinking

1. Why can the Articles of Confederation be considered a major achievement, even though the government proved too weak to last? Consider the following issues in your answer:
   a. Americans' limited experience in governing their nation
   b. the effect of wartime problems on Americans' ability to plan for the nation's future
2. Was the Northwest Ordinance a wise plan of government? Why or why not? Consider the following points in your answer:
   a. the flexibility of the ordinance in allowing the government to change over time

b. the ordinance's protection of people's rights
c. the value of the ordinance as a model for governing other territories
3. What, in your opinion, were the most important arguments in favor of ratifying the Constitution? What were the most important arguments against ratification? What might have happened if the Constitution had been rejected or if not all the states had ratified it?

## Understanding History

1. Reread the section "The Confederation suffers economic troubles" on page 192. Then answer these questions.
   a. **Economics.** How did the variety of currencies in use after the Revolution hurt the nation?
   b. **Economics.** Why did the government lack funds to pay its debts and expenses?
2. Reread the section "The Ordinance of 1785 arranges for the sale of land" on page 193. Then answer these questions.
   a. **Citizenship.** How did the ordinance support public education?
   b. **Citizenship.** Do you think the government should take an interest in education? Why or why not?
3. Reread the section "Jefferson has praise and criticism for the Constitution" on page 201. Then answer these questions.
   a. **Primary Sources.** What parts of the Constitution did Jefferson say he liked?
   b. **Citizenship.** Why did Jefferson think a bill of rights should be included in the Constitution?

## Projects and Activities

1. **Making a Chart.** Make a chart comparing the Articles of Confederation with the Constitution. Include information under the following headings: "Branches of Government," "Organization of Congress," "Representation in Congress," and "Powers of Congress."

2. **Making a Map.** Make a map of the 13 original states. Number the states to show the order in which they ratified the Constitution.
3. **Giving an Oral Report.** Find out more about one of the Framers of the Constitution. Share your findings with the class in an oral report.
4. **Analyzing a Document.** Read a copy of your state constitution. Present to the class a summary of the rights of citizens in your state.

## Practicing Your Skill

Copy the outline below onto a separate sheet of paper. Then complete the outline by replacing each blank line with one of the topics from the list that follows.

---

Compromises Made at Constitutional Convention

I. **Issue of Representation in Congress**
   A. _____
      1. Bicameral Congress
      2. States' Representation based on population
   B. **New Jersey Plan**
      1. _____
      2. _____
   C. **Great Compromise**
      1. _____
      2. States' representation in House based on population
      3. States allowed equal number of representatives in Senate

II. **Other Issues**
   A. **Population Count**
   B. **Congress's Power to Control Trade**
   C. _____

---

**Bicameral Congress**
**Unicameral Congress**
**Election of the President**
**Equal number of representatives**
**Virginia Plan**

# THE CONSTITUTION OF THE UNITED STATES

## 1787

**The Great Seal has an olive branch (for peace), arrows (for war), and 13 stars and stripes (for the 13 original states).**

Starting on this page, you will find the complete text of the United States Constitution. The actual text of the Constitution appears in the column that is printed on a color background on each page. In the other column you will find explanations of each part of the Constitution.

Headings and subheadings have been added to the Constitution to help you identify its different parts. Those parts of the original document that are no longer in effect are enclosed in brackets and printed in gray type.

## PREAMBLE

The Preamble states the purposes for which the Constitution was written: (1) to form a union of states that will benefit all, (2) to make laws and establish courts that are fair, (3) to maintain peace within the country, (4) to defend the nation against attack, (5) to help the people lead happy and useful lives, and (6) to make sure that this nation's people and their descendants remain free.

The opening words of the Preamble make clear that it is the people themselves who have the power to establish a government or change it.

## ARTICLE I

### SECTION 1

All national laws must be made by Congress. But Congress can make no laws except those permitted under the Constitution. Congress is made up of two houses—the Senate and the House of Representatives.

### SECTION 2

Clause 1.   Members of the House of Representatives are elected in each state every two years. Any person who has the right to vote for representatives to the

## PREAMBLE

We the people of the United States, in order to form a more perfect union, establish justice, insure domestic tranquillity, provide for the common defense, promote the general welfare, and secure the blessings of liberty to ourselves and our posterity, do ordain and establish this Constitution for the United States of America.

## ARTICLE I
## LEGISLATIVE BRANCH

### SECTION 1   Congress

All legislative powers herein granted shall be vested in a Congress of the United States, which shall consist of a Senate and House of Representatives.

### SECTION 2   The House of Representatives

**Clause 1.   Election and term of members.** The House of Representatives shall be composed of members chosen every second year by the people of the several states, and the electors in each state shall have the qualifications requisite for electors of the most numerous branch of the state legislature.

**Clause 2. Qualification of members.** No person shall be a representative who shall not have attained to the age of twenty-five years, and been seven years a citizen of the United States, and who shall not, when elected, be an inhabitant of that state in which he shall be chosen.

**Clause 3. Apportionment of representatives and of direct taxes.** Representatives and direct taxes shall be apportioned among the several states which may be included within this Union, according to their respective numbers, [which shall be determined by adding to the whole number of free persons, including those bound to service for a term of years, and excluding Indians not taxed, three fifths of all other persons.] The actual enumeration shall be made within three years after the first meeting of the Congress of the United States, and within every subsequent term of ten years, in such manner as they shall by law direct. The number of representatives shall not exceed one for every thirty thousand, but each state shall have at least one representative; [and until such enumeration shall be made, the State of New Hampshire shall be entitled to choose three; Massachusetts, eight; Rhode Island and Providence Plantations, one; Connecticut, five; New York, six; New Jersey, four; Pennsylvania, eight; Delaware, one; Maryland, six; Virginia, ten; North Carolina, five; South Carolina, five; and Georgia, three.]

**Clause 4. Filling vacancies.** When vacancies happen in the representation from any state, the executive authority thereof shall issue writs of election to fill such vacancies.

**Clause 5. Officers; impeachment.** The House of Representatives shall choose their Speaker and other officers; and shall have the sole power of impeachment.

larger house of the state legislature has the right to vote for the state's representatives in the House of Representatives. This is the only qualification for voting listed in the original Constitution. It made sure that the House would be elected by the people themselves.

**Clause 2.** A representative must be at least 25 years old, a United States citizen for at least seven years, and a resident of the state from which he or she is elected.

**Clause 3.** The number of representatives each state has is determined by the state's population. Direct taxes are to be collected from the states according to the number of people living in each state. (Amendment 16 made the income tax an exception to this rule.) A direct tax is one paid to the government by the person who is taxed. Since there now are no slaves or indentured servants in the United States and Indians are citizens, all the people of a state are counted in determining the number of representatives a state shall have. Congress decides how the population is to be counted, but a census must be taken every ten years. The House of Representatives cannot have more than one member for every 30,000 persons in the nation. But each state is entitled to one representative, no matter how small its population. In 1910 Congress limited the number of representatives to 435.

**Clause 4.** When a state does not have all the representatives to which it is entitled—for example, when a representative resigns or dies—the governor of that state must call a special election to fill the vacancy.

**Clause 5.** The House of Representatives elects its presiding officer (the Speaker) and other officers such as the chaplain and the sergeant at arms. Only the House has the right to impeach, that is, to bring charges of misdeeds in office against an official of the United States.

**Clause 1.** The Senate is made up of two senators from each state. Senators are no longer chosen by the legislatures of their states. Amendment 17 states that they are to be elected by the people. A senator serves a six-year term.

**Clause 2.** Senators were divided into three groups so that their terms would not all end at the same time. Today all senators are elected for six-year terms, but only one third are elected in any election year. The provision for filling vacancies in the Senate was changed by Amendment 17.

**Clause 3.** A senator must be at least 30 years old, a United States citizen for nine years, and a resident of the state from which he or she is elected.

**Clause 4.** The Vice President of the United States serves as the president of the Senate, but cannot vote except in case of a tie. This is the only duty that the Constitution assigns to the Vice President. In recent years the Vice President has been given more responsibilities by the President.

**Clause 5.** The Senate chooses its other officers, including a President pro tempore. *Pro tempore* means "for the time being." The President pro tempore presides in the Senate when the Vice President is absent or when the Vice President is serving as President of the United States.

**Clause 6.** The Senate tries the case when a federal official is impeached by the House of Representatives. The senators must formally declare that they will be honest and just. If the President of the United States is tried, the Chief Justice presides over the Senate. Two thirds of the senators present must

## *SECTION 3* The Senate

**Clause 1. Number and election of members.** The Senate of the United States shall be composed of two senators from each state, chosen [by the legislature thereof,] for six years; and each senator shall have one vote.

**Clause 2. Choosing senators.** Immediately after they shall be assembled in consequence of the first election, they shall be divided as equally as may be into three classes. [The seats of the senators of the first class shall be vacated at the expiration of the second year, of the second class at the expiration of the fourth year, and of the third class at the expiration of the sixth year,] so that one third may be chosen every second year; [and if vacancies happen by resignation, or otherwise, during the recess of the legislature of any state, the executive thereof may make temporary appointments until the next meeting of the legislature, which shall then fill such vacancies.]

**Clause 3. Qualifications of members.** No person shall be a senator who shall not have attained to the age of thirty years, and been nine years a citizen of the United States, and who shall not, when elected, be an inhabitant of that state for which he shall be chosen.

**Clause 4. President of Senate.** The Vice President of the United States shall be President of the Senate, but shall have no vote, unless they be equally divided.

**Clause 5. Other officers.** The Senate shall choose their own officers, and also a President pro tempore, in the absence of the Vice President, or when he shall exercise the office of President of the United States.

**Clause 6. Trials of impeachment.** The Senate shall have the sole power to try all impeachments. When sitting for that purpose, they shall be on oath or affirmation. When the President of the United States is tried, the Chief Justice shall preside; and no person shall be convicted without the concurrence of two thirds of the members present.

**Clause 7. Punishment.** Judgment in cases of impeachment shall not exceed further than to removal from office, and disqualification to hold and enjoy any office of honor, trust, or profit under the United States; but the party convicted shall nevertheless be liable and subject to indictment, trial, judgment, and punishment, according to law.

## SECTION 4 Elections and Meetings of Congress

**Clause 1. Method of holding elections.** The times, places, and manner of holding elections for senators and representatives shall be prescribed in each state by the legislature thereof; but the Congress may at any time by law make or alter such regulations, [except as to the places of choosing senators.]

**Clause 2. Meeting of Congress.** The Congress shall assemble at least once in every year, [and such meeting shall be on the first Monday in December, unless they shall by law appoint a different day.]

## SECTION 5 Organization and Rules of Each House

**Clause 1. Organization.** Each house shall be the judge of the elections, returns, and qualifications of its own members, and a majority of each shall constitute a quorum to do business; but a smaller number may adjourn from day to day, and may be authorized to compel the attendance of absent members, in such manner, and under such penalties as each house may provide.

**Clause 2. Rules.** Each house may determine the rules of its proceedings, punish its members for disorderly behavior, and with the concurrence of two thirds, expel a member.

agree that the charge is true for the impeached person to be found guilty.

**Clause 7.** If the Senate finds an impeached official guilty, it may only punish that official by keeping him or her from ever holding a government job again. Once out of office, however, the former official may be tried in a regular court and, if found guilty, punished like any other person.

### SECTION 4

**Clause 1.** The legislature of each state has the right to determine how, when, and where senators and representatives are elected, but Congress may pass election laws which the states must follow. For example, a federal law requires that secret ballots be used. Congressional elections are held on the Tuesday following the first Monday in November of even-numbered years.

**Clause 2.** Congress must meet at least once a year. Amendment 20 made January 3 the day for beginning a regular session of Congress.

### SECTION 5

**Clause 1.** Each house of Congress has the right to decide whether its members are qualified and fairly elected. Either house may by a majority vote refuse to seat a newly elected member. A *quorum* is the number of members that must be present for official business to be carried on. The Constitution states that a majority—half the members plus one—is a quorum in either the Senate or the House. When fewer than a quorum are present, that house may adjourn until the next day and may use penalties to force absent members to attend.

**Clause 2.** Each house of Congress has the right to make rules to follow in its work. Over the years many rules have grown up concerning the duties of officers and committees and the procedures used in conducting business. Each house may punish its members for wrongdoing or even expel them by a two-thirds vote.

Clause 3. Each house of Congress must keep a record of what goes on at its meetings and must publish the record. The *Congressional Record* is issued daily during sessions of Congress. Parts of the record that the members of Congress believe should be kept secret may be withheld. How members of either house vote on a question may be entered in the record if one fifth of those present in that house wish this to be done.

Clause 4. When Congress is meeting, neither house may stop work for more than three days without the consent of the other house. Neither house is allowed to hold its sessions in another city without the consent of the other house.

## SECTION 6

Clause 1. Senators and representatives are paid out of the United States Treasury. Their salary is determined by laws passed by Congress. At the present time the salary is $60,662 annually, plus allowances for travel, office staff, stationery, and other expenses. Members of Congress also enjoy *franking privilege,* that is, the right to send free any mail stamped with their name. Members of Congress may not be arrested at meetings of Congress or while going to or from such meetings unless they are suspected of treason, other serious crimes, or disturbing the peace. They may not be punished for anything they say in Congress, except by the house of which they are a member.

Clause 2. Until after their terms have ended, senators or representatives may not hold offices created by the Congress of which they are members. The same restriction applies to jobs for which Congress has voted increased pay. No person may be a member of Congress without first giving up any other federal office he or she may hold.

## SECTION 7

Clause 1. Bills for raising money for the federal government must start in the House of Representatives, but the Senate may make changes in such bills. Actually, the Senate has as much influence over revenue bills as does the House.

**Clause 3. Journal.** Each house shall keep a journal of its proceedings, and from time to time publish the same, excepting such parts as may in their judgment require secrecy; and the yeas and nays of the members of either house on any question shall, at the desire of one fifth of those present, be entered on the journal.

**Clause 4. Adjournment.** Neither house, during the session of Congress, shall without the consent of the other adjourn for more than three days, nor to any other place than that in which the two houses shall be sitting.

## SECTION 6 Privileges and Restrictions

**Clause 1. Pay and privileges of members.** The senators and representatives shall receive a compensation for their services, to be ascertained by law, and paid out of the Treasury of the United States. They shall in all cases, except treason, felony, and breach of the peace, be privileged from arrest during their attendance at the session of their respective houses and in going to and returning from the same; and for any speech or debate in either house, they shall not be questioned in any other place.

**Clause 2. Holding other offices prohibited.** No senator or representative shall, during the time for which he was elected, be appointed to any civil office under the authority of the United States which shall have been created, or the emoluments whereof shall have been increased during such time; and no person holding any office under the United States shall be a member of either house during his continuance in office.

## SECTION 7 Method of Passing Laws

**Clause 1. Revenue bills.** All bills for raising revenue shall originate in the House of Representatives; but the Senate may propose or concur with amendments as on other bills.

**Clause 2. How bills become laws.** Every bill which shall have passed the House of Representatives and the Senate shall, before it become a law, be presented to the President of the United States; if he approves he shall sign it, but if not he shall return it, with his objections, to that house in which it shall have originated, who shall enter the objections at large on their journal, and proceed to reconsider it. If after such reconsideration two thirds of that house shall agree to pass the bill, it shall be sent, together with the objections, to the other house, by which it shall likewise be reconsidered, and if approved by two thirds of that house, it shall become a law. But in all such cases the votes of both houses shall be determined by yeas and nays, and the names of the persons voting for and against the bill shall be entered on the journal of each house respectively. If any bill shall not be returned by the President within ten days (Sundays excepted) after it shall have been presented to him, the same shall be a law, in like manner as if he had signed it, unless the Congress by their adjournment prevent its return, in which case it shall not be a law.

**Clause 3. Approval or disapproval by the President.** Every order, resolution, or vote to which the concurrence of the Senate and House of Representatives may be necessary (except on a question of adjournment) shall be presented to the President of the United States; and before the same shall take effect, shall be approved by him, or being disapproved by him, shall be repassed by two thirds of the Senate and House of Representatives, according to the rules and limitations prescribed in the case of a bill.

## SECTION 8 Powers Granted to Congress

The Congress shall have power

**Clause 1.** To lay and collect taxes, duties, imposts, and excises; to pay the debts and provide for the common defense and general welfare of the United States; but all duties, imposts, and excises shall be uniform throughout the United States;

**Clause 2.** A bill (except one for raising revenue) may start in either the Senate or the House of Representatives. However, exactly the same bill must be passed by a majority vote in both houses of Congress. Differences are usually ironed out in a conference committee made up of members of both houses. When both the Senate and House have voted in favor of the bill, it is sent to the President. The President can then do one of two things: sign the bill or veto it. If the bill is vetoed, it must then be discussed again in Congress. If two thirds of both houses of Congress vote for the bill after reconsidering it, the bill becomes law without the President's signing it. In such cases, the vote of each member of Congress is recorded.

The President has ten days (not counting Sundays) to study any bill. If the President keeps a bill more than ten days without signing or vetoing it and Congress continues to meet, the bill becomes a law. But if Congress adjourns before the ten-day period ends, the bill is dead. This is known as a "pocket veto."

**Clause 3.** Other acts that require approval of both houses of Congress take effect only if they are signed by the President or passed over a presidential veto by a two-thirds vote of both houses. However, a vote to adjourn Congress requires only a majority vote of both houses.

SECTION 8

**Clause 1.** Congress may pass laws for collecting various kinds of taxes. All federal taxes must be the same in all parts of the nation.

**Clause 2.** Congress has the power to borrow money that the federal government may need and to promise to repay this money. Borrowing is generally done by issuing government bonds or certificates of indebtedness that are bought by people or organizations.

**Clause 3.** Congress has the power to pass laws concerning trade between this country and foreign countries and between one state and another state.

**Clause 4.** Congress has the power to make laws determining how citizens of other countries may become citizens of the United States. Congress also makes laws to protect those to whom a person or organization owes debts that cannot be paid. Such bankruptcy laws must be the same throughout the country.

**Clause 5.** Congress controls the minting of money and decides how much each coin is worth. And it may determine the value of foreign coins used in the United States. Congress also sets up standards for measuring weight and distance.

**Clause 6.** Congress passes laws punishing people who make counterfeit money and government bonds.

**Clause 7.** Congress provides for a postal system and may build and maintain roads over which the mail is carried.

**Clause 8.** Congress encourages art, science, and invention by passing laws that protect artists and inventors. Copyright laws make it illegal for a person to use the work of an artist, musician, or author without permission. In the same way, patent laws protect inventors and those who discover new methods and procedures in business, industry, and transportion.

**Clause 9.** Congress has the power to establish federal courts other than the Supreme Court.

**Clause 10.** Congress may specify what acts committed on American ships violate United States laws or international laws. The accused will stand trial in a federal court when the ship returns to port.

**Clause 11.** Congress alone has the power to declare war. *Letters of marque and reprisal* are government licenses authorizing the holders to fit out armed ships for use in capturing enemy merchant ships. This power to commission privateers to prey upon enemy commerce was used extensively in the War of 1812. The practice is no longer followed.

**Clause 12.** Congress may create an army for the nation. But Congress may not vote money to support the army for more than two years in advance.

**Clause 2.** To borrow money on the credit of the United States;

**Clause 3.** To regulate commerce with foreign nations, and among the several states, and with the Indian tribes;

**Clause 4.** To establish a uniform rule of naturalization, and uniform laws on the subject of bankruptcies throughout the United States;

**Clause 5.** To coin money, regulate the value thereof and of foreign coin, and fix the standard of weights and measures;

**Clause 6.** To provide for the punishment of counterfeiting the securities and current coin of the United States;

**Clause 7.** To establish post offices and post roads;

**Clause 8.** To promote the progress of science and useful arts by securing for limited times to authors and inventors the exclusive right to their respective writings and discoveries;

**Clause 9.** To constitute tribunals inferior to the Supreme Court;

**Clause 10.** To define and punish piracies and felonies committed on the high seas and offenses against the laws of nations;

**Clause 11.** To declare war, grant letters of marque and reprisal, and make rules concerning captures on land and water;

**Clause 12.** To raise and support armies, but no appropriation of money to that use shall be for a longer term than two years;

**Clause 13.** To provide and maintain a navy;

**Clause 14.** To make rules for the government and regulation of land and naval forces;

**Clause 15.** To provide for calling forth the militia to execute the laws of the Union, suppress insurrections, and repel invasions;

**Clause 16.** To provide for organizing, arming, and disciplining the militia, and for governing such part of them as may be employed in the service of the United States, reserving to the states respectively the appointment of the officers and the authority of training the militia, according to the discipline prescribed by Congress;

**Clause 17.** To exercise exclusive legislation in all cases whatsoever over such district (not exceeding ten miles square) as may, by cession of particular states and the acceptance of Congress, become the seat of the government of the United States, and to exercise like authority over all places purchased by the consent of the legislature of the state in which the same shall be for the erection of forts, magazines, arsenals, dock-yards, and other needful buildings; and

**Clause 18.** To make all laws which shall be necessary and proper for carrying into execution the foregoing powers, and all other powers vested by this Constitution in the government of the United States, or in any department or officer thereof.

## *SECTION 9* **Powers Denied to the Federal Government**

**Clause 1.** [The migration or importation of such persons as any of the states now existing shall think proper to admit shall not be prohibited by the Congress prior to the year one thousand eight hundred and eight, but a

**Clause 13.** Congress may create a navy for the United States and vote the money necessary to operate it.

**Clause 14.** Congress may make rules for our armed forces. While on active duty, members of the armed forces are under military law and regulation rather than civil law.

**Clause 15.** Congress may determine when and how the militia, the citizen soldiers of the various states, may be called into the service of the national government. The militia may be used to enforce law, to put an end to rebellion, and to drive back an invasion of the country.

**Clause 16.** Congress provides for organizing, arming, and disciplining the militia. The states appoint the officers and train the militia under the regulations set up by Congress. When called out by the national government, however, the militia is part of the national armed forces.

**Clause 17.** Congress has the power to make laws for the District of Columbia. Because it contains the national capital, the District of Columbia is not under the control of any state. Congress also makes laws regulating the use of all other property belonging to the national government—forts, arsenals, etc.

**Clause 18.** Congress also has the power to pass all laws needed to carry out the responsibilities assigned it by the Constitution. This is the so-called "elastic clause." It can be stretched to meet the changing needs of the nation. It is the basis for much legislation not authorized in any other provision of the Constitution. The taxing power and the commerce clause, in particular, have led to legislation that the authors of the Constitution did not foresee.

SECTION 9

**Clause 1.** In 1808 Congress prohibited further importation of slaves.

tax or duty may be imposed on such importation, not exceeding ten dollars for each person.]

**Clause 2.** Congress may not take away a person's right to the writ of habeas corpus except in time of great national danger. (A *writ of habeas corpus* is a court order directing that a prisoner be given a hearing so that the court can decide whether that person should be held and charged with a crime or released.)

**Clause 2.** The privilege of the writ of habeas corpus shall not be suspended, unless when in cases of rebellion or invasion the public safety may require it.

**Clause 3.** Congress may not pass a bill of attainder. (A *bill of attainder* is a legislative act that condemns a person without a trial in court.) Neither can Congress pass an *ex post facto* law. Such a law makes an act a crime after the act has been committed.

**Clause 3.** No bill of attainder or ex post facto law shall be passed.

**Clause 4.** Congress may not levy a direct tax that is not in proportion to population. Amendment 16 provides an exception in the case of the income tax.

**Clause 4.** No capitation or other direct tax shall be laid, unless in proportion to the census or enumeration herein before directed to be taken.

**Clause 5.** Congress may not tax goods sent from one state to another or goods sent to other countries.

**Clause 5.** No tax or duty shall be laid on articles exported from any state.

**Clause 6.** In laws concerning commerce, Congress may not favor one port over other ports. Congress must not tax goods being sent by water from one state to another state.

**Clause 6.** No preference shall be given by any regulation of commerce or revenue to the ports of one state over those of another; nor shall vessels bound to or from one state be obliged to enter, clear, or pay duties in another.

**Clause 7.** Money can be paid out of the Treasury only if Congress has voted the appropriation. (An *appropriation* is money granted for a given purpose.) An account of money received and money spent must be published from time to time.

**Clause 7.** No money shall be drawn from the treasury, but in consequence of appropriations made by law; and a regular statement and account of the receipts and expenditures of all public money shall be published from time to time.

**Clause 8.** The United States may not grant a title of nobility. Federal officials may not accept titles, gifts, or honors from any foreign ruler or government unless Congress gives its permission.

**Clause 8.** No title of nobility shall be granted by the United States; and no person holding any office of profit or trust under them shall, without the consent of Congress, accept of any present, emolument, office, or title, of any kind whatever, from any king, prince, or foreign state.

## SECTION 10

## *SECTION 10* Powers Denied to the States

**Clause 1.** States may not make treaties, enter into agreement with foreign countries, or grant their citizens the right to make war. States cannot issue their

**Clause 1.** No state shall enter into any treaty, alliance, or confederation; grant letters of marque and reprisal; coin money;

214

emit bills of credit; make any thing but gold and silver coin a tender in payment of debts; pass any bill of attainder, ex post facto law, or law impairing the obligation of contracts; or grant any title of nobility.

**Clause 2.** No state shall, without the consent of the Congress, lay any imposts or duties on imports or exports, except what may be absolutely necessary for executing its inspection laws; and the net produce of all duties and imposts, laid by any state on imports or exports, shall be for the use of the treasury of the United States; and all such laws shall be subject to the revision and control of the Congress.

**Clause 3.** No state shall, without the consent of Congress, lay any duty of tonnage; keep troops or ships of war in time of peace; enter into any agreement or compact with another state or with a foreign power; or engage in war, unless actually invaded or in such imminent danger as will not admit of delay.

# ARTICLE II
# EXECUTIVE BRANCH

## SECTION 1  President and Vice President

**Clause 1. Term of office.** The executive power shall be vested in a President of the United States of America. He shall hold his office during the term of four years, and, together with the Vice President chosen for the same term, be elected as follows:

**Clause 2. Electors.** Each state shall appoint, in such manner as the legislature thereof may direct, a number of electors, equal to the whole number of senators and representatives to which the state may be entitled in the Congress; but no senator or

own money or declare that any money other than that of the United States can be used as legal money.

The states as well as the national government are forbidden to punish people without giving them a trial, to pass laws that would punish people for acts that were not against the law at the time they were committed, and to grant titles of nobility. State governments must not pass any laws that would make contracts or other legal agreements less binding on the people who agreed to them.

**Clause 2.** States may not tax goods leaving or entering their territory. However, they may charge fees to cover the costs of inspection. Any profit from such inspection fees must be turned over to the United States Treasury. Congress has the power to change the inspection laws of a state.

**Clause 3.** Unless Congress gives permission, a state may not tax ships entering its ports, keep an army or navy—except the militia—in time of peace, make treaties with other states or foreign countries, or make war except when it is invaded.

## ARTICLE II

### SECTION 1

**Clause 1.** The President of the United States enforces or executes the nation's laws and is elected, as is the Vice President, for a four-year term.

**Clause 2.** The President and Vice President are elected by electors chosen by the states according to rules established by the legislatures. Each state has as many electors as it has senators and representatives in Congress. No senator or representative or other person holding a federal job may be an elector. Today electors usually are important party members whose votes are pledged to a given candidate.

215

representative, or person holding an office of trust or profit under the United States, shall be appointed an elector.

**Clause 3.** This clause did not work well in practice and was changed by Amendment 12.

**Clause 3. Former election method.** [The electors shall meet in their respective states and vote by ballot for two persons, of whom one at least shall not be an inhabitant of the same state with themselves. And they shall make a list of all the persons voted for and of the number of votes for each; which list they shall sign and certify, and transmit sealed to the seat of government of the United States, directed to the President of the Senate. The President of the Senate shall, in the presence of the Senate and House of Representatives, open all the certificates, and the votes shall then be counted. The person having the greatest number of votes shall be the President, if such number be a majority of the whole number of electors appointed; and if there be more than one who have such majority, and have an equal number of votes, then the House of Representatives shall immediately choose by ballot one of them for President; and if no person have a majority, then from the five highest on the list the said house shall in like manner choose the President. But in choosing the President the votes shall be taken by states, the representation from each state having one vote; a quorum for this purpose shall consist of a member or members from two thirds of the states, and a majority of all the states shall be necessary to a choice. In every case, after the choice of the President, the person having the greatest number of votes of the electors shall be the Vice President. But if there should remain two or more who have equal votes, the Senate shall choose from them by ballot the Vice President.]

**Clause 4.** Congress determines when electors are chosen and when they vote. The day is the same throughout the United States. The popular vote for electors takes place on the Tuesday after the first Monday of November in each "leap year." In mid-December the electors meet in their state capitals and cast their electoral votes.

**Clause 4. Time of elections.** The Congress may determine the time of choosing the electors, and the day on which they shall give their votes; which day shall be the same throughout the United States.

**Clause 5.** To be President, a person must be a citizen of the United States by birth, at least 35 years old,

**Clause 5. Qualifications for President.** No person except a natural-born citizen, [or a citizen of the United States, at the time of the adoption of this Constitution,] shall be eligible to the office of President; neither shall any person be eligible to that office who shall not have attained the age of thirty-five years, and been fourteen years a resident within the United States.

and a resident of the United States for at least 14 years.

**Clause 6. Vacancy.** In case of the removal of the President from office or of his death, resignation, or inability to discharge the powers and duties of the said office, the same shall devolve on the Vice President; and the Congress may by law provide for the case of removal, death, resignation, or inability, both of the President and Vice President, declaring what officer shall then act as President; and such officer shall act accordingly, until the disability be removed or a President shall be elected.

Clause 6. If the presidency becomes vacant, the Vice President becomes the President of the United States. If neither the President nor the Vice President is able to serve, Congress has the right to decide what government official shall act as President. Amendment 25 practically assures that there always will be a Vice President to succeed to the presidency.

**Clause 7. The President's salary.** The President shall, at stated times, receive for his services a compensation, which shall neither be increased nor diminished during the period for which he shall have been elected, and he shall not receive within that period any other emolument from the United States, or any of them.

Clause 7. The President is paid a salary fixed by Congress. That salary may not be increased or decreased during the term of office. The President may not receive any other salary from the United States or from one of the states. The salary of the President is now $200,000 a year, plus additional amounts for expenses.

**Clause 8. Oath of office.** Before he enter on the execution of his office, he shall take the following oath or affirmation: "I do solemnly swear (or affirm) that I will faithfully execute the office of President of the United States, and will to the best of my ability, preserve, protect, and defend the Constitution of the United States."

Clause 8. In taking the oath of office, the President promises to preserve, protect, and defend the Constitution of the United States.

## SECTION 2 Powers of the President

SECTION 2

**Clause 1. Military powers; Cabinet; reprieves and pardons.** The President shall be Commander-in-Chief of the Army and Navy of the United States, and of the militia of the several states, when called into the actual service of the United States. He may require the opinion, in writing, of the principal officer in each of the executive departments, upon any subject relating to the duties of

Clause 1. The President is commander-in-chief of the armed forces and of the militia when it is called out by the national government. As commander-in-chief, the President has great power, especially in time of war. The President may ask the heads of the executive departments for advice and for reports on the work of the various departments. No provision is made in the Constitution for the Cabinet or for Cabinet meetings. But the existence of executive departments is implied here. The President may pardon persons convicted of crimes against the federal government or delay the punishment of such persons, except in cases of impeachment.

**Clause 2.** The President may make treaties, but all treaties must be approved in the Senate by a two-thirds vote of the senators present. The President may also appoint important government officials. Such appointments must be approved in the Senate by a majority of the senators present. Congress may, however, pass laws giving the President, the courts, or the heads of departments power to appoint less important officials without the consent of the Senate.

**Clause 3.** If the Senate is not meeting, the President may make temporary appointments to fill vacancies. These appointments end at the close of the next session of Congress unless the Senate approves them. Congress, with the approval of the President, has given the Office of Personnel Management responsibility for determining the fitness of job applicants and for ranking them on civil service lists from which appointments to many federal positions are made.

## SECTION 3

The President must report to Congress from time to time on conditions within the United States. The President may also suggest that Congress act to pass certain laws or to solve problems facing the nation. The President may call a special session of Congress if a situation arises that requires action by Congress when that body is not in regular session. In case the Senate and House cannot agree when to end a session, the President may adjourn Congress. The President receives representatives of foreign nations, sees that the laws of the nation are enforced, and commissions officers in the armed services.

their respective offices, and he shall have power to grant reprieves and pardons for offenses against the United States, except in cases of impeachment.

**Clause 2. Treaties and appointments.** He shall have power, by and with the advice and consent of the Senate, to make treaties, provided two thirds of the senators present concur; and he shall nominate and, by and with the advice and consent of the Senate, shall appoint ambassadors, other public ministers and consuls, judges of the Supreme Court, and all other officers of the United States, whose appointments are not herein otherwise provided for, and which shall be established by law; but the Congress may by law vest the appointment of such inferior officers as they think proper in the President alone, in the courts of law, or in the heads of departments.

**Clause 3. Filling vacancies.** The President shall have power to fill up all vacancies that may happen during the recess of the Senate, by granting commissions which shall expire at the end of their next session.

## *SECTION 3* Duties of the President

He shall from time to time give to the Congress information of the state of the Union, and recommend to their consideration such measures as he shall judge necessary and expedient; he may, on extraordinary occasions, convene both houses, or either of them, and in case of disagreement between them with respect to the time of adjournment he may adjourn them to such time as he shall think proper; he shall receive ambassadors and other public ministers; he shall take care that the laws be faithfully executed, and shall commission all the officers of the United States.

## SECTION 4 Impeachment

The President, Vice President and all civil officers of the United States shall be removed from office on impeachment for, and conviction of, treason, bribery, or other high crimes and misdemeanors.

# ARTICLE III
# JUDICIAL BRANCH

## SECTION 1 The Federal Courts

The judicial power of the United States shall be vested in one Supreme Court and in such inferior courts as the Congress may from time to time ordain and establish. The judges, both of the Supreme and inferior courts, shall hold their offices during good behavior and shall, at stated times, receive for their services a compensation which shall not be diminished during their continuance in office.

## SECTION 2 Jurisdiction of the Federal Courts

**Clause 1. Federal courts in general.** The judicial power shall extend to all cases, in law and equity, arising under this Constitution, the laws of the United States, and treaties made, or which shall be made, under their authority; to all cases affecting ambassadors, other public ministers, and consuls; to all cases of admiralty and maritime jurisdiction; to controversies to which the United States shall be a party; to controversies between two or more states; [between a state and citizens of another state;] between citizens of different states; between citizens of the same state claiming lands under grants of different states, and between a state, or the citizens thereof, and foreign states, citizens, or subjects.

**Clause 2. Supreme Court.** In all cases affecting ambassadors, other public ministers, and consuls, and those in which a state shall be a party, the Supreme Court shall have

## SECTION 4

The President, Vice President, and other important government officials may be removed from office if impeached and found guilty of treason, bribery, or other serious crimes.

## ARTICLE III

## SECTION 1

The power to interpret the laws of the United States belongs to the Supreme Court and the other federal courts established by Congress. District courts and courts of appeal are now part of the regular court system. Federal judges are appointed by the President with the approval of the Senate. They hold office as long as they live, unless they retire, resign, or are impeached and found guilty. Judges are paid salaries which cannot be lowered during their terms of service.

## SECTION 2

**Clause 1.** Federal courts may try cases concerning (1) the Constitution and federal laws and treaties, (2) representatives of foreign nations, (3) laws governing ships and sailors, (4) disputes between the United States and a person or another government, (5) disputes between states, (6) disputes between citizens of different states, (7) disputes in which citizens of the same state claim lands granted by different states, and (8) disputes between a state or its citizens and a foreign state or its citizens.

**Clause 2.** Any case involving a representative of a foreign country or one of the states is first tried in the Supreme Court. Any other case is first tried in a lower court. But the Supreme Court may hear a case from a lower court on appeal. Since the Supreme Court is the highest court in the land, its decision cannot be appealed.

**Clause 3.** Except in cases of impeachment, the accused has a right to a trial by jury in the state in which the crime was committed. If the crime did not take place within a state, a law passed by Congress determines where the trial is to be held.

## SECTION 3

**Clause 1.** A citizen who makes war on the United States or aids this country's enemies is guilty of treason. To be judged guilty of treason, one must confess in court or be convicted by the testimony of two or more persons.

**Clause 2.** Congress decides what the punishment for treason will be. But the family or descendants of a guilty person may not be punished.

## ARTICLE IV

## SECTION 1

The records and court decisions of one state must be accepted in all states. Congress has the power to see that this is done.

original jurisdiction. In all the other cases before mentioned, the Supreme Court shall have appellate jurisdiction, both as to law and fact, with such exceptions and under such regulations as the Congress shall make.

**Clause 3. Rules respecting trials.** The trial of all crimes, except in cases of impeachment, shall be by jury; and such trial shall be held in the state where the said crimes shall have been committed; but when not committed within any state, the trial shall be at such place or places as the Congress may by law have directed.

## *SECTION 3* Treason

**Clause 1. Definition of treason.** Treason against the United States shall consist only in levying war against them or in adhering to their enemies, giving them aid and comfort. No person shall be convicted of treason unless on the testimony of two witnesses to the same overt act, or on confession in open court.

**Clause 2. Punishment for treason.** The Congress shall have power to declare the punishment of treason, but no attainder of treason shall work corruption of blood, or forfeiture except during the life of the person attainted.

## *ARTICLE IV*
## THE STATES AND THE FEDERAL GOVERNMENT

## *SECTION 1* State Records

Full faith and credit shall be given in each state to the public acts, records, and judicial proceedings of every other state. And the Congress may by general laws prescribe the manner in which such acts, records, and proceedings shall be proved, and the effect thereof.

## SECTION 2 Privilege Rights

**Clause 1. Privileges and immunities.** The citizens of each state shall be entitled to all privileges and immunities of citizens in the several states.

**Clause 2. Extradition.** A person charged in any state with treason, felony, or other crime who shall flee from justice and be found in another state shall, on demand of the executive authority of the state from which he fled, be delivered up, to be removed to the state having jurisdiction of the crime.

**Clause 3. Fugitive workers.** [No person held to service or labor in one state, under the laws thereof, escaping into another shall, in consequence of any law or regulation therein, be discharged from such service or labor, but shall be delivered upon claim of the party to whom such service or labor may be due.]

## SECTION 3 New States and Territories

**Clause 1. Admission of new states.** New states may be admitted by the Congress into this Union; but no new state shall be formed or erected within the jurisdiction of any other state; nor any state be formed by the junction of two or more states, or parts of states, without the consent of the legislatures of the states concerned, as well as of the Congress.

**Clause 2. National territory.** The Congress shall have power to dispose of and make all needful rules and regulations respecting the territory or other property belonging to the United States; and nothing in this Constitution shall be so construed as to prejudice any claims of the United States, or of any particular state.

## SECTION 4 Guarantees to the States

The United States shall guarantee to every state in this Union a republican form of government, and shall protect each of them

## SECTION 2

**Clause 1.** The citizens of all states have in a given state the rights and privileges granted to the citizens of that state. For example, a citizen of Oregon going into California would be entitled to all the privileges of citizens of California.

**Clause 2.** If the governor makes the request, a person charged with a crime in one state may be returned from another state to stand trial. Such action is called *extradition*. A request for extradition may be denied, however.

**Clause 3.** This clause referred to slaves. Amendment 13 abolished slavery.

## SECTION 3

**Clause 1.** Congress has the power to add new states to the Union. However, no state can have some of its territory taken away without its consent as well as the consent of Congress.

**Clause 2.** Congress has the power to make rules and regulations concerning the property and the territory of the United States.

## SECTION 4

It is the duty of the federal government to see that each state (1) has a republican form of government, (2) is protected from invasion, and (3) receives help to put

221

down riots and other disorders when such help is requested by the legislature or the governor of the state.

against invasion; and on application of the legislature, or of the executive (when the legislature cannot be convened), against domestic violence.

## ARTICLE V

The Constitution may be changed by amendment. An amendment may be proposed by a two-thirds vote of both houses of Congress or by a convention called at the request of the legislatures of two thirds of the states. Proposed amendments must be approved by the legislatures of three fourths of the states or by conventions called in three fourths of the states. When an amendment is approved, it becomes part of the Constitution. However, no amendment may take away equal state representation in the Senate.

## ARTICLE V
# AMENDING THE CONSTITUTION

The Congress, whenever two thirds of both houses shall deem it necessary, shall propose amendments to this Constitution, or, on the application of the legislatures of two thirds of the several states, shall call a convention for proposing amendments, which, in either case, shall be valid to all intents and purposes, as part of this Constitution, when ratified by the legislatures of three fourths of the several states or by conventions in three fourths thereof, as the one or the other mode of ratification may be proposed by the Congress; provided that [no amendments which may be made prior to the year one thousand eight hundred and eight shall in any manner affect the first and fourth clauses in the ninth section of the first article; and that] no state, without its consent, shall be deprived of its equal suffrage in the Senate.

## ARTICLE VI

## ARTICLE VI
# SUPREMACY OF FEDERAL LAWS

**Clause 1.** The framers of the Constitution agreed that the United States would be responsible for all debts contracted by the Confederation government.

**Clause 1. Public debt.** All debts contracted and engagements entered into, before the adoption of this Constitution, shall be as valid against the United States under this Constitution as under the Confederation.

**Clause 2.** The Constitution and the laws and treaties of the United States are the supreme law of the nation. If state law is in conflict with national law, it is the national law that must be obeyed.

**Clause 2. Supremacy of the Constitution.** This Constitution, and the laws of the United States which shall be made in pursuance thereof, and all treaties made, or which shall be made, under the authority of the United States, shall be the supreme law of the land; and the judges in every state shall be bound thereby, anything in the Constitution or laws of any state to the contrary notwithstanding.

**Clause 3. Oath of office; no religious test.** The senators and representatives before mentioned, and the members of the several state legislatures, and all executive and judicial officers, both of the United States and of the several states, shall be bound by oath or affirmation to support this Constitution; but no religious test shall ever be required as a qualification to any office or public trust under the United States.

## ARTICLE VII
# RATIFICATION OF THE CONSTITUTION

The ratification of the conventions of nine states shall be sufficient for the establishment of this Constitution between the states so ratifying the same.

**Clause 3.** All government officials, federal and state, must take an oath to support the Constitution. But no religious test can ever be required for an official to hold office.

### ARTICLE VII

The Constitution went into effect when nine states voted to accept it.

## Signers of the Constitution

On September 17, 1787, the following delegates, representing twelve states, signed the Constitution.

George Washington—
President
and delegate
from Virginia

**NEW HAMPSHIRE**
John Langdon
Nicholas Gilman

**MASSACHUSETTS**
Nathaniel Gorham
Rufus King

**CONNECTICUT**
William Samuel Johnson
Roger Sherman

**NEW YORK**
Alexander Hamilton

**NEW JERSEY**
William Livingston
David Brearley
William Paterson
Jonathan Dayton

**PENNSYLVANIA**
Benjamin Franklin
Thomas Mifflin
Robert Morris
George Clymer
Thomas FitzSimmons
Jared Ingersoll
James Wilson
Gouveneur Morris

**DELAWARE**
George Read
Gunning Bedford, Junior
John Dickinson
Richard Bassett
Jacob Broom

**MARYLAND**
James McHenry
Daniel of St. Thomas Jenifer
Daniel Carroll

**VIRGINIA**
John Blair
James Madison, Junior

**NORTH CAROLINA**
William Blount
Richard Dobbs Spaight
Hugh Williamson

**SOUTH CAROLINA**
John Rutledge
Charles Cotesworth Pinckney
Charles Pinckney
Pierce Butler

**GEORGIA**
William Few
Abraham Baldwin

# AMENDMENTS

## AMENDMENT 1

Congress must not pass laws that stop people from worshiping as they see fit. Congress cannot stop people from speaking, writing, or printing anything they want to, except that they must not slander or libel others nor urge violent overthrow of the government. Congress must not take away the people's right to meet together for any lawful purpose provided they do not interfere with the rights of others. And Congress must not take away the people's right to ask the government to correct grievances or abuses.

## AMENDMENT 2

The federal government cannot deny states the right to enlist citizens in the militia and to provide them with training in the use of weapons.

## AMENDMENT 3

In time of peace the government may not force people to have soldiers live in their homes. In wartime people cannot be compelled to do this without passage of a law.

## AMENDMENT 4

The government may not search a home or arrest a person without good cause and then only after the official who makes the search or arrest has obtained a *warrant*—an official order from a judge. Judges may not issue warrants unless they believe such action is necessary to enforce the law.

# AMENDMENTS

## AMENDMENT 1
## FREEDOM OF RELIGION, SPEECH, PRESS, ASSEMBLY, AND PETITION (1791)

Congress shall make no law respecting an establishment of religion or prohibiting the free exercise thereof; or abridging the freedom of speech, or of the press; or the right of the people peaceably to assemble, and to petition the government for a redress of grievances.

## AMENDMENT 2
## RIGHT TO BEAR ARMS (1791)

A well-regulated militia being necessary to the security of a free state, the right of the people to keep and bear arms shall not be infringed.

## AMENDMENT 3
## QUARTERING OF SOLDIERS (1791)

No soldier shall, in time of peace, be quartered in any house without the consent of the owner, nor in time of war, but in a manner to be prescribed by law.

## AMENDMENT 4
## SEARCH AND SEIZURE (1791)

The right of the people to be secure in their persons, houses, papers, and effects, against unreasonable searches and seizures, shall not be violated, and no warrants shall issue but upon probable cause, supported by oath or affirmation and particularly describing the place to be searched and the persons or things to be seized.

# AMENDMENT 5
## RIGHTS OF ACCUSED PERSONS (1791)

No person shall be held to answer for a capital or otherwise infamous crime, unless on a presentment or indictment of a grand jury, except in cases arising in the land or naval forces, or in the militia, when in actual service in time of war or public danger; nor shall any person be subject for the same offense to be twice put in jeopardy of life or limb; nor shall be compelled in any criminal case to be a witness against himself, nor be deprived of life, liberty, or property, without due process of law; nor shall private property be taken for public use without just compensation.

# AMENDMENT 6
## JURY TRIAL IN CRIMINAL CASES (1791)

In all criminal prosecutions, the accused shall enjoy the right to a speedy and public trial by an impartial jury of the state and district wherein the crime shall have been committed, which districts shall have been previously ascertained by law, and to be informed of the nature and cause of the accusation; to be confronted with the witnesses against him; to have compulsory process for obtaining witnesses in his favor; and to have the assistance of counsel for his defense.

# AMENDMENT 7
## RULES OF COMMON LAW (1791)

In suits at common law, where the value in controversy shall exceed twenty dollars, the right of trial by jury shall be preserved, and no fact tried by a jury shall be otherwise reexamined in any court of the United States than according to the rules of common law.

## AMENDMENT 5

No person may be tried in a federal court for a serious crime unless a grand jury decides that the person ought to be tried. (But members of the armed forces may be tried in military court under military law.) People who have been tried for a crime and judged innocent cannot be tried again for the same crime. Neither can they be forced to give evidence against themselves. And no person may be executed, imprisoned, or fined except as punishment after a fair trial. A person's private property may not be taken for public use without a fair price being paid for it.

## AMENDMENT 6

A person accused of a crime is entitled to a prompt public trial before an impartial jury. The trial is held in the district where the crime took place. The accused must be told what the charge is. The accused must be present when witnesses give their testimony. The government must help the accused bring into court friendly witnesses. The accused must be provided a lawyer.

## AMENDMENT 7

If a lawsuit involves property or settlement worth more than twenty dollars, the case may be tried before a jury.

## AMENDMENT 8

Persons accused of crimes may in most cases be released from jail by posting a bond that they will not run away. This is called "being out on bail." Bail, fines, and punishments must be reasonable.

## AMENDMENT 9

Since it is impossible to list in the Constitution all the rights of the people, the listing of certain rights does not mean that people do not have other rights.

## AMENDMENT 10

The powers which the Constitution does not give to the United States and does not deny to the states belong to the states and to the people.

## AMENDMENT 11

No federal court may try a case in which a state is being sued by a citizen of another state or of a foreign country. Amendment 11 changes a provision of Article III, Section 2, Clause "1."

## AMENDMENT 12

Amendment 12 describes the present-day procedure in the electoral college. The most important change made by this amendment was that the presidential electors would vote for President and Vice President

## AMENDMENT 8
## PROTECTION FROM EXCESSIVE PENALTIES (1791)

Excessive bail shall not be required, nor excessive fines imposed, nor cruel and unusual punishments inflicted.

## AMENDMENT 9
## OTHER RIGHTS OF THE PEOPLE (1791)

The enumeration in the Constitution of certain rights shall not be construed to deny or disparage others retained by the people.

## AMENDMENT 10
## POWERS KEPT BY STATES AND THE PEOPLE (1791)

The powers not delegated to the United States by the Constitution, nor prohibited by it to the states, are reserved to the states respectively, or to the people.

## AMENDMENT 11
## SUITS AGAINST A STATE (1798)

The judicial power of the United States shall not be construed to extend to any suit in law or equity commenced or prosecuted against one of the United States by citizens of another state or by citizens or subjects of any foreign state.

## AMENDMENT 12
## ELECTION OF PRESIDENT AND VICE PRESIDENT (1804)

The electors shall meet in their respective states and vote by ballot for President and Vice President, one of whom, at least, shall not be an inhabitant of the same state with themselves; they shall name in their ballots the person voted for as President, and in distinct ballots the person voted for as Vice President, and they shall make distinct lists of all persons voted for as President, and of all persons voted for as Vice President, and of the number of votes for each, which lists they shall sign and certify, and transmit sealed to the seat of the government of the United States, directed to the President of the Senate; the President of the Senate shall, in the presence of the Senate and House of Representatives, open all the certificates and the votes shall then be counted; the person having the greatest number of votes for President shall be the President, if such number be a majority of the whole number of electors appointed; and if no person have such majority, then from the persons having the highest numbers not exceeding three on the list of those voted for as President, the House of Representatives shall choose immediately, by ballot, the President. But in choosing the President, the votes shall be taken by states, the representation from each state having one vote; a quorum for this purpose shall consist of a member or members from two thirds of the states, and a majority of all the states shall be necessary to a choice. And if the House of Representatives shall not choose a President whenever the right of choice shall devolve upon them, [before the fourth day of March next following,] then the Vice President shall act as President, as in the case of the death or other constitutional disability of the President. The person having the greatest number of votes as Vice President shall be the Vice President, if such number be a majority of the whole number of electors appointed, and if no person have a majority, then from the two highest numbers on the list, the Senate shall choose the Vice President; a quorum for the purpose shall consist of two thirds of the whole number of senators, and a majority of the whole number shall be necessary to a choice. But no person constitutionally ineligible to the office of President shall be eligible to that of Vice President of the United States.

on separate ballots. In 1800, when only one ballot was used, Thomas Jefferson and Aaron Burr received the same number of votes, and the election had to be decided by the House of Representatives. To guard against this possibility in the future, Amendment 12 calls for separate ballots.

The electors meet in their state capitals and cast their separate ballots for President and Vice President. They send them to the President of the Senate, showing the votes for each candidate. They are opened, and the electoral votes for President are counted in the presence of both houses. The candidate having a majority is declared elected. If no candidate for President receives a majority, the election goes to the House. The members of the House then vote for one of the three highest candidates. Each state casts one vote. A quorum consists of at least one member from two thirds of the states. The candidate who receives a majority of the votes of the states is elected President. If the House fails to elect a President, the Vice President acts as President.

The electoral votes for Vice President are also counted in the presence of both houses. The candidate having a majority is declared elected. If no candidate for Vice President receives a majority, the Senate chooses a Vice President from the two highest candidates. For this purpose, a quorum consists of two thirds of the total membership of the Senate. A majority of the whole number of the Senate is necessary to elect a Vice President. No person can be Vice President who does not meet the qualifications for President.

## AMENDMENT 13

**Section 1.** Slavery cannot exist in the United States or its territories. No one may be forced to work, except as punishment for committing a crime.

**Section 2.** Congress may pass whatever laws are necessary to enforce Amendment 13. Many amendments include such an *enabling act*.

## AMENDMENT 14

**Section 1.** All persons born or naturalized in the United States and subject to this country's laws are citizens of the United States and of the state in which they live. No state may take away the rights of citizens or take any person's life, liberty, or property except according to law. All state laws must apply equally to everyone in the state.

**Section 2.** In counting population to determine a state's representation, all people in the state are counted. But if the right to vote is denied to any male inhabitants of a state who are entitled to vote, that state's representation can be reduced accordingly. This section abolished the provision in Article I, Section 2, Clause 3, which said that only three fifths of the slaves should be counted as population.

## AMENDMENT 13
## SLAVERY ABOLISHED (1865)

**Section 1. Abolition of slavery.** Neither slavery nor involuntary servitude, except as a punishment for crime whereof the party shall have been duly convicted, shall exist within the United States or any place subject to their jurisdiction.

**Section 2. Enforcement.** Congress shall have the power to enforce this article by appropriate legislation.

## AMENDMENT 14
## CIVIL RIGHTS GUARANTEED (1868)

**Section 1. Definition of citizenship.** All persons born or naturalized in the United States, and subject to the jurisdiction thereof, are citizens of the United States and of the state wherein they reside. No state shall make or enforce any law which shall abridge the privileges or immunities of citizens of the United States; nor shall any state deprive any person of life, liberty, or property, without due process of law; nor deny to any person within its jurisdiction the equal protection of the laws.

**Section 2. Apportionment of representatives.** Representatives shall be apportioned among the several states according to their respective numbers, counting the whole number of persons in each state, [excluding Indians not taxed.] But when the right to vote at any election for the choice of electors for President and Vice President of the United States, representatives in Congress, the executive and judicial officers of a state, or the members of the legislature thereof, is denied to any of the [male] inhabitants of such state, [being twenty-one years of age] and citizens of the United States, or in any way abridged, except for participation in rebellion, or other crime, the basis of representation therein shall be reduced in the proportion which the number of such [male] citizens shall bear to the whole number of [male] citizens [twenty-one years of age] in such state.

**Section 3. Restrictions on holding public office.** No person shall be a senator or representative in Congress, or elector of President and Vice President, or hold any office, civil or military, under the United States, or under any state, who, having previously taken an oath as a member of Congress, or as an officer of the United States, or as a member of any state legislature, or as an executive or judicial officer of any state, to support the Constitution of the United States, shall have engaged in insurrection or rebellion against the same, or given aid or comfort to the enemies thereof. But Congress may by vote of two thirds of each house remove such disability.

**Section 4. Public debt of the United States valid; Confederate debt void.** The validity of the public debt of the United States, authorized by law, including debts incurred for payment of pensions and bounties for services in suppressing insurrection or rebellion, shall not be questioned. But neither the United States nor any state shall assume or pay any debt or obligation incurred in aid of insurrection or rebellion against the United States, or any claim for the loss or emancipation of any slave; but all such debts, obligations, and claims shall be held illegal and void.

**Section 5. Enforcement.** The Congress shall have power to enforce by appropriate legislation the provisions of this article.

## AMENDMENT 15
## RIGHT TO VOTE (1870)

**Section 1.** The right of citizens of the United States to vote shall not be denied or abridged by the United States or by any state on account of race, color, or previous condition of servitude.

**Section 2.** The Congress shall have power to enforce this article by appropriate legislation.

## AMENDMENT 16
## INCOME TAX (1913)

The Congress shall have power to lay and collect taxes on incomes, from whatever

Section 3. Persons who hold appointed or elective offices or commissions in the armed forces which required an oath to support the Constitution of the United States violate that oath by taking up arms against the United States. They cannot hold any office that would again require them to take such an oath. Congress may abolish this rule by a two-thirds vote of each house. This provision was designed to bar leaders of the Confederacy from holding federal offices.

Section 4. All debts contracted by the United States are to be paid. But neither the United States nor any state government is to pay the debts of the Confederacy. Neither is any payment to be made as compensation for slaves who were set free.

## AMENDMENT 15

Citizens may not be kept from voting because of their race or color or because they were once slaves.

## AMENDMENT 16

Congress may tax incomes. The total amount in federal income tax paid by people in the various states does not have to be determined by the number of people who live in the states.

## AMENDMENT 17

**Section 1.** The original Constitution provided that senators were to be elected by the state legislatures. Amendment 17 changed that to election by popular vote. Anyone qualified to vote for a state representative can vote for United States senators.

**Section 2.** If a vacancy occurs in the United States Senate, the governor of the state affected may call a special election to fill the vacancy. The state legislature, however, may permit the governor to appoint someone to fill the vacancy until an election is held.

**Section 3.** Senators chosen by state legislatures before Amendment 17 was added to the Constitution could complete their terms.

## AMENDMENT 18

**Section 1.** Amendment 18 forbade the manufacture, sale, or shipment of intoxicating beverages within the United States. The importation or exportation of such beverages was also forbidden. Amendment 18 was repealed by Amendment 21.

source derived, without apportionment among the several states and without regard to any census or enumeration.

## AMENDMENT 17
## DIRECT ELECTION OF SENATORS (1913)

**Section 1. Election by the people.** The Senate of the United States shall be composed of two senators from each state, elected by the people thereof, for six years; and each senator shall have one vote. The electors in each state shall have the qualifications requisite for electors of the most numerous branch of the state legislatures.

**Section 2. Vacancies.** When vacancies happen in the representation of any state in the Senate, the executive authority of such state shall issue writs of election to fill such vacancies: provided that the legislature of any state may empower the executive thereof to make temporary appointments until the people fill the vacancies by election as the legislature may direct.

**Section 3. Effective date.** This amendment shall not be so construed as to affect the election or term of any senator chosen before it becomes valid as part of the Constitution.

## AMENDMENT 18
## PROHIBITION (1919)

**Section 1.** [After one year from the ratification of this article the manufacture, sale, or transportation of intoxicating liquors within, the importation thereof into, or the exportation thereof from the United States and all territory subject to the jurisdiction thereof for beverage purposes is hereby prohibited.]

**Section 2.** [The Congress and the several states shall have concurrent power to enforce this article by appropriate legislation.]

**Section 3.** [This article shall be inoperative unless it shall have been ratified as an amendment to the Constitution by the legislatures of the several states, as provided in the Constitution, within seven years from the date of the submission hereof to the states by the Congress.]

# AMENDMENT 19
## WOMEN'S VOTING RIGHTS (1920)

**Section 1.** The right of citizens of the United States to vote shall not be denied or abridged by the United States or by any state on account of sex.

**Section 2.** The Congress shall have power to enforce this article by appropriate legislation.

# AMENDMENT 20
## TERMS OF OFFICE (1933)

**Section 1. Terms of President, Vice President, and Congress.** The terms of the President and Vice President shall end at noon on the 20th day of January, and the terms of senators and representatives at noon on the 3rd day of January, of the years in which such terms would have ended if this article had not been ratified; and the terms of their successors shall then begin.

**Section 2. Sessions of Congress.** The Congress shall assemble at least once in every year, and such meeting shall begin at noon on the 3rd day of January, unless they shall by law appoint a different day.

**Section 3. Presidential succession.** If, at the time fixed for the beginning of the term of the President, the President-elect shall have died, the Vice President-elect shall become President. If a President shall not have been chosen before the time fixed for the beginning of his term, or if the President-elect shall have failed to qualify, then the Vice President-elect shall act as President until a President shall have qualified; and the Congress may by law provide for the case wherein neither a President-elect nor a Vice President-elect shall have qualified, declaring who shall then act as President, or the

---

**AMENDMENT 19**

**Section 1.** No citizen may be denied the right to vote because she is a woman.

**AMENDMENT 20**

**Section 1.** The terms of the President and Vice President end at noon on January 20 following a presidential election. The terms of one third of the senators and of all representatives end at noon on January 3 in years ending in odd numbers. The new terms begin when the old terms end.

**Section 2.** Congress meets at least once a year. The regular session begins on January 3 unless Congress sets a different day.

**Section 3.** If the President-elect dies before being sworn in, the Vice President-elect becomes President. If the Vice President-elect has not been chosen or does not qualify for office, the Vice President-elect acts as President until a President is chosen or qualifies. If neither the President-elect nor Vice President-elect qualifies to hold office, Congress decides who shall act as President until a President or Vice President is chosen or qualifies.

**Section 4.** In cases in which the election is thrown into Congress because no candidate for either President or Vice President receives a majority of the electoral votes, Congress may make a law to decide what to do if one of the candidates dies.

**Section 5.** Section 5 set the date on which the first two sections of Amendment 20 were to take effect after the amendment had been approved by the states.

**Section 6.** To become a part of the Constitution, Amendment 20 had to be approved within seven years.

## AMENDMENT 21

**Section 1.** Amendment 21 repeals the Eighteenth Amendment.

**Section 2.** Intoxicating liquors may not be transported or imported into any state or territory of the United States if the laws of that state or territory prohibit the sale of liquor.

**Section 3.** Section 3 set a time limit of seven years for approval of Amendment 21.

manner in which one who is to act shall be selected, and such person shall act accordingly until a President or a Vice President shall have qualified.

**Section 4. Choice of President by the House.** The Congress may by law provide for the case of the death of any of the persons from whom the House of Representatives may choose a President whenever the right of choice shall have devolved upon them, and for the case of the death of any of the persons from whom the Senate may choose a Vice President whenever the right of choice shall have devolved upon them.

**Section 5. Date effective.** Sections 1 and 2 shall take effect on the fifteenth day of October following the ratification of this article.

**Section 6. Limited time for ratification.** [This article shall be inoperative unless it shall have been ratified as an amendment to the Constitution by the legislatures of three fourths of the several states within seven years from the date of its submission.]

## AMENDMENT 21
## REPEAL OF PROHIBITION (1933)

**Section 1. Repeal of Amendment 18.** The eighteenth article of amendment to the Constitution of the United States is hereby repealed.

**Section 2. States protected.** The transportation or importation into any state, territory, or possession of the United States for delivery or use therein of intoxicating liquors, in violation of the laws thereof, is hereby prohibited.

**Section 3. Limited time for ratification.** [This article shall be inoperative unless it shall have been ratified as an amendment to the Constitution by conventions in the several states, as provided in the Constitution, within seven years from the date of the submission hereof to the states by the Congress.]

# AMENDMENT 22
## TWO-TERM LIMITATION ON PRESIDENCY (1951)

**Section 1. Definition of limitation.** No person shall be elected to the office of the President more than twice, and no person who has held the office of President, or acted as President, for more than two years of a term to which some other person was elected President shall be elected to the office of the President more than once. [But this article shall not apply to any person holding the office of President when this article was proposed by the Congress, and shall not prevent any person who may be holding the office of President, or acting as President, during the term within which this article becomes operative from holding the office of President, or acting as President during the remainder of such term.]

**Section 2. Limited time for ratification.** [This article shall be inoperative unless it shall have been ratified as an amendment to the Constitution by the legislatures of three fourths of the several states within seven years from the date of its submission to the states by the Congress.]

# AMENDMENT 23
## VOTING IN THE DISTRICT OF COLUMBIA (1961)

**Section 1.** The District constituting the seat of government of the United States shall appoint, in such manner as the Congress may direct:

A number of electors of President and Vice President equal to the whole number of senators and representatives in Congress to which the District would be entitled if it were a state, but in no event more than the least populous state; they shall be in addition to those appointed by the states, but they shall be considered, for the purposes of the election of President and Vice President, to be electors appointed by a state; and they shall meet in the District and perform such duties as provided by the twelfth article of amendment.

AMENDMENT 22

**Section 1.** No person may be elected President more than twice. A person who has served more than two years in the place of an elected President may be elected President only once. This limitation did not apply to President Truman, who was in office when Amendment 22 was proposed. Before this amendment was added, the Constitution placed no limit on the number of terms a President might serve. Presidents Washington and Jefferson, however, decided against a third term. This practice had been observed until 1940, when Franklin D. Roosevelt was elected for a third term.

**Section 2.** Section 2 called for the approval of Amendment 22 within seven years.

AMENDMENT 23

**Section 1.** People who live in the District of Columbia may vote in presidential elections. They may choose as many electors as does the state with the smallest population. Before this amendment was adopted, residents of the District of Columbia had not voted for President and Vice President because the Constitution provided that only states should choose presidential electors.

## AMENDMENT 24

Section 1. Citizens may not be prevented from voting in a national election because they have not paid a state poll tax or other tax.

## AMENDMENT 25

Section 1. If the President dies or resigns, the Vice President becomes President.

Section 2. When there is a vacancy in the office of Vice President, the President may appoint a person to be Vice President. The appointment must be approved by a majority vote in both houses of Congress.

Section 3. A President who is ill or unable to carry out official duties may assign those duties to the Vice President by notifying the Speaker of the House and the President pro tempore of the Senate. The Vice President then acts as President until the President is again able to serve.

Section 4. If the President is ill or unable for other reasons to carry out official duties and is unable or unwilling to assign those duties to the Vice President,

Section 2. The Congress shall have power to enforce this article by appropriate legislation.

# AMENDMENT 24
## POLL TAX PROHIBITION (1964)

Section 1. The right of citizens of the United States to vote in any primary or other election for President or Vice President, for electors for President or Vice President, or for senator or representative in Congress, shall not be denied or abridged by the United States or any state by reason of failure to pay any poll tax or other tax.

Section 2. The Congress shall have power to enforce this article by appropriate legislation.

# AMENDMENT 25
## PRESIDENTIAL DISABILITY (1967)

Section 1. **Accession of the Vice President.** In case of the removal of the President from office or of his death or resignation, the Vice President shall become President.

Section 2. **Replacing the Vice President.** Whenever there is a vacancy in the office of the Vice President, the President shall nominate a Vice President who shall take office upon confirmation by a majority vote of both Houses of Congress.

Section 3. **Vice President as Acting President.** Whenever the President transmits to the President pro tempore of the Senate and the Speaker of the House of Representatives his written declaration that he is unable to discharge the powers and duties of his office, and until he transmits to them a written declaration to the contrary, such powers and duties shall be discharged by the Vice President as Acting President.

Section 4. **Determining presidential disability.** Whenever the Vice President and a majority of either the principal officers of the executive departments or of such other body as Congress may by law provide, transmit to the President pro tempore of the Senate and the Speaker of the House of Representatives their written declaration that the President is unable to discharge the powers and duties of his office, the Vice President shall immediately assume the powers and duties of the office as Acting President.

Thereafter, when the President transmits to the President pro tempore of the Senate and the Speaker of the House of Representatives his written declaration that no inability exists, he shall resume the powers and duties of his office unless the Vice President and a majority of either the principal officers of the executive department or of such other body as Congress may by law provide, transmit within four days to the President pro tempore of the Senate and the Speaker of the House of Representatives their written declaration that the President is unable to discharge the powers and duties of his office. Thereupon, Congress shall decide the issue, assembling within forty-eight hours for that purpose, if not in session. If the Congress, within twenty-one days after receipt of the latter written declaration, or, if Congress is not in session, within twenty-one days after Congress is required to assemble, determines by two-thirds vote of both Houses that the President is unable to discharge the powers and duties of his office, the Vice President shall continue to discharge the same as Acting President; otherwise, the President shall resume the powers and duties of his office.

the Vice President and a majority of the Cabinet must notify the Speaker of the House and the President pro tempore of the Senate. The Vice President then acts as President. The President cannot again assume official duties unless the Vice President and a majority of the Cabinet agree that he is fit to do so. If the Vice President and a majority of the Cabinet do not believe that the President is fit, Congress must meet and make a decision within 21 days. If two thirds of both houses of Congress feel that the President is unable to carry out the duties of his office, the Vice President continues to act as President. Otherwise, the President again takes over the duties of the presidency.

# AMENDMENT 26
# VOTING AGE (1971)

**Section 1.** The right of citizens of the United States who are eighteen years of age or older to vote shall not be denied or abridged by the United States or by any state on account of age.
**Section 2.** The Congress shall have power to enforce this article by appropriate legislation.

## AMENDMENT 26

**Section 1.** The right to vote may not be denied because of age to any citizen who is 18 or older.

# 10 The Federalists Launch the New Government
## 1789–1800

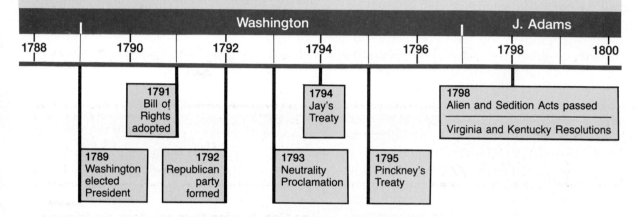

Washington | J. Adams

1788 — 1790 — 1792 — 1794 — 1796 — 1798 — 1800

**1791** Bill of Rights adopted

**1794** Jay's Treaty

**1798** Alien and Sedition Acts passed

Virginia and Kentucky Resolutions

**1789** Washington elected President

**1792** Republican party formed

**1793** Neutrality Proclamation

**1795** Pinckney's Treaty

New York citizens cheer George Washington as he rides to Federal Hall to be sworn in as the first President of the United States.

## Preparing to Read

George Washington, the first President of the United States, faced the task of putting the Constitution into practice. Washington, with the help of Congress and his advisers, set up the government outlined in the Constitution. In its early years, the government wrestled with economic problems and foreign affairs. Americans soon formed sharp differences of opinion about the course the nation should follow. Yet in its first eight years, the federal government steadily gained respect at home and abroad. As you read this chapter, try to answer the following questions:

1. What kind of government did the Constitution establish?
2. How did the new government solve economic problems?
3. What issues in politics and foreign affairs faced America?
4. How did conflict with France affect the nation?

# 1 What kind of government did the Constitution establish?

## Vocabulary

republic
tyranny
bill

veto
unconstitutional
amend
amendment

"We the people ... establish this Constitution for the United States of America." By beginning the Constitution with these words, the Framers expressed a new idea. At the time, kings and queens ruled many of the world's countries. The United States, however, was to be governed by the people. The Constitution created a **republic** —a country with a representative government, in which the supreme power rests with the nation's citizens.

## Powers and Limits

The Framers of the Constitution hoped to make "a more perfect union" of the 13 states. In other words, they wanted the states to be more firmly united than they had been under the Articles of Confederation.

The Constitution thus set clear guidelines to help the national and state governments do their work well.

**The Constitution arranges for the division of powers.** In writing the Constitution, the Framers thought about each level of government. They spelled out the powers of the national government and the states.

*Federal powers.* The Constitution gave Congress a number of powers that it had lacked under the Confederation. These included the power to collect taxes and to control trade among the states. Congress also gained the power to organize a court system and to raise armies and navies. Congress was also given sole authority to issue money and regulate its value.

*State powers.* While the federal government was to control matters involving the whole nation, the states kept certain powers. For example, each state can make its own laws about education and about trade within its borders. Each state can also set its own punishments for most crimes.

*Shared powers.* The Constitution allows the federal government and the states to

# The Federal System

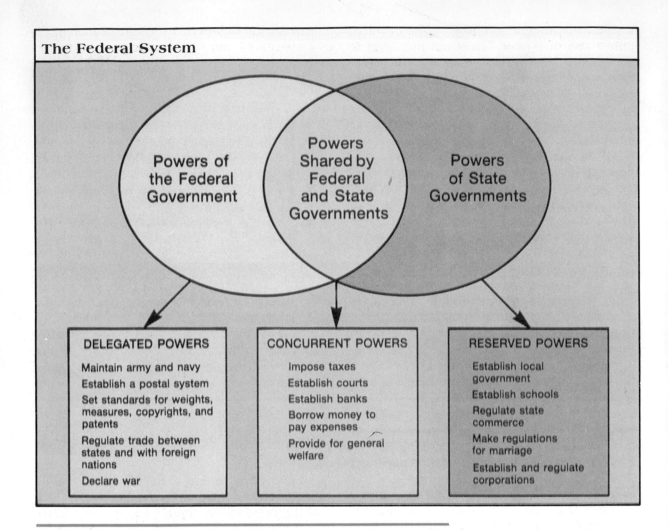

**Powers of the Federal Government**

**Powers Shared by Federal and State Governments**

**Powers of State Governments**

**DELEGATED POWERS**

Maintain army and navy

Establish a postal system

Set standards for weights, measures, copyrights, and patents

Regulate trade between states and with foreign nations

Declare war

**CONCURRENT POWERS**

Impose taxes

Establish courts

Establish banks

Borrow money to pay expenses

Provide for general welfare

**RESERVED POWERS**

Establish local government

Establish schools

Regulate state commerce

Make regulations for marriage

Establish and regulate corporations

## Chart Study

Powers of government are divided between the state and federal governments. Examples of powers appear on the chart. What name is given to powers shared by both levels of government? Which level of government has the power to establish schools?

share a number of powers. Both, for example, can set taxes, borrow money, maintain courts and prisons, and build roads. However, if conflicts arise between state and national laws, the states must follow the national laws.

**The federal government has three branches.** The Constitution divides the United States government into three separate branches. The legislative branch, which makes the laws, consists of the Senate and the House of Representatives. Senators are elected for six years, while representatives serve for two. The executive branch, which enforces the laws, is headed by the President and the Vice President. Both serve four-year terms. The judicial branch, which interprets the laws, consists of the **Supreme Court** and other federal courts. Supreme Court judges receive lifetime appointments.

The **separation of powers,** division of the government into separate branches, developed from very careful planning. The members of the Constitutional Convention wanted to prevent **tyranny** —the cruel or unjust use of power. They did not want to put too much power in the hands of one official or even a few officials. If a select group made all the rules, enforced them, and judged their fairness, they could persecute people at will. In the American system of government, therefore, a group of elected legislators makes the laws. Another group of government officials sees that citizens obey the laws. A third group judges the innocence or guilt of accused lawbreakers and decides how the guilty should be punished.

**Each branch checks the others.** By providing for separation of powers, the Constitution reduced the chance for tyranny. However, the Framers worried that each branch of the government might still misuse its power. If left to act completely on its own, Congress, for example, could pass laws favoring one state over another. The executive branch and the federal courts could also act unfairly.

To prevent such problems from occurring, the Constitution provides a system of **checks and balances**—a means of limiting the power of the three branches by having each branch monitor the others. The President, for example, must approve all of Congress's **bills** —proposed laws—before they can take effect. If the President chooses to **veto** —reject—a bill, it does not become law. The President checks the power of the judicial branch because it is the President who appoints federal judges.

The Senate, however, must approve the President's choices for judges. This is one way Congress checks both the executive and the judicial branches. The Senate must also approve all treaties made by the President. In addition, Congress may overturn a presidential veto, refuse to fund presidential activities, and even remove a President who seriously misbehaves.

The judicial branch has the power to strike down laws and actions of the other two government branches. If the Supreme Court decides that Congress or the President has violated the Constitution, it may declare the law or act to be **unconstitutional** —contrary to the Constitution. Because of the system of checks and balances, no single branch of the government can become too powerful.

## The Flexibility to Change

The Framers planned the Constitution as thoroughly as they could. They knew, however, that as times changed, their plan of government might need updating. As a result, they provided a way for government leaders to **amend** —improve or alter—the Constitution. Article V of the Constitution explains that Congress or the states may propose **amendments** —additional changes. These become laws if the legislatures in three fourths of the states approve. (See page 222.) Because the Constitution was well planned, it has been amended only 26 times in 200 years.

**The first 10 amendments protect basic liberties.** Even before the first state ratified the Constitution, many Americans called for

One of James Madison's contributions to the new country was drafting the Bill of Rights.

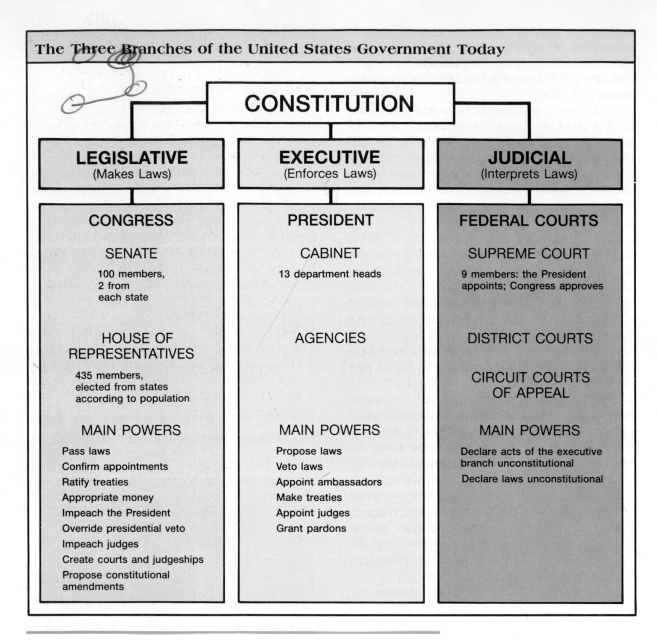

## The Three Branches of the United States Government Today

### CONSTITUTION

| LEGISLATIVE (Makes Laws) | EXECUTIVE (Enforces Laws) | JUDICIAL (Interprets Laws) |
| --- | --- | --- |
| **CONGRESS** | **PRESIDENT** | **FEDERAL COURTS** |
| SENATE<br>100 members,<br>2 from<br>each state | CABINET<br>13 department heads | SUPREME COURT<br>9 members: the President<br>appoints; Congress approves |
| HOUSE OF REPRESENTATIVES<br>435 members,<br>elected from states<br>according to population | AGENCIES | DISTRICT COURTS<br><br>CIRCUIT COURTS<br>OF APPEAL |
| MAIN POWERS<br>Pass laws<br>Confirm appointments<br>Ratify treaties<br>Appropriate money<br>Impeach the President<br>Override presidential veto<br>Impeach judges<br>Create courts and judgeships<br>Propose constitutional amendments | MAIN POWERS<br>Propose laws<br>Veto laws<br>Appoint ambassadors<br>Make treaties<br>Appoint judges<br>Grant pardons | MAIN POWERS<br>Declare acts of the executive branch unconstitutional<br>Declare laws unconstitutional |

## Chart Study

**The three branches of government have specific responsibilities.
What is the main responsibility of the legislative branch?**

the addition of a bill of rights. Some states, including Massachusetts and Virginia, refused to ratify until they were promised that a bill of rights would be written. James Madison brought up this matter when Congress first met in 1789. Congress quickly proposed 12 amendments to the Constitution. Ten of these were approved by the states in 1791. These first 10 amendments, written chiefly by James Madison, make up the **Bill of Rights.** (See pages 224–226.)

The Bill of Rights lists the rights of citizens under the United States government. The First Amendment protects freedom of religion, freedom of speech, and freedom of the press. It also says that citizens may meet peacefully in groups. In addition, they may ask the government for changes when something is wrong.

The next seven amendments guarantee additional freedoms. These include the right to bear arms and the right to a fair trial. The Bill of Rights also protects citizens from having their property confiscated or their homes searched without reason. It even states that people accused or convicted of crimes must not be treated too severely.

The first eight amendments in the Bill of Rights prevent the government from taking advantage of the American people. The ninth and tenth amendments further limit the federal government's power. They grant to the states and to the people any powers not specifically listed in the Constitution.

**Customs and court decisions expand the Constitution.** The amendment process provides a way of formally changing the Constitution. Certain government customs, however, are not discussed in the Constitution or in any amendments. These practices have been followed so long they have become an unwritten part of government. For example, all Presidents appoint a **Cabinet**— board of advisers. The Constitution, however, makes no mention of such a group. It simply says that the President may set up departments to help run the government. The President may also name people to run the departments. It is by custom, not by law, that these people are called the Cabinet. By custom, they meet as a group to advise the President on many matters.

Like customs, court decisions also add to the basic framework laid out in the Constitution. The Constitution is considered the supreme law of the land. Yet sometimes the meaning of words in the Constitution is vague. The Supreme Court must then interpret the Framers' ideas. The Constitution states, for example, that Congress may make any laws "necessary and proper" for carrying out its duties. (See page 213.) The Supreme Court has interpreted this statement, the **elastic clause,** to mean that Congress may take more powers than the Constitution

## LINKING PAST AND PRESENT

## ★★★ *The Government*

The federal government began in 1789 with just three departments—State, War, and Treasury—and fewer than 2,000 employees. The elastic clause of the Constitution, however, gave the government the flexibility to expand. As the United States has grown in size, population, and power, the government has kept pace. Today the President and Congress have more duties and powers than ever before. They also have more than a dozen agencies and 3 million federal workers to help them.

Much of the growth has come about because of new technology. Televisions, automobiles, computers, spaceships, nuclear power plants—none of these existed 200 years ago. Today, however, the federal government regulates all these matters and more.

lists. For example, the Constitution says nothing about airplane traffic. Yet because Congress can control interstate trade, it can also regulate airlines.

SECTION REVIEW

1. **Vocabulary**   republic, tyranny, bill, veto, unconstitutional, amend, amendment
2. **People and Places**   Massachusetts, Virginia, James Madison
3. **Comprehension**   How does the Constitution make tyranny unlikely?
4. **Comprehension**   What does the Bill of Rights protect?
5. **Critical Thinking**   The system of checks and balances discourages government officials from acting rapidly. How might this be an advantage? How might it be a drawback?

# 2 How did the new government solve economic problems?

## Vocabulary

inaugurate          interest
justice             speculator
bond                tariff

The government that began in 1789 faced a great challenge. The first President and the new Congress had to prove that the United States could succeed under the Constitution. They had to find ways to pay the country's debts and raise taxes. The President needed to show firm leadership so that states would respect the federal government.

## Launching the Government

Early in 1789 the members of the Electoral College voted in the country's first presidential election. Each elector wrote down two names. The top vote-getter would become President. The runner-up would be named Vice President.

**Washington takes office.** In April 1789 the Senate counted the electoral votes. To no one's surprise, George Washington was the unanimous choice for President of the United States. John Adams, another leader in the Revolution, won election as Vice President.

The new government leaders met in New York City, the nation's first capital. It took Washington eight days to travel there from his home in Virginia. On April 30, 1789, he was **inaugurated** —officially sworn to service. With his hand on the Bible, Washington promised to "preserve, protect, and defend the Constitution of the United States."

**The government establishes courts.** Although Americans had now elected their President and Congress, the new government had no judicial system. The Constitution called for a Supreme Court and other federal courts. Therefore in 1789 Congress passed the **Federal Judiciary Act.** This act declared that the Supreme Court would consist of five **justices** —judges—plus a **Chief Justice.** * Washington decided to appoint John Jay, a well-known lawyer from New York, as Chief Justice.

**Washington chooses a Cabinet.** Congress also created three executive departments to help the President govern. Washington named three talented men to run these departments. He chose the brilliant Thomas Jefferson as head of the **Department of State.** This office handles relations between the United States and other countries. Henry Knox, a trusted soldier and Patriot during the Revolution, became head of the **War Department.** He took charge of military matters, including the national army and navy. Alexander Hamilton was named to run the **Treasury Department.** He had responsibility for raising money and handling government finances.

In addition, Washington appointed Edmund Randolph as **Attorney General.** Randolph's job was to advise the government on legal matters. The three department heads and the Attorney General made up Washington's Cabinet. Today the Cabinet has several more members—the heads of new departments created over the years.

## Economic Difficulties

The new government's most pressing problem centered on money matters. The United States owed a great deal of money at home and abroad. During the Revolutionary War the Continental Congress had borrowed

---

* The number of justices on the Supreme Court has changed several times. At present there are nine, including the Chief Justice.

to meet its expenses. The Congress of the Confederation also ran short of money. By 1789 the sums that had been borrowed still had not been paid back.

A government, like a person, cannot succeed if it fails to pay its bills. It loses the faith and respect of its citizens and other countries. Washington knew that the government would have to find ways of paying the money it owed.

**Hamilton brings valuable experience to his job.** Washington had put a skilled man in charge of the United States' finances. Alexander Hamilton, Secretary of the Treasury, had served on George Washington's military staff during the American Revolution. He later became a lawyer and a key member of the Constitutional Convention. His essays in *The Federalist* helped bring about the adoption of the Constitution. Hamilton was 32 years old when he became Secretary of the Treasury. Hardworking, intelligent, and shrewd about money, he proved well suited for his job.

**Hamilton tackles the nation's debts.** Hamilton found that he had to deal with not one but many debts. The United States owed millions of dollars to France, the Netherlands, and Spain. The separate states had borrowed, too, to finance the Revolution. The national government had also borrowed from private citizens. When a government borrows, it gives the lender a **bond** —a paper promising to repay the loan at a certain time. When the bond becomes due, the government returns the sum it borrowed, plus **interest.** Interest is an extra payment in return for the use of money loaned.

Soon after the Revolution, many Americans who had bought bonds lost faith in the government's ability to repay them. Some people sold the bonds at a reduced price to **speculators** —people who take business risks in the hope of profiting. Often the speculators paid only a quarter of the original value of the bonds. They stood to gain large profits if the United States paid back the full value of the bonds plus interest.

## Creative Solutions

When Hamilton became Secretary of the Treasury, he presented a financial plan to Congress. He proposed to combine all state

The executive branch of government includes the President's Cabinet. President Washington (right) chose (right to left) Thomas Jefferson as Secretary of State, Alexander Hamilton as Secretary of the Treasury, Henry Knox (seated) as Secretary of War, and Edmund Randolph as Attorney General.

# AMERICAN HIGHLIGHTS

## CULTURE • The Capital

In 1790, when Congress agreed to locate the nation's capital on the banks of the Potomac, it left final plans to George Washington. Washington chose the actual site for the District of Columbia. He also hired Pierre L'Enfant to design the capital. L'Enfant imagined a city of monuments, parks, and wide avenues. At the heart of the city would stand the domed Capitol Building where Congress would work. Nearby, at a spot chosen by Washington, the President's mansion would be built.

Workers did not complete the President's home, today called the White House, until after Washington left office. The next President, John Adams, moved in while building was still in progress. As his wife, Abigail, wrote to their daughter:

> The house is upon a grand and superb scale ... but there is not a single room finished. We have not the least fence, yard, or other convenience outside, and the great unfinished [East Room] I make a drying room of, to hang up the clothes in....

Still, she added, "It is a beautiful spot ... and, the more I view it, the more I am delighted with it."

**The Nation's Capital**

and national debts into one large debt. The government could issue new bonds for all the money owed. The government could then pay off these bonds with tax money it would collect. In this way, Hamilton hoped to preserve the nation's honor.

**Southerners oppose the plan.** Many southerners in Congress objected to Hamilton's idea. They argued that speculators should not receive full value for bonds bought so cheaply. Most speculators lived in northern cities. Southerners worried that the North would grow rich at the expense of the South.

Southerners also saw no reason for the national government to pay all state debts.

Every state had borrowed to meet the war costs. However, some southern states, such as Virginia, had already repaid their debts. It was only fair, they argued, that the other states do the same.

**Hamilton strikes a bargain.** Hamilton knew that the southern members of Congress could defeat his plan. Therefore he proposed a compromise. Congress had temporarily established the nation's capital at New York City. Many southerners, however, wished to move the capital south. Hamilton discussed the matter with James Madison and other southern leaders. If these men voted for his financial plan, Hamilton said, he would push for a capital in the south.

Hamilton's offer was accepted. Congress approved his plan in 1790, agreeing to pay all state and national debts. Congress also voted to locate the nation's capital between Maryland and Virginia. These states gave some of their land along the Potomac River to the federal government. This area, called the District of Columbia in honor of Columbus, thus became the permanent capital site. The new capital city, Washington, was designed by a French-born engineer, Pierre L'Enfant (law-FAW). Benjamin Banneker, a black mathematician and surveyor, helped in the planning. On December 1, 1800, Washington, D.C., officially became the nation's capital. Before this time New York City and Philadelphia each served as the nation's capital.

**Hamilton proposes a banking system.** Another part of Hamilton's program involved setting up a national chain of banks. Hamilton wanted to build one central bank in Philadelphia with branches in other cities. These banks would give the government a safe place to keep the tax money it raised. The banks could also loan money to the United States Treasury and to American business owners and merchants.

Again Hamilton met stiff opposition. Thomas Jefferson, among others, argued that the Constitution did not give Congress the power to create a national bank. Hamilton, however, reminded these critics that Congress could borrow money and regulate the money system. He said that a national bank was "necessary and proper" to help in these tasks. Congress agreed and the first **Bank of the United States** was established in 1791.

**Hamilton suggests a new tax.** The government had another important worry: paying its bills. Soon after Congress first met, it passed a law establishing a tariff —a tax on imports from other countries. For example, nails brought into the country were taxed one cent a pound. Molasses, which came from the West Indies, was taxed two and a half cents a gallon.

The tariff encouraged Americans to buy from American merchants rather than foreigners. Some of the manufactured goods,

John Trumbull painted Alexander Hamilton's portrait in the 1790's. Hamilton's plans gave the United States a firm financial foundation by paying debts, establishing taxes, and creating a national bank.

however, were not readily available in the United States. People in the South, especially, continued to import needed products from countries overseas.

The tariff raised enough money to cover the government's expenses. Yet far more money was needed to pay off the United States' debts. Hamilton thus recommended a tax on certain American-made goods. At his suggestion, Congress taxed all whiskey made and sold in the United States.

**A rebellion against the whiskey tax fails.** The tax on whiskey angered frontier farmers. These farmers had trouble bringing

In this painting by Frederick Kemmelmeyer, President Washington reviews troops assembled in 1794 to crush the Whiskey Rebellion. By persuading Pennsylvania farmers to pay the whiskey tax, the new government proved its ability to enforce federal laws.

their crops to markets on the eastern seacoast because of poor roads. To get around this problem, they made their grain into whiskey. Whiskey was easier to transport and brought a better price in the East. The whiskey tax, then, came as a hard blow.

In western Pennsylvania in 1794, a group of farmers refused to pay the tax. In an outbreak called the **Whiskey Rebellion,** the farmers took up arms and chased away the tax collectors. President Washington responded by leading about 13,000 soldiers to Pennsylvania. At this show of force, the farmers gave in and agreed to pay the tax.

Washington's firm action proved the power of the new government. With no bloodshed, the government had swiftly put down the first challenge to its authority. It had also found a way to fill the Treasury.

## SECTION REVIEW

1. **Vocabulary**   inaugurate, justice, bond, interest, speculator, tariff
2. **People and Places**   George Washington, John Adams, John Jay, Thomas Jefferson, Henry Knox, Alexander Hamilton, Edmund Randolph, Potomac River, Washington, D.C., Pierre L'Enfant, Benjamin Banneker
3. **Comprehension**   What economic problems did the new government face?
4. **Comprehension**   How did the government try to solve its economic problems?
5. **Critical Thinking**   In his day, Alexander Hamilton was considered both a financial genius and a villain. What might account for such divided opinions?

## CRITICAL THINKING: Reading Tables

In studying the past, facts will often be expressed as numbers, or **data.** Sentences full of numbers, however, can be quite difficult to understand. To show information more clearly, historians often present data in a **table.** In a table, information is arranged in columns (going down) and in rows (going across).

To read a table, follow these guidelines. First, look at the title of the table. This tells you what information is presented in the table. Next, carefully read the column headings to see what kinds of information are contained in each column and how the columns are arranged. Often the information in a column is presented in alphabetical order. In other tables, data are arranged in numerical order, beginning with the smallest or the largest numbers. Finally, compare and contrast the information in the table to find out if it shows any general direction or change in direction.

The table on this page shows the results of a **census**—a count of the population—for the original 13 states of the Union. The first census was taken by the United States government in 1790 to determine how many seats each state would have in the House of Representatives. Since that time, a census has been taken in the United States every 10 years. Study the table. Then answer the following questions on a separate sheet of paper.

1. How is this table arranged?
2. What was the population of Georgia in 1790?
3. Which state had the smallest population in 1790?
4. In which state did more people live in 1790, North Carolina or South Carolina?

### The 1790 Census

| State | Population |
| --- | --- |
| Connecticut | 238,000 |
| Delaware | 59,000 |
| Georgia | 83,000 |
| Maryland | 320,000 |
| Massachusetts | 476,000 |
| New Hampshire | 142,000 |
| New Jersey | 184,000 |
| New York | 340,000 |
| North Carolina | 394,000 |
| Pennsylvania | 434,000 |
| Rhode Island | 69,000 |
| South Carolina | 249,000 |
| Virginia | 748,000 |

5. Which two states had the largest populations in 1790? What fact concerning the early English colonization of North America might explain why these two states had more people than the other states?
6. Draw another table using the 1790 census figures. Arrange it by population size, from the largest state to the smallest state.
7. Because representation is based on population size, which five states would be entitled to the greatest number of seats in the House of Representatives, as a result of the 1790 census?

## Vocabulary

| | |
|---|---|
| political party | impress |
| democracy | effigy |
| neutral | precedent |

Returning to solid financial ground was the United States' most urgent problem. However, the nation also wanted to gain the respect of foreign countries. In addition, the government knew that it could not please all Americans with its decisions.

## The Growth of Political Parties

During Washington's presidency, Americans often held conflicting ideas about the direction of government policy. By 1792 they divided into two rival **political parties** — groups organized to promote specific goals and candidates for office. Thomas Jefferson, Washington's Secretary of State, led one group. Alexander Hamilton, Secretary of the Treasury, guided the other.

**Political parties develop.** From the time he proposed the financial plan, Hamilton had opponents. Thomas Jefferson and others believed that Hamilton was making the federal government too powerful and too favorable toward business. Therefore Jefferson, with the assistance of James Madison, formed the **Democratic-Republican party.** This name showed their strong belief in **democracy** —government by the people— and in the republican system.

Jefferson's followers were mainly farmers and artisans. Often called Republicans, they thought taxes and government regulations should be kept to a minimum. They wanted the federal government limited to the role outlined for it in the Constitution. Republicans believed that ordinary people and the states, not Congress, should control most government matters.

Hamilton, meanwhile, supported a strong federal government. His ideas appealed mostly to business and manufacturing people from the East. Hamilton and Vice President John Adams formed the **Federalist party.** The Federalists believed that the new nation could not function without taxes and regulations. They favored a loose interpretation of the Constitution. Congress, they said, could make laws that were "necessary and proper" to carry out the principles of the Constitution. In other words, the federal government could take powers not clearly listed in the Constitution.

**Washington remains popular with both parties.** President Washington hoped that Americans could work together without forming political parties. Although he tended to agree with the Federalists, he refused to join either party. In one of his speeches Washington warned against the party spirit:

> It serves always to distract the public councils and [weaken the government]. It [upsets] the community with ill-founded jealousies and false alarms; kindles the [hostility] of one part against another....

Both the Federalists and the Republicans held Washington in great respect. In 1792, at the end of his first four years in office, Washington was reelected president and John Adams was reelected Vice President.

## Problems with France and Britain

During Washington's second term in office, foreign affairs became a great concern. In 1789 people in France had started the **French Revolution.** This was a rebellion by peasants and middle class people against the nobles. At first many Americans sympathized with the revolt in France. They compared the struggle in France to their own American Revolution. Soon, however, Americans risked being drawn into the conflict, and public opinion grew divided.

**The French Revolution leads to wars within Europe.** By the start of Washington's second term, the French Revolution had become uncontrolled and violent. The revolutionaries began executing the nobles, and in 1793 they beheaded the king and queen. Most Americans disapproved of such violence. Still, many believed, the French people had a right to fight for self-government.

As Americans watched the situation in France, so did people all over Europe. The rulers of Great Britain, Austria, and Prussia grew greatly alarmed. They feared that their own citizens, following the example of the French, might stage rebellions. As a result, these leaders all declared war on France.

Americans now had a good reason to take interest in the French Revolution. The United States had signed a treaty of alliance with France in 1778. If France went to war, the United States was expected to go to war, too. President Washington and his advisers had to decide whether or not the United States should aid France.

**The United States stays out of the war.** The Republicans were in favor of helping the French. Thomas Jefferson and others felt bound by the alliance to France. They believed, too, that the United States had a duty to help people overthrow unfair systems of government. The Federalists, on the other hand, opposed sending aid to France. They thought that France was heading toward mob rule rather than democracy. Also, they did not want to fight Britain, an important partner in trade.

After consulting his Cabinet, President Washington decided to take the Federalists' advice. Early in 1793 Washington issued the **Neutrality Proclamation.** This document declared that the United States would remain **neutral** —taking no one's side—in the war. Both Jefferson and Hamilton agreed with Washington's decision. However, the French ambassador, "Citizen" Edmond Genêt

## Our Presidents

### GEORGE WASHINGTON

★ **1789–1797** ★

**1**ST PRESIDENT

NO PARTY

★ Born February 22, 1732, in Virginia

★ Married Martha Custis in 1759; no children

★ Surveyor; delegate to First and Second Continental Congresses; commander-in-chief of Continental Army

★ Lived in Virginia when elected President

★ Nicknamed "The Father of His Country"

★ Vice President: John Adams

★ Died December 14, 1799, in Virginia

★ Key events while in office: Bill of Rights; Kentucky, Tennessee, and Vermont became states; Whiskey Rebellion; Jay's Treaty

(zhuh-NAY), tried to stir up support for France behind Washington's back. Counting on the popularity of the French cause, Genêt urged Americans to send ships to France. Washington finally asked France to call Genêt home.

**The British seize American ships and sailors.** The United States had trouble remaining neutral in the European wars. The chief threat to American neutrality came from Great Britain, which had the world's most powerful navy. Britain did not intend to let the United States aid the French by shipping supplies to them. The British navy, therefore, set out to block such trade.

British warships began illegally stopping American ships bound for French ports.

The British seized American ships and cargoes, and forced American sailors to serve in Britain's royal navy. Jay's Treaty prevented war between Britain and the United States.

Some British officers seized the ships they stopped. Others just demanded to go on board and look over the crew. Any crew members who had been born in England were then **impressed** into—forced to serve in—the British navy. Even worse, the British often impressed American-born sailors. The United States government grew outraged at this lack of respect for American citizens and property.

**Britain maintains forts on the American border.** Americans also felt angry about the presence of British forts on the northwest border of the United States. The British had agreed to give up these posts in the Treaty of Paris. Ten years had now passed, and they had not kept their word.

The British were able to hold the forts because they had the support of nearby Indians. They gave the Indians arms and other gifts. The British secretly tried to create an Indian barrier to the United States' westward growth. They hoped that one day the Northwest Territory would again belong to Great Britain.

**The Indians suffer a defeat.** When Washington became President, fighting had already broken out between American Indians and white settlers in the Northwest Territory. Washington sent two expeditions against the Indians, both of which failed. Finally he ordered General Anthony Wayne, a hero of the Revolutionary War, into action. With well-trained troops and Indian guides, Wayne marched into northwest Ohio. On August 20, 1794, Wayne scored a victory. He and his soldiers defeated about 2,000 Shawnee, Ottawa, and Chippewa on a log-covered field. The **Battle of Fallen Timbers** crushed the Indians' hopes of keeping their land. They signed the Treaty of Greenville, agreeing to surrender their homelands and move westward.

## Settling Differences with Foreign Powers

Without the Indians, the British could not hope to recover the lands of the Northwest. They asked the United States to negotiate a treaty. The United States quickly agreed to talk. President Washington did not want the young nation involved in a war.

**John Jay makes a treaty to keep peace.** In 1794 Washington sent Chief Justice John Jay to Great Britain. There Jay worked out the agreement known as **Jay's Treaty.** In the treaty, the British promised to give up the forts along the northwest border.

Most Americans complained that Jay had been too easy on the British. He had not made them promise to stop seizing American ships and impressing American sailors. For the most part, Jay's Treaty simply restated what Britain had agreed to earlier in the Treaty of Paris. Some angry Americans made effigies —rough models—of Jay, which they burned publicly. Nevertheless, President Washington felt that Jay's Treaty would prevent war with Great Britain. He

helped persuade the Senate to ratify the document in 1795.

**Pinckney's Treaty settles differences with Spain.** The Spanish grew worried when they heard about Jay's Treaty. They feared that if the United States and Britain were on good terms, the two countries might jointly try to take over Spain's American colonies. The Spanish decided that they needed a treaty with the United States, too.

President Washington sent Thomas Pinckney to work out a treaty with Spain in 1795. **Pinckney's Treaty** gave Americans the right to travel on the Mississippi and to store goods at New Orleans. It also set the boundary line between Georgia and Spanish Florida. The treaty was more favorable to the United States than to Spain. The Spanish had accepted American demands because of their eagerness to reach agreement.

Native American attacks on white settlements, encouraged by the British, led to the Battle of Fallen Timbers in 1794. After the battle the Shawnee leader Little Turtle surrendered to General Anthony Wayne.

**Washington retires.** When the presidential election of 1796 drew near, Washington made a farewell statement. In this **Farewell Address,** he announced that he would not seek a third term as President. His decision set a precedent —an example that becomes standard practice—for those who followed him. Until the time of Franklin D. Roosevelt in the 1940's, no President served more than two terms. (Congress later made this custom a law by passing the Twenty-second Amendment to the Constitution.)

As the nation's first President, Washington set the nation on a sure course toward success. When he left office, he went back to his beloved Virginia plantation, Mount Vernon. There he died in 1799 at the age of 67.

## SECTION REVIEW

1. **Vocabulary**    political party, democracy, neutral, impress, effigy, precedent
2. **People and Places**    Edmond Genêt, Anthony Wayne, Thomas Pinckney, Mississippi River, New Orleans, Spanish Florida
3. **Comprehension**    How did the first two political parties differ?
4. **Comprehension**    What foreign-policy issues faced the United States during Washington's second term?
5. **Critical Thinking**    Do you agree with President Washington that two terms are enough for a President? Explain.

# 4 How did conflict with France affect the nation?

## Vocabulary

nominate            sedition
alien               nullify

After Washington left office, the Republicans and the Federalists grew more bitterly divided. Both political parties supported United States policies when an undeclared war began with the French nation. They strongly disagreed, however, about the government's policies at home.

## An Unofficial War

In the 1796 election, the Republicans and the Federalists were rivals for power. John Adams stood as the Federalist candidate for President. The Republicans nominated — chose as a candidate—Thomas Jefferson. When the electors' votes were counted, Adams won 71 votes to Jefferson's 68. Adams thus became the second President, and Jefferson became Vice President. The two parties would have to try to work together in the executive branch.

**Trouble brews with France.** France had been angered by Jay's Treaty with Great Britain. The French were still fighting the British in Europe, and France resented American friendliness to Britain. As a result, the French took hostile action against American ships at sea. The French navy captured American ships and prevented them from carrying goods to the enemies of France. In a short time the French seized more than 300 American vessels.

**The XYZ Affair stirs American patriotism.** President Adams wished to continue the policy of neutrality that Washington had set. Hoping to avoid war, Adams sent three diplomats to France to negotiate a treaty. At the beginning of the talks, the French demanded that the United States government furnish them a large loan. The three diplomats also insisted on a $250,000 gift to French officials.

The Americans proudly refused to pay what they considered a bribe. Highly insulted, they sent a full report to President Adams. When Adams told Congress about this affair, he did not use the real names of the French representatives. Instead he called them X, Y, and Z. Hence this event is known as the **XYZ Affair.**

**The United States fights an undeclared war with France.** American citizens reacted with outrage to the XYZ Affair. Many people repeated the slogan, "Millions for defense, not one cent for tribute!" In other words, they would rather fund and fight a war than pay a bribe. In 1798 Congress canceled the alliance it had made with France 20 years earlier. The situation grew so tense that fighting broke out at sea.

At the time, the American navy included only 22 ships. Yet these vessels attacked and captured French ships whenever they could. The United States government also began to recruit an army. In less than three years, the French lost 84 ships. Despite the fighting, however, the United States and France were not officially at war. Neither Congress nor the French government ever declared that a state of war existed.

As relations worsened between the United States and France, Americans began to build a navy. This 1800 etching by William Birch shows shipbuilders working on the hull of a navy warship, the *Philadelphia.*

# Our Presidents

## JOHN ADAMS

★ **1797–1801** ★

**2ND PRESIDENT**

**FEDERALIST**

★ Born October 30, 1735, in Massachusetts

★ Married Abigail Smith in 1764; 5 children

★ Lawyer; delegate to First and Second Continental Congresses; Vice President under Washington

★ Lived in Massachusetts when elected President

★ Vice President: Thomas Jefferson

★ Died July 4, 1826, in Massachusetts

★ Key events while in office: French Revolution; XYZ Affair; Alien and Sedition Acts; Washington, D.C., became the nation's capital

**France and the United States reach an agreement.** In 1800 Adams again sent representatives to France to discuss peace. By this time a new French leader, Napoleon Bonaparte, had come to power. Napoleon had no wish to continue fighting with the United States. The two countries signed an agreement to stop all naval attacks. This agreement, the Convention of 1800, cleared the way for American and French ships to sail the ocean in peace.

President Adams saved the country from more bloodshed, but he paid a price for his actions. Many members of his own party favored outright war with France. They accused Adams of weakness. The President, however, believed that he had served his country well. He later said that he wished to be remembered as "John Adams, who took upon himself the responsibility of peace with France."

## Trouble at Home

While the American-French conflict was still at its height, Americans were also struggling bitterly against one another in the United States. This was not a military struggle but a heated contest for power between the two political parties.

**Congress limits personal freedoms.** In 1798 Congress passed a set of laws known as the **Alien and Sedition Acts.** The Federalists, who outnumbered the Republicans, proposed these laws. They said that supporters of the French posed a threat to the United States. Therefore, the federal government had to unify the country and protect it from **aliens** —foreigners. Actually, the Federalists feared losing their majority in Congress. They used the Alien and Sedition Acts to silence their Republican rivals.

The first act increased the length of time newcomers had to live in the United States to gain citizenship. An earlier law required 5 years of residence. Now Congress set 14 years as the waiting period. Many Republicans had only recently settled in America from Europe. If they could not become citizens, then they could not vote. Thus Republican candidates would get fewer votes in the next election.

Two other acts gave the President power to arrest dangerous aliens or order them out of the country. Finally, the Sedition Act outlaws **sedition** —saying anything false or critical about the government. Federalists used this law to keep their opponents from speaking out. They arrested 25 Republican newspaper editors and sent 10 to jail. In this way, the law restricted freedom of speech and freedom of the press.

**Jefferson leads opposition to the Alien and Sedition Acts.** Republicans saw the Alien and Sedition Acts as a clear threat to American freedom. Thomas Jefferson and other party leaders had protested the acts in speeches to Congress. One Republican suggested that the Federalists aimed to frighten ... all presses which they consider as contrary to their views; to prevent a free [exchange] of opinion; ... and, through those means, to [keep] themselves in power.

In 1798 Jefferson and Madison wrote resolutions challenging the federal government's power. Passed by the legislatures of Kentucky and Virginia, they are known as the **Kentucky and Virginia Resolutions.** They said states do not have to accept unconstitutional laws passed by Congress. The Kentucky Resolution further declared that states can **nullify** —cancel—such laws.

Neither Kentucky nor Virginia actually nullified the Alien and Sedition Acts. Within a few years, Congress changed the laws or let them expire. Thus the question of the states' right to disobey federal laws was left unresolved. Jefferson, meanwhile, gained new supporters. His bold stand to defend the Constitution made him popular with many voters. Jefferson was now in a strong position to run for President in 1800.

## SECTION REVIEW

1. **Vocabulary**    nominate, alien, sedition, nullify
2. **People and Places**    John Adams, Thomas Jefferson, Napoleon Bonaparte
3. **Comprehension**    What caused trouble between the United States and France during John Adams's presidency?
4. **Comprehension**    What did the Alien and Sedition Acts do?
5. **Critical Thinking**    Why might Adams have chosen not to declare war on France?

# Chapter 10 Summary

The Constitution divided power among three branches of the federal government, each having checks and balances on the others. The Bill of Rights, added in 1791, protects people's individual liberties. Other amendments, customs, and court interpretations of the Constitution have expanded the framework of American government.

George Washington became President in 1789, with John Adams as his Vice President. Washington's talented Cabinet included Thomas Jefferson as Secretary of State and Alexander Hamilton as Secretary of the Treasury. Hamilton arranged to pay federal and state debts and to start the Bank of the United States. Although farmers in Pennsylvania rebelled against one of his policies, the whiskey tax, Hamilton improved the country's finances.

Hamilton and Jefferson disagreed often and formed rival political parties. The Federalists, led by Hamilton, favored business interests and a powerful federal government.

Jefferson's Democratic-Republican party argued for the interests of ordinary citizens and the states. The two parties also quarreled about helping France in its war with Great Britain. In 1793 Washington issued his Neutrality Proclamation, declaring that the United States would remain neutral. Jay's Treaty prevented war with Great Britain in 1794, and Pinckney's Treaty in 1795 settled differences with Spain.

John Adams was elected President in 1796, with Thomas Jefferson as his Vice President. In 1798 Adams tried to make a treaty with France for the safety of American ships. After the French demanded a bribe, the conflict between the United States and France became an undeclared war. At the same time, Federalists in Congress passed the Alien and Sedition Acts. These anti-Republican laws took away some of the freedoms guaranteed by the Constitution. The Republicans responded by writing the Virginia and Kentucky Resolutions.

# Chapter 10 REVIEW

## Vocabulary and Key Terms

Use the following terms to complete the sentences below. Write your answers on a separate sheet of paper.

**Alien and Sedition Acts**
**Bank of the United States**
**bill**
**Bill of Rights**
**bonds**
**Cabinet**
**checks and balances**
**impress**
**neutral**
**political parties**
**tariffs**
**unconstitutional**
**veto**

1. The President's power to _____ a _____ passed by Congress is part of the system of _____.
2. Hamilton collected _____ on imports, started the _____, and made sure the country repaid its _____ and other debts.
3. Two members of Washington's _____ formed rival _____.
4. The United States found it hard to stay _____ when Britain began to _____ American sailors.
5. Jefferson argued that the _____ violated the _____ and thus were _____.

## Recalling the Facts

1. How does the Constitution divide power between the federal government and the states?
2. What is one way each branch of government can check the others?
3. What is the Bill of Rights?
4. What was the Whiskey Rebellion?
5. How did the United States respond to the war between France and Great Britain in the early 1790's?

6. What problems did Jay's Treaty address? Pinckney's Treaty?
7. What was the XYZ Affair?
8. Why did Federalists pass the Alien and Sedition Acts?

## Places to Locate

Match the letters on the map with the places listed below. Write your answers on a separate sheet of paper.

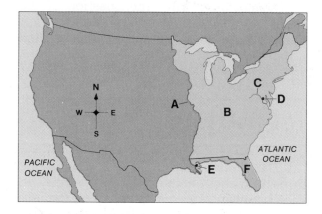

1. United States in 1795
2. Potomac River
3. District of Columbia
4. Mississippi River
5. New Orleans
6. Spanish Florida

## Critical Thinking

1. Analyze the Bill of Rights on pages 224–226. Consider the following questions in your analysis:
   a. What amendments are most meaningful now? Explain.
   b. Which amendments most closely reflect the times in which they were written? Explain.
   c. Are there other freedoms and rights that you would add to the Bill of Rights? Explain.

2. Was it possible for the United States to be truly neutral in the struggle between Great Britain and France? Consider the following points in your answer:
   a. British and French respect for the American decision
   b. Americans' feelings toward Britain and France
   c. American actions toward Britain and France
3. In his Farewell Address, President Washington offered Americans some advice for the future. Listed below are some of his ideas. Which suggestions do you agree with and which do you disagree with? Why? How successful has the United States been in following Washington's advice?
   a. Cherish and guard freedom.
   b. Avoid forming political parties.
   c. Try not to build up a national debt.
   d. Avoid permanent alliances with foreign countries.

## Understanding History

1. Reread the section "Hamilton strikes a bargain" on page 244. Then answer these questions.
   a. **Geography.** Considering the size and shape of the early United States, why was the location of Washington, D.C., advantageous?
   b. **Geography.** Is geographical location important for a capital today? Why or why not?
2. Reread the section "Hamilton proposes a banking system" on page 245. Then answer these questions.
   a. **Economics.** How would the national bank spur business growth in the United States?
   b. **Citizenship.** How did Hamilton justify creating a bank?
3. Reread the section "Political parties develop" on page 248. Then answer these questions.
   a. **Citizenship.** How did political parties form?
   b. **Citizenship.** What are the benefits of a two-party system?

## Projects and Activities

1. **Making a Chart.** Design a flow chart showing how a bill becomes a law.
2. **Expressing Points of View.** Imagine that you and your classmates are members of Congress in the 1790's. President Adams has just told you about the XYZ Affair. Discuss how you should respond.
3. **Outlining Information.** Review Sections 2, 3, and 4 of Chapter 10. Create an outline summarizing the key events while Washington and Adams were President.

## Practicing Your Skill

The table below shows the value of American trade over a 70-year period. The "Imports" column tells how many millions of dollars Americans spent on goods from abroad. The "Exports" column shows income from the sale of goods to foreign countries. Study the table and answer the following questions.

### Value of United States Trade
1790–1860

| Year | Imports (in millions) | Exports (in millions) |
|------|------------------------|------------------------|
| 1790 | $ 23 | $ 20 |
| 1810 | 91 | 71 |
| 1820 | 74 | 70 |
| 1830 | 71 | 74 |
| 1840 | 107 | 132 |
| 1850 | 178 | 152 |
| 1860 | 362 | 400 |

1. What was the value of American exports in 1790? in 1820?
2. What was the value of American imports in 1790? in 1840?
3. Which had greater value in most years—imports or exports? Which years are the exceptions?
4. Did trade generally increase, decrease, or remain steady over the years? Why?

# CHAPTER 11 The United States Grows Stronger 1800–1815

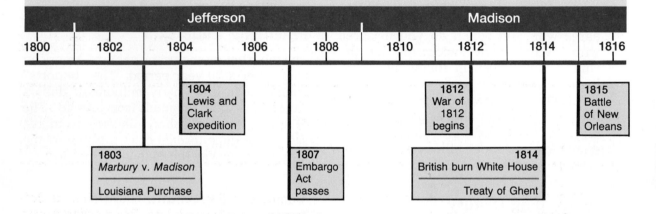

| Jefferson | | | | | Madison | | | |
|---|---|---|---|---|---|---|---|---|
| 1800 | 1802 | 1804 | 1806 | 1808 | 1810 | 1812 | 1814 | 1816 |

1804
Lewis and Clark expedition

1803
*Marbury* v. *Madison*

Louisiana Purchase

1807
Embargo Act passes

1812
War of 1812 begins

1814
British burn White House

Treaty of Ghent

1815
Battle of New Orleans

The American warship *Constitution* defeats a British vessel during the War of 1812. This 1832 painting is by Thomas Chambers.

## Preparing to Read

The turn of the century brought changes to the United States and to its government. Thomas Jefferson's election in 1800 marked a shift in power from the Federalists to the Democratic-Republicans. An age of greater democracy began, and the United States grew stronger and larger. The next President, James Madison, tried to build on the foundation Jefferson laid. Madison, however, could not escape the growing troubles with Britain and France, nor the steadily rising tensions with Native Americans. As you read this chapter, try to answer the following questions:

1. What trends emerged during the presidency of Thomas Jefferson?
2. How did lands west of the Mississippi become part of the United States?
3. What drew the United States into another war with Britain?

# 1 What trends emerged during the presidency of Thomas Jefferson?

## Vocabulary

ballot

administration

writ of mandamus

judicial review

Thomas Jefferson liked to think of his election to the presidency as the "Revolution of 1800." He set a new style of governing, cut taxes, and lowered federal spending. Yet to the relief of the Federalists, Jefferson continued many policies set by Washington and Adams.

## A Smooth Transfer of Power

The man sworn in as President on March 4, 1801, stands out as one of America's greatest leaders. Thomas Jefferson had a searching mind and many interests. He read widely in art, science, religion, and government. He also showed skill as an inventor, an architect, a musician, and a writer. Jefferson, however, chose a career in politics.

**Jefferson wins a hard-fought election.** In the election of 1800 the Federalists again nominated John Adams for President. The Democratic-Republicans chose Thomas Jefferson as their candidate. They asked Aaron Burr, a Revolutionary War hero from New York, to run for Vice President.

When the electors' votes were counted, the result was an unexpected tie. Adams won only 65 votes to Jefferson's 73, but Burr also received 73 votes. Of course the Republicans had wanted Jefferson to be President and Burr to be Vice President. Under the Constitution, however, the House of Representatives had to break the tie.

In the House voting, Republicans backed Jefferson. Federalists, fearing that Jefferson might reverse all Federalist policies, threw their support to Burr. For 35 votes, the election remained a tie. At last, on the thirty-sixth vote, some Federalists changed their minds. Jefferson was elected President, and Burr became Vice President.

Because of the 1800 election, Congress passed the Twelfth Amendment in 1804. The amendment called for separate **ballots** — sheets of paper used to mark votes—for the President and Vice President. In the future, there would be no disputes about which offices candidates were to fill.

# Our Presidents

## THOMAS JEFFERSON

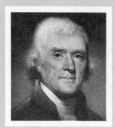

★ **1801–1809** ★

### 3RD PRESIDENT
DEMOCRATIC-
REPUBLICAN

★ Born April 13, 1743, in Virginia

★ Married Martha Skelton in 1772; 6 children

★ Lawyer; author of the Declaration of Independence; governor of Virginia; Secretary of State; Vice President under Adams

★ Lived in Virginia when elected President

★ Vice Presidents: Aaron Burr; George Clinton

★ Died July 4, 1826, in Virginia

★ Key events while in office: Ohio became a state; Louisiana Purchase; *Marbury* v. *Madison;* Lewis and Clark expedition; Embargo Act

**Jefferson brings a new style to the White House.** Born in 1743 to a wealthy Virginia family, Jefferson had every advantage as a child. He received a fine education and later mingled with royalty in Paris. Still, Jefferson had simple tastes. When he became President, he avoided ceremony and show. Instead of riding in a fancy carriage to his inauguration, he walked. He entertained at the White House with friendly dinners instead of grand parties. He signed his invitations "Mr. Jefferson" rather than "The President of the United States."

Despite his casual style, Jefferson took his job seriously. He came to office with a great deal of experience in government. Jefferson had been a member of the Virginia House of Burgesses and the Second Continental Congress. He had served as governor of Virginia, ambassador to France, Secretary of State under Washington, and Vice President under Adams. Jefferson, however, felt proudest of having written the Declaration of Independence.

## A Small but Strong Government

Jefferson had clear views on the federal government. He wanted to limit its power as much as possible. He preferred to give ordinary citizens most of the power to govern themselves.

**Jefferson limits the government's role.** The third President of the United States disagreed with Federalist ideas about a strong, active government. In Jefferson's mind, the federal government existed mainly to keep peace. At his inauguration, he said Americans needed a wise government "which shall [keep] men from injuring one another, which shall leave them otherwise free to regulate their own pursuits...."

Jefferson did his best to limit government involvement in people's lives. He encouraged Congress to end the Alien and Sedition Acts. He repealed the taxes on whiskey and other American-made goods. He favored free trade and no special rules or privileges for anyone. Jefferson did, however, try to encourage farming. He felt that America's future depended on building strength as a nation of small farmers.

**Jefferson lowers government spending.** Under Washington and Adams, the federal government had grown steadily. The costs of running the government had risen, too. President Jefferson, in his first message to Congress, said, "We may well [ask] whether our organization is not too complicated, too expensive; whether offices and officers have not been multiplied unnecessarily."

Jefferson dissolved a number of positions within the executive branch. He also cut out waste in the military. With Congress's approval, he reduced the size of the navy and stopped the building of new ships. He trimmed the army as well, from 4,000 to 2,500 soldiers.

Meanwhile, Jefferson worked to lower the federal debt. He and Albert Gallatin, Secretary of the Treasury, thought the national debt should be repaid without delay. Under Washington and Adams, Congress had given the different departments large sums of money to spend as they chose. Jefferson opposed this practice and recommended a change. Although Congress moved slowly, Gallatin managed to reduce the national debt from $83 million to $57 million by 1809.

**Jefferson takes a tough stand against piracy.** To Jefferson, a small government did not mean a weak government. Early in his **administration** —term in office—he proved that the United States would fight for its rights. At the time, the United States enjoyed a healthy trade with Europe. Shipping goods on the Mediterranean Sea, however, involved risks. Pirates from the Barbary Coast—the North African states of Morocco, Algeria, Tunis, and Tripoli—seized many merchant ships.

For years, American and European governments paid the Barbary pirates to leave their ships alone. The pirates often attacked anyway. In 1801 the ruler of Tripoli demanded more "protection money" from the United States. President Jefferson reacted with a show of force. He sent a fleet of warships to protect American merchant vessels.

In 1801 President Jefferson sent warships to fight the Barbary pirates along the North African coast. In a battle at Tripoli, Americans set fire to a captured ship, the *Philadelphia,* thus robbing the pirates of their booty.

261

For the next four years, America's small navy clashed with enemy ships in the Mediterranean. Early in 1804, Stephen Decatur led a bold raid against an American ship, the *Philadelphia*, that Barbary pirates had captured. Decatur's crew burned the ship, thus keeping the pirates from using it. The following year the ruler of Tripoli signed a treaty promising not to interfere with American ships. The other Barbary Coast states later did the same.

## A Stronger Judicial Branch

Jefferson was able to push many of his ideas through Congress because Republicans controlled the House and the Senate.

**The decisions of Chief Justice John Marshall strengthened the national government and enlarged the role of the Supreme Court. His decision in *Marbury* v. *Madison* firmly established the Supreme Court's power to interpret and uphold the Constitution.**

Federalists, however, held power in the judicial branch. John Adams, the country's second President, had made sure of this. Just before he left office, he named a number of Federalist judges to key government posts. He also chose a loyal Federalist, John Marshall, to be Chief Justice of the United States.

**Marshall's ideas conflict with Jefferson's.** Chief Justice Marshall had served as a member of Congress and as Secretary of State under Adams. Though they were distant cousins, Marshall and Jefferson disliked each other heartily. Marshall wished to expand the federal government's power, while the President wished to limit it. Jefferson often felt frustrated by the Federalists' control of the courts. Unfortunately, there was little he could do. As he once remarked about judges, "... few die and none resign." John Marshall remained Chief Justice for 34 years. During that time, he did much to shape the form of American government.

**The Supreme Court gains great power.** One of the Supreme Court's most important decisions came early in 1803, in a case called ***Marbury* v. *Madison.****\* William Marbury, a justice of the peace in the District of Columbia, was a "midnight judge." He was one of the officials President Adams appointed in the last hours of his administration.

Adams left office before Marbury's judgeship became official. When Jefferson took over, he wanted to stop Marbury from taking office. He ordered James Madison, the new Secretary of State, to withhold the papers that would make Marbury's appointment official. Marbury asked the Supreme Court to force Madison to issue the papers. Marbury based his request on a law passed by Congress. The law gave the Court the power to issue **writs of mandamus** (man-DAY-muhs). A writ of mandamus is a legal paper ordering a government worker to carry out his or her duties.

In its decision, the Supreme Court said it could not give Madison a writ of mandamus. Marshall, who wrote the Court's decision,

---

\* Court cases are identified by naming the parties involved. The *v.* stands for *versus*, meaning "against."

explained that the law Congress had passed went against the Constitution. He said that Congress had no power to pass such a law.

Marshall's decision was the first time the Supreme Court used **judicial review** —its power to review laws and declare them unconstitutional. Fifty-four years passed before the Court judged another law to be invalid. Still, Marshall had taken a key step toward balancing power in the government. His ruling in *Marbury* v. *Madison* gave the Supreme Court a strong voice in lawmaking. Since that 1803 decision, the Court has used its power of judicial review to strike down more than 100 congressional acts.

## SECTION REVIEW

1. **Vocabulary**  ballot, administration, writ of mandamus, judicial review
2. **People and Places**  Thomas Jefferson, Aaron Burr, Barbary Coast, John Marshall, William Marbury, James Madison
3. **Comprehension**  How did President Jefferson reduce the role of the government?
4. **Comprehension**  Why was *Marbury* v. *Madison* an important case?
5. **Critical Thinking**  Do you think Jefferson was right in calling his election a revolution? Explain.

# 2  How did lands west of the Mississippi become part of the United States?

## Vocabulary
flatboat
continental divide

President Jefferson encouraged farmers to go west in order to strengthen the United States' position in the frontier regions. He also made important decisions that doubled the size of the United States. In addition, he sent explorers to find out about this area.

## Westward Expansion

Years before President Jefferson took office, Americans had begun pushing west. Many pioneers spread into the Northwest Territory. Others moved into the region south of the Ohio River, between the Appalachians and the Mississippi River. This land was later organized into the Mississippi Territory. (See map on page 268.)

**Americans push beyond the Appalachian Mountains.** In 1769 a group of pioneer families from North Carolina crossed over the Appalachian Mountains to present-day Tennessee. They settled on the Watauga River, which flows into the Tennessee River. Other settlements grew up along nearby rivers. In 1779 pioneers started the town of Nashville on the Cumberland River.

The settlement of present-day Kentucky was spurred by Daniel Boone, an expert hunter and frontier scout. In 1775 Boone began opening an old Indian trail into central Kentucky. This **Wilderness Road,** as it was called, went through the Cumberland Gap, a narrow pass in the Cumberland Mountains, and then wound along the Kentucky River. At a site on the river, Boone and his followers built a village named Boonesborough.

In the late 1700's more and more pioneers followed the Wilderness Road west. In 1792 Kentucky became the fifteenth state in the Union. Tennessee gained statehood in 1796.

**Ohio settlements grow steadily.** In April 1788 a group of 47 settlers floated down the Ohio River to the place where the Muskingum River joins the Ohio. There they started the town of Marietta. Marietta soon became the capital of the Northwest Territory. The town grew rapidly, and within two

**Trailblazer Daniel Boone travels the Cumberland Trail to Kentucky in this nineteenth-century painting by William Ranney. By 1800 thousands of pioneers had pushed west across the Appalachian Mountains.**

years the town had churches, schools, and a population of about 1,000. Soon after Marietta was founded, other settlers established Cincinnati farther down the Ohio River. By 1790 the town boasted about 900 inhabitants. Settlers continued to pour into the region. In 1803 Ohio became the seventeenth state to join the Union.

## Buying Louisiana

By 1800 nearly one fifth of all Americans lived between the Appalachian Mountains and the Mississippi River. Most of these people earned a living by trapping or farming. To sell their furs and crops, they sent them down the Ohio and Mississippi rivers on rafts or **flatboats** —flat-bottomed boats with square ends. At the port of New Orleans, the goods were loaded onto ocean-going ships and taken to far-off buyers.

**France gains control of New Orleans.** Pinckney's Treaty in 1795 had given the United States and Spain equal rights to the Mississippi River. (See Chapter 10.) New Orleans, however, belonged to Spain. Spain also owned all of Louisiana, the vast region between the Mississippi and the Rocky Mountains.

In 1800 Spain signed a secret treaty that gave New Orleans and Louisiana to France. When Jefferson learned of the treaty, the news distressed him. France was then governed by Napoleon Bonaparte, a powerful military leader who wished to conquer all of Europe. Napoleon also planned to build a French empire in America. Jefferson saw the danger at once. If the French took control of New Orleans, they might close this valuable port to Americans. As Jefferson wrote to Robert Livingston, the American ambassador in France:

> The [transfer] of Louisiana ... by Spain to France works most sorely on the United States.... There is on the globe one single spot, the possessor of which is our natural and habitual enemy. [The spot] is New Orleans, through which the produce of three eighths of our territory must pass to market, and [this western territory] will [soon] yield more than half of our whole produce and contain more than half of our inhabitants.

Jefferson added that to keep the French out of New Orleans, Americans might have to join forces with the British. He did not want to depend on Britain, however. Nor did he want to fight Napoleon. Jefferson decided to try negotiation first.

**Jefferson tries to purchase New Orleans.** In March 1803 the President sent James Monroe to join Robert Livingston in France. He instructed them to offer to buy New Orleans for $7.5 million. If France refused, they would ask for permanent permission to pass through New Orleans. If all else failed, Monroe and Livingston were to begin secret talks with Great Britain.

The Americans made their offer at just the right time. Napoleon's dreams of an American empire had been spoiled by trouble in Haiti, a French island in the Caribbean Sea. Black slaves there, led by Toussaint L'Ouverture (too-SAN loo-vayr-TYOOR), revolted against the French. Nearly 35,000 French soldiers sent to put down the revolution were killed. Many died in the fighting. Others fell victim to yellow fever, a tropical disease carried by mosquitoes.

In Europe, Napoleon was on the brink of war with Britain. He needed money to fight, and he wanted no more problems in America. He decided to sell Louisiana. In April Napoleon sent an aide, Talleyrand, to meet with Livingston and Monroe. "What will you give," asked Talleyrand, "for the *whole* of Louisiana?" Though they were startled, the Americans recognized a good opportunity. They agreed to a price of $15 million.

**The United States gains Louisiana.** Jefferson worried that the purchase of Louisiana might be unconstitutional. The Constitution, after all, said nothing about the government's power to buy new land. To be safe, Jefferson wanted to amend the Constitution. Livingston, however, warned that any delay might cause Napoleon to change his mind. The President and Congress decided to overlook the legal question. A treaty with France made the **Louisiana Territory** part of the United States on December 20, 1803.

Toussaint L'Ouverture led a successful slave revolt against French rule in Haiti. He declared the slaves free and established Haiti as an independent republic.

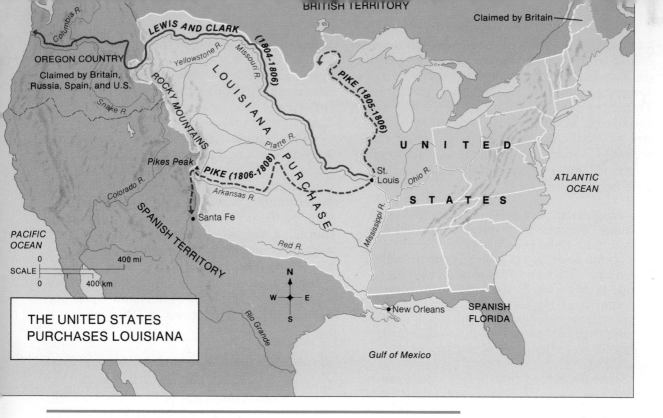

THE UNITED STATES PURCHASES LOUISIANA

## Map Study

The purchase of the Louisiana Territory set the stage for the exploration and settlement of vast new lands. What natural features bounded the Louisiana Territory on the east and west? What body of water did explorers Lewis and Clark reach? What natural feature is named for the explorer Zebulon Pike?

## Paving the Way for Settlement

The **Louisiana Purchase** doubled the size of the country. Along with New Orleans, the United States gained about 828,000 square miles (2.1 million square kilometers) of land. (See map on this page). Forests rich in game stretched across the northern part of the Louisiana Territory. Farther south and west lay great rolling prairies where shaggy buffaloes roamed. Americans were eager to settle this land. In doing so, however, they forced many Native Americans from their homes.

**Trailblazers explore the Louisiana Territory.** Even before the Louisiana Purchase was final, Jefferson sent a small expedition to explore the Louisiana Territory. The leaders were Captain Meriwether Lewis and

Lieutenant William Clark. Their main goal was to find an all-water route across the continent. Jefferson also asked Lewis and Clark to gather scientific information about the region and to befriend the Indians they met. Lastly, they were to explore Oregon, a vast area on the Pacific coast claimed by several countries.

The expedition started from St. Louis, Missouri, in May 1804. In three small boats the party followed the Missouri River north into present-day Montana. They passed through Sioux territory without incident and spent the winter among the Mandan Indians in North Dakota. There they met Sacajawea (sak-uh-juh-WEE-uh), a Shoshone woman married to a French-Canadian trader. When Lewis and Clark continued their journey in

## GEOGRAPHY • The Louisiana Territory

On May 4, 1804, about 40 men and a dog climbed into 3 small boats loaded with supplies. Leaving from St. Louis, they headed northwest on the Missouri River. These hardy adventurers were on an important mission for the United States. President Jefferson had asked the group's leaders, Meriwether Lewis and William Clark, to find the most direct water route between the Missouri River and the Pacific Ocean. In addition, the explorers were to learn as much as possible about the Louisiana Territory and its Indian inhabitants.

Lewis and Clark faced an enormous—and dangerous—task. The men traveled across unknown country filled with raging rivers and towering mountains. They lost equipment along the way. Grizzly bears ate their food and thieves stole their horses. Through the difficult journey, Lewis and Clark kept a journal describing everything they saw. They collected samples of plants, rocks, and wildlife, observed the stars, and noted the customs of the Indians. When they returned in 1806, they brought back a wealth of useful information.

**A page from the journal**

the spring of 1805, Sacajawea went along as their guide and interpreter.

Sacajawea led the explorers to her tribe in the Rocky Mountains. Her brother, the chief, gave Lewis and Clark fresh horses and supplies. As Sacajawea led them across the high mountains, the explorers realized they had crossed the **continental divide**. A continental divide is a long stretch of high land where the river systems on either side flow in opposite directions.

From the Rockies, the expedition continued west to the Snake and Columbia rivers. Finally, traveling in canoes borrowed from Nez Perce Indians, the group reached the Pacific Ocean. In 1806 Lewis and Clark returned to St. Louis. They had covered 8,000 miles (12,800 kilometers), and all but one member of their party survived.

Although Lewis and Clark found no waterway through the Rockies, the expedition succeeded in its other aims. The explorers began friendly relations with the Indians and learned much about the land. They also strengthened the United States' claim to Oregon. Jefferson was so pleased with the expedition that he appointed Meriwether Lewis as governor of the Louisiana Territory.

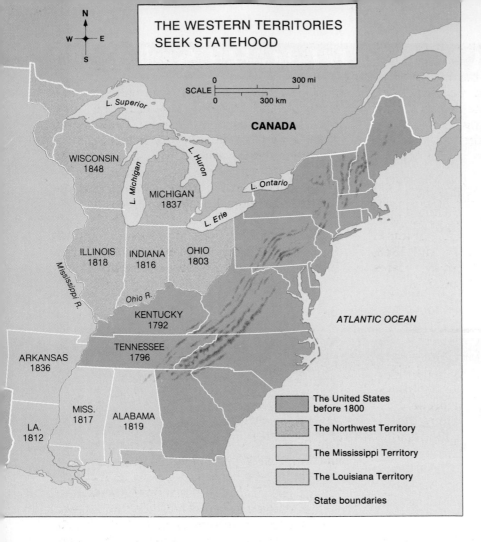

## THE WESTERN TERRITORIES SEEK STATEHOOD

N W E S

SCALE

0        300 mi

0        300 km

CANADA

L. Superior

L. Michigan

L. Huron

L. Ontario

L. Erie

WISCONSIN
1848

MICHIGAN
1837

ILLINOIS
1818

INDIANA
1816

OHIO
1803

Mississippi R.

Ohio R.

KENTUCKY
1792

ATLANTIC OCEAN

TENNESSEE
1796

ARKANSAS
1836

MISS.
1817

ALABAMA
1819

LA.
1812

The United States
before 1800

The Northwest Territory

The Mississippi Territory

The Louisiana Territory

State boundaries

**Map Study**

As people settled the western territories, more areas became eligible for statehood. Which state was the first to be formed from the Northwest Territory? By what year was the Mississippi Territory no longer a territory? Before statehood, Arkansas was part of which territory?

**Pike leads explorers north and west.** Meanwhile, in 1805, Zebulon Pike began an expedition north along the Mississippi River. Pike hoped to find the river's source. Although he did not succeed, he learned a great deal about the upper Mississippi Valley. The next year Pike set out west from St. Louis to explore the Louisiana Territory. He headed south of the Lewis and Clark route, following the Arkansas River for many weeks. Finally Pike came to the Rockies. There he discovered the mountain that now bears his name—Pikes Peak in present-day Colorado.

It was winter when Pike and his group reached the Rockies. Cold and tired, they turned south in search of the Red River. Instead they entered Spanish territory along the Rio Grande. Spaniards took Pike and his followers prisoner and brought them before the Spanish governor. When Pike was later released, he returned to Louisiana with valuable maps and much useful information. He published reports of his travels in 1810.

**Pioneers head west.** When Americans read about Lewis and Clark's expedition and about Pike's explorations, many decided to head west. They dreamed of making homes for themselves in a region of unspoiled beauty and plentiful resources. Some people floated down rivers in flatboats. Others crossed the country in covered wagons. Within a few years, pioneers could travel by steamboat down the Ohio River to the Mississippi. At several points along the Mississippi, ferries waited to take families from the east bank to the west. Thousands of eager settlers crossed into the new territory.

Before long, new towns began to appear west of the Mississippi River. Some of them, such as Des Moines, Iowa, and Leavenworth, Kansas, grew around forts that the first settlers built for protection. Other towns, such as Davenport, Iowa, began as fur-trading centers.

In a few years several new states bordered the western shores of the Mississippi. Louisiana entered the Union in 1812. Missouri became a state in 1821, and Arkansas followed 15 years later. In 1846 and 1858, Iowa and Minnesota joined the row of states along the west bank of the Mississippi.

## SECTION REVIEW

1. **Vocabulary**   flatboat, continental divide
2. **People and Places**   Daniel Boone, Wilderness Road, New Orleans, Napoleon Bonaparte, Louisiana Territory, Meriwether Lewis, William Clark, Sacajawea, Rocky Mountains, Zebulon Pike
3. **Comprehension**   How did the United States gain the Louisiana Territory?
4. **Comprehension**   How did Lewis and Clark pave the way for western settlers?
5. **Critical Thinking**   What advantages and disadvantages might Americans have expected with the purchase of Louisiana?

# 3 What drew the United States into another war with Britain?

## Vocabulary

embargo
blockade

Jefferson won great popularity during his first term in office. He eased Federalist fears that he would overturn the government. He doubled the size of the United States. For the most part, the country enjoyed peace and prosperity. Later, however, trouble developed with Native Americans, and, in 1812, a new war began with Britain.

## Growing Conflict

The United States owed much of its prosperity to its busy trade with Europe. In 1803, when war broke out between France and Britain, Jefferson said the United States would stay neutral. Americans would keep trading with both European powers.

France and Britain, however, had other ideas. Each side tried to prevent American ships from carrying supplies to the enemy.

The British Navy stopped American vessels and impressed American sailors. France also captured American ships when it could, though the French did not seize the crews.

**Jefferson tries to avoid war.** Jefferson, reelected for a second term in 1804, hated war. Yet he could not ignore the British and French attacks. Somehow he had to force European countries to respect the rights of American ships at sea. Jefferson decided to pressure Great Britain and France by using an **embargo** —a government order to stop foreign trade. The **Embargo Act,** passed in 1807, banned American ships from sailing to any foreign ports. It also closed American ports to ships from other countries.

Jefferson tried to enforce the Embargo Act without success. The law proved more crippling to the United States than to France or Britain. Americans went without the sugar, tea, and other goods they ordinarily imported. Farmers suffered from the loss of their foreign customers. Sailors and shipbuilders had little work. Many Eastern merchants simply ignored the embargo and sailed for Europe anyway. As a result,

France and Great Britain took the opportunity to seize more American ships.

In 1809 the American government gave in to pressure at home. Congress repealed the Embargo Act and replaced it with the **Non-Intercourse Act.** This act gave merchants the freedom to trade with any countries except Britain and France. Trade with these two nations would resume only when they agreed to respect American ships.

**Indian troubles stir anti-British feelings.** France and Britain were both guilty of interfering with American shipping. Yet Americans felt more anger toward Britain. They blamed the British for another problem—conflicts with Native Americans. Many frontier settlers believed that the British gave weapons to the Indians and encouraged them to make war on white pioneers. The Indians actually had good reasons of their own for fighting. They believed that the United States was robbing them of their lands by unfair treaties.

## LINKING PAST AND PRESENT

## ★ ★ ★ *Sanctions*

When American colonists boycotted British goods in the 1760's and 1770's, they were using an **economic sanction—** a penalty designed to cause policy changes. An embargo is another kind of economic sanction. By passing the Embargo Act in 1807, the United States hoped to persuade Britain and France to stop seizing American ships.

Governments today still use embargos as economic weapons. During the early 1970's Arab countries placed an oil embargo on the United States. The Arabs wanted to punish America for supporting Israel. Americans suffered keenly from the resulting oil and gasoline shortages.

The United States declared an embargo in early 1980. Angry about the Soviet invasion of Afghanistan, Congress forbade the sale of grain to the Soviet Union.

As pioneers moved west, they forced Native Americans off the land east of the Mississippi. Sometimes they tricked chiefs into signing treaties that gave away their tribes' lands forever. William Henry Harrison, governor of the Indiana Territory, persuaded the Indians of that region to give up about 48 million acres (19.4 million hectares) between 1795 and 1809.

**Indians resist the land takeovers.** Around 1808 the sons of a Shawnee chief joined forces to save their land and people. One brother, Tecumseh (tih-KUHM-suh), was a respected warrior. The other brother, known as the Prophet, was a religious leader and healer. From their headquarters at Tippecanoe Creek in present-day Indiana, the two men tried to unite all the tribes east of the Mississippi.

Governor Harrison took swift action against the Indians. He met with a few tribes and persuaded them to sign a treaty selling land in the heart of the Indiana Territory. These Indians parted with about 3 million acres (1.2 million hectares) for less than one-half cent per acre. Tecumseh declared the treaty meaningless. In a speech he said,

The white people have no right to take the land from the Indians, because the Indians had it first. It is theirs. The Indians may sell, but they must join together. Any sale not made by all is not valid.

Tecumseh then set off to rally more Native Americans to his cause. In his absence, the Prophet led an attack on Harrison's camp. After two hours of fighting, Harrison defeated the Indians and destroyed their village. This **Battle of Tippecanoe,** on November 7, 1811, put an end to Indian unity. Still, scattered Native Americans continued to raid white settlements.

**Some Americans favor war with Britain.** Settlers in the West and South held the British responsible for the Indian attacks. Many frontier farmers also wanted the United States to expand its territory. Hungry for land, they looked north to Canada, which belonged to Great Britain, and south to Florida, which belonged to Spain. At that time, Spain and Great Britain were allies. Some

Americans hoped that if war with Britain broke out, the United States could conquer Canada and Florida.

Several young Republicans in Congress showed keen interest in developing the West. They wanted to stop the British from supporting Native Americans and keeping outposts in the Northwest Territory. These leaders included Henry Clay of Kentucky and John C. Calhoun of South Carolina. The lawmakers talked so much about going to war that they earned the nickname "War Hawks."

## The War of 1812

Pushed on by the War Hawks, Congress declared war against Britain on June 19, 1812. By this time the United States had a new President, James Madison. Madison had already gained Napoleon's promise that France would stop bothering American ships. Britain, too, was taking steps toward peace. Unfortunately, Britain's new policy came too late to avoid war.

**The United States faces disadvantages.** The United States was not prepared for a war. Fewer than 7,000 soldiers made up the army, and most of the officers had little wartime experience. Even with troops from the state militias, the American soldiers were greatly outnumbered by the British. The American navy, too, could not compare with Britain's. The United States had only 16 ships when the war began, and Congress voted no funds to build more.

The United States was also weakened by divided public opinion. Many New Englanders opposed what they called "Mr. Madison's War." The merchants of this region had disliked Jefferson's embargo because it interfered with their trade. They wanted to send their ships to sea in spite of the danger of British capture. Even if only a few ships reached foreign ports, the goods they carried sold at such high prices that the traders made large profits. When the **War of 1812** started, the British used their superior naval forces to **blockade** —close off—American ports. In this way, Britain cut off shipping along the Atlantic coast.

**Neither side triumphs on land.** Early in the war, the United States launched an invasion of Canada. The plan called for American soldiers to attack from three directions: from Detroit, Niagara Falls, and Lake Champlain. All three efforts failed in the end. However, American soldiers did set fire to the government buildings in York. This city, present-day Toronto, was the Canadian capital at the time.

The British, meanwhile, attacked the northern United States. In 1814 they raided the Atlantic coast and burned some towns. In August of that year, British ships sailed up Chesapeake Bay and sent soldiers to seize Washington, D.C. In revenge for the burning of York, the British set fire to the Capitol and the White House. President Madison and his wife, Dolley, fled just before the enemy arrived. Fortunately, Dolley Madison managed to carry some important government papers and a portrait of George Washington with her to safety.

After capturing Washington, D.C., British troops marched north toward Baltimore, Maryland. At nearby Fort McHenry they began their attack. The American forces defended the fort bravely. Francis Scott Key, an American prisoner aboard a British ship in the harbor, watched the battle. Bombs and cannonballs flew all night long. The next morning—September 14, 1814—the fighting ended. Key, seeing the American flag still flying, wrote the poem "The Star-Spangled Banner." Key's poem was later set to music, and the song became the American national anthem.

**The United States wins several naval battles.** At first Americans had more success at sea than on land. One early victory came in August 1812. An American ship, the *Constitution*, met the British *Guerrière* off the coast of Nova Scotia. The *Constitution* withstood enemy fire so well that it earned the nickname "Old Ironsides." In a matter of half an hour the Americans, led by Captain Isaac Hull, destroyed the *Guerrière*.

The following year Captain Oliver H. Perry scored another naval success. Perry built a fleet of small ships on Lake Erie during the winter of 1812 to 1813. British Commodore R. H. Barclay stopped the fleet temporarily with a blockade, but in late summer Perry's ships broke free. They met Barclay's ships on the western end of the lake. After a fierce three-hour fight, Perry reported his victory with the message: "We have met the enemy and they are ours."

★ ★ ★     PRIMARY SOURCE

# THE STAR-SPANGLED BANNER  1814

A young American lawyer, Francis Scott Key, wrote the words to "The Star-Spangled Banner" as he was being held prisoner aboard a British ship during the attack on Fort McHenry. After Key's release, the stirring poem was set to music. The song soon became a source of inspiration to all Americans. In 1931 Congress made "The Star-Spangled Banner" the national anthem of the United States.

## Read to Find Out
1. What questions does the poem ask?
2. What do you think the sight of the flag after the night's battle meant to Key?

O say! can you see, by the dawn's early light,
What so proudly we hail'd at the twilight's last gleaming,
Whose broad stripes and bright stars, thro' the perilous fight,
O'er the ramparts we watch'd were so gallantly streaming?
And the rockets' red glare, the bombs bursting in air,
Gave proof thro' the night that our flag was still there.
O, say, does that Star-Spangled Banner yet wave
O'er the land of the free and the home of the brave?

*Francis Scott Key*

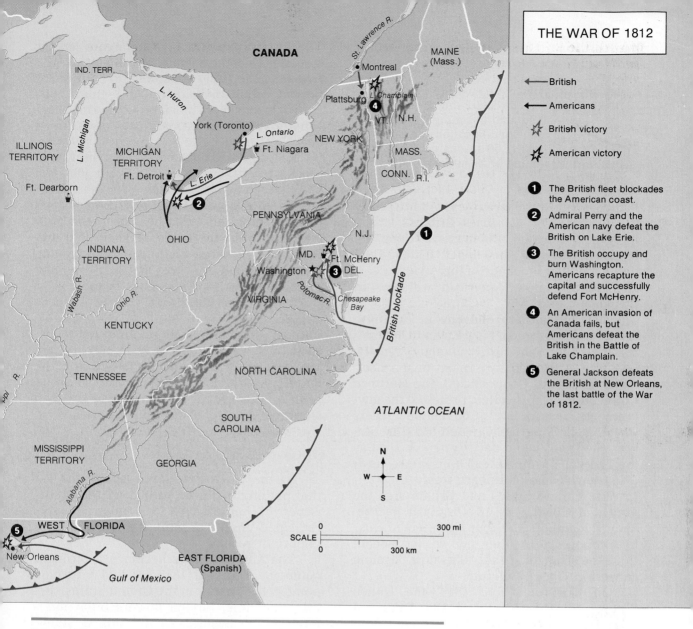

THE WAR OF 1812

→ British
← Americans
✧ British victory
✦ American victory

1. The British fleet blockades the American coast.
2. Admiral Perry and the American navy defeat the British on Lake Erie.
3. The British occupy and burn Washington. Americans recapture the capital and successfully defend Fort McHenry.
4. An American invasion of Canada fails, but Americans defeat the British in the Battle of Lake Champlain.
5. General Jackson defeats the British at New Orleans, the last battle of the War of 1812.

SCALE
0          300 mi
0          300 km

## Map Study

**The War of 1812 was fought in lakes bordering Canada and in ports along the British blockade line. What American victory prevented the British from invading the northeastern United States? By what waterways did the British reach Washington, D.C.?**

**American sailors win praise.** American sailors proved to be steadfast fighters. The words of Captain James Lawrence show the American spirit. Although his vessel was badly battered and he was dying of a wound, Captain Lawrence ordered his crew, "Don't give up the ship!"

At least one of every six members of the United States Navy was black. Many slaves and free blacks already had experience working as sailors on merchant vessels. Now they fought alongside white sailors on privateers and navy fleet ships. They served their country loyally and earned respect for

273

their bravery. One American naval officer said the blacks were

> not surpassed by any seamen we have in the fleet and I have yet to learn that the color of the skin or the cut and trimming of the coat can affect a man's qualifications or usefulness. I have nearly 50 blacks on board of this ship, and many of them are among my best men.

The United States' success at sea amazed the British. For centuries Britain's strong navy had defeated all enemies. Soon the British recovered the upper hand. They tightened their blockade of the Atlantic coast and trapped most American warships in their home ports.

**New Englanders convene at Hartford.** As the war continued, New England Federalists grew more and more unhappy. Finally, late in 1814, the Federalist party held a meeting at Hartford, Connecticut. The **Hartford Convention,** as it is called, protested the government's war policy. Convention leaders said that if Congress violated the Constitution, the states could defy Congress. Just as the Federalists announced their views, however, news came of a peace treaty.

**The United States and Britain sign the Treaty of Ghent.** By 1814 the war had become a stand-off. Neither side seemed close to winning, and neither side wished to continue the struggle. Peace talks now began in earnest in Ghent, Belgium.

On Christmas Eve 1814, the United States and Britain signed the **Treaty of Ghent.** The treaty ignored the issues of impressment, blockades, and neutral rights. Instead it simply called an end to the war and restored prewar boundaries. It also set up a commission to settle disputes over the border between Canada and the United States.

**Jackson scores a final victory at New Orleans.** News of the Treaty of Ghent took time to travel from Europe to America. Meanwhile the fighting continued. On December 24, 1814—the very day that the treaty was signed—American General Andrew Jackson surprised British troops outside New Orleans. After making a quick attack, Jackson withdrew to build his defenses.

Then, on January 8, 1815, he again led his forces against the enemy. This **Battle of New Orleans** lasted only about half an hour, but it proved costly to Britain. More than 2,000 British troops were killed or wounded. Jackson's losses included only 8 soldiers killed and 13 wounded.

Among Jackson's forces were many free blacks from New Orleans. About 400 had volunteered when Jackson promised them equal treatment and equal pay. Slaves from nearby plantations also helped defend New Orleans. After the battle Jackson said that the British general, Sir Edward Pakenham, had been killed by "the bullet of a free man of color, who was a famous rifle-shot."

By the time the Battle of New Orleans ended, peace had already been made. Though the battle had no military value, Jackson's reputation as a war hero helped him become President later. In addition, the battle gave Americans a strong sense of pride. The War of 1812 had ended with a stunning victory for the United States.

## Outcomes of the War

At the war's end, some Americans felt that nothing had been gained. After all, the issues of impressment and neutral rights remained unsettled. Still, the war did have important results.

**The United States becomes a stronger country.** The year 1815 marked a turning point in the history of the United States. Before that time, foreign powers often interfered in the business of the United States. Now Europeans treated the United States with more respect. Americans had proved, once again, that they would fight if their rights were threatened. They could now afford to pay less attention to events in Europe and concentrate on matters at home.

Nationalism swept the country after the War of 1812. Americans felt pride and confidence in the strength of the nation. They cheered the armed forces and the leaders who had made victory possible. As peace settled over the land, the people of New England, the South, and the West forgot many of their differences.

Unfortunately, the people of Canada were left with a feeling of bitterness toward Americans. Canada had taken no part in the troubles between the United States and Great Britain. Canadians felt angry to learn that their American neighbors wanted to seize their territory.

**The economy grows.** Economically, the War of 1812 left the United States in a strong position. The war had helped build up American manufacturing. Until the early 1800's, Americans imported most of their manufactured goods. Then, with Jefferson's embargo and the dangers of wartime shipping, overseas trade nearly ended. People in the United States began to manufacture items they could no longer get from abroad.

After the war, manufacturing businesses kept growing steadily. Shipping and trade also revived. The country found itself with a small national debt and much open land waiting to be settled. Americans could look forward to peace and prosperity.

## SECTION REVIEW

1. **Vocabulary**   embargo, blockade
2. **People and Places**   William Henry Harrison, Tecumseh, the Prophet, Tippecanoe Creek, War Hawks, Canada, Isaac Hull, Oliver H. Perry, Hartford, Ghent, Andrew Jackson
3. **Comprehension**   Why did some Americans favor war with Great Britain in 1812?
4. **Comprehension**   What important outcomes resulted from the War of 1812?
5. **Critical Thinking**   Did either side truly "win" the War of 1812? Explain.

# Chapter 11 Summary

Thomas Jefferson, elected President in 1800, believed in an informal style of leadership and in a small but strong government. He cut taxes, reduced the armed forces, and kept the federal government's activity to a minimum. At the same time, he showed strength by fighting the Barbary Coast pirates who interfered with American shipping in the Mediterranean Sea.

Jefferson also used his presidential powers to buy the Louisiana Territory from France in 1803. The Louisiana Purchase doubled the size of the United States. Many settlers followed the explorers Lewis and Clark and Zebulon Pike into this area.

Meanwhile, Federalists controlled the judicial branch. Under Chief Justice John Marshall, the Supreme Court became a powerful force. The Court set an important precedent in *Marbury* v. *Madison* by using its powers of judicial review to declare a law unconstitutional.

When Britain and France went to war in 1803, neither nation respected American neutrality. To avoid war, Congress passed the Embargo Act in 1807 and, in 1809, the Non-Intercourse Act. These unpopular measures, however, did not end the trouble. In 1812 Congress declared war on Britain. Americans blamed the British for seizing American ships and encouraging Indian attacks on western settlements. War Hawks hoped to gain Florida and Canada. After an American invasion of Canada failed, the British burned Washington, D.C., and attacked Baltimore. Meanwhile, Isaac Hull and Oliver Perry scored American victories at sea.

Neither side, however, seemed to be winning the war. At the Hartford Convention in 1814, Federalists voiced their opposition to the war. At about the same time, the United States and Britain agreed to peace under the Treaty of Ghent. The fighting did not end, however, until Andrew Jackson defeated the British at the Battle of New Orleans in 1815. The United States, ill-prepared when it began the war, emerged from the conflict with new pride and strength.

## CRITICAL THINKING: Recognizing Points of View

Identifying points of view is an important skill for historians. Favorable points of view often can be recognized by the use of **positive language.** For example, the writer who described George Washington as "useful and virtuous" certainly viewed him favorably. **Negative language** indicates an unfavorable point of view. When Thomas Paine called King George III the "Royal Brute," he was expressing a negative viewpoint.

Points of view are **subjective.** That is, they involve a person's opinions, attitudes, beliefs, or feelings. In reading historical material, historians look carefully for **bias**—personal preferences—on the part of the writer. In this way, historians separate the truth from subjective viewpoints.

The quotations that follow show two different points of view of the War of 1812. The first is from President Madison's war message to Congress.

> The conduct of [Britain's] Government presents a series of acts hostile to the United States as an independent and neutral nation.
>
> British cruisers have been in the continued practice of violating the American flag on the great highway of nations, and of seizing and carrying off persons sailing under it....
>
> Under pretended blockades,... our commerce has been plundered in every sea....
>
> We behold ... on the side of Great Britain a state of war against the United States, and on the side of the United States ... peace toward Great Britain.

A different point of view was expressed by Britain's Prince Regent George IV. Read this leader's statement and then answer the following questions on a separate sheet of paper.

> The earnest endeavours of the Prince Regent to preserve the relations of peace and amity with the United States of America having unfortunately failed, his Royal Highness ... deems it proper publicly to declare the causes, and origin of the war, in which the government of the United States has compelled him to engage ...
>
> His Royal Highness can never acknowledge any blockade whatsoever to be illegal.... His Royal Highness can never admit, that ... the ... right of searching neutral merchant vessels in time of war, the impressment of British seamen, when found therein, can be deemed any violation of a neutral flag ...
>
> Such are the causes of war which have been put forward by the government of the United States. But the real origin of the present contest will be found in that spirit, [found in] the councils of the United States: their marked partiality in ... assisting the aggressive tyranny of France....

1. In Madison's first paragraph, what kind of language is used to describe Britain's actions? Give an example.
2. What kind of language does George IV use in his first paragraph to describe Britain's actions? Give an example.
3. What three charges does President Madison make against the British?
4. Why, according to George IV, did the United States declare war?
5. How do the two points of view presented in these quotations differ?

# CAUSES and EFFECTS

# The Constitution ★★★

States fear strong central government

New states want to preserve self-government

States have different needs and interests

Fight for independence builds unity

## CONTRIBUTING CAUSES

Confederation has no power to tax, enforce laws, or protect property

Articles of Confederation are too weak

America cannot respond to foreign attack

Economic problems plague the new nation

## MAIN CAUSES

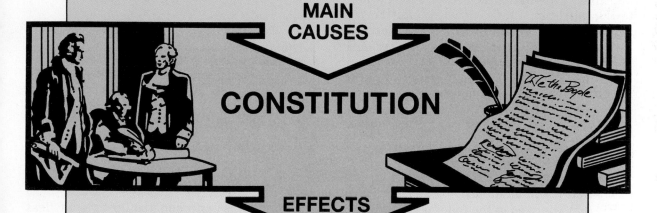

# CONSTITUTION

## EFFECTS

Three-branch government is established

Federalist power increases

Central government becomes stronger

States learn to compromise for common goal

## LONG-TERM EFFECTS

Federal Bill of Rights is enacted

Slave trade remains legal

Political parties form

Regions conflict over role of central government

# Chapter 11 REVIEW

## Vocabulary and Key Terms

Choose the italicized term in parentheses that best completes each sentence. Write your answers on a separate sheet of paper.

1. President Jefferson ordered the (*blockade/embargo*) in 1807 to stop foreign trade.
2. (*Judicial review/Writ of mandamus*) is the power of federal courts to declare laws unconstitutional.
3. France sold the (*Mississippi Territory/ Louisiana Territory*) to the United States in 1803.
4. Sacajawea led Lewis and Clark across the (*continental divide/Wilderness Road*).
5. Tecumseh and William Henry Harrison fought at the (*Battle of New Orleans/ Battle of Tippecanoe*).
6. The (*Hartford Convention/Treaty of Ghent*) expressed Federalist opposition to the War of 1812.

## Recalling the Facts

1. What events led to the passage of the Twelfth Amendment?
2. What changes in the federal government did Thomas Jefferson make when he became President?
3. How did the Supreme Court rule in *Marbury* v. *Madison*? Why was this decision important?
4. Why did Napoleon sell the Louisiana Territory to the United States?
5. What resulted from the Lewis and Clark expedition in 1804?
6. How did Jefferson try to avoid war with Britain in the early 1800's?
7. What happened at Tippecanoe?
8. What were three causes of the War of 1812?
9. How did the United States benefit from the War of 1812?

## Places to Locate

Match the letters on the map with the places listed below. Write your answers on a separate sheet of paper.

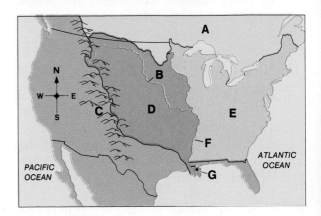

1. United States before 1803
2. New Orleans
3. Mississippi River
4. Louisiana Purchase
5. Missouri River
6. Rocky Mountains
7. Canada

## Critical Thinking

1. What was Jefferson's philosophy of "less government"? Did the Louisiana Purchase and the Embargo Act contradict that philosophy? Why or why not?
2. Do you think Jefferson was wise to make cutbacks in the military when he became President. Why or why not? How heavily do you think the nation should spend for military purposes today? Explain.
3. When President Jefferson sent Lewis and Clark to explore Louisiana, he told them to offer the Native Americans peace and friendship. Did they do so? Did American policy toward Native Americans later change? Do you think the government treated the Indians fairly? Explain your answers.

4. Analyze the issues involved in the Hartford Convention. Consider the following questions in your analysis:
   a. What reasons did the Federalists have to be unhappy with the government's war policy?
   b. Did the Hartford Convention represent a switch in Federalists' support for a strong central government? Explain.
   c. What other examples of protest against the American government had there been to date?

## Understanding History

1. Reread the section "Jefferson takes a tough stand against piracy" on page 261. Then answer these questions.
   a. **Geography.** What interest did the United States have in the Mediterranean Sea?
   b. **Economics.** What did the United States stand to gain economically from fighting the Barbary pirates?
2. Reread the section "France gains control of New Orleans" on page 264. Then answer these questions.
   a. **Geography.** What natural features formed the eastern and western boundaries of Louisiana?
   b. **Primary Sources.** According to Jefferson, why was New Orleans important to the United States?
3. Reread the section "Jefferson tries to avoid war" on page 269. Then answer these questions.
   a. **Economics.** Did the Embargo Act have the desired effect? Explain.
   b. **Citizenship.** Do you think Eastern merchants were right to ignore the embargo? Explain.

## Projects and Activities

1. **Writing a Biography.** Choose one of the following people to research: John Marshall, Dolley Madison, Daniel Boone, Zebulon Pike, Tecumseh. Write and illustrate a biography about your subject's life and his or her achievements.
2. **Researching Place Names.** Use an atlas to find out how many places in the United States bear the names of people mentioned in this chapter.
3. **Performing a Skit.** As a group project, act out an imaginary meeting between the Lewis and Clark party and a group of Native Americans. Try to find out about each other's lives and customs.
4. **Making a Time Line.** Find out the dates of important battles and events during the War of 1812. Create a time line to show this information.
5. **Making a Poster.** Imagine that you are a War Hawk in 1811 or a New England Federalist in 1814. Design a poster to express your views.

## Practicing Your Skill

The passages below express different points of view about the courts' power of judicial review. The first passage is from an 1803 newspaper article. The second is part of a letter written by Thomas Jefferson. Read the passages, and then answer the following questions on a separate sheet of paper.

> [If] a law conflict[s] with the Constitution, the judges are bound to declare which is [to be obeyed]. The judges here take no power. It is not they who speak—it is the Constitution, or rather, the people.
>
> The *Washington Federalist*
>
> The Constitution ... is a mere thing of wax in the hands of the judiciary, which they may twist and shape into any form they please. ... My [view] of the Constitution is ... that each department is truly independent of the others and has an equal right to decide for itself what is the meaning of the Constitution. ...
>
> Thomas Jefferson

1. Does the newspaper article support or criticize the courts for using judicial review? Which point of view does Jefferson take?
2. Which passage says that judges express the will of the people?
3. What phrase suggests the viewpoint that judges' decisions are based on whim?

# UNIT 4 REVIEW

## Unit Summary

★ **The Articles of Confederation formed America's first government.**

- The Confederation created a weak central authority and left many powers to the states.
- Inadequate power at the federal level resulted in unsolved national problems.
- In 1787 delegates abandoned the Confederation and wrote the Constitution of the United States.
- The Constitution was ratified by the states in 1789.

★ **The Constitution established a successful system of government.**

- A separation of powers at the federal level created the legislative, executive, and judicial branches.
- The Bill of Rights guaranteed basic freedoms to citizens.
- President George Washington selected a Cabinet of advisers, and set the precedent of two terms of office.
- During Adams's presidency, Congress passed laws that threatened American civil rights.

★ **As President, Thomas Jefferson strengthened the United States.**

- Jefferson reduced government spending and the national debt.
- The United States purchased the Louisiana Territory from France and doubled the nation's size.
- The Supreme Court gained power under John Marshall's leadership.
- By fighting Britain in the War of 1812, the United States earned the respect of many nations.

## Understanding Chronology

Study the Unit 4 time line on page 185. Then complete the following activity on a separate sheet of paper.

The Unit 4 time line includes events that occurred during the administrations of the nation's first four Presidents. Copy the time line and add to it the dates that Washington, Adams, Jefferson, and Madison served as President. Then add at least one more event that happened during each presidency.

## Writing About History

1. **Comparing Viewpoints.** Write two paragraphs comparing Jefferson's and Hamilton's views about government. Then write another paragraph explaining which view you would have supported and why.
2. **Preparing a Journal.** Imagine that you were a member of the Lewis and Clark expedition. Keep a detailed journal describing the land, the plants and animals, and the Native Americans of the area you explored. Include a description of your most interesting discovery, and your feelings about the entire journey.
3. **Writing an Essay.** Write an essay on the spirit of nationalism in the United States today. Describe the way Americans feel about their country and give evidence to support your views. Compare nationalism today with the way Americans felt about the United States after winning the War of 1812.
4. **Expressing a Viewpoint.** Write an editorial that might have appeared in a newspaper in 1788. Briefly outline arguments for and against your state's ratification of the Constitution. Then close the editorial by supporting a point of view that is favorable to ratification.

*OGRABME, or. The American Snapping-turtle.*

5. **Interpreting a Cartoon.** The cartoon above deals with the Embargo Act of 1807. Note that *Ograbme,* or "Oh! Grab Me," is embargo spelled backwards. Explain the meaning of the cartoon and what each figure represents. Explain the purpose of the embargo and the reasons why some Americans disagreed with it.

## Projects

1. **Making A Chart.** Thomas Jefferson and John Adams both died on July 4, 1826—the fiftieth anniversary of the Declaration of Independence. Make a chart and compare the lives of these two outstanding Americans. Point out the ways in which they were similar, and the ways in which they were different.

2. **Drawing Historical Maps.** Draw two or more maps to show how the territorial United States changed between 1783 and 1803. Show land areas originally claimed by other nations and indicate the dates that states were admitted to the Union.

3. **Plotting a Diagram.** Draw a diagram of the township system used to organize the Northwest Territory. Then explain how this system encouraged the settlement of the western lands.

4. **Giving a Speech.** Present a speech to celebrate the Constitution's Bicentennial. Explain the document's strengths, how it has changed, and why it has endured.

5. **Presenting Information.** Work in groups to organize a class presentation titled "Our Government in Action." Using charts, pictures, or posters show how the Constitution works. Explain the separation of powers, the election of government leaders, the qualifications for candidates, government terms of office, the system of checks and balances, and amending the Constitution.

6. **Creating Advertisements.** Imagine that you owned a land company in the 1780's and you wish to sell some property. Make five advertisements promoting settlement in the Northwest Territory. Explain the township system and the cost and availability of good farmland. Make sure your advertisements promote interest in the Northwest Territory.

## Finding Out More

Cabral, Olga. *So Proudly She Sailed: Tales of Old Ironsides.* Houghton Mifflin, 1981. Find out how the *USS Constitution* gained its nickname.

Gilfond, Henry. *The Executive Branch of the United States Government.* Watts, 1981. This book examines the presidency, the Cabinet, and controversial topics like impeachment and executive privilege.

Hilton, Suzanne. *We the People: The Way We Were.* Westminster, 1981. The author describes the way Americans lived after the Revolution and sets the scene for the new nation.

Phelan, Mary Kay. *The Story of the Louisiana Purchase.* Harper & Row, 1979. Illustrations from original documents and excerpts from letters, diaries, and newspapers of the time are used in this exciting account of the Louisiana Purchase.

Tunis, Edwin. *The Young United States, 1783 to 1830.* Crowell, 1976. In this book, the early years of the nation are described as a time of change, a time of growth, and a time of learning about democracy. Historical events as well as travel, education, and kinds of settlements are examined.

# UNIT 5
# THE YOUNG NATION
## 1815–1846

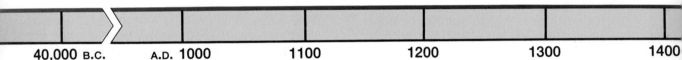

40,000 B.C.    A.D. 1000    1100    1200    1300    1400

In the early 1800's New Orleans was a thriving port city. It was one of many centers of commerce of the young United States.

1815 – 1846

| 1500 | 1600 | 1700 | 1800 | 1900 | 2000 |

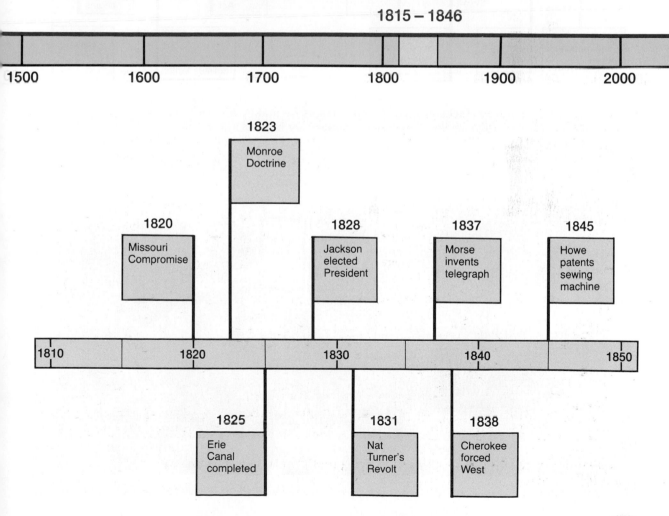

1823 Monroe Doctrine

1820 Missouri Compromise

1828 Jackson elected President

1837 Morse invents telegraph

1845 Howe patents sewing machine

| 1810 | 1820 | 1830 | 1840 | 1850 |

1825 Erie Canal completed

1831 Nat Turner's Revolt

1838 Cherokee forced West

# 12 National and Sectional Interests Compete

## 1815–1846

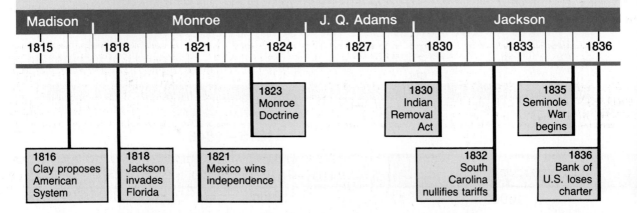

| Madison | | Monroe | | J. Q. Adams | | Jackson | |
|---|---|---|---|---|---|---|---|
| 1815 | 1818 | 1821 | 1824 | 1827 | 1830 | 1833 | 1836 |

1823
Monroe
Doctrine

1830
Indian
Removal
Act

1835
Seminole
War
begins

1816
Clay proposes
American
System

1818
Jackson
invades
Florida

1821
Mexico wins
independence

1832
South
Carolina
nullifies tariffs

1836
Bank of
U.S. loses
charter

**President-elect Andrew Jackson greets supporters as he makes his way to his inauguration in 1829. Jackson expanded democracy in the United States.**

## Preparing to Read

After the War of 1812, Americans felt a new confidence in the strength of their nation. The United States warned European nations to stay out of the Western Hemisphere, and a stronger federal government increased feelings of American unity. In the 1820's democracy grew under the strong leadership of President Andrew Jackson. As you read this chapter, try to answer the following questions:

1. How did nationalism and sectionalism shape policy after the War of 1812?
2. What led to the American foreign policy known as the Monroe Doctrine?
3. How did the Jacksonian Era begin?
4. What issues arose during Jackson's second term?

 **1 How did nationalism and sectionalism shape policy after the War of 1812?**

### Vocabulary
oratory
sectionalism

In the early 1800's, Congress granted the federal government greater powers over the economy. This policy was intended to make the United States a strong nation, able to hold its own against the nations of Europe. Soon, however, the new national unity was strained by regional quarrels over slavery.

### The Growth of Federal Power

In the years after the War of 1812, only one political party existed in the United States. Members of Congress from all three sections of the country agreed on policies that strengthened federal power.

**A new era begins in the United States.** The successful ending of the War of 1812 gained new support for the Republican party. James Monroe, a Republican from Virginia, was elected President in 1816. The Republicans adopted many Federalist policies, and the Federalist party soon disappeared completely. It seemed that one political party could satisfy all Americans. For this reason, people called the Monroe presidency the **Era of Good Feelings.**

---

### LINKING PAST AND PRESENT
### ★★★ *Sectional Interests*

During the 1800's, members of Congress often defended sectional interests. Southerners tried to protect agriculture and northeasterners worked to protect industry. Together they made compromises that served the whole nation.

Today members of Congress still represent the interests of home regions. Representatives from the Southwest, for example, are concerned about water shortages. Lawmakers from the Midwest worry about the welfare of farmers. The states in the South and the West must provide new services for steadily growing populations. Just as in the past, members of Congress work to balance sectional needs with the good of the whole United States.

## JAMES MONROE

★ **1817–1825** ★

**5**TH PRESIDENT

DEMOCRATIC-REPUBLICAN

★ Born April 28, 1758, in Virginia

★ Married Elizabeth Kortright in 1786; 3 children

★ Senator from Virginia; governor of Virginia; ambassador to Great Britain; Secretary of State; Secretary of War

★ Lived in Virginia when elected President

★ Vice President: Daniel Tompkins

★ Died July 4, 1831, in New York

★ Key events while in office: The Era of Good Feelings; Florida purchased from Spain; Mississippi, Illinois, Alabama, Maine, and Missouri became states; Missouri Compromise; Monroe Doctrine

Three strong-minded Congressmen helped shape the events of the new era. John Calhoun of South Carolina, Daniel Webster of Massachusetts, and Henry Clay of Kentucky were well known for their powerful **oratory** —public speaking. They often debated United States policy in the early 1800's. At times **sectionalism** —loyalty to local interests—influenced the three leaders. Calhoun spoke for the South, Webster for the Northeast, and Clay for the West. At other times, nationalism won out. Henry Clay believed strongly in nationalist policies.

**Clay proposes the American System.** In 1816, while President Madison was still in office, Henry Clay proposed a new economic program to Congress. Later known as the **American System,** the program was aimed at making the United States independent of the rest of the world. First, Clay called for a tariff to discourage the sale of foreign goods in the United States. Next, he asked for new roads and canals to improve trade between the states. Finally, he urged Congress to set up a second national bank. The charter of the first Bank of the United States had run out five years earlier.

Clay's American System gained wide support in Congress. In 1816 Congress passed a tariff on manufactured goods shipped into the United States. The tariff kept British manufacturers from driving the growing northeastern industries out of business. Congress also drew up a bill proposing improvements in transportation throughout the country. President Madison vetoed the bill, however, and James Monroe continued to oppose such plans when he became President. Finally, in 1816 Congress passed the bill that established the second Bank of the United States.

**The Bank of the United States strengthens federal power.** After the charter of the first Bank of the United States ran out, private banks throughout the states began to print their own money and set their own loan policies. Some people believed that a new national bank was needed to regulate the private banks. According to the charter granted it by Congress, the second Bank of the United States could print a standard currency for the whole country. It was also permitted to lend money to businesses and private banks.

Hoping for loans, the business leaders of the Northeast were in favor of the new Bank of the United States. The bank increased federal power, and for that reason some Americans in the South and the West opposed it. When hard times hit the nation in 1819, people blamed the bank, referring to it as "the Monster." That same year, however, the Supreme Court decided a case in favor of the bank. In the *McCulloch v. Maryland* decision, Supreme Court Justice John Marshall wrote that, under the Constitution, the federal government has the authority to establish and maintain a bank without interference from the states.

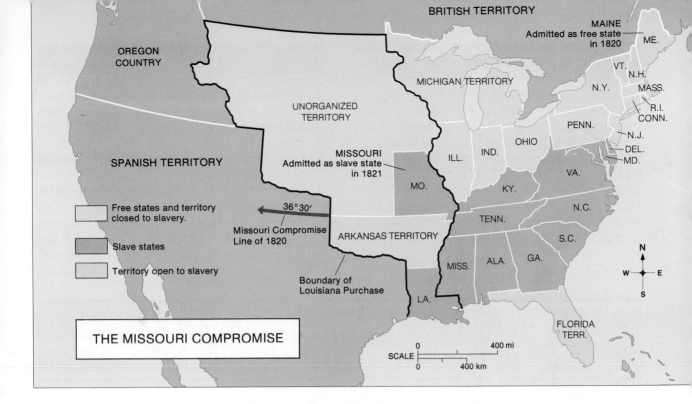

OREGON COUNTRY

BRITISH TERRITORY

MAINE
Admitted as free state
in 1820
ME.

MICHIGAN TERRITORY

UNORGANIZED TERRITORY

SPANISH TERRITORY

MISSOURI
Admitted as slave state
in 1821

MO.

ILL. IND. OHIO PENN.

VT.
N.H.
N.Y. MASS.
R.I.
CONN.
N.J.
DEL.
MD.

VA.

KY.

N.C.

Free states and territory closed to slavery.

Slave states

Territory open to slavery

36°30'

Missouri Compromise Line of 1820

Boundary of Louisiana Purchase

ARKANSAS TERRITORY

TENN.

MISS. ALA. GA. S.C.

LA.

FLORIDA TERR.

N
W E
S

THE MISSOURI COMPROMISE

SCALE

0          400 mi
0      400 km

## Map Study

**The Missouri Compromise permitted slavery in Missouri and in states south of the Missouri Compromise Line. What free state joined the Union to balance the number of free and slave states?**

## The Missouri Compromise

The question of Missouri's admission to the Union as a slave state caused problems between the Northeast and the South. A compromise settled the question by extending the power of both the free and the slave states.

**Sectional differences prompt a debate over slavery.** Between 1810 and 1820, the population west of the Appalachian Mountains grew from about 1 million to more than 2 million. Five new states entered the Union—Louisiana (1812), Indiana (1816), Mississippi (1817), Illinois (1818), and Alabama (1819). Before gaining admission from Congress, each new state had to declare whether or not it would allow slavery within its boundaries.

By 1819 the number of slave states in the Union equaled the number of free states. That same year, however, Missouri applied

to enter the Union as a slave state. Members of Congress from the Northeast did not want slavery to spread. They demanded that Missouri enter the Union as a free state. Southern members of Congress refused to give way. They wanted to protect southern political power from the attacks of the Northeast.

**The Missouri Compromise settles the question.** In late 1819 Maine, which had been part of Massachusetts, applied for admission to the Union as a free state. This development prompted Senator Jesse Thomas of Illinois to propose a bill that was known as the **Missouri Compromise.** The bill provided for Maine and Missouri to enter the Union at the same time. In this way, the number of free and slave states could be kept equal. The bill also settled the question of slavery in the rest of the Louisiana Territory. It allowed slavery south of the parallel 36°30'N and barred it north of that line.

287

Speaker of the House Henry Clay worked long and hard to convince the members of Congress to accept the Missouri Compromise. Clay was well aware that a quarrel over the slavery issue could become a major threat to national unity. Some people from the South were reluctant to support the bill, because they did not believe that Congress had the authority to place limits on the spread of slavery. Nevertheless, in 1820, the United States Congress approved the Missouri Compromise, and President Monroe signed it into law. Missouri finally became a slave state on August 10, 1821.

## SECTION REVIEW

1. **Vocabulary**   oratory, sectionalism
2. **People and Places**   James Monroe, John Calhoun, Daniel Webster, Henry Clay, Missouri
3. **Comprehension**   What was the American System?
4. **Comprehension**   What were the powers of the Bank of the United States?
5. **Critical Thinking**   Was the Missouri Compromise a good way to settle the quarrel over slavery? Why or why not?

# 2 What led to the American foreign policy known as the Monroe Doctrine?

## Vocabulary

reimburse
diplomatic recognition
doctrine

Between 1810 and 1824, Spain lost its empire in the Americas. The United States gained Spanish Florida, and Spain's South American colonies won independence. President Monroe launched a new policy to make sure that European nations would never again try to establish colonies in the Western Hemisphere.

## Changes in Spanish America

At the height of its power, Spain had founded many colonies in the Americas. In 1808 Napoleon, the ruler of France, conquered Spain, leaving the Spanish too weak to resist challenges to their ruling power in the colonies.

**The United States expands into West Florida.** In the early 1800's, Spain owned present-day Florida, which was then known as East Florida. Spain also owned West Florida, a strip of land along the Gulf of Mexico, in present-day Mississippi and Alabama. West Florida included several useful ports, and the United States was eager to obtain it.

In 1810 President Madison took advantage of a rebellion in the colony to declare part of West Florida to be United States territory. During the War of 1812, Congress claimed another portion of West Florida for the United States. Spain lacked the military power to resist these claims.

**The United States gains control of East Florida.** The few Spanish troops in East Florida were unable to prevent trouble on the border between Georgia and Florida. The Seminole Indians were crossing the border to make raids on settlements in Georgia. Also, runaway Georgia slaves were escaping to East Florida.

In 1818 President Monroe sent General Andrew Jackson to Georgia with orders to stop the Indian raids. Jackson decided to lead his forces in an invasion of East Florida. He captured two Spanish forts and claimed Florida for the United States. Many Americans applauded Jackson's boldness, but Congress was angry that he had acted without

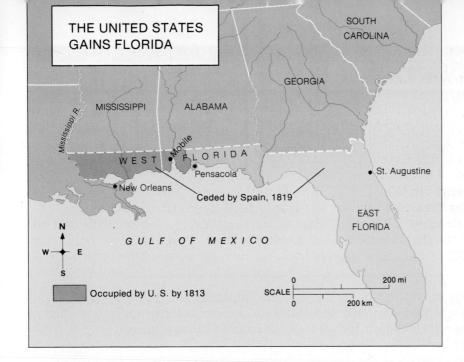

THE UNITED STATES GAINS FLORIDA

SOUTH CAROLINA
GEORGIA
MISSISSIPPI
ALABAMA
Mississippi R.
WEST FLORIDA
Mobile
Pensacola
New Orleans
Ceded by Spain, 1819
St. Augustine
EAST FLORIDA
GULF OF MEXICO
N
W E
S
Occupied by U. S. by 1813
SCALE
0          200 mi
0          200 km

## Map Study

Until 1819 Spain disputed American claims to West Florida. By what date had Americans occupied Mobile, Alabama? Which states gained access to the Gulf of Mexico through West Florida?

proper authority. Spain and other European nations protested this unlawful seizure of Spanish territory.

Monroe withdrew the American troops from East Florida, but the incident convinced Spain that it could no longer defend the Floridas. In the **Adams-Onís Treaty** of 1819, Spain sold East and West Florida to the United States for $5 million. The $5 million was used to **reimburse** —repay—American citizens for property lost in the Seminole raids. Spain also gave up its claim to the Oregon region, and the United States gave up its claim to Texas.

**Latin American nations win independence from Spain.** Like the North American colonists in 1776, the Latin American colonists of the 1800's were hungry for freedom. Latin American merchants were tired of strict Spanish trade laws. Creoles— Spanish people born in the Americas—were angry at being denied positions in government. (Most government jobs were reserved for people born in Spain.) The Indians of Latin America also hoped that revolution would give them a voice in government.

Mexico's struggle for independence began in 1810, when Father Miguel Hidalgo (hih-DAHL-go), a village priest, led Indians in the capture of several towns. Hidalgo was executed by the Spanish, but the revolution continued, and Mexico gained independence in 1821.

Another leader in the Latin American struggle for freedom was Simón Bolívar (bo-LEE-vahr), the son of a wealthy Creole family in Venezuela. Known as the "Liberator" of South America, Bolívar freed Colombia in 1819 and Venezuela in 1821. He then joined forces with José de San Martín (sahn mahr-TEEN), an Argentinian soldier who freed Chile of Spanish control. In 1824 the armies of Bolívar and San Martín defeated the Spanish at the Battle of Ayacucho (ah-yah-KOO-cho) in Peru. This battle marked the successful end of the struggle for independence in Spanish South America.

## The Monroe Doctrine

In response to threats of foreign interference in the Americas, President Monroe announced a new plan for foreign policy. The United States would stay out of European affairs, and Europe in turn would keep out of the Western Hemisphere.

**Foreign nations threaten to interfere in the Americas.** After Napoleon's defeat in 1815, the nations of Europe joined together in an alliance to keep the peace. The European

289

# THE MONROE DOCTRINE 1823

President Monroe announced the Monroe Doctrine in his annual message to Congress in 1823. The Monroe Doctrine became one of the most important statements in United States history. It has influenced American foreign policy to the present day.

## Read to Find Out
1. What does President Monroe say would be dangerous to the peace and safety of the Americas?
2. According to the Monroe Doctrine, what is the United States policy toward European powers?

---

The American continents, by the free and independent condition which they have assumed and maintain, are henceforth not to be considered as subject for future colonization by any European powers....

The political system of the [European] powers is essentially different ... from that of America.... We owe it, therefore, to candor ... to declare that we should consider any attempt on their part to extend their system to any portion of this hemisphere as dangerous to our peace and safety....

Our policy in regard to Europe, which was adopted [many years ago], nevertheless remains the same, which is, not to interfere in the internal concerns of any of its powers....

*James Monroe*

---

alliance worked to protect existing governments and to oppose revolutions. Americans became alarmed at rumors that France planned to help Spain recover its Latin American colonies.

To add to American concern, in 1821 Russia tried to strengthen its claim to the Oregon region. It warned the ships of other nations to avoid the Pacific coast from Alaska to Oregon. The United States and Great Britain had already jointly claimed Oregon, and American ships often visited the area to trade with the Indians.

The United States opposed European involvement in the Americas. In 1822 the United States gave **diplomatic recognition** to the new Latin American nations. Diplomatic recognition is formal acceptance of a nation's government. In this way, the United States demonstrated to the European alliance that it would regard any attempts to restore Spanish rule in Latin America as unlawful. The United States also sent a strong letter of protest to Russia, asserting American rights to sail the waters of the Pacific Ocean.

**President Monroe forbids foreign interference in the Americas.** The United States sent its strongest message to Europe in 1823, when President Monroe announced a new **doctrine** —principle—of American foreign policy. This principle, known as the **Monroe Doctrine,** had three main points. First, the Western Hemisphere would no longer be open to colonization by European powers. Next, the United States would oppose any attempt to interfere with the new Latin American governments. Third, the United

States would not interfere in the affairs of any European countries nor would it become involved in the affairs of their existing American colonies.

The Monroe Doctrine showed the determination of the United States to maintain its independence from European nations. The Doctrine became a lasting principle of American foreign policy. The Monroe Doctrine could not, however, have been enforced without the backing and support of the British Navy. Great Britain carried on a profitable trade with the new Latin American nations. For this reason, Britain wanted to make sure the Americas were free from Spanish control.

## SECTION REVIEW

1. **Vocabulary**   reimburse, diplomatic recognition, doctrine
2. **People and Places**   West Florida, East Florida, Andrew Jackson, Mexico, Father Miguel Hidalgo, Simón Bolívar, Colombia
3. **Comprehension**   What were the terms of the Adams-Onís Treaty?
4. **Comprehension**   Why was the Battle of Ayacucho important?
5. **Critical Thinking**   Do you think that President Monroe acted wisely in announcing the Monroe Doctrine? Why or why not?

# 3 How did the Jacksonian Era begin?

## Vocabulary

spoils system
secede

More than any other President before him, Andrew Jackson believed in the right of ordinary people to take part in government. Jackson also believed, however, in giving strong powers to the federal government. This led him to quarrel with southerners who defended the rights of states.

### The Rise of Jackson

Andrew Jackson lost the close race for the presidency in 1824. Four years later, however, he defeated John Quincy Adams and became President, beginning what would one day be known as the Jacksonian Era.

**The election of 1824 is marked by sectional rivalry.** In the election of 1824, each section of the United States was determined to get control of the White House. The

## Our Presidents

### JOHN QUINCY ADAMS

★ 1825–1829 ★

**6**TH PRESIDENT

NATIONAL REPUBLICAN

★ Born July 11, 1767, in Massachusetts
★ Married Louisa Catherine Johnson in 1797; 4 children
★ Lawyer; senator from Massachusetts; ambassador to Russia and to England
★ Lived in Massachusetts when elected President
★ Vice President: John Calhoun
★ Died February 23, 1848, in Washington
★ Key events while in office: Erie Canal

Northeast backed John Quincy Adams, the son of President John Adams. The South supported William Crawford of Georgia. The West put forward two candidates, Henry Clay of Kentucky and Andrew Jackson of Tennessee.

When the electoral votes were counted, no candidate had a majority. In such a case, the House of Representatives must choose the President. Henry Clay asked his supporters to vote for John Quincy Adams. When Adams was chosen by the House, he rewarded Clay by appointing him Secretary of State.

John Quincy Adams's four years in office were troubled ones. A stern, cold man, he never gained the popularity he needed to get his policies passed by Congress. He also never overcame the distrust inspired by his election. Jackson had won a larger popular vote and more electoral votes than Adams. He still fell short of the required majority, however. Jackson's followers became furious when they learned that the House of Representatives had chosen Adams to be President. They claimed that Jackson had been robbed of the presidency and charged that Adams had made a "corrupt bargain" with Henry Clay.

**Andrew Jackson becomes President.** In the election of 1828, Jackson ran as the candidate of the new **Democratic party,** which had grown out of the old Democratic-Republican party. Jackson won an easy victory over the unpopular John Quincy Adams. The new President's inaugural party soon became a mob scene. Crowds pressed into the White House, muddying the floor and smashing china teacups in their eagerness to shake Jackson's hand. The day left little question that Andrew Jackson was truly a man of the people.

A hero to many Americans, Andrew Jackson had overcome poverty and hardship. He was born of Scotch-Irish parents on the Carolina frontier, and at only 13 he was taken prisoner by British soldiers during the Revolution. To his dying day he bore the scar of the saber cut he received when he refused to shine the boots of a British officer. As a young man, Jackson moved to the Tennessee frontier, where he became a judge and later won election as a member of Congress. In addition, he gained fame as a general in the War of 1812, winning an important victory at the Battle of New Orleans. (See Chapter 11.)

Jackson was a decisive leader, loyal to his friends and unbending to his enemies. As soon as he took office, he dismissed a large number of government officeholders, most of them postmasters. He replaced them with members of his own party, who had worked on his campaign. Many people were against this use of the **spoils system**—the practice of giving government jobs to political supporters. Jackson, however, refused to change his mind.

# Our Presidents

## ANDREW JACKSON

★ **1829–1837** ★

**7**TH PRESIDENT

DEMOCRAT

★ Born March 15, 1767, in South Carolina

★ Married Rachel Donelson Robards in 1791; no children

★ Lawyer; representative and senator from Tennessee; major-general in War of 1812

★ Lived in Tennessee when elected President

★ Vice Presidents: John Calhoun; Martin Van Buren

★ Nicknamed "Old Hickory"

★ Died June 8, 1845, in Tennessee

★ Key events while in office: Bank of the United States controversy; "Trail of Tears"; nullification crisis; Arkansas and Michigan became states

# The Tariff Debate

During Jackson's first term, the Northeast and the South quarreled over tariff duties. South Carolina threatened to leave the Union over the issue, until a compromise tariff satisfied both sides.

**Southerners protest against high tariffs.** In 1828 Congress passed a high tariff, and President Adams signed it into law. When Andrew Jackson took office, debate over the tariff increased. The Northeast supported the tariff of 1828, which protected its manufacturing from foreign competition. The South, on the other hand, did little manufacturing. It opposed the tariff, which raised prices on imported goods at a time when crop prices were falling.

The South Carolina legislature drew up a statement protesting the tariff of 1828. This statement was largely the work of John Calhoun, Vice President at the time. Calhoun declared that the Constitution did not give Congress the power to pass tariff laws that favored one section of the United States over another. According to Calhoun, the states could nullify any law that they believed to be unfair.

**Webster defends national unity.** In 1830 Robert Hayne of South Carolina and Daniel Webster of Massachusetts debated the doctrine of **states' rights** on the Senate floor. States' rights was the idea that state governments were more powerful than the federal government. Hayne argued that the rights of the states came before the unity of the whole nation. Webster defended the powers of the national government.

A brilliant orator with dark, deep-set eyes and a thundering voice, Webster argued that the laws made by Congress were not subject to the approval of each individual state. Instead the laws represented the will of the people as a whole. "It is, Sir," he declared, "the people's Constitution, the people's government, made for the people, made by the people, and answerable to the people." He scolded Hayne for wanting "Liberty first, and Union afterwards," and demanded "Liberty *and* Union, now and forever, one and inseparable!"

South Carolina Senator John C. Calhoun is the subject of this 1830's cartoon. By portraying Calhoun commanding the sun to stand still, the cartoonist is criticizing the senator's stand on the nullification issue.

**Jackson threatens to use force.** Jackson tried to satisfy the South by recommending that the tariff be lowered. In 1832 Congress passed a reduced tariff. South Carolina's legislature still thought it was too high. The legislature nullified the tariff laws of 1828 and 1832. It declared that if the federal government tried to force the state to accept the tariff laws, South Carolina would **secede** —withdraw—from the Union.

This 1851 painting by G.P.A. Healy shows Massachusetts Senator Daniel Webster debating Senator Robert Hayne of South Carolina in 1830. The two senators argued whether states could disregard federal laws.

Jackson was furious when he learned what South Carolina had done. "If one drop of blood be shed [in South Carolina] in defiance of the laws of the United States," he said, "I will hang the first man of them I can get my hands on to the first tree I can find." He announced that he would enforce the tariff laws and prepared to send an army to South Carolina.

**A compromise ends the conflict.** To avoid an unpleasant showdown, Henry Clay proposed a compromise tariff that would lower tariff duties gradually over a period of 10 years. Congress passed the new bill in 1833, and President Jackson signed it into law.

Both sides felt they had won a victory. South Carolina had made Congress lower the tariff, and Jackson had forced South Carolina to back down. South Carolina did not,

however, give up its claim that states had the right to nullify laws and secede from the Union.

# 4 What issues arose during Jackson's second term?

## Vocabulary
credit
panic

President Andrew Jackson became a stronger leader than ever during his second term. He exercised his veto power often and pushed for the relocation of Native Americans. His opponents complained that he behaved more like a king than a President. His great changes in economic policy seemed successful at first, but they later caused a financial collapse that carried his opponents to power.

## Native American Policy

During Jackson's presidency, many Native American peoples signed treaties giving up their lands in the East. Some groups resisted, but the government sent federal troops to move them west.

**Native Americans are forced to move west.** In 1825 President Monroe proposed that all Native American groups remaining in the East should move to lands west of the Mississippi. This policy gained wide support from white Americans, who wanted new lands east of the Mississippi opened for settlement. At that time, few people thought that white settlers would ever want to live on the western plains.

# AMERICAN HIGHLIGHTS

## PROFILE • Sequoya

A Cherokee Indian of mixed ancestry, Sequoya was a bold warrior in his youth. After an injury in a hunting accident, he worked as a silversmith and studied European and Indian languages.

Determined to preserve the Cherokee culture, Sequoya spent 12 years developing a way to write his native language. He used symbols from Greek, Hebrew, and English to represent the syllables of spoken Cherokee. In 1828 the Cherokee started their own newspaper, the *Cherokee Phoenix*.

Sequoya was named "president" of the tribe in honor of his invention of the Cherokee alphabet. He spent the rest of his life traveling, studying Indian speech. He died in Mexico in 1843.

The giant redwood trees of Sequoia National Park in California were named in his honor. A statue of Sequoya stands in the United States Capitol in Washington, D.C.

**Sequoya**

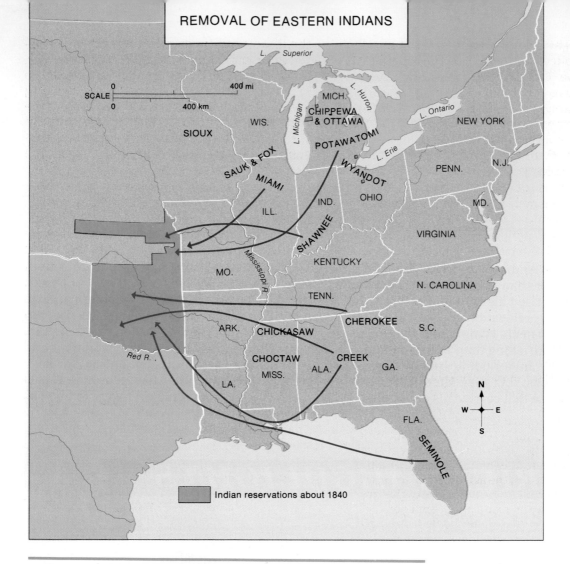

## REMOVAL OF EASTERN INDIANS

SCALE

0      400 mi

0      400 km

Indian reservations about 1840

## Map Study

**President Jackson supported the Indian Removal Act of 1830, forcing eastern Indians to move west of the Mississippi River. What were lands set aside for Indians called? What Native American groups were confined near their homelands east of the Mississippi River?**

When Jackson took office, he pushed for faster Indian removal. He thought that whites and Indians would be better off apart. In 1830 Congress passed the Indian Removal Act, authorizing Jackson to give Indians western lands in exchange for their lands in the East. During Jackson's presidency, 94 treaties providing for relocation were negotiated with Indian peoples.

**The Cherokee struggle to keep their homeland.** The Cherokee Indians adopted many of the ways of white society, founding their own schools, factories, and plantations. When the state of Georgia decided to take over their lands, the Cherokee appealed to the Supreme Court. In 1832 Chief Justice John Marshall ruled in favor of the Cherokee. He declared that the state of Georgia had no right to take Cherokee lands and that the Cherokee could not be forced to relocate. Under the Constitution, President Jackson should have obeyed the Supreme Court decision. Instead he chose to ignore it. "John Marshall has made his decision," Jackson said, "now let him enforce it."

Some Cherokee gave up and moved west, but most remained in Georgia. In 1838 federal troops rounded up the 15,000 remaining Cherokee and forced them to march west in the cold and rain of winter. Nearly one quarter of the people died during the harsh journey, which became known to the Cherokee as the **Trail of Tears.** A settler moving westward wrote the following account of what he saw:

On Tuesday evening we fell in with a detachment of the poor Cherokee Indians ... about eleven hundred Indians—sixty wagons—six hundred horses, and perhaps forty pairs of oxen. We found them in the forest camped for the night by the road side ... under a severe fall of rain accompanied by heavy wind. With their canvas for a shield from the ... weather, and the cold wet ground for a resting place, ... they spent the night.... Many of the aged Indians were suffering extremely from the fatigue of the journey, and the ill health consequent upon it ... Several were then quite ill, and one aged man we were informed was then in the last struggles of death....

One lady passed [with] her youngest child about three years old ... sick in her arms, and all she could do was to make it comfortable as circumstances would permit.... She could only carry her dying child in her arms a few miles farther, and then she must stop in a stranger-land and [give up] her much loved babe to the cold ground, and that too without pomp or ceremony, and pass on with the multitude....

**Some Native Americans resist relocation.** Not all Native Americans peacefully accepted the move west. The Sauk and Fox Indians of southern Wisconsin and northern Illinois were forced to move into the Iowa Territory. In 1832 a Sauk chief named Black Hawk tried to lead his people back to their original homes. The United States Army and the Illinois militia quickly crushed this uprising in a clash known as the Black Hawk War.

In 1835 the Seminole Indians refused to leave their lands in Florida. Led by a young chief named Osceola (ahs-ee-O-luh), the Seminoles fought a seven-year war against the United States Army. In 1842, after thousands of lives had been lost on both sides, the Seminoles moved west.

## The End of the Jacksonian Era

During Jackson's second term, new economic policies created prosperity. Still highly popular, Jackson supported Martin Van Buren in the next presidential election. The economy collapsed shortly after Van Buren took office, and Jackson's old opponents used public discontent to ride to power.

## Our Presidents

### MARTIN VAN BUREN

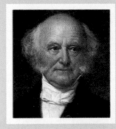

★ 1837–1841 ★

**8TH PRESIDENT**

**DEMOCRAT**

★ Born December 5, 1782, in New York

★ Married Hannah Hoes in 1807; 4 children

★ Lawyer; senator from New York; governor of New York; Secretary of State; Vice President under Jackson

★ Lived in New York when elected President

★ Vice President: Richard Johnson

★ Nicknamed "The Magician"

★ Died July 24, 1862, in New York

★ Key events while in office: Panic of 1837

# Our Presidents

## WILLIAM HENRY HARRISON

### ★ 1841 ★

### 9TH PRESIDENT

### WHIG

★ Born February 9, 1773, in Virginia

★ Married Anna Symmes in 1795; 10 children

★ Governor of Indiana Territory; defeated the Shawnee in Battle of Tippecanoe; general in War of 1812; representative and senator from Ohio

★ Lived in Ohio when elected President

★ Vice President: John Tyler

★ Died April 4, 1841, in Washington, D.C.

★ Nicknamed "Tippecanoe"

★ Served the shortest presidential term in American history; first President to die in office

**Jackson attacks the Second Bank of the United States.** Andrew Jackson never trusted the Bank of the United States, which was owned largely by eastern business leaders. He firmly believed that the officers of such a powerful bank could influence members of Congress. Jackson considered it undemocratic for a few wealthy people to have so much power. Like many westerners, he also believed that the bank's high interest rates made it difficult for the average person to borrow money. Jackson planned to get rid of the bank as soon as its charter ran out in 1836.

In 1832 Henry Clay and Daniel Webster convinced the bank president to apply to Congress for a new charter. This was the year that Jackson was running for reelection, and the two men hoped that the bank issue would damage his campaign. Congress approved a bill renewing the bank's charter. Sick in bed when he heard the news, Jackson was furious. "The Bank is trying to kill me," he declared, "but I will kill it." Jackson vetoed the bank bill, and soon after he was overwhelmingly reelected to a second term as President.

Jackson judged his reelection to mean that the American people wanted him to continue his war against the Bank of the United States. He made the decision to destroy the bank even before its charter had run out. He withdrew all government funds from the Bank of the United States. He then deposited the money in selected state banks, known as "pet banks" because people considered them to be favorites of the federal government. These pet banks began to offer people **credit** —money on loan—on easier terms, causing a wave of speculation and a sharp rise in property prices. Jackson pointed with pride to the prosperity he had been able to create for the country.

The Bank of the United States (B.U.S.), established in 1791, was rechartered in 1816. In 1832, when the B.U.S. sought its third charter, President Jackson moved to destroy it. He believed the bank favored eastern interests.

**Martin Van Buren becomes President.**
Jackson's highhanded actions alarmed many of his opponents, who thought he was taking more power than the Constitution allowed him. They called Jackson "King Andrew" and named themselves the Whig party, after the English political party that had opposed King George III. The Whigs ran three candidates in the 1836 presidential election, but they were defeated by the Democratic candidate, Martin Van Buren. Jackson had chosen Van Buren, his Vice President, to follow him as President.

At the time of Van Buren's election, the nation was still enjoying prosperity. This prosperity rested, however, on an unstable foundation. For years state banks had been printing more currency than they could back with gold or silver. Speculators had been using such currency to buy land. In 1836 Jackson signed the Specie Circular, an order providing that public lands could be paid for only in specie.

Soon after President Van Buren took office in 1837, a **panic** —an economic crisis— spread throughout the country. Worried by the Specie Circular, people were bringing their currency to the banks and demanding specie in exchange for it. Many banks were forced to close down because they ran out of gold and silver. Other banks refused to take back their currency. By fall almost 90 percent of the country's factories had shut down, causing many unemployed Americans to suffer desperately difficult times. This financial collapse came to be known as the **Panic of 1837.**

**The Whigs elect Harrison and Tyler.**
Many Americans blamed President Van Buren for the Panic of 1837. The Whigs made use of this shift in public opinion in the election of 1840. They chose William Henry Harrison of Ohio to run for President, and John Tyler of Virginia to run for Vice President. Harrison had commanded the army that defeated the Indians at Tippecanoe in 1811. He had also fought bravely in the War of 1812. The Whigs made the most of Harrison's military record and his nickname "Old Tippecanoe." They conducted a rousing campaign with noisy parades and stirring rallies,

## Our Presidents

### JOHN TYLER

★ 1841–1845 ★

**10**TH PRESIDENT

WHIG

★ Born March 29, 1790, in Virginia
★ Married Letitia Christian in 1813; 8 children
★ Married Julia Gardiner in 1844;
★ 7 children
★ Lawyer; governor of Virginia; representative and senator from Virginia; Vice President under Harrison
★ Lived in Virginia when elected Vice President
★ Vice President: none
★ Died January 18, 1862, in Virginia
★ First Vice President to become President upon the death of the President
★ Key events while in office: Webster-Ashburton Treaty; annexation of Texas; Florida became a state

using "Tippecanoe and Tyler too!" as their slogan.

Harrison was the first member of the Whig party to be elected President. An elderly man tired out by the exhausting campaign, he died of pneumonia only one month after taking the oath of office. Harrison was the first President to die in office. Vice President John Tyler took his place. Tyler had been nominated for Vice President chiefly to win electoral votes in the South. Tyler had been a popular Virginia governor and senator, as well as a member of the United States House of Representatives. As the President,

General William Henry Harrison's victory at the Battle of Tippecanoe is commemorated on this 1840 presidential campaign banner.

however, he failed to get along either with Whig party leaders or with Congress. Beginning with Tyler's term as the nation's President, sectional interests grew as the North and the South developed wide economic and social differences.

## SECTION REVIEW

1. **Vocabulary**   credit, panic
2. **People and Places**   Black Hawk, Osceola, Martin Van Buren, William Henry Harrison, John Tyler
3. **Comprehension**   What was the Indian Removal Act?
4. **Comprehension**   Why did President Jackson dislike the Bank of the United States?
5. **Critical Thinking**   How did Jackson's economic policies help cause the Panic of 1837?

# Chapter 12 Summary

The Era of Good Feelings began with the 1816 election of James Monroe. That year Henry Clay proposed a plan later called the American System. This economic program included plans for a national bank and a tariff law. Sectionalism increased with Missouri's application to the Union, but in 1820 the Missouri Compromise settled this quarrel over the spread of slavery.

In 1818 Andrew Jackson invaded East Florida, and the following year Spain sold Florida to the United States in the Adams-Onís Treaty of 1819. President Monroe issued the Monroe Doctrine in 1823, warning Europe not to interfere in the Americas.

In 1824 John Quincy Adams beat Andrew Jackson in a close race for the presidency. In 1828, however, Jackson became President and made use of the spoils system to reward his supporters. In a quarrel over

the tariffs of 1828 and 1832, South Carolina threatened to nullify the tariff laws and to secede from the Union if necessary. Henry Clay worked out a compromise tariff, however, in 1833.

Congress passed the Indian Removal Act in 1830, authorizing Jackson to force Native Americans to accept western lands in return for their lands in the East. Jackson attacked the Bank of the United States, withdrawing its government funds and depositing the money in state banks. This policy brought quick prosperity and easy credit to the country, but during the presidency of Martin Van Buren it caused a financial collapse known as the Panic of 1837. In 1840 the Whig candidate William Henry Harrison was elected President. Harrison died after only one month in office, and Vice President John Tyler then became President.

# CRITICAL THINKING: Developing an Essay

An **essay** is a short composition on a single subject, usually giving the writer's personal view of that subject. An essay consists of three parts: the **introduction,** the **body,** and the **conclusion.** Each part is made up of one or more paragraphs. Study the diagram at the bottom of this page as you read the following guidelines.

An essay begins with an introduction. The introduction has two purposes. First, it should interest people in reading the whole essay. Second, it should state the general subject of the essay and the author's particular view or opinion on the subject. The rest of the essay is developed to support this viewpoint or opinion.

The body of the essay consists of one or more development paragraphs. These paragraphs present arguments and evidence— facts and examples—that support the specific point or opinion in the introduction. For example, suppose a nationalist in the 1820's were writing an essay in support of a new bank of the United States. One argument for the bank might be that it would print a standard currency and restore public trust in the money supply.

Another way to support an opinion is to present an opposing viewpoint and then use evidence to disprove it. Using the same essay about the bank, here is an example:

Opponents of the new bank say that it will only help the manufacturing states of the Northeast. Nothing could be further from the truth. The new bank will make loans to businesses and state banks. This can only encourage the growth of all our sections.

Remember that each paragraph in an essay should be linked to the next paragraph by a **transition.** A transition is a sentence that relates one idea to the next. An essay should end with a conclusion that restates and supports the writer's opinion.

Now write your own essay. Choose between these subjects: *Henry Clay's American System; the Monroe Doctrine;* or *Andrew Jackson and the Tariff of 1832.* When you have enough information to begin writing, organize it into an outline. Then write your essay using the guidelines. When you have finished, edit your essay. Finally, check for grammar and spelling errors.

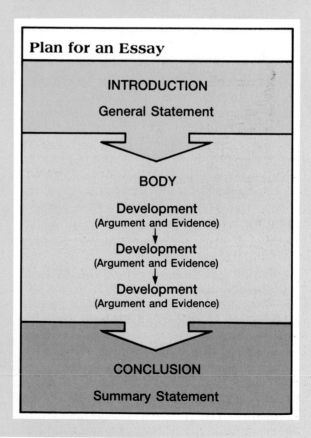

**Plan for an Essay**

**INTRODUCTION**

**General Statement**

**BODY**

**Development**
(Argument and Evidence)

**Development**
(Argument and Evidence)

**Development**
(Argument and Evidence)

**CONCLUSION**

**Summary Statement**

# Chapter 12 REVIEW

## Vocabulary and Key Terms

Match each of the following terms with its correct definition. Write your answers on a separate sheet of paper.

credit
panic
Whig party
American System
Missouri Compromise

spoils system
sectionalism
Democratic party
Monroe Doctrine
secede

1. the political party of President William Henry Harrison
2. the practice of giving government jobs to political supporters
3. loyalty to local or regional interests
4. money on loan
5. an economic crisis
6. an economic plan proposed by Henry Clay
7. an 1820 law concerned with the spread of slavery
8. to withdraw from the Union
9. a warning to Europe against interfering in the Americas
10. the political party of President Andrew Jackson

## Recalling the Facts

1. What was the Era of Good Feelings?
2. What were the three major parts of Henry Clay's American System?
3. What were the terms of the Missouri Compromise?
4. How did the United States get Florida?
5. What roles did Simón Bolívar and José de San Martín play in winning Latin American independence?
6. Why did President Monroe issue the Monroe Doctrine?
7. Why were southern states against a high tariff?
8. What was the theory of states' rights?
9. What was the Trail of Tears?

## Places to Locate

Match the letters on the map with the places listed below. Write your answers on a separate sheet of paper.

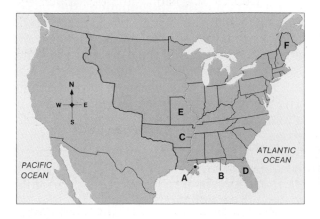

1. Missouri
2. Mississippi River
3. New Orleans
4. East Florida
5. West Florida
6. Maine

## Critical Thinking

1. Why did the dispute over slavery grow as new states and territories joined the Union in the early 1800's? Consider these points in your answer:
   a. the balance of power in Congress between North and South
   b. the importance of compromise
2. Would each of the following people probably want new United States territories to be slave or free? Explain.
   a. a Mississippi cotton planter
   b. a representative from Missouri
   c. a northern business leader
3. What do you think the United States had to gain from the Monroe Doctrine?
4. President Jackson took strong stands on issues. Did this make him a good President? Consider his stand on these issues in your answer:
   a. the spoils system     c. nullification
   b. Indian relocation

## Understanding History

1. Reread the section "The Bank of the United States strengthens federal power" on page 286. Then answer these questions.
   a. **Economics.** Why did some people believe that a new national bank was necessary?
   b. **Economics.** How did the Supreme Court's decision in *McCulloch* v. *Maryland* strengthen the federal government?
2. Reread the excerpt from the Monroe Doctrine on page 290. Then answer these questions.
   a. **Primary Sources.** What does President Monroe say about further colonization of the American continents?
   b. **Primary Sources.** According to President Monroe, why is the political system of the European nations dangerous to the United States?
3. Reread the section "The Cherokee struggle to keep their homeland" on page 296. Then answer these questions.
   a. **Culture.** In what ways did the Cherokee adopt the lifestyles of white Americans?
   b. **Primary Sources.** What conditions did the Cherokee face along the Trail of Tears?

## Projects and Activities

1. **Writing a Report.** Write a brief report showing the importance of compromise in settling difficult issues. Be prepared to present your report to the class.
2. **Summarizing Information.** Write five newspaper headlines about how the United States gained Florida. Include military concerns and diplomatic issues.
3. **Analyzing an Issue.** Imagine that you are a reporter covering the nullification crisis of 1832. Write a brief article analyzing the issue and explaining its background. End your article with a report on South Carolina's plan to secede from the Union. Use reference materials to find information for your report.

4. **Staging a News Conference.** Take the position of President Monroe about to sign the Monroe Doctrine. Hold a news conference in class to announce the reasons for the policy. Be prepared to answer questions from the class.
5. **Expressing Point of View.** Imagine that you are an Indian on the Trail of Tears. Express your feelings in a diary entry.

## Practicing Your Skill

Read the incomplete essay below. Then complete the items that follow.

> Andrew Jackson's military record helped him become President.
>
> Jackson brought a new political style to office.
>
> As President, Jackson took strong stands on issues.

1. The essay includes three topic sentences. In which paragraph would the following topics best fit?
   a. inauguration of 1828
   b. War of 1812
   c. spoils system
   d. Second Bank of the United States
   e. gaining Florida
2. Write a title for the essay.
3. Complete the essay.

# CHAPTER 13

# The Northeast Becomes the Center of Commerce
## 1815–1846

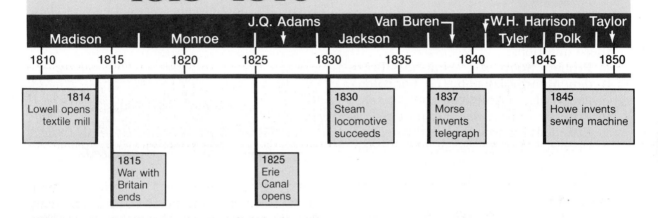

| Madison | | Monroe | | J.Q. Adams ↓ | Jackson | Van Buren ↓ | W.H. Harrison ↓ Tyler | Polk | Taylor ↓ |

| 1810 | 1815 | 1820 | 1825 | 1830 | 1835 | 1840 | 1845 | 1850 |

**1814**
Lowell opens textile mill

**1815**
War with Britain ends

**1825**
Erie Canal opens

**1830**
Steam locomotive succeeds

**1837**
Morse invents telegraph

**1845**
Howe invents sewing machine

Smoke from the factories in Bridgewater, Massachusetts, was a daily reminder that the Northeast was a center of manufacturing and trade.

## Preparing to Read

Inventions of the early 1800's began to quicken the pace of American life. Northeasterners built factories using machines for the production of goods. British and American inventors discovered faster methods of transportation, and soon manufactured goods could be shipped easily from the Northeast to the West. Westerners sent farm products back to the Northeast, where merchant ships could carry them to foreign markets. As you read this chapter, try to answer the following questions:

1. Why did trade and manufacturing grow in the Northeast?
2. How did machines change ways of living in the Northeast?
3. How did changes in travel and communication help the nation grow?

 # 1 Why did trade and manufacturing grow in the Northeast?

Cut off from British markets after the Revolutionary War, Northeastern merchants had to find markets for American goods. Northeastern business leaders began to manufacture goods by machine, as British inventions found their way into the United States. The Northeast became the trade and manufacturing center of the United States.

### The Growth of Commerce

In the 1800's, American merchants sought markets in such places as Asia and California. Shipping prospered, and Americans built some of the fastest ships afloat.

**American trade slows after the Revolution.** The brisk sea trade of colonial days declined in the years following the Revolution. The British Navy had destroyed or captured many American ships. A number of sailors had lost their lives, and others had given up seafaring to join the pioneers going west. Even after the Revolutionary War, Britain barred American ships from many British empire ports. This was a blow to New England merchants, who had made large profits in markets such as the West Indies.

**Americans begin to trade with China.** Searching for markets, American merchants turned to China and other Asian nations. A ship, the *Empress of China*, sailed from New York to China in 1784, returning a year later with tea and silks. Another ship, the *Grand Turk*, soon left Salem for the Orient.*

At first American merchants did not know what cargoes would bring the highest profits in Asian ports. In 1793, however, Captain Robert Gray sailed his ship *Columbia* from Boston to China. He went by way of the Oregon coast, where he bought a cargo of furs from the Indians. When he reached China, he found that these furs were highly prized by the Chinese. Gray returned to New England by sailing around Africa and across the Atlantic. He was the first American sea captain to sail around the world.

---

\* The term *Orient* was used to refer to the countries and islands of East Asia.

# AMERICAN HIGHLIGHTS

## ECONOMICS • The China Trade

As the early New England traders carried cargoes to China, they had to consider Chinese tastes. The Chinese, proud of their own culture, had little interest in American foods and textiles. The first ships that sailed to China carried ginseng, a root that the Chinese valued as a medicine. After the price of ginseng began to fall, American traders switched to selling the fox, raccoon, and otter furs they carried from the Pacific coast. These soft, rich furs appealed to Chinese buyers who liked delicacy and luxury.

On their return journey, the American merchants often carried ivory and silk. Once considered luxuries that Americans could do without, these items soon became popular in the United States. Americans were also eager to buy Chinese porcelain. Skillful Chinese artists made tea sets, vases, and tableware in traditional Chinese patterns or in patterns that appealed to American tastes.

**A chinaware vase**

After Gray's return, other American ships bound for China began to make stops on the west coast of North America. The Indians traded furs in exchange for knives, needles, kettles, and other manufactured articles. The traders then sailed to China, where they exchanged the furs for tea, silk, china, and other luxury goods.

**Merchants trade with California.** In the early 1800's, California was still under Spanish rule. Americans first came to the California coast to hunt fur-bearing sea otters. American ships docked in California's harbors for repairs and supplies, even though Spain had barred foreign ships from trading in California. After Mexico won independence from Spain in 1821, the ports of California opened to all ships. American merchants began a busy trade in cattle hides with the Mexican ranchers of California.

Richard Henry Dana, a young Bostonian, worked for two years on a ship that traded in California. He later wrote a book, *Two Years Before the Mast,* about his voyage. In it he described goods that were traded for hides in ports such as San Francisco:

Our cargo was an assorted one; that is, it consisted of everything under the sun. We had spirits of all kinds (sold by the cask), teas, coffee, sugar, spices, raisins, molasses, hardware, crockery-ware, tin-ware, cutlery, clothing of all kinds, boots and shoes, . . . calicoes and cottons, . . . silks; also shawls, scarfs, necklaces, jewelry, and combs for the women; furniture; and, in fact, everything that can be imagined. . . .

A keen observer, Dana realized that the tiny settlement of San Francisco would one day be a great city. After leaving, he wrote:

If California ever becomes a prosperous country, this bay will be the center of its prosperity. The abundance of wood and water; the extreme fertility of its shores; the excellence of its climate, which is as near to being perfect as any in the world; and its facilities for navigation, affording the best anchoring-grounds in the whole western coast of America—all fit it for a place of great importance.

**Whaling brings good profits.** While American merchant vessels were trading in foreign ports, fleets of New England whaling ships were chasing whales in all the oceans of the world. Whalers sailed from ports such as Nantucket and New Bedford, Massachusetts, on voyages that lasted as long as two or three years. They brought back whale oil, which was in great demand for lamps, candles, and cosmetics.

Whaling became more profitable as sailors learned to identify the best whaling grounds. They also developed better tools for capturing the whales. A Massachusetts blacksmith, Lewis Temple, invented a toggle harpoon, which would not slip out once it had pierced the whale's flesh. As a result, sailors began to capture more of the whales that they harpooned.

**The prosperity of the Northeast depends on trade.** The far-flung voyages of American merchant ships, fishing vessels, and whalers made shipping in the Northeast even more important than it had been before the Revolution. Shipping centers such as New York, Boston, and Salem hummed with activity. Harbor warehouses stored merchandise imported from all over the world.

The Northeast had suffered hard times during the War of 1812 because American merchant vessels were kept off the high seas. As trade came to an end, warehouses overflowed with goods, sailors lost their jobs, and ships rotted in the ports. A traveler reported that the streets along the New York waterfront were deserted and that grass had begun to grow on the wharves.

Once the War of 1812 was over, however, people of the Northeast turned again to the sea to seek their fortunes. Yankee ships and sailors soon were to be found on all the seas and in many distant ports. **Packet ships** — ships carrying passengers and freight at

## ★ ★ ★ *Whaling*

During the early 1800's, New England whaling ships sailed the oceans of the world. When a whale was sighted, sailors lowered small boats into the water and rowed after it. They had to be within a few yards of the whale to harpoon it. The whales often escaped.

By 1900 whalers were using harpoon guns and motorized whaling boats. More whales were killed from 1900 to 1940 than had been taken in the previous 400 years. Whaling countries formed a council to control the number of whales taken, but the council was not effective.

By the 1960's, many species of whales were in danger of disappearing. Alarmed scientists protested, and in 1971 the United States banned whaling and whale products.

fixed dates—began sailing between American and European ports.

**Clipper ships set speed records.** In the 1840's, New England shipbuilders began building **clipper ships** —sailing vessels especially designed for speed. These ships carried great towering sails and covered long distances at record speed. Often used in the China trade, the clipper ships became the pride of America.

The most famous clippers were designed by Donald McKay of Boston. His *Flying Cloud* made a voyage from New York around Cape Horn to San Francisco in 89 days. Sailing before a strong wind, the ship could cover 375 miles (634 kilometers) in a day.

The heyday of the clipper ships lasted only a few years. By the early 1850's, the British began using iron steamboats. At first, American sailors scorned the ugly steam-powered vessels. Before the end of the decade, however, Americans also began building steamboats. The graceful clipper ships gave way to these new rulers of the sea.

America's fast new ships—with tall masts and narrow hulls—were called *clipper ships* for the way they "clipped off" the miles. The clipper *Hurricane,* shown here with sails fully set, carried tea between China and the United States in the mid-1800's.

## The Growth of Manufacturing

In the late 1700's, English inventors developed machines for the quick production of goods. This sudden and dramatic change in the methods of production was known as the **Industrial Revolution.** It soon spread to the United States, as Americans copied and improved the English machines.

**English inventors lead the way for the Industrial Revolution.** The Industrial Revolution began with new machines for spinning thread and weaving cloth. Before the mid-1700's, most homes had both a spinning wheel for making thread and a hand loom for weaving cloth. A spinner using a spinning wheel could produce only one thread at a time. In the 1760's, the English inventor

James Hargreaves built a spinning jenny. It could spin eight threads instead of one. With later improvements, it could spin 80 threads at a time.

A few years later another English inventor, Edmund Cartwright, built a loom run by water power. The power loom worked faster and produced wider cloth than the old hand loom. In time, steam as well as water power was used to drive the loom.

**The first factories are started.** By the late 1700's, many people had stopped weaving cloth by hand in their homes. It was easier for them to buy cloth made by machine. The first factory for spinning thread and weaving cloth was set up by the English inventor Richard Arkwright. He installed several spinning jennies and looms in one big building—a factory. He then hired workers to run the machines. It was a profitable business, and soon other factories sprang up across Britain. They were often built near streams to take advantage of water power. Because they manufactured **textiles** — woven fabrics—they were known as textile factories.

**Samuel Slater starts the first American textile factory.** English manufacturers did not want foreign competitors to begin making cloth by machine. For this reason, the British government forbade the sale of textile machines to other countries. It even passed a law forbidding textile workers to leave the country.

In 1789 an English textile worker, Samuel Slater, managed to slip out of the country and travel to the United States. Only 21 years old, Slater was already a skilled mechanic. He built textile machines from memory and even improved them. In Pawtucket, Rhode Island, he opened a textile factory known as Slater's Mill in 1790.

**The Industrial Revolution takes hold in America.** The Industrial Revolution started slowly in the United States. At first few Americans had the large amounts of money needed to buy machines and build factories. The United States continued to import manufactured goods from Europe in exchange for food and raw materials. During the War of 1812, however, the United States was cut off from British goods. Americans then began to manufacture the articles they needed. No longer spending money on shipping, they could afford to build new factories.

In 1814 Francis Lowell opened a textile factory in Waltham, Massachusetts. This was the first American factory in which all the steps involved in turning raw cotton into finished cloth were carried on under one roof. Soon American textile factories were producing not only cotton cloth but woolen and linen fabrics. Other factories began to produce goods made from cloth, felt, leather, and iron. James Forten, a black inventor, started a Philadelphia factory for the production of sails.

**New England and the Middle Atlantic states take the lead in manufacturing.** Most textile mills and other early American factories were located in New England. There were three advantages to building factories in this region. First, New England had swift-running streams to supply water power.

Samuel Slater started the first American textile mill in Pawtucket, Rhode Island. Textile mills quickly spread throughout New England. What natural resource did Slater use to power his mill?

James Forten began his career as a sailmaker and became the wealthy owner of a Philadelphia sail factory. Forten was also a leading speaker for the rights of black Americans in the early 1800's.

Next, New England had a large labor force available. The soil was stony and poor, and farmers were willing to leave their farms to work in the factories. Finally, New England was already a center of shipping. Its ships could carry products to ports along the Atlantic coast and to other countries.

The Middle Atlantic states—New York, Pennsylvania, and New Jersey—had rich deposits of iron ore. People in these states built factories to produce such iron goods as guns, stoves, axes, and wagon-wheel rims.

**Americans develop new machines and processes.** Industry in the Northeast would not have grown rapidly if Americans had only copied English machines. Instead, American inventors improved many machines. They also introduced more efficient methods of production.

The sewing machine was a key American invention. For years, inventors had tried to provide the textile industry with a machine for sewing cloth. In 1845 a New England farmer, Elias Howe, developed a sewing machine run by a hand-turned wheel. Howe's invention was later improved and marketed by an inventor, Isaac Singer. The sewing machine made it possible to produce garments faster and to sell them at lower prices.

Another significant development in the American manufacturing industry was the use of **standardized parts** —parts made to be exactly the same so they could be interchanged. Eli Whitney, a New Englander, invented standardized parts. In 1798 Whitney signed a contract to produce 10,000 guns for the United States Army within a two-year period. Such a task would have been impossible in earlier times, when every gun was fashioned from start to finish by a single skilled worker. Under that system, the parts varied from one gun to another.

With standardized parts, all triggers or gun barrels manufactured for a certain model of gun would be exactly the same. Because the parts were identical, new guns could be put together more quickly, and damaged guns could be easily repaired. The use of standardized parts was essential to the growth of the factory system.

## SECTION REVIEW

1. **Vocabulary**   packet ship, clipper ship, textile, standardized parts
2. **People and Places**   Robert Gray, China, California, Richard Henry Dana, San Francisco, Donald McKay, Samuel Slater, Francis Lowell, James Forten, Elias Howe, Isaac Singer, Eli Whitney
3. **Comprehension**   What new markets did American merchant ships find after the Revolutionary War?
4. **Comprehension**   Why did New England become the center of manufacturing in the United States?
5. **Critical Thinking**   Was the Industrial Revolution really a "revolution"? Why or why not?

### Vocabulary

labor union
union dues

The Industrial Revolution changed the lives of Northeastern workers. Business leaders built factories to produce textiles and other goods, and farming lost importance. Many factory towns grew into cities, as people moved to be close to work.

## The Lives of Factory Workers

The early factories of the Northeast drew many young women and other workers away from farms and into manufacturing jobs. At first, working conditions were fairly good, but after a few decades conditions worsened. Some workers organized groups to press for shorter hours and higher pay.

**Early New England factories hire many women.** When textile mills first opened in New England, the owners made a great effort to get people to leave their farms or trades to become factory workers. Some factories hired whole families and provided houses for them. Francis Lowell set up dormitories for the young women mill workers. Other owners also tried to make factory life pleasant for their workers.

Factory owners preferred to hire women. Women worked just as hard as men, but were paid only half as much. A young New Hampshire woman wrote the following letter home, describing her experience working in a textile mill in Lowell, Massachusetts:

At first the hours seemed very long, but I was so interested in learning that I endured it very well. When I went out at night, the sounds of the mill were in my ears—all mingled together in strange discord. It makes my feet ache and swell to stand so much, but I suppose I shall get accustomed to that too. The right hand, which is used in stopping and starting the loom, becomes larger than the left, but in other respects the factory is not detrimental [harmful] to a young girl's appearance.

These mills are not such dreadful places as you imagine them to be. You think them dark damp holes. They are no such thing. They are spacious, well-built edifices, with neat paths around them and beautiful plots of greenery and flowers. Inside, the rooms are high, very light, kept nicely white-washed, and extremely neat, with many plants in the window seats. The machinery is very handsomely made and painted, and is placed in regular rows, presenting a beautiful and uniform appearance.

**The factory system changes the lives of American workers.** Before the Industrial Revolution, most American workers had great freedom in their jobs. A woman cultivating a small farm could keep the profits of the crops it produced. A man who made carriage wheels by hand could take pride in the careful work he had accomplished.

When they went to work in factories, workers no longer gained profits from the goods that they made. They also felt less pride in their work, because the goods they produced were all alike. The only stake the workers had in the factory was the labor they had to sell. In short, if factory workers wanted to keep their jobs, they had to accept the hours and the wages set by the employer. As time went on, factory owners became less interested in the living and working conditions of the factory hands.

**Working conditions become worse.** By the 1830's and 1840's, more factories had been built in America, and the competition between them had increased. To gain an edge, owners kept work hours long and wages low. Factory hands often worked

Edwin Billings of Massachusetts painted this scene of his family's wagon shop in the 1800's. The shopworkers were skilled artisans, shown here making a wagon wheel by hand. How is Billings's shop different from a factory?

from 12 to 15 hours a day. Men were paid about $5 a week, women about $2 dollars for the same work, and children only $1 a week.

The Panic of 1837 caused some businesses to close and made jobs more scarce. (See Chapter 12.) At the same time, immigrants were pouring into the United States from Europe. With plenty of people to choose from, factory owners could make great demands on workers. If one worker left, another could always be found.

**Early labor unions try to improve conditions.** To improve conditions, Americans began to form **labor unions** —groups of workers who join together to protect their rights and interests. The first unions were formed in the 1830's and 1840's. Most were only for members of one skilled craft, such as bricklaying or carpentry. A few unions included factory workers. Led by Sarah Bagley, the textile workers in Lowell, Massachusetts, formed the Female Labor

Reform Association. It was the first American women's group to work for improved labor conditions. There was also a nationwide union, the National Trades Union.

The goal of the unions was shorter hours and higher wages. They also demanded free education for workers' children. Many of these early unions failed during the Panic of 1837, when workers could not afford to pay **union dues** —union membership fees. Other unions lasted through the 1840's, but achieved few reforms. At that time, many Americans felt the plan to make the workday only 10 hours was an outrageous demand. Not until after the Civil War were lasting labor unions formed.

## The Rise of Cities

The number of large cities in the United States increased as factories spread. In the mid-1800's, immigrants from Ireland and elsewhere in Europe settled in the growing cities. City life was inconvenient by modern standards, but city dwellers had many comforts that people on farms and in villages did not have.

**The factory system leads to the growth of cities.** As more factories were built, larger numbers of people left the countryside and moved to factory towns. Such towns were often located along canals or railroad lines, and they became centers for trading and transportation. As the towns grew, business leaders built new stores, banks, and warehouses. Many small factory towns quickly became busy industrial cities.

During the Revolutionary War, there were only 5 towns of more than 8,000 people in the United States. In 1840 there were 44 towns of more than 8,000, and by 1860, there were 141. Most of the large cities, such as New York, Philadelphia, and Boston, were in the Northeast. New cities were also springing up in the West. By 1860, Cincinnati, St. Louis, and Chicago ranked among the 10 largest American cities. In spite of this fast growth, the majority of Americans still lived on farms or in small villages.

**Immigrants help to swell the population of cities.** After 1820 a rising number of immigrants settled in the cities and factory towns of the Northeast. Irish farmers driven from their homes by British landlords formed the first large group of immigrants. This flow of Irish immigrants increased greatly in the 1840's, when disease destroyed Ireland's potato crop. One million Irish people starved and more than one million others left the country. Those who came to the United States took jobs wherever they could find them. They often worked in factories and on canals and railroads.

Other European immigrants also came to the United States during the 1840's. To escape from the unsettled or unhappy conditions at home, many Europeans fled their countries for the United States. Like the Irish, they settled in large cities, where they could find jobs and keep in touch with others who had come from their native lands.

**Immigrants face prejudice.** The immigrants made many important contributions to American life. Skilled workers brought knowledge of their trades. Others brought food, music, and customs that enriched American life. For example, the custom of the Christmas tree came from German immigrants. In spite of these contributions, many Americans were alarmed by the flood of immigrants. Native-born Protestants were suspicious of Irish and German Catholics. Some people feared having to compete with immigrants for jobs.

## Graph Study

The population of the United States more than tripled between 1820 and 1860. By how much did the population increase between 1820 and 1860?

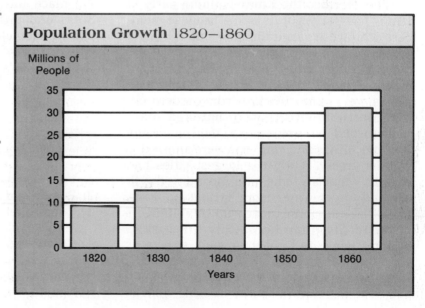

**Population Growth** 1820–1860

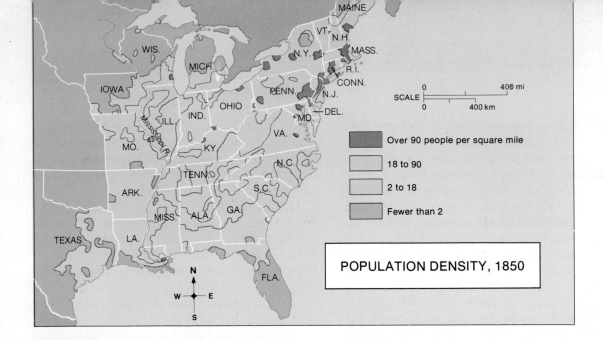

POPULATION DENSITY, 1850

SCALE

0 — 400 mi
0 — 400 km

Over 90 people per square mile

18 to 90

2 to 18

Fewer than 2

## Map Study

Workers in the 1800's crowded into areas where the nation's new factories were located. As a result, these areas increased in population density—the average number of people in a given area. In what section of the country were the most thickly settled areas located? What was the number of people per square mile in these areas?

Americans who opposed immigrants were called **Nativists,** because they wanted the country to be for native born citizens. Nativists formed the **Know-Nothing party** in 1846. The party got its name because members who were asked about it said, "I know nothing." The party died in 1856.

**American cities are in the midst of change.** The growing cities of the mid-1800's were very different from modern cities. Most city streets were unpaved roads that turned to ankle-deep mud in rainy weather. Hogs and chickens were allowed to wander freely. Only the largest cities had regular water systems, and most city dwellers had to get water from springs or wells. Rival fire companies made up of volunteers provided fire protection. Only a few cities had gas lamps to light their main streets.

American city life also had advantages. City dwellers had more conveniences than people living on farms or in villages. Instead of candles, city dwellers used oil-burning lamps. Instead of fireplaces, stoves were used for cooking and heating. Tinware took the place of heavy iron and copper pans. Sofas and armchairs replaced the benches and wooden chairs of country homes. These comforts drew many people to the cities. By the mid-1800's the cities were centers of population as well as trade.

## SECTION REVIEW

1. **Vocabulary**   labor union, union dues
2. **People and Places**   Lowell, Sarah Bagley
3. **Comprehension**   Why did many early textile mills hire women?
4. **Comprehension**   What caused a wave of immigration in the 1840's?
5. **Critical Thinking**   How useful were the early labor unions?  Explain.

## CRITICAL THINKING: Determining Relevance

Suppose you were writing a report on how machines changed the working lives of Americans. You would probably find a huge amount of information on that subject, but not all of it would be **relevant**—applicable or to the point. Relevant information is essential to your understanding of your particular subject. Non-relevant information may be interesting, but it does not advance your understanding of the subject.

Determining what is relevant and what is non-relevant is very important to the study of history. It helps you make decisions about what kinds of evidence are likely to support a historical statement or theory. Also, when preparing for a test, determining relevance helps you decide what material you should review.

Keeping in mind your task—to determine how machines changed the working lives of Americans—read the following sentences about the sewing machine. Be sure to look for information that is relevant to your subject.

---

Elias Howe, who invented the sewing machine, was born in Scotland. The sewing machine created opportunities for women to earn wages.

---

The first sentence tells you where the inventor of the sewing machine, Elias Howe, was born. This information may be somewhat interesting, but it does not add anything to your understanding of how machines changed the working lives of Americans. The last sentence, however, does contain certain relevant information. It points out that the sewing machine provided opportunities for many women to earn wages. This information is essential to understanding the effect machines had on changing the working lives of many Americans during the first part of the nineteenth century.

Now make a decision about whether each of the following statements is relevant or non-relevant to your understanding of how machines changed the working lives of Americans. Then on a separate sheet of paper, write an **R** if you think the statement is relevant. If you think the statement is non-relevant, write an **N**.

1. Samuel Slater kept the plans of English textile machines in his head when he left the country.
2. Samuel Slater was an English textile worker who opened Slater's Mill in Pawtucket, Rhode Island.
3. The British government passed a law forbidding all textile workers to leave the country.
4. Before Eli Whitney developed standardized parts, each handmade gun, for example, was different from every other gun.
5. Water power, and later steam power, was used to drive the new machines.
6. Some factories employed children or families with children.
7. Although factory workers worked as long as 12 to 15 hours a day, their pay was quite low.
8. Some factory workers organized groups for the purpose of pressing for shorter hours and higher pay.
9. Before the widespread use of machines, many people worked in their homes or in small workshops.
10. Because they were all alike, the goods produced in factories did not fill the workers with as much pride as the goods they had made by hand.

# How did changes in travel and communication help the nation grow?

## Vocabulary

turnpike
toll
Morse code

In the 1800's, canals and surfaced roads improved American transportation. Steamboats and steam railroads made trade and travel even faster. With the invention of the telegraph, businesses could send instant messages that kept up with the busy pace of American life.

## New Roads and Canals

As trade between the West and the Northeast grew, Americans looked for ways to transport goods more quickly. The national government joined private companies in building and maintaining surfaced roads. Americans also built canals linking important rivers and lakes.

**Poor roads hamper American travelers.** In 1800 there were few paved roads in the United States. Most roads were little more than paths cleared of trees and brush. They were dusty in the summer and muddy in rainy weather, with deep holes in which carriage wheels could easily break. The American historian Henry Adams wrote the following account of overland travel of the time:

> Even the lightly equipped traveller found a short journey no slight effort. Between Boston and New York was a tolerable highway, along which thrice a week, light stagecoaches carried passengers and the mail, in three days. From New York a stage-coach started every week-day for Philadelphia, consuming the greater part of two days in the journey.... South of Philadelphia the

road was tolerable as far as Baltimore, but between Baltimore and the new city of Washington it meandered through forests; the driver chose the track which seemed least dangerous, and rejoiced if in wet seasons he reached Washington without miring or upsetting his wagon. In the Northern States, four miles an hour was the average speed for any coach....

**The National Road links East and West.** The flow of settlers westward across the Appalachian Mountains drew attention to the need for better overland transportation. In 1811 the United States government began building the **National Road.** The first section of this road ran from Cumberland, Maryland, to the eastern border of Ohio. (See map on page 317.) New sections were later added, until the road reached Vandalia, Illinois. The National Road became the main overland route to the West. It was paved with crushed rock, which made travel faster. Wagons, coaches, riders on horseback, packhorses, and people on foot journeyed westward over the new road.

**Private companies build turnpikes.** Many Americans wanted the states as well as the national government to build improved roads. The state governments, however, had little money to spare. Soon private companies began building roads for profit. These turnpikes —roads that travelers must pay to use—were most common in the East. The owners of turnpikes collected a toll —tax— at toll gates along the road to help pay the costs of building and repair.

Because paving was expensive, companies often surfaced turnpikes with planks of wood. Wet weather rotted the wood, making turnpikes dangerous when not in good repair. The turnpikes were still a big improvement over old colonial roads. In 1790 there had not been a single important stretch of hard-surfaced road in the entire nation. By

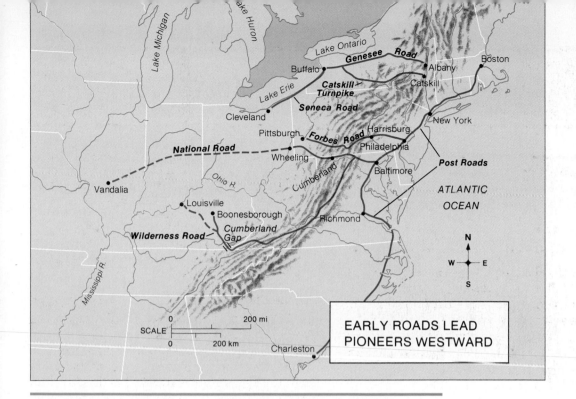

EARLY ROADS LEAD
PIONEERS WESTWARD

## Map Study

During the early 1800's, newly built surfaced roads encouraged settlers to move west. The new roads also provided trading links between the West and cities in the East. What road connected Baltimore, Maryland, and Vandalia, Illinois? About how many miles long was the Seneca Road? About how many kilometers?

1860 there were more than 88,000 miles (141,000 kilometers) of surfaced roads in the United States.

**Canals provide cheap water routes.** Western farmers and Northeastern manufacturers needed a means of transportation that was cheaper than the turnpikes. For this reason, Americans in the 1800's began to build canals between important rivers and lakes. The canals provided a link between Atlantic port cities and waterways far inland. They were especially useful for transporting heavy cargoes, which could be moved more easily by water than by land. Barges were towed by horses or mules driven along a path on the canal bank. So many canals were built from 1825 to 1850 that this period has been called the **Canal Era.**

**The Erie Canal increases trade.** When the National Road brought additional trade to Baltimore, New Yorkers began to fear that Baltimore would become the leading Atlantic port. Under the leadership of Governor DeWitt Clinton, the New York legislature proposed to build a canal from Albany to Buffalo. The new canal would connect the Hudson River with the Great Lakes. In this way, the Erie Canal would make possible the first all-water route from New York City to the Great Lakes. The Erie Canal was completed in 1825, after eight years of hard work.

The Erie Canal soon became the most important route between the West and the Atlantic seaboard. Before the canal, the cost of moving goods between Buffalo and New York City was about $100 a ton. The canal reduced the cost to $10 a ton. Goods were also moved three times as fast. New York City, the largest city in the United States, grew more rapidly due to the canal trade.

317

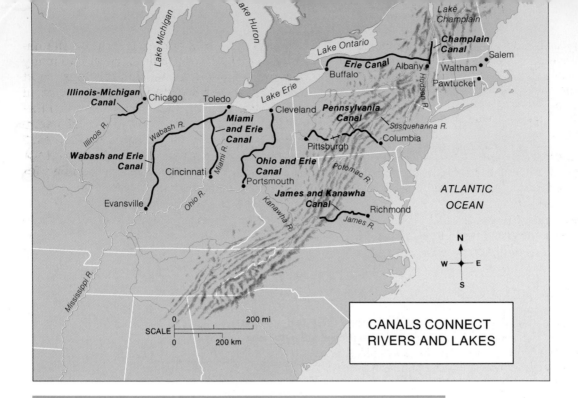

Map showing canals connecting rivers and lakes. Labels include: Lake Michigan, Lake Huron, Lake Ontario, Lake Erie, Lake Champlain, Champlain Canal, Erie Canal, Albany, Salem, Waltham, Pawtucket, Buffalo, Illinois-Michigan Canal, Chicago, Toledo, Cleveland, Pennsylvania Canal, Susquehanna R., Columbia, Miami and Erie Canal, Pittsburgh, Wabash R., Illinois R., Wabash and Erie Canal, Cincinnati, Miami R., Ohio and Erie Canal, Portsmouth, Potomac R., James and Kanawha Canal, Richmond, Ohio R., Kanawha R., James R., Evansville, Mississippi R., ATLANTIC OCEAN. Scale: 0–200 mi, 0–200 km.

CANALS CONNECT RIVERS AND LAKES

## Map Study

**Between the 1820's and the 1850's canals were built linking major waterways. How many canals linked the Great Lakes with the Ohio River? Which canal linked the Great Lakes with the Hudson River?**

## Steam Transportation

The steam engine revolutionized trade and travel in the United States. The Scottish inventor James Watt built the first practical steam engine in 1769. Factory owners began to use steam engines to run machines. By the early 1800's, inventors had built steamboats and steam locomotives.

**Americans build steamboats.** In 1787, John Fitch, a Philadelphia metalworker, launched a crude steam-driven vessel on the Delaware River. The next year he built a second steamboat, which he operated in a passenger service between Philadelphia and Burlington, New Jersey. Few people rode the boat, however, and Fitch went out of business. People thought the steamboat was a crazy and dangerous invention.

Robert Fulton built the first commercially successful steamboat. Fulton was a Pennsylvania painter who went to Europe to study art. He soon became more interested in machines than in painting, and in 1803 he launched his first steamboat. The boat sank, but Fulton did not give up. That same year he built a second steamboat, which remained afloat.

Confident that his invention could make money, Fulton returned to the United States. The people of New York laughed at Fulton as he constructed his third steamboat, which they called "Fulton's Folly." In August 1807, Fulton launched his boat, the *Clermont,* on the Hudson River. The *Clermont* traveled 300 miles (480 kilometers), from New York City to Albany and back again, in 62 hours. After the journey, Fulton wrote:

The power of propelling boats by steam is now fully proved. The morning I left New York there were not perhaps 30 persons in the city who believed that the boat would ever move one mile per hour or be of the least [use]; and, while we were putting off from the wharf, which was crowded with spectators, I heard a number of sarcastic remarks. This is the way ignorant men compliment [inventors].

Fulton later used the *Clermont* in regular passenger service on the Hudson. His concern for passenger comfort helped make the business a financial success.

**Steamboats increase river trade.** Less than a decade after Fulton launched the *Clermont*, steamboats loaded with goods and passengers were a common sight on the nation's big rivers. Steamboat travel had many dangers. Hidden rocks, floating logs, swift currents, and exploding boilers often caused accidents. Sparks flew out of the smokestack and set fires on board, and rival steamboats sometimes collided as they raced each other. In spite of these hazards, the brightly-painted river steamboats were popular for their comfort and speed.

Steamboats could sail against the current, so they were of special importance to westerners. Once, westerners floated their farm products on rafts down the Mississippi

Steam-powered boats provided fast cheap, transportation on the nation's lakes and rivers. H.D. Manning's painting shows an 1850's race between steamboats on the Mississippi River. Races between steamboats became a popular custom. What dangers of steamboat travel does the picture suggest?

River to New Orleans. They then made the long return journey by land. Steamboats could carry crops and stock down the river and return with manufactured products.

**Steam railroads are invented.** As the steamboat gained popularity, inventors in the United States and abroad began trying to use the steam engine for travel on land. An American inventor, Oliver Evans, made the following prediction in 1812:

> The time will come when people will travel in stages moved by steam engines from one city to another as fast as birds fly—fifteen to twenty miles an hour.... A carriage will set out from Washington in the morning, and the passengers will breakfast at Baltimore, dine in Philadelphia, and sup at New York the same day.
>
> To accomplish this, two sets of railways will be laid ... nearly level ... made of wood or iron, on smooth paths of broken stone or gravel, with a rail to guide the carriages so that they may pass each other in different directions and travel by night as well as by day....

Most people scoffed at Evans's ideas at the time, but even then wooden rails had been laid for short distances. Later the wooden rails were covered with strips of iron. Horses were used to pull the carriages over these makeshift railroads.

In 1814 the English inventor George Stephenson built a steam-driven engine to haul coal in the mines of northern England. Stephenson continued to experiment with steam engines, and in 1829 he built a passenger locomotive called the *Rocket*. The American business leader Peter Cooper built the first United States locomotive, the *Tom Thumb,* in 1830. During its trial run, the *Tom Thumb* raced a horse-drawn coach on the Baltimore and Ohio Railroad. The *Tom Thumb* led the race at first, but its engine broke down and the horse won. Within a few years, however, railroads were a new method of transportation.

**Early railroad travel was uncomfortable.** The first American locomotives burned wood instead of coal. Smoke and soot streamed out of the smokestack and blew back into the faces of the passengers. Poor springs and uneven tracks gave passengers a bad jolting. Farmers along the railroad complained that the noise of the locomotives stopped hens from laying eggs and cows from giving milk.

By the mid-1800's, railroads were rapidly becoming the nation's most important form of transportation. Linking East and West, coal-burning steam locomotives hauled passengers, mail, and freight at speeds boats could not match.

The English novelist Charles Dickens wrote the following description of a train ride he took during his visit to the United States in 1842:

The train calls at stations in the woods, where the wild impossibility of anybody having the smallest reason to get out is only to be equaled by the apparently desperate hopelessness of there being anybody to get in. It rushes across the turnpike road, where these is no gate, no policeman, no signal: nothing but a rough wooden arch, on which is painted "WHEN THE BELL RINGS, LOOK OUT FOR THE LOCOMOTIVE." On it whirls headlong, dives through the woods again, emerges in the light, clatters over frail arches, rumbles upon the heavy ground, shoots beneath a wooden bridge which intercepts the light for a second like a wink, suddenly awakens all the slumbering echoes in the main street of a large town, and dashes on haphazard, pell-mell, neck-or-nothing, down the middle of the road.... On, on, on tears the mad dragon of an engine with its train of cars; scattering in all directions a shower of burning sparks from its wood fire; screeching, hissing, yelling, panting; until at last the thirsty monster stops beneath a covered way to drink [to take on water], the people cluster round, and you have time to breathe again.

**The railroads gain importance.** The discomforts of rail travel did not stop Americans from building new railroads at a rapid pace. In 1830 there were about 30 miles (48 kilometers) of railroad track in the United States. Ten years later, there were 2,800 miles (4,505 kilometers). By 1850 there were about 9,000 miles (14,000 kilometers) in the United States. Most early railroads ran short distances connecting two cities. In the 1850's, larger railroad systems began to take shape. The most important were the Baltimore and Ohio, the Pennsylvania, and the New York Central systems. (See map on page 322.) Most railroad lines ran east and west. Few railroads connected the North and South.

Of all the new methods of transportation developed in the early 1800's, railroads proved to be the most important. Goods

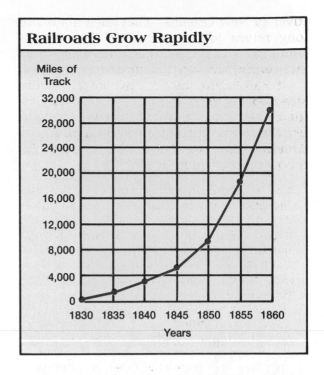

## Railroads Grow Rapidly

### Graph Study

Within 30 years railroad workers laid more than 30,000 miles (48,000 kilometers) of track. About how many miles of track existed in 1840? About how many kilometers? In what 10-year period did the miles of track more than double?

could be moved faster by rail than by road or even by canal. Railroads also provided transportation between points where water travel was impossible. The railroads were used to ship manufactured goods to the West. They also carried western farm products to markets in the Northeast. In this way, the railroads helped the West and the Northeast to be bound together.

## Rapid Communication

The different changes in methods of transportation speeded up the pace of American life. More than ever before, Americans seemed to have a need to send messages quickly. Samuel Morse filled this need by inventing the telegraph.

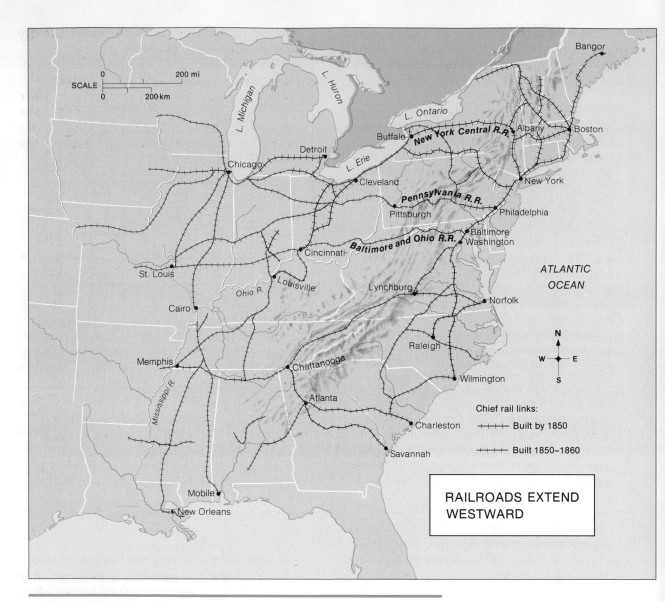

RAILROADS EXTEND WESTWARD

Chief rail links:
++++++ Built by 1850
++++++ Built 1850–1860

## Map Study

Between 1850 and 1860 thousands of miles of new track extended railroads westward. What railroad line carried travelers between Baltimore, Maryland, and Cincinnati, Ohio? By what year could goods be shipped by rail between Savannah, Georgia and Chattanooga, Tennessee?

**The need for rapid communication increases.** After methods of transportation improved, trade was carried on over long distances. Businesses needed to send messages faster than their goods could travel by rail. The railroads needed a way to send quick messages from station to station. Most early railroads had only a single track, so rapid communication could help avoid collisions. Finally, ordinary Americans wanted to be able to send messages to relatives in distant parts of the country.

**Samuel Morse invents the telegraph.** Samuel F.B. Morse discovered a way to provide rapid communication. Morse was a successful artist with a keen interest in science. He believed that he could use electricity to send messages through a wire, and began a series of experiments to prove his idea. By 1837 he had developed the telegraph, which could send signals through copper wire. To transmit messages, Morse invented **Morse code** —a system of signals representing the letters of the alphabet.

In order to test the usefulness of his invention, Morse had to raise money to build a long telegraph line. For several years, Morse and his friends tried unsuccessfully to interest Congress in the telegraph. During this time, Morse was so poor that he could hardly support his family. At last Congress voted the money to build a 40-mile (64-kilometer) telegraph line between Washington, D.C., and Baltimore.

**The telegraph is successful.** In May 1844, Morse sent the first message from Washington over the line to Baltimore. "What hath God wrought?" he tapped out on the telegraph key. His friends in Baltimore received the message and sent it back clearly over the wire.

Within ten years, telegraph lines connected the larger cities on the east coast. Telegraph service allowed newspapers to have up-to-date news. Private and business messages could be sent rapidly, and railroads could organize the movement of trains. The telegraph was a success.

## SECTION REVIEW

1. **Vocabulary** turnpike, toll, Morse code
2. **People and Places** Cumberland, Vandalia, DeWitt Clinton, Erie Canal, Albany, Buffalo, James Watt, John Fitch, Robert Fulton, Samuel F.B. Morse
3. **Comprehension** How did transportation in the United States improve in the 1800's?
4. **Comprehension** Why was the telegraph an important invention?
5. **Critical Thinking** How did improvements in transportation and communication help to bring Americans closer together?

# Chapter 13 Summary

Barred from British ports after the Revolutionary War, Northeastern clipper ships visited new ports in places such as China and California. The Northeast soon became the center of trade and manufacturing in the United States. Northeastern manufacturers copied British machines for the rapid production of textiles and other goods. Eli Whitney's invention of standardized parts also speeded American manufacturing.

The new factories changed Northeastern life, drawing workers away from farms and into manufacturing jobs. In the 1830's, some workers formed labor unions to press for shorter hours and higher pay. The spread of manufacturing led to the population growth of Northeastern cities, as American and immigrant workers established homes close to the factories.

Transportation improved in the early 1800's as Americans built surfaced roads such as turnpikes and dug canals linking important lakes and rivers. The invention of the steam engine by James Watt led to even greater advances in transportation. Steamboats and steam railroads made trade and travel faster, helping eastern manufacturers and western farmers to exchange goods. In 1837 Samuel F.B. Morse invented the telegraph, and soon Americans were able to use Morse code to send instant messages over long distances.

# Chapter 13 REVIEW

## Vocabulary and Key Terms

Choose the italicized term in parentheses that best completes each of the following sentences. Write your answers on a separate sheet of paper.

1. (*Packet ships*/*Clipper ships*) first carried passengers and freight at fixed dates.
2. (*Textiles*/*Standardized parts*) made it possible for workers to assemble and repair products quickly.
3. In the 1830's and 1840's, the first (*union dues*/*labor unions*) were formed in the United States.
4. Private companies maintained (*tolls*/*turnpikes*) by charging travelers a fee for the use of the road.
5. The (*Industrial Revolution*/*Canal Era*) was a sudden and dramatic change in the methods of production.
6. The (*National Road*/*Erie Canal*) ran through New York state from Albany to Buffalo.

## Recalling the Facts

1. Why did American trade slow down after the Revolution?
2. For what reason did some China traders make frequent stops along the coast of Oregon?
3. How did the Industrial Revolution begin in England?
4. Why did early factory owners prefer to hire women as workers?
5. Why did working conditions become increasingly worse during the 1830's and 1840's?
6. What caused a wave of immigration to the United States in the 1840's?
7. For what reason did New York Governor DeWitt Clinton want to build the Erie Canal?
8. How did steamboats affect western trade?
9. Why were railroads considered to be the most important means of transportation that had been developed in the early 1800's?
10. What two cities did the first telegraph line link?

## Places to Locate

Match the letters on the map with the places listed below. Write your answers on a separate sheet of paper.

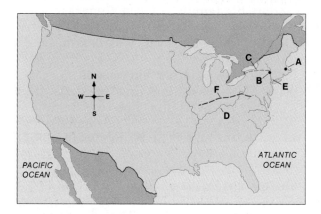

1. Albany, New York
2. Ohio River
3. Lowell, Massachusetts
4. National Road
5. Erie Canal
6. Hudson River

## Critical Thinking

1. Explain those factors that caused trade and manufacturing to grow in the Northeast. Address the following issues in your answer:
   a. What natural geographic features made the Northeast a good place for building factories?
   b. What part did the Northeast play in the American economy before the Revolutionary War?

2. Explain how advances in transportation affected the United States in the early 1800's. Consider the following issues in your answer:
   a. What were some of the effects that the new methods of transportation had on American trade?
   b. Was it necessary for advances in transportation to occur before the West could be settled? Explain why you answered as you did.
   c. In what ways did the construction of new canals, new roads, and new railroads affect the employment of large numbers of people in the United States?

## Understanding History

1. Reread the section "English inventors lead the way for the Industrial Revolution" on page 308. Then answer these questions.
   a. **Technology.** How was cloth made before the mid-1700's?
   b. **Technology.** What are some ways that the invention of the spinning jenny and the power loom changed the production of textiles?
2. Reread the letter that was written by a young Lowell, Massachusetts, factory worker on page 311. Then answer these questions.
   a. **Primary Sources.** What did the writer list as the disadvantage of factory work?
   b. **Primary Sources.** How does the writer describe the appearance of the factory?
   c. **Primary Sources.** How do you know that the writer of the letter is describing one of the very first textile mills in New England?
3. Reread the section "The National Road links East and West" on page 316. Then answer these questions.
   a. **Geography.** What two American cities did the National Road connect when it was finished?
   b. **Geography.** What was the importance of the National Road?

## Projects and Activities

1. **Researching Information.** See if you can find out more about the construction of the Erie Canal. What problems did the workers on the canal have as they built it? How was the opening of the Erie Canal celebrated?
2. **Making a Chart.** Organize facts about the Industrial Revolution into a chart. Make sure to include inventions, inventors, dates, and the effects of each invention.
3. **Keeping a Journal.** Suppose you are a worker in an early textile mill. Make journal entries describing what your life is like at the factory. Include the reasons why you took the job, what your work is like, and what you hope to gain from working in a mill.
4. **Writing a Report.** Find out more about New England whaling ships in the mid-1800's. Write a brief report describing the best whaling grounds and the methods the whalers used to capture and process whales. Be sure to include those products that came from whales that made them valuable to people.

## Practicing Your Skill

Assume that you are researching the topic "Why early labor unions failed." Decide whether each of the following statements is relevant or non-relevant to your topic. On a separate sheet of paper, write an *R* if you think the statement is relevant. Write an *N* if you think the statement is non-relevant.

1. During the Panic of 1837, many factory workers were unable to afford to pay their union dues.
2. Sarah Bagley is known as the founder of the Lowell Female Labor Reform Association, the first American women's organization to work for improved labor conditions.
3. In the 1840's, most American factory workers refused to believe that working hours should be made shorter.
4. One of the demands of the early labor unions was free education for the children of factory workers.

# 14 Cotton Shapes Southern Life
## 1815–1846

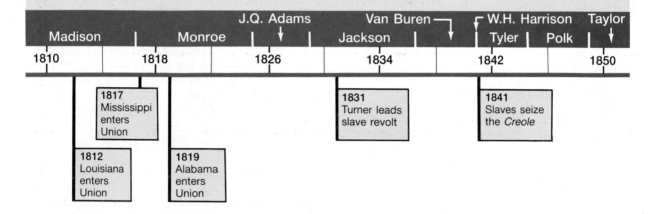

Madison | Monroe | J.Q. Adams | Jackson | Van Buren | W.H. Harrison / Tyler | Polk | Taylor

1810 — 1818 — 1826 — 1834 — 1842 — 1850

**1817** Mississippi enters Union

**1812** Louisiana enters Union

**1819** Alabama enters Union

**1831** Turner leads slave revolt

**1841** Slaves seize the *Creole*

**Cotton quickly became the leading crop of the South. Slaves worked the huge cotton plantations, as this painting by Winslow Homer shows.**

## Preparing to Read

While northeasterners were building businesses and factories, southerners were turning to cotton production. Cotton brought high profits to the planters and farmers who raised it, and it soon became the chief export of the United States. The increase in cotton production led to the spread of slavery in the South. As a result, the gap between the South and the antislavery North widened. As you read this chapter, try to answer the following questions:

1. How did cotton become the leading crop in the South?
2. What was life like in the South before 1860?
3. What differences divided the North and the South?

---

 # How did cotton become the leading crop in the South?

---

## Vocabulary

cotton boll

patent

---

As textile factories sprang up throughout Great Britain and the Northeast, the demand for raw cotton increased. At the same time, a dramatic improvement in the methods of processing cotton made cotton the most profitable southern crop. Planters cleared the fertile lands of the Lower South and set up farms and plantations for cotton production.

## The Invention of the Cotton Gin

In the late 1700's, southern farmers grew large crops of tobacco, rice, and indigo. Some also grew cotton, but they did not make a good profit on it. Each **cotton boll**—cotton pod—is full of seeds that must be removed before the cotton can be used for making thread. In the early days of cotton farming, the seeds were picked out by hand. It took one person a whole day to clean a pound of cotton fiber. Farmers knew that cotton would not become profitable until a fast method of cleaning it was invented.

**Eli Whitney invents the cotton gin.** In 1793 Eli Whitney invented a machine for cleaning cotton quickly. A recent graduate of Yale College, Whitney had accepted a job

---

This portrait of Eli Whitney was painted about 1820 by the artist and inventor Samuel F.B. Morse.

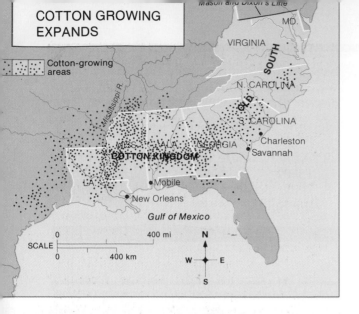

## COTTON GROWING EXPANDS

Cotton-growing areas

SCALE

0 — 400 mi

0 — 400 km

N W E S

## Map Study

**As profits increased, planters bought more land for growing cotton. In what general direction from the Old South did cotton growing spread? What states made up the Cotton Kingdom?**

as a teacher in a South Carolina school. In a letter to his father, he explained what happened on his journey south:

> I went from New York with the family of the late Major General Green ... to their plantation about twelve miles from Savannah with an expectation of spending four or five days and then proceeding into Carolina to take the school as I have mentioned in former letters. During this time I heard much said of the extreme difficulty of ginning cotton, that is, separating it from its seeds. There were a number of very respectable gentlemen at Mrs. Greene's who all agreed that if a machine could be invented which would clean cotton [rapidly], it would be a great thing both to the country and to the inventor. I ... happened to be thinking on the subject and struck out a plan of a machine in my mind.... In about ten days I made a little model, for which I was offered, if I would give up all right and title to it, a hundred guineas [about $500]. I concluded to [give up] my school and turn my attention to perfecting the machine. I made one before I came away which required the labor of one

man to turn it and with which one man will clean ten times as much cotton as he can in any other way before known and also cleanse it much better than in the usual mode. This machine may be turned by water or with a horse, with the greatest of ease, and one man and a horse will do more than fifty men with the old machines.

After inventing the cotton gin, Whitney took out a **patent** —a government license guaranteeing the inventor all profits from his or her invention for a certain length of time. People ignored the patent, however, and built thousands of copies of Whitney's cotton gin.

**Cotton cultivation spreads rapidly in the South.** The invention of the cotton gin was a history-making event. It happened just as textile factories were being built in England and in the Northeast. (See Chapter 13.) The factories created a steadily growing demand for cotton, and the cotton gin allowed the South to meet that demand.

With the cotton gin to speed up work, profits from cotton cultivation were high. Planters and farmers in the **Old South**— Maryland, Virginia, the Carolinas, and Georgia—began turning from other crops to plant cotton. They found, however, that cotton did not grow well in much of Maryland, Virginia, and North Carolina. Good cotton-growing soil was often ruined by planters eager for quick profits. Cotton wears out the soil if it is planted on the same land year after year. Instead of raising other crops, planters often grew as much cotton as possible and then moved on to other lands.

## The Cotton Kingdom

Southern farmers continually needed new land where cotton would grow well. Many left the Old South and moved southwest, clearing and planting the lands of the **Lower South**—Alabama, Mississippi, and Louisiana. Within decades cotton made the Lower South one of the most prosperous regions in the country.

**Southerners seek better land for cotton.** To the southwest of the older settled South lay vast stretches of fertile land covered with thick forests. Well suited to cotton cultivation, these rich lands extended from Georgia into the lower Mississippi Valley. After the invention of the cotton gin, settlers poured into the lands of the Lower South. Some of the new settlers were plantation families from Virginia and the Carolinas. Others came from the small farms and the backwoods of the Old South, hoping to build up plantations. The newcomers pushed out Native American groups such as the Cherokee, the Creek, and the Choctaw. Under the Indian removal policies of the federal government, Native Americans were forced to move west. (See Chapter 12.)

Slaves cleared and planted much of the new land. In 1808 Congress had passed a law forbidding the importation of slaves, but settlers could still buy slaves already living in the United States. The nation's slave population continued to grow, as more children were born into slavery. Many of the plantation owners who remained in the Old South sold slaves to settlers moving to the southwest. Also, those planters who left the Old South brought their slaves with them to the Lower South.

**Cotton is king.** As the population of the Lower South grew, new states entered the Union. Louisiana joined the United States in 1812, Mississippi in 1817, and Alabama in 1819. Along with part of Georgia, these states were called the **Cotton Kingdom** because their main crop was cotton. The Cotton Kingdom soon became richer than the Old South. Mobile, Alabama, grew into a major port of the Lower South. Mobile and New Orleans became busier centers of trade than Charleston and Savannah.

By 1850 cotton was the most important southern crop. Farmers still grew tobacco in Virginia and North Carolina, rice in South Carolina and Georgia, and sugar cane in Louisiana. Cotton, however, was produced on a much larger scale. In 1790, just before the introduction of the cotton gin, the United States produced about 4,000 bales of cotton. By 1850 the output of cotton had climbed to more than 2 million bales, and cotton had become the chief export of the United States. Because there were few mines or factories in

## LINKING PAST AND PRESENT

## ★★★ Southern Farming

"King Cotton" ruled the South in the mid-1800's. Because the South depended on agriculture, it had few factories.

After the Civil War, manufacturers began to build textile mills in the southern states. Later, in the early 1900's, the rich supply of labor and raw materials prompted many business leaders to build factories in the South.

Today the southern states make the greater part of their income through manufacturing. Yet the South is still a fertile agricultural region. The southern states grow a wide variety of fruits and vegetables. Peanuts and pecans come from Georgia, soybeans and sweet potatoes thrive in Mississippi, and oranges grow in Florida. No longer king, cotton today is only one of many products of the South.

the South, most southerners believed that their prosperity depended on cotton. Many even felt that the prosperity of the whole nation relied on the production and export of cotton. That is why they said, "Cotton is King."

## SECTION REVIEW

1. **Vocabulary**   cotton boll, patent
2. **People and Places**   Eli Whitney, Old South, Lower South, Cotton Kingdom, Mobile, New Orleans
3. **Comprehension**   How did the cotton gin speed up cotton production?
4. **Comprehension**   What led to the settlement of the Lower South in the early 1800's?
5. **Critical Thinking**   How did the Industrial Revolution help make the southern economy dependent on cotton?

## MAPS AND GRAPHS: Interpreting a Bar Graph

When studying history, it is useful to compare numerical facts. This enables you to see changes over time or to compare differences between places. A **bar graph** is one way to illustrate these relationships.

A bar graph uses bars, or columns, to present numerical information. To interpret a bar graph, first read the title to see what the graph shows. Next, look at the **horizontal axis**—the information shown along the bottom of the graph. Here, the horizontal axis lists years to show how cotton production changed over time.

Find the **vertical axis** along the left side of the graph. This axis shows the number of bales of cotton grown in millions. Finally, look at both axes. Note that the intervals between the numbers and between the years are equal, and that numbers and years are evenly spaced.

By studying its parts, you know that this graph shows how many million bales of cotton were grown in particular years in the 1800's. To further interpret the graph, answer the following questions.

1. For which years does the graph give information?
2. Does the graph tell exactly how much cotton was produced in these years?
3. About how many million bales of cotton were grown in 1850?
4. In which year did cotton production first increase to more than 1 million bales?
5. Compare the bars for 1830 and 1840. Between these years, did cotton production **(a)** double, or **(b)** more than double?
6. Compare the bars for 1840 and 1860 to see if cotton production **(a)** nearly doubled, or **(b)** nearly tripled.

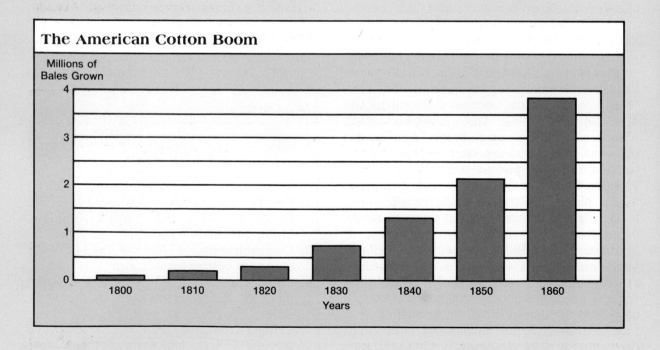

The American Cotton Boom

# What was life like in the South before 1860?

## Vocabulary
spiritual
extended family

Agriculture was the center of the southern economy, but not all southerners shared the same way of life. Some white southerners owned small farms and others controlled vast plantations. Some settled in the towns and cities of the South. Most black southerners were slaves who labored in the fields, but some were skilled craftsworkers who lived in cities.

## The Plantation System

The rich planters of the South were a small but powerful group. Many were leaders in their states, and their plantations became social centers.

**Planters lead the South.** The planters of the South used slave labor to make cotton plantations profitable. Slaves were expensive, and not all southerners could afford to buy them. In 1860, only one white southern family out of four owned slaves. The price of a strong field hand ranged from $1,200 to $1,500. Cotton required more field hands than any other southern crop because it had to be tended and picked carefully by hand. Planters had to spend a great deal of money buying slaves in order to set up a cotton plantation. In return, however, they won large profits.

Cotton brought political power as well as wealth to a small group of planters. In 1860, out of a population of more than 8 million whites, only about 10,000 southerners owned 50 or more slaves. These rich planters became the leaders of their states. Because their views were respected, planters also spoke for the South in Congress.

**Plantations have a standard method of cotton production.** All cotton plantations were managed in much the same way. At the end of the short southern winter, field hands plowed the land and planted the cotton. They tended the plants day by day through the long summer, keeping out weeds and preventing damage by insects. In early autumn the slaves walked through the fields with long bags slung over their shoulders, picking cotton. A former slave wrote the following account of how the field hands worked:

> The hands are required to be in the cotton field as soon as it is light in the morning.... With the exception of ten or fifteen minutes, which is given them at noon to swallow their

## Graph Study

In 1850 most slaveowners held between 1 and 9 slaves. In 1850, what percent of slaveowners owned 50 or more slaves? What percent owned 10 to 49 slaves?

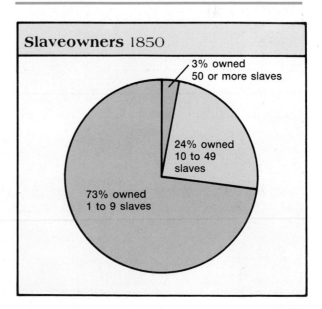

**Slaveowners** 1850

3% owned 50 or more slaves

24% owned 10 to 49 slaves

73% owned 1 to 9 slaves

allowance of cold bacon, they are not permitted to be a moment idle until it is too dark to see, and when the moon is full, they oftentimes labor till the middle of the night. They do not dare to stop even at dinner time, nor return to the quarters, however late it be, until the order to halt is given by the driver.

Most large plantations owned a cotton gin, worked in the early days by horses or water power, and later by steam. Field hands carried the picked cotton to the gin, which cleaned the seeds out of the fiber. They packed the clean cotton into bales. If the plantation was located on a river, the bales were piled on a wharf and left ready to be loaded on steamboats. From other plantations the bales were hauled in wagons to the river bank.

Steamboats carried the bales of cotton down the river to a port city. Some sailed down the Mississippi River to New Orleans. Others sailed down such waterways as the Alabama River and the Mobile River to Mobile. From these ports on the Gulf of Mexico, the cotton was shipped to textile factories in the Northeast and in Great Britain.

**Plantation families live in comfort.** The family of a wealthy planter usually lived in a large, stately house shaded by spreading trees. Graceful pillars supported the roof of a front porch. The rooms were large, with high ceilings and tall windows.

Plantation life was not all leisure. Each day the plantation owner either gave instructions to the overseer or directed the slaves in person. Plantation owners included both men and women, but most were men. The

Steamboats carried cotton bales to river ports. The bales were piled on the wharves and then loaded onto ships bound for cotton mills in New England and Great Britain.

Wealthy plantation owners built tall, spacious homes. Entertaining guests was an important part of plantation life. What feature of plantation-house architecture does the picture show?

owner's wife usually directed the house servants and gave medical care to the slaves. It required a great deal of organization to keep a large plantation going. One woman recalled the way her grandparents handled the supplies for the slaves on their South Carolina plantation:

Bales and bales of woolen goods and unbleached cotton cloth were bought for clothing the slaves. Grandfather bought all his staple groceries by the wholesale—barrels of sugar and flour, sacks of coffee, chests of tea, [tubs] of salt mackerel, and shoes by the gross. These purchases were made once a year through his factors in Charleston, who bought his cotton. The goods were shipped up the [river] to Hunt's Bluff, the nearest landing. For days, wagons were hauling the goods to the Three Creeks Plantation.

The commissary where supplies were kept resembled a country store. Every Wednesday at sundown the heads of all the Negro families gathered at this store to get their weekly allowance of provisions. Each allotment had been weighed and measured in advance and was ready to be delivered. . . .

Making the clothing for such a large number of Negroes was a never-ending task. Grandmother and a sewing woman cut out the garments from the bales of cloth, and they were made up in the sewing room by women trained for this work under a supervising sewing woman. As a rule the women who sewed were the less robust workers who were not strong enough to work in the fields. On rainy days or in the bitter cold weather of winter all the Negro women on the place were expected to work in the sewing room. . . .

The sons of planters did not learn to run the plantation until they had finished college. Daughters, however, learned to supervise the work of the household at an early age. Expected to marry young, they had to be ready to run households of their own. Both sons and daughters had time for such entertainment as riding, hunting, and attending parties. Visiting relatives and neighbors was an important part of the life of plantation families.

## Slave Life

The carefree and elegant life of the plantation family sharply contrasted with the lives of the plantation slaves. Some slaves were house servants. On a large plantation, each member of the family had a slave as a personal servant. Other slaves worked in the kitchen or were maids, butlers, and coach drivers. Skilled slaves served as carpenters, blacksmiths, and gardeners. The great majority, however, were field hands. Their lot was the hardest, especially on plantations in the Lower South.

**Slaves lead hard lives.** The slaves lived in log cabins not far from the owner's house. Most slave cabins had no windows and only a single room. The bed was usually a plank of wood with a coarse blanket. At one end of the cabin was a fireplace for heating and cooking. The slaves ate pork, corn meal, and molasses provided by the planter. The planter also gave each slave a few pieces of clothing, which had to last all year.

**In this 1852 painting, slaves wait to be sold at a slave auction in Richmond, Virginia. The artist, Eyre Crowe, opposed slavery. His painting shows the dignity of the slaves, despite their bondage.**

In Eastman Johnson's 1862 painting, a young family flees slavery on a stolen horse. Johnson, a northerner, believed slavery should be abolished.

Some slaveowners gave slaves extra comforts, allowing them to hunt, fish, plant gardens, and raise chickens. Even with a kind master, however, slavery was a heavy burden. Slaves could not forget that they had been robbed of their freedom. The master kept the products of their work and could reward or punish them as he or she saw fit. Harsh masters often brutally whipped slaves who misbehaved or ran away.

**Slaves develop a unique culture.** Slaves lacked freedom and property, but they did possess a rich culture of their own. The most important aspect of slave culture was religion. Faced with many hardships in everyday life, slaves found comfort in Christianity and the hope of reward in heaven. Most slaves attended Methodist or Baptist churches run by white congregations. Some formed all-black churches, such as the African Baptist Church, where they could conduct their own services.

Inspired by by Protestant hymns and by African music, slaves developed a new style of music. They sang **spirituals** —religious folk songs—such as "Go Down, Moses" and "Swing Low, Sweet Chariot." The spirituals expressed the slaves' yearning for freedom. They also made up slow chants to sing as they worked. At night in their cabins they told each other folktales, using the forms of African fables to tell stories set in the American South.

**Slave families struggle to stay together.** Family life was also important to the slaves. Families often worked together on their own gardens during their precious time away from the master's demands. They tried to preserve the traditional African custom of living in **extended families** . An extended family is a close-knit group made up of grandparents, parents, children, aunts, uncles, and cousins.

One of the most cruel features of slavery was the breakup of black families. When members of a family were sold to different masters, they rarely saw each other again. Slaves in the Old South especially feared being sold "down the river" to the newly settled lands of the Lower South. Slaves outnumbered whites in many parts of the Lower South, and masters fearful of slave revolts kept discipline strict. Far away from towns and churches, they could overwork slaves

335

without drawing criticism from their neighbors. A Kentucky slave wrote the following account of being sold down the river to New Orleans:

> My wife and children accompanied me to the landing, where I bade them an adieu which might be for life, and then stepped into the boat. . . . On our way down the river, we stopped at Vicksburg, and I got permission to visit a plantation a few miles from the town, where some of my old companions from Kentucky were living. It was the saddest visit I ever made. Four years in an unhealthy climate and under a hard master had done the ordinary work of twenty. Their cheeks were literally caved in with starvation and disease. They described their daily life, which was to toil . . . in malarious marshes, under a burning, maddening sun, exposed to poison of mosquitoes and black gnats. And they said they looked forward to death as their only deliverance. Some of them fairly cried at seeing me there, and the thought of the fate which they felt awaited me. Their worst fears of being sold down South had been more than realized. I went away sick at heart.

**Slaves lead rebellions.** Slaves showed the desire for freedom in their actions as well as in their culture. Some slaves ran away, attempting to visit family members or to escape to the North. Other desperate slaves planned to rebel against the slaveowners. About 200 slave rebellions took place during the years that slavery existed in the United States. These revolts seldom won freedom

Most white southerners lived on small farms. Working their own land, the farmers grew food crops and cash crops. This nineteenth-century painting by Louis Hoppe shows the Meyenberg family farm in southeastern Texas.

for the slaves involved, but they showed that blacks did not meekly accept slavery.

A Virginia slave named Nat Turner led one of the bloodiest of the slave rebellions. Turner believed that God had chosen him to free the slaves and take revenge on whites. In 1831 Turner judged an eclipse of the sun to be a divine signal for action. He and his band of slaves killed 57 white people before being captured by state and federal troops. More than 100 blacks—many of them innocent of any connection with the uprising—were killed by whites in the panic that was stirred up by the rebellion. Other major slave rebellions of the early 1800's were led by Gabriel Prosser in Virginia and Denmark Vesey in South Carolina.

One successful revolt took place on board a ship. In 1841 more than 100 slaves were being transported from Virginia to Louisiana on a ship called the *Creole*. Led by a slave named Madison Washington, the slaves seized control of the *Creole*. They sailed it to the British West Indies, where they lived out their lives in freedom.

## Small Farmers and City Dwellers

Plantations were an important part of southern life, but only a minority of southerners lived on them. The rest of the southern population ran small farms or held jobs in cities.

**The majority of southerners live on small farms.** Most southern whites farmed small plots of land and lived in modest frame houses. Many of their farms were located in the less fertile areas of the South, or on land that was just being cleared. Other small farms were located on land that had been abandoned by the big planters. Some small farmers owned one or two slaves, but most worked the land with the help of family members.

Small farmers raised corn, potatoes, and vegetables to feed themselves. They usually grew a small crop of cotton as well. The crop amounted to only a few bales of cotton each year, but it provided the farmer with a cash income. If crops were good several years in a row, then the farmer could use the profits

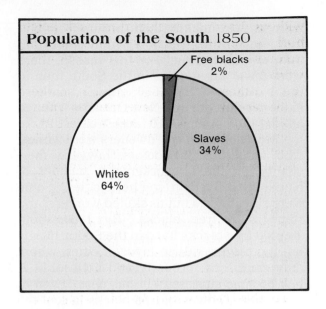

**Population of the South 1850**

Free blacks 2%

Slaves 34%

Whites 64%

Graph Study

By 1850 more than 3 million slaves lived in the South. What percent of the South's population were slaves? What percent of the population were free blacks?

to buy more land. Many small farmers dreamed of owning large plantations and numerous slaves. For this reason, farmers without slaves were often strongly in favor of slavery.

**Mountain whites lead simple lives.** The mountain people were a group of southern whites who lived apart from the rest of the population. They were descendants of the hardy pioneers who had first settled in the valleys of the Appalachian Mountains. Like their parents and grandparents, the mountain people led a rough frontier life. Some lived on the food that they grew. Others lived by fishing in mountain streams and hunting wild game.

The mountain people were proud and independent in spite of their poverty. They had little interest in slavery or in other matters that concerned the big planters.

**Some southerners live in cities.** The growth of manufacturing in the Northeast prompted many people to give up farming in favor of city jobs. In the South, however, farmers were making high profits from cotton, and farming remained more important than manufacturing. For this reason, there were fewer large cities in the South than in the Northeast. By 1860 only 2 southern cities—Baltimore and New Orleans—ranked among the country's 10 largest cities.

Most southern city dwellers were whites, who held jobs as doctors, lawyers, merchants, or skilled workers. A number of blacks also lived in southern cities. Some were slaves hired out as skilled workers, and some were free blacks. By 1860 about 260,000 free blacks lived in the South. Many left the countryside in favor of cities, where they could own property and hold jobs. A few became successful in business. Even in large cities, however, free blacks lacked the opportunity to vote and to get an education.

They also ran the risk of being kidnapped by slave traders and sold back into slavery.

## SECTION REVIEW

1. **Vocabulary**   spiritual, extended family
2. **People and Places**   Alabama River, Nat Turner, Gabriel Prosser, Denmark Vesey, Madison Washington
3. **Comprehension**   How did planters transport their cotton to market?
4. **Comprehension**   Why did slaves fear being sold "down the river" to the Lower South?
5. **Critical Thinking**   What factors enabled a minority of people—the planters—to maintain political leadership in the South?

# 3 What differences divided the North and the South?

## Vocabulary
abolish
abolitionist

The differences between the North and the South increased as time passed. The North became a center of manufacturing, where slavery was no longer necessary or profitable. One by one the northern states outlawed slavery. The South remained a center of agriculture, where slave labor made high profits possible. The **Mason and Dixon Line,** the boundary between Pennsylvania and Maryland, divided slave from free states.

## Differences in Economic Growth

As the northern and southern economies changed, the political views of the two sections moved farther apart. The rise of cotton production in the South made southerners reluctant to give up slavery.

**The North and the South disagree on many matters.** When people in different areas have different ways of life, their opinions on issues are also likely to differ. For example, northerners usually favored high tariffs. They reasoned that high tariffs would keep out foreign goods and help them to sell their own products at a higher price. Southerners usually opposed high tariffs. Few of them had manufactured goods for sale, and they did not want to pay higher prices on imported goods.

**The North and the South draw apart over the issue of slavery.** Both northerners and southerners had begun to question slavery during the 1700's. Slavery had been profitable when the colonies were new and laborers were hard to find. As the supply of labor increased, many farmers began to believe that it would be more profitable to hire

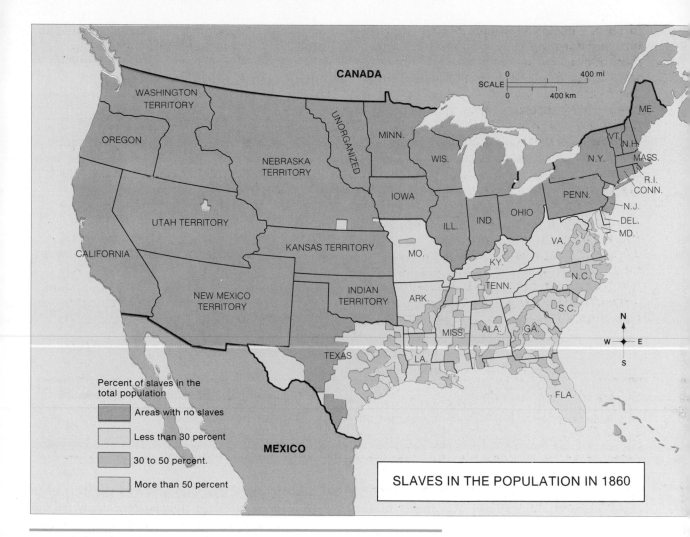

CANADA

WASHINGTON
TERRITORY

OREGON

UNORGANIZED

MINN.

WIS.

ME.

VT. N.H.

N.Y.

MASS.

R.I.
CONN.

NEBRASKA
TERRITORY

UTAH TERRITORY

IOWA

ILL.

IND.

OHIO

PENN.

N.J.

DEL.

MD.

CALIFORNIA

KANSAS TERRITORY

MO.

VA.

KY.

N.C.

NEW MEXICO
TERRITORY

INDIAN
TERRITORY

ARK.

TENN.

S.C.

MISS.

ALA.

GA.

TEXAS

LA.

FLA.

Percent of slaves in the
total population

Areas with no slaves

Less than 30 percent

30 to 50 percent

More than 50 percent

MEXICO

SCALE
0   400 mi
0   400 km

N
W   E
S

SLAVES IN THE POPULATION IN 1860

## Map Study

**By 1860 slavery existed mainly in southern states. Which five states
had large areas in which slaves made up more than half the
population?**

daily workers than to keep slaves. Some
southern slaveowners also began to believe
that it was wrong for one person to keep another in bondage. George Washington
hoped that slavery would one day cease to
exist in the United States, and he made arrangements to have his own slaves freed at
the time of his death. Patrick Henry and
Thomas Jefferson also had doubts about
slavery, because it was contrary to the ideas
that are plainly expressed in the Declaration
of Independence.

The northern states took the lead in outlawing slavery. By 1804 most areas north of
the Mason and Dixon Line had passed laws
freeing their slaves. Active anti-slavery societies sprang up in the South as well as the
North. The southern attitude toward slavery
changed, however, with the invention of the
cotton gin in 1793. The cotton gin made
slave labor highly profitable once again.
Cotton production went on almost all year
round, and many workers were needed to
plant, tend, and pick the cotton. It was work

Many slaves had faith in the ideal of freedom and equality, even though they were held in bondage. Slaves who escaped to the North or to Canada often voiced their opposition to slavery by writing accounts of their own lives.

In the mid-1800's, abolitionist journals often published slave narratives. Some whites believed that blacks did not suffer as slaves. By reading slave narratives, however, many learned what life was like for a slave persecuted by a harsh master. Other slave narratives recounted the hazardous journey north.

A number of slave narratives were published as books in Great Britain as well as in the United States. The most famous slave narrative, Frederick Douglass's *My Bondage and My Freedom*, was not only an account of his personal experiences, but also an attack on the institution of slavery. Douglass wrote, "It did not entirely satisfy me to *narrate* wrongs; I felt like *denouncing* them...."

**Frederick Douglass**

that children as well as adults could do, and it was easy to supervise. All these factors made slave labor ideal for cotton production. To many southerners, slavery no longer looked like an outdated institution. It looked instead like the economic future of the South.

## Differences over Slavery

The North and the South argued over slavery, but neither side managed to convince the other. The quarrel over slavery further divided the two sections.

**White southerners defend slavery.** After slavery had been banned throughout the North, many northerners began to urge the South to **abolish** —end—slavery as well. The more the **abolitionists** — opponents of slavery—attacked slavery, the more strongly white southerners defended it. There were still some white southerners who doubted that slavery was right or even profitable, but their voices were drowned out by the majority. Most southerners especially resented criticisms of slavery made by northerners. They believed that people in the North did not understand their southern way of life.

Many white southern leaders wrote books and made speeches claiming that slavery was a good thing. They pointed out that the Bible mentions slavery and that slavery had existed since earliest times. John C. Calhoun, the well-known southern political leader, declared that "there has never yet existed a wealthy and civilized society in which one portion of the community did not in fact live on the labor of the other." Even many southern churches began to defend slavery. Some church organizations that had members throughout the country broke into separate northern and southern branches.

A few white southerners even claimed that slavery was a benefit to black people. They said that slavery exposed Africans to a "higher" culture and argued that southern slaves were better off than northern factory workers. White southerners paid little attention to the views of black people on the subject of slavery. They ignored the fact that many abolitionists were former slaves who had escaped to freedom in the North.

**Southerners and northerners have different views of the United States.** Thomas Jefferson had viewed the United States as a nation of independent farmers, and many southerners in the 1800's still had faith in that tradition. They wanted the national government policy to favor southern agriculture. They also believed that the national government should not interfere with the affairs of the states. Northerners often did not agree with these southern views. Most northerners believed that the United States had to keep up with the social and economic changes of the rest of the world. They wanted the national government policy to favor business, and they were more willing to have any important decisions made by the national government.

The people of the North and those of the South found it hard to compromise on the issue of slavery. Northerners could not ignore what they felt to be the injustice of slavery in the South. Yet most southerners would not even consider abolishing slavery. One determined southerner declared that "rather than yield our dearest rights and privileges"—meaning slavery—"we should see the Union scattered to the winds." This was not just empty speechmaking. These different feelings about slavery would one day soon threaten to divide the Union.

## SECTION REVIEW

1. **Vocabulary**   abolish, abolitionist
2. **People and Places**   Mason and Dixon Line, John C. Calhoun
3. **Comprehension**   Why did slavery disappear in the North?
4. **Comprehension**   Why did slavery become profitable for the South?
5. **Critical Thinking**   Why did white southerners defend slavery?

# Chapter 14 Summary

In 1793 Eli Whitney invented the cotton gin, the first machine for removing the seeds from the cotton boll. The cotton gin made it possible to increase the amount of cotton southern planters could grow, just when American and English textile factories were calling for more and more raw cotton. High profits prompted many planters to leave the Old South and settle the fertile lands of the Lower South, which was also known as the Cotton Kindgom.

A small number of white southerners owned vast plantations. Wealthy and politically powerful, these planters lived in grand plantation houses. The cotton that they raised was cultivated by field hands who lived in rough cabins. The slaves developed a culture of their own, which centered around religion. Slave culture also included the development of spirituals and the telling of folktales. Some blacks escaped slavery by running away to the North, and others such as Nat Turner of Virginia organized slave revolts. Some of the free blacks lived along with whites in southern cities.

By 1804 most areas north of the Mason and Dixon Line had voted to abolish slavery. Southerners resented northern calls for abolition and argued that the South was justified in maintaining slavery. The slavery issue continued to drive the North and the South further apart.

# Chapter 14 REVIEW

## Vocabulary and Key Terms

Use the following terms to complete the sentences below. Write your answers on a separate sheet of paper.

**extended family**
**abolitionists**
**Spirituals**
**Cotton Kingdom**
**Mason and Dixon Line**
**Old South**

1. The _____ included Maryland, Virginia, North Carolina, South Carolina, and most of Georgia.
2. The states of Louisiana, Mississippi, Alabama, and part of Georgia were considered to be part of the _____.
3. In the United States, many black slaves maintained the African tradition of the _____.
4. _____ were slave songs that were inspired both by African music and by Protestant hymns.
5. The opponents of slavery were known as _____.
6. The _____ was a boundary between the slave and free states.

## Recalling the Facts

1. How did the cotton gin make cotton farming more profitable?
2. Why did planters settle the lands of the Lower South?
3. In what way did Congress limit the slave trade in 1808?
4. How did plantation owners transport their cotton to market?
5. What Virginia slave led a bloody rebellion in 1831?
6. Why did slavery disappear in the northern states?
7. Why did slavery remain important to the South's economy?

## Places to Locate

Match the letters on the map with the places listed below. Write your answers on a separate sheet of paper.

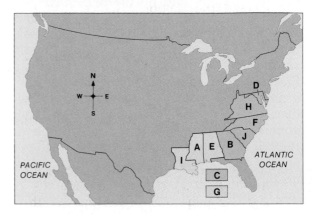

1. Virginia
2. Louisiana
3. Lower South
4. South Carolina
5. Old South
6. Alabama
7. Mississippi
8. Georgia
9. North Carolina
10. Maryland

## Critical Thinking

1. In 1860 less than 1 percent of southerners owned large plantations. Why did these plantation owners have so much political power? Consider the following points in your answer:
   a. the social position of the planters
   b. the wealth of the planters
   c. the importance of cotton to United States trade
2. What factors kept blacks in slavery in the South? Consider these questions in your answer:
   a. What happened to slaves caught escaping or planning a revolt?
   b. What was the most common southern attitude toward slavery?
   c. How did plantation owners work to maintain slavery?

## Understanding History

1. Reread the section "Eli Whitney invents the cotton gin" on page 327. Then answer these questions.
   a. **Science and Technology.** What were the power sources of the cotton gin?
   b. **Science and Technology.** How did Whitney try to protect his right to his invention?
2. Reread the section "Slaves lead hard lives" on page 334. Then answer these questions.
   a. **Culture.** Why did slaves fear being sold "down the river" to the Lower South?
   b. **Primary Sources.** According to the account written by a Kentucky slave, what were the hardships of a slave in the Lower South?
3. Reread the section "The North and the South draw apart over the issue of slavery" on page 338. Then answer these questions.
   a. **Citizenship.** Why did Patrick Henry and Thomas Jefferson doubt the justice of slavery?
   b. **Economics.** Why was slave labor useful for cotton cultivation?

## Projects and Activities

1. **Writing a Report.** Find out more about the life of Denmark Vesey, the leader of a South Carolina slave revolt in 1822. Read about Vesey's plans for the revolt and how they were discovered. Write a report on your findings.
2. **Making a Chart.** Review this chapter and make a chart with three headings: Facts about the importance of cotton; Facts about life in the South; Facts about the debate over slavery. Classify facts from the chapter into these categories. Compare completed charts in a discussion in class.
3. **Researching and Drawing a Map.** Use textbooks and historical atlases to find out the important southern crops of 1850 and where they were grown. Draw a map of the southern states and add symbols that stand for each crop. Include a map key to show the meaning of each symbol.
4. **Writing a Fictional Account.** Imagine you are a slave sold "down the river" from Tennessee to Louisiana. Describe your frame of mind as you begin the journey, the route you follow, and the experiences you have along the way.

## Practicing Your Skill

Study the bar graph below and then answer the questions that follow.

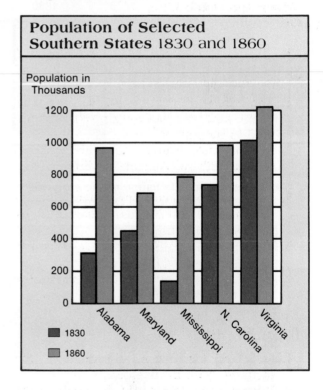

**Population of Selected Southern States** 1830 and 1860

1. What was Maryland's population in 1830? in 1860?
2. Which two states showed the greatest increase in population between 1830 and 1860?
3. How did Mississippi's growth compare with that of North Carolina during the years shown?
4. What conclusion can you draw about the rate of population growth in the Old South and the Lower South?

# 15 Americans Call for Social Change

## 1815–1846

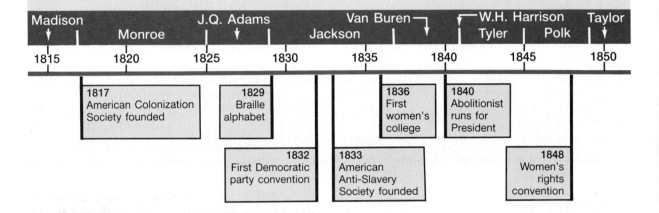

Madison | Monroe | J.Q. Adams | Jackson | Van Buren | W.H. Harrison Tyler | Polk | Taylor

1815    1820    1825    1830    1835    1840    1845    1850

1817
American Colonization
Society founded

1829
Braille
alphabet

1836
First
women's
college

1840
Abolitionist
runs for
President

1832
First Democratic
party convention

1833
American
Anti-Slavery
Society founded

1848
Women's
rights
convention

An important social change of the early 1800's was the growth of democracy, as this painting of Election Day by George Caleb Bingham shows.

## Preparing to Read

During the 1800's Americans worked to change many aspects of political and social life. New laws extended the vote to more people than ever before. Election reforms gave people a larger share in the government. The largest and most far-reaching reform movement of the time was the crusade for the abolition of slavery. Women also began to call for increased legal and social rights. Other social campaigns sought to help the American people make improvements in their lives in many different ways. As you read this chapter, try to answer the following questions:

1. How did democracy expand in the 1800's?
2. How did the antislavery movement develop?
3. What movements for social reform arose in the 1800's?

# 1 How did democracy expand in the 1800's?

## Vocabulary

caucus
normal school
revival

Throughout his years in office, President Jackson worked to give voters a greater share in government. This period, sometimes called the Jacksonian Era, reflected Jackson's faith that ordinary people could govern themselves. Still, many people were excluded from taking part in the more democratic government.

## Election Methods

During the 1800's, many states wrote new laws giving the vote to a greater number of people than ever before. New laws also gave the people a stronger voice in state and national elections.

**New laws extend the vote.** The 13 original states granted the vote only to men who owned property. In the 1800's, many Americans felt that the property requirement was unfair. They felt that the right to vote should not depend on whether a person had enough money to buy land. Most of the new western states wrote constitutions granting the vote to all white males over 21. These states brought greater democracy to the nation. Western voters helped elect Andrew Jackson, the candidate of the "common man," to the presidency in 1828.

As western states entered the Union, many of the 13 original states took steps to extend the vote. Most of the northeastern states wrote new state constitutions abolishing the property requirement. In the South voting laws changed more slowly. Nevertheless, by 1860 the property requirement had been abolished in 23 of the 30 states.

In spite of these reforms, the voting laws still did not treat all Americans equally. Women were denied the vote in every state. Native Americans and slaves were also denied the vote. Free blacks could vote in some states, but the opponents of abolitionism were working to take away the rights of free blacks. During the mid-1800's, free blacks actually lost the vote in some states. By 1860 they could vote in only five states.

New Jersey, the first state allowing women to vote, outlawed the practice in 1807. The voting-rights reforms of the Jacksonian Era did not extend to women.

**Elections become more democratic.** As states extended the vote, they made election reforms. Many states took power away from the state legislatures. For example, each state legislature could choose the governor. In the 1830's and 1840's, many states passed laws allowing voters to choose the governor in a direct election.

State legislatures also held great power in presidential elections. The legislatures chose the members of the Electoral College, who, in turn, elected the President. In the 1820's, many Americans began to call for new laws giving the people a stronger voice in presidential elections. By 1828 every state except Delaware and South Carolina held direct elections in which the people chose the members of the Electoral College.

Until the 1830's, each political party chose a presidential candidate in a closed **caucus** —meeting of important party members. Ordinary people had little influence in their political parties. In 1832, however, the major political parties began using nominating conventions to choose candidates. Party members in each state elected delegates to represent them at the convention. These delegates then chose the party candidates for President and Vice President. In this way, conventions gave ordinary people a stronger voice in the party's nominations.

At the first Democratic convention, President Jackson was renominated and Martin Van Buren was nominated for Vice President. The National Republicans chose Henry Clay as their presidential candidate.

## Educational Changes

As more Americans gained the vote, reformers worked to make education available to more children. Many reformers believed that Americans could not use their democratic privileges wisely if they were not well informed. For this reason, free elementary schools became common in the North, and new high schools and colleges were opened.

**Public education needs reform.** In the early 1800's, few American children were able to get a good education. New England schools had been neglected since the Revolutionary War. Buildings were run down, and teachers were poorly trained. Conditions were worse in the West. Families had to work so hard to make a living that there was little time or money left for schooling. In the South, education was often limited to the children of wealthy planters.

In many states, public schools required parents to pay part of the cost of their children's education. Poor children could attend such public schools only if their parents took a "pauper's oath," declaring that they had no money to give the school. Most poor people kept their children out of school, because they were unwilling to take such an oath.

**Free public schools are established.** During the 1830's, Americans began to demand better public education for their children. The Massachusetts lawyer Horace Mann was a leader in the fight for free elementary schools. Mann believed that education was important for democracy. He called free public education "the great equalizer," saying that it united the rich and the poor. Leaders in other states joined Mann in working for public education, and by 1850 elementary schools supported by public taxes were common in the northern states. As secretary of the first Massachusetts Board of Education, Horace Mann also worked to set up **normal schools** —schools for educating teachers.

During this time of change, more young people gained the opportunity to attend high school and college. Boston established the first public high school in 1821, and other

## LINKING PAST AND PRESENT

## ★ ★ ★ *Public Education*

Reformers of the 1800's demanded excellence in public education. They knew that educated citizens were needed for the nation's economic and social well-being. Public education has steadily expanded because of reformers' efforts.

After 1850 many states passed compulsory school-attendance laws. These laws require that children attend school until they complete a certain grade or reach a certain age. Today, education is compulsory in all states.

Public schools have changed to meet the demands of a growing nation. At first, most schools were one-room schoolhouses. Today, however, most schools have classrooms, science labs, libraries, and gymnasiums as well as special rooms for art, music, and vocational classes.

northern cities soon followed its example. Some states founded universities and provided them with public funds. Private colleges began to offer a wider range of subjects, preparing students not only for the ministry, but also for careers in law, medicine, and business.

Young women were barred from public high schools and most colleges. Some attended private high schools known as seminaries. Wesleyan College, the first American women's college, opened in Macon, Georgia, in 1836. The following year another women's college, Mount Holyoke, was opened in Massachusetts, and Ohio's Oberlin College decided to accept women as well as men. For most women, however, higher education was still out of reach.

**Blacks face obstacles to education.** In most states black families were required to pay taxes to support public schools. Black children, however, were barred from those schools. A few elementary schools for

The class of 1855 at Ohio's Oberlin College included one black woman. In the early 1800's, educational opportunities were denied to most black Americans.

blacks were opened in northern cities and in Washington, D.C. Most northern black children, however, were educated at home or not at all. There were no schools for black children in slave states, where it was illegal to teach blacks to read.

Few American colleges would accept blacks, and those that did often took only one or two black students at a time. The first black graduate of an American college was Alexander Twilight, who graduated from Middlebury College in 1823. Three years later, the first blacks graduated from Amherst College and Bowdoin College. Oberlin College, founded in 1833, accepted more than 200 blacks within the next 30 years.

## A New American Culture

The 1800's saw a blossoming of American culture. Writers and painters turned away from older European styles. They began to create works of art that reflected a particularly American view of life and the world.

**Painters develop an American style.** Before the 1800's most American painters followed the European styles in art. Around 1825 Thomas Cole began painting landscapes in a simple, direct style. Cole became the leader of a group of American artists that was called the Hudson River school. The Hudson River school artists frequently painted scenes of the Hudson River valley in New York state. Other American artists began painting landscapes of the western plains and mountains. George Caleb Bingham painted scenes of frontier life in the Mississippi Valley. Together, these new artists expressed hope and confidence in the nation and its future.

**New writers enrich American literature.** Before 1820 the United States had produced few poets or novelists of worldwide importance. Some people even doubted that the United States was capable of producing writers that were equal to the great writers of England. These doubts proved false in the mid-1800's, when a group of brilliant new American writers began to publish their poems and novels.

The poet and author Edgar Allan Poe often wrote mystery stories with European settings. Most of the new American writers, however, set their works in America. Washington Irving wrote such stories as the "Legend of Sleepy Hollow" and "Rip Van Winkle," about the people of the Hudson Valley in New York. James Fenimore Cooper wrote frontier novels such as the *The Last of the Mohicans* and *The Deerslayer,* which described the adventures of Indians and backwoods people. In Salem, Massachusetts, Nathaniel Hawthorne wrote *The Scarlet Letter* and *The House of the Seven Gables,* in which he explored the Puritan heritage of New Englanders. The American past inspired the poet Henry Wadsworth Longfellow to write such poems as *Hiawatha, Paul Revere's Ride,* and *The Courtship of Miles Standish.*

Two of the greatest American writers of the 1850's and 1860's were not able to achieve much literary success during their lifetimes. Herman Melville wrote novels that were inspired by his adventures as a sailor on voyages that had taken him around the world. His greatest novel, *Moby Dick,* describes the voyage of a Nantucket whaling ship. Walt Whitman wrote *Leaves of Grass,* a book of poems expressing his faith in democracy and in the young American nation. Because of his unconventional style, Whitman won little praise for his work when it was published.

**Women writers achieve success.** Many of the most successful writers of the time were women. Fanny Fern wrote novels about young women who achieved success through honesty and hard work. Her best-selling books made her wealthy. Other women also wrote important works. Margaret Fuller's *Woman in the Nineteenth Century* had great influence in the movement for women's rights.

**New England writers cherish independence.** Several New England writers had a lasting influence on American literature and thought. Ralph Waldo Emerson, trained as a minister, proclaimed that every person's life should be guided by a divine "inner light." Emerson's essays and poems also showed great faith in the nation's future. Through his forceful and original ideas, Emerson greatly contributed to American intellectual life in the 1800's.

Another New England writer, Henry David Thoreau, attacked social institutions that he thought to be immoral. Thoreau believed that people must be free to act by their own idea of right and wrong. He urged people to refuse to obey unjust laws. Thoreau's work helped shape many reform movements of his time.

**Religion encourages reform movements.** The spirit of reform was also spurred by religion. The life of American Protestants in the early 1800's was marked by a strong religious **revival** —a reawakening of religious faith. Ministers went from town to town, preaching to large crowds at outdoor gatherings called camp meetings. Listeners were urged to renew their own faith and to cure the evils of society. The revival movement often led to emotional demonstrations of religious faith. It also filled many Americans with determination to make needed social reforms.

## SECTION REVIEW

1. **Vocabulary** caucus, normal school, revival
2. **People and Places** Horace Mann, Wesleyan College, Georgia, Edgar Allan Poe, Nathaniel Hawthorne, Fanny Fern, Henry David Thoreau
3. **Comprehension** How did voting laws change in the early 1800's?
4. **Comprehension** How did the election of officials change?
5. **Critical Thinking** How might limited public education have made democracy hard to achieve?

## Vocabulary

compensate
militant

As the 1800's progressed, American reformers focused on ending slavery. They argued that it was wrong for one person to own another, and insisted that slavery be abolished. Abolitionists gave speeches, printed newspapers, and sometimes broke the law to reach their goal.

## Early Efforts Against Slavery

A few American colonists had opposed slavery, but vigorous antislavery activity did not begin until after the Revolutionary War. By the 1790's several antislavery societies sprang up. Abolitionists, however, remained few in number.

**Strong beliefs spur the antislavery movement.** In the early 1800's abolitionist views spread more rapidly, especially in the North. People had different reasons for believing slavery was wrong. For some, antislavery sentiment grew out of their religion. Since colonial days, Quakers were against slavery. They believed all people are equal before God. It was sinful, therefore, for one person to own another. Others argued against slavery for political reasons. The Declaration of Independence said all people are endowed with unalienable rights—life, liberty, and the pursuit of happiness. Some people believed that a society was not democratic if slavery existed.

Others gained intense feeling against slavery from their own experience with it. Black people, slave and free, held a particular hatred for a social system that kept them in bondage. A society that allowed slavery, they believed, was unjust and inhumane.

By 1804 most northern states abolished slavery. In the South, however, the abolition movement faced a difficult situation. Under the Constitution, each state could decide whether to allow slavery within its borders. Most white citizens in the South supported the slave system. They believed that the health of the southern economy depended on slave labor. Also, most white southerners worried that freeing the slaves would disrupt southern society.

**Liberia is established.** Early on, some abolitionist groups sought ways to gradually free slaves and **compensate** —pay—the slaveholders for their losses. Some groups freed slaves by raising money to buy them from their owners. Others supported colonization—sending former slaves to settle in Africa—as a way to win support for abolition. In 1817 the American Colonization Society was founded. With help from President Monroe, the society bought a strip of land in West Africa. This territory, established as Liberia in 1822, later became an independent nation.

At first, the society members recruited free black people to settle in Liberia. They promoted colonization as a way for blacks to gain greater freedom and independence. After 1827 a few slaveholders freed their slaves for the purpose of sending them to Liberia.

Some black people believed they would always be denied their full rights in the United States. They saw colonization as a way to better their lives. One such person was Paul Cuffe, a wealthy merchant. Even before the American Colonization Society was formed, Cuffe had sent 38 people to Africa at his own expense. Cuffe hoped to continue his colonization program, but he died before he could carry out his plan.

Despite these efforts, most black people rejected colonization. They knew that the

American Colonization Society's most influential members were southern planters who favored slavery. These planters, black people believed, wanted to get rid of free blacks so they could tighten their grip on slavery. In speeches and pamphlets, black people declared that they were in the United States to stay. One anticolonization statement read:

This is our home and this is our country. Beneath its soil lie the bones of our fathers; for it, some of them fought, bled, and died. Here we were born, and here we will die.

In the end, only a few thousand black Americans settled in Africa.

**Free blacks act against slavery.** From the start, free blacks were the backbone of the antislavery movement. They formed antislavery societies and attacked slavery through lawsuits, lectures, and pamphlets. In 1800 a group of black people in Philadelphia submitted an antislavery petition to Congress. In 1827 Samuel Cornish and John Russwurm started the first black newspaper, *Freedom's Journal.* Through articles about the brutal treatment of slaves, they exposed the evils of slavery.

In 1829 David Walker, a black living in Boston, wrote a fiery pamphlet called *An Appeal to the Colored Citizens of the World.* In his *Appeal,* Walker advised black people to revolt against slavery. He warned whites: "We must and shall be free.... Will you wait until we shall, under God, obtain our liberty by the crushing arm of power?"

Walker's message overshadowed earlier, more moderate antislavery activity. Most northern whites, including abolitionists, condemned the pamphlet as dangerous. Southerners, alarmed to find the *Appeal* circulating among slaves, offered a reward for Walker's capture.

**Abolitionists call for immediate action.** Walker's *Appeal* marked a turning point in the antislavery movement. William Lloyd Garrison, a white abolitionist in New England, best expressed this mood. Garrison opposed violence, but he called for the immediate—not gradual—freeing of the slaves. Moreover, he rejected the idea of compensating slaveholders for their losses.

Paul Cuffe, part black and part Indian, encouraged blacks to colonize Sierra Leone in West Africa.

In 1831 Garrison launched *The Liberator,* an abolitionist newspaper. In the first issue, Garrison made his position clear. He declared:

I *will* be as harsh as truth.... I am in earnest—I will not [mislead]—I will not excuse— I will not retreat a single inch—AND I WILL BE HEARD.

Garrison's angry attacks against slavery aroused bitter feeling in the North and South. Many southerners blamed Nat Turner's rebellion on Garrison. Turner led his revolt a few months after Garrison started his newspaper. (See Chapter 14.)

Garrison was often mobbed by angry crowds. He was once nearly killed by a mob in Boston. Nevertheless, Garrison continued to fight slavery. In 1833 Garrison joined with other abolitionists to form the American Anti-Slavery Society.

## A Great Crusade

By the mid-1830's the abolition movement was a great force. Abolitionist agents established local antislavery societies. By 1840 a network of nearly 2,000 societies stretched across the North. They included black and white members.

**Former slaves are active abolitionists.** Black men and women gave a powerful voice to the abolition movement. Many black abolitionists were former slaves. When they escaped to free states, many spoke out against the pain and cruelty of slavery. Several became leaders in the abolition movement.

Frederick Douglass was one such leader. In 1838 Douglass escaped from slavery in Maryland and fled to Massachusetts. At an antislavery meeting, he spoke about what freedom meant to him. Douglass so impressed the audience that he was hired to lecture about his experience as a slave. A powerful orator, Douglass was probably the most effective of all abolitionist lecturers. He also spoke against the injustices faced by free blacks.

William Wells Brown, another abolitionist leader, also escaped from slavery. He became a famous lecturer and writer. Both Douglass and Brown went to England to seek support for the abolitionist movement.

Sojourner Truth was among the first black women to speak publicly against slavery. Originally named Isabella Baumfree, she was born a slave in New York, but gained her freedom when New York abolished slavery. She took her new name and vowed to tell the truth about slavery. Traveling widely through the North, Sojourner Truth was a tireless crusader for justice.

Some black abolitionists were born into freedom. One such person was James Forten. Forten, a veteran of the Revolutionary War, gained a fortune manufacturing sails. He contributed large amounts of money to abolitionist activities, especially to William Lloyd Garrison and *The Liberator*.

**The movement spreads.** Garrison remained a leader in the American Anti-Slavery Society, but many others gained importance. One major figure was Theodore D. Weld, a minister. Weld gave moving sermons that sometimes converted entire communities to the abolitionist cause. Many of these converts became abolitionist agents.

Some southerners also contributed to the abolition movement. Among them were two sisters, Sarah and Angelina Grimké (GRIM-kee) of Charleston, South Carolina. The Grimké sisters came from a prominent family of slaveholders. They detested slavery, however, and left the South and moved to Philadelphia. The Grimké sisters' antislavery speeches drew large crowds.

**Slaves flee on the Underground Railroad.** Some abolitionists took direct action by helping runaway slaves escape. Many slaves made their way to the North and to Canada by means of the **Underground Railroad.** This was not really a railroad, but a network of people who helped runaway

As a slave, Frederick Douglass taught himself to write by secretly copying the schoolbooks of his master's son. After escaping to freedom, Douglass wrote about his experiences as a slave. His writings exerted a powerful influence on the antislavery movement.

PROFILE • Harriet Tubman and Her Times

Harriet Tubman was born a slave around 1821. When she was a child, Tubman was struck across the head by a cruel overseer. The resulting injury caused Tubman to suffer spells of drowsiness for the remainder of her life.

As a slave, Tubman was a field hand. She plowed, loaded, and unloaded wood with great strength and endurance. In 1849 Tubman escaped from slavery. Shortly afterwards she became a conductor for the Underground Railroad. In 1857 she led her aged parents to freedom.

Harriet Tubman was a brave, skilled leader. During her journeys, she took many precautions. She threatened with death any passenger who thought of surrender or attempted to return. By outwitting armed patrols and vicious tracking dogs, Tubman helped more than 300 passengers survive the dangerous trip. Rewards for her capture mounted to $40,000.

For Tubman, freedom was worth fighting and dying for. She stated:

I had reasoned this out in my mind. There was one of two things I had a right to, liberty or death. If I could not have one, I would have the other. For no man would take me alive. I would fight for my liberty as long as my strength lasted.

**Harriet Tubman**

slaves reach safety. Most escape routes ran through Illinois, Indiana, and Ohio.

Underground Railroad "conductors" led escaping slaves to "stations"—the homes of people who secretly sheltered the runaways. By night the slaves traveled north from one station to the next. On the way, other slaves, free blacks, and sympathetic whites provided food, shelter, and clothing.

The most famous conductor of the Underground Railroad was a former slave named Harriet Tubman. She risked her life and her freedom at least 19 times by returning to the South to help others escape. Through her efforts, more than 300 slaves gained freedom.

Levi Coffin, a Quaker in Indiana, was known as the president of the Underground Railroad. If he knew that blacks in his town lacked money to help escaped slaves, Coffin hid runaways in his home.

**Differences cause a split in the movement.** By the late 1830's, the American Anti-Slavery Society was split by differences

Runaway slaves stop at an Indiana farmhouse in this 1850's painting by Charles T. Webber. Between 1830 and 1860 about 50,000 slaves escaped to northern states and Canada on the Underground Railroad.

among its members. William Lloyd Garrison was in the center of many disagreements. Garrison's **militant** —aggressive—stand on abolition made him uncompromising in his demands.

Garrison attacked church leaders and others for failing to speak against slavery. He called the Constitution "a covenant with Death and an agreement with Hell" because it protected slavery. Garrison believed that the northern states should separate from the South. He also insisted that abolitionists refuse to vote, hold office, or take any other political action as long as slavery existed.

Other abolitionists felt that political action was necessary for the success of the abolition movement. Many abolitionists also disagreed with Garrison's efforts to give women equal rights in the American Anti-Slavery Society. In 1839 many people broke off from Garrison's society and formed a moderate antislavery organization. Soon after, they began a campaign of political action by forming an antislavery political party—the **Liberty party.** The next year, the Liberty party nominated James G. Birney, a former Alabama slaveowner, as its presidential candidate. Birney lost the election, but the Liberty party made abolition an important political issue.

At the same time, an outspoken group of abolitionists called for militant action. They believed that the laws protecting slavery should be defied. One such person was Henry Highland Garnet, a former slave from Maryland. At a national black convention, Garnet proclaimed:

> Brethren, arise, arise! Strike for your lives and liberties. Now is the day and the hour. . . . Rather die free men than live to be slaves. . . . Let your motto be resistance!

## SECTION REVIEW

1. **Vocabulary**   compensate, militant
2. **People and Places**   Liberia, Paul Cuffe, William Lloyd Garrison, Frederick Douglass, Sojourner Truth, James Forten, Sarah and Angelina Grimké, Indiana, Ohio, Harriet Tubman, James G. Birney
3. **Comprehension**   Why was Liberia established?
4. **Comprehension**   How did abolitionists help in the Underground Railroad?
5. **Critical Thinking**   How were William Lloyd Garrison's activities different from those of the Liberty party?

# CRITICAL THINKING: Comparing Primary and Secondary Sources

If you were writing a report of an event in the 1850's, you might consult **primary sources** and **secondary sources.** As you recall, primary sources are records from the past, such as newspapers, diaries, letters, and government documents.

A secondary source is an account of an event written by someone who did not witness or take part in that event. This textbook, for example, is a secondary source.

Both primary and secondary sources are important to the study of history. Primary sources often give detailed accounts of past events and record how people felt about them at the time. Secondary sources are written later, so they often give a clearer picture of the causes and effects of past events.

The excerpts on this page illustrate some differences between primary and secondary sources. Both are about William Lloyd Garrison, a leader of the antislavery movement. Read the excerpts carefully. Then answer the questions that follow.

---

Excerpt A

[At a Fourth of July meeting in 1854, Mr. Garrison performed an action which would, he said, make clear . . . how he regarded the proslavery laws.] Producing a copy of the Fugitive Slave Law, he set fire to it and burnt it to ashes. . . . Then, holding up a copy of the *U.S. Constitution*, he branded it as the source and parent of all the other [outrages. He called it] "a covenant with death. . . . [Thereupon, he burned] it to ashes on the spot, exclaiming: "So perish all compromises with tyranny! And let all the people say, Amen!" A tremendous shout of "Amen!" went up to heaven in ratification of the deed.

---

Excerpt B

Garrison . . . refused to compromise with fellow reformers and . . . it was very hard for others to work with him. . . . His solution to the slavery problem was nonviolent secession of New England from the Union, if nothing else. He burned a copy of the Constitution in public to show his contempt for a government that protected slavery.

Some historians have argued that Garrison did the cause more harm than good. He soon helped drive the South into a singleminded defense of slavery. He divided abolitionists while making the label so [hateful] that reasonable people shrank from it. Garrison and his followers created the no-compromise atmosphere that made peaceful solutions impossible. . . .

---

1. Which of the two excerpts is the primary source? Which of the excerpts is the secondary source?
2. What are some of the different kinds of primary sources that the author might have used to write the account in the secondary source?
3. Which of the sentences in Excerpt B refers to an incident that was described in Excerpt A?
4. Which excerpt tells you how Garrison's speech and actions were received by his audience?
5. According to the author of Excerpt B, what were some of the effects of Garrison's actions?
6. The author of Excerpt B states that Garrison created a no-compromise atmosphere around the slavery issue. What words and actions in Excerpt A support this statement?

# What movements for social reform arose in the 1800's?

## Vocabulary

suffrage

temperance

rehabilitation

Abolition was by far the largest reform movement in the 1800's. There were, however, many other crusades for social change. Reformers sought ways to help others live useful, happy lives. They also battled against what they considered to be injustices in American society.

## Women's Rights

Many women took a special interest in the abolition movement. When they tried to participate actively, however, they often met with resistance.

**Public action by women meets disapproval.** Abolitionists, clergy, and others often fiercely attacked women who spoke out against slavery. In the 1800's most people disapproved of women's involvement in public affairs. It was considered unfeminine for women to speak in public places. Women could not even offer prayers in church. For a woman to address a mixed audience—one that included men and women—was viewed as shocking.

**Abolitionists call for women's rights.** Sarah and Angelina Grimké were criticized for their part in the abolition movement. In response to their critics, the Grimké sisters spoke out on women's rights. Some abolitionists considered the women's rights issue to be unrelated to abolitionism. The Grimké sisters, however, continued to crusade for both. They argued that both issues dealt with basic rights.

In 1840 a group of American women, including Elizabeth Cady Stanton and Lucretia Mott, went to London for the World Anti-Slavery Convention. Although these women were delegates, the men in charge refused them the right to participate. Mott and Stanton realized that they could not bring about social change if they themselves lacked full social and political rights. They decided to launch a vigorous campaign for women's rights.

**Women lack important rights.** Equal rights for women would require major reform. In the 1800's women had few legal or political rights. Women could not vote, sit on juries, or hold public office.

Many people believed that a woman's place was in the home. As a result, most women of the mid-1800's were also denied opportunities for education. For this reason, jobs that required education and training were usually closed to them.

Many laws treated women—particularly married women—as dependents. In most states, a husband controlled any property his wife inherited and any wages she earned. A husband could also punish his wife, as long as he did not seriously harm her. Single women had greater freedom. They had more control over their own lives and could manage their own property.

**Women demand equal rights.** Stanton and Mott set out to draw attention to problems faced by women. In 1848 they organized a women's rights convention at Seneca Falls, New York. This was the first national convention of its kind.

Both the women and the men at the Seneca Falls Convention adopted a plan of action—the **Seneca Falls Declaration**—that was modeled on the Declaration of Independence. (See pages 180–183.) The Seneca Falls Declaration proclaimed that "all men and women are created equal." The history of mankind, the document maintained, "is a history of repeated injuries . . . on the part of

# THE SENECA FALLS DECLARATION  1848

Elizabeth Cady Stanton was one of the earliest and most respected leaders of the women's suffrage movement. In 1848 Stanton helped organize a convention for women's rights at Seneca Falls, New York. The delegates to the convention drew up the following document, called the Seneca Falls Declaration, asking for the rights that women had been denied.

## Read to Find Out

1. Upon what famous American document is the Seneca Falls Declaration based?
2. What does the declaration tell about women's rights in Stanton's time?

---

... We hold these truths to be self-evident: that all men and women are created equal; that they are endowed by their Creator with certain unalienable rights; that among these are life, liberty, and the pursuit of happiness; that to secure these rights governments are instituted, deriving their just powers from the consent of the governed....

The history of mankind is a history of repeated injuries and [seizing of rights] on the part of man toward woman, having as its direct object the establishment of an absolute tyranny over her....

He has never permitted her to vote....

He has taken from her all right to property, even ... wages....

In marriage, she must promise obedience to her husband, he becoming ... her master....

He has kept for himself nearly all the profitable jobs....

He has denied her the opportunity of ... education....

He only allows her the lowest positions in the Church, and the State....

He has tried, in every way possible, to destroy her confidence, lessen her self-respect, and make her a dependent person....

### *Elizabeth Cady Stanton*

man toward woman." The historic statement closed with the demand that women "have immediate admission to all the rights and privileges which belong to them as citizens of the United States."

The convention delegates passed many resolutions. They demanded equality for women at work, church, school, and before the law. The only resolution that delegates hesitated to pass was one that called for women's **suffrage** —right to vote. To most of the delegates, this seemed like a bold step. After a lengthy discussion, the delegates passed the suffrage resolution, but only by a very narrow margin.

Women's rights leaders were often ridiculed for their ideas. In 1851 at a meeting in Ohio, a minister suggested that women were weak and helpless and therefore should not be allowed to vote. Sojourner Truth, a leader in the movement, replied:

> That man over there says women need to be helped into carriages and lifted over ditches, and to have the best place everywhere. Nobody ever helps me into carriages or over puddles, or gives me the best place. And ain't I a woman? Look at my arm! I have ploughed and planted and gathered into barns, and no man could head me! And ain't I a woman? I could work as much and eat as much as a man—when I could get it—and bear the lash as well! And ain't I a woman?.... I have borne thirteen children, and seen most of them sold off into slavery, and when I cried out with my mother's grief, none but Jesus heard me! And ain't I a woman?

**Sojourner Truth, born into slavery, won freedom in 1827. She became famous for her inspiring speeches against slavery. She also spoke in support of women's rights.**

In the 1850's many national women's rights conventions took place. Among those who joined the movement was Susan B. Anthony. Anthony, a powerful organizer, soon became the most influential leader in the suffrage movement. She also worked to secure equal pay for women teachers and the right of women to control their property.

**Women's rights advance slowly.** The reform movement that began at Seneca Falls did help women gain some ground, but progress was slow. A few states gave married women control over their property and earnings. Many women also made gains from increasing educational opportunities. Still, women were denied many rights—including suffrage—for years to come.

## Social Reforms

Americans of the mid-1800's also worked for many social reforms. Hundreds of groups sought changes in such areas as alcohol abuse, treatment of the mentally ill, and prison conditions.

**Reformers crusade against alcohol.** In the 1800's heavy drinking was a common problem. People drank liquor at most social events. Habitual drinking caused crises for many families.

In the 1830's reformers began to recognize problems caused by alcohol. They urged **temperance** —moderation—in the use of alcohol. Later, temperance groups insisted that people stop drinking altogether. In 1836 the first national convention of the American Temperance Union was held. In 1846 the Maine legislature passed a law banning the sale of liquor, and 13 states soon followed. There were many people opposed to these laws, however, and most of them were repealed.

**Conditions improve in prisons and mental institutions.** In the early 1800's people who had committed minor crimes were sent to prison. Conditions in the prisons were usually filthy, and the prisoners frequently lacked adequate food, medical care, and exercise. Young people who had committed minor crimes were often housed with hardened criminals.

The early 1800's was a period of religious re-awakening, as this 1836 engraving by E.W. Clay shows. Many religious leaders urged their followers to support the reform movements of the times.

A number of people became concerned about the treatment of prisoners. Chief among them was Dorothea Dix of Massachusetts. In speeches and writings, Dix insisted that prisoners needed **rehabilitation** —help to return to normal, useful lives. As a result of Dix's efforts, prisons became less brutal.

Dix was also determined to improve conditions at mental institutions. In the 1800's mental illness was looked upon as a disgrace, and the mentally ill were harshly treated. They were usually locked in institutions and sometimes chained to walls. Mental patients were poorly fed and received little medical care.

Dix traveled across the United States speaking about the problems of the mentally ill. Through Dorothea Dix's efforts, associations were formed to study better methods of treating mental illness.

**Disabled Americans seek greater opportunities.** Reformers also worked to improve conditions for disabled people. In the 1830's Samuel G. Howe founded the Perkins Institute for the Blind in Boston. There Howe trained blind people to earn their living and to lead independent lives. Blind Americans also learned to use the braille (brayl) alphabet, a raised alphabet that could be read by touch. This method was invented in 1829 by

Louis Braille of France. It greatly improved methods for educating blind people. Another reformer, Thomas H. Gallaudet (gal-uh-DET) worked with the deaf. In 1817 Gallaudet started the first American school for deaf children, the American Asylum for Deaf-Mutes, in Hartford, Connecticut.

These students at the Perkins Institute for the Blind in the late nineteenth century are reading geography textbooks in braille. The school also taught its students trades.

## SECTION REVIEW

1. **Vocabulary**  suffrage, temperance, rehabilitation
2. **People and Places**  Elizabeth Cady Stanton, Lucretia Mott, Seneca Falls, New York, Sojourner Truth, Susan B. Anthony, Maine, Dorothea Dix, Samuel G. Howe, Louis Braille
3. **Comprehension**  How did the World Anti-Slavery Convention lead to the cause for women's rights?
4. **Comprehension**  What are some legal rights that women did not have in the nineteenth century?
5. **Critical Thinking**  In what ways, do you think, might better treatment of prisoners and of the mentally ill have impoved society as a whole?

# Chapter 15 Summary

During the 1800's many states ended property requirements for voters. This gave more people a say in government, but many groups were still denied the vote. Nominating conventions replaced caucuses as the way to select presidential candidates. Elections also became more democratic. Governors and members of the Electoral College were chosen through direct elections. The major parties began using nominating conventions to choose presidential candidates.

As democracy increased, many people saw the need for greater reform. Abolitionism was the largest reform movement. Some reformers called for gradual abolition through colonization in Liberia. Abolitionists like William Lloyd Garrison, Frederick Douglass, and Sarah and Angelina Grimké called for immediate abolition. Many abolitionists helped run the Underground Railroad. In 1840 there was a split in the movement. One group formed the Liberty party. More militant abolitionists called for revolt. There were many other reform movements in the 1800's. At the Seneca Falls Convention women asked for suffrage. Other reformers sought rehabilitation for prisoners and for temperance. Some of the reformers worked to improve the unsatisfactory conditions for the disabled.

# CAUSES and EFFECTS

## Sectional Differences ★ ★ ★

South has good
soil and climate
for farming

North has good
harbors and
rivers for trade

Industrial
Revolution brings
new machines

### CONTRIBUTING CAUSES

Cotton gin makes
cotton production
profitable

Slavery provides
cheap farm labor

New markets
open for
American products

New inventions
lead to growth
of factories

### MAIN CAUSES

# SECTIONAL DIFFERENCES

### EFFECTS

Abolitionism
grows in North

Plantation system
dominates South

Conflicts over
slavery and
tariffs deepen

South threatens
to secede

Union is
preserved by
compromise

### LONG-TERM EFFECTS

Improved
transportation
binds West
to Northeast

Labor unions and
reform movements
develop

Conflicts lead
to Civil War

Democratic and
Republican
parties emerge

# Chapter **15** REVIEW

## Vocabulary and Key Terms

Use the following terms to complete the sentences below. Write your answers on a separate sheet of paper.

militant
rehabilitation
Liberty party
caucus

compensate
temperance
suffrage

1. The closed _____ gave ordinary people little influence in choosing presidential candidates.
2. Some abolitionists sought to _____ slaveholders whose slaves were freed through colonization.
3. Henry Highland Garnet was a more _____ abolitionist than were members of the _____.
4. Susan B. Anthony worked to secure _____ and other rights for women.
5. Reformers of the 1800's demanded _____ in the use of alcohol and _____ for prisoners.

## Recalling the Facts

1. How did the laws of some western states help elect Andrew Jackson to the presidency in 1828?
2. In what condition were schools after the Revolutionary War?
3. What obstacles in education did black people face in the 1800's?
4. Why did Henry David Thoreau urge people to defy unjust laws?
5. What effect did the revival movement have on many Americans?
6. Why did many black people reject the efforts of the American Colonization Society?
7. What led to the split in the American Anti-Slavery Society?
8. How did most people react to women's involvement in public activities?

9. Why did reformers start the temperance movement?
10. What conditions in prisons and mental institutions did Dorothea Dix try to change?
11. How did the efforts of Louis Braille and Samuel G. Howe improve conditions for blind people?

## Places to Locate

Match the letters on the map with the places listed below. Write your answers on a separate sheet of paper.

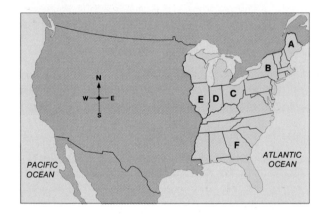

1. Georgia
2. Illinois
3. Maine
4. Ohio
5. Indiana
6. New York

## Critical Thinking

1. Some abolitionists called for militant action in the mid-1800's. Do you think militant action was necessary? Why or why not? Consider these questions in your answer:
   a. Why did abolitionists believe slavery was wrong?
   b. What attitude did southerners have toward the abolition of slavery?
   c. What demands did militant abolitionists make?

2. Reformers called for changes in the treatment of prisoners. Do you think these reforms were necessary? Consider these questions in your answer:
   a. What is the purpose of imprisoning criminals?
   b. What were conditions like in nineteenth-century prisons?
   c. What changes in prison conditions did reformers demand?

## Understanding History

1. Reread the section "New laws extend the vote" on page 345. Then answer these questions.
   a. **Citizenship.** Why might the laws of some of the western states have prompted the original 13 states to extend the vote?
   b. **Citizenship.** By 1860 what factors kept voting laws from being truly democratic?
2. Reread the section "Women demand equal rights" on page 356. Then answer these questions.
   a. **Primary Sources.** How did the Seneca Falls Declaration point out injustices toward women?
   b. **Primary Sources.** What aspects of Sojourner Truth's life experience showed that women were not weak or helpless?

## Projects and Activities

1. **Writing a Fictional Account.** Imagine you are a slave escaping on the Underground Railroad. Write a diary of your journey. Describe your reasons for escaping and the experiences you have along the way.
2. **Giving an Oral Report.** Find out more about one of the following topics: Walt Whitman, women's colleges, nineteenth-century American painters, Liberia, the Underground Railroad, women's suffrage, Samuel G. Howe, Louis Braille. Prepare an oral report and present it to the class using the information you have gathered.

3. **Researching Literature.** Use the library to find a poem by Walt Whitman. In front of the class, read the poem and then explain its meaning.
4. **Writing a Report.** Research one of the following important figures of the 1800's: Henry David Thoreau, William Lloyd Garrison, Frederick Douglass, James Forten, Sojourner Truth, Susan B. Anthony, Dorothea Dix. Write a report based on the information you find.

## Practicing Your Skill

Below are two excerpts. Read them, then answer the questions that follow.

> **Excerpt A**
> On the day of the inauguration it seemed to [some people] as though their worst fears had come true. Jackson was followed from the Capitol to the White House by a motley mob, black and white, of all sorts, who pressed into the Mansion to see the new President of the people.

> **Excerpt B**
> ... [S]uch a cortege as followed him! Country men, farmers, gentlemen, mounted and dismounted, boys, women and children, black and white. Carriages, wagons and carts all pursuing him to the President's house.... What a scene did we witness [inside]! The Majesty of the People had disappeared, and a rabble, a mob, of boys, [blacks], women, children, scrambling, fighting, romping. What a pity; what a pity.

1. Which of the two accounts is the primary source? Which is the secondary source?
2. What kinds of primary sources might the author have used to write the secondary source?
3. Which sentence in Excerpt A summarizes the events in Excerpt B?
4. Excerpt A states that some people regretted the events described. In what way does Excerpt B support this idea?

# UNIT 5 REVIEW

## Unit Summary

★ **Sectional interests began to grow after the War of 1812.**

- Conflict arose over the issues of land, tariffs, and slavery.
- The Missouri Compromise settled the slavery question in the Louisiana Purchase.
- The Monroe Doctrine warned Europe against interference in the Western Hemisphere.

★ **The Northeast became the center of manufacturing.**

- Use of the factory system increased industrial production.
- Canals and improved roads expanded trade and travel.
- The steam engine marked a new era in transportation.
- Long-distance communication was made possible by the telegraph.

★ **Cotton became the leading crop in the South.**

- The cotton gin made cotton growing more profitable.
- The use of slave labor increased on southern plantations.
- Economic and social differences divided the North and the South.

★ **The 1800's brought greater democracy and social change.**

- Voter participation was increased.
- The abolition movement gained strength in the North.
- Social reforms improved educational opportunities.
- The women's movement worked for equal opportunities for women.

## Understanding Chronology

Study the Unit 5 time line on page 283. Then complete the following activity on a separate sheet of paper.

Use your text to find the dates of the following events. Arrange the events in chronological order. Then explain how each one is related to an event shown on the Unit 5 time line.

**Indian Removal Act**
**Statehood of Maine**
**Independence of Mexico**
**Invention of the cotton gin**

## Writing About History

1. **Creating a Letter.** Imagine that you moved from a farm to work in an urban factory during the 1840's. Write a letter to your family describing working conditions, what people in the city are like, and how city life differs from farm life. Close your letter with a description of your feelings about your new life.
2. **Organizing Information.** Write a report summarizing the differences between the North and the South in the 1800's. Include northern and southern occupations, geography, living conditions, and attitudes toward slavery and abolition.
3. **Writing an Editorial.** Choose one of the social-reform issues important in the 1800's. Write an editorial for a newspaper explaining the purpose of the reform, why it is needed, and what practical steps can be taken to accomplish the reform. Then write another editorial expressing the opposite point of view.
4. **Writing a Biography.** Write a biography of President Andrew Jackson. Find information about his years as a soldier, his popularity with frontier citizens, and his use of the spoils system.

**5. Interpreting a Cartoon.** The political cartoon above shows how some people thought of Andrew Jackson during his presidency. Explain the cartoon and list reasons why Jackson had become unpopular with some Americans.

## Projects

**1. Making a Crossword Puzzle.** In the textbook find important names, places, ideas, and other data about the North and the South. Use this information to make a crossword puzzle. Ask your classmates to complete the puzzle.

**2. Presenting a Speech.** Imagine that you were a supporter of one of the following movements: abolition, women's rights, temperance, or prison reform. Prepare a speech for an audience in the 1840's. Use posters or other props when giving your presentation to the class.

**3. Planning a Presentation.** With a partner, plan a presentation about travel and communication advances in the 1800's. Make posters showing turnpikes, canals, steamboats, railroads, and the telegraph system. Explain how they affected American economic and social life. Present your project in class.

**4. Doing Research.** Find information about the results of the Indian removal policy during the early 1800's. Explain the reasons for the Indian Removal Act, the methods used to force Native Americans to relocate, and how the removal policy changed their lives. Present your information in a written report.

**5. Making a Speech.** Imagine that you were a supporter of Henry Clay's American System in 1816. Write a speech to Congress outlining the American System and why it should be adopted. Present your speech to the class.

## Finding Out More

Blos, Joan W. *A Gathering of Days: A New England Girl's Journal, 1830–32.* Scribner, 1979. A fictional diary of a 13-year-old girl's life in New Hampshire.

Fisher, Leonard Everett. *The Factories.* Holiday House, 1979. The beginning of the factory system in the United States and the factory's contribution to America's industrial growth are explored.

Levinson, Nancy Smiler. *The First Women Who Spoke Out.* Dillon, 1983. A book about early women's rights leaders.

Wilson, Dorothy Clarke. *I Will Be a Doctor! The Story of America's First Woman Physician.* Abingdon, 1983. Elizabeth Blackwell, who faced incredible odds to graduate from medical school, grew to prominence in America as a physician, an educator, and a social worker.

# UNIT 6

# EXPANSION AND CIVIL WAR

## 1840–1877

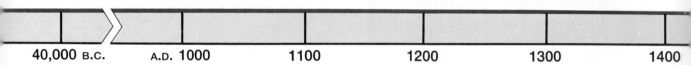

| 40,000 B.C. | A.D. 1000 | 1100 | 1200 | 1300 | 1400 |

As America spread westward, disagreement about the nation's future led the North and the South into a bitter Civil War.

1840 – 1877

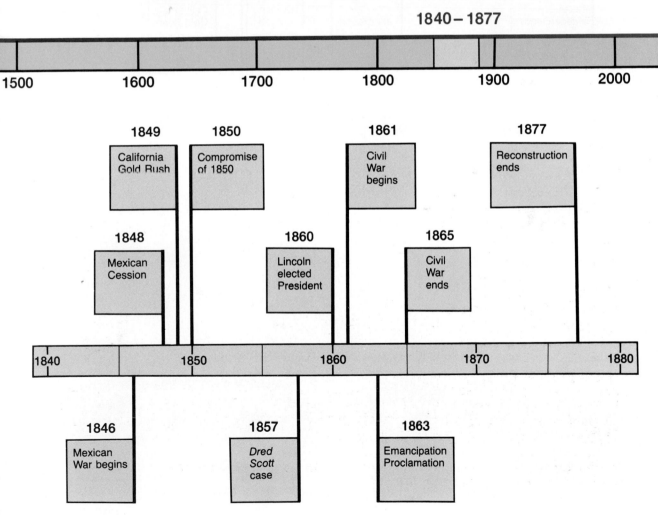

| 1500 | 1600 | 1700 | 1800 | 1900 | 2000 |

**1849** California Gold Rush

**1850** Compromise of 1850

**1861** Civil War begins

**1877** Reconstruction ends

**1848** Mexican Cession

**1860** Lincoln elected President

**1865** Civil War ends

| 1840 | 1850 | 1860 | 1870 | 1880 |

**1846** Mexican War begins

**1857** *Dred Scott* case

**1863** Emancipation Proclamation

# CHAPTER
# 16 The United States Reaches from Sea to Sea
## 1840–1853

| Jackson | Van Buren | W. H. Harrison / Tyler | Polk | Taylor | Fillmore | Pierce |
|---------|-----------|------------------------|------|--------|----------|--------|

1835　　　　　　1840　　　　　　1845　　　　　　1850　　　　　　1855

- Texan independence
- Texas annexation
- Oregon divided
- Mexican War begins
- California Gold Rush
- Treaty of Guadalupe Hidalgo
- Gadsden Purchase

**Wagon trains crossed many rivers on the long journey west. River crossings were only one of many hazards on the trail.**

## Preparing to Read

As American pioneers marched steadily westward, they looked eagerly at the lands beyond the Louisiana Territory. Step by step these lands were added to the United States, like the pieces of a giant jigsaw puzzle. The familiar outline of the present-day United States was filled in as each piece was added. This chapter explains how the United States gained more and more territory, until it reached from the Atlantic Ocean across the entire continent to the Pacific. As you read this chapter, try to answer the following questions:

1. How did the United States gain part of the Oregon Country?
2. How did the United States gain Texas, the Southwest, and California?
3. How did the discovery of gold bring California into the Union?

# 1 How did the United States gain part of the Oregon Country?

## Vocabulary
expansionist
joint occupation
prairie schooner

During the 1840's many Americans were excited by reports of the area west of the Rocky Mountains. Adventurous pioneers dreamed of taming this frontier and gaining new lands for the United States. James K. Polk, who was elected President in 1844, was a strong believer in growth. During his four years in office, a huge amount of territory was added to the United States.

Polk and those who shared his ideas were called **expansionists.** Expansionists wanted to expand or enlarge the territory of the United States. These people believed that the young nation should reach from the Atlantic Ocean to the Pacific Ocean. Indeed, they felt that such expansion was clearly bound to happen. This view—that the United States was meant to span the whole North American continent—was known as **Manifest Destiny.**

## Settlement of Oregon

All the land between Alaska and California, sometimes referred to as the Pacific Northwest, was once called the **Oregon Country.** This beautiful region of mountains, rivers, and fertile valleys was home to many different Native American groups. There was an abundance of wildlife as well, including many fur-bearing animals.

**Four nations claim Oregon.** In the early 1800's Oregon was claimed by Spain, Britain, Russia, and the United States. Explorers from all four countries had sailed along the Oregon coast or made their way inland.

During the early part of the century, both British and American traders began to see possibilities of a rich fur trade in Oregon. In 1811 John Jacob Astor, a leader in the American fur business, established a fur-trading post near the mouth of the Columbia River. The British already had a post near present-day Spokane, Washington. For a short time, the British and American companies were rivals for the Oregon fur business. The War of 1812, however, ruined Astor's plans. At that time, the Americans sold their holdings to the British.

369

Oxen were more valuable than horses on the Oregon Trail. Though oxen were slower, they were stronger and able to pull the heavy wagons longer distances. Families with fewer than three span, or pairs, of oxen often had to lighten their wagons by discarding property.

**Britain and the United States share Oregon.** After the war, both the United States and Great Britain maintained their claims to Oregon. In 1818 the two countries agreed to **joint occupation**—shared ownership—of Oregon. Shortly afterward, Spain and Russia gave up their claims to Oregon. Spain agreed to claim no land north of the forty-second parallel, while Russia gave up any claim south of the latitude 54°40′N.* (See map on page 372.) Thus the United States and Great Britain were free to try to work out their plan for joint occupation of Oregon.

**Settlers travel to Oregon.** For about 20 years after 1818, not many Americans went to Oregon. The British, on the other hand, were making good profits from the Oregon fur trade. In Fort Vancouver, a Canadian named John McLoughlin was employed by the Hudson's Bay Company to act as governor. McLoughlin treated the Indians fairly and welcomed the few Americans who found their way to Oregon.

News of this Pacific Northwest region did not attract many Americans until the late 1830's. Among the early settlers were missionaries, such as Henry and Eliza Spalding and Marcus and Narcissa Whitman, who wanted to teach Christianity to the Indians. Narcissa Whitman and Eliza Spalding were the first white women to cross the western mountains into the Pacific Northwest.

The Whitmans started a mission at Walla Walla near the Columbia River. They worked among the Cayuse Indians for about 11 years. They wrote enthusiastic letters to friends back East, describing the rich farmlands, plentiful rainfall, thick forests, and good salmon fishing in Oregon.

Another leading pioneer was George Washington Bush. Bush was a free black who had fought bravely for the United States during the War of 1812. In 1844 he guided his family and a handful of whites into the Oregon Country. They settled on land north of the Columbia River, where Bush became a wealthy farmer.

**Americans follow the Oregon Trail.** Reports from the Whitmans and others

---

* This line of latitude, read as "fifty-four forty north," lies 54 degrees and 40 minutes north of the equator.

reached the East at a time when many people there were out of work and feeling discouraged. Soon **prairie schooners**—large covered wagons—were rolling westward over the **Oregon Trail.** (See map on page 385.)

The pioneers gathered at Independence or St. Joseph, Missouri, or at Omaha, Nebraska, where they banded together in large caravans for protection. When the spring grass was high enough to feed the horses and cattle, they set out on their 2,000-mile (3,200-kilometer) journey.

Scouts went far ahead of the wagons to see what lay beyond. For many days the long lines of prairie schooners, horses, cattle, and oxen crawled westward from dawn to dusk. Each night the wagons were drawn up in a circle to keep the animals from wandering away. If all went well, there was time to reach Oregon before snow fell in the Rockies and made the mountains impassable. Yet if anything delayed the pioneers, they knew they would be in serious trouble.

The trail left the Missouri River and followed the Platte River along its north branch into the Rockies. From here the pioneers climbed a steep grade to the South Pass, a broad, level valley that cut through the Rockies. To the west they found the Green River and from there they crossed to the Snake River. The Snake took them north and west to the great Columbia River. They had reached Oregon at last!

## Gaining the Oregon Country

By the early 1840's several thousand Americans had made their way to Oregon, where they had become farmers and started little villages. But these settlers were not satisfied to have Oregon shared by the United States and Great Britain. They wanted a

During the 1860's and 1870's the Plains Indians resisted the westward flow of settlers. The settlers' fears are reflected in this attack scene painted by Frederic Remington.

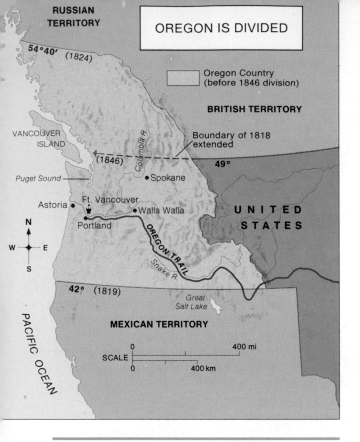

**OREGON IS DIVIDED**

54°40' (1824)

☐ Oregon Country (before 1846 division)

**BRITISH TERRITORY**

VANCOUVER ISLAND

Boundary of 1818 extended

(1846)

49°

Puget Sound

• Spokane

Astoria •

Ft. Vancouver

**UNITED STATES**

• Walla Walla

Portland

OREGON TRAIL

Snake R.

42° (1819)

Great Salt Lake

**MEXICAN TERRITORY**

PACIFIC OCEAN

SCALE

0                400 mi

0      400 km

## Map Study

The dispute between Great Britain and the United States over the Oregon Country was settled by extending the border between Canada and the United States to the Pacific Ocean. What parallel was used as the boundary? Use the map in this book's atlas to determine what states were made from the Oregon Territory.

government of their own, and they wanted to be part of the United States. Soon the governments of Great Britain and the United States began to realize that the plan of joint occupation would no longer work. A new way of governing the Oregon Country would have to be found.

**Oregon is divided.** Many Americans insisted that the United States should claim all of Oregon. James K. Polk was their champion. When he ran for President in 1844, he strongly supported their cause. Two of his campaign slogans were "All of Oregon or none" and "Fifty-four forty or fight."

After his election, President Polk set out to gain the Oregon Country for the United States.

So many Americans had settled in Oregon that the British fur trade was no longer as profitable as it had been. The British government, realizing this, was willing to compromise but not to give up all of Oregon. The United States also decided to compromise. Representatives from the United States and Great Britain met for many months. Finally, in June 1846 an agreement was reached to divide Oregon at the forty-ninth parallel of latitude. The border between Canada and the United States had previously been set at that latitude from the Great Lakes to the Rocky Mountains. The agreement of 1846 extended this line of latitude west to the Pacific Ocean. (See map on this page.)

The land in the Pacific Northwest south of the forty-ninth parallel was organized by Congress as the Oregon Territory. Its population continued to grow rapidly, and in 1859 part of the territory was added to the Union as the state of Oregon. The rest of the territory was then called Washington, in honor of the country's first President. Years later, it was divided into the states of Washington and Idaho.

## SECTION REVIEW

1. **Vocabulary**  expansionist, joint occupation, prairie schooner
2. **People and Places**  James Polk, Oregon Country, John Jacob Astor, Marcus and Narcissa Whitman, Oregon Trail, forty-ninth parallel
3. **Comprehension**  How did the United States and Great Britain resolve their claims to Oregon in 1818?
4. **Comprehension**  What did candidate Polk's campaign slogan "Fifty-four forty or fight" mean?
5. **Critical Thinking**  How were compromise and peaceful negotiation important in settling the Oregon claims? Explain your answer.

# MAPS AND GRAPHS: Latitude and Longitude

Some of the maps in this book are marked with a crisscross pattern of lines called a grid. The lines that run in an east-west direction are called **latitude lines,** or **parallels.** Parallels are measured in degrees (°) and parts of degrees called minutes ('). There are 60 minutes in each degree. These measurements tell how far a parallel is from the **equator**—the imaginary line at 0° latitude. The letters *N* and *S* tell whether the parallel lies north or south of the equator.

The lines that run in a north-south direction are called **longitude lines,** or **meridians.** Meridians are labeled in degrees east (*E*) or west (*W*) of a baseline of 0° longitude, called the **prime meridian.**

A grid on a map is a great help in finding places. The location of a place can be described by its **coordinates**—the point where lines of latitude and longitude meet. For example, the coordinates of Salt Lake City, Utah, are 41°N, 112°W. (Note that the latitude is always given first.) By finding the point where these two lines would meet on the grid, you can find Salt Lake City.

Sometimes it is necessary to estimate latitude and longitude because maps do not have space to show every parallel and meridian. These lines are usually shown at intervals of 5, 10, 15, or 20 degrees.

In 1846 the United States and Great Britain divided the Oregon Country at the 49°N parallel. At various times, latitude and longitude lines have been used to help solve other border problems.

The map on this page shows the western United States in 1850. Study the map, and then answer the following questions on a separate sheet of paper.

1. Which territory lies entirely north of the 40°N parallel?

2. The 120°W meridian forms part of the border between what two areas?
3. In which territory do the lines 35°N and 110°W meet?
4. What places are located at the following coordinates?
   **a.** 45°N, 123°W        **c.** 39°N, 105°W
   **b.** 36°N, 106°W
5. The city of Denver, Colorado, was founded in 1859 at approximately 40°N, 105°W. Locate these coordinates on the map. Is Denver north or south of Salem? About how many degrees of latitude separate the two cities?

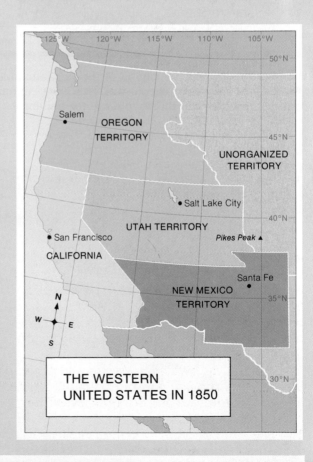

THE WESTERN
UNITED STATES IN 1850

# 2 How did the United States gain Texas, the Southwest, and California?

## Vocabulary
annex
cede

Mexico declared its independence from Spain in 1821. The new Republic of Mexico claimed all the land colonized by the Spaniards in what is now the southwestern part of the United States. American pioneers, however, were beginning to move into that region, and many people thought this land, as well as the Pacific Northwest, should belong to the United States.

## American Movement into Texas

In 1820 the land known as Texas was a vast area that included fertile farmland, grassy prairies, dry plains, mountains, and deserts. This land, however, was thinly settled. Most of the inhabitants were Native Americans, such as the Wichita, the Apache, the Kiowa, and the Comanche. Spanish priests had founded several missions, and a handful of military posts existed. There were few communities, however, and these were mainly in southeastern Texas.

**Americans settle in Texas.** The first American colonists came to Texas in 1822, led by Stephen F. Austin. They settled on

In 1840 Austin was the capital of the Republic of Texas. How does the picture show that Austin was a thriving community? What natural resource did the people use for building?

land that the Spanish government had promised Austin's father two years earlier. By the time of their arrival, Mexico had won its independence from Spain and was in control of the region. The new Mexican government was eager for growth in Texas, and it welcomed American settlers. The newcomers, however, had to agree to belong to the Catholic faith, become Mexican citizens, and obey Mexican laws.

Austin was able to offer land to settlers for very little money, and the colony grew rapidly. Soon the Mexican government opened other parts of Texas for settlement by Americans. Many small farmers from the United States bought land, and plantation families from the South moved to Texas with their slaves. Free blacks who settled in Texas worked as farmers, ranchers, or cowhands. Some of them, like Sam McCulloch, later fought for Texan independence. By 1835 there were 30,000 colonists from the United States in Texas. This was a much greater number of settlers than Spain had sent in more than 300 years.

**Texans declare their independence.** Mexico realized too late that it had been a mistake to allow Americans to settle in its territory. The Americans were different in language, religion, and ways of living. Furthermore, they were independent in spirit and disliked many of the Mexican laws. Quarrels developed between the American colonists and the Mexican government. One disagreement was about slavery. Mexico had laws forbidding slavery in its territory, but many Americans brought their slaves into Texas anyway.

To prevent these disputes from growing more serious, the Mexican government tried to stop more American colonists from entering Texas. This only added to the anger of the Americans already there. When an ambitious general named Antonio López de Santa Anna seized control in Mexico, matters went from bad to worse. The American colonists and many Mexicans in Texas resented Santa Anna's harsh rule. Finally, they revolted against Mexico. On March 2, 1836, they declared Texas an independent nation.

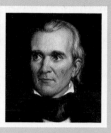
Mexico tried to crush the revolt. General Santa Anna led troops into Texas to punish the Americans. The Texans suffered two severe defeats but won a final victory.

The first defeat was at the **Alamo** (AL-uh-mo) in the city of San Antonio. The Alamo was an old Spanish mission surrounded by high walls. A force of fewer than 200 Texans, under the command of Colonel William Barrett Travis, barricaded themselves in the mission. Most of the defenders were recent settlers from the United States. They were joined by a small number of Mexicans who opposed Santa Anna. Santa Anna, however, led 3,000 Mexican soldiers. In spite of these unequal odds, the Texans refused to surrender and held out for 13 days. When the battle was over, the only survivors were a slave and a handful of women and children.

Soon after the fall of the Alamo, Mexican troops attacked a small Texan force at Goliad (GO-lee-ad). Although the Texans surrendered, Santa Anna ordered them all executed. His cruelty aroused all Texans.

**Texas wins independence.** In the battle of San Jacinto (san juh-SIN-toh) on April 21, 1836, the Texans avenged these defeats. A force of 800 Texans under General Sam Houston surprised a larger Mexican army. Shouting their battle cry, "Remember the Alamo! Remember Goliad!" they killed, wounded, or captured almost all of the enemy force. Santa Anna himself was made prisoner. The Mexicans were forced to withdraw across the Rio Grande. Texas had won its independence.

In September 1836 the American settlers raised a flag with a single star. Adopting the nickname the **Lone Star Republic,** they proclaimed Texas a self-governing country. Sam Houston, once governor of Tennessee, became the first president of Texas. Later, the capital was established at a site on the Colorado River and called Austin, in honor of Stephen F. Austin, the "Father of Texas."

**Texas joins the Union.** The Texans had no intention of remaining an independent republic for long. They considered themselves Americans, and they wanted to be a part of the United States. Furthermore, they did not feel safe, because Mexico had refused to recognize their independence. In 1836 Texas asked Congress to be annexed — added—to the United States.

Many Americans objected to admitting Texas into the Union. Texas, they said, would become a slave state. With its entrance into the Union, slave states would outnumber free states and gain a voting advantage in the Senate. Another objection was that Mexico still ·claimed Texas and threatened to go to war if the United States annexed Texas. As a result, the Senate refused to make Texas a state.

For nearly 10 years the Lone Star Republic remained independent. By 1845, however, after the election of President Polk, the feeling against admitting Texas was weaker. In December 1845 Texas became the twenty-eighth state of the United States. Today Texans call their state the Lone Star State and fly the Lone Star flag together with Old Glory (the United States flag). They are proud of their heroic fight for independence and of their history as an independent republic.

Robert Onderdonk's painting of the Battle of the Alamo shows the Texans defending themselves against Santa Anna's army. In the center, with his rifle raised overhead, stands the famous frontier hunter and scout Davy Crockett. Crockett had moved from Tennessee to Texas in 1835.

The United States gained control of California during the Mexican War. This painting, of a battle fought near Los Angeles, shows the methods of fighting used at the time.

## War Between the United States and Mexico

For many Americans, the news that Texas had become a state was cause for celebration. This turn of events, however, added to the trouble that was brewing between the United States and Mexico.

**Mexico resents the annexation of Texas.** The government of Mexico had never recognized the independence of Texas. Furthermore, Santa Anna had informed the United States government that annexing Texas would mean war with Mexico. As a result, when Texas joined the United States, the Mexican government became very angry. To make matters worse, Texas boldly claimed the Rio Grande as its southern boundary. Mexico insisted that the Texas Republic had included only the land as far south and west as the Nueces (noo-AY-ses) River. (See map on page 379.)

**Americans eye New Mexico.** American expansionists now looked beyond Texas to other lands belonging to Mexico. For years

American traders had been making their way toward Santa Fe, New Mexico, over the **Santa Fe Trail.** Each year a caravan of wagons creaked out of Independence, Missouri, and crawled across the plains of present-day Kansas. In Santa Fe the traders found eager customers. New Mexico was so far from the sources of Mexican goods that its settlers would buy almost anything that American merchants brought. Although most of the traders took their profits and returned home, a few stayed in Santa Fe. Many Americans began to think it was part of the Manifest Destiny of the United States to take over this whole region.

**Americans show interest in California.** The region of California, which also belonged to Mexico, stretched along the Pacific Coast. Its vast lands included tall, jagged mountains, wide valleys, and barren deserts. California had more people than the other Mexican possessions. Spanish missions stretched from San Diego to San Francisco. In time, towns grew up around the missions. Wealthy Spanish families had also settled in

377

California on large plots of land. There, with the help of Indian servants, they farmed or raised horses and cattle. They had little contact with the outside world, however, for Spain allowed only Spaniards to settle in its colonies and did not permit them to trade with other countries.

When Mexico took over the Spanish territories, the new government encouraged foreign trade. Soon European ships were rounding Cape Horn at the tip of South America and making the long trip to California ports. American traders set up business in California, and other Americans became ranchers there. By 1846 several hundred Americans lived in California. People began to talk about adding California and New Mexico to the United States, and some Americans were quite willing to fight for these territories if necessary.

**War begins with Mexico.** With so much bad feeling between Mexico and the United States, the stage was set for war. In late 1845, President Polk had sent a representative to Mexico City with an offer to buy California and New Mexico. The Mexican government refused to see the American representative. When Polk heard about this, he decided to take action.

For several months General Zachary Taylor had been guarding the Nueces River with a small army. In January 1846, President Polk ordered Taylor to take a position on the Rio Grande—inside the disputed territory. (See map on page 379.) Mexico regarded that advance as an act of war. As a result, a Mexican force crossed the river and attacked the American troops. When this news reached the United States, Congress acted on the recommendation of President Polk and declared war on Mexico early in May 1846.

**The United States invades Mexico.** General Taylor marched across the Rio Grande into northern Mexico, and early in 1847 he defeated Santa Anna's troops at Buena Vista (BWAY-nuh VEES-tuh). Meanwhile, General Winfield Scott had landed at Veracruz on the coast of Mexico. From there he fought his way up the mountains toward Mexico City, the capital.

Just outside the city, Scott demanded the surrender of Chapultepec (chuh-POOL-tuh-pek), an ancient palace and fortress. About 1,000 Mexican soldiers and 50 brave cadets from the national military school fought to defend the fortress. Some of those who lost their lives were as young as 13 years old. These heroic children, or *Los Niños Heroícos* (los NEEN-yos huh-RO-ih-kos), have become heroes of Mexico, just as the defenders of the Alamo are remembered as heroes of the United States. On September 14, 1847, American troops entered Mexico City. The war was practically over.

**California and the New Mexico region are conquered.** While fighting was taking place in Mexico, the United States had seized control of California and New Mexico. This was not difficult because these regions were far from Mexico City and were defended only by small groups of Mexican soldiers.

Soon after the war began, an American force under General Stephen W. Kearny had set out for Santa Fe. After capturing that city without a struggle, part of his small army headed west across the desert to California.

Meanwhile, in 1846, Americans who lived in California had already overthrown the Mexican government. Their rebellion was called the **Bear Flag Revolt** because the Americans carried a flag showing a grizzly bear. John C. Frémont, a United States Army officer, became a leader of the new Bear Flag Republic proclaimed by the Californians. General Kearny arrived soon after the revolt began. Despite stiff resistance from Mexican settlers near San Diego who opposed the Bear Flag Republic, he was able to take over all of California.

## Adding Territory in the Southwest

In Mexico, meanwhile, it was clear that the tide had turned in favor of the Americans. American forces under General Scott had occupied Mexico City for several months. Santa Anna had resigned as president and had fled the country. The Mexican government had to make peace. In February 1848 the **Treaty of Guadalupe Hidalgo** (GWAHD-uhl-oop hih-DAL-go) was signed.

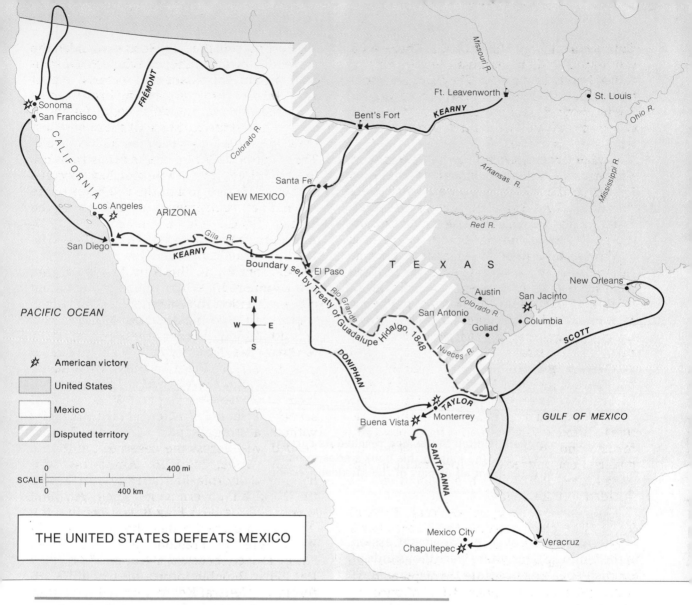

THE UNITED STATES DEFEATS MEXICO

## Map Study

The Mexican War was fought in Mexico, the present-day Southwest, and California. Find the boundary established by the Treaty of Guadalupe Hidalgo. What rivers form part of the boundary? What lands came under American control?

**The war brings a vast territory to the United States.** Under the terms of the peace treaty, Mexico had to accept the Rio Grande as its border. In so doing, it recognized Texas as belonging to the United States. Mexico also **ceded** —gave up—a huge amount of land to the United States. This land, called the **Mexican Cession,** amounted to almost half of Mexico's territory. In return, the United States government agreed to give Mexico $15 million in cash. It also paid American citizens $3.25 million, which they claimed the Mexican government owed them.

**Some people in the Mexican Cession oppose change.** When Mexico signed the

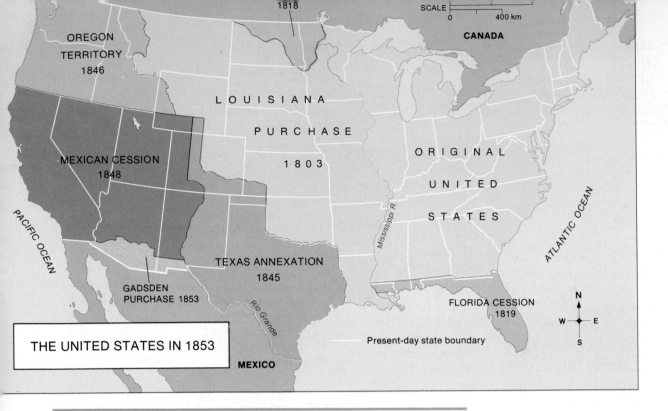

1818

SCALE |———————|
0        400 km

CANADA

OREGON
TERRITORY
1846

LOUISIANA

PURCHASE

1803

ORIGINAL

UNITED

STATES

MEXICAN CESSION
1848

PACIFIC OCEAN

ATLANTIC OCEAN

Mississippi R.

GADSDEN
PURCHASE 1853

TEXAS ANNEXATION
1845

Rio Grande

FLORIDA CESSION
1819

N
W ◆ E
S

THE UNITED STATES IN 1853

Present-day state boundary

MEXICO

## Map Study

**By 1853 the continental United States had reached its current national boundaries. Use the map in this book's atlas to name the states that were made from all or part of the Mexican Cession.**

treaty that turned over the Mexican Cession to the United States, there were thousands of Spanish-speaking people in the region. Mexico insisted that the rights of these people be respected. The United States agreed that the Spanish-speaking people could keep their language, religion, and culture. Their property and political rights would be respected as well.

**The United States buys more land from Mexico.** In 1853 the United States paid Mexico $10 million for a stretch of land in the southern part of present-day New Mexico and Arizona. This area was needed to provide a route for a railroad that the United States wanted to build to the West Coast. Because the arrangements were made by an American diplomat named James Gadsden, this land was called the **Gadsden Purchase.** (See map on this page.) In a few short years,

the United States had reached its present boundary in the Southwest. It had gained rich land resources and strengthened its power in North America.

## SECTION REVIEW

1. **Vocabulary**  annex, cede
2. **People and Places**  Stephen Austin, General Santa Anna, Alamo, Sam Houston, Rio Grande, Lone Star Republic, Mexican Cession, Gadsden Purchase
3. **Comprehension**  Why were there bad feelings between Mexico and the United States in the 1830's and 1840's?
4. **Comprehension**  What were the peace terms of the Treaty of Guadalupe Hidalgo?
5. **Critical Thinking**  Did the United States trigger the Mexican War? Explain.

# How did the discovery of gold bring California into the Union?

## Vocabulary

prospector    claim

discrimination    vigilante

The Mexican Cession opened up vast stretches of new land for restless pioneers. But not many American settlers were interested in the dry and mountainous regions that made up much of the Southwest. They did not yet realize the value of these lands for cattle raising. Nor did they know that rich deposits of copper, gold, and silver were located here. The story of California, on the other hand, is quite different. An exciting discovery brought adventurous Americans stampeding into California soon after it became part of the United States.

## California Gold Fever

Gold had long been mined throughout Spain's colonies. After Mexico gained its independence from Spain, Mexicans continued to mine in California. It was not until California had become a United States territory, however, that richer mines were found.

**Gold is discovered in California.** John Sutter had left his native Switzerland and settled in California. He acquired much land and made a good living by farming and raising livestock. In January 1848, James Marshall, a carpenter who had been building a sawmill for Sutter, came to Sutter's office. He was breathless with excitement and demanded to see his employer alone. This is how Sutter described Marshall's visit:

I was surprised to see him. Only the day before I had sent him all the supplies he could possibly need.... I could not [understand] the purpose in this unexpected visit. Yet I conducted him from my office to my private rooms—parlor and bedroom—where we shut the door.

"Is the door locked?" said Marshall.

"No," I answered, "but I will lock it if you wish." He was a [strange] fellow and I only supposed he took this way of telling me some secret.

Then he said distinctly: "Are we alone?"

"Surely," I answered.

[Marshall then asked for some scales.]

Shrugging, and thinking to humor him, I went myself and fetched the scales. On my return I failed to lock the door. Then Marshall dug feverishly into his pantaloon pockets and pulled forth a white cotton rag which

## Our Presidents

### ZACHARY TAYLOR

★ **1849–1850** ★

**12**TH PRESIDENT

WHIG

★ Born November 24, 1784, in Virginia

★ Married Margaret Smith in 1810; 6 children

★ Major-general in army; won the Battle of Buena Vista

★ Lived in Louisiana when elected President

★ Vice President: Millard Fillmore

★ Nicknamed "Old Rough and Ready"

★ Died July 9, 1850, in Washington, D.C.

★ Key events while in office: California gold rush

had something rolled up in it. Just as he was unfolding it to show me the contents, the door was opened by a clerk. . . .

"There!" screamed Marshall, "did I not tell you we had listeners!"

Quickly he thrust the rag back into his pocket. I [quieted] him, my curiosity aroused. Ordering the surprised clerk to retire, I locked the door.

Then he drew out the rag again. Opening the cloth carefully, he held it before me in his hand. It held what might have been an ounce and a half of gold dust—dust, flakes and grains. The biggest piece was not as large as a pea and varied from that down to less than a pinhead in size.

"I believe it is gold!" whispered Marshall, his eyes wild and restless. "But the people at the mill laughed at me—said I was crazy!" I examined his find closely.

"Yes, it looks like gold," I admitted slowly. "Come let us test it. . . ."

---

**James Beckwourth was a black explorer, hunter, trapper, and scout who helped blaze trails through the Old West. He discovered a mountain pass, now known as Beckwourth Pass, through the Sierra Nevada range.**

Sutter and Marshall tested the shiny yellow metal. The test showed that Marshall had indeed discovered gold!

## A Gold Rush

The news of the discovery of gold could not be kept behind locked doors for long. Quickly it spread through the neighborhood, and then through all of California. By 1849 the news had leaped across the United States and around the world.

**Gold seekers soon race to California.** Adventurous people by the thousands deserted shops, farms, and offices to head for California. The dream of getting rich from a few weeks of work in the California gold fields lured them on. Great crowds of **prospectors** —miners—rushed to John Sutter's land. They camped in his fields, trampled down his crops, and stole his horses and cattle. Sacramento was started on part of Sutter's land. From a settlement of just four houses in April 1848, it soon grew to a booming city of almost 10,000 people.

Those who rushed to California for gold were called **forty-niners,** for the year 1849 in which many of them came. Although some forty-niners were women, most were men without families, adventurers seeking to make a fortune. Free blacks came by the hundreds, and many struck it rich. By 1855 the blacks living in California were the wealthiest in the country.

The forty-niners included not only Americans but also people from Mexico, Europe, and Asia. The Chinese were the largest group of gold seekers to come from another nation. Chinese miners called the California ranges the "Gold Mountains." Although they often suffered **discrimination** —unfair treatment—because of their race, many stayed in California. The area of San Francisco known as Chinatown is a lasting reminder of the Chinese prospectors.

**The forty-niners come by land and sea.** The forty-niners had a choice of several routes to California. (See map on page 385.) The overland route from Independence, Missouri, to the southern part of California took more than two months. Those who followed it suffered from heat and thirst. Other adventurous travelers followed the Oregon Trail to the Great Salt Lake, and then struggled across deserts and mountains to northern California. They ran the dreadful risk of being caught in the mountains by deep winter snow.

The gold seekers could also go to California by sea. The safest but longest trip was around South America and north to San Francisco. Because this journey took from six to nine months, many of the forty-niners chose a faster route by way of Panama. Ships of every kind, jammed with passengers, sailed from the Atlantic Coast of the United States to the east coast of Panama. From there the travelers crossed the Isthmus of Panama through jungle and swamp to the Pacific Coast. Many died of fever or diseases caused by insect bites. Those who survived boarded ships for San Francisco.

**Life was rough in California in 1849.** After reaching California, the prospectors rushed to the rivers and mountainsides where gold had been found. There they staked out their **claims** —small plots of land—and started digging gravel and washing it for gold. Life at the mines and the diggings was rough. Anyone who attempted to take over another person's claim was tried by a court of miners. People found guilty of stealing were hanged. Fighting, robbery, and murder became common in the mining camps.

The camps often had odd names, such as Hangtown, You-Bet, Red Dog, and Ground Hog Glory. Within 10 years about $500 million worth of gold was found in California. Some of the miners who came the first year, when gold was plentiful, became rich. Most of the latecomers were no better off than they had been back home.

Some people realized that they could make more money by selling food and supplies to the miners than by looking for gold. A Jewish man named Levi Strauss made a fortune by producing the rugged denim work pants that became known as blue jeans. Many storekeepers charged high prices because goods were scarce. A sack of onions or a loaf of bread cost far more in California

## LINKING PAST AND PRESENT

### ★★★ *The Western*

Dusty cattle drives, stagecoach robberies, and dramatic shootouts are vivid images of the Old West. Westerns—books and movies that recreate such scenes—bring the Old West to life again.

Westerns have been popular since the 1870's, when "dime novels" that sold for 10 cents painted a colorful picture of life in the West. The legends have lived on in movies like *High Noon* and *How the West Was Won*. Television, too, has had its share of westerns, with programs like *Gunsmoke* and *Bonanza*.

One of the most famous radio and television heroes of the West was the mysterious Lone Ranger. Accompanied by his Indian friend Tonto, the Lone Ranger rode through the West helping people in trouble. His trademarks were the mask he wore over his face and the silver bullets he used.

than in other parts of the United States. The miners carried bags of gold dust and paid for goods in ounces of gold instead of dollars.

The miners' chief amusements were gambling, racing, and drinking. It was hard to keep law and order when thousands of gold seekers were determined to make fortunes by any means possible. Crime was especially troublesome in San Francisco. Adventurers from all over the world passed through that city on their way to the diggings. San Francisco grew rapidly as boarding houses, hotels, and saloons were hastily put up to serve the crowds of gold seekers. Gamblers, drifters, and criminals flocked there, and the law was often ignored.

In self-defense, some citizens formed **vigilante** (vij-uh-LAN-tee) groups to keep order. The vigilantes were volunteers who took it upon themselves to capture and punish lawbreakers. They arrested, tried, and hanged some desperate criminals. Many

## GEOGRAPHY • Mine Sites and the Land

For American pioneers making their way westward, one of the greatest challenges was getting over the rugged peaks of the Rockies, the Sierra Nevada, and the Cascade Range. To many settlers, these mountains meant nothing but hardship.

Then, in 1848, gold was discovered in the California foothills of the Sierra Nevada. News of the find spread quickly, bringing a new kind of pioneer to the West: the forty-niner, a rough-and-tumble mining prospector.

Within months, prospectors in the mountains of western Nevada discovered vast silver deposits. Another rich silver-bearing area was the Pikes Peak region of the Colorado Rockies. During the next 15 years, prospectors set up mining camps and then mining towns all over the mountainous areas of present-day Idaho, Montana, and South Dakota.

The discovery of precious minerals in the West led to a new appreciation of the mountains. Mining soon became an important industry, providing raw materials for manufacturing many goods.

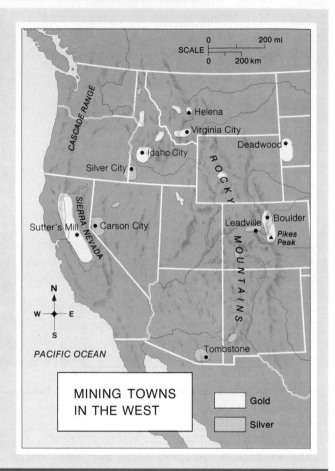

MINING TOWNS IN THE WEST

Gold

Silver

---

innocent people were punished, however, because the vigilantes' methods were not always fair.

## Becoming a State

The gold rush brought rapid population growth to California. Without the discovery of gold, it might have taken several decades to reach the 60,000-population mark necessary for statehood. However, more than 80,000 people arrived in California within two years after gold was found on John Sutter's land.

**California enters the Union.** By the end of 1849, Californians were ready to draw up a state constitution. In September of the following year, California was admitted to the Union as a free state. Californians did not celebrate immediately, however. Travel was so slow that it took more than a month before the news of statehood arrived from the nation's capital, Washington, D.C.

By 1860 there were 380,000 people in California—four times the population of 1850. Most Californians lived in the northern part of the state. The gold rush had not affected Los Angeles or San Diego in the

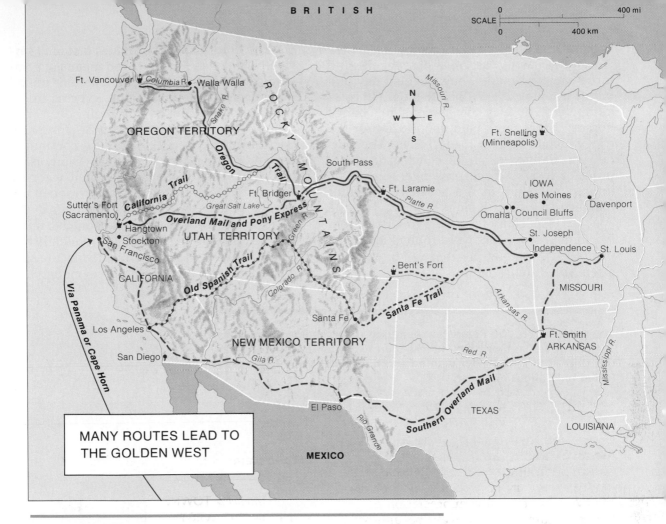

MANY ROUTES LEAD TO
THE GOLDEN WEST

## Map Study

**Study the route of the Overland Mail and Pony Express. Where did this route begin and end? About how many miles did it cover? How many kilometers? Name the route that passed through El Paso.**

south. These towns remained sleepy little communities for many years.

In the north, meanwhile, San Francisco had grown into an important city with more than 50,000 residents. When gold was no longer plentiful, many of the mining camps became deserted ghost towns. Others, however, developed into flourishing communities. Stockton and Sacramento, located at the heart of the mining region, grew rapidly. Hangtown changed its name to Placerville and became a settled community. Along with growing order, Californians were soon enjoying improvements in transportation and communication.

**The overland stage connects California with the East.** California was 2,000 miles (3,200 kilometers) away from the eastern part of the United States. Better and faster means of transportation were needed to link California with the rest of the nation. In 1857 stagecoach lines were established from cities on the Missouri River to points in California. The most important of these was the Overland Mail Company. It carried mail and passengers from St. Joseph and St. Louis, Missouri, to San Francisco.

The stagecoaches, called Concord coaches, had wide wheels, springs made of leather, and curtains to protect passengers from rain. Pulled by four or six horses, they carried as many as nine passengers and three sacks of mail. They traveled day and night, stopping every 10 or 15 miles (16 or 24 kilometers) at wayside stations to change horses. Passengers paid about $200 for the trip, which took from 20 to 25 days. The journey was dangerous. If the coaches hit something or lost a wheel, passengers might be injured or killed in the accident. Another danger came from bandits who waylaid the coaches, especially those carrying gold from the mines. Travelers were robbed and bags of gold were stolen by these outlaws, who often killed their victims.

**The Pony Express provides fast mail service.** The need for improved means of communication led to the establishment of the **Pony Express** in 1860. Pony Express riders were carefully picked for their job. They could cover the distance from St. Joseph to Sacramento in 8 to 12 days. By continuing day and night, riders could deliver important mail much faster than if the mail went by stagecoach. The mail was wrapped in leather pouches for protection against the weather. Each rider covered about 100 miles (160 kilometers), stopping frequently to change horses. A rider would throw the saddlebags of mail on a fresh horse, mount, and

The painter Frederic Remington captured the excitement at a Pony Express relief station when, in less than two minutes, the mail was transferred to a new rider with a fresh horse. The Pony Express lasted only about one year.

speed away. Riders galloped across the rugged land at speeds of up to 25 miles (40 kilometers) per hour.

The writer Mark Twain, traveling west on the overland stagecoach, described the thrill of seeing a Pony Express rider:

> We had had a ... desire, from the beginning, to see a pony-rider, but somehow or other all that passed us and all that met us managed to streak by in the night, and so we heard only a whiz and a hail, and the swift phantom of the desert was gone before we could get our heads out of the windows. But now we were expecting one along every moment, and would see him in broad daylight. Presently the driver exclaims:
> "Here he comes!"
> Every neck is stretched further, and every eye strained wider. Away across the endless dead level of the prairie a black speck appears against the sky, and it is plain that it moves. Well, I should think so! In a second or two it becomes a horse and rider, rising and falling, rising and falling—sweeping toward us nearer and nearer—growing more and more distinct, more and more sharply defined—nearer and still nearer—and the flutter of the hoofs comes faintly to the ear—another instant a whoop and a hurrah from our upper deck, a wave of the rider's hand, but no reply, and man and horse burst past our excited faces, and go winging away....

After only a little more than a year, the Pony Express went out of business. A telegraph line to San Francisco was completed, and messages could be sent in minutes. Regular mail continued to go by stagecoach until the first cross-country railroad was completed in 1869.

## SECTION REVIEW

1. **Vocabulary**   prospector, discrimination, claim, vigilante
2. **People and Places**   John Sutter, James Marshall, Sacramento, San Francisco
3. **Comprehension**   By what routes did prospectors travel to California?
4. **Comprehension**   Why was the Pony Express important?
5. **Critical Thinking**   How did rapid population growth affect life in California?

# Chapter 16 Summary

The 1840's were a time of great expansion for the United States. Many Americans felt that it was the nation's Manifest Destiny to stretch from the Atlantic Ocean to the Pacific. Pioneers followed the Oregon Trail to the rich farmlands and forests of the Pacific Northwest. By 1846 the United States had gained the Oregon Territory and had established the nation's northern boundary at the forty-ninth parallel from the Great Lakes to the Pacific Ocean.

American settlement of Texas began in the 1820's, when Stephen F. Austin led a number of families there to start a colony. In 1836 Texas won its independence from Mexico and became a republic. The annexation of Texas as a state in 1845 led to war with Mexico. As a result of this war, the United States gained the Mexican Cession, a huge territory extending from Texas to the Pacific. In 1853 the United States filled in its present border in the Southwest by buying a small strip of land known as the Gadsden Purchase.

Gold seekers from all over the world rushed to California in 1849 after gold was discovered on John Sutter's land near Sacramento. California grew rapidly and became a state in 1850. Stagecoach lines, the Pony Express, and the telegraph improved transportation and communication between California and the rest of the nation.

# Chapter 16 REVIEW

## Vocabulary and Key Terms

Use the following terms to complete the sentences below. Write your answers on a separate sheet of paper.

**Alamo**                    **joint occupation**
**Bear Flag Revolt**         **Lone Star Republic**
**expansionists**            **Manifest Destiny**
**forty-niners**             **Oregon Country**

1. People called _____, who believed in _____, thought that the United States should extend its boundaries to the Pacific Ocean.
2. In 1818 the United States and Great Britain agreed to _____ of the region known as the _____.
3. Although Texans lost the battle at the _____ in 1836, Texas later won independence as the _____.
4. Americans overthrew Mexican rule in California in the _____ of 1846.
5. The _____ rushed to California to search for gold.

## Recalling the Facts

1. What natural resources attracted settlers to Oregon?
2. What two countries claimed Oregon in the 1840's? How was the dispute finally settled?
3. Why did Texans revolt against Mexican rule?
4. What territory did the United States gain as a result of the Treaty of Guadalupe Hidalgo?
5. Why did great numbers of people come to California between 1848 and 1850?
6. What was life like in the California mining camps?
7. In what ways did cross-country transportation and communication improve after 1850?

## Places to Locate

Match the letters on the map with the places listed below. Write your answers on a separate sheet of paper.

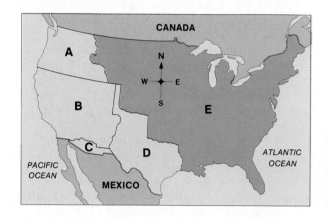

1. United States in 1819
2. Oregon Territory
3. Texas annexation
4. Mexican Cession
5. Gadsden Purchase

## Critical Thinking

1. Many Americans in the 1830's and 1840's believed it was the Manifest Destiny of the United States to expand to the Pacific. Do you think expansion was good for the United States at the time? Why or why not? Consider these points in your answer:
   a. other countries' claims to western lands
   b. the rights of people already living on western lands
   c. the difficulties settlers faced
   d. the benefits of westward expansion for the United States
2. What factors made territorial expansion possible for the United States in the 1840's? Consider these questions in your answer:

a. Could the United States have grown so greatly if President Polk had opposed expansion?

b. How did earlier westward movement pave the way for further expansion?

c. How did other countries contribute to American growth?

## Understanding History

1. Reread the section "Americans follow the Oregon Trail" on page 370. Then answer these questions.

   a. **Geography.** Why did the pioneers start out on the Oregon Trail in the spring?

   b. **Geography.** Why was the South Pass an important part of the Oregon Trail?

2. Reread the section "Texans declare their independence" on page 375. Then answer these questions.

   a. **Culture.** How did American and Mexican cultures differ?

   b. **Citizenship.** Do you think Americans should have followed Mexican laws? Explain your answer.

3. Reread the section "Gold is discovered in California" on page 381. Then answer these questions.

   a. **Primary Sources.** Why, do you suppose, was James Marshall so excited about his discovery?

   b. **Primary Sources.** Why might people at the mill have thought Marshall was crazy?

## Projects and Activities

1. **Reviewing Information.** Make flash cards to quiz classmates on the vocabulary words and key terms found in this chapter.

2. **Giving an Oral Report.** Find out more about one of the following topics: John Jacob Astor, Marcus and Narcissa Whitman, Stephen Austin, gold rush towns in California, the Pony Express. Present an oral report to the class using the information you have gathered.

3. **Writing a Fictional Account.** Imagine you are one of the pioneers traveling to Oregon. Write a diary of your journey. Describe the route you are following, the supplies you have taken, your reasons for going, and the experiences you have along the way.

4. **Analyzing a Problem.** Imagine that you and your classmates are living in California during the gold rush days. Form a committee to discuss the crime problem and propose ways to maintain law and order.

## Practicing Your Skill

Use the map below to answer the questions that follow. Write your answers on a separate sheet of paper.

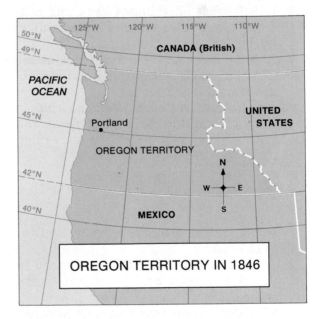

OREGON TERRITORY IN 1846

1. Between what two degrees of latitude did the Oregon Territory lie?

2. What is the approximate latitude and longitude of Portland?

3. How many degrees of latitude are there between the northern and southern boundaries of the Oregon Territory? If each degree of latitude is equal to about 70 miles (112 kilometers), what is the distance between these boundaries?

| Fillmore | | Pierce | | Buchanan | | Lincoln |
|---|---|---|---|---|---|---|
| 1850 | 1852 | 1854 | 1856 | 1858 | 1860 | 1862 |

**1852**
*Uncle Tom's Cabin*

**1857**
*Dred Scott* decision

**1859**
Brown raids Harpers Ferry

**1850**
Compromise of 1850

Fugitive Slave Act

**1854**
Kansas-Nebraska Act

Republican party forms

**1860**
South Carolina secedes

**1861**
Confederacy attacks Fort Sumter

**During the Lincoln-Douglas debates in 1858, Abraham Lincoln (standing) opposed the spread of slavery to the western territories.**

## Preparing to Read

By the 1850's, people in the North and in the South had different ways of living. Not surprisingly, they disagreed on many matters. As Americans moved west, the issue of slavery sharply split the North and South. Northerners wanted to end the practice of slavery while southerners tried to extend it. The quarrel grew so bitter that compromise broke down, and the United States moved steadily toward war. As you read this chapter, try to answer the following questions:

1. How did the North and the South try to settle their differences?
2. How did the North and the South move closer to conflict?
3. What events led to the outbreak of war?

# 1 How did the North and the South try to settle their differences?

## Vocabulary
homestead
fugitive

The American victory in the Mexican War opened up new lands in the West. As settlers moved into these territories from the North and the South, they brought different ways of living and thinking. Southern planters came with their slaves, while northerners came with a fierce opposition to slavery.

## Deep Divisions

Sectional tensions between the North and the South had been building for many years. Yet Americans had always found ways to compromise. In the 1850's, however, slavery became a constant source of conflict.

**The issue of slavery divides Americans.** In 1820 northerners and southerners had both accepted the Missouri Compromise. (See Chapter 12.) They had agreed that slavery could continue in the Louisiana Purchase south of the 36°30′N parallel. North of that line, owning slaves would be against the law. For a time the Missouri Compromise of 1820 settled the slavery quarrel. Yet it did not end the bitter feelings between northerners and southerners.

Most people in the North thought that slavery was morally wrong. The cotton economy of the South, however, depended upon slave labor. Southern planters knew that cotton crops wore out the soil quickly. The need for new cotton fields drew southerners west. There they continued to keep slaves, defending their actions on economic grounds. A lawmaker from South Carolina said to a northern critic:

> Have the Northern States any idea of the value of our slaves? . . . If we lose them, the value of the lands they [farm] will [shrink] . . . and an annual income of at least 40 millions of dollars will be lost to your citizens. . . . In [an economic] view, therefore, it must ever be the policy of the Eastern and Northern States to continue connected with us.

Some Americans, however, worried that the country would not stay together. The nation already had a long history of sectional quarrels, as the time list on page 392 shows. At the time of the Missouri Compromise,

| 1787 | Northerners and southerners disagree on counting slaves in the population |
| 1790 | Southerners oppose Hamilton's plan to repay state debts |
| 1815 | New Englanders call the Hartford Convention to protest the War of 1812 |
| 1820 | Northerners oppose Missouri's admission to the Union as a slave state |
| 1830 | Southerners advance the idea of states' rights |
| 1832 | South Carolina threatens to secede over tariff laws |

Thomas Jefferson had written that the slavery question, "like a firebell in the night, awakened and filled me with terror." If Americans could not reach agreement on slavery, bitterness might tear the Union apart.

**The Mexican War brings new quarrels.** By the Missouri Compromise, all territory owned by the United States in 1820 was to be either "free" or "slave." The addition of new territories after 1820, however, reopened debate about slavery. In the 1830's and early 1840's, the question of admitting Texas as a free state had divided Americans. (See Chapter 16.) More problems arose when the Mexican War broke out in 1846.

Americans knew they stood to win vast lands from Mexico. At once they asked whether the new territories would become slave states or free states. The war had hardly begun when a representative from Pennsylvania, David Wilmot, made a suggestion to Congress. Wilmot hated slavery. He proposed that Congress agree beforehand that no slavery "shall ever exist in any part" of any territory that might be won from Mexico. This proposal, called the **Wilmot Proviso** (pruh-VY-zo), came up in Congress again and again. Each time, it was defeated. Northern representatives who disliked slavery voted for it, but southerners outvoted them.

**The Free-Soil party emerges.** When the Wilmot Proviso failed again in 1848, some northerners decided to form a new political party. Calling themselves **Free-Soilers,** they demanded an end to slavery. The Free-Soil party also urged Congress to give western settlers free **homesteads** —land on which to settle and build houses. Candidates ran for office with the slogan "Free soil, free speech, free labor, and free men." In the 1848 elections, 13 Free-Soilers won seats in Congress.

**Southerners become alarmed.** The Free-Soilers' success worried southerners. They felt threatened for another reason too.

## Chart Study

Northerners outnumbered southerners in the House of Representatives. As a result, free states had more votes than slave states. What percentage of House members represented free states in 1850?

### Northern and Southern Representation in Congress

| Year | Members from free states | Members from slave states | Percentage of southern members |
|------|--------------------------|---------------------------|--------------------------------|
| 1800 | 76 | 65 | 46 |
| 1810 | 96 | 79 | 45 |
| 1820 | 123 | 90 | 42 |
| 1830 | 141 | 99 | 41 |
| 1840 | 135 | 88 | 39.5 |
| 1850 | 142 | 90 | 38.8 |

In 1848 there were 30 states in the Union. Exactly half allowed slavery, while the other half did not. Thus the free states and the slaves states had an equal number of senators in Congress. The situation was different in the House of Representatives. Population was growing faster in the North than in the South. As a result, the number of northern, antislavery representatives was rapidly climbing.

Southerners knew they could be outvoted in the House. They feared that someday they might be outnumbered in the Senate, too. This could happen if new territories in the West someday became free states. Southerners hated the idea of a Congress controlled by northerners. In addition to halting slavery, northerners might set high tariffs on imports. Then southerners would have to pay more for the clothes, furniture, and other finished goods they bought from Europe. Southerners decided they must do everything possible to keep new territories from entering the Union as free states.

**California asks for statehood.** After the Mexican War ended in 1848, the dispute over slavery in the Mexican Cession grew more heated. Passions rose especially high in 1850, when California asked to join the Union as a free state. Northerners backed California's request. White southerners, however, protested loudly. They saw no reason to close California to slavery.

The question of statehood for California brought matters to a head. If California became a free state, the balance of power between free and slave states would shift. Southerners would not accept such a change. They might even leave the Union.

## Reaching a Compromise

Congress saw that the issue of slavery threatened to split the country. Fortunately, wise lawmakers found a solution.

**Great leaders speak out in Congress.** Senators Daniel Webster, Henry Clay, and John C. Calhoun all played key roles in the

Senate debate over the Compromise of 1850 featured three great political leaders representing the North, the South, and the West. The leaders were Daniel Webster of Massachusetts (left, with hand cupped to ear), Henry Clay of Kentucky (standing, center), and John C. Calhoun of South Carolina (right, near Senate president's chair).

# Our Presidents

## MILLARD FILLMORE

★ 1850–1853 ★

**13TH PRESIDENT**

**WHIG**

★ Born January 7, 1800, in New York
★ Married Abigail Powers in 1826; 2 children
★ Married Caroline McIntosh in 1858; no children
★ Lawyer; representative from New York; Vice President under Taylor
★ Lived in New York when elected Vice President
★ Vice President: none
★ Died March 8, 1874, in New York
★ Key events while in office: Compromise of 1850; California became a state

congressional debates. Each had already served nearly 40 years in Congress.

Webster, the Massachusetts orator and politician, disliked slavery intensely. More than anything, however, he wanted to keep the country united. Clay, the "Great Compromiser" from Kentucky, felt the same way. In 1820 Clay had helped work out the Missouri Compromise. Now, 30 years later, he was making his last effort to bring about an understanding between the North and the South. Calhoun, the champion of states' rights from South Carolina, urged southerners not to compromise. Although now in poor health, Calhoun led the fight to extend slavery into the West.*

---

\* Calhoun died March 31, 1850. After his death, other senators were more willing to compromise.

There were young leaders in Congress too, whose names would later become famous. Stephen A. Douglas from Illinois believed that people in the territories should settle the question of slavery for themselves. William H. Seward, a New Yorker, said that God's law made all people free and was a "higher law" than the United States Constitution. Brilliant young southerners, meanwhile, spoke out in favor of slavery. Among them were Jefferson Davis of Mississippi and Alexander H. Stephens of Georgia. When the South later formed its own government, these two men became its president and vice president.

**Congress passes the Compromise of 1850.** Debate about slavery raged for nine months. Finally Congress voted to accept the **Compromise of 1850,** proposed by Henry Clay. The Compromise had not won favor with President Taylor. When Taylor died, however, the new President, Millard Fillmore, supported the measure. So did Daniel Webster. Webster helped sway Congress with these simple words:

> I wish to speak to-day, not as a Massachusetts man, nor as a northern man, but as an American.... I speak to-day for the preservation of the Union.... Instead of speaking of the possibility or [usefulness] of secession,... let us enjoy the fresh air of Liberty and Union....

The Compromise of 1850 settled the question of slavery in the lands won from Mexico. It was agreed that California would enter the Union as a free state. The rest of the land in the Mexican Cession was divided into the New Mexico Territory and the Utah Territory. (See middle map on page 397.) The question of slavery there was left to the people. In other words, those who lived on the land could decide for themselves whether slavery would be permitted.

The Compromise of 1850 had other provisions as well. First, it set a firm boundary between Texas and New Mexico. Texas gave disputed land to New Mexico and received, in return, $10 million. Second, the Compromise forbade the sale of slaves in the District of Columbia. Slavery itself, however, could continue there. Third, Congress agreed to pass a strict law regarding **fugitive** — runaway—slaves. This **Fugitive Slave Law** said that people in the free states had to help catch and return escaped slaves. Anyone caught aiding a runaway could be jailed or given a heavy fine.

Congress hoped that the Compromise of 1850 would settle the slavery question forever. The lawmakers wanted no more angry debates that might endanger the nation. Both the North and the South supported the compromise in hopes that the trouble over slavery could be forgotten.

## SECTION REVIEW

1. **Vocabulary**   homestead, fugitive
2. **People and Places**   David Wilmot, Free-Soilers, California, Daniel Webster, Henry Clay, John C. Calhoun
3. **Comprehension**   What issues contributed to sectionalism in the late 1840's?
4. **Comprehension**   What were the terms of the Compromise of 1850?
5. **Critical Thinking**   Do you think the Compromise of 1850 was fair to both sides? Why or why not?

# 2  How did the North and the South move closer to conflict?

## Vocabulary

sovereign

martyr

For a brief period the Compromise of 1850 cooled hot tempers. Peace, however, did not last long. Certain events over the next 10 years made quarrels more common, more angry, and more bitter.

## The Deepening Crisis

In 1852 a New Hampshire Democrat, Franklin Pierce, became President. Pierce wanted to calm the tensions that still divided northerners and southerners. Events during his administration, however, only drove Americans further apart.

**Northerners defy the Fugitive Slave Law.**  Many people in the North viewed the Fugitive Slave Law as a great evil. The law made it highly risky for slaves to flee the South. Slave-catchers, on the other hand, earned a fine living by tracking down fugitives for the reward money. In some cases,

greedy slave-catchers kidnapped free blacks and claimed they were runaways.

In spite of the dangers, many southern blacks managed to escape slavery. In the North they found sympathetic people who refused to obey the Fugitive Slave Law. Abolitionists continued to shelter runaways and help them reach freedom. The Underground Railroad remained strong. (See Chapter 15.) Some northern states even passed laws forbidding citizens to cooperate with slave-catchers.

**The written word becomes a powerful weapon.**  Anger over the Fugitive Slave Law inspired one New England woman to write a novel. In 1852 Harriet Beecher Stowe published *Uncle Tom's Cabin*. The book told of a kind, hardworking slave, Uncle Tom, and his mistreatment by a cruel master. The moving story touched the hearts of thousands of northerners. They accepted its description of suffering slaves and heartless owners as a true picture of life in the South.

*Uncle Tom's Cabin* stirred northerners against slavery as nothing else had. Within a year, the book sold about 300,000 copies. In the South, however, *Uncle Tom's Cabin*

# Our Presidents

## FRANKLIN PIERCE

★ 1853–1857 ★

**14TH PRESIDENT**

**DEMOCRAT**

★ Born November 23, 1804, in New Hampshire

★ Married Jane Means Appleton in 1834; 3 children

★ Lawyer; representative and senator from New Hampshire; brigadier general in Mexican War

★ Lived in New Hampshire when elected President

★ Vice President: William King

★ Died October 8, 1869, in New Hampshire

★ Key events while in office: Gadsden Purchase; Kansas-Nebraska Act; Republican party started

sparked a storm of protest. Southerners felt that the book misled readers about slavery. They grew more bitter toward abolitionists.

**The Kansas-Nebraska Act reopens the slavery quarrel.** Differences between the North and the South worsened in 1854. Early that year the Senate began considering the **Kansas-Nebraska Act.** This bill, proposed by Stephen A. Douglas of Illinois, called for dividing the Nebraska Territory into two parts—Kansas and Nebraska. (See bottom map on page 397.)

All this land was part of the Louisiana Purchase. Because it lay north of the Missouri Compromise Line, it was closed to slavery. The Kansas-Nebraska Act would allow people living in the territories to be **sovereign** —self-governing—with regard to

slavery. By a local vote they could choose to permit slavery or decide to forbid it. This idea—letting residents decide whether their territory would be slave or free—was called **popular sovereignty.**

Douglas hoped to become President someday. To do so he needed the support of the South as well as the North. He expected the Kansas-Nebraska Act to please people in both regions. As he said:

> The bill does equal and exact justice to the whole Union and to every part of it. It violates the rights of no state or territory. Instead, it ... leaves the people of them to the free enjoyment of all their rights under the Constitution.

Congress passed the Kansas-Nebraska Act in May 1854. People in the South rejoiced. Northerners, however, viewed the new law as a betrayal. They had agreed to the Missouri Compromise years earlier to limit the spread of slavery. Now they had lost their guarantee that slavery would be kept out of the West.

**Violence breaks out in Kansas.** Kansas soon became the scene of a bitter struggle between proslavery and antislavery forces. Settlers from the North began moving across the Kansas border, vowing to keep the territory free. Southerners also poured in, promising to vote for slavery. Each side formed its own government. With no single authority to keep peace, arguments quickly led to fighting.

In May 1856 a proslavery group attacked the town of Lawrence, burning homes and stores. Several people died in the blaze. A short time later, an abolitionist named John Brown led several companions to a proslavery settlement at Pottawatomie Creek. There, in the middle of the night, Brown and his followers brutally murdered five men.

The violence prompted newspapers to call the territory "Bleeding Kansas." Bands of fighters on horseback began to roam the roads. More people from the North and the South streamed in, not to farm but to fight. By late 1856 more than 200 people had lost their lives, and millions of dollars worth of property had been destroyed.

**A senator suffers a beating.** The violence even extended into the stately halls of the nation's Capitol. In a speech before Congress in May 1856, Senator Charles Sumner of Massachusetts blamed southerners for the trouble in Kansas. Sumner criticized South Carolina's senator, Andrew Butler, especially harshly. The next day Butler's nephew, Representative Peter Brooks, took revenge. He found Sumner in his office and beat him with a heavy cane until the senator collapsed. The attack kept Sumner away from Congress for more than three years. No action, however, was taken against Brooks. Many southerners actually applauded Brooks's behavior. To show their support, they sent him dozens of new canes.

In Kansas, the struggle over slavery went on. Because of their greater numbers, the antislavery settlers finally won. In 1861 Kansas entered the Union as a free state.

## Political Responses and More Bloodshed

Most Americans opposed violence as a means of settling their differences. Instead they turned to political and legal channels. At the voting booths and in the courts, they made their voices heard.

**Opponents of slavery form the Republican party.** Anger over the Kansas-Nebraska Act rocked American politics. The slavery question had already begun to divide the Whigs. The split grew wider, however, when southern Whigs backed the idea of popular sovereignty in the West.

Many northern Whigs felt the time had come to leave their party. In 1854 they held a meeting with antislavery Democrats and Free-Soilers in Ripon, Wisconsin. Here the **Republican party** was born. Its leaders

## Map Study
The Compromise of 1850 settled the issue of slavery in the West. What territories were left open to slavery? How did the Kansas-Nebraska Act overrule the Missouri Compromise?

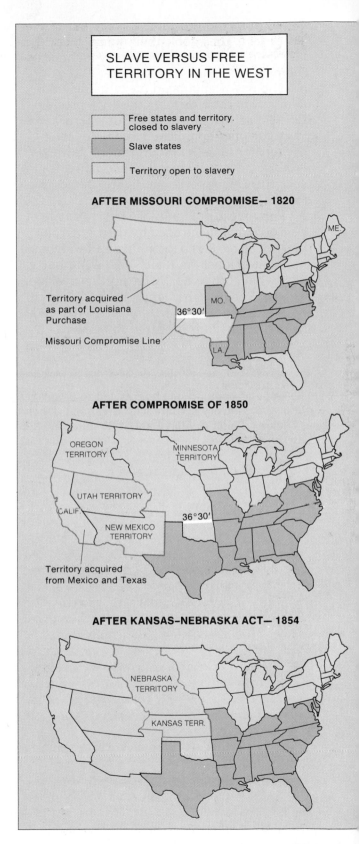

SLAVE VERSUS FREE TERRITORY IN THE WEST

- Free states and territory, closed to slavery
- Slave states
- Territory open to slavery

AFTER MISSOURI COMPROMISE— 1820

Territory acquired as part of Louisiana Purchase

Missouri Compromise Line

36°30'

ME.
MO.
LA.

AFTER COMPROMISE OF 1850

OREGON TERRITORY
MINNESOTA TERRITORY
UTAH TERRITORY
CALIF.
NEW MEXICO TERRITORY
36°30'

Territory acquired from Mexico and Texas

AFTER KANSAS–NEBRASKA ACT— 1854

NEBRASKA TERRITORY
KANSAS TERR.

shared one goal: keeping slavery out of the territories. They took their name from the old Democratic-Republican party founded by Thomas Jefferson. (See Chapter 10.)

The new Republican party gained many members in the North. In the 1856 presidential election, two thirds of the northern states voted for the Republican candidate, John C. Frémont. Almost all southerners, however, were Democrats. They had enough votes to elect the Democratic candidate, James Buchanan, as President.

Republicans did not lose heart in spite of their defeat. Encouraged by their good start, they hoped to send a Republican President to the White House in 1860. The Whig party, meanwhile, broke up. Most northern Whigs became Republicans, while many Whigs in the South rejoined the Democrats. By 1860 the Whig party disappeared altogether.

**The Supreme Court decides the *Dred Scott* case.** In 1857 an important legal question came before the United States Supreme Court. The case concerned Dred Scott, a slave from Missouri. Scott's owner had taken him north of the Missouri Compromise Line in 1834. For four years they lived in free territory in Illinois and Wisconsin. Later they returned to Missouri, where Scott's owner died. Scott then began a lawsuit to gain his freedom. He claimed that he had become a free person by living in free territory for several years.

When the *Dred Scott* case reached the Supreme Court, the justices considered three issues. First, was Dred Scott a United States citizen with the right to sue in the federal courts? Second, did living in free territory make Scott a free person? Third, was the Missouri Compromise constitutional?

The issue of popular sovereignty led to bloodshed in Kansas. In this picture, proslavery settlers with a cannon attack antislavery settlers at Hickory Point, a village about 25 miles (40 kilometers) north of Lawrence, Kansas.

## CULTURE • The Impact of *Uncle Tom's Cabin*

Harriet Beecher Stowe's antislavery novel, *Uncle Tom's Cabin,* was an overnight bestseller. Its popularity quickly spread overseas as well. Translations of the book appeared in dozens of countries, including France, Germany, Russia, Denmark, and Portugal. In England readers bought more than 1 million copies.

In 1852 George Aiken wrote a version of *Uncle Tom's Cabin* for the stage. The play drew thousands of people to the theater in New York. Soon traveling troupes of actors were performing Uncle Tom's story for audiences across America.

*Uncle Tom's Cabin* helped bring respectability to the theater. In the 1850's some people viewed theater-going as immoral. Harriet Beecher Stowe, who was married to a minister, never gave permission for her book to be made into a play. When she saw a performance of *Uncle Tom's Cabin,* however, her companion said, "I never saw such delight upon a human face as she displayed."

An advertisement for *Uncle Tom's Cabin*

Chief Justice Roger B. Taney (TAW-nee) handed down the decision for the majority of the Court. The Court ruled that slaves did not have the rights of citizens. Furthermore, Dred Scott had no claim to freedom, because he was living in Missouri, a slave state, when he began his suit. His earlier stay in the North had no bearing on the matter. Finally, the Court said, the Missouri Compromise was unconstitutional. Congress could not forbid slavery in any part of the territories. Doing so would interfere with slaveholders' right to own property, a right protected by the Fifth Amendment.

Southerners cheered the Court's decision. Northerners, on the other hand, were stunned. By striking down the Missouri Compromise, the Supreme Court had cleared the way for the extension of slavery. Opponents of slavery now pinned their hopes on the Republican party. If the Republicans became strong enough, they could still keep slavery in check.

**The Lincoln-Douglas debates draw national interest.** Abraham Lincoln, a young Illinois lawyer, became one of the key figures in the Republican party. In 1858 Lincoln decided to run for the United States Senate. His opponent was Democratic Senator Stephen A. Douglas, the man responsible for the Kansas-Nebraska Act.

Between August 21 and October 15, 1858, the two candidates met for seven debates in towns around the state. Audiences immediately noticed outward differences between the men. The tall, thin Lincoln cared little for

## Our Presidents

### JAMES BUCHANAN

★ 1857–1861 ★

**15TH PRESIDENT**

**DEMOCRAT**

★ Born April 23, 1791, in Pennsylvania

★ Never married

★ Lawyer; representative and senator from Pennsylvania; ambassador to Russia; Secretary of State; ambassador to England

★ Lived in Pennsylvania when elected President

★ Vice President: John Breckinridge

★ Died June 1, 1868, in Pennsylvania

★ Key events while in office: *Dred Scott* decision; Panic of 1857; John Brown's raid on Harpers Ferry; Minnesota and Oregon became states

---

fashion. His coat sleeves did not reach to his wrists, nor his trousers to his shoes. He moved awkwardly and spoke with a country accent. Douglas, on the other hand, dressed stylishly and carried himself with grace. Though only about five feet tall, Douglas was called "The Little Giant" because of his powerful oratory.

Lincoln and Douglas differed almost as sharply in ideas as they did in appearance. Lincoln viewed slavery as "a moral, a social, and a political wrong." He did not suggest abolishing slavery where it already existed, but he opposed its spread. To Douglas slavery was a political concern, not a question of right or wrong. Douglas continued to favor popular sovereignty in the territories. The local people, he thought, should decide whether to make slavery legal or illegal.

Douglas won reelection to the Senate by a slight margin. He had, however, lost fans in the South by stating that the voters in a territory could outlaw slavery. Lincoln, meanwhile, had come into the national spotlight. People all over the country now knew his name, and many shared his views. In one speech, Lincoln had warned Americans, "A house divided against itself cannot stand. I believe this government cannot endure permanently half slave and half free." Lincoln's words echoed the widespread fear that the nation might split apart. Violence had erupted before, and it would do so again.

**John Brown attacks Harpers Ferry.** The abolitionist John Brown had gone unpunished for the murders of proslavery people in Kansas. In 1859 Brown struck again. This time he and 18 followers seized the federal arsenal in Harpers Ferry, Virginia. Brown planned to take weapons stored there to arm slaves. He hoped to start a slave revolt that would end in freedom for all southern blacks.

---

## LINKING PAST AND PRESENT

### ★ ★ ★ *Political Debate*

Throughout American history, debate has been part of political life. Face-to-face debates give candidates a chance to directly challenge each other's ideas. In addition, voters have a chance to compare the positions of those running for office.

When Abraham Lincoln and Stephen A. Douglas competed for a Senate seat in 1858, they held seven debates. The two men spoke before crowds of as many as 12,000 people. Today, thanks to television, candidates can reach even larger audiences. In the presidential race of 1960, more than 70 million people tuned in to the debates between Richard M. Nixon and John F. Kennedy. Some historians credit Kennedy's election to his strong showing in these debates.

John Brown's capture after his 1859 raid at Harpers Ferry, Virginia, ended his plans to free the slaves. This 1884 painting by Thomas Hovendon shows Brown leaving the courthouse after being sentenced to death. Brown's raid alarmed the nation.

News of Brown's raid quickly reached Washington, D.C. President Buchanan ordered federal troops to set out at once for Harpers Ferry. The soldiers, led by Colonel Robert E. Lee, soon captured Brown and his followers. This time Brown was brought to trial, found guilty of treason, and hanged. Some abolitionists looked upon Brown as a hero and a martyr —someone who dies or suffers for a cause. Most northerners, however, considered him a madman. Many white southerners felt shock and dread. They were afraid that northern abolitionists would stop at nothing to end slavery, even if it meant destroying the Union in the process.

## SECTION REVIEW

1. **Vocabulary**   sovereign, martyr
2. **People and Places**   Harriet Beecher Stowe, Stephen A. Douglas, Nebraska Territory, John Brown, "Bleeding Kansas," Dred Scott, Abraham Lincoln, Harpers Ferry
3. **Comprehension**   What events split the North and the South in the 1850's?
4. **Comprehension**   Why did antislavery groups form the Republican party?
5. **Critical Thinking**   Do you agree with Lincoln that the United States could not remain half slave and half free?

**401**

## CRITICAL THINKING: Distinguishing Fact From Opinion

When studying history, you need both facts and opinions to get a full picture of what happened. Facts tell exactly what happened, where and when it happened, and who was involved. Facts are based on information that can be checked for accuracy. Opinions, on the other hand, express people's feelings, beliefs, and attitudes.

In this chapter, for example, the facts about the Compromise of 1850 are stated on pages 394–395. All the terms of the agreement listed there could be checked in other sources of information and proven true. However, the statement "Congress hoped that the Compromise of 1850 would settle the slavery question forever" gives you opinions rather than facts. It tells you what personal beliefs and feelings about the Compromise the lawmakers held.

Although both facts and opinions are useful in studying history, it is important to distinguish between them. Opinions are not always based on the truth. Yet sometimes opinions are stated so strongly that they are accepted as facts. Mistaking opinions for facts can lead to a less accurate understanding of a subject.

When writers state facts, they use neutral language that is free of bias or personal judgments. On the other hand, when writers express opinions, they use subjective language that shows their point of view. Another good way to recognize opinions is to look for phrases such as "I believe" and "in my view."

The excerpt on this page is from the journal of Charlotte L. Forten, a 16-year-old free black girl living in Boston in 1854. She is discussing the arrest and conviction of Anthony Burns, a fugitive slave. Read the passage.

Then on a separate sheet of paper, answer the questions that follow.

> Our worst fears are realized. The [court's] decision was against poor [Anthony] Burns, and he has been sent back to a [slavery] worse, a thousand times worse than death.
>
> With what scorn must that government be regarded, which cowardly assembles thousands of soldiers to satisfy the demands of slave holders; to deprive of his freedom a man, created in God's own image, whose sole offense is the color of his skin! And if resistance is offered to this outrage, these soldiers are to shoot down American citizens without mercy; and this by the express orders of a government which proudly boasts of being the freest in the world; this on the very soil where the Revolution of 1776 began.
>
> I can write no more. A cloud seems hanging over me, over all our persecuted race, which nothing can dispel.

1. In the first paragraph, what facts does Charlotte L. Forten give about the day's events?
2. What opinion about slavery does Forten give in the first paragraph?
3. In the second paragraph, what fact does Forten give about the orders that soldiers must follow?
4. In the second paragraph, what opinions does Forten express about the federal government?
5. What is the "outrage" to which Forten refers? Does the word "outrage" express a fact or an opinion?

# 3 What events led to the outbreak of war?

## Vocabulary

civil war

platform

The events of the 1850's had driven a deep wedge between the North and South. *Uncle Tom's Cabin*, the Kansas-Nebraska Act, John Brown's trial—all aroused strong feelings. It became clear that northerners and southerners were no longer thinking and acting like citizens of one nation. The United States seemed on the brink of **civil war** — war between different groups in the same country.

## A Fateful Election

By 1860 the mood of the country was tense. Americans nervously prepared for the upcoming elections. Their choice of a President would decide the future of the nation.

**Four candidates compete for the presidency.** The election of 1860 was a four-way race. The Democratic party, unable to agree on its goals, split in two. One part, the southern Democratic party, nominated John C. Breckinridge of Kentucky. The southern Democrats believed in states' rights and wanted slavery protected in the territories. The northern Democrats favored popular sovereignty. Stephen A. Douglas was their choice for President.

## Map Study

In 1860 Abraham Lincoln was elected President. How many rivals did he have? What regions voted for Lincoln? The number of a state's electoral votes is the same as the number of its representatives in Congress. Why did northern states have more electoral votes than southern states?

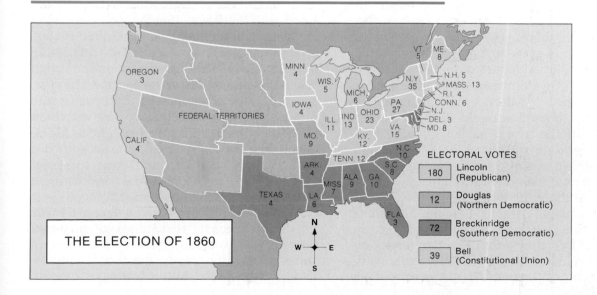

THE ELECTION OF 1860

ELECTORAL VOTES

180 — Lincoln (Republican)

12 — Douglas (Northern Democratic)

72 — Breckinridge (Southern Democratic)

39 — Bell (Constitutional Union)

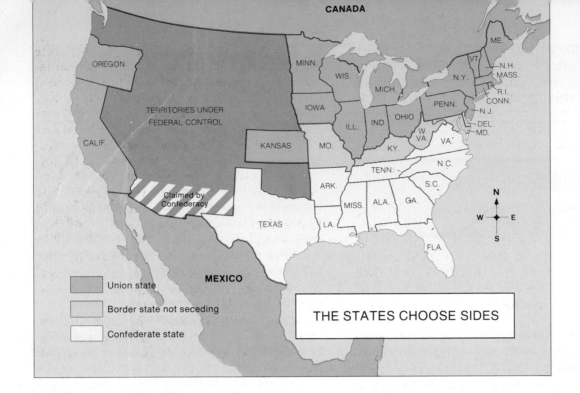

CANADA

OREGON
MINN.
WIS.
MICH.
ME.
VT
N.H.
MASS.
N.Y.
R.I.
CONN.
PENN.
N.J.
DEL.
MD.

TERRITORIES UNDER
FEDERAL CONTROL

IOWA
ILL. IND. OHIO
W. VA.
VA.

CALIF.
KANSAS
MO.
KY.

Claimed by
Confederacy
TENN.
N.C.

ARK.
S.C.

TEXAS
MISS. ALA. GA.

LA.

FLA.

N
W — E
S

MEXICO

Union state

Border state not seceding

Confederate state

THE STATES CHOOSE SIDES

## Map Study

**When the Civil War war began, most Southern states quickly joined
the Confederacy. Which border states remained in the Union? How
many states joined the Confederate States of America?**

A third party, the Constitutional Union party, nominated John Bell of Tennessee. Bell wanted to find some peaceful way of holding the Union together. He hoped for another compromise over slavery.

Finally there were the Republicans. They demanded what they had demanded in 1854: that slavery be kept out of the territories. The Republicans also included other ideas in their **platform** —statement of beliefs and intended policies. To gain support in the North and the West, they favored a tariff, free land for settlers in the West, and the construction of a railroad to the Pacific. The Republicans named Abraham Lincoln as their candidate for President.

**Americans elect Lincoln.** Lincoln's nomination alarmed many people in the South. They considered him dangerous because of his strong stand against slavery. Most southern states did not even put his

name on the ballot. However, because support for his rivals was so divided, Lincoln won the election. He did not receive the vote of a single slave state, but he carried the North and the West. (See map on page 403.)

The man who became the United States' sixteenth President was a most remarkable person. Lincoln had grown up on the rough Indiana frontier. Before he became a lawyer, he split rails, worked on a flatboat on the Mississippi, and tended store. He educated himself, often reading by firelight at night. When Lincoln entered politics, he gained a reputation for fairness and clear thinking. People respected "Honest Abe" and warmed to his friendly sense of humor.

Although Lincoln hated slavery, he was not an abolitionist. He said again and again that he would not interfere with slavery in states where it already existed. Doing so would only cause bitter feelings. Lincoln firmly believed, however, that the western territories should be kept free. In a speech before his election, Lincoln promised to stand up for his beliefs. He closed with these words: "Let us have faith that right makes might; and in that faith let us to the end dare to do our duty as we understand it."

## The Outbreak of Civil War

The election of a northerner, a Republican, was the final straw for the South. White southerners no longer felt safe. They feared for their way of life, which depended on slavery. Earlier the southern states had warned that if Lincoln became President, they would leave the Union. They now prepared to take action.

**The southern states secede.** Not all southerners wanted to break away from the Union. Senator John Crittenden of Kentucky proposed instead that the Missouri Compromise Line be extended to the Pacific Ocean. Slavery would be permitted south of the line but outlawed north of it.

The time for compromise, however, had passed. Even before Lincoln was sworn in as President, southern states began to carry out their threats to secede. On December 20, 1860, South Carolina became the first state to withdraw from the Union. By February 1, 1861, Mississippi, Florida, Alabama, Georgia, Louisiana, and Texas had also seceded.

President Buchanan, who was nearing the end of his term, seemed unsure what to do. Buchanan knew that if he used force, war would result. He took no steps to stop the seceding states. Many northerners approved of this policy. Said one newspaper editor in the Indianapolis *Daily Journal:*

We are a divided house. And we are none the worse for it. . . . We are well rid of South Carolina. . . . She can do far less harm out of the Union if we let her go quietly, than she has always done in it, and can now do in double measure if she is forcibly kept in. . . . If other States follow her, . . . let them go in peace. . . . [A] war, we believe, is a thousand times worse evil than the loss of a State, or a dozen States, that hate us, and will not stay with us without ruling us.

**Southerners establish a separate government.** In February 1861 representatives from the seven states that had seceded met in Montgomery, Alabama. There they drew up a constitution for a new government, and declared themselves a separate nation. They called themselves the Confederate States of America, or the **Confederacy.**

The Confederate constitution was much like that of the United States. It had a few important differences, however. First, it said that within the Confederacy, each state was "sovereign and independent." Second, it held that the Confederate Congress could not interfere with slavery. Third, it banned tariffs on imports. Finally, it limited the president to a single six-year term.

**Jefferson Davis leads the Confederacy.** The next step for the representatives in Montgomery was to choose government

Jefferson Davis of Mississippi married Varina Howell in 1845. In 1847 he became a senator, but he resigned rather than accept the Compromise of 1850.

leaders. They elected Jefferson Davis of Mississippi as president of the Confederacy. Alexander H. Stephens of Georgia was voted vice president.

Jefferson Davis had grown up on a large plantation with many slaves. After graduating from military school, he went on to distinguish himself as an officer in the Mexican War. He also served in both houses of Congress and as Secretary of War under President Pierce. Davis had always defended the rights of slave-owners in the South. Now he accepted the challenge of helping the Confederacy become an independent nation.

**Lincoln hopes for peace.** When Abraham Lincoln took over the United States presidency on March 4, 1861, he faced serious troubles. The Union he had sworn to "preserve, protect, and defend" was already shattered. Lincoln did not want war. In his inaugural speech, he told southerners:

> In your hands, my dissatisfied fellow countrymen, and not in mine, is the momentous issue of civil war. The government will not [attack] you.... We are not enemies, but friends. We must not be enemies....

In spite of Lincoln's plea, the country remained divided.

**War draws near.** In the eyes of Confederates, the United States was now a foreign power. To protect themselves, Confederate troops took over several federal forts in the South. United States soldiers, however, refused to leave Fort Sumter in South Carolina. The fort stood on an island in

In April 1861, Confederate troops fired on Fort Sumter, a federal outpost in Charleston, South Carolina. Aid sent by President Lincoln did not arrive in time, and after 34 hours of bombardment, Fort Sumter's defenders surrendered. On May 6 the Confederate Congress declared war on the United States.

Charleston Harbor. Though its location made it easy to defend, the troops there were low on food. Major Robert Anderson, commander of the Union force, asked Lincoln to send supplies and reinforcements.

Lincoln found himself with a hard choice to make. Sending troops and weapons would surely provoke the Confederacy. Yet Lincoln could not ignore the seizure of federal property. Acting upon the advice of his Cabinet, he made a cautious move. He ordered ships to take food—but no other relief—to Fort Sumter.

**The first shots are fired.** When the Confederate leaders learned that supplies were on the way, they suspected that soldiers might follow. On the morning of April 12, 1861, before help from the Union could arrive, Confederate cannon fired on Fort Sumter. The long period of uneasy waiting was over, and the **Civil War** had begun. After more than 30 hours of intense bombardment, the Union forces at Fort Sumter surrendered.

The outbreak of fighting led four more southern states to dissolve their ties with the North. Within a few days, Virginia, Arkansas, Tennessee, and North Carolina joined the Confederacy. Lincoln, meanwhile, began preparing an army. The Civil War was now a reality—but few imagined what a long, terrible war it would be.

## SECTION REVIEW

1. **Vocabulary**   civil war, platform
2. **People and Places**   Abraham Lincoln, Confederate States of America, Jefferson Davis, Fort Sumter
3. **Comprehension**   Why did southern states start seceding in late 1860?
4. **Comprehension**   How did war begin?
5. **Critical Thinking**   How was the secession of the southern states an extreme example of the principle of states' rights?

# Chapter 17 Summary

Differences between the northern and southern economies and ways of life had begun to split the nation by 1850. During the next decade, slavery in the territories became a heated issue. The Compromise of 1850 provided a temporary solution to sectional quarrels. California became a free state, and the question of slavery in New Mexico and Utah was left to the people who settled there. The Compromise also provided for a strict Fugitive Slave Law, which proved unpopular in the North.

The 1852 publication of *Uncle Tom's Cabin*, an antislavery book, added to the growing unrest. The Kansas-Nebraska Act of 1854, which allowed popular sovereignty in these two territories, led to more troubles. Proslavery and antislavery forces soon began fighting in Kansas. They also struggled in the courts. In the *Dred Scott* case of 1857, the Supreme Court ruled that Congress could not forbid slavery in the territories. The decision outraged northerners. They looked to the newly formed Republican party to keep slavery from spreading.

Slavery became the central issue in the 1858 Senate race between Democrat Stephen A. Douglas and Republican Abraham Lincoln. Douglas favored popular sovereignty, while Lincoln opposed the extension of slavery outside slave states. Douglas won the election but Lincoln gained national fame.

The events of the 1850's, capped by John Brown's raid at Harpers Ferry in 1859, put the nation on the brink of war. When Abraham Lincoln was elected President in 1860, the southern states carried out their threat to secede. They formed the Confederacy and elected Jefferson Davis as their president. The following year, on April 12, the Civil War began when Confederate forces fired on Fort Sumter.

## Vocabulary and Key Terms

Choose one term from the following list to replace each blank in the paragraph below. Write your answers on a separate sheet of paper.

**Compromise of 1850**
*Dred Scott* **case**
**fugitive**
**Fugitive Slave Law**
**Kansas-Nebraska Act**
**platform**
**popular sovereignty**
**Republican party**

Even after the ___1___, quarrels arose over slavery. In 1854 Congress passed the ___2___, allowing people in the territories to decide the matter of slavery by ___3___. Congress also passed the ___4___, making it harder for ___5___ slaves to escape. In 1857 the Supreme Court made an important proslavery ruling in the ___6___. Northerners, meanwhile, formed the ___7___. Abraham Lincoln, their candidate for President in 1860, ran on an antislavery ___8___.

## Recalling the Facts

1. How did the Mexican War stir debate over slavery?
2. What was the Compromise of 1850?
3. How did *Uncle Tom's Cabin* affect the mood of the country in the 1850's?
4. Why did the Kansas-Nebraska Act lead to violence among settlers?
5. How did Abraham Lincoln and Stephen Douglas differ on the issue of slavery? What results did the Lincoln-Douglas debates have?
6. What did the Supreme Court decide in the *Dred Scott* case?
7. What was the outcome of the 1860 election, and what effect did it have?
8. Who was president of the Confederacy?

## Places to Locate

Match the letters on the map with the places listed below. Write your answers on a separate sheet of paper.

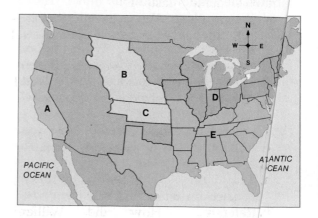

1. Free states in 1850
2. Slave states in 1850
3. California
4. Kansas Territory
5. Nebraska Territory

## Critical Thinking

1. How did the sectionalism of the 1850's build on past events? Consider the following points in your answer:
   a. past disagreements over slavery
   b. past disagreements over tariffs
   c. the nullification crisis of 1830
2. In the *Dred Scott* case, the Supreme Court upheld the view that slaves were property. How did such thinking contradict ideas stated in the Declaration of Independence?
3. When Abraham Lincoln met Harriet Beecher Stowe during the Civil War, he greeted her with these words: "So you're the little woman who wrote the book that made this great war!" To what extent do you think *Uncle Tom's Cabin* shaped the course of history?

4. Harriet Beecher Stowe and John Brown both became heroes to many abolitionists. Compare their goals, their methods, and their successes. Do you approve or disapprove of what they did? Explain.

## Understanding History

1. Reread the section "The issue of slavery divides Americans" on page 391. Then answer these questions.
   a. **Geography.** What geographic factors made southerners seek to extend slavery?
   b. **Primary Sources.** According to the southerner who is quoted, why would the North maintain its ties to the South?
2. Reread the section "Great leaders speak out in Congress" on page 393. Then answer these questions.
   a. **Geography.** Debate over slavery focused on which region?
   b. **Religion.** How did William Seward's religious beliefs influence his views on slavery?
3. Reread the section "The Kansas-Nebraska Act reopens the slavery quarrel" on page 396. Then answer these questions.
   a. **Citizenship.** How was popular sovereignty a compromise?
   b. **Citizenship.** Is popular sovereignty a democratic concept? Explain.
   c. **Citizenship.** Do you think popular sovereignty was a good idea? Why or why not?

## Projects and Activities

1. **Making a Poster.** Design a poster advertising a community meeting to discuss popular sovereignty. Your poster should reflect either a northern or a southern viewpoint.
2. **Analyzing Primary Sources.** Find excerpts from the Lincoln-Douglas debates of 1858. Review the arguments presented and summarize them in your own words. Share your information with the rest of the class.

3. **Presenting a Reading.** Find a copy of *Uncle Tom's Cabin* and read all or parts of the novel. Select an appropriate scene for a class reading. With a few classmates, choose parts to rehearse and present to the class. Have a narrator introduce the scene and explain what is happening.
4. **Staging an Interview.** Imagine that you are a reporter interviewing Chief Justice Roger Taney after the *Dred Scott* decision. Do some background research on the case, including biographical research on Taney. Prepare questions for the Chief Justice about the decision and its probable impact.
5. **Making a Time Line.** Arrange the important events of the chapter in a time line that shows the coming of the Civil War. Compare your time line with a classmate's and discuss how each event listed helped lead to war.

## Practicing Your Skill

The passage below expresses the reaction of former slave Frederick Douglass to the *Dred Scott* decision. Read the passage, and then answer the questions that follow.

> [The decision] declares that Congress has no right to prohibit slavery anywhere.... A decision like this cannot stand.... The whole history of the antislavery movement is studded with proof that all measures taken to [weaken] antislavery [forces] have only made [those forces] greater and bolder. It was so with the Fugitive Slave bill. It was so with the Kansas-Nebraska bill and it will be so with this last and most shocking of all proslavery devices, this Taney decision.

1. Is Douglass's first sentence a fact or an opinion? How do you know?
2. Is the second sentence a fact or an opinion? How do you know?
3. What factual statement does Douglass make about the Fugitive Slave Law and the Kansas-Nebraska Act?
4. What opinions does Douglass express about the *Dred Scott* decision?

# 18 The North and the South Fight a Bitter War
## 1861–1865

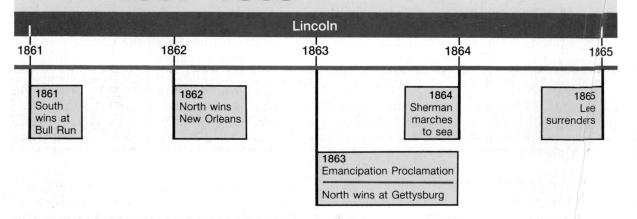

Lincoln

| 1861 | 1862 | 1863 | 1864 | 1865 |

1861
South wins at Bull Run

1862
North wins New Orleans

1864
Sherman marches to sea

1865
Lee surrenders

1863
Emancipation Proclamation

North wins at Gettysburg

**The Battle of Gettysburg was one of the bloodiest fights of the Civil War. The Union victory at Gettysburg marked a turning point in the war.**

## Preparing to Read

Few people in the United States were surprised when the Civil War began. Sectional tensions had been building for so long that war seemed bound to result. For four years, from 1861 to 1865, Americans fought against one another. Bloody battles took their toll on both sides before the South finally surrendered. At the war's end, the United States was still a single nation, but the conflict had disrupted the lives of nearly all Americans. As you read this chapter, try to answer the following questions:

1. What strengths and strategies did each side have?
2. How did the fighting proceed in the Civil War?
3. How did the war end, and how did it affect American life?

# 1 What strengths and strategies did each side have?

## Vocabulary

| | |
|---|---|
| defensive | enlist |
| offensive | strategy |

The North and the South entered the Civil War with different goals, strengths, and battle plans. Each side, however, felt a keen determination to win.

## Setting the Stakes

After the Confederate attack on Fort Sumter, there was no turning back from war. Americans saw two possibilities for the future. If the Confederate States of America won the war, it would become a separate nation. If the United States triumphed, it would force the seceding states to remain in the Union.

**The sections fight for different goals.** People in both the North and the South had powerful reasons to fight. For southerners the Civil War was a struggle for independence. Many whites in the South believed that slavery was an economic necessity for their region. They also felt that their way of life, based on cotton growing, clashed with the trading and manufacturing economy of the North. These southerners fought for the right to secede from the Union.

Northerners had opposite aims. Some fought because they hated slavery and hoped the war would put an end to it. Most northerners wanted above all to preserve the Union. Abraham Lincoln, at his inauguration, had said, "Physically speaking, we cannot separate." He believed that legally, too, the North and South were linked under the Constitution. No state, he said, "can lawfully get out of the Union."

**Some slave states side with the Union.** When the Confederacy first declared its independence, it included seven states. Four more states seceded after the Union surrendered Fort Sumter. (See Chapter 17.) However, the four northernmost slave states—Maryland, Missouri, Kentucky, and Delaware—waited to take action. President Lincoln realized the importance of these states. If they left the Union, the Confederacy would gain strength. Lincoln did his best to reassure slaveholders in these states that the war was not about slavery but about saving the Union.

411

## Our Presidents

### ABRAHAM LINCOLN

★ 1861–1865 ★

**16**TH PRESIDENT
**REPUBLICAN**

★ Born February 12, 1809, in Kentucky

★ Married Mary Todd in 1842; 4 children

★ Lawyer; representative from Illinois

★ Lived in Illinois when elected President

★ Vice Presidents: Hannibal Hamlin;
Andrew Johnson

★ Nicknamed "Honest Abe"

★ Died April 15, 1865, in Washington,
D.C., after being shot by an assassin
April 14, 1865

★ Key events while in office: Civil War;
Emancipation Proclamation; Gettysburg
Address; Kansas, West Virginia, and
Nevada became states

---

Delaware quickly made its decision. It would stay with the North. The other three states thought seriously about seceding, but they, too, finally gave the Union their loyalty.

In Virginia, meanwhile, not everyone accepted the legislature's decision to join the Confederacy. People living in the mountainous northwestern part of the state broke away from their fellow Virginians. They formed the free state of West Virginia, which entered the Union in 1863. With the addition of West Virginia, the North had 23 states to the South's 11.

**Americans choose sides.** The Civil War divided not only the nation but neighborhoods and even families. Some northerners went south to fight for the Confederacy. Some southerners supported the Union. Loyalties were most sharply divided in the border states—those on the dividing line between the North and the South. (See map on page 415.) In those states, neighbors often marched off to fight on opposite sides. Sons sometimes met their fathers, and brothers sometimes faced each other, as enemies on the battlefield. The wife of Confederate President Jefferson Davis had close relatives who fought for the Union. The war also separated members of President Lincoln's family. Three of his wife's brothers died for the Confederacy.

## Strengths and Weaknesses

Each side in the Civil War had certain strengths. The North outstripped the South in terms of people and resources. The South, however, had other factors in its favor.

**The North has material advantages.** When the Civil War began, more than twice as many Americans lived in the North as in the South. The North had about 22 million people, while the South had roughly 9 million. Of those southerners, more than 3.5 million were slaves. As such, they could not serve in the Confederate Army. Thus the North had a much larger population from which to draw soldiers. The North also had plenty of people to support the war effort by producing food and supplies.

In addition to human resources, the North had the means to equip its soldiers. Most of the factories that could make guns, ammunition, and uniforms were in the North. The North had more railroads, too, and could move goods readily. In addition, the United States already had a working government, a sizable navy, and secure banks. The South had to build these things as it went along.

**The South has fine leaders and a will to win.** On the surface, the North seemed stronger than the South. Southerners, however, planned to fight mostly on their own soil. This meant that they would know the terrain much better than the enemy did. Furthermore, people tend to fight harder when they are on the **defensive** —protecting themselves—rather than when they are on the **offensive** —attacking an enemy. With their homeland at stake, southerners showed a fierce spirit to succeed.

The South had another important advantage over the North. Most southerners had good outdoor-living skills. Men in the South grew up learning how to handle guns and ride horses. As a result, they were better prepared for the life of soldiers than were northern city dwellers. The South's military leaders, too, were among the nation's finest. Many Confederate officers had been trained at West Point and other military schools. They had served in the United States Army before they resigned their posts to fight for the Confederacy.

The South's greatest leader was Robert E. Lee. Lee, a Virginian, had faced a hard decision at the start of the war. Although he was a southerner, he opposed slavery and secession. When Virginia joined the Confederacy, however, Lee turned down an offer to command the Union troops. He could not bring himself to bear arms against his beloved state. Lee instead volunteered to serve with the Confederacy. Thus the South gained a brilliant general whose skill gave the Confederacy a key advantage.

## Battle Plans and Preparations

Both the North and the South expected the war to be short. Each side laid its plans confidently, sure that it could win in a matter of months.

**The North and the South recruit troops.** After the attack on Fort Sumter, both the Union and the Confederate States began to raise armies. On April 15, 1861, President Lincoln called for 75,000 volunteers to serve for three months. By July the army had swelled to more than twice that number. Many blacks were among those who rushed to enlist —sign up—for service in the armed forces. Blacks, however, were turned away. Union leaders insisted that the purpose of the war was to preserve the Union, not to free the slaves. Therefore, they said, blacks had no place in the army.

Confederate President Jefferson Davis meanwhile asked for 100,000 volunteers for 12 months. Southerners quickly met his request. In these early days of the war, enthusiasm ran high on both sides. Northern soldiers were proud to wear the blue uniforms of the United States Army. Similarly,

## Graph Study

At the start of the Civil War, the North and the South had unequal resources. In what resources was the South at a disadvantage? What percent of the total exports came from the South?

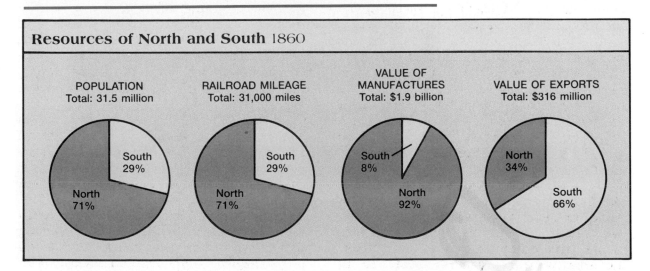

**Resources of North and South** 1860

POPULATION
Total: 31.5 million

South 29%
North 71%

RAILROAD MILEAGE
Total: 31,000 miles

South 29%
North 71%

VALUE OF MANUFACTURES
Total: $1.9 billion

South 8%
North 92%

VALUE OF EXPORTS
Total: $316 million

North 34%
South 66%

Confederate men were eager to dress in Confederate gray. Troops marched and drilled with great spirit. Southerners adopted the rousing "Dixie" as a favorite marching tune, while northerners patriotically sang "The Union Forever."

**Both sides make plans for winning the war.** Southerners believed that if they held out long enough, people in the North would tire of the war and give up fighting. The Confederates planned to wear out their enemies by waging a defensive war. They would keep most of their troops in the South, forcing the North to make the attacks. They would, however, send a small force north to capture Washington, D.C. From there the Confederates would march into Maryland and central Pennsylvania. They would weaken the North by splitting it in two.

Southern leaders expected to get foreign help in carrying out their plans. The South already shipped much of its cotton to Britain and France, where it was needed by textile factories. The Confederates now counted on exchanging cotton for European guns, ammunition, and medical supplies. They also hoped for money and direct military aid.

The North's aim was to win the war by invading the South. General Winfield Scott, commander of the Union army, came up with a three-part strategy —military plan. The first step was to sap Confederate strength with a "divide and conquer" policy. Much of the Confederacy lay west of the Mississippi River. By gaining control of the Mississippi, the Union could cut off the western states from the rest of the Confederacy.

Second, the North planned to blockade southern ports. In this way, goods could not be shipped to or from the South. The third part of Scott's proposal involved seizing the Confederate capital at Richmond, Virginia.

**Confederate General Robert E. Lee salutes his troops in this painting by N.C. Wyeth. Many historians consider Lee one of the most brilliant soldiers in American history.**

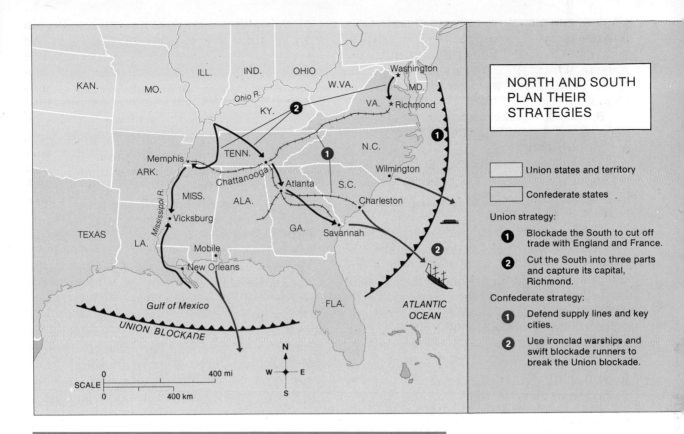

NORTH AND SOUTH PLAN THEIR STRATEGIES

Union states and territory
Confederate states

Union strategy:
1. Blockade the South to cut off trade with England and France.
2. Cut the South into three parts and capture its capital, Richmond.

Confederate strategy:
1. Defend supply lines and key cities.
2. Use ironclad warships and swift blockade runners to break the Union blockade.

## Map Study

At the beginning of the Civil War, the North and the South made plans to secure victory. How did the Union plan to prevent European goods from reaching the South? Why was Richmond important for the Confederates to defend? Why did Union plans include controlling the Mississippi River?

Northerners were sure the Confederacy would surrender once the capital fell. Thus, the capture of Richmond was the Union's first goal.

Winfield Scott's Union strategy was often called the "anaconda plan." Like the anaconda snake, the North would defeat its enemies by squeezing them.

At the beginning of the Civil War, the North was hard pressed to put its strategies into effect. The North's navy was not large enough to completely blockade southern ports. In addition, the Union army's recruits needed to be trained. Unfortunately for the South, its defensive strategy gave the Union time to train its army and build up its navy.

## SECTION REVIEW

1. **Vocabulary** defensive, offensive, enlist, strategy
2. **People and Places** West Virginia, Robert E. Lee, Winfield Scott
3. **Comprehension** What advantages did the North and the South have in the Civil War?
4. **Comprehension** How did the strategies of the North and the South differ during the Civil War?
5. **Critical Thinking** Would it have been wiser for the South to fight an offensive war? Explain.

## 2 How did the fighting proceed in the Civil War?

### Vocabulary

blockade runner    emancipate

ironclad    casualty

The North hoped to win a quick victory. One reason was that Confederate territory lay within easy striking distance. The Confederate capital at Richmond, Virginia, was only about 100 miles (160 kilometers) south of Washington, D.C. Although the inexperienced Union troops were far from ready for battle, northerners began to call for action.

### A Sobering Start

In the spring of 1861, the cry "On to Richmond!" rang through the North. Union troops were ordered south to capture the Confederate capital.

**Confederates turn back northern soldiers at Bull Run.** The Union forces crossed the Potomac River into Virginia early in July. Chaos marked the advance into enemy territory. Many people from Washington, D.C., trailed behind the army, eager to see the Union win a victory. Members of Congress, newspaper reporters, and ordinary citizens all came to share in the excitement. The troops, unused to military discipline, often fell out of line to pick berries and search for water.

Meanwhile, Confederate troops had assembled at Manassas Junction, Virginia, on a small stream called Bull Run. Near this point, about 30 miles (48 kilometers) from Washington, D.C., the two armies met in battle. At first the Confederate forces seemed to be losing. They held firm, however, until fresh reinforcements arrived under the command of General Thomas Jackson. Jackson's steady fighting earned him the nickname "Stonewall."

After a few hours, the Union lines broke and the soldiers retreated in great confusion. As they fled, said an observer, they littered the ground "with coats, blankets, firelocks, cooking tins, caps, belts, bayonets...." The Confederates, instead of pursuing the enemy into Washington, scrambled to pick up the cast-off supplies.

**Events at Bull Run awaken the North.** The **Battle of Bull Run** shocked people in the North and discouraged the Union troops. One young soldier said, "I've had enough of fighting to last my lifetime." Even the Union leaders were stunned. They saw clearly that their soldiers needed more training. They also realized that Washington, D.C., needed better defenses against the Confederates.

### LINKING PAST AND PRESENT

### ★ ★ ★ Photography

Until the mid 1800's, newspaper reporters relied on vivid word descriptions to capture the events of the day. During the Civil War, however, advances in photography allowed Mathew Brady to tell stories with a camera. Brady and a team of assistants traveled with the Union army, taking dramatic pictures of battlefields and war-weary soldiers.

By the 1880's, newspapers and magazines often used photographs to inform the public about important issues. Photographs helped persuade people to create national parks, to clean up city slums, and to pass laws protecting child workers. More recently photographs have recorded peace marches, astronauts landing on the moon, and America's 200th birthday celebration.

Volunteers eagerly enlisted in the armies of the North and the South. This painting by Thomas Nast shows Union troops leaving New York City for Washington, D.C. A large crowd cheers the soldiers as they march to war.

The South, too, learned a lesson from the battle. Though joyful about its success, the Confederate army was still disorganized. The South had missed a chance to chase the Yankees and seize the Union capital.

## The War in the West

For months after the Battle of Bull Run, the main fighting took place not in the East but west of the Appalachians. (See map on page 418.) During this time the Union army and navy worked together to win control of the Mississippi River.

**Farragut captures New Orleans.** In order to secure the Mississippi, the North needed to seize Confederate cities and forts along the river. Most important was the city of New Orleans near the mouth of the Mississippi. David Farragut, a navy captain, took charge of capturing New Orleans.

Farragut had begun his naval career in the War of 1812, when he was quite young. Now 60 years old, Farragut commanded a fleet of wooden ships. In the spring of 1862 he led his sailors up the Mississippi. Boldly they raced past the gunfire of Confederate forts on each side of the river. Then Farragut

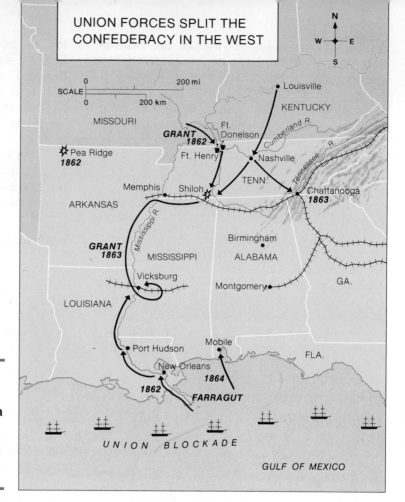

UNION FORCES SPLIT THE CONFEDERACY IN THE WEST

## Map Study

Early victories by Ulysses S. Grant and David Farragut helped the North achieve its goal of splitting the Confederacy. What three cities were keys to controlling the southern Mississippi River?

defeated a Confederate fleet guarding New Orleans. He captured the city, giving the Union control of the lower Mississippi.

**Grant gains early victories for the North.** Meanwhile, other Union forces were moving against Confederate forts farther north on the Mississippi. Union troops also advanced along the Tennessee and Cumberland rivers. The leader of these forces was Ulysses S. Grant, a West Point graduate who had fought in the Mexican War. Although Grant had resigned from the army in 1854, he reenlisted at the start of the Civil War. Grant's quiet personality masked his iron will. He showed a knack for planning strategy and an ability to make wise and quick decisions.

Early in 1862 Grant attacked Fort Henry and Fort Donelson in western Tennessee. With the help of navy gunboats, the Union forces captured both forts. When the commander of Fort Donelson asked for the terms of surrender, Grant replied, "Immediate and unconditional surrender." From then on, U.S. Grant was nicknamed "Unconditional Surrender" Grant.

After the capture of the two forts in Tennessee, Grant's armies moved southward. In April the Confederate forces made a surprise attack at Shiloh (SHY-lo) in southern Tennessee. The Confederates came close to winning the battle. When fresh Union soldiers arrived, however, Grant forced the outnumbered Confederate troops to retreat.

Shiloh was one of the war's bloodiest battles. About 11,000 Confederate soldiers fell during the two days of fighting. Of the Union troops, about 13,000 were wounded or killed. These heavy losses came as a shock to both sides.

**The North wins control of the Mississippi River.** The Union victory at Shiloh brought the North closer to its goal of controlling the Mississippi. Then, in June 1862, the river city of Memphis, Tennessee, fell into northern hands. The Union now could keep southerners from using the upper Mississippi as well as New Orleans. The Confederates, however, held a 250-mile (400-kilometer) strip of land between Vicksburg, Mississippi, and Port Hudson, Louisiana. (See map on page 418.)

Early in 1863 General Grant made repeated tries to capture Vicksburg. The city stood on high bluffs on the east bank of the river, surrounded by swampy ground. This put the Confederates in an excellent position to shell enemy forces. When Grant found he could not take Vicksburg by direct attack, he prepared for a long siege. For six weeks his forces bombarded the city. Meanwhile, Union gunboats guarded the river and blocked incoming supplies. On July 4, 1863, the Confederate commander surrendered Vicksburg on Grant's terms. A short time later, Port Hudson also surrendered to Union forces.

The Union forces now had control of the Mississippi. One part of the North's strategy had succeeded. The Confederacy had been cut in two.

## The War at Sea

Meanwhile, the Union pursued another part of its strategy: blockading southern ports. When the Civil War began, the navy was not prepared for such a large task. It took several months before the blockade became effective.

The Union's *Monitor* (left, foreground) battled the Confederacy's *Merrimack* (right) off the coast of Virginia in March 1862. Neither ironclad ship could damage the other. What was the advantage of ironclads over wooden ships?

**The Union navy cuts off southern shipping.** When the war started, the Union navy had only about 90 ships. Vessels of every kind, however, were hastily prepared for blockade duty. Robert Smalls, a slave who piloted a Confederate gunboat, managed to sneak the ship out of Charleston Harbor and deliver it to the Union fleet. Soon Union ships were guarding important Confederate ports from Virginia to Texas.

Because the southern coastline stretched more than 3,500 miles (5,600 kilometers), the Union navy could not seal off every port. A small number of blockade runners —ships that slip through a blockade—managed to evade capture. Under cover of night these Confederate ships stole into southern ports with badly needed ammunition, guns, and other supplies. Yet in spite of all attempts to break the blockade, the North kept its stranglehold over the South's shipping. Southern people found it almost impossible to get tea, coffee, and matches. Cotton could not be exported, and countless bales piled up on the docks.

To tighten the blockade, the Union army and navy took steps to capture southern ports. David Farragut added to his fame by taking Mobile, Alabama. By the end of the war, all Confederate ports except Charleston, South Carolina, and Wilmington, North Carolina, were in Union hands. The Union blockade did more harm to the South than any other tactic.

**The *Merrimack* and the *Monitor* battle to a draw.** One of the first major naval clashes of the war took place in March 1862. At the outset of the war the Confederates had seized a United States ship, the *Merrimack*, docked in a Virginia navy yard.* On March 8, 1862, they used this vessel to attack Union ships blockading the coast. Shells fired by the Union sailors had no effect on the strange-looking *Merrimack*, which had been covered with iron plates. The *Merrimack* destroyed two Union ships and ran another one aground before it withdrew.

On the next day the *Merrimack* returned to destroy the remaining Union ships. This time, however, it met the Union's *Monitor*, another ironclad —armored—ship. The *Monitor* looked even more odd than the *Merrimack*. Smaller in size, it had a low, flat deck and two powerful guns mounted in a revolving tower. According to one observer, the *Monitor* looked like a "tin can on a shingle."

In the fight that followed, neither ship damaged the other seriously. The battle ended in a draw, but it marked a new age in naval warfare. Before this time, the navy's ships had all been built of wood. The new ironclads proved that wooden warships were a thing of the past.

## The War in the East

While Union forces were busy gaining control of the Mississippi and blockading the southern coast, other Union forces tried to capture Richmond. This was the third part of the Union strategy to defeat the Confederates. For some time, however, the South held the edge in the East. (See map on page 421.)

**McClellan's attack on Richmond fails.** The Union had already been stopped once— at Bull Run—from seizing the Confederate capital. After this defeat, Lincoln put General George B. McClellan in charge of reorganizing and drilling the troops. In a few months the army became a well-trained, well-equipped body of about 100,000 soldiers. Yet McClellan was cautious in attacking the enemy. He did not move until Lincoln impatiently ordered him to Richmond in March 1862.

McClellan's troops approached Richmond from the east, by way of the peninsula between the James and York rivers. They advanced so slowly, however, that the Confederates decided to attack first. In the famous Seven Days' Battles, fought from June 26 to July 2, Generals Robert E. Lee and Stonewall Jackson forced the Union army to retreat. The second Union attempt to capture Richmond had failed.

**The Union wins a key victory.** In August 1862 another Union advance against Richmond ended in defeat. At this second

---

* The Confederates renamed the ship the *Virginia*, but it is still better known as the *Merrimack*.

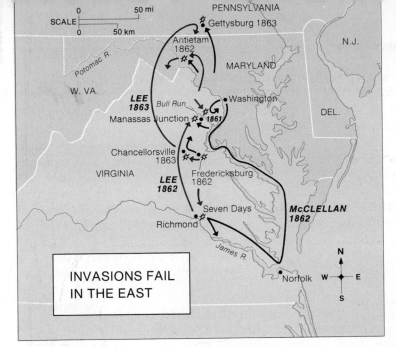

INVASIONS FAIL IN THE EAST

Battle of Bull Run, the Union soldiers outnumbered the Confederates three to two but suffered twice as many losses.

On the heels of this fierce conflict came an even bloodier battle. Lee had led about 40,000 soldiers across the Potomac River into Maryland. He hoped to destroy northern railroad lines and capture Washington, D.C. A copy of Lee's plans, however, had fallen into the hands of Union soldiers under McClellan. McClellan and about 70,000 troops met Lee's forces at Antietam (an-TEE-tuhm) Creek on September 17. Heavy fighting followed, and Lee returned to Virginia. By then more than 23,000 soldiers from both sides had been killed or wounded.

The North's success at the Battle of Antietam sent an important message abroad. The British and French governments had shown sympathy for the Confederates. Britain had even built ships for the Confederates, and France planned to do the same. Now, however, these countries worried about backing the South. They did not want to support a losing cause and they had already found other sources of cotton.

At home, President Lincoln made the most of the Union's narrow victory. Five days after the battle, he announced a bold new policy.

**Lincoln proclaims an end to slavery in the South.** All along Lincoln had said that the North's goal in the Civil War was simply to save the Union. Many northerners, however, thought the chief purpose of the war should be to **emancipate** —free—the slaves. In reply to the demands of abolitionists, Lincoln said:

My [foremost] object in this struggle is to save the Union.... If I could save the Union without freeing any slave, I would do it; if I could save it by freeing all the slaves, I would do it; and if I could save it by freeing some and leaving others alone, I would also do that.

Nevertheless, when Lincoln wrote these words, he had already decided to take a step toward ending slavery. He realized that freeing the slaves in the Confederacy would be a serious blow to the South. Thus, on September 22, 1862, he issued the **Emancipation Proclamation.** He announced that beginning January 1, 1863, "all persons held as slaves within any state ... in rebellion against the United States, shall be then, thenceforth, and forever free."

The Emancipation Proclamation did not apply to the slave states that had stayed loyal to the Union. Nor did it actually take effect

**421**

# THE GETTYSBURG ADDRESS  1863

Soon after the Battle of Gettysburg, President Lincoln was asked to dedicate part of the battlefield as a cemetery for the brave soldiers who had died there. Lincoln's brief speech told what the Union was struggling to preserve.

## Read to Find Out

1. What does Lincoln say the world can never forget?
2. What is the great task, or cause, to which Lincoln says Americans must dedicate themselves?

---

Four score and seven years ago our fathers brought forth on this continent a new nation, conceived in liberty and dedicated to the proposition that all men are created equal.

Now we are engaged in a great civil war, testing whether that nation or any nation so conceived and so dedicated can long endure. We are met on a great battlefield of that war. We have come to dedicate a portion of that field as a final resting place for those who here gave their lives that that nation might live. It is altogether fitting and proper that we should do this.

But, in a larger sense, we cannot dedicate—we cannot consecrate—we cannot hallow—this ground. The brave men, living and dead, who struggled here have consecrated it far above our poor power to add or detract. The world will little note nor long remember what we say here, but it can never forget what they did here. It is for us, the living, rather, to be dedicated here to the unfinished work which they who fought here have thus far so nobly advanced.

It is rather for us to be here dedicated to the great task remaining before us—that from these honored dead we take increased devotion to that cause for which they gave the last full measure of devotion; that we here highly resolve that these dead shall not have died in vain; that this nation, under God, shall have a new birth of freedom; and that government of the people, by the people, for the people shall not perish from the earth.

*Abraham Lincoln*

---

in the Confederacy on January 1. Slaves were set free only as Union forces gained control of Confederate lands.

Still, Lincoln's statement clearly broadened the North's goals. The Civil War was being fought not only to save the Union but also to free the slaves. In addition, the Emancipation Proclamation helped turn British and French sympathies against the South.

**Further defeats discourage the North.** During the months that followed the Emancipation Proclamation, the Confederates won battle after battle in the East. At Fredericksburg, Virginia, in December 1862, General Lee soundly thrashed Union attackers. At nearby Chancellorsville the following May, Lee and a force of less than 60,000 beat more than twice that number of Union soldiers.

These were dark days for the North. Robert E. Lee had outfought Union forces much larger than his own. Lincoln had put several generals in charge after McClellan's failures, but he had not found one who could match Lee in military skill. The President himself drew harsh criticism. Many people blamed him for the army's poor record.

The South, meanwhile, paid dearly for its victories. At Chancellorsville it suffered more than 10,000 casualties —people killed or injured. Among the casualties was Stonewall Jackson. Accidentally shot by one of his own soldiers, Jackson died within a few days.

## A Turning Point

After his victory at Chancellorsville, General Lee decided to try invading the North again. He hoped to strike a blow that would end the war. Lee swung north through Maryland and into Pennsylvania. Watchful Union armies followed a parallel route, keeping between Lee's troops and Washington, D.C.

**The Battle of Gettysburg stops the Confederate advance.** On July 1, 1863, the two armies met at Gettysburg in the rolling hills of southern Pennsylvania. Under their newly appointed commander, General George Meade, the Union forces took up a hillside position opposite the Confederates. Bitter fighting continued for two and a half days. On the afternoon of July 3, General Lee decided to make a bold and desperate attack. He ordered General George Pickett to lead about 15,000 brave Confederates toward the center of Union forces on Cemetery Ridge.

In neat lines the soldiers in gray marched across an open field. As they charged through steady Union fire, thousands were shot down. A handful succeeded in planting the Confederate flag high on the hill among the Union positions. However, cannon and musket fire had left three fourths of the attackers dead or wounded. Pickett's charge had failed. The battle was a staggering loss for the Confederacy. The next day Lee turned back south.

**The President speaks at Gettysburg.** Soon after the **Battle of Gettysburg,** the United States government set aside 17 acres (about 7 hectares) of the battlefield as a soldiers' cemetery. President Lincoln agreed to make "a few appropriate remarks" at the dedication ceremony.

Lincoln listened patiently as the main speaker went on for more than two hours. Finally Lincoln had his turn. He spoke just 10 sentences, claiming, "The world will little note, nor long remember what we say here." Yet Lincoln's few words—the **Gettysburg Address**—are among the most memorable in American history.

**Gettysburg becomes the turning point of the war.** The news of the victory at Gettysburg caused great joy in the North. From the West came more news. Vicksburg had surrendered to Ulysses S. Grant on July 4. While Grant's victory cut the Confederacy in two, the Union success at Gettysburg blocked the Confederate invasion of the North. These Union triumphs marked the turning point of the Civil War. In America and overseas, people understood that the South might fight on, but it was not likely to win. Although England and France had favored the South, they decided not to aid the Confederacy.

## SECTION REVIEW

1. **Vocabulary** blockade runner, ironclad, emancipate, casualty
2. **People and Places** Richmond, Bull Run, Thomas "Stonewall" Jackson, David Farragut, New Orleans, Ulysses S. Grant, Vicksburg, Robert Smalls, George B. McClellan, Antietam, Gettysburg
3. **Comprehension** How did the Emancipation Proclamation affect slaves and the Union cause?
4. **Comprehension** Why were the Union victories at Vicksburg and Gettysburg important?
5. **Critical Thinking** Why, do you think, did Lincoln wait until 1863 to free the slaves?

# MAPS AND GRAPHS: Special-Purpose Maps

Maps that present specific types of information are called **special-purpose maps.** Some special-purpose maps present economic information, such as the kinds of industries found in a particular area. Others provide political information, such as population figures or election results. Other special-purpose maps distort—alter the shape of—some geographical features to make the information clearer. For example, on a population map of the United States, New York might appear as a very large state because it has a large population.

The special-purpose map below gives military information about the Battle of Gettysburg. Like other kinds of maps, this map shows important information in the form of **symbols** that are explained in the map **key,** or **legend.** The key explains the meaning of the different colored bars, arrows, and lines on the map. Study the map and key carefully. Then, on a separate sheet of paper, answer the following questions.

1. What do the red arrows on this special-purpose map represent?
2. What do the black bars represent? The black arrows?
3. Did most of the fighting take place to the north or south of Gettysburg?
4. Which high points near Gettysburg did the Union forces hold?
5. From which ridge did Pickett lead his charge?
6. Based on information in the map and in this chapter, what advantage did the Union troops have in overcoming Pickett's charge?

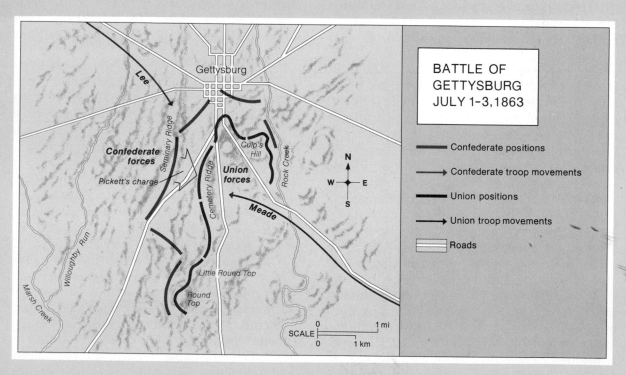

BATTLE OF
GETTYSBURG
JULY 1–3, 1863

Confederate positions
Confederate troop movements
Union positions
Union troop movements
Roads

# How did the war end, and how did it affect American life?

## Vocabulary

| | |
|---|---|
| income tax | bounty |
| greenback | draft |
| inflation | habeas corpus |

When the Civil War began, Americans had no idea how much agony and destruction it would cause. By the war's end, nearly everyone—soldier, slave, ordinary citizen—had been touched by this terrible struggle.

## The Final Phase

The Battle of Gettysburg had shifted the tide in favor of the North. At Vicksburg, meanwhile, General Grant had proven himself an extraordinary leader. The North, however, was still almost two years away from winning the war.

**General Grant commands the military.** After the surrender of Vicksburg in 1863, General Grant took charge of the Union forces in Tennessee. He defeated Confederate troops at Chattanooga, forcing them to retreat toward Atlanta, Georgia. Lincoln was impressed by Grant's successes in the West. On March 9, 1864, he gave Grant command of all the Union armies. At last Lincoln had found a general who might be able to lead the North to final victory.

Grant believed that the only way to win was by relentlessly pounding the enemy. He began making plans that he hoped would end the war. Grant's strategy was to wage a campaign of destruction in the South. To accomplish this he relied on Generals William Tecumseh Sherman and Philip Sheridan, who had aided in the capture of Chattanooga. Sheridan was to march through Virginia's Shenandoah Valley, burning the rich farmland there. Sherman would slash through the Confederacy from Chattanooga to Atlanta. At the same time Grant himself would attack Lee in Virginia. No matter what the cost, General Grant would capture Richmond.

**Sherman's march to the sea divides the South.** In the summer and fall of 1864, Sheridan's forces swept through the Shenandoah region. They set fire to buildings and fields, chased away livestock, and changed the fertile valley into a wasteland. Meanwhile, in May 1864, Sherman left Chattanooga with about 100,000 soldiers. Although Confederate troops fought them every step of the way, Sherman's army advanced slowly but surely.

In September Sherman captured Atlanta. Soon afterward, he took a bold step to divide the South further. With 60,000 soldiers, he struck out for Savannah, Georgia, more than 200 miles (320 kilometers) away on the Atlantic coast. Frightful destruction marked this march from Atlanta to the sea. To deprive southern forces of food and supplies, the Union soldiers burned houses and barns, towns and crops. They tore up railroad tracks and killed farm animals as they went along. Ordinary people in the South now suffered as directly as soldiers did.

Late in December 1864, Sherman captured Savannah. (See map on page 426.) Behind him, stretching all the way from Atlanta, lay a bleak and blackened strip of land about 60 miles (96 kilometers) wide.

**The end comes.** Meanwhile, General Grant was locked in battle with General Lee's armies in Virginia. The fighting began northwest of Richmond in a thickly wooded area called the Wilderness. Grant was unable to break through Lee's lines, but he kept up the attack through the fall and winter. In spite of heavy losses among his own troops, he hammered away at the Confederates. Step by step the armies moved east and then

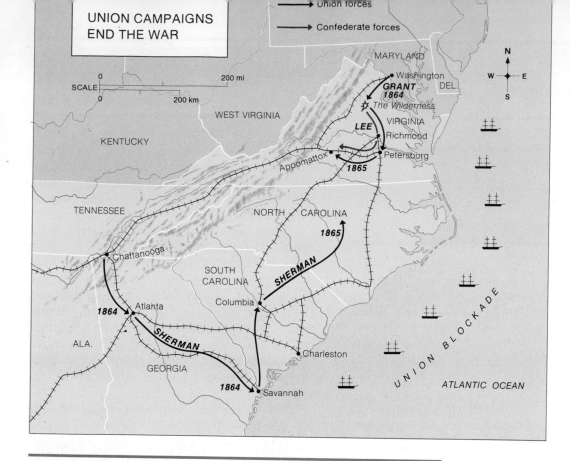

→ Union forces
→ Confederate forces

MARYLAND
• Washington DEL.
GRANT
1864
☆ The Wilderness
VIRGINIA
LEE
• Richmond
Appomattox • Petersburg
1865

WEST VIRGINIA

KENTUCKY

SCALE
0 ——— 200 mi
0 ——— 200 km

TENNESSEE

NORTH CAROLINA
1865

Chattanooga

SOUTH
CAROLINA

SHERMAN

Atlanta
1864          Columbia

ALA.
SHERMAN

GEORGIA
Charleston

1864
Savannah

UNION BLOCKADE

ATLANTIC OCEAN

N
W ✦ E
S

## Map Study

Union campaigns by Generals Sherman and Grant brought the Civil War to an end. In what direction did General Sherman proceed after he marched to Savannah, Georgia? Where did Lee surrender to Grant?

south in a half-circle around Richmond. At last, hard-pressed by the enemy, Lee left Richmond to head southwest. (See map on this page.) He hoped to travel by train to North Carolina, but Union armies blocked his way. Lee thus had no choice but to surrender all of the Confederate armies to General Grant.

The formal surrender took place at Appomattox (ap-uh-MAT-uhks) Court House, Virginia, on April 9, 1865. Grant treated Lee with the respect due a great leader. He refused to follow the custom of taking the losing general's sword. Grant also allowed Lee's officers to keep their swords and pistols. He let the soldiers keep the horses they would need for spring plowing. Learning

that Lee's troops were hungry, Grant sent food to them. He even stopped his soldiers from firing their guns in celebration of the victory.

After four long years, the Civil War was over. The results of the war were clear. The North had triumphed, and the Union had been saved. Furthermore, the slaves were freed, and the question of secession was settled once and for all.

Both sides, however, paid a heavy price. The cost of the war will never be known, but it is estimated to be more than $20 billion. The fighting claimed the lives of at least 200,000 soldiers. Thousands more died from disease or went home wounded. The war also took its toll on those who did not fight.

## ECONOMICS • Women in Wartime

The Civil War presented economic challenges for women across the nation. While their fathers, husbands, and brothers were off fighting, women had to provide for their families and supply the armies. They worked in stores, in factories, in government offices, and in the fields. When goods became scarce in the South, women found clever ways to cope with the shortages. They melted church bells to make cannon. Instead of buying coffee at $2.50 or more a pound, they roasted and brewed cornmeal, available for only pennies a pound.

Women also gave generously to the federal and Confederate governments. In the North women bought thousands of dollars worth of war bonds. Southern women sold their jewels and finery to fund the Confederate cause. A woman in Charleston, South Carolina, donated her silverware, and a widow in Arkansas sent the government 400 bales of cotton. Without such sacrifices on the part of women, neither side could have met the costs of the war.

**Women making bullets**

## The Home Front

In both the North and the South, most healthy white men went into the army. This meant that non-combat work fell mostly to women and, in the South, to slaves.

**Women fill new roles.** In the absence of the men, southern women took over the job of managing plantations. They replaced cotton with food crops and kept the fields productive. When the naval blockade cut off the South's imports of machinery, medicines, and household items, women turned out war goods in their homes. They cut up draperies to make clothes. They used linen sheets and towels to make bandages for the wounded.

In the North, meanwhile, women replaced the factory workers who went off to war.

While thousands of women worked to supply the armies, others worked close to the battlefields. Several southern women helped the Confederacy by serving as spies. Blacks in the North, like Susie King Taylor, served as teachers, launderers, and cooks for the Union troops.

Many women on both sides cared for sick and wounded soldiers. Medical care at the time was quite primitive, and trained doctors and supplies were in short supply. Sally Louisa Tompkins used her own money to open a hospital in Richmond, Virginia. Her work was so valuable that Jefferson Davis

**427**

At the start of the Civil War many soldiers reported to camp accompanied by wives, children, and even family pets. Women took part in the war as cooks, laundry workers, nurses, scouts, and spies.

made her a captain in the Confederate army. In the North, Dorothea Dix persuaded Lincoln to accept women as army nurses. Dr. Elizabeth Blackwell set up a training program for nurses, and Clara Barton organized supply and nursing services.

**Slaves embrace freedom cautiously.** Like women, blacks found themselves thrust into new roles during the war. Southern slaves at first remained loyal to their owners. As the war went on, some slaves left the plantations to work in the iron and salt mines of the South. Others built roads for the Confederate troops. Many slaves, however,

aided Union soldiers behind Confederate lines. They served secretly as scouts and guides and passed on information about the movements of Confederate troops.

When Lincoln issued the Emancipation Proclamation, many slaves kept their joy to themselves. They saved their celebrating until Union troops arrived and made their new freedom a reality.

**Northern blacks make vital contributions.** In July 1862 Congress decided to let blacks enlist in the United States army. By the end of the war, about 200,000 free blacks and freed slaves had served in the

Union forces. These black soldiers and sailors fought bravely. One newspaper described their heroism in an early battle:

At Helena, they bore the brunt of the fighting, and defeated a superior force of the enemy.... Wherever the Negroes have had a chance they have given evidence of the [greatest] gallantry.

Blacks also endured hardships not shared by white soldiers. Black troops usually received less pay, less training, and fewer supplies than did whites. Blacks faced special danger if they were captured by Confederates. They were often sold into slavery or put to death rather than held as prisoners of war. In spite of the discrimination and hardships, blacks fought loyally. More than 40,000 black soldiers lost their lives in the war. At least 20 blacks received the Medal of Honor, the country's highest military honor.

## Economic Changes

The Civil War affected not only individuals but also the economies of the North and South. For the South, the costs of fighting severely strained the economy. The North, however, grew more prosperous.

**The North and the South raise funds.** Both the United States and the Confederacy needed money to support the war. One financial measure adopted by both sides was an **income tax** —a tax on yearly earnings.†  In the past, Americans had paid taxes on property and on goods. Now, for the first time, they also had to pay a fraction of their wages to the government.

Even with more tax money coming in, the North and the South still had trouble paying their bills. Both governments began printing more paper money. Many people feared that these paper dollars might never bring their full worth in gold and silver. In the dark days of 1864, when it seemed that the war would never come to an end, the northern **greenback** —paper dollar—was worth only about 40 cents. Because it took more paper dollars to pay for goods, prices soared higher. The result was **inflation** —a sharp, steady rise in prices.

---

† This income tax ended in 1872. The present-day income tax came after the passage of the Sixteenth Amendment in 1913.

About 200,000 blacks served in the Union forces. Black regiments won recognition for their bravery and their contributions to major victories.

The South was much worse off. Without the reserves of gold and silver that the North had, the South found it harder to finance the war. As a result, while the North printed about $432 million in paper bills, the South printed more than $1.5 billion. Prices for food and housing quickly doubled and tripled. Toward the end of the war, the South's paper dollar was worth about three cents.

These conditions created severe inflation in the South. Prices rose so high that ordinary people could no longer afford goods like butter, sugar, and tea. A clerk in the Confederate army complained that a few merchants took unfair advantage of the situation: "Our danger is from within, not without. We are distressed more by the [speculators] than by the enemy."

**The troubles in the South worsen.** As the Civil War went on, southern farms, plantations, and buildings became run-down. Roads and railroad tracks were damaged and never fixed. Railroad cars and locomotives wore out and could not be replaced. It grew difficult to send food and supplies to the armies. When Union forces invaded the South, they caused even more damage. By the war's end, much of the South lay in ruins.

**By the war's end, most of the South's cities lay in ruins, as this 1865 photograph of Charleston, South Carolina, shows. Rebuilding the destroyed cities was a major problem for the South after the war.**

**The North prospers during the war.** For several reasons, the hardships caused by the war were much less severe in the North than in the South. First, very little fighting took place on northern soil. Second, because of its large population, the North had plenty of workers to carry on at home. The North also had more railroads and telegraph lines than the South, making it easier to transport goods and communicate. Finally, because of its many factories, the North did not depend on outside suppliers of finished goods. Manufacturers worked at top speed to make the clothes, food, blankets, tents, guns, and ammunition needed by the army. Recent inventions also boosted the North's ability to produce food and supplies. (See time list on this page.)

The boom in northern business opened up many new jobs. As the demand for workers rose, wages went up. So did prices. High prices brought greater profits to factory owners, shopkeepers, and others with something to sell. Thus many people in the North grew richer during the war, and the economy grew stronger.

## Political Affairs

Although the war effort boosted the North's economy, not all northerners supported the war. Political unrest soon surfaced. The South, too, had its share of political troubles.

**Enlistments decline.** At the start of the Civil War, neither side found it hard to attract soldiers. As hopes of a swift victory faded, however, fewer and fewer men volunteered for service. Promises of travel and glory carried little weight when balanced against the low pay of military service and the risks of fighting.

In July 1861 the North began offering a $100 **bounty** —bonus—to anyone who joined the Union forces. Later the government tripled this bounty. This only encouraged "bounty jumpers" to enlist, claim their reward, desert, and then enlist again somewhere else. The army, unfortunately, remained short of soldiers. The South had the same problem.

In April 1862 the Confederate Congress began the first **draft** in American history. A draft is a process of selecting persons for required military duty. In the South, white men between 18 and 35 years of age became subject to the draft. The North passed its own draft law in March 1863. Names were drawn from a list of men between the ages of 20 and 45. Draftees could escape military service, however, by paying $300 or by hiring substitutes.

**New Yorkers resist the draft.** Many people in the North opposed the draft. Poor citizens were especially angry because the law favored the rich. On July 13, mobs began to riot in New York City. They set fire to buildings, attacked police officers, cut down telegraph wires, and looted stores. The rioters singled out blacks for some of the worst beatings.

After four days, state troops and heavy thunderstorms brought an end to the raging violence. The draft continued, but it never proved a great success. Only a small percentage of northerners entered the Union army as draftees.

**The Confederacy faces opposition.** The draft also proved unpopular in the South. As in the North, rich men could pay a fee to avoid army duty. Certain other people, such as those who supervised at least 20 slaves, were also freed from service. These rules seemed unfair to small farmers.

Southerners also disliked the heavy taxes they had to pay. They grew angry as President Davis tried to make the government still stronger. His critics began calling

President Lincoln was criticized by many northerners for his handling of the war. He was reelected in 1864. After the war's end, Americans recognized his wise leadership.

**Lincoln battles opposition.** The North had its own problems with disunity. Some people did not think Lincoln could lead the Union to victory. Other people did not believe the North should be fighting at all. Those with the most extreme antiwar views were known as **Copperheads.** Copperheads spoke against the Union cause and actively aided the Confederacy. The most outspoken of the Copperheads was Clement L. Vallandigham, a member of Congress from Ohio. Because of Vallandigham's disloyalty to the Union, Lincoln banished him to the Confederacy.

Lincoln proved to be a tough opponent. He took criticism well, but he would not stand for disloyalty. When necessary, he had rebels arrested and held in jail. During the course of the war, about 13,000 people were arrested for their anti-Union activities. Sometimes formal charges were never filed against the prisoners, sparking complaints from Lincoln's foes. They said that all citizens had a right to **habeas corpus** (HAY-bee-uhs KOR-puhs)—protection from being illegally jailed. Lincoln argued that in times of war the government could lift this right. In time, however, Lincoln pardoned many of the people who were arrested.

**Lincoln wins reelection.** As the 1864 election drew near, the Republicans nominated Lincoln for a second term. To unify the North's support for the war, they called themselves the National Union party. For Vice President they nominated Andrew Johnson, a Democrat from Tennessee. Johnson was the only southerner still in the United States Senate.

The Democrats' candidate was George McClellan, former commander of the Union army. For a time, the vote promised to be close. Then, about two months before the vote, General Sherman took Atlanta. The fall of Atlanta sealed the public's faith in Lincoln. Lincoln won the election, winning 212 electoral votes to McClellan's 21. Lincoln was sworn into office for a second term on March 4, 1865.

By this time victory for the North lay just around the corner. Lincoln looked ahead to the task of bringing the South back into the

him "King Jeff the First" and refused to cooperate. The governors of Georgia, North Carolina, and South Carolina, for example, lagged when asked to provide money and troops. There was little that President Davis could do. The Confederate constitution, after all, guaranteed states' rights. Thus, the weak structure of the Confederate government hurt the southern war effort.

Union. He knew that rebuilding the nation would take hard work. Yet he felt sure that all Americans could put the horrible war behind them. At his inauguration, he spoke of the future:

> Fondly do we hope—fervently do we pray—that this mighty ... war may speedily pass away....
>
> With malice toward none; with charity for all; with firmness in the right, as God gives us to see the right, let us strive on to finish the work we are in; to bind up the nation's wounds; to care for him who shall have borne the battle and for his widow, and his orphan— to do all which may achieve and cherish a just and lasting peace among ourselves, and with all nations.

# Chapter 18 Summary

The Civil War proved to be a long, bitter struggle. Southerners fought to preserve slavery and to win independence from the Union. Northerners fought to save the Union and to end slavery. The North had the advantages of a larger population, more resources, an established government, and an army and navy. The North planned to crush the Confederacy by gaining control of the Mississippi River, blockading southern ports, and seizing the capital at Richmond, Virginia.

The South's strengths were its defensive position and its outstanding military leaders. Its strategy was to hold out until the North tired of the war. The Confederates also hoped to capture Washington, D.C., and to get help from Europe.

In 1861 the first Battle of Bull Run ended with a victory for the South. The North had more success in the West and at sea. Early attempts to take Richmond, however, failed. Then, in September 1862, the North narrowly won the Battle of Antietam. This gave Lincoln a chance to issue the Emancipation Proclamation, freeing the slaves.

In the following months the picture brightened for the South. Robert E. Lee defeated Union forces in several key battles. The Battle of Gettysburg, however, proved to be a turning point. The Confederates lost badly and never regained their advantage. Ulysses S. Grant took command of all Union armies and carried out the final defeat of the South. After Sherman's march through Atlanta and the fall of Richmond, General Lee surrendered at Appomattox Court House on April 9, 1865.

The Civil War meant many casualties among soldiers and hardship for those at home. Political discontent and opposition to the draft troubled both sides. The South suffered more than the North, however, because most of the fighting took place on southern soil. While the South's economy withered, the North's grew. Abraham Lincoln was renominated for the presidency in 1864. At first the election outcome was uncertain, but Sherman's taking of Atlanta ensured Lincoln's reelection. When he began his second term in 1865, he knew that reuniting the nation would be no easy task.

# Chapter 18 REVIEW

## Vocabulary and Key Terms

Choose the italicized term in parentheses that best completes each sentence. Write your answers on a separate sheet of paper.

1. The (*income tax/strategy*) used by the North was (*an offensive/a defensive*) one.
2. When volunteers dwindled, both sides began to (*enlist/draft*) soldiers.
3. The *Merrimack* and the *Monitor* were (*blockade runners/ironclads*).
4. In the (*Gettysburg Address/Emancipation Proclamation*), Lincoln honored the war dead.
5. (*Greenbacks/Copperheads*) in the North objected when Lincoln denied people (*habeas corpus/bounties*).

## Recalling the Facts

1. What strengths did each side have in the Civil War?
2. What happened to the North at the Battle of Bull Run?
3. How did the Union win control of the Mississippi River?
4. Why was the naval blockade a key part of the North's strategy?
5. Why did Lincoln issue the Emancipation Proclamation?
6. What was the outcome of the Battle of Gettysburg?
7. How did Grant lead the North to a final victory?
8. What role did women play in the Civil War?
9. What economic effects did the war have for each side?
10. What political problems surfaced for the North during the war? For the South?
11. How did President Lincoln react to the Copperheads during the war?
12. What event ensured President Lincoln's reelection in 1864?

## Places to Locate

Match the letters on the map with the places listed below. Write your answers on a separate sheet of paper.

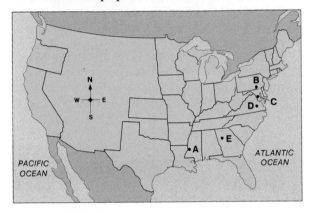

1. Washington, D.C.
2. Richmond, Virginia
3. Vicksburg, Mississippi
4. Gettysburg, Pennsylvania
5. Atlanta, Georgia

## Critical Thinking

1. The Civil war brought great bloodshed, hardship, and bitterness to the nation. In your opinion, were the results worth the costs? Do you think the North and the South would have gone to war if they had known how terrible it would be? Consider these points in your answer:
   a. a state's right to secede
   b. the loss of life and damage to property
   c. the ending of slavery
   d. the likely results of not fighting
2. How did leadership issues affect the course of the Civil War? Discuss these topics in your answer:
   a. the strength of Robert E. Lee
   b. the North's difficulty finding a capable military commander
   c. the public's views of Abraham Lincoln and Jefferson Davis

3. Both General Grant and President Lincoln treated the defeated Confederacy with generosity and respect. Why do you think they took this approach? Address these questions in your answer:
   a. How did people in the North and South feel about each other?
   b. Who suffered most in the war?
   c. What was the best way to reunite both sides after the war?

## Understanding History

1. Reread the section "The sections fight for different goals" on page 411. Then answer these questions.
   a. **Economics.** What economic differences divided the North and the South?
   b. **Culture.** In what sense was the Civil War a fight over cultural beliefs?
   c. **Citizenship.** How were southerners challenging the Constitution?
   d. **Geography.** According to Lincoln, what geographic fact made secession unthinkable?
2. Reread the section "Both sides make plans for winning the war" on page 414. Then answer these questions.
   a. **Economics.** Why did the South expect help from overseas?
   b. **Geography.** Why did the North want to gain control of the Mississippi River?
   c. **Economics.** How would a blockade put pressure on the South?
3. Reread "The Gettysburg Address" on page 422. Then answer these questions.
   a. **Primary Sources.** What is the "unfinished work" that Lincoln mentions in his speech?
   b. **Primary Sources.** What is the main idea of this speech?
4. Reread the time list on page 431. Then answer these questions.
   a. **Science and Technology.** Which invention made it possible for fewer people to raise more wheat?
   b. **Science and Technology.** How might the North have benefited from the other inventions listed?

## Projects and Activities

1. **Listing Biographical Information.** Make up a "Who's Who" list of all the people mentioned in this chapter. Identify key facts about each person.
2. **Giving an Oral Report.** Find out more about one of the following topics: the ironclad ships, black soldiers in the Civil War, Sherman's march through the South, medical care during the war. Present an oral report to the class.
3. **Staging a Debate.** Prepare an answer to this question: Should the North's main goal in the Civil War have been saving the Union or freeing the slaves? Debate your position with another student who has taken the opposite view.

## Practicing Your Skill

The special-purpose map below shows General Grant's movements along the Mississippi and Tennessee rivers in 1862 and 1863. Study the map, and then answer the following questions on a separate sheet of paper.

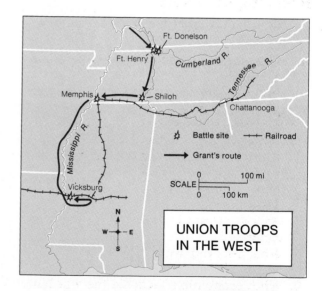

UNION TROOPS IN THE WEST

1. In what direction did Grant head when he left Fort Henry?
2. Which battle came first—the Batttle of Vicksburg or the Battle of Shiloh?
3. Where did Grant cross the Mississippi?
4. How many times did Grant cross southern railroad lines?

# CHAPTER
# 19 The Nation Heals Its Wounds
## 1865–1877

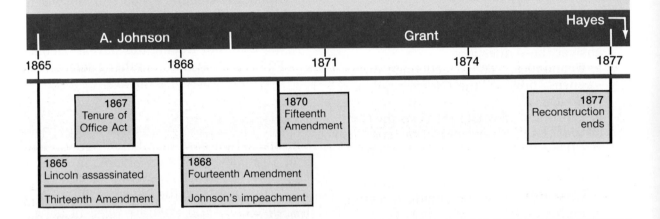

| A. Johnson | | Grant | | Hayes ↴ |
|---|---|---|---|---|
| 1865 | 1868 | 1871 | 1874 | 1877 |

**1867**
Tenure of
Office Act

**1870**
Fifteenth
Amendment

**1877**
Reconstruction
ends

**1865**
Lincoln assassinated

Thirteenth Amendment

**1868**
Fourteenth Amendment

Johnson's impeachment

After the Civil War the South began to rebuild. The workers in this Birmingham, Alabama, factory are casting iron into blocks.

## Preparing to Read

The years following the Civil War were troubled ones for the United States. The country's leaders disagreed over how to restore American unity and rebuild the South. Some favored forgiveness while others wanted to punish the ex-Confederates. Some worked to protect blacks while others fought against them. Bitter feelings lasted for more than a decade. Yet hand in hand with the problems came changes for the good. As you read this chapter, try to answer the following questions:

1. How did the nation approach its problems after the Civil War?
2. How did Reconstruction proceed under Congress's control?
3. What changes occurred as Reconstruction came to an end?

# 1 How did the nation approach its problems after the Civil War?

## Vocabulary

| | |
|---|---|
| amnesty | radical |
| assassinate | civil rights |
| | override |

After the disorder and destruction of the Civil War, Americans turned to the task of rebuilding. For four years northerners and southerners had been enemies. Now they tried to put aside their bitter feelings to solve the problems they jointly faced.

### Early Plans for Rebuilding

Soon after the surrender at Appomattox, Confederate General Robert E. Lee urged northerners and southerners to work together. "I believe it to be the duty of everyone," he wrote, "to unite in the restoration of the country and the re-establishment of peace and harmony." Recovery, however, would be a long, rough process.

**War leaves its mark on the South.** When Union soldiers returned north after the Civil War, they found their homes undamaged and their cities thriving. Southerners faced much grimmer conditions. Weeds grew in the fields. Houses and barns had been burned down. Bridges lay broken, and two thirds of the railroad lines were destroyed. Damage had been especially severe in southern cities. A newspaper reporter told what he saw in Charleston, South Carolina:

A city of ruins, of desolation, of vacant houses, of widowed women, of rotting wharves, of deserted warehouses, of weed-wild gardens, of miles of grass-grown streets, of acres of pitiful and voiceless barrenness—that is Charleston.

In addition, the southern economy had collapsed. Confederate money was worthless. Former slave owners had lost billions of dollars because of property damage. Without their slaves, they had no labor force to get the fields back into production. The heavy casualties of the war also thinned the number of white workers. The South had lost about 25 percent of its white male population between the ages of 18 and 40. Many other men had been permanently disabled.

**Problems must be solved.** All over the country, men and women wondered how to rebuild the South. Somehow southerners had to repair the war damage, revive the economy, and return to peacetime living. With huge debts and little money, this would not be easy.

Another important problem concerned the ties between the seceded states and the national government. Some northerners wanted to treat the South generously. Others insisted that the Confederate states should be punished as defeated enemies. Americans also argued about whether those who had fought against the Union should be allowed to vote and hold office. Many northerners still mistrusted southerners and could not imagine sharing the reins of government with them.

Freed blacks tend a cabbage patch on their farm in this 1879 painting by Thomas P. Anshutz. For former slaves, freedom meant working for themselves to make a new life.

Finally, the situation of freed slaves posed a serious problem. Thousands of black people in the South were without homes or work. They wandered from place to place, hoping to start a new life. Most were poor and unable to read or write. Decisions about their future had to be made.

**Lincoln plans for peace.** Even before the war ended, President Lincoln began planning a recovery program for the nation. On December 8, 1863, he explained his ideas for the period of **Reconstruction**—rebuilding—that would follow the war. First, Lincoln offered **amnesty** —official pardon— to southerners who swore loyalty to the Union. Second, he agreed to recognize state governments in the South under two conditions. The states had to accept emancipation of the slaves, and at least 10 percent of the voters had to take an oath of loyalty.

Lincoln did not live to put his plans into effect. On April 14, 1865, just five days after peace was declared, Lincoln and his wife decided to see a play at Ford's Theater in Washington, D.C.. They sat in box seats reserved for the President. Meanwhile, John Wilkes Booth, an actor from Virginia, paced outside. Booth was upset over the South's defeat. He had decided to **assassinate** —kill—Lincoln during the play.

**Lincoln is assassinated.** Midway through the last act, Booth crept into the theater. Quietly he opened the door to Lincoln's box, stepped inside, and shot Lincoln in the back of the head. Then he leaped to the stage, crying in Latin, "Thus be it ever to tyrants!" Before anyone fully realized what had happened, Booth limped out the back door of the theater and fled on his horse. A few days later, soldiers tracked him to Virginia where they shot and killed him.

Meanwhile, the wounded President had been carried to a house across the street from the theater. There, early on the morning of April 15, Lincoln died. Northerners were overcome by grief. Even people in the South mourned the loss of this great, kindhearted man. Jefferson Davis himself said, "Next to the defeat of the Confederacy, the heaviest blow that fell upon the South was the assassination of Lincoln."

## Conflict in the Capital

After Abraham Lincoln's death, the heavy duties of the presidency fell upon Andrew Johnson, the former Vice President. Johnson intended to carry out Lincoln's generous plans for restoring the seceded states to the Union. The Republican Congress, however, was not willing to leave Reconstruction in the hands of President Johnson—a Democrat and a southerner.

**Andrew Johnson follows Lincoln.** The new President, like the man he replaced in office, came from a simple background. Born in North Carolina, Johnson grew up in poverty in Tennessee. He never attended school, but after working as a tailor he started his own business. His wife taught him to read and write. Johnson's honesty and determination earned him the respect of the people in his home state. He entered politics and was elected to the Senate in 1857. When Tennessee seceded in 1861, Johnson refused to go along. He was the only southern senator to remain loyal to the Union during the Civil War.

Johnson lacked the popularity that Lincoln had achieved. He also lacked Lincoln's ability to compromise. An honest but stubborn man, Johnson soon made enemies in Congress.

**Johnson launches Reconstruction.** When Johnson took over the presidency, Congress was not in session. Johnson therefore began to carry out Lincoln's plan for Reconstruction. He granted amnesty to all but a few of those who had fought against the United States. He named temporary governors for the seceded states. He ordered the states to hold conventions to draw up new state constitutions. Johnson also asked each state to ratify the **Thirteenth Amendment,** which outlawed slavery in the United States. When these steps were taken, southern voters could elect state officials and new representatives to Congress.

Johnson's plan for Reconstruction, which basically followed Lincoln's, had the support of some Republicans in Congress. However, a number of members, known as **Radical Republicans,** were discontent. A

**radical** is someone who favors extreme changes. The Radical Republicans insisted that Congress, not the President, should decide how to deal with the South.

**Congress seeks to punish the South.** In the House of Representatives, Thaddeus Stevens of Pennsylvania and Henry Davis of Maryland led the Radical Republicans. Charles Sumner of Massachusetts and Benjamin Wade of Ohio were leaders in the Senate. Radical Republicans felt the President had offered overly generous terms to the South. They favored punishing anyone who had supported the Confederacy.

In 1864, while Lincoln was still in office, the Radicals had sponsored the Wade-Davis

Bill. Under this plan, Confederate government officials and those who had voluntarily fought against the Union would not be allowed to vote or hold office. Also, the bill said that a majority—not 10 percent—of the voters in each state had to pledge loyalty to the Union. Lincoln had stopped the Wade-Davis Bill from becoming law. This step, however, did not weaken the Radicals.

When Congress met in December 1865, most southern states had met Johnson's terms for rejoining the Union. Newly elected southern senators and members of the House of Representatives were waiting to take their seats. To the shock of northerners, these members included four former Confederate generals and Alexander H. Stephens, the former vice president of the Confederacy. Only a few months earlier these same people had led the fight against the Union.

Congress angrily refused to seat the southern delegations. Congress then set up the Joint Committee on Reconstruction. Six senators and nine representatives, including Thaddeus Stevens, served on the committee. Their task was to report on conditions in the South so that Congress could make its own Reconstruction policies.

**Southern blacks suffer discrimination.** The committee found little evidence that southerners felt truly loyal to the Union. The committee also said that blacks in the South were often denied their rights. The former slave states got around the Thirteenth Amendment by passing **black codes.** These were laws that sharply limited the rights of blacks. The codes made it hard for blacks to own property, earn a living, and get an education. The codes also kept blacks from voting. Although blacks had certain limited

**This engraving shows blacks voting in an 1867 election in New Orleans. Later, some southern legislatures prevented blacks from voting.**

The Freedmen's Bureau established schools to help freed slaves.
What help are the women in this Freedmen's Bureau school
providing?

rights, their lives were not much different from those of slaves. Blacks were required to work, but they had few opportunities apart from farming and household service jobs.

**President Johnson clashes with Congress.** Republicans in Congress were determined to aid the former slaves. Early in 1866 they passed a bill to keep funds going to the **Freedmen's Bureau.** This agency, started in March 1865, provided education, medical care, and other help to blacks and poor whites. In its first year, the Bureau gave out thousands of dollars worth of food and clothing. It ran hospitals and started schools and colleges for blacks. It also brought separated families back together and helped former slaves find jobs.

The bill to extend the Freedmen's Bureau had broad support in Congress. To the surprise of many, however, President Johnson vetoed the bill. Johnson felt that the Freedmen's Bureau was a wartime measure and should not continue in peacetime. He also said that the job of helping blacks belonged to the state and local governments, not the federal government.

**Johnson vetoes the Civil Rights Act.** President Johnson's veto of the Freedmen's

Bureau bill angered members of Congress. In April 1866 they passed the **Civil Rights Act,** which granted citizenship to blacks. It promised them the same civil rights — personal freedoms guaranteed by the Constitution—that whites enjoyed. The Civil Rights Act also said the federal government could step into state matters to protect the rights of blacks. Nearly all the Republicans in Congress supported the Civil Rights Act. Again, however, President Johnson vetoed the act, saying it was unconstitutional.

Johnson's vetoes outraged Congress, and the President lost many of his supporters. Johnson seemed completely unwilling to consider opposing views. He began to make speeches attacking the Radical Republicans. Johnson's stubbornness caused other members of Congress to side with the Radicals. As a result, the Radicals won enough votes to override —set aside—the President's vetoes. Congress restored both the Freedmen's Bureau bill and the Civil Rights Act.

The Radicals had now challenged the President and won an important victory. They proved that they had the support to undo Johnson's Reconstruction policies. Still, they feared that the Civil Rights Act might be repealed or judged unconstitutional. To guard against this possibility, the Radicals drew up a new proposal.

**The Radicals draft the Fourteenth Amendment.** The proposed **Fourteenth Amendment** had four main parts. First, it said that all persons born in the United States are citizens. Almost all former slaves thus became citizens. The amendment further said that no state could use unlawful means to take away a citizen's life, liberty, property, or civil rights.

The second part of the Fourteenth Amendment did away with the Three-Fifths Compromise. (See Chapter 9.) From now on, blacks would be fully counted in the population. Any state that kept blacks from voting would lose some of its seats in the House of Representatives. The Republicans hoped that a Republican party, supported by black voters, could be built in the largely Democratic South.

Another part of the Fourteenth Amendment kept former Confederate officials from holding federal or state office. They could serve only if they were approved by a two-thirds vote of Congress. Finally, the amendment said that the debts of the Confederate government were not to be paid. Southerners thus had no way of recovering their financial losses.

**Johnson presses the South to reject the Fourteenth Amendment.** Congress demanded that the southern states accept the Fourteenth Amendment as a condition for taking their seats in Congress. President Johnson, however, was very much against the amendment. He urged southerners not to ratify it. Ten southern states followed Johnson's advice. Tennessee gave the only vote of approval in the South, so the measure failed in 1866.

The defeat of the Fourteenth Amendment at this time only added to the Republicans' hard feelings toward the President. Many Radical Republicans saw Johnson as the major roadblock to Reconstruction. They eagerly waited for the congressional elections in November 1866. At that time, they hoped, they could add to their numbers and put their programs into effect.

## SECTION REVIEW

1. **Vocabulary**   amnesty, assassinate, radical, civil rights, override
2. **People and Places**   Ford's Theater, John Wilkes Booth, Andrew Johnson, Radical Republicans, Thaddeus Stevens, Charles Sumner, Tennessee
3. **Comprehension**   What steps were taken to help blacks and to protect their rights after the Civil War?
4. **Comprehension**   How did President Johnson's plans for Reconstruction differ from Congress's?
5. **Critical Thinking**   Which approach to dealing with the South—punishment or forgiveness—do you think was better for the nation? Why?

### Vocabulary

moderate

impeach

In the elections of 1866 many opponents of President Johnson won seats in Congress. Republicans now controlled two thirds of both houses. The majority took a tough stand toward the former Confederate states— much to the dismay of Johnson and people in the South.

## Congress in Charge

Not all the Republicans in Congress were Radical Republicans. Some were **moderates** —people who avoid extreme views and actions. The moderates wanted to keep the Republican party strong. To stay in power, they worked with the Radicals to begin a harsher Reconstruction program.

**The Republicans deal a heavy blow to the South.** In March 1867, Congress passed the **First Reconstruction Act** over the veto of President Johnson. Congress followed this act with three more over the next year. These laws made up the plan for Radical Reconstruction — the period from 1867 to 1877.

Under the Reconstruction acts, the governments of the 10 states that had refused to ratify the Fourteenth Amendment were declared illegal. Congress had total authority over these states. The government divided them into five military districts and placed them under army rule. Soldiers were sent to keep order while new state governments were formed.

The acts also spelled out the steps that southern states had to follow to rejoin the Union. Each state had to call a constitutional convention with members elected by blacks as well as whites. Former Confederate officials, however, could not vote. The convention would draw up a state constitution to be ratified by the voters and approved by Congress. The state legislature elected under the new state government had to accept the

After the Civil War, blacks were elected to Congress for the first time. Shown in this picture (from left to right) are Senator Hiram T. Revels and Representatives Benjamin Turner, Robert DeLarge, Josiah Walls, Jefferson Long, Joseph Rainy, and R. Brown Elliot.

443

"How say you, Senator Ross?" boomed the Chief Justice.

Senator Edmund G. Ross of Kansas looked at his fellow senators. They were waiting for his vote in the impeachment trial of Andrew Johnson. Thirty-five senators, all Republicans, had already found the Democratic President guilty of high crimes against the government. Ross, also a Republican, felt pressure to join them. He had received both bribes and threats to sway his vote. Yet Ross thought the case against Johnson was weak. After weighing all the evidence, he made his decision: "Not guilty."

By a single vote, Ross saved the President from being unfairly forced out of office. The senator's courage, however, cost him his political career. Branded as disloyal by members of his party, he never won election to public office again. Still, Ross had reason to be proud. He had been true to his conscience and prevented a serious injustice.

**President Johnson accepts the impeachment trial summons.**

Fourteenth Amendment. When all these steps had been taken, the state could rejoin the Union. Its senators and representatives could then take their seats in Congress.

**The Republicans restrict the President.** As much as Johnson disliked the new laws, he had a duty to enforce them. Republicans, however, worried that Johnson might find other ways to interfere in Reconstruction. In March 1867 Congress passed the **Tenure of Office Act** to curb the President's power.

The Tenure of Office Act said that the President could not remove members of the Cabinet without the Senate's approval. Johnson decided to test the constitutionality of the law. In February 1868 he fired Secretary of War Edwin Stanton, the only Radical in his Cabinet. This was the chance the Radicals had been awaiting. If they could remove the President from office for breaking the law, they would have more freedom to enact their policies.

## A Challenge to the President

The Constitution provides a way for the House of Representatives to **impeach** — accuse and try—elected officials. The Senate sits as a jury in impeachment trials. To convict and remove a President from office, two thirds of the Senate must agree that the President is guilty.

**The House impeaches Johnson.** Shortly after Stanton's firing, the House voted to impeach the President. Johnson was tried before the Senate, with the Chief Justice of the Supreme Court presiding. The Radicals felt certain that Johnson would be removed from office. After all, Republicans controlled the necessary two-thirds vote.

Most of the charges against the President had to do with his violation of the Tenure of Office Act. The House also charged Johnson with making speeches against Congress. The trial lasted two months. Crowds packed

444

the hearing room at first, but then thinned out. The Senate listened carefully to all the evidence. When the vote was taken, Johnson was fount not guilty. Seven Republicans had joined with 12 Democrats to vote against conviction. Johnson stayed in office by one vote!

**Grant becomes President.** By clearing Johnson, the Senate showed that Presidents have the right to disagree with Congress. If Johnson had been forced out, future Presidents might have had less independence. However, while Johnson escaped dismissal, he lost influence within his party. Near the end of his term in 1868, the Democrats chose Horatio Seymour to run for President.

Republicans nominated General Ulysses S. Grant, a Civil War hero to northerners. Grant also won the votes of most southern blacks. Grant won a sweeping victory in the Electoral College.

**Congress proposes the Fifteenth Amendment.** Republicans knew that Grant's election would not have been possible without the support of blacks. To protect the voting rights of blacks, Congress quickly proposed the **Fifteenth Amendment** in 1869, which forbids any state from denying citizens the right to vote on account of race.

Approval of the Fifteenth Amendment quickly became another condition that southern states had to meet to rejoin the Union. By this time, all but four of the southern states had been readmitted. Only Georgia, Mississippi, Texas, and Virginia remained under military rule. By 1870, however, these states ratified the Fifteenth Amendment. The Union was again whole.

## Changes in the South

The new status of blacks did not sit well with those whites in the South who had considered blacks to be inferior. They were shocked by the idea of blacks voting or holding office. As one explained:

> They've always been our owned servants, and we've been used to having them mind us without a word of objection, and we can't bear anything else from them now.

**Blacks take part in government.** After the Civil War, for the first time, blacks held positions in government. Some, like Robert Elliott of South Carolina, helped to frame the new state governments. Elliott also served in the South Carolina legislature. Others won election to Congress. Hiram R. Revels and Blanche K. Bruce from Mississippi served in the United States Senate. Robert Smalls of South Carolina won five terms in the House of Representatives.

Whites still dominated governments, however. No blacks served as governors. Only a few states elected black lieutenant governors. Only two—South Carolina and Mississippi—had more blacks than whites in the state legislatures.

**Other groups play a role in Reconstruction.** Many southerners resented the new state governments and disliked the people

## ★ ★ ★ *The Vote*

Today, every adult American has the right to vote in political elections. Yet this has not always been so. In most parts of the United States, for almost 100 years, only free white males who owned property could vote.

After the Civil War Congress took the first step toward guaranteeing voting rights for all. In 1870, the Fifteenth Amendment assured black men of the right to vote. Fifty years later the Nineteenth Amendment made it possible for women to vote. Three later amendments further extended voting rights. The Twenty-third Amendment gave the vote to people in Washington, D.C. The Twenty-fourth said that no one must pay a tax to vote. The Twenty-sixth Amendment lowered the minimum voting age from 21 to 18. Today the ballot gives all American adults a voice in government.

---

who supported these governments. They called white southerners who cooperated **scalawags.** Some scalawags were loyal to the Union during the war. Others were former Democrats with political aims. They switched parties because the Republicans now controlled Congress.

Southerners felt **carpetbaggers** were as bad as scalawags. Carpetbaggers were northern whites who moved south after the Civil War. They got their name because they carried their belongings in small suitcases made of a carpet-like cloth.

Carpetbaggers went south for different reasons. Some had been Union soldiers and had developed strong feelings for the South. Others were northern business leaders eager to take advantage of new opportunities. They had money to buy plantations and mines from southerners who could not afford to keep them. Still others came as teachers or to help the former slaves. Also, the federal government sent tax collectors, customs officers, and other government workers to the South. Although some were greedy and dishonest people, many had good intentions.

**Reconstruction governments improve life in the South.** Southern whites charged that Reconstruction governments were dishonest and inefficient. They often exaggerated, however. Most legislators, black or white, had little experience in government. They made mistakes, but they brought needed changes to the war-torn South.

The new state legislatures passed fairer voting laws and gave women more property rights. They set up public schools for whites and for blacks. They improved the court system and stopped putting debtors in prison.

The legislatures also voted large sums of money for buildings, schools, roads, and railroads. These changes were costly, and taxes had to be increased. The heaviest taxes fell on southern whites with property. Many had to sell their lands because they could not pay the taxes. This caused more resentment. One southerner summed up the feelings of many with these words:

I tell you, no free people in the history of the world were ever treated with such indignity.... Our people feel that you [northerners] are cruelly and senselessly trifling with us—yes, insulting us. They feel that, having conquered, you have not the [generosity] of brave conquerers, but are bent upon heaping humiliation on your unfortunate victims.

## SECTION REVIEW

1. **Vocabulary**    moderate, impeach
2. **People and Places**    Edwin Stanton, Ulysses S. Grant, Robert Elliott, Robert Smalls, Mississippi, scalawags, carpetbaggers
3. **Comprehension**    How did Congress try to limit President Johnson's power?
4. **Comprehension**    How did southerners react to Radical Reconstruction?
5. **Critical Thinking**    What might Congress have gained and what might Congress have lost by delaying passage of the Fourteenth Amendment?

## CRITICAL THINKING: Presenting an Argument

History books may frequently include such phrases as "The President argued for the measure by saying,..." or "The senator's argument against the policy was..." In these phrases, an **argument** consists of reasons given to support or oppose an opinion or action. The purpose of an argument is to attempt to persuade other people to accept the speaker's position.

A written argument is really a form of essay. Like other essays, it has an introduction, a body, and a conclusion. (See the Chapter 12 Gaining Skill.) The introduction of an argument is called a **premise.** It expresses the main idea behind your argument. You should always state your premise strongly and clearly in order to gain your readers' attention.

The body of the argument consists of the evidence that supports or backs up your premise. The important ideas may be repeated, but only if each repetition promotes or advances your argument. You may also, if you wish, include some viewpoints that oppose your opinion. If you do, then you should offer **rebuttals** to, or arguments against, those opposing viewpoints. Make sure that you do this in an open and fair way, avoiding sarcastic or insulting remarks.

Close your argument with a short conclusion that restates your premise and then briefly summarize the evidence you have to support it.

These guidelines will enable you not only to write arguments, but also to evaluate the arguments put forth by others. On this page is an argument by Thaddeus Stevens that supports the First Reconstruction Act. One part of this act gave the vote to blacks living in the former Confederate states. Read the argument carefully, and then answer the questions that follow.

> There are several good reasons for the passage of [the First Reconstruction Act].
>
> In the first place, it is just. I am now confining my argument to Negro suffrage in the rebel [Confederate] states. Have not loyal blacks as good a right to choose rulers and make laws as rebel whites?
>
> In the second place, it is [necessary] in order to protect the loyal white [Union] men in the seceded states. The white Union men are in a great minority in each of those states. With them the blacks would act in a body,... the two united would form a majority, control the states, and protect themselves. Now they are the victims of daily murder....
>
> Another good reason is that it would insure the [rising power] of the Union [Republican] Party. "Do you admit to a party purpose?" exclaims some horror-stricken [hothead]. I do. For I believe, on my conscience, that on the continued rise of that party depends the safety of this great nation....
>
> For these, among other reasons, I am for Negro suffrage in every rebel state. If it be just, it should not be denied; if it be necessary, it should be adopted; if it be punishment to traitors, they deserve it.

1. What is the premise of Thaddeus Stevens's argument?
2. What three reasons does Stevens offer for giving blacks in the former Confederate states the vote?
3. What opposing viewpoint does Stevens say might be raised?
4. What rebuttal does Stevens make to this opposing view?
5. Based on the above guidelines, do you think this is a strong argument? Explain your answer.

Southern whites found it hard to forgive the North for its Reconstruction policies. They worked steadily to regain political power in their region. Some also resisted Reconstruction with violence against blacks.

## Setbacks for Blacks

In the South, many whites still showed hostility to blacks. A South Carolina man wrote of his struggle to alter his attitudes:

> The new relation in which we now stand toward the Negroes, our former slaves, is a matter for grave and serious consideration, if we desire to act justly toward them. We are very apt to retain former feelings.... I must ask aid from above so I may perform all the duties and obligations of my position....

Yet not all whites were so willing to treat blacks fairly.

**White southerners turn to violence.** Unable to accept blacks as equals, some whites formed secret societies to work against them. The strongest, the **Ku Klux Klan,** began in Tennessee in 1866. Branches of the Klan were soon all over the South.

The Klan had two aims: to weaken the Republicans and to spread the idea of white superiority. Terror was the Klan's main tactic. At night, dressed in ghostly white robes and hoods, members rode to the homes of black political leaders, black farmers, and teachers at black schools. The Klan burned crosses and warned blacks not to vote or support Republican activities. They often beat their victims and sometimes **lynched** them— hanged them without a trial.

Blacks could usually identify their attackers, but few Klan members were tried in court. Sheriffs could not make arrests because other whites gave Klan members alibis or did not believe the charges. Governors could not keep order because white militias often sympathized with the Klan. The southern states finally asked the federal government for help. In 1870 and 1871 Congress passed laws against the Klan's activities. The violence slowly died down, but only after hundreds of people had suffered.

**Northerners withdraw their support.** Meanwhile, many people in the North tired

Organizations such as the White League tried to prevent blacks from exercising their civil rights. What right is shown being denied in this 1880's political cartoon?

of the South's racial troubles. They felt that the federal government had done enough for blacks by passing the Thirteenth, Fourteenth, and Fifteenth amendments.

Northerners were also dismayed by reports of **corruption** —dishonesty—in Reconstruction governments. They wondered if these Republican-controlled governments were worth protecting. Besides, they had troubles of their own. Corruption plagued government in the North, and people sought reform. They worried about inflation, tariffs, and other economic matters. As northerners wrestled with these issues, many lost interest in helping southern blacks.

## The Democrats' Comeback

Until Congress stepped in, societies like the Ku Klux Klan kept many blacks from voting. Republicans lost power without black voters, and were further weakened by the **Amnesty Act of 1872.** This law restored the right to vote and hold office to most former Confederates. Southern whites now had greater voting strength. They made plans to control the government.

**Democrats rule in the South.** Most white Southerners had become strong supporters of the Democratic party. A group of Democrats called the Conservatives led the party. In state elections during the 1870's, they vowed to overthrow the carpetbaggers, scalawags, and blacks.

Often this meant scare tactics. Whites threatened to fire black workers who voted for Republicans. Democrats came to the polls armed and drove away their opponents. The goal, said one Mississippi newspaper, was "A white man's Government, by white men, for the benefit of white men." Soon people began to speak of the "Solid South," meaning that the South usually voted solidly for Democrats.

**The election of 1876 is decided by compromise.** In 1876, Democrats had a chance to expand their power beyond the South. They chose Samuel Tilden, governor of New York, as their candidate. The Republicans nominated Ohio Governor Rutherford B. Hayes, a man known for honesty. Tilden

"Another such victory and I am undone," says the wounded Republican elephant. This cartoon was published after the election of 1876.

won more popular votes than Hayes. A dispute arose, however, over who received the majority of electoral votes.

Congress appointed a special commission to decide the results of the election. The commission had 15 members—seven Democrats and eight Republicans. By an eight-to-seven decision, the commission gave the election to Hayes. Southern Democrats were very angry over the outcome, but agreed to a compromise. They would support the decision in return for three promises from Hayes. First, Hayes pledged to withdraw federal troops from the South. Second, he agreed to name a southerner to his Cabinet. Third, he promised to spend federal money to make improvements in the South.

**Reconstruction comes to an end.** President Hayes kept his word. He supported the building of railroads and schools in the South. He named a Tennessee Democrat to be Postmaster General. Most importantly, Hayes ordered all federal troops home. The withdrawal of the last soldiers

449

### RUTHERFORD B. HAYES

★ 1877–1881 ★

**19**TH PRESIDENT

**REPUBLICAN**

★ Born October 4, 1822, in Ohio

★ Married Lucy Ware Webb in 1852; 8 children

★ Lawyer; representative from Ohio; governor of Ohio

★ Lived in Ohio when elected President

★ Vice President: William Wheeler

★ Died January 17, 1893, in Ohio

★ Key events while in office: Reconstruction ended; Edison invented electric light bulb

from the South, in April 1877, marked the end of Reconstruction.

A troubled decade in American history was over. On the positive side, the nation had been reunited and rebuilding the South had begun. On the negative side, blacks still faced problems despite the legal gains they had made. Radical Reconstruction did nothing to end **segregation** —separation—of the races. In the North and the South, blacks were kept apart from whites in schools, restaurants, and other public places. Senator Charles Sumner introduced bills in Congress to outlaw segregation, but failed. It would be nearly a century before the nation honored the full rights of blacks.

**Blacks head west to seek a better life.** Discrimination caused many southern blacks to leave their homes. The first large migration of blacks took place in the late 1870's. Many blacks moved from one part of the South to another, seeking rich farmlands. Others moved to northern cities, hoping to work in factories and businesses. They had trouble finding jobs, however, and often ended up no better off than they had been in the South. Most blacks who migrated during the late 1870's went west. The West offered new opportunities and a better life.

### The New South

Reconstruction left behind problems and bitter feelings. Yet important economic growth occurred during this period, too. Cities were rebuilt, railroads were repaired, and business and trade expanded. The South that developed after the war was very different from the old "land of cotton." It was, in the words of the Atlanta *Constitution* editor, Henry Woodfin Grady, a **"New South."**

**Large plantations begin to disappear.** One economic change was the breakdown of the old plantation system. After the Civil War, planters had neither the money nor the slave labor to work their lands as before. Nor did most freed slaves want to stay on large plantations and work for wages. Instead they hoped to own, or at least rent, farms of their own. "Forty acres and a mule" became the dream of many southern blacks.

High taxes and the lack of workers soon forced many plantation owners to sell part of their property. Most land was sold in lots of a few acres. As a result, the number of large plantations in the South decreased, while the number of small farms increased.

**A new farming system develops.** Some plantation owners rented their land instead of selling it. Their tenants were usually poor whites or blacks called **sharecroppers** — renters who paid the landowners with a share of the crops they raised. In exchange they received plots of land, seeds, tools, and cabins. This system provided a way for landowners to keep their land, and it gave landless families a place to farm.

Many sharecroppers, however, barely made a living. They often had to give the landowner 50 percent or more of their crops. Because the sharecroppers had no money, they bought food and other supplies on credit. When harvests were bad or farm prices were low, their crops did not bring enough money to pay their bills. Most sharecroppers found themselves deeply in debt to the landowners or to merchants who had sold them goods on credit.

Some states passed laws to keep sharecroppers from leaving the state until their debts were paid. It became almost impossible for sharecroppers to escape the system.

**Southern farmers raise new crops.** Changes also took place in the crops grown in the South after the war. Cotton remained the chief crop. Large quantities of tobacco, rice, and sugar cane also continued to be raised. As transportation improved, however, farmers began to branch out. They found they could make good profits from fruits and vegetables that were suited to the southern soil and climate. Thanks to the railroads, they could ship their produce north

and west before it spoiled. Oranges and grapefruits began to flow out of Florida. Strawberries came from South Carolina and peaches from Georgia. Melons and corn also grew well in the South.

**Industry gets a start in the South.** While most southerners made their living from the land, many believed that dependence on farming had been the Confederacy's downfall. After the Civil War, southerners grew more interested in business and industry. Their region was rich in natural resources that had never been developed because growing cotton seemed more profitable. For example, there were great stretches of forest that could provide lumber. Beneath southern soil lay large deposits of coal, iron, and oil—all needed in industry. Plentiful cotton and a large supply of workers encouraged the building of mills to manufacture cloth.

This 1872 firefighters' parade shows the pride that New Orleans residents had in their city during the Reconstruction era. New Orleans was not heavily damaged by the Civil War.

A network of railroad lines crisscrossed the nation. In addition to improving transportation, the spurt in railroad building created a demand for iron and steel. Birmingham, Alabama, with resources of coal and iron ore, soon became a thriving industrial center.

Factory towns grew up in many regions, drawing many workers into the manufacture of cotton cloth, tobacco, and cottonseed products. Ports such as Galveston, Texas; Mobile, Alabama; and Norfolk, Virginia became centers of trade and commerce.

**The United States enters a new era.** The South was not the only region that changed after the Civil War. The growth of industry was reshaping the whole country. Farmers were using new methods and new machines to increase their production. Cities were growing by leaps and bounds. More people spilled west, and newcomers flooded in from Europe. As new concerns gained public attention, the bitterness caused by the Civil War and Reconstruction slowly faded from people's memories.

## SECTION REVIEW

1. **Vocabulary**   lynch, corruption, segregation, sharecropper
2. **People and Places**   Ku Klux Klan, Samuel Tilden, Rutherford B. Hayes, Florida, South Carolina, Georgia, Birmingham
3. **Comprehension**   How did whites regain control of southern state governments?
4. **Comprehension**   What changes marked the New South?
5. **Critical Thinking**   Did the breakup of plantations have positive or negative results for blacks? Explain.

# Chapter 19 Summary

The period of Reconstruction was a troubled time in American history. The South had to be rebuilt, the seceded states had to be restored to the Union, and new southern state governments had to be formed. In addition, the future of freed slaves was threatened by southern whites who wanted to deny blacks their rights.

After Abraham Lincoln's assassination in 1865, Andrew Johnson became President. Radical Republicans in Congress opposed his Reconstruction plan and took harsher action against the South. Johnson responded by vetoing laws designed to aid blacks and by breaking the Tenure of Office Act. As a result, Congress impeached him. Johnson stayed in office, but Republican Ulysses S. Grant won the presidency in 1868.

All the southern states rejoined the Union by 1870. Outwardly they accepted the Thirteenth, Fourteenth, and Fifteenth amendments, which protected blacks' rights. Yet many white southerners resented the new role of blacks in government. They also disliked the carpetbaggers and scalawags who supported Reconstruction governments. White groups like the Ku Klux Klan kept blacks and white Republicans from voting. The Democratic party regained control in the South, but Republicans held onto the presidency. Their candidate in 1876, Rutherford B. Hayes, took office after working out a compromise with southerners. Hayes withdrew federal troops from the South in 1877, ending Reconstruction.

The changes after the Civil War led to the development of the New South. Large plantations were broken into smaller farms. Poor blacks and whites became sharecroppers. Southerners began to raise new crops and to develop industries based on their natural resources. As the South continued its recovery, however, segregation became firmly planted in society.

# CAUSES and EFFECTS

## The Civil War ★ ★ ★

New states
form in West

Population of
North increases

North and South
develop different
ways of life

Abolition
gains support

North and South
want more seats
in Congress

**CONTRIBUTING
CAUSES**

Confederacy
is formed

Conflicts erupt
over slavery
in new states

North protests
Fugitive Slave Law

Lincoln's election
alarms South

South attacks
Fort Sumter

**MAIN
CAUSES**

## CIVIL WAR

**EFFECTS**

Slavery is
abolished

South is badly
damaged by war

Republicans
impose harsh
Reconstruction
plans on South

Lincoln is
assassinated

Nation is
reunited

South becomes
solidly Democratic

**LONG-TERM
EFFECTS**

South is rebuilt
with new crops
and industry

Northern
industry booms

Blacks become
citizens and vote

Segregation
takes hold

# Chapter 19 REVIEW

## Vocabulary and Key Terms

Choose one term from the following list to replace each blank in the paragraph below. Write your answers on a separate sheet of paper.

**amnesty**
**black codes**
**carpetbaggers**
**Freedmen's Bureau**
**Ku Klux Klan**
**Radical Republicans**
**Reconstruction**
**Thirteenth Amendment**

During the period known as __1__, Americans disagreed about how to treat the South. President Johnson supported __2__ for ex-Confederates. The __3__ in Congress favored punishment. They also wanted to help blacks. To do this they funded the __4__ and passed the __5__, outlawing slavery. White southerners tried to defy Congress by passing __6__ and forming secret groups like the __7__. Eventually Democrats regained power in the South, pushing blacks and northern __8__ out of office.

## Recalling the Facts

1. What were the main problems to be solved during Reconstruction?
2. What purpose did the Freedmen's Bureau serve?
3. How did Abraham Lincoln die?
4. What caused conflict between President Johnson and the Radical Republicans?
5. How did southern whites react to Radical Reconstruction?
6. How did the Democratic party win power in the South?
7. What happened in the presidential race of 1876?
8. How did the southern economy change during Reconstruction?

## Places to Locate

Match the letters on the map with the places listed below. Write your answers on a separate sheet of paper.

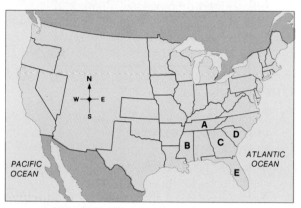

1. Tennessee
2. South Carolina
3. Mississippi
4. Florida
5. Georgia

## Critical Thinking

1. Some historians believe that if Lincoln had not been assassinated, Reconstruction would have proceeded more smoothly. Do you agree? Why or why not? Compare the following points in your answer:
   a. Lincoln's and Johnson's plans for Reconstruction
   b. differences between Lincoln and Johnson in personality, party, and influence
   c. the strength of southerners' and northerners' feelings toward each other and toward blacks
2. One of the goals of the Reconstruction period was to improve conditions for southern blacks. How would you rate Reconstruction policies in this regard? What kept blacks from gaining greater rights? Address these questions in your answer:

a. What did northern political leaders do to help blacks, and what were their motives?

b. How did southerners react to the idea of blacks' rights?

c. How and why did northern attitudes toward civil rights change over time? Were political parties a factor?

3. Many southerners felt Congress's policies during Radical Reconstruction were too harsh. Many historians argue that rarely have conquerors treated their enemies so mildly. Would you judge Congress's policies as fair? Explain.

## Understanding History

1. Reread the section "War leaves its mark on the South" on page 437. Then answer these questions.

a. **Geography.** How did the war affect the South's population?

b. **Economics.** How did the emancipation of the slaves affect the southern economy?

2. Reread the section "Northerners withdraw their support" on page 448. Then answer these questions.

a. **Citizenship.** What did blacks gain from the Thirteenth, Fourteenth, and Fifteenth amendments?

b. **Economics.** What economic matters turned northerners' attention away from the South?

3. Reread the section "Industry gets a start in the South" on page 451. Then answer these questions.

a. **Geography.** How did southerners take fuller advantage of their geographic resources after the Civil War?

b. **Science and Technology.** What did the spread of railroads mean for the South?

## Projects and Activities

1. **Making a Chart.** Create a chart showing legislation passed during Reconstruction. Fill in information under these headings: "Law," "Year Passed," and "Effects."

2. **Analyzing a Problem.** Imagine that you and your classmates live in the South during Reconstruction. Discuss the activities of the Ku Klux Klan and what should be done about them.

3. **Writing a Letter.** Imagine you are a carpetbagger new to the South. Write to your family back home, telling where you are, why you are there, what the South is like, and how southerners react to you. Give as much detail as possible.

4. **Giving a Speech.** Imagine that you are Robert Elliot or another southern black legislator during Reconstruction. Write a speech to give on your first day in office, telling how you feel about your position and what you hope to accomplish. Present your speech to the class.

## Practicing Your Skill

Francis Cardoza, a black member of South Carolina's constitutional convention, made the statement below in 1868. Read the statement, and answer the questions that follow.

What is the main cause of the prosperity of the North? It is because every man has his own farm and is free and independent. Let the lands of the South be similarly divided.... We will never have true freedom until we abolish the system of [farming] which existed in the Southern States.... If [the lands] are sold, ... the chances are that the colored man and the poor [white] man would be the purchasers. I will prove this ... by facts. About one hundred poor colored men of Charleston met together and formed themselves into a Charleston Land Company.... They have been meeting for a year. Yesterday they purchased some 600 acres of land.... This is only one instance of thousands of others that have occurred in this city and State.

1. What is Cardoza proposing?

2. What sentence expresses the premise, or main idea, behind his argument?

3. How does Cardoza support his argument that small farms will bring prosperity?

4. How does he support his argument that blacks would buy small farms?

# UNIT 6 REVIEW

## Unit Summary

★ **The United States expanded westward to the Pacific Ocean.**

- The Oregon Territory was gained by an agreement with Britain.
- Texas joined the Union in 1845, 10 years after its independence.
- America's war with Mexico added vast lands to the nation.
- In 1850 California became a state after gold attracted settlers.

★ **Conflicts between the North and the South split the nation.**

- Differences on states' rights and slavery were settled by compromise.
- Increased sectional hostility could not be solved by agreement.
- The South seceded from the Union after Lincoln's election in 1860.
- The Civil War began on April 12, 1861, at Fort Sumter.

★ **The North and the South fought a bitter war between 1861 and 1865.**

- Despite early losses, Union forces defeated the Confederacy.
- The South surrendered at Appomattox on April 9, 1865.
- President Lincoln was assassinated before he could implement his Reconstruction policy.

★ **The nation experienced many changes after the Civil War.**

- President Andrew Johnson was impeached, but remained in office.
- The plantation system ended, and industry developed in the South.
- American industry experienced uneven growth and labor problems.

## Understanding Chronology

Study the Unit 6 time line on page 367. Then complete the following activity on a separate sheet of paper.

Choose one of the chapters from Unit 6. Make a time line showing the major events and their dates that are discussed in the chapter. Use the dates shown in the *Chapters in this Unit* list on page 367 and the events on the Unit 6 time line as a guide.

## Writing About History

1. **Describing an Event.** Imagine that you were a witness to the South's surrender at Appomattox Court House on April 9, 1865. Describe the surrender by writing three paragraphs—one from the viewpoint of a Confederate soldier, one from a Union soldier, and one from a newspaper reporter.
2. **Summarizing Views.** Write two paragraphs summarizing the northern and the southern views on the issue of states' rights. Then choose one point of view and write a speech defending it.
3. **Writing a Report.** Write a report tracing the abolitionist movement. In your report, explain how the following topics expressed the growth of antislavery sentiment: legislation dealing with slavery, *Uncle Tom's Cabin*, the Underground Railroad, the *Dred Scott* case, violence in Kansas and at Harpers Ferry, and important abolitionists.
4. **Developing a Story.** Write a story about a family who traveled west in a prairie schooner to settle in the Oregon Territory. Include information about how a prairie schooner was built and what it was like to travel for weeks in a covered wagon. Describe the hardships faced by the family and the excitement of finally reaching their new home.

**5. Interpreting a Cartoon.** Study the cartoon above. Write an explanation of what the cartoonist was saying about Mayor Tweed and the methods the cartoonist used to express his opinions. Describe how such cartoons affected popular opinion in the 1870's.

## Projects

1. **Advertising a Region.** Draw a poster to advertise either the Oregon or the Texas Territory in the 1800's to attract settlers to the region. Base the advertisement on the geographic and economic advantages of the region.
2. **Making Maps.** Prepare one or more maps to show the expansion of the United States between 1840 and 1853. Include territories that were added and states that joined the Union during that time.
3. **Making Charts.** Prepare a series of charts comparing the North and the South during the Civil War. Include charts that compare the strengths and weaknesses of both sections at the beginning of the war, the military advantages of each, the battles each section won and lost, and the territory gained or surrendered by each side.
4. **Presenting Biographical Sketches.** Work with a partner to compare the lives of famous people in the Civil War. You might write a biography of Abraham Lincoln and compare his life with Jefferson Davis's, or compare Robert E. Lee with Ulysses Grant. You might include a dialogue between the individuals showing their backgrounds and viewpoints.

## Finding Out More

Beatty, Patricia. *Turn Homeward Hannalee.* Morrow, 1984. This is a story of mill workers during the Civil War.

Haugaard, Erik Christian. *Orphans of the Wind.* Houghton Mifflin, 1966. This is the story of 12-year-old Jim, who is signed on as a deckboy for a Civil War blockade runner.

Hunt, Irene. *Across Five Aprils.* Tempo Books, 1965. The youngest son of an Illinois farm family remains at home when his brothers leave to fight in the Civil War. The story traces the effects of the war on the lives of each family member.

Santrey, Laurence. *Young Frederick Douglass: Fight for Freedom.* Troll, 1983. This is an easy-to-read story of the slave who became an abolitionist leader.

Stein, R. Conrad. *The Story of the Monitor and the Merrimac.* Childrens Press, 1983. This easy-to-read account describes the fateful encounter of two Civil War ships.

Sterling, Dorothy, ed. *The Trouble They Seen: Black People Tell the Story of Reconstruction.* Doubleday, 1976. Freed slaves tell their views of life after the Civil War.

Wisler, G. Clifton. *Thunder on the Tennessee.* Dutton, 1983. The horror of war is experienced by a young boy who joins the Confederate Army.

# UNIT 7
# MODERN AMERICA TAKES SHAPE
## 1865–1898

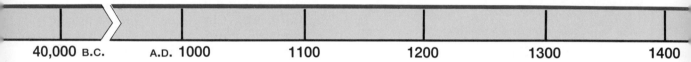

40,000 B.C.    A.D. 1000    1100    1200    1300    1400

Advances in transportation and communication led to the rapid growth of cities after the Civil War, as this painting of Indianapolis shows.

1865–1898

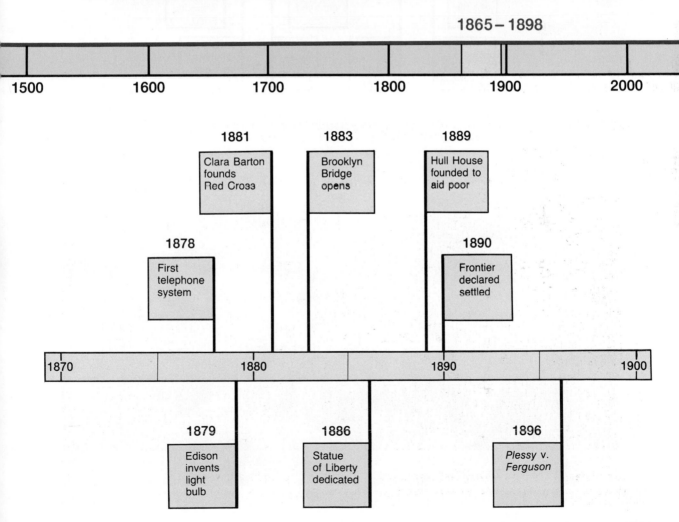

# CHAPTER
# 20 Pioneers Settle the West
## 1865–1898

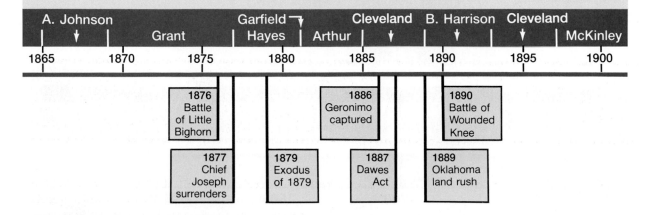

A. Johnson    Garfield    Cleveland    B. Harrison    Cleveland

Grant    Hayes    Arthur    McKinley

1865   1870   1875   1880   1885   1890   1895   1900

**1876** Battle of Little Bighorn

**1877** Chief Joseph surrenders

**1879** Exodus of 1879

**1886** Geronimo captured

**1887** Dawes Act

**1890** Battle of Wounded Knee

**1889** Oklahoma land rush

**A train heading west across the Great Plains symbolizes the movement of settlers into the western Indians' homelands.**

## Preparing to Read

Pioneers first settled those parts of the United States that had both trees and water transportation. By 1860 few people had settled the Great Plains, the Rocky Mountains, or the deserts of the West—a region that was home to several hundred thousand Indians. During the 1870's and 1880's, however, the western United States was settled by waves of miners, ranchers, and farmers. In time, the western Indians were forced to surrender their lands and their traditional way of life. As you read this chapter, try to answer the following questions:

1. What led people to settle the West?
2. What happened to the Indians who tried to keep their lands?
3. How did miners, ranchers, and farmers settle the last frontier?

# 1 What led people to settle the West?

### Vocabulary

public lands
semiarid
transcontinental

In the decades before the Civil War several hundred thousand people had settled along the Pacific Coast. Few people, however, had settled in the deserts, mountains, and plains of the West. The pioneers traveling to Oregon and California had crossed this expanse quickly because they saw no way to make a living there. The land was left to the Indians, most of whom hunted the buffaloes that grazed on the plains. After the Civil War the western United States was rapidly settled. A new law and new technology brought about this change.

## The Homestead Act

Large numbers of the American people had increasingly called for free or cheap land. Poor farm families were unable to afford land available in the eastern states. City workers hoped that free land in the West would reduce the number of surplus workers. Before the Civil War, abolitionists thought that many small farms would prevent the spread of large plantations. Finally, in 1862 Congress passed the **Homestead Act.**

**The Homestead Act aids western settlement.** The Homestead Act provided a program for giving **public lands**—lands owned by the national government—to American citizens. The Homestead Act made public lands easy to get. Any person who was the head of a family or was at least 21 years old could become the owner of a farm, or homestead, of 160 acres (65 hectares). The only requirement was that the settler live on the land and work it for five years. Married couples were entitled to two shares, or 320 acres (130 hectares). People who settled the West after the Homestead Act was passed were called homesteaders.

At the end of the Civil War the Homestead Act played an important part in the lives of many soldiers who left the army. Many of the discharged soldiers wished to strike out on some bold new venture rather than return home. The land grants under the Homestead Act gave them a chance to start a new life on the frontier.

Later, at the end of Reconstruction, black Americans also took part in the westward migration. When federal troops were withdrawn from the South, many former slaves feared that their newly won civil rights would no longer be protected. As a result, thousands of blacks joined the "Exodus of 1879," migrating west in search of a better life.

## New Technology

Millions of people eventually homesteaded in the West. The Homestead Act gave them the legal right to do so. Technology gave them the means to do so.

**New methods of steel production encourage railroad building.** After the establishment of Samuel Slater's mill in 1790, manufacturing in the Northeast became much more important. New inventions and new ways of manufacturing caused American industry to grow at tremendous rates. The growth of iron and steel manufacturing was essential to the development of American industry. The major inventions of the nineteenth century depended on good-quality iron and steel. The telegraph, for example, first used iron wires. The steam engines that powered boats, locomotives, and factories depended on parts that were made of iron and steel.

For centuries, steel was known to have qualities of strength and toughness not found in iron. Steel, however, was too expensive to be widely used. Impurities had to be removed from iron to make steel, and no cheap way of removing these impurities was known. Then, in the 1850's, the British inventor Henry Bessemer and the American scientist William Kelly each discovered a startling fact. Working on the same problem

**Blacks who migrated to Kansas, Nebraska, Colorado, and Wyoming after Reconstruction called themselves Exodusters. An exodus is the departure of a large number of people. The black pioneers in the Exodus of 1879 contributed to the development of the West.**

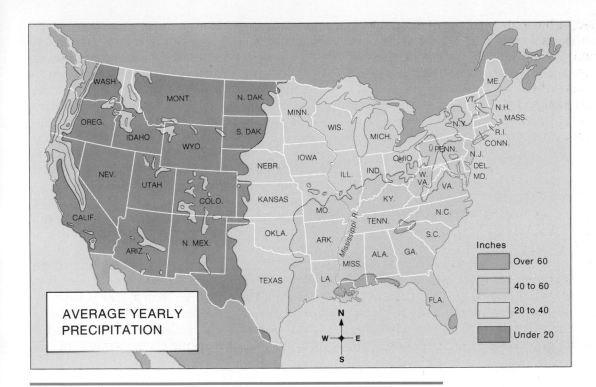

AVERAGE YEARLY PRECIPITATION

Inches

Over 60

40 to 60

20 to 40

Under 20

## Map Study

**Great Plains farmers needed at least 20 inches (50.8 centimeters) of precipitation—rainfall and snowfall—to grow grain. In areas with less precipitation, crops required irrigation. What was the average yearly precipitation in Iowa? Name three western states in which farmers would most likely irrigate their fields.**

separately, they found that a blast of air directed at melted iron would remove its impurities. This new process of making steel, now called the Bessemer process, was so cheap and easy that steel could be produced in large quantities and at low cost.

Before the Bessemer process of producing steel, railroad tracks were made of iron and had a life of about three years. With the Bessemer process, it became economical to produce miles of steel tracks that lasted for many years. The Bessemer process thus contributed to a great surge of railroad building. After the Civil War railroads led the way west.

**New inventions aid western settlement.** The iron and steel industries gave rise to other inventions that would help settle the West. These inventions helped settlers adapt

to an environment that was quite different from what they had known in the East or in Europe. The **semiarid** —somewhat dry— Great Plains lie west of the ninety-eighth meridian, the line of longitude that runs through the center of the United States. On the Great Plains rainfall averages between 10 and 20 inches (25.4 and 50.8 centimeters) a year. For many years, the main vegetation on the Great Plains was buffalo grass, which was short and tough but highly nutritious. Early pioneers did not settle the area. Their plows could not cut the tough sod, water was scarce, and there was not enough timber for fences.

In the 1860's and 1870's, however, a series of inventions made farming possible in the Great Plains. James Oliver of Indiana invented a steel plow that could slice through

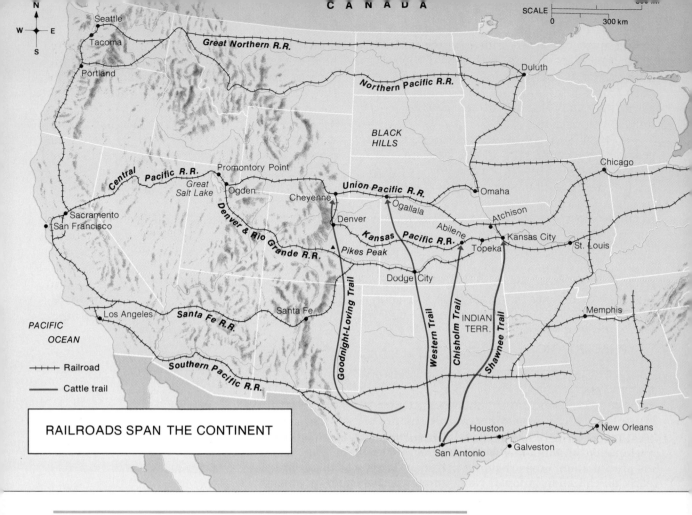

CANADA

SCALE
0    300 km

RAILROADS SPAN THE CONTINENT

## Map Study

**Ranchers drove cattle to cow towns for shipment to meat-packing plants in the East. Many cow towns became prosperous cities. What city thrived at the junction of the Kansas Pacific Railroad and the Chisholm Trail?**

and easily turn the prairie sod. Joseph Glidden invented barbed wire, which could be used to fence cattle in pastures or out of crops. The invention of the water-pumping windmill made it possible to bring water to the surface.

## The Transcontinental Railroad

The construction of the first American **transcontinental**—cross-country—railroad did more than anything else to encourage settlement of the West. For years Americans

had dreamed of linking the East and West by railroad. In 1862, the same year as the Homestead Act, Congress passed a law authorizing a transcontinental railroad.

**Two companies race to build a transcontinental railroad.** The Union Pacific and the Central Pacific railroad companies were organized to build a railroad from Omaha, Nebraska, to Sacramento, California. The Union Pacific was to push westward from Omaha, while the Central Pacific would build eastward from Sacramento. Somewhere in the vast region between, the two would meet. For every mile of track laid, the government gave the railroad companies both loans of money and large pieces of land. Thus, the company that laid the longest stretch of track would receive the most land and money.

A race started between the two railroads. Thousands of workers were hired to lay track across broad prairies and through narrow mountain passes. At the height of the race nearly 20,000 laborers toiled through scorching heat and blinding snowstorms. Mile by mile the two roads crept closer together. Finally, on May 10, 1869, two locomotives—*Number 119* of the Union Pacific and *Jupiter* of the Central Pacific— met at Promontory Point near Ogden, Utah. The race had been won by the Union Pacific,

which had the easier task of crossing mostly level terrain. When Governor Leland Stanford of California drove a golden spike into the final railroad tie, telegraph wires flashed the news all over the country. In cities such as Chicago, New York, and Boston, people celebrated with parades, gun salutes, and prayer services. The dream of spanning the continent by rail had come true.

**Railroads bring settlers to the West.** By 1884 three more railroads—the Southern Pacific, the Northern Pacific, and the Santa Fe—had lines stretching to the Pacific Coast. The transcontinental railroads actively encouraged settlement of the West. The railroads advertised heavily in eastern and European newspapers. They paid newswriters to travel through the West and

## Map Study

Standard time zones were first proposed in the 1860's to make railroad schedules easier to follow. Schedules were confusing because local time often differed from city to city. Americans finally accepted standard time zones in 1883. When it is 3:00 P.M. on the West Coast, what is the time on the East Coast?

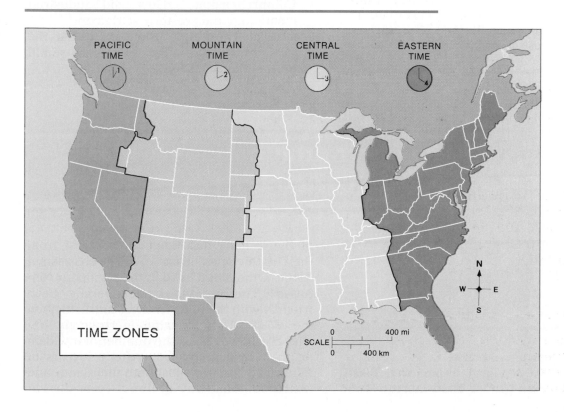

TIME ZONES

In this 1867 photograph, Chinese workers haul dirt to enclose a Central Pacific railroad trestle at Sierra Point, California. In 1869 the Central Pacific joined the Union Pacific to form the nation's first cross-country railroad.

describe what they saw. As a result, thousands of eastern farmers as well as immigrants from Germany, Sweden, Norway, Denmark, Holland, and Russia went west on the railroad.

The railroads had several reasons for such advertising. The government had awarded them thousands of square miles of land, which they now wanted to sell to settlers. More settlers also meant more business. Farmers would use the railroad to ship their products to eastern markets. In turn, manufacturers would ship goods west to meet the needs of the new settlers.

## SECTION REVIEW

1. **Vocabulary** public lands, semiarid, transcontinental
2. **People and Places** Henry Bessemer, Great Plains, James Oliver, Joseph Glidden, Promontory Point
3. **Comprehension** How did the Homestead Act encourage western settlement?
4. **Comprehension** How did industrial technology aid western settlement?
5. **Critical Thinking** Pioneers called the train whistle the most welcoming sound on the plains. Why?

# 2 What happened to the Indians who tried to keep their lands?

## Vocabulary

reservation
administer
assimilate

The American pioneers faced a major obstacle as they migrated into the West. Dozens of Indian groups lived there. Some of the Indians had been forced west from their homelands east of the Mississippi River. Others had lived in the region for centuries. The Indians had generally been friendly with the first travelers and settlers to the West. They became increasingly unfriendly, however, as the number of invaders on their land increased. After 25 years of fighting, the Indians lost both their lands and their traditional way of life.

# The Indian Wars

As more settlers moved west, the Indians became desperate. In many cases, settlers took lands that had been granted to the Indians by treaty. Even worse, the Indians faced the loss of their homes and their means of making a living. Fast-growing white settlements cut down the areas in which the Indians could roam freely.

Just as important to the Indian way of life, the buffalo were being killed off at a tremendous rate. Hunters armed with powerful rifles could easily kill this slow-moving, shaggy beast. William F. Cody, better known as "Buffalo Bill," killed more than 4,000 animals in less than two years. Cody hunted buffalo to provide food for the workers building railroads across the West.

Other hunters slaughtered the animals merely for sport, leaving them where they fell. The buffalo, which numbered about 16 million in the early 1860's, began to disappear from the plains. That meant starvation for the Indians. They took up arms in a desperate attempt to save their lands and their way of life. At first, bands of warriors struck at wagon trains and stagecoaches. Then, growing bolder, they attacked trains, farms, trading posts, and settlements.

**Government troops break the resistance of the Indians.** Because each side believed so strongly in its cause, the Indian wars went on for many years. Some of the fiercest fighting took place between United States troops and Sioux tribes. In 1862 an Indian war broke out in Minnesota. Led by a chief named Little Crow, a group of Sioux killed

George Catlin's painting suggests the importance of buffalo hunting to the Plains Indian way of life. As railroads and settlers moved into the Great Plains, buffalo herds almost disappeared.

# ★ ★ ★ *Little Big Horn*

On June 26, 1876, General George A. Custer and his 210 men attacked an Indian encampment of 7,000 people near the Little Big Horn River. Two days later, back-up troops found Custer and all his men dead. There were different accounts about what happened at Little Big Horn. Some were stories and paintings by Indians who fought in the battle.

In 1985 an archeological team studied bones and artifacts that had been uncovered by a fire at the Little Big Horn National Monument. The team fed information about bullets, guns, and fallen bodies into a computer. The archeologists have concluded that Indian accounts of the battle are generally accurate. The Indians won the battle because of their superior numbers and firearms.

more than 700 settlers before they were defeated and forced onto new lands in the Dakota Territory.

The discovery of gold in the Black Hills, however, brought miners into the Dakota Territory during the mid-1870's. When the Plains Indians began to gather under the Sioux leaders, Crazy Horse and Sitting Bull, federal troops were sent to round them up. Among the officers leading these troops was General George A. Custer. In June 1876, on the banks of the Little Bighorn River, Custer and more than 200 of his men were killed in an unsuccessful attack on the Indian camp. Despite their victory, the Indians were short of ammunition and food, and in October they surrendered.

Other groups also waged a heroic and bitter fight. In 1877 Chief Joseph led the Nez Perce in a brilliant campaign against the better-equipped government forces. Forced to leave their beautiful ancestral valley in northeastern Oregon, the Nez Perce decided to fight rather than go quietly to a government **reservation** —a tract of land set aside for Indians. The band of men, women, and children headed into the mountains of Idaho and Wyoming. Along their route they successfully defeated the army troops that relentlessly pursued them.

Chief Joseph finally realized the Nez Perce would find peace only if they could reach Canada. He led the Indians north across Montana, but just 30 miles (48 kilometers) from the border, he was forced to surrender to army troops. He surrendered, saying,

> I am tired of fighting. The chiefs are killed.... The little children are freezing to death. My people, some of them have run away to the hills and have no blankets, no food.... Hear me my chiefs, I am tired; my heart is sick and sad. From where the sun now stands, I will fight no more forever.

The last wars with the western Indians were fought against the Apache in New Mexico. When the Apache leader, Geronimo, was captured in 1886, Indian warfare came to an end. There was still one final tragedy, however. Some Indian groups wanted their lands back. In 1890 some of the Sioux began to follow a religious leader who taught that the performance of certain dances would lead to the return of their lands. These "Ghost Dances" alarmed settlers in South Dakota. Fearing renewed warfare, they called in the army. On December 29, 1890, United States soldiers began the **Battle of Wounded Knee** in South Dakota. They killed most of the 350 unarmed Sioux living there.

**The Indian wars are an unhappy chapter in American history.** Thousands of people were killed during the 25 years of warfare. Families were broken up, homes destroyed, and men, women, and children slaughtered on both sides. There seemed to be no way of preventing these wars because each side felt it was right. The Native Americans were fighting for their lives, their lands, and their way of life. They could point to a long history of broken treaties and promises on the part of the white settlers and government

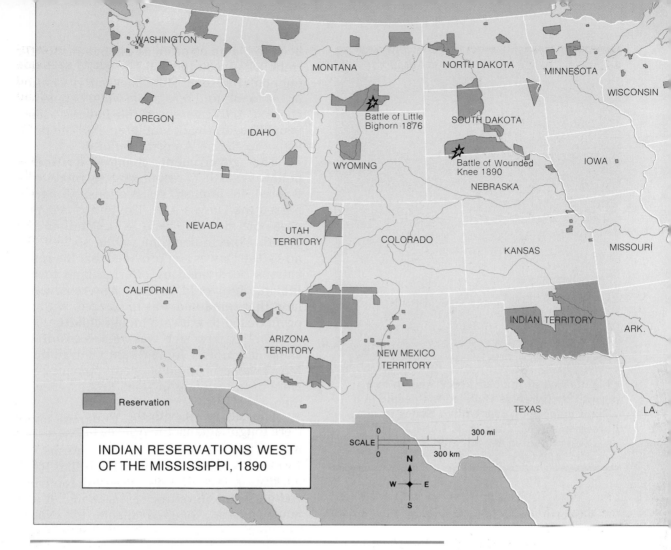

INDIAN RESERVATIONS WEST OF THE MISSISSIPPI, 1890

Reservation

SCALE

0 — 300 mi
0 — 300 km

N W E S

## Map Study

**By 1890 most Western Native Americans had been forced onto reservations. In 1890, which territory had the largest Indian reservations? In which states were the last Indian Wars fought?**

agents. The white people, on the other hand, felt there would be no peace until the power of the Indians was completely broken.

In the end, the Indians lost to superior technology. The same weapons used to kill the buffalo gave the pioneers a great advantage in battle. In addition, the Indians could not compete with the trains that puffed across the plains or with the almost instant communication of the telegraph. The technological resources of the United States provided the people with the means and the motivation to destroy the Indians. Indian resistance, in turn, was also weakened by exposure to diseases and alcohol, both brought by white settlers.

## Government Policy Toward Indians

In the late 1860's, the government placed the defeated tribes on reservations. The government promised to protect the Indians who lived on the reservations and to give them food and supplies.

Chief Joseph of the Nez Perce, shown in a portrait by Cyrenius Hall, led his people in a valiant defense against United States troops. Forced to surrender in 1877, Chief Joseph died on a reservation in Washington in 1904.

**Government officials oversee the Indian reservations.** To deal with the Indians, the **Bureau of Indian Affairs** was established as part of the Department of the Interior. Within the Bureau, the Commissioner of Indian Affairs was responsible for supervising the reservation system. This person, appointed by the President, often had little knowledge of or experience with Indians. The same could be said of most of the agents appointed to **administer** —manage—each reservation.

The reservation system did not work very well. The Indians felt hemmed in and longed for the freedom of the plains. In addition, many government agents cheated the Indians and treated them cruelly.

**The attitude of white people toward Indians changes.** Meanwhile, many Americans began to take a different view of Native American affairs. Investigations made by the government showed that the settlers had been to blame as often as the Indians for the trouble between the two. In 1881 a best-selling book by Helen Hunt Jackson, *A Century of Dishonor*, told how some white people had cheated and mistreated the Indians. More people began to take an interest in the problems the Native Americans faced.

**The government changes its Indian policy.** In 1887, responding to those who wanted to abolish reservations, Congress passed the Dawes Act. The underlying purpose of the act was to **assimilate** — absorb—the Indians into white society. To do so, the Dawes Act provided that the reservations be divided by offering land to any Indian who would farm it. Any reservation land that remained was to be sold, with the profits used to educate Indian children.

The Dawes Act was unsuccessful because it ignored Indian cultural traditions. Most western Indians were nomads who were used to living in small groups. Few of them wanted to become farmers.

Finally, in the 1930's, Congress abandoned the policies of the Dawes Act and began new reforms. These reforms respected Indian traditions. The Indian Reorganization Act of 1934 provided for tribal self-government on the reservations. It also made federal loans available for Native American businesses and gave Indians help in making the best use of their lands.

## SECTION REVIEW

1. **Vocabulary**    reservation, administer, assimilate
2. **People and Places**    William F. Cody, Crazy Horse, Sitting Bull, George A. Custer, Chief Joseph, Wounded Knee
3. **Comprehension**    How did the disappearance of the buffalo contribute to the defeat of the western Indians?
4. **Comprehension**    How did the Dawes Act reverse previous Indian policy? Why was it in turn reversed?
5. **Critical Thinking**    Despite the determined resistance of the Plains Indians, why was their way of life doomed?

# How did miners, ranchers, and farmers settle the last frontier?

## Vocabulary

boomtown                    cow town
open range                  brand

In 1890 the federal government reported that the frontier had disappeared. According to the 1890 census, an average of two Americans lived on every square mile of the West. That did not mean that the American West was thickly settled with cities and towns. It did mean, however, that the frontier line that had been moving steadily westward since the 1600's was now gone.

In the settlement of the last frontier, three groups of people—miners, cattle ranchers, and farmers—played key roles. They led lives of hardship and danger, of heartbreaking failure, and of high adventure.

## Mining Settlements in the Mountains

Prospectors first went west during the California gold rush of 1849. (See Chapter 16.) At first these fortune seekers found plenty of gold in California. As gold became harder to find, many prospectors turned to the rugged mountain country. Always on the lookout for precious minerals, they prospected in both the desert mountains and the Rocky Mountains.

**Miners find gold and silver in the western mountains.** The hopes of many prospectors were rewarded during the 1850's and 1860's when rich deposits of silver were found in the mountains of Nevada, Idaho, and Montana. In 1858 gold was discovered in Colorado. Fortune seekers headed for Colorado in wagons bearing the sign "Pikes Peak or Bust." Pikes Peak was the first Colorado mountain most travelers sighted as they trudged west across the plains. The luckier

ones struck gold. Others were disappointed. They changed their signs to "Busted, by Gosh!" and moved on. Gold was later discovered in Wyoming, Arizona, New Mexico, and in the Black Hills of South Dakota.

**The mining rush causes the mountain states to grow rapidly.** Wherever adventurers swarmed hoping to find gold or silver, **boomtowns** sprang up almost overnight. Boomtowns were instant towns where even the stores, saloons, and banks were likely to be set up in tents or hastily constructed

## Graph Study

In 1850, about 179,000 settlers lived in the western territories. By how much did the population increase between 1850 and 1890?

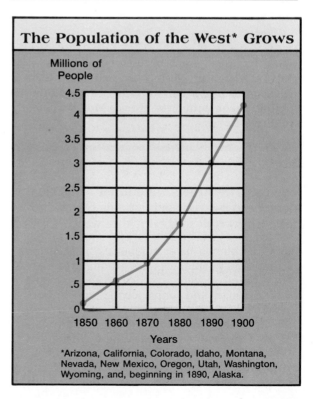

### The Population of the West* Grows

Millions of People

*Arizona, California, Colorado, Idaho, Montana, Nevada, New Mexico, Oregon, Utah, Washington, Wyoming, and, beginning in 1890, Alaska.

Helena, Montana, got its start as a boomtown named Last Chance Gulch after prospectors discovered gold there in 1864. By the 1880's, mining towns dotted the Rocky Mountains and the silver-rich Southwest.

cabins. The streets were filled with choking dust, deep ruts, or oozing mud. One visitor to a boomtown described it this way:

> This human hive, numbering at least ten thousand people, was the product of ninety days. Into it were crowded all the elements of a rough and active civilization. Thousands of cabins and tents ... were seen on every hand. Every foot of the gulch [a narrow rocky valley] ... was already disfigured by huge heaps of gravel. ... Gold was abundant, and every possible device was employed by the gamblers, the traders, the vile men and women that had come in with the miners into the locality, to obtain it. Nearly every third cabin was a saloon where vile whiskey was peddled out for fifty cents a drink in gold dust. Many of these places were filled with gambling tables and gamblers. ... Not a day or night passed which did not yield its full [amount] of vice, quarrels, wounds, or murder. The crack of the revolver was often heard above the merry notes of the violin. Street fights were frequent, and as no one knew when or where they would occur, every one was on his guard against a random shot.

In time, reserves of other minerals were found in the West, including copper, coal, lead, and zinc. Mining these, as well as the gold and silver, required expensive machinery. After many years, the lone prospector gave way to the large mining company.

Many frontier boomtowns became ghost towns when the gold or silver ran out. The mining boom, however, had stimulated many economic activities—farming, trade, building, lumbering, banking, and transportation. Some boomtowns turned into permanent communities that served the needs of farmers, traders, ranchers, and miners. The boomtown at the site of Colorado's first gold discovery was Denver, today one of the largest cities in the West.

The mountain regions would have been settled even without minerals. The mining rush of the 1850's and 1860's, however, sped settlement and statehood for Nevada (1864), Colorado (1876), Montana (1889), Idaho (1890), and Wyoming (1890).

## Cattle Raising on the Western Plains

Just as mining helped to settle the mountain regions of the Far West, so cattle raising helped to develop the western plains. When the Spaniards had settled Mexico and, later, parts of the present-day Southwest, they brought with them cattle and horses. On their ranchos, the Spaniards raised steers with long, spreading horns. Skilled ranch hands used small but swift horses called broncos to herd the cattle. Many of the first American settlers in Texas, New Mexico, and California raised cattle primarily for their hides. Getting live cattle to eastern markets was almost impossible because of the lack of transportation.

**Cattle raising begins to boom.** After the Civil War, cattle raising developed into a major industry. When railroads began crossing the prairies, ranchers found that they could drive their cattle over the plains to

**W.H.D. Koerner's painting shows a cowhand driving Texas longhorns through the vast open range in Wyoming. By the mid-1880's the open range disappeared and was replaced by fenced-in ranches.**

Before photography became widespread in the 1850's, many people looked to different forms of artwork—painting, sculptures, and sketches—for realistic "pictures" of the world around them. Nowhere was this more true than in the United States, where a number of artists participated in and kept a permanent record of the expansion of the frontier.

Some artists traveled with the first expeditions that headed westward. Among the famous American artists who practiced their craft on the frontier was John James Audubon, famous for his paintings of North American birds. In the 1830's George Catlin and Karl Bodmer each painted impressions of the Plains Indians. A half-century later, painters Frederic Remington and Charles M. Russell each succeeded in capturing moments of action in the life of American Indians, cowhands, and soldiers. Because of these artists of the West, we can experience part of the life and legend of the Old West.

**A bronze statue by Charles M. Russell**

railroad points in Kansas and Nebraska. Each year Texas ranchers would collect huge herds of cattle and start them northward on what was called the **long drive.**

Often a herd numbered 2,000 or 3,000 cattle. Grazing leisurely across the prairies, the animals finally reached the **cow towns** —towns where cattle could be shipped east on the railroad. From there they were loaded on railroad cars bound for meat-packing centers such as Omaha, Kansas City, or Chicago.

The success of the long drive encouraged cattle raising throughout the West. The killing of the buffalo had made available great stretches of grass-covered prairie, stretching from Texas to Montana. Ranchers discovered that buffalo grass was good food for their cattle. Before long, the cattle of many different ranchers were grazing together on the **open range** —vast areas of unfenced land owned by the government.

In the spring all of the cattle that had been grazing on the open range were rounded up. Then they were sorted according to their **brand** —a ranch owner's mark burned into the hide. The newborn calves were branded and then the cows and their calves were returned to the open range. The remaining cattle were gathered for the long drive to the cow towns.

**The American cowhand becomes part of the western scene.** The long drive would have been impossible without the cowhand. The cowhand's job was to protect the cattle from wild animals and rustlers and to keep the cattle from straying away. It was often dangerous, uncomfortable work.

The cowhands came from a variety of ethnic backgrounds. Many were Hispanic, for it was in Mexico that longhorns were first raised. About one fourth of the cowhands were black. As slaves in Texas, some blacks had served as cowhands. Other blacks became cowhands after getting their freedom and heading west.

The cowhands developed special clothes for their work. They wore boots with pointed toes and narrow heels that would not get stuck in the stirrups of their saddles. Wide-brimmed hats provided protection against sun and rain. Cowhands protected their necks from the hot sun with silk kerchiefs. The kerchiefs could also be worn as masks on long, dusty rides. With their distinctive costume and colorful way of life, the cowhands quickly became a lasting part of American folklore.

**The open range comes to an end.** Cattle raising on the open range lasted for only a few decades. As increasing numbers of people entered the cattle business, good grazing lands became scarce. Ranchers then began to fence off the range in order to protect their pastures from newcomers. The land was often public land, but the ranchers defended their fences with "gun law." Many homesteaders also staked out their homesteads on the range. To protect their crops from roving cattle, the farmers fenced in their property with barbed wire. The cattle ranchers fought the homesteaders in every way they could, but the open range continued to shrink.

**James Walker's 1877 corral scene shows Hispanic cowhands training wild horses called mustangs. Spanish ranchers began raising cattle and horses in the Southwest in the 1600's. Spanish contributions to the cowhands' way of life included wide-brimmed hats and chaps—wide, leather trouser-legs worn to protect against thorns.**

A chuckwagon provided food for cowhands on the open range. J.C.H. Grabill's 1887 photograph shows trail herders in the Dakota Territory stopped for a meal.

The death blow to the open range came in the winter of 1886 to 1887 when the West experienced one of the worst winters in memory. The November snow became so deep that animals could not paw through it to graze. Then in January a terrible blizzard howled across the plains. Drifting with the winds, cattle piled up at the fences and died. Finally, there was a period of extreme cold with temperatures as low as -55°F (-48°C). When spring came, the western plains were littered with millions of dead animals. Most cattle owners went bankrupt. The era of the open range was over.

## The Last Wave of Settlement

Both the miner and the cowhand, who helped to open the unsettled West, were restless figures, often on the move. When farmers took up land, however, they intended to stay and settle down.

**Homesteaders meet new challenges.** Pioneer life on the plains was not easy. Those farm families that came to the Great Plains faced an environment for which most were unprepared. Instead of timber for housing, the homesteaders had to use a resource that was easily available—sod. They cut the prairie sod into blocks, which they used to construct their homes.

Until homesteaders could dig a well and afford a windmill, finding clean drinking water was usually their most serious concern. A member of a Kansas pioneer family later recalled:

The spring, about half a mile or more distant, was the nearest source of good water. Happily this was clear, cold and of good quality, without tang.... A yoke was made to place across the shoulders, so as to carry at each end a bucket of water, and then water was brought a half mile from spring to house.

Homesteaders suffered unforeseen dangers and hardships. Blizzards often destroyed livestock. In some years clouds of grasshoppers gobbled up crops within minutes. Dry spells, floods, tornadoes, and prairie fires were other hazards. Many farmers discovered that the railroad advertisements were misleading. The plains were not a meadow that needed only plowing to become a garden. Many people gave up. Heading back east, one Kansas farmer wrote on his wagon: "From Kansas, where it rains grasshoppers, fire and destruction." The ones who stayed were those who learned to farm in a semiarid, often fickle, environment.

In spite of the many hardships they faced regularly, the early western farmers developed a deep attachment to their land and the way of life they had developed. One pioneer woman had this to say about living and farming on the Great Plains:

> It might seem a cheerless life, but there were many compensations: the thrill of conquering a new country; the wonderful atmosphere; the attraction of the prairie, which simply gets into your blood and makes you dissatisfied away from it; the low-lying hills and the unobstructed view of the horizon; and the fleecy clouds driven by the never-failing winds.

**Nebraska homesteaders stand by their windmill and their sod house on the Great Plains. Sod was used for building because wood was scarce on the prairie. What purpose did windmills serve?**

**Westerners recognize the equality of women.** For the most part, mining and cattle ranching in the West had been jobs for men. Although women lived and worked in the boomtowns and cow towns, they were rare in the mining digs or on the long drives. In contrast, homesteading would have been impossible without women. Pioneering men and women were partners, each contributing equally to the difficult daily task of providing for a family. Westerners recognized this equality, and thus western states became the first to grant women the right to vote.

**Oklahoma is settled.** In 1889 the government opened to settlers much of the Indian Territory in present-day Oklahoma. A great land rush resulted. More than 50,000 eager settlers lined up to compete for 6,000 free homestead lots. When a gun shot was fired at noon one spring day, they rushed across the boundary in a wild scramble to stake out desirable homesteads. Those who jumped the gun were called "sooners" because they started out sooner than the others.

In the next few years more Native American lands were added to the Oklahoma Territory, and in 1907, Oklahoma became a state. Other western states that entered the Union as a result of the settlement of the last frontier were Utah (1896), North Dakota and South Dakota (1889), and New Mexico and Arizona (1912).

## SECTION REVIEW

1. **Vocabulary**   boomtown, cow town, open range, brand
2. **People and Places**   Colorado, Kansas, Oklahoma
3. **Comprehension**   How did the mining frontier differ from the cattle frontier? In what ways were they similar?
4. **Comprehension**   What challenges did homesteaders face?
5. **Critical Thinking**   How did the railroad both create and destroy the cattle frontier?

# Chapter 20 Summary

Between 1865 and 1900 the deserts, mountains, and plains of the West changed from a frontier to a settled region. This was made possible by the Homestead Act, which gave public land to settlers, and by advances in technology. The Bessemer process resulted in the economical production of steel rails, which in turn stimulated railroad building. The completion of the transcontinental railroad in 1869 opened up the West to pioneers. Inventions such as the steel plow, barbed wire, and the windmill made it possible for settlers to live on the treeless, semiarid Great Plains.

The settlement of the West led to wars with the Indians, who resented the loss of their land and the killing of the buffalo on which they depended. By 1890, however, the army had defeated the Indians, many of whom were starving and had no choice but to go to the reservations the government assigned them.

Miners discovered rich finds of gold, silver, copper, coal, and other minerals in the mountainous West. Their first settlements were boomtowns, which in turn drew other settlers. As the railroad began to span the continent, cattle ranchers drove huge herds of longhorn cattle to the cow towns for shipment to the East. For several decades cattle tended by cowhands grazed on the open range. The use of barbed wire fences, the increasing number of homesteaders, and a killing winter brought the period of the open range to an end. The homesteaders who settled on the Great Plains experienced extreme hardship as they struggled to make a living in a difficult environment.

# CRITICAL THINKING: Evaluating Evidence

Historians obtain evidence from many sources. Different sources often provide different views of the same historical event. In these cases, historians have to **evaluate**—judge the accuracy and fairness of—these different views. Evaluating evidence involves the use of several skills you have already learned. These skills include analyzing primary and secondary sources, recognizing points of view, distinguishing fact from opinion, and analyzing arguments.

To begin evaluating historical evidence, ask yourself the following questions:

*1. Is the information from primary or secondary sources?* It is important to identify the kind of source you are using and the kind of information that source can provide.

*2. Is the information accurate?* One way to determine accuracy is to check the information against facts given in other sources. For example, if a pioneer's diary told of conflicts with Native Americans, you could read newspapers written at that time to see whether those incidents were reported. Another way to check accuracy is to judge the writer's knowledge and expertise.

*3. Is the information reliable?* Newspapers are usually reliable. Other sources may not be so trustworthy. Sometimes more than one source reports the same information. For example, two pioneers' diaries may note the same incident, with the same details. When two sources agree, their accounts are considered more reliable.

*4. Is the information a statement of fact or opinion?* Almost all historical evidence includes statements of both fact and opinion. Facts are more reliable than opinions.

The following two excerpts provide information about frontier schools in the late 1800's. Evaluate the information by answering the questions below the excerpts.

---

**Excerpt A**

I was employed to teach ... on Oak Creek about four and one-half miles from Cora. The school building was a sod 'dugout,' about fourteen feet long with dirt floor, unplastered walls, two small windows in front, heated by a small fireplace about one yard across. It had neither blackboard, teacher's desk nor chair. The seats were small logs split and supported by pegs, and were placed at the sides of the room. I taught in five districts and in all there were no outbuildings, but some schools had teacher's desks and chairs, also blackboards and lights. The Cora school had a small frame building with floor and stove. I think at the time I was teaching, not more than three or four schools had floors.

---

**Excerpt B**

The school classrooms [where I taught] had a few bare benches, flat, without backs, and so far off the floor that little legs, dangling high in the air, would ache cruelly before a change of position was possible. An extra-brave or desperate pupil might lie down a bit to relieve the strain, but the season of relief would be short lived. No charts, no maps, no pictures, no books but a Speller. They would have 'numbers' later, but some of the little fellows would never get that far. The miracle was that a love of 'learning' ever survived the rigors of school days then ...

---

1. Are the two excerpts from primary or secondary sources?
2. Do you think the information in Excerpt A is accurate? Explain your answer.
3. Do you think the information in Excerpt B is reliable? Why or why not?
4. Would these excerpts be useful sources of information for a study of frontier schools? Why or why not?

## Vocabulary and Key Terms

Use the following terms to complete the sentences below. Write your answers on a separate sheet of paper.

assimilate      open range
Homestead Act      public lands
administer      reservations
long drive

1. The _____, passed by Congress, gave _____ to settlers.
2. Most of the agents appointed to _____ the reservations had little or no knowledge of the Indians.
3. Under the Dawes Act, the federal government tried to _____ Indians into white society, instead of forcing them to go to _____.
4. Cattle grazed on the _____ before and during the _____ to the cow towns.

## Recalling the Facts

1. When was the Homestead Act passed, and what did it say?
2. What inventions helped the settlement of the West?
3. How did the federal government encourage the building of the first transcontinental railroad?
4. Why did western Indians fight against the settlement of whites? What was the result of this fighting?
5. Why was the reservation system not more successful?
6. What differences were there in the ways the miners, the cattle ranchers, and the farmers lived?
7. What caused the disappearance of the open range?
8. In what ways did homesteaders adapt to the environment of the Great Plains?
9. In what way were men and women partners on the farming frontier?

## Places to Locate

Match the letters on the map with the places listed below. Write your answers on a separate sheet of paper.

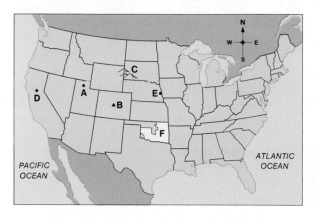

1. Indian Territory
2. Omaha, Nebraska
3. Sacramento, California
4. Pikes Peak
5. Promontory Point
6. Black Hills

## Critical Thinking

1. In the warfare between pioneers and Native Americans, was one side more to blame than the other? Why? Address these questions in your answer:
   a. What did the settlers want, and how did they achieve it?
   b. How did the Indians react to the westward migration of pioneers?
2. The government tried various measures to deal with Native Americans. Why were these policies not more successful? What might have worked better? Consider these points in your answer:
   a. the federal policy toward the Native Americans
   b. Native American traditions
   c. the white attitudes toward the Native Americans

3. How did economic interests affect the settlement of the frontier? Consider these points in your answer:
   a. types of settlers and their motives
   b. the role played by railroads and other companies
   c. the federal government's financial support of frontier settlement

## Understanding History

1. Reread the section "New methods of steel production encourage railroad building" on page 462. Then answer these questions.
   a. **Science and Technology.** In what ways were the iron and steel industries important to the major inventions of the nineteenth century?
   b. **Economics.** Why did the invention of steel rails make railroad building more economical?
2. Reread the section "The government changes its Indian policy" on page 470. Then answer these questions.
   a. **Culture.** What assumptions did the Dawes Act make? What did it ignore about many Indian cultures?
   b. **Citizenship.** Why did the Indian Reorganization Act of 1934 have a better chance to succeed than the Dawes Act?
3. Reread the section "Cattle raising begins to boom" on page 473. Then answer these questions.
   a. **Economics.** What was the purpose of the long drive?
   b. **Geography.** Why did cattle thrive on the Great Plains?

## Projects and Activities

1. **Preparing a Bulletin-Board Display.** Work with your classmates to prepare a display about the American cowhand. Divide into groups and choose an aspect of cowhand life to investigate, such as clothing, food, shelter, or work. Cut pictures from magazines and combine them with written information to create a display on cowhand culture.

2. **Drawing a Map.** Draw a map of the western United States before 1860. Show areas occupied by such Native Americans as the Sioux, Apache, Comanche, Nez Perce, and Cheyenne. Use an encyclopedia or other information source.
3. **Writing a Fictional Account.** Imagine you are a prospector heading west to Colorado in 1858. Write an account of your trip, telling why you are going, what you see, and what life is like in a Colorado boomtown. Be very descriptive.
4. **Giving an Oral Report.** Find out more about one of these people: William F. Cody, George A. Custer, Sitting Bull, Crazy Horse, Chief Joseph, Geronimo. Present an oral report to the class.

## Practicing Your Skill

Read the excerpt below. Then answer the questions that follow.

> My people have never first drawn a bow or fired a gun against the whites. It was you who sent out the first soldier and we who sent out the second. . . .
>
> You said that you wanted to put us upon a reservation, to build us houses and make us medicine lodges. I do not want them. I was born upon the prairie, where the wind blew free and there was nothing to block the light of the sun. I was born where there were no enclosures and where everything drew a free breath. . . .
>
> When I was at Washington the Great White Father told me that all the Comanche land was ours, and that no one should hinder us in living upon it. So, why do you ask us to leave the rivers, and the sun, and the wind, and live in houses? . . .
>
> Ten Bears, Comanche chief

1. Does the speaker support his argument that the white soldiers were responsible for the fighting? Explain your answer.
2. What evidence is given that the reservation system is not good for the Comanches? Is it believable? Explain.
3. How does the speaker support his tribe's claim to the land? Could this evidence be verified?

# CHAPTER
# 21 Industrial Growth Changes the Nation
## 1865–1898

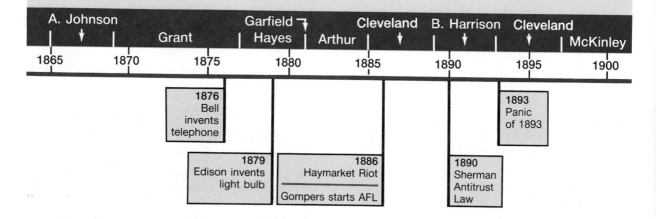

A. Johnson | Grant | Garfield, Hayes | Arthur | Cleveland | B. Harrison | Cleveland | McKinley

1865   1870   1875   1880   1885   1890   1895   1900

1876
Bell invents telephone

1879
Edison invents light bulb

1886
Haymarket Riot

Gompers starts AFL

1890
Sherman Antitrust Law

1893
Panic of 1893

**Industrial growth made American cities into great centers of transportation and communication.**

## Preparing to Read

In the years between 1865 and 1900, the United States became one of the world's leading industrial nations. Industrialization made possible the final settlement of the West. In the East, industrialization resulted in the development of large cities. There factories and mills turned out products for the nation. Industrialization raised the standard of living for many Americans. It also caused problems, including poor working conditions, low wages, periods of high unemployment, and powerful monopolies. New state and federal laws, as well as the organization of labor, were important in addressing some of these problems. As you read this chapter, try to answer the following questions:

1. What made the United States an industrial leader?
2. How did business leaders affect the growth of industry?
3. How did industrialization affect American workers?
4. How did industrialization affect the economy?

# 1  What made the United States an industrial leader?

## Vocabulary

| | |
|---|---|
| free enterprise | capitalist system |
| dividend | mass production |
| capital | division of labor |
| entrepreneur | assembly line |
| | merchandising |

The United States had many advantages that spurred industrial growth. It was rich in natural resources. It had hard-working and inventive people. The economic system encouraged people to organize and to invest in businesses. Good transportation and communication systems helped the country grow. In addition, people developed new methods of producing and selling goods. This, in turn, increased the demand for manufactured products.

## National Resources

Throughout the early years of the country, most Americans depended on the resources of soil, water, and timber. Good soil was the source of food and cash crops. Rivers provided waterpower to turn machinery. The nation's transportation system depended on rivers and ocean harbors. Timber was the principal fuel and the main building material.

As industries grew, soil, water, and timber continued to be important resources. Rich soil, particularly in the Midwest, produced crops large enough to feed millions of city people. Waterways remained essential for transporting industrial products. Timber was used to build railroad cars, factories, ships, and apartment houses.

**The United States develops rich mineral resources.** As industry grew, Americans used more and more mineral resources. In the nineteenth century the most important minerals were coal and iron ore. The nation had large supplies of both. Coal provided fuel for steam engines to drive machinery. Coal was also used to produce iron and steel. Steel mills were usually located near plentiful supplies of coal and iron ore.

The technology of the late 1800's led to the development of other resources, such as

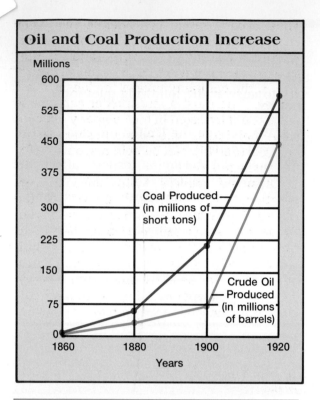

## Oil and Coal Production Increase

## Graph Study

Oil and coal were essential to America's industrialization. How many short tons of coal were produced in 1880? In 1900? How much crude oil was produced in 1880? In 1900?

oil and aluminum. The United States is rich in oil and aluminum ore. It has large deposits of copper and lead, which are important to industrial production. The nation's gold and silver provided the money for factories, mines, and other businesses. In addition, the nation is rich in human resources.

**The United States has millions of hardworking people.** Industrialization was helped greatly by the large supply of people willing to work in American factories and mines. Between 1860 and 1900, the number of Americans grew from 31 million to almost 80 million. Many of these new Americans were immigrants who came to the United States after the Civil War.

Most immigrants came from southern and eastern Europe. Others migrated from Latin America, the Caribbean region, China, and Japan. Whether they had been farmers or factory workers in their native countries, these immigrants were accustomed to hard work. They were eager to succeed in their new country. Their labor helped turn raw materials into finished industrial products.

Furthermore, Americans have always been a practical people, eager to find better ways to do things. Inventions helped the United States become an industrial giant.

**Thomas Edison illustrates the American inventive spirit.** Among the many inventors active in the late 1800's, no one stands out more than Thomas Alva Edison. Born in Ohio in 1847, Edison showed an interest in science and electricity from an early age. At 21, he patented his first invention. From then until his death in 1931, Edison produced a steady stream of inventions. His genius lay in putting scientific ideas to practical use.

Edison's greatest gift to the world was probably the electric lightbulb, which he perfected in 1879. In the following 50 years, Edison developed dozens of inventions that shaped the modern industrial world. At his laboratory in Menlo Park, New Jersey, Edison invented or improved on the telegraph, the phonograph, generators and power stations, the electric streetcar, motion pictures, and the microphone.

## A Free Economic System

The business and economic traditions of the United States fostered the growth of industry. These traditions include an economic system that encourages change, new technology, and freedom of choice.

**Economic rights aid the growth of industry.** The heart of the American economic system is **free enterprise.** A free-enterprise system is one that recognizes the rights to own private property, to undertake private business activities, and to make a profit from them.

A business may be a small family farm, or it may be a huge manufacturing company. Whatever its size, the goal of a business is to make a profit. A business may be owned by one person, by a partnership of two or more persons, or by a corporation. A corporation is a form of business organization that has many owners. Most large businesses are corporations.

When a corporation is formed, it offers for sale shares of stock in the corporation. Those who buy the shares of stock are called stockholders. Stockholders own the corporation. They choose a board of directors, which is responsible for managing the business. For each share of stock they own, stockholders may receive a **dividend** —a share of the profits — once a year.

**Corporations have many advantages.** One advantage of corporations is that the sale of stock can raise **capital** —money needed to start and operate large businesses. Another advantage is that stockholders are free to sell their shares to someone else.

Thus, a corporation can operate year after year without depending on any one owner. A third advantage of a corporation is that stockholders are not held personally responsible if the company breaks the law or owes money. The most a stockholder can lose is the amount invested in the company. In contrast, individuals who own a business alone or in partnership can be held responsible for the business's debts.

**Business leaders build powerful corporations.** The industrial growth of the United States also depended on the inventiveness of American **entrepreneurs** (ahn-truh-pruh-NURZ). Entrepreneurs are individuals who take risks to start new businesses. In the early nineteenth century, American entrepeneurs began to build corporations that had large amounts of capital.

American industrial growth depended on the labor of hardworking people, including millions of immigrants. By 1870, more than 5 million foreign-born people lived in the United States.

## Firsts in Technology 1850–1900

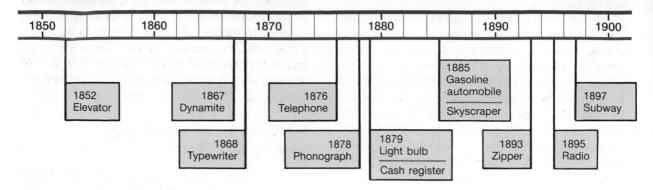

## Chart Study

The United States was a leader in new inventions during the late 1800's. In what year was the typewriter invented? How did the invention of the elevator affect the growth of cities?

Banks, insurance companies, and turnpike companies were the first corporations. Later, other corporations formed to build railroads and canals. By the end of the 1800's, many manufacturing companies had also become corporations. The American economy had become a **capitalist system** —a free-enterprise system that depends on large concentrations of capital. Some corporations became so large and powerful that as a group they became known as **big business.**

### Advances in Transportation and Communication

American business benefited greatly from the development of new means of transportation and communication. With better transportation, people and cargo could travel greater distances more cheaply. New methods of communication permitted information to be sent faster than ever before.

**A vast railroad system is developed.** A great burst of railroad construction took place after the Civil War. In addition to the transcontinental railroads, Americans built many shorter lines connecting cities and towns. As more people used railroads, they realized that the many separate lines needed to be linked together.

Cornelius Vanderbilt, a steamship owner, became the leader in linking the railroads. In the 1860's and 1870's, he bought small railroad lines between Chicago and New York, and combined them into the giant New York Central System. Other business leaders formed the Pennsylvania Railroad and the Baltimore and Ohio Railroad. Tying the railroads together meant fewer delays and cheaper fares for passengers.

The improved railroad system also made it cheaper to ship goods to distant markets. City dwellers in the East could eat bread made from South Dakota wheat, and South Dakota farmers could buy iron skillets and other goods made in eastern factories. Railroads also transported raw materials such as coal and iron ore to mills, mines, and factories. Finished goods could then be shipped by rail to port cities. From there the goods were sent to other countries.

**Inventions make railroad travel safer and more comfortable.** Railroad service improved as a result of new products of the late 1800's. These included air brakes, invented by George Westinghouse, and automatic couplers, invented by Eli H. Janney for joining two railroad cars. In addition, the use of track signals helped to cut down accidents between trains. Better springs and

486

methods of heating and lighting increased riding comfort.

**New inventions speed up communications.** Improvements in the telegraph and the invention of the telephone greatly speeded up communications. The telegraph had been in use since the 1840's. Inventions before the Civil War had made it possible to send several messages over the same wire at the same time. In 1866, an American named Cyrus Field successfully laid a telegraph cable on the floor of the Atlantic Ocean between the United States and Europe. As a result, important messages could be sent in a few moments across thousands of miles of ocean.

In 1876 Alexander Graham Bell invented the telephone. When Bell first introduced the telephone, many people thought the invention was just a toy. By 1878, however, the first telephone exchange in the United States was set up at New Haven, Connecticut. By 1880, more than 80 towns had local telephone networks. In 1900, there were about 1,356,000 telephones in the United States, twice the total for all of Europe. The use of telephones rapidly became an important means of business communication.

## New Methods of Making and Selling Goods

New business methods were also important to the nation's industrial growth. In the years after the Civil War, American business leaders learned how to produce vast quantities of goods at low cost and to sell them to large numbers of people.

**New manufacturing methods speed production.** The reason for the success of

Working at a switchboard as a telephone operator was one of many new job opportunities for women in the communications industry. The telephone operator's importance grew as new telephone lines were opened.

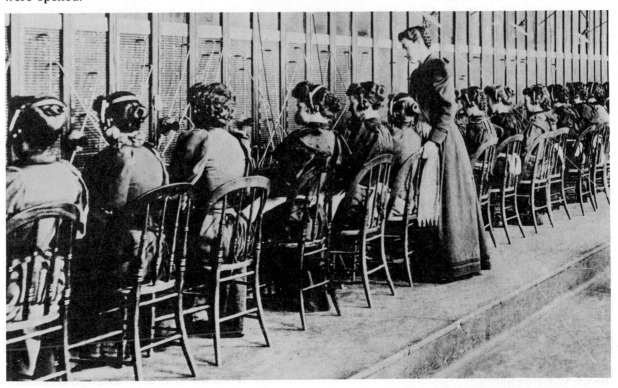

American industry is **mass production** — making large quantities of goods quickly and cheaply. Eli Whitney took an important step toward mass production with the development of standardized parts. (See Chapter 13.) Another important step forward was the **division of labor** —breaking one highly skilled job into many simpler ones. Before the Industrial Revolution one skilled worker usually did every task in changing raw material into a finished product. One shoemaker, for example, would do all the work to turn a piece of leather into a pair of shoes. After the invention of the sewing machine, however, shoes could be made in factories. Then, the labor of making shoes was divided among many workers. One person would cut the leather, another would make the heel and sole, and a third would sew the parts together. This method speeded production and lowered costs in many industries.

The most important step in mass production came early in the twentieth century. This was the **assembly line** —a new system for manufacturing products. A slow-moving conveyor belt carried the parts of products to workers at fixed stations. Each worker did one task putting together the product. The assembly line was used successfully by Henry Ford to manufacture cars. Ford's assembly line combined on a large scale the use of standardized parts and the division of labor. Each worker did one task as the automobile passed on the conveyor belt. When

**In the years after the Civil War, specialty stores became common in the cities. What goods were sold in this store?**

the end of the line was reached, the car was complete.

The mass production of cars and other products brought down their cost, with the result that many Americans could buy them. As people demanded more goods, business and industries produced greater quantities. This helped the American economy to grow rapidly.

**Businesses find new ways to sell products.** Entrepreneurs also developed new methods of **merchandising** —selling— in the years after the Civil War. These new methods—department stores, chain stores, and mail-order houses—are still in use today.

In large cities, department stores began to appear in the 1870's and 1880's. Here, in different departments, customers could find almost anything they might want. Because the stores bought and sold large quantities of goods, they were able to give customers lower prices than smaller stores could. Pioneers in the department store business included John Wanamaker, who established a store in Philadelphia in 1877, and Marshall Field, who opened his famous store in Chicago in 1881.

Chain stores—a number of almost identical stores owned by the same company— also began in the late 1800's. Chain stores, like department stores, could sell their goods at low prices. The first chain store was the Atlantic and Pacific Tea Company, founded in 1859. Then in 1879, F.W. Woolworth opened the first of his hundreds of "dime stores," where no item cost more than a dime.

A third form of merchandising, the mail-order house, brought manufactured goods to rural Americans. In 1872 Aaron Montgomery Ward started the first mail-order company. He sent out catalogs with descriptions and pictures of goods that people could buy by mail. People in small towns and on farms quickly began ordering from Ward's catalog. In 1886 Sears, Roebuck, another mail-order company, was founded. In rural areas throughout the United States, the arrival of mail-order catalogs became one of the year's most exciting events.

## LINKING PAST AND PRESENT

## ★ ★ ★ *Advertising*

Advertising has always been part of American life. In early colonial times, many merchants often peddled their goods in the streets. They advertised by calling out to passers-by, telling them what goods they had for sale. In addition, they placed printed advertisements outside shop windows. In 1704, the first newspaper advertisement in the American colonies appeared in *The Boston News-Letter.* Many of the nation's newspapers, however, would not accept any advertisements until the mid-1800s. In 1880, Americans spent about $200 million on advertising.

The growth of the radio and television industry made it possible for advertisers to reach millions of people at once. Today, the United States has the largest advertising industry in the world, and advertisers spend more than $95 billion each year.

## SECTION REVIEW

1. **Vocabulary**   free enterprise, dividend, capital, entrepreneur, capitalist system, mass production, division of labor, assembly line, merchandising
2. **People and Places**   Thomas Edison, Cornelius Vanderbilt, Cyrus Field, Alexander Graham Bell, Henry Ford, Marshall Field, F.W. Woolworth, Aaron Montgomery Ward
3. **Comprehension**   What mineral resources were important to the growth of industry in the United States?
4. **Comprehension**   What new forms of production and merchandising came about in the nineteenth century?
5. **Critical Thinking**   How does free enterprise encourage change, new technology, and freedom of choice?

## MAPS AND GRAPHS: Interpreting a Line Graph

The rapid industrialization of the United States was helped by a growing population. The expanding population provided plenty of workers to fill factory jobs. The graph that appears on this page shows how much the country's population increased between the years 1860 and 1900. Because the information is shown by a line, this kind of graph is called a **line graph.**

Reading a line graph is similar to reading a bar graph. Read the title and the information that is given along the horizontal and vertical axes to find out what information the graph contains. (To review these steps, re-read the Gaining Skill lesson that appears in Chapter 14.)

Bar graphs show numerical information in sets of bars or columns. They are useful for answering such questions as *How much?* On a line graph, each piece of information is shown by a dot or a point. Then a line is drawn connecting the dots or points. Line graphs are especially helpful for answering such questions as *How have things changed over time?*

Use the information that appears on the line graph on this page to answer the following questions.

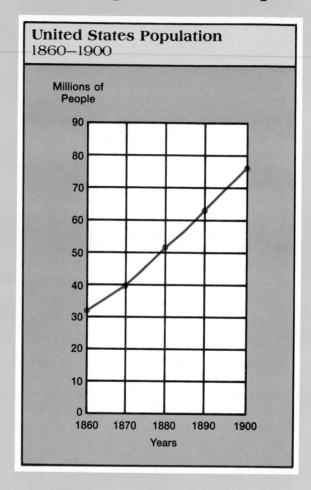

**United States Population 1860–1900**

Millions of People

Years

1. What is the subject of the line graph shown here?
2. What does the horizontal axis of the graph show?
3. What does the vertical axis of the graph show?
4. About how many people lived in the United States in 1860?
5. In which year did the nation's 1860 population double?
6. In which year was the population of the United States more than 50 million for the first time?

7. During which ten-year period did the population of the United States grow more — 1860 to 1870 or 1890 to 1900? How can you tell?
8. Between which two years shown on the graph did the greatest increase in the nation's population take place?
9. Between which two years did the smallest population increase occur?
10. According to the graph, how did the population of the United States change over time? Explain your answer.

# 2 How did business leaders affect the growth of industry?

## Vocabulary

business consolidation

industrialist

refine

The second half of the nineteenth century was a time of **business consolidation** — the merging of several small companies into one large company. This consolidation happened in every major industry. One result of the consolidation of business was that huge, nationwide companies were established. Another result was that many of these companies became monopolies, exercising complete control over an industry or, as in the case of railroads, over a particular region. The business leaders who controlled these huge companies were called "captains of industry."

## A Railroad Builder

A key figure in the American railroad industry was James J. Hill. He was born in 1838 in a log cabin on a frontier farm in Canada. After the death of his father, Hill decided to strike out for himself. He came to St. Paul, Minnesota, where he worked for a steamboat company and a railroad.

**James J. Hill builds a railroad empire in the Northwest.** Until he was about 40 years old, Hill had done nothing out of the ordinary. He had great ideas, but others did not take them seriously. One of Hill's ideas was to develop the northwestern part of the United States. Hill had traveled through this sparsely settled area on foot, by wagon, and by dog sled. In 1878 he persuaded a small group of business leaders to take over the railroad where he worked. Hill was then appointed general manager. The railroad was in poor condition and seemed about to fail. From this modest beginning, however,

Hill built a railroad empire that spanned more than half the continent.

**Hill promotes his railroad.** Hill understood that the Northwest had to have many prosperous farms for his railroad to succeed. He arranged for settlers to take trips to view the country. He imported fine cattle from Europe to encourage cattle raising. Hill also helped farmers obtain seeds and farm machinery on reasonable terms. Later, he arranged for hundreds of young people to be sent to agricultural schools.

By 1893 the Great Northern railway system, under Hill's direction, spanned the country between St. Paul, Minnesota, and Seattle, Washington. Later, Hill controlled most of the railroad lines in the Northwest, totalling about 20,000 miles (32,000 kilometers) of track.

## The Steel Business

The rapid growth of the steel industry in the United States was largely brought about by Andrew Carnegie. Carnegie was not a steelmaker by trade. He and his parents came from Scotland in 1848, when Carnegie was 13 years old. Carnegie worked in a Pennsylvania cotton mill, where he earned $1.20 a week. Later, he worked for the Pennsylvania Railroad, where he advanced from telegraph operator to branch manager.

**Andrew Carnegie uses the Bessemer steel process.** From his work for the railroad, Carnegie moved into the business of building iron railroad bridges. On a trip to Britain, Carnegie learned about the Bessemer process for making high-quality, low-cost steel. He then decided to concentrate all his energy and money in the production of steel. Carnegie soon became a successful **industrialist** —one who owns or manages a manufacturing business. By 1890, the Carnegie Steel Company was the leading producer

J.P. Morgan built a monopoly by combining many small companies into one huge corporation. What exaggerated claim does this cartoon make about the goals of business leaders like J.P. Morgan?

of steel in the United States. In 1893 the company's profits totaled $3 million. By 1900, profits mounted to $40 million.

Carnegie was a hardworking and shrewd business leader who used his profits to expand his business. To keep costs down and blast furnaces working at full speed, Carnegie bought vast deposits of iron ore in the upper Great Lakes region. To carry the ore to the steel mills that were located in Pittsburgh, he bought a fleet of vessels on the Great Lakes and a railroad.

**Carnegie shares his fortune.** In 1901 Andrew Carnegie decided to retire. After his retirement, Carnegie gave away vast amounts of his personal fortune to charities and other worthy causes. Many cities and towns in the United States have public libraries built with funds donated by Carnegie. When asked why he gave away so much of his money, he said, "I started life as a poor

man, and I wish to end it that way." Carnegie was hardly a poor man when he died, yet he had given away $350 million!

**The steel industry grows under J.P. Morgan.** When Andrew Carnegie retired, he sold his steel company to J.P. Morgan, a wealthy investment banker. Morgan purchased several other steel companies and then combined them into the world's largest steel company, the United States Steel Corporation. Morgan's investments in railroads, steel, and banks made him one of the richest and most powerful men in the world.

## The Oil Business

The American oil business grew during the same years that Carnegie was building his fortune. Petroleum, or oil, lay in great quantities below the earth's surface in Pennsylvania. In some places it seeped through the rock and floated to the surface of creeks. Farmers sometimes skimmed off the oil to grease their wagons. No one knew the value of petroleum, however, until a scientist, Benjamin Silliman, tested it. He found that it can be **refined** —purified—into kerosene and used for lighting homes and buildings.

**An oil boom begins in Pennsylvania.** In 1859 the first oil well was drilled at Titusville, Pennsylvania. The news had much the same effect as the discovery of gold had in California. People flocked by the thousands to Pennsylvania. The area near Titusville became the center of a new industry. Towns and cities sprang up, and refineries for producing kerosene appeared.

**John D. Rockefeller controls the oil business.** The growing oil industry interested John D. Rockefeller, a young merchant in Cleveland, Ohio. In 1863 Rockefeller started his business with one refinery in Ohio. In 1870, he formed the Standard Oil Company and either built or bought out more refineries. By the 1880's, Rockefeller's Standard Oil controlled 90 percent of all the refining plants in the United States. He did not stop there, however. He bought factories to make barrels, and he gained control of most of the pipelines that carried oil to the refineries. Rockefeller also organized a vast sales

Advances in the iron and steel industries made possible the building of the Brooklyn Bridge in New York. The bridge, which opened in 1883, was an engineering marvel.

force to market his products throughout the country. By 1900, Rockefeller and his Standard Oil Company had a monopoly on the nation's oil business.

Some Americans criticized Rockefeller for being a ruthless competitor in business. Like Carnegie, Rockefeller had put most of the profits back into his company. As a result, Rockefeller had enough capital to buy out rival companies. If his rivals refused to sell, he lowered the price of his own kerosene. Rockefeller's rivals then were not able to make a profit and they were driven out of business.

Such "cutthroat" competition was common in the early years of big business. Like Rockefeller, other leaders who consolidated American industries often used ruthless methods. In some cases, they used techniques that present-day laws forbid. These captains of industry were among the most powerful and best-known Americans of their time. They were sometimes hated for their great wealth and for their harsh business methods. Nevertheless, their boldness, energy, and ability helped make the United States an industrial giant.

## SECTION REVIEW

1. **Vocabulary** business consolidation, industrialist, refine
2. **People and Places** James J. Hill, St. Paul, Seattle, Andrew Carnegie, Pittsburgh, J.P. Morgan, John D. Rockefeller
3. **Comprehension** What steps did Hill take to be sure his railroad succeeded?
4. **Comprehension** In what way was the growth of the American steel and oil industries similar?
5. **Critical Thinking** Should John D. Rockefeller have been prevented from forcing his rivals out of business? Why or why not?

# How did industrialization affect American workers?

## Vocabulary

| | |
|---|---|
| tenement | trade union |
| strike | federation |
| local | collective bargaining |

Millions of workers made possible the industrialization of the United States. Even though they shared some benefits of industrialization, they also worked for low wages in unsafe conditions and lived in crowded, unhealthy places. In response to these conditions, workers organized to fight for better wages and working conditions.

## Problems Faced by Workers

People who toiled in the nation's factories, mines, and mills in the late 1800's worked under harsh conditions. Workers labored 11 to 12 hours a day, and the work was often exhausting. The factories were also dangerous. In many factories little attention was paid to the health and safety of the employees. For example, those who worked in steel mills could easily be burned by red hot iron. Workers in textile mills might lose fingers or hands in machinery.

**Workers receive low wages.** Unskilled factory workers received very low wages in the late 1800's. Company owners were competing to make products at the lowest possible cost. One way to reduce costs was to keep wages low. Wages remained low because the thousands of immigrants pouring into the United States would accept almost any job at any wage. Most unskilled workers received $1.50 to $3.00 a day—just enough to feed a family and pay the rent. Children often worked in the mills or factories to help their parents pay the bills.

Skilled workers with special training were somewhat better paid. Blacksmiths, carpenters, machinists, and painters often earned as much as 70 percent more than unskilled workers. There were fewer skilled workers than unskilled workers in the cities. Because the talents of skilled workers were in demand, employers had to pay them higher wages.

Wages for all workers improved slowly. Between 1860 and 1880, unskilled workers' wages were raised about 30 percent. Wages for skilled workers were increased by about 40 percent.

**Urban workers live in overcrowded, unhealthy conditions.** With industrialization, millions of people streamed into American cities to live and work. Many working people lived in tenements —large apartment buildings often kept in a run-down condition. Life in the tenements was crowded, unhealthy, and often miserable. Several families frequently shared one apartment, and most tenement buildings had no plumbing. With no running water or flush toilets, germs thrived and diseases spread rapidly. Because of the smoky air in the cities, many thousands of workers died from lung disease each year.

The poor conditions in which millions lived and worked did not go unnoticed. The labor leader Samuel Gompers, who had once lived in a New York City tenement, wrote this to a judge in 1894:

Inquire from the thousands of women and children whose husbands or fathers were suffocated or crushed in the mines through the . . . [great] greed of stockholders clamoring for more dividends. Investigate the sweating dens of the large cities. Go to the mills, factories, through the country. Visit the modern tenement houses or hovels in which thousands of workers are compelled to [live a bare] existence.... [Ask] employers whether the laborer is not regarded the same as a machine, thrown out as soon as all the work possible has been squeezed out of him.

## The Formation of Labor Unions

Low wages, long working hours, industrial accidents, and uncertain employment led American workers to organize to improve working conditions. A single worker or a small group of workers did not have the power to make an employer improve working conditions. When numbers of workers joined together to demand changes, however, employers were often forced to make improvements.

**A railroad strike is called in 1877.** In the summer of 1877, railroad companies east of the Mississippi River announced that the wages of all railroad employees would be cut 10 percent. In response, the workers went out on **strike** —a work stoppage. This was the first major strike in the United States. During the strike, trains could not run because there were no workers to operate them. Railroad companies were determined to break the strike, and events soon turned bitter. In city after city—Baltimore, Pittsburgh, Buffalo, Columbus, Chicago, and St. Louis—fierce riots took place. In Pittsburgh 26 people were killed and many more were wounded. Casualties mounted in several other cities, too.

The strike lasted about a month. Federal soldiers were finally called in to restore order. The railroad workers then unhappily accepted the lower wages and went back to work. The strike convinced many workers that they needed powerful unions to get better working conditions.

**The Knights of Labor wins victories for workers.** In 1869 a Philadelphia tailor, Uriah S. Stevens, founded a union known as the **Knights of Labor.** Stevens's union was open to all workers—men and women, blacks and whites, skilled and unskilled. The branches of Stevens's labor union were called **locals.** At first the union grew slowly. In the 1880's, however, the Knights made important gains under the leadership of Terence V. Powderly.

In general, the Knights of Labor did not approve of strikes. Strikes, however, gave the union some great successes. In 1884 and

In this 1925 painting by Grant Wood, a skilled machine-shop worker shapes a truck part. Skilled workers were highly trained for their trades and earned better wages than unskilled workers.

495

The leadership of Terrence Powderly (center) led to the growth of the Knights of Labor. The Knights' goals included bringing all workers—skilled and unskilled, black and white, men and women—into one large union.

1885 the railroads again tried to lower wages. The Knights organized strikes and made the railroads back down. In one case, a railroad not only restored the old wages but also agreed to pay extra for overtime work. As a result of the union's victories, thousands of workers joined the Knights. Membership increased from about 28,000 in 1880 to 104,000 in 1885, and then jumped to about 700,000 in 1886.

**The Knights of Labor collapses.** The peak year for the Knights of Labor was 1886. After that year the union steadily lost power until it collapsed seven years later. Two causes of the Knights' decline were loss of public support and the organization of competing labor unions.

In 1886 the Knights held a rally in Chicago's Haymarket Square to show support for the workers' demand for an eight-hour day. When the police arrived to break up the rally, someone threw a bomb that killed seven police officers and injured dozens of people. No one could discover who threw the bomb, but the violence was blamed on the Knights of Labor. Public opinion, which had supported the Knights against the railroads, turned against the union.

In the same year, locals of the Knights of Labor also called several strikes that did not have the support of the national union. These strikes often ended in violence. Many skilled workers, upset at the violence, withdrew from the Knights to start their own separate unions.

**The American Federation of Labor is organized.** Samuel Gompers, of Dutch-Jewish background, came as a young boy to

New York where he took a job as a cigar maker. Gompers became an enthusiastic supporter of the Cigar Makers Union. This was a **trade union** —a union of skilled workers in a single craft. Gompers realized that the Cigar Makers Union would be in a much stronger bargaining position if it had ties with other trade unions. In 1881, with Gompers's help, several unions organized themselves into a **federation** —an organization made up of separate groups. The federation included different unions representing printers, glassworkers, iron and steelworkers, and cigar makers.

When skilled workers left the Knights of Labor in 1886, many of them became members of the new federation, now named the **American Federation of Labor** (AFL). Before long, the AFL replaced the Knights of Labor as the largest union organization in the United States. Samuel Gompers became its first president. Except for one year, Gompers continued to hold that position until his death in 1924.

**Conditions improve under the American Federation of Labor.** The AFL fought to achieve better wages and better working conditions for skilled workers. Among its goals were an eight-hour day, a six-day week, and an end to child labor. Although the AFL called strikes when necessary, it also used **collective bargaining** —talks held between an employer and a labor union to settle disputes. As the American Federation

Union leaders held outdoor rallies to gain public support. As the unions gained strength, workers gradually won improvements in hours, wages, benefits, and job safety.

of Labor gained strength, the wages of skilled workers increased to more than double those of unskilled workers. Unskilled workers did not have a union of their own until the 1930's.

**The states pass labor laws.** Responding to the demands of labor, the states began to pass laws that would protect workers. These state laws included limits for the number of hours a child could work and provided for healthier and safer working conditions. Other new labor laws required an employer to pay a worker for injuries that were suffered on the job. The Massachusetts legislature passed a minimum wage law in 1912, and other state legislatures soon followed its lead.

# 4 How did industrialization affect the economy?

## Vocabulary
depression
business cycle
trust

With the development of new products, industrialization made life better and easier for millions of people. Industrialization also created economic problems for Americans. The nation had periods of high unemployment, and powerful monopolies controlled prices and limited people's choices.

## Economic Problems

One of the worst problems of industrialization was unemployment. On two occasions during the late 1800's, severe unemployment affected the whole country.

**Economic growth is followed by a downturn.** In the late 1860's the American economy grew rapidly. Existing businesses expanded their operations, and many new businesses and industries began. These new businesses hired new workers, bought new machinery, and built new factories. The money to pay for this growth was often borrowed from banks or raised by selling new stock. Company managers decided to borrow in order to expand because they believed customers would keep buying their products. Confidence in the economy was high, and businesses prospered. Such a period of rapid economic growth is called a **boom.**

In 1873, however, a panic began. Companies had produced too many goods. Unable to sell their products, they could not pay their debts or give dividends to stockholders. To reduce costs, the factories let some workers go, lowered wages for others, and slowed down production. Lenders and stockholders started to panic when this happened, fearing that they would lose their investment. Lenders demanded their money back, and stockholders sold their shares. Companies that could not pay their bills had to sell out or close down. Workers at these companies lost their jobs.

## ECONOMICS • The Business Cycle

The United States has had a remarkably prosperous history. Yet the country has also been through lean times. During the panics of 1873 and 1893, for example, many people lost their jobs and their savings. Each time, however, the economy recovered and new business booms began.

Economists keep a close watch on the business cycle by plotting its ups and downs on a graph. Several **indicators,** or signs, help economists judge the health of the economy. When the economy is strong, people buy and sell goods in great volume. Production rates are high, and few people are out of work. On the other hand, when the economy is in a downturn, commerce slows, production drops, and unemployment rises.

During the 1800's and early 1900's, the business cycle swung wildly up and down. Today, the swings are less dramatic because the government encourages economic stability.

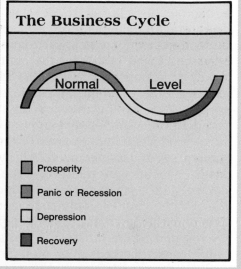

Business cycle

**The economy slows down.** Following the Panic of 1873, the American economy entered a **depression** —a period of economic decline. The depression following the Panic of 1873 lasted until 1878. During these years, many workers were unemployed.

Even before industrialization, the American economy experienced booms and depressions. In earlier times, however, depressions had less impact on the country. Farmers took care of basic needs even when the nation's business was poor. With industrialization, however, an increasing number of people depended on wages for food and rent. Wage earners who lost their jobs had no way to provide for their families.

In the 1880's the economy entered another period of growth and confidence. This boom led to the Panic of 1893. The depression following the Panic of 1893 lasted until 1896. Unemployment at this time was severe. In 1894, for example, 18 percent of American workers were unemployed. In 1892, only 3 percent had been out of work.

This repeated pattern of booms and depressions may be called a **business cycle.** As the United States became more industrialized, more Americans became victims of changes in the economy.

## Monopolies and Trusts

Those corporations that survived depressions often had large reserves of capital. Using this capital, they bought out their competition. Finally, as in the case of Standard Oil, many large firms became monopolies.

At the end of the nineteenth century, business leaders developed another way to create monopolies. They formed **trusts** — groups of people who controlled the stock in the major corporations in one industry. By controlling many corporations in one industry, trusts could control prices and policies in the whole industry. By 1900, powerful trusts held monopolies of the nation's largest industries—steel, oil, tobacco, flour, sugar, and meat packing.

**499**

**Monopolies have benefits and drawbacks.** Monopolies and trusts are usually huge organizations. Their size gives them certain advantages. They can afford to buy raw materials in huge quantities and modern and expensive machinery. They can hire scientists and engineers to develop products and to make factories more efficient. These advantages may mean lower manufacturing costs and lower prices for the public.

A large monopoly can, on the other hand, create serious problems. It can force smaller companies out of business. With little or no competition, a monopoly can raise the price of its products without fear of losing its customers. A monopoly may hold back new ideas or technology that might challenge its control. In a free-enterprise economy, like the United States, only fair competition keeps prices down and gives people choice. By the end of the nineteenth century many Americans realized that monopolies and trusts prevented fair competition and forced prices up. People clamored for monopolies to be controlled or broken up.

**The government regulates some monopolies.** The government recognized that some monopolies were useful. Railroad service, for example, is more efficient if it is provided by a single large company rather than by a number of smaller, competing companies. Instead of forbidding the monopolies in such cases, Congress decided that it would regulate them. In 1887, Congress passed the **Interstate Commerce Act** controlling the rates that railroads could charge when hauling freight between states. Later, Congress also passed laws regulating electric, telegraph, and telephone companies. In such cases, monopolies had to give good service at fair rates to the public.

**Harmful monopolies prove difficult to outlaw.** The public began to demand that trusts be prevented from setting up harmful monopolies. Senator John Sherman of Ohio proposed a law making it illegal for big businesses to form monopolies. In 1890 Congress passed the **Sherman Antitrust Act.** This law stated that no trust should be in control of the production or sale of oil, steel,

This 1889 political cartoon criticizes Congress for failing to control the growing power of monopolies and trusts. Why are the figures representing the trusts and monopolies larger than the members of Congress?

sugar, beef, or other products, in more than one state.

The Sherman Act, however, was hard to enforce. The federal government attempted to break up monopolies by taking them to court. The law was not strong enough, however, and court decisions usually went against the government.

As the twentieth century began, the United States had become one of the world's great industial nations. Monopolies and bold business leadership had helped make the nation's industrial growth possible. At the same time, industrial growth had caused serious economic problems. Americans had taken some steps toward solving those problems. Attempts had been made to regulate big business, and the working conditions of many men and women had been improved.

Yet much remained to be done. In the years to come, reformers would still look for a better life for all Americans.

## SECTION REVIEW

1. **Vocabulary**  depression, business cycle, trust
2. **People and Places**  John Sherman
3. **Comprehension**  How does a depression cause unemployment?
4. **Comprehension**  What steps did the United States Congress take to control or break up monopolies?
5. **Critical Thinking**  How did industrialization encourage the growth of trusts and monopolies?

# Chapter 21 Summary

Between the Civil War and the first years of the twentieth century, industrialization brought far-reaching changes to American life. Several factors caused the United States to become a leading industrial nation. Among these factors were rich reserves of natural resources, a plentiful supply of willing workers, and a tradition of inventiveness and free enterprise. In addition, advances in transportation and communication, the development of mass production, and new methods of merchandising goods also aided industrialization.

Inventive and forceful individuals were especially important to the growth of American industry. People such as Thomas Edison, Alexander Graham Bell, and Henry Ford developed new products or new ways of manufacture. James J. Hill, Andrew Carnegie, J. P. Morgan, and John D. Rockefeller were among those responsible for the organization and consolidation of large nationwide corporations.

Millions of workers also made industrialization possible in the United States. So

many immigrants were willing to work that wages remained low, particularly for unskilled workers. Workers, including children, labored and lived in unsafe and unhealthy environments. To better their lot, workers began to organize into labor unions. Terence Powderly led the Knights of Labor, a union open to all workers. This union, however, fell apart after 1886. About the same time Samuel Gompers took over leadership of the successful American Federation of Labor, a union of skilled workers.

Industrialization raised the standard of living for most Americans, but it also resulted in greater economic insecurity. Economic depressions resulted in business bankruptcies, in factory close-downs, and in unemployment.

By the end of the nineteenth century trusts controlled most big industries. To regulate monopolies that were in the public interest, such as railroads, Congress passed the Interstate Commerce Act. To break up monopolies and trusts, Congress passed the Sherman Antitrust Act.

# Chapter 21 REVIEW

## Vocabulary and Key Terms

Choose the italicized term in parentheses that best completes each sentence. Write your answers on a separate sheet of paper.

1. The money raised to start or operate a business is called (*dividends/capital*).
2. The economic system based on private ownership of businesses operated for profit is called (*merchandising/free enterprise*)
3. People who start businesses are (*entrepreneurs/industrialists*).
4. Henry Ford developed (*standardized parts/the assembly line*).
5. A union of organizations is (*a federation/collective bargaining*).
6. (*Trusts/Depressions*) usually cause high unemployment.
7. A period of rapid economic growth is a (*boom/depression*).

## Recalling the Facts

1. What mineral resources became important in the nineteenth century?
2. What was a major reason for the rapid increase in the population following the Civil War?
3. What advantages does a corporation have over other forms of business?
4. Why did advances in communication and transportation encourage the growth of industry?
5. How did John D. Rockefeller gain control of the oil business?
6. Why were workers' wages particularly low in the United States during the nineteenth century?
7. What were the goals of the American Federation of Labor?
8. What serious problems can result from a monopoly?
9. What was the purpose of the Interstate Commerce Act?

## Places to Locate

Match the letters on the map with the cities listed below. Write your answers on a separate sheet of paper.

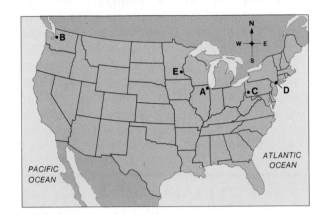

1. St. Paul
2. Chicago
3. New York City
4. Pittsburgh
5. Seattle

## Critical Thinking

1. In the late 1800's the United States became one of the world's leading industrial nations. How did this happen? What factors gave the United States an advantage over many other countries? Consider these points in your answer:
   a. human and natural resources
   b. business practices and technology
   c. the American economic system
2. Industrialization brought many social and economic changes. How were working people affected? Was life for workers better or worse than before? Address these questions in your answer:
   a. How did the worker's role in production change?
   b. What were working and living conditions like?

**c.** How did worker-employer relations change?

**d.** How did economic cycles affect workers?

## Understanding History

1. Reread the section "Thomas Edison illustrates the American inventive spirit" on page 484. Then answer these questions.
   **a. Science and Technology.** How do scientists differ from inventors?
   **b. Science and Technology.** How can inventions create industries?
2. Reread the section "Economic rights aid the growth of industry" on page 484. Then answer these questions.
   **a. Citizenship.** What rights do people have in a free-enterprise system?
   **b. Economics.** Is it likely that the owners of a corporation also share in its management? Explain your answer.
3. Reread the section "Urban workers live in overcrowded, unhealthy conditions" on page 494. Then answer these questions.
   **a. Culture.** How did industrialization affect workers' living conditions?
   **b. Primary Sources.** What charges does Samuel Gompers make against stockholders? Against employers?
4. Reread the section "Harmful monopolies prove difficult to outlaw" on page 500. Then answer these questions.
   **a. Economics.** What was the purpose of the Sherman Antitrust Act?
   **b. Economics.** Why was the government unable to break up monopolies after the passage of the Sherman Antitrust Act?

## Projects and Activities

1. **Reviewing Information.** With flash cards quiz others on the vocabulary words and key terms in this chapter.
2. **Analyzing Political Cartoons.** Study the cartoons on pages 492 and 500. Then write an essay comparing the cartoons. In your essay discuss the point of view of the cartoonists, how they express that view, and the probable effect of the cartoons on public opinion.
3. **Supporting an Argument.** Imagine that you are Samuel Gompers. You wish to get a group of skilled workers to join an AFL union. Prepare an argument of why those workers should join the union, emphasizing their problems and how a union can help them. Present your argument in class.
4. **Making a Poster.** Make a poster that illustrates why the United States became an industrial leader.

## Practicing Your Skill

Use the graph below to answer the questions that follow.

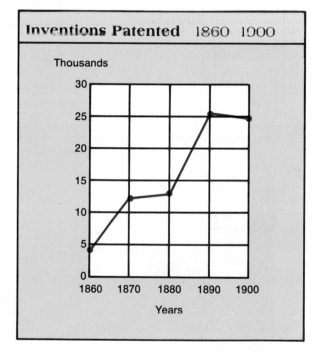

**Inventions Patented** 1860–1900

1. What is the purpose of this graph?
2. About how many patents for inventions were granted in 1870?
3. In what decade did the number of patents almost triple? Almost double?
4. In what decade was there the greatest increase in the total number of patents?
5. Is it accurate to say that the number of inventions grew steadily between 1860 and 1900? Explain your answer.

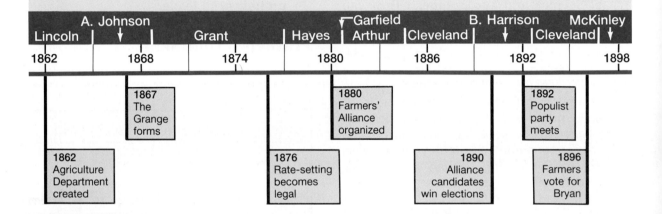

| Lincoln | A. Johnson | Grant | Hayes | Garfield / Arthur | Cleveland | B. Harrison | Cleveland | McKinley |
|---|---|---|---|---|---|---|---|---|
| 1862 | 1868 | 1874 | 1880 | | 1886 | 1892 | | 1898 |

**1862** Agriculture Department created

**1867** The Grange forms

**1876** Rate-setting becomes legal

**1880** Farmers' Alliance organized

**1890** Alliance candidates win elections

**1892** Populist party meets

**1896** Farmers vote for Bryan

New machines such as this harvester helped cause great changes in the lives of most American farmers during the late 1800's.

MANUFACTURED BY THE
FREMONT HARVESTER CO.
FREMONT, OHIO.

## Preparing to Read

During the nineteenth century, farming in the United States underwent many changes. New ideas, advances in technology, and more western farmland led to higher agricultural production than at any time before. This production made industrialization possible because fewer people could produce food for many. Changes in farming also changed life on many American farms. Several of these changes helped the farmers. Other changes caused problems, and farmers throughout the country joined together to try to find solutions. As you read this chapter, try to answer the following questions:

1. What forces changed farm production?
2. What problems did changes in farming bring?
3. How did farmers try to overcome their problems?

# 1 What forces changed farm production?

### Vocabulary
sheaves
thresher
combine
divert
groundwater

At the beginning of the nineteenth century, most American farms were small, family-run farms. The exceptions were the large southern plantations that depended on slave labor to grow cotton and other crops.

A farm was not a means of *earning a living* in the present-day sense. Instead, the farm *provided a living*. Farm families raised most of their own food, as well as most of the materials from which they made their clothes. They sold a few hogs and cattle and some wheat or corn or oats. With the little cash they received, they bought the things they could not raise or make at home.

## Changes in Farm Technology

In the early 1800's farmers used simple, handmade tools. These included a wooden plow to turn the soil and a scythe to cut hay or grain. For plowing and hauling, farmers primarily used oxen. During the next century one change after another occurred on the American farm. A farmer's most important tools came to be machinery—machinery that had been made possible by the industrialization of the United States.

**New inventions change farming methods.** The first farming tool to undergo rapid change was the plow. The colonial plow was a wooden plow in the shape of a *V*. It was so heavy that as many as a dozen oxen were required to pull it. In the 1810's, however, a better, lighter plow was developed. This was an iron plow that had been designed by Thomas Jefferson. The plow worked well in sandy, eastern soil, but not in the heavy soil of the Midwest. In 1837 an Illinois blacksmith named John Deere produced the first steel plow. It sliced through heavy soil more easily than existing plows and therefore took less animal power to pull.

Other inventions of the 1830's were also important in making farm work easier and faster. A Virginia farmer named Cyrus McCormick patented a successful horse-drawn grain reaper. The reaper swept the grain stalks against a cutter and then dropped

Before the invention of harvesting machines, grain had to be cut, raked, and bundled by hand. The development of machinery enabled farmers to plant and harvest many more acres of crops.

them in **sheaves** —bundles of grain stalks. With a reaper, farmers were able to cut as much wheat in one day as they could in two weeks with a scythe. The next step in harvesting was to separate the grain from the husks. This was made easier by another 1830's invention, the **thresher** .

John Deere and Cyrus McCormick both became industrialists. Their farm-equipment factories in the Midwest turned out a steady supply of machines that helped revolutionize farm methods.

**More advances in farm machinery take place after 1865.** After the Civil War, far-reaching improvements in farm tools and machinery continued to change farming. In 1869 James Oliver perfected a method of casting steel plows. Oliver's plows were stronger and tougher than earlier steel plows. Other farm machines called planters were developed. They could cut furrows into the earth, break up the dirt clods, and then plant the grain in several different rows at one time. Other machines called seeders could plant the seed, cover it with soil, and spread fertilizer on the soil.

Even more striking changes took place in reapers. In the 1860's reapers were developed that not only cut the wheat but also tied it into sheaves without the farmers' help.

Finally, **combines** —huge machines that both cut and threshed wheat—made it possible to harvest tons of wheat quickly and easily. In 1830 it took three hours of labor to produce a bushel of wheat. By 1896 that time had dropped to one-half hour.

**The sources of power change.** Many of the new machines were lighter and better designed. They could be pulled easily by horses. In the second half of the nineteenth century, horses replaced oxen on American farms. Between 1865 and 1900 the number of horses more than doubled.

Steam-powered tractors had also been invented, but they were so heavy that their use was limited. The invention of the gasoline-powered tractor in 1892 gave farmers another source of power. Tractors, powered first by gasoline and later by diesel fuel, pulled the plows, seeders, and combines. By 1920 tractors were replacing horses on most farms. Barns quickly became places to store farming equipment as well as to house animals and livestock.

## Changes in Farming Practices

Because the new farm machines made it possible for farmers to do their work faster and more efficiently, farm production rose.

Increased farm production, however, brought changes in the way American farmers lived.

**Agricultural science improves farming.** In 1862, Congress passed the Morrill Act to encourage agricultural and mechanical science. The act provided that federal land grants be given to each state. The states were to sell the land and then use the money to build colleges. The colleges were to teach, among other things, agricultural and mechanical sciences. Those who attended these land-grant colleges learned about scientific ways of farming. The colleges also researched and promoted new methods of preserving food.

The United States Department of Agriculture, set up in 1862, dealt with farming issues throughout the nation. With the support of the Department of Agriculture, scientists found new ways to improve soil and fight damage to crops by insects and diseases. Scientists improved agriculture in other ways, too. They found more uses for

**The combine cut and threshed grain. Farm hands bundled the sheaves into bales. The first combines were heavy—requiring as many as 30 horses to move them. Later, harvesting machines became lighter and more efficient.**

certain crops. They improved farming methods, and they developed hardier kinds of seed and livestock.

**Farmers turn to cash crops.** With the advances in farm technology, a farm family was able to plant and harvest larger amounts of land. Large farms also became more economical than small ones. Few farmers could afford to buy machines and let them stand idle. They had to keep the machines in use so that they could earn cash to pay for the machines. As a result, farmers devoted their land and time to cash crops rather than crops for their own use. Farm families also needed cash to buy the manufactured goods that were being produced in American factories.

Farmers began to specialize in the cash crops and livestock best suited to where they lived. For example, the climate and soil in the Midwest is ideal for growing corn.

Therefore, many farmers in the Midwest chose corn as a cash crop. Thus, farming became more a means of earning a living rather than a way to provide directly for the farm family's needs. In time, farming became a business, and farmers became business managers. They depended on profits to earn their livings.

## Farming in the West

New farm machines made possible the development of lands that before were impossible to farm. In the semiarid and dry climates of the Great Plains, farmers also found new ways to cope with the lack of rain.

**Farmers begin to irrigate.** Irrigation was used in areas that had too little moisture. Irrigation was not new. For centuries, the Indians in Arizona and New Mexico had

## Graph Study

The dollar value of American farm products has risen steadily. How much were farm products worth in 1880? In 1920?

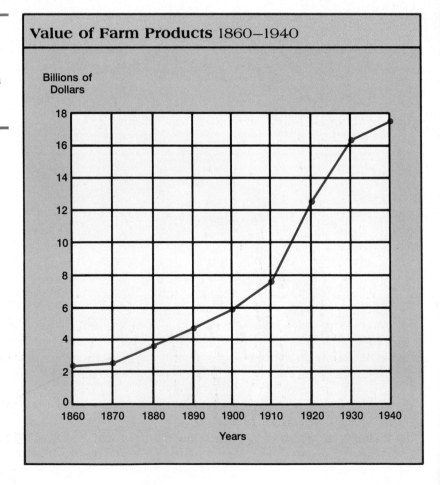

**Value of Farm Products** 1860–1940

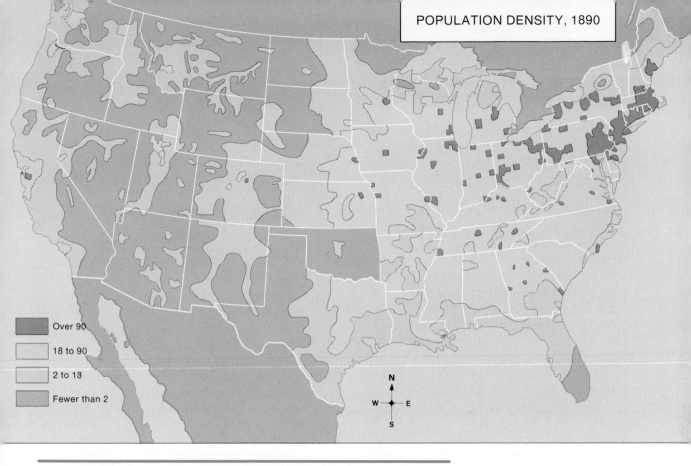

## Map Study

**By 1890 the population density in western farming regions had increased greatly. Which region of the United States—eastern or western—had the greater population density?**

successfully irrigated dry lands. The **Mormon** settlers in Utah also practiced irrigation. The Mormons belonged to the Church of Jesus Christ of Latter-day Saints. In 1847, under the leadership of Brigham Young, Mormons had begun settlements in the valley of Utah's Great Salt Lake.

Methods of irrigation were most successful when a flowing stream or river could be **diverted** — turned aside. The Mormons diverted water from mountain streams.

In parts of the West, irrigation did not begin until the middle of this century. The development of hydroelectric projects created vast reservoirs of water that could be diverted to fields far away. The invention of irrigation systems resulted in the large-scale

pumping of **groundwater** —the water under the earth's surface—for irrigation.

**Western farmers learn new ways to grow new crops.** Another way farmers adapted to western conditions was to change what they grew and how they grew it. Department of Agriculture scientists became explorers. They searched for plants that grew well in other semiarid parts of the world. From Russia, China, and Turkey they brought back varieties of wheat, alfalfa, and clover. These imports grew well on the Great Plains. They helped make the region into one of the most productive farming areas in the world.

Farming practices that were suitable to moisture-rich areas did not work where

## ★ ★ ★ *Farming Methods*

In the 1800's American scientists looked for new ways to grow crops in soil that contained little water. Their work helped to make the Great Plains one of the world's greatest farming areas.

Today scientists are studying ways to grow crops in water without soil. This technique is called **hydroponics** (hy-druh-PAHN-iks). Plants are held in place in shallow pans or troughs filled with water. The roots of the plants spread out in the pan and absorb needed food from chemicals mixed in the water.

Today farmers use hydroponics in areas where the soil is poor or where it harbors plant diseases. Scientists believe that in the future, hydroponics may also be used to grow food in outer space.

moisture was scarce. Successful farmers took care to preserve the moisture in the soil. After decades of experimenting, western farmers learned that it was best not to plow their fields. Instead, they sliced under the surface so as not to turn the soil.

## SECTION REVIEW

1. **Vocabulary**   sheaves, thresher, combine, divert, groundwater
2. **People and Places**   John Deere, Cyrus McCormick, James Oliver, Arizona, New Mexico, Mormons, Utah
3. **Comprehension**   How did new inventions result in greater farm production?
4. **Comprehension**   How did the lives of farmers change as they began to grow cash crops?
5. **Critical Thinking**   Do you think the changes brought by industrialization were good for farmers?  Why or why not?

# 2 What problems did changes in farming bring?

## Vocabulary

supply and demand        conservation
erosion                  nutrient

Farmers must struggle against forces that they cannot control, such as too much or too little rain. Their crops may be destroyed by frost, hail, dust storms, or insects. In the 1800's, farmers had to fight economic forces, too.

## Low Prices and Rising Costs

Low prices for farm goods caused great difficulties for farmers in the late 1800's. Farmers in earlier years provided for most of

their needs. They had not been greatly troubled by changes in prices for their products. Industrialized farmers, however, depended on cash crops. If the price of those crops was high, the farmers received a good income. If the price was low, the farmers' incomes fell. Yet farmers could not control the prices their crops could bring. Prices rose and fell according to the rule of **supply and demand**. The rule of supply and demand says that when the demand is great for something that is in short supply, prices are high. When the supply becomes greater, however, prices go down. For example, when fresh strawberries first appear in summer, the price is high because they are scarce and people want them. As the berries become plentiful, the price drops.

## GEOGRAPHY • Saving Open Lands

During America's early years, pioneers and settlers used the land and what they found on it as they saw fit. They cleared and burned forests. They mined coal, gold, and other resources wherever they found them. Meanwhile, the federal government sold or gave away thousands of acres of public lands.

During the nineteenth century, some people realized that government action was needed to conserve, or save, public lands. A leader of these conservationists was Gifford Pinchot (PIN-sho). Pinchot had studied forestry in Europe. He was aware that the loss of forested land could lead to floods, the washing away of soil, and the loss of fish and game. Pinchot strongly urged the United States government to take the lead in saving open lands.

In 1898 Pinchot became the head of the federal government's Division of Forestry. Pinchot persuaded the government to set aside millions of acres of public lands. Many large areas of scenic beauty became part of the new National Park System. Today millions of American and foreign visitors travel to these national parks to enjoy the breathtaking beauty of unspoiled wilderness.

An unspoiled wilderness area

**Farmers receive lower prices for their crops.** Because farmers were producing huge crops of wheat, oats, barley, corn, and cotton, the price of these products went down. For example, between 1867 and 1887 the price of a bushel of wheat fell from 2 dollars to 68 cents. Because more and more farmers were depending on cash crops, lower prices caused hardship.

**Farmers take on large debts.** Most farmers borrowed money in order to purchase land or buy new farm equipment. Farmers could repay their debts as long as crop prices were high. When prices for farm products began to fall, however, many farmers could not meet the payments on their debts. These farmers were then in danger of losing their machinery and their farms.

**Transportation costs rise.** Transportation was another cost over which farmers had little control. Most farmers depended almost entirely on the railroads to carry their crops to market. Whatever the railroads charged for this service, farmers had to pay. Farmers, particularly in the West, believed that the railroads charged higher freight rates than were necessary. Many farmers had to sell their crops at low prices and still pay high shipping costs. They found they had little or nothing to show for their year's labor. Resentment against the railroads began to grow.

George Washington Carver developed new products from peanuts, sweet potatoes, and pecans. Carver's discoveries helped southern farmers make their farms profitable.

## The Effects of Overproduction

Faced with low crop prices and rising costs, American farmers reacted by producing even more. This overproduction made problems even worse.

**Overproduction causes prices to fall further.** As farmers faced dropping farm prices and increasing debts, many concluded that they must produce even more crops to make ends meet. They reasoned that increased production would make up for the lowered prices of farm products. As farmers increased production, however, the supply of farm goods increased, and prices dropped even lower.

**Intense production ruins the soil.** The larger crops also wore out the soil. In their push to produce more and more crops, farmers cut down more trees and plowed up their grasslands. Thus exposed to rain and wind, the soil often washed or blew away. This wearing away of the soil is called **erosion**. Millions of acres of topsoil were destroyed by erosion before farmers began to practice methods of soil **conservation**—protection of a resource.

Soil also became ruined because its fertility was lost. When farmers planted the same soil over and over again with the same crop, the important **nutrients** (NOO-tree-uhnts) in the soil were exhausted or used up. Nutrients are those essential ingredients in the soil that provide the food that is necessary to nourish growing plants. If farmers failed to add fertilizer to their soil or to take care of it in other ways, the soil would eventually begin to wear out. Then the soil would not be capable of growing crops anymore. This is what happened in the American South where successive plantings of corn, cotton, and tobacco led to the wearing out of the soil so that no crops at all could be grown.

George Washington Carver was a black scientist who taught agriculture at Tuskegee Institute, a well-known black college in Alabama. Carver was responsible for helping southern farmers reclaim their lost farmland. Carver discovered that farmers could give new life to worn-out soil by growing peanuts and sweet potatoes. In addition, Carver found many uses for peanuts and sweet potatoes, which became important cash crops for southern farmers.

## SECTION REVIEW

1. **Vocabulary**   supply and demand, erosion, conservation, nutrient
2. **People and Places**   George Washington Carver, Tuskegee Institute
3. **Comprehension**   Why, when crop prices fell, were farmers unable to solve the problem by growing more?
4. **Comprehension**   What effects did overproduction have on the soil?
5. **Critical Thinking**   How might farmers have solved the problems of high costs and low prices?

# MAPS AND GRAPHS: Analyzing Trends

In this chapter you read that American farmers in the 1800's were raising cash crops instead of food that would be used directly by the farmer's family. This change did not happen all at once. Instead, it happened slowly as more farmers began to plant more cash crops. In time, farming as a way of life became more like a business. Such a change that happens gradually over a long period is called a **trend.**

Understanding trends is important in studying history. If you understand how people's lives were changing during a particular period, you will be better able to understand specific events of the time. For example, knowing that farmers were raising more cash crops can help you understand why farmers began trying to control the rates charged by railroads for shipping crops.

Trends can often be shown graphically. The line graphs below show trends in agricultural production and farm prices in the

second half of the 1800's. Study these graphs and then analyze the trends by answering the following questions.

1. What information does each graph show? What time period do both graphs cover?
2. About how many bushels of wheat and oats were produced in 1885?
3. What general trend does Graph A show for agricultural production? What general trend is shown by Graph B for agricultural prices?
4. During which five-year period did wheat prices and production change most?
5. From the information given in the graphs, what can you conclude about the relationship between crop production and crop prices in the late 1800's?
6. Based on the trends shown in the two graphs, why did farmers in the late 1800's try to boost crop prices?

Graph A

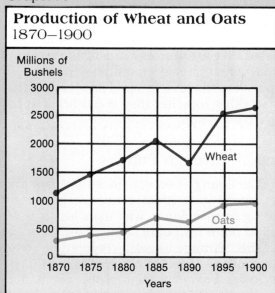

Graph B

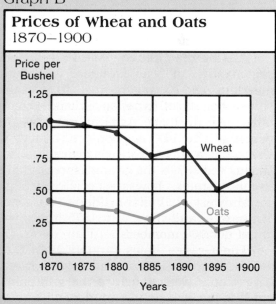

# 3 How did farmers try to overcome their problems?

In the last decades of the nineteenth century, thousands of farmers faced falling crop prices, high shipping costs, and increasing debts. Their common problems led farmers to organize to bring about change.

## The Grange Movement

American farmers realized that the problems they faced were too big for individual farmers to solve by themselves. As a result, farmers joined together to seek solutions to their troubles.

**The Grange unites farmers.** One man who believed that farmers should work together to solve their common problems was Oliver H. Kelley. In 1867 Kelley founded an organization known as the National Grange of the Patrons of Husbandry, commonly called the **Grange.**

At first the Grange was mostly a social organization of farm families. At monthly meetings the Grangers met to socialize, share their farm experiences, and listen to talks on agriculture. As farm problems grew worse in the 1870's, people turned to the Grange as a way to express their discontent. During the 1870's the Grange spread rapidly to many states. It was especially strong in the Midwest—in Indiana, Illinois, Wisconsin, Minnesota, and Iowa. By 1875, there were about 800,000 members.

**The Grange helps farmers help themselves.** As the Grange grew more powerful, it developed ways to help farmers. It pointed out that farmers should not depend on a single cash crop. The Grange particularly encouraged farmers to work as a group to meet some of their economic problems. It showed them that better prices could be obtained by marketing their crops in groups rather than as individuals. The Grange explained that farmers, as a united force, could better fight the high freight rates charged by the railroads. The Grange also pointed out that, as a group, farmers could demand lower interest rates from the banks on loans for farms and farm machinery.

One way for farmers to work together was through a **cooperative** —an association that buys and sells products for its members. Cooperatives had more power than individual members to get higher prices for crops. A farmers' cooperative could also buy large quantities of farm goods from manufacturers and then sell the goods directly to farmers. Through cooperatives farmers saved one third to one half the price on such goods as reapers, wagons, and sewing machines.

Farmers' cooperatives then expanded into other farm-related businesses. They built grain elevators, flour mills, and packing plants. They started banks, insurance companies, and even factories. Many of these cooperative businesses lacked good business management, however, and they went bankrupt. Nevertheless, farmers had learned that by working together they could bring about effective change.

## Action Through Politics

The Grange had convinced farmers that they could gain great economic power by uniting in groups. It was then just a short step to unite for political purposes.

**The Grange seeks regulation over monopolies.** The Grange had helped farmers lower some of their costs, but it also aimed to control the causes of high costs. It especially wanted regulation of the monopolies. The two monopolies that most affected

This 1870's Grange poster promotes the virtues of farm life. What words on the poster point out the country's dependence on farmers?

Grain had to be shipped by rail and stored in grain elevators—
mechanical silos. This picture shows the platforms that raised or
lowered grain inside the silos. Railroad and grain elevator
monopolies often hurt farmers by charging high rates.

farmers were the grain elevators and the railroads. Farmers depended on these monopolies for storage and shipment of their crops. If the monopolies could be forced to lower their prices, almost all farmers would benefit. Through the Grange, farmers helped elect governors and members of state legislatures who were sympathetic to their views. As a result, the legislatures of several states passed laws that regulated the rates charged by railroads and grain elevators. Such rate-setting laws were often called Granger laws.

The railroads and grain elevators resisted the new laws. In some cases the railroads responded by providing poor service. The railroads and grain elevators went to court saying that the laws were illegal. They said that rate-setting denied them their constitutional right to private property. In 1876 the Supreme Court decided the issue in the case of *Munn* v. *Illinois*. The Court disagreed with the monopolies. Private property, the Court said, was not completely private if it affected the public interest. Rate-setting by the states was legal.

**The federal government regulates railroads.** Most of the railroads, however, ran through more than one state. That made it difficult for any single state to regulate the cost of shipping goods by rail. It became increasingly clear that the railroads could be effectively regulated only by the federal government. After a congressional committee had investigated and found many examples of abuse by the railroads, Congress acted. In 1887 it passed the Interstate Commerce Act to regulate railroads operating in more than one state. The act established the Interstate Commerce Commission—a special committee of five members. The Commission was responsible for seeing that railroads obeyed the new law.

**Farmers organize into alliances.** In the 1870's the Grange was the most powerful farmers' group. By the 1880's a new group, the **Farmers' Alliance,** had become the most important farmers' organization. The Farmers' Alliance was actually several alliances of farmers in different parts of the country. The primary purpose of these alliances was to rouse the political power of farmers. Western farmers in particular continued to face the combination of low prices and crushing debts. They wanted the federal government to take action to solve their problems. They called for an income tax, government ownership of railroads, and a change in the government's money policy.

The government's money policy was based on the **gold standard**. The gold standard stated that every paper dollar was worth a specific amount of gold and could be exchanged for gold. That meant that the amount of money in circulation was tied directly to the amount of gold held by the government. The government could not print more money than the amount of gold it held. The nation's economy, however, was expanding faster than the nation's gold supply. As a result, there were fewer dollars to go around. The fewer the dollars, the more valuable they became. As the dollar rose in value, it could buy more wheat, corn, or bacon. That meant that farmers received less for their products. Farmers hoped that if there were more money in circulation, prices would rise, and they could pay their debts more easily.

As the 1890 elections drew near, farm families turned their cause into a crusade. The Farmers' Alliance supported candidates who backed the farmers' causes. Alliance-backed candidates made fiery speeches attacking the railroads, monopolies, banks, and the gold standard. Their enthusiasm and

organization paid off. In the election, Alliance-supported candidates won 55 congressional seats and 6 governorships. Alliance candidates took control of 12 state legislatures as well.

**The People's party is organized.** From the success of the Farmers' Alliance a new political party—the People's party—was born. Those who belonged to the People's party were called **Populists.** The People's party held its first national convention in Omaha, Nebraska, on Independence Day, 1892, to nominate a presidential candidate. The members listened to the stirring words of a Minnesota Populist, Ignatius Donnelly. The intention of the People's party, he said, was to "restore the government of the Republic to the hands of the 'plain people.'"

The party's platform called for government ownership of railroads and telegraph and telephone companies. The Populists also demanded more money in circulation, unlimited coinage of silver, and a Federal

The People's party attracted support from many groups. How does the cartoon show that the Populists represented many interests?

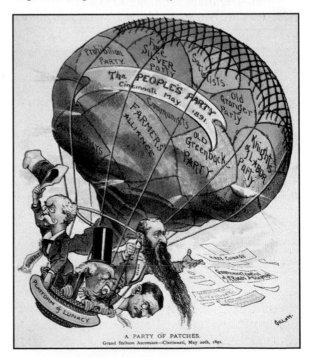

A PARTY OF PATCHES.
Grand Balloon Ascension—Cincinnati, May 20th, 1891.

income tax. Other changes called for by the Populists included rural mail delivery, the direct election of United States senators, and the **secret ballot.** A secret ballot is a vote that is cast privately.

The People's party chose former Union General James B. Weaver of Iowa as their candidate for President. Populists such as Mary Elizabeth Lease of Kansas supported Weaver with spellbinding campaign speeches. Blaming many of the farm problems on eastern bankers and industrialists, she declared: "We want money, land, and transportation.... The people are at bay. Let the bloodhounds of money who have dogged us thus far beware."

Grover Cleveland, a Democrat and former President, was elected President again in 1892, but the Populist party did well. James Weaver received 8 percent of the popular vote—a good showing for a third-party candidate. A number of Populist candidates were also elected to the House of Representatives and to state legislatures.

In 1896, the Populists and the Democrats both nominated William Jennings Bryan for President. Bryan, a great orator, was a defender of farmers' interests.

**Farmers look to William Jennings Bryan for leadership.** In the 1896 election, farmers rallied behind William Jennings Bryan from Nebraska. For four years Bryan had served in the House of Representatives, where he had worked for policies that would help farmers. Although Bryan supported many of the Populists' ideas, he was a member of the Democratic party.

At the Democratic National Convention in Chicago in 1896, Bryan made a powerful speech in which he attacked the gold standard. In this speech he also stressed the country's dependence on farmers. A great orator, Bryan, who was just 36 years old, delivered one of the most famous speeches in American history:

> ... You come to tell us that the great cities are in favor of the gold standard; we reply that the great cities rest upon our broad and fertile prairies. Burn down your cities and leave our farms, and your cities will spring up again as if by magic; but destroy our farms and the grass will grow in the streets of every city in the country....
> ... You shall not press down upon the brow of labor this crown of thorns, you shall not crucify mankind upon a cross of gold.

When Bryan finished this speech, there was a moment of silence at first. And then, in Bryan's own words, "bedlam broke loose." The delegates shouted and clapped for almost an hour. The next day the Democratic party nominated Bryan to be its candidate for President.

Bryan's nomination by the Democrats surprised the Populists and caught them off guard. The Democrats had absorbed part of their platform and had nominated a Populist sympathizer for President. At their national nominating convention the Populists decided that they, too, would nominate Bryan as their presidential candidate.

**Bryan loses to William McKinley.** Bryan campaigned throughout the country on the issue of **free silver** —the unlimited coinage of silver. Opposing Bryan was the Republican nominee, William McKinley. In general Bryan spoke for farmers in the South and West. He attracted people who were in debt and people who wanted the federal government to do more to solve their problems. McKinley was supported by those who opposed change and who feared that free silver would bring economic ruin to the nation. McKinley's strength lay primarily in the industrial Northeast.

Bryan was defeated in the election of 1896 by William McKinley. McKinley won the industrial states and such important farming states as Iowa, Illinois, and Minnesota. As the "silver-tongued orator," however, William Jennings Bryan continued to have a strong influence on American politics.

**The People's party disappears.** It was a measure of the success of the People's party that so many of its ideas were adopted by the Democrats. In that success, however, the party itself lost strength and soon disappeared. The nation never adopted free silver, but many Populist proposals did become laws in the twentieth century. These included the secret ballot, the direct election of United States senators, and the income tax. Such laws helped strengthen democracy in the United States.

# Chapter 22 Summary

In the nineteenth century new farm machinery made it possible for farmers to produce more crops with less work. Such machines included steel plows, reapers, threshers, and combines. Scientific advances led to new farming methods. Farm production increased and farmers came to depend on cash crops for their living. Farmers adapted to the dry lands of the West by using irrigation and new crop varieties.

Overproduction caused problems with the rule of supply and demand. The more farmers raised, the less they received. As crop prices fell, costs for farming supplies rose. Many farmers went deeply in debt. High shipping rates charged by railroads added to the farmers' problems. Overproduction also led to soil destruction. Scientists such as George Washington Carver taught farmers how to restore their soil and to practice soil conservation.

To deal with their problems, farmers joined together. In the 1870's the Grange established cooperatives and used political power to get new laws passed. These Granger laws included state regulation of railroads and grain elevators. Later the federal government began to regulate the railroads. In the 1880's the Farmers' Alliance supported candidates for political office. The Populists called for government ownership of railroads, more money in circulation, free silver, and an income tax. In the 1896 election, farmers backed William Jennings Bryan, the Presidential candidate of both the Democratic and Populist parties. Bryan campaigned against the gold standard and for free silver. Bryan lost the election to William McKinley, who had strong support in the East. After the Democratic party adopted much of the Populist platform, the People's party faded.

## Vocabulary and Key Terms

Use the following terms to complete the sentences below. Write your answers on a separate sheet of paper.

combine
cooperatives
erosion
free silver
gold standard

Grange
Populist
supply and demand
thresher

1. The invention of the _____ and the _____ made farming more productive.
2. The rule of _____ helps explain why prices for farm crops stayed low.
3. Overproduction often resulted in _____ of the land.
4. In the 1870's the most important farmers' organization was the _____, which encouraged farmers to form _____.
5. The platform of the _____ party called for government ownership of railroads.
6. Western farmers blamed many of their problems on the _____ and urged a government policy of _____.

## Recalling the Facts

1. Why did farming become more productive in the 1800's?
2. What was the significance of the Morrill Act to farmers?
3. Why did farmers raise cash crops?
4. What economic problems did many farmers face in the late 1800's?
5. What effect did overproduction have on the soil?
6. What were Granger laws?
7. What did the Supreme Court decide in *Munn* v. *Illinois* ?
8. Why did western farmers attack the gold standard?
9. What changes did the Populists demand?
10. What caused the Populist party to fade away after the election of 1896?

## Places to Locate

Match the letters on the map with the places listed below. Write your answers on a separate sheet of paper.

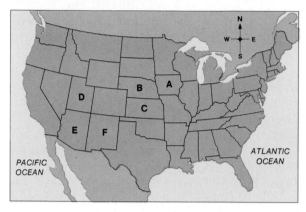

1. Arizona
2. Iowa
3. Nebraska
4. New Mexico
5. Kansas
6. Utah

## Critical Thinking

1. In the late 1800's American farming became a business. What was the effect on farmers and on society? Consider these questions in your answer:
   a. How did farming change during the nineteenth century?
   b. What were the benefits and costs of changes in farm practices?
   c. How and why did farmers work for changes in the society? How successful were they in bringing change?
2. The nineteenth-century American farmer experienced and reacted to industrialization. Explain how this was so. Consider these questions in your answer:
   a. How did industrialization affect farm technology?
   b. How did business affect farmers?
   c. Why would farmers want government ownership of railroads, an income tax, and the secret ballot?

## Understanding History

1. Reread the section "Western farmers learn new ways to grow new crops" on page 509. Then answer these questions.
   a. **Geography.** Why did scientists visit Russia, China, and Turkey?
   b. **Geography.** Why is it important not to plow in a semiarid region?
2. Reread the section "The Grange seeks regulation over monopolies" on page 514. Then answer these questions.
   a. **Citizenship.** What step did farmers in the Grange take to get regulation over monopolies?
   b. **Government.** Why did the railroads and grain elevators appeal the Granger laws to the courts? How did the Supreme Court rule on the issue?
3. Reread the section "Farmers look to William Jennings Bryan for leadership" on page 518. Then answer these questions.
   a. **Primary Sources.** Whom is Bryan addressing as "you"? Who is "we"?
   b. **Economics.** What does Bryan imply about the economic importance of farming to the rest of the nation?

## Projects and Activities

1. **Analyzing a Problem.** Imagine that you and a classmate are farmers in the late 1800's. You want to promote farm issues and the Populist platform in American cities. Devise a strategy for presenting your problems to city dwellers and gaining their support.
2. **Making a Table.** Make a table entitled "Farm Life, 1860–1900." Divide the table into four vertical columns headed "Decade," "Changes in Technology," "Farm Organization or Party," "Important Farm Issues." Enter the appropriate information under each heading. If you wish, add to information in the text with readings from other sources.
3. **Drawing a Cartoon.** Consider the point of view expressed in the political cartoon on page 517. Then imagine that you are a political cartoonist sympathetic to the Populists. Draw a cartoon that expresses part of the Populist platform.

4. **Writing an Essay.** Consider the Grange poster on page 515. Then write an essay that explains what this poster tells about American farm life in the 1870's. In your essay, tell what you learned about Grange values, farm work, and leisure time on a farm.
5. **Writing a Report.** Write a report on one of the following persons: John Deere, Cyrus McCormick, George Washington Carver, James B. Weaver, Mary Elizabeth Lease, William Jennings Bryan. Include what you think the person's most important character trait was and how that character trait affected the person's success.

## Practicing Your Skill

Use the graph to answer the questions that follow.

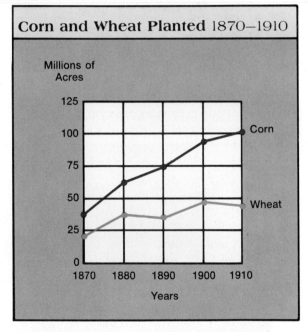

**Corn and Wheat Planted** 1870–1910

1. What is the purpose of this graph?
2. About how many million acres of corn were planted in 1870? In 1880?
3. How does the trend in corn acreage between 1880 and 1890 differ from that of wheat acreage?
4. What differences exist between the trends for wheat and corn acreage?
5. What would you expect the trend lines to show for the year 1920? Explain.

# 23 Urban Growth Brings Social Change
## 1865–1898

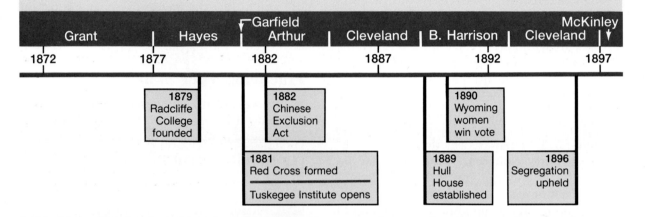

| Grant | Hayes | Garfield Arthur | Cleveland | B. Harrison | McKinley Cleveland |
|---|---|---|---|---|---|
| 1872 | 1877 | 1882 | 1887 | 1892 | 1897 |

**1879** Radcliffe College founded

**1882** Chinese Exclusion Act

**1890** Wyoming women win vote

**1881** Red Cross formed

Tuskegee Institute opens

**1889** Hull House established

**1896** Segregation upheld

**Rapid advances in transportation spurred the growth of cities during the late 1800's, as this painting of New York City shows.**

## Preparing to Read

During the late 1800's millions of new immigrants came to America. Unlike most earlier immigrants, these new citizens settled in the nation's growing cities. Their labor helped industry grow, and their social and religious customs brought new variety to American life. As they adjusted to their new lives, immigrants faced problems of poverty, crowding, and unfair treatment. As they worked to improve their own lives, the new immigrants in the United States transformed and enriched American society. As you read this chapter, try to answer the following questions:

1. Who were the immigrants, and how did they affect American life?
2. How was the United States becoming an urban nation?
3. What opportunities existed for minorities and women?
4. What changes occurred in education, the arts, and leisure?

## 1  Who were the immigrants, and how did they affect American life?

### Vocabulary

| | |
|---|---|
| ghetto | genocide |
| czar | steerage |
| | ethnic |

Between 1870 and 1920 more than 26 million immigrants came to the United States from many different countries. Some came in search of work. Others came to find greater political or religious freedom, or to escape overcrowding or hunger in their native lands. Arriving in the United States, many immigrants did find greater opportunities. At the same time they and their children shaped modern America.

### A Flood of Immigrants

The immigrants who came before the Civil War were primarily from Germany, Great Britain, and Ireland. Until the 1880's most immigrants continued to come from these countries as well as from Scandinavia and France. Immigration before 1880 is often called the Old Immigration. Most of the immigrants before 1880 settled on open land. This was because the land was cheap and available.

**A new wave of immigration begins.** In 1881 another wave of immigration began, bringing millions of newcomers from southern and eastern Europe, particularly Italy, Russia, and Austria-Hungary. This wave is sometimes called the New Immigration. Open land was no longer as cheap. Instead, there was a growing demand for industrial workers. Thus, most European immigrants after 1880 stayed in the cities to work.

**Economic opportunity draws immigrants to America.** Most immigrants hoped to find jobs in the mines, mills, and factories of a booming America. Others saw the United States as a place to practice a trade or profession. Nearly all believed that the move would help their children better themselves through work and education.

Cheap passage to America also encouraged immigration. Before the Civil War most people crossed the Atlantic on sailing ships. After the war, regularly scheduled steamship service was established and grew common.

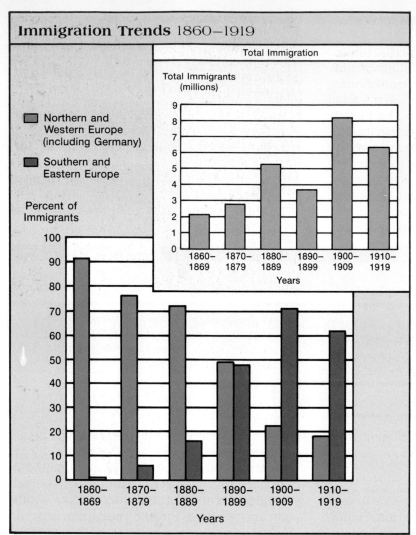

**Immigration Trends** 1860–1919

Northern and Western Europe (including Germany)

Southern and Eastern Europe

Total Immigration

Total Immigrants (millions)

Percent of Immigrants

Years

**Graph Study**

Immigration trends changed after 1880. What percent of immigrants came from southern and eastern Europe between 1870 and 1879? What percent came from southern and eastern Europe between 1900 and 1909?

The steamships offered passage from Europe to America for as little as $25.

**Economic pressures cause many Europeans to leave.** Powerful economic pressures were pushing Europeans away from their homes and villages. Among these pressures was overpopulation. The population of Europe increased by about 50 percent between 1850 and 1900. There was not enough land to support the growing number of European farmers. At the same time, agricultural prices in Europe were falling. Those farmers who had land often were not able to earn enough to live.

**Jews flee religious persecution in Russia.** Many immigrants came to America to escape persecution. Among these were Jews from the Russian Empire. For hundreds of years Jews had lived throughout Europe and the Middle East. They were held together by their shared heritage. At one time most European cities had a **ghetto.** A ghetto was a separate section of a city in which a minority group was forced to live.

In 1881 a new **czar** —king—came to power in Russia and began to persecute the Jews. "Russia for the true Russians" became the slogan of the new government. Ruthless gangs of thugs entered the ghettos to beat up, rob, and sometimes murder Jews. To escape this horrible persecution, Jews fled to America where they could be safe. Between 1880 and 1914 about 3 million Jewish people came to the United States.

**Armenians flee Turkish persecution.** Armenians also came to America because of persecution. The Armenians were a Christian people who lived south of the Black Sea under Turkish rule. In 1894 the Turks began a campaign of **genocide** against the Armenians. Genocide is the deliberate destruction of a racial, cultural, or national group. By 1918 almost 2 million Armenians were killed. Thousands fled to America to escape the massacres.

## Immigrants from Asia and North America

After the Civil War, most immigrants to the United States came from Europe. Thousands more, however, came from Asia and other parts of North America. Like most of the European immigrants, these new Americans were seeking economic opportunity.

**The Chinese labor on the West Coast.** Chinese people first came to California during the gold rush. (See Chapter 16.) Later they continued to seek employment on the West Coast. The Chinese provided most of the labor on western railroads and on projects to drain swamps and build canals.

Most of the Chinese who came to America were men whose families remained in China. The men themselves usually planned to return to China. In 1880 only 5 percent of the Chinese in the United States were women. The Chinese sought to keep their traditional ways. This in turn made Americans suspicious. Hostility to the Chinese increased when labor organizations blamed the Chinese for low wages. Because the Chinese would work for less money than others, it was said, wages remained low for everyone. Some Americans called for the government to stop Chinese immigration. As a result, Congress in 1882 passed the **Chinese Exclusion Act.** This law forbade further Chinese immigration.

**Japanese immigrants arrive in the 1880's.** In the 1880's Japan was experiencing a population boom greater than that of Europe. In response to the growing

In this photograph by Lewis Hine, a Slovak family awaits processing at Ellis Island. After entering the country, many immigrants faced difficulties and hardships.

competition for jobs and land, many Japanese began to leave Japan. At first Japanese laborers went to Hawaii to work on sugar plantations. Many later came to the continental United States. In California the Japanese became excellent farmers.

**Immigrants come from Canada, Mexico, and the Caribbean area.** Among immigrants from North America, the majority were French-Canadians. Between 1860 and 1900 about 1 million French-Canadians moved to New England where they were able to find work in the textile mills and in the shoe factories.

After 1900, other immigrants entered the United States from the Caribbean area and Mexico. Mexicans came to the United States to take jobs in the Southwest, particularly on the railroads and in agriculture. Immigrants from the Caribbean area came mostly from the British West Indies, especially Jamaica and the Bahamas. Most settled in New York or Boston. The West Indian blacks spoke English and included numbers of skilled workers.

Chinese youths studied American history in this San Francisco classroom. Education helped many immigrants learn American ways. Chinese immigrants, however, often preferred to keep their traditional culture.

## The Immigrant Experience

The immigrants often suffered great hardship in order to reach American shores. Once they arrived, they were not always welcomed. Many Americans felt threatened by the immigrants, whose ways were often so different. In time, the immigrants and their children thrived, and they enriched America by their contributions.

**Immigrants face a difficult journey.** To come to the United States, immigrants had to take many risks. Few knew much about America except what they might have read in letters or in steamship advertisements. Reaching a port sometimes took weeks of

hazardous travel. Once in port, the travelers often faced a long wait for a place on one of the steamships. Most immigrants traveled in steerage —the lowest deck on the ship. This is how one writer described it:

Crowds everywhere, ill smelling bunks, uninviting washrooms—this is steerage. The odors of scattered orange peelings, tobacco, garlic and disinfectants meeting but not blending. No lounge or chairs for comfort, and a continual [mix of languages]— this is steerage.

In such close and often unclean conditions, disease spread rapidly. Some immigrants did not survive the trip. By the end of the nineteenth century, however, steerage conditions improved somewhat. Instead of expecting steerage passengers to provide and cook their own food, the steamship lines began to include meals in the price of passage. Some lines began to supply medical services.

The passage was not all dreary. When the weather was pleasant, passengers gathered on deck for conversation, music, and even dancing. Good friendships and even marriages resulted.

**The Statue of Liberty becomes a symbol for immigrants.** Most immigrants landed at New York City. Those who arrived after 1886 were greeted by the Statue of Liberty, the world's tallest monument at the time.

The statue, a gift from France, became a symbol of the freedom that immigrants sought in America. The day of its dedication in October 1886 was a public holiday in New York. President Grover Cleveland gave the signal to light the lamp in the statue's hand. People celebrated to the noise of sirens, whistles, boat horns, and cheering. The souvenir program that day contained a poem by Emma Lazarus with these lines:

> Give me your tired, your poor,
> Your huddled masses yearning to breathe
>   free,
> The wretched refuse of your teeming shore;
> Send these, the homeless, tempest-tost to
>   me,
> I lift my lamp beside the golden door!

These lines were later inscribed on the base of the statue.

**Millions enter the United States through Ellis Island.** After 1892, immigrants were taken to a federal facility at Ellis Island in New York Harbor for processing. Officials there were charged with keeping criminals, the insane, and the diseased from entering the United States. The facility handled as many as 1 million immigrants a year.

Once cleared to leave Ellis Island and enter the United States, the immigrants faced a whole new set of problems. They had to find jobs and places to live. They had to get along in a land where the language and customs were foreign.

## LINKING PAST AND PRESENT

## ★★★ *Lady Liberty*

The Statue of Liberty raising her lamp has stood on Liberty Island in New York Harbor since 1886. The years, however, took their toll. By the time Liberty was 100 years old, she had cracks in her face, and the internal iron structure had rusted.

For the statue's 100th birthday in 1986, it was thoroughly restored. Scientists, architects, and engineers studied the original plans. The statue's copper skin was removed, and in some places new plates were made from the original molds. On the inside, stainless-steel bars replaced the old iron ones. A whole new torch was made, with a flame covered in gold.

On July 4, 1986, a giant birthday celebration was held. President Ronald Reagan gave the signal, and, to cheers and fireworks, Liberty's lamp was relit.

The writer Isaac Asimov described his father's awe at being in New York:

> For my parents to go from a small [town] in western Russia to the enormous city of New York was very much like going from Earth to Mars. The simple scale of the city struck my father dumb with astonishment. He tells me he stood for a long time watching successive trains pass by . . . and wondering where all the people came from to fill all those cars.

Most immigrants found their way to the part of the city where others spoke their language. There they received help and advice in their efforts to adapt to a new land.

**Americans question unlimited immigration.** Not all Americans welcomed the new immigrants. Because the newcomers were willing to work for lower wages, they sometimes took jobs that Americans wanted. They tended to keep workers' wages low. Groups such as the American

# THE PLEDGE OF ALLEGIANCE 1892

The Pledge of Allegiance was written in 1892 by Francis Bellamy, an editor for a magazine called *The Youth's Companion.* Americans who first read the Pledge felt that it expressed in a few words the deep loyalty that they felt toward their country. The words "under God" were later added by Congress. By saying the Pledge of Allegiance, Americans promise their loyalty to the United States and to its democratic ideals.

## Read to Find Out

1. What does the flag represent?
2. Why do people feel it is important to pledge allegiance to our nation's flag?

---

I pledge allegiance to the flag of the United States of America and to the Republic for which it stands, one nation under God, indivisible, with liberty and justice for all.

*Francis Bellamy*

Federation of Labor and the People's party called for an end to unlimited immigration.

Some Americans also regarded the newcomers with prejudice. This hostility to the immigrants usually arose because they came from a different **ethnic** —racial or cultural— background. The immigrants also had different religious and social customs from many Americans. While most Americans were Protestant, most of the immigrants after 1880 were Jewish or Catholic.

**The immigrant experience enriches the United States.** The millions of newcomers became part of American life. They did not, however, simply abandon their old ways. Many immigrants held on to their native culture while learning American ways. Immigrants and their children became industrialists, scientists, engineers, inventors, writers, musicians, artists, and political leaders. They helped to make the United States a world leader in agriculture and industry. Mario Cuomo, who became governor of New York in 1982, has compared America to a mosaic. A mosaic is a design made of many small pieces of colored glass or tile. Cuomo said:

They never asked my mother to stop being Italian when she came here. They told her to start being an American. And so we took her culture and other peoples' cultures, and married it all together and in the harmonizing of those fragments, in a magnificent mosaic, is the real beauty of this country. That's what we are: we're a mosaic.

## SECTION REVIEW

1. **Vocabulary**    ghetto, czar, genocide, steerage, ethnic
2. **People and Places**    Italy, Russia, Austria-Hungary, China, Japan, Mexico, New York City, Grover Cleveland, Emma Lazarus, Ellis Island
3. **Comprehension**    What were the differences between the Old Immigration and the New Immigration?
4. **Comprehension**    What were the main causes of European immigration after 1880?
5. **Critical Thinking**    Why, do you think, have historians sometimes said that the immigrants *were* American history?

# 2 How was the United States becoming an urban nation?

## Vocabulary

masonry
settlement house
political machine
ward
patronage

Together, industrialization and immigration caused American cities to grow rapidly in the late 1800's. At the end of the Civil War, most Americans lived in the countryside. By 1900, however, 4 out of 10 Americans lived in cities. This rapid development offered exciting opportunities, but it also brought new problems.

## Influences on City Growth

Geography played an important part in the growth of most cities. Factories were built where they could get raw materials or where they could ship goods to market. As a result, cities usually grew up around transportation centers or near important resources.

**Railroads help cities to grow.** Before the Civil War, cities were located on good harbors because water transportation was important. After the Civil War, cities also grew where railroad lines crossed. Cities such as Birmingham, Atlanta, Kansas City, Indianapolis, and Denver grew because they became railroad centers.

The railroad also helped the growth of older cities such as New York, Philadelphia, and Chicago. These cities became major manufacturing and shipping centers because they had access to both water and rail transportation. In 1880 each of the three cities had more than 500,000 residents. Ten years later they each had populations of 1.5 million or more.

**Development of new resources helps cities grow.** Some cities developed where iron and steel mills were located. The mills sprang up near sources of raw materials. Steel production depends on iron ore, coal, and limestone. Cities such as Pittsburgh, Chicago, and Birmingham grew partly because they were close to these resources.

The cities of the Midwest also grew because they were close to the country's rich agricultural region. Meat-packing and food-processing industries located in such cities as Cincinnati, Omaha, Chicago, Milwaukee, and Minneapolis. Businesses that sold goods to farmers were also likely to locate in midwestern cities.

**Improvements in local transportation help cities.** Until the late 1800's most city dwellers walked to work. That meant that working people had to live within a few miles of their jobs. As a result, cities could not grow and spread out. Starting in the 1870's, however, Americans developed streetcars and cable cars. These new transportation systems made it possible for people to live

## Chart Study

This chart shows the 10 largest cities in the United States in 1880. How many cities had populations of more than 250,000 people? Which city was the third largest?

| Cities 1880 | Population |
| --- | --- |
| New York | 1,773,000 |
| Philadelphia | 847,000 |
| Chicago | 503,000 |
| Boston | 363,000 |
| St. Louis | 351,000 |
| Baltimore | 332,000 |
| Cincinnati | 255,000 |
| San Francisco | 234,000 |
| New Orleans | 216,000 |
| Washington, D.C. | 178,000 |

529

J.J. Fogerty's painting shows New York's Broadway in the 1880's. Tall buildings lined the streets, and telephone and telegraph wires crossed overhead. Within a few years, electric streetcars shared the streets with horse-drawn vehicles.

farther from their work. This contributed to the growth of cities.

The first streetcars were pulled by horses. By the 1890's, however, electrical power replaced horses. In some cities the streetcars ran on tracks elevated above the city streets. These elevated systems were often called "the el."

**Bridges affect city growth.** As railroads grew, Americans built bridges across the nation's rivers. The addition of a bridge often improved a city's transportation network and therefore spurred its growth.

Bridges caused problems, however. Boats and ships sometimes ran into the bridge piers. As a result, people tried to build bridges with as few piers as possible. One such bridge, designed in a series of arches, crossed the Mississippi River at St. Louis. It was designed by James Buchanan Eads, a self-taught engineer. St. Louis had long been an important river port. Eads's bridge, completed in 1874, made the city an important railroad center as well.

Probably the most famous of nineteenth-century bridges was constructed in New York City. Completed in 1883, the Brooklyn

Bridge joined Brooklyn to Manhattan Island. The designer of the bridge was John A. Roebling, an immigrant engineer from Germany. The bridge's single span of 1,595 feet (486 meters) allowed ship traffic to flow freely on the river below.

**Cities grow upward.** City land quickly became more expensive as the populations of the cities increased. This expensive land caused people to build taller buildings. Earlier buildings were constructed of wood or **masonry** —bricks or stones. They were only a few stories high. Two new inventions made the construction of taller buildings possible. They were the elevator and iron-and-steel construction.

Elisha Otis designed the first elevator that worked. The first passenger elevator designed by Otis was installed in a New York City department store in 1857. The pioneer in the design of tall buildings was James Bogardus. Bogardus used iron-and-steel beams to construct the building's framework. Such frameworks were much stronger than wood or masonry walls. As a result, buildings constructed of iron and steel were able to soar upward.

## Dealing with City Problems

As cities doubled and tripled in population, they faced serious problems. Overcrowding led to unhealthy living conditions. The millions of immigrants needed help to adjust to city life. Many cities also suffered from poor and unjust government.

**Unhealthy living conditions cause disease.** Often several thousand people squeezed into the tenements on a single city block. Cities were seldom able to provide adequate sewage and water systems for so many people. Often there were not enough facilities to collect and dispose of garbage. City dwellers complained loudly. "The stink is enough to knock you down," declared a New Yorker. Far worse than the stink, however, was disease. Contagious diseases such as tuberculosis, scarlet fever, typhoid, diphtheria, and whooping cough spread rapidly through tenement districts. These problems continued throughout the late 1800's. It was not until the twentieth century that better sanitation and medical care reduced death by infectious disease.

**Terrible fires sweep through cities.** One of the worst hazards of city life in the nineteenth century was fire. Most tenements were poorly built wooden buildings. People depended on kerosene lanterns for light. Streets were narrow, and fire-protection services were inadequate. Almost every city had a major fire. The worst was the Great Chicago Fire in 1871.

The fire started in wooden tenements and then spread through the heart of the city. An observer wrote:

> Billows of fire were rolling over the business palaces of the city and swallowing up their contents. Walls were falling so fast that the quaking of the ground under our feet was scarcely noticed, so continuous was the [shaking]. . . . Everybody in this quarter was hurrying toward the lake shore.

In the late 1800's, in the rapidly growing cities, professional firefighters raced to fires in horse-drawn firewagons.

## JAMES A. GARFIELD

★ 1881 ★

**20**TH PRESIDENT

REPUBLICAN

★ Born November 19, 1831, in Ohio

★ Married Lucretia Rudolph in 1858; 7 children

★ Representative and senator from Ohio

★ Lived in Ohio when elected President

★ Vice President: Chester A. Arthur

★ Died September 19, 1881, in New Jersey after being shot by an assassin July 2, 1881

immigrant families learned English, sewing, and cooking. A nursery provided child care for mothers who had jobs or were sick. Nourishing food was served to the underfed children of the neighborhood. Addams also helped provide clean, inexpensive rooms for working women.

**Reformers seek to change laws.** Other reformers followed Addams's example. Some organized boys' or girls' clubs to involve children in healthy activities such as swimming, hiking, and team sports. As a result of their work with the immigrant poor, reformers saw the need for new laws. They began to work for such goals as an end to child labor, an eight-hour work day for women, better sanitation, better schools, and parks.

**Cities are poorly governed.** Reformers often had difficulty in bringing about needed change because of the way cities were governed. **Political machines** —groups of people organized to achieve and keep power in

The Great Chicago Fire left about 90,000 people homeless, destroyed roughly 18,000 buildings, and killed about 300 people.

**Social reformers fight for better living conditions.** Beginning about 1890, American reformers began trying to solve the problems of urban poverty. Jacob Riis (rees) came to the United States from Denmark when he was 21. Riis lived on the streets and in the slums of New York City. Later he worked as a reporter and became famous for his articles and books describing city problems. Riis's most important book, *How the Other Half Lives,* gave a stirring description of the overcrowded and dirty slums in New York City.

Another reformer who sought to improve slum conditions was Jane Addams. Brought up in a comfortable midwestern home, Addams was deeply troubled when she first saw the slums of Chicago. She began Hull House, a **settlement house** in the Chicago slums in 1889. A settlement house was a combination home, school, and clubhouse. At Hull House

**This Hull House cooking class taught skills to youths from disadvantaged homes. Reformers established settlement houses such as Hull House to help immigrants and the poor.**

## PROFILE • Jane Addams and the Ward Boss

In 1889 Jane Addams and her friend Ellen Starr rented a four-story mansion in Chicago's nineteenth ward, then one of its worst slum districts. The women had decided to help poor immigrants help themselves. They quickly realized the seriousness of the problem. Houses were not connected to sewers. Streets were filthy. Thousands of children did not attend school. Why, asked Jane Addams, was something not done? The answer, she found out, lay with Johnny Powers, the ward boss. Powers was one of the most corrupt politicians in Chicago, and as alderman, ruled the nineteenth ward.

In 1898 Addams and her fellow reformers challenged Powers by supporting another candidate for the elected position of alderman. Powers was furious. On Election Day, the voters made their choice. John Powers stayed in office and remained ward boss most of his life. In the long run, however, Addams won. She became a national figure, influencing reform across the nation. For her achievements, she received the Nobel Peace Prize in 1931.

**Jane Addams**

government—controlled many cities. At the head of a city machine was the political "boss," who was often the mayor. The city was divided into **wards** —political districts. In charge of each ward was a ward boss. The ward boss looked out for the people in the ward, going to their baptisms and funerals, getting them jobs, giving them turkeys at Christmas.

In return for these favors, the ward boss asked for the people's votes at election time. Sometimes people were paid for their vote or asked to vote twice in the same election. Ballots were sometimes falsified to make sure that the machine's candidates won.

**Boss Tweed controls New York.** The most famous political machine came to power in New York City in the 1860's. It was run by William Marcy "Boss" Tweed. The Tweed Ring may have stolen as much as $200 million from the city. Members of the Tweed Ring took money in exchange for giving people city jobs. They also accepted bribes from companies that wanted contracts to perform city services. Tweed juggled city accounts to hide the personal use of public funds. The Tweed machine often provided housing, jobs, or other services for newly arrived immigrants. In return, the politicians could count on the votes of these new citizens on Election Day.

Thomas Nast, a young cartoonist for *Harper's Weekly*, began to attack Tweed through the use of humorous drawings. Tweed offered him one half million dollars to stop. Nast refused, and his political cartoons eventually helped put Tweed and his friends in jail.

# Our Presidents

## CHESTER A. ARTHUR

★ 1881–1885 ★

**21**ST PRESIDENT

REPUBLICAN

★ Born October 5, 1829, in Vermont
★ Married Ellen Lewis Herndon in 1859; 3 children
★ Lawyer; Port of New York customs official; Vice President under Garfield
★ Lived in New York when elected Vice President
★ Vice President: none
★ Died November 18, 1886, in New York
★ Key events while in office: Standard time zones established; Pendleton Civil Service Act

**Congress reforms the civil service system.** Many federal government positions were also filled by patronage. As a result, federal government service was frequently poor and sometimes civil servants were found to be corrupt. In 1877 President Rutherford B. Hayes made a real effort to make appointments to federal jobs that were truly based on merit. President Hayes's action offended many of his supporters.

The next American President, James A. Garfield, was assassinated early in his term. Garfield served for only 200 days before being shot by a disappointed office seeker. The assassination underscored the need for civil-service reform.

Vice President Chester A. Arthur succeeded Garfield and immediately called for civil-service improvements. As a result, Congress passed the **Pendleton Act** in 1883. The Pendleton Act provided for open examinations for public-service jobs. The next two Presidents, Grover Cleveland and Benjamin Harrison, each extended the positions that would be covered by civil-service examinations. Gradually, civil-service reform managed to reduce corruption at both the national and local levels of government.

**Professional city services develop.** The power of political machines was based on **patronage** —granting of jobs and favors. Patronage helped many individual immigrants as well as many other city dwellers. The machines, however, failed to provide many of the services that were needed for the general urban population. Beginning in the 1880's, some reformers campaigned for professional city government. They believed that city offices that were run by professional people would solve many of their urban problems.

By 1900 some American cities had established professional police and fire departments. Publicly owned water and sewage systems also became quite common. Measures such as these greatly restricted the power of certain political bosses and at the same time helped to improve the living conditions for many people.

## SECTION REVIEW

1. **Vocabulary**   masonry, settlement house, political machine, ward, patronage
2. **People and Places**   Chicago, St. Louis, Jacob Riis, Jane Addams, "Boss" Tweed, Thomas Nast, Rutherford B. Hayes, James A. Garfield, Chester A. Arthur, Benjamin Harrison
3. **Comprehension**   What are some factors that contributed to the growth of large cities?
4. **Comprehension**   What were some of the problems that American cities faced during the second half of the nineteenth century?
5. **Critical Thinking**   Why, do you think, might some immigrants and some reformers disagree about the value of a patronage system?

# MAPS AND GRAPHS: Comparing Maps

During the last decades of the 1800's, America's **urban population**—the number of people living in towns and cities—grew rapidly. In 1870 only about 25 percent of Americans lived in towns or cities. Just 30 years later, 40 percent of Americans were urban dwellers. Also during this time period, the number of large towns and cities in the United States grew significantly. These kinds of trends or patterns can be identified by comparing and contrasting maps from different time periods.

The two maps below show the growth of cities in the United States at the end of the nineteenth century. For each map, note the year for which it gives information. Also check the key to interpret the kinds of information shown on the map. Then compare and contrast the two maps, noting similarities and differences. Identify any trends or patterns in the growth of cities shown by the maps. Then answer the following questions.

1. How many cities had a population of more than 500,000 in 1880?
2. How many cities grew from less than 500,000 people to more than 500,000 between 1880 and 1900?
3. In 1880, which region had most of the cities with populations over 100,000?
4. Which two regions had the largest increase in the number of big cities between 1880 and 1900?
5. Which region had the smallest increase in the number of big cities between 1880 and 1900?
6. Based on what you have read in this chapter, why do you think that cities grew so rapidly in the last part of the nineteenth century?

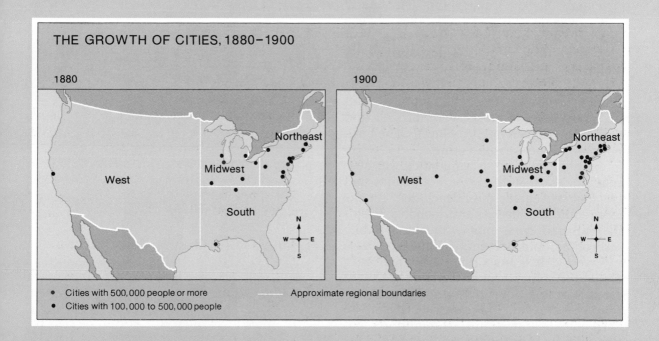

THE GROWTH OF CITIES, 1880–1900

1880

1900

West · Midwest · Northeast · South

• Cities with 500,000 people or more
• Cities with 100,000 to 500,000 people
—— Approximate regional boundaries

## Vocabulary

poll tax
literacy test

Reforms in the late nineteenth century helped to improve opportunities for minority groups and women. Nonetheless, prejudice against many groups remained a problem in the United States.

## Unfair Treatment

During Reconstruction many blacks took part in the rebuilding of the South. (See Chapter 19.) After federal troops left the southern states, however, new laws limited the rights of black citizens.

**Prejudice against black people takes several forms.** Some new laws in the South prevented blacks from voting. In many states, laws established **poll taxes** —fees that had to be paid in order to vote. Poll taxes kept poor people, black and white, from voting because they could not pay the fee. Other state laws required voters to pass **literacy tests** —tests of the ability to read and write. Literacy tests were difficult and were usually given only to blacks. The tests kept many blacks from voting.

Another form of discrimination was segregation. By 1890 most southern states had laws that segregated public facilities. Blacks were required to use separate schools, hospitals, railroad cars, movie theaters, public washrooms, and drinking fountains. These laws were called **Jim Crow laws.** In a bitter defeat for black Americans, the United States Supreme Court ruled in 1896 that segregation was legal. In **Plessy v. Ferguson** the Court upheld a Louisiana law requiring separate railroad cars for blacks and whites, as long as equal service was provided. For the next half-century "separate-but-equal" laws were used throughout the South to segregate the races. The facilities provided for blacks, however, were rarely equal to those for whites. Southern blacks were also denied many kinds of jobs reserved for white people. When they did work alongside whites, blacks usually received less pay.

**Blacks also face prejudice in the North.** Many southern blacks moved north hoping to find a freer life. In the North, blacks had legal and political rights that were denied them in the South. The large number of

Northern cities offered blacks more opportunities than did Southern cities. By 1900, black members of the New York City Police Department directed traffic in black neighborhoods.

manufacturing jobs in northern cities also attracted black workers.

Black people found, however, that racial prejudice was almost as strong in the North as in the South. Many jobs were denied to black workers, and for the same work blacks earned less money. Black workers were excluded from most unions. During times of economic trouble, they were the first to be fired. Segregation was not the law in northern states, but most northern cities were in fact segregated.

**Black Americans work to expand their opportunities.** In both the North and the South, black reformers fought racial discrimination. One of the best-known leaders of the time was Booker T. Washington. He argued that blacks could succeed in American society by learning useful skills. He wanted to help blacks become skillful farmers, mechanics, and industrial workers. In 1881, Washington started Tuskegee Institute in Alabama to put his ideas into practice.

Not all black leaders agreed with Washington. Some reformers wanted immediate political equality and economic opportunity for black Americans. Two such black leaders were W.E.B. Du Bois (doo-BOYS) and Ida Wells-Barnett. Du Bois, the first black man to receive a doctoral degree from Harvard University, was a professor at Atlanta University. Wells-Barnett was a newspaperwoman from Tennessee. She campaigned to end lynchings and other acts of violence against blacks. Her work led to the founding of many anti-lynching organizations.

## Gains for Women

The mid-1800's marked the beginning of a movement among American women to gain full rights and opportunities. Throughout the rest of the century, women became increasingly active in the affairs of the nation.

**Women tackle social problems.** Jane Addams's work in helping the urban poor encouraged other women to follow her example. Clara Barton, who had helped nurse sick and wounded soldiers during the Civil War, organized the American Red Cross in

## Our Presidents

### GROVER CLEVELAND

★ **1885–1889** ★
★ **1893–1897** ★

**22**ND and
**24**TH PRESIDENT

DEMOCRAT

★ Born March 18, 1837, in New Jersey

★ Married Frances Folsom in 1886; 5 children

★ Lawyer; governor of New York

★ Lived in New York when elected President

★ Vice Presidents: Thomas Hendricks; Adlai Stevenson

★ Died June 24, 1908, in New Jersey

★ Only President to serve two nonconsecutive terms of office

★ Key events while in office: (*First term*) AFL formed; United States Centennial; Statue of Liberty dedicated; Geronimo surrendered; Dawes Act; (*Second term*) Panic of 1893; *Plessy* v. *Ferguson*; Utah became a state

1881. Many children were helped by programs started by Frances Xavier Cabrini, a Catholic nun. Mother Cabrini founded hospitals, orphanages, and schools in both the United States and South America.

Many Americans in the 1800's blamed alcohol for the country's social problems. In the early 1870's women joined together to invade and close saloons. Carrie Nation, a crusader against alcohol, sometimes used an ax to smash saloons. The best-known anti-alcohol organization was the **Woman's Christian Temperance Union** (WCTU), founded in 1874. Hundreds of thousands of women joined the WCTU, which also fought against political corruption.

Members of the National Woman Suffrage Association marched to call attention to their cause. The movement to extend voting rights to women continued through the late 1800's and early 1900's.

The leader of the WCTU during the 1880's and 1890's was Frances Willard. Under her leadership, the WCTU worked for laws to improve prisons, start kindergartens, end child labor, and give the vote to women.

**More women work in business and industry.** With the growth of business and industry, more women had a chance to work outside the home. Department stores created many sales jobs for women. The invention of the telephone and the typewriter also created jobs for women. Women replaced men in many office jobs, becoming secretaries, bank clerks, and telephone operators.

Women were usually paid less than men. As early as 1866, Congress set the salaries of women clerks in government jobs at $900 a year. Men doing the same work were paid $1,200 to $1,800. At the end of the century, men working in manufacturing were paid an average of $587 a year, and women $314.

**Women work in the professions.** In the late 1800's teaching and nursing remained the chief professions for women. About two thirds of elementary school teachers were women. The creation of many new public schools in the southern states created teaching jobs open to both black and white women.

The first American schools of nursing opened in 1873. By 1880 there were more than 3,000 trained nurses in the United States. Almost all were women.

**Women gain opportunities for higher education.** After the Civil War, many men's colleges began to accept female students. The number of women's colleges also increased. Women's colleges founded after the Civil War included Vassar (1865), Smith (1871), Radcliffe (1879), and Bryn Mawr (1885). By 1901 there were about 200 women's colleges in the United States. Because of increased educational opportunities, more women were able to enter medicine, law, and scientific professions.

**Women work for the right to vote.** Many women in the late 1800's demanded suffrage. In 1869 Elizabeth Cady Stanton and Susan B. Anthony organized the National Woman Suffrage Association. This organization sought to amend the Constitution to allow women the right to vote.

The first victory for women's suffrage came the same year. In 1869 Wyoming Territory granted women the right to vote. When Wyoming asked to become a state, in 1889, many members of Congress objected to women's suffrage in Wyoming's proposed constitution. The Wyoming legislature declared, "We may stay out of the Union for 100 years, but we will come in with our women." In 1890 Congress narrowly approved Wyoming's statehood.

By 1900, three other western states—Utah, Colorado, and Idaho—had joined Wyoming in guaranteeing women's right to vote in state elections. Still, it would be another 20 years before this right had been extended to all American women.

# 4  What changes occurred in education, the arts, and leisure?

## Vocabulary

dialect
columnist

The growth of cities and industry led to changes in education, the arts, and the use of leisure time. Americans showed more interest in reading and learning. The arts flourished, and outdoor sports became more popular.

## Progress in Education

After the Civil War, Americans began to see education as a way to get ahead. As a result, the national and state governments began to spend more tax money to support schools.

**Elementary education changes.**  By the late 1800's more American children were attending school than ever before. Many communities established public schools paid for by taxes. By the end of the century, more than 30 states required attendance at school. Between 1870 and 1900 the number of children in public schools grew from about 4 million to almost 11 million.

**Colleges and universities increase in number.**  The number of college students also increased. In 1870 there were 52,000 college students. By 1900 that figure had leaped to 238,000. The number of colleges and universities also increased greatly.

Early American colleges had been primarily supported by churches. After the Civil War, however, many wealthy men and women donated funds to colleges. Sophia Smith gave much of her inherited fortune to found Smith College, a women's school. Ezra Cornell, who had made a fortune in the telegraph business, gave money to establish Cornell University. Private funds were also used to establish colleges for black students. These schools included Fisk University in Nashville, Tennessee, and Howard University in Washington, D.C.

Some states founded large universities with federal land grants given them by the

## BENJAMIN HARRISON

★ 1889–1893 ★

**23RD PRESIDENT**

**REPUBLICAN**

- ★ Born August 20, 1833, in Ohio
- ★ Married Caroline Lavinia Scott in 1853; 2 children
- ★ Married Mary Scott Lord Dimmick in 1896; 1 child
- ★ Lawyer; senator from Indiana
- ★ Lived in Indiana when elected President
- ★ Vice President: Levi Morton
- ★ Died March 13, 1901, in Indiana
- ★ Key events while in office:
- ★ Sherman Silver Purchase Act; Sherman Antitrust Act; Populist party formed; North Dakota, South Dakota, Montana, Washington, Idaho, and Wyoming became states; Battle of Wounded Knee

Morrill Act. (See Chapter 22.) California, Wisconsin, Illinois, and Minnesota used the land grant in this way. Once a state had established a university, the state legislature provided funds for its continued support.

The course of study also changed during these years. Early colleges emphasized training for the clergy. After the Civil War, colleges began to emphasize knowledge needed in the changing world. Courses included foreign languages, science, modern history, and engineering. The training of lawyers and doctors also improved.

**Public libraries expand.** Public libraries played an important part in the spread of education. Before the Civil War there were few libraries open to the public. The gifts by Andrew Carnegie, however, made possible the building of more than 2,000 libraries in communities across the United States.

## Reading and Literature

The spread of education helped more people to enjoy reading. As the audience for literature grew, writers began to write about America. They portrayed people and ways of life that seemed typically American.

**Writers tell about life in different regions.** One group of writers described experiences in the American West. The most famous of these writers was Mark Twain. Twain, whose real name was Samuel Langhorne Clemens, spent his boyhood in Hannibal, Missouri. He later worked as a riverboat pilot on the Mississippi River. Twain drew on these experiences when he wrote *The Adventures of Tom Sawyer, The Adventures of Huckleberry Finn,* and other stories.

American writers also wrote about other regions. Ellen Glasgow of Virginia described the changes in southern society after the Civil War. Sarah Orne Jewett vividly portrayed the people of New England.

**Poets contribute to American literature.** Among the poems Americans loved were those of James Whitcomb Riley, a poet from Indiana. Riley's poems used **dialect** —the speech of a particular region. He described farm life with humor and sympathy.

The poems of a New England woman, Emily Dickinson, were mostly unknown until after her death. Dickinson wrote hundreds of short, witty poems that are considered some of the finest in American literature.

**Books are written especially for young people.** Some authors wrote books meant for young readers. Louisa May Alcott's *Little Women* became a lasting favorite. Among the most popular children's books after the Civil War were those of Horatio Alger. Alger wrote more than 100 books about boys who rose from rags to riches. In 1900, one of this country's most popular children's books was published. It was *The Wizard of Oz,* by L. Frank Baum.

**Newspapers and magazines change to meet new conditions.** In the late 1800's, newspapers began to reach many more people. The number of daily papers grew from about 600 in 1870 to almost 2,500 in 1900.

Using the telephone and the transatlantic cable, papers printed news from all over the world. News services such as the Associated Press and the United Press gathered and distributed news. **Columnists** —people who interpret or comment on the news—began writing for papers from coast to coast.

Magazines also became more popular. By the 1880's magazines were reaching millions of readers. The *Ladies' Home Journal* featured articles on such topics as gardening and child care as well as on the issues of the day. *McClure's* was the first magazine to print articles attacking monopolies, corruption, and other evils.

## Art and Music

Interest in art and music also increased after the Civil War. American artists and musicians began to study in Europe. Americans started private art collections and the Metropolitan Museum of Art in New York City became one of the world's largest museums. Americans also began to develop distinctly American art and music.

**American artists gain fame.** Four well-known American painters of the late 1800's were Frederic Remington, Winslow Homer, Mary Cassatt (kuh-SAT), and Edward Bannister. Remington painted scenes of life in the Far West. Homer painted pictures of the sea and the New England coast, while Cassatt explored the theme of mothers and their children. Bannister was the best-known black painter of his day. His landscapes won praise for their strong, original style.

**America develops its own music.** After the Civil War, Americans began to develop new forms of music. John Philip Sousa (SOO-zuh), a famous bandmaster, composed popular march tunes. His best-known march was "The Stars and Stripes Forever."

The musical influence of black Americans also began to grow. James A. Bland, a well-known black musician, wrote hundreds

This painting by Thomas Eakins shows members of the Philadelphia Athletics, one of the first professional baseball teams. The Athletics joined the National League in 1876.

of popular melodies, including "In the Evening by the Moonlight" and "Carry Me Back to Old Virginny." The latter song became the official state song of Virginia. Around 1900, a new kind of music appeared. Ragtime, as it was called, expressed the vigor and fast movement of modern life.

## Sports and Recreation

When people worked hard on farms, on fishing boats, or in lumber camps, they had limited interest in outdoor sports. As people began to work indoors, they turned to sports for fun and exercise. The colleges also encouraged organized sports.

**Baseball becomes a favorite sport.** Baseball is often called the national pastime. It began in the early 1800's with such games as "one o' cat" and "rounders." About 1840, rules were proposed that led to baseball as Americans know it today. By the late 1800's, baseball clubs had formed in many cities.

**541**

The first professional team, the Cincinnati Red Stockings, began in 1869. By 1900, two major leagues, the National and the American, had been formed. Three years later, the first World Series was played.

**Football wins popularity.** Football had its beginnings in the British game of rugby. At first, as played by Americans, it was largely a game of kicking the ball. The first college football game was played between Princeton and Rutgers in 1869.

**Basketball catches up with baseball and football in popularity.** Basketball was not played until the 1890's. James Naismith, a physical education teacher in Springfield, Massachusetts, wanted a sport for students to play indoors in winter. He worked out the rules for a game, which he named basketball. Players scored points by tossing a ball into peach baskets, set up at each end of a hall. The referee had to climb a ladder to get the ball after each "basket" had been made. This problem was solved by cutting a hole in the bottom of the basket.

**The bicycle is invented.** The bicycle was invented in the late nineteenth century. It had a huge front wheel turned directly by the pedals. By 1885 chain-driven safety bicycles were being made. The bicycle gave city dwellers a new freedom. Bicycle riding quickly became a new form of recreation for both men and women.

## SECTION REVIEW

1. **Vocabulary**    dialect, columnist
2. **People and Places**    Mark Twain, James Whitcomb Riley, Emily Dickinson, Frederic Remington, Winslow Homer, Mary Cassatt, John Philip Sousa
3. **Comprehension**    What changes in education took place in the late 1800's?
4. **Comprehension**    What sports became popular in the late 1800's?
5. **Critical Thinking**    The most popular literature of the day is not always the best literature of the time. Why?

# Chapter 23 Summary

The last third of the nineteenth century was a time of large-scale immigration and rapid city growth. After 1880 most immigrants came from southern and eastern Europe. This change marked the start of the New Immigration. Most of the new immigrants were Roman Catholic or Jewish. Most settled in the cities.

The growth of cities was spurred by industrial needs, transportation, and inventions. Important inventions were the Brooklyn Bridge, iron-and-steel buildings, and the elevator. The growing cities faced new challenges. These included absorbing the millions of new immigrants, providing healthy living conditions, and stopping political corruption. Reformers like Jacob Riis, Thomas Nast, and Jane Addams worked to expose bad conditions and bring about change.

During these years, opportunities for black people were restricted. In the South poll taxes and literacy tests kept blacks from voting, and Jim Crow laws forced them to use segregated facilities. Discrimination was also felt by such minorities as Asians, Native Americans, Jews, and Catholics.

Women became active in business and in public affairs. They found jobs in stores, offices, and telephone exchanges. They worked to improve city life, to stop alcohol use, and to achieve women's suffrage.

With the rise of industrialism, people sought better education. The number of people attending schools and colleges increased rapidly. Writers, artists, and musicians explored many aspects of American life. Americans also developed new sports. By 1900 baseball, football, basketball, and bicycling were important forms of recreation.

# CAUSES and EFFECTS

# The Urbanization of America ★ ★ ★

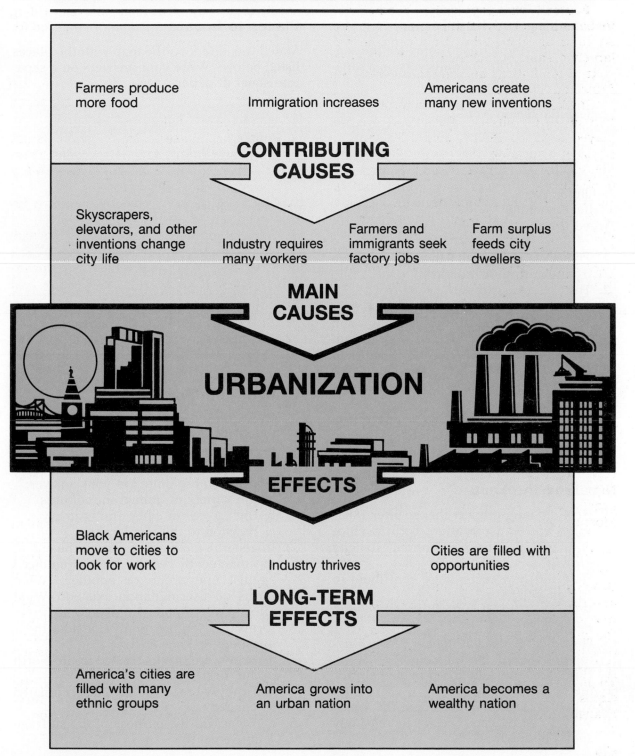

Farmers produce more food

Immigration increases

Americans create many new inventions

**CONTRIBUTING CAUSES**

Skyscrapers, elevators, and other inventions change city life

Industry requires many workers

Farmers and immigrants seek factory jobs

Farm surplus feeds city dwellers

**MAIN CAUSES**

**URBANIZATION**

**EFFECTS**

Black Americans move to cities to look for work

Industry thrives

Cities are filled with opportunities

**LONG-TERM EFFECTS**

America's cities are filled with many ethnic groups

America grows into an urban nation

America becomes a wealthy nation

# Chapter 23 REVIEW

## Vocabulary and Key Terms

Use the following terms to complete the sentences below. Write your answers on a separate sheet of paper.

**Chinese Exclusion Act**
**dialect**
**ethnic**
**Jim Crow laws**
**patronage**
**Pendleton Act**
**political machine**
**Tweed Ring**

1. The _____ prevented this _____ group from entering the country.
2. The _____ restricted the system of _____ through civil-service reform.
3. In the South one form of discrimination was _____, which created a system of segregation.
4. In the 1860's a _____ known as the _____ controlled the government in New York City.
5. James Whitcomb Riley, an American poet, used _____ to express how people actually talked.

## Recalling the Facts

1. How did immigration change after 1880?
2. Why was transportation, both to cities and within cities, important to city growth?
3. How did new technology contribute to city growth?
4. What was the significance of *Plessy* v. *Ferguson* ?
5. How did the ideas of Booker T. Washington and W.E.B. Du Bois differ?
6. How did Jane Addams provide help for the poor?
7. What writer told about life in the West?
8. Why did Americans become increasingly sports-minded?

## Places to Locate

Match the letters on the map with the places listed below. Write your answers on a separate sheet of paper.

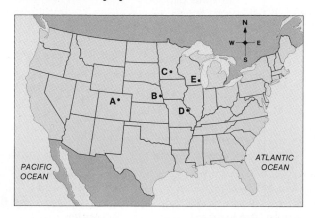

1. St. Louis
2. Milwaukee
3. Denver
4. Minneapolis
5. Omaha

## Critical Thinking

1. During the late nineteenth and early twentieth centuries, millions of immigrants came to the United States. How did these people affect American life? Consider these points in your answer:
   a. the variety of immigrant cultures
   b. the growth of cities and industry
   c. reaction to the immigrants
2. In general, most Americans at the end of the nineteenth century were prejudiced against one group or another. What forms of discrimination existed? What efforts were made to overcome these forms of discrimination? Consider these questions in your answer:
   a. How were blacks treated in the North and in the South?
   b. How were women discriminated against?
   c. What was the purpose of the suffrage movement?

3. How did the growth of the cities affect city government? Consider these questions in your answer:
   a. How did political machines operate?
   b. What health and safety problems did cities face?
   c. Why did reformers try to change how cities were governed? How successful were they?

## Understanding History

1. Reread the section "The Statue of Liberty becomes a symbol for immigrants" on page 527. Then answer these questions.
   a. **Primary Sources.** What does "give me your tired, your poor" mean in Lazarus's poem?
   b. **Primary Sources.** What is the "golden door"?
2. Reread the section "Social reformers fight for better living conditions" on page 532. Then answer these questions.
   a. **Citizenship.** How was the work of Jacob Riis and Jane Addams similar, and how was it different?
   b. **Citizenship.** How did Jane Addams's work help immigrants become part of their new land?

## Projects and Activities

1. **Making a Chart.** Make a chart with information on the writers, artists, and musicians covered in this chapter. Write these column headings across the top of your chart: "Name," "Occupation," "Characteristics," "Noted Works." Fill out the chart as completely as possible.
2. **Writing a Letter.** Imagine that it is 1890 and that you are an immigrant who has recently arrived in the United States. Write a letter to your relatives back home, describing where you are, what you are doing, and how customs differ in your new land.
3. **Analyzing a Problem.** Imagine that you and your classmates are living during the late 1800's and are part of the movement for women's suffrage. Form a committee to discuss ways to convince the American public and Congress that women should have the vote. Present your report to the class.
4. **Doing Research and Writing a Report.** Find out what your community was like 100 years ago. Ask a librarian or a local historical society to suggest sources for researching the topic. If there is a great amount of information, focus on just one part of your community's history, such as an important event or the establishment of professional city services. Write a report on what you learned and share it with the class.

## Practicing Your Skill

Use the map to answer the following questions.

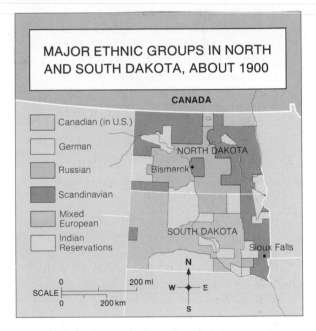

MAJOR ETHNIC GROUPS IN NORTH AND SOUTH DAKOTA, ABOUT 1900

1. What were the two major ethnic groups in North Dakota?
2. What ethnic group lived in northeast North Dakota? What ethnic group lived in northeast South Dakota?
3. Would it be likely for German-speaking people to live in Sioux Falls? Explain.
4. What generalization can you make comparing ethnic groups in North Dakota with those in South Dakota?

# UNIT 7 REVIEW

## Unit Summary

★ **Low-cost public lands encouraged western settlement.**

- The Homestead Act of 1862 made public lands available to settlers.
- Mining and cattle raising attracted many people to the West.
- Native Americans lost their lands to western settlers.

★ **The United States became a leading industrial nation.**

- Rich natural resources, a large labor force, and changes in technology aided industrialization.
- Mass production lowered the prices of goods and helped economic growth.
- Workers formed unions to fight labor problems.
- The government passed laws to regulate business and industry.

★ **New farming technology led to increased production.**

- Improved farm machinery and new methods made farming possible in western lands.
- The Grange and the Farmers' Alliance fought for benefits.
- The Populist party worked to solve farmers' problems.

★ **The arrival of millions of immigrants changed the nation.**

- Many immigrants from eastern and southern Europe settled in cities.
- Industry, railroads, and immigration led to rapid urban growth.
- Women and minority groups gained opportunities in the late 1800's.

## Understanding Chronology

Study the Unit 7 time line on page 459. Then answer the following questions on a separate sheet of paper.

1. Alexander Graham Bell was 25 years old when he opened a school in Boston in 1872. How old was he when the first telephone system began operating?
2. Thomas Edison was born in 1847. How old was he when he invented the light bulb?
3. Clara Barton was 60 years old when she founded the Red Cross. In what year was she born?
4. Jane Addams died in 1935 at the age of 74. How old was she when she founded Hull House?

## Writing About History

1. **Describing a Region.** Imagine that you were a writer who lived during the late 1800's. Write a story about the region in which you live and the way of life there. Describe the work that people do, the houses of the area, and how people spend their leisure time. Include facts and descriptions that make your region different from others.
2. **Writing a Speech.** Write a speech encouraging farmers to join alliances or workers to join unions. Explain the problems of farmers or workers in the late 1800's and how alliances or unions might help solve the problems.
3. **Preparing a Documentary.** Write the script for a television documentary telling about the destruction of the buffalo in the late 1800's. Explain why and how the buffalo were killed by the white settlers. Then describe the changes in the Plains Indians' lifestyle caused by the buffalo's extinction. Describe the pictures you would use for your documentary.

4. **Interpreting a Cartoon.** Study the political cartoon above. Write a paragraph explaining what the octopus represents and then describe the artist's feelings about business practices in the late nineteenth century.

## Projects

1. **Making Models.** Prepare a three-dimensional model showing life in the late nineteenth-century United States. You might create a scene of a mining town, a cattle ranch, a homestead on the plains, or a city tenement. Include models of the kinds of houses people had, what they did to earn a living, and what their environment was like.

2. **Writing Biographical Sketches.** Work in groups to prepare brief biographies for a book titled *Who's Who in America in the Late 1800's.* Each of the book's chapters should include the biographies of a particular group of famous people, such as reformers, politicians, capitalists, writers, or artists. Assemble the biographical sketches into a book for a classroom display.

3. **Presenting an Oral Report.** Prepare an oral report on one aspect of American culture in the late nineteenth century. You might report on a famous artist, a particular painting, a book or a poem, a sports event, the popular music, or American architecture. Show pictures or give examples of your subject and explain how this form of culture expressed an American style.

4. **Making Maps and Graphs.** Prepare a series of maps and graphs to show changes that took place in the late nineteenth-century United States. Maps can show the expansion of railroads, the routes of cattle drives, and the movement of the frontier. Graphs can illustrate population growth, numbers of immigrants, or agricultural production.

5. **Making a Chart.** Make a chart comparing the mining, ranching, and homesteading lifestyles. Compare each group's work, the place where each group lived, the hardships of each lifestyle, as well as the goals and values of each way of life. Use your chart as a source for review.

## Finding Out More

Claypool, Jane. *Manufacturing*. Watts, 1984. This book covers the history of manufacturing and the use of mass production today.

Fisher, Leonard Everett. *The Unions*. Holiday House, 1982. This story traces the history of labor unions in the United States, especially in the late 1800's, and explains the establishment of Labor Day as a national holiday.

Freedman, Russell. *Immigrant Kids*. Dutton, 1980. This book discusses the experiences of immigrant children journeying to America and living in the United States. Photographs of nineteenth-century children enliven the narrative.

Lasky, Kathryn. *Beyond the Divide*. Macmillan, 1983. This story tells of an Amish girl and her father who travel west on a wagon train.

Talbot, Charlene Joy. *The Sodbuster Venture*. Atheneum, 1982. Two young women experience hardships and independence on the Kansas prairie.

# UNIT
# 8

# AMERICA REACHES OUTWARD

## 1898–1919

40,000 B.C.    A.D. 1000    1100    1200    1300    1400

American naval power helped spread the influence of the United States overseas. This painting was done by Fred Pansing in 1899.

1898 – 1919

| 1500 | 1600 | 1700 | 1800 | 1900 | 2000 |
|------|------|------|------|------|------|

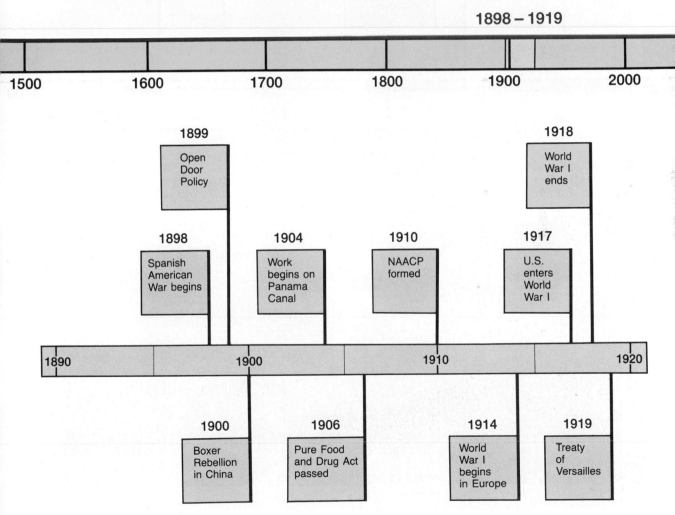

**1899** Open Door Policy

**1918** World War I ends

**1898** Spanish American War begins

**1904** Work begins on Panama Canal

**1910** NAACP formed

**1917** U.S. enters World War I

1890 — 1900 — 1910 — 1920

**1900** Boxer Rebellion in China

**1906** Pure Food and Drug Act passed

**1914** World War I begins in Europe

**1919** Treaty of Versailles

# 24 American Influence Spreads Overseas
## 1898–1917

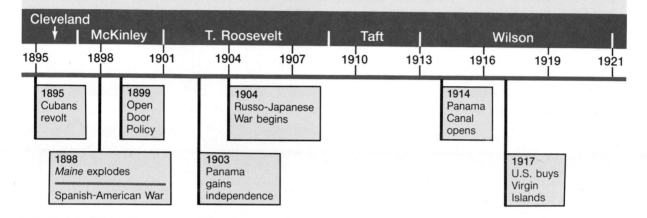

Cleveland

McKinley | T. Roosevelt | Taft | Wilson

1895 | 1898 | 1901 | 1904 | 1907 | 1910 | 1913 | 1916 | 1919 | 1921

1895
Cubans
revolt

1899
Open
Door
Policy

1904
Russo-Japanese
War begins

1914
Panama
Canal
opens

1898
*Maine* explodes

Spanish-American War

1903
Panama
gains
independence

1917
U.S. buys
Virgin
Islands

**American troops charge in the Battle of San Juan Hill. Victory in the Spanish-American War helped make the United States a colonial power.**

## Preparing to Read

By the 1890's, Americans were talking of the closing of the frontier. It was growing more difficult to go west and still find good land for farming or ranching. The nation was now settled from coast to coast, the population was growing, and the economy had expanded greatly since the Civil War. A nation so large and productive was bound to take a greater interest in world affairs. At the turn of the century, this interest led the United States to acquire some territory and influence outside its borders. As you read this chapter, try to answer the following questions:

1. What ideas and events led to American expansion in the Pacific?
2. Why did the United States fight a war with Spain?
3. What was America's foreign policy in Asia in the early 1900's?
4. How did expansion affect relations with Latin America?

# 1 What ideas and events led to American expansion in the Pacific?

## Vocabulary
isolationism
imperialism

Following the Civil War, most Americans thought the United States should stay out of world affairs. There was much to do to rebuild the country, and events during the war had made Americans uneasy about trusting European nations. Both Great Britain and France had meddled in affairs of the Western Hemisphere, ignoring the Monroe Doctrine. During the Civil War Britain had aided the Confederacy by building 3 warships that captured 140 northern merchant vessels. France had taken over Mexico and set up a government with Austrian Archduke Maximilian as its ruler. Eventually the British paid the United States $15.5 million in damages and the French left Mexico. Nevertheless, many Americans still preferred to isolate the United States from any further dealings with the countries of Europe. Their position was known as **isolationism**.

## From Isolationism to Expansionism

Oddly enough, it was Americans' success in building up their own resources that eventually led to expansion overseas. In the 30 years following the Civil War, people were busy building railroads, digging mines, and farming more land. Through hard work, Americans began to produce a surplus of goods. Farmers, for example, grew more cotton and wheat and produced more ham and bacon than other Americans could consume. Miners dug more copper and more coal than factories could use. Manufacturers produced more goods than people could buy.

**Americans look overseas.** To sell this surplus, American producers also began to look for new markets overseas. Successful business leaders began to think about investing overseas. They had more money than they could invest at home, and they wanted to make large profits in mining, industry, and business abroad.

Other nations, however, were already in competition for world markets. Britain, France, and Germany had set up colonies in

Africa, Asia, and the Pacific region to provide markets for their goods. European nations also controlled many of the best trading ports throughout the world.

**Attitudes begin to change.** To enter this competition, many Americans realized, the government would have to adopt expansionist policies. In the 1840's the idea of Manifest Destiny had led the country to grow westward. Now, many people believed, the United States should reach out to other parts of the world.

In addition to those who favored expansion for business reasons, there were Americans who wanted the United States to be a great power with its own colonies. These people, following the lead of European countries, favored imperialism —the creation of an empire. Still other Americans believed the United States had a duty to teach people in distant lands about the Christian religion and the American way of life. They spoke of bringing the "blessings of civilization" to people living in poverty.

**Some Americans favor a strong navy.** Many expansionists believed that a strong navy would further their interests. An influential speaker for expansionism was Captain Alfred Thayer Mahan of the Naval War College. In his 1890 book *The Influence of Sea Power upon History,* he argued that the most powerful nations were those that controlled the seas. If the United States wished to be a world power, Mahan said, it must build a large merchant fleet and a strong navy to protect it. He also urged the United States to set up naval bases and coaling stations in the Caribbean and the Pacific.

Acting on the advice of Mahan and of leaders like Senator Henry Cabot Lodge of Massachusetts, Congress strengthened the navy during the 1890's. By 1907 the United States had developed the Great White Fleet— the second largest fleet in the world.

## New American Possessions

Long before the Great White Fleet, William H. Seward favored overseas expansion. As Secretary of State for Presidents Lincoln and Johnson, Seward argued that the United States' power in North America was linked to its power on the seas. He wanted the nation to play a larger role in world affairs, and he realized that more territory in the Pacific would make this possible.

**The United States purchases Alaska.** When Russia offered to sell Alaska to the United States in 1867, Seward jumped at the chance. Acting quickly, he persuaded the Senate to approve the necessary treaty. The price for Alaska was set at $7.2 million—less than two cents an acre for about 0.6 million square miles (1.5 million square kilometers).

Many Americans joked about Seward's purchase of Alaska. They called it "Seward's Folly" and "Seward's Icebox." Seward, however, turned out to be right. The seals off the Alaskan coast were of great value because seal fur was highly prized at the time. Later, gold, oil, and other minerals were discovered there. Alaska turned out to be a great bargain.

Russian settlements dotted the Alaskan coast in the early 1800's. This 1840's painting shows the village and fort of Michaelovski, a fur-trading center. The United States purchased Alaska in 1867.

**Seward makes other plans for expansion.** Seward's dreams did not end with Alaska. In 1867 he arranged for the United States to take possession of Midway Island in the middle of the Pacific Ocean. Here Seward hoped to obtain still more territory, especially the Danish West Indies and the Dominican Republic. The Senate, however, would not approve his plans. Thirty years were to pass before the United States again gained a sizeable amount of territory.

**American involvement in Hawaii grows.** One of Seward's dreams was to acquire the Hawaiian Islands for the United States. Since 1786, American trading vessels and whaling ships had been stopping at the islands for fresh water and supplies. American missionaries began to settle in Hawaii in the 1820's. Many of their children stayed in Hawaii and bought large amounts of land, which they developed into plantations of sugar cane and pineapples.

Gradually the Americans took control of most of the land and businesses. They also influenced Hawaiian politics, advising the king to adopt a constitution similar to that of the United States.

It was in the planters' economic interest to maintain ties with the United States. Many Americans at home could also see the strategic value of Hawaii. In 1875 Hawaii signed an agreement with the United States. Hawaiians gained the right to sell sugar in the United States without paying any tariffs. The United States gained the exclusive use of Pearl Harbor, which was the best seaport in the islands. In addition, Hawaii agreed that no part of the islands should be given to any foreign country.

American planters in Hawaii profited enormously from this treaty. By 1885 Hawaii's sugar exports to the United States had grown nearly 10 times. Five years later, however, Congress removed import taxes on all sugar, thus destroying Hawaii's favored position. Facing economic ruin, the planters decided to seek annexation to the United States.

**Hawaii is annexed.** Until 1891, Americans had great influence in Hawaii. Queen Liliuokalani (lee-lee-oo-oh-kah-LAH-nee)

Queen Liliuokalani ruled Hawaii from 1891 to 1893. American settlers, who wanted the United States to annex Hawaii, overthrew her.

took the throne in that year. She had clear antiforeign views and wanted Hawaiians to regain economic control of the islands. In 1893 she took away many of the powers held by the American sugar planters. In turn, the planters staged a revolt. With the help of marines from an American warship, they overthrew the queen.

The American ambassador to Hawaii immediately recognized the revolutionary government. The United States, however, refused to annex the islands. President Grover Cleveland discovered that the uprising was not supported by the Hawaiian people themselves. Furthermore, Cleveland disapproved of the role the Americans had played in the revolt.

Disappointed by the failure of their plan, the leaders of the revolt declared Hawaii a republic. Then in 1898, after William McKinley became President, Congress voted to annex the islands. Hawaii was established as an American territory, and American citizenship was granted to the residents of the islands.

Hawaii was able to prosper under American rule. The people raised sugar and pineapples and sold them to the mainland. They bought large amounts of manufactured goods from American companies. Pearl Harbor became the country's most important naval base in the Pacific.

1. **Vocabulary**  isolationism, imperialism
2. **People and Places**  William Seward, Alaska, Hawaii, Queen Liliuokalani, William McKinley
3. **Comprehension**  What were three reasons why some Americans supported expansionist policies?
4. **Comprehension**  Why did the United States become interested in Hawaii?
5. **Critical Thinking**  Are colonies necessary if a nation is to become a great power? Explain.

# 2 Why did the United States fight a war with Spain?

## Vocabulary

yellow journalism
antiexpansionist

In 1898 war broke out between the United States and Spain. The war had been fueled by events in Cuba, an island that is located just 90 miles (145 kilometers) south of Florida. The United States was not fighting to gain territory, but the outcome of the war would increase the size of American holdings overseas. It would also strengthen the importance of the United States in world affairs.

## Background to the Conflict

Spain had ruled Cuba since 1492, when Christopher Columbus discovered the island. The Spanish strictly controlled not only the government and the military, but also the economy of Cuba. While they reaped the profits of the sugar cane plantations, native Cubans lived in poverty.

**Cuba revolts against Spain.**  By the late 1800's, however, many Cubans resented Spanish rule. Several times they rebelled and tried to win their independence. Each time, Spanish soldiers overpowered them. In 1895 rebellion broke out again. The rebels declared Cuba an independent country.

To crush the uprising, Spain placed a new governor-general, Valeriano Weyler, in charge. Weyler's policies were brutal. He declared martial law, destroyed property that might be of use to the rebels, and imprisoned Cuban civilians. He ordered his troops to march against the rebels and put an end to the revolt.

The Cuban forces, however, avoided open battle. Under the leadership of Maximo Gomez, they carried out surprise attacks against the Spanish soldiers. They did whatever damage they could and then dashed away. They also burned supplies and fields of sugar cane, hoping to force the Spanish out of Cuba through economic losses.

**Americans react to the Cuban conflict.** The United States watched the struggle between Cuba and Spain with deep, though divided, concern. American businesses had invested great sums of money in Cuban sugar plantations, mines, and other ventures. The United States also carried on heavy trade with Cuba. Because of the revolt, however, the United States could neither import Cuban sugar nor export meat, flour, and manufactured goods to the island. More fighting in Cuba would mean a greater loss of trade.

The conflict was bad for business, but most Americans sided with the Cubans for another reason. Americans remembered how the 13 colonies had revolted and won their independence from Great Britain. Their sympathies for the Cubans were further aroused by reports of Spanish cruelty.

American newspapers carried pages of reports about the revolt. Most newspapers were highly critical of Spanish policy. Two papers in particular—William Randolph Hearst's *Journal* and Joseph Pulitzer's *World*—helped fuel American anger toward the Spanish. These papers were competing against each other and realized that exciting stories about the Cuban revolt could affect readers. Both the *Journal* and the *World* practiced **yellow journalism** —sensational, and often false, reporting. As Hearst once told his news correspondent in Cuba, "You furnish the pictures and I'll furnish the war."

**The battleship *Maine* blows up.** As the Cuban revolt continued, the United States government feared that the lives and property of Americans in Cuba were in danger. To protect them, an American battleship, the *Maine*, steamed into the harbor of Havana, Cuba, late in January 1898.

For three weeks the *Maine* remained at anchor. Suddenly on one hot, still night, there was a dull roar and an explosion shook the city. The *Maine* had blown up! It sank immediately, and 260 of its crew died.

**The United States declares war on Spain.** Nobody knows for certain what caused the explosion on the *Maine*. Yet angry Americans blamed the Spanish. "Remember the *Maine*!" became a rallying cry. Many Americans felt that Spain should be taught a lesson and that the Cuban people should be freed from Spanish rule.

## Our Presidents

### WILLIAM McKINLEY

★ **1897–1901** ★

**25TH PRESIDENT**

**REPUBLICAN**

★ Born January 29, 1843, in Ohio
★ Married Ida Saxton in 1871; 2 children
★ Lawyer; representative from Ohio; governor of Ohio
★ Lived in Ohio when elected President
★ Vice Presidents: Garrett Hobart; Theodore Roosevelt
★ Died September 14, 1901, in New York after being shot by an assassin September 6, 1901
★ Key events while in office: Spanish American War; Philippines, Puerto Rico, and Guam acquired; Hawaii annexed; Open Door Policy proposed; Boxer Rebellion

Many Americans wanted war, but McKinley tried to preserve the peace. His efforts failed. On April 24, 1898, Spain declared war on the United States. The next day Congress declared war on Spain. Thus began the **Spanish-American War.**

## The "Splendid Little War"

President McKinley had tried to keep the United States out of a war with Spain. Popular opinion, however, was all for crushing Spain in a "splendid little war," as soon-to-be Secretary of State John Hay called it.

**The United States makes its battle plans.** Achieving victory over the Spanish took careful strategy. Spain had about 80,000 troops in Cuba alone, but the United States had fewer than 30,000 soldiers in its entire army. The Spanish Navy, however, was weak and ill prepared. On the other hand, the United States Navy was powerful and ready for war.

McKinley took immediate steps to strengthen the army and prepare it for battle. Plans were made for American forces to invade and occupy the Caribbean islands held by Spain. The American navy was to blockade Cuba. In this way Spain would be prevented from landing troops and supplies in Cuba. The navy would also try to destroy the enemy's ships, wherever they might be found.

**Dewey destroys the Spanish fleet at Manila.** Surprisingly, the first important battle of the war took place thousands of miles from Cuba. Immediately after war had been declared, Commodore George Dewey set sail with several American warships from Hong Kong. His goal was the Spanish fleet stationed in the Philippine Islands.

Early on the morning of May 1, 1898, Dewey's ships sailed into Manila Bay. As the sky lightened, the American ships readied for battle. The attack on the Spanish fleet lasted only a few hours. Within that time, the superior American force destroyed the wooden Spanish fleet. The Americans did not lose a single sailor or ship.

In spite of Dewey's victory, the Philippines could not be conquered until American soldiers arrived to defeat the Spanish land forces. Dewey blockaded the capital city of Manila during the two months it took to send an army from the United States. In August

Commodore Dewey led the American fleet to victory in the Battle of Manila Bay in 1898. A Japanese artist in the Philippines painted this scene of the first important battle in the Spanish-American War.

1898, after an attack by American soldiers and Filipino patriots who were eager to win freedom from Spain, Manila surrendered.

**Americans win swift victories in Cuba.** Late in June, American troops landed in Cuba. There they faced many hardships. Their woolen uniforms proved too warm for Cuba's tropical climate. Much of their food spoiled in the heat. The troops also had no defense against malaria and yellow fever. Because of widespread disease, more American soldiers in Cuba died from sickness than were killed in battle.

Slowly, the American army advanced toward Santiago, a city in the eastern part of the island. There the most famous battle of the Spanish American War took place. The American army unit known as the **Rough Riders,** led by Colonel Leonard Wood and Lieutenant Colonel Theodore Roosevelt, joined several units of black troops. Together they stormed and captured San Juan Hill near Santiago. Roosevelt, already a well-known government official, became a national hero after this battle. Roosevelt later praised the black soldiers for their bravery in battle.

Soon the American forces had Santiago surrounded. Shortly afterward, an American naval squadron attacked and destroyed all the Spanish warships in Santiago harbor. With that defeat, the city surrendered.

After the victory at Santiago, American forces invaded Puerto Rico, an island about 500 miles (800 kilometers) east of Cuba. The Americans met little resistance from Spanish forces. Within a short time, the Americans had occupied the island.

## The Philippine Question

Having suffered heavy losses, the Spanish government sought to end the conflict. On August 12, 1898, less than four months after Congress had declared war, the United States and Spain agreed to end the fighting. Representatives from the two nations met to work out the terms of the peace treaty. Spain granted independence to Cuba and gave the United States the islands of Puerto Rico and Guam (gwahm), a Spanish possession in the Pacific. Still, the representatives could not settle the troublesome question of what to do with the Philippines.

**Americans debate the merits of expansion.** The American people were deeply divided over the Philippine question. On one side were **antiexpansionists** —people who believed that the United States should not expand its territory and impose its rule on foreign lands. On the other side were expansionists who believed that the United States had the right to gain colonies, as well as a duty to help the Filipinos develop their country. This group also wanted to use the islands as a base from which to extend American trade and power in Asia, especially in China.

Debate raged in Congress while President McKinley decided what to do. As he later said,

> I walked the floor of the White House night after night until midnight; and I am not ashamed to tell you . . . that I went down on my knees and prayed Almighty God for light and guidance more than one night. And one night late it came to me this way—I don't know how it was but it came: (1) that we could not give them back to Spain—that would be cowardly and dishonorable; (2) that we could not turn them over to France and Germany—our commercial rivals in the Orient—that would be bad business and discreditable; (3) that we could not leave them to themselves—they were unfit for self-government—and they would soon have . . . misrule over there worse than Spain's was; and (4) that there was nothing left for us to do but to take them all, and to educate the Filipinos, and uplift and civilize and Christianize them, and by God's grace do the very best we could by them. . . . And then I went to bed, and went to sleep and slept soundly.

McKinley then ordered the Americans at the peace conference to offer Spain $20 million for the Philippines. Possession of the islands was transferred to the United States in a treaty signed on December 10, 1898.

**The United States governs the Philippines.** The Filipino people did not want their country to become a possession of the United States. Most of the citizens of the

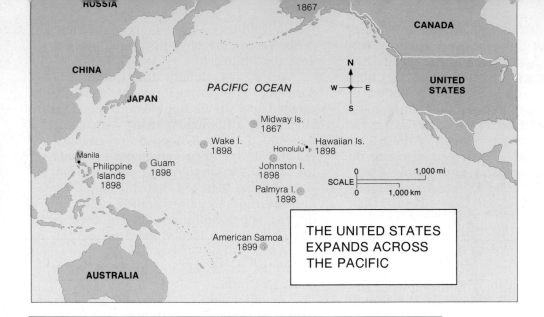

THE UNITED STATES EXPANDS ACROSS THE PACIFIC

## Map Study

**Between the mid-1800's and the early 1900's, the United States extended its influence across the Pacific. Which possessions did the United States acquire before 1898? In what year did the United States acquire the Philippines? Which island group was the southernmost American possession?**

Philippines had expected that the United States would give the islands their freedom after the Spanish government had surrendered. When that did not happen, Filipino patriots, led by Emilio Aguinaldo (ah-gee-NAHL-doh), fought for their independence. Bitter jungle warfare lasted for more than three years and took many lives. Peace was not restored to the islands until Aguinaldo was finally captured in 1901. He then took an oath of loyalty to the American government and asked his people to put an end to their rebellion.

The United States brought order to the islands by establishing a temporary government. It also tried to improve conditions in the Philippines by setting up a bureau of health, training teachers, and building schools. Some Filipinos received land and new farming tools. They were also introduced to new methods of farming. The United States further aided the people of the Philippines by buying large quantities of Philippine sugar, hemp, and tobacco. It was not until 1946 that the Philippines was able to gain its independence.

## SECTION REVIEW

1. **Vocabulary** yellow journalism, antiexpansionist
2. **People and Places** William Randolph Hearst, Joseph Pulitzer, Havana, John Hay, George Dewey, Manila, Rough Riders, Puerto Rico, Guam, Emilio Aguinaldo
3. **Comprehension** Why did Americans sympathize with the Cubans in the struggle against Spain?
4. **Comprehension** What did the United States gain as a result of the Spanish-American War?
5. **Critical Thinking** Did the United States go to war with Spain for selfish or unselfish reasons? Explain.

## CRITICAL THINKING: Interpreting Political Cartoons

While reading newspapers or magazines you may have noticed political cartoons. Some political cartoons call attention to public issues or problems. Other cartoons make us laugh at our mistakes. Any political cartoon, however, expresses an opinion or point of view on an important issue of the day. Political cartoons are meant to influence as well as to inform.

To make their viewpoint clearer or more forceful, cartoonists often exaggerate the facts. For example, Abraham Lincoln was tall, and many cartoonists exaggerated his height by drawing him with very long legs and a tall stovepipe hat. A drawing that exaggerates certain features for effect is called a **caricature.**

Cartoonists also use **symbols.** Some famous symbols used in American political cartoons are the donkey, representing the Democratic party; the elephant, representing the Republican party; and Uncle Sam, representing the United States. To fully understand a political cartoon, you must understand its symbols.

The cartoon below examines the subject of American expansionism in the late nineteenth century. Study the cartoon, particularly its use of symbols and exaggeration. Then answer the following questions.

1. Who is the central character in the cartoon and what does he represent?
2. How is expansionism represented in the cartoon?
3. Does the cartoonist support or oppose American expansion? Support your answer with evidence from the cartoon.
4. In your opinion, would this cartoon give historians an accurate picture of how Americans of the late 1800's felt about expansion? Explain your answer.

# What was America's foreign policy in Asia in the early 1900's?

## Vocabulary

sphere of influence

legation

The Spanish American War marked a turning point in relations between the United States and the rest of the world. As a result of the war, the United States gained possessions and now had important interests in the Pacific. Theodore Roosevelt noted that it was no longer a question of whether the country would take part in world affairs, but whether it would "play the part well or ill." One of the first places the United States exercised its new power was in Asia.

## The Open Door Policy

The acquisition of the Philippine Islands increased American interest in Asia, especially in China. Americans were eager to expand their trade into China, as European nations were already doing. The United States wanted to make sure that it, too, would have an equal trading opportunity there.

**China resists Westerners.** China was a unified and powerful empire for centuries before the European nations were formed. The Chinese people called their emperor the "Son of Heaven" and believed their culture to be the highest form of civilization. Foreigners were generally not welcome in China. All foreign traders were restricted to using the port city of Canton to lessen the influence of the Westerners.

Traders looked on China as a vast, untapped market because it had not gone through an industrial revolution. Merchants believed that China's millions of people would want to buy the products of industrialized nations.

**European powers and Japan take over parts of China.** Because China held on to its traditional ways of life, it did not advance technologically. This technological backwardness left China increasingly defenseless against the strength of Western nations seeking trade and colonies. In the 1840's, Great Britain fought and won a war against the Chinese. In settlement, China gave Britain the island of Hong Kong and permission for English people to live and trade in five other Chinese cities. Later France gained trading rights in southern China. Russia forced China to give it special privileges in the territory of Manchuria and the city of Port Arthur. Then in the 1890's, Japan waged war on China and won a sweeping victory. As a result of this war, China was forced to recognize the independence of Korea and to cede the island of Formosa (present-day Taiwan) to Japan.

During the nineteenth century, the emperors of China were weakened by internal rebellions as well. After the defeat of China by Japan, several foreign powers divided the country into **spheres of influence**. Spheres of influence were areas in which each country would have exclusive rights to trade and invest. Great Britain, France, Russia, Japan, and Germany each claimed a region of China. Gradually all of the outlying parts of China, it seemed, were being nibbled away.

**The Chinese strike back.** Patriotic Chinese became angry. They saw their country and its riches being handed out bit by bit to foreigners. Some Chinese patriots formed secret societies with such names as the "Great Sword Society," the "Plum-Blossom Fists," and the "Fists of Public Harmony." Because the members of these Chinese societies practiced gymnastics, foreigners called them "boxers." In their secret meetings the boxers talked of driving the foreigners out of China.

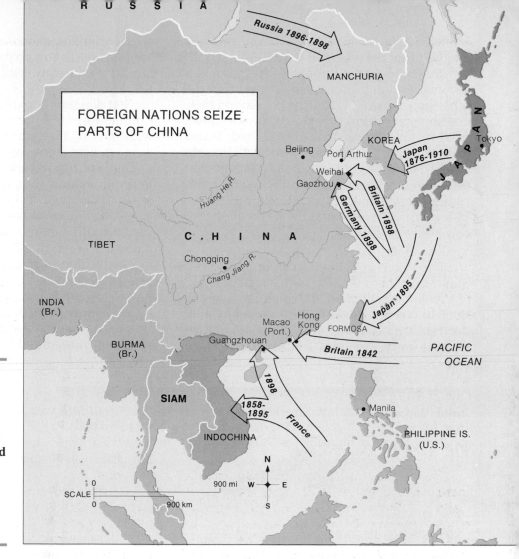

RUSSIA

Russia 1896-1898

MANCHURIA

FOREIGN NATIONS SEIZE
PARTS OF CHINA

KOREA

Beijing

Port Arthur

Japan
1876-1910

JAPAN

Tokyo

Weihai

Gaozhou

Britain 1898

Germany 1898

Huang He R.

C H I N A

TIBET

Chongqing

Chang Jiang R.

Japan 1895

INDIA
(Br.)

Macao
(Port.)

Hong
Kong

FORMOSA

BURMA
(Br.)

Guahgzhouan

Britain 1842

PACIFIC
OCEAN

SIAM

1898

1858-
1895

France

Manila

PHILIPPINE IS.
(U.S.)

INDOCHINA

N

0          900 mi      W      E
SCALE
0          900 km              S

**Map Study**
In the late 1800's, competing nations seized parts of China. Which areas did Japan seize? Which region did France seize? Which nation took over Manchuria? Which country ruled Hong Kong?

In 1900, the boxers rose in revolt, killing hundreds of foreigners and destroying their property. They also attacked **legations** — the official residences of diplomats—in the capital city of Peking (present-day Beijing). This outbreak of violence became known as the **Boxer Rebellion.**

**Foreign soldiers crush the Boxer Rebellion.** European countries, Japan, and the United States sent soldiers to stop the rioting in Peking and restore order. The Chinese government was forced to pay large sums of money for the damages suffered by foreigners and the trouble the rioting had caused. The European powers and Japan kept their shares of this money, but the United States later returned above $17 million, more than

half of its share. This money was used to send Chinese students to American schools and colleges.

**The Open Door Policy urges fair play in China.** Events in China aroused American concern even before the Boxer Rebellion. When China was being partitioned into spheres of influence, Secretary of State John Hay sought to protect American interests by sending a message to Britain, France, Germany, Russia, and Japan. He asked these countries to agree that all nations be given equal opportunity to trade in China. No country, in other words, was to receive special favors. Because Hay's idea meant that China should be open to all, it was called the **Open Door Policy.** The other powers did not

561

immediately accept Hay's ideas, but he claimed that they agreed with him.

After the Boxer Rebellion, Hay issued a second open door note. Hay feared that the other powers would again try to expand their holdings in China. He told the European powers and Japan that the United States opposed any further division of China. In effect, Hay's Open Door Policy meant that the United States would protect equal trade rights for all and independence for China. These principles became the basis of American policy in China.

## American Policy Toward Japan

Japan was another Asian nation that had long interested the United States. For hundreds of years Japan, like China, had had little to do with foreigners. It would not allow any foreigners, except a few Dutch ships, to enter its ports to carry on trade. Japan was almost completely shut off from the rest of the world.

**Perry opens Japan to the world.** In 1854 Commodore Matthew Perry visited Japan with part of the American fleet. The Japanese government was impressed by the strength of the American navy. It agreed to Perry's demand that Japan sign a treaty allowing American ships to trade in its ports.

Soon, other countries negotiated similar treaties with Japan. Quick to recognize what made the Western nations powerful, the Japanese decided to modernize their nation. In less than 50 years, Japan became a great power and a strong industrial nation.

**Theodore Roosevelt helps settle Japan's war with Russia.** For many years after Perry's visit, the United States and Japan were

In this Japanese painting, Americans led by Commodore Perry (third from left) arrive in Tokyo in 1854. How does the picture show that the Japanese were unfamiliar with the American flag?

on friendly terms. Japan had taken control of parts of China, but it seemed to accept the Open Door Policy of the United States.

Russia, on the other hand, was trying to take greater control of Manchuria, China's large northern territory. Japan wanted to keep Manchuria open because the region was rich in iron and other minerals needed for Japanese industry. In 1904 Japan went to war against Russia. In this war, called the Russo-Japanese War, Americans generally sympathized with Japan.

To the surprise of many people, Japan won victory after victory over Russia, both on land and at sea. President Roosevelt became concerned, fearing that a total victory would give Japan too much power in Asia and hurt American interests there. So Roosevelt offered to help end the war. Both Russia and Japan agreed. A peace treaty was signed, granting Japan special rights in Manchuria and Korea. The Japanese were disappointed. They expected their victories to bring them even greater gains.

**Problems develop between the United States and Japan.** With the end of the Russo-Japanese War, a change took place in relations between Japan and the United States. The Japanese felt that President Roosevelt had favored Russia in the peace settlement. The Japanese were also offended by American restrictions on Asian immigrants. Chinese immigration had been stopped in

1882, and politicians and labor leaders were urging a halt to Japanese immigration. Some western states were passing laws that discriminated against the Japanese living in the United States. In 1906, when San Francisco ordered all Japanese children to attend separate schools, Japan appealed to President Roosevelt to end this "national insult."

In 1907 Japan and the United States reached an understanding known as the Gentlemen's Agreement. California's school segregation ended, but only after Japan promised to allow no more Japanese workers to enter the United States. The Japanese resented this agreement, and relations between the two nations remained troubled.

## SECTION REVIEW

1. **Vocabulary**    sphere of influence, legation
2. **People and Places**    Canton, Hong Kong, Korea, Formosa, Matthew Perry
3. **Comprehension**    What was the goal of the Open Door Policy in China?
4. **Comprehension**    Why were relations between the United States and Japan strained in the early years of this century?
5. **Critical Thinking**    Compare China's response to the West with Japan's. What was the outcome in each case?

# 4 How did expansion affect relations with Latin America?

## Vocabulary
arbitration
autonomy

As the United States was shaping its new policies toward Asia, it was also redefining its policies toward Latin America. Since 1823, the Monroe Doctrine had guided United States foreign policy in keeping the European nations out of Western Hemisphere affairs. Not only did the United States want Europeans out of its affairs, it wanted no interference in Latin America. As the United States grew more powerful, it began to explore what its own involvement should be in the countries of Latin America.

## Concerns to the South

A serious challenge to the Monroe Doctrine occurred in 1895. A border dispute developed between Venezuela and its eastern neighbor, the British colony of British Guiana (gee-AH-nuh). The Monroe Doctrine forbade the establishment of new colonies in the Americas. The United States interpreted this to mean that enlarging existing colonies was also forbidden. It demanded that Great Britain agree to **arbitration** —settling a dispute by a board of neutral persons. At first Britain felt the United States had no right to interfere. Eventually, it agreed to arbitration and actually got most of the land it wanted. Acceptance of the broader version of the Monroe Doctrine showed increasing American power in the hemisphere's affairs.

**Problems in Cuba are addressed.** Although the Spanish American War freed Cuba from Spain, the newly independent country faced many problems. The nation lacked an organized government. Many Cubans were homeless and starving, and disease was widespread. As a result, American troops stayed in Cuba to maintain order and improve living conditions.

One of the most pressing problems in Cuba was yellow fever. Yellow fever had long been a dreaded disease in tropical countries, but no one knew what caused it. A Cuban doctor, Carlos Finlay, believed that the disease was carried by mosquitoes. To test this theory, a number of American doctors and soldiers, under the supervision of Dr. Walter Reed, allowed themselves to be bitten by mosquitoes that had previously bitten yellow fever victims. As a result, army doctors were able to prove that the disease was carried by a certain kind of mosquito.

The army then began to drain swamps and pour oil over stagnant water so there would be no place for the mosquitoes to breed. In three months, Major William C. Gorgas, the officer in charge of health conditions in Cuba, was able to rid Havana of yellow fever.

**Americans influence the Cuban government.** When Congress declared war against Spain in 1898, it had promised that the United States would not take control of Cuba. Once the war was over, however, many members of Congress did not think that Cubans were ready for self-government. General Leonard Wood was appointed military governor of Cuba. Under his leadership, Americans helped the Cubans build roads, bridges, hospitals, and schools. They also helped Cuba establish a government.

This government, however, was subject to limits imposed by the United States. Before the United States would agree to withdraw its troops from Cuba, the Cubans had to include four provisions in their new constitution. First, Cuba could make no treaties with foreign governments that would compromise its independence. Second, Cuban debt would be limited. Third, the United States had the right to intervene in Cuban affairs to maintain independence and peace and to protect American lives and property. Finally, Cuba had to grant land to the United States for naval stations.

In 1902, after the Cuban people adopted their new constitution, American troops left the island. American forces returned to Cuba more than once, however, when rebellions broke out and threatened growing American investments. Most Cubans resented American interference and saw it as similar to the European interference forbidden by the Monroe Doctrine.

**The United States improves conditions in Puerto Rico.** The United States also faced social, economic, and political problems in Puerto Rico. Like Cuba, Puerto Rico was a small, impoverished island. The United States worked to improve living conditions by building roads, starting health programs, and setting up schools. It also allowed Puerto Rican products to enter the United States without tariffs. As a result, sugar, tobacco, and banana production boomed.

Although increasing trade brought more wealth to the island, very little of it reached the common people. Unemployment and poverty continued to be major problems. In addition, some Puerto Ricans resented American control. They were not familiar with American ways and customs or forms of government. Some of the islanders began to demand **autonomy** —self-government.

Americans at home debated whether Puerto Rico should remain a colony or someday become independent. Congress adopted a form of partial self-rule for the island. Puerto Rico would have a governor and executive council appointed by the President of the United States, along with a legislature elected by Puerto Ricans. In 1917 Puerto Ricans gained American citizenship.

## The Panama Canal

At the beginning of the 1900's, United States territory stretched not only from the Atlantic to the Pacific, but halfway around the world. Yet the only sea route between the east and west coasts of the United States was around South America, a journey of about 12,000 miles (19,200 kilometers). To protect American possessions in the Pacific and to help American commerce, it became increasingly important to shorten this trip. Thus, interest in building a canal across the isthmus connecting North and South America grew. (See map on page 567.)

**The United States decides to dig a canal.** The idea of building a canal across Central America was not a new one. France, England, and the United States had all considered such a project, but these early attempts had failed. During the Spanish American War, it took the battleship *Oregon* 67 days to sail from San Francisco to Key West, Florida. Americans then became convinced that a canal was necessary, and that the United States must build it.

**The United States secures land for a canal.** In 1850 the United States and Great Britain had signed a treaty agreeing to build a canal together. This agreement prevented the United States from acting on its own. As a result, the United States and Britain worked out a new treaty in 1901. This treaty permitted the United States to build a canal, as long as all nations were allowed to use it.

The next steps were to choose a location and get local approval for the canal. Two routes for the canal were possible—one across Nicaragua and one across Panama,

## ★ ★ ★ *Puerto Rico*

Puerto Rico became territory of the United States in 1898 after the Spanish American War. Although Puerto Ricans received citizenship in 1917, progress toward self-government was slow. Until 1947 the President of the United States appointed the island's governor and other major officials. In 1952 the island became a **commonwealth**—a territory with a constitution and a great deal of self-government.

Since the early 1970's some people have wanted to make Puerto Rico the fifty-first state. Statehood is a matter of great debate in Puerto Rico. Polls indicate that a majority of the people want statehood. A large minority want to stay a commonwealth, and a few want independence. In years to come, the Puerto Rican people and Congress will decide the question.

then part of Colombia. In 1902 Congress approved the route across Panama.

The United States then began to negotiate terms for the canal with Colombia. An agreement was reached, but the Colombian senate refused to accept it. Local Panamanians, angry at the treaty's failure, staged a revolt against Colombia. This revolt had the support of the United States and President Roosevelt. The small group of rebels quickly established Panama as a new, independent republic.

The United States immediately made an agreement with Panama. For a down payment of $10 million and rent of $250,000 a year, the United States leased a strip of land 10 miles (16 kilometers) wide. This Canal Zone would become home to thousands of Americans, most having some connection to the canal.

Colombia deeply resented the actions of the United States. Many Americans thought

When Theodore Roosevelt celebrated its completion in 1914, he called it "one of the great works of the world." It was an engineering triumph, a 51-mile long artificial waterway linking two oceans. It was the Panama Canal.

Three obstacles stood in the way of building the canal—mosquitoes, mountains, and a river. Even before work began, many workers fell ill with malaria and yellow fever, tropical diseases spread by mosquitoes. Only after the mosquitoes were controlled could construction proceed.

The workers then had to blast their way through the mountainous Continental Divide. The flood waters of the Chagres River made a sea-level passage impossible. Thus a dam and locks had to be built. More than 43,000 workers toiled on the canal project. Their efforts serve as a lasting reminder of the human spirit's ability to triumph over natural adversity.

**A ship in the Panama Canal**

that President Roosevelt had been high-handed. Later, the United States paid Colombia $25 million to make up for supporting the Panamanian revolt.

**The United States builds the Panama Canal.** American Army engineers were given the tremendous task of building the **Panama Canal.** Because high mountains rose in the interior of Panama, it was decided that the engineers should build a canal 85 feet (25 meters) above sea level, in the middle of the isthmus. Locks would be built to raise and lower ships where necessary.

For seven years, using huge steam shovels and other powerful machinery, workers blasted, dug, and dredged. At one point, a channel nearly 9 miles (14.4 kilometers) long had to be cut through mountains of solid rock. Most of the workers were black laborers from the Caribbean. Thousands died from disease and construction accidents.

In August 1914 the great engineering feat was finally completed. In Washington, D.C.,

President Wilson pushed a switch that released the dammed-up waters and filled the canal. Soon ships were passing from one ocean to the other.

**The canal leads to another American purchase.** To defend the canal, the United States decided that it needed a base in the Caribbean Sea. As a result in 1917 the United States paid Denmark $25 million for three islands in the Virgin Islands group. In 1927, the residents of these islands were declared citizens of the United States.

## Relations with Latin America

During the years of expansion and growth, the influence of the United States spread throughout the Western Hemisphere. Many Latin Americans, however, resented having a powerful neighbor to the north.

**Latin Americans grow suspicious of the Monroe Doctrine.** At first, the countries of Latin America had accepted the protection

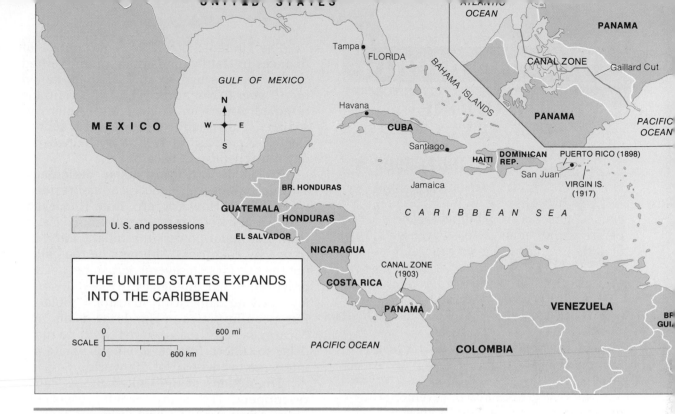

MEXICO

GULF OF MEXICO

Tampa

FLORIDA

Havana

CUBA

Santiago

HAITI DOMINICAN REP.

Jamaica

San Juan

PUERTO RICO (1898)

VIRGIN IS. (1917)

BAHAMA ISLANDS

CANAL ZONE

Gaillard Cut

PANAMA

PANAMA

PACIFIC OCEAN

BR. HONDURAS

GUATEMALA

HONDURAS

EL SALVADOR

NICARAGUA

CANAL ZONE (1903)

COSTA RICA

PANAMA

CARIBBEAN SEA

VENEZUELA

BR. GUI

COLOMBIA

U. S. and possessions

**THE UNITED STATES EXPANDS INTO THE CARIBBEAN**

SCALE

0                    600 mi

0              600 km

PACIFIC OCEAN

## Map Study

**After the Spanish-American War, American influence spread in the Caribbean. Name three United States possessions in the Caribbean.**

that was offered by the Monroe Doctrine. They knew that they would not be able to defend themselves against the stronger European nations that might want to gain territory in the Americas.

As time went on, Latin American countries began to regard the United States with suspicion. They had seen the United States government annex Mexican territory as a result of the Mexican War. (See Chapter 16.) Then they saw it take control of Puerto Rico, interfere in Cuban affairs, and obtain the Panama Canal Zone.

American businesses also had bought up hundreds of thousands of acres in Central America. To many Latin Americans, these were acts of imperialism. Some people feared that the United States would look south for yet more territory. In the early 1900's, certain events made it seem that their fears were coming true.

**The Roosevelt Corollary expands the Monroe Doctrine.** Many governments of Central American and Caribbean countries had a history of instability. Some had piled up large debts to European countries. Soon after 1900, conditions became desperate in several of these countries, and there were frequent revolts. Furthermore, European countries began demanding repayment of their loans. They were even threatening to send warships to collect the money. A European military presence, however, would be a threat to the Panama Canal Zone.

President Theodore Roosevelt reminded Congress that the Monroe Doctrine did not allow European interference in the Western Hemisphere. He declared that the United States should step in and manage the affairs of any Latin American country that could not keep order or pay its debts. This policy was known as the **Roosevelt Corollary** to the

567

## THEODORE ROOSEVELT

★ **1901–1909** ★

**26TH PRESIDENT**

**REPUBLICAN**

- ★ Born October 27, 1858, in New York
- ★ Married Alice Hathaway Lee in 1880; 1 child
- ★ Married Edith Kermit Carow in 1886; 5 children
- ★ Colonel of the "Rough Riders" in Spanish American War; governor of New York; Vice President under McKinley
- ★ Lived in New York when elected Vice President
- ★ Vice President: Charles Fairbanks
- ★ Died January 6, 1919, in New York
- ★ Key events while in office: Russo-Japanese War ended; Panama Canal begun; Pure Food and Drug Act; Oklahoma became a state

Monroe Doctrine. In effect, President Roosevelt wanted the United States to become an "international police power" in the Western Hemisphere. Roosevelt's methods of enforcing this policy came to be known as "gunboat diplomacy."

**The United States polices Latin America.** In 1905 the United States intervened in the Dominican Republic to straighten out that nation's tangled affairs. American officials took charge of the country's finances and arranged for the payment of its debts. Conditions improved greatly, but the people of the Dominican Republic resented American interference.

The United States also took control of finances in Haiti. To maintain order, United States Marines arrived in Haiti and stayed for 19 years. Not surprisingly, the Haitians resented American control and American soldiers. American troops were also sent to Central America. In 1912, they helped put down a rebellion in Nicaragua.

**President Taft tries dollar diplomacy.** Theodore Roosevelt's successor as President was William Howard Taft. Like Roosevelt, Taft wanted to protect the Panama Canal from European powers that might interfere in nearby countries. Although he too called out the marines on several occasions, he also practiced **dollar diplomacy.** Under this policy, private American investors replaced European investors in Honduras, Haiti, and Nicaragua. Taft reasoned that with no more debts to collect, European nations would not intervene in this part of the world.

**The actions of the United States cause resentment.** To many people, especially Latin Americans, the United States seemed to be depriving these countries of their independence. They began to wonder if the United States intended to use the Monroe Doctrine as an excuse to gain control of all of Latin America. Bitter feelings arose in most countries. These feelings would affect relations between the United States and Latin America for years to come.

## American Involvement in Mexico

The policy of intervention in Latin American affairs begun by Theodore Roosevelt continued throughout the early 1900's. In 1912 Woodrow Wilson became President. Soon Wilson faced problems in Mexico, and intervened to protect American interests there.

**A revolution takes place in Mexico.** From 1877 to 1911, Mexicans lived under the rule of a harsh dictator, Porfirio Diaz (DEE-ahs). Diaz had allowed foreign businesses to buy large tracts of land, build railroads, and develop Mexico's rich oil deposits. In return, the Mexican government received a share of the large profits made by the foreign companies. Foreign businesses and some Mexican politicians grew rich, but conditions worsened for most of the Mexican people.

At last the Mexican people rose in revolt. American investments, which by 1913 totaled $1 billion, were threatened by the unstable situation. Soon there were demands in Congress for American intervention.

**The United States sends troops to Mexico.** During the Mexican revolution, the country was in a state of great confusion. The Mexican government could not protect the property and lives of Americans and other foreigners who lived there. The United States encouraged the establishment of an orderly government. The Mexicans, however, complained of American interference. In 1916 an incident brought about direct American involvement in Mexico. A Mexican revolutionary leader, Pancho Villa (VEE-yuh), seized 18 Americans from a train and killed them. Two months later, Villa's men crossed the Rio Grande and killed 17 more Americans in Columbus, New Mexico.

President Wilson sent American soldiers under General John J. Pershing into Mexico to catch Villa. For almost a year Pershing's troops searched northern Mexico for Villa. Finally, in 1917, Wilson ordered the troops withdrawn. The United States was about to enter World War I and needed all its soldiers in Europe. The departure of the American forces, however, did not end the bitterness felt by Mexicans toward the United States.

## SECTION REVIEW

1. **Vocabulary**   arbitration, autonomy
2. **People and Places**   Venezuela, British Guiana, Walter Reed, Isthmus of Panama, Pancho Villa
3. **Comprehension**   What problems did the United States face in Cuba and Puerto Rico?
4. **Comprehension**   What was the Roosevelt Corollary to the Monroe Doctrine?
5. **Critical Thinking**   How did the acquisition of the Panama Canal influence American foreign policy in Latin America?

# Chapter 24 Summary

Until the late 1800's Americans were too busy developing their own country to take much interest in foreign affairs. As the economy grew, they began to look for markets overseas. Some people felt the United States should acquire colonies of its own. In 1867 the United States purchased Alaska from Russia, and in 1898 it annexed Hawaii.

In 1895 a revolt broke out against Spanish rule in Cuba. Sympathy for the Cubans, exaggerated reports in the American press, and the sinking of the *Maine* led to war between the United States and Spain in 1898. As a result of the Spanish-American War, the United States acquired Puerto Rico, Guam, and the Philippines. Cuba was granted independence, but the United States retained great influence on the island.

The United States also expanded its influence in Asia. To preserve equal trading rights and independence in China, the United States developed the Open Door Policy. The United States also helped put down the Boxer Rebellion, a revolt against foreigners in China. Americans had opened Japan to trade in 1854. When Japan fought a war against Russia, the United States helped to settle the dispute.

In the early 1900's the United States intervened in several Central American and Caribbean countries to restore order. It also built the Panama Canal, after helping Panama gain its independence from Colombia. Latin American nations soon came to resent interference in their affairs and accused the United States of imperialism.

# Chapter 24 REVIEW

## Vocabulary and Key Terms

Use the following terms to complete the sentences below. Write your answers on a separate sheet of paper.

autonomy
Spanish-American War
imperialism
arbitration

yellow journalism
Rough Riders
antiexpansionists
Panama Canal

1. Sensational reporting, known as _____, was one of the factors that brought the United States into the _____.
2. The United States urged Russia and Japan to accept _____ to settle their war.
3. Theodore Roosevelt is remembered for his role in the army unit known as the _____ and for his efforts to secure the _____ for the United States.
4. People against America's acquisition of lands overseas were called _____.
5. In time, Puerto Rico was granted self-government, or _____.
6. The policy that seeks to create an empire is called _____.

## Recalling the Facts

1. How was the United States' acquisition of Alaska different from its acquisition of Hawaii?
2. What overseas possessions did the United States get by winning the Spanish-American War?
3. What did the Open Door Policy seek to do?
4. What problems did the United States have in the Philippines?
5. Why did the United States build the Panama Canal?
6. How did Theodore Roosevelt expand the Monroe Doctrine?
7. What was dollar diplomacy?
8. Why did President Wilson send troops into Mexico?

## Places to Locate

Match the letters on the map with the places listed below. Write your answers on a separate sheet of paper.

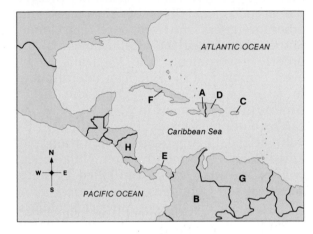

1. Panama
2. Cuba
3. Nicaragua
4. Haiti
5. Venezuela
6. Dominican Republic
7. Colombia
8. Puerto Rico

## Critical Thinking

1. By the early 1900's, a little more than 100 years after throwing off colonial rule, the United States was itself a colonial power. How and why did this happen? Was it a good idea for the United States? Address these questions in your answer:
   a. Where did the United States expand?
   b. What methods did it use to acquire territory?
   c. What motives lay behind American expansion?
   d. What were the benefits and costs for the United States?
2. Was American influence in Asia more beneficial than harmful for Asian countries? Consider these points in your answer:
   a. the results for those countries
   b. how they viewed the United States

3. During the first part of the twentieth century many Latin Americans began to change their opinion of the United States. How and why did their attitude change? Were their feelings justified? Consider these points in your answer:
a. earlier feelings toward the United States
b. American actions in Latin America and the Caribbean
c. Latin American culture and national pride

## Understanding History

1. Reread the section "Americans react to the Cuban conflict" on page 554. Then answer these questions.
a. **Citizenship.** What concerns about Cuba do you think were most important to the average American? Why?
b. **Primary Source.** What was the meaning of Hearst's statement?
2. Reread the section "Americans influence the Cuban government" on page 564. Then answer these questions.
a. **Citizenship.** Did the United States honor its earlier pledge to leave control of Cuba to the Cuban people? Explain.
b. **Economics.** What role might economic interests have had in the United States' policy toward Cuba?
3. Reread the section "The United States improves conditions in Puerto Rico" on page 564. Then answer these questions.
a. **Economics.** How did control by the United States affect the Puerto Rican economy?
b. **Economics.** What economic problems remained in Puerto Rico despite American influence?
4. Reread the section "The United States secures land for a canal" on page 565. Then answer these questions.
a. **Citizenship.** Should the United States have supported the Panamanian revolt? Why or why not?
b. **Geography.** How wide was the Panama Canal Zone? Why was it important to the United States?

## Projects and Activities

1. **Making a Time Line.** Make a time line showing important American events and actions discussed in this chapter.
2. **Writing a News Article.** Imagine that you are a reporter covering the Battle of San Juan Hill during the Spanish-American War. Write a news story that accurately describes the battle.
3. **Preparing a Panel Discussion.** Prepare a panel discussion with a group of five classmates. Two students should act as expansionists and two as antiexpansionists. The fifth student should act as moderator. In front of the class, discuss American control over the Philippines after the Spanish-American War.

## Practicing Your Skill

Use the political cartoon below to answer the questions that follow.

1. What does the eagle represent?
2. What symbols does the cartoonist use to indicate the eagle's identity?
3. Where is the eagle spreading its wings?
4. Do you think this cartoon expresses an expansionist or an antiexpansionist view? Explain your answer.

# 25 The Progressives Reform American Life 1900–1917

McKinley | T. Roosevelt | Taft | Wilson

1900 | 1903 | 1906 | 1909 | 1912 | 1915

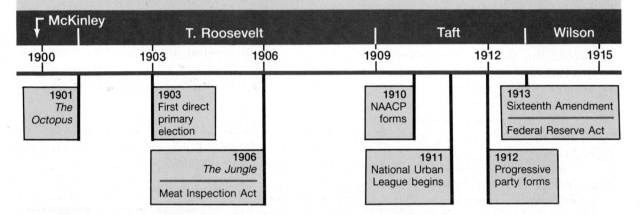

| | |
|---|---|
| **1901** *The Octopus* | |
| **1903** First direct primary election | |
| | **1906** *The Jungle* — Meat Inspection Act |
| **1910** NAACP forms | |
| | **1911** National Urban League begins |
| **1913** Sixteenth Amendment — Federal Reserve Act | |
| **1912** Progressive party forms | |

A candidate presents his views on the issues of the early 1900's. A key concern of the Progressives was a more-responsive government.

## Preparing to Read

At the same time the United States was becoming a world power, the American people were troubled by many problems at home. The late 1800's had been a time of rapid growth for American business and for American cities. The changes brought about by that growth had helped make the United States a stronger, more confident nation. The changes had also increased the power of big business and the amount of corruption in government. The condition of urban workers also grew worse. Many people feared that basic American values, even democracy itself, might be threatened. As a result, a great reform movement arose in the early 1900's to face these nagging issues. As you read this chapter, try to answer the following questions:

1. What were the achievements of the Progressive Movement?
2. What problems did President Theodore Roosevelt try to solve?
3. How did President Taft differ from President Roosevelt?
4. What reforms did President Woodrow Wilson undertake?

# 1 What were the achievements of the Progressive Movement?

## Vocabulary

strike-breaking
exposé
muckraker
direct primary

initiative
referendum
recall
prohibition

By the turn of the century, serious problems in American society had become evident to just about everyone. Grangers and Populists had pointed out the stranglehold of banks and railroads over farmers. Labor unions had brought to light the unsafe and inhuman working conditions of factories. Jane Addams had called attention to the needs of immigrants in America's large cities. And the struggle for civil-service reform had focused on corruption in government at the national, state, and local levels. It was more than just a small group of reformers who wanted to bring change to these conditions. Reform had become a movement all across the United States.

## The Progressive Movement

The core of the great reform movement of the early 1900's, called the **Progressive Movement,** was middle-class city dwellers. These people included teachers and professors, lawyers, social workers, and rising numbers of women who had leisure time. Well-educated and well-informed, they grew offended by the evils they found around them. Political decay followed as party bosses took control of local and state governments. Social problems multiplied as poor immigrants were packed into tenements, slums spread, and disease and crime increased. All of these issues aroused middle-class citizens to work for reform. These reformers soon began calling themselves progressives.

**Progressive reforms have broad appeal.** The progressives were not a political party with a sharply defined platform. Instead, they were both Republicans and Democrats. They shared the belief that government

At the beginning of the twentieth century, a group of artists began to paint or draw realistic scenes of city life. These scenes included city streets and parks, urban women hanging laundry to dry, and life in the slums. These artists' critics gave them the name "the Ashcan school."

These artists often worked independently, but they were thought of as a group because they shared a single purpose—creating art with a social message. Like the muckraking writers of the era, the Ashcan artists had clear political and social ideas. Through their art, they brought their ideas to life.

In 1913 many Ashcan artists organized a huge exhibition of paintings at the New York City Armory. The Armory Show of 1913 is now recognized as a major event in our country's art history. Many viewers were shocked by the paintings, but they could not deny the troublesome social problems the artists portrayed.

**"Woman's Work" by John Sloan**

should protect not only the rights but also the well-being of all citizens.

Members of other groups also supported the progressive causes. The Populist farmers of the western and southern states demanded more responsible government and limits to monopolies. Many former Populists, like William Jennings Bryan, contributed to the Progressive Movement. Industrial workers also joined in the fight to improve working conditions. Their demands included a shorter workweek, higher wages, safer factories, and accident insurance. These workers also sought some protection against **strike-breaking** —the use of force by employers to end strikes. Writers, artists, journalists, and educators also used their work to speak out for needed reforms.

**Writers point out social problems.** Despite opposition from powerful groups in business and government, progressive causes attracted great national interest. The movement was fueled by the popular press— low-cost magazines and newspapers that reached a mass readership. Magazines like *McClure's, Cosmopolitan,* and *Everybody's* published **exposés** (ex-po-ZAYZ)—articles that uncovered wrongdoing in government, business, and politics.

The journalists who wrote these articles were called **muckrakers.** This term, originally an insult, suggested that reporters dug around in the muck, or dirt, for their stories. Progressive journalists adopted the term with pride. Their work brought problems to public attention. One muckraker, Lincoln Steffens, stunned the nation with "The Shame of the Cities." This magazine series exposed corruption in city governments. Ida Tarbell's *History of the Standard Oil Company* described the ruthless methods Standard Oil used to ruin its competitors.

Other writers also focused on social and political problems of the early 1900's. Frank

574

Norris told of the struggle in California between wheat farmers and powerful railroads in his novel *The Octopus*. *The Woman Who Toils* described the problems of women in industry. It was written by two wealthy sisters-in-law, Marie and Bessie Van Vorst, who disguised themselves as workers to gather information. Another novelist, Upton Sinclair, exposed shameful practices in the meat-packing industry in *The Jungle*. The political cartoonist and writer Finley Peter Dunne made fun of politicians and attacked corruption through his popular fictional character Mr. Dooley. Photographers like Jacob Riis and Lewis Hine used their cameras to document such social ills as child labor and urban poverty.

## Progressive Reforms

Progressives believed that government was the only force powerful enough to make the changes necessary in American society. First, they believed, government itself had to be reformed to make it more democratic and responsible to the people.

**Progressives at the local level show the way.** Most progressive reforms started at the local level. Two heroes of the reform movement gained national attention for cleaning up political corruption in the Ohio cities of Cleveland and Toledo. Tom Johnson, mayor of Cleveland, broke the control of the bosses over the city streetcar system. He also reformed taxes and put honest officials in city government. A colorful business leader, Samuel "Golden Rule" Jones, made similar reforms as mayor of Toledo.

One of the biggest tasks faced by local reformers was curbing the power of political bosses. To do this, some cities turned to new forms of government. The **commission plan,** first tried in Galveston, Texas, replaced the mayor and city council with a commission of officials. Each official oversaw a different department of the city, such as police, fire, or

In this photograph by Lewis Hine, children play stickball in a narrow alley. Hine photographed tenement life to call attention to the problems of the urban poor.

sanitation. Another new form of local government was the **city manager plan.** Under it, a paid city manager, free of political ties, was responsible to a commission or a city council. These plans helped rid local government of political bosses. They were soon adopted by cities throughout the country.

**Reforms continue at the state level.** In the states, a number of governors also carried out reforms. Charles Evans Hughes of New York created a commission to regulate public utilities, which often overcharged for water, electricity, and gas. In California, Hiram Johnson fought the great power of the Southern Pacific Railroad. Meanwhile, Governor Woodrow Wilson of New Jersey supported reforms to limit the state's powerful trusts. Progressive governors worked to break the ties between big-business interests and political machines in state government.

In this cartoon, Governor Robert M. La Follette displays a poster showing the effects of state reforms. The poster shows Wisconsin as a model state after new laws curbed the power of railroad trusts. How does the poster portray the railroads before reform?

Perhaps the most famous of the progressive governors was Robert "Fighting Bob" La Follette of Wisconsin. His state was described as a "laboratory of progressivism" because of the many reforms passed there.

In 1903 the first **direct primary** was adopted by the state of Wisconsin. The direct primary is an election in which the voters, not the political bosses, choose the candidates to run for state office. The direct primary was popular in Wisconsin and soon spread to other states. Every state now uses some form of the direct primary.

States also introduced the direct election of senators. Previously, senators had been elected by their state legislatures, which were often influenced by the political machines. The direct election of senators by the people of the state became the law of the nation after the **Seventeenth Amendment** was ratified in 1913.

In addition to the direct primary and the direct election of senators, progressives were in favor of the adoption of the secret ballot. Until the 1890's, voters had chosen from among ballots that were printed in different colors. How a person voted, therefore, was easy to determine. By using the secret ballot, voters could go to the polls and make their choices in private.

State governments also carried out reforms to give the public greater control over government. One of these reforms was the **initiative.** This procedure lets a state's citizens suggest new laws or amendments to the state constitution. Another reform was the **referendum.** Under this plan, voters are given the opportunity to either approve or turn down laws passed by the state legislature. Some states also adopted the **recall.** This reform enables the voters to remove from office a public official whose work they consider to be unsatisfactory.

**Social reforms are passed by the states.** Progressives also worked at the state level to improve social conditions. Many states passed laws to extend protections to workers. These included accident insurance, limits on child labor, minimum-wage laws, and regulations on hours and wages for working women.

These children worked as coal sorters, laboring as long as 12 hours a day in hazardous conditions. During the 1890's, progressive state governments passed laws restricting child labor.

**The Prohibition movement gains strength.** Some states, under a great deal of pressure from reformers, also outlawed alcoholic beverages. Many people believed that drinking alcohol lowered worker productivity and contributed to poverty, crime, and disease. The crusade to limit the drinking of alcohol had begun in the 1830's and 1840's. In 1846 the Maine legislature had passed the first state prohibition law, forbidding the manufacture and sale of alcohol. By 1874 the prohibition movement had gained considerable strength. In that year, the Woman's Christian Temperance Union (WCTU) was organized. (See Chapter 23.) The WCTU attempted to bring the Protestant churches into the effort to limit the use of alcohol.

## SECTION REVIEW

1. **Vocabulary**   strike-breaking, exposé, muckraker, direct primary, initiative, referendum, recall, prohibition
2. **People and Places**   Lincoln Steffens, Ida Tarbell, Frank Norris, Upton Sinclair, Ohio, New Jersey, Robert La Follette, Wisconsin
3. **Comprehension**   What were the main goals of the progressives?
4. **Comprehension**   How did the muckrakers help the progressive cause?
5. **Critical Thinking**   What made the progressives reformers rather than revolutionaries?

## MAPS AND GRAPHS: Interpreting Circle Graphs

In addition to line and bar graphs, historians often use **circle graphs** to present statistics. A circle graph is also called a **pie graph** because it is divided into pie-shaped sections. Each section represents a **percentage,** or so many hundredths, of the whole circle. In the circle graphs shown below, it is clear which groups were largest and smallest. Circle graphs serve a special purpose. They show the relationship of the sections to the whole.

Circle graphs can also be used to compare the same kind of information over time. Look at the two circle graphs below. They show information about women in the American labor force. The first graph gives this information for 1900, while the second graph provides the same kind of information for 1920. In both of these cases, the whole graph represents the total number of women in the American labor force. The sections represent the different kinds of work done by women in the labor force. Study the two circle graphs carefully and then answer the following questions.

1. What percentage of women in the labor force worked in managerial and professional jobs in 1900? In 1920?
2. How many more women were working in 1920 than in 1900?
3. In what kind of jobs were most women employed in 1900?
4. Which group of women workers showed the greatest increase between 1900 and 1920?
5. Which group showed the greatest decrease between 1900 and 1920?

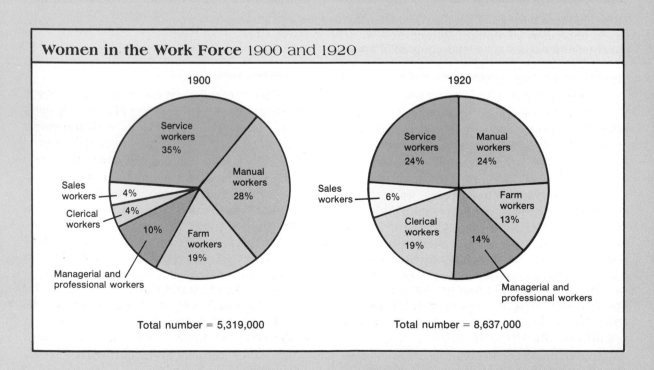

**Women in the Work Force** 1900 and 1920

1900

Service workers 35%
Manual workers 28%
Sales workers 4%
Clerical workers 4%
10%
Farm workers 19%
Managerial and professional workers

Total number = 5,319,000

1920

Service workers 24%
Manual workers 24%
Sales workers 6%
Farm workers 13%
Clerical workers 19%
14%
Managerial and professional workers

Total number = 8,637,000

# 2 What problems did President Theodore Roosevelt try to solve?

## Vocabulary
merit system
special interest

Theodore Roosevelt became President in 1901, at the beginning of the Progressive Era. Like the progressives, Roosevelt believed that government should be efficient and act for the public good. This belief led him to carry out many reforms. Roosevelt's accomplishments and personal qualities made him one of the most popular Presidents in American history.

## Roosevelt's Career

Theodore Roosevelt was born to wealthy parents in New York City in 1858. As a boy he suffered from asthma. Determined to overcome his weakness, Theodore exercised regularly in the family gymnasium and built up his strength. This energy and determination to reach his goals later contributed to his successful political career.

**Roosevelt enters public service.** During Roosevelt's youth, most people of wealth looked on politics as a dirty business and wanted nothing to do with it. Roosevelt, however, wanted to clean up the corruption he saw in government and business.

After graduating from Harvard College, Roosevelt began his career in government. He was elected to the New York legislature in 1881, at the age of 23. He later served on the United States Civil Service Commission. There he improved the merit system —the practice of awarding government jobs on the basis of ability rather than political favoritism. Later, he became head of the police department of New York City.

In spring 1897 Roosevelt was appointed Assistant Secretary of the Navy. When the United States declared war on Spain in 1898, Roosevelt resigned his government post to form the cavalry regiment known as the Rough Riders. (See Chapter 24.)

**Roosevelt enters national politics.** Roosevelt's war record made him a popular hero, and he was elected governor of New York in November 1898. In 1900 he was nominated for the vice presidency by the Republican party. Many people believed that Theodore Roosevelt made a mistake in accepting the nomination. In those days an American Vice President did not have great responsibilities.

The Republicans won the election of 1900. William McKinley was elected to a second term as President, and Theodore Roosevelt became Vice President. Soon thereafter McKinley was shot and killed by an assassin. Roosevelt thus became President of the United States at the age of 42, the youngest person ever to hold that office.

## Roosevelt's Record in Domestic Affairs

Theodore Roosevelt brought a fresh burst of energy to the White House. As President, he was quick-witted, well-informed, and eager to get things done. In addition to expanding American influence in Latin America and Asia, he was also active in affairs at home. His feeling that the American people deserved a "square deal" from their government made progressives regard him as their leader. They were encouraged by several steps taken by Roosevelt during his presidency.

**Arbitration settles the coal strike of 1902.** One of the earliest challenges Roosevelt faced was a strike by coal miners. In May 1902, about 150,000 miners stopped work. Their union, the United Mine Workers, demanded a 20-percent raise in wages

When he took office in 1901, President Theodore Roosevelt brought his young family to the White House. Roosevelt, a man of great energy, worked for reforms that he believed would benefit the American people.

and a 9-hour workday. Mine owners did not accept these demands, and the strike dragged on for five months.

As winter approached, the public's need for coal grew urgent. Roosevelt called the two sides together for a meeting. When the mine owners refused to budge, he said he would appoint an investigating commission. Roosevelt even suggested he might use the army to operate the mines. Such action would benefit neither side. Eventually the owners agreed to the commission, and the miners went back to work. By the next year, the miners had secured a 9-hour day, a 10-percent raise, and an established procedure for resolving disputes.

This solution was a great victory for Roosevelt, who had not supported either side. He emerged from the strike a hero. He had placed the needs of the people above the interests of either labor or management.

**Roosevelt tackles the trusts.** The coal strike was yet another reminder to the public of the great wealth and power of big business, monopolies, and trusts. Business monopolies were steadily growing larger and more powerful. Small businesses, industrial workers, and farmers often had no protection against high prices and unfair competition. In addition, monopolies influenced many government decisions. They spent large sums of money to fund the campaigns of candidates likely to be friendly to them.

Roosevelt believed that in a democracy it was wrong for monopolies to have such power. He also appreciated the benefits of industrialization. To him the solution to the problem was to distinguish between "good trusts" and "bad trusts." The government should regulate, rather than destroy, the bad trusts, according to Roosevelt.

The Sherman Antitrust Act had been passed in 1890, but earlier Presidents had done little to enforce it. Under Roosevelt, however, the government went to court against several great trusts to make them obey the Sherman Antitrust Act. Because of his fight against these trusts, Roosevelt was called a "trustbuster." His success in fighting the trusts, however, was mixed. Some trusts were better controlled, but the number of monopolies actually increased during Roosevelt's presidency.

**Conservation becomes a national issue.** As a young man, Roosevelt had owned cattle ranches in the West. He was troubled by the careless use of much of the nation's natural wealth—its forests, soil, water power, and minerals. Experts who studied this problem predicted that in a few years most of the country's resources would be used up.

Roosevelt took measures to save these resources. Laws were passed to set aside millions of acres as national forests and parks. Other laws encouraged the building of dams to make use of water power and to

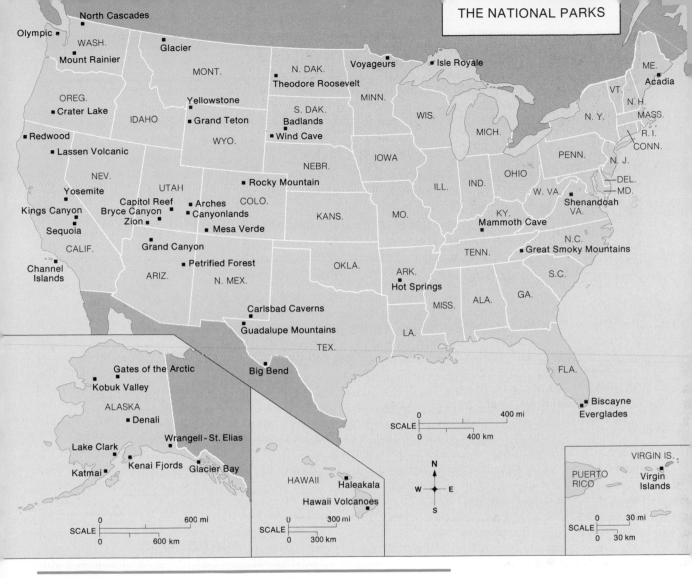

## Map Study

**During Theodore Roosevelt's presidency, the National Park System was expanded. In which state is the Grand Canyon National Park? Which state has the most parks today?**

provide irrigation for dry western lands. Roosevelt also supported laws to conserve mineral resources. At a conference in 1908, he met with national leaders to study the conservation of land. Roosevelt made many people aware for the first time of the need to use natural resources wisely.

**Laws protect the public from harmful products.** The President also wanted to prevent the sale of certain harmful products. After reading *The Jungle,* Roosevelt ordered his own investigation of the meat-packing industry. The results shocked him, and he pushed for laws to protect the public from unhealthy meat products. In 1906 Congress passed the Meat Inspection Act. This law allowed government officials to inspect meat sold in interstate trade. Under the terms of this law, meat that passed inspection would be given a government stamp. Another important law, the Pure Food and Drug Act, prohibited the manufacture and sale of any

**581**

# OUR NATIONAL PARKS 1901

John Muir was an explorer, naturalist, and writer who campaigned for forest conservation in the United States. Muir's efforts influenced Congress to pass laws to protect our nation's forests. In 1892 Muir formed the Sierra Club, a leading conservation organization in the United States.

## Read to Find Out

1. Why does Muir say that planting new trees will not replace the trees that are being cut down?
2. What do you think Muir means when he says that only Uncle Sam can save trees from fools?

---

... Any fool can destroy trees. They cannot run away; and if they could, they would still be destroyed,—chased and hunted down as long as fun or a dollar could be got out of their bark hides, branching horns, or magnificent [trunks]. Few that fell trees plant them; nor would planting avail much towards getting back anything like the noble primeval forests. During a man's life only saplings can be grown, in the place of the old trees—tens of centuries old—that have been destroyed. It took more than three thousand years to make some of the trees in these Western woods,—trees that are still standing in perfect strength and beauty, waving and singing in the mighty forests of the Sierra. Through all the wonderful, eventful centuries since Christ's time— and long before that—God has cared for these trees, saved them from drought, disease, avalanches, and a thousand straining, leveling tempests and floods; but he cannot save them from fools,— only Uncle Sam can do that.

*John Muir*

---

impure or dishonestly labeled foods and drugs. Roosevelt said, "No man may poison the people for his private profit."

**Roosevelt supports better government.** Many Americans believed that the people should participate more in government. They felt that too many government officials listened only to **special interests**. Special interests are groups who pressure government officials to favor or oppose certain issues. Roosevelt supported reforms like the direct primary, the initiative, the referendum, and the recall. None of these was adopted at the national level, but Roosevelt's support helped them gain approval in many states.

## SECTION REVIEW

1. **Vocabulary**   merit system, special interest
2. **People and Places**   William McKinley, Theodore Roosevelt
3. **Comprehension**   How did Roosevelt deal with trusts and monopolies?
4. **Comprehension**   Why was Theodore Roosevelt interested in the conservation of the nation's natural resources?
5. **Critical Thinking**   Was Roosevelt successful in carrying out progressive reforms? Explain your answer.

# How did President Taft differ from President Roosevelt?

When the election of 1908 drew near, Theodore Roosevelt was completing his second term in the White House. He was still popular with the voters, but he declared that he would not run for reelection. Instead Roosevelt recommended that the Republicans select William Howard Taft of Ohio. Taft had held several government offices and had been Roosevelt's Secretary of War.

## Taft and the Progressives

With Roosevelt's support, Taft was elected President in 1908. The progressives expected him to be their leader, and in many ways, Taft continued the work begun by Roosevelt. Taft took more trusts and monopolies to court than Roosevelt had. He also extended federal control over public lands.

**Taft angers the progressives over the tariff.** Taft did not have Roosevelt's energetic personality. Instead, he was cautious and made decisions slowly. The progressives soon grew upset with Taft when he did not support their position on the tariff issue.

William Howard Taft was appointed governor of the Philippines in 1901. He served as Theodore Roosevelt's Secretary of War before being elected President in 1908.

# Our Presidents

## WILLIAM H. TAFT

★ **1909–1913** ★

**27**TH PRESIDENT

REPUBLICAN

★ Born September 15, 1857, in Ohio

★ Married Helen Herron in 1886; 3 children

★ Lawyer; first civil governor of Philippines; Secretary of War

★ Lived in Ohio when elected President

★ Vice President: James Sherman

★ Died March 8, 1930, in Washington, D.C.

★ Only former President to be appointed Chief Justice of the United States

★ Key events while in office: Mexican Revolution started; NAACP formed; New Mexico and Arizona became states

For years, many people had called for the tariff on imported goods to be lowered. Tariffs had been passed to make foreign items more expensive and thus make American goods more appealing to consumers. Now many people believed the need to protect and encourage American industry had passed. Western farmers and others who resented the rising cost of living were especially against the tariff. They saw the tariff as a kind of taxation on buyers that was helpful to manufacturers.

In his campaign, Taft had promised to lower the tariff. Soon after his inauguration, he called Congress into session to work on a new tariff bill. The bill that Congress eventually passed actually raised the tariff. Taft, not wanting to anger the conservative Republicans, agreed to sign the Payne-Aldrich Tariff in 1909. Although eastern industrialists were satisfied, midwestern progressives were furious with Taft.

**Taft appears to be a foe of conservation.** Supporters of Roosevelt's conservation policies also lost patience with Taft. Gifford Pinchot had been head of the United States Forest Service under Roosevelt and continued in this job under Taft. Pinchot openly criticized the Secretary of the Interior for removing sales restrictions on federal lands in Montana and Wyoming. Taft then fired Pinchot. Conservationists viewed this action by Taft as undermining progressive goals.

## Reactions to Taft

These conflicts with the progressives tended to obscure the many important reforms Taft brought about. One of the most significant was the Mann-Elkins Act. This law gave the federal government the right to regulate the rates railroads were charging. Some of Taft's other accomplishments included setting up the Children's Bureau within the Department of Labor and limiting the workday to eight hours for federal employees. Taft also supported the **Sixteenth Amendment** allowing an income tax, and the Seventeenth Amendment giving voters the power to elect senators directly.

Even with these accomplishments, Taft lost support among Republicans. One group, including Senator La Follette, called themselves **insurgents.** An insurgent is a member of a political party who rebels against its leadership. The insurgents believed that Taft did not do enough for the progressive cause.

**Roosevelt turns against Taft.** After he left office, Theodore Roosevelt went to Africa on a **safari** —a hunting expedition. When he returned in the summer of 1910, he was disappointed by Taft's actions. Roosevelt felt let down by Taft and went on a speaking tour to promote his own ideas, which he called the **New Nationalism.** He wanted to increase the power of the federal government to oversee industry and carry out social reforms.

**Taft is challenged by Roosevelt.** In the next two years, the split between President

584

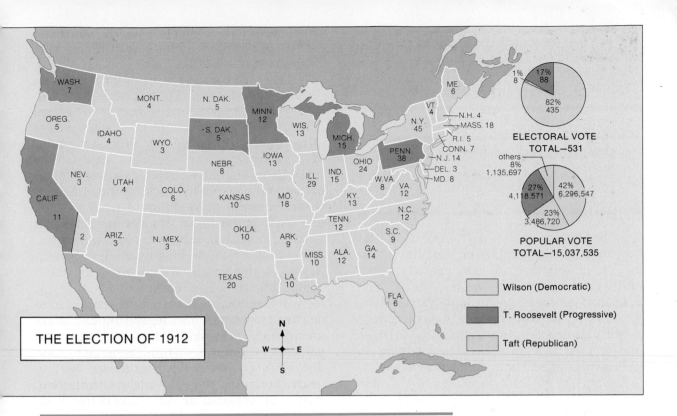

THE ELECTION OF 1912

ELECTORAL VOTE
TOTAL—531

1% 8
17% 88
82% 435

POPULAR VOTE
TOTAL—15,037,535

others 8% 1,135,697
27% 4,118,571
42% 6,296,547
23% 3,486,720

Wilson (Democratic)

T. Roosevelt (Progressive)

Taft (Republican)

## Map Study

**This map shows the results of the 1912 election. How many electoral votes did the winner receive? What percent of the popular vote did the winner receive? Which states cast their electoral votes for the Republican candidate?**

Taft and former President Roosevelt grew very deep. In 1912 Roosevelt decided to seek the Republican party's presidential nomination. When Taft was renominated instead, Roosevelt and his followers left the convention. They formed the Progressive party and met in Chicago to nominate their own candidate for President. Naturally, Roosevelt was the delegates' choice. When he arrived in Chicago, reporters asked him how he felt. Roosevelt exclaimed, "I feel as strong as a bull moose!" From then on, the bull moose was the official symbol of the Progressive party. The party was often called "the Bull Moose party."

Roosevelt's strength seriously weakened the Republican party in 1912. Thus, because of the split between the Republicans and the Progressives, the Democratic candidate, Woodrow Wilson, won a clear-cut victory.

## SECTION REVIEW

1. **Vocabulary**   insurgents, safari
2. **People and Places**   Gifford Pinchot, Montana, Wyoming
3. **Comprehension**   What position did the progressives take on the tariff?
4. **Comprehension**   Why were the progressives disappointed with President Taft?
5. **Critical Thinking**   Did Roosevelt's third-party candidacy ensure that the Democratic nominee would be elected President in 1912? Why or why not?

## Vocabulary

lobbyist

levy

The winner of the election of 1912 was the Democratic candidate, Woodrow Wilson. Like Roosevelt, Wilson wanted the federal government to solve social and economic problems. Wilson, however, disagreed with Roosevelt on how to do this. Roosevelt had urged tighter regulation of trusts and unions. Wilson advocated breaking up monopolies to promote competition.

## LINKING PAST AND PRESENT

### ★ ★ ★ Tariffs Today

Two hundred years ago, the United States traded with only a few other countries. Today, America has trading agreements with more than 90 countries. Most of these agreements center on tariffs.

Most tariffs are protective. They try to protect their own country's products by making imported goods cost more. But sometimes tariffs are so high that trade between countries stops.

The United States and its trading partners often try to lower tariffs. After World War II, many countries signed agreements to cut tariffs. Again in the 1960's and 1970's, tariffs were lowered.

During the early 1980's, however, many countries raised their tariffs. Now the United States and its trading partners are seeking new tariff agreements. They want to protect their own goods as well as lower tariffs.

## The New Freedom

Wilson shared Roosevelt's desire for a better America, but his background and temperament were quite different from the active and enthusiastic Roosevelt. Thomas Woodrow Wilson was born in Virginia in 1856, the son of a Presbyterian minister. Raised in the South, Wilson was calm and composed. He was a thinker whose most effective weapons were words. A scholar and teacher for most of his life, Wilson had been president of Princeton University. His only political experience was one term as governor of New Jersey. Nevertheless, he intended to be a strong President, offering an ambitious program that he called the **New Freedom.**

**Wilson works for change.** In his inaugural address, Wilson described his plans to protect ordinary people from big business. In Congress he launched his first assault on what he saw as three evils—the tariff, the trusts, and the banking system. He struck his first blow at tariffs.

*The tariff.* Laws passed in the 1890's and early 1900's had increased tariff duties. President Wilson believed that lower tariffs would force American industries to be more competitive. He asked Congress to lower the tariff duties on many articles so that trade could flow more freely between the United States and other nations. He believed that foreign countries would not buy American goods unless they could sell their own goods in the United States.

The House followed Wilson's wishes and quickly passed the Underwood Tariff bill to lower tariff rates. The bill became bogged down in the Senate, where **lobbyists** — people who put pressure on government for special interests—tried to weaken it. President Wilson then appealed to the American people. Mounting public pressure finally forced the passage of the bill, and average tariff rates dropped from almost 41 percent to 27 percent.

*The income tax.* Lower tariff rates would mean smaller revenues for the federal government. To make up for this loss, progressives added an amendment to the Underwood Tariff that provided for a personal income tax. This new tax was to be graduated. In other words, the percentage of tax paid would increase for people with higher incomes. The progressives believed that those people with large incomes should pay a higher rate of tax than those people that had low incomes.

Congress had tried to pass an income tax law in 1894, but the Supreme Court had declared it unconstitutional. In 1913, however, just before Wilson took office, the Sixteenth Amendment was added to the Constitution, permitting Congress to **levy** —impose—an income tax. Thus the Underwood Tariff also became a tax law.

*Banking reforms.* President Wilson also asked for changes in the banking system. The nation had suffered an economic panic in 1907. During the panic large numbers of bank depositors tried to withdraw their savings. Many banks had run out of money and were forced to close their doors. Wilson wanted to set up a banking system that would prevent such problems in the future. At Wilson's request Congress passed the Federal Reserve Act in 1913. This law set up a **Federal Reserve Bank** in each of 12 regions of the country. Each of these banks was under the control of the Federal Reserve Board. The Federal Reserve Banks had broad powers to regulate the supply of money. They could also be of benefit to those local banks that were in danger of having to close their doors.

*Business and monopolies.* Woodrow Wilson, like other progressives, believed that powerful monopolies were dangerous because they blocked free competition. He therefore urged Congress to pass laws to control such monopolies. One of these laws, the Clayton Antitrust Act, listed things that big corporations could not do. Another law set up the Federal Trade Commission, which

## Our Presidents

### WOODROW WILSON

★ **1913–1921** ★

**28TH PRESIDENT**

**DEMOCRAT**

★ Born December 29, 1856, in Virginia
★ Married Ellen Louise Axson in 1885; 3 children
★ Married Edith Bolling Galt in 1915; no children
★ Lawyer; president of Princeton University; governor of New Jersey
★ Lived in New Jersey when elected President
★ Vice President: Thomas Marshall
★ Died February 3, 1924, in Washington, D.C.
★ Key events while in office: Sixteenth, Seventeenth, Eighteenth, and Nineteenth amendments; Panama Canal opened; Clayton Antitrust Act; World War I; League of Nations formed; Treaty of Versailles defeated

was given the power to seek out facts about businesses and to prevent the establishment of monopolies.

*Farmers and workers.* President Wilson also took action to aid farmers and workers. New federal programs made it possible for farmers to borrow money more easily and for longer periods of time. The government also sponsored programs designed to teach farmers better farming methods. A new federal law reduced the regular working day on interstate railroads to eight hours. Individual states also passed laws to limit child labor and to improve health and safety conditions in mines and factories.

The Federal Reserve Act was designed to stabilize the American banking system. These women in New York's Federal Reserve Bank recorded banking transactions.

## Black Americans During the Progressive Era

When he took office, Wilson promised to treat black Americans fairly. Nevertheless, during his presidency the practice of segregation became more widespread, even in the federal government.

**Black Americans face prejudice.** The Progressive Era was a difficult time for blacks. The discrimination that blacks faced in the late 1800's continued into the 1900's. Cities in both the North and the South remained segregated, and black workers were often treated unfairly.

Blacks met new setbacks in the federal government. Black clerks had worked along-side white clerks in the Treasury and Post Office departments since the 1870's. President Wilson, however, ordered partitions put up to separate the black clerks from the whites. Booker T. Washington, visiting the capitol in 1913, noted, "I have never seen the [blacks] so discouraged and bitter as they are at the present time."

**Black Americans work to overcome obstacles.** Despite the setbacks, black leaders campaigned to end discrimination. W.E.B. Du Bois and Ida Wells-Barnett continued the struggle for civil rights that they began in the late 1800's. (See Chapter 23.) In 1909–1910 Du Bois and Wells-Barnett were among 60 prominent Americans who formed the **National Association for the Advancement of Colored People** (NAACP). The purpose of the NAACP was to help blacks secure legal equality throughout the United States. NAACP lawyers, both black and white, defended people accused of crimes merely because of their race. Within 10 years, NAACP lawyers were winning cases before the Supreme Court.

Another organization, the National Urban League, was started by Dr. George Edmund Haynes and others in 1911. This group helped blacks overcome the discrimination they faced in cities. The National Urban League asked whites and blacks to cooperate to solve their common problems.

**War halts reform at home.** Just how far-reaching the reforms of President Wilson's New Freedom might have been will never be known. War broke out in Europe a little more than a year after Wilson took office. Increasingly the nation's attention centered on that conflict. When the United States entered the combat in 1917, the nation had to give its full attention to winning the war.

## SECTION REVIEW

1. **Vocabulary**  lobbyist, levy
2. **People and Places**  Woodrow Wilson, Princeton University, George Edmund Haynes
3. **Comprehension**  Why did some Americans favor a graduated personal income tax?
4. **Comprehension**  How did President Wilson reform the banking system?
5. **Critical Thinking**  How successful was Wilson in carrying out his progressive ideas? Explain.

# Chapter 25 Summary

During the early 1900's people known as progressives called for reforms in American business and government. Progressives came from all walks of life, but the core of the movement was the urban middle class. Progressives were concerned about the power of big business, especially monopolies and trusts. They were also troubled by corruption and inefficiency in government. They felt that the average citizen was losing out to special interests and believed that reforms were necessary to restore American values of fair competition and democracy. They thought that government should be strengthened to carry out those reforms.

With the help of the press and journalists known as muckrakers, progressives worked for change. At the local level, progressive mayors attacked the power of political bosses and brought back clean government. Cities reorganized their governments to make them more responsive to the people. At the state level, governors fought powerful trusts and passed laws to improve working conditions. States also adopted measures to ensure greater public participation in government, and ratified amendments that made prohibition the law of the land and that gave women the right to vote.

The Progressive Movement received national leadership from Presidents Theodore Roosevelt, William Howard Taft, and Woodrow Wilson. All three believed in strong, efficient government, and they supported laws to limit the power of big business and to help working people. Roosevelt tried to break up the trusts, promote conservation, protect the public from impure food and medicine, and get people more involved in government. Taft also brought trusts to court and secured federal regulation of railroad rates. Wilson lowered tariffs, created the Federal Reserve Bank, imposed an income tax, and promoted laws to protect workers and children. Blacks still faced unfair treatment and formed organizations to help them gain equality. Wilson's reform efforts ended as war in Europe drew his attention.

## Vocabulary and Key Terms

Use the following terms to complete the paragraph below. Write your answers on a separate sheet of paper.

exposés
direct primary
muckrakers
recall
special interests

initiative
merit system
Progressive Movement
referendum

During the late 1800's and early 1900's many people supported reforms that made up the __1__. Reformers tried to make the American government more responsive to the will of the people and reduce the influence of __2__. They also supported the __3__, which helped place qualified people in public service. In addition, they backed measures like the __4__, which allowed voters to nominate candidates for office; the __5__, which let them propose laws; the __6__, which let them approve laws passed by the legislature; and the __7__, which gave them the power to remove officials from office. Reformers were aided in their efforts by crusading journalists known as __8__, who wrote __9__ detailing corruption and inefficiency in government.

## Recalling the Facts

1. What was the commission plan of government?
2. Why were Roosevelt and the progressives concerned about monopolies?
3. Why was Theodore Roosevelt called a "trustbuster"?
4. What laws were passed under Roosevelt to protect the public from harmful products?
5. Why did President Taft sign the Payne-Aldrich Tariff?
6. Who were the three presidential candidates in the election of 1912?
7. Why did President Wilson lower tariffs?
8. What tariff law permitted Congress to levy an income tax?

## Places to Locate

Match the letters on the map with the places listed below. Write your answers on a separate sheet of paper.

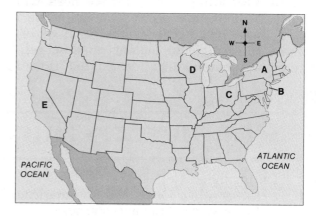

1. Ohio
2. New Jersey
3. Wisconsin
4. New York
5. California

## Critical Thinking

1. Progressives focused much of their attention on three areas. These areas were making government more efficient and responsive, regulating business to control monopolies and promote fair competition, and improving social conditions. In which of these three areas were reformers most successful? Why do you think that was? Consider these questions in your answer:
   a. Who were the progressives and what was their vision of society?
   b. What changes most suited the progressives' interests?
   c. What obstacles might the progressives have encountered in each area?

2. President Taft continued the reforms started by President Roosevelt. Yet many progressives turned against Taft. Why did this happen? Consider these points in your answer:
   a. the tariff issue
   b. Taft's firing of Gifford Pinchot
   c. the role of the insurgents

## Understanding History

1. Reread the section "Progressives at the local level show the way" on page 575. Then answer these questions.
   a. **Citizenship.** Why did reforms begin at the local level?
   b. **Citizenship.** How did the commission plan and the city manager plan make local government more responsive to the people?
2. Reread the section "Conservation becomes a national issue" on page 580. Then answer these questions.
   a. **Geography.** Why were the country's natural resources being used up so quickly?
   b. **Geography.** What did Roosevelt do to conserve national resources?
3. Reread the section "Wilson works for change" on page 586. Then answer these questions.
   a. **Economics.** What three economic areas did Wilson seek to change?
   b. **Economics.** What were the purposes of the Clayton Antitrust Act and the Federal Trade Commission?

## Projects and Activities

1. **Following Current Events.** Research current magazines or newspapers for an exposé article on American government, business, or society. Write a paragraph summarizing the article. Present your summary to the class.
2. **Analyzing a Problem.** Imagine that you and your classmates are living during the Progressive Era in a city dominated by a political machine. Write an exposé of the problem. Include possible ways of cleaning up the city government.

3. **Writing a Report.** Find out more about one of the following: Upton Sinclair, Robert La Follette, the election of 1912, W.E.B. Du Bois, Ida Wells-Barnett, or the NAACP. Write a report on the information you gather.

## Practicing Your Skill

Use the graphs to answer the questions that follow.

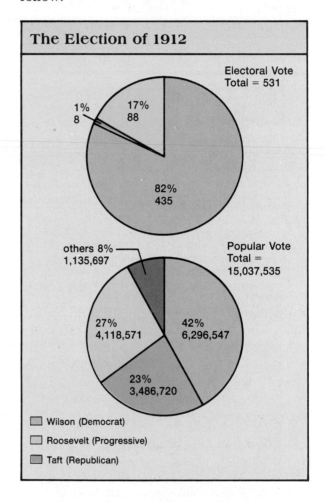

The Election of 1912

1. Who won the election of 1912? Did he win the electoral and the popular vote?
2. Who was the second-place candidate in both the electoral vote and the popular vote? How many electoral votes did he receive? How many popular votes?
3. Who was the third-place candidate? How did his popular vote compare with his percentage of the electoral vote?

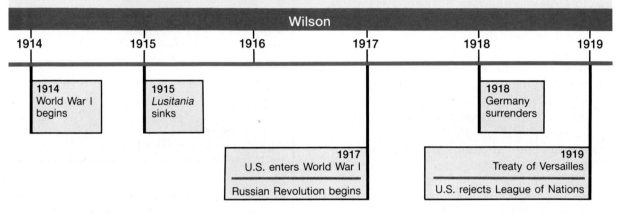

Wilson

| 1914 | 1915 | 1916 | 1917 | 1918 | 1919 |

**1914**
World War I
begins

**1915**
*Lusitania*
sinks

**1918**
Germany
surrenders

**1917**
U.S. enters World War I

Russian Revolution begins

**1919**
Treaty of Versailles

U.S. rejects League of Nations

The display of the Allies' flags in this 1917 painting of New York's Fifth Avenue shows strong pro-Allied feelings.

## Preparing to Read

In the first years of the twentieth century, the nations of Europe competed fiercely with one another. Their rivalry soon drew the continent into one of history's most destructive wars. The United States tried but failed to stay out of the conflict. In the final year of the war, millions of American troops crossed the Atlantic to fight for freedom and democracy. America's soldiers won a great victory. After the war ended, however, America's leaders were less successful in their efforts to build a lasting peace. As you read this chapter, try to answer the following questions:

1. What led the United States to enter World War I?
2. How did the United States help win World War I?
3. What part did the United States play in making the peace?

# 1 What led the United States to enter World War I?

## Vocabulary

militarism
aggression
mobilize
propaganda

In 1914 the nations of Europe were teetering on the edge of war. The murder of a prominent European leader set off a chain of violent attacks, and within days most of the countries of Europe were declaring war on one another. The United States tried to steer clear of the conflict, but the war affected the American people in many ways. The nation gradually became more and more entangled in the struggle.

## Causes of War

Tension had been building among the countries of Europe for a number of years, as rival nations competed for empires and military power. Fearing attacks, Europeans formed complicated alliances with one another. Once violence began, most of the continent of Europe was quickly drawn into the conflict.

**European powers compete for empires.** During the 1800's, the powerful nations of Europe tried to add to their wealth and power by building empires. Empires enriched the parent countries by providing cheap raw materials and larger markets for finished goods. Britain, Germany, France, and Italy sought to build their empires by making colonies in Africa and Asia. Russia and Austria-Hungary built their empires by taking over neighboring lands in Europe. The scramble for empires led to a number of bitter rivalries, especially between France and Germany and between Russia and Austria-Hungary.

**Competition leads to a military buildup.** As they competed with one another, the rival European nations grew deeply nationalistic. Each country was determined to protect its own interests. To do so, the nations of Europe built large armies and navies. The policy of building strong armed forces to prepare for war is called **militarism**. Militarist governments in Germany, France, and Russia each assembled armies of more than 4 million soldiers. Great Britain built up the world's largest navy. Uniforms grew more elaborate, and were often trimmed with gold braid, fur, or feathers. Frequent military parades showed each country's national pride.

**Rival alliances take shape.** To further protect themselves, European powers formed alliances with one another. By 1914 there were two major alliances in Europe. The **Triple Alliance** included Germany, Austria-Hungary, and Italy. The **Triple Entente** (ahn-TAHNT) included France, Russia, and Great Britain. Within each alliance, the members promised to help one another in case of an enemy attack. In addition, some powerful nations agreed to protect smaller countries from aggression —attack. For example, Great Britain promised to protect Belgium, and Russia promised that it would protect Serbia.

With all of Europe heavily armed, and nations connected by promises to defend one another, Europe was like a powder keg. "It requires only a spark to set the whole thing off," noted an American diplomat.

**The Archduke of Austria-Hungary is murdered.** On June 28, 1914, Archduke Francis Ferdinand of Austria-Hungary was visiting the city of Sarajevo (SAH-rah-yeh-vo). The Archduke was the heir to the throne of Austria-Hungary. Thousands of people crowded the streets of Sarajevo to see the future ruler. As the Archduke's car drove through the crowded streets, two shots rang out, killing the Archduke and his wife Sophie. The killer was Gavrilo Princip (PREEN-seep), a nationalist from the neighboring country of Serbia. Austria-Hungary had recently taken over the area around Sarajevo, called Bosnia, where many Serbs lived. Princip and other nationalist Serbs had plotted the murder to avenge the takeover of Bosnia, which they resented.

**War erupts.** Austria-Hungary blamed Serbia for the crime. On July 28, 1914, Austria-Hungary declared war on Serbia. Russia, keeping its agreement to protect Serbia, mobilized —prepared—its military forces for war. As a result, Germany, which was allied with Austria-Hungary, declared war on Russia on August 1. On August 3 Germany also made a declaration of war on Russia's ally France.

Germany feared having to fight a war on its eastern and western borders at the same time. The Germans were hopeful of taking France out of the war quickly. German armies invaded Belgium, heading toward France. Great Britain, which was Belgium's ally, then declared war on Germany. Thus, within a few days after the murder of Archduke Francis Ferdinand at Sarajevo, most of the European nations were at war.

The Great War, or **World War I,** was to last until 1918. On one side were Germany and Austria-Hungary. These countries were also called the **Central Powers** because of their location in the center of Europe. Bulgaria and Turkey later joined the Central Powers. On the other side were the **Allied Powers** of France, Russia, and Great Britain. Italy joined the Allies in 1915, and 20 other nations joined the Allies before the fighting finally ended.

## War in the Trenches

The German army nearly succeeded in winning a quick victory against France. German troops poured through Belgium and advanced to within 15 miles (24 kilometers) of Paris, the French capital. In September, however, French and British troops stopped the German advance at the Marne River. After the **Battle of the Marne,** the fighting bogged down. Neither side was able to win a clear victory. For three years the two armies faced each other and fought without making a move forward or backward more than a few miles.

**A new kind of warfare develops.** With no victory in sight, both sides dug trenches for protection. These long ditches stretched for 400 miles (640 kilometers) across Belgium and France. The line of trenches was called the **Western Front.** Soldiers on both sides lived for months in the muddy trenches, with enemy shells exploding continually nearby. Between the trenches of the two sides was "no man's land"—a wasted zone of mud, barbed wire, and land mines. In trench warfare, troops from one side or the other would go "over the top"—rush out of the trenches— and try to break through the enemy lines.

Soldiers lived in the trenches, eating and sleeping during the day and digging more trenches during the night. Troops had no way to protect themselves from bad weather, enemy shells, or poison gas.

Such attacks met with machine-gun fire and seldom succeeded. As the war went on, new weapons—poison gas and tanks—increased the number of dead and wounded. Millions of soldiers were lost on both sides. In the east, the armies of the Central Powers and the Russian forces also faced each other along miles of trenches, with neither side able to win a clear victory.

## American Policy

The outbreak of war in 1914 had shocked Americans. Still, Europe and its quarrels seemed far away. Americans hoped to stay out of the war and avoid Europe's problems.

**The President asks Americans not to take sides.** As soon as World War I began, President Woodrow Wilson urged all Americans to be "neutral in fact as well as in name ... impartial in thought as well as in action." By not taking sides, Wilson believed the nation could avoid the war. Most Americans supported the President's position. Slowly, however, and for various reasons, the United States drew closer and closer to involvement in the conflict.

**American sympathies are divided.** Americans from the start found it hard to be neutral. It seemed to most people that Germany and Austria-Hungary were chiefly responsible for the war. Also, many people had emotional ties to one side or the other. The majority of Americans were of British descent and were tied to Great Britain by common customs and language. Some Americans also remembered France's aid in the Revolutionary War. On the other hand, many German Americans sympathized with Germany and the Central Powers. Many Irish Americans, who bitterly opposed Great Britain, also tended to give their support to the Central Powers.

**American opinion swings toward the Allies.** As the war dragged on, American support for the Allies grew. Most of the war news that reached the United States came from Allied sources and was favorable to the Allied cause. The Allies also influenced American opinion through **propaganda.** Propaganda is the spreading of opinions that favor a cause or point of view. Allied propaganda called the Germans "Huns" and pictured them as bloodthirsty savages. The

595

propaganda spread by the Central Powers made the British seem equally horrible. In general, however, Allied propaganda had a greater effect on American opinion.

The growing trade between America and the Allies also helped build sympathy for the Allied cause. The British Navy blockaded Germany, making it difficult for American ships to reach German ports. Americans found it easier to trade with Britain and France. The United States shipped huge amounts of arms, food, oil, and other supplies to the Allies. This trade created an economic boom in the United States. Americans naturally favored those nations that bought American goods.

**The Germans start submarine warfare.** Perhaps the greatest influence on American opinion was Germany's use of submarines, called U-boats. Submarines were new, and for several reasons people considered their use unfair. First, submarines attacked from hiding to avoid the guns of enemy ships. Second, submarines could not take captives

Torpedoed ships sank very quickly and U-boat crews could not rescue survivors from the sinking vessels.

or rescue survivors. People of the time considered it monstrous not to rescue survivors from a sinking ship. Finally, submarines often sank the ships of neutral countries. According to international law, a warring nation had the right to stop neutral ships and seize war goods being shipped to the enemy. The German U-boats could not follow this rule. Instead, submarines attacked and sank neutral ships without warning.

Early in the war, Germany warned the United States that it would attack neutral ships sailing to Great Britain. President Wilson responded to this threat with another warning. He said the Germans would be held to account if American lives were lost in U-boat attacks. In the view of German leaders, however, cutting Great Britain's supply lines was worth the risk of angering the neutral countries.

**The Germans sink the *Lusitania*.** On May 7, 1915, a German U-boat sank the British liner *Lusitania* near the coast of southern Ireland. The *Lusitania*—then one of the largest and fastest ships in the world—was heading from New York to Liverpool, on the west coast of England. Hit by a single torpedo, the huge liner tilted sharply and sank within 18 minutes. Of nearly 2,000 passengers and crew members, 1,198 died. Among the dead were 128 Americans.

Americans were outraged by the sinking of the *Lusitania*. The United States issued strong warnings to the German government not to endanger the lives of American citizens. For a time Germany agreed to limit its submarine warfare.

**Wilson wins reelection.** In spite of the growing anti-German feeling, most Americans still wanted to stay out of the war. Wilson agreed. "There is such a thing as a man being too proud to fight," he said. In 1916 Wilson ran for reelection as President. His campaign slogan was "He kept us out of war." The Republicans chose Charles Evans Hughes, a Supreme Court justice, to run against Wilson. The election was close, and Hughes went to bed believing he was the new President. When election returns came in from California, however, President Wilson was the victor.

Without warning, a German U-boat torpedoed the *Lusitania,* a British liner carrying American passengers. The sinking of the *Lusitania* contributed to anti-German feeling in the United States.

## Declaration of War

Following his reelection, Wilson tried to arrange peace talks between the warring powers. The effort failed. Instead, Germany decided to gamble on a quick victory.

**Germany resumes submarine attacks.** By the start of 1917 Germany was becoming desperate. The British blockade created serious shortages of supplies. In February 1917 the Germans announced that they would again attack any ship nearing Britain. The Germans expected this decision to bring the United States into the war. Germany, however, hoped to gain the victory before American troops could get to Europe.

In response to the German announcement, Wilson broke off diplomatic relations with Germany. Wilson had kept the United States out of war for two and a half years. He now began to believe that Germany was a threat to the United States.

**The Zimmermann telegram pushes the United States closer to war.** Near the end of February, Americans learned of a secret German message involving the United States. The message was sent by Germany's foreign minister, Arthur Zimmermann, to the German ambassador in Mexico City. In it Zimmermann suggested an alliance between Germany and Mexico. If war broke out between the United States and Germany, Mexico would be invited to join with Germany. In return, Germany would help Mexico recover its "lost territory in Texas, New Mexico, and Arizona." British agents had intercepted and decoded the **Zimmermann telegram** and had passed it on to President

# THE AMERICAN'S CREED 1917

William Tyler Page, a clerk of the House of Representatives, wrote the American's Creed in 1917. The Creed includes phrases from the Constitution, the Declaration of Independence, and certain famous speeches.

## Read to Find Out

1. Upon what principles is the government of the United States established?
2. According to the Creed, what are the duties of an American citizen?

I believe in the United States of America as a Government of the people, by the people, for the people; whose just powers are derived from the consent of the governed; a democracy in a Republic; a sovereign Nation of many sovereign States; a perfect Union, one and inseparable; established upon those principles of freedom, equality, justice, and humanity for which American patriots sacrificed their lives and fortunes. I therefore believe it is my duty to my country to love it; to support its Constitution; to obey its laws; to respect its flag; and to defend it against all enemies.

*William Tyler Page*

Wilson. When Wilson made the message public, the American people were outraged. Anti-German feeling increased greatly.

**The United States enters the war.** In March 1917 German U-boats sank several more American ships. Wilson decided that the United States could no longer stay neutral. On April 2 he asked Congress to declare war on Germany. "The world must be made safe for democracy," Wilson told Congress. He said that the war had become a contest to secure the rights of democratic countries:

It is a fearful thing to lead this great, peaceful people into war, into the most terrible and disastrous of all wars, civilization itself seeming to be in the balance. But the right is more precious than peace, and we shall fight for the things which we have always carried nearest our hearts—for democracy, for the right of those who submit to authority to have a voice in their own government, for the rights and liberties of small nations.

On April 6, 1917, Congress declared war on Germany.

## SECTION REVIEW

1. **Vocabulary** militarism, aggression, mobilize, propaganda
2. **People and Places** Archduke Francis Ferdinand, Sarajevo, Belgium, Paris, Marne River, Woodrow Wilson, Arthur Zimmermann
3. **Comprehension** What conditions in Europe led to the start of World War I?
4. **Comprehension** What effect did Germany's use of submarine warfare have on the United States?
5. **Critical Thinking** Do you think President Wilson was right when he decided the United States should enter World War I? Explain your answer.

The United States had entered the war, but the nation was not prepared for battle. Throughout 1917, Americans worked to mobilize the country. In 1918 thousands of American troops arrived in Europe and helped turn the tide of war in favor of the Allies. By the end of the year the Central Powers were defeated.

## Preparing for War

President Wilson realized that to win the war in Europe, Americans had to organize at home. Wilson quickly took steps to muster support for the fighting.

**A draft law strengthens the armed forces.** When the United States declared war, the army had only about 200,000 troops. The country had to create a large fighting force quickly. On May 18, 1917, Congress passed the **Selective Service Act.** This draft law required all men between 21 and 30 years old to register for the draft. These age limits were later expanded to 18 and 45.

In the next 18 months, almost 5 million Americans entered military service. About 3 million were drafted. Others volunteered or belonged to National Guard units that were called for duty. About 370,000 black Americans were among those who joined the armed forces. Blacks, however, suffered discrimination in many ways. They were not permitted to enlist in the Marine Corps. In the army, blacks were assigned to segregated, all-black units led by white officers. In spite of discrimination, black soldiers fought bravely, and many were among the war's most decorated troops.

Soldiers also joined the army from every other American ethnic group, including Puerto Ricans, Mexican Americans, Native Americans, and Asians. In addition, thousands of women served in the armed forces as nurses, ambulance drivers, and clerks.

**The government spurs production of war resources.** The millions of draftees had to be quickly equipped with food, clothing, and weapons. The nation also had to produce vast amounts of heavy weapons and equipment, including locomotives, freight cars, railroad tracks, trucks, and cannon. Ships had to be built to transport troops and supplies to Europe. In addition, Americans knew early in 1917 that Britain and France were almost out of food and supplies. To win the war, the United States would have to supply the Allies as well as its own troops.

The government set up dozens of agencies and committees to spur production of needed war goods. The Food Administration, headed by Herbert Hoover, urged Americans to conserve and expand food supplies. Families grew their own vegetables in backyard "victory gardens." Farmers planted extra crops. Americans observed "wheatless Mondays" and "meatless Tuesdays." Another agency, the War Industries Board, regulated industry. It decided which factories would receive supplies of steel and other resources, and told the factories what to produce. The War Labor Board was set up to prevent strikes and labor problems. It regulated wages and working hours.

To pay for the cost of the war, the government increased taxes. It also raised $21 billion through the sale of **Liberty Bonds.** Americans bought the bonds as a way of loaning money to the government. Movie stars and athletes helped sell the bonds. The government also organized thousands of "Four-Minute Speeches" to build support for the war. Speakers at clubs, theaters, churches, and union meetings spread the message that the war was necessary to defend democracy.

**New workers join the labor force.** As men joined the armed forces, millions of women found opportunities to work outside their homes. Women ran elevators and streetcars, made ammunition and heavy machinery, directed traffic, and delivered mail. These had been considered men's jobs. With so many women working, Americans began to change their view that women could only do certain kinds of work.

Black Americans had new job opportunities as the nation mobilized. Many left farms in the south to move to northern cities. They found work in factories making goods for the war. Black ghettos began to develop in such northern cities as New York, Philadelphia, Chicago, and Detroit.

**Opponents of the war are harshly treated.** Most Americans supported the war effort, but a few spoke out against it. Most of them were pacifists —people who oppose all wars. Pacifists were treated harshly because of their views. The government passed the Sedition Act in 1918, making it illegal to speak against the government or the war. More than 1,500 people were arrested under this law.

Harsh treatment was also directed at many German Americans. Some were fired from their jobs. Others were attacked on the streets. Schools stopped teaching German, and many Americans refused to use German words such as *hamburger* and *sauerkraut*.

**American troops train under General Pershing.** As the nation built up supplies, the army trained for battle. The President put General John J. Pershing in command. Pershing was nicknamed "Black Jack" because he led an all-black unit in the Spanish-American War. He was famous as the leader of the army that hunted for Francisco "Pancho" Villa in Mexico. (See Chapter 24.) He planned to have 1 million troops ready to fight in France by the spring of 1918.

**Convoys protect American ships.** To send supplies and troops to Europe, the United States had to find a way to protect its ships from German submarines. The navy began using convoys . A convoy was a group of ships surrounded and protected by naval destroyers and cruisers. Using this system, Americans shipped 5 million tons of supplies and millions of soldiers to Europe.

## Winning the War

American troops arrived in Europe in June 1917. These "Yanks" brought new hope to the Allies, who cheered as the Americans marched through Paris. More Americans arrived in the fall and winter, but their numbers increased slowly. Throughout 1917 the Allies lost huge numbers of soldiers.

This World War I-era poster asks Americans to buy savings stamps. The money raised from the sale of the stamps helped to pay for the war. The poster shows Allied fighter planes flying under the protection of an American eagle.

KEEP HIM FREE

W.S.S.

BUY

WAR SAVINGS STAMPS

ISSUED BY THE UNITED STATES TREASURY DEPT.

## CITIZENSHIP • Freedom and National Security

Since the nation began, free speech has been a treasured right of Americans. There have been times in the nation's history, however, when limits have been placed on freedom of speech. This has happened most often when the country has been at war. During wartime, the need for national security may conflict with the right to speak freely.

During World War I, the government strove to build up public support for the war. Speeches and recruiting posters were used to "sell the war to the American people." To silence critics, Congress passed the Espionage Act and the Sedition Act. These laws made it illegal to speak or write anything against the war effort. One antiwar critic imprisoned under the Espionage Act was Eugene Debs, a labor leader and a Socialist. Debs disagreed with the Espionage Act and declared that free speech should never be prohibited. Many Americans agreed with Debs. While in prison, Debs was nominated as the Socialist candidate for President. He received more than 1 million votes in the 1920 election.

**World War I recruitment poster**

**Russia withdraws from the war.** The situation grew worse as a result of two revolutions in Russia. In March 1917 the Russians overthrew the czar, or emperor. They established a democratic government that promised to bring new freedom and reforms. In November 1917, however, the new government was overthrown by the **Bolsheviks.** This small party, led by V.I. Lenin, had intended to establish **communism** in Russia.*

---

* The Bolsheviks established Russia as the Union of Soviet Socialist Republics (USSR) in 1922. The nation is often called the Soviet Union.

Communism is a social and political system based on the ideas of the German thinker Karl Marx. Marx predicted that the workers of the world would overthrow the ruling classes. Then, Marx believed, private property would be abolished, and the workers would set up a classless society.

The Bolshevik leaders wanted peace so they could set up the new Communist system. They signed a peace treaty with Germany in March 1918. The Treaty of Brest-Litovsk gave up huge amounts of Russian territory to Germany. It also made it possible for Germany to move its troops from the eastern front to the western front.

601

THE UNITED STATES
ENTERS WORLD WAR I

**Map Study**

In 1917 the United States entered World War I on the side of the
Allies. Trace the line of trench warfare in 1918. What river does the
line approach? Which Central Power invaded Belgium? Which
Central Power invaded Serbia after the assassination of Archduke
Ferdinand?

**The Germans start a new attack.** With
all its troops in the west, Germany began a
new attack against the Allies. The Germans
hoped to capture Paris and win a final victory. From March until June the Germans
hammered at the Allied lines, pushing them
back toward Paris. By June 3 the Germans
had advanced to within 50 miles (80 kilometers) of the French capital.

**American and Allied forces turn back
the German advance.** American forces
reached full strength in Europe in the spring
of 1918. The Allies wanted to use American
soldiers to replace their lost troops. General
Pershing refused. With President Wilson's
backing, Pershing insisted that the Americans fight as a separate unit. In June the
Americans helped the French turn back the

Germans at Château-Thierry (shah-TOH tyeh-REE) on the Marne River. Pershing's troops then advanced against the Germans in nearby Belleau (BEL-o) Wood. After three weeks of fierce fighting the Americans won the Battle of Belleau Wood on June 25.

**The Allies win the final battles.** In July the Germans attacked again along the Marne River. After three days of fighting, the Allies stopped the Germans. Then a counterattack by the Americans forced the Germans to retreat. This battle, General Pershing wrote, "turned the tide of the war."

The Allies were now on the offensive. In September, American troops attacked German positions at St. Mihiel (SAN mee-YEL). (See map on page 602.) After four days, the Germans were driven out. This battle marked the first time airplanes were used to support ground troops. Many of the planes were flown by Americans.

In late September more than 1 million American troops joined the Allies in the Battle of the Argonne Forest. In the thick forest soldiers could see only a few yards, and their advance was hindered by rain, mud, barbed wire, and heavy German machine-gun fire. More than 120,000 Americans were killed or wounded. After 47 days of fighting, the Germans were driven back. The battle produced one of the war's most popular heroes, Alvin C. York of Tennessee. York destroyed a German machine-gun nest and then, acting alone, captured over 100 prisoners.

**The war ends.** The Central Powers had no hope of winning. Germany's allies surrendered one by one. On November 11 Germany signed an armistice —a cease-fire agreement. Europe's Great War was over.

As the battlefields fell silent, the world counted the losses caused by the war. Altogether, 8.5 million soldiers had died. An equal number of civilians lost their lives. The United States had lost about 50,000 troops in battle and about the same number to disease. These losses, however, were small compared to those of European nations. Britain had lost 1 million soldiers, and France 1.3 million. Germany lost 1.8 million. The war had almost wiped out a generation of European men.

American troops, led by General Pershing, wait at St. Mihiel before driving the German forces from the city. The battle lasted four days and about 7,000 American soldiers died in the heavy fighting.

## SECTION REVIEW

1. **Vocabulary** pacifist, convoy, communism, armistice
2. **People and Places** John J. Pershing, Bolsheviks, V.I. Lenin, Karl Marx, Marne River, St. Mihiel, Argonne Forest, Alvin C. York
3. **Comprehension** How did the United States prepare for World War I after war was declared?
4. **Comprehension** Why was the United States' role in the war critical?
5. **Critical Thinking** At the end of the war, why might Americans' feeling about the war have differed from those of the Allies?

# CRITICAL THINKING: Drawing Conclusions

As you read history, you may not find all the information needed to understand the ideas presented. If so, you may have to draw a conclusion about the intended meaning. A **conclusion** is a judgment or opinion based on careful thought and consideration of available information.

When drawing conclusions, first review what is stated directly. Next, add your own knowledge and experience to this information to arrive at a judgment. Finally, get more information to check your conclusion. In Section 1, for example, you read:

> Early in the war, Germany warned the United States that it would attack neutral ships sailing to Great Britain. President Wilson responded to this threat with another warning. He said the Germans would be held to account if American lives were lost in U-boat attacks.
> ... On May 7, 1915, a German U-boat sank the British liner *Lusitania* near the coast of southern Ireland. ... Among the dead were 128 Americans.

The excerpt does not say what the American response was. Yet if you review President Wilson's warning and make a judgment about how seriously he meant his words, you will probably conclude that the United States took some action. You can check your conclusion by reading the next paragraph in Section 1:

> Americans were outraged by the sinking of the *Lusitania*. The United States issued strong warnings to the German government not to endanger the lives of American citizens. For a time Germany agreed to limit its submarine warfare.

From this passage, you learn that the United States did make demands on Germany. Your conclusion is correct.

In June 1919, as you will read in Section 3, the Treaty of Versailles set the terms for peace between Germany and the Allies. Read the following excerpt about the Treaty of Versailles, and draw some conclusions about its effects. Then answer the questions that follow.

> The Germans were not asked to sign the Treaty of Versailles; they were told to sign it. If they refused, the Allies warned them, their country would be torn apart. The ceremony took place on June 23, 1919, in the Hall of Mirrors in the Trianon Place in Versailles, near Paris. In this very same hall ... at the end of the Franco-Prussian War in 1871, a victorious Germany had proclaimed her empire.... Now France held the whip over her old enemy. Revenge was in the very air.
>
> The Germans were sure that, by the terms of the peace, the Allies meant to destroy them utterly. This was no justice, they said, but bitterness and hate. Never would they forget it.
>
> The Germans never did forget. One German in particular, [Adolf Hitler], was to keep the memory of Versailles ... alive.

1. What facts are stated about what the Allies told the Germans?
2. What does the author say about the French attitude toward the Germans?
3. What conclusion can you draw about how the Germans felt about the treaty?
4. What conclusion can you draw about Adolf Hitler?
5. How could you check to find out if your conclusions are accurate?

## Vocabulary

self-determination
reparation

With the war over, President Wilson turned his attention to making peace. He had called the war "the war to end all wars." He hoped that the terms of settlement would assure freedom and peace for all nations.

## The Peace Conference

Wilson sailed for Europe in December 1918 to attend the peace conference. He was the first American President to leave the country while in office. In Paris thousands of people lined the streets to cheer *"Vive Wilson!"*—"Long live Wilson!" The President hoped this reception would help him achieve "peace with honor."

**The Allies disagree over terms of peace.** Wilson and representatives from the victorious Allied countries met at Versailles (vuhr-SY), just outside Paris, to negotiate the peace treaty. The conference lasted from January to June 1919. More than 30 countries were represented at the conference, but the important decisions were made by four people, known as the Big Four. They included President Wilson, Prime Minister David Lloyd George of Great Britain, Premier Georges Clemenceau (kleh-mahn-SO) of France, and Prime Minister Vittorio Orlando of Italy.

Wilson soon realized that the other three leaders did not share his hopes for "peace without victory." The Europeans came from countries worn out by the war. They wanted revenge, and they wanted to crush Germany so that it could never make war again. In the discussion of payment for war damages and the location of new boundary lines, the Allied leaders wanted severe terms for Germany and the other Central Powers. Wilson believed that forcing harsh terms on the Central Powers would be a mistake. He felt that a policy of revenge would lead to more wars in the future.

**Wilson seeks a peace based on his Fourteen Points.** Wilson had already proposed terms for what he believed would be a lasting peace. His plan for a better world was contained in a speech delivered before Congress on January 8, 1918. Wilson's statement became known as the **Fourteen Points.**

The fourteen points, or proposals, in Wilson's speech were intended to prevent the kinds of international problems that led to World War I. The most important proposals were: (1) Agreements among nations should be arrived at openly through public discussion, not made in secret. (2) There should be freedom of the seas "alike in peace and war." (3) Trade barriers between nations should be broken down. (4) Nations should reduce the size of their armies and navies. (5) Colonial claims should be settled as fairly as possible. (6) National groups should have the right to **self-determination** —the right to decide how they will be governed. (7) "A general association of nations" should be set up to promise independence and safety "to great and small nations alike."

**The Treaty of Versailles is written.** At first the Allies accepted the Fourteen Points as the basis for peace. As the talks continued, however, the other members of the Big Four did not support Wilson's peace plans. The chief concern of Lloyd George, Clemenceau, and Orlando was to gain advantages for their own countries. Reluctantly, Wilson was forced to give up most of his Fourteen Points. On one point, however, President Wilson refused to budge. He insisted that the peace treaty should set up an association of nations to help keep peace.

605

## NEW NATIONS APPEAR IN POSTWAR EUROPE

FINLAND

NORWAY

SWEDEN

NORTH SEA

ESTONIA

LATVIA

LITHUANIA

DENMARK

BALTIC SEA

GREAT BRITAIN

Danzig

E. PRUSSIA

NETH.

GERMANY

POLAND

BELG.

LUX.

CZECHOSLOVAKIA

• Versailles

FRANCE

SWITZ.

AUSTRIA

HUNGARY

RUMANIA

YUGOSLAVIA

BLACK SEA

SPAIN

ITALY

BULGARIA

ALBANIA

GREECE

TURKEY

MEDITERRANEAN SEA

**Prewar extent of**
German Empire
Austria-Hungary
Russian Empire
Postwar boundary

SCALE
0    600 mi
0    600 km

### Map Study

Under the terms of the Treaty of Versailles many new nations were created in Europe. Which countries gave up land to form Poland? Which former Central Power gave up land to form Czechoslovakia and Yugoslavia?

The **Treaty of Versailles** was completed in June 1919. The harsh terms of the treaty shocked the Germans, who had not been represented in the peace talks. Germany and the other defeated countries were forced to sign the treaty, however. The agreement included the following points: (1) Germany had to accept responsibility for starting the war. The Germans would also have to make huge **reparations** —payments for damages—to the Allied countries. (2) The Allies would occupy that part of Germany west of the Rhine River to make sure the Germans met their obligations under the treaty. (3) Germany was disarmed and had to agree not to own or build battleships, warplanes, or tanks. Its army was to remain small. (4) Germany had to give its colonies, as well as some of its territory in Europe, to other countries. (5) Several new European nations were formed from land taken from the defeated countries and Russia. These new nations included Poland, Czechoslovakia, and Yugoslavia. (See map above.) These homelands would permit self-determination for such national groups as Poles, Czechs, and Slavs. (6) The treaty created a world organization known as the **League of Nations.**

**The treaty outlines the plan for the League of Nations.** Each country to sign the Treaty of Versailles would be a member of the planned League of Nations. The League was to include an Assembly in which all member nations would have a vote. There would also be a Council of the five Allied powers (the United States, Great Britain, France, Italy, and Japan), plus four other members chosen by the Assembly. A World Court, organized by the League, would judge disputes between nations.

The purpose of the League was to promote cooperation among nations and bring about international peace. If a country attacked another country and continued fighting in spite of the League's orders, the members could act against it. They could stop lending money to such a nation or cut off trade with it. In some cases, the League might use force against a warring country. One negative vote in the Assembly could block such action.

## The Campaign for the League

President Wilson returned to the United States certain that the League of Nations was a means of preserving peace. He found, however, that many Americans did not share his views. Some felt the treaty did not punish the defeated nations enough. Many German Americans, on the other hand, thought the terms were unfair to Germany.

**The Senate debates the treaty.** The United States Constitution requires that treaties be approved by a two-thirds vote of the Senate. Wilson therefore had to seek the Senate's approval of the new treaty. Many senators strongly opposed the treaty and the League of Nations. Some senators were angry because the President had ignored them in working out the peace treaty. Others did not think the peace treaty supported the plan for peace set forth in the Fourteen Points. Still others were tired of Europe and its troubles and wanted to avoid any further involvement overseas. Many Americans shared these isolationist views after World War I. Their isolationism led them to oppose the League of Nations. They feared the League would draw the United States into new European quarrels.

Two main groups of senators opposed the League of Nations. The "bitter-enders" would not accept the League under any conditions. A second group, led by Henry Cabot Lodge of Massachusetts, was willing to accept the League with some compromises. Lodge especially disliked one section of the plan for the League. This section called on members to act together against nations that threatened the peace. Under the Constitution only Congress has the authority to declare war. Lodge believed that Congress should be able to decide whether or not the United States would take part in any action against another nation.

## LINKING PAST AND PRESENT

## ★ ★ ★ *The Nobel Prize*

Dynamite was invented in 1867 by Alfred Nobel, a Swedish chemist. Nobel later invented other explosives, and his inventions made him one of the world's richest people. He was greatly disturbed that his inventions were used for war and destruction, however. His original purpose had been to stop accidental deaths by inventing safer explosives. Nobel used $9 million of his fortune to set up a fund to award several yearly prizes, including a prize for contributions toward international peace.

The Nobel Peace Prize quickly became one of the world's most valued awards. In 1919 the peace prize was given to Woodrow Wilson for his part in establishing the League of Nations. Other American winners of the Nobel Peace Prize have included Theodore Roosevelt, Jane Addams, Martin Luther King, Jr., and Henry Kissinger.

**Wilson asks the people for support.** Wilson would not accept Lodge's restrictions on American membership in the League. Instead, Wilson decided to take his case to the people. In September 1919 he began a national speaking tour to explain the League of Nations. He visited 29 cities and asked people to support the League.

On September 25, as his train sped from Colorado to Kansas, Wilson became seriously ill. The trip was canceled and Wilson returned to the White House. There, on the night of October 2, 1919, he suffered a stroke that left him partially paralyzed. Although he stayed in office until the end of his term, Wilson never fully regained his health.

**The Senate rejects the League.** In spite of Wilson's efforts, many Americans still wanted to steer clear of affairs outside the Americas. In November the Senate voted not to accept the Treaty of Versailles. As a result, the United States never joined the

League of Nations. America signed a separate peace agreement with Germany in 1921. The League was set up without the United States in 1920, but it proved too weak to bring about Wilson's dream of lasting peace.

## SECTION REVIEW

1. **Vocabulary**   self-determination, reparation
2. **People and Places**   Versailles, David Lloyd George, Georges Clemenceau, Vittorio Orlando, Henry Cabot Lodge
3. **Comprehension**   Why did the Allied leaders disagree over peace terms?
4. **Comprehension**   Why did many senators oppose the Treaty of Versailles?
5. **Critical Thinking**   Should the United States have joined the League of Nations? Why or why not?

# Chapter 26 Summary

Imperialism, militarism, and competing alliances created political tension in Europe. In 1914 the murder of the Archduke of Austria-Hungary sparked World War I. For three years the Allies and the Central Powers waged trench warfare, at great cost in human life. At first the United States adopted a policy of neutrality. Public opinion turned against Germany as a result of submarine warfare and the Zimmermann telegram. Early in 1917 the United States declared war against Germany.

The nation mobilized for war by rapidly building up its armed services and increasing industrial production. Mobilization gave new opportunities to women and minorities, but it also led to attacks on pacifists and others who disagreed with national policy. The Allied situation in the war worsened when Bolsheviks took over the Russian government, and Russia withdrew from the war to establish communism. In 1918 American

troops helped the Allies stop the German advance toward Paris and then won fierce battles at St. Mihiel and the Argonne Forest. In November Germany signed an armistice ending the fighting.

President Wilson hoped for generous peace terms based on his Fourteen Points. The other members of the Big Four at the Paris peace conference wanted revenge and sought huge reparations from Germany. Wilson compromised on most of his proposals, but the Treaty of Versailles included his plan for the League of Nations. The treaty also established new nations in central Europe to promote self-determination for national groups there. Many members of the United States Senate opposed the League of Nations. Wilson toured the nation seeking support for ratification of the treaty, but illness forced him to end the tour. The Senate rejected the treaty, and the United States never joined the League of Nations.

# CAUSES and EFFECTS

# The Spanish American War ★ ★ ★

United States
uphold the
Monroe Doctrine

American business
seeks new markets
and investments

United States
competes for
colonies

## CONTRIBUTING CAUSES

Yellow
journalists fan
opposition to
Spain

Cuba rebels
against Spain

The *Maine*
explodes

Americans
support Cuban
independence

## MAIN CAUSES

# SPANISH AMERICAN WAR

## EFFECTS

United States
gains Guam,
the Philippines,
and Puerto Rico

Theodore Roosevelt
becomes a hero

Cuba wins
independence

United States has
strong influence
in Cuba

## LONG-TERM EFFECTS

United States
plays a greater role
in world affairs

Panama Canal
is built

World trade
increases

United States
polices
the Americas

# Chapter 26 REVIEW

## Vocabulary and Key Terms

Match each of the following terms with its correct definition. Write your answers on a separate sheet of paper.

Bolsheviks
League of Nations
Central Powers
communism
Fourteen Points

Treaty of Versailles
reparations
armistice
militarism

1. payments for war damages
2. a political system based on the ideas of Karl Marx
3. an organization of nations set up to preserve world peace
4. policy of building up armed forces to prepare for war
5. Communist group that took over the government of Russia
6. proposals made by President Wilson as a basis for peace
7. cease-fire agreement
8. countries that fought against the United States in World War I
9. agreement written at the peace conference at the end of World War I

## Recalling the Facts

1. What policies caused tension among certain European nations before the outbreak of World War I?
2. How did World War I begin?
3. What two groups of nations fought each other in World War I?
4. What was trench warfare?
5. Why did the American policy of neutrality eventually fail?
6. How did the United States mobilize for World War I?
7. What was the importance of the convoy system?
8. How did the arrival of American troops change the war in Europe?

## Places to Locate

Match the letters on the map with the places listed below. Write your answers on a separate sheet of paper.

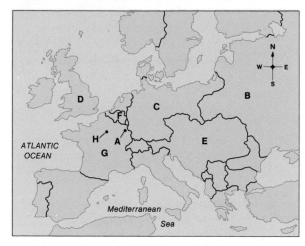

1. Germany
2. Belgium
3. Paris
4. Russia
5. St. Mihiel
6. Austria-Hungary
7. Great Britain
8. France

## Critical Thinking

1. American life changed greatly after World War I. Do you think the war's effect on the country was good? Consider these points in your answer:
   a. the role of women and minorities
   b. treatment of opponents of the war
   c. the nation's role in the settlement of the war
2. If you had been a member of the United States Senate in 1919, would you have voted to ratify the Treaty of Versailles? Why or why not? Consider these questions in your answer:
   a. Was the Treaty of Versailles a fair settlement of the war?
   b. Did the plan for the League of Nations conflict with Congress's right to declare war?

## Understanding History

1. Reread the section "War erupts" on page 594. Then answer these questions.
   a. **Geography.** What geographic factors prompted the Germans to invade Belgium?
   b. **Geography.** How did Germany's location in the center of Europe affect the start of the war?
2. Reread the section "The government spurs production of war resources" on page 599. Then answer these questions.
   a. **Economics.** What steps did the government take to control the production of industrial goods?
   b. **Citizenship.** In what ways did Americans support the effort to mobilize for war?
3. Reread the section "The Senate debates the treaty" on page 607. Then answer these questions.
   a. **Citizenship.** Do you think Wilson should have involved the Senate in working out the peace treaty?
   b. **Citizenship.** Why did some senators think the treaty conflicted with the Constitution?

## Projects and Activities

1. **Making a Time Line.** List events in World War I, with their dates, from the time the United States declared war until the time Germany signed the armistice. Then use your list to make a time line of the war.
2. **Giving a Speech.** Imagine that you are Woodrow Wilson on a tour of the United States to gain support for the Treaty of Versailles and the League of Nations. Prepare a speech outlining the reasons you think the United States should sign the treaty and join the League. Give your speech in front of the class.
3. **Drawing a Political Cartoon.** Draw a political cartoon that either supports or opposes American entry into World War I. Your cartoon might express the view that the war was necessary to defend democracy, or it might express the idea that America should stay out of Europe's problems.

4. **Creating a Map.** Research the Battle of the Argonne Forest or another battle of World War I. Create a map showing details of the battle. Include geographical features and explain how the shape of the land influenced the battle.
5. **Writing a Fictional Account.** Imagine that you are an American soldier or nurse in France during World War I. Write an account of your daily activities and how you feel about the war.

## Practicing Your Skill

Use the primary source below to answer the questions that follow.

War brings no prosperity to the great mass of common and patriotic citizens.... War brings prosperity to the stock gambler on Wall Street....

We are going into war upon the command of gold. We are going to run the risk of sacrificing millions of our countrymen's lives in order that other countrymen may coin their lifeblood into money....

We ought to remember the advice of the Father of our Country and keep out of entangling alliances. Let Europe solve her problems as we have solved ours.... In the greatest war of our history and at the time it occurred, the greatest war in the world's history, we were engaged in solving an American problem. We settled the question of human slavery and washed our flag clean by the sacrifice of human blood. It was a great problem and a great burden, but we solved it ourselves. Never once did we think of asking Europe to take part in its solution.

Senator George W. Norris

1. To what war is the speaker referring? Is he in favor of American involvement in the war? How do you know?
2. What other war does the speaker talk about? What makes you conclude that?
3. What does the speaker regard as the main motive for American involvement in World War I? How do you know?
4. Who does the phrase "the Father of our Country" describe?

# UNIT 8 REVIEW

## Unit Summary

★ **The United States adopted an active, expansionist world role.**

- American producers sought new markets for surplus goods.
- The United States bought Alaska from Russia and annexed Hawaii.
- As a result of the Spanish-American War, the United States gained new territories.
- The Open Door Policy was issued to keep China open for trade.
- The Monroe Doctrine was used in a dispute between Great Britain and Venezuela.
- The Panama Canal, completed in 1914, shortened the route between the east and the west coasts.

★ **The Progressive Movement sought to reform American life.**

- Muckrakers publicized social problems and aided reforms.
- The Nineteenth Amendment gave women the right to vote in 1920.
- Theodore Roosevelt and Woodrow Wilson gave national leadership to the Progressive Movement.

★ **The United States supported the Allies during World War I.**

- Political rivalries in Europe led to World War I in 1914.
- Germany's hostile actions toward the United States increased public sympathy for the Allied Powers.
- The United States entered the war in 1917, and Germany surrendered in 1918.
- Congress rejected the League of Nations as a plan for peace.

## Understanding Chronology

Study the Unit 8 time line on page 549. Then complete the following activity on a separate sheet of paper.

Copy the Unit 8 time line, adding, next to each date, the name of the President who served at that time. Then write each of the following events under the correct presidency: the United States annexes Hawaii, the Nineteenth Amendment becomes law, and the Progressive party is formed.

## Writing About History

1. **Keeping a Journal.** Imagine that you helped to build the Panama Canal. Find information about problems encountered by the workers. Then write journal entries describing the hardships and the satisfaction of completing the great engineering feat.

2. **Preparing a Nomination Speech.** Write a speech to nominate one of the following presidential candidates at their 1912 conventions: Democrat Woodrow Wilson, Progressive Theodore Roosevelt, or Republican William H. Taft. Include some information about the candidate's background, leadership qualities, and presidential goals.

3. **Identifying Issues.** Use the style of the muckrakers to publicize a current problem. Research the problem to make sure that your facts are accurate. Then write about the problem using emotional appeal to promote reform.

4. **Writing a Report.** Write a report on Alaska and Hawaii. Find information on their geography, climate, natural resources, people, and what distinguishes them from the rest of the nation. Conclude your report with a paragraph explaining which of the two states you would like to visit and why.

**5. Interpreting a Cartoon.** Study the cartoon above. By 1898, when this cartoon first appeared, the tall figure of Uncle Sam was a familiar symbol of the United States. Give an explanation of what Uncle Sam is doing and how the cartoon expresses the idea of imperialism. Does the cartoon present an expansionist view or an antiexpansionist view? Explain your answer.

## Projects

**1. Making a Map.** Draw a map of the world that shows the expansion of the United States between 1867 and 1920. Identify all of the territories that were gained by the United States and the dates of each acquisition.

**2. Presenting a Play.** Work in small groups to prepare and present a play about Theodore Roosevelt, one of America's most popular and colorful Presidents. The play might be divided into acts dealing with Roosevelt's childhood, his early political career and military service, his presidency, his family, and his later life. Try to include primary source material that shows President Roosevelt's personality and humor.

**3. Comparing Information.** Prepare a chart that compares President Roosevelt's "square deal" with President Wilson's New Freedom. Include each administration's goals, its policies, and its successes and failures. Draw conclusions about which presidential administration best represented the Progressive Movement and explain your opinions.

**4. Preparing a Chart.** Prepare a cause-and-effect chart of American foreign involvements between 1865 and 1898. Categorize each incident as a trade agreement, a dispute, an acquisition of territory, or a war. Then identify the primary cause that led the United States to become involved in each incident.

**5. Analyzing a World Event.** Work in groups to study different aspects of World War I. Investigate several of the following topics: causes of the war, wartime alliances, battles and weapons, the home front, why the United States became involved, and results of the war. Use newspapers, posters, music, and first-person accounts to gain an understanding of the times. Present your information to the class using reports, charts, pictures, or posters.

## Finding Out More

Asimov, Isaac. *The Golden Door; the United States from 1865 to 1918.* Houghton Mifflin, 1977. The author shows the development of the American nation from Reconstruction to the close of World War I. Important political and social attitudes of the times are discussed in this easy-to-read book.

Blumberg, Rhoda. *Commodore Perry in the Land of the Shogun.* Lothrop, Lee & Shepard Books, 1985. The expeditions of Commodore Matthew Perry are described and a view of nineteenth-century Japan is presented in this fascinating, informative text.

Constant, Alberta Wilson. *Does Anybody Care About Lou Emma Miller?* Harper, 1979. This story tells about Kansas family life in the early years of the twentieth century.

Schwartz, Alvin, ed. *When I Grew Up Long Ago.* Harper, 1978. Oral histories report about life in the United States between 1890 and 1914.

Stein, R. Conrad. *The Story of Lafayette Escadrille.* Childrens Press, 1983. This account of famous American fliers in World War I is easy to read.

# UNIT 9 TURBULENT DECADES
## 1919–1945

40,000 B.C.    A.D. 1000    1100    1200    1300    1400

In the prosperous years of the 1920's, well-dressed theater-goers flocked to the bright lights of New York City's Times Square.

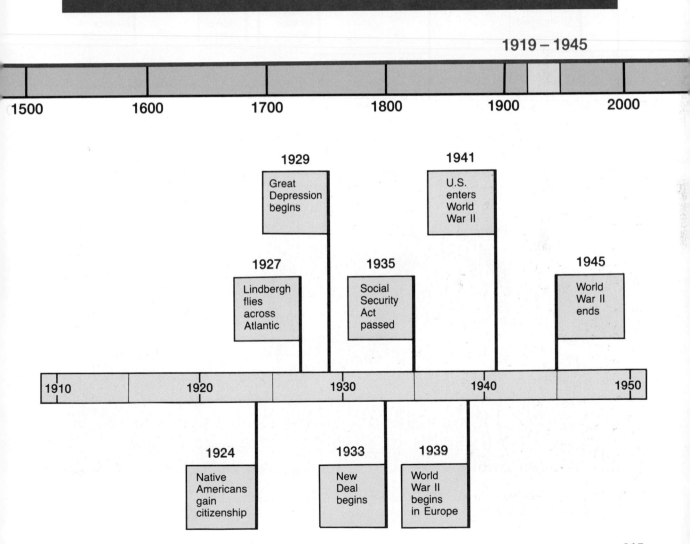

1919 – 1945

1500     1600     1700     1800     1900     2000

**1929**
Great Depression begins

**1941**
U.S. enters World War II

**1927**
Lindbergh flies across Atlantic

**1935**
Social Security Act passed

**1945**
World War II ends

1910     1920     1930     1940     1950

**1924**
Native Americans gain citizenship

**1933**
New Deal begins

**1939**
World War II begins in Europe

| Wilson | Harding | Coolidge | | Hoover | F.D. Roosevelt |
|---|---|---|---|---|---|
| 1919 | 1922 | 1925 | 1928 | 1931 | 1934 |

1920
Nineteenth
Amendment

1927
Lindbergh
crosses
Atlantic

1929
Stock
market
crash

1932
Reconstruction
Finance
Corporation begins

1919
Eighteenth
Amendment

1924
Teapot Dome scandal

Immigration Act

The increased use of the automobile and new styles of clothing reflected the rapidly changing lifestyles of the 1920's.

## Preparing to Read

With World War I over, Americans turned their attention to matters at home. They struggled to adjust to the rapid growth of cities and other social changes. During the 1920's business and industry boomed. Millions of Americans enjoyed great prosperity, and new wealth sparked new manners and lifestyles. In rural areas and in large cities, however, many people still suffered in poverty. In 1929 the economic boom collapsed, and the decade of the Roaring Twenties gave way to extremely hard times. As you read this chapter, try to answer the following questions:

1. How did American life change after World War I?
2. How did an economic boom lead to the "Roaring Twenties"?
3. How did prosperity give way to the Great Depression?

# 1 How did American life change after World War I?

## Vocabulary

| | |
|---|---|
| foreclose | quota |
| cost of living | anarchist |
| deport | bootlegging |

After the war, Americans hoped for a calm and settled life. The first years after the war, however, were not settled ones. The nation faced economic problems and large shifts in population.

## Changing Times

The shift to peacetime production caused problems for many farmers and workers. Cities grew rapidly, as black Americans and immigrants joined the urban work force.

**Crop surpluses cause a crisis for farmers.** During the war, the demand for wheat and other crops was high at home and abroad. To meet the demand, many farmers borrowed money from banks to buy more equipment and land. When the war ended, however, European farmers resumed planting. The increased supply of food caused a market surplus, and crop prices went down. Many American farmers were unable to repay their loans. When this happened, the banks **foreclosed** —canceled the loans and took over the farmers' property. As a result, thousands lost their farms.

**Unemployment rises after the war.** Urban workers also faced problems. Most American industries reduced output after the war and thus required fewer laborers. As a result, unemployment increased during the early 1920's. About 550,000 people were unemployed in 1919. By 1920 more than 2 million Americans were out of work.

For those who had jobs, wages were down. Also, the **cost of living** —the average cost of food, housing, and clothing—nearly doubled between 1916 and 1920. When companies failed to meet their workers' demands for better pay, many labor unions called for strikes.

**The government responds to labor unrest.** In 1919 more than 1,100 Boston police officers went on strike. People feared the strike would lead to lawlessness. Governor Calvin Coolidge of Massachusetts used the state militia to patrol the streets. He then fired the strikers, stating: "There is no right to strike against public peace by anybody, anywhere, any time." The governor's actions made him a public hero.

There were nearly 4,000 other strikes in 1919. The government and public opinion tended to sympathize more with business than with labor. Resentful strikers frequently became violent. Though many of these strikes failed, working conditions did gradually improve.

**The United States becomes an urban nation.** In spite of labor problems, many new workers moved to American cities. The 1920 census revealed that, for the first time, most Americans lived in cities or towns. Before that time, most Americans had lived in rural areas. Throughout the 1920's, the cities continued to swell. Millions of immigrants came to American cities from Europe. Thousands of American farmers also came to urban areas to seek work. By 1930 urban dwellers outnumbered rural dwellers by nearly 15 million.

**Many southern blacks head north.** Black Americans also contributed to the growth of cities. Between 1916 and 1921, more than 500,000 southern blacks moved to northern and midwestern cities. Many sought to escape the sharecropping system and Jim Crow laws of the South. They hoped to find better jobs, higher wages, freer lives, and better education for their children.

Many blacks, especially men, did find work in northern industries. Their jobs, however, tended to be the hardest and poorest paid. Many unions excluded blacks. Also, most industries preferred to hire recent European immigrants rather than blacks. Consequently, many black men suffered frequent unemployment. Most black women were limited to domestic work as washerwomen or servants.

**Women work outside of the home.** Another important social change was the growing number of working women. During World War I, many white women had begun to work in factories and other businesses.

## Graph Study

The United States rapidly changed from a rural nation to an urban one. In what year shown on the graph did the urban population first exceed the rural population? In what year did the urban population outnumber the rural one by about 2 to 1?

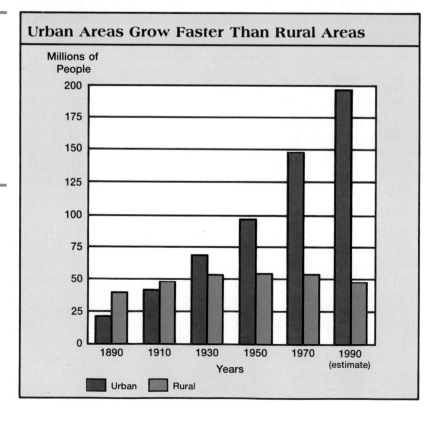

**Urban Areas Grow Faster Than Rural Areas**

Millions of People

Years

■ Urban  ■ Rural

Black artist Jacob Lawrence's painting shows blacks migrating north in the 1920's. How does Lawrence show that blacks were moving north?

They filled in for millions of men who joined the armed forces. After the war, women continued to work. By 1930 more than 10 million women had jobs outside the home, usually as factory workers or office clerks.

## Reactions to Change

Many Americans were disturbed by the rapid changes in society. Rural Protestants especially wanted to keep the nation as it had been before the war. Fear of changes led to trouble for immigrants and black Americans.

**The nation fears Communists.** In 1917 Americans had been shocked when Communists took control of the government of Russia. (See Chapter 26.) The Russian Communist leader V.I. Lenin predicted that other Communist revolutions would take place around the world. Americans were alarmed when a Communist party emerged in the United States. A series of terrorist bombings in 1919 led to widespread fears of a Communist revolution. Because Communists were sometimes called Reds, the fear and distrust of communism became known as the **Red Scare.**

Many Americans associated the Communist threat with new immigrants, especially those from eastern and southern Europe. Some immigrants were radicals, and many native-born Americans felt suspicious of immigrants as a whole.

Attorney General A. Mitchell Palmer was a leading anti-Communist. He ordered mass raids against those thought to be Communists. Beginning in 1919, more than 6,000 people were arrested. Many of them were

**619**

Some Americans blamed immigrants for the economic problems of the early 1900's. What economic problem is identified in this cartoon? Why might a flood of immigrants add to the problem?

recent immigrants. Some were imprisoned or **deported** —sent out of the country. Yet most of those arrested were not involved in Communist activities.

**The Red Scare leads to action against immigrants.** Palmer proclaimed that a Communist revolution would begin on May 1, 1920. When the day passed without incident, the Red Scare panic began to die down. Many Americans were still suspicious of immigrants, however, and wanted to reduce their number. In response to public pressure, Congress passed the **National Origins Act** of 1924. This law set **quotas** —limits—on immigration. The quotas allowed only a certain number of immigrants to enter the United States from each country.

The National Origins Act favored immigration from western and northern Europe. It limited immigration from eastern and southern Europe, and nearly ended immigration from Asia and Africa. Immigration from Canada and from Latin American countries remained unrestricted.

Fear of foreigners continued throughout the 1920's. This feeling reached a high point during the trial of Italian immigrants Nicola Sacco (NIH-ko-lah SAH-ko) and Bartolomeo Vanzetti (bar-tah-lo-MAY-o van-ZEH-tee). Sacco and Vanzetti were both well-known **anarchists** —people who oppose organized government. In 1920 they were arrested and charged with robbery and murder at a Massachusetts shoe factory. Though there was little evidence to support the charges, Sacco and Vanzetti were found guilty and sentenced to death. Many people believed that the two immigrants had been sentenced because of their beliefs. Despite widespread protests, Sacco and Vanzetti were executed in 1927.

**Black Americans face racial violence.** The years after the war were also marked by violence toward black Americans. Black soldiers returned from Europe with pride and hope. They had fought bravely, and many had been treated as heroes in France. Many whites, however, received black veterans with hostility. Whites did not want to compete with blacks for jobs and housing. When black citizens demanded fair treatment, they were threatened and sometimes killed. More than 70 lynchings were reported in 1919 alone.

Many attacks against blacks were led by the Ku Klux Klan. The Klan had reappeared in the South in 1915, and in the 1920's it gained millions of members in the South and Midwest. Only white Protestants born in the United States could join the Klan. Klan members did not attack only blacks. They also terrorized Jews, Catholics, and immigrants. In the early 1920's the Klan gained considerable political power. In 1925, however, the leader of the Klan in Indiana was charged with murder. After that year the power of the Klan declined rapidly.

**Black leaders seek solutions to racial strife.** The tension between blacks and whites also led to riots. In summer 1919, race riots broke out in Chicago, Omaha, Washington, D.C., and other cities. Many black leaders and organizations such as the National Association for the Advancement of Colored People looked for solutions to racial violence, poverty, and other problems facing black Americans. Jamaican immigrant Marcus Garvey argued that blacks would never gain economic or political equality in the United States. Garvey wanted blacks to reclaim their heritage and return to Africa. Garvey's **Back-to-Africa Movement** was particularly popular among poor blacks. Though his plan did not work, Garvey's movement inspired pride and dignity among many black Americans.

**Prohibition becomes law.** Since the mid-1800's some reformers had tried to prohibit the use of liquor. Prohibitionists argued that alcohol led to broken marriages, unemployment, disease, violence, and crime. After World War I, Prohibition grew in popularity, particularly among rural Americans. In 1919, the states ratified the **Eighteenth Amendment,** which outlawed the manufacture, sale, and transport of alcoholic beverages. In the same year Congress passed the **Volstead Act,** giving the government the power to enforce Prohibition.

The law did not work. **Bootlegging** — manufacturing illegal liquor—grew into a big business. Many Americans produced home-made liquor, and alcohol was also smuggled into America from other countries. Secret bars known as **speakeasies** sold drinks to patrons. Organized crime grew when some gangsters made huge profits by supplying liquor to speakeasies. Gangsters like Chicago's Al Capone and Philadelphia's Maxie Hoff bribed government officials and sometimes shot down rival gangsters in the streets.

The government found that it was impossible to enforce a law that so many Americans would not obey. Officials feared that people would begin to disregard other laws as well. In time Americans realized that Prohibition was a mistake. In 1933 the nation repealed the Eighteenth Amendment. It is the only amendment to the Constitution to have been repealed.

## The 1920 Election

As the 1920 election neared, many Americans were ready for a rest from change and turmoil. They wanted to turn away from public issues and to start to focus on their private lives.

**Harding is elected President.** The Republicans were well aware that many American voters were tired of war, reforms, and social change. They were quite confident of winning the 1920 election. Republican leaders chose Warren G. Harding to be their presidential nominee.

Harding was a senator from Ohio. He was not well-known, but he was a handsome, friendly man and was considered to be a good speaker. As his running mate Senator Harding selected Calvin Coolidge of Massachusetts, who was famous for ending the Boston police strike.

Harding ran his campaign from the porch of his Ohio home. He promised Americans a return to **normalcy.** "America's present need is not heroism but healing; not [cures] but normalcy; not revolution but restoration," Harding declared. *Normalcy*—a word invented by Harding—seemed to

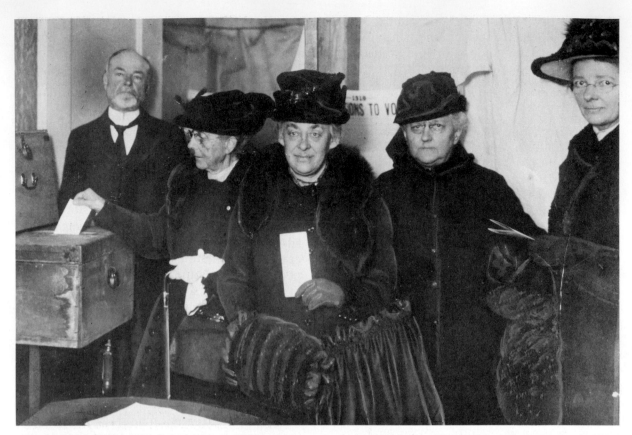

After the ratification of the Nineteenth Amendment, more than 9 million women voted in the 1920 presidential election. This newspaper photograph shows leaders in the suffrage movement voting for the first time.

express what people wanted in 1920. It suggested a simpler time, when government did not interfere in people's lives and businesses. Harding's slogan also recalled a time when Americans were not involved in Europe's affairs.

The 1920 presidential election was the first one in which all American women could vote. The women's suffrage movement had gained ground during World War I. A suffrage amendment, submitted to Congress in 1917, was approved in 1919. In August 1920 it was ratified by the states and became the **Nineteenth Amendment.** Most Americans, including women, liked Harding's promise to return to normalcy. Harding won the election by a large majority.

## SECTION REVIEW

1. **Vocabulary**    foreclose, cost of living, deport, quota, anarchist, bootlegging
2. **People and Places**    Boston, Calvin Coolidge, V.I. Lenin, A. Mitchell Palmer, Sacco and Vanzetti, Marcus Garvey, Chicago, Al Capone, Warren G. Harding
3. **Comprehension**    What economic and social changes caused unrest in America after World War I?
4. **Comprehension**    Why did the United States government limit immigration?
5. **Critical Thinking**    Do you think Americans were wise in wanting to return to normalcy in 1920?

# How did an economic boom lead to the "Roaring Twenties"?

## Vocabulary

kickback
suburb
synthetic

improvise
expatriate
materialism

Warren G. Harding was the first of three Republican Presidents elected during the 1920's. All three of these Presidents had similar ideas about government. Unlike the progressives, they thought government should encourage business but not interfere with it. During most of the 1920's, business boomed. Many Americans—but not all—enjoyed great prosperity, and the decade came to be called the **Roaring Twenties.**

## Economic Recovery

Following Harding's election the economy began to improve. Harding was credited for improving conditions, but his presidency ended in a scandal.

**Harding provides weak leadership.** President Harding was not a strong decision-maker. Complex issues often confused him. Rather than solve problems, he avoided making decisions.

Harding knew he was not a strong leader, so he tried to choose experienced and respected people to serve in his Cabinet. Secretary of the Treasury Andrew Mellon and Secretary of Agriculture Henry C. Wallace were among Harding's best choices for key posts. In other appointments Harding proved to be a poor judge of character. He brought many of his friends to Washington, where they were known as the "Ohio gang." Some turned out to be dishonest.

Despite his shortcomings, Harding was a popular President. He had good relations with the press. He also allowed visitors to tour the White House for the first time since before the war. Harding's openness made Americans feel close to him.

**The Harding administration works to help business.** Harding and his advisers made economic growth a top priority. To achieve this, they planned to lower taxes. They also planned to reduce government control over business and to protect business from foreign competition.

Secretary of the Treasury Mellon was a key figure in developing Harding's economic program. Mellon, a banker and aluminum manufacturer, proposed that the Congress

## Our Presidents

### WARREN G. HARDING

★ 1921–1923 ★

**29**TH PRESIDENT

REPUBLICAN

- ★ Born November 2, 1865, in Ohio
- ★ Married Florence Kling DeWolfe in 1891; no children
- ★ Newspaper editor and publisher; senator from Ohio
- ★ Lived in Ohio when elected President
- ★ Vice President: Calvin Coolidge
- ★ Died August 2, 1923, in California
- ★ Key events while in office: Washington Arms Conference; World Court organized; Teapot Dome scandal

## CALVIN COOLIDGE

★ **1923–1929** ★

**30**TH PRESIDENT

REPUBLICAN

- ★ Born July 4, 1872, in Vermont
- ★ Married Grace Anna Goodhue in 1905; 2 children
- ★ Lawyer; governor of Massachusetts; Vice President under Harding
- ★ Lived in Massachusetts when elected Vice President
- ★ Vice President: Charles Dawes
- ★ Nicknamed "Silent Cal"
- ★ Died January 5, 1933, in Massachusetts
- ★ Key events while in office: Lindbergh flew nonstop from New York to Paris; Jazz Age

lower income taxes on wealthy Americans. He argued that if wealthy people paid lower income taxes, they would invest in old businesses and start new ones. These investments, he reasoned, would cause growth in industry and an increase in jobs. Mellon used the same reasoning to argue for lower taxes on business profits.

Secretary Mellon's plan was criticized for disregarding the needs of lower-income Americans. Also, because Mellon was a millionaire himself, many people strongly distrusted his reasons for lowering the taxes of wealthy people. Mellon pushed for his tax program, however, and Congress passed a series of laws that greatly reduced taxes on wealthy Americans and on business profits. Lower-income taxpayers received only a minor tax cut.

**The Harding administration seeks to help farmers.** Harding and Secretary of Agriculture Wallace also planned measures to ease the problems of farmers. In 1921 Congress passed the Emergency Tariff Act. This act protected farmers by placing duties on wheat, wool, sugar, meat, and corn. In 1922 the Fordney-McCumber Tariff Act set new tariffs on manufactured goods and farm goods. These duties were the highest in the nation's history.

**The economy improves.** Harding's economic program seemed to work. By 1922, business improved, wages were up, and unemployment was going down. Farming, however, did not fare as well as other businesses. While some farmers benefited from the new tariffs, most farmers remained in crisis throughout the 1920's.

**Harding dies in office.** President Harding received disturbing news in the spring of 1923. There were indications that a number of his "Ohio gang" friends were taking part in certain illegal activities. Harding was alarmed, but he took no action. Shortly afterwards, Harding began his reelection campaign. The farm crisis had caused the Republicans to lose congressional seats in the 1922 elections. Harding hoped to revive confidence in his administration by making a cross-country speaking tour.

During the tour, Harding was distressed by further news of corruption among his friends. Investigations had begun and a major scandal seemed certain. Harding was crushed by his friends' betrayal of his trust. With little warning, Harding fell ill with pneumonia and died in August 1923. His death stunned the nation.

**The corruption surfaces.** The scandals exploded soon after Harding's death. Harding's friends had used their positions to get money from bribes and **kickbacks** — payments in exchange for official favors.

The most damaging case of corruption, known as the **Teapot Dome Affair,** involved Secretary of the Interior Albert Fall. Fall arranged for his department to control naval oil reserves in Elk Hills, California, and Teapot Dome, Wyoming. Fall then allowed private oil companies to use the reserves. In return, he received more than $400,000 in kickbacks. Fall was convicted for his crime. He was the first Cabinet member to serve a jail term.

Teapot Dome and other scandals severely tarnished President Harding's image. Even though he was not directly involved in the schemes, he did little when he learned of them. Many people blamed him for not taking effective action against corruption in his administration.

## Coolidge Prosperity

Vice President Calvin Coolidge was sworn in as President shortly after Harding's death. In 1924 he was elected President in his own right. Coolidge's years in office were a time of economic growth and confidence for most Americans. This period came to be called "Coolidge Prosperity."

**Coolidge supports business.** Coolidge did not have Harding's charm. He was known for saying as few words as possible and was nicknamed "Silent Cal." Americans, however, liked Coolidge's simple, honest approach. To restore public confidence, he quickly ordered investigations of the Harding administration scandals. He summed up his philosophy of government by declaring, "The business of America is business." Coolidge continued Harding's practice of encouraging private enterprise.

From 1923 to 1929 the output of industry nearly doubled and wages were steady. Growing industries created new careers and new forms of enjoyment and convenience. Much of this wave of prosperity was spurred by the growing automobile industry.

**Ford puts America on wheels.** Automobile production had begun before 1900, but the industry came of age in the

The use of the assembly line became widespread during the 1920's, especially in the automobile industry. How did the assembly line increase production?

1920's. The key was efficient production. Henry Ford started using the assembly line in his factory in 1914. By 1916 he was producing a new car every three minutes. By 1925 Ford's production was so efficient he could sell his Model T's for only $260. Automobiles had previously been playthings for rich people, but now many families could afford them. Ford sold more than 15 million Model T's by 1927. Other companies copied Ford's methods, and the auto industry continued to grow.

The auto industry started other businesses growing as well. Drivers needed oil and gas, service stations, highways, and roadside restaurants. Businesses sprang up to meet these demands. Automakers needed steel, rubber, glass, and paint. The industries that produced these materials expanded and hired thousands of new workers. By the late 1920's about 3 million Americans worked in jobs related to automobile production.

**The automobile changes American life.** The automobile gave many people new opportunities. Young people spent less time at home with their parents and had more personal freedom. Many Americans began to drive to work. As a result, they had a wider choice of places to live. Some people began to move farther out from the cities, and suburbs —residential areas on the outskirts of cities—began to grow. The housing industry expanded to meet the need for new suburban homes.

The automobile also changed American vacations and leisure time. Family cars enabled many people to travel farther from home and to visit other parts of the country. Also, the Sunday drive became a popular part of American family life.

**The automobile changed the way Americans spent their leisure time. By the 1920's, going for a drive in the family car became an American custom.**

**Other developments alter American life.** The use of electric power also increased rapidly during the 1920's. As the decade progressed, electricity surpassed coal and steam in the efficient output of energy. By the end of the 1920's, electricity was the nation's primary source of energy.

Electric power brought new forms of enjoyment and convenience to American homes. People eagerly bought refrigerators, electric irons, washing machines, vacuum cleaners, and countless other household items.

These new products took hours off the time that was needed to do household chores. With fewer hours spent doing household duties, many people, especially women, had considerably more free time. In many cases, women used this time to work outside the home. Their additional income made it possible for many families to buy cars, houses, and other items.

The spread of electricity also encouraged the use of radios. The first radio broadcast was made in 1920. Radio quickly became an enormously popular form of entertainment. By the end of the decade, about 11 million American families owned radios.

**Advertising creates new consumers.** With many new products on the market, manufacturers had to compete for the money Americans were spending. Businesses turned to advertising as a way to encourage sales. Most advertising was done through newspapers and magazines. Billboards and radio broadcasts also became useful advertising tools.

Advertisers began to use pictures of attractive people and catchy slogans to suggest that their products would make life better. In many ways, advertising convinced Americans that they had new needs and that they should adopt new ways of living.

The "credit plan" also boosted sales. By making regular payments, Americans were able to buy cars and other goods that might normally have been too expensive.

**Science plays an important role in industry.** Advances in science also spurred industrial growth. During World War I American scientists had begun to develop

synthetics —materials made by humans, not by nature. In the 1920's, researchers introduced a number of synthetic materials.

One of the best-known researchers was George Washington Carver. Carver devoted years of research to finding industrial uses for farm products. Among other things, Carver developed paints from soybeans, axle grease and shaving lotion from peanuts, and shoe polish from sweet potatoes. Other new materials included plastics, light metals, and synthetic fibers. By the end of the decade, Americans could buy such new products as aluminum cookware, artificial silk stockings, and cameras.

## The Jazz Age

The prosperity of the 1920's inspired Americans to explore new ways of living. New styles of dress and behavior were often zany and sometimes shocking. A number of

627

writers, artists, and entertainers gained great popularity. Several sports stars became national heroes.

**Americans are in the mood to experiment.** F. Scott Fitzgerald, a novelist of the 1920's, nicknamed the decade the **Jazz Age.** Jazz, developed by black musicians in New Orleans, was the popular music of the time. Jazz was an inventive new musical form. Musicians **improvised** —made up—the music as they played. To Fitzgerald, jazz expressed the spirit of the 1920's. The mood was rebellious and experimental, and many people were eager to break with tradition.

Many young people of the 1920's seemed determined to part with accepted rules of conduct. Young women shocked older Americans by having their hair "bobbed," or cut very short. They wore short dresses, rolled their stockings below their knees, and draped themselves with long strings of beads. These women, known as **flappers,** broke customs that limited women's social independence. Not all women were flappers, but flappers set new standards for women's dress and conduct.

Young men also adopted new styles. Many wore their hair long and slicked down, in a fashion made popular by movie star Rudolph Valentino. Young Americans also took up many unusual fads during the 1920's. One of the fads that was very popular was flagpole sitting—balancing on top of flagpoles.

**Art and literature thrive.** Not all Americans of the time behaved in zany ways. Artists and writers produced important works in the 1920's. Many of these works were critical of American society, and some artists and writers became **expatriates** —people who leave their countries to live elsewhere. The largest group of expatriates followed writer Gertrude Stein to live in Paris, France. One of the best-known expatriates was Ernest Hemingway. His novels described how World War I had shattered traditional ideas of heroism. At home, F. Scott Fitzgerald wrote about the lives of wealthy Americans. Novelist Sinclair Lewis criticized growing **materialism** —focus on possessions as life's highest value.

Other artists and writers took more positive views of America. Georgia O'Keeffe depicted the vast beauty of the southwestern desert in her paintings. Willa Cather wrote about the fierce courage of Americans in the Midwest. William Faulkner's novels explored the complex beauty of southern life.

**Writers explore black American culture.** The Harlem section of New York became the center of a literary and artistic movement known as the **Harlem Renaissance.** Novelists Jessie Redmond Fausset and Walter White wrote about the black American sense of racial identity. Zora Neale Hurston wrote stories based on southern black folklore.

In his poem "I, Too, Sing America," Langston Hughes wrote about the dignity that American blacks maintained against great odds:

I, too, sing America.

I am the darker brother.
They send me to eat in the kitchen
When company comes,
But I laugh,
And eat well,
And grow strong.

Tomorrow,
I'll be at the table
When company comes.
Nobody'll dare
Say to me,
"Eat in the kitchen,"
Then.

Besides,
They'll see how beautiful I am
And be ashamed—

I, too, am America.

Poets Claude McKay and Countee Cullen also wrote of the rich culture, joys, and sorrows of black American life.

**New popular heroes emerge.** The 1920's also gave rise to new interest in entertainment, especially movies and professional sports. Movie stars and athletes became heroes to millions of Americans. Silent movie fans idolized Clara Bow, Mary Pickford, Douglas Fairbanks, Rudolph Valentino, and

## CULTURE • Bessie Smith, Empress of the Blues

Singer Bessie Smith dazzled audiences of the 1920's with her powerful, earthy voice. She also introduced many Americans to a new musical form called the blues. This simple and powerful form grew out of a southern tradition, but Smith brought blues singing to the urban north. Her lyrics, pace, and tone expressed feelings of agony and joy. People identified with the situations she sang about.

Bessie Smith was born in Chattanooga, Tennessee, in 1898. She was orphaned at an early age, and joined a traveling minstrel show when she was 11 years old. Gertrude "Ma" Rainey and Cora Fisher, early blues singers, influenced Smith's singing style.

Having sung all over the country, Smith recorded "Down Hearted Blues" in 1923. More than 800,000 copies of the record were sold at 75 cents each. "Down Hearted Blues" was an enormous hit, and Bessie Smith became known as the "Empress of the Blues." Other singers began to copy her style.

Smith's popularity declined in the 1930's. She had a brief comeback, but was killed in a car accident in 1937. Bessie Smith's life was brief, but she greatly influenced American music for many years to come.

**Blues singer Bessie Smith**

other film stars. The first talking movie, *The Jazz Singer,* was released in 1927. The "talkies" started a great new wave of interest in movies. Hollywood, California, became world-famous as the center of the American motion-picture industry.

Baseball player George Herman "Babe" Ruth joined the New York Yankees in 1920. He was soon hitting longer home runs than baseball fans had ever seen before. In 1927 he hit a record 60 homers. Millions of Americans filled the ballparks to see Babe Ruth play. Others flocked to watch tennis star Helen Wills, boxer Jack Dempsey, golfer Bobby Jones and other athletes. Radio and newspapers helped spread the popularity of these athletes. Americans listened and read in awe in August 1926 when Gertrude Ederle became the first woman to swim the English Channel.

**Lindbergh flies the Atlantic.** Some people thought the greatest of all the decade's heroes was the shy young aviator, Charles Lindbergh. In May 1927 Lindbergh set out to capture a $25,000 prize for flying alone nonstop across the Atlantic Ocean. Lindbergh flew in a single-engine plane called the **Spirit of St. Louis.** At a speed of about 110 miles per hour, he completed his historic flight in a little more than 33 hours when he arrived in Paris. "Lucky Lindy" came home to a huge parade, and Americans all over the country began a new dance called the "Lindy" in his honor.

In many ways, Charles Lindbergh symbolized the decade of the 1920's. Americans admired his courage and independence. His flight also made most people feel optimistic about the future.

**The Republicans win again.** With the nation enjoying great prosperity, Coolidge could easily have been reelected. In his usual blunt way, however, Coolidge announced, "I do not choose to run for President in 1928." The Republicans then nominated Herbert C. Hoover, who was Secretary of Commerce under Presidents Harding and Coolidge. Orphaned as a child, Hoover had become a famous engineer. Many Americans had faith in Hoover's ability to get things accomplished. Hoover easily defeated the Democratic candidate, Governor Al Smith of New York, and was elected President. When Hoover took office in March 1929, many Americans expected the prosperity of the Coolidge years to continue. It was not to be so. Before the year ended, the nation was plunged into the worst depression in its history.

Anne and Charles Lindbergh, pioneers in air travel, were photographed before taking off on one of many flights to chart new air routes. The Lindberghs helped show Americans that air travel was practical.

## SECTION REVIEW

1. **Vocabulary**   kickback, suburb, synthetic, improvise, expatriate, materialism
2. **People and Places**   Andrew Mellon, Henry C. Wallace, Teapot Dome, Albert Fall, Calvin Coolidge, Henry Ford, George Washington Carver, F. Scott Fitzgerald, New York, Langston Hughes, Babe Ruth, Charles Lindbergh, Herbert Hoover
3. **Comprehension**   How did the automobile industry help the American economy grow?
4. **Comprehension**   In what ways did American social life change during the 1920's?
5. **Critical Thinking**   Do you think President Coolidge was right when he said, "The business of America is business"? Why or why not?

# How did prosperity give way to the Great Depression?

## Vocabulary

| | |
|---|---|
| stockbroker | run |
| margin | mortgage |

In spite of the business boom, there were problems in the American economy. In October 1929 the stock market crashed. Following the crash, the nation slid into a deep depression. President Hoover sought to restore confidence in the economy, but the depression grew steadily worse.

## Signs of Warning

As Hoover was sworn in as President, he said, "I have no fear for the future of the country." Some people were beginning to worry, however, that the economic boom of the 1920's was nearing its end.

**The economy slows down.** Toward the middle of 1929 the boom in automobile sales slowed down. Americans throughout the nation were beginning to buy fewer goods, and builders were starting to construct fewer new buildings. A few economic experts began to warn that stock prices were much too high.

In spite of these warnings, Americans were continuing to buy more stock. Stock prices were rising rapidly. Many people had made a great deal of money by buying stocks and then selling them at a higher price. Every day there were more reports of ordinary Americans making fortunes overnight simply by investing in the stock market. Encouraged by these stories, more than 2 million Americans became stockholders. Many of these people were not seeking to invest in American business. Instead they were hoping to make large and quick profits by speculating.

**Buying on margin encourages speculation.** Normally, a person buying stock paid a **stockbroker** —an agent who buys and sells stocks for others—the entire cost. In the late 1920's, however, stockbrokers allowed many people to buy stocks for a **margin** —percentage—of the price. The stockholder then owed the broker the balance. Stockholders usually paid the balance when they sold the stock. In the meantime, stockbrokers borrowed from banks to cover the cost of the stocks.

Buying on margin enabled many more Americans to purchase stocks. Boosted by speculation and by margin buying, stock prices sailed higher and higher. In many cases, stocks rose so high that they cost much more than the worth of the companies that issued them. This was a sign that the rising stock market might soon decline.

## The Stock Market Crash

In the fall of 1929, Americans began to lose confidence that the high prices in the stock market would continue. Prices began to drop, and in October the market collapsed.

**Stock values begin to drop.** In the summer and early fall of 1929 some investors began to sell their stocks. This caused prices in the market to flutter, and stockholders began to worry.

On October 23, 1929 stock prices dropped sharply. Stockbrokers began asking investors to pay for stocks that had been bought on margin. Many stockholders could not pay, and they began to sell their stocks instead. The sales of so much stock caused prices to drop further between October 24 and October 29.

**Investors panic.** A group of bankers led by J.P. Morgan tried to restore confidence in the weak stock market. They spent millions

## HERBERT C. HOOVER

### ★ 1929–1933 ★

**31ST PRESIDENT**

**REPUBLICAN**

★ Born August 10, 1874, in Iowa

★ Married Lou Henry in 1899;
2 children

★ Engineer; Chairman of the Commission for Relief in Belgium during World War I; Secretary of Commerce

★ Lived in California when elected President

★ Vice President: Charles Curtis

★ Died October 20, 1964, in New York

★ Key events while in office: Great Depression started; Hitler seized power in Germany

of dollars buying new stock. President Hoover also tried to reassure people. He told Americans that the nation's business was on "a sound and prosperous basis." The attempt to restore confidence failed, however. On October 29, 1929—also known as **Black Tuesday**—panic struck. Thousands of investors ordered their stockbrokers to sell. On New York City's **Wall Street,** where stocks are bought and sold, there was a stampede to sell before prices fell further. More than 16 million shares were sold that day. Stock prices fell far below their original value. People who had owned millions of dollars worth of stock were suddenly poor.

For weeks after Black Tuesday, stock prices continued downward. Over a two-week period, for example, stock values in major corporations were cut in half. Nearly 2 million ordinary Americans saw their dreams of wealth quickly disappear. Many lost their life savings and had nothing to fall back on.

## The Great Depression

The stock market crash marked the start of the **Great Depression.** This period of economic decline lasted from 1929 to 1941. It was the longest and most severe depression in the nation's history.

**Overproduction helps cause the Great Depression.** Even today, economists do not agree about what caused the Great Depression. Most do agree, however, that overproduction was part of the problem. During most of the 1920's, industry and farms had been producing as much as they could. By 1929, most Americans had already purchased the major items that they could afford, such as automobiles, refrigerators, and phonographs. Sales then began to slow down. With a surplus of consumer goods, many large corporations attempted to cut their expenses by laying off workers and reducing production.

Laid-off workers had less money to spend. Reduced consumer spending in turn led to more industry cutbacks. About a million and a half workers were unemployed during 1929. Three months after Black Tuesday, more than 4 million Americans were out of work.

**Many banks fail.** Another cause of the Depression resulted from problems in the nation's supply of money. During the 1920's the Federal Reserve Board had increased the country's money supply. This made it easier for people to borrow money and encouraged banks to make loans for speculation. After the stock market crashed, many investors were not able to repay their loans, and banks began to run seriously short of money. People hurried to withdraw their money from the banks before it was too late. The result was a **run** —too many withdrawals in too short a period—on banks. One bank after another failed because of the run. These bank failures caused many people to lose all of their savings. Other banks closed their doors in an effort to avoid failure. Because so many banks had closed, there was not enough currency in circulation to keep the economy going.

**The economy spirals downward.** Some workers were laid off and lost savings, while others had to accept lower wages or less work. The result was that millions of Americans could not meet their obligations. Many people were unable to repay mortgages — loans made to homebuyers—and automobile loans. Families lost homes, farms, and other property because they could not repay loans. Many businesses also failed. Investors had lost their money in the stock market crash and could no longer buy stock. As a result, businesses could not raise money they needed to keep operating. With sales of consumer goods falling, many factories had to close their doors.

**The farm crisis worsens.** American farmers had been in economic trouble throughout the 1920's. With the start of the Depression, prices for farm products fell drastically. Farmers wanted help from the federal government. They called on the government to loan money to farmers, or to take action that would raise prices for farm goods. President Hoover attempted to ease

As rumors of bank failures spread, people rushed to their banks to withdraw their savings. In the early 1930's thousands of banks failed and millions of people lost their life savings.

the farm crisis with the Agricultural Marketing Act of 1929. This act provided about $500 million that could be used for loans or for buying surplus crops to keep prices high. The Agricultural Marketing Act also encouraged farmers to maintain high production, however. The result was still greater overproduction by farmers, and the government aid ran out by 1932.

**The Depression becomes worldwide.** Many foreign economies were intertwined with the American economy. As the American economy declined, the Depression spread throughout the world. After World War I, American investors had made large loans to European countries to speed their economic recovery. The investors hoped that the loans would encourage these countries to buy American products. American investors had also loaned money to Latin American and Asian nations who wanted to buy American goods. These American investments were boosting the entire world economy. When American investment suddenly stopped, many foreign economies fell rapidly. In addition, a number of wealthy Europeans had invested heavily in American stocks. European investors lost large sums of money when the American stock market crashed.

**Tariffs discourage foreign trade.** Before the Depression, many foreign countries bought American farm goods and manufactured goods. In 1930, however, Congress passed the Hawley-Smoot Tariff to reduce foreign competition. The tariffs were so high that other nations reacted by raising tariffs on American goods. As a result of these tariffs, international trade rapidly declined. This decline further slowed the world's economy.

## Hoover's Policies

As the United States sank deeper into the Great Depression, many people looked to the government for help. President Hoover, however, did not believe that government involvement would end the Depression. He thought that what Americans needed most was a boost in confidence.

**Hoover encourages "rugged individualism."** Hoover believed that the American economic system was based on **rugged individualism.** In his view, all Americans had equal opportunity, and success went to those who earned it. Hoover called such people "rugged individualists." The President was himself a self-made millionaire. He believed that all Americans could get ahead as he had. All the nation needed to recover from the Depression was renewed confidence. Hoover held conferences with business leaders and made speeches designed to boost public confidence.

**Hoover urges voluntary action.** As the Depression deepened, Hoover took stronger action. He lowered taxes, cut his own salary, and urged employers to halt layoffs. The President also urged Americans to take voluntary action to help those in need. He asked Americans to give more money to charity, and to provide jobs for people who were out of work. Hoover also asked the states to start more public works projects, such as roads and bridges, to create jobs. He called on state and local governments to provide emergency relief for the needy.

**Many demand direct government aid.** Few state or local governments had the money to follow Hoover's suggestions. Some cities could provide only one or two cents per person per day for food relief. The promises of business leaders to keep their employees became meaningless as one company after another went bankrupt.

Faced with hunger and homelessness, many people demanded aid from the federal government. Hoover refused. He was convinced that direct aid would lead to a loss of self-reliance and independence. As the suffering continued, many Americans came to blame Hoover for their plight. The President's inaction, they believed, showed that he did not care about people's suffering. The newspapers that homeless people covered themselves with at night came to be called "Hoover blankets." Outside many cities, families who had lost their homes built shacks from scrap tin, lumber, and tarpaper. They called these settlements **Hoovervilles,** reflecting their anger toward the President.

During the Great Depression millions of Americans could not find work. Isaac Soyer's 1937 painting shows job seekers waiting at an employment agency. What feelings do the job seekers seem to express?

**The government aids corporations and banks.** Hoover believed that if business picked up, the nation's problems would be solved. His major goal, therefore, was to get business moving again. To accomplish this, he called for the creation of the Reconstruction Finance Corporation (RFC). The RFC, started in 1932, acted as a loan company, providing money for banks, railroads, insurance companies, and home mortgage associations. Despite granting more than $2 billion in loans, the RFC did not create an upsurge in the economy. It did, however, save many companies from bankruptcy. The Great

Depression probably would have been even worse without the RFC loans. Many people, however, still opposed Hoover's approach. They felt his program had failed to help American citizens.

**Hoover uses force against veterans.** The disagreements with Hoover's policies were dramatized when veterans marched on Washington, D.C., in 1932. World War I veterans were scheduled to receive bonuses for their wartime service. These bonuses were to be paid in 1945. In June 1932 more than 15,000 veterans marched on Washington demanding the immediate payment of their bonuses. When Congress refused, about 2,000 members of the **Bonus Army** set up tents and shacks and took over unused buildings in the city. They announced that they would stay until the bonuses were paid.

Hoover opposed the bonus program because he felt it was financially unsound. When city police tried to force the veterans to leave, a battle broke out. Hoover then called in the army to drive the veterans from the city. The army, under General Douglas Mac-Arthur, invaded the veterans' camp with tanks and tear gas and burned the camp down. Many Americans were shocked that Hoover had used force against the veterans. These events cost Hoover many votes in the 1932 election.

## SECTION REVIEW

1. **Vocabulary**   stockbroker, margin, run, mortgage
2. **People and Places**   J.P. Morgan, Wall Street, Washington, D.C., Douglas Mac-Arthur
3. **Comprehension**   What happened to the American economy after the stock market crash in 1929?
4. **Comprehension**   Why did some Americans blame President Hoover for the poverty of the Depression?
5. **Critical Thinking**   Was Hoover's plan for fighting the Depression a good policy? Why or why not?

# Chapter 27 Summary

American life changed rapidly after World War I. Workers faced high unemployment, and there were many strikes. Cities grew rapidly as southern blacks, immigrants, and women sought urban jobs. Fear of Communists and foreigners led to the Red Scare and the Sacco-Vanzetti trial. The Ku Klux Klan terrorized blacks, Catholics, Jews, and immigrants. Prohibition led to bootlegging, speakeasies, and organized crime. In 1920, voters elected Warren G. Harding, who promised a return to normalcy.

Harding and his Cabinet reduced taxes and passed the Emergency Tariff Act to help farmers. During Harding's presidency, the economy grew stronger. Harding was a weak leader, however, and he failed to stop his "Ohio gang" friends' corrupt schemes. These schemes included the Teapot Dome scandal. After Harding's death, Calvin Coolidge became President in 1923. Coolidge supported business, and the economy grew rapidly. The automobile industry, led by Henry Ford, spurred economic growth. In the Jazz Age, young Americans broke many social traditions. Expatriate writers in France and black artists of the Harlem Renaissance created important works. Americans idolized movie stars and athletes. Charles Lindbergh's transatlantic flight thrilled the nation.

The economy began to slow down in 1929, but speculators kept buying stocks on margin. In October 1929, many investors lost everything in the stock market crash. After the crash, the economy declined steadily as the Great Depression took hold. Banks failed, people lost their homes and jobs, and farm prices fell sharply. President Hoover tried to restore confidence and urged Americans to take voluntary action to improve the economy. As hunger and homelessness spread, Americans built Hoovervilles and demanded aid from the federal government. Hoover's Reconstruction Finance Corporation loaned money to businesses. Veterans in the Bonus Army marched on Washington, D.C., demanding early payment of war bonuses. Americans were shocked when Hoover called out the army to drive the veterans from the city. As the Great Depression deepened, Hoover lost support.

# CRITICAL THINKING: Interpreting Statistics

Historians use many kinds of **statistics.** Statistics are facts in number form that measure population, social conditions, and economic and business activities.

Statistics can be used to support a historical statement. For example, the statement that immigration increased rapidly in the early 1900's can be supported by showing the numbers of immigrants arriving during that time period.

Historians also use statistics to interpret past events. Statistics could help explain how the population of the United States was changing. By comparing these statistics to figures showing changes in rural and urban populations, historians could draw conclusions about where these immigrants now lived.

Historians must take great care, however, when using statistics to interpret the past. Many important events occur that are never recorded or reflected in statistics. Thus statistics cannot accurately tell the whole story of the past. They must always be compared with other kinds of information.

Historians carefully evaluate any statement based on statistics.

Below are five kinds of economic statistics for 1928 to 1933. These statistics are called **economic indicators** because they measure, or indicate, the level of economic activity. Study these statistics, and then answer the following questions.

1. In which year was unemployment the highest?
2. In which year were the average weekly wages for production workers the highest? By how much did wages fall between that year and 1933?
3. What happened to the value of United States exports between 1928 and 1933? How might the value of exports and unemployment statistics be related?
4. Why do you think federal government spending increased during this time?
5. In your opinion, which economic indicator best shows the decline in economic activity during the years of the Great Depression? Explain your answer.

## Some Economic Indicators of the Great Depression

| Indicator | 1928 | 1929 | 1930 | 1931 | 1932 | 1933 |
|---|---|---|---|---|---|---|
| 1. Unemployment (in thousands) | 1,982 | 1,550 | 4,340 | 8,020 | 12,060 | 12,830 |
| 2. Average weekly earnings for production workers in manufacturing (constant dollars) | 27.80 | 28.55 | 25.84 | 22.62 | 17.05 | 17.71 |
| 3. Bank suspensions because of financial difficulties | 499 | 659 | 1,352 | 2,294 | 1,456 | 4,004 |
| 4. Federal government spending (in millions of dollars) | 2,933 | 3,127 | 3,320 | 3,578 | 4,659 | 4,623 |
| 5. Value of United States exports (in millions of dollars) | 5,776 | 5,441 | 4,013 | 2,918 | 2,343 | 2,061 |

## Vocabulary and Key Terms

Use the following terms to complete the sentences below. Write your answers on a separate sheet of paper.

stockbrokers
Great Depression
normalcy
Teapot Dome
Bonus Army
kickbacks
Jazz Age

synthetics
Wall Street
flappers
quota
anarchists
mortgages
margin

1. Stocks are traded on _____ in New York City.
2. In the 1920's, Americans developed new kinds of materials called _____.
3. During the _____, many families could not pay their home loans, or _____.
4. During the _____, women called _____ set new standards of social freedom.
5. Veterans in the _____ marched on Washington, D.C., in 1932.
6. Americans liked Harding's promise of a return to _____.
7. In the _____ scandal, Albert Fall took _____ from oil companies.
8. People who oppose organized government are called _____.
9. Congress set a limit, or _____, on immigration from each country.
10. Many _____ sold stock on a _____, or percentage, of the cost.

## Recalling the Facts

1. What ended the Boston police strike?
2. What was the Sacco-Vanzetti case?
3. In what ways were the hopes of black Americans disappointed in the 1920's?
4. Why was Prohibition unsuccessful?
5. What did Presidents Harding, Coolidge, and Hoover believe about business and the economy?
6. How did the automobile industry spur economic growth in the 1920's?
7. In what ways did American customs and behavior change in the Jazz Age?
8. How did speculation help cause the stock market crash in 1929?
9. In what ways did the American economy slow down in the Great Depression?
10. Why were Americans angry at President Hoover's treatment of the Bonus Army?

## Places to Locate

Match the letters on the map with the places listed below. Write your answers on a separate sheet of paper.

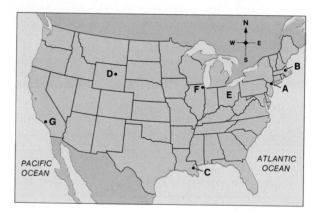

1. Boston
2. Teapot Dome, Wyoming
3. Chicago
4. New York City
5. New Orleans
6. Ohio
7. Hollywood, California

## Critical Thinking

1. The Roaring Twenties were a time of prosperity in the United States, but they gave way to the worst depression the country has ever known. Why did the country go from one extreme to the

other? Do you think the depression could have been prevented? Address these questions in your answer:

a. What were American attitudes toward business and wealth in the 1920's?

b. Why did the stock market crash?

c. What effect did government economic policies have before and during the Depression?

2. At the start of the 1920's, Americans liked the promise of a "return to normalcy." To what extent did the decade of the 1920's fulfill this promise? Consider these questions in your answer:

a. How did the nation's economy grow?

b. What new kinds of social behavior arose?

c. What was life like for women and minorities during this period?

## Understanding History

1. Reread the section "The nation fears Communists" on page 619. Then answer these questions.

a. **Politics.** Why did many Americans fear the possibility of a Communist revolution in the United States?

b. **Citizenship.** In what ways did Attorney General Palmer's actions violate people's rights?

2. Reread the section "The automobile changes American life" on page 626. Then answer these questions.

a. **Geography.** How did the increasing use of automobiles affect where people lived?

b. **Social History.** How did the automobile affect American family life?

## Projects and Activities

1. **Making a Line Graph.** Make a line graph showing sales of stock on the New York Stock Exchange from 1920 to 1932. The following figures show how many million shares were sold during each year: **1920**—227; **1921**—173; **1922**—259; **1923**—236; **1924**—282; **1925**—454; **1927**—577; **1928**—920; **1929**—1,125; **1930**—810; **1931**—577; **1932**—425.

2. **Making a Scrapbook.** Make a scrapbook on the history of jazz. Find pictures of jazz artists, including the important musicians of the "Jazz Age," and combine them with text providing information on these people. Share your scrapbook with your classmates.

3. **Writing a Report.** Find out about one of the following: Prohibition, the first American automobiles, flappers, a famous person of the 1920's, Hoovervilles, women's rights in the 1920's. Write a report based on what you find.

## Practicing Your Skill

The table below shows statistics indicating the number and the percent of American workers who were unemployed from 1919 to 1932. Study the table and answer the questions that follow on a separate sheet of paper.

### Unemployment 1919–1932

| Year | Number of Unemployed (thousands) | Percentage of Civilian Labor Force |
|---|---|---|
| 1919 | 950 | 2.3 |
| 1920 | 1,670 | 4.0 |
| 1921 | 5,010 | 11.9 |
| 1922 | 3,220 | 7.6 |
| 1923 | 1,380 | 3.2 |
| 1924 | 2,440 | 5.5 |
| 1925 | 1,800 | 4.0 |
| 1926 | 880 | 1.9 |
| 1927 | 1,890 | 4.1 |
| 1928 | 2,080 | 4.4 |
| 1929 | 1,550 | 3.2 |
| 1930 | 4,340 | 8.7 |
| 1931 | 8,020 | 15.9 |
| 1932 | 12,060 | 23.6 |

1. How many and in what year were the most people unemployed?

2. In what two years were 4 percent of American workers unemployed?

3. In which seven-year period was unemployment below 6 percent? How do these figures relate to what you have read about the 1920's?

4. In what way did unemployment figures change in the years from 1929 to 1932?

# 28 The United States Battles the Great Depression

## 1932–1940

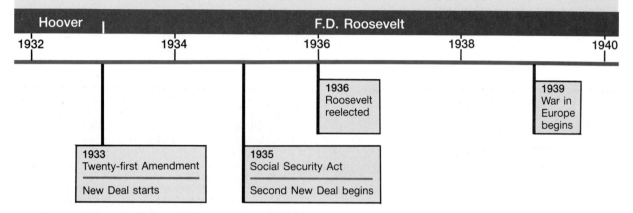

Hoover | F.D. Roosevelt

1932 1934 1936 1938 1940

**1936**
Roosevelt
reelected

**1939**
War in
Europe
begins

**1933**
Twenty-first Amendment

New Deal starts

**1935**
Social Security Act

Second New Deal begins

**This 1930's mural shows workers building a dam—one of many public-works projects financed by the federal government.**

## Preparing to Read

The Great Depression that began in 1929 was far worse than any downturn Americans had experienced before. The Depression changed the lives of millions of people, and raised fears about the country's economic future. In the 1932 elections, worried voters sought new and active leadership. With Congress's support, President Franklin Roosevelt made sweeping changes to fight the Depression. These changes helped millions of American people, but the Great Depression continued. By the late 1930's, some people began to criticize President Roosevelt and his programs. As you read this chapter, try to answer the following questions:

1. How did Roosevelt fight the Depression?
2. How did Americans react to the New Deal?
3. What effect did the New Deal have on American life?

# 1 How did Roosevelt fight the Depression?

## Vocabulary

| | |
|---|---|
| drought | direct relief |
| migrant worker | work relief |
| lame duck | parity |

As millions of people lost their jobs, farms, and homes, public confidence declined. During the 1920's, Americans had hoped that hard work would bring a better standard of living. Instead, the Depression had caused widespread poverty. After Franklin Roosevelt was elected President, he worked to restore people's belief in the American economy, and more importantly, in themselves.

## Effects of the Depression

The Depression years were difficult for most Americans. American life changed as people found different ways to cope with hard times.

**Jobless Americans live in poverty.** By 1932 nearly 13 million people were jobless. Bank failures left many others penniless. Without money, people could not afford basic needs. Millions faced hunger. Unable to pay rents and mortgages, many of the jobless lost their homes.

People did their best to help each other by sharing whatever food they had. Charity groups and local governments also tried to help. They set up breadlines, soup kitchens, and lodging houses to provide food and shelter. Local efforts, however, could not help the huge numbers of people in need.

Family life also suffered during the Depression. Families were often forced to split up. Some breadwinners left their homes and families to look for work far away. Children as young as 13 years old sometimes left home rather than burden their families.

The jobless did what was necessary to survive. To make ends meet, some people stood on street corners selling apples or shining shoes. Others begged for money or picked through garbage in search of food. Still others stood in long breadlines. Many of the jobless felt ashamed to accept charity.

With no money and no place to live, thousands of Americans took to the road. Many of these homeless people hitched rides

*Drought-stricken Area* is the title of this 1934 painting by Alexander Hogue. How does the painting show that Dust Bowl conditions caused despair?

in railroad boxcars, drifting from one town to another looking for work. Often, their pay was little more than a decent meal and a place to sleep for the night.

**The Depression changes American life.** Many Americans kept their jobs and businesses during the Depression. Yet people still faced the possibility of unemployment. With the future so uncertain, people changed their lifestyles. Families greatly cut down on spending, and many couples postponed their marriages.

Americans found cheap ways to have fun. Radio brought free entertainment into millions of homes. People also played board games, card games, and bingo. Many went to the movies, where they could attempt to forget their problems.

**Disaster hits the Great Plains.** In the Great Plains, a **drought** (drowt)—period of dry weather—added to the other problems that were caused by the Great Depression. The farmers who lived in this region plowed vast areas of land, exposing the soil to the wind. The long drought turned miles upon miles of topsoil into dust. High winds swept across the open plains, creating huge, dark clouds of dust.

The windstorms hurled dust for miles. One farmer told of "counting Kansas farms as they came by." Great piles of dust buried farmland, homes, and equipment. Throughout a vast region called the **Dust Bowl,** farming became impossible. With farms gone, many people packed their belongings into cars and trucks and left the region. Many poor farmers from Oklahoma and Arkansas, known as "Okies" and "Arkies," headed to California. There, as **migrant workers** — farmhands who move from farm to farm— they planted and harvested crops.

## Roosevelt Offers a New Deal

By 1932 Americans had struggled through three years of the Depression. They looked to the Democratic party to lift the nation out of the Depression and to restore the economy.

**Democrats win the 1932 election.** No President ever suffered as great a loss of popularity as did Herbert Hoover after 1929. Hoover's policies had failed to end the Depression, and many Americans felt that Hoover did not care about their poverty and suffering. Though defeat was certain, the Republicans chose Hoover to run for reelection in 1932.

The Democrats, confident of victory, chose Franklin Delano Roosevelt as their candidate. Roosevelt, known as FDR, was the successful governor of New York and a distant cousin of Theodore Roosevelt.

Roosevelt campaigned with cheerful optimism. He pledged "bold, persistent experimentation" to end the Depression. He avoided stating a clear-cut plan of action, but he promised "a new deal for the American people." The government would provide relief for the jobless, the elderly, and the farmers. It would help the average American, whom Roosevelt called "the forgotten man."

Roosevelt's message of hope was what Americans wanted to hear. His program to fight the Depression promptly became known as the **New Deal.** In addition to relief from the Depression, the Democrats also called for an end to Prohibition.

Roosevelt scored a landslide victory. He won 22.8 million popular votes to Hoover's 15.8 million. Roosevelt's electoral-vote victory was also great—472 to 59. The Democrats also gained a majority of seats in Congress.

**Roosevelt conquers personal tragedy.** Roosevelt's personal life had prepared him for the task of restoring confidence to the

Franklin D. Roosevelt refused to let a severe disability stop his political career. He was elected governor of New York in 1928 and reelected in 1930. As governor, many of his policies for fighting the Depression were successful. In 1932 Roosevelt was nominated as the Democratic presidential candidate.

nation. He was born in Hyde Park, New York, to a wealthy family. In 1905 he married Anna Eleanor Roosevelt, a distant cousin. Roosevelt's swift rise in politics began in 1910. He served as a state senator and as Assistant Secretary of the Navy during World War I. In 1920 Roosevelt ran unsuccessfully for Vice President.

In 1921 tragedy struck. Afflicted with polio, Roosevelt was paralyzed in both legs. At 39 years old, his career seemed to be over. Roosevelt, however, fought to regain his strength. He recovered from his illness, but was never able to walk without braces and crutches. With encouragement from his family, Roosevelt returned to politics. In 1928 he became governor of New York.

Frances Perkins, Secretary of Labor, served as a member of President Roosevelt's Brain Trust. This 1935 photograph shows Perkins shaking hands with steel workers in Pittsburgh, Pennsylvania.

Roosevelt had faced his illness with courage and patience, and he seldom lost his warmth or good humor. Americans sensed that through his illness, Roosevelt had gained a deep understanding of problems that ordinary people faced each day.

**Roosevelt prepares to take office.** By law, Roosevelt could not enter office until March 4, 1933. Roosevelt's victory made President Hoover a lame duck —a person who is finishing a term of office after failing to win reelection.

While waiting to take office, Roosevelt organized an unofficial group of advisers known as the **Brain Trust.** Made up mostly of college professors, the Brain Trust helped Roosevelt plan the details of the New Deal. Later, the President chose his Cabinet, which included Secretary of the Interior Harold Ickes and Secretary of Labor Frances Perkins. Perkins was the first woman to serve in the Cabinet.

One of the President's closest advisers was Eleanor Roosevelt. She tirelessly traveled the country, visiting hospitals, coal mines, and private homes. She found out what Americans were thinking and reported her findings to the President. Many of the New Deal programs were based on Eleanor Roosevelt's suggestions.

Before Roosevelt took office, Congress proposed two amendments to the Constitution. The **Twentieth Amendment,** ratified in early 1933, shortened the lame-duck period between a President's election and inauguration. Thus, Inauguration Day is now January 20. The **Twenty-first Amendment,** ratified in December 1933, repealed Prohibition.

## The New Deal Takes Shape

In his inaugural address, Roosevelt spoke directly to the American people. In a rich, strong voice he declared, "The only thing we have to fear is fear itself." He asked for faith, courage, and belief in American democracy. He believed that the government should use all of its wealth and power to fight the Depression. Roosevelt knew, however, that government action could succeed only by conquering public fear.

**Roosevelt restores confidence in banks.**
The first challenge facing the new President
was the banking crisis. Hundreds of banks
had failed because of bank runs. (See Chapter 27.) A major banking panic took place
just before Roosevelt took office. Throughout the nation, depositors rushed to withdraw their cash. The entire banking system
was near collapse.

On March 6, 1933, two days after he took
office, Roosevelt declared a **Bank Holiday.**
He closed all of the nation's banks for four
days. In the meantime, Roosevelt asked
Congress to pass the Banking Relief Act.
Under this act, the government would examine all banks. Those banks that seemed safe
and reliable would open again. Unsound
banks would stay closed. To show its support of the President, Congress passed the
Banking Relief Act in two hours.

On Sunday, March 12, Roosevelt spoke
to the American people on the radio. The
President's radio broadcasts became known
as **fireside chats.** In this first fireside chat, the
President told the nation what steps the government was taking. "It is safer to keep your
money in a reopened bank," he assured listeners, "than under a mattress."

The President's informal fireside chat
gave people greater confidence in banks.
Over the next few days, nearly all banks reopened. Depositors slowly returned their
money, and the banking system grew
stronger. Fireside chats became an important feature of Roosevelt's presidency, because they were valuable for gaining public
support.

**Congress holds a special session.**
Roosevelt also asked Congress to meet in a
special emergency session. This period became known as the **Hundred Days.** From
March 9 to June 16, Roosevelt sent Congress
a flood of proposals. Congress enacted most
of them into law.

## New Deal Programs

The flurry of laws passed during the
Hundred Days gave shape to the New Deal.
These laws created many new government
agencies. These agencies had three major

The Civilian Conservation Corps provided
young men jobs in forestry and engineering.
The CCC was one of the most successful New
Deal programs.

goals. The first goal was to provide relief for
the jobless. The second goal was to help
business, industry, and agriculture recover.
The third goal was to reform the American
economy to prevent future depressions.

**Programs provide jobs and aid.** Many
New Deal acts set up programs to help the
jobless. One such program, a personal favorite of Roosevelt, was the **Civilian Conservation Corps** (CCC). In the CCC, men from 17
to 25 years old worked to conserve natural
resources. CCC projects included planting
trees, stopping soil erosion, controlling
floods, and fighting forest fires. Participants
lived in camps and were paid $30 a month.
More than 2 million men took part in the
CCC. It was one of the most successful New
Deal programs.

Another program, the Federal Emergency Relief Administration (FERA) gave
more than $500 million to the states. The
states in turn gave **direct relief** —cash
grants—to people in need. Roosevelt, however, was not satisfied with direct relief.

Norris Dam, started in 1933 and completed in 1936, was the first dam built by the Tennessee Valley Authority. The dam contains two power plants for generating electricity.

Though many people were aided, their lives did not change. The President liked programs of work relief —work in return for aid. People's confidence, he believed, was helped by involvement in work projects. The projects also improved the nation.

**A new agricultural program aids farmers.** Since World War I ended, farmers had raised more crops than people could buy. Farm surpluses had caused prices to drop and reduced farmers' income. (See Chapter 27.) To spur recovery in agriculture, Congress created the **Agricultural Adjustment Administration** (AAA). Under the AAA, the government paid farmers to reduce production of certain crops. The aim of the AAA was to raise farm prices and to help farmers reach parity —equal spending power—with other consumers. By 1934, crop prices were beginning to rise.

**Recovery measures help business.** To help the sluggish economy, Congress approved the creation of the **National Recovery Administration** (NRA). The NRA asked each industry to draw up codes of fair competition. The codes, or rules, stated the amount of goods to be produced in the industries. They also set prices and wages and guaranteed the right of workers to form unions. The codes were intended to help businesses operate more fairly, raise their profits, and end worker layoffs.

The NRA encouraged buyers to do business with only those companies that followed the codes. Companies that used the codes displayed the NRA emblem, a Blue Eagle with the motto "We Do Our Part." The emblem soon became a symbol of pride. All across the United States it appeared in the windows of shops, mills, and factories. Some smaller companies, however, ignored these codes. They believed that the NRA seriously hurt competition by giving big businesses an advantage.

Other New Deal programs sought to help industry in less direct ways. The **Public Works Administration** (PWA) was set up to boost the construction industry and provide jobs. The PWA spent more than $3 billion on such public-works projects as schools, hospitals, and dams. The **Federal Housing Administration** (FHA) provided loans for building and repairing houses.

**Reform measures protect investments.** Roosevelt proposed several acts to reform the nation's financial system. One such act created the **Federal Deposit Insurance Corporation** (FDIC). The FDIC insured bank deposits. If an insured bank failed, depositors would not lose their savings. Later, the **Securities and Exchange Commission** (SEC) was set up to regulate stock exchanges. Other measures helped end some of the business practices that contributed to the stock market crash.

**Roosevelt tries a bold experiment.** One of the most ambitious New Deal programs was the **Tennessee Valley Authority** (TVA). The TVA was set up to develop the economy of the Tennessee River Valley. This farming region covered all of Tennessee and parts of six other states. To stop disastrous floods, the TVA built a string of 40 dams throughout the area. The dams also produced cheap electric power, which was sold to people living in the Tennessee Valley. The TVA improved farmland, attracted industries to the region, and helped set up schools and health centers.

The TVA sparked heated debate. Private power companies complained that they could not compete with low government prices. Moreover, many critics questioned the government's right to own utilities. Still, the TVA was a remarkable success. It greatly raised the standard of living in the region.

## SECTION REVIEW

1. **Vocabulary**   drought, migrant worker, lame duck, direct relief, work relief, parity
2. **People and Places**   Dust Bowl, Herbert Hoover, Franklin Roosevelt, Frances Perkins, Eleanor Roosevelt, Tennessee River Valley
3. **Comprehension**   How did Roosevelt end the banking crisis?
4. **Comprehension**   What were the three main goals of the New Deal?
5. **Critical Thinking**   How might public fear have made it difficult to fight the Depression?

# 2 How did Americans react to the New Deal?

## Vocabulary

coalition          conservative
liberal            recession

Roosevelt generally enjoyed broad-based support for his programs. Many Americans applauded the government's willingness to help them. Not everyone, however, supported the New Deal. A major defeat in 1935 brought about its decline.

## Sources of Criticism

Some business and political leaders attacked Roosevelt's program. They charged that the government was interfering with people's lives and businesses. While some critics wanted less reform, others wanted more. Many of Roosevelt's opponents had been early supporters of the New Deal.

**Critics oppose increased government activity.** By 1934 there was a growing mood of opposition toward the New Deal, even within Roosevelt's own party. A number of Democrats joined with Republican opponents of the New Deal. Together they formed the Liberty League. This group charged that the government was spending too much money and was pampering people with its New Deal agencies. They also opposed the power that the government had given to labor unions. Calling New Deal programs "alphabet soup," they said that the government had become too big and would destroy independence and free enterprise.

Some critics believed that Roosevelt was becoming too powerful. They charged that he had taken too much authority away from Congress and from local government. They saw this as a danger to democracy and to the system of checks and balances.

**Other critics call for more reforms.** The New Deal was also attacked for not doing enough to end the Depression. One powerful critic was Senator Huey Long of Louisiana. Long, who was nicknamed "Kingfish," called for a tax on the rich. The tax would be used to provide all families with a minimum yearly income of $2,000. Long's "Share Our Wealth" plan gained a huge following.

Some critics believed the New Deal brought too many new programs. According to this cartoon, what effect might the New Deal have on government?

Another outspoken critic of Roosevelt was Father Charles Coughlin (KAWG-lin), a Catholic priest. Millions tuned into Father Coughlin's weekly radio broadcast. Known as the "Radio Priest," he called for government ownership of banks, utilities, and natural resources.

Francis Townsend, a retired California doctor, called for a monthly pension of $200 for everyone who was over 60 years old. According to Townsend's plan, the people that received the pension would be required to retire, thereby opening up jobs for others. They would also be required to spend the money within 30 days in order to boost the economy.

**Americans show their approval of the New Deal.** Despite growing opposition, voters showed their approval of the New Deal. In the 1934 elections, the Democrats gained even more seats in Congress. President Roosevelt was confident of support from the majority of Americans. He knew, however, that he would not be able to ignore the growing opposition.

## The Second New Deal

Despite New Deal efforts, the Depression held its grip on the nation. Unemployment dropped by about 4 million, but it was still very high. Roosevelt sought to improve the economic well-being of more Americans. He also saw a need for more government regulation of business. Roosevelt proposed greater reforms in 1935 and 1936. These measures became known as the **Second New Deal.**

**Roosevelt proposes more work relief.** In 1935 Congress approved the creation of the **Works Progress Administration** (WPA). Roosevelt chose Harry Hopkins, his trusted friend and adviser, to run the program. Hopkins and his staff developed an amazing array of projects.

One major goal of the WPA was to employ people in jobs that suited their interests and talents. The WPA hired artists to paint colorful murals in public buildings. Symphony orchestras and community theaters were formed. Photographers such as Dorothea Lange roamed the country and produced vivid images of life during the 1930's. The WPA also hired writers and scholars, many of whom were black Americans. Many artists made lasting contributions under the WPA. Other WPA projects included the construction of airports, public buildings, and roads. Nearly every city and town had a WPA project.

Another work relief program, the **National Youth Administration** (NYA), provided part-time work for high school and college students. The NYA helped thousands of young people stay in school.

**Roosevelt seeks to improve conditions for farmers.** A number of reform measures were geared to improving farm life. Under the **Rural Electrification Administration** (REA), the government helped bring electricity to rural areas. In 1935 only 10 percent of American farms had electricity. Within 20 years, the efforts of the REA, TVA, and WPA brought electricity to about 90 percent of American farms. Two projects that contributed to rural electrification were the Hoover Dam on the Colorado River and the Grand Coulee Dam on the Columbia River.

President Roosevelt greets supporters in Warm Springs, Georgia, in this 1933 photograph. While some Americans criticized the New Deal, most people admired Roosevelt's personality and leadership.

Most early New Deal programs helped farm owners. By creating the Farm Security Administration (FSA), Roosevelt sought to help tenant farmers, sharecroppers, and migrant workers. The FSA offered loans to poor farmers who wanted to buy farms.

**Reform measures help the elderly.** The Depression seriously affected older Americans. Many lost their savings through bank failures. The **Social Security Act** of 1935 set up a pension system for older people. Secretary of Labor Frances Perkins played a key role in developing social security.

During their working years, workers and their employers made payments into a special fund. When the workers retired, they were given monthly benefits. The Social Security Act also set up benefit programs for unemployed workers, disabled people, and dependent children. Social security was one of the most far-reaching of New Deal reforms. In the years since social security began, there have been numerous changes in the program. The basic system, however, operates much as it did in 1935.

**Roosevelt increases controls on business.** As the New Deal progressed, Roosevelt grew more opposed to the power of big corporations. A number of new reforms extended government control over business. One law set up agencies to regulate gas and electric companies. Another law increased

## Some New Deal Programs

| Program | | Purpose |
| --- | --- | --- |
| **FINANCE** | | |
| FDIC | Federal Deposit Insurance Corporation 1933– | To protect money of depositors in insured banks |
| SEC | Securities and Exchange Commission 1934– | To regulate the stock exchanges |
| FHA | Federal Housing Authority 1934– | To insure loans to homeowners for mortgages or home repairs |
| **AGRICULTURE** | | |
| AAA | Agricultural Adjustment Act 1933–1936 | To regulate farm production and promote soil conservation |
| FSA | Farm Security Administration 1937–1945 | To help tenant farmers and migrant workers to own farms |
| **BUSINESS AND LABOR** | | |
| NRA | National Recovery Administration 1933–1935 | To regulate industry, raise wages and prices, and permit workers to organize unions |
| NLRB | National Labor Relations Board 1935– | To regulate and protect unions |
| **EMPLOYMENT AND PUBLIC WORKS** | | |
| CCC | Civilian Conservation Corps 1933–1942 | To employ young men to plant trees, stock fish, build trails, and restore historic sites |
| TVA | Tennessee Valley Authority 1933– | To create jobs building dams to generate electricity |
| PWA | Public Works Administration 1933–1939 | To create jobs building roads, sewers, schools, post offices, hospitals, and tunnels |
| WPA | Works Progress Administration 1935–1942 | To create jobs for writers, artists, actors, and musicians |
| **RELIEF** | | |
| SSI | Social Security Insurance 1935– | To provide direct relief (public assistance), unemployment insurance, and retirement benefits |

## Chart Study

**New Deal programs affected many areas of American life. Which program regulated the stock exchanges? Which program created jobs for artists? Which programs are still in effect?**

taxes on corporations and wealthy individuals. Many Americans cheered Roosevelt's efforts to distribute taxes more fairly. Those against them, however, called the measure a plan to "soak the rich."

## A Blow to the New Deal

Roosevelt was confident that the New Deal was working better than ever. In 1935, however, the Supreme Court dealt the President a serious defeat.

**A New Deal program is struck down.** Some business leaders challenged the legality of a number of New Deal programs in court. In 1935 the United States Supreme Court declared that the National Recovery Administration was unconstitutional. The Supreme Court found that Congress had granted too much power to the President by allowing the NRA to set minimum wages and prices.

Roosevelt was furious with the Supreme Court's decision. It not only struck down one of his major programs, but it also brought an end to the use of the Blue Eagle that had become a symbol of pride. The episode started a long feud between the President and the Court.

**New acts protect workers.** Roosevelt and his advisers wanted to keep those parts of the NRA that protected workers. In 1935 Congress approved the **Wagner Act.** This act guaranteed the right of workers to join unions and bargain collectively. The act also set up the **National Labor Relations Board** (NLRB), which settled disputes and made sure that union activity could continue without interference from employers. Protections under the Wagner Act and the NLRB led to a surge in union organizing. Union membership soared from 3 million to about 9 million workers. Other measures helped nonunion workers. Among them were laws that set minimum wages and ended child labor.

**Roosevelt is reelected in 1936.** In the 1936 elections, many people—business leaders in particular—wanted Roosevelt out of office. They put their money and support behind the Republican candidate, Governor Alfred Landon of Kansas. Most of the nation's newspapers, owned by wealthy business leaders, also demonstrated support for Landon for President.

Roosevelt had support from every major group, except the wealthy. Farmers, young people, black Americans, immigrants, unions, and many others all supported Roosevelt. The groups that backed Roosevelt formed a **coalition** —a temporary alliance to promote a common cause. The coalition firmly established the Democrats as the majority party. Roosevelt won an easy victory. The electoral-vote total was not even close. There were 523 electoral votes for Roosevelt and 8 for Landon.

## Decline of the New Deal

In his second inaugural address, Roosevelt promised to continue the New Deal. He showed even greater concern for the poor, stating, "I see one third of a nation ill-housed, ill-clad, ill-nourished." President Roosevelt had many ideas for further reform, but he gradually lost support in both houses of Congress.

**Roosevelt battles the Supreme Court.** As Roosevelt began his second term, the government was divided. The President and the majority of Congress held **liberal** political views. Liberal views generally favor progressive change and reform in government. The views of the Supreme Court were more **conservative** —in favor of preserving the existing political order. Seven of the nine justices currently sitting on the Supreme Court had been appointed by Republican Presidents during the 1920's.

The Court had already hurt the New Deal by striking down the NRA. In 1936 the Court declared the AAA unconstitutional. Fearing that the Court would strike down other New Deal measures, Roosevelt tried to reform the Court system. He proposed that the Supreme Court be enlarged from 9 to 15 members. This would allow him to appoint 6 new justices.

Roosevelt's proposal drew wide criticism. Americans realized that Roosevelt wanted new justices who would support his

**651**

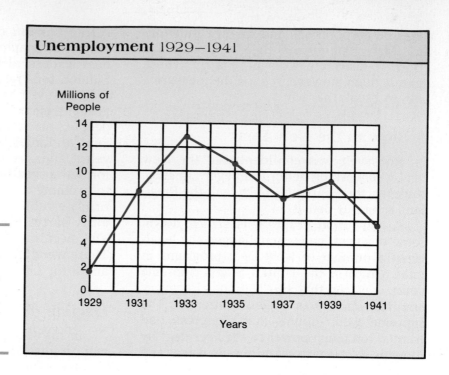

**Unemployment** 1929–1941

Millions of People

Years

**Graph Study**

Unemployment rose after the stock market crash of 1929. In what year was unemployment the highest? How did the New Deal affect unemployment between 1933 and 1937?

policies. They knew, too, that this "court-packing" scheme could destroy the balance of power. Many people worried that Roosevelt was becoming too powerful. Congress finally rejected his plan without ever bringing it to a vote.

While Congress debated the Court plan, the Court upheld the Wagner Act and the Social Security Act. In later years, the justices who opposed New Deal programs died or resigned. In time, President Roosevelt appointed nine justices to the Supreme Court. Nevertheless, the Court fight was a serious defeat for Roosevelt. It cost him a great deal of political support, which was vital for getting his New Deal measures passed in Congress.

**The New Deal ends.** In 1937 the New Deal faced another setback. Roosevelt reduced funding for relief programs in order to balance the federal budget. At the same time, the Federal Reserve Board raised interest rates. This led businesses to reduce borrowing and investment. Production slowed down, and approximately one million people lost their jobs. Roosevelt's plans had caused a deep **recession** —temporary decline in economic activity.

In 1938 the Democrats lost several seats in Congress. Many people were growing tired of the New Deal and were discouraged by the continuing Depression. At the same time, Americans were becoming alarmed by threats of conflict in Europe and Asia. As the decade closed, the nation's attention turned from the New Deal to the possibility of another great war.

## SECTION REVIEW

1. **Vocabulary**   coalition, liberal, conservative, recession
2. **People and Places**   Huey Long, Charles Coughlin, Francis Townsend, Harry Hopkins, Dorothea Lange, Colorado River, Columbia River, Alfred Landon
3. **Comprehension**   Why did most Americans support New Deal policies?
4. **Comprehension**   Why did some Americans oppose the New Deal?
5. **Critical Thinking**   Were people justified in fearing that President Franklin Roosevelt was gradually becoming too powerful? Why or why not?

## CRITICAL THINKING: Analyzing a Newspaper Article

To use newspapers as source material, learn how to find articles and get information from them. If you want to read newspaper articles on Franklin D. Roosevelt's "Hundred Days" as President, find newspapers from January through March 1933. They will probably be organized into sections. Most newspapers also have at least one page for editorials, giving opinions on particular topics. Articles about Roosevelt's "Hundred Days" would probably appear in a section about world and national events.

Once you find the right section, skim the headlines—titles in large type—for articles about your subject. A headline usually gives a story's main idea in a short punchy statement. If you find an article on the "Hundred Days," see if it has a **byline**—the writer's name. Also, see if it has a **dateline**—the first line of the article telling where and when the story was written. The dateline may name the news service that supplied the story. A news service writes and sells stories to newspapers. Two common news services are the Associated Press (AP) and United Press International (UPI).

News stories give the most important information in the **lead**—first—paragraph. You should be able to understand the main idea of a news story by reading the headline and the lead paragraph. The other paragraphs provide supporting and explanatory details. News stories usually answer the following questions: who, what, where, when, why, and how. Look for answers to these questions when reading newspaper articles.

This news story, from the *Chicago Daily News*, 1933, describes a Public Works Administration (PWA) project. Read the article, and then answer the questions that follow.

### ROAD BUILDING EXPECTED TO AID DOZEN-ODD LINES

Washington, D.C., July 5.—(AP)—A dozen-odd industries are expected by the public works administration to benefit from the building of $400,000,000 worth of highways.

In fact, the administration figures that more men will be employed in industry than in actual construction of the roads. Where there are 11,000 man hours of work required for the actual laying of one mile of highway, the administration said yesterday, 19,000 man hours are needed to supply the materials.

The industries listed included steel, cement, explosives, gravel, crushed stone, fuels, sacks and bags, ore, gypsum, limestone, sand, power, asphalt, brick and wire. Around 12,000,000 tons of freight must be transported, he added.

1. Does this story have a byline or a dateline?
2. Where and when was this story written? Which of the news services provided this story?
3. In which section of the newspaper did this story most likely appear—news, sports, or fashion?
4. From reading only the headline and the lead paragraph, what is the main idea of the article?
5. How does the second paragraph further explain the main idea?
6. What details are added in the last paragraph?
7. What does this article add to your understanding of the New Deal?

## Vocabulary

industrial union
sit-down strike
welfare state

Despite its failure to end the Depression, the New Deal brought important changes to American life. Since the 1930's, Americans have debated the significance of the New Deal, its successes, and its failures.

## Effects of the New Deal

Many different groups were affected by New Deal programs. Most people supported Roosevelt and the Democrats. For many people, however, hardship remained.

**Workers form new unions.** The 1930's saw the growth of a new type of labor union. The American Federation of Labor (AFL) was based on trade unionism. Trade unions, however, excluded factory workers and unskilled laborers. In the 1930's a group of union leaders, led by John L. Lewis of the United Mine Workers, favored organizing **industrial unions** —unions that represent workers in the same industry, regardless of their jobs. When AFL leaders refused to organize industrial unions, Lewis and others formed the **Congress of Industrial Organizations** (CIO).

Industrial unions began to form in the steel, textile, and automobile industries. They included many more blacks and women than did the trade unions. Eventually, the CIO competed with the AFL in size and power.

**Labor unions become powerful.** Under the Wagner Act, the government protected union activity. Even with the Wagner Act, many businesses refused to recognize unions. To gain recognition, workers launched

bitter fights against big automobile, textile, and steel companies. Workers found a new weapon with the **sit-down strike** . In a sit-down strike, workers take over a plant, refusing to work or to leave. Companies were often reluctant to act against sit-down strikes. In time, many companies agreed to recognize industrial unions, and unions gained more economic and political power than ever before.

**Black Americans seek gains from the New Deal.** Poverty and discrimination made the Depression years difficult for black Americans. Tenant farmers and sharecroppers were badly hurt by falling crop prices. In the cities, black factory workers were usually the first to lose their jobs. During the worst years of the Depression, about one half of all black workers were jobless. In urban and rural areas, local efforts often denied aid to blacks.

In the early years of his presidency, Roosevelt was slow to attend to issues facing black people. He feared that he would lose the support of white southern Democrats. By the mid-1930's, however, Roosevelt's administration focused more on the concerns of black Americans.

Roosevelt appointed a number of black people to federal positions. Most of these posts were set up to protect the interests of blacks in New Deal programs. Among those appointed were Mary McLeod Bethune, Dr. Ralph Bunche, and Robert Weaver. These and other black leaders formed the Black Cabinet, which advised the President on issues concerning blacks.

Relief and employment from such programs as the WPA, NYA, and CCC helped thousands of black people. Most New Deal programs, however, still paid black workers lower wages than white workers. Also, Social Security excluded farm workers and household workers from coverage. Many

In the struggle to end discrimination, black Americans found an ally in Eleanor Roosevelt. After her husband became President, Mrs. Roosevelt spoke out strongly for civil rights and other social causes.

black workers were thus denied pension benefits. Despite these problems, most black Americans were quite enthusiastic about the New Deal. They recognized President Roosevelt's efforts to help disadvantaged Americans. They also admired Eleanor Roosevelt, who was very active in the fight to end race discrimination. Black voters slowly shifted away from the Republican party. By the end of the 1930's, they gave the Democratic party their solid support.

**The New Deal changes policy toward Native Americans.** Government policy had long failed to meet the needs of Native Americans. One positive step came in 1924, when Native Americans were granted citizenship. Still, they suffered high unemployment and poor living conditions.

The New Deal made an important change in government policy toward Native Americans. The Indian Reorganization Act of 1934 reversed the policy of breaking up tribal lands. The federal government also supported local, tribal government. Later measures encouraged efforts to improve farming and reestablish traditional ways of life among Native Americans.

**The government takes action against Mexican immigrants.** Immigration from Mexico was high during the 1920's. Mexican

## PROFILE • Eleanor Roosevelt and Her Times

Eleanor Roosevelt was shy as a young girl, but she became an active public figure as an adult. Her crusades for social causes won respect and admiration the world over.

Eleanor Roosevelt began to work on her husband's behalf when he was stricken with polio in 1921. By traveling and speaking in public forums, she became well known and soon had a political life of her own. She used her role as First Lady to promote many causes.

Deeply concerned with injustices facing black Americans and women, Eleanor Roosevelt constantly spoke out on these issues. She also became a powerful voice on behalf of youth employment, and sought ways to end poverty. She expressed her views in her radio program, in her daily newspaper column, and in her many books.

Eleanor Roosevelt believed that every American has the right and responsibility to be a public servant. She was fond of saying, "It is today that we must create the world of the future." By using her position to voice her concerns, she made her contribution to that cause.

**Eleanor Roosevelt**

---

workers, like other immigrants, sought jobs in farming and industry. Many Mexicans became migrant workers in the Southwest. They usually faced discrimination in jobs, housing, and schools.

When the Depression hit, government officials wanted to keep Mexicans from taking scarce jobs and aid. Between 1930 and 1940, nearly 500,000 people were deported to Mexico. Most were Mexican citizens, but some were American citizens by birth.

## Changes in Government

Since early in the nation's history, American Presidents have advanced their ideas about the role of government. One idea—government for the welfare of all people—was first put forth by Thomas Jefferson and later expanded by Theodore Roosevelt and Woodrow Wilson. Franklin Roosevelt, however, went far beyond these leaders in turning this idea of government into policy.

**The government assumes new responsibilities.** Before the New Deal, people who lost their jobs had no income until they were working again. Retired people lived off their savings or their families. The disabled, the homeless, and the poor often relied on help from private charities.

President Roosevelt believed that all Americans are entitled to the basic necessities—food, clothing, shelter, and security. Roosevelt also believed that the government is responsible for protecting those rights. To Roosevelt, government action was especially important during the Depression, when people suffered problems caused by forces outside their control.

In the New Deal, the American government stepped in to protect people's jobs, housing, and economic security. Many people opposed this development. Americans today still disagree about whether the country should be a **welfare state** —a nation where the government takes responsibility for the well-being of its citizens. Nevertheless, most Americans today look to the government to protect and improve their living and working conditions. Such benefits as unemployment payments, social security, and insured bank deposits are taken for granted.

**The government takes part in economic planning.** The New Deal also brought government involvement in economic planning. The TVA, for example, involved planning many aspects of economic life for a large section of rural America. Economic planning was also needed for farm programs. Paying farmers to reduce production reduced the amount of food reaching the market. This, in turn, raised the prices of farm goods.

The government became more involved in planning the national economy as well. For example, by increasing or decreasing public-works projects, the President could put greater or lesser sums of money into the economy.

**The New Deal calls for big government.** The responsibilities taken on by the government in the New Deal were enormous. The American economy was complex and deep in crisis. To carry out government programs,

## Our Presidents

### FRANKLIN D. ROOSEVELT

★ **1933–1945** ★

**32ND PRESIDENT**

DEMOCRAT

★ Born January 30, 1882, in New York
★ Married Anna Eleanor Roosevelt in 1905; 6 children
★ Lawyer; governor of New York
★ Lived in New York when elected President
★ Vice Presidents: John Garner; Henry Wallace; Harry S Truman
★ Died April 12, 1945, in Georgia
★ Only President elected to four terms
★ Key events while in office: Twentieth and Twenty-first amendments; New Deal; CIO formed; Social Security Act; World War II; Atlantic Charter; UN formed

Roosevelt created many boards and agencies. Government departments expanded in power and size. While Roosevelt was in office, the federal government swelled from 600,000 to nearly 4 million employees.

**Big government creates shifts in power.** Many New Deal measures helped establish government control over business. Since the growth of powerful corporations in the nineteenth century, business leaders had greatly influenced government. The New Deal significantly decreased the influence of business in the government.

Increased federal power also took power away from state and local governments. Many of Roosevelt's opponents were particularly opposed to these shifts in power.

**657**

# ★ ★ ★ *Depression Art*

The New Deal touched many aspects of American life, including art. During the Depression few people could afford to sponsor art projects or buy expensive paintings. Many artists had problems continuing their work. The Works Progress Administration hired artists to take part in special projects or to continue their own work. With help from the WPA, such painters as Jackson Pollock, Jacob Lawrence, Mark Rothko, and others produced thousands of paintings.

Depression-era paintings are often exhibited in museums. A number of WPA projects, however, were large murals painted on the walls of libraries, airports, and post offices.

## An Ongoing Debate

During the early 1930's, few people doubted the success of the New Deal. Roosevelt's programs worked far better than had been expected. Some people, however, regarded the New Deal as a failure. Americans still debate whether the New Deal succeeded.

**Some people consider the New Deal a failure.** Critics charge that the New Deal failed to end the Depression. At the end of the 1930's, the American economy was still facing many of the problems it faced in 1932. Critics also charge that the New Deal failed to change conditions for people who were locked in extreme poverty.

Some opponents believe the New Deal caused Americans to lose personal freedom. Increases in federal power, they argue, involve a loss of personal liberties. Opponents also charge that government control of business harmed the free-enterprise system.

Roosevelt's spending policy is considered by many critics to be his biggest failure. In order to pay for New Deal measures, the government spent more money than it collected through taxes. The government began to borrow huge sums of money. The national debt rose each year of Roosevelt's presidency. In 1933 the national debt was about $22.5 billion. By 1940 it had nearly doubled.

**Supporters point to successes.** Those who see the New Deal as a success point out that most of its programs produced almost

The gloom and despair of the Great Depression was a common subject of the art of the times. Lily Furedi's painting *Subway,* completed around 1934, is typical of Great Depression art.

immediate benefits. Work-relief programs put millions of people back to work. Many Americans' homes and farms were saved, and thousands of farmers learned better farming methods.

Many people felt the most important result of the New Deal involved people's feelings. Public-works projects beautified the nation and inspired pride. The New Deal lifted people out of the despair of the Depression by helping them to support themselves.

From 1930 to 1933, many Americans faced poverty, hunger, and starvation. With the New Deal, supporters say, the suffering was far less. In their view the New Deal was important in softening the worst effects of the Depression.

## SECTION REVIEW

1. **Vocabulary** industrial union, sit-down strike, welfare state
2. **People and Places** John L. Lewis, Mary McLeod Bethune, Dr. Ralph Bunche, Robert Weaver
3. **Comprehension** What led to increased power for labor unions?
4. **Comprehension** How did the role of the federal government change as a result of the New Deal?
5. **Critical Thinking** How did President Franklin Roosevelt's beliefs have an influence on the way he fought the Great Depression?

# Chapter 28 Summary

As the Great Depression continued, Americans lost their jobs, farms, and homes. Local charities set up breadlines, soup kitchens, and lodging houses to help people in need. Times were even harder in the Great Plains, where a long drought created the Dust Bowl.

In 1932 voters turned to the Democrats for leadership. President Franklin Roosevelt worked with his Brain Trust to develop the New Deal, Roosevelt's program to fight the Depression. Roosevelt's first action was to end the banking crisis. He declared a Bank Holiday and asked Congress to pass the Banking Relief Act. In the meantime, Roosevelt assured Americans in a fireside chat that the banks were safe.

During the Hundred Days, Congress passed a flood of laws that established New Deal agencies. The main goals of the New Deal were relief, recovery, and reform. New Deal programs provided work relief, sought recovery in business and agriculture, and established reforms to regulate the economy.

Many people criticized the New Deal. Members of the Liberty League thought that the government had become too powerful and was overspending. Other critics felt that more reform was needed to end the Depression. In 1935 Roosevelt launched the Second New Deal, a program of still greater reforms. The most important measure was the Social Security Act.

The Supreme Court declared the National Recovery Administration unconstitutional. Fearing that the Court would seriously damage the New Deal, Roosevelt proposed to reform the Supreme Court. His proposal was highly criticized. After 1938, Roosevelt lost some of his support in Congress. By 1939 the President turned his attention to world affairs.

Despite its failure to end the Depression, the New Deal changed many aspects of American life. Many groups, such as industrial unions, black Americans, Mexican Americans, and Native Americans, were affected. By creating a welfare state, President Roosevelt changed the government's role in American life. Even today, there is an ongoing debate about the successes and failures that resulted from the New Deal.

# Chapter 28 REVIEW

## Vocabulary and Key Terms

Choose one term from the following list to replace each blank in the paragraph below. Write your answers on a separate sheet of paper.

**fireside chats**
**National Recovery Administration**
**work relief**
**Hundred Days**
**Rural Electrification Administration**
**direct relief**
**New Deal**
**Social Security Act**
**coalition**
**Brain Trust**

The __1__ was Roosevelt's program to fight the Depression. During the __2__, Congress passed laws that Roosevelt planned with the help of the __3__. For the jobless, the government provided __4__, which Roosevelt preferred to __5__. To boost the economy, the __6__ helped industries write up codes of fair competition. The __7__ improved life in farming regions.

## Recalling the Facts

1. What caused the Dust Bowl?
2. What types of projects did the Civilian Conservation Corps sponsor?
3. How did the Agricultural Adjustment Administration raise crop prices?
4. How were conditions in the Tennessee River valley improved?
5. What was the major goal of the Works Progress Administration?
6. What was the function of the National Labor Relations Board?
7. Why did Roosevelt try to reform the Supreme Court?
8. What caused the recession in 1937?
9. Why was the Congress of Industrial Organizations formed?
10. How did black Americans fare in the New Deal?
11. Why did the government deport Mexican workers?

## Places to Locate

Match the letters on the map with the places listed below. Write your answers on a separate sheet of paper.

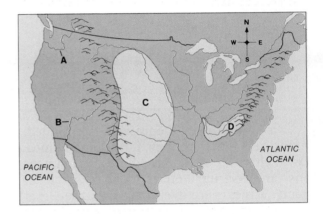

1. Great Plains
2. Tennessee River valley
3. Colorado River
4. Columbia River

## Critical Thinking

1. New Deal policies greatly expanded the power and size of the federal government. Do you think this expansion of government power was necessary? Why or why not? Consider these questions in your answer:
   a. How did the federal government's role change as a result of the policies of the New Deal?
   b. What circumstances prompted these changes?
   c. Were government policies productive or harmful for business? Explain why you answered as you did.

2. The New Deal had a tremendous impact on American government and society. Do you think this impact was generally positive or negative? Consider these questions in your answer:
   a. What were the short-term effects of the New Deal?
   b. What impact did long-term reforms have?
   c. How did the policies of the New Deal affect the nation's workers, black Americans, Native Americans, and Mexican Americans?

## Understanding History

1. Reread the section "Recovery measures help business" on page 646. Then answer these questions.
   a. **Economics.** What were the major purposes of the codes of fair competition set up by industries?
   b. **Citizenship.** Why was the emblem of the Blue Eagle considered to be a symbol of pride?
2. Reread the section "The New Deal changes policy toward Native Americans" on page 655. Then answer these questions.
   a. **Geography.** In what ways did the New Deal encourage better use of tribal land?
   b. **Culture.** How did the policies of the New Deal signal a change in the national government's view of Native American culture?

## Projects and Activities

1. **Making a Chart.** Make a chart outlining the main programs that were produced by the New Deal. Use the following column headings on your chart: Program, Purpose, Results. Fill out the chart as completely as possible.
2. **Researching Periodicals.** Look through old newspapers or magazines at your community library for an article relating to the New Deal. Read and then summarize the article. Present your summary in class.

3. **Giving an Oral Report.** Find out about a work-relief project that was carried out in your community, region, or state during the time of the New Deal. Present an oral report on the project to your classmates. Include pictures in your report, if available.
4. **Writing a Report.** Research one of the following important figures of the New Deal period: Eleanor Roosevelt, Frances Perkins, Huey Long, Harry Hopkins, John L. Lewis, Mary McLeod Bethune. Write a report based on the information you are able to find.

## Practicing Your Skill

Below is an excerpt from a February 3, 1936 newspaper article. Read the excerpt, then answer the questions that follow.

### 'FIRST LADY' BACKS WORK BY WOMEN

Special to the New York Times.

WASHINGTON, Feb. 2.—The right of women, even married women, to work outside the home was asserted tonight by Mrs. Franklin D. Roosevelt in an address before the Town Hall, a public forum here. . . . .

The First Lady said that there was no proof that women [take the place of] men in jobs . . . and added that "most women do the work they do because they do it better than men."

Mrs. Roosevelt said that this was a good time to discuss the problem "Should women be allowed to work," because, in many countries, the right of women [to] work had lately been questioned.

1. What is the headline of the story?
2. Is there a byline?
3. Where was the story written? When was it written?
4. How does this news story answer the questions *who, what, when, where, why* and *how*?
5. Is the story objective? Explain.

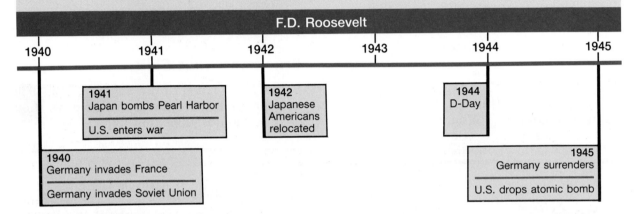

F.D. Roosevelt

| 1940 | 1941 | 1942 | 1943 | 1944 | 1945 |

**1941**
Japan bombs Pearl Harbor

U.S. enters war

**1942**
Japanese
Americans
relocated

**1944**
D-Day

**1940**
Germany invades France

Germany invades Soviet Union

**1945**
Germany surrenders

U.S. drops atomic bomb

**American B-24 bombers played a key role in fighting the aggression of Germany, Italy, and Japan during World War II.**

## Preparing to Read

In the United States, democracy had remained strong throughout the Great Depression. In other parts of the world, however, the Depression gave birth to new, warlike political systems. In the late 1930's these aggressive governments plunged the world into history's most destructive war. In Europe and then in Asia, American military strength helped gain the victory for freedom and democracy. At the end of the fighting, the United States of America emerged as the most powerful nation in the world. As you read this chapter, try to answer the following questions:

1. What events led to the outbreak of World War II?
2. How did the United States become involved in World War II?
3. How did the United States gain victory in World War II?

# 1 What events led to the outbreak of World War II?

### Vocabulary

dictator
fascism
totalitarian
demilitarize
appeasement

The Great Depression caused economic problems throughout the world. In Europe, economic worries added to feelings of bitterness remaining from World War I. Together these troubles caused democratic governments to collapse in Italy, Germany, and other countries. Aggressive new governments arose that threatened the world's peace.

### The Rise of Dictators

Promising to make their nations rich and powerful, **dictators** —rulers with absolute authority—took control as democratic governments collapsed. Once in power, they took away many freedoms and began to threaten other nations.

**A new government forms in Italy.** Many Italians were rather unhappy with their lives after World War I. Italy's democratic government was weak, and many of the people suffered unemployment. Italians also felt bitter about the terms of the Treaty of Versailles. They thought the treaty had not granted enough territory to Italy. Finally, many people feared that there might be a Communist revolution in Italy.

In Italy in 1919 Benito Mussolini formed the **Fascist party** (FASH-ist). This party practiced **fascism** —a system of government that emphasizes military power and total control over people's lives. Mussolini was a fiery speaker who glorified power. He convinced many Italians to join the Fascist party to stop communism and to restore the ancient glory of Italy. In 1922 Mussolini and his followers seized control of the government and established a dictatorship. Italians who opposed Mussolini were imprisoned, killed, or driven out of the country. The government built up the armed forces, and Mussolini proclaimed that Italy would become a great world power. He boasted that Italians would control the Mediterranean lands as they had in the days of ancient Rome.

**Hitler preaches hatred in Germany.** Many Germans also felt discontented after World War I. They blamed their government

**663**

By the mid-1930's Nazi leader Adolf Hitler became dictator of Germany. The swastika on Hitler's arm band came to symbolize the persecution of Jews and others that Hitler blamed for Germany's problems.

Socialist Worker's party. Its members were called **Nazis** (NAHT-seez). Hitler preached hatred of Jews and Communists, and he claimed that Germans were a superior "master race" that should control all of Europe. In imitation of Mussolini, Hitler sought to establish fascism in Germany.

**Hitler takes power.** During the 1920's Hitler built up the Nazi party, often using violence against its opponents. He was a good organizer and a powerful speaker, and many Germans accepted his ideas. When conditions became worse in the Great Depression, Hitler's influence grew rapidly. In 1933 he became the chancellor, or prime minister, of Germany.

During the next two years, Hitler ended democratic government in Germany and made himself dictator. He threw out the German constitution and rapidly built up the armed forces, in violation of the Treaty of Versailles. The Nazi party used threats and violence to take control of newspapers and schools. Those who dared to speak out against Hitler were thrown into prison, tortured, or killed. Laws were passed that took away the legal rights of Jews. By the late 1930's thousands of Jews were sent to prison camps. Other minorities in Germany were also harshly treated. In a few years, Germany had become a **totalitarian** country—a country in which a single authority controls the nation and its people. With the nation completely under his power, Adolf Hitler began to make claims that Germany had the right to expand its territory.

**Stalin controls the Soviet Union.** During World War I the Bolshevik party under Lenin took control of the Soviet Union. (See chapter 26.) The Bolsheviks used secret police and murder to silence those who opposed their plans to establish communism. After Lenin's death in 1924, Joseph Stalin became the new dictator of the Soviet Union. Under Stalin the use of violence and terror reached staggering levels. Stalin forced Soviet peasants to give up their land and join collective farms run by the government. The millions who resisted were executed or were sent to prison camps. Millions more Soviet citizens were arrested and

for signing the Treaty of Versailles, which had stripped Germany of much of its land and power. Unemployment was widespread, and the German economy suffered from trade problems and inflation. When the Great Depression began, these conditions grew worse.

Adolf Hitler, a former soldier, took advantage of the country's troubles. He organized a new political party, the National

imprisoned because they were suspected of disagreeing with the government. People were urged to report to the secret police any activities of friends and neighbors that might be considered disloyal.

**Military leaders take over in Japan.** The Great Depression also led to changes in the government of Japan. Many Japanese felt that their democratic government was too weak to solve the economic problems of the Depression. Japan was also industrializing rapidly and needed a steady supply of coal, oil, and other raw materials. The Japanese islands lacked raw materials, and military leaders wanted to take over parts of Asia that were rich in natural resources. Before 1930 Japan had already acquired Korea and a number of Pacific islands. In the early 1930's military leaders took control of the Japanese government. Soon after, in 1931, the Japanese army invaded Manchuria, a section of northern China. (See map on page 670.) Within a short time Japan had turned Manchuria into a Japanese-controlled state called Manchukuo.

## American Policy

Americans preferred to ignore the growing power of dictatorships in Europe and Asia. Isolationist views were strong, and the nation took steps to prevent involvement in any future war in Europe.

**The United States seeks to limit ties with other nations.** Many Americans regretted American involvement in World War I. They believed that the nation had been drawn into that war by uncontrolled events. Isolationists wanted to prevent those kinds of incidents from happening again. Under pressure from isolationists, Congress passed the first Neutrality Act in 1935. This act outlawed loans or sales of weapons to warring nations. A second Neutrality Act, passed two years later, prohibited Americans from traveling on ships of nations at war. It also attempted to limit trade with warring countries. Such countries could buy American nonmilitary goods only if they sent their own ships and paid in cash. This was known as the "cash and carry" plan.

**Relations with Latin America improve.** As America sought to avoid war in Europe, the nation also improved its relations with Latin American neighbors. President Hoover made a good-will tour of Latin America in the early 1930's. He signed an agreement promising to withdraw American troops from Haiti. When Franklin Roosevelt became President in 1933, he announced that the United States would not interfere in Latin American affairs. Instead, he promised, America would follow the "policy of the good neighbor—the neighbor who respects the rights of others." Roosevelt soon put the **Good Neighbor Policy** into effect. He carried out Hoover's agreement to withdraw American troops from Haiti, and he also withdrew troops from Nicaragua. In 1934 the United States signed a treaty giving up the right to interfere in Cuban affairs.

## Heading Toward War

During the late 1930's the world's dictators began a series of military attacks. Japan took over much of China. Italy and Germany overpowered neighboring countries. At first the peaceful countries of Europe tried to ignore the problem of aggression. Finally, however, the dictators' attacks led to war.

**Italy invades Ethiopia.** In 1935 Mussolini's troops attacked Ethiopia in North Africa. The Ethiopians were armed with bows and arrows and old-fashioned rifles, and their cavalry was unable to stand up to Italy's tanks and airplanes. In eight months Ethiopia was defeated. The emperor of Ethiopia called on the League of Nations for help, but the League failed to take strong action. Individual countries also failed to oppose Italy's aggressive actions. Britain and France did not want to anger Mussolini. In the United States, President Roosevelt did not want to offend the isolationists, and the government steered clear of the issue.

**Germany and Italy become allies.** In 1936 Hitler's troops moved into the Rhineland, a part of Germany lying west of the Rhine River and bordering France. Under the Treaty of Versailles, Germany had agreed that this area would be **demilitarized** —kept free of troops and weapons. Neither Britain nor France took action against Hitler's breaking of the treaty.

Soon afterward, Germany and Italy signed a treaty of alliance. Mussolini boasted that Rome and Berlin, the capitals of Italy and Germany, would be the new axis on which the world turned. As a result, the new military alliance became known as the **Axis Powers.** Japan later joined the Axis alliance.

**Japan attacks China.** In Asia, Japan launched a full-scale attack on China in 1937. Japanese airplanes bombed Chinese cities, railroads, and supply networks. The Chinese fought back bravely, but they lacked weapons and supplies. They could not prevent Japanese troops from capturing coastal cities and river valleys. Before long Japan controlled almost all of northern and central China.

**Germany seizes land in Europe.** In 1938 Hitler's army moved into the neighboring country of Austria. In the face of German threats, Austria gave up its independence without fighting and became a part of Germany. Later the same year, Hitler demanded that Czechoslovakia give up the Sudetenland (soo-DAYT-uhn-land), an area with many German-speaking people. Great Britain and France had signed treaties to protect Czechoslovakia. They wanted to avoid war. At the Munich Conference in 1938 they agreed to Hitler's demand. Many people were shocked by this act of appeasement —giving in to preserve the peace. The British and French leaders, however, believed Hitler's promise that he would take no more territory in Europe. The promise was broken within six months. In March 1939 Hitler's troops took over the rest of Czechoslovakia.

**Hitler ordered German tank divisions to invade Poland on September 1, 1939. As a result of Hitler's action, Great Britain and France declared war on Germany on September 3.**

## The Start of World War II

With Germany and Italy determined to take what they wanted, war seemed unavoidable. Britain and France began to prepare for the coming fight. They increased the size of their armies. They had far to go, however, to catch up with the Axis Powers.

**War begins.** In the late summer of 1939 Hitler demanded a strip of Polish territory that separated East Prussia from the rest of Germany. Britain and France promised to help Poland if Germany attacked. Britain also sought an alliance with the Soviet Union. Instead, Stalin signed a neutrality agreement with Germany. Secretly, the two countries agreed to divide Poland. The Nazi-Soviet Pact left Hitler free to attack Poland without worrying about starting a war with the Soviet Union. Then on September 1, 1939, Hitler ordered the German invasion of Poland. Great Britain and France declared war on Germany two days later. **World War II** had begun.

| SECTION REVIEW |
| --- |

1. **Vocabulary**  dictator, fascism, totalitarian, demilitarize, appeasement
2. **People and Places**  Benito Mussolini, Adolf Hitler, Joseph Stalin, Manchuria, Ethiopia, Rhineland, Austria, Czechoslovakia, Poland
3. **Comprehension**  How did the Great Depression lead to threats to world peace in the 1930's?
4. **Comprehension**  Why did the United States try to follow isolationist policies in the 1930's?
5. **Critical Thinking**  Do you think World War II could have been prevented? Explain your answer.

# 2 How did the United States become involved in World War II?

## Vocabulary

blitzkrieg

rationing

The Nazi armies quickly took over large parts of Europe at the start of World War II. The United States, realizing the Nazi threat to freedom, offered increasing support to the **Allies**—the nations that opposed the Axis. A surprise attack by the Japanese in 1941 brought the United States into the war.

## Nazi Attacks

The German forces attacked Poland in 1939 in a fierce **blitzkrieg** —the German word for "lightning war." The German troops moved so fast that the British and French were unable to furnish any aid to Poland. At the same time, Soviet troops invaded eastern Poland. Against these odds, Polish resistance was soon overcome.

**The war spreads over western Europe.** For a few months after the conquest of Poland there was little real fighting. In the spring of 1940, however, the Nazis unleashed an all-out attack to the west. They quickly overran Norway and Denmark. Then the blitzkrieg turned south. In a lightning campaign, Hitler's forces took over the Netherlands and Belgium and pushed into France. British forces arrived to help the French, but the Germans moved quickly and caught the Allies in a trap at Dunkirk on the English Channel. In a frantic effort, Great Britain sent every boat that was available across the

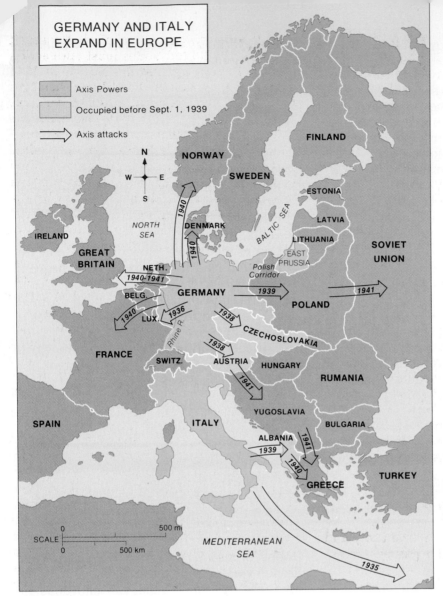

**GERMANY AND ITALY EXPAND IN EUROPE**

Axis Powers

Occupied before Sept. 1, 1939

Axis attacks

Channel to rescue the trapped troops. About 338,000 British and French soldiers were ferried to safety in warships, merchant vessels, tugboats, fishing boats, and even pleasure yachts. With Allied troops out of the way, the Germans marched on Paris. On June 22, 1940, France surrendered.

**The Germans bomb Britain.** For a time it seemed that Great Britain would be the next country to fall. Led by their new prime minister, Winston Churchill, the British prepared to resist a German invasion. Said Churchill, "We shall defend our island whatever the cost may be.... We shall never surrender." The Germans chose to begin the

attack by air. In the Battle of Britain, waves of German bombers hammered at London and other British cities. Whole sections of the cities were destroyed. The British Royal Air Force fought back using a new weapon, radar. With radar to locate approaching bombers, British pilots shot down thousands of German planes. By the end of 1940, Hitler abandoned his plan to invade Britain.

**Hitler attacks on other fronts.** Elsewhere in Europe, however, the German armies met with great success. Most of the countries of eastern Europe were forced to join the Nazis or were conquered and enslaved. In 1941, in spite of the Nazi-Soviet

Pact, Hitler launched a full-scale attack against the Soviet Union. Although the Soviet forces fought fiercely, German armies poured into western Russia. The battle line extended from near Leningrad in the north to near Stalingrad on the Volga River before the German advance came to a halt. (See map on page 676.) After the defeat of France, the Nazis occupied French colonies in North Africa. German forces then pushed to take over the British colony of Egypt.

## America's Response

When the war broke out in Europe, the United States maintained its official policy of neutrality. Most Americans, however, sympathized with the French, British, and Polish victims of Hitler's attacks. Gradually the nation moved closer to war.

**Americans respond to the threat of war.** In 1939 President Roosevelt stated that the United States would remain neutral. At the same time, he noted that Americans did not have to be "neutral in thought." Roosevelt persuaded Congress to change the Neutrality Act to allow arms sales to the Allies. The Allies still had to pay cash and transport the arms in their own ships.

By 1940 Americans realized that the country had to be prepared for war. Congress took steps to strengthen the army and navy. The government also passed a draft law, establishing the first peacetime draft in the nation's history. In the election of 1940, Roosevelt ran for a third term as President. Isolationist feelings were still strong, and Roosevelt wanted to reassure the nation. "Your boys are not going to be sent into any foreign wars," he told American voters. The threat of war was growing daily, however, and the voters chose to keep Roosevelt, an experienced leader, in the White House. Wendell Willkie, the Republican candidate, was badly defeated. Roosevelt's election to a third term as President broke the two-term tradition set by George Washington.

**America extends loans to Britain.** Following the election, Roosevelt urged the nation to lend Britain needed supplies and weapons. By this time Britain was running out of money to pay for supplies. Roosevelt believed the United States must take action to help Britain against the Nazis. In 1941 Congress approved the **Lend-Lease Act.** This act allowed the President to sell or lend war materials to any nation whose defense was "vital to the defense of the United States."

Under the Lend-Lease Act the United States sent tanks, airplanes, and ammunition to the British. The Lend-Lease Act was later extended to include aid to the Soviet Union. Roosevelt did not approve of Stalin's dictatorship, but he believed Hitler's invasion of the Soviet Union had to be stopped.

**Churchill and Roosevelt make plans.** During summer 1941 the United States moved closer to war. The United States Navy began escorting British vessels carrying Lend-Lease aid across the Atlantic. As a result, German submarines began attacking American ships. In August Roosevelt and Churchill met on a British battleship at sea. The two leaders drew up the **Atlantic Charter** stating the war aims of the Allies. They agreed to work to defeat the Nazis and to seek no new territory. They also agreed that all peoples should have the right to choose their own form of government.

Soon after the Atlantic Charter was signed, a German submarine fired on an American destroyer. Roosevelt responded with an order for American vessels to "shoot on sight" any German vessel that threatened the shipping lanes between the United States and Britain. Americans now realized that war was almost certain.

## A Surprise Attack

While Americans anxiously watched the war in Europe, the conflict had also been growing in Asia. In 1940, Japanese armies had occupied French Indochina. (See map on page 679.) The United States government worried that Japan would try to take over still more territory in the Pacific.

**Roosevelt acts against Japan.** President Roosevelt sought to stop Japanese aggression. He warned the Japanese that the United States would take "any and all steps" to protect its interests in Asia. He also cut off

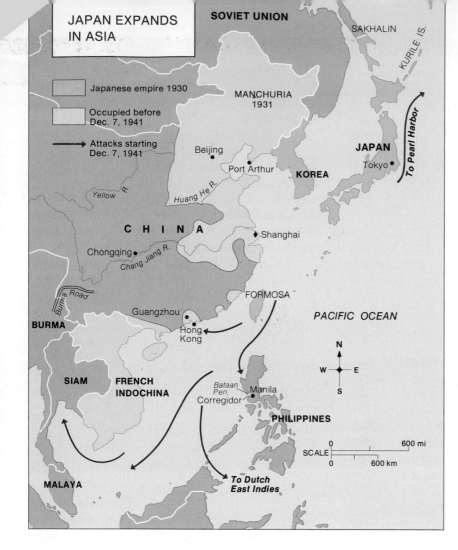

**JAPAN EXPANDS IN ASIA**

Japanese empire 1930

Occupied before Dec. 7, 1941

Attacks starting Dec. 7, 1941

SOVIET UNION

SAKHALIN

KURILE IS.

MANCHURIA 1931

Beijing

Port Arthur

KOREA

JAPAN

Tokyo

To Pearl Harbor

Yellow R.

Huang He R.

C H I N A

Shanghai

Chongqing

Chang Jiang R.

Burma Road

FORMOSA

PACIFIC OCEAN

Guangzhou

Hong Kong

BURMA

SIAM

FRENCH INDOCHINA

Bataan Pen.
Corregidor

Manila

PHILIPPINES

N
W E
S

SCALE

0        600 mi
0        600 km

MALAYA

To Dutch East Indies

**Map Study**

By 1930 the Japanese Empire included Korea and Formosa. What regions became part of the Japanese Empire before December 7, 1941? What areas did Japan attack starting December 7, 1941?

sales of oil and steel to Japan. Roosevelt's action angered the Japanese, who badly needed the oil. In November 1941 Japanese and American leaders met to discuss their disagreements. Neither country would accept the other's demands. Meanwhile, Japan planned a surprise attack against the United States.

**Japan bombs Pearl Harbor.** On the morning of December 7, 1941, Japanese dive bombers struck suddenly at **Pearl Harbor,** Hawaii. The American Pacific fleet, lying peacefully at anchor in its home port, was caught completely by surprise. In two hours the Japanese bombers destroyed 19 ships and 150 American airplanes. About 3,500 Americans were killed or wounded. The Japanese attack had crippled the American

forces in the Pacific, except for three aircraft carriers. By luck, they were at sea.

**The United States declares war.** Americans, stunned by the Japanese attack, quickly united in the nation's defense. At Roosevelt's request, Congress declared war on Japan on December 8, the day after the bombing. Three days later Germany and Italy declared war on the United States.

## The War Effort

Americans quickly turned to the task of mobilizing for war. Millions of men and women joined the armed forces. Others helped to produce food, weapons, and supplies. Almost every American became involved in the war effort.

# PRESIDENT ROOSEVELT'S WAR MESSAGE 1941

On December 7, 1941, about 360 Japanese divebombers attacked Pearl Harbor, Hawaii, surprising the American fleet anchored there. More than 2,300 Americans were killed and almost 1,200 others were wounded. On December 8, 1941, President Roosevelt asked Congress to recognize that a state of war existed between the United States and Japan.

## Read to Find Out

1. Why does President Roosevelt say it was obvious that the Japanese attack on Pearl Harbor was planned?
2. What is President Roosevelt asking of Congress?

*To the Congress of the United States:*

Yesterday, December 7, 1941—a day which will live in infamy—the United States of America was suddenly and deliberately attacked by naval and air forces of the Empire of Japan.

The United States was at peace with . . . Japan . . . looking toward . . . peace in the Pacific. . . . The distance of Hawaii from Japan makes it obvious that the attack was deliberately planned many days or even weeks ago. . . .

Japan has . . . undertaken a surprise offensive extending throughout the Pacific area. . . . The people of the United States . . . understand the implications to the very life and safety of our nation. . . . I ask that the Congress declare that, since the unprovoked and dastardly attack by Japan on Sunday, December 7, a state of war has existed between the United States and the Japanese Empire.

*Franklin D. Roosevelt*

**The armed forces prepare.** The army, navy, and air force quickly established new bases across the country to train millions of recruits. During the war, about 6 million men and women enlisted, and another 10 million men were drafted. Women took over many non-combat jobs. In the air force, women pilots flew bombers and other planes to bases overseas.

**Minority groups join in the war effort.** About 1 million black men and women served in the armed forces. Discrimination was widespread, and most blacks were placed in segregated units led by white officers. As in World War I, black units served with great bravery in spite of prejudice. The armed forces did take some new steps toward equal treatment. For the first time, blacks could join the Marine Corps. Also, many more blacks became officers than in the past. A black doctor, Charles Drew, helped save the lives of thousands of American soldiers. Drew developed the blood bank, which provided needed supplies of blood for the wounded.

Other minority groups also served bravely. Many Americans of Hispanic descent fought in the armed services. These included thousands of Mexican Americans and Puerto Ricans. Among Native Americans, one of three men served in the war—a higher proportion than from any other ethnic

# AMERICAN HIGHLIGHTS

## ECONOMICS • Wartime Inventions

World War II was the most costly and destructive conflict in history. At the same time, however, the war led to many creative inventions and new ways of doing things. Radar, invented as a weapon of war, soon made flying safer for commercial passengers. Diving became a popular sport after the invention of underwater breathing equipment used by navy divers during the war.

Another important wartime development was the widespread use of plastics. Soldiers carried plastic radios and telephones and used plastic chairs and tables. Wires were covered with plastic insulation, and uniforms were pressed with irons that had plastic handles.

After the war, Americans began to use plastics for all kinds of consumer goods. Today Americans consume about 25 million tons of plastics each year for such things as dishes, furniture, toys, tools, sports equipment, and automobile parts.

**Plastic radios**

group. Navajos played a particularly important role in fighting in the Pacific. Using their native language, Navajo "code talkers" transmitted vital military messages by radio. The Japanese thought the Navajo language was a secret code. They were never able to solve the mystery.

**The economy shifts to wartime production.** To provide needed war materials, American mines and factories speeded up operations. They hired millions of new workers, and wages quickly rose. Farm incomes also improved as prices for farm products increased. Wartime production quickly ended the Great Depression, and many New Deal relief programs came to an end.

New government agencies were set up to organize production for war. Auto companies stopped making cars and began to turn out tanks, trucks, and airplanes. Production of other consumer goods also halted. By 1942, American factories were making close

to 60,000 airplanes a year—10 times as many as in 1939. To make sure industrial output continued, the government controlled prices and wages. Many items such as meat, sugar, gasoline, and tires became scarce at home because they were needed in combat. The government controlled the use of these items by **rationing** —limiting the amount each person could buy.

**The work force expands.** With millions of men joining the armed services, many women took jobs in industry. In many cases they did jobs previously considered suitable only for men. Women operated cranes and welding torches. They worked in aircraft factories, steel mills, shipyards, and offices. In many defense factories, the majority of workers were women. About 6 million women took new jobs during the war.

The nation's critical need for workers was a factor in helping black Americans in the fight against discrimination. At the start

During World War II, millions of women (left) entered the work force, and posters (right) encouraged cooperation.

of the war, many jobs were not open to blacks. Black leaders told President Roosevelt that they would organize a protest march on Washington unless he acted to assure fair treatment. The President ordered defense factories to put an end to discrimination in their hiring practices. As a result, many black Americans were able to find new work opportunities.

## Relocation of Japanese Americans

Japanese Americans were not very well treated during World War II. Most of the Japanese Americans lived on the Pacific Coast of the United States. They had long been subjected to racial prejudice. This was partly because of the successes they had made in business and in farming.

**Distrust leads to relocation.** After the Japanese bombing of Pearl Harbor, many Americans feared that Japan might attack the West Coast of the United States. This fear led to suspicion that some Japanese Americans might be acting as spies and would assist the Japanese in another attack. As a result, a number of military leaders and others urged that Japanese Americans be moved inland away from the coast.

In 1942 President Roosevelt bowed to public pressure. He ordered the army to move about 115,000 Japanese Americans to "relocation centers." These relocation centers were really camps that had been set up mostly in desert locations. In the camps the Japanese Americans were required to live under guard and behind barbed wire. About 70,000 of the Japanese Americans who were forced to relocate were American citizens who had been born in the United States. The Japanese Americans were not allowed to leave the camps until late in the war, when an Allied victory was certain. Years later, the United States government agreed to

After the bombing of Pearl Harbor, some Americans questioned the loyalty of Japanese Americans living near the West Coast. As a result, many Japanese Americans were forced to relocate to camps inland. Many Japanese Americans lost their homes and businesses.

repay the Japanese Americans for the loss of their homes and property caused by the relocation. The payments, however, covered only a small part of what these Japanese Americans had lost.

**Japanese American soldiers serve with bravery.** In spite of unfair treatment, Japanese Americans made many valuable contributions to the war effort. At the beginning of the war, Japanese Americans were not accepted in the armed forces. In 1943, when this policy was changed, thousands signed up for military service. One Japanese-American unit became the most decorated combat group in the entire army. Its slogan, "Go for broke," became a popular American expression.

# 3 How did the United States gain victory in World War II?

At the time the United States entered the war, the outlook for the Allies was grim. Italy and Germany controlled most of Europe, and Japan was winning victories in Asia. The Allied forces had to settle on a plan for winning the war.

## Allied Strategy

The Allies decided that they must defeat Germany and Italy first, and then turn their attention to the war in the Pacific. After some early defeats, the plan was successful.

**The Philippines fall to Japan.** The decision to focus on Europe meant fewer troops and supplies in Asia. As a result, the United States suffered a severe blow in May 1942, when Japan took the Philippines. American and Filipino troops under General Douglas MacArthur fought bravely but were overpowered. "I shall return," MacArthur promised the Filipinos as American troops withdrew.

**The Allies face problems in Europe.** The situation in Europe in 1942 was desperate. German troops had taken Greece and Yugoslavia and were nearing Moscow in the Soviet Union. The Soviets fought back fiercely but were forced to retreat. To keep the Germans from getting supplies, the Soviets destroyed crops and equipment in front of the advancing German army. In the Atlantic, German submarines sank Allied ships faster than the Allies could build them.

**The Allies defeat the Germans in North Africa.** An important first step in the Allies' plan was to drive the Axis forces from North Africa. Late in 1942 British forces defeated the Germans at El Alamein in Egypt. The Germans, led by General Erwin Rommel, the "Desert Fox," were driven westward. At the same time, Americans under General Dwight D. Eisenhower landed in North Africa to the west of Rommel's troops. Caught between the British and the Americans, Rommel's army surrendered in May 1943.

**The Allies head north to Italy.** From North Africa, Allied forces crossed the Mediterranean to the Italian island of Sicily in July 1943. The Axis forces were driven from Sicily in a few weeks, and Allied troops then landed on the Italian mainland. (See map on page 676.) As the Allies advanced, the Italian people drove Mussolini from power, and set up a new government. This new government surrendered to the Allies. The Germans still controlled much of the country, however. The Allied conquest of Italy was a long and bitter struggle that lasted almost until the end of the war in Europe.

**The Soviets win a decisive battle.** In the Soviet Union the Germans also began to lose. Late in 1942 Soviet forces, aided by American Lend-Lease supplies, stopped the German attack at Stalingrad. The Soviets then counterattacked. After months of fierce fighting, the Germans surrendered. Hitler's army lost more than 250,000 soldiers in this important battle. After the victory at Stalingrad, Soviet troops began to drive the Germans out of Soviet territory.

## Victory in Europe

With the Soviets pushing back the Germans in eastern Europe, the Allies laid plans to open a second front in the west. In late 1943 Roosevelt and Churchill agreed to send troops across the English Channel to invade German-occupied France. General Eisenhower was appointed commander of the Allied forces.

Farthest extent of Axis occupation

Allied nations

Neutral nations

→ Allied advance

SCALE

0       400 mi

0       400 km

ICELAND

U.S. SUPPLY LINE TO SOVIET UNION

Murmansk

FINLAND

NORWAY

SWEDEN

ESTONIA

Leningrad

LATVIA

Moscow

LITH.

SOVIET UNION

IRELAND

NORTH SEA

DENMARK

BALTIC SEA

Volga R.

ATLANTIC OCEAN

GREAT BRITAIN

London

Berlin

1945

1943

English Channel

Dunkirk

BELG.

NETH.

1945

Warsaw

1944

Stalingrad

Normandy

1944

LUX.

GERMANY

POLAND

Don R.

Paris

1942-1943

FRANCE

Rhine R.

CZECHOSLOVAKIA

SWITZ.

AUSTRIA

1945

Budapest

1944

PORTUGAL

SPAIN

1944

HUNGARY

RUMANIA

1944

ITALY

YUGOSLAVIA

Danube R.

BLACK SEA

Rome

Anzio

Salerno

ALBANIA

BULGARIA

1942

MEDITERRANEAN SEA

GREECE

TURKEY

SICILY

1943

NORTH AFRICA

## Map Study

**Allied troops battled Axis forces in Africa and Europe. In what year
did the invasion of Sicily begin? In what year did Allied forces land
at Normandy? Soviet troops fought Axis forces in Poland. Near what
German city did the Western Allies and the Soviets meet?**

**The Allies prepare for the invasion.** To
weaken the German war machine, the Allies
bombed Germany. Day and night, the American and British bombers dropped tons of
bombs on German cities and large factories.
Thousands of tons of bombs were dropped

on Germany. The bombing did not stop Axis
production of weapons and supplies. It did,
however, weaken defenses against the coming Allied invasion. Meanwhile, the Allies
assembled almost 3 million troops for the
invasion. Plans had to be made to ferry these

On June 6, 1944—D-Day—British, Canadian, and American troops invaded Normandy, France. Within one month about 1 million Allied troops crossed the English Channel and had begun pushing Hitler's troops back toward Germany.

troops across the English Channel and to supply them with food, ammunition, and supplies. The Allies also took care to prevent the Germans from learning where the planned landing would take place. The Germans, meanwhile, fortified the French coast with barbed wire, ditches, mines, and machine guns.

**The Allies invade.** June 6, 1944—D-Day—was the day chosen for the Allied landing. In a fleet of 4,000 ships, Allied troops crossed the English Channel. They landed in Normandy on the northern coast of France.

Naval guns bombarded the coast, and planes provided air support as the soldiers scrambled ashore. Day after day, despite heavy losses on some beaches, the Allied invasion continued. Within a month, more than 1 million troops landed. By August 25 the Allies entered Paris, freeing the French capital from four years of Nazi rule.

**Germany surrenders.** After freeing Paris, the Allies turned east toward Germany. France and Belgium were nearly cleared of Axis troops by the end of September. On December 16 the Germans made a last desperate stand. In the **Battle of the Bulge,** they counterattacked against Allied troops. The attack created a bulge 60 miles (96 kilometers) deep in the Allied lines, but the Germans failed to break through. The Allies went back on the offensive.

By March 1945 they crossed the Rhine River, heading toward Berlin, the German capital, from the west. At the same time, Soviet troops neared Berlin from the East. On April 25, the two forces met south of the German capital. Hitler committed suicide five days later as Soviet troops entered Berlin. Within a week Germany surrendered, and the Allies joyfully celebrated **V-E Day—** the day of victory in Europe.

**Nazi death camps are discovered.** The joy of victory was tarnished by the news of Nazi **concentration camps** —prison camps. Earlier in the war the Allies had heard reports of these camps. Their full horror came to light as Allied troops marched into Germany and eastern Europe. At the camps, millions of Jews had been starved, tortured, and murdered. Soldiers sickened at the sight of gas chambers and ovens where the Nazis had carried out the mass killings known as the **Holocaust.** About 6 million Jews had been murdered. As many as 6 million others—gypsies, Poles, Slavs, political enemies of the Nazis, and handicapped people— also perished.

The discovery of the death camps led the Allies to put some Nazi leaders on trial. In the **Nuremberg Trials,** thousands of Nazis were found guilty of war crimes. Death sentences were passed against 12 Nazi leaders, and many others received long prison terms.

## The War in the Pacific

In the Pacific, the task of defeating Japan fell mainly to the United States. While the Allies concentrated on Europe, Japan had taken over most of the western Pacific. (See map on page 679.) Slowly, however, the tide turned in favor of the Americans. In 1942 the American navy won two important military victories that stopped Japanese advances. The Battle of the Coral Sea blocked an invasion of Australia, and the Battle of Midway saved Hawaii.

**Americans capture Pacific Islands.** After the Battle of Midway, American troops pushed toward Japan, using Pacific islands

**When news of Germany's surrender reached the United States, happy crowds of people celebrated in the streets.**

678

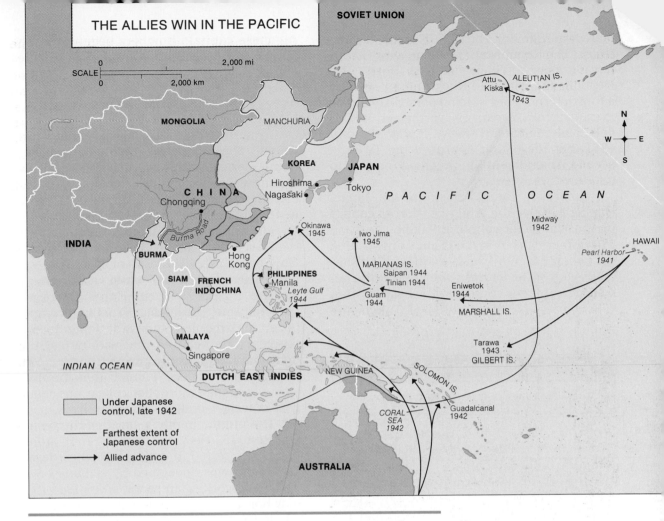

THE ALLIES WIN IN THE PACIFIC

SCALE
0        2,000 mi
0        2,000 km

SOVIET UNION

MONGOLIA        MANCHURIA

KOREA        JAPAN

Hiroshima        Tokyo
Nagasaki

CHINA
Chongqing

PACIFIC        OCEAN

ALEUTIAN IS.
Attu
Kiska
1943

Midway
1942

INDIA

Burma Road

BURMA

Okinawa
1945

Iwo Jima
1945

Pearl Harbor
1941

HAWAII

Hong
Kong

PHILIPPINES
Manila
Leyte Gulf
1944

MARIANAS IS.
Saipan 1944
Tinian 1944

Eniwetok
1944

SIAM        FRENCH
INDOCHINA

Guam
1944

MARSHALL IS.

MALAYA

Singapore

INDIAN OCEAN

DUTCH EAST INDIES

NEW GUINEA

Tarawa
1943
GILBERT IS.

SOLOMON IS

Under Japanese
control, late 1942

Farthest extent of
Japanese control

Allied advance

CORAL
SEA
1942

Guadalcanal
1942

AUSTRALIA

## Map Study

**Japan controlled a vast area of the Pacific. Allied forces moved closer to Japan by island-hopping across the Pacific. What battle brought the Allies closest to Japan? In what year did the Allies regain the Philippines?**

as steppingstones. The Americans were able to seize some Japanese-held islands and leapfrogged others. This strategy was known as **island hopping.** Many island landings were among the most deadly battles of the war. After navy ships shelled an island, marines and soldiers waded ashore, often under heavy fire.

An early victory in the island-hopping campaign came at Guadalcanal north of Australia in 1942. By 1944, American troops under General MacArthur returned to the Philippines. In a few months they controlled

the islands. One of the greatest naval battles in history took place in the Gulf of Leyte (LAY-tay) in October 1944. At Leyte the Japanese lost a large part of their fleet, and Japan's sea power was crushed.

**Roosevelt wins a fourth term.** In autumn 1944 Americans divided their attention between war news and the upcoming presidential election. Roosevelt was tired and suffering from ill health. He wanted to retire. Yet his duty, he said, was to run for a fourth term and avoid a change in leadership during wartime. President Roosevelt's running mate was Senator Harry S Truman of Missouri. The Republican candidate was Governor Thomas E. Dewey of New York. The Republicans criticized Roosevelt for seeking a fourth term. They said no person should be President for 16 years. Nevertheless, Roosevelt easily defeated Dewey. It was not until 1951 that the nation approved the **Twenty-second Amendment** limiting the President to two terms in office.

**American forces close in on Japan.** During the election American forces continued to win victories in the Pacific. Early in 1945 Americans took the islands of Iwo Jima (EE-wo JEE-muh) and Okinawa (o-kuh-NAH-wuh). The battles were very costly, but American planes could now be based within 750 miles (1,170 kilometers) of Tokyo, the

---

## LINKING PAST AND PRESENT

### ★★★ *Nuclear Energy*

In the early 1900's Albert Einstein, a German scientist, showed that atoms contain huge amounts of energy. The energy in an atom can be released by splitting its center, or **nucleus.**

In 1939 Einstein wrote to President Franklin Roosevelt. He explained that the nuclear energy released by splitting atoms could make an enormously powerful bomb. Einstein's letter persuaded Roosevelt to fund the secret **Manhattan Project** that developed the atomic bombs used at the end of World War II.

After World War II scientists looked for peaceful ways to use nuclear energy. In 1954 the first nuclear-powered ship—the submarine *Nautilus*—was launched. The first nuclear power plant opened three years later. Today nuclear power provides about 16 percent of the nation's energy. Many Americans are concerned, however, about the safety of nuclear power plants. In 1986 an accident at a nuclear plant in the Soviet Union heightened these concerns.

---

Japanese capital. Bombers began to attack Tokyo and other important Japanese cities almost daily.

## Atomic Warfare

In spring 1945 Japan was clearly near defeat. The Japanese people were starving, and American ships were bombarding the Japanese coast. Japan's leaders, however, considered surrender a disgrace and continued to fight. Their refusal to give up led to one of history's most fateful decisions.

**Harry S Truman becomes President.** On April 12, 1945, President Roosevelt suffered a stroke and died while vacationing in Georgia. Vice President Harry S Truman then became President. Truman promptly began making plans to invade Japan later in the year. He believed that without such an invasion Japan would not surrender. Military experts advised Truman that the invasion would take more than a year and would cost at least 1 million American lives.

**The atomic bomb is successfully tested.** On June 16, 1945, the world's first atomic bomb was tested in the New Mexico desert. The bomb was developed by scientists who had been working in secret since 1943. The new bomb was powerful enough to destroy a whole city.

The news of the successful test reached Truman in Potsdam, outside Berlin. The President was meeting there with Churchill and Stalin. On July 26 the Allied leaders warned Japan to surrender or face "prompt and utter destruction." The Japanese did not know about the atomic bomb and ignored the warning. Some scientists advised Truman not to use the fearful new weapon. Truman, however, decided that the bomb should be used if it would bring the war to an end and save American lives.

**Japan surrenders.** On August 6, 1945, an American bomber dropped a single atomic bomb on Hiroshima, Japan. The bomb wiped out almost the entire city and killed at least 70,000 people. The Soviet Union declared war on Japan two days later. When the Japanese still did not surrender, the United States dropped a second bomb on

Nagasaki. This time 40,000 people were killed. Many more in both cities later died from exposure to radiation. On August 14 the emperor of Japan ordered the country's military leaders to surrender. The formal surrender was signed two weeks later aboard the battleship *Missouri* in Tokyo Bay.

**Americans celebrate the end of the war.** In the United States, Americans rejoiced at the news that the war was over. Some offered prayers of thanksgiving. Others celebrated in the streets with victory parades, music, and honking horns. In spite of the celebrations, however, the war's cost had been staggering. The United States alone had lost about 405,000 people in the armed forces. The nation had also spent about $320 billion on the war. Around the world, World War II had cost about 60 million casualties, and much of Europe and Asia lay in ruins.

For Americans, the war produced another burden. America was the war's great victor and the only country to possess atomic weapons. Clearly, the United States was now the world's leading nation. Americans were to discover that world leadership was a difficult and troublesome job.

## SECTION REVIEW

1. **Vocabulary**   concentration camp, island hopping
2. **People and Places**   Douglas MacArthur, Erwin Rommel, Dwight D. Eisenhower, Sicily, Stalingrad, Normandy, Harry S Truman, Iwo Jima, Okinawa, Hiroshima, Nagasaki
3. **Comprehension**   What were the major steps in the Allied victory in Europe?
4. **Comprehension**   How did island hopping contribute to the defeat of Japan?
5. **Critical Thinking**   Do you think the American decision to use the atomic bomb in Japan was a good decision? Why?

# Chapter 29 Summary

During the Great Depression, Benito Mussolini and Adolf Hilter set up totalitarian governments in Italy and Germany. They took away democratic freedoms and threatened neighboring countries. Meanwhile, Japan invaded China and established the state of Manchukuo. The United States followed isolationist policies toward the fascist dictatorships, but improved Latin American relations with the Good Neighbor Policy. After setting up the Axis alliance Hitler took over Austria and Czechoslovakia. World War II began when the Nazis invaded Poland in 1939.

The Germans overran Europe in a blitzkrieg, but Allied troops escaped at Dunkirk. Hitler then bombed Britain and invaded the Soviet Union. The United States supported Britain through the Lend-Lease Act and the Atlantic Charter. After the Japa-nese attack at Pearl Harbor the United States declared war. The Depression ended as American industry expanded to meet wartime production needs. Job opportunities improved for women and minorities, but about 115,000 Japanese Americans were forcibly moved to relocation centers.

The Allies defeated the Germans in North Africa and then invaded Italy. After the Soviet victory at Stalingrad, the Allies landed in Normandy on D-Day. The Germans lost the Battle of the Bulge and then surrendered when Allied troops reached Berlin. The horror of the Holocaust led to the Nuremberg Trials. In the Pacific, island hopping brought American troops close to Japan. After President Roosevelt died, President Truman decided to use the atomic bomb on Japan. After bombs destroyed Hiroshima and Nagaski, Japan surrendered.

# CRITICAL THINKING: Making Decisions

In this chapter, you read about the role of the United States in World War II. Many decisions directed America's actions in the war. These decisions were not made suddenly or haphazardly. The President and his advisers established goals. Then they carefully reviewed the alternatives for meeting those goals. They weighed the advantages and disadvantages of each alternative, and then decided which course of action to follow. This process of considering and evaluating alternative courses of action is called decision making.

Effective decision making involves a series of steps or questions. Some of these questions are listed here.

*1. Is a decision necessary?* Before you begin the decision-making process, ask yourself if a decision is needed. Consider what would happen if no decision were made. No decision can be a good course of action.

*2. What goals do you hope to achieve by this decision?* Setting goals at the outset helps evaluate the alternatives later.

*3. What alternatives are available?* List your possible courses of action. Then collect information on the advantages and disadvantages of each alternative.

*4. Which alternative will bring you closest to your goals?* Compare your alternatives with the goals set earlier. Choose the alternative that best matches these goals.

*5. How can the decision be improved?* Consider the disadvantages of your choice of action. Make adjustments to reduce or to avoid the weaknesses of this alternative.

This process can help you to make effective decisions. It also can be used as a tool for evaluating decisions made by other people, both in the present and the past.

In the summer of 1945, President Truman struggled with the problem of ending the war against Japan. He had several possible courses of action to follow. These alternatives are listed in the chart. Study the chart, and then answer the following questions.

**President Truman's Decision to End the War**

| Alternatives | Effects |
|---|---|
| A. Drop the atomic bomb | • Quick end to the war<br>• Massive destruction<br>• Heavy Japanese civilian casualties<br>• Limited American casualties |
| B. Demonstrate the atomic bomb as a threat | • Japanese generals may ignore it<br>• War prolonged<br>• Avoid destruction and civilian casualties<br>• Possible heavy American casualties |
| C. Invade Japan | • War prolonged<br>• Heavy American casualties<br>• Avoid destruction and civilian casualties |

1. In your opinion, what did President Truman want to achieve by this decision?
2. What alternatives did Truman consider?
3. Which of the effects of Alternative A would be disadvantages?
4. Look at the effects of Alternative B. Which of these would be advantages?
5. For Alternative C, which effects are disadvantages?
6. What other courses of action might have been open to President Truman?
7. If you were in the President's position, what alternative would you choose? Follow the decision-making guidelines to explain your answer.

# CAUSES and EFFECTS

## The Great Depression ★ ★ ★

Government has "hands-off" policy toward business

Spending power increases

Americans expect endless prosperity

Many Americans do not share in growing wealth

**CONTRIBUTING CAUSES**

Americans speculate on the stock market

Stock market crashes

Industry slows down

Panic causes banks to fail

Unemployment rises and spending power falls

**MAIN CAUSES**

**GREAT DEPRESSION**

**EFFECTS**

Americans face widespread hunger, poverty, and unemployment

Worldwide depression occurs

Roosevelt starts the New Deal

Work-relief and social security programs begin

**LONG-TERM EFFECTS**

Government takes active role in economy

Social-welfare programs develop

Labor unions gain more power

Dictators take power in Europe

# Chapter 29 REVIEW

## Vocabulary and Key Terms

Use the following terms to complete the sentences below. Write your answers on a separate sheet of paper.

| | |
|---|---|
| Holocaust | D-Day |
| Nazi | totalitarian |
| Axis Powers | *blitzkrieg* |
| rationing | V-E Day |
| appeasement | Allied |
| dictator | Fascist |

1. In a _____ government, a single authority controls the nation.
2. While Hitler organized the _____ party in Germany, Mussolini was leading the _____ party in Italy.
3. Germany, Italy, and Japan formed an alliance known as the _____.
4. The British and French policy of _____ did not stop Hitler from launching a fierce _____ against Poland.
5. During the war, the United States government used _____ to limit the use of scarce goods and resources.
6. The _____ invasion of France began on _____.
7. Millions of Jews were murdered in the _____, or mass killings ordered by the Nazi _____ Adolf Hitler.
8. _____ ended the war in Europe.

## Recalling the Facts

1. What dictators came to power in Italy and Germany after World War I?
2. Why did the United States pass the Neutrality Act in 1935?
3. How did Germany's actions in Austria, Czechoslovakia, and Poland lead to war?
4. What was the Lend-Lease Act?
5. What event caused the United States to enter World War II?
6. Why was D-Day important to Allied strategy?
7. What was island-hopping?
8. What caused Japan to surrender?

## Places to Locate

Match the letters on the map with the places listed below. Write your answers on a separate sheet of paper.

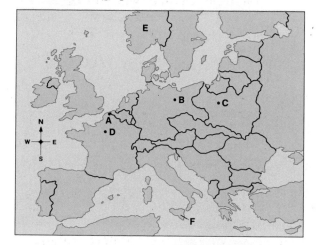

| | |
|---|---|
| 1. Paris | 4. Norway |
| 2. Berlin | 5. Sicily |
| 3. Warsaw | 6. Dunkirk |

## Critical Thinking

1. Was neutrality a reasonable policy for the United States to follow in the 1930's? Consider the following points in your answer:
   a. Americans' view of World War I
   b. The effect of the Depression on the United States and other nations
   c. The aggressive actions of the German and Italian governments
2. The decision to use the atomic bomb against Japan is considered to be one of the most important decisions in American history. Was it the best action for the nation to take? Consider these questions in your answer:

a. Why did the United States decide to use the atomic bomb?

b. What were the effects of using the atomic bomb?

c. Were there alternatives to using the atomic bomb?

## Understanding History

1. Reread the section "The Germans bomb Britain" on page 668. Then answer these questions.
   a. **Geography.** How did Britain's location affect German war strategy?
   b. **Science and Technology.** What helped the British survive German air attacks?
2. Reread the section "Distrust leads to relocation" on page 673. Then answer these questions.
   a. **Citizenship.** Why did many Americans feel suspicious of Japanese Americans?
   b. **Citizenship.** How did relocation violate Japanese Americans' rights?
3. Reread the section "Americans celebrate the end of the war" on page 681. Then answer these questions.
   a. **Geography.** How did the location of the United States help limit the war damage it sustained?
   b. **Science and Technology.** How did technology help to make the United States the world's leading nation at the end of World War II?

## Projects and Activities

1. **Conducting an Interview.** Interview someone who took part in World War II, either as a member of the armed forces or as a citizen who helped in the war effort at home. Discuss your findings with the class.
2. **Writing a News Story.** Imagine that you are a reporter during World War II. Write a news story on an aspect of the war that you feel is especially important. Make sure your story answers these questions: Who? What? When? Where? Why?
3. **Review Information.** Make flash cards to quiz classmates on the vocabulary words and key terms in the chapter.
4. **Creating an Advertisement.** Imagine that you are living during World War II and that your job is to persuade other Americans to conserve a resource such as gasoline, sugar, meat, or tires. Create an advertisement explaining that the resource is needed for the war effort. Appeal to people's patriotism and loyalty.

## Practicing Your Skill

A key decision in World War II was to invade Italy in 1943. This decision was reached by Winston Churchill and Franklin D. Roosevelt. Before reaching their decision, they considered the alternatives and the possible effects of each alternative. Study the chart and then answer the questions that follow.

### The Decision to Invade Italy

| Alternatives | Effects |
| --- | --- |
| A. Do not invade in 1943 | • Axis power would grow<br>• Germans would continue attacks on Great Britain and Soviet Union<br>• Allied forces would have more time to prepare for a later invasion |
| B. Invade Italy in 1943 | • Axis troops would have to fight on another front<br>• An Allied victory would give the Allies a foothold in Europe |
| C. Invade Germany in 1943 | • Direct attack on Axis forces<br>• Almost impossible to gain a foothold in Germany<br>• Heavy Allied casualties |

1. In your opinion, what did the Allied leaders hope to gain by their decision?
2. Look at the effects of Alternative A. Which of these would be an advantage?
3. Look at the effects of Alternative C. Which of these would be disadvantages?
4. Given the three alternatives listed in this chart, what recommendations would you have given to the Allied leaders? Why?

# UNIT 9 REVIEW

## Unit Summary

★ **The prosperous 1920's gave way to the Great Depression.**

- President Harding encouraged economic and business growth.
- Industrial growth, higher wages, and new career opportunities created an economic boom.
- Increased automobile use caused widespread economic and social changes.
- Music, literature, and fashion reflected the Jazz Age lifestyles.
- The 1929 stock market crash started the Great Depression.
- President Hoover's policies were unable to relieve widespread unemployment and poverty.
- Franklin D. Roosevelt's election brought hope to many Americans.

★ **The New Deal sought to help Americans and to end the Depression.**

- Government programs offered jobs to the unemployed and loans to farmers and homeowners.
- The New Deal helped Americans but did not end the Depression.
- Roosevelt's policies had long-range governmental effects.

★ **The United States fought in World War II from 1941 to 1945.**

- After the Japanese attacked Pearl Harbor, the United States joined the Allied Powers.
- American forces helped to bring Allied victory in Europe.
- The atomic bomb was dropped on Japan in 1945, ending the war.

## Understanding Chronology

Study the Unit 9 time line on page 615. Then answer the following questions on a separate sheet of paper.

1. Imagine that you were born in 1915. How old would you have been when the Great Depression began? When the United States entered World War II?
2. How would these major events have affected your life?
3. How would these events have affected you differently if you had been born in 1900 or 1930 rather than in 1915?

## Writing About History

1. **Finding Cause and Effect.** Use your textbook to review the economic, social, and political changes in the nation after World War I. Write a paragraph summarizing the changes and then write a second paragraph explaining how these changes affected the American people.
2. **Identifying Heroes.** Choose several individuals who might have been considered heroes in the 1920's, the 1930's, or the 1940's. The people may have been politicians, sports figures, members of the armed forces, movie stars, or others. Write a brief description of each person's achievements. Then summarize the qualities that made these individuals heroes of their time.
3. **Preparing Interviews.** Interview relatives or neighbors who lived during the Great Depression and World War II. Ask those interviewed to tell you when they were born, where they lived, and what they remember about that time. Tape record the interviews or take careful notes. Then use the interviews to write a report summarizing the first-person accounts of the 1930's and the 1940's.

4. **Interpreting a Cartoon.** The cartoon above shows Uncle Sam being tied down by the New Deal agencies. What story in literature was used as the basis of this cartoon? What point of view does the cartoon express about the New Deal? Using the same symbols in the cartoon above, draw another cartoon to express the opposite point of view.

## Projects

1. **Advertising Products.** Create advertisements for products that changed American life after World War I. Include a description of each product, why it is useful, and how it will improve the consumer's life. Draw examples or find pictures to illustrate the product. Display your advertisements in class.

2. **Comparing Periods of History.** Work in groups to present a comparison of the 1920's Jazz Age with the 1930's Great Depression. Research the social, political, economic, and cultural trends of the periods and then compare the two decades. Presentations might consist of plays, interviews, posters, or pictures.

3. **Making Military Maps.** Make a map showing the strategies and the troop movements for one of the World War II military campaigns. Then write a brief summary of the battle and the results of the campaign.

4. **Analyzing Popular Culture.** Work in groups to present a 1930's radio broadcast. Listen to recordings of radio shows and news broadcasts from that period to get information about the shows and performers. Create a 1930's radio broadcast including a news report, sports information, and a drama or skit. Draw conclusions about the impact of radio on American life in the 1930's.

5. **Debating Issues.** Work in teams to stage a debate between those who supported Roosevelt's New Deal and those who opposed it. Debate the purposes, the successes, and the failures of Roosevelt's policies, basing your arguments on the immediate and long-term effects of the New Deal. Arguments should represent the viewpoints of Americans today and those who lived in the 1930's.

## Finding Out More

Davis, Daniel S. *Behind Barbed Wire: The Imprisonment of Japanese Americans During World War II.* Dutton, 1982. This account traces the World War II internment of Japanese Americans to earlier discrimination and explores the consequences for those confined.

Frank, Anne. *Anne Frank: The Diary of a Young Girl.* Doubleday, 1967. Anne, a 13-year-old Jewish girl in Nazi Germany, recorded what she experienced and how she felt about hiding from the Nazis with her family and others.

Jacobs, William J. *Eleanor Roosevelt: A Life of Happiness and Tears.* Putnam, 1983. This is a well-rounded portrait of an outstanding First Lady.

Lawson, Don. *An Album of World War II Home Fronts.* Watts, 1980. This story tells of civilian activities in many countries during World War II.

Lawson, Don. *FDR's New Deal.* Harper, 1979. This is a well-written account of a difficult time in history.

Olsen, Violet. *The Growing Season.* Atheneum, 1982. The difficulties of growing up on an Iowa farm during the Depression are told by a young girl.

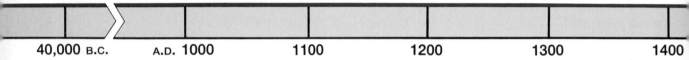

40,000 B.C.          A.D. 1000          1100          1200          1300          1400

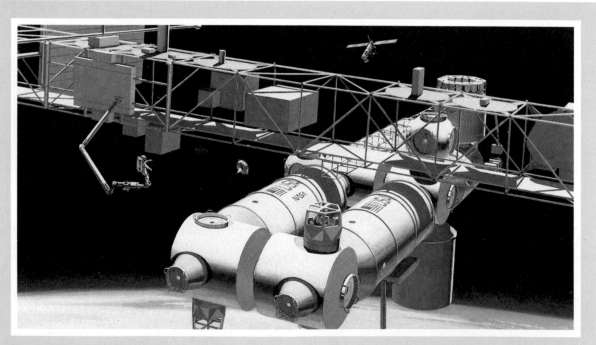

The United States maintains its leadership role on earth and in space, as this model of a planned 1990's space station shows.

1945 –

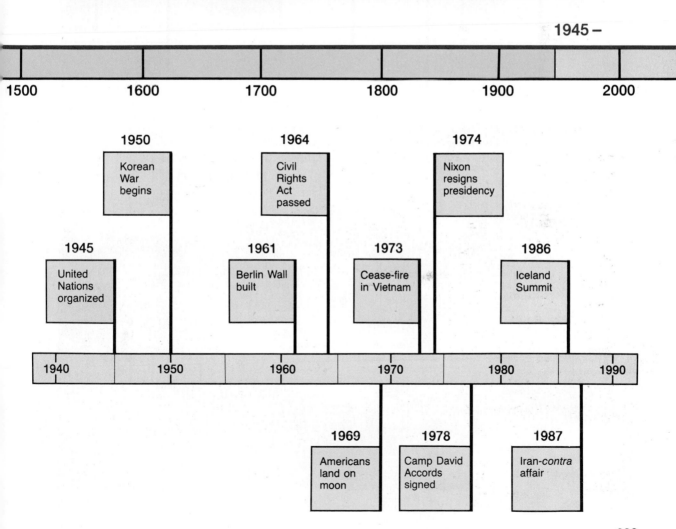

| 1500 | 1600 | 1700 | 1800 | 1900 | 2000 |

**1950**
Korean War begins

**1964**
Civil Rights Act passed

**1974**
Nixon resigns presidency

**1945**
United Nations organized

**1961**
Berlin Wall built

**1973**
Cease-fire in Vietnam

**1986**
Iceland Summit

| 1940 | 1950 | 1960 | 1970 | 1980 | 1990 |

**1969**
Americans land on moon

**1978**
Camp David Accords signed

**1987**
Iran-*contra* affair

# 30 The Cold War Shapes Postwar Life
## 1945–1960

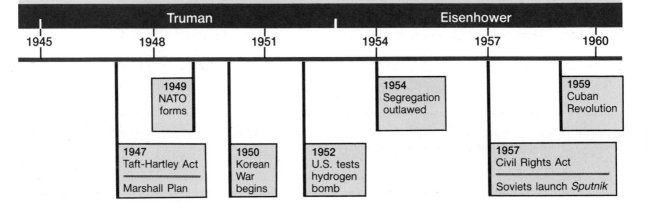

Truman | Eisenhower

1945     1948     1951     1954     1957     1960

**1949** NATO forms

**1954** Segregation outlawed

**1959** Cuban Revolution

**1947** Taft-Hartley Act

Marshall Plan

**1950** Korean War begins

**1952** U.S. tests hydrogen bomb

**1957** Civil Rights Act

Soviets launch *Sputnik*

**The building of new suburban communities—often with very similar homes—was a key social development of the 1950's.**

## Preparing to Read

The end of World War II did not bring the true and lasting peace that Americans longed for. Instead, the United States entered a period of steady tension with the Soviet Union and other Communist countries. As the leader of the world's democracies, the United States tried to keep communism from spreading in Europe, Asia, and Latin America. The tension led to war in Korea and military clashes in other parts of the world. At home, though, the 1950's were a time of great prosperity. They were also years of progress for black Americans, as they battled against discrimination and fought to gain more rights. As you read this chapter, try to answer the following questions:

1. How did the cold war shape American foreign policy?
2. How did the war in Korea affect the United States?
3. What problems did Americans face at home after World War II?
4. How did President Eisenhower meet the challenges of the 1950's?

## 1 How did the cold war shape American foreign policy?

### Vocabulary

| | |
|---|---|
| cold war | iron curtain |
| satellite | containment |

As World War II ended, the United States and other nations made plans for an era of peace and cooperation. These hopes were broken, however, as the Soviet Union sought to spread communism in Europe and elsewhere. Americans soon found themselves facing the Soviets in a **cold war** —an uneasy peace marked by constant tension.

### Hopes for Peace

Even before the end of World War II, world leaders laid plans for keeping peace in the postwar world. The most important plan was to build a new organization that would help countries settle their differences.

**The United Nations is organized.** In 1943 leaders of the United States, the Soviet Union, Great Britain, and China decided to form a new world organization to help keep peace after the war. In April 1945, representatives from 50 countries gathered in San Francisco to draw up the plans for the **United Nations** (UN). Two months later, they had finished writing the UN charter.

The charter set up several groups to carry out the work of the United Nations. The chief groups are the General Assembly, the Secretariat, and the Security Council. The Security Council is the UN's most powerful group. Its purpose is to keep the world at peace.

The Security Council is made up of 5 permanent members and 10 other members chosen for two-year terms. The permanent members of the Security Council are the United States, Great Britain, the Soviet Union, France, and China. If all 5 members agree, the UN may act, by force if necessary, to settle disputes between countries. Each of the permanent members, however, can veto any action of the Security Council. This veto power often limits the effectiveness of the United Nations.

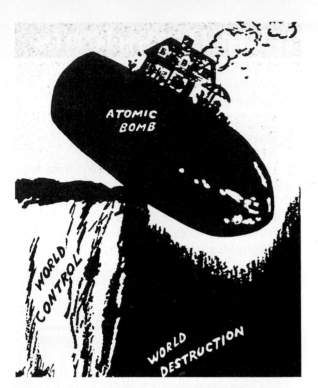

Rube Goldberg's 1947 cartoon pointed to the dangers of atomic weapons. According to Goldberg, what two choices does the world have in the atomic age?

**The Yalta Conference produces plans for the future.** In February 1945, Allied leaders met at Yalta, in the southern Soviet Union. There they talked over plans for the postwar world. Roosevelt, Churchill, and Stalin agreed to divide Germany into four zones. They also decided to divide the city of Berlin the same way. These areas would be controlled by the Americans, the British, the French, and the Soviets.

The leaders at Yalta worked out another plan for the countries of Eastern Europe. Though the Soviets controlled most of these countries, Stalin promised to allow free elections there.

## Communist Expansionism

It soon became clear that the Soviet Union would aggressively seek to build its power and influence in the world. The United States took steps to keep communism in check.

**Communist influence spreads farther.** Americans became uneasy about the Soviets soon after World War II ended. Soviet troops refused to leave the countries that they had occupied in Eastern Europe. The promise of free elections was forgotten. These Eastern European countries became satellites of the Soviet Union. A satellite is a country that is dominated politically by another country.

Under Soviet control, the people of Eastern Europe lost their freedom and the right to govern themselves. They could no longer exchange goods and ideas with Western Europe. Harsh punishments made people afraid to speak out against Soviet control. The Soviets had isolated the Eastern European countries behind an iron curtain —an invisible barrier that divided Eastern and Western Europe.

The Communists also hoped to spread their influence beyond Eastern Europe. In 1947 Communist rebels, aided by Soviet satellite nations, tried to overthrow the Greek government. American leaders feared that if Greece turned Communist, other Mediterranean countries might do the same. Turkey, for example, was already facing a Communist threat. At the same time, the Communist party was growing strong in Italy.

**The United States aids free countries.** To combat Soviet influence in the world, President Harry Truman favored a policy of containment —keeping communism from spreading beyond the Soviet satellite nations. He and his advisers knew that poor and hungry people were more likely than others to choose communism. They decided, therefore, to send aid to the war-weary countries of Western Europe.

President Truman proposed a $400-million aid package for Greece and Turkey early in 1947. Much of this money was for weapons to defend against the Communists who threatened those countries. At the same time, the President introduced what became known as the **Truman Doctrine.** This doctrine stated that the United States would support free people who were being attacked by small groups from within or large armies from outside countries. Clearly, the Truman Doctrine was aimed at Communists and the Soviet Union.

Another program was proposed by George Marshall, Truman's Secretary of State. The goal of the **Marshall Plan** was to rebuild the European economies that were severely weakened by World War II. The plan even offered aid to the Soviet Union. In a speech on June 5, 1947, Marshall outlined the plan to the public:

> Our policy is directed not against any country or doctrine, but against hunger [and] poverty.... Its purpose should be the revival of a working economy ... so ... free institutions can exist.

Most European leaders applauded the Marshall Plan. The Soviet Union, however, refused to participate.

The Marshall Plan was a great success. By 1949 voters in Italy and France had rejected Communist candidates. The economies of all the Western European nations were improving. In addition, the countries of Western Europe now enjoyed a new spirit of cooperation.

**The policy of containment is put to the test in Berlin.** Berlin was located deep within the Soviet zone of divided Germany. On June 24, 1948, the Soviets blockaded the city. They closed all land and water routes linking Berlin to the zones held by the United States, Britain, and France. The Soviets did this to force the Western Allies out of the city.

To counter the blockade, President Truman ordered the **Berlin airlift.** The Allies sent planes carrying food, clothing, medicine, and even coal to the Western sections of the city. The airlift lasted 321 days, until Stalin reopened the routes to Berlin. To this day, West Berlin is independent of Soviet-controlled East Germany.

**Communists rise to power in China.** The United States' policy of containment could not stop communism from spreading to China. Since 1927, Communist rebels had been fighting the Nationalist Chinese government. After World War II the struggle became more intense.

The Nationalist Chinese, led by Chiang Kai-shek (chang ky-shek), were supported by the United States. The United States sent the Nationalists more than $3 billion in aid between 1945 and 1949. Chiang's government, however, was thought to be corrupt and wasteful. The Communist rebels, led by Mao Zedong (mow zuh-DUNG), were supported by the Soviet Union. The Communists also had the backing of most of the Chinese people.

Slowly, Mao's army won more and more territory. By the middle of 1949, the rebels controlled the entire Chinese mainland. In October, Mao set up the People's Republic of China. The Nationalists fled to Taiwan, an island off the mainland. The largest country in Asia was now Communist.

EUROPE AFTER WORLD WAR II

FINLAND

NORWAY

SWEDEN

NORTH SEA

Moscow •

IRELAND

GREAT BRITAIN

DENMARK

• London

NETH.

• Berlin

SOVIET UNION

ATLANTIC OCEAN

BELG.

E. GERMANY

POLAND

W. GERMANY

Paris • LUX.

CZECHOSLOVAKIA

CASPIAN SEA

FRANCE

SWITZ.

AUSTRIA

HUNGARY

RUMANIA

YUGOSLAVIA

BLACK SEA

PORTUGAL

SPAIN

ITALY

Rome •

BULGARIA

ALBANIA

TURKEY

MEDITERRANEAN SEA

GREECE

SCALE

0        400 mi

0      400 km

## Map Study

After World War II the Soviets seized control of Eastern Europe. To halt Communist influence, the United States and Western European nations formed the NATO alliance. **What NATO countries border Bulgaria? What Soviet satellites border West Germany?**

## Forging New Alliances

Ill feelings continued to grow between Communist and Western leaders. President Truman and his advisers decided to strengthen ties with old allies.

**NATO is formed.** In 1949 the United States, Canada, and 10 European countries agreed to form the **North Atlantic Treaty Organization** (NATO). (See map on this page.) Four more countries joined later. The NATO members declared their support for the United Nations and their desire to settle all disputes peacefully. They agreed, though, that an attack on any member would be jointly fought by all.

**The Warsaw Pact is signed.** In response to NATO, the Communist countries of Europe formed their own organization. The **Warsaw Pact** of 1955 put eight Communist countries under the same military command. The pact ensured that if one country was attacked, all members would defend it.

## SECTION REVIEW

1. **Vocabulary**    cold war, satellite, iron curtain, containment
2. **People and Places**    Yalta, Stalin, Berlin, Harry Truman, Greece, Turkey, China, Chiang Kai-shek, Mao Zedong
3. **Comprehension**    How did the Marshall Plan help contain communism?
4. **Comprehension**    How are the the NATO treaty and the Warsaw Pact similar?
5. **Critical Thinking**    Should the United States have given more aid to Nationalist China? Why or why not?

## Vocabulary

evacuate

stalemate

demilitarized zone

In Asia as in Europe, American foreign policy focused on the struggle to contain communism. Korea was divided into Communist and non-Communist sectors, and conflict between the two systems of government led to war. Similar tensions also arose in another divided Asian country, Vietnam.

## Conflict in Korea

After World War II the Soviet Union occupied the northern part of Korea. The United States held southern Korea. The dividing line between the north and the south was the 38th parallel. Talks aimed at reuniting the two Koreas lasted for two years, but no agreement was reached. Meanwhile, United States officials helped establish a non-Communist government in South Korea. The Soviets organized a Communist government in North Korea.

**The conflict begins.** On June 25, 1950, the North Koreans began an invasion of South Korea. The invading troops pushed steadily southward and soon took over Seoul (sohl), the capital of South Korea. (See map on page 696.) South Korean troops tried to make a stand at the Han River, south of Seoul. The South Korean army, however, was very weak.

**The United Nations gives help to South Korea.** When the invasion began, President Truman asked the United Nations Security Council to take action. The UN demanded that the North Koreans withdraw their forces. The UN also voted to send troops to help South Korea.

At the time, the representative of the Soviet Union was not sitting with the council. The Soviets were boycotting the UN because its members refused to admit the People's Republic of China. As a result, the Soviets could not veto the Security Council's decision.

**American troops arrive in Korea.** President Truman quickly ordered American soldiers to South Korea. He placed General Douglas MacArthur in command. Truman also told MacArthur to help **evacuate** —get out—any Americans in Korea. The United States Congress backed Truman's actions. Congress did not, however, make a formal declaration of war against North Korea. American soldiers made up most of the UN force in Korea. With UN approval, General MacArthur became commander of all the UN troops.

**The North Koreans continue to advance.** At first, the UN troops had trouble stopping the North Korean advance. The North Koreans greatly outnumbered UN forces, sometimes by as much as eight to one. Most of the American soldiers had never been in battle. In addition, their World War II weapons were no match for the Soviet-built tanks used by the North Koreans.

The North Koreans forced the UN and South Korean troops to retreat. Finally, General MacArthur's troops held only a small area around Pusan, a port at the southern end of the Korean peninsula.

**UN forces strike back.** From Pusan, MacArthur launched a surprise attack against the North Koreans. On September 15, 1950, UN forces landed by sea at Inchon. This city lay on the west coast just below the 38th parallel. From Inchon, UN troops fought their way east, cutting off North Korean troops to the south from their source of supplies. Before long, UN forces had recaptured Seoul.

THE KOREAN WAR

CHINA

Yalu River

Farthest advance
of UN forces,
November 1950

NORTH KOREA

◉ Pyongyang

SEA OF JAPAN

Truce line, July 1953

38th parallel

Panmunjom
Inchon    ◉ Seoul

UN attack,
Sept. 1950

YELLOW SEA

SOUTH KOREA

Farthest advance of
North Korean forces,
July 1950

● Pusan

N
W ◆ E
S

SOVIET
UNION

JAPAN

SCALE
0 ————————— 200 mi
0 ————————— 200 km

## Map Study

**United Nations forces helped South Korean troops fight against North Korean invaders. What city lay south of the farthest North Korean advance? What city did UN forces attack in September 1950? What country lay north of the Yalu River?**

**MacArthur tries to take the offensive.** Following their success at Inchon, General MacArthur and his troops drove the enemy back across the 38th parallel. MacArthur then wanted to pursue them into North

Korea. President Truman feared that an invasion of North Korea would widen the war. He thought the Communist Chinese might join North Korea to protect their common border. MacArthur argued that even if the Chinese came into the war, UN forces would be able to win. President Truman finally agreed. With the support of the UN General Assembly, Truman ordered General MacArthur to cross into North Korea.

**China enters the war.** UN soldiers pushed their way north toward the Yalu River, the border between North Korea and China. The Chinese Communists warned UN forces to stop, but the warning was ignored. When UN troops kept marching ahead, thousands of Chinese soldiers crossed the Yalu. They joined other Chinese who had been hiding in the mountains of North Korea. The Chinese began to push the outnumbered UN forces south.

## Ending the Conflict

General MacArthur wanted to blockade the Chinese coast and bomb the Chinese side of the Yalu River. Truman and his advisors, however, did not agree with MacArthur's plan. They believed that war with China would sap the resources of the United States. Truman's advisers also believed that the real enemy in the conflict was the Soviet Union, not China.

**President Truman fires MacArthur.** Many Americans opposed expansion of the war in Korea. They feared that war with China would lead to another world war. General MacArthur, however, wanted to pursue a policy of total victory. When the President did not give in to the general's demands, MacArthur openly criticized Truman and the government's policies. Because the President is also the Commander-in-Chief of the armed forces, some people viewed MacArthur's actions as a refusal to follow orders. Other Americans supported MacArthur's position.

President Truman found General MacArthur's behavior unacceptable. Truman also felt that an important democratic ideal was at stake. The armed forces had to be ruled by the nation's elected leaders. Finally, on April 11, 1951, President Truman fired MacArthur and ordered him to return home. At first, many Americans sided with MacArthur. Some of them even accused President Truman of treason. After a Senate investigation, however, the public threw its support behind Truman. Americans realized that a President could not allow a general to set policy for the whole country.

**Neither side wins the war.** The Chinese troops pushed UN soldiers back across the 38th parallel. However, the Communists could not break through the UN line, and the war soon reached a **stalemate.** A stalemate occurs when neither side in a conflict is able to gain the victory. After a year of fighting, leaders from both sides met to plan a cease-fire. These meetings dragged on for more than two years.

Finally, on July 27, 1953, both sides signed an agreement at Panmunjom (pahn-mun-JOM). The fighting was over, but no winner was declared. The agreement set a new border between North and South Korea. It also called for the establishment of a **demilitarized zone** along the border. A demilitarized zone is an area in which no military activity is allowed.

**Both sides suffer heavy losses.** The cost of the Korean war was high. More than 30,000 Americans and 45,000 South Koreans died in battle. About 3,000 soldiers from other countries in the UN force were killed. The North Koreans and Chinese Communists lost more than 1.4 million soldiers. Millions more civilians died as well.

**Korea remains divided.** The three years of fighting made little change in the political situation of Korea. Neither side gained much

In winter 1950, UN troops withdrew from North Korea along difficult mountain trails. UN forces were ordered to retreat after China suddenly entered the war.

territory. The tensions between North and South Korea did not ease. Today troops still guard both sides of the dividing line between North and South Korea. North Korea continues as a Communist country. South Korea remains non-Communist.

## Revolution in Southeast Asia

In Southeast Asia the United States also tried to stop communism from spreading. Indochina, which included the countries of Vietnam, Laos, and Cambodia, had been a colony of France since the 1860's. After World War II, Communists wanted to free Indochina from French control. The United States supported the French against the Communists.

**Communists oppose the French in Vietnam.** The most powerful Communist group in Indochina was the **Vietminh,** or Vietnamese Communists, led by Ho Chi Minh. For years Ho Chi Minh and his followers had opposed French rule. In 1945 the Vietminh captured the northern city of Hanoi (hah-NOY), the capital of Vietnam. They formed a Communist government that ruled the northern part of the country.

Ho Chi Minh wanted to unify Vietnam under his control. The French, however, continued to support the non-Communist government in southern Vietnam. This government was centered in the city of Saigon (sy-GAHN).

**Major powers supply aid.** In the 1950's, the Soviets and Chinese sent weapons to the Vietminh to aid in their fight against the French. The United States sent weapons and advisers to help the French.

By 1954 the Americans were spending more money in Vietnam than the French were. The United States' policy was based on the **domino theory.** This theory held that if one country in the region fell to Communism, then others would follow, like dominoes toppling in a row. Containment in Southeast Asia meant winning in Vietnam.

**The French withdraw from Southeast Asia.** In March 1954 the Vietminh attacked the French fort at Dien Bien Phu (dyen byen FOO) in northern Vietnam. The siege lasted

55 days. About 6,000 French were wounded or killed during the fighting. On May 8 the French surrendered.

Following the French surrender, peace talks were held in Geneva, Switzerland. The French agreed to withdraw from Indochina. Laos and Cambodia were to become independent countries. The peace agreement also divided Vietnam. The Communists would rule the area north of the 17th parallel. The government in Saigon would rule the southern part of the country. Ngo Dinh Diem (no din dee-EM) was made the leader of South Vietnam. Diem later set himself up as South Vietnam's dictator.

**The United States supports South Vietnam.** In 1954 leaders of the United States and its allies signed an agreement forming the **Southeast Asia Treaty Organization** (SEATO). All eight members of the organization promised to help contain communism in Southeast Asia. With this goal in mind, President Eisenhower sent weapons and advisers to South Vietnam. Many people, however, believed that the United States should not aid South Vietnam because it was a dictatorship. Support of that dictatorship would eventually draw the United States into a major conflict.

## SECTION REVIEW

1. **Vocabulary**   evacuate, stalemate, demilitarized zone
2. **People and Places**   South Korea, North Korea, Seoul, Douglas MacArthur, Yalu River, Panmunjom, Indochina, Vietnam, Ho Chi Minh, Saigon, Ngo Dinh Diem
3. **Comprehension**   How did the United States become involved in the Korean War?
4. **Comprehension**   Why did President Eisenhower send weapons and advisers to South Vietnam?
5. **Critical Thinking**   Do you think the United States would have aided South Korea even if the UN had refused to help? Explain.

### Vocabulary
closed shop        blacklist
perjury            censure

At the end of World War II, Americans faced problems at home as well as overseas. Millions of American soldiers returned to civilian life. The nation had to deal with veterans' issues, rising prices, and labor unrest.

### Shifting to a Peacetime Economy

In 1945 and 1946, most members of the armed forces returned home. Americans welcomed them with parties and parades. The adjustment to peacetime life, however, brought changes for many people.

**Millions of soldiers become civilians.** The federal government wanted to ease the way for the many veterans returning to civilian life. In 1944 Congress had passed the Servicemen's Readjustment Act. The act became known as the **GI Bill of Rights.** Under this law, the government paid the expenses of veterans who attended college. It also loaned money to veterans who started businesses.

As the veterans returned, the government urged women to leave their jobs in factories. Government posters read: "Give your job to a veteran! Go back home!" Some women wanted to keep on working. Many others, however, left their jobs to become full-time homemakers.

Most industries quickly shifted from producing war materials to making peacetime goods. Factories turned out millions of automobiles, radios, televisions, and home appliances. Builders put up hundreds of thousands of new homes.

At the end of World War II, Americans welcomed home millions of veterans. The veterans' need for housing and peacetime jobs spurred changes in the American economy.

Meanwhile, veterans married and started families. Millions of babies were born between 1945 and 1960. This rapid expansion of the population is often called the **baby boom.** The growing population meant a growing demand for goods.

**Inflation becomes a worry.** During the war, goods had been rationed. Many items, including cars and appliances, had not been available to consumers. Now that the war was over, Americans wanted to buy everything at once. They demanded more goods than factories could produce. With goods in great demand yet in short supply, prices rose quickly. The end of wartime price controls added to the problem. To pay the higher prices of goods, workers needed more money.

**Unions seek higher wages.** During the war, labor unions had agreed not to strike. Now the unions wanted pay hikes for their members. Many companies, however, refused to raise wages. As a result, strikes broke out across the country.

Americans were alarmed about these strikes and about creeping inflation. Many voters blamed the Democrats for these troubles. In the congressional election of 1946, Republicans gained a majority of seats in both houses.

The Republicans quickly drafted a new measure limiting the power of unions. Senator Robert A. Taft of Ohio and other Republican leaders in Congress argued that the law gave unfair advantages to labor unions. Under Taft's leadership, Congress passed the **Taft-Hartley Act,** over President Truman's veto.

The Taft-Hartley Act weakened unions. Among other things, it made **closed shops** against the law. A closed shop is a workplace where all workers must be union members. Another part of the Taft-Hartley Act called for an 80-day "cooling-off" period before a strike could begin. The law also gave employers the right to sue a union for breaking a contract.

## Dealing with Social Problems

With the war over, President Truman hoped to carry on with some of the social reforms that President Roosevelt had begun. Truman favored minority rights and aid for the poor. Congress often disagreed with the President, however, and many of Truman's ideas failed.

**Racial barriers begin to fall.** President Truman called for an end to racial discrimination in hiring federal workers. He also

This 1950 advertisement shows brand-new cars at a filling station. As millions of Americans bought new cars, service stations spread to cities and highways from coast to coast.

Many people predicted that Thomas Dewey would win the election of 1948. Yet President Truman won by more than 2 million popular votes. In this photograph, Truman displays a newspaper published before the final votes were counted. What mistake did the newspaper make?

ordered an end to segregation in the armed forces. The Republican-controlled Congress, however, defeated many other civil rights measures that the President suggested.

Still, Truman worked hard to help blacks share more fully in American life. He appointed the first black federal judge in the United States and the first black American governor, who presided over the Virgin Islands. Truman was also the first President to invite black Americans to take part in his inaugural celebration.

**Truman faces a challenge in 1948.** Many Democrats were displeased with Truman's policies. Before the 1948 presidential election, southern Democrats had formed the States' Rights party. Other Democrats who were sympathetic to the Soviet Union had formed the Progressive party.

Newspapers and public opinion polls predicted that Truman would lose to Thomas E. Dewey, the Republican candidate. Experts said that Truman could not win because he did not have the full support of his party. All during the campaign, Truman made speeches across the country and brought his message to the people. In November the voters surprised political experts by electing Truman to a full term.

**Truman asks for a Fair Deal.** After his election victory in 1948, Truman pressed even harder for social reform. He introduced the **Fair Deal,** his program to continue the changes started in the New Deal.

Truman persuaded Congress to pass some of his bills, such as those to clear slums and to build low-income housing. Congress also passed Truman's new immigration law, which allowed more people from eastern and southern Europe into the country. Many southern Democrats, however, objected to the Fair Deal measures that were meant to

In the early 1950's, Senator Joseph McCarthy charged that many government officials and other prominent Americans were Communists. After televised hearings in 1954, McCarthy was discredited.

end discrimination. These Democrats joined with the Republicans in Congress to defeat Truman's civil rights bill.

## Anti-Communism at Home

Toward the end of the Truman years, American attention at home focused on national security. In late 1949, the Soviet Union announced that it had developed an atomic bomb. Americans were shocked. Previously the United States had been the only country with atomic weapons.

**The government acts for national security.** Some people wondered whether a traitor in the American government might have leaked atomic secrets to the Soviets. To uncover any traitors, Congress turned to the House Un-American Activities Committee. The committee began hearings in which it questioned many Americans about their political views and activities.

One of the best-known people to be questioned was Alger Hiss. Hiss had been a respected government official under President Roosevelt. The committee asked Hiss about the sale of government secrets to the Soviet Union in the 1930's. He was not charged with selling secrets, but he was accused of lying about his activities. In January 1950, after a long trial, Hiss was found guilty of **perjury** —lying under oath.

The Hiss trial filled many Americans with fear. They worried that government workers might be spying for the Communists. The fear of communism at home was heightened by Joseph McCarthy, a Republican senator from Wisconsin. McCarthy led an alarming drive to uncover Communists and force them out of the government.

**McCarthy names suspected Communists.** Senator McCarthy began his campaign against Communists in February 1950 in a speech to a women's club. In this speech, McCarthy claimed that the State Department was "thoroughly infested with Communists."

The Truman administration insisted that these charges were false. All the same, many frightened Americans believed Senator McCarthy and supported his efforts to root out traitors. Even some who agreed with McCarthy, however, disliked his methods. He gave name after name to the House Un-American Activities Committee. He offered no proof, however, to back up his claims.

Besides government officials, McCarthy also accused writers, actors, scientists, and others. Because they were **blacklisted** — placed on a list of people thought to be disloyal—many were unable to find work. McCarthy often ruined people's lives just by adding their names to this list.

In time, Senator McCarthy became so powerful that few members of Congress dared go against him. Some who did were defeated at reelection time. President Truman did stand up to McCarthy, calling him "a political gangster." Still, McCarthy held on to his power.

In 1954 McCarthy charged that several high-ranking officers in the United States Army were Communists. The resulting committee hearings were shown on television. For the first time, the American public saw how McCarthy bullied his victims. Many of his supporters turned against him. Finally, in December 1954, the Senate voted to **censure** —condemn—McCarthy. This step brought a swift end to McCarthy's influence. Yet Americans continued to worry about protecting military secrets from other nations.

## SECTION REVIEW

1. **Vocabulary**   closed shop, perjury, blacklist, censure
2. **People and Places**   Robert A. Taft, Virgin Islands, Thomas E. Dewey, Alger Hiss, Joseph McCarthy
3. **Comprehension**   What were some effects of American soldiers' coming home after World War II?
4. **Comprehension**   How did the members of Congress respond to President Truman's Fair Deal?
5. **Critical Thinking**   Do you think America's national security was threatened in the early 1950's? Why or why not?

# 4 How did President Eisenhower meet the challenges of the 1950's?

## Vocabulary

affluent
civil disobedience
massive retaliation

President Truman chose not to run for another term in 1952. When the new President, Dwight D. Eisenhower, took office in 1953, the Korean War was slowly drawing to a close. Yet Eisenhower was to face new crises, both at home and elsewhere. The threat of atomic war hovered over almost every international dispute. At home, in spite of great growth and widespread prosperity, many Americans still faced poverty and discrimination.

## Coping with Rapid Change

Dwight D. Eisenhower was born in Texas and grew up in Kansas, where he was nicknamed "Ike." During World War II, Eisenhower served as the Supreme Commander of the Allied Forces in Europe. Later he became the president of Columbia University. In 1950 President Truman put Eisenhower in charge of the NATO forces. In 1952 the Republican party chose him to run as their candidate for President.

**Americans put a Republican in office.** Eisenhower's strong leadership during World War II had made him well known and well liked. His broad grin and self-assured manner appealed to Democrats and Republicans alike. Eisenhower won the election of

# Our Presidents

## DWIGHT D. EISENHOWER

★ 1953–1961 ★

**34TH PRESIDENT**

REPUBLICAN

★ Born October 14, 1890, in Texas

★ Married Mamie Geneva Doud in 1916; 2 children

★ Commander of Allied forces in Europe; president of Columbia University; commander of NATO forces in Europe

★ Lived in New York when elected President

★ Vice President: Richard M. Nixon

★ Died March 28, 1969, in Washington, D.C.

★ Key events while in office: Korean War ended; Space Age started; *Brown* v. *Board of Education of Topeka;* Alaska and Hawaii became states

---

1952 by a landslide. He defeated the Democratic candidate, Adlai Stevenson, to become the first Republican President in 20 years. In 1956 he beat Stevenson again, by an even wider margin.

**The 1950's are a time of good fortune.** During the Eisenhower years, more Americans than ever joined the work force. Wages climbed, and the United States became an **affluent** (AF-loo-uhnt)—wealthy—society. The buying spree that had started after World War II showed no signs of slowing down in the 1950's.

The automobile industry flourished in this affluent society. Americans bought more cars than ever before. To accommodate all the motorists, Congress approved a

huge road-building program in 1956. The plans called for more than 40,000 miles (64,000 kilometers) of new roads to be laid over the next 13 years.

Across the country new communities arose on the outskirts of cities. These suburbs showed the prosperity of many Americans. People could afford to buy new homes outside the city and still drive into the city to work. Before long, businesses were moving to the suburbs, too. Shopping centers seemed to spring up everywhere.

Americans in the 1950's were buying not only new cars and homes but also boats, appliances, cameras, and televisions. By 1960 nearly 90 percent of American homes had at least one television set.

As Americans became more affluent, they also became more mobile. Many people moved long distances to take better jobs. Families looking for cheap housing and a warm climate moved to such states as Texas and California. As a result, states in the South and West became more important in national elections.

The two westernmost states entered the Union during President Eisenhower's second term. On January 3, 1959, Eisenhower signed a proclamation announcing that Alaska had become the forty-ninth state. Eight months later, Hawaii was admitted as the fiftieth state.

**New technology changes society.** The 1950's also were a time of exciting technological advances. New products appeared that revolutionized the way Americans lived. Synthetic "wash and wear" clothing replaced natural fabrics. Pocket-sized transistor radios amazed the listening public. Plastics were used in countless goods as a substitute for wood and metal. For those who could afford it, the color television was a prized possession.

Rapid advances also took place in science and medicine. Scientists made discoveries about DNA—the material that passes on traits, such as eye color, from parents to children. Other researchers developed lasers, which later led to breakthroughs in communications and medicine. Electronic computers were built. Doctors used new

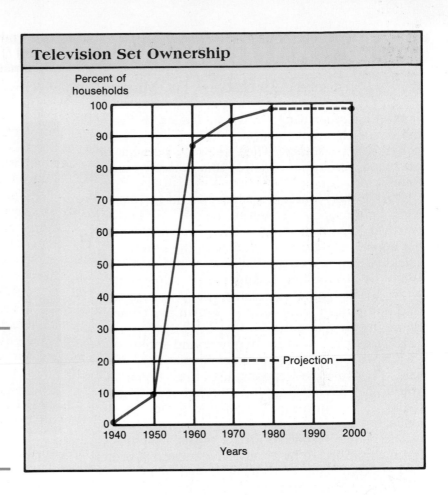

## Television Set Ownership

Percent of households

*(vertical axis: 0, 10, 20, 30, 40, 50, 60, 70, 80, 90, 100)*

– – – Projection

1940  1950  1960  1970  1980  1990  2000

Years

### Graph Study

In 1940 about 1 percent of American households had television sets. What percent had television sets in 1950? In 1980? What projected trend in television set ownership does the graph show?

machines, such as the iron lung, to help sick people live longer. Dr. Jonas Salk discovered a vaccine to prevent polio. At one time, this disease had crippled or killed thousands of young people each year.

## Dealing with Poverty and Discrimination

President Eisenhower believed the American government had grown too large. When he ran for office, he spoke about reducing government control of Americans' lives. After his election, however, Eisenhower avoided large government cutbacks. In many cases, he actually expanded the role of the government.

**Eisenhower makes social reforms.** President Eisenhower worked closely with Congress to extend Social Security to cover millions more Americans. He helped raise

the minimum wage to $1 an hour. He asked for more aid for hospitals, medical research, low-cost housing, and rebuilding run-down city areas. In addition, Eisenhower set up the **Department of Health, Education, and Welfare** (HEW) to care for the needs of children, the sick, and the poor.

**Eisenhower enforces civil rights laws.** In 1954 the Supreme Court made a landmark ruling in a case called **Brown v. Board of Education of Topeka.** The Court stated that laws requiring separate schools for blacks were unconstitutional. As a result, states could no longer legally segregrate children in public schools.

The school board in Little Rock, Arkansas, made plans to place blacks and whites in the same schools. Arkansas Governor Orval Faubus objected, however. He tried to stop black students from attending Central High School in Little Rock. Many angry white

## PROFILE • Dr. Martin Luther King, Jr.

Martin Luther King, Jr., was a leader. He gave the civil rights movement a philosophy— nonviolent resistance. Then he practiced what he preached, setting an example that others would follow.

During the Montgomery bus boycott in 1955, King's philosophy was put to the test. While King was attending a meeting, a bomb was thrown at his house. The bomb exploded on the porch. Luckily, King's wife and baby were not hurt. When he arrived home, King saw hundreds of angry blacks gathered outside. They wanted to find and punish whoever had thrown the bomb. Some people had guns.

King quickly went to the porch and spoke to the crowd. "Now let's not become panicky," he said. "If you have weapons, take them home. If you do not have them, please do not seek to get them.... We must meet violence with nonviolence."

The people respected King's words. Nonviolence continued to be an effective means of protest and the civil rights movement spread. The movement owed much of its success to the philosophy of its leader—Dr. Martin Luther King, Jr.

**Martin Luther King, Jr.**

---

protesters agreed with the governor. Then President Eisenhower sent troops to Little Rock to uphold the law. Under the soldiers' protection, black students began to attend classes at the high school.

**The civil rights movement spreads.** The Supreme Court's *Brown* ruling was an important victory for blacks. Yet segregation was still a problem in many places. For example, blacks in Montgomery, Alabama, were forced to ride in the rear of buses. They had to stand if whites wanted their seats.

On December 1, 1955, a black woman named Rosa Parks refused to give her seat on the bus to a white man. As a result, she was arrested. To protest the arrest of Rosa Parks, blacks in Montgomery refused to ride the

buses. They planned to keep up their boycott until they were promised the same treatment as white passengers.

The leader of the boycott was Dr. Martin Luther King, Jr. King was a Baptist minister from Montgomery. He insisted that his followers use nonviolent means to seek equal treatment. He also believed in protesting through **civil disobedience** —refusal to obey unjust laws.

The year-long boycott nearly put the Montgomery bus company out of business. Finally, in November 1956, the Supreme Court said that it was unconstitutional for a city to run a segregated bus system.

This victory encouraged Dr. King and other black leaders. They began a drive to

Rosa Parks was arrested in 1955 for refusing to give up her seat to a white passenger on a bus in Montgomery, Alabama. In protest, black community leaders organized the Montgomery bus boycott.

end other kinds of discrimination. They started boycotts against stores, theaters, and restaurants that were segregated. The boycotts worked. Because most businesses did not want to lose customers, they began to serve black people.

**New policies affect other minorities.** President Eisenhower wanted Native Americans to enter the mainstream of American life. He asked Congress to end federal aid to Indian reservations. Eisenhower hoped that the Indians would leave their reservations and take jobs in cities. Many Native Americans who did move found it hard to get used to city life. They lacked job skills and missed their homes and native cultures.

Many Puerto Rican people faced similar troubles when they migrated to the United States. Puerto Ricans had been American citizens since 1917, and in 1952 Puerto Rico became a commonwealth protected by the United States. All the same, Puerto Ricans who came to American cities often met with unfair discrimination in jobs and housing. In time, Puerto Ricans began to organize to gain better treatment.

## Rivalry in Weapons and Space

In foreign affairs, President Eisenhower faced continued tension with the Soviet Union. In November 1952 the United States tested the world's first hydrogen bomb. This atomic weapon was thousands of times more powerful than the bomb that leveled Hiroshima in 1945. (See Chapter 29.) Then, in August 1953, the Soviets tested their own hydrogen bomb. For the first time in history, two countries had the power to completely destroy each other.

**A new policy raises world tensions.** Faced with the possibility of nuclear destruction, the United States set a new policy for dealing with the Soviets. American leaders wanted to guard against a nuclear war. To do this, the United States announced in 1954 that it would respond to any Communist nuclear attack with **massive retaliation.** Massive retaliation meant all-out use of atomic weapons directed at the Soviet Union. By guaranteeing such a response, the United States hoped to keep atomic weapons from ever being used.

707

In this 1950's photograph, Puerto Rican Americans study English in a New York City classroom. Puerto Rican immigrants numbered more than 74,000 during 1953, the year after Puerto Rico became a commonwealth.

**East and West compete for supremacy.** The fear of nuclear war led both Soviets and Americans into an **arms race.** Each country tried to protect itself by building more and better atomic weapons. Both countries stockpiled atomic bombs. They also developed missiles that could carry the bombs thousands of miles. Soon both countries had enough weapons to destroy the world several times over.

The Soviets and Americans also competed in space. In October 1957 the Soviets launched *Sputnik I*—the first artificial space satellite. In response, the United States hurried to set up its own space program. In 1958 the first American satellite, *Explorer I*, orbited Earth. This same year, the United States organized the **National Aeronautics and Space Administration** (NASA). At first, NASA designed and launched only satellites. Later it built spaceships and trained astronauts to pilot them.

The launch of *Sputnik I* by the Soviets caused another reaction in the United States. Many people feared that American schools taught too little science. The educational system seemed unable to produce the engineers that the space program needed. To calm these fears, Congress voted to spend more money to improve the teaching of science and technology.

## Other International Problems

Meanwhile, the Soviet Union tried to extend its influence in other countries. This led to friction in the Middle East and Latin America. The Soviets also faced a major problem in a country already under their control.

**Hungarians rise in revolt.** In October 1956, people in Hungary rebelled against their Soviet rulers. Soviet Premier Nikita Khrushchev (KRUSH-chef) sent tanks and thousands of soldiers to crush the revolt. Many Americans urged their government to help the Hungarian "freedom fighters." President Eisenhower, however, thought that

American interference might lead to another world war. He refused to send help. Thousands of Hungarians were killed, and the Soviets kept control of Hungary.

**Conflicts arise in the Middle East.** In 1948 Israel had been established as a Jewish homeland. Arab countries in the Middle East refused to accept Israel and threatened to destroy the new nation. This conflict became a constant source of trouble in the Middle East. It also gave the Soviets a chance to play a stronger role in the region. They offered aid to Israel's Arab neighbors, including Egypt.

A crisis developed in 1956 when Egypt took over the Suez Canal and closed this important waterway to Israeli shipping. War soon broke out. Israel, joined by France and Great Britain, attacked Egypt and seized control of the canal. In time, a cease-fire was called and United Nations soldiers arrived to keep peace.

People in the United States still worried about Soviet interference in the Middle East. As a result, Congress in 1957 gave President Eisenhower the power to send American armed forces if a Middle Eastern country asked for them. This policy became known as the **Eisenhower Doctrine.**

In 1958 President Eisenhower used the new policy. Christians and Muslims were waging a civil war in Lebanon. At the wish of the Lebanese government, Eisenhower sent several thousand United States marines into Lebanon to restore order. The marines established an uneasy peace and then returned home.

**The cold war reaches Latin America.** In January 1959 Fidel Castro, a revolutionary leader, overthrew the dictator who ruled Cuba. Americans watched this revolution closely, because Cuba is just 90 miles (145 kilometers) from Florida. At first, Americans supported Castro, who promised the Cubans a democratic government.

As time went on, however, American sympathy for Castro faded. Castro refused to hold elections. He also accepted aid from the Soviets. Finally, Americans realized that Castro was a Communist and that Cuba had become a Communist country. Americans

## LINKING PAST AND PRESENT

### ★ ★ ★ *Oral History*

The decade of the 1950's was a golden time for many people. World War II was over, and the economy was healthy. Dwight Eisenhower, a popular war hero, was President.

There are hundreds of books about the 1950's. Some of the best history of the period, however, is not written down. It exists in the memories of people who lived then. These people fought in the Korean War, they bought the first television sets, and they joined America's move to the suburbs. Their stories present an oral history of the decade.

Oral history—spoken accounts of a time by the people who lived then—can be a valuable source of information. Today many historians use tape recorders to preserve people's memories of events and their feelings about them. These recordings help us understand how ordinary people coped with changing times.

were alarmed that a Communist nation lay so close to the United States. The government began making secret plans to bring down the Castro government.

**East-West tensions vary.** For a time during the late 1950's, the cold war seemed to ease. Groups of Soviet and American citizens visited each other's countries. In 1959 Khrushchev himself came to the United States. Plans were made for a meeting of top world leaders to be held in Paris. President Eisenhower also arranged to visit the Soviet Union.

Just before the Paris meeting, however, the Soviets shot down an American U-2 spy plane over their country. The Soviets were outraged that Americans had been spying on Soviet territory. Khrushchev then refused to meet with Western leaders. The cold war continued to threaten world peace.

This photograph shows President and Mamie Eisenhower relaxing on their farm in Gettysburg, Pennsylvania.

# Chapter 30 Summary

After World War II Harry Truman became President. He faced many crises. The United States and the Soviet Union engaged in a cold war as the Soviets sought to extend their influence. The Soviets dropped an iron curtain that sealed off their satellite countries in Eastern Europe and threatened other countries, too. Truman followed a policy of containment to try to stop Soviet expansion and the spread of communism. Through the Truman Doctrine and the Marshall Plan the United States helped to maintain democracy in Western Europe.

In 1950 American troops were sent to help South Korea defend itself against a North Korean invasion. They were part of a United Nations force under General Douglas MacArthur. By the war's end, thousands of Americans had died in battle.

At home, Truman faced other challenges. The baby boom had begun. Inflation was a problem and unions demanded higher wages. Civil rights also became a national issue. Truman's Fair Deal program sought to aid black Americans.

During Dwight D. Eisenhower's presidency, the United States became an affluent society. People bought new cars and new homes in the suburbs. There were many advances in science and technology. Black Americans, however, still faced discrimination. The Supreme Court decision in *Brown* v. *Board of Education of Topeka* opened the doors of schools once closed to blacks. Dr. Martin Luther King, Jr., and his followers used civil disobedience to break down more racial barriers.

In the 1950's, the United States and the Soviet Union began an arms race and both nations competed in space. Conflicts in the Middle East and in Latin America helped prolong the cold war.

# MAPS AND GRAPHS: Population Changes

At the time of the first census in 1790, the population of the United States was about 4 million people. By the time of the seventeenth census in 1950, that figure had risen to more than 150 million. Population growth is one aspect of **demography**—the study of population statistics.

**Demographers**—people who study population—are interested in other kinds of statistics, too. They examine **population shifts,** or the movement of populations from one place to another. Several kinds of maps can reveal population shifts. One kind shows **population density**—how close together or how far apart people live. The population density is highest in urban areas. It is lowest in rural areas. A population density map might use colors to show differences in density. Urban areas might be a dark color. The surrounding suburbs would be a lighter color. The open countryside would be an even lighter color. By comparing such maps for different years, demographers can predict how the population is shifting.

Another kind of map shows **population distribution.** This is a measure of where people live. A population distribution map for the United States might show the percentage of people living in each state. The maps on this page show population distribution in another way—by region. They give the percentage of the total United States population living in each region in a certain year. By comparing these two maps, you can see how regional population changed in 30 years.

Study the maps, and then answer the following questions on a separate sheet of paper.

1. Which region of the United States had the highest population in 1950?
2. Which regions had a smaller share of the population in 1980 than they had in 1950?
3. Which regions had a larger share of the population in 1980 than in 1950?
4. What conclusion can you draw about where the population is moving, based on these two maps?

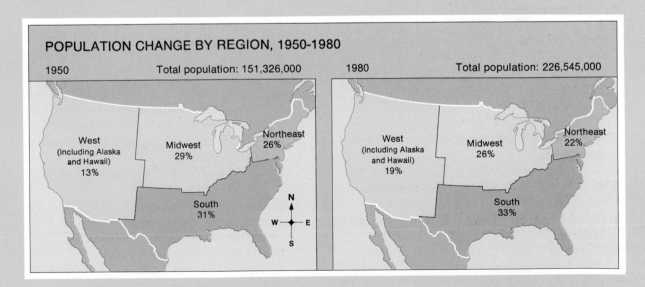

**POPULATION CHANGE BY REGION, 1950-1980**

1950 — Total population: 151,326,000

West (including Alaska and Hawaii) 13%
Midwest 29%
Northeast 26%
South 31%

1980 — Total population: 226,545,000

West (including Alaska and Hawaii) 19%
Midwest 26%
Northeast 22%
South 33%

# Chapter 30 REVIEW

## Vocabulary and Key Terms

Use the following terms to complete the sentences below. Write your answers on a separate sheet of paper.

affluent
civil disobedience
cold war
containment
domino theory

Fair Deal
iron curtain
Truman Doctrine
United Nations

1. President Truman began the _____ to continue New Deal reforms, and he tried to halt communism through his policy of _____.
2. The _____ separated Eastern European countries from the West.
3. The _____ said that America would aid any free people under attack from inside rebels or outside countries.
4. Blacks protested unjust laws through _____.
5. By the 1950's, with wages rising, America had become an _____ society.
6. The _____ was organized to seek world peace.
7. The Americans and the Soviets engaged in a _____, a period of uneasy peace.
8. The _____ was based on the belief that if one country in a region fell to communism, the others would also fall.

## Recalling the Facts

1. What impact did the Marshall Plan have on Europe?
2. What action resulted in the Berlin airlift?
3. Why did President Truman fire General MacArthur?
4. Who were the Vietminh, and who was their leader?
5. What did the GI Bill of Rights do for American veterans?
6. What was the Supreme Court decision in *Brown* v. *Board of Education of Topeka*?

## Places to Locate

Match the letters on the map with the places listed below. Write your answers on a separate sheet of paper.

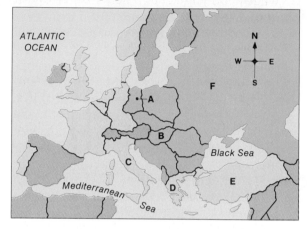

1. Italy
2. Hungary
3. Greece
4. Soviet Union
5. Berlin
6. Turkey

## Critical Thinking

1. During the 1950's Senator Joseph McCarthy led an effort to rid the United States of Communists. Why did this happen, and what effects did it have? Consider these questions in your answer:
   a. What were relations like between the United States and the Soviet Union?
   b. How did Americans respond to McCarthy's campaign, and why?
   c. How did the campaign affect freedom of expression?
   d. What happened to people who were blacklisted?
2. In the 1950's the United States and the Soviet Union began an arms race. Why was this a problem? Consider these questions in your answer:
   a. Why did the arms race develop? Could it have been avoided?
   b. What effects has the arms race had?

## Understanding History

1. Reread the section "Inflation becomes a worry" on page 700. Then answer these questions.
   a. **Economics.** Why did Americans want more goods after the war?
   b. **Economics.** How had the government kept prices low during the war?
2. Reread the section "Unions seek higher wages" on page 700. Then answer these questions.
   a. **Citizenship.** How did Americans show that they did not like Democratic policies?
   b. **Citizenship.** How were American voters indirectly responsible for the Taft-Hartley Act?
3. Reread the section "The 1950's are a time of good fortune" on page 704. Then answer these questions.
   a. **Geography.** How did the automobile affect the growth of suburbs?
   b. **Culture.** Do you think there were many shopping centers outside of cities before World War II? Explain.
4. Reread the section "New technology changes society" on page 704. Then answer these questions.
   a. **Culture.** Why, do you think, did "wash and wear" fabrics replace natural fabrics?
   b. **Science and Technology.** Why was the polio vaccine so important?

## Projects and Activities

1. **Making a Time Line.** Create a time line showing the important events of the Korean War.
2. **Supporting an Opinion.** Imagine that you are one of Harry Truman's advisers. Do you favor firing or retaining General MacArthur? Write a report to President Truman supporting your opinion.
3. **Making a Bulletin-Board Display.** Create a bulletin-board display with your classmates on present-day civil rights issues in the United States. Clip pictures from magazines and newspapers. Add captions that explain the issues.

4. **Giving an Oral Report.** Find out more about one of the following subjects: the Alger Hiss case, the United Nations, Ho Chi Minh, Dr. Martin Luther King, Jr., the space race, or Fidel Castro. Present an oral report to the class, based on the information you have gathered.

## Practicing Your Skill

Use the map below to answer the questions that follow. Write your answers on a separate sheet of paper.

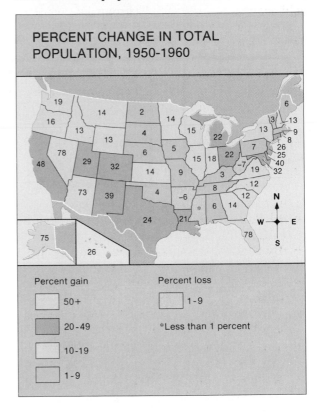

PERCENT CHANGE IN TOTAL POPULATION, 1950-1960

Percent gain
- 50+
- 20-49
- 10-19
- 1-9

Percent loss
- 1-9

*Less than 1 percent

1. What does this map show?
2. What is the highest percentage of population gain that the map key shows? How many states gained this much?
3. How many states showed a loss of population? How can you determine this without looking at every number?
4. Which part of the country showed the greatest percentage of increase in the population—the Southwest, the Northeast, or the Southeast?
5. What does the asterisk (*) mean?

# 31 The Nation Faces Stormy Times
## 1960–1976

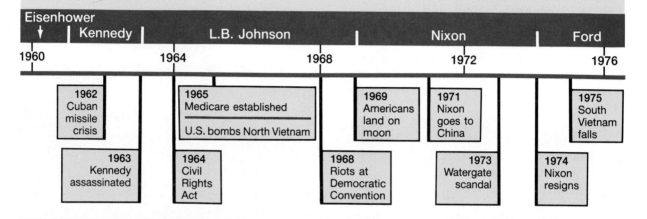

Eisenhower

Kennedy    L. B. Johnson    Nixon    Ford

1960    1964    1968    1972    1976

**1962** Cuban missile crisis

**1965** Medicare established

U.S. bombs North Vietnam

**1969** Americans land on moon

**1971** Nixon goes to China

**1975** South Vietnam falls

**1963** Kennedy assassinated

**1964** Civil Rights Act

**1968** Riots at Democratic Convention

**1973** Watergate scandal

**1974** Nixon resigns

The United States space program was highly successful in the 1960's and early 1970's. *Apollo 15* astronauts explored the moon's surface in 1971.

## Preparing to Read

Important events shook the world during the 1960's and the early 1970's. The United States and the Soviet Union teetered on the brink of nuclear war. American astronauts landed on the moon. The fighting in Vietnam grew and spread to other countries in Southeast Asia.

In the United States, the period brought both pain and progress. One President was assassinated. Another left office in the wake of scandal. Protests by young people and minorities made daily headlines. Yet during these years, women, blacks, and other minority groups made great strides forward. The poor received more help, and the last American soldiers in Vietnam returned home. As you read this chapter, try to answer the following questions:

1. What important issues marked the Kennedy years?
2. How did the 1960's challenge President Johnson?
3. What triumphs and setbacks did the Nixon and Ford years bring?

# 1  What important issues marked the Kennedy years?

## Vocabulary

| | |
|---|---|
| intelligence | fallout |
| guerrilla | disarmament |

For the most part, the 1950's had been calm, secure times for Americans. Dwight D. Eisenhower had become a very popular President. He might well have been reelected in 1960, but the Twenty-second Amendment limits Presidents to two terms. The 1960's thus meant the start of a new administration. The decade also brought unexpected challenges and heartache.

## A Young Leader in the White House

In the 1960 election, the Republican party nominated Vice President Richard M. Nixon to follow Eisenhower. Nixon's Democratic opponent was Massachusetts Senator John F. Kennedy. Kennedy came from a large family of successful politicians. From an early age, he seemed to be in training for a political career.

**Kennedy runs for office.** John F. Kennedy graduated from Harvard University in 1940. He then joined the United States Navy, winning a medal for bravery in World War II. In 1946, Massachusetts voters elected Kennedy to the United States House of Representatives. Six years later, Kennedy became a senator.

As early as 1956, Kennedy started planning for the 1960 presidential race. At first it seemed that Kennedy's Roman Catholic faith might hurt his chances. Never before had a Catholic become President. Some Americans feared that a Catholic would let the Pope interfere in the government. Kennedy assured people that he believed in keeping church and state separate. He went on to win his party's nomination.

At the start of the campaign, Nixon was better known than Kennedy. Television changed things, however. In four televised debates, Kennedy proved his knowledge of major issues.

**Kennedy becomes President.** The 1960 election was one of the closest in American history. Nixon lost by a margin of less than 120,000 popular votes. Kennedy, only 43 years of age, became the youngest President ever elected.

At his inauguration, Kennedy called for all people to join in the "struggle against the common enemies of man: tyranny, poverty, disease, and war itself." Kennedy ended his speech with these words:

And so, my fellow Americans: Ask not what your country can do for you—ask what you can do for your country.

My fellow citizens of the world: Ask not what America will do for you, but what together we can do for the freedom of man.

**Kennedy reaches out to developing countries.** The new President quickly began putting his ideas into action. On March 1, 1961, Kennedy set up the **Peace Corps.** Under this program, American volunteers spent time living and working overseas. They served as teachers, health-care workers, and technical advisers in developing countries. The Peace Corps is still active today.

Just a few weeks after the Peace Corps began, President Kennedy launched another aid program, the **Alliance for Progress.** Through the Alliance, the United States hoped to encourage economic growth and democracy in Latin America.

## The Communist Threat

President Kennedy had planned to focus more on domestic issues than on foreign policy. Almost at once, however, he had to deal with crises in Berlin, Cuba, and Southeast Asia.

**The Soviets build the Berlin Wall.** West Germans had prospered during the 1950's. East Germans, on the other hand, faced hard times under Communist rule. By 1960 thousands of people were leaving East Germany each week. Most of these refugees passed from East Berlin to West Berlin. (See Chapter 30.)

East Germany was losing skilled workers. In addition, the flight of so many East Germans embarrassed the Soviets. Soviet Premier Nikita Krushchev decided to take action. In August 1961 he had the East Germans build a wall between East and West Berlin. The wall was high, made of concrete, and topped with barbed wire. Guards on the wall shot anyone who tried to escape to the West.

In 1961 the Soviets built the Berlin Wall to keep East German people from entering West Berlin. The building of the Berlin Wall greatly increased tensions between the United States and the Soviet Union.

The Soviets' decision to build the **Berlin Wall** made Americans uneasy. President Kennedy decided to add 1,500 more soldiers to the 5,000 American troops already in Berlin. Though no fighting broke out, Berlin remained a trouble spot. Many East Germans, including border guards, tried to scale the wall and escape to freedom.

**Crises develop in Cuba.** The Soviets, meanwhile, were also active in Cuba. They gave support to Fidel Castro, the Communist leader of the country. (See Chapter 30.) The United States did not want communism to gain a foothold in the Americas. In 1960, under Eisenhower, the **Central Intelligence Agency** (CIA) had worked out a plan to overthrow Castro. The CIA's responsibility is to gather intelligence —political and military information—about foreign countries. It also carries out secret operations to support America's foreign policy.

The CIA's plan for Cuba was to help anti-Castro Cubans in the United States to invade their homeland. One of Kennedy's first decisions as President was to go ahead with the plan. In April 1961 about 1,500 anti-Castro fighters landed at the Bay of Pigs in southern Cuba. Within 48 hours, Castro's troops captured most of this force. Before he would release the prisoners, Castro demanded food

and medical supplies worth about $52 million. The **Bay of Pigs invasion** was a disaster for President Kennedy.

In the fall of 1962, more trouble arose between Cuba and the United States. President Kennedy learned that the Soviet Union was arming Cuba with nuclear missiles. The Soviets had aimed the missiles at American cities such as Boston, New York, and Washington, D.C.

President Kennedy demanded that the Soviets remove the missiles. He also sent American ships to blockade Cuba and stop the Soviets from delivering military supplies. For several tense days, Americans waited to see what the Soviets would do. In late October, Premier Krushchev agreed to remove the missiles. In return, the United States promised not to invade Cuba. President Kennedy won respect for his firm handling of this **Cuban missile crisis.**

**Southeast Asia remains unstable.** President Kennedy faced another Communist challenge farther from home. Since 1957 the **Vietcong**—Communist fighters in South Vietnam—had been trying to overthrow the government under President Ngo Dinh Diem. The Vietcong had support from North Vietnam and from many peasants in South Vietnam. They used guerrilla warfare to

President Kennedy warned that the United States would use armed force to prevent Communist takeovers in Southeast Asia. What was the purpose of the map shown in this 1961 photograph?

# Our Presidents

## JOHN F. KENNEDY

★ 1961–1963 ★

**35**TH PRESIDENT

DEMOCRAT

★ Born May 29, 1917, in Massachusetts
★ Married Jacqueline Lee Bouvier in 1953; 2 children
★ Representative and senator from Massachusetts
★ Lived in Massachusetts when elected President
★ Vice President: Lyndon B. Johnson
★ Assassinated November 22, 1963, in Texas
★ Key events while in office: Bay of Pigs invasion; Berlin Wall built; Cuban missile crisis; Peace Corps and Alliance for Progress created; Twenty-third Amendment; American involvement in Vietnam War increased

made their government even weaker. By this time the number of United States soldiers in Vietnam had grown to about 15,000. They were taking part in the fighting, and slowly the **Vietnam War** was becoming an American war.

**The threat of nuclear war alarms Americans.** Events in Vietnam and Cuba made Americans keenly aware of the dangers of war. Many people were already worried about the health hazards of nuclear weapons. They knew that **fallout** —the radioactive particles that fill the air after a nuclear explosion—would burn skin and cause a deadly illness. Victims of fallout might die at once or suffer for years.

In the 1950's the United States had begun talks with other world powers on the subject of **disarmament** —doing away with weapons. The United States and the Soviet Union did not reach agreement to disarm completely. They did agree, though, to limit their testing of new nuclear weapons. In July 1963, representatives from the United States, the Soviet Union, and Great Britain met in the Soviet capital of Moscow. There they signed a treaty arranging for a test ban. They pledged not to test nuclear weapons in the atmosphere, in outer space, or under water. Underground testing, though, was still allowed. The treaty took effect on October 10. By that time, 99 other countries had also promised to join in the test ban.

attack the South Vietnamese forces. Guerrillas are soldiers who fight in small, roving bands and use hit-and-run methods to surprise the enemy.

The situation in Southeast Asia alarmed many Americans. To help prevent a Communist takeover of South Vietnam, the United States had sent military advisers there in the late 1950's. President Kennedy sent another 100 advisers and 400 special Green Beret forces in 1961.

South Vietnam continued to lose, however. Conflict among South Vietnamese leaders hurt their efforts to fight the Communists. Then in 1963 President Diem was assassinated. South Vietnamese officials disagreed over who would replace him. This

## Domestic Affairs and Civil Rights

Along with challenges in foreign policy, President Kennedy faced challenges at home. He saw the need for new policies on health care, immigration, and civil rights. Kennedy also wanted a strong space program that could compete with the Soviets' space program.

Kennedy called his plan to meet these challenges the **New Frontier.** In a key campaign speech, Kennedy noted:

[We] stand today on the edge of a new frontier—the frontier of the 1960's, a frontier of unknown opportunities and paths, a frontier of unfulfilled hopes.

**The New Frontier program has limited success.** Congress was fully behind the space program. In May 1961 astronaut Alan Shepard became the first American launched into space. Less than a year later, John Glenn orbited the earth.

Apart from the space program, however, Congress showed little enthusiasm for Kennedy's New Frontier. Congress did agree to pass the Housing Act of 1961, which funded low-cost housing in American cities. Congress also raised the minimum wage for workers and passed two important amendments to the Constitution. The **Twenty-third Amendment** allowed people living in the District of Columbia, most of whom were black, to vote. The **Twenty-fourth Amendment** ended poll taxes.

Yet Kennedy could not get Congress to back most of his New Frontier ideas. Democrats from the South joined Republicans to defeat his bills. Kennedy's efforts to provide health care to the aged failed. So did his proposals to loosen immigration laws, cut taxes, and aid the public schools.

President Kennedy also made slow progress in the area of civil rights. Many members of Congress believed that civil rights was a matter for the states, not the federal government. Because he did not wish to anger Congress, Kennedy hesitated to propose strong civil rights laws. Instead he moved quietly, appointing many blacks to government offices. For example, he made Thurgood Marshall a federal judge. Marshall later became the first black justice of the Supreme Court.

**The civil rights movement gains strength.** People outside the government worked for civil rights, too. Groups of brave blacks and whites called **freedom riders** made bus trips together throughout the South to protest segregation. Though the segregation of buses was against the law, it still existed in practice. (See Chapter 30.) Mobs sometimes attacked freedom riders, and police sometimes arrested them. In support of the freedom riders, the federal government ordered that all southern bus stations be desegregated.

In 1963 Dr. Martin Luther King, Jr., proclaimed "I have a dream" to a crowd of more than 200,000 people in Washington, D.C. Dr. King won the Nobel Peace Prize in 1964 for his contributions to the civil rights movement.

# I HAVE A DREAM 1963

In 1963 more than 200,000 Americans of all races met in Washington, D.C., to rally for equal rights. In a moving speech, the Reverend Martin Luther King, Jr., expressed his dream of an America where all people are truly free.

## Read to Find Out

1. What is the "American dream" to which King refers?
2. What is King's dream for his children?

---

I say to you . . . in spite of the difficulties and frustrations of the moment I still have a dream. It is a dream deeply rooted in the American dream. I have a dream that one day this nation will rise up and live out the true meaning of its creed: "We hold these truths to be self-evident: that all men are created equal. . . ."

I have a dream that my four little children will one day live in a nation where they will not be judged by the color of their skin but by the content of their character.

I have a dream today. . . .

From every mountainside, let freedom ring. And when we allow freedom to ring . . . we will . . . speed up that day when all God's children, black men and white men, Jews and Gentiles, Protestants and Catholics, will . . . sing . . . "Free at last! Free at last! Thank God almighty, we are free at last!"

### *Martin Luther King, Jr.*

---

Individuals also did their part for civil rights. In October 1962 James Meredith, a black veteran of the Korean War, enrolled at the all-white University of Mississippi. Whites who opposed integration took up arms and tried to keep Meredith from entering the university. After riots broke out, President Kennedy sent federal troops to keep order. Meredith became the first black graduate of the University of Mississippi.

Violence went on elsewhere, too. In May 1963 Martin Luther King, Jr., led peaceful marches in Birmingham, Alabama. King wanted to end segregation in the city's hotels and restaurants. The Birmingham police turned dogs and fire hoses on the marchers. Millions of Americans watched the terrible scene on television. This coverage helped win public sympathy for civil rights.

In June President Kennedy called for new civil rights laws. Kennedy wanted to end segregation in public places and discrimination in hiring. To show support, Martin Luther King, Jr., led a "March on Washington" in August 1963. More than 200,000 blacks and whites flocked to the capital. There King spoke of his dream—a country where Americans of all races would be united. After King's speech, the crowd sang a black spiritual entitled "We Shall Overcome." This song became the theme song of the civil rights movement.

## A National Tragedy

President Kennedy did not live to see the fruits of his civil rights work. On November 22, 1963, Kennedy and his wife, Jacqueline,

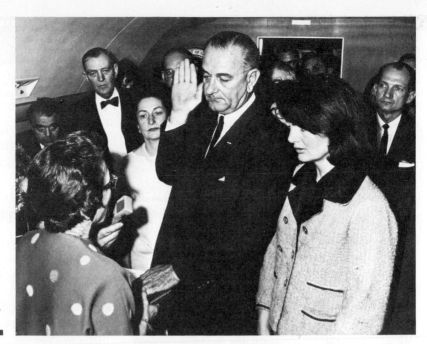

Lyndon Johnson took the oath of office aboard Air Force One, the presidential jet, shortly after the assassination of President Kennedy. By his side were Lady Bird Johnson (left) and Jacqueline Kennedy (right).

were riding through Dallas in an open car. Crowds waved and cheered. Then shots rang out, and two bullets struck Kennedy. The President died almost at once.

**Kennedy's death stuns the world.** The sudden shooting caused widespread shock. America's friends and foes alike paid tribute to the slain President. In Communist Yugoslavia, President Tito ordered flags flown at half-mast. In the Soviet Union, televisions broadcast the President's funeral. In Washington, D.C., a flame was kept burning over Kennedy's grave in Arlington Cemetery.

Meanwhile, the Dallas police had arrested a suspect, Lee Harvey Oswald. Oswald said he was innocent, but the evidence against him appeared strong. Oswald never stood trial, however. On November 24, as he was being moved to a new jail, he was shot and killed by Jack Ruby, a Dallas nightclub owner.

**Johnson becomes President.** On the afternoon of the assassination, Vice President Lyndon B. Johnson was sworn in as President. Few Presidents have had more political experience than Johnson. A Texan, he served several terms in the House of Representatives. In 1948 he was elected to the Senate. As Senate Majority Leader, Johnson

was the driving force behind many of the laws passed during the Eisenhower years.

After the shock of Kennedy's death, Americans were relieved by Johnson's promise to keep working for the goals that Kennedy had proposed. Other world leaders praised the smooth changeover from one presidency to another.

## SECTION REVIEW

1. **Vocabulary**   intelligence, guerrilla, fallout, disarmament
2. **People and Places**   Richard M. Nixon, John F. Kennedy, Berlin, Bay of Pigs, Thurgood Marshall, James Meredith, Martin Luther King, Jr., Lee Harvey Oswald, Lyndon B. Johnson
3. **Comprehension**   What two major problems did President Kennedy have with Cuba?
4. **Comprehension**   What gains did blacks make during Kennedy's administration?
5. **Critical Thinking**   Why, do you think, did Congress support the space program and block so much other New Frontier legislation?

721

### Vocabulary

controversy

activist

Lyndon B. Johnson's long service in the House and Senate proved useful to him as President. He was able to push many bills through Congress to bring social reforms to the United States. In foreign policy, though,

## Our Presidents

### LYNDON B. JOHNSON

★ 1963–1969 ★

**36**TH PRESIDENT

DEMOCRAT

★ Born August 27, 1908, in Texas

★ Married Claudia Alta "Lady Bird" Taylor in 1934; 2 children

★ Representative and senator from Texas; Majority Leader of the Senate; Vice President under Kennedy

★ Lived in Texas when elected Vice President

★ Vice President: Hubert H. Humphrey

★ Died January 22, 1973, in Texas

★ Key events while in office: Twenty-fourth and Twenty-fifth amendments; Great Society programs; Civil Rights Act of 1964; Voting Rights Act of 1965; Vietnam War

Johnson was less successful. American involvement in the Vietnam War divided the country and led to trouble for Johnson's presidency.

### Promising Times

As Kennedy's Vice President, Johnson had spoken out strongly for social reforms. Now, as the new President, Johnson held fast to these goals. He proposed sweeping new changes as part of his **Great Society** plan. In one speech, he described the Great Society this way:

> In a land of great wealth, families must not live in hopeless poverty. In a land rich in harvest, children just must not go hungry. In a land of healing miracles, neighbors must not suffer and die unattended. In a great land of learning . . . young people must be taught to read and write.

**Johnson works smoothly with Congress.** President Johnson was determined to follow through on Kennedy's call for a civil rights bill. He persuaded many members of Congress to vote for such a measure. On July 2, the **Civil Rights Act of 1964** became law. This far-reaching act outlawed race discrimination in public places, on the job, and at the polls.

Johnson also declared a "War on Poverty." In August 1964 Congress passed the **Economic Opportunity Act.** This measure set aside almost $1 billion for job-training and preschool programs. It created a system of food stamps to help the needy buy groceries. It also gave funding to **Volunteers in Service to America** (VISTA). VISTA was much like the Peace Corps but its aim was to aid poor Americans.

**Johnson wins the 1964 election.** Lyndon Johnson was eager to take even bolder action. In 1964 he ran for reelection

## CITIZENSHIP • Freedom and Opportunity

The Civil Rights Act of 1964 and the Voting Rights Act of 1965 meant equal treatment for all Americans in public places, at work, and at the polls. Yet laws alone could not always guarantee minority citizens a fair chance to share fully in American life. As President Johnson said in 1965, "It is not enough to open the gates of opportunity. All our citizens must have the ability to walk through those gates." Johnson knew that for many Americans, especially members of minority groups, poor schools and poor living conditions were hurdles to getting ahead.

The government tried to help in several ways. It funded community health clinics and job-training and placement programs. It began Project Head Start, a preschool program for children from low-income families. It built new, affordable housing in urban areas. These efforts, along with the tireless work of civil rights leaders and community members, began to make a difference. More minority citizens reached positions of leadership in America. Equal opportunity was becoming a reality in life as well as in law.

**A Head Start classroom**

---

as the Democratic candidate for President. Republican Senator Barry Goldwater of Arizona ran against him. Goldwater criticized the government's policies to help black Americans and the poor. He also urged the United States to end the Vietnam War by bombing North Vietnam.

Goldwater's ideas seemed dangerous to many people. Johnson won the election by a landslide. The President received almost 16 million more votes than Goldwater, and he carried 44 states. Johnson now felt that the American people were fully behind him. As a result, he doubled his efforts to make the Great Society a reality.

**Great Society laws improve American life.** A spirit of reform marked the Johnson years. The President proposed several bills that Congress passed into law. In 1965 two education acts provided funds for schools and loans for college students. Another act set up **Medicare**—a health-care program for people 65 or older.

Also in 1965, President Johnson established the **Department of Housing and Urban Development** (HUD). Its role was to improve city life. To head the department, Johnson chose Robert C. Weaver. Weaver became the first black Cabinet member. In 1966 Johnson set up another Cabinet agency—the **Department of Transportation.**

Protecting consumers and the environment was also important to Johnson. New laws called for product safety and truth in advertising. Other laws set standards for clean air and water. The President's wife, Lady Bird Johnson, worked hard to beautify American highways. Another determined

President Johnson asked Congress for many new government programs. Some Americans worried about the long-term effects of the changes taking place. According to this cartoon, to what could Johnson's program be compared?

woman, scientist Rachel Carson, warned Americans about overusing pest-killers. Her book *Silent Spring* inspired a law against DDT and other harmful poisons.

**Minorities make gains.** Ending racial injustice remained a key goal in the Great Society. Congress funded special programs for Native Americans. The Immigration Act of 1965 did away with quotas that worked against certain groups.

Another major step forward came with the **Voting Rights Act of 1965.** Before this act became law, many states used unfair literacy tests to keep blacks from voting. Martin Luther King, Jr., called attention to this situation. On March 7, 1965, he planned a peaceful march between Selma and Montgomery, Alabama. Outside Selma, state police met the marchers with tear gas and clubs. Many marchers were badly beaten, and Americans

who watched the scene on television were shocked. After two days, President Johnson sent in the National Guard. A short time later, he signed the Voting Rights Act. This act put an end to literacy tests. Thousands of blacks could now register to vote for the first time.

**A new amendment is added to the Constitution.** Another development during the Johnson years was the passage of the **Twenty-fifth Amendment.** According to this amendment, the President can choose a Vice President if that office becomes vacant. The amendment also outlines when and how a Vice President should take over the duties of the presidency.

**The Supreme Court acts on social issues.** The Chief Justice of the Supreme Court during the Johnson administration was Earl Warren. Warren took a liberal position on many social issues. Under his leadership the Court made many decisions that aroused public **controversy** —dispute between sides with opposite views.

Two controversial cases concerned prayers and Bible readings in the public schools. The justices ruled that neither practice should be allowed. The Constitution, they said, calls for separation of church and state. Yet some Americans objected to the decision. They felt that it weakened religion in the United States.

*Miranda* v. *Arizona* was another landmark case. The Court decided that persons accused of a crime must be informed of their rights before being questioned by the police. If the police fail to do this, and the accused person confesses, the confession cannot be used in court. Some Americans cheered the *Miranda* decision as necessary for the protection of citizens' rights. Other Americans took a more critical view. They thought the Court was putting the rights of the criminal before the rights of the victim.

Americans also disagreed over the Supreme Court's stand on school busing. In some school districts, busing was used as a way to end school segregation. White children were bused to schools in black neighborhoods, and black children were bused to white schools. Many parents disliked the busing plan. They worried for their children's safety in unfamiliar neighborhoods. They also objected to the extra time students spent getting to and from school. These views did not sway the Supreme Court. The justices said that integration was needed, that busing was proper, and that those involved had to cooperate.

The Supreme Court also ruled in favor of **affirmative action**—policies that give minorities special consideration for job positions and college admissions. The Court hoped that by taking affirmative action, society could make up for past discrimination. Again the Court had opponents. Some people argued that affirmative action would discriminate against whites.

## Discontent at Home

New laws failed to satisfy all groups of Americans. Many people still felt unjustly treated. Some of these people found strength in numbers. By organizing and working together, they tried to right the wrongs they suffered.

**The women's movement continues.** During the Johnson years, women began to speak out because they did not have the same opportunities men did. Many women felt pressure to marry and spend their lives as homemakers. Women who worked outside the home were usually limited to low-level, low-paying jobs. Though women made up nearly half the work force, few held top positions in business. Only a small number of women had professional jobs. One reason for this was that medical and law schools accepted only a small number of female students. Even with the proper training, women made less money than men who did the same work.

Many women decided the time had come for change. The Civil Rights Act of 1964 made it illegal to discriminate on the basis of sex. Now more and more women sued the schools and businesses that discriminated against them. They also joined forces in the **National Organization for Women** (NOW). This group, led by Betty Friedan, worked to pass more laws giving women equal rights.

During the 1960's many Americans protested job discrimination against women. The message on this woman's poster became law under the Equal Employment Opportunity Act of 1972.

**Mexican-American citizens speak out.** Chicanos, or Mexican-Americans, also made demands during the Johnson years. Under the leadership of Cesar Chávez, Chicano farm workers in the Southwest formed a union. They persuaded people around the country to boycott grapes and lettuce grown on nonunion farms. As a result, the farm owners agreed to provide higher pay and better working conditions to the workers.

Other Mexican-Americans fought for government aid to relieve poverty. Chicano activists —people who believe in strong action to solve problems—began a political movement called La Raza, meaning "The People." This movement helped Mexican-Americans gain election to public office on the local, state, and national levels.

In this 1973 photograph, Cesar Chávez (center) talks to migrant farm workers in California. Chávez helped migrant farm workers form labor unions to protect their rights.

coined the term *black power.* The **black-power movement** had a clear-cut goal: to build strength among blacks by organizing politically and starting all-black schools and businesses. The movement also boosted racial pride. African styles of dress swept into fashion, and "Black is beautiful" became a popular slogan.

Most blacks still supported the goals and peaceful methods of Martin Luther King, Jr. As some black activists became more aggressive, however, many Americans stopped supporting civil rights.

**Young people rebel.** During the Johnson years, almost 40 percent of the population was under the age of 20. Millions of young Americans were concerned about injustices. They began to challenge many aspects of American life.

Some young people shocked older Americans by "dropping out" of American life. They turned their backs on mainstream society and proclaimed peace, love, and greater personal freedom as their main values. This spirit ran through much of the music of the times. The Beatles sang "All You Need Is Love," and Bob Dylan scored a hit with "The Times, They Are A-Changin'."

Meanwhile, other young people took political action. Some joined the civil rights movement. Some spoke out against war, big business, and those in power. Student protests rocked campuses from the University of California at Berkeley to Columbia University in New York.

## Trouble Overseas

One of the chief targets of student protest was American foreign policy. Many young people believed that the United States' military involvement in Vietnam was wrong. They also objected to President Johnson's actions in Latin America.

**Johnson sends troops to the Dominican Republic.** In April 1965 a civil war broke out in the Dominican Republic, an island nation southeast of Cuba. President Johnson sent in about 22,000 United States troops. He hoped to stop Communist rebels from taking over the Dominican government.

**Blacks riot in American cities.** For urban blacks, the new civil rights laws brought few improvements in day-to-day life. Blacks still lived in crowded ghettos, paying high rents for poor housing. Adults had trouble finding jobs. Children went to inferior schools. As anger mounted, minor incidents often touched off acts of violence.

In August 1965, six days of looting and burning followed a traffic arrest in the Watts district of Los Angeles. Over the next three summers, riots broke out in black neighborhoods in New York, Detroit, and more than 100 other cities. The riots caused thousands of injuries and deaths and about $112 billion in damage.

New black leaders also spoke out angrily against racial injustice. Malcolm X argued for separation, rather than integration, of the races. Nonviolent protest, he said, had not succeeded in bringing about equality. Another black leader, Stokely Carmichael,

On May 6 a cease-fire was called. Yet American soldiers stayed on the island for more than a year, until new democratic leaders were elected. Many Americans had mixed feelings about their government's intervention. Some people said the Communists had never posed a threat to the Dominican Republic. They also criticized the United States for acting without consulting neighboring countries.

**The United States builds up its forces in Southeast Asia.** During this same period, the United States' role in Vietnam was growing. Like Eisenhower and Kennedy, President Johnson believed in the domino theory. He feared that if Vietnam fell to Communists, then other Southeast Asian countries would fall, too. As a result, he continued to send American soldiers to fight the Vietcong.

In August 1964 the United States received reports that North Vietnamese torpedo boats had attacked two American destroyers in the Tonkin Gulf. (See map on page 728.) Immediately President Johnson ordered the bombing of North Vietnam. Then he asked Congress to pass the **Tonkin Gulf Resolution.** This bill gave the President power "to take all necessary measures ... to prevent further aggression."

The Resolution passed both houses of Congress with only two votes against it. The stage was now set for a major war. In late 1964 about 23,000 American troops were in Vietnam. That number rose to about 500,000 within 3 years.

The fighting grew steadily heavier, too. The Americans and South Vietnamese struck at enemy territory with bombs, rockets, and Agent Orange—a chemical that killed plant life. The Vietcong and North Vietnamese, who had less air power, depended more on ground attacks by guerrilla fighters. South Vietnamese peasant farmers often suffered heavily in the fighting. Some of their villages were destroyed, and many peasants were mistreated by soldiers from both sides.

United States marines jump from a helicopter to secure a hilltop battle position during the Vietnam War. Helicopters were used for moving troops, locating the enemy, and evacuating the wounded.

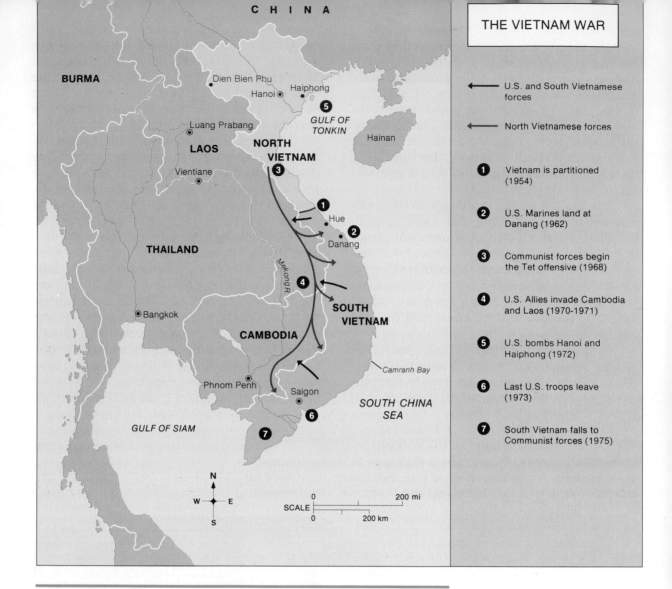

THE VIETNAM WAR

⬅ U.S. and South Vietnamese forces

⬅ North Vietnamese forces

**1** Vietnam is partitioned (1954)

**2** U.S. Marines land at Danang (1962)

**3** Communist forces begin the Tet offensive (1968)

**4** U.S. Allies invade Cambodia and Laos (1970-1971)

**5** U.S. bombs Hanoi and Haiphong (1972)

**6** Last U.S. troops leave (1973)

**7** South Vietnam falls to Communist forces (1975)

## Map Study

**This map shows Southeast Asia and the key events of the Vietnam War. Into what two countries was Vietnam partitioned in 1954? What countries lay in the path of the Tet Offensive? Across what body of water did American forces attack Hanoi and Haiphong?**

**The Vietnam War stirs controversy.** Every day, American newspapers and televisions carried stories about the war. As Americans followed the conflict and saw the casualties mount, many people began to question President Johnson's policies. "Hawks"—those who approved of the war—thought America should take stronger action. They believed that the country's full military power should be unleashed against the Communists. "Doves"—those in favor of peace—urged Johnson to pull all American troops out of Southeast Asia.

Between 1965 and 1967, Johnson tried a number of times to end the Vietnam War. None of his efforts succeeded. Meanwhile, the United States sent more soldiers and supplies to South Vietnam. In the fall of 1967,

American military leaders felt sure that victory was near. Then the Vietcong launched the **Tet Offensive**—a series of attacks on South Vietnam during February 1968.* The Tet Offensive caught the Americans and South Vietnamese off guard. Thousands of soldiers were killed or wounded. In addition, the battles severely shook Americans' belief that the United States could win the war.

## The Terrible Year of 1968

The Tet Offensive was an early blow in a troubled year. As 1968 unfolded, two murders shocked the American public and political disorder grew.

**Johnson makes a surprising announcement.** Most Democrats assumed that Lyndon Johnson would be their candidate for President in the 1968 election. Many Democrats, however, were against the war. One antiwar leader, Senator Eugene McCarthy of Minnesota, decided to challenge Johnson for the nomination.

To the surprise of most political experts, McCarthy won 42 percent of the votes in the New Hampshire primary. Soon afterward, Senator Robert Kennedy of New York also entered the race. Kennedy had been Attorney General under his brother, the late President John F. Kennedy.

On March 31, 1968, President Johnson told Americans that he would not run for reelection. "I shall not seek," he said, "and I will not accept the nomination of my party for another term as President." In the same speech, Johnson announced that he was stopping the bombing of North Vietnam. His advisers had told him that the United States could not win the war without sending at least 200,000 more soldiers.

**The spring and summer of 1968 bring more upheaval.** On April 4, an assassin shot Martin Luther King, Jr., in Memphis, Tennessee. King's killer was James Earl Ray, a white escaped convict. About two months after King's death, a Middle Eastern immigrant named Sirhan Sirhan shot Robert Kennedy in Los Angeles. Kennedy had just won the California Democratic primary.

After Kennedy's death, most Democrats decided to back Vice President Hubert Humphrey for President. Humphrey, a former senator from Minnesota, had moderate views. In August, at the Democratic National Convention in Chicago, Humphrey easily won his party's nomination.

Meanwhile, outside the convention hall, thousands of young people gathered to protest the Vietnam War. Their violent clashes with the Chicago police were seen by television audiences across the country.

**Nixon wins by a narrow margin.** Humphrey's rivals for the office of President were Republican Richard Nixon and third-party candidate George Wallace. Wallace, the governor of Alabama, called for segregation and a return to more law and order. Nixon, who had been Vice President under Eisenhower, also campaigned for law and order. In addition, he promised a balanced budget and "an honorable end to the war in Vietnam."

The popular vote in the 1968 election was close. Nixon, however, received a clear majority. Though the mood of the country was still unsettled, Americans were ready for a change in leadership.

## SECTION REVIEW

1. **Vocabulary**   controversy, activist
2. **People and Places**   Barry Goldwater, Rachel Carson, Earl Warren, Betty Friedan, Cesar Chávez, Malcolm X, Stokely Carmichael, the Dominican Republic, Tonkin Gulf, Hubert Humphrey, Richard Nixon, George Wallace
3. **Comprehension**   How did Great Society laws help Americans build a better future?
4. **Comprehension**   What troubles at home and abroad overshadowed Johnson's achievements?
5. **Critical Thinking**   Do you think Congress gave up its war-making powers by passing the Tonkin Gulf Resolution? Why or why not?

---

* Tet is the Vietnamese New Year's holiday.

# MAPS AND GRAPHS: Reading an Election Map

An election map is a special-purpose map that shows how people voted in a given election. By studying an election map, you can see at a glance where each candidate had the most support. From this information, you can draw conclusions about regional voting patterns.

Presidential elections, as you know, begin with a popular vote in which citizens vote for electors from their candidate's party. Then the winning electors from each state choose the President. Generally, all the electoral votes of each state go to the candidate whose party won the most popular votes. This is only a tradition, though, and not law. Sometimes electors go against the popular majority when they vote.

The map below uses color to show how electors voted in the 1968 presidential election. The numbers on the states tell how many electoral votes each state had. In addition, the map key gives you information about the popular vote.

Study the map below carefully. Then answer the questions that follow.

1. Which state had the most electoral votes? Which candidate carried this state?
2. Which candidate received the votes of Florida? Does this mean that all Florida voters favored this candidate? Explain.
3. In which area of the country did George Wallace make the strongest showing?
4. Who was most successful in the West?
5. Which state did not give all its electoral votes to a single candidate?
6. Was the race between Nixon and Humphrey closer in the popular vote or the electoral vote?
7. To become President, a candidate must receive a majority of the electoral votes. In 1968 this meant winning at least 270 out of a possible 538 votes. What would have happened if Humphrey had won California's votes?

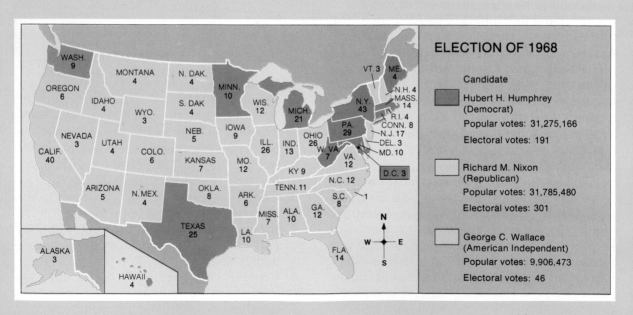

ELECTION OF 1968

Candidate

Hubert H. Humphrey (Democrat)
Popular votes: 31,275,166
Electoral votes: 191

Richard M. Nixon (Republican)
Popular votes: 31,785,480
Electoral votes: 301

George C. Wallace (American Independent)
Popular votes: 9,906,473
Electoral votes: 46

# What triumphs and setbacks did the Nixon and Ford years bring?

## Vocabulary
deficit

draft evader

Richard Nixon faced many challenges as President. He had to deal with the Vietnam War and other troubles from the Johnson years. During his first term, Nixon achieved some startling successes, especially overseas. A scandal during his second term, however, forced him out of office.

### Ending the Vietnam War

When President Nixon took office, the country was deeply divided over the Vietnam War. Nixon believed that peace at home depended on peace in Southeast Asia. He and his adviser on foreign policy, Henry Kissinger, soon announced a plan to end the war.

**Nixon withdraws troops from Vietnam.** Nixon and Kissinger agreed that American troops should be brought home. Yet they did not want the United States to let down its South Vietnamese allies. Nixon decided to pull American soldiers out of the region gradually. As they left, South Vietnamese soldiers would be trained to take their places.

The first withdrawal of United States forces began in the summer of 1969. By early 1972, fewer than 140,000 American troops remained in Vietnam. There had been about four times that many two years before.

**Renewed involvement sparks fresh protests.** Unfortunately, the plan to turn over the fighting to the South Vietnamese did not work well. With less American aid, the South Vietnamese began losing to the Communists. As a result, President Nixon again expanded the war. On April 30, 1970, he sent American troops to Cambodia to destroy North Vietnamese supply bases there.

College students protested at once. At Kent State University in Ohio, the National Guard had to be called in to keep order. When the students began throwing objects and shouting insults, some of the soldiers panicked. They fired into the crowd, killing four students. The tragedy at Kent State stirred even stronger antiwar feelings. Yet in

## Our Presidents

### RICHARD M. NIXON

★ **1969–1974** ★

**37**TH PRESIDENT

REPUBLICAN

★ Born January 9, 1913, in California

★ Married Thelma Catherine Patricia "Pat" Ryan in 1940; 2 children

★ Lawyer; representative and senator from California; Vice President under Eisenhower

★ Lived in New York when elected President

★ Vice Presidents: Spiro Agnew; Gerald R. Ford

★ Living

★ Resigned in 1974 to avoid impeachment

★ Key events while in office: American astronauts landed on the moon; Twenty-sixth Amendment; better relations with the People's Republic of China; American withdrawal from Vietnam War; Watergate scandal

February 1971 Nixon approved an invasion of Laos, the country north of Cambodia. About 200,000 angry Americans poured into Washington, D.C., to protest. Soon afterward, the State Department admitted:

> It is clear that a majority of Americans now favor the withdrawal of United States combat forces from Vietnam and an end to the Vietnam war.

**A peace treaty is signed in Paris.** While fighting continued in Vietnam, peace talks also got under way. In late September 1972, Henry Kissinger met with a North Vietnamese representative in Paris. When they were unable to reach an agreement, President Nixon decided to apply more pressure to North Vietnam. He ordered American troops to bomb Hanoi, the capital city, around the clock. Within two weeks, North Vietnam agreed to renew the peace talks.

In January 1973, leaders from the United States and North and South Vietnam signed a peace treaty. A cease-fire began at once. Within 60 days, most American troops returned home. Though fighting broke out again later, the peace treaty ended the Vietnam War for most Americans.

**Problems linger.** The bitter feelings sparked by the war proved long-lasting. More than 56,000 Americans lost their lives in the conflict, and five times that many came home wounded. These veterans rarely got a hero's welcome back home. The public saw the war as a dark chapter in American history, and returning soldiers received little thanks for their service. It was not until 1982 that a memorial to those who fought in Vietnam was built in Washington, D.C.

While some Americans wanted only to forget about the war, others tried to make sense of it. Many people thought the United States had made a mistake by fighting a distant war without clear support from the whole public. Many people also agreed that future Presidents should work more closely with Congress during military crises. As a result, Congress passed the **War Powers Act** in 1973. This law says that the President must have approval from Congress to send troops into combat for more than 60 days.

Another concern after the Vietnam War was the situation of POW's—prisoners of war—and MIA's—soldiers listed as missing in action. Though the North Vietnamese had agreed to free all POW's and help find MIA's, they did not fully cooperate. Some people believe there may still be American prisoners held in Southeast Asia.

## Tackling Other Tough Problems

As matters in Southeast Asia grew more settled, new concerns arose in the Middle East. Problems at home also demanded more attention.

**The Vietnam Veterans Memorial, designed by Maya Yang Lin, includes the name of every American soldier who died in the Vietnam War. Thousands of visitors have visited the memorial in Washington, D.C., since its dedication in November 1982.**

**The United States aids Israel in a Middle Eastern war.** In October 1973 the uneasy peace between Israel and its Arab neighbors broke down. Egypt and Syria attacked Israeli soldiers, and Israel struck back a few days later. This war is sometimes called the **Yom Kippur War** because it started on the Jewish holiday of Yom Kippur.

The fighting lasted only a few weeks. During this time, the Soviets helped Egypt and Syria while the United States sent planeloads of supplies to Israel. In response, some Arab nations cut off oil shipments to the United States. Though a cease-fire soon ended the war, the Arabs did not lift the oil embargo. Americans soon faced serious shortages of oil and gas.

**Nixon addresses the country's energy needs.** President Nixon proposed several ways to make up for the loss of Middle Eastern oil. He asked Congress to pass laws limiting outdoor lighting and reducing speed limits on highways. He also asked for a higher tax on oil. With these measures, Nixon hoped to conserve oil. At the same time, the United States began to produce more oil. The federal government helped drill offshore oil wells and build the **Alaska pipeline.** This pipeline carried oil from the north coast to tankers in southern Alaska.

Along with its energy problem, the United States had a pollution problem. The air was clouded by smoke from cars and factories. Waste was often dumped into rivers and lakes. To help keep pollution in check, the government decided to set up a new office, the **Environmental Protection Agency (EPA)**, in 1970.

**Nixon tries to strengthen the economy.** The economy presented another challenge to the President. The worst economic problem in the 1970's was inflation. In 1950 a bag of groceries might have cost about $10. In 1975 the same bag cost about $22—an increase of 220 percent. As prices rose, workers demanded higher wages to cover their cost of living. To pay these wages, companies had to raise the prices of their goods. As a result, inflation kept climbing.

President Nixon tried to halt inflation. He proposed price controls and wage freezes. Neither strategy worked. People cut back on their spending, so businesses lost money. To make up for their losses, businesses cut back their production and fired workers. This resulted in a recession. The unemployment rate doubled.

For the government as well as the people, times were hard. Federal officials had spent vast sums on the Great Society, the Vietnam War, and energy development. The government had created a huge budget **deficit** — debt—because it spent more money than it took in. Many Americans were alarmed. They wanted the government to balance its budget. Yet they did not want to give up social, scientific, and defense programs.

## Rebuilding American Pride

One of the government's costliest efforts was the space program. Successes in space, however, boosted Americans' pride. So did progress made in relations with the Soviets and Chinese. Gains for women and minorities also gave people a sense of triumph.

**The exploration of space continues.** Since 1960 the goal of the United States space program had been to put an American on the moon. On July 20, 1969, the dream came true. Millions of people watched on television as *Apollo 11* astronaut Neil A. Armstrong set foot on the moon. He spoke these memorable words: "That's one small step for a man, one giant leap for mankind." Between 1969 and 1972, five more crews of American astronauts landed on the moon.

**Nixon opens talks with China and the Soviet Union.** With Americans outshining the Soviets in space, and with strong armed forces at home, Nixon began trying to ease world tensions.

The United States had broken off relations with the People's Republic of China in 1949. (See Chapter 30.) In February 1972 Nixon visited Beijing, the Chinese capital. He was the first President ever to travel to China. After a week of talks, Nixon and China's Premier Zhou En-lai (jo en-LY) made a joint statement. Both leaders promised to develop trade and to work out their differences peacefully.

President and Mrs. Nixon dined with Premier Zhou En-lai (left) during their 1972 visit to Beijing. As a result of this visit, relations between the United States and the People's Republic of China improved. In 1979 the United States extended diplomatic recognition to China.

A few months after the China trip, President Nixon visited the Soviet capital, Moscow. There he and Soviet leader Leonid Brezhnev (BREZH-nef) signed a treaty to limit the use of missiles. Since 1969, Soviets and Americans had been working toward such an agreement. Their meetings were named the **Strategic Arms Limitation Talks** (SALT).

President Nixon remained firmly anti-Communist. By meeting with Communist leaders, though, he hoped to reduce the threat of another world war. Nixon called this policy **détente** (day-TAHNT), borrowing a French word for "the relaxing of tensions."

**Women press for equality.** Meanwhile, changes were also taking place at home. Since 1923, women had been trying to amend the Constitution to prevent sex discrimination. Finally, in 1972, Congress proposed the **Equal Rights Amendment** (ERA). The ERA said that "Equality of rights under the law shall not be denied . . . by the United States or by any state on account of sex."

Before the ERA could become law, 38 states had to approve it. Twenty-one states did so within six months. In some parts of the country, however, many people campaigned against the ERA. Some said that the Constitution already did enough to protect women's rights. Others feared that under the ERA, women might be drafted into the army. In the end, only 35 states passed the ERA, and the measure failed.

Meanwhile, women were breaking new ground as political leaders. In 1972 New York Representative Shirley Chisholm made a bid to become the Democratic candidate for President. In 1974 Ella Grasso was elected governor of Connecticut. Other women earned appointments as judges, ambassadors, and presidential advisers. One such woman was Romana A. Bañuelos, a Mexican-American. President Nixon named her to be Treasurer of the United States.

**Minorities make advances.** Women were not the only Americans gaining more rights. Many Native Americans were calling attention to the discrimination they suffered in jobs and housing. To press for more government protection, a group of Native Americans began the **American Indian Movement** (AIM) in 1968.

AIM members and other Indians sometimes used extreme means to force change. In 1972, activists took over the Bureau of Indian Affairs in Washington, D.C. The next year a group of armed Sioux seized the town of Wounded Knee, South Dakota. Meanwhile, other Native Americans brought suits in court. By 1976 the Indians had won about $640 million in settlement payments.

Legal action also helped the handicapped gain more opportunities. During the 1970's Congress set up job-training programs for the disabled and banned discrimination in hiring. Other new laws said that public buildings had to have ramps or elevators for people in wheelchairs.

The young also made gains in the 1970's. In 1971 the **Twenty-sixth Amendment** became law. This amendment extended voting rights to those between 18 and 21 years old.

## The Watergate Crisis

The positive changes during Nixon's first term helped the President win reelection in 1972. Nixon's Democratic opponent, Senator George McGovern of South Dakota, carried only one state and the District of Columbia. Nixon viewed his landslide victory as a vote of confidence from the American people. Soon, however, scandal about the election forced the President out of office.

**Nixon approves illegal activities.** Almost from the start of his administration, Nixon worried about government workers leaking sensitive information to the press. He sought help from the **Federal Bureau of Investigation** (FBI). The FBI's job is to enforce federal laws and protect the country's security. In May 1969 Nixon ordered the FBI to spy on staff people he mistrusted.

By 1972 the White House was spying on its Democratic opponents as well. The Democratic party had its headquarters in the Watergate building in Washington, D.C. In June 1972, police caught five men breaking into Watergate. One of these burglars turned out to be a campaign worker for the President.

At once the White House tried to cover up its part in the break-in. President Nixon ordered the FBI and the CIA not to look into the matter. Then he arranged to pay the people involved as much as $1 million to keep quiet.

**The nation learns about Watergate.** Meanwhile, a secret source in the White

---

## ★★★ *Watergate*

On August 9, 1974, Richard M. Nixon made history as the first President ever to resign. The House of Representatives was ready to impeach him, and the Senate seemed certain to convict him. A number of White House officials had already confessed to crimes of wiretapping, theft, and tampering with evidence. Nixon, they said, had been a part of these activities.

Nearly 200 years earlier, the Framers of the Constitution had feared such abuses of power. For just this reason, they had set up the system of checks and balances. They had created three branches of government—Congress, the presidency, and the Supreme Court— each with the power to check the others.

The Watergate scandal stunned and angered Americans. Yet it proved without doubt that the system of checks and balances still works today.

---

House was giving information to Carl Bernstein and Bob Woodward, two reporters at the *Washington Post*. The *Post* broke the news that the White House had been involved in the **Watergate scandal.** President Nixon denied the story, but the Senate began an investigation in May 1973.

In July the Senate committee, chaired by Sam Ervin of North Carolina, learned that the President had recorded all his telephone conversations. The committee members realized that these tapes might prove that the President knew about Watergate. Nixon, however, refused to hand over the tapes. Finally, in October, he released 7 out of more than 60 tapes. On one of these, 18 minutes of key evidence had been erased.

**The Vice President resigns.** All through this time, the press reported more stories about dishonesty in the White House. Some said that the President had traded political

## GERALD R. FORD

★ 1974–1977 ★

**38TH PRESIDENT**

REPUBLICAN

★ Born July 14, 1913, in Nebraska

★ Married Elizabeth "Betty" Bloomer Warren in 1948; 4 children

★ Lawyer; representative from Michigan; Minority Leader of the House of Representatives; Vice President under Nixon

★ Lived in Michigan when appointed Vice President

★ Vice President: Nelson A. Rockefeller

★ Living

★ First President not elected to either the vice presidency or the presidency

★ Key events while in office: Nixon pardon; *Mayaguez* rescue; United States Bicentennial

---

favors for campaign contributions. Americans also learned that Nixon owed almost $500,000 in back taxes. Spiro T. Agnew, the Vice President since 1969, was also accused of cheating on his taxes. Agnew resigned in October to avoid standing trial.

President Nixon then nominated Representative Gerald Ford of Michigan to take Agnew's place. Congress approved the appointment. Ford officially became Vice President on December 6, 1973.

**Nixon resigns.** By mid-1974 Congress had grown angry enough to begin the process of impeaching President Nixon. A committee of the House of Representatives charged Nixon with standing in the way of justice and abusing his power.

On August 5, 1974, the President released the rest of his tapes. The tapes made it clear that Nixon had known about the break-in and the cover-up. He had also lied to the public at least 17 times. President Nixon now faced almost certain conviction on impeachment charges. To avoid such disgrace, he resigned on August 9. That same day Gerald Ford became President.

**Ford tries to bury the past.** One of the new President's first acts was to pardon Richard Nixon. This meant that Nixon could not be tried for any crimes he might have committed.† Many Americans disagreed with Ford's decision. However, some felt that Watergate should be forgotten.

President Ford took other steps to heal past wounds. He softened the punishments for Vietnam War **draft evaders** —people who had refused to join the armed forces. Some draft evaders had already served time in jail and were freed. Others had fled to Canada and now returned home.

**Congress moves to prevent future misdeeds.** During the Watergate hearings, investigators found that the CIA and FBI had taken part in crimes. They had illegally tapped telephone lines and destroyed evidence. As a result, Congress put the two agencies under stricter control. Congress also passed the **Freedom of Information Act.** This act gave the press easier access to government documents.

Congress also decided to set rules about campaign contributions. It passed a reform act that changed the way campaigns were funded. This law limited the dollar amount that people can give to a campaign. It also provided a way for presidential candidates to obtain federal funds.

Congress and President Ford worked hard to bring more openness to government. Yet the memory of Watergate was slow to fade. Other troubles persisted, too. Inflation stayed high. Oil and gasoline were still in short supply. Overseas, Southeast Asia remained a troubled region.

---

† Most of Nixon's key aides were tried, convicted, and sentenced to prison.

**South Vietnam falls.** Even after American troops left Vietnam, the United States sent billions of dollars to help the South Vietnamese. The aid was not enough. In April 1975 the North Vietnamese captured Saigon, South Vietnam's capital. Thereafter, Vietnam became a united country under Communist rule.

Shortly after the fall of Saigon, American forces made a brief return to Southeast Asia. In May 1975, Communists from Cambodia seized an unarmed United States ship, the *Mayaguez*. President Ford quickly sent troops to rescue the ship and its crew.

**The United States celebrates a birthday.** The year 1976 marked a milestone for the United States. On July 4, the country celebrated its **Bicentennial**, or two-hundredth birthday. The occasion gave Americans a chance to reflect on the past. Recent events— the Watergate scandal, the Vietnam War, social protests—had severely shaken the nation. Yet Americans had weathered these crises, just as they had done many times before. In 1976 the country was again at peace.

## SECTION REVIEW

1. **Vocabulary**   deficit, draft evader
2. **People and Places**   Henry Kissinger, Kent State University, Israel, Neil A. Armstrong, Beijing, Zhou En-lai, Moscow, Leonid Brezhnev, George McGovern, Watergate, Spiro Agnew, Gerald Ford
3. **Comprehension**   What were President Nixon's main achievements in détente?
4. **Comprehension**   How did President Ford and Congress try to heal the nation's wounds after Watergate?
5. **Critical Thinking**   Did Richard Nixon's contributions as President outweigh his mistakes? Explain.

# Chapter 31 Summary

In the early 1960's President John F. Kennedy took a tough stand against communism. He sent more troops to Vietnam, approved the flawed Bay of Pigs invasion in Cuba, and won praise for his handling of the Cuban missile crisis. At the same time, Kennedy worked for world peace. He launched both the Peace Corps and the Alliance for Progress, and he worked out a test-ban treaty with the Soviet Union. Kennedy had less success at home, however, with his proposals for civil rights.

After Kennedy's assassination in 1963, Lyndon B. Johnson met many of Kennedy's goals. Through Great Society legislation like the Voting Rights Act of 1965, the Economic Opportunity Act, and Medicare, Johnson helped blacks, the young, the poor, the aged, and other minorities. However, many Americans turned against Johnson when he involved the United States more heavily in the Vietnam War. Unrest surfaced among the young and other groups. Women formed NOW to press for equal rights. Martin Luther King, Jr., led civil rights marches, while Stokely Carmichael and Malcolm X led the black-power movement.

Richard M. Nixon became President in 1968. Nixon's greatest successes were in foreign policy. He withdrew American forces from Vietnam, and his détente policy improved relations with Communist China and the Soviet Union. Meanwhile, minorities made gains at home, and American astronauts landed on the moon. After Nixon won reelection in 1972, Americans learned about the Watergate scandal. Nixon resigned from office in 1974, and Gerald Ford became President. Highlights of Ford's administration included his pardon of Nixon, his bold action in the *Mayaguez* incident, and the country's Bicentennial.

# Chapter 31 REVIEW

## Vocabulary and Key Terms

Choose the italicized terms in parentheses that best complete each sentence. Write your answers on a separate sheet of paper.

1. Volunteers in (*VISTA*/*the Peace Corps*) serve overseas, but those in (*VISTA*/*the Peace Corps*) work in the United States.
2. The "War on Poverty" was part of President Johnson's (*New Frontier*/*Great Society*) program.
3. (*Affirmative action*/*Medicare*) gives special consideration to minorities who have suffered discrimination.
4. American forces in Vietnam fought against the (*freedom riders*/*Vietcong*).
5. Many antiwar (*activists*/*guerrillas*) felt that the (*Tonkin Gulf Resolution*/*War Powers Act*) gave President Johnson too much power.
6. Arab countries placed an oil embargo on the United States after the (*Tet Offensive*/*Yom Kippur War*).

## Recalling the Facts

1. What was the Cuban missile crisis?
2. What changes came about as a result of the Great Society program?
3. How did the black-power movement differ from the civil rights movement led by Martin Luther King, Jr.?
4. How did Cesar Chávez help Mexican-Americans?
5. Why did many Americans criticize President Johnson's policies toward Vietnam?
6. Why was the Tet Offensive important?
7. What troubles plagued the American economy in the 1960's and 1970's?
8. What achievements did Americans make in space during the 1960's?
9. How did President Nixon put détente into practice?
10. What was the Equal Rights Amendment?
11. What led President Nixon to resign?

## Places to Locate

Match the letters on the map with the places listed below. Write your answers on a separate sheet of paper.

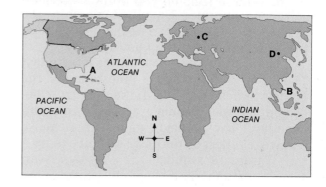

1. Beijing
2. Cuba
3. Moscow
4. Vietnam

## Critical Thinking

1. The Supreme Court under Chief Justice Earl Warren made a number of controversial decisions. Was the Warren court too liberal, as critics charged? Evaluate the following rulings in your response:
   a. school prayer
   b. the *Miranda* decision
   c. busing
   d. affirmative action
2. Should the United States have followed a different policy in Vietnam? Why or why not? Consider the following questions in your answer:
   a. What was the nature of the Vietnam War, and why was the United States involved?
   b. What might have happened if Johnson had followed the advice of "hawks" to increase the war effort?
   c. What might have happened if the United States had not aided South Vietnam or had withdrawn its forces earlier in the war?

3. Watergate became a major political scandal in the early 1970's. Some people, however, felt it was blown out of proportion. Was Watergate a serious crime? Why or why not? Consider these questions in your responses:
   a. What was the main issue?
   b. Are dishonesty and spying a normal part of politics?
   c. Should Nixon have been pardoned?
   d. What effects do you think Watergate had on Americans' views toward public officials? On other countries' views of the United States?

## Understanding History

1. Reread the section "Kennedy runs for office" on page 715. Then answer these questions.
   a. **Religion.** Why was Kennedy's religion an issue?
   b. **Science and Technology.** How did television help Kennedy's campaign?
2. Reread Martin Luther King's speech, "I Have a Dream," on page 720. Then answer these questions.
   a. **Primary Sources.** What do you think King meant by "the difficulties and frustrations of the moment"?
   b. **Citizenship.** What document does King quote in the first paragraph?
3. Reread the section "Nixon addresses the country's energy needs" on page 733. Then answer these questions.
   a. **Economics.** What economic step did Nixon take to discourage oil use?
   b. **Geography.** Why is it important to control pollution?

## Projects and Activities

1. **Reviewing Information.** Make flash cards to quiz classmates on key people and places discussed in this chapter.
2. **Researching Popular Culture.** Find out more about the music, books, movies, and styles of dress that were popular in the 1960's. Gather your findings into a scrapbook showing how the popular culture captured the mood of the times.

3. **Writing a Fictional Account.** Imagine that you were a witness to one of the following events: the "March on Washington" in 1963, the Democratic National Convention in 1968, the Indian takeover of Wounded Knee in 1973, or a Bicentennial celebration in 1976. Write a description of why you were there, what you saw, and how you felt.
4. **Analyzing Primary Sources.** Find a copy of President Kennedy's inaugural speech, the Tonkin Gulf Resolution, or President Johnson's speech on March 31, 1968, announcing an end to the bombing of North Vietnam. Read the document, and then summarize the key points in your own words.

## Practicing Your Skill

Study the presidential election map below. Then answer the questions that follow.

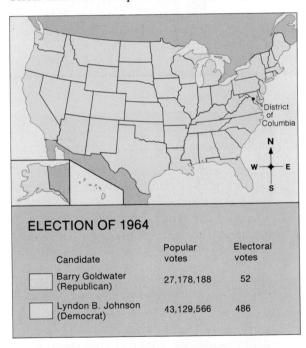

ELECTION OF 1964

| Candidate | Popular votes | Electoral votes |
|---|---|---|
| Barry Goldwater (Republican) | 27,178,188 | 52 |
| Lyndon B. Johnson (Democrat) | 43,129,566 | 486 |

1. Who won the 1964 election?
2. How many states did the losing candidate carry?
3. In what part of the country did the loser have the greatest strength?
4. Which was closer—the electoral vote or the popular vote?

# CHAPTER
# 32 America Reaches for New Horizons
## 1976–present

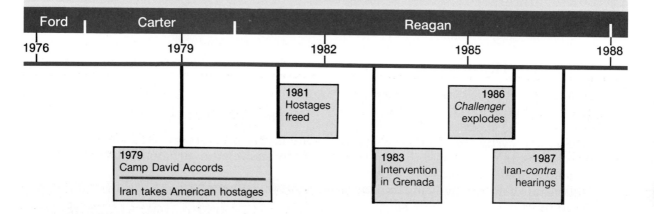

| Ford | Carter | | Reagan | | |
|---|---|---|---|---|---|
| 1976 | 1979 | 1982 | 1985 | | 1988 |

1981
Hostages
freed

1986
*Challenger*
explodes

1979
Camp David Accords

Iran takes American hostages

1983
Intervention
in Grenada

1987
Iran-*contra*
hearings

**In 1987 Americans celebrated the two-hundredth birthday of the United States Constitution with shows, parades, and balloons.**

## Preparing to Read

In 1976 the United States entered its third century as a free country. Americans had a history of growth and success, but they still faced challenges. Economic troubles and certain social problems needed attention. World tensions posed a threat to peace. Dwindling resources raised new concerns about the environment. Yet in spite of such worries, Americans looked to the future with hope. The quality of life was still improving for many people. As you read this chapter, try to answer the following questions:

1. What issues posed challenges for President Carter?
2. How did conservatism in the 1980's move the country in new directions?
3. What do recent developments suggest about the future?

# 1 What issues posed challenges for President Carter?

## Vocabulary

trade deficit

stagflation

deregulate

human rights

During the 1960's and early 1970's, the United States had experienced great social turmoil. In the late 1970's unrest gave way to calm, but many problems did not go away. An unstable economy, a serious energy crisis, and relations with other countries were all matters of pressing concern.

## A New Face in the White House and Familiar Problems

In 1976, two years after replacing Richard Nixon as President, Gerald Ford prepared to run for a full term in office. Ford won the Republican party's nomination. The Democrats chose Jimmy Carter, a Georgia peanut farmer, as their candidate. Carter had been almost unknown to the country when he set out to run for President. Yet he soon met with great success in state primary elections.

## Our Presidents

### JIMMY CARTER

★ 1977–1981 ★

**39**TH PRESIDENT

DEMOCRAT

★ Born October 1, 1924, in Georgia
★ Married Rosalynn Smith in 1946; 4 children
★ Peanut farmer; officer in the navy; governor of Georgia
★ Lived in Georgia when elected President
★ Vice President: Walter F. Mondale
★ Living
★ Key events while in office: Camp David Accords; Iran hostage crisis

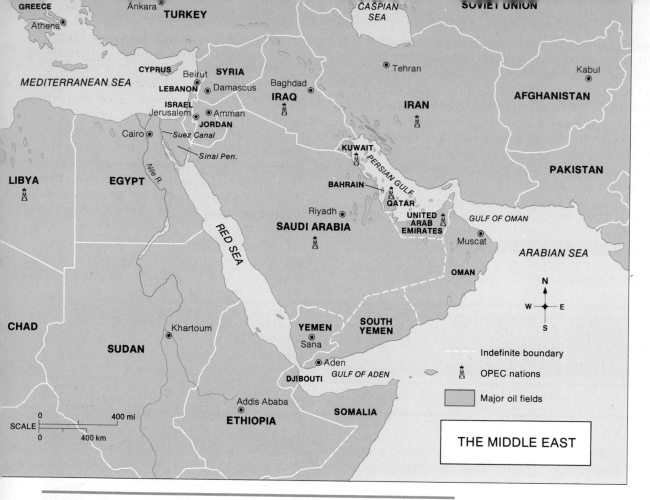

## Map Study

Rich oil reserves make the Middle East a region of great importance to the United States and other nations. Which Middle Eastern countries are members of OPEC? By what waterways does oil reach Europe from Kuwait?

**Carter wins a close race.** Carter, a former naval officer, had served as a state senator and governor of Georgia. Yet he was an "outsider" in national government, untouched by the Watergate affair. Carter's sincerity and simple manner appealed to many people. He gained wide support when he declared to the American public, "I will never lie to you."

By Election Day, experts said the race between Ford and Carter was "too close to call." The results of the popular vote were indeed close, but Carter won a clear victory in the Electoral College. The Democrats also kept control of Congress. This meant that for the first time in eight years, the country had a President whose political party held power in the legislature.

Carter, however, did not have strong ties to the Democratic leaders in Congress. Nor did he have experience with the way Congress worked. This made it hard for him to win votes for his programs.

**Economic troubles persist.** When Carter took office, inflation and unemployment were both on the rise. Another worry was the trade deficit —the imbalance that occurs when a country imports more than it exports. By the mid-1970's Americans were buying many goods from other countries. Japan, especially, offered strong competition to American manufacturers of cars, cameras, televisions, and small electronic goods. As a result, American factory owners cut back production and laid off workers. These unemployed workers had less money to spend, so other businesses suffered and still more workers lost their jobs.

At the same time that many Americans were out of work, prices of goods continued to rise. Businesses that were forced to cut production raised prices to protect their profits. A jump in the price of oil forced Americans to pay more for gasoline. Prices for other petroleum products, such as plastics, also rose. Such inflation combined with stagnant, or slow, business activity came to be called **stagflation.**

**The President attacks the problem.** To deal with the problem of unemployment, President Carter tried to create new jobs. He set up some public-works projects and cut taxes to encourage business growth. After Carter's first two years in office, however, about 6 million Americans were still out of work.

Carter's efforts to halt inflation also fell short of his goals. Carter planned to bring down the cost of living with a system of voluntary price and wage controls. He asked companies to hold down price increases, and he urged workers to settle for only small pay raises. Still, inflation kept climbing. The 1979 inflation rate was the highest since 1946, after World War II.

**The United States faces an energy crisis.** Soaring energy costs were a big part of the inflation problem. The 1973 Arab oil embargo had shown Americans the danger of relying on foreign oil. (See Chapter 31.) Yet in the late 1970's the United States still imported more than 40 percent of its oil. Most of this came from the **Organization of Petroleum Exporting Countries** (OPEC)—a league of 13 oil-rich countries mainly in the Middle East and Africa. OPEC kept the price of oil high, causing hardship for American motorists and American industry. In 1979 a world oil shortage made the situation even

worse. Gasoline prices reached new highs, and motorists sometimes waited an hour or more to fill their tanks at service stations.

**Carter calls for a national energy program.** The President suggested several bold steps to ease the energy crisis. He asked for higher taxes on gasoline so that Americans would drive less. He sought penalties on automakers who produced "gas guzzlers"—cars that use too much gas. He wanted to give tax credits to homeowners and businesses that cut oil use by putting in better insulation or solar-heating units.

Carter also encouraged the development of nuclear power plants. The plants are costly to build but they can be run cheaply and they do not pollute the air.

President Carter's proposals for an energy program met with opposition in Congress. Debates and compromises delayed

## LINKING PAST AND PRESENT

## ★ ★ ★ *Energy Sources*

As the United States has grown larger, meeting the nation's energy needs has become a greater challenge. For years Americans have relied chiefly on fossil fuels—coal, oil, and natural gas—to produce heat and electricity. Yet because the supply of fossil fuels is limited, Americans have also explored ways to create energy from renewable resources like water and sunlight.

The first water-powered electric plant was built in Wisconsin in 1882. In the 1930's, scientists at Harvard University and the Massachusetts Institute of Technology began studying solar energy. During the 1970's, oil shortages spurred research into wind-powered electric plants and **geothermal energy**—energy created from heat below the earth's surface. Scientists will keep trying to harness renewable resources of energy, to be sure that future generations have enough energy supplies.

action for many months. Only late in 1978 did Congress pass bills to help save energy and explore alternate sources of fuel. At President Carter's urging, Congress also set up a new Cabinet office, the **Department of Energy.** The department took over most federal energy agencies.

By the end of the 1970's, Americans were conserving more energy. They bought smaller cars, drove fewer miles, and used energy-saving practices such as car-pooling. Americans were also exploring nuclear power with interest. In 1979, however, the country's growing nuclear energy industry suffered a setback. An accident inside the Three Mile Island plant in Pennsylvania raised fears about the safety of nuclear power. Three Mile Island had to be shut down, and the opening of other plants was delayed.

**The government loosens controls on business.** By the late 1970's many Americans felt that the government regulated business too tightly. The public, they thought, would benefit more if companies could compete freely with one another. Thus Congress began to **deregulate** —end government control of—some businesses.

The airlines, banking, and trucking industries were among the first to be deregulated. Many companies within these industries soon lowered their rates to attract more customers. At the same time, though, some companies cut back on services.

## New Foreign Policy Goals

When President Carter took office, the memory of the Vietnam War was still fresh. Carter believed that fear of communism had led the United States to make mistakes in Vietnam. Carter said he would be guided not by fear but by moral concerns.

**The President offers a new direction in foreign policy.** During his first year in office, Jimmy Carter stated his strong support for **human rights.** By human rights, Carter meant people's basic rights to freedom, justice, and security. Carter criticized countries that denied freedom of speech. He spoke out against foreign governments that did not

allow fair trials and treated prisoners cruelly. To back up his words, President Carter cut off military aid to countries that did not respect the rights of their people.

In other ways, too, the United States showed its support for human rights. In 1977, for example, President Carter agreed to welcome Cuban refugees into the United States. The Cuban dictator Fidel Castro allowed many thousands of people to leave their island on small boats. Most of them arrived in the United States with only the clothes they wore and the hope of a better life.

Carter insisted that the ideals of freedom and democracy were the basic difference between the free world and the Communist world. He wanted the United States to be respected not only as a military power but also as a moral leader. Some countries, however, especially those ruled by dictators, saw Carter's human-rights policy as meddling.

**Carter works out a new plan for the Panama Canal.** In Panama, meanwhile, many people were pressing for full control of the Panama Canal. Americans had built the canal in the early 1900's and had operated it ever since. (See Chapter 24.) While Americans regarded the Canal Zone as United States property, many Panamanians felt it was part of their country. In the interests of good relations with Latin America, President Carter worked out two new treaties with Panama. The first gave Panama control of the canal by 1999. The second treaty assured that the waterway would remain neutral and open to all countries.

**Carter works for peace in the Middle East.** One of President Carter's greatest foreign policy successes had to do with the Middle East. Because of American dependence on Middle Eastern oil, and because of concern for world peace, President Carter tried hard to reduce tension between Israel and the Arab nations.

In 1978 the President helped bring together Prime Minister Menachem Begin (men-AH-kem BAY-gin) of Israel and President Anwar Sadat of Egypt. Israel and Egypt had often been at war since 1948. President Carter, however, invited the two Middle East leaders to hold talks at Camp David, the

President Carter successfully mediated an agreement between Egypt's President Anwar Sadat (left) and Israel's Premier Menachem Begin (right). After a tense 13-day conference at Camp David, Sadat, Begin, and Carter signed a plan for peace in the Middle East.

presidential retreat in Maryland. In March 1979 all three leaders signed the **Camp David Accords**—a set of principles for peace between Israel and Egypt.

**Carter and Brezhnev move forward in arms control.** The United States also made progress in relations with the Soviet Union. In 1979 President Carter and Soviet Premier Leonid Brezhnev held new Strategic Arms Limitation Talks and signed the SALT II treaty. The treaty aimed to slow the arms race by limiting each country's supply of nuclear weapons.

Though SALT II seemed to be a positive step, some Americans believed it might leave the Soviet Union in a more favorable position than the United States. The Senate debated approval of the treaty for some time without reaching any decision. SALT II never became law, but both superpowers unofficially abided by its terms for several years.

## Difficult Times

In 1979, fresh troubles broke out in Iran and Afghanistan. President Carter tried for months to resolve these problems, with little success. Many Americans slowly lost confidence in his leadership.

**A revolution in Iran ends in crisis for Americans.** In early 1979 a revolution in Iran brought to power a Muslim leader, the Ayatollah Khomeini (ko-MAY-nee). He replaced the Shah, or king, of Iran, a friend of the United States who had tried to modernize his country. Khomeini called for a return to the strict teachings of Islam. He also demanded that the Shah, who was receiving medical treatment in the United States, be sent back to Iran to stand trial. When President Carter refused to cooperate, the Ayatollah became furious.

Anger soon led to action by Khomeini's followers. On November 4, 1979, Muslim students stormed the American embassy in Iran's capital, Tehran (teh-RAHN). There they took 66 Americans as hostages. This act violated international law, which protects embassies even in time of war.

The **Iran hostage crisis** drew American protest at once. President Carter quickly put a hold on Iranian deposits in American banks. He also stopped all imports from Iran and placed a ban on travel to that country. Yet these measures did not bring the desired outcome. The Iranians released 13 hostages in late November, but they continued to hold the others for months.

In April 1980 President Carter approved a secret rescue mission. The operation ended in disaster even before the rescuers reached Tehran. One of the rescue helicopters crashed in the Iranian desert, killing eight people and wounding five.

**The Soviet Union invades Afghanistan.**
As the hostage crisis dragged on in Iran, new trouble arose in nearby Afghanistan. In December 1979, Soviet soldiers marched into that country. Soviet leaders said they wanted to prevent disorder in case the Muslims in Afghanistan chose to follow the Ayatollah Khomeini. The United States, however, saw the Soviet invasion as a threat. The occupation of Afghanistan placed the Soviets within a short distance of the Persian Gulf—the gateway to Middle Eastern oil.

President Carter responded with a call for more American military power. He withdrew the SALT II treaty from further Senate consideration. Carter also forbade sales of American grain to the Soviets, and he led 67 countries in a boycott of the 1980 Olympics in Moscow. None of these measures worked, however. The Soviets stayed in Afghanistan, propping up a Communist government there.

**Joyful American hostages came home to freedom after 444 days of captivity in Iran. The last hostages returned on January 25, 1981.**

**Carter faces a tough challenge in the 1980 election.** Events in Iran and Afghanistan created a tense climate for the 1980 presidential election. Opinion polls showed that less than 25 percent of the public was satisfied with Carter's leadership. In spite of his faltering popularity, however, the Democrats nominated Carter for another term.

The Republican party chose Ronald Reagan as its candidate. Reagan was a former movie star who had been governor of California. He promised to build up the nation's military forces, reduce taxes, and cut waste in government.

On Election Day, Americans gave Ronald Reagan 44 million votes and Jimmy Carter 35 million. Reagan won an even more striking victory in the Electoral College—489 votes to Carter's 49. The Republicans also gained control of the Senate for the first time since 1954.

**The hostages are released.** Just before he left office, President Carter succeeded in ending the Iran hostage crisis. In exchange for the hostages' return, the United States promised to lift the economic sanctions it had placed on Iran. It also agreed to stay out of Iran's domestic affairs. After 444 days as captives, the Americans were finally released on January 20, 1981. People at home heard the news with joy. That same day, Ronald Reagan was sworn in as President.

## SECTION REVIEW

1. **Vocabulary**  trade deficit, stagflation, deregulate, human rights
2. **People and Places**  Jimmy Carter, Three Mile Island, Panama, Menachem Begin, Anwar Sadat, Iran, Ayatollah Khomeini, Afghanistan, Ronald Reagan
3. **Comprehension**  How did President Carter deal with the energy crisis of the late 1970's?
4. **Comprehension**  What was Carter's human-rights policy?
5. **Critical Thinking**  Do you think President Carter should have handled the Iran hostage crisis differently? Explain.

## CRITICAL THINKING: Understanding a Public Opinion Poll

The opinions of citizens are essential to a representative form of government. Elected officials must know these opinions in order to pass laws that express the will of the people. Officials learn and measure **public opinion**—the beliefs, views, and attitudes of the people—in various ways. One way is to meet with citizens, asking questions about issues and listening to the responses. Many citizens express opinions in letters to their representatives or to local newspapers. Another way to discover people's attitudes is through public opinion polls.

In an opinion poll, a **sample**—a selected group of people—is chosen and asked their views on certain questions. The sample should represent, as closely as possible, the population as a whole. For example, the sample should have the same percentages of males and females, whites and minorities, young people and old, as in the whole population. Furthermore, larger samples give more reliable results than smaller samples.

Although opinion polls can indicate how people feel on certain issues, poll results sometimes can be misleading. For example, a small or unrepresentative sample might result in biased findings. Poor wording of the questions is another common problem. Sometimes questions are stated so that people are likely to respond in only one way. Other times, the questions oversimplify the issues.

During the 1980's, public education in the United States became an important issue. The public opinion polls at the right ask questions about how to raise money for schools and how that money should be spent. Study the polls and then answer the following questions.

| | 1982 | 1985 |
|---|---|---|
| 1. How do you feel about raising taxes to fund public schools? | | |
| Favor raising taxes | 30% | 38% |
| Opposed to raising taxes | 60% | 52% |
| Do not know | 10% | 10% |
| 2. How much money should be spent on programs for students with learning disabilities? | | |
| More | 42% | 51% |
| About the same | 48% | 40% |
| Less | 4% | 2% |
| Do not know | 6% | 7% |
| 3. How much money should be spent on programs for gifted students? | | |
| More | 19% | 30% |
| About the same | 64% | 58% |
| Less | 11% | 5% |
| Do not know | 6% | 7% |

1. What percentage of the American people were opposed to raising taxes to fund public schools in 1982? How had people's attitudes changed by 1985?
2. Did the percentage of people who wanted more money spent on programs for gifted students increase or decrease between 1982 and 1985? By how much?
3. What trend is shown by these two opinion polls? Do the polls tell you why people's attitudes changed? Explain.

## Vocabulary

| | |
|---|---|
| loophole | terrorism |
| summit | feminist |

In Ronald Reagan's words, "the 70's were years of rising problems and falling confidence." In 1981 President Reagan promised to put the country back on the road to prosperity. His approach was a conservative one. He called for tax and spending cuts to revive the economy, a build-up of military defenses, and a reduction in the role of the federal government.

## New Economic Policies

When Ronald Reagan took office as President, the United States faced its most serious economic problems since the Great Depression. American industry was struggling to keep up with foreign competitors. Unemployment and inflation, along with high interest rates and high taxes, caused widespread suffering.

Americans looked to Reagan's programs as the answer to the country's troubles. Their hopes were temporarily shaken when they learned the shocking news of an attempt on the President's life. While leaving a Washington, D.C., hotel in March 1981, the President was hit by a would-be assassin's bullet. Reagan, however, quickly made a full recovery.

**The President launches his economic program.** One of Reagan's campaign promises had been to balance the federal budget. He pledged, in other words, that federal spending would not be more than the government's income. Reagan also promised to bring inflation under control.

Reagan developed a two-part strategy to meet these goals. First, he called for cuts in government spending. His chief targets were social programs such as Medicare, Social Security, and veterans' benefits. These programs, he thought, should be turned over to the states. Reagan also asked Congress to cut federal funds for the arts, mass transit, and energy conservation. The Environmental Protection Agency (EPA) lost nearly one third of its budget and had to end much of its research into alternative fuels.

Along with budget cuts, Reagan asked for tax cuts. Reagan reasoned that lower taxes would leave Americans with more money to invest. New investments would stimulate the economy, causing businesses to grow and unemployment to drop. With more Americans working and paying taxes, the government's income would go up. Thus it would be possible to balance the country's budget.

**Reagan plans to boost military spending.** While **Reaganomics**—the President's economic program—rested in part on cuts in government spending, there was one budget item that Reagan wanted to increase. That item was money for defense. In President Reagan's view, a military build-up was vital to the country's security. Reagan pointed out that during the 1970's the Soviet Union had built the strongest navy in the world. The Soviets also had more bombers and tanks than the United States did. America could compete with the Soviets in nuclear missiles, but the use of such weapons meant a risk of massive destruction.

President Reagan believed that the only way to be sure of peace was to match the military power of the Soviet Union. Reagan asked for huge budget increases to build such weapons as B-1 bombers and MX missiles. In addition, the navy would be given large sums for new ships. To pay for the arms build-up, Reagan planned to borrow money rather than raise taxes.

**Liberals criticize Reaganomics.** The President's policies caused much debate through the early 1980's. Critics feared that cuts in government spending would mean the loss of social services, jobs, and environmental programs. They worried that an arms build-up would add to the threat of direct conflict between the United States and the Soviet Union. They also pointed out that the national debt would swell if the government borrowed money for military purposes.

**Reaganomics has mixed results.** Some of Reagan's economic policies succeeded. Congress passed tax cuts, and government spending was reduced. The inflation rate dropped from 10 percent to about 6 percent. Even so, business did not get better.

By 1982 the United States was in a deep recession. American automakers faced strong competition from overseas, and unemployment rose. Interest rates rose, too, discouraging people from buying new homes. The most serious economic problem resulted from the government's heavy borrowing to pay for the arms build-up. By the end of 1982, the budget deficit had reached a record high of more than $110 billion.

**Farmers and union workers struggle during the 1980's.** Farmers were among those hardest hit by the recession. Overproduction caused crop prices to drop, while farm costs continued to rise. Many farmers lost land that their families had owned for generations. President Reagan tried a number of remedies. One plan gave farmers surplus grain from government storage bins in exchange for not planting crops. In spite of such help, many small farmers were forced out of business.

Union workers also faced hard times. With the nation's factories in a slowdown, employers had to lay off many workers. Autoworkers signed new contracts, giving up wage increases in return for job security. The union of air traffic controllers, on the other hand, went on strike for better pay and shorter hours. President Reagan quickly reminded them that it is against the law for government workers to strike. He ordered them back to work, and fired more than 11,000 controllers who refused to return.

## Our Presidents

### RONALD W. REAGAN

★ 1981–1989 ★

**40**TH PRESIDENT

REPUBLICAN

★ Born February 6, 1911, in Illinois
★ Married Jane Wyman in 1940; 2 children
★ Married Nancy Davis in 1952; 2 children
★ Actor; governor of California
★ Lived in California when elected President
★ Vice President: George Bush
★ Living
★ Oldest President to hold office
★ Key events while in office: First woman appointed to the Supreme Court; "Reaganomics"; income tax reform; Iran-*contra* affair

## A Vote of Confidence

Early in 1984, Ronald Reagan announced that he would run for a second term. The Republicans renominated both President Reagan and George Bush, the Vice President. The Democrats, meanwhile, had trouble agreeing on their candidate. The leaders in the race included Senator Gary Hart from Colorado and the Reverend Jesse Jackson, a black civil rights leader. The Democrats finally chose Walter Mondale, who had served as Vice President under Jimmy Carter. Mondale asked Congresswoman Geraldine Ferraro of New York to be his running mate. Ferraro was the first woman ever nominated for Vice President by a major political party.

Jesse Jackson sought the Democratic presidential nomination in 1984. Jackson was the first black American to gain wide support in a campaign for national office.

**President Reagan wins a second term.** Issues in the 1984 campaign included federal spending and budget cuts, foreign policy, and arms-control talks. Yet the candidates' personalities seemed to interest people almost as much as their views on the issues did. Opinion polls showed that most Americans responded more warmly to President Reagan than to Mondale. They liked Reagan's humor, patriotism, and optimism.

At the voting booths as well, Reagan won the approval of a sweeping majority. He carried 49 states and received 525 electoral votes. Reagan saw this landslide victory as a hearty endorsement of his policies.

**The President achieves tax reform.** President Reagan made tax reform a key goal of his second term. In 1984 he and his supporters in Congress proposed four main reforms. First, people with very low incomes would not be required to pay any taxes. Second, taxes for wealthy Americans would be reduced. Third, the new law would close many **loopholes** in the tax laws—ways to avoid paying taxes. Finally, Reagan asked that income tax forms be made easier to understand and simpler to fill out.

Both Democrats and Republicans joined in backing the tax reform legislation. The Reagan administration achieved the most sweeping change in the American tax system since World War II.

## A New Approach to Foreign Affairs

President Reagan felt that the United States had to "stand tall" to keep communism from spreading in the world. Reagan's early build-up of the military moved the country away from détente and toward a tougher foreign policy.

**Relations with the Soviet Union are troubled.** Soon after Reagan took office in 1981, Americans grew worried about affairs in Poland. The Polish government was trying to suppress Solidarity, an independent labor union that wanted more freedom for Poland's workers. The Reagan administration believed that the Soviet Union was behind the crackdown.

In 1983 another incident increased tension between the United States and the Soviet Union. A Soviet fighter jet shot down an unarmed South Korean passenger plane over Soviet territory. The attack resulted in the deaths of 269 people, including many Americans. The Soviet Union claimed that the Korean jet had been on a spy mission for the United States. President Reagan denied this charge, and countries around the world condemned the Soviet action.

Nuclear arms control continued to be another stumbling block in American-Soviet relations. A movement had begun in the United States for a "nuclear freeze"—an end to production of nuclear weapons. More than 500,000 people gathered in New York City in June 1982 to show their support for a freeze. Yet arms-control talks with the Soviet Union broke down in 1983.

Then a new leader, Mikhail Gorbachev (gor-buh-CHAWF), became premier of the Soviet Union. He and President Reagan held a **summit** —a meeting between heads of state—in Geneva, Switzerland, in 1985. They met again the next year in Reykjavik (RAY-kyuh-veek), Iceland. The talks ended, however, when Reagan refused to give up work on his Strategic Defense Initiative (SDI). Popularly called "star wars," SDI was a space-based anti-missile defense system being developed by the United States.

**Conflicts develop in Latin America.** In addition to strained dealings with the Soviets, President Reagan had worries closer to home. (See map on page 752.) The Falkland Islands, off the coast of Argentina, had been held by Great Britain since 1771. Argentina, however, also claimed the Falklands, and invaded them in 1982. War soon broke out between Britain and Argentina. The British, with American help, quickly defeated the Argentinians. The conflict, however, was not forgotten by America's neighbors to the south.

New trouble arose in 1983. The socialist government of Grenada (gruh-NAY-duh), an island nation in the Caribbean Sea, had begun building an airstrip capable of handling combat aircraft. The United States and some of Grenada's neighbors grew fearful of hostile action. In December, Caribbean forces and American troops jointly invaded Grenada and drove out the Communists. In a free election held in 1984, the people of Grenada gave overwhelming support to pro-American candidates.

**The United States faces problems in El Salvador and Nicaragua.** Meanwhile, civil war raged in El Salvador, the smallest Central American country. Communist guerrillas were trying to topple the country's government. Reagan was firmly committed to keeping the Communists out of power. The Reagan administration began to send more economic and military aid to El Salvador. Some people, however, feared that the President's policy in El Salvador would lead Americans into the war.

Critics were also alarmed about American military involvement in Nicaragua. A group of Nicaraguan revolutionaries, called

President Reagan and Soviet leader Gorbachev paint a picture of their 1985 summit talks on arms reduction. How does the cartoon express the view that the talks did not measure up to expectations?

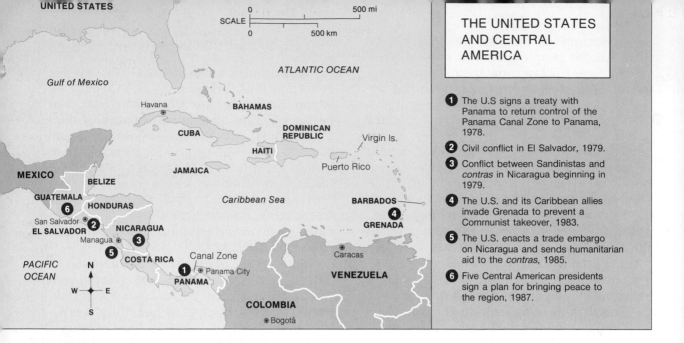

UNITED STATES

SCALE
0 ___ 500 mi
0 ___ 500 km

Gulf of Mexico

Havana

ATLANTIC OCEAN

BAHAMAS

CUBA

DOMINICAN
REPUBLIC

HAITI

Virgin Is.

Puerto Rico

JAMAICA

MEXICO

BELIZE

GUATEMALA

HONDURAS

Caribbean Sea

BARBADOS

San Salvador
EL SALVADOR

NICARAGUA

GRENADA

Managua

PACIFIC
OCEAN

N

COSTA RICA

Canal Zone

Caracas

Panama City

VENEZUELA

W      E

PANAMA

S

COLOMBIA

Bogotá

### THE UNITED STATES AND CENTRAL AMERICA

1 The U.S signs a treaty with Panama to return control of the Panama Canal Zone to Panama, 1978.

2 Civil conflict in El Salvador, 1979.

3 Conflict between Sandinistas and *contras* in Nicaragua beginning in 1979.

4 The U.S. and its Caribbean allies invade Grenada to prevent a Communist takeover, 1983.

5 The U.S. enacts a trade embargo on Nicaragua and sends humanitarian aid to the *contras,* 1985.

6 Five Central American presidents sign a plan for bringing peace to the region, 1987.

## Map Study

The United States frequently played a role in events in Central American and Caribbean nations. What region did the United States cede to Panama in 1978? On what island did American troops land to oppose communism in 1983? How was the United States involved in Nicaragua in 1985?

---

Sandinistas, took over their country's government in 1979. They promised to bring democracy to Nicaragua, but soon adopted communism instead.

Led by President Daniel Ortega, the Sandinista government began to limit the rights of its citizens. The government took away freedom of speech and freedom of the press. It crushed labor unions that did not agree with its views. For arms and supplies, Nicaragua turned to the Soviet Union and Cuba.

The United States feared the rise of communism in the Americas. President Reagan called for aid to the *contras*—Nicaraguan rebels who opposed the Sandinistas. Congress was reluctant to support the *contras* at first. Some people charged that the *contras* were as dangerous as the Sandinistas. In 1984, when Americans learned that the CIA had already secretly helped plant mines in Nicaraguan harbors, Congress banned *contra* aid. Two years later, however, after a long and bitter struggle, Congress approved $100 million for the *contras*.

**The United States becomes more active in the Middle East.** The Middle East was another hot spot in the 1980's. (See map on page 753.) A key problem was **terrorism** — the use of violence to frighten people or a government into meeting the demands of a group. Libya's dictator, Muammar Qaddafi (kuh-DAHF-ee), promoted terrorist attacks against Americans. In 1986, American planes bombed key terrorist bases in Libya. After the bombing raid, terrorist activity slowed down.

One of the most troubled Middle Eastern countries was Lebanon, where Christian and Muslim forces were waging civil war. Lebanon was also the home base for the **Palestine Liberation Organization** (PLO). The PLO, an Arab group, was waging guerrilla warfare against Israel and seeking to create a homeland for the Palestinian people.

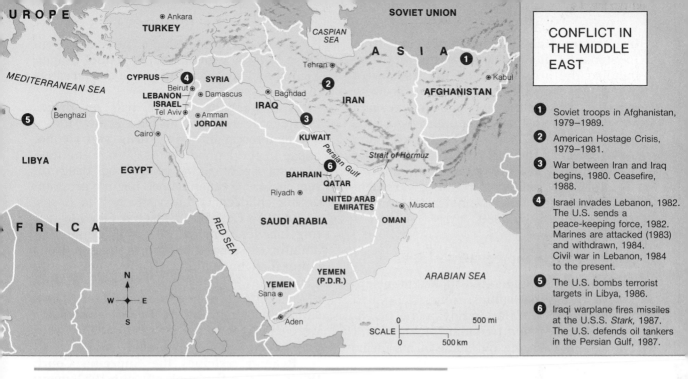

**SOVIET UNION**

**TURKEY**

Ankara

CASPIAN SEA

A S I A

Tehran

Kabul

**CYPRUS** ④ **SYRIA**

MEDITERRANEAN SEA

Beirut
**LEBANON**
**ISRAEL**
Tel Aviv

Damascus

Baghdad

**IRAN**

**AFGHANISTAN**

Amman
**JORDAN**

**IRAQ**

③

Benghazi

⑤

Cairo

**KUWAIT**

Persian Gulf

Strait of Hormuz

**LIBYA**

**EGYPT**

**BAHRAIN**
**QATAR**

Riyadh

**UNITED ARAB EMIRATES**

Muscat

F R I C A

RED SEA

**SAUDI ARABIA**

**OMAN**

N
W E
S

**YEMEN**
Sana

**YEMEN (P.D.R.)**
Aden

*ARABIAN SEA*

SCALE

0        500 mi
0    500 km

### CONFLICT IN THE MIDDLE EAST

❶ Soviet troops in Afghanistan, 1979–1989.

❷ American Hostage Crisis, 1979–1981.

❸ War between Iran and Iraq begins, 1980. Ceasefire, 1988.

❹ Israel invades Lebanon, 1982. The U.S. sends a peace-keeping force, 1982. Marines are attacked (1983) and withdrawn, 1984. Civil war in Lebanon, 1984 to the present.

❺ The U.S. bombs terrorist targets in Libya, 1986.

❻ Iraqi warplane fires missiles at the U.S.S. *Stark,* 1987. The U.S. defends oil tankers in the Persian Gulf, 1987.

## Map Study

Conflicts in the Middle East continued to threaten world peace in the 1970's and 1980's. What country did the Soviet Union invade in 1979? What country did Israel invade in 1982? In what country did the United States attack terrorist bases in 1986? Which two Middle Eastern countries were at war during the 1980's?

In June 1982, Israeli soldiers invaded Lebanon to drive out the PLO. They succeeded in pushing the PLO into Beirut (bay-ROOT), the Lebanese capital. Then the United States stepped in, working out plans to send a peacekeeping force of American, French, and Italian soldiers into Beirut. These soldiers kept order as hundreds of PLO fighters left Lebanon.

Peace, however, did not come to Lebanon. Late in 1982, Lebanese Christians massacred more than 1,000 Palestinians in a refugee camp. Then in April 1983, Muslim forces blew up the American embassy in Beirut. Sixty-three people were killed. The following October, 241 American marines died when Muslim terrorists drove a truck full of explosives into their headquarters.

The American people demanded an end to United States involvement in Lebanon. In 1984 all American troops came home. Still, unrest continued in the Middle East, and Americans became prime targets for terrorist kidnappings. At least 10 Americans were believed to be hostages in Lebanon in 1985.

**Secret deals come to light.** The safe return of American citizens concerned President Reagan deeply. Yet the United States had a firm policy of not bargaining with terrorists. Then, late in 1986, Americans learned that the Reagan administration had secretly sold arms to Iran the year before. A short time later, two American hostages had been released in Lebanon. People began to talk of an "arms-for-hostages" deal. The matter was further complicated by the news that some of the profits from the arms sale had been given to the *contras* in Nicaragua. This was at a time when Congress had forbidden *contra* aid.

The President and Congress both launched lengthy investigations into the

**Iran-*contra* affair.** Key testimony came from Lieutenant Colonel Oliver North, who had handled the arms sale and the transfer of money to the *contras*. National Security Adviser John Poindexter said that he, and not President Reagan, had approved of the transfer of funds. In the end, while claiming to have been in the dark about much of what went on, Reagan accepted responsibility for his staff's wrongdoing. The government charged North with criminal acts, and his trial began early in 1989.

## Support for Conservative Ideas

President Reagan often spoke out in support of traditional values. Americans liked his emphasis on "faith, family, work, neighborhood, peace, and freedom." Reagan still had trouble carrying out some of his ideas.

---

# Our Presidents

## GEORGE BUSH

★ **1989 –** ★

**41ST PRESIDENT**

**REPUBLICAN**

★ Born June 12, 1924, in Massachusetts

★ Married Barbara Pierce in 1945; 5 children

★ Businessman (oil); representative from Texas; director of Central Intelligence Agency; Vice President under Reagan

★ Lived in Texas when elected President

★ Vice President: Dan Quayle

★ Living

★ First sitting Vice President to be elected President since Martin Van Buren (1836)

---

He could not, for example, persuade Congress to pass a law allowing school prayer. Yet he did lead the country in a conservative direction.

**The Reagans declare war on drugs.** President Reagan and his wife, Nancy, took a strong interest in ending drug and alcohol abuse in the United States. While the government spent more money on drug research, Mrs. Reagan helped begin a program urging children to "Just say no" to drugs.

In 1986 Congress passed a new law setting heavier penalties for drug crimes. In addition, it stepped up efforts to keep drugs out of the United States. Many states passed stronger laws against drunk drivers. In spite of these efforts, drug abuse continued to be a serious problem. By 1989 many Americans were calling for stronger action to end what they called a "drug epidemic."

**Reagan reshapes the Supreme Court.** When Reagan first took office in 1981, many of the members of the Supreme Court were considered moderates or liberals. By the end of his second term, however, several justices had retired, and Reagan had replaced them with conservatives. His appointees included Sandra Day O'Connor, the first woman to serve on the bench, Antonin Scalia, the first Italian-American justice, and Anthony Kennedy.

Though O'Connor's appointment pleased some **feminists** —supporters of women's rights—some liberals were worried. They saw the Court leaning toward more conservative decisions. For example, in a 1984 case about police procedures for collecting evidence, the Court moved away from past trends of protecting suspects' rights. Liberals feared that in the future the Supreme Court might also reverse its support for affirmative action and people's privacy rights.

**Religious groups make themselves heard.** Another sign of growing conservatism in the United States was the rise of religious groups like the Moral Majority. The Moral Majority, founded in 1979, wanted to focus political attention on moral issues and family values. The organization also took a tough stand against communism and pressed for a strong defense system for the United States.

**George Bush is elected President.** In 1988 Ronald Reagan's Vice President, George Bush, fought hard to win the Republican nomination for President. To become the Democratic nominee, Governor Michael Dukakis of Massachusetts had to overcome another strong primary campaign by the Reverend Jesse Jackson. Despite an early lead in the polls, Dukakis soon fell behind as Bush promised to continue in the tradition of Ronald Reagan and to balance the budget without raising taxes. When election night was over, Bush had won 426 of 538 electoral votes and 54 percent of the popular vote. Still, the Democrats strengthened their hold on Congress, picking up one seat in the Senate and five in the House. In his inauguration speech, Bush vowed to work closely with Congress to balance the federal budget.

## SECTION REVIEW

1. **Vocabulary**   loophole, summit, terrorism, feminist
2. **People and Places**   George Bush, Walter Mondale, Geraldine Ferraro, Mikhail Gorbachev, El Salvador, Nicaragua, Lebanon, Oliver North, John Poindexter, Sandra Day O'Connor, Michael Dukakis
3. **Comprehension**   What economic goals did the Reagan administration have?
4. **Comprehension**   How did President Reagan change the direction of American foreign policy?
5. **Critical Thinking**   A witness at the Iran-*contra* hearings said there are times when people "have to go above the written law." Do you agree? Explain.

# 3 What do recent developments suggest about the future?

**Vocabulary**

humanitarian
apartheid

dissident
poverty level
acid rain

The world has changed greatly in recent times. New governments have come to power in many countries. Shifts have taken place in the world economy. New technology has changed the environment and affected people's living patterns. In the years ahead Americans will certainly face more changes. They must be prepared for trying times, but they can also look forward to continued growth and progress.

## Challenges in Foreign Relations

Since the end of World War II, industrialized countries have played the lead role in world affairs. These countries are divided into two camps—those that believe in freedom and democracy, like the United States, and those that practice communism, like the Soviet Union. There is, however, a **Third World** as well. The Third World is made up of the developing countries of Africa, Asia, and Latin America. Since the 1970's, Americans and Soviets have both tried to gain influence in the Third World.

**The United States forges ties with Third World Countries.** American aid to developing nations has taken several forms. Some of it has been **humanitarian** —promoting human welfare. In 1984, for example, an extended drought in Ethiopia caused millions of people to face starvation and death. Americans quickly joined a worldwide relief effort. In July 1985 a 14-hour rock concert called "Live Aid" was broadcast on radio and television in more than 100 countries. The broadcast raised about $70 million to help the starving people of Africa.

## CULTURE • The Volunteer Spirit in the 1980's

Americans have always been willing to help others. In frontier times, settlers often depended on one another for survival. In the 1980's, the volunteer spirit is still strong. Statistics show that Americans spend more time and money on volunteer activities than people in most other countries. American volunteers help neighbors, friends, schools, and thousands of religious and community organizations. In the 1980's they have also worked to feed starving children in Africa and to help bankrupt farmers in the United States.

One of the most talked-about charitable events of the 1980's was Hands Across America. This fund raiser, held on May 25, 1986, was planned to help feed the nation's hungry and homeless persons. Almost 6 million people, including President Reagan, paid $10 or more to take part. Joining hands, they formed a human chain that stretched 4,150 miles (6,640 kilometers) across the United States from New York to California.

Hands Across America distributed about $15.5 million to nearly 2,000 charities all over the country. Many needy people benefited from their fellow Americans' willingness to lend a hand.

**Hands Across America**

United States banks have also loaned developing countries huge sums of money to help them industrialize. By the 1980's, Third World debts had soared to hundreds of billions of dollars. To ease the burden, United States banks have written off large portions of their Third World loans.

**The United States supports change in South Africa and in the Philippines.** Americans have also taken a special interest in South Africa and the Philippines in recent years. South Africa has long had a policy of **apartheid** (uh-PAHRT-hyt)—official segregation of the races. Though blacks make up the majority of the population, the ruling government is white. Whites in South Africa enjoy more freedom, better schools and jobs, and a higher standard of living than blacks.

In the 1980's the United States showed its opposition to apartheid by limiting trade with South Africa. In addition, many American businesses left the country. In spite of such pressure, the South African government did little to change its racial policy.

In the Philippines, meanwhile, political change was also an issue. Many Filipinos felt that President Ferdinand Marcos, who had ruled for 20 years, ran a corrupt government. In 1986 Marcos fled the country after his attempt to rig an election failed. The new President, Corazon Aquino (ah-KEE-no), pledged to make the Philippines more democratic. She faced economic troubles, however, and a Communist uprising. The United States helped by giving Aquino military and economic aid.

**Relations with the Soviet Union show hope.** In the late 1980's, Soviet Premier Gorbachev began a new policy of *glasnost*, or "openness." He gave the press greater freedom and lifted some controls on artists and writers. He allowed more **dissidents** —people who opposed the political system— to leave the country. Gorbachev also agreed to resume arms-control talks.

Americans liked Gorbachev's policies, and the relationship between the two countries improved. The growing warmth was briefly threatened by an accident at a Soviet nuclear power plant in 1986. The accident, at Chernobyl, caused radiation hazards in much of northern Europe.

Despite Chernobyl, however, the relationship continued to warm up. President Reagan and Gorbachev met two more times, in Washington in 1987 and in Moscow in 1988. Cooperation marked both summits. One result was a treaty to eliminate intermediate-range nuclear forces (INF). Another hopeful step came in 1989 when all Soviet troops withdrew from Afghanistan.

**Unstable conditions continue in the Middle East.** Conflicts in the Middle East remained major worries. In 1980 Iran and Iraq went to war over disputed territory. The fighting spread to the Persian Gulf, an oil shipping area. In 1987, 37 Americans died there when Iraqi planes mistakenly fired at the U.S.S. *Stark*. A ceasefire between Iran and Iraq began in August 1988, but peace talks soon stalled.

Violence also continued between Arabs and Israelis. Throughout 1988 Israel sought to end an uprising of Palestinians in part of Israel. Late in 1988 PLO leader Yasir Arafat declared a Palestinian state in this area. He also agreed to Israel's right to exist. The United States favored talks with the PLO, but Israel declined.

## Challenges at Home

Throughout its history, the United States has been viewed as the land of promise. Millions of immigrants have come seeking freedom. Today there are still rich opportunities for those who are willing to work hard.

**The United States immigration policy changes.** More than 500,000 immigrants entered the United States each year during the 1980's. Special consideration was given to refugees fleeing from Communist countries. Thousands of these newcomers were "boat people" from Indochina. When Vietnam, Cambodia, and Laos fell to the Communists, these people left their homelands in small fishing boats.

Meanwhile, thousands more immigrants slipped into the United States illegally. Many crossed the border from Mexico and got low-paying jobs in American cities and on farms. The government spent large sums of money to patrol the border and to send illegal workers back home.

In 1987 a new immigration law went into effect. Under the law, illegal aliens who had settled in the country before January 1, 1982, could stay and become citizens. Employers who knowingly hired illegal workers, however, would have to pay large fines. The new immigration law protected American workers and still aided thousands of people who sought a better life in the United States.

**Opportunities for women and minorities expand.** The 1980's brought women closer to full equality in American life. More women rose to high-level positions in business. Athletes like tennis champion Martina Navratilova (nah-vruh-tuh-LO-vuh) brought new respect to women's sports. More women joined the armed forces and entered such fields as engineering and medicine— fields long dominated by men. In addition, more women held political office in the 1980's than ever before. By the mid-1980's more than 1,000 women were elected to state legislatures. About 15,000 women served in city and county government.

The push for equal opportunities also continued among America's minorities. In some cases, the power and influence of minorities grew as their numbers grew. For example, Hispanics now make up almost 8 percent of the population. They have more buying power and more political clout than ever before. The people of San Antonio and Miami have elected Hispanic mayors, and Florida has a Hispanic governor.

Asian Americans are another fast-growing minority. They have become leaders in business, science, and many other fields. In 1987, four Asian Americans served in Congress. Blacks, too, have made important contributions to society and gained a stronger voice in government. In 1984 and 1988 the Reverend Jesse Jackson was a key contender in the race for President.

Yet minority groups still face problems. In the 1980's, blacks and Hispanics still lagged behind whites in education, employment, and earnings. About 30 percent of non-white Americans had earnings below the **poverty level** —the income needed to have a decent standard of living. At the same time, only about 12 percent of the white population fell below the poverty level.

## Advances in Technology

Americans have long been leaders in technology. By the 1980's, Americans had entered the computer age. Space exploration had become common. Clearly, the United States was now a "high-tech" society.

**New technology changes the way Americans live.** Computers first began to be mass-produced in the 1950's. Today hardly any part of American life remains untouched by these amazing machines. Schools, businesses, and banks depend on computers to keep records and process information. Engineers design buildings with them. Newspapers set type by computer and many factories use computers to control assembly lines and other equipment.

## Graph Study

**Patterns of immigration to the United States changed dramatically in the 1980's. From which region did the percentage of immigrants show the greatest increase between 1941 and 1986? What percent of American immigrants came from Asia between 1941 and 1960? What percent came from Asia between 1981 and 1986?**

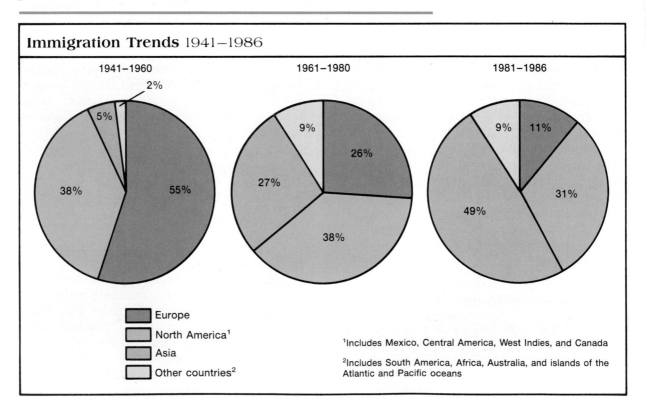

**Immigration Trends** 1941–1986

1941–1960

2%
5%
38%
55%

1961–1980

9%
26%
27%
38%

1981–1986

9%  11%
31%
49%

■ Europe
□ North America[1]
■ Asia
□ Other countries[2]

[1]Includes Mexico, Central America, West Indies, and Canada

[2]Includes South America, Africa, Australia, and islands of the Atlantic and Pacific oceans

The increased use of computers has brought changes to the American labor force. For example, more Americans now work in service industries than in manufacturing. Home life, too, has changed because of new technology. In 1987 almost one in five families owned a home computer. Many Americans also bought videocassette recorders, compact disc players, and microwave ovens.

**The space program makes great progress before a major setback.** During President Reagan's first term in office, Americans took pride in the space shuttle. This was a new kind of vehicle that, unlike most earlier spacecraft, could be reused and sent on more than one voyage. The first space shuttle, the *Columbia*, was launched from Cape Canaveral, Florida, in April 1981. The *Columbia* circled the globe for three days and then returned to earth, landing like an airplane.

This was the dawn of a new age in space exploration. A series of shuttle flights carried astronauts, scientific experiments, and communications satellites into space. Among the astronauts who took part in the space-shuttle program were Sally Ride, the first American woman in space, and Guion Bluford, the first black American in space.

Tragedy struck the space-shuttle program in January 1986. The shuttle *Challenger* exploded about one minute after liftoff from Cape Canaveral. All seven crew members died. Among them was social studies

★ ★ ★   **PRIMARY SOURCE**

# *A CHALLENGER* CREW MEMORIAL 1986

On January 28, 1986, Americans excitedly watched the launch of the space shuttle *Challenger*. Their excitement turned to horror as the *Challenger* exploded a mere 73 seconds after takeoff, killing the 7 astronauts aboard. President Reagan delivered this speech at a memorial service for the *Challenger* crew.

### Read to Find Out

1. What is the "profound truth" that President Reagan mentions?
2. According to President Reagan, how will Americans commemorate the *Challenger* astronauts?

... The sacrifice of [the seven astronauts] has stirred the soul of our nation and through the pain our hearts have been opened to a profound truth: The future is not free; the story of all human progress is one of a struggle against all odds.... This America ... was built by men and women like our seven star voyagers, who answered a call beyond duty, who gave more than was expected or required....

We think back to the pioneers of an earlier century ... who ... set out into the frontier of the American West. Often they met with terrible hardship.... But grief only steeled them to the journey ahead....

Man will continue his conquest of space. To reach out for new goals and ever greater achievements—that is the way we shall commemorate our seven *Challenger* heroes....

*Ronald Reagan*

Scientists collect water samples to test for acid-rain damage. Acid rain, caused by air pollution, damages forests and destroys fresh-water ponds. International cooperation may be needed to solve the problem.

teacher Christa McAuliffe. Investigations showed that NASA officials launched the shuttle in spite of technical problems. As a result of the *Challenger* disaster, NASA spent $2.4 million improving shuttle safety. On September 29, 1988, the space shuttle *Discovery* lifted off, returning the United States to space for the first time since January of 1986.

**Americans deal with environmental problems.** As Americans work to make new technology safer, they also want to protect the environment from further harm. Several new steps have been taken to limit air and water pollution. In 1986 Congress set stricter rules for the use of harmful chemicals. Congress also approved funds for cleaning up polluted sites. In addition, the United States signed an agreement with Canada to try to prevent **acid rain** —polluted rain caused by burning coal and other fossil fuels. Acid rain from the United States has killed millions of fish and trees in eastern Canada.

## Trends in American Life

According to census figures, the population of the United States was 227 million in 1980. By 1987 the population had grown to more than 242 million. By 1990 it was expected to reach between 245 million and 255 million. As the population has risen, it has changed in other ways, too.

**Americans live longer than before.** A child born in 1930 could expect to live about 60 years. By 1988 the life expectancy had reached about 75 years. Americans are thus living longer than ever before. This development is partly due to advances in medicine. Many diseases that were common only a few generations ago have now been completely wiped out.

Americans are living healthier lives as well. They have cut back on fats, sugars, and salt in their diet. They exercise more today, and they have a greater awareness of health hazards. As a result of studies linking lung cancer to smoking, many Americans have quit smoking. Smoking has also been restricted or banned in many offices, restaurants, and public places.

**Living patterns change.** One of the most striking trends of the 1980's has been a move toward smaller families. Couples are marrying at a later age and having fewer children. The fastest-growing age groups in the 1980's were people between 35 and 44 years old and people 85 years and older. The maturing of the population has had far-reaching effects, as senior citizens have gained a greater voice in government.

Americans have also been on the move. Mild weather, low heating costs, and plentiful jobs have attracted many people to the **Sunbelt**—the South and Southwest. Arizona, Nevada, Florida, Texas, Utah, Colorado, and California are among the fastest growing states. As southern and southwestern states gain more residents, they also gain more representatives in Congress. Issues important in the Sunbelt, such as water conservation, are beginning to receive more attention from the federal government.

## Stepping into the Future

The desire to move forward is one of the strengths of the American people. Whatever challenges may lie ahead, Americans will face them with courage and confidence.

**The United States faces economic challenges at home and abroad.** At the end of the 1980's, the American economy faced serious challenges. While inflation had slowed and unemployment was low, the federal budget deficit continued to grow steadily. At the same time, the trade deficit was also increasing each year. This meant that Americans were spending more on foreign-made goods than other countries were spending on American-made goods. One of the reasons for this was the ability of other countries, especially Japan, to produce certain items more cheaply, and sometimes better, than American companies. As a result of this, some questioned the ability of the United States to maintain its position as a world economic leader. Others, however, maintained that the United States would find ways to overcome these latest challenges.

**Americans expect much from their leaders.** Since the beginnings of the United States, the American people have had faith in their ability to govern themselves. At first they gave the reins of government mostly to well-to-do white men. Today America's leaders reflect the broad mix of people in the United States. Men and women of all ages, races, religions, and social backgrounds serve at every level of government.

As the United States has grown more crowded and more complex, the job of public servants has become harder. Their chief duty is to provide for the health and welfare of the people. At the same time they must manage new technology carefully and spend public money wisely. They face tough decisions about how best to meet competing needs of different groups.

George Bush faced many challenges as President, among them the huge trade deficit with Japan. In talks with Prime Minister Takeshita, Bush insisted that Japan help by opening its markets to American goods.

Perhaps no one faces more challenges than the President of the United States. The President is expected to help shape laws, command the armed forces, and set foreign policy. The demands of the job are heavy. Yet many civic-minded men and women still dream of holding the highest office in the land.

**Americans balance their personal interests with the public good.** The right to choose their leaders is a right that American citizens take seriously. During elections, voters play two roles. First, they are private persons with concerns for their individual happiness. They want good jobs, comfortable homes, fine schools, and safe neighborhoods. They seek laws and leaders who will work to improve life for themselves and their families.

At the same time, voters are part of a larger community—the United States. As such, they must think about what is best for the whole country. Clean air and water, a strong economy, peace with other countries— these are dreams that all Americans share. They know, too, that if the United States' success story is to continue, there must be equal opportunity and equal rights for all.

Studying the past can help Americans build a better future. The American people have always been pioneers, exploring the new. Their willingness to cooperate and compromise, and, when necessary, to fight for what they believe in, has helped them prosper. Their democratic traditions and respect for the rights of the individual have helped make the United States a great nation. It will remain one, so long as Americans remember the lessons of their history.

## SECTION REVIEW

1. **Vocabulary**  humanitarian, apartheid, dissident, poverty level, acid rain
2. **People and Places**  Third World, South Africa, Philippines, Corazon Aquino, Persian Gulf, Sally Ride, Guion Bluford, Christa McAuliffe, Yasir Arafat
3. **Comprehension**  What foreign-policy issues have concerned American leaders in recent years?
4. **Comprehension**  How has the American population changed in recent years?
5. **Critical Thinking**  Do you think the American space program should continue to expand? Why or why not?

# Chapter 32 Summary

Democratic President Jimmy Carter, elected in 1976, faced many challenges. Severe inflation, high unemployment, and sluggish business activity led to stagflation. Oil shortages resulted in an energy crisis for the United States. In 1979 the Iran hostage crisis and the Soviet invasion of Afghanistan overshadowed Carter's success in negotiating the Camp David Accords.

In 1980 Carter lost his bid for a second term to Republican Ronald Reagan. President Reagan set the country on a more conservative path. He cut federal spending on social and environmental programs, boosted the military budget, and made sweeping tax cuts. Inflation dropped during the 1980's, but the budget deficit reached record highs.

In foreign affairs Reagan focused less on human rights and more on fighting communism. The United States gave aid to anti-Communist forces in Grenada, El Salvador, and Nicaragua. Meanwhile, the Iran-Iraq war, fighting in Lebanon, and terrorist bombings and kidnappings raised worries about the Middle East. Efforts to free American hostages in Lebanon soon led the White House into the Iran-contra affair. The President drew sharp criticism for this matter, but Americans continued to support him.

In 1988 Reagan's Vice President, George Bush, was elected President. He pledged to uphold traditional values and to work with Congress to reduce the federal budget deficit.

At the end of the 1980's, arms control and world peace remained a great challenge. Relations with the Soviet Union, the Middle East, Third World nations, and South Africa were of special interest. Key concerns at home included stabilizing the economy, giving full equality to women and minorities, and protecting the environment. Hispanic Americans and older Americans were increasing in number, and many people were moving to the Sunbelt.

# CAUSES and EFFECTS

## The Vietnam War ★ ★ ★

Treaty divides Vietnam into Communist North and non-Communist South

United States opposes Communist expansion in Southeast Asia

United States sends military advisers to aid South Vietnam

### CONTRIBUTING CAUSES

North Vietnam wages guerrilla war in South Vietnam

American troops fight alongside South Vietnamese

President Johnson orders bombing of North Vietnam

Tonkin Gulf Resolution gives President broad war powers

### MAIN CAUSES

### VIETNAM WAR

### EFFECTS

Many Americans oppose expansion of United States' involvement

Television shows Americans the horrors of war

Antiwar protests lead to bitterness and violence at home

### LONG-TERM EFFECTS

Americans debate the nation's role as a world leader

American veterans readjust to civilian life

United States withdraws from Vietnam

North Vietnamese Communists take over South Vietnam

## Vocabulary and Key Terms

Use one of the following terms to replace each underlined phrase in the sentences below. Write your answers on a separate sheet of paper.

apartheid        OPEC
Camp David Accords    summits
deregulated       Sunbelt
dissidents        terrorism

1. During the 1970's, 13 oil-rich nations set high prices for oil.
2. President Carter ended government control of the airlines.
3. The peace agreement between Egypt and Israel did not end sudden violence in the Middle East.
4. Between 1985 and 1988, President Reagan and Soviet Premier Gorbachev held four top-level meetings.
5. Some Soviet citizens who oppose the political system have been allowed to leave the country.
6. The United States has pressed for an end to racial segregation in South Africa.
7. The population of the southern and southwestern states has grown steadily.

## Recalling the Facts

1. What economic problems did President Carter face during his administration?
2. How did the United States show concern for human rights in the 1970's?
3. What led up to the Iran hostage crisis?
4. Why was President Reagan's economic program controversial?
5. What was the Iran-*contra* affair?
6. How did the Supreme Court change during Reagan's administration?
7. How did Geraldine Ferraro and Sandra Day O'Connor open doors for women?
8. In what ways is the American population changing?

## Places to Locate

Match the letters on the map with the places listed below. Write your answers on a separate sheet of paper.

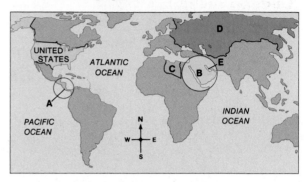

1. Central America
2. Soviet Union
3. Persian Gulf
4. Middle East
5. Libya

## Critical Thinking

1. In the 1980's the United States has played a number of different roles in international affairs. What has the United States done to promote world peace? To promote human rights and democracy? To help developing countries?
2. In 1983 President Reagan created a committee to suggest a national policy toward Latin America. In its report the committee said, "The 1980's must be the decade in which the United States recognizes that its relationships with Mexico and Central and South America rank in importance with its ties to Europe and Asia." Do you think Reagan took this advice to heart? Explain.
3. How do you think the United States should deal with terrorists? Consider the pros and cons of the following strategies:
   a. meeting terrorists' demands
   b. responding with diplomatic and economic pressures
   c. responding with military force

4. Have Americans used new technology wisely? Consider these points in your answer:
   a. accidents at nuclear power plants
   b. advances in medical research
   c. pollution problems and acid rain
   d. the widespread use of computers
   e. the space-shuttle program

## Understanding History

1. Reread the section "Economic troubles persist" on page 742. Then answer these questions.
   a. **Economics.** How did slow business activity contribute to inflation?
   b. **Citizenship.** Do you think Americans should buy American-made goods even if foreign manufacturers offer lower prices or better quality?
2. Reread the section "Living patterns change" on page 760. Then answer these questions.
   a. **Culture.** How are American family patterns changing?
   b. **Geography.** Why is water conservation important in the Sunbelt?

## Projects and Activities

1. **Making a Map.** On a map of the world, color those countries that the United States aided during the Carter and Reagan administrations. Consult an almanac and add symbols to show what system of government each country has.
2. **Writing a Report.** Find out more about one of the following subjects: the nuclear power industry, the farm crisis of the 1980's, the movement to end apartheid in South Africa, American immigration reform, computer technology. Write a report on what you learn.
3. **Debating an Issue.** Organize a debate on United States policy toward Nicaragua. First study news clippings to learn more about the struggle in that country. Then take a position on the question of whether the United States should support the *contras*, the Sandinista government, or neither side.

4. **Giving a Newscast.** Imagine that it is the year 2000. With a few classmates, prepare a broadcast for a nightly news program. In addition to covering political events at home and overseas, you should report on the economy, cases before the Supreme Court, and science news. You might also discuss the latest in entertainment or lifestyles.

## Practicing Your Skill

Below are the results of an opinion poll about government spending for national defense and military purposes. In four different years, Americans were asked to answer this question: "Do you think we are spending too little, too much, or about the right amount?" Study the responses carefully. Then tell whether each of the statements that follows is true or false. Write your answers on a separate sheet of paper.

| Year | Too much | About right | Too little | No opinion |
|------|----------|-------------|------------|------------|
| 1981 | 15% | 22% | 51% | 12% |
| 1983 | 37 | 36 | 21 | 6 |
| 1985 | 46 | 36 | 11 | 7 |
| 1987 | 44 | 36 | 14 | 6 |

1. A majority of Americans have no opinion on defense spending.
2. In 1981 a majority of Americans believed the government was spending too little on defense.
3. In most years, those who thought the government was spending too much outnumbered those who thought the government was spending too little.
4. In 1987 a majority of Americans thought the government was spending about the right amount.
5. The percentage of Americans who believe that the government is spending about the right amount has been steady since 1983.

# UNIT 10 REVIEW

## Unit Summary

★ **The postwar years brought rapid changes to the nation.**

- American foreign policy sought the containment of communism.
- Competition between the United States and the Soviet Union resulted in a cold war.
- The United Nations, established to preserve world peace, intervened in the Korean War.
- Inflation and labor problems accompanied the shift to a peacetime economy.

★ **Crises and progress marked the 1960's and 1970's.**

- President Kennedy's New Frontier sought economic and social advances at home and in developing nations.
- A war on poverty, civil rights legislation, and growing involvement in Vietnam marked Lyndon Johnson's administration.
- President Nixon improved relations with China and the Soviet Union.
- The Watergate scandal led to Nixon's resignation from office.
- American involvement in the Vietnam War ended.

★ **The nation's Bicentennial began a new era for Americans.**

- Economic problems continued during Jimmy Carter's administration.
- President Reagan reduced the federal government's role and sought ways to stimulate the economy.
- As the 1980's ended, President Bush and America faced new challenges.

## Understanding Chronology

Study the Unit 10 time line on page 689. Then complete the following activity on a separate sheet of paper.

Create a time line to show important events in your family's history from 1945 to the present. You might include the birthdates of family members, school graduations, marriages, jobs, relocations, or other significant events. Compare your family time line with the Unit 10 time line on page 689. Write a paragraph describing how national and world events during this time period affected your family.

## Writing About History

1. **Writing Newspaper Headlines.** Find information about the United States' space program, its goals, and its successes. Then write a series of newspaper headlines about outstanding achievements in the space program since 1961. Choose one of the headlines and write an article to explain it.
2. **Gaining Historical Perspective.** Choose a topic or event currently in the news. Find information about the event from television, newspapers, and news magazines. Then write two or three paragraphs explaining the topic or event for an American history textbook that will be used five years from now.
3. **Analyzing Personal Style.** Work in groups to write a book titled *The American Presidency Since 1945.* Find information about each person who was President from 1945 to the present time. Research each President's goals, personal style, relationship with the public, and leadership qualities. Then write a brief biographical chapter for each President and assemble them into a book. Display your books in class.

Nobody wins a war.

**4. Interpreting a Cartoon.** Study the political cartoon above. Using the cartoon as a guide, write an essay on world peace. Consider how the caption "Nobody Wins a War" applies to Americans as well to Vietnamese. Conclude your essay by answering the question, "Do you think the world is closer to peace now than it was in 1973? Why or why not?"

## Projects

**1. Comparing Social Trends.** Work in groups to compare the major social trends in the 1950's, the 1960's, and the 1970's. Find information on the interesting fads, the popular heroes, the favorite movies and songs, and the best-selling books for each decade. Draw conclusions about the important ideas and social concerns for each time period, and then present your conclusions in the form of a skit, a collage, or a report.

**2. Making a Survey.** Prepare a survey to determine the impact of television on American society. Ask questions to find out the number of hours per week people spend watching television and the types of shows people watch. Distribute the survey to your classmates, or to other classes within your school. Make a chart showing the results of your survey, listing the most popular television shows for each group surveyed and the average amount of time people watch television. Analyze the results and write a brief summary of your findings.

**3. Planning a Time Capsule.** Make a list of items for a 1980's time capsule. Choose items that will help future generations understand the American way of life in the 1980's. Compare your list with those of your classmates and then decide which suggestions best represent life in the 1980's.

**4. Presenting Panel Discussions.** Work in groups to trace the civil rights movement from the 1950's to the present. Find information on civil rights legislation, civil rights leaders, Supreme Court cases, and demonstrations. Summarize the progress that has been made and determine what problems remain to be solved. Present your research to the class in a panel discussion.

**5. Organizing Information.** Use your textbook to find the goals and the major accomplishments of each President from Harry Truman to Ronald Reagan. Organize the information in a chart, noting the differences between foreign and domestic policy. Then compare each President's goals and successes. Present your findings to the class.

## Finding Out More

Emmens, Carol A. *An Album of the Sixties.* Watts, 1981. Highlights of the decade are presented in text and photographs.

Fincher, E. B. *The War in Korea.* Watts, 1981. This book gives a complete account of the background and the aftermath of the Korean War.

Hoobler, Dorothy, and Thomas Hoobler. *An Album of the Seventies.* Watts, 1981. This book provides an introduction to the events of the 1970's.

Kiefer, Irene. *Poisoned Land: The Problem of Hazardous Waste.* Atheneum, 1981. This timely book discusses toxic wastes and disposal problems.

Lawson, Don. *The War in Vietnam.* Watts, 1981. The author traces the Vietnam conflict from the French withdrawal through increasing American involvement, the protest movement, and the final disengagement.

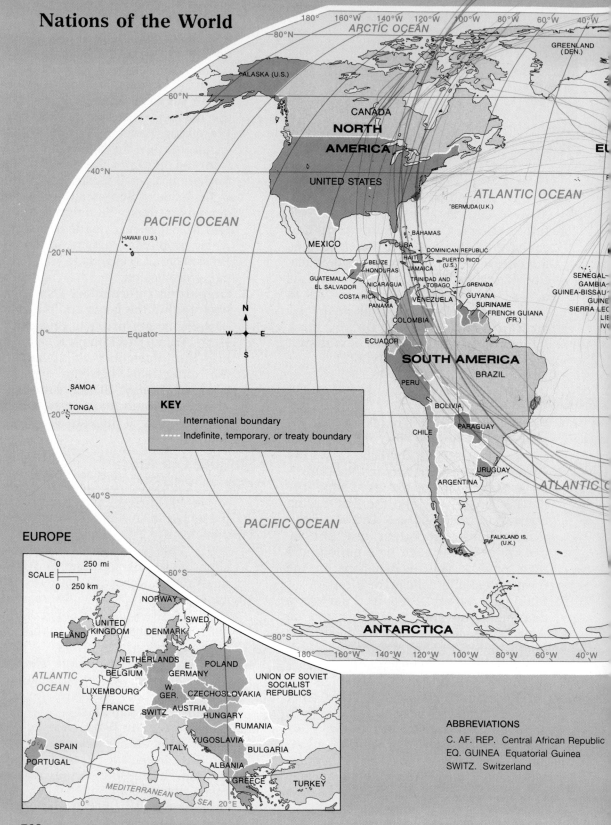

# Nations of the World

**KEY**
— International boundary
···· Indefinite, temporary, or treaty boundary

ARCTIC OCEAN
180° 160°W 140°W 120°W 100°W 80°W 60°W 40°W
80°N

GREENLAND
(DEN.)

ALASKA (U.S.)
60°N

CANADA

**NORTH AMERICA**

40°N

UNITED STATES

*PACIFIC OCEAN*

*ATLANTIC OCEAN*

HAWAII (U.S.)
20°N

MEXICO

BAHAMAS
CUBA
*BERMUDA (U.K.)*
DOMINICAN REPUBLIC
HAITI
PUERTO RICO
(U.S.)
BELIZE
HONDURAS
JAMAICA
GUATEMALA
EL SALVADOR  NICARAGUA
TRINIDAD AND
TOBAGO
GRENADA
COSTA RICA
PANAMA
VENEZUELA
GUYANA
SURINAME
FRENCH GUIANA
(FR.)

SENEGAL
GAMBIA
GUINEA-BISSAU
GUINEA
SIERRA LEO
LIB
IVO

COLOMBIA

N
W E
S

ECUADOR

0°  Equator

**SOUTH AMERICA**

BRAZIL

PERU

SAMOA

TONGA
20°S

BOLIVIA

PARAGUAY

CHILE

URUGUAY

ARGENTINA

*ATLANTIC O*

40°S

*PACIFIC OCEAN*

FALKLAND IS.
(U.K.)

60°S

**ANTARCTICA**

80°S
180° 160°W 140°W 120°W 100°W 80°W 60°W 40°W

## EUROPE

0    250 mi
SCALE
0    250 km

NORWAY

SWED.

UNITED
KINGDOM        DENMARK

IRELAND

NETHERLANDS
BELGIUM

E.
POLAND
GERMANY

UNION OF SOVIET
SOCIALIST
REPUBLICS

*ATLANTIC
OCEAN*

LUXEMBOURG
W.
GER.  CZECHOSLOVAKIA

FRANCE
SWITZ.  AUSTRIA
HUNGARY

RUMANIA

YUGOSLAVIA

SPAIN
ITALY
BULGARIA

PORTUGAL
ALBANIA

GREECE
TURKEY

*MEDITERRANEAN*
*SEA*  20°E

## ABBREVIATIONS

C. AF. REP.  Central African Republic
EQ. GUINEA  Equatorial Guinea
SWITZ.  Switzerland

ARCTIC OCEAN

80°N

FINLAND

60°N

UNION OF SOVIET SOCIALIST REPUBLICS

**ASIA**

POLAND

HUNG.
UGO.
RUMANIA
BULGARIA

MONGOLIA

40°N

LB.
GREECE
TURKEY
CYPRUS
SYRIA
LEBANON
ISRAEL
JORDAN
IRAQ
IRAN
AFGHANISTAN

PEOPLE'S REPUBLIC
OF CHINA

N. KOREA
S. KOREA
JAPAN

KUWAIT
QATAR
PAKISTAN

NEPAL
BHUTAN

LIBYA
EGYPT
SAUDI
ARABIA
U. ARAB EMIR.
OMAN

INDIA

BANGLADESH
BURMA

LAOS

TAIWAN

20°N

CHAD
SUDAN
YEMEN
YEMEN (P.D.R.)

DJIBOUTI

THAILAND

VIETNAM

PHILIPPINES

PACIFIC OCEAN

**AFRICA**

C.AF.REP.

ETHIOPIA

SRI LANKA

CAMBODIA

UGANDA
KENYA
SOMALIA

MALDIVES

MALAYSIA

SINGAPORE

Equator

0°

RWANDA
BURUNDI
ZAIRE
TANZANIA

SEYCHELLES

INDONESIA

PAPUA
NEW GUINEA

NAURU

SOLOMON
ISLANDS

NGOLA
MALAWI
COMOROS

ZAMBIA
ZIMBABWE
MOZAMBIQUE
MADAGASCAR

*INDIAN OCEAN*

FIJI

20°S

MBIA
BOTSWANA
MAURITIUS

SOUTH
AFRICA
SWAZILAND
LESOTHO

**AUSTRALIA**

NEW
ZEALAND

40°S

SCALE

0        2,000 mi
0        2,000 km

60°S

**ANTARCTICA**

80°S

40°E  60°E  80°E  100°E  120°E  140°E  160°E  180°

MIDDLE EAST

SCALE
0          1,000 mi
0          1,000 km

UNION OF SOVIET
SOCIALIST REPUBLICS

40°N

TURKEY

GREECE

TUNISIA

CYPRUS
LEBANON
ISRAEL
SYRIA

IRAQ

IRAN

AFGHAN.

JORDAN

KUWAIT
BAHRAIN
QATAR

PAK.

ALGERIA
LIBYA
EGYPT

SAUDI
ARABIA

U. ARAB
EMIR.

OMAN

20°N

NIGER
CHAD
SUDAN

RED SEA

YEMEN
YEMEN
(P.D.R.)

ETHIOPIA

20°E        40°E        60°E

60°N

U. ARAB EMIR.  United Arab Emirates

W. GER.  West Germany

YEMEN (P.D.R.)  People's Democratic Republic of Yemen

ATLAS

# The United States: *Cities and States*

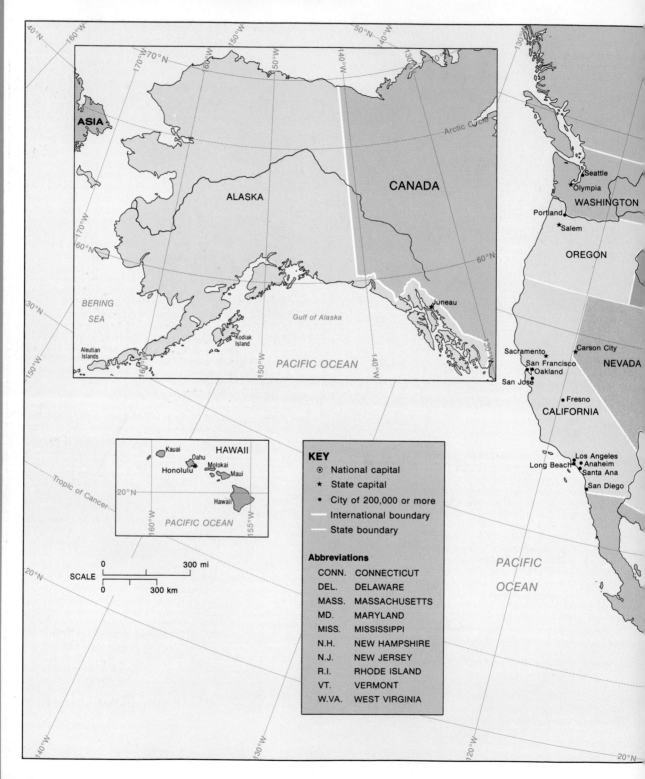

ASIA

ALASKA

CANADA

Arctic Circle

BERING
SEA

Gulf of Alaska

Juneau

Kodiak
Island

Aleutian
Islands

PACIFIC OCEAN

Seattle
★Olympia

WASHINGTON

Portland

★Salem

OREGON

Sacramento★
San Francisco
Oakland
San Jose

Carson City
NEVADA

• Fresno

CALIFORNIA

Long Beach
Los Angeles
• Anaheim
Santa Ana

San Diego

Kauai
Oahu     HAWAII
Honolulu   Molokai
Maui

Hawaii

PACIFIC OCEAN

Tropic of Cancer

PACIFIC
OCEAN

## KEY

⊙ National capital

★ State capital

• City of 200,000 or more

— International boundary

— State boundary

## Abbreviations

| | |
|---|---|
| CONN. | CONNECTICUT |
| DEL. | DELAWARE |
| MASS. | MASSACHUSETTS |
| MD. | MARYLAND |
| MISS. | MISSISSIPPI |
| N.H. | NEW HAMPSHIRE |
| N.J. | NEW JERSEY |
| R.I. | RHODE ISLAND |
| VT. | VERMONT |
| W.VA. | WEST VIRGINIA |

SCALE

0          300 mi

0          300 km

CANADA

*Hudson Bay*

MONTANA

NORTH DAKOTA
Bismarck

MINNESOTA

*Lake Superior*

MICHIGAN

*Lake Huron*

MAINE

Augusta

WYOMING

SOUTH DAKOTA
Pierre

Minneapolis   St. Paul

WISCONSIN

Madison
Milwaukee

Lansing

*Lake Michigan*

Detroit

*Lake Ontario*

Rochester

Buffalo

Montpelier   N.H.
NEW   VT.   Concord
YORK          Boston
Albany   MASS.
Hartford   Providence
R.I.
CONN.

NEBRASKA

IOWA
Des Moines

Chicago

Cleveland

*Lake Erie*

PENNSYLVANIA

Harrisburg

Jersey City
Newark
Trenton
Philadelphia
N.J.

New York

Cheyenne

Omaha

ILLINOIS   INDIANA   OHIO

Toledo   Akron

Pittsburgh

Dover
DEL.

Denver

Lincoln

Springfield

Columbus
Dayton
Cincinnati

Baltimore

Washington, D.C.
MD.   Annapolis

COLORADO
Colorado
Springs

KANSAS

Kansas
City

Indianapolis

W.VA.

Richmond

Topeka

Jefferson
City

St.
Louis

Louisville

Frankfort
Lexington

Charleston

VIRGINIA

Norfolk
Virginia
Beach

NEW MEXICO

Santa Fe

querque

Wichita

MISSOURI

KENTUCKY

Raleigh

ATLANTIC

OCEAN

Tulsa

Nashville

NORTH CAROLINA

Charlotte

Oklahoma
City

ARKANSAS

Memphis

TENNESSEE

SOUTH
CAROLINA

Columbia

El Paso

OKLAHOMA

Little
Rock

Birmingham

Atlanta

Fort Worth   Dallas

Shreveport

MISS.   ALABAMA

GEORGIA

Jackson

Montgomery

TEXAS

Baton
Rouge

Mobile

Tallahassee

Jacksonville

Austin

LOUISIANA   New Orleans

FLORIDA

San Antonio   Houston

Tampa
St. Petersburg

Corpus Christi

BAHAMAS

MEXICO

N
W   E
S

*Gulf of Mexico*

Miami

*Tropic of Cancer*

CUBA

50°N

40°N

30°N

20°N

110°W   100°W   80°W   70°W   60°W   90°W

# The United States: *Physical Features*

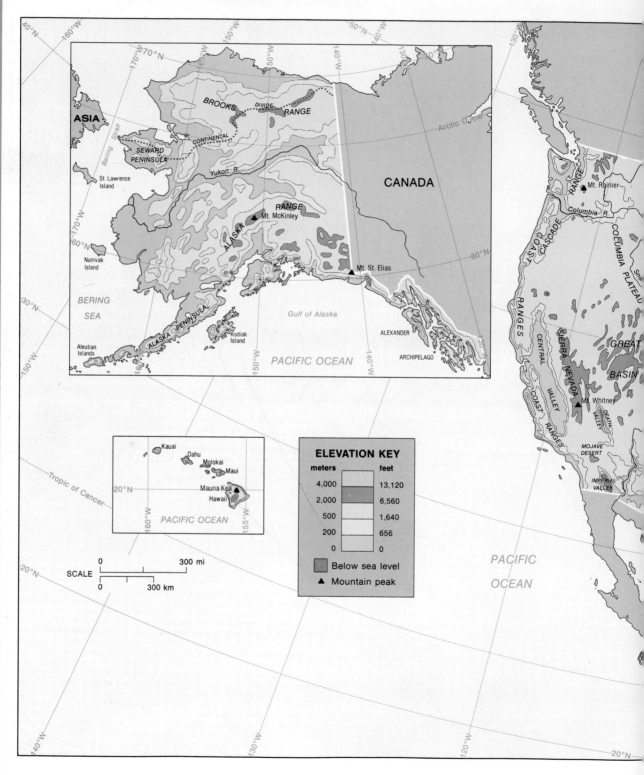

ASIA

BROOKS RANGE

DIVIDE

CONTINENTAL

SEWARD PENINSULA

St. Lawrence Island

Yukon R.

Bering Strait

RANGE

Mt. McKinley

ALASKA

Nunivak Island

BERING SEA

ALASKA PENINSULA

Kodiak Island

Aleutian Islands

Mt. St. Elias

Gulf of Alaska

PACIFIC OCEAN

CANADA

Arctic Circle

ALEXANDER

ARCHIPELAGO

Mt. Rainier

Columbia R.

COAST

CASCADE

RANGE

COAST RANGES

CENTRAL VALLEY

COAST RANGES

SIERRA NEVADA

Mt. Whitney

DEATH VALLEY

MOJAVE DESERT

IMPERIAL VALLEY

COLUMBIA PLATEAU

GREAT BASIN

Sn

Kauai

Oahu

Molokai

Maui

Mauna Kea

Hawaii

PACIFIC OCEAN

Tropic of Cancer

**ELEVATION KEY**

| meters | | feet |
|--------|--|------|
| 4,000 | | 13,120 |
| 2,000 | | 6,560 |
| 500 | | 1,640 |
| 200 | | 656 |
| 0 | | 0 |

Below sea level

▲ Mountain peak

SCALE

0   300 mi

0   300 km

PACIFIC

OCEAN

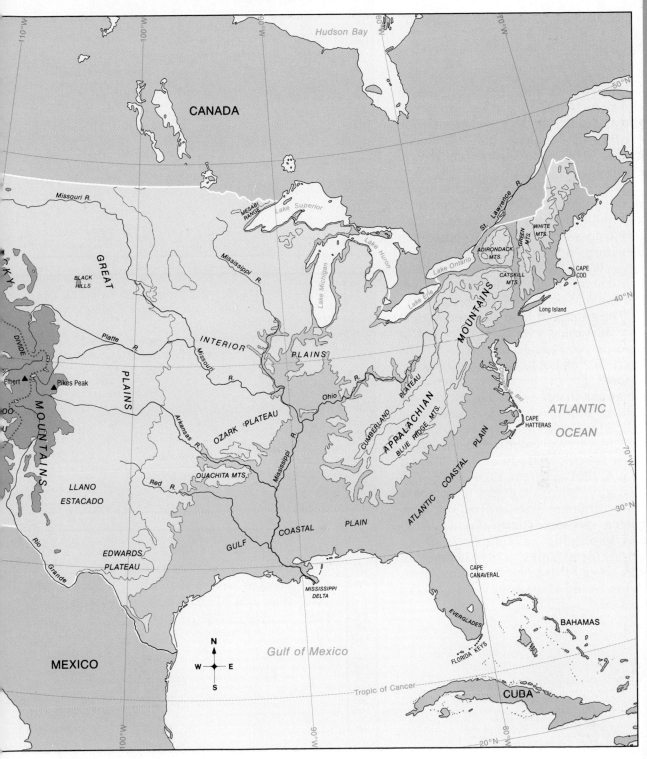

CANADA

*Hudson Bay*

*Lake Superior*

MESABI RANGE

Missouri R.

Mississippi R.

GREAT

BLACK HILLS

*Lake Michigan*

*Lake Huron*

St. Lawrence R.

WHITE MTS.

GREEN MTS.

ADIRONDACK MTS.

*Lake Ontario*

CATSKILL MTS.

CAPE COD

40° N

*Lake Erie*

Long Island

Platte R.

INTERIOR

PLAINS

P L A I N S

Missouri R.

Ohio R.

CUMBERLAND PLATEAU

APPALACHIAN

M O U N T A I N S

*Chesapeake Bay*

ATLANTIC OCEAN

DIVIDE

Elbert

Pikes Peak

OZARK PLATEAU

Arkansas R.

BLUE RIDGE MTS.

CAPE HATTERAS

70° W

MOUNTAINS

OUACHITA MTS.

Mississippi R.

ATLANTIC COASTAL PLAIN

LLANO ESTACADO

Red R.

30° N

EDWARDS PLATEAU

Rio Grande

GULF

COASTAL

PLAIN

CAPE CANAVERAL

MISSISSIPPI DELTA

EVERGLADES

BAHAMAS

MEXICO

N
W   E
S

*Gulf of Mexico*

FLORIDA KEYS

Tropic of Cancer

CUBA

20° N

100° W

90° W

80° W

# TIME CHART

This 8-page time chart presents a chronology of important historical events from 1400 to the present. The events are divided into *American Events*, *American Culture*, and *World Events*.

*American Events* includes milestones in American political, military, and judicial history. *American Culture* traces American achievements in literature, art, science, and technology. *World Events* notes important political and cultural developments in Europe and elsewhere in the world.

The chart can help you understand how historical events are related in time. If you read across the top of the chart, for example, you can trace the chronology of important events in American history. Reading across the bottom of the chart, you can trace events in world history.

The vertical columns of the chart show specific periods of time, for example, 1601–1650, or 1776–1800. You can read down a column to compare many different events that occurred during the same time period. What was happening in other parts of the world, for example, when Jamestown was being settled, or when the Constitution of the United States was being ratified?

## 1400–1500

### AMERICAN EVENTS

1438   Inca empire at its height in Peru.
1492   Columbus's first voyage to the Americas.
1493   Papal Line of Demarcation established.
1497–1498   Cabot reaches North America.

### AMERICAN CULTURE

1400–1500   Aztecs and Incas build cities, roads, schools, temples, and irrigation canals.
1400–1500   Native Americans of Mexico and South America develop metalworking in copper, silver, and gold.

### WORLD EVENTS

1400's   Portuguese explore African coast.
1455   Gutenberg's printing press in use.
1468   Songhai capture Timbuktu.
1488   Días sails around southern tip of Africa.
1498   Vasco da Gama reaches India.

## 1501–1600

**early 1500's** African slave trade begins across the Atlantic.

**1513** Balboa reaches the Pacific Ocean. Ponce de León explores Florida.

**1521** Cortés conquers the Aztecs.

**1532** Pizarro conquers the Incas.

**1535** Cartier explores the St. Lawrence River.

**1540** Coronado explores the Southwest.

**1542** Cabrillo explores California.

**about 1570** Iroquois League formed.

**1577–1580** Drake sails around the world.

**1584** English land at Roanoke Island.

---

**mid-1520s** Spaniards begin to build cities, missions, cathedrals, libraries, and museums in New Spain. They also introduce horses, steel, sugar refining, and cattle ranching.

**1514** Las Casas begins lifelong defense of Native Americans.

---

**1503** Leonardo da Vinci paints the *Mona Lisa.*

**1508–1512** Michelangelo paints Sistine Chapel ceiling.

**1517** Protestant Reformation begins.

**1519–1522** Magellan's crew circumnavigates the globe.

**1543** Copernicus publishes his theory that the earth revolves around the sun.

**1588** England defeats the Spanish Armada.

**1596** Shakespeare's *Romeo and Juliet* is first performed.

## 1601–1650

**1607** English settle Jamestown.

**1609** French settle Quebec.

**1609–1615** Voyages of Hudson and Champlain.

**1610** Spanish establish Santa Fe.

**1619** Virginia House of Burgesses established.

**1620** *Mayflower* lands at Plymouth.

**1630** Puritans settle Boston.

**1632–1636** Maryland, Rhode Island, New Hampshire, and Connecticut colonies begin.

---

**1608–1624** John Smith's books on Virginia and New England.

**1631** First American-built ship launched.

**1636** Harvard College founded.

**1647** First public schools in Massachusetts.

**1650** Anne Bradstreet's poems published.

---

**1604** Galileo demonstrates law of gravity.

**1608** Telescope invented.

**1628** English Petition of Right.

**1642** Rembrandt paints *Night Watch.*

**1642–1653** English Civil War.

**1643** Louis XIV begins his reign as king of France.

**1650** India's Taj Mahal completed.

**CHRONOLOGY**

| 1651–1700 | 1701–1750 |
|---|---|

### AMERICAN EVENTS

**1651** First Navigation Act.

**1663** Carolina becomes a proprietary colony.

**1664** New York becomes an English colony. Dutch surrender New Jersey to England.

**1673** Marquette and Joliet explore the Mississippi valley.

**1682** William Penn and Quakers found Pennsylvania.
La Salle claims Louisiana.

**1691–1692** Salem witchcraft trials.

**1704** First Delaware legislature is assembled.
Colonists are massacred at Deerfield, Massachusetts.

**1719** South Carolina becomes a royal colony.

**1729** North Carolina becomes a royal colony.

**1733** Georgia colony founded.

**1733–1740** Jonathan Edwards's preaching spurs the Great Awakening.

**1735** Peter Zenger defends freedom of the press.

### AMERICAN CULTURE

**1659** Joseph Jencks's fire engine.

**1661** John Eliot translates the Bible into the Algonquin language.

**1690** Benjamin Harris's *New England Primer*.

**1693** College of William and Mary founded.

**1701** Yale College founded.

**1704** *Boston News-letter*, North America's first newspaper.

**1723** Building begins on Boston's Old North Church.

**1728** Jews build first American synagogue.

**1732** Benjamin Franklin's *Poor Richard's Almanac*.

### WORLD EVENTS

**1664** Isaac Newton explains laws of gravity.

**1665–1666** Plague and fire of London.

**1667** Milton's *Paradise Lost*.

**1689** English Bill of Rights.

**1690** John Locke's *Essay Concerning Human Understanding*.

**1705** Halley predicts comet's return.

**1714** Fahrenheit invents mercury thermometer.

**1719** Daniel Defoe's *Robinson Crusoe*.

**1726** Jonathan Swift's *Gulliver's Travels*.

**1729** J.S. Bach's *St. Matthew's Passion* first performed.

**1736** Linnaeus classifies plants and animals.

**1741** Handel composes the *Messiah*.

## 1751–1775

**1754–1763** French and Indian War.

**1763** British prevent settlement west of the Appalachian Mountains.

**1765** Stamp Act.

**1767** Daniel Boone crosses the Appalachian Mountains.

**1769** Junípero Serra starts first California mission.

**1770** Boston Massacre.

**1773** Boston Tea Party.

**1774** Intolerable Acts.
First Continental Congress.

**1775** Paul Revere's ride.

## 1776–1800

**1776** Declaration of Independence.

**1781** Battle of Yorktown.

**1783** Treaty of Paris.

**1787** Northwest Ordinance.

**1788** Ratification of the Constitution.

**1789** George Washington becomes first President of the United States.

**1791** Bill of Rights.

**1800** Washington, D.C., becomes the nation's capital.
Thomas Jefferson elected President.

---

**1751–1775** Benjamin West and Charles Willson Peale recognized as important American painters.

**1754** Columbia University founded as King's College.

**1773** Oliver Evans proposes a steam-driven "horseless carriage."

**1776–1800** John Singleton Copley recognized as an important American painter.

**1776** Thomas Paine's *Common Sense*.

**1787** John Fitch's steamboat.

**1787–1788** *The Federalist* essays.

**1790** Samuel Slater's textile mill.

**1793** Eli Whitney's cotton gin.

**1800** Library of Congress founded.

---

**1757** British take control of India.

**1762** Catherine the Great begins her rule of Russia.

**1765** James Watt improves the steam engine.

**1775** First shots fired in Lexington, Massachusetts, mark start of Revolutionary War.

**1776** Adam Smith's *Wealth of Nations*.

**1778** James Cook discovers Hawaii.

**1786** Mozart's first opera.

**1789** French Revolution begins.

**1799** Napoleon begins rule of France.

**1800** Beethoven's first symphony.

## 1801–1825

## 1826–1850

**AMERICAN EVENTS**

| | |
|---|---|
| **1803** | Louisiana Purchase. *Marbury* v. *Madison*. |
| **1804** | Lewis and Clark expedition begins. |
| **1812–1814** | War of 1812. |
| **1817–1825** | Erie Canal built. |
| **1819** | Florida added to the U.S. |
| **1820** | Missouri Compromise. |
| **1823** | Monroe Doctrine. |

| | |
|---|---|
| **1827** | *Freedom's Journal*, first U.S. black newspaper. |
| **1828** | Andrew Jackson elected President. |
| **1830** | Indian Removal Act. |
| **1831** | Nat Turner's Rebellion. |
| **1836** | The Battle of the Alamo. |
| **1838** | Trail of Tears. |
| **1846** | Bear Flag Revolt. |
| **1846–1848** | Mexican War. |
| **1848** | Seneca Falls Declaration. |
| **1849** | California gold rush. |
| **1850** | Compromise of 1850. |

**AMERICAN CULTURE**

| | |
|---|---|
| **1807** | Robert Fulton's steamboat. |
| **1811** | National road begun. |
| **1814** | Francis Scott Key's "Star-Spangled Banner." Francis Lowell's factory system. |
| **1820** | Washington Irving's "Rip Van Winkle," "Legend of Sleepy Hollow." |
| **1821** | Sequoya's Cherokee alphabet. |
| **1825** | Thomas Cole starts Hudson River school of painting. |

| | |
|---|---|
| **1826** | James Fenimore Cooper's *Last of the Mohicans*. |
| **1830** | *Tom Thumb*, the first American-built steam locomotive. |
| **1832** | Samuel F.B. Morse's telegraph. |
| **1834** | Cyrus McCormick's reaper. |
| **1840** | Edgar Allen Poe's "The Fall of the House of Usher." |
| **1845** | Frederick Douglass's autobiography. |
| **1846** | Elias Howe's sewing machine. |
| **1850** | Nathaniel Hawthorne's *The Scarlet Letter*. |

**WORLD EVENTS**

| | |
|---|---|
| **1810–1826** | Latin American countries seek independence from Spain. |
| **1812** | Grimm's *Fairy Tales* published. |
| **1818** | Mary Shelley's *Frankenstein*. |

| | |
|---|---|
| **1831** | Victor Hugo's *The Hunchback of Notre Dame*. |
| **1835** | Alexis de Tocqueville's *Democracy in America*. |
| **1837** | Charles Dicken's *Oliver Twist*. Queen Victoria begins her rule of the British Empire. |
| **1839** | Daguerre develops photography. |
| **1847** | Charlotte Bronte's *Jane Eyre*. |
| **1848** | Karl Marx and Friedrich Engels publish *Communist Manifesto*. |

## 1851–1875

| | |
|---|---|
| **1857** | *Dred Scott* decision. |
| **1859** | John Brown's attack at Harpers Ferry. |
| **1860** | Abraham Lincoln elected President. Pony Express begins operation. |
| **1861–1865** | Civil War. |
| **1862** | Homestead Act. |
| **1863** | Emancipation Proclamation. Gettysburg Address. |
| **1867** | The United States buys Alaska. |
| **1869** | Transcontinental railroad completed. |

## 1876–1900

| | |
|---|---|
| **1876** | Battle of Little Big Horn. |
| **1877** | Chief Joseph surrenders. |
| **1886** | American Federation of Labor (AFL) formed. Statue of Liberty dedicated. |
| **1889** | Jane Addams's Hull House. |
| **1896** | William Jennings Bryan's "Cross of Gold" speech. *Plessy* v. *Ferguson.* |
| **1898** | The U.S. annexes Hawaii. |
| **1898–1899** | Spanish-American War. |

| | |
|---|---|
| **1851** | Herman Melville's *Moby Dick.* |
| **1852** | Harriet Beecher Stowe's *Uncle Tom's Cabin.* |
| **1854** | Henry David Thoreau's *Walden.* |
| **1855** | Walt Whitman's *Leaves of Grass.* |
| **1856** | Henry Bessemer invents new steel-making process. |
| **1869** | Louisa May Alcott's *Little Women.* |
| **1875** | Alexander Graham Bell invents the telephone. |

| | |
|---|---|
| **1876** | Mark Twain's *Adventures of Tom Sawyer.* |
| **1879** | Thomas Edison's light bulb. |
| **1883** | Brooklyn Bridge completed. |
| **1889** | Scott Joplin's "Maple Leaf Rag." |
| **1890** | *Poems by Emily Dickinson* published. |
| **1895** | Stephen Crane's *Red Badge of Courage.* Radio invented. |

| | |
|---|---|
| **1859** | Charles Darwin's *Origin of Species.* |
| **1864** | Louis Pasteur discovers pasteurization. |
| **1865** | Lewis Carroll's *Alice's Adventures in Wonderland.* |
| **1866** | Feodor Dostoevsky's *Crime and Punishment.* |
| **1867** | Alfred Nobel invents dynamite. |
| **1870** | Jules Verne's *20,000 Leagues Under the Sea.* |

| | |
|---|---|
| **1876** | Renoir recognized as French Impressionist painter. |
| **1880** | Rodin's sculpture, *The Thinker.* |
| **1883** | Robert Louis Stevenson's *Treasure Island.* |
| **1887** | Arthur Conan Doyle's first Sherlock Holmes story. |
| **1889** | Van Gogh's painting, *Starry Night.* |
| **1894** | Rudyard Kipling's *The Jungle Book.* |
| **1897** | Discovery of the electron. |
| **1898** | Marie Curie discovers radium. |

## 1901–1925

## 1926–1950

### AMERICAN EVENTS

| | |
|---|---|
| **1906** San Francisco earthquake. | **1929** Stock market crash. |
| **1909** Robert Peary reaches North Pole. | **1929–1941** Great Depression. |
| **1910** NAACP founded. | **1933** FDR's New Deal begins. |
| **1914** Panama Canal completed. | **1941** Japanese attack Pearl Harbor. |
| **1916** National Park Service founded. | **1941–1945** Lend-Lease aids Allies. |
| **1917** The U.S. enters World War I. | **1945** United Nations proposed. |

**1906** San Francisco earthquake.
**1909** Robert Peary reaches North Pole.
**1910** NAACP founded.
**1914** Panama Canal completed.
**1916** National Park Service founded.
**1917** The U.S. enters World War I.
Puerto Ricans become U.S. citizens.
**1919** President Wilson signs Versailles Treaty.
**1924** Indians become U.S. citizens.
J. Edgar Hoover becomes F.B.I. chief.

**1929** Stock market crash.
**1929–1941** Great Depression.
**1933** FDR's New Deal begins.
**1941** Japanese attack Pearl Harbor.
**1941–1945** Lend-Lease aids Allies.
**1945** United Nations proposed.
First atomic bomb tested.
**1947** Truman Doctrine.
**1950** Senator Joseph McCarthy starts Red scare.
American troops in Korea.

### AMERICAN CULTURE

**1903** Wright brothers' airplane.
**1906** Upton Sinclair's *The Jungle.*
**1908** Henry Ford builds first Model T.
**1909** First completely synthetic plastic invented.
**1911** Irving Berlin's "Alexander's Ragtime Band."
**1920** Sinclair Lewis's *Main Street.*
First radio-broadcasting station.
**1925** F. Scott Fitzgerald's *The Great Gatsby.*

**1926** Ernest Hemingway's *The Sun Also Rises.*
**1927** Charles Lindbergh's trans-Atlantic flight.
First sound movie.
**1928** Walt Disney's Mickey Mouse.
**1936** Jesse Owens wins four Olympic gold medals.
**1939** First commercial television broadcast.
First jet plane.
**1947** Jackie Robinson, major league baseball's first black player.
**1948** Transistor invented.

### WORLD EVENTS

**1905** Albert Einstein's *Special Theory of Relativity.*
**1912** Sinking of the *Titanic.*
**1914** Edgar Rice Burrough's *Tarzan.*
**1914–1918** World War I.
**1915** Sinking of the *Lusitania.*
**1917–1918** Russian Revolution.
**1920** League of Nations established.
**1923** Sigmund Freud's *The Ego and the Id.*

**1928** Penicillin discovered.
**1933** Hitler and Nazis assume power in Germany.
**1933–1945** The Holocaust.
**1936–1939** Spanish Civil War.
**1939–1945** World War II.
**1944** D-Day, Normandy invasion.
**1945** Nuremberg trials begin.
Atomic bombs dropped on Japan.
**1947** Anne Frank's *Diary of a Young Girl.*
**1948** State of Israel proclaimed.
**1950** Korean War begins.

## 1951–1970

1954    *Brown* v. *Board of Education.*

1957    School integration in Little Rock, Arkansas.
Eisenhower Doctrine.

1958    *Explorer I* launched.

1959    Alaska and Hawaii become states.

1961    Bay of Pigs invasion of Cuba.

1962    Cuban missile crisis.

1963    Nuclear test-ban treaty.
President Kennedy assassinated.

1965    Voting Rights Act.

1968    Martin Luther King, Jr. and Robert Kennedy assassinated.

## 1971–Present

1971    Supreme Court upholds busing to achieve school integration.

1973    U.S. Troops withdraw from Vietnam.
Watergate hearings begin.
Start of Arab oil embargo.

1976    American Bicentennial.

1979–1981    Iranian hostage crisis.

1983    Bomb kills U.S. Marines in Lebanon.
U.S. forces help invade Grenada.

1986    Space shuttle *Challenger* explodes.
Iran-*contra* scandal uncovered.

1987    Bicentennial of U.S. Constitution.
Gorbachev visits U.S.

---

1951    First mass-produced computer.

1952    First hydrogen bomb tested.
Jonas Salk's polio vaccine.

1956    Elvis Presley's television debut.

1959    First television pictures of Earth from space.

1960    First laser perfected.

1961    Alan Shepard becomes first American in space.

1962    Rachel Carson's *Silent Spring.*

1964    Beatles make U.S. debut.

1967    Successful heart transplant.

1969    Neil Armstrong walks on moon.

---

1972    CAT-scan machine invented.
Miami Dolphins go undefeated.

1975    U.S.-Soviet link-up in space.

1976    Alex Haley's *Roots.*

1977    George Lucas's *Star Wars.*

1979    *Voyager* space probes take pictures of Jupiter.

1980's    Superconductors and fiber optics developed.

1981    Space shuttle *Columbia* launched.

1982    First artificial heart transplant.

---

1953    Workings of DNA discovered.

1955    Warsaw Pact signed.

1956    Suez Canal crisis.

1957    Soviets launch *Sputnik I* and *II.*
Vietnam War begins.

1959    Fidel Castro begins rule of Cuba.

1966–1969    Cultural Revolution in China.

1967    Six-Day Arab-Israeli War.

1967–1970    Civil War in Nigeria.

1969    Muammar Qadaffi seizes power in Libya.
Golda Meir becomes prime minister of Israel.

---

1973    Yom Kippur Arab-Israeli War.
OPEC formed.

1976–1979    Pol Pot regime in Cambodia.

1979    USSR invades Afghanistan.
Islamic Revolution in Iran.
Sandinistas begin rule in Nicaragua.

1980    Iran-Iraq War begins.

1983    Start of famine in Ethiopia.

1986    Corazon Aquino assumes power in Philippines.
Chernobyl nuclear accident.

1987    U.S. warships patrol Persian Gulf.

The American Flag

Flags that have flown over the United States are shown to the left and below. Patriot forces fought under the Grand Union flag during the first days of the Revolution. In 1777 Congress approved a new flag, with 13 stripes and 13 stars. After independence was won, an additional stripe and star were added each time a state entered the Union. In 1818 Congress decided to set the number of stripes at 13 and to add a star for each new state. That practice has been followed ever since.

The Grand Union Flag

The First Stars and Stripes

The Flag of 1818

Alabama

Alaska

Arizona

Arkansas

California

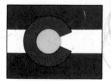

Colorado

Connecticut

Delaware

Florida

Georgia

Hawaii

Idaho

Illinois

Indiana

Iowa

Kansas

Kentucky

Louisiana

Maine

Maryland

Massachusetts

Michigan

Minnesota

Mississippi

Missouri

Montana

Nebraska

Nevada

New Hampshire

New Jersey

New Mexico

New York

North Carolina

North Dakota

Ohio

Oklahoma

Oregon

Pennsylvania

Rhode Island

South Carolina

South Dakota

Tennessee

Texas

Utah

Vermont

Virginia

Washington

West Virginia

Wisconsin

Wyoming

FLAGS

783

| | State Name | Date of Admission | Population (1986 Estimate) | Number of Representatives | Capital |
|---|---|---|---|---|---|
| 1 | Delaware | 1787 | 633,000 | 1 | Dover |
| 2 | Pennsylvania | 1787 | 11,889,000 | 23 | Harrisburg |
| 3 | New Jersey | 1787 | 7,620,000 | 14 | Trenton |
| 4 | Georgia | 1788 | 6,104,000 | 10 | Atlanta |
| 5 | Connecticut | 1788 | 3,189,000 | 6 | Hartford |
| 6 | Massachusetts | 1788 | 5,832,000 | 11 | Boston |
| 7 | Maryland | 1788 | 4,463,000 | 8 | Annapolis |
| 8 | South Carolina | 1788 | 3,376,000 | 6 | Columbia |
| 9 | New Hampshire | 1788 | 1,027,000 | 2 | Concord |
| 10 | Virginia | 1788 | 5,787,000 | 10 | Richmond |
| 11 | New York | 1788 | 17,772,000 | 34 | Albany |
| 12 | North Carolina | 1789 | 6,331,000 | 11 | Raleigh |
| 13 | Rhode Island | 1790 | 975,000 | 2 | Providence |
| 14 | Vermont | 1791 | 541,000 | 1 | Montpelier |
| 15 | Kentucky | 1792 | 3,728,000 | 7 | Frankfort |
| 16 | Tennessee | 1796 | 4,803,000 | 9 | Nashville |
| 17 | Ohio | 1803 | 10,752,000 | 21 | Columbus |
| 18 | Louisiana | 1812 | 4,501,000 | 8 | Baton Rouge |
| 19 | Indiana | 1816 | 5,503,000 | 10 | Indianapolis |
| 20 | Mississippi | 1817 | 2,625,000 | 5 | Jackson |
| 21 | Illinois | 1818 | 11,553,000 | 22 | Springfield |
| 22 | Alabama | 1819 | 4,053,000 | 7 | Montgomery |
| 23 | Maine | 1820 | 1,174,000 | 2 | Augusta |
| 24 | Missouri | 1821 | 5,066,000 | 9 | Jefferson City |
| 25 | Arkansas | 1836 | 2,372,000 | 4 | Little Rock |
| 26 | Michigan | 1837 | 9,145,000 | 18 | Lansing |
| 27 | Florida | 1845 | 11,675,000 | 19 | Tallahassee |
| 28 | Texas | 1845 | 16,682,000 | 27 | Austin |
| 29 | Iowa | 1846 | 2,851,000 | 6 | Des Moines |
| 30 | Wisconsin | 1848 | 4,785,000 | 9 | Madison |
| 31 | California | 1850 | 26,981,000 | 45 | Sacramento |
| 32 | Minnesota | 1858 | 4,214,000 | 8 | St. Paul |
| 33 | Oregon | 1859 | 2,698,000 | 5 | Salem |
| 34 | Kansas | 1861 | 2,461,000 | 5 | Topeka |
| 35 | West Virginia | 1863 | 1,919,000 | 4 | Charleston |
| 36 | Nevada | 1864 | 963,000 | 2 | Carson City |
| 37 | Nebraska | 1867 | 1,598,000 | 3 | Lincoln |
| 38 | Colorado | 1876 | 3,267,000 | 6 | Denver |
| 39 | North Dakota | 1889 | 679,000 | 1 | Bismarck |
| 40 | South Dakota | 1889 | 708,000 | 1 | Pierre |
| 41 | Montana | 1889 | 819,000 | 2 | Helena |
| 42 | Washington | 1889 | 4,463,000 | 8 | Olympia |
| 43 | Idaho | 1890 | 1,003,000 | 2 | Boise |
| 44 | Wyoming | 1890 | 507,000 | 1 | Cheyenne |
| 45 | Utah | 1896 | 1,665,000 | 3 | Salt Lake City |
| 46 | Oklahoma | 1907 | 3,305,000 | 6 | Oklahoma City |
| 47 | New Mexico | 1912 | 1,479,000 | 3 | Santa Fe |
| 48 | Arizona | 1912 | 3,280,000 | 5 | Phoenix |
| 49 | Alaska | 1959 | 534,000 | 1 | Juneau |
| 50 | Hawaii | 1959 | 1,062,000 | 2 | Honolulu |
| | District of Columbia | | 626,000 | 1 (non-voting) | |
| | | | 241,038,000 | 435 | |

This glossary gives definitions for vocabulary words and key historical terms used in *America's Story*. These words and terms are printed in dark type the first time they are used in the text. In addition, vocabulary words are highlighted in blue where they are first used. The page number following each definition tells you on what page the word is first used in the text. Remember that many words have more than one meaning. The definitions given here are the ones that will be most helpful to you in reading this book. You will find other references in the index.

Words that are difficult to pronounce are respelled where they first appear in the text. These words also have a special spelling in this glossary. You can find out the correct pronunciation of these words by using the pronunciation key at the bottom of each left-hand page. The full pronunciation key below shows how to pronounce each letter in a special spelling. The key also shows the difference between syllables with primary and secondary stress marks. The pronunciation key at the bottom of each left-hand page is a short form of the full key.

## Pronunciation Key

| | | | | | | | |
|---|---|---|---|---|---|---|---|
| ă | pat | hw | which | ô | alter, caught, for, paw | ŭ | cut, rough |
| ā | aid, they, pay | ĭ | pit | oi | boy, noise, oil | û | circle, firm, heard, term, turn, word |
| â | air, care, wear | ī | by, guy, pie | ou | cow, out | | |
| ä | father | î | dear, deer, fierce, mere | o͞o | took | v | cave, valve, vine |
| b | bib | | | o͞o | boot, fruit | w | with |
| ch | church | j | judge | p | pop | y | yes |
| d | deed | k | cat, kick, pique | r | roar | yo͞o | abuse, use |
| ě | pet, pleasure | l | lid, needle | s | miss, sauce, see | z | rose, size, xylophone, zebra |
| ē | be, bee, easy | m | am, man, mum | sh | dish, ship | zh | garage, pleasure, vision |
| f | fast, fife, off phase, rough | n | no, sudden | t | tight | | |
| | | ng | thing | th | path, thin | ə | about, silent, pencil, lemon |
| g | gag | ŏ | horrible, pot | *th* | bathe, this | | |
| h | hat | ō | go, row, toe | | | ər | butter |

Copyright © 1986 by Houghton Mifflin Company. Adapted and reprinted by permission from *The American Heritage Student's Dictionary.*

# A

**abolish** to put an end to (p. 340)

**abolitionist** an opponent of slavery (p. 340)

**acid rain** polluted rain caused by burning fossil fuels (p. 760)

**activist** a person who believes in taking strong action to solve problems (p. 725)

**Act of Toleration** a Maryland law of 1649 forbidding the religious persecution of Christians (p. 83)

**Adams-Onís Treaty** an agreement of 1819 in which Spain sold East and West Florida to the United States (p. 289)

**administer** to manage (p. 470)

**administration** the President's term in office (p. 261)

**adobe** (ə·dō′bē) a sun-dried clay brick (p. 6)

**affirmative action** a policy that gives minorities and women special consideration for jobs and educational opportunities, aiming to make up for past discrimination (p. 725)

**affluent** (ăf′lo͞o·ənt) wealthy (p. 704)

**aggression** an enemy attack (p. 594)

**Agricultural Adjustment Administration** (AAA) a New Deal agency established to spur recovery in agriculture (p. 646)

**Alamo** (ăl′ə·mō′) a mission in San Antonio, Texas, where in 1836, Texans seeking independence were defeated by Mexican forces (p. 375)

**Alaska pipeline** a pipeline that carries oil from the north coast of Alaska to tankers in southern Alaska (p. 733)

**Albany Plan of Union** a short-lived agreement of 1754, calling for a joint defense of the colonies from common dangers (p. 188)

**alien** a foreign resident of a country (p. 254)

**Alien and Sedition Acts** a set of laws, passed in 1798, limiting the rights of foreigners and outlawing words or actions disloyal to or critical of the government (p. 254)

**alliance** a formal agreement by two or more nations to act together in a cause (p. 165)

**Alliance for Progress** an aid program established by President John F. Kennedy in 1961 that encouraged economic growth and democracy in Latin America (p. 716)

**Allied Powers** an alliance between France, Russia, Great Britain, and later Italy and other countries opposed to the Central Powers during World War I (p. 594)

**Allies** the nations that opposed the Axis Powers in World War II, including the United States, Great Britain, France, and the Soviet Union (p. 667)

**ally** a partner in a common cause (p. 36)

**ambassador** a government's official spokesperson in a foreign country (p. 18)

**amend** to change or add to (p. 239)

**amendment** a legally adopted change in or revision of the Constitution (p. 239)

**American Federation of Labor** (AFL) a union of skilled workers, the largest American labor union by 1886 (p. 497)

**American Indian Movement** (AIM) an effort started in 1968 by Native Americans to gain more government protection from discrimination (p. 734)

**American System** a program proposed by Henry Clay in 1816, aimed at making the United States economically unified and self-sufficient (p. 286)

**amnesty** an official pardon (p. 438)

**Amnesty Act of 1872** a law restoring to most former Confederates the right to vote and hold office (p. 449)

**anarchist** a person who opposes organized government (p. 620)

**Anglican Church** the Church of England (p. 74)

**annex** to add to an existing country or area (p. 376)

**antiexpansionist** one who believed the United States should not expand its territory or impose its rule in foreign lands (p. 557)

**Antifederalists** the people who opposed the ratification of the Constitution, fearing a strong central government (p. 201)

**apartheid** (ə·pärt′hīt′) the official policy of racial segregation in South Africa (p. 756)

**appeasement** the policy of giving in to enemies to preserve peace (p. 666)

**apprentice** a person who works for another, without pay, in return for instruction in a skill or trade (p. 98)

**arbitration** a process in which a dispute is settled by a board of neutral persons (p. 564)

**archeologist** (är′kē·ŏl′ə·jĭst) a scientist who recovers and studies the remains of past human life (p. 4)

**armistice** a cease-fire agreement (p. 603)

**arms race** efforts by the United States and the Soviet Union to outdo each other in possessing weapons (p. 708)

**arsenal** a government storehouse of weapons (p. 195)

**Articles of Confederation** the first United States constitution, adopted by 1781 (p. 189)

**artifact** a human-made tool, ornament, or other object of archeological interest (p. 4)

**artisan** a skilled worker (p. 14)

**assassinate** to kill, especially a public official or a famous person (p. 438)

**assembly line** a system by which products are put together as they pass from worker to worker, often on a conveyor (p. 488)

**assimilate** to absorb and make similar to the dominant culture (p. 470)

**Atlantic Charter** a statement, written in 1941, of the Allies' aims during World War II (p. 669)

**Attorney General** the Cabinet member who advises the government on legal matters (p. 242)

**autonomy** the right of self-government (p. 565)

**Axis Powers** the alliance between Germany, Italy, and Japan during World War II (p. 666)

# B

**baby boom** the rapid expansion of the American population after World War II (p. 700)

**Backcountry** a hilly frontier region inland from the Tidewater, settled in the mid-1700's by former tenant farmers (p. 102)

**Back-to-Africa Movement** a movement for black Americans to return to Africa, led by Marcus Garvey in the 1920's (p. 621)

**Bacon's Rebellion** an attack on Jamestown in 1676 by Virginia frontier farmers protesting the government's refusal to protect them from Indians (p. 125)

**ballot** a piece of paper on which a vote is marked (p. 259)

---

ă pat ā pay â care ä father ě pet ē be ĭ pit ī pie î fierce ŏ pot ō go ô paw, for oi oil
o͞o book o͞o boot ou out ŭ cut û fur th thin *th* the hw which zh vision ə ago, item, pencil, atom

**Bank Holiday** a weekday on which banks are officially closed (p. 645)

**Bank of the United States** a national bank created in 1791 to help Congress borrow money and regulate the money system (p. 245)

**barter** to trade goods and services without exchanging money (p. 143)

**Battle of Bull Run** a significant Civil War battle at Manassas Junction, Virginia, in 1861, won by the Confederacy (p. 416)

**Battle of Bunker Hill** a battle of 1775 near Boston, a victory for the British in the Revolutionary War (p. 158)

**Battle of Fallen Timbers** a conflict won by government troops in 1794, forcing Native Americans to give up lands in the Northwest Territory (p. 250)

**Battle of Gettysburg** a long and costly battle of 1863 in Pennsylvania that was won by Union troops, creating a turning point in the Civil War (p. 423)

**Battle of New Orleans** the last battle of the War of 1812, won by American troops in 1815 (p. 274)

**Battle of Quebec** a conflict won by the British in 1759, creating a turning point in the French and Indian War (p. 114)

**Battle of Saratoga** a conflict won by the Patriots in New York in 1777, marking a turning point in the Revolutionary War (p. 169)

**Battle of the Bulge** the last major stand, made unsuccessfully, by the German army against the Allies in World War II (p. 678)

**Battle of the Marne** a battle won by French and British troops in 1914 that prevented a German advance at the Marne River in France (p. 594)

**Battle of Tippecanoe** a conflict of 1811 that resulted in a government victory over Shawnee Indians who were resisting land takovers in the Indiana Territory (p. 270)

**Battle of Wounded Knee** an army attack in 1890 on unarmed Sioux Indians in South Dakota, most of whom were killed (p. 468)

**Battle of Yorktown** a battle of 1781 in Virginia, a Patriot victory that ended the Revolutionary War (p. 173)

**Bay of Pigs invasion** an unsuccessful invasion of Cuba in 1961 by anti-Castro Cubans who were aided by the United States (p. 717)

**Bear Flag Revolt** an uprising in 1846 in which Americans living in California rebelled against the Mexican government and formed an independent republic (p. 378)

**Berlin airlift** efforts by the United States to send food and supplies by air to Soviet-blockaded Berlin, Germany, in 1948 (p. 693)

**Berlin Wall** a concrete wall separating East Berlin from West Berlin, constructed by the Soviets in 1961 (p. 717)

**bicameral** having two legislative houses (p. 198)

**big business** a name for large, powerful corporations, taken as a group (p. 486)

**bill** a draft of a law presented for approval to a legislature (p. 239)

**bill of rights** a list of essential freedoms guaranteed to all citizens (p. 189)

**Bill of Rights** the first 10 amendments of the Constitution, which guarantee the basic rights of American citizens (p. 240)

**black codes** the laws that former slave states passed after the Civil War, limiting the rights of black Americans (p. 440)

**blacklist** to list names of people thought to be disloyal to the government (p. 703)

**black-power movement** a movement started in the 1960's to build strength among blacks through political, economic, and educational organization and through racial pride (p. 726)

**Black Tuesday** October 29, 1929, the day the stock market crashed, beginning the Great Depression (p. 632)

**blitzkrieg** a German word meaning "lightning war," a sudden military effort (p. 667)

**blockade** to close off an area, such as a port or city (p. 271)

**blockade runner** a ship that attempts to get past enemy blockades (p. 420)

**Bolsheviks** members of the political party that took over the Russian government in 1917 to establish a Communist system (p. 601)

**bond** a government certificate of debt promising repayment with interest, on a specified date, of money borrowed from the purchaser of the certificate (p. 243)

**Bonus Army** the World War I veterans who marched on Washington in 1932 demanding early payment of war bonuses that were to be paid in 1945 (p. 636)

**boom** a period of rapid economic growth (p. 498)

**boomtown** a town that sprang up from sudden growth and prosperity during the mining rush (p. 471)

**bootleg** to make, sell, or transport illegal liquor, as during Prohibition (p. 621)

**booty** a collection of stolen goods (p. 56)

**border states** the states on the dividing line between the North and the South, where loyalties were sharply divided during the Civil War (p. 412)

**Boston Massacre** an incident in 1770 that started when angry colonists taunted British soldiers who then fired into the crowd, killing several colonists (p. 144)

**Boston Tea Party** a protest in 1773 of the Tea Act by American colonists, who boarded British East India Company ships and dumped tea overboard (p. 145)

**bounty** a bonus, often for performing a service for the government (p. 431)

**Boxer Rebellion** an outbreak of violence by Chinese nationalists hoping to drive foreigners out of China in 1900 (p. 561)

**boycott** a refusal to buy goods or services, used as a means of protest (p. 143)

**Brain Trust** a group of advisers who helped Franklin Roosevelt plan New Deal programs (p. 644)

**brand** a mark, burned into an animal's hide, that identifies the owner (p. 474)

**breadbasket colonies** the name used to characterize the Middle Colonies because they exported so much grain in the 1700's (p. 107)

**Brown v. Board of Education of Topeka** a landmark Supreme Court decision of 1954 declaring racial segregation in public schools to be unconstitutional (p. 705)

**Bureau of Indian Affairs** a government agency responsible for supervising the reservation system (p. 470)

**business consolidation** the merging of several small companies into one large company (p. 491)

**business cycle** a repeated pattern of booms and depressions in an economy (p. 499)

## C

**Cabinet** a group of people appointed by the President to head executive departments and act as advisers (p. 241)

**Camp David Accords** a set of principles for peace between Israel and Egypt agreed upon in the United States in 1979 (p. 745)

**Canal Era** the period from 1825 to 1850, when many canals were built to link major waterways (p. 317)

**Cape of Good Hope** the southern tip of Africa, which Portuguese explorers sailed around in the late 1400's, thus establishing an all-water route to Asia (p. 19)

**capital** the money and property needed to start and operate a business (p. 485)

**capitalist system** a free-enterprise economy that depends on large concentrations of capital in corporations (p. 486)

**caravan** a group of people traveling together, often merchants in desert regions (p. 17)

**carpetbaggers** the name given to northern whites who went to the South after the Civil War, often for political or financial advantage (p. 446)

**cash crop** a crop that is grown to be sold (p. 107)

**casualty** a person killed or injured in wartime (p. 423)

**caucus** a meeting of important members of a political party, often for the purpose of nominating candidates (p. 346)

**cede** to give up officially or formally (p. 379)

**censure** to condemn (p. 703)

**Central Intelligence Agency** (CIA) a federal agency responsible for gathering political and military information about foreign countries (p. 717)

**Central Powers** an alliance between Germany and Austria-Hungary during World War I (p. 594)

**charter** a legal paper granted by a monarch giving certain rights to a person or group (p. 63)

**charter colonies** the colonies that were governed by the terms of their charters and gave the people an indirect voice in choosing their governors (p. 122)

**checks and balances** a system in which each branch of government monitors the others, thereby preventing the misuse of power (p. 239)

**Chief Justice** the head of the Supreme Court (p. 242)

**Chinese Exclusion Act** an 1882 law forbidding Chinese immigration (p. 525)

**circumnavigate** to sail completely around (p. 30)

**city manager plan** a form of city government in which a nonpolitical, paid city manager is responsible to a commission or a city council (p. 576)

**civil disobedience** the refusal to obey laws regarded as unjust, usually through nonviolent protest (p. 706)

**Civilian Conservation Corps** (CCC) a New Deal agency that employed jobless young men to work to conserve natural resources (p. 645)

**civilization** a culture that has reached an advanced level of development (p. 8)

**civil rights** the personal freedoms guaranteed to all citizens by the Constitution (p. 442)

**Civil Rights Act** a law passed in 1866 granting citizenship to blacks and guaranteeing personal freedoms to all citizens (p. 442)

ă pat   ā pay   â care   ä father   ĕ pet   ē be   ĭ pit   ī pie   î fierce   ŏ pot   ō go   ô paw, for   oi oil
ŏŏ book   ōō boot   ou out   ŭ cut   û fur   th thin   th the   hw which   zh vision   ə ago, item, pencil, atom

**Civil Rights Act of 1964** a federal law that outlaws race discrimination in public places, on the job, and at the polls (p. 722)

**civil war** a conflict between different groups in the same country (p. 403)

**Civil War** a war between the Union and the Confederacy, lasting from 1861 to 1865 (p. 407)

**claim** a plot of land staked out by a miner (p. 383)

**clipper ship** a sailing vessel of the mid-1800's, designed for great speed (p. 307)

**closed shop** a workplace where union membership is required (p. 700)

**coalition** a temporary alliance to promote a common cause (p. 651)

**cold war** an uneasy peace after World War II, marked by constant tension between the United States and the Soviet Union (p. 691)

**collective bargaining** a process of negotiation between an employer and a labor union to settle disputes (p. 497)

**colony** a settlement ruled by a distant parent country (p. 34)

**columnist** a newspaper writer who interprets or comments on the news (p. 541)

**combine** a farm machine that cuts and threshes grain (p. 506)

**commerce** the buying and selling of goods (p. 99)

**commission plan** a form of city government in which the duties of the mayor and city council are performed by department heads (p. 575)

**Committee of Correspondence** a local group of Patriots who shared information with other colonists and organized protests against the Intolerable Acts (p. 148)

**common** a tract of land belonging to or used by the whole community, often for grazing farm animals (p. 98)

**communism** a social and political system based on Karl Marx's ideas of eliminating private ownership and establishing a classless society (p. 601)

**compensate** to reimburse (p. 350)

**compromise** to reach an agreement by having each side give up some of its demands (p. 198)

**Compromise of 1850** an agreement that admitted California as a free state, let the people of other parts of the Mexican Cession decide whether to admit slavery, forbade the slave trade in the District of Columbia, and passed a strict Fugitive Slave Law (p. 394)

**concentration camp** a prison camp in which Nazis confined millions of Jews and others they considered undesirable before and during World War II (p. 678)

**Concord** a town in Massachusetts, where in 1775, the first shots of the Revolutionary War were fired (p. 151)

**Confederacy** the Confederate States of America, 11 southern states that seceded from the Union by 1861 and formed a separate nation (p. 405)

**confederation** a loose union of independent states (p. 189)

**confiscate** to take away personal property, as by a government (p. 75)

**Congress** the Senate and House of Representatives, the two assemblies whose members are elected to make the laws of the United States (p. 198)

**Congress of Industrial Organizations** (CIO) an organization of industrial unions (p. 654)

**conquistador** (kŏn·kē′stə·dôr) a Spanish adventurer who explored and conquered the Americas during the 1500's (p. 34)

**conservation** the process of protecting a natural resource (p. 512)

**conservative** tending to favor preserving the existing political order (p. 651)

**constitution** a written plan of government (p. 189)

**Constitution** the plan of government for the United States, written in 1787 (p. 197)

**Constitutional Convention** a meeting in Philadelphia in 1787 that gave birth to the Constitution of the United States (p. 198)

**containment** the policy of keeping communism from spreading beyond Soviet satellite nations after World War II (p. 692)

**Continental Army** the military force of the Patriots during the Revolutionary War (p. 157)

**continental divide** a long stretch of high land where rivers on either side flow in opposite directions (p. 267)

**controversy** a dispute between sides holding differing views (p. 724)

**convention** a formal meeting of delegates (p. 195)

**convert** to bring about a change in beliefs (p. 35)

**convoy** an accompanying and protecting force, as with ships (p. 600)

**cooperative** an organization owned and run by those using its services, often an association that buys and sells products for its members (p. 514)

**Copperheads** northerners who spoke against the Union cause and actively aided the Confederacy (p. 432)

**corruption** dishonest practices (p. 449)

**cost of living** the average cost of food, housing, and clothing (p. 617)

**cotton boll** the seed pod of a cotton plant (p. 327)

**Cotton Kingdom** the Lower South in the mid-1800's, when cotton was the region's main crop (p. 329)

**cow town** a town from which cattle could be shipped by train (p. 474)

**Creole** (krē′ōl) a member of the second most privileged social class in Spanish America, of Spanish ancestry born in Spanish America (p. 50)

**Crown** the authority or government of a monarch (p. 29)

**Crusaders** the European soldiers who took part in the Crusades (p. 14)

**Crusades** a series of wars fought by European Christians in the Middle Ages to recover the Holy Land from the Muslims (p. 14)

**Cuban missile crisis** an incident in 1962 in which the United States stopped the Soviets from arming Cuba with missiles, agreeing not to invade Cuba in return (p. 717)

**culture** a people's way of life, including certain customs, tools, and knowledge (p. 4)

**currency** anything circulating as money (p. 141)

**Currency Act** a British law of 1764 prohibiting colonists from issuing their own money and requiring colonial debts to be paid in gold or silver (p. 141)

**czar** a king or emperor, especially in the Russian Empire (p. 524)

# D

**Daughters of Liberty** a group of women organized in 1765 to protect British colonists' rights in America (p. 143)

**D-Day** June 6, 1944, the day the Allies landed in Normandy, France, freeing France from German rule (p. 677)

**Declaration of Independence** a document signed by the delegates of the Second Continental Congress in 1776, setting forth certain principles of government and breaking all ties with Britain (p. 160)

**Declaratory Act** a British law of 1766 stating that Parliament had the power to pass laws governing the colonies (p. 143)

**defensive** protecting from attack (p. 412)

**deficit** a shortage in the amount of money taken in compared to the amount spent (p. 733)

**delegate** an official representative (p. 143)

**demilitarize** to remove troops and weapons from an area (p. 665)

**demilitarized zone** an area in which all military activity is banned (p. 697)

**democracy** a system of government by the people (p. 248)

**Democratic party** a political party that grew out of the Democratic-Republican party in 1828 (p. 292)

**Democratic-Republican party** a political party formed in 1792 that promoted a limited role for the federal government (p. 248)

**Department of Energy** a Cabinet agency established in 1978 to oversee most federal energy agencies (p. 744)

**Department of Health, Education, and Welfare** (HEW) a Cabinet agency established to care for the needs of the nation's children, sick, and poor (p. 705)

**Department of Housing and Urban Development** (HUD) a Cabinet agency established in 1965 to improve conditions in the nation's cities (p. 723)

**Department of State** the executive office handling foreign relations (p. 242)

**Department of Transportation** a Cabinet agency established in 1966 to promote safer and more efficient transportation (p. 723)

**deport** to expel from a country (p. 620)

**depression** a period of drastic decline in economic activity, marked by widespread unemployment (p. 499)

**deregulate** to end government control of (p. 744)

**détente** (dā·tänt′) a policy designed to relax tensions between nations (p. 734)

**dialect** the speech of a particular region (p. 540)

**dictator** a ruler with absolute authority over the government (p. 663)

**diplomatic recognition** the formal acceptance of another nation's government (p. 290)

**direct primary** an election in which candidates for public office are nominated by popular vote (p. 576)

**direct relief** cash grants given by New Deal agencies to people in need (p. 645)

**disarmament** the act of doing away with weapons (p. 718)

**discrimination** an unfair act or attitude based on prejudice toward a particular group of people (p. 382)

**dissent** to disagree (p. 74)

**dissident** a person who opposes the existing political system (p. 757)

**divert** to turn aside, as with streams or rivers (p. 509)

---

ă pat  ā pay  â care  ä father  ĕ pet  ē be  ĭ pit  ī pie  î fierce  ŏ pot  ō go  ô paw, for  oi oil
o͝o book  o͞o boot  ou out  ŭ cut  û fur  th thin  *th* the  hw which  zh vision  ə ago, item, pencil, atom

**dividend** a share of profits paid to stockholders (p. 485)

**divine right** a monarch's claim to rule by a right given to him or her by God (p. 75)

**division of labor** the breaking of one highly skilled job into many simpler ones to share the work among a group (p. 488)

**doctrine** a principle put forth, as by a government (p. 290)

**document** an official paper (p. 119)

**dollar diplomacy** a policy used by President William Howard Taft, encouraging American investment in Latin America (p. 568)

**domino theory** the belief that if one nation in a region (as in Southeast Asia) falls to communism, neighboring nations will soon follow (p. 698)

**draft** a process of selecting people for required military duty (p. 431)

**draft evader** a person who refuses to join the armed forces when called upon to do so by the government (p. 736)

***Dred Scott* case** a Supreme Court decision in 1857 declaring that slaves did not have the rights of citizens, the Missouri Compromise was unconstitutional, and Congress could not forbid slavery in the territories (p. 398)

**drought** (drout) a long period of dry weather (p. 642)

**Dust Bowl** an area of the south-central United States, where a long drought in the 1930's turned topsoil to dust (p. 642)

**duty** a tax on imported goods (p. 144)

# E

**Economic Opportunity Act** a federal law passed in 1964 that set aside government money for job training, preschool programs, food stamps, and VISTA (p. 722)

**economy** the system of producing and distributing goods and services (p. 51)

**effigy** a crude model of a hated person (p. 251)

**Eighteenth Amendment** a change in the Constitution, ratified in 1919, that outlawed the manufacture, sale, and transport of alcoholic beverages (p. 621)

**Eisenhower Doctrine** a policy established in 1957 giving the President authority to send troops to Middle Eastern countries requesting help (p. 709)

**elastic clause** a statement in the Constitution allowing Congress to make any laws "necessary and proper" for carrying out its duties (p. 241)

**elector** a qualified voter (p. 199)

**Electoral College** a group of electors chosen by each state, based on the number of senators and representatives it has, to elect the President and Vice President (p. 199)

**emancipate** to free from bondage (p. 421)

**Emancipation Proclamation** an order issued by President Abraham Lincoln in 1863, freeing all slaves in the states still fighting against the Union in the Civil War (p. 421)

**embargo** a government order to stop foreign trade (p. 269)

**Embargo Act** a law of 1807 banning American ships from sailing to foreign ports and closing American ports to foreign ships (p. 269)

**empire** a group of lands ruled by a single leader (p. 9)

**enclosure movement** the fencing of property in England by nobles during the late 1500's (p. 73)

***encomienda*** (ĕn′kō·mĭ·ĕn′də) a Spanish American landowner's right to demand labor from Native Americans on the land (p. 51)

**English Bill of Rights** a document written in 1689 forbidding cruel and unusual punishment and declaring the rights of citizens to bear arms, to have frequent elections, and to be tried by ⌐ jury (p. 120)

**enlist** to sign up for a term of service in the armed forces (p. 413)

**enlistment** a term of service in the armed forces (p. 163)

**entrepreneur** (ŏn′trə·prə·nûr′) a person who organizes and operates a new business, often taking risks (p. 485)

**Environmental Protection Agency** (EPA) a federal agency established in 1970 to control pollution (p. 733)

**Equal Rights Amendment** (ERA) a proposed change in the Constitution, not ratified, that protects people's rights against discrimination on the basis of sex (p. 734)

**equator** the imaginary circle around the center of the earth, dividing the Northern and Southern hemispheres (p. 19)

**Era of Good Feelings** the name used to characterize James Monroe's presidency (p. 285)

**erosion** a wearing away of soil (p. 512)

**ethnic** of a racial or cultural group (p. 528)

**evacuate** to withdraw from a threatened area (p. 695)

**expansionist** a person of the 1800's who wanted to enlarge the territory of the United States (p. 369)

**expatriate** a person who has left his or her homeland to reside in another country (p. 628)

**export** to send goods to another country for trade or sale (p. 107)

GLOSSARY

**exposé** (ĕk′spō·zā′)  a sensational article that reveals wrongdoing in government, business, or politics (p. 574)

**extended family**  a close-knit group made up of parents, children, and other relatives such as grandparents and cousins (p. 335)

**external tax**  a tax on colonial trade outside the colonies (p. 143)

## F

**Fair Deal**  President Harry Truman's program of social reforms (p. 701)

**fallout**  the radioactive particles that fill the air after a nuclear explosion (p. 718)

**Farewell Address**  an announcement by George Washington that he would not seek a third term as President (p. 252)

**Farmers' Alliance**  a political organization promoting the interests of farmers in the late 1800's (p. 517)

**fascism**  a system of government that emphasizes military power and total control over people's lives (p. 663)

**Fascist party** (făsh′ĭst)  the ruling political party in Italy from 1922 to 1943 (p. 663)

**federal**  a form of government in which states keep certain powers but give final authority to a central government (p. 198)

**Federal Bureau of Investigation** (FBI)  the government agency responsible for enforcing federal laws and protecting the country's security (p. 735)

**Federal Deposit Insurance Corporation** (FDIC)  a government agency that insures bank deposits (p. 646)

**Federal Housing Administration** (FHA)  an agency established under the New Deal to provide loans for building and repairing houses (p. 646)

**Federalist party**  a political party, formed in 1792, that promoted a strong federal government (p. 248)

**Federalists**  the people who favored the ratification of the Constitution, believing in the need for a strong central government (p. 201)

**Federal Judiciary Act**  a law of 1789 declaring that the Supreme Court would consist of five justices and a Chief Justice (p. 242)

**Federal Reserve Bank**  one of 12 banks given broad powers to regulate the supply of money in the United States (p. 587)

**federation**  an association formed by the joining of separate groups (p. 497)

**feminist**  a person who supports women's rights (p. 754)

**feudalism**  a system of interlocking loyalties in medieval society (p. 12)

**Fifteenth Amendment**  a change in the Constitution that forbids states from denying citizens the right to vote on account of race (p. 445)

**fireside chat**  one of Franklin Roosevelt's radio broadcasts to the American people (p. 645)

**First Continental Congress**  a meeting in Philadelphia in 1774, attended by delegates from all colonies except Georgia, where colonists demanded a change in British policy and recognition of colonists' rights (p. 148)

**First Reconstruction Act**  a law of 1867, the first of four laws that made up the plan for Radical Reconstruction (p. 443)

**flappers**  young women in the 1920's who set new standards of freedom in dress and conduct (p. 628)

**flatboat**  a flat-bottomed boat with square ends (p. 264)

**foreclose**  to cancel a loan when a person is unable to repay and to take possession of his or her property (p. 617)

**forty-niner**  a person who took part in the California gold rush of 1849 (p. 382)

**Fourteen Points**  a statement by President Woodrow Wilson in 1918 proposing terms for peace after World War I (p. 605)

**Fourteenth Amendment**  a change in the Constitution that gave blacks citizenship, repealed the Three-Fifths Compromise, and punished the Confederacy (p. 442)

**Freedmen's Bureau**  an agency that provided aid to blacks and poor whites after the Civil War (p. 441)

**Freedom of Information Act**  a law passed in 1974 giving the press easier access to government documents (p. 736)

**freedom rider**  a person who took part in bus trips through the South to protest segregation in the 1960's (p. 719)

**free enterprise**  a system that allows private businesses to operate in competition with one another with little government regulation (p. 484)

**freemen**  in feudal times, people who were not slaves or serfs, but were often landholders (p. 119)

**free silver**  the unlimited coinage of silver (p. 518)

---

ă pat    ā pay    â care    ä father    ě pet    ē be    ĭ pit    ī pie    î fierce    ŏ pot    ō go    ô paw, for    oi oil
o͞o book    o͞o boot    ou out    ŭ cut    û fur    th thin    th the    hw which    zh vision    ə ago, item, pencil, atom

**Free-Soilers**    a political party formed in 1848 by northerners opposing slavery and favoring homesteads for western settlers (p. 392)

**French and Indian War**    a conflict between the British and the French from 1754 to 1763, fought for the control of North America (p. 112)

**French Revolution**    an uprising in France, from 1789 to 1799, that brought about the downfall of the monarchs and nobles (p. 248)

**frontier**    an unsettled area at the edge of the wilderness (p. 89)

**fugitive**    runaway (p. 395)

**Fugitive Slave Law**    a part of the Compromise of 1850 requiring people in free states to help capture escaped slaves (p. 395)

**Fundamental Orders of Connecticut**    an agreement written in 1639 establishing a government in Connecticut (p. 82)

# G

**Gadsden Purchase**    the territory, part of present-day New Mexico and Arizona, that the United States bought from Mexico in 1853 (p. 380)

**game**    wild animals that are hunted for food (p. 74)

**genocide**    the deliberate destruction of a racial, cultural, or national group (p. 525)

**Gettysburg Address**    a speech delivered by Abraham Lincoln in 1863 after the Battle of Gettysburg (p. 423)

**ghetto**    a poor, run-down part of a city, usually occupied by members of one minority group (p. 542)

**GI Bill of Rights**    a federal bill that provides financial aid to returning soldiers entering college or starting businesses (p. 699)

**glacier**    a large, slow-moving mass of ice (p. 3)

**gold standard**    a government money policy under which every paper dollar is equal in value to and exchangeable for a certain amount of gold (p. 517)

**Good Neighbor Policy**    a policy established by Franklin Roosevelt ending the United States' involvement in Latin American affairs (p. 665)

**grammar school**    an advanced educational program in colonial times, preparing older boys for college (p. 101)

**Grange**    an organization of farmers, founded for social, political, and economic purposes in 1867 (p. 514)

**Great Awakening**    a religious movement from 1720 to 1750, in which traveling ministers emphasized personal religious experience (p. 101)

**Great Compromise**    an agreement reached at the Constitutional Convention, creating the Senate and House of Representatives (p. 198)

**Great Depression**    a period of severe national economic decline from 1929 to 1941 (p. 632)

**Great Society**    Lyndon Johnson's program of social reform (p. 722)

**greenback**    a United States paper dollar (p. 429)

**groundwater**    the water under the earth's surface (p. 509)

**guerrilla**    a soldier who fights in small groups and uses hit-and-run methods (p. 717)

# H

**habeas corpus** (hā′bē·əs kôr′pəs)    a writ that protects a person from being jailed illegally by requiring that the arrested person be brought before a court (p. 432)

**hacienda** (hä′sē·ĕn′də)    a large estate (p. 51)

**Harlem Renaissance**    a black literary and artistic movement of the 1920's (p. 628)

**Hartford Convention**    a meeting in 1814 where the Federalist party protested the government's war policy (p. 274)

**heathen**    one who is regarded as being unreligious or uncivilized (p. 89)

**Holocaust**    the mass killing of millions of people, including 6 million Jews, by Nazis during World War II (p. 678)

**Holy Land**    the area where Jesus Christ lived, at the eastern end of the Mediterranean Sea (p. 13)

**homestead**    a plot of land on which to settle and build (p. 392)

**Homestead Act**    a law passed in 1862 that gave plots of public land to the heads of families who had lived on and worked the land for five years (p. 461)

**Hooverville**    the name, after President Herbert Hoover, given to a settlement of shacks built at the edge of a city, in which homeless and jobless people lived during the Great Depression (p. 634)

**hornbook**    an elementary reader commonly used in colonial times (p. 100)

**House of Burgesses**    a body of representatives that made governmental decisions during the 1600's in colonial Virginia (p. 79)

**House of Representatives**    the lower house of Congress, with each state represented according to population (p. 198)

**Huguenots** (hyōo′gə·nŏts′)    French Protestants of the 1500's and 1600's (p. 75)

**humanitarian**    concerned with human welfare (p. 755)

**GLOSSARY**

**human rights** people's basic rights to freedom, justice, and security (p. 744)

**Hundred Days** an emergency session of Congress in 1933, called to enact New Deal programs (p. 645)

## I

**Ice Age** a period of time characterized by very cold temperatures and glaciers (p. 3)

**impeach** to accuse and try an elected official (p. 444)

**imperialism** a policy of creating an empire by acquiring territory or by establishing economic or political control over other nations (p. 552)

**import** a good brought from one country for trade or sale in another (p. 107)

**impress** to force to serve in the military (p. 250)

**improvise** to make up (p. 628)

**inaugurate** to formally admit to service in office (p. 242)

**income tax** a tax on a person's yearly earnings (p. 429)

**indentured servant** an English man or woman who exchanged usually four to seven years of labor for passage to American colonies (p. 64)

**indigo** a plant used to make blue dye (p. 102)

**industrialist** a person who owns or manages a large manufacturing business (p. 491)

**Industrial Revolution** a shift from hand tools and home manufacturing to machines and large-scale factory production, beginning in England in the late 1700's and spreading to the United States (p. 308)

**industrial union** a labor union that represents workers in the same industry (p. 654)

**inflation** a sharp, steady rise in prices (p. 429)

**initiative** a procedure through which citizens can propose a law or an amendment to a state's constitution (p. 576)

**insurgent** a member of a political party who rebels against its leadership (p. 584)

**intelligence** military and political information about foreign countries (p. 717)

**interest** an extra payment in return for the use of money loaned (p. 243)

**internal tax** a tax on colonial trade within the colonies (p. 143)

**Interstate Commerce Act** a law passed in 1887 that, by controlling rates, regulates monopolies that benefit the public (p. 500)

**intolerable** unbearable (p. 148)

**Intolerable Acts** the four laws that were passed by Parliament in 1774 as punishment for the Boston Tea Party (p. 148)

**investor** a person who puts money into a project in order to earn a profit (p. 63)

**invincible** incapable of being beaten (p. 58)

**Invincible Armada** the Spanish fleet thought to be unconquerable but defeated in 1588 by the English (p. 58)

**Iran-*contra* affair** the incidents that led to a scandal in 1986, when it became known that members of Ronald Reagan's staff had secretly sold arms to Iran and illegally used some of the profits as aid to the *contras* (p. 754)

**Iran hostage crisis** the takeover of the American embassy in Tehran by Iranian students in 1979 (p. 745)

**ironclad** a nineteenth-century warship with metal-armored sides (p. 420)

**iron curtain** an invisible barrier between Eastern and Western Europe after World War II (p. 692)

**irrigate** to bring water to crops by means of streams, canals, or pipes (p. 6)

**Islam** a religion based on the teachings of Mohammed (p. 13)

**island hopping** an American military strategy in the Pacific Ocean in 1945, where islands were used as steppingstones to reach Japan (p. 679)

**isolationism** a policy of avoiding political and economic entanglements with other countries (p. 551)

## J

**Jay's Treaty** an agreement of 1795 in which the British promised to give up forts along the United States' northwest border (p. 251)

**Jazz Age** a nickname for the 1920's (p. 628)

**Jim Crow laws** laws that promoted segregation in public facilities (p. 536)

**joint occupation** shared ownership of a territory (p. 370)

**joint-stock company** a company owned by several investors through shares of stock (p. 63)

**judicial review** the Supreme Court's power to declare laws unconstitutional (p. 263)

**jury** a group of citizens who hear trials and hand down judgments in courts of law (p. 119)

**justice** a judge (p. 242)

---

ă pat   ā pay   â care   ä father   ĕ pet   ē be   ĭ pit   ī pie   î fierce   ŏ pot   ō go   ô paw, for   oi oil
o͞o book   o͞o boot   ou out   ŭ cut   û fur   th thin   *th* the   hw which   zh vision   ə ago, item, pencil, atom

**justice of the peace** a local official given authority to judge court cases, collect taxes, and perform other official duties (p. 123)

# K

**Kansas-Nebraska Act** a law passed in 1854 that divided the Nebraska Territory into Kansas and Nebraska, whose residents would decide whether to permit slavery (p. 396)

**Kentucky and Virginia Resolutions** a law passed in 1798 declaring that states do not have to accept unconstitutional laws passed by Congress (p. 255)

**kickback** an illegal payment in exchange for an official favor (p. 624)

**knight** a noble of inferior wealth trained to fight on horseback (p. 12)

**Knights of Labor** a large, powerful labor union of the late 1800's, open to skilled and unskilled workers (p. 495)

**Know-Nothing party** a political group, active from 1846 to 1856, formed by Nativists (p. 314)

**Ku Klux Klan** a secret society formed after the Civil War to spread the idea of white superiority, often by terrorizing blacks (p. 448)

# L

**labor union** an organization of workers formed to protect their rights and interests concerning wages and working conditions (p. 312)

**lame duck** a person who is finishing a term of office after failing to win reelection (p. 644)

**League of Nations** an organization established by the Treaty of Versailles to keep peace in the world (p. 607)

**legation** an official residence of a diplomat in a foreign country (p. 561)

**legislator** a member of the government body that makes laws (p. 122)

**legislature** a group of people given the power to make and change laws (p. 121)

**Lend-Lease Act** a law passed in 1941 allowing the President to sell or lend war materials to any nation whose defense is vital to the United States (p. 669)

**levy** to impose, as with a tax (p. 587)

**Lexington** the town in Massachusetts to which Paul Revere rode to warn Patriot leaders of a British advance (p. 151)

**liberal** tending to favor progressive change and reform in government (p. 651)

**Liberty Bonds** the government bonds that were sold to help pay for World War I (p. 599)

**Liberty party** an antislavery political party of the mid-1800's (p. 354)

**Lima** (lē′mə) a city in Peru, founded by Francisco Pizarro in 1535 (p. 38)

**limited monarchy** a monarchy where the king or queen does not have complete power (p. 120)

**Line of Demarcation** a boundary through the North and South poles, established by the Pope in 1493 to divide unsettled lands between Spain and Portugal (p. 27)

**literacy test** a test of the ability to read and write (p. 536)

**lobbyist** one who tries to influence legislators to vote for a special interest (p. 586)

**local** a branch of a labor union (p. 495)

**London Company** a joint-stock company formed to develop trade in America (p. 77)

**Lone Star Republic** the nickname given to Texas when it became an independent country (p. 376)

**long drive** the movement of huge cattle herds from Texas north to Kansas and Nebraska, for shipping east by train (p. 474)

**loophole** a means of escape, as with an unclear provision in a law (p. 750)

**lord** a noble who owned a manor (p. 12)

**Louisiana Purchase** a treaty of 1803 in which the United States bought the Louisiana Territory from France (p. 266)

**Louisiana Territory** the region between the Mississippi River and the Rocky Mountains (p. 265)

**Lower South** the states of Alabama, Mississippi, and Louisiana (p. 328)

**Loyalists** the American colonists who wanted to remain British subjects (p. 158)

**lynch** to hang someone without a trial (p. 448)

# M

***McCulloch* v. *Maryland*** a Supreme Court decision of 1819 allowing the federal government to establish and maintain a bank without interference from the states (p. 286)

**Magna Charta** (măg′nə kär′tə) a charter granted by King John in 1215, limiting the English monarchs' power by extending certain rights to the citizens (p.119)

**Manifest Destiny** a doctrine of the 1800's stating that the United States was meant to span the entire North American continent from east to west (p. 369)

**man-of-war** a warship (p. 170)

**manor** a large estate in the Middle Ages, often including a castle, church, village, and farmland (p. 12)

**manufacture**　to make goods (p. 107)

*Marbury* v. *Madison*　a Supreme Court decision of 1803, the first case in which the Court declared unconstitutional a law passed by Congress (p. 262)

**margin**　the money given to a stockbroker as a deposit against any losses made on an account (p. 631)

**Marshall Plan**　an American economic aid program to Europe following World War II (p. 693)

**martyr**　a person who suffers or dies for a cause (p. 401)

**Mason and Dixon Line**　the boundary between Maryland and Pennsylvania that divided slave states from free states (p. 338)

**masonry**　a structure of bricks or stone (p. 530)

**massive retaliation**　a strategy calling for the all-out use of atomic weapons against the Soviet Union in response to a nuclear attack by a Communist nation (p. 707)

**mass production**　the making of large quantities of goods quickly and cheaply (p. 488)

**materialism**　the theory that possessions constitute life's highest value (p. 628)

**Mayflower Compact**　an agreement signed by Pilgrim leaders aboard the *Mayflower* in 1620, providing for local government in America (p. 80)

**Medicare**　a federal health-care program established in 1965 for people 65 or older (p. 723)

**medieval**　belonging to the Middle Ages (p. 12)

**melting pot**　a place where people of different cultures or races live together and influence each other (p. 109)

**mercantilism**　a system of foreign trade practiced in Europe after 1500, based on gaining wealth, establishing colonies, and regulating colonial trade so that the home country remained more powerful than the colonies (p. 54)

**mercenary**　a soldier paid to fight for a foreign army (p. 159)

**merchandising**　the selling of goods (p. 489)

**merit system**　the practice of awarding government jobs based on ability rather than political favoritism (p. 579)

**mestizo** (mĕs·tē′zō)　a member of a lower social class in Spanish America, of mixed Spanish and Native American ancestry (p. 50)

**Mexican Cession**　the land that Mexico ceded to the United States in 1848 under the terms of the Treaty of Guadalupe Hidalgo, nearly half of Mexico's territory (p. 379)

**Middle Ages**　the period in European history from about A.D. 500 to 1400 (p. 12)

**Middle Passage**　the journey across the Atlantic in the African slave trade, during which many Africans died from harsh treatment (p. 76)

**migrant worker**　a hired laborer who moves from farm to farm to help plant and harvest crops (p. 643)

**migration**　a movement from one region and settlement in another (p. 4)

**militant**　aggressive (p. 354)

**militarism**　a policy of building strong armed forces to prepare for war (p. 593)

**militia** (mə·lĭsh′ə)　a citizen army (p. 139)

**minutemen**　the armed Patriots who pledged to fight on a minute's notice (p. 151)

*Miranda* v. *Arizona*　a Supreme Court decision of 1966 ruling that suspects of crime must be advised of their rights to an attorney and to remain silent or police questioning would be considered illegal (p. 724)

**mission**　a settlement founded for the purpose of spreading religion in another land (p. 51)

**missionary**　a person sent to spread religion in another land (p. 35)

**Missouri Compromise**　an act of 1820 admitting Missouri as a slave state, Maine as a free state, and barring slavery north of the parallel 36°30′N (p. 287)

**mobilize**　to prepare for war (p. 594)

**moderate**　one who avoids extreme views and actions, as with politics (p. 443)

**monarch**　a king or queen who rules a country (p. 16)

**monopoly**　the complete control over the means of producing or selling a product or service (p. 17)

**Monroe Doctrine**　a principle announced in 1823, whereby the United States would stay out of European affairs and European countries would keep out of affairs in the Western Hemisphere (p. 290)

**Mormons**　members of the Church of Jesus Christ of Latter-day Saints, who, led by Brigham Young, began settlements in the valley of Utah's Great Salt Lake (p. 509)

**Morse code**　a system of sending messages, using short and long signals to represent letters and numbers (p. 323)

**mortgage**　a loan made to a homebuyer (p. 633)

**Mound Builders**　the prehistoric Native American tribes who built huge earthen mounds for religious ceremonies and for burial (p. 6)

---

ă pat　ā pay　â care　ä father　ĕ pet　ē be　ĭ pit　ī pie　î fierce　ŏ pot　ō go　ô paw, for　oi oil
ōō book　ōō boot　ou out　ŭ cut　û fur　th thin　*th* the　hw which　zh vision　ə ago, item, pencil, atom

**muckraker** a journalist who searches for and exposes corruption (p. 574)

**Muslims** the followers of Islam (p. 13)

# N

**National Aeronautics and Space Administration** (NASA) the organization in charge of space programs in the United States (p. 708)

**National Association for the Advancement of Colored People** (NAACP) a group formed in 1910 to help black Americans secure legal equality (p. 588)

**nationalism** devotion to one's country (p. 16)

**National Labor Relations Board** (NLRB) a government agency designed to settle labor disputes and to protect unions from interference from employers (p. 651)

**National Organization for Women** (NOW) a group that advocates equal rights for women, started in the 1960's (p. 725)

**National Origins Act** a law passed in 1924 that set immigration quotas (p. 620)

**National Recovery Administration** (NRA) a New Deal agency established to help business recover (p. 646)

**National Road** the main overland route to the West in the 1800's, running from Maryland and eventually reaching Illinois (p. 316)

**National Youth Administration** (NYA) a New Deal agency that provided work for high school and college students (p. 648)

**Nativists** the Americans of the mid-1800's who favored the interests of native inhabitants over those of immigrants (p. 314)

**navigation** the science of sailing ships (p. 15)

**Navigation Acts** a series of laws, passed in the 1660's, protecting English colonial trade (p. 127)

**Nazi** (nät′sē) a member of the National Socialist Workers' party, which was founded by Adolf Hitler in Germany in 1919 (p. 664)

**negotiate** to discuss arrangements in order to reach an agreement (p. 174)

**neutral** taking no one's side (p. 249)

**Neutrality Proclamation** a document of 1793 declaring that the United States would not take sides in the French Revolution (p. 249)

**New Deal** Franklin Roosevelt's program for economic and social recovery from the Depression (p. 643)

**New Freedom** Woodrow Wilson's program of change, especially regarding tariffs, trusts, and the banking system (p. 586)

**New Frontier** John F. Kennedy's plan to handle foreign and domestic issues (p. 718)

**New Jersey Plan** a proposal offered at the Constitutional Convention, calling for three branches of government, including a unicameral legislature in which all states would be equally represented (p. 198)

**New Nationalism** Theodore Roosevelt's plan for economic and social reforms (p. 584)

**New South** the name used to characterize the South after Reconstruction (p. 450)

**New Spain** a part of Spain's empire in the 1500's, including Venezuela and all Spanish claims north of the Isthmus of Panama (p. 49)

*Niña* (nē′nyä) the ship accompanying the *Santa María* and the *Pinta* on Columbus's voyage to America (p. 21)

**Nineteenth Amendment** a change in the Constitution that gives women suffrage (p. 622)

**noble** a person born to a high position in medieval society (p. 12)

**nomad** a member of a group that has no fixed home and moves about in search of food (p. 3)

**nominate** to choose as a candidate (p. 252)

**Non-Intercourse Act** a law passed in 1809 allowing Americans to trade with all countries except Britain and France (p. 270)

**normalcy** normality (p. 621)

**normal school** a school that trains teachers (p. 347)

**North Atlantic Treaty Organization** (NATO) a defensive alliance between the United States and 15 other countries on or near the Atlantic Ocean (p. 694)

**Northwest Ordinance** a plan of 1787 for settling the Northwest Territory that provided for eventual self-government (p. 193)

**Northwest Passage** a waterway through North America providing a direct route between Europe and Asia, for which explorers in the 1500's searched in vain (p. 31)

**Northwest Territory** the land north of the Ohio River to the Great Lakes and west to the Mississippi River (p. 193)

**nullify** to cancel formally (p. 255)

**Nuremberg Trials** the court proceedings after World War II in which the Allies tried Nazi leaders for war crimes (p. 678)

**nutrient** (noo′trē·ənt) a nourishing ingredient (p. 512)

# O

**offensive** attacking (p. 412)

**Old South** the states of Maryland, Virginia, North Carolina, South Carolina, and Georgia (p. 328)

**GLOSSARY**

**Olive Branch Petition** an unsuccessful attempt by the Second Continental Congress to avoid war with Britain, urging the Crown to protect the colonists from the unfair policies of Parliament (p. 157)

**Open Door Policy** a policy set forth by Secretary of State John Hay in 1899, advocating that all nations have an equal opportunity to trade with China (p. 561)

**open range** the vast areas of unfenced land owned by the government and used by ranchers for grazing cattle (p. 474)

**oratory** the skill of public speaking (p. 286)

**ordinance** a government regulation (p. 193)

**Ordinance of 1785** a plan for settling the Northwest Territory, dividing the land into townships (p. 193)

**Oregon Country** an early 1800's name for the land between Alaska and California, now called the Pacific Northwest (p. 369)

**Oregon Trail** the main route to the Oregon Country from Missouri in the 1840's (p. 371)

**Organization of Petroleum Exporting Countries** (OPEC) a league of 13 oil-rich countries mainly in the Middle East and Africa (p. 743)

**override** to set aside or nullify (p. 442)

**overseer** a person who directs the work of others, often a supervisor of slaves (p. 103)

# P

**pacifist** a person who opposes war (p. 600)

**packet ship** a ship carrying passengers and freight on fixed dates (p. 307)

**Palestine Liberation Organization** (PLO) a terrorist Arab group waging guerrilla war against Israel in an effort to create in its place a homeland for Palestinians (p. 752)

**Panama Canal** a waterway built in 1914 across the isthmus that connects North and South America (p. 566)

**panic** a sudden fear of financial loss among investors (p. 299)

**Panic of 1837** a period of bank closings and rising unemployment caused by state banks printing more currency than they could back with specie (p. 299)

**parity** a level of farm prices maintained through government support, giving farmers the same purchasing power as other consumers (p. 646)

**Parliament** the law-making body of England (p. 63)

**patent** a government license guaranteeing an inventor the sole right to make, use, and sell his or her invention for a certain length of time (p. 328)

**Patriots** the colonists who engaged in activities designed to further the cause of resistance to British policies in America (p. 148)

**patronage** the granting of political jobs and favors (p. 534)

**Peace Corps** a government organization, established by President John F. Kennedy in 1961, in which American volunteers work with people in developing countries (p. 716)

**Pearl Harbor** a Hawaiian seaport, the site of a surprise Japanese attack on the American fleet on December 7, 1941, leading the United States to enter World War II (p. 670)

**Pendleton Act** a law passed in 1883 providing for open examinations for public-service jobs (p. 534)

**peninsula** a finger of land nearly surrounded by water (p. 40)

*peninsulares* (pənĭn′sōō·lär′āz) members of the most privileged social class in Spanish America, Spaniards born in Spain (p. 50)

**perjury** lying under oath (p. 702)

**persecute** to mistreat (p. 75)

**Peru** a part of Spain's empire in the 1500's, including all Spanish claims in South America except Venezuela (p. 49)

**petition** a written request for a right (p. 157)

**Petition of Right** a document of 1628 stating that English citizens could not be taxed without the consent of Parliament (p. 120)

**Pilgrims** the group of English Separatists who founded Plymouth in 1620 (p. 79)

**Pinckney's Treaty** an agreement with Spain, signed in 1795, that allowed Americans to travel on the Mississippi River and to store goods in New Orleans (p. 251)

*Pinta* the ship accompanying the *Santa María* and the *Niña* on Columbus's voyage to America (p. 21)

**pioneers** the early settlers of a frontier region (p. 89)

**piracy** an act of robbery at sea (p. 56)

**plantation** a large estate or farm on which crops were raised, often by slaves in the South (p. 102)

**planter** a plantation owner (p. 102)

**platform** a formal statement of a group's beliefs and intentions (p. 404)

**plaza** a public square (p. 54)

---

ă pat  ā pay  â care  ä father  ĕ pet  ē be  ĭ pit  ī pie  î fierce  ŏ pot  ō go  ô paw, for  oi oil
ōō book  ōō boot  ou out  ŭ cut  û fur  th thin  *th* the  hw which  zh vision  ə ago, item, pencil, atom

*Plessy* v. *Ferguson* a Supreme Court decision of 1896 ruling that segregation was legal, leading to "separate-but-equal" laws in the South (p. 536)

**plunder** to rob of goods (p. 56)

**Plymouth** the settlement of Pilgrims in Massachusetts, founded in 1620 (p. 80)

**political machine** a group of people, often corrupt, organized to achieve and keep power in a government (p. 532)

**political party** a group organized to promote specific goals and candidates for office (p. 248)

**poll tax** a fee paid by a person in order to vote (p. 536)

**Pontiac's War** an unsuccessful attempt by several Native American tribes to stop British colonists from settling west of the Allegheny Mountains (p. 139)

**Pony Express** a fast mail service from Missouri to California involving relays of horse riders, lasting from 1860 to 1861 (p. 386)

**popular sovereignty** the principle that the voters who lived in a territory should decide for themselves whether to permit slavery (p. 396)

**Populists** the People's party, founded in the 1890's to promote the needs of ordinary people (p. 517)

**poverty level** a line of income below which one cannot maintain a decent standard of living (p. 758)

**prairie schooner** a large covered wagon (p. 371)

**precedent** a previous decision that becomes a rule to be followed in similar cases (p. 252)

**prehistory** the time before events were recorded in writing (p. 4)

**President** the head of the executive branch of the United States government (p. 199)

**presidio** a fort protecting Spanish claims in the Southwest (p. 43)

**prime minister** a head of a government, often serving as the leader of the parliament (p. 114)

**privateer** a privately-owned ship authorized by the government during wartime to attack and capture enemy ships (p. 170)

**proclamation** an official public announcement (p. 140)

**Proclamation of Rebellion** a statement by George III in 1775 declaring the American colonies to be in open revolt (p. 159)

**Proclamation of 1763** an act by King George III of Britain forbidding settlement west of the Allegheny Mountains and maintaining government control over trade with the Indians (p. 140)

**profit** all money made in a business exchange after expenses are paid (p. 17)

**Progressive Movement** a movement, beginning around 1900, aimed at reforming political, economic, and social problems in America (p. 573)

**prohibition** a law forbidding the manufacture and sale of alcohol (p. 577)

**propaganda** the spreading of ideas that can influence a point of view (p. 595)

**proprietary colonies** the colonies whose governors were chosen by the proprietors and approved by the Crown (p. 122)

**proprietor** a noble granted a charter to use personal funds to start a colony (p. 63)

**prospector** one who explores an area for mineral deposits such as gold (p. 382)

**Protestants** the members of Christian churches founded as a result of the mid-1500's protest against Catholic teachings (p. 58)

**public lands** the land owned by the national government (p. 461)

**Public Works Administration** (PWA) a New Deal agency established to aid the construction industry and provide jobs (p. 646)

**pueblo (pwĕb'lō)** an adobe village, several stories high and with hundreds of rooms, used by certain Native American tribes of the Southwest (p. 6)

**Puritans** the group that tried to simplify the worship services of the Church of England in the 1600's (p. 74)

# Q

**Quaker** a member of the religious group that settled Pennsylvania and was opposed to war, ministers, and elaborate church ceremonies (p. 85)

**quarter** to furnish with food and housing (p. 148)

**quota** the maximum number of persons that may be admitted, as to a country (p. 620)

# R

**radical** one who favors extreme changes (p. 439)

**Radical Republicans** the opponents of Andrew Johnson's Reconstruction plan who advocated harsher action against the South and greater rights for blacks (p. 439)

**rancho** a cattle ranch (p. 53)

**ratify** to approve officially (p. 189)

**rationing** making goods available in fixed, limited amounts during a period of scarcity (p. 672)

**raw materials** natural resources used to make goods (p. 54)

**Reaganomics** the nickname given to Ronald Reagan's economic program (p. 748)

**recall** a procedure by which a public official can be removed from office by direct popular vote (p. 576)

**recession** a temporary decline in economic activity (p. 652)

**Reconstruction** a period of recovery and rebuilding from the end of the Civil War until 1877 (p. 438)

**Reconstruction Finance Corporation** (RFC) a government loan company set up in 1932 to provide funds to banks and businesses in an effort to recover from the Depression (p. 635)

**Red Scare** the fear and distrust of communism in the United States following World War I (p. 619)

**referendum** the submission of legislation to direct popular vote (p. 576)

**refine** to purify (p. 492)

**reform** to improve (p. 84)

**refuge** a safe place (p. 83)

**rehabilitation** a return to useful life through education or therapy (p. 359)

**reimburse** to repay (p. 289)

**Renaissance** (rĕn′ĭ·säns′) the period from A.D. 1400 to 1600, when Europeans' interest in art, literature, and science was revived (p. 14)

**reparation** a payment by a defeated nation as compensation for damages during a war (p. 606)

**repeal** to officially withdraw a law (p. 143)

**representative** a person selected to speak for others in matters of government (p. 79)

**representative government** a system where those who make laws are chosen by the people (p. 79)

**republic** a nation in which supreme power rests with the people (p. 237)

**Republican party** a political party opposed to slavery, formed in 1854 by northern Whigs, antislavery Democrats, and Free-Soilers (p. 397)

**reservation** a tract of land set aside by the government for Native Americans (p. 468)

**resolution** a formal statement or decision to be voted on by delegates (p. 160)

**revenue** the income of a government (p. 140)

**revival** a reawakening of religious faith (p. 349)

**Revolutionary War** a conflict, lasting from 1775 to 1781, in which the Patriots defeated the British and won independence for the United States (p. 149)

**Roanoke Island** (rō′ə·nōk) the first English settlement in North America, which was established in 1585 and later vanished (p. 60)

**Roman Catholic Church** the Christian religious body headed by the Pope in Rome (p. 13)

**Roosevelt Corollary** a policy of President Theodore Roosevelt declaring the right of the United States to intervene militarily in Latin American affairs (p. 567)

**Rough Riders** an American army unit, led by Theodore Roosevelt, that aided in the capture of San Juan Hill during the Spanish-American War (p. 557)

**royal colonies** the colonies whose governors were appointed by the Crown (p. 122)

**rugged individualism** the doctrine that success comes with self-reliance (p. 634)

**run** a banking term for too many withdrawals in too short a period of time (p. 632)

**Rural Electrification Administration** (REA) a New Deal agency responsible for bringing electricity to rural areas (p. 648)

# S

**safari** a hunting expedition in Africa (p. 584)

**St. Lawrence River** a Canadian river, discovered by Jacques Cartier in 1535 (p. 32)

**Salem Witchcraft Trials** the cases in which several people were hanged as witches from 1691 to 1692 in Salem, Massachusetts (p. 100)

**salutary neglect** a British policy of the 1700's allowing the colonies to develop their own economies with little interference (p. 129)

**San Salvador** a Bahama island, the traditional site of Columbus's first landing in America (p. 21)

**Santa Fe Trail** an overland route between Missouri and New Mexico in the 1800's (p. 377)

**Santa María** the ship on which Columbus sailed on his voyage to America (p. 21)

**satellite** a nation that is politically dominated by another (p. 692)

**scalawags** the name given to white southerners who supported Reconstruction (p. 446)

**sea dogs** the English sea captains who plundered Spanish ships in the 1500's (p. 57)

**secede** to formally withdraw from membership (p. 293)

**Second Continental Congress** the delegates who became the governing body of the colonies during the Revolutionary War (p. 157)

---

ă pat　ā **pay**　â care　ä father　ĕ pet　ē be　ĭ pit　ī pie　î fierce　ŏ pot　ō go　ô paw, for　oi oil
ōō book　ōō boot　ou out　ŭ cut　û fur　th thin　*th* the　hw which　zh vision　ə ago, item, pencil, atom

GLOSSARY

**Second New Deal** President Franklin Roosevelt's proposals of 1935-1936 that called for even greater economic reforms than were offered in the original New Deal (p. 648)

**secret ballot** a vote that is cast privately (p. 518)

**sectionalism** the practice of giving loyalty to local interests over those of the country (p. 286)

**Securities and Exchange Commission** (SEC) a government agency set up to regulate stock exchanges (p. 646)

**sedition** any words or actions that stir rebellion against the authority of the government (p. 254)

**segregation** the policy and practice of the social separation of races (p. 450)

**Selective Service Act** a law of 1917 requiring men between certain ages to register for the draft (p. 599)

**self-determination** the right of a people to decide how they will be governed (p. 605)

**self-reliance** a confidence in one's own abilities (p. 93)

**self-sufficient** able to provide all the goods that are needed without help from others (p. 104)

**semiarid** having light annual rainfall (p. 463)

**Senate** the upper house of Congress, with each state having equal representation (p. 199)

**Seneca Falls Declaration** a plan of action adopted at the 1848 women's rights convention in New York (p. 356)

**separation of powers** the division of government responsibilities into the legislative, executive, and judicial branches (p. 238)

**Separatists** the group that broke away from the Church of England during the 1600's (p. 74)

**serf** a peasant laborer who was born on the manor and was not free to leave (p. 13)

**settlement house** a center providing such services as education, housing, and food in a poor area (p. 532)

**Seventeenth Amendment** a change in the Constitution providing for the direct election of senators by popular vote (p. 576)

**sharecropper** a tenant farmer who pays rent to the landowner with a share of the crops raised (p. 450)

**shares of stock** the units of ownership of a company (p. 63)

**sheaves** a collection of bundled grain stalks (p. 505)

**Sherman Antitrust Act** a law of 1890 making it illegal for big business to form monopolies and trusts (p. 500)

**sit-down strike** a work stoppage in which workers take over a plant, refusing to work or to leave (p. 654)

**Sixteenth Amendment** a change in the Constitution allowing the income tax (p. 584)

**smuggling** to bring in or out illegally (p. 130)

**social class** a group holding a particular position in society (p. 14)

**Social Security Act** a federal law passed in 1935 that established a government pension system for older citizens (p. 649)

**Sons of Liberty** a group of men organized in 1765 to protect British colonists' rights (p. 143)

**Southeast Asia Treaty Organization** (SEATO) an organization formed in 1954 by the United States and its allies to contain communism in Southeast Asia (p. 698)

**sovereign** self-governing (p. 396)

**Spanish-American War** a war in 1898 in which the United States defeated Spain and demanded that Spain grant Cuba its independence and turn over the Philippines, Guam, and Puerto Rico to the United States (p. 555)

**speakeasy** a place that sold alcohol illegally during Prohibition (p. 621)

**special interest** a group that pressures government officials to favor or oppose certain issues (p. 582)

**specie** (spē'shē) coined money (p. 163)

**speculator** a person who takes a business risk in hopes of greatly profiting (p. 243)

**sphere of influence** an area in which a foreign power has exclusive rights to trade and invest (p. 560)

***Spirit of St. Louis*** the airplane that Charles Lindbergh flew nonstop across the Atlantic Ocean in 1927 (p. 630)

**spiritual** a religious folk song of black American origin (p. 335)

**spoils system** the practice of giving government jobs to political supporters (p. 292)

**sponsor** one who supports and helps pay for a project (p. 21)

**stagflation** inflation combined with stagnant business activity and unemployment (p. 743)

**stalemate** a deadlock (p. 697)

**Stamp Act** a British law of 1765 placing a tax on various colonial materials and requiring that these materials bear a stamp showing that the tax was paid (p. 141)

**Stamp Act Congress** a group of delegates from nine colonies who formally protested the Stamp Act in 1765 (p. 143)

**standardized parts** any parts that are identical and interchangeable so that goods can be easily assembled or repaired (p. 310)

**states' rights** the idea that the powers of states should be extended and the powers of the federal government should be limited (p. 293)

**GLOSSARY**

**steerage** the lowest deck aboard a ship, usually the cheapest class of travel (p. 526)

**stockade** a barrier, often a high fence, used for protection (p. 112)

**stockbroker** an agent who buys and sells stocks for others (p. 631)

**strait** a narrow passage of water (p. 30)

**Strategic Arms Limitation Talks** (SALT) periodic meetings since 1969 between Soviet and American leaders to try to reach agreement on how best to limit the use of missiles (p. 734)

**strategy** a plan of action (p. 414)

**strike** a work stoppage by employees, usually for higher pay or better working conditions (p. 495)

**strike-breaking** any action designed to make a workers' strike ineffective (p. 574)

**suburb** a residential area on the outskirts of a city (p. 626)

**suffrage** the right to vote (p. 357)

**Sugar Act** a British law of 1764 establishing a revenue-producing tax on sugar, coffee, indigo, and molasses (p. 141)

**summit** a meeting between heads of state (p. 751)

**Sunbelt** the south and southwestern regions of the United States (p. 760)

**supply and demand** a rule of economics stating that when demand is great for scarce goods, prices are high, but when the supply becomes greater, prices go down (p. 510)

**Supreme Court** the highest federal court in the United States (p. 238)

**surplus** the amount in excess of what is needed (p. 97)

**survey** to measure for the purpose of setting boundaries (p. 193)

**synthetics** materials made by humans (p. 627)

# T

**Taft-Hartley Act** legislation passed after World War II that weakened unions (p. 700)

**tariff** a tax on imports (p. 245)

**Tea Act** a law of 1773 allowing the British East India Company to ship tea directly from Asia to America (p. 145)

**Teapot Dome Affair** a scandal during Warren Harding's presidency that involved kickbacks to Secretary of the Interior Albert Fall by private oil companies (p. 624)

**technology** the means of putting scientific knowledge to practical use (p. 37)

**temperance** moderation, as with the use of alcohol (p. 358)

**tenant farmer** a person who works the land owned by another and pays rent in cash or crops (p. 102)

**tenement** a run-down apartment building, usually in a city (p. 494)

**Tennessee Valley Authority** (TVA) a New Deal agency designed to develop the economy of the Tennessee River valley (p. 646)

**Tenure of Office Act** a law passed in 1867 stating that the President could not remove Cabinet members without the Senate's approval (p. 444)

**tepee** a cone-shaped tent of skins or bark, used by some Native American groups (p. 7)

**terra incognita** a Latin phrase meaning "unknown land" (p. 23)

**terrorism** the use of terror or violence to achieve an end (p. 752)

**Tet Offensive** a series of strong attacks by the Vietcong on South Vietnam in 1968 (p. 729)

**textile** a woven fabric (p. 309)

**Third World** the developing countries of Africa, Asia, and Latin America (p. 755)

**Thirteenth Amendment** a change in the Constitution outlawing slavery (p. 439)

**Three-Fifths Compromise** an agreement between southern and northern states in 1787, stating that five slaves would count as three persons for purposes of representation (p. 199)

**thresher** a farm machine that separates grain from husks (p. 506)

**Tidewater** a flat, southern coastal plain whose rivers are affected by far-reaching ocean tides (p. 102)

**toll** a tax collected on turnpikes to help pay building and repair costs (p. 316)

**Tonkin Gulf Resolution** a bill passed in 1964 by Congress giving the President broad powers to respond to enemy attack, thus authorizing the expansion of American involvement in the Vietnam War (p. 727)

**Tories** a name for the Loyalists (p. 158)

**totalitarian** designating a form of government in which a single authority controls a nation and its people (p. 664)

**town meeting** a form of local government in which people speak for themselves instead of electing representatives (p. 123)

| ă pat | ā **pay** | â care | ä father | ĕ pet | ē be | ĭ pit | ī pie | î fierce | ŏ pot | ō go | ô paw, for | oi oil |
|---|---|---|---|---|---|---|---|---|---|---|---|---|
| ōō book | ōō boot | ou out | ŭ cut | û fur | th thin | *th* the | hw which | zh vision | ə ago, item, pencil, atom | | | |

**GLOSSARY**

**Townshend Acts** the laws of 1767 that extended Britain's economic and legal control over the colonies (p. 144)

**trade deficit** the imbalance that occurs when a country imports more than it exports (p. 742)

**trade union** a labor union consisting of skilled workers in a single craft (p. 497)

**Trail of Tears** the harsh westward journey of Cherokee Indians from Georgia, forced to leave their homelands in 1838 (p. 297)

**transcontinental** spanning the continent (p. 464)

**Treasury Department** the executive office responsible for raising money and handling government finances (p. 242)

**treaty** a formal written agreement (p. 27)

**Treaty of Ghent** the agreement of 1814 that ended the War of 1812 (p. 274)

**Treaty of Guadalupe Hidalgo** (gwŏd′l·o͞op′ hĭ·dăl′gō) an agreement of 1848 in which Mexico accepted the Rio Grande as its border and ceded much of its land to the United States, ending the Mexican War (p. 378)

**Treaty of Paris of 1763** an agreement in which Britain gained control of all French territory east of the Mississippi River except New Orleans, ending the French and Indian War (p. 115)

**Treaty of Paris of 1783** an agreement recognizing the United States as an independent nation and granting the new nation territory from Canada to Florida and from the Atlantic Ocean to the Mississippi River (p. 174)

**Treaty of Tordesillas** (tôr·dä·sē′·yəs) an agreement between Spain and Portugal in 1494, shifting the Line of Demarcation slightly west (p. 27)

**Treaty of Versailles** an agreement of 1919, rejected by the United States, establishing terms for peace between the Allied Powers and the Central Powers at the end of World War I (p. 606)

**triangular trade** a three-way pattern of colonial trade, as with the trade of rum, slaves, and molasses between Boston, the west coast of Africa, and the West Indies (p. 127)

**Triple Alliance** a pact between Germany, Austria-Hungary, and Italy before World War I (p. 594)

**Triple Entente** (ŏn·tŏnt′) a pact of union between France, Russia, and Great Britain before World War I (p. 594)

**Truman Doctrine** a principle brought forth in 1947 that free people being attacked would be supported by the United States (p. 692)

**trust** a group that, by controlling large shares of stock in one industry, works to create a monopoly (p. 499)

**turnpike** a road that travelers must pay to use (p. 316)

**Tweed Ring** a corrupt New York City political machine of the 1860's (p. 533)

**Twentieth Amendment** a change in the Constitution that shortened the lame-duck period between a President's election and inauguration (p. 644)

**Twenty-fifth Amendment** a change in the Constitution that explains and clarifies the office of Vice President (p. 724)

**Twenty-first Amendment** a change in the Constitution that repealed Prohibition (p. 644)

**Twenty-fourth Amendment** a change in the Constitution that ended poll taxes (p. 719)

**Twenty-second Amendment** a change in the Constitution limiting the President to two terms in office (p. 680)

**Twenty-sixth Amendment** a change in the Constitution that set the voting age at 18 (p. 735)

**Twenty-third Amendment** a change in the Constitution that allows the citizens of the District of Columbia to vote (p. 719)

**tyranny** a cruel or unjust use of power (p. 239)

# U

**unanimous** being in complete agreement (p. 197)

**unconstitutional** contrary to the Constitution (p. 239)

**Underground Railroad** a secret network of people who helped runaway slaves escape, often to Canada (p. 352)

**unicameral** having one legislative house (p. 189)

**union dues** a labor union's membership fees (p. 312)

**United Nations** (UN) a world organization formed in 1945 to help maintain peace (p. 691)

# V

**V-E Day** May 8, 1945, the day of Allied victory in Europe during World War II (p. 678)

**veto** an action of the President to prevent a bill from becoming law by exercising authority over the legislative body (p. 239)

**Vice President** the second in command of the executive branch of the United States government (p. 200)

**viceroy** (vīs′roi′) a governor in the Spanish empire, ruling as the representative of the monarch (p. 50)

**Vietcong** Communist fighters in South Vietnam (p. 717)

**Vietminh** Vietnamese Communists (p. 698)

**GLOSSARY**

**Vietnam War** an undeclared war from the 1950's to 1973 in which the United States and other nations tried to prevent a Communist take-over of South Vietnam (p. 718)

**vigilante** (vĭj′ə·lăn′tē) a volunteer citizen who, without legal authority, works to capture and punish lawbreakers (p. 383)

**Vikings** the Scandinavian seafaring adventurers who were the first Europeans to visit North America (p. 12)

**Vinland** the part of northeastern North America visited and named by the Vikings in A.D. 1000 (p. 12)

**Virginia Plan** a proposal for a federal government, offered at the Constitutional Convention, calling for a legislature of two houses, an executive branch, and a judiciary branch (p. 198)

**Volstead Act** a law passed in 1919 giving the government power to enforce Prohibition (p. 621)

**Volunteers in Service to America** (VISTA) a government organization in which volunteers aid poor Americans (p. 722)

**Voting Rights Act of 1965** an act that outlawed literacy tests as voting requirements (p. 724)

# W

**Wagner Act** a federal law passed in 1935 that guaranteed workers the right to join unions and bargain collectively (p. 651)

**Wall Street** the street in New York City where stocks are bought and sold (p. 632)

**ward** a political district in a city (p. 533)

**War Department** the executive office in charge of military matters (p. 242)

**War of 1812** a three-year conflict started because of British interference with American ships (p. 271)

**War Powers Act** a law passed in 1973 that requires a President to have approval from Congress before sending troops into combat for more than 60 days (p. 732)

**Warsaw Pact** an organization of eight Communist countries who agree to come to each other's defense (p. 694)

**Watergate scandal** the illegal activities and abuses of office, some by high-ranking government officials, that led to the resignation of Richard Nixon from the presidency in 1974 (p. 735)

**welfare state** a nation where the government takes responsibility for the well-being of its citizens (p. 657)

**Western Front** a line of trenches 400 miles across France and Belgium during World War I (p. 594)

**Whiskey Rebellion** an unsuccessful attempt by farmers to avoid paying the whiskey tax in 1794 (p. 246)

**Wilderness Road** a trail through the Cumberland Mountains and along the Kentucky River (p. 263)

**Wilmot Proviso** (prə·vī′zō) a resolution, defeated in Congress many times in the mid-1800's, proposing that slavery be banned in any territory won from Mexico (p. 392)

**Woman's Christian Temperance Union** (WCTU) a women's organization of the 1800's opposed to alcohol (p. 537)

**work relief** providing people with work projects in return for aid under the New Deal (p. 646)

**Works Progress Administration** (WPA) a New Deal agency that provided work-relief projects (p. 648)

**World War I** a conflict, lasting from 1914 to 1918, in which the Allied Powers defeated the Central Powers (p. 594)

**World War II** a conflict, lasting from 1939 to 1945, in which the Allies defeated the Axis Powers (p. 667)

**writ of assistance** a general search warrant allowing British officers to search any building in the colonies for smuggled goods (p. 144)

**writ of mandamus** (măn·dā′məs) a legal paper ordering a government worker to carry out a duty (p. 262)

# X Y Z

**XYZ Affair** an attempt by the French in 1798 to bribe American diplomats trying to negotiate a treaty for neutrality (p. 253)

**yellow journalism** a type of reporting, often inaccurate, that creates a sensation (p. 555)

**Yom Kippur War** a battle started on the Jewish holiday of Yom Kippur in 1973, in which Egypt and Syria attacked Israel, who counterattacked a few days later (p.733)

**Zimmermann telegram** a message, intercepted by British agents in 1917, encouraging an alliance between Germany and Mexico against the United States (p. 597)

---

ă pat　ā pay　â care　ä father　ĕ pet　ē be　ĭ pit　ī pie　î fierce　ŏ pot　ō go　ô paw, for　oi oil
o͝o book　o͞o boot　ou out　ŭ cut　û fur　th thin　th the　hw which　zh vision　ə ago, item, pencil, atom

The purpose of the index is to help you locate quickly information on any topic in this book. The index includes references not only to the text but to maps, pictures, charts, and graphs as well. A page number with *m* before it, such as *m*143, refers to a map. Page numbers with *p*, *c*, and *g* refer to pictures, charts, and graphs. Page numbers with H, such as H9, refer to the Handbook of Basic Review.

# A

**AAA.** *See* Agricultural Adjustment Administration.
**abolitionists,** 340, 350–354, 395–396, 401
**acid rain,** 760, *p*760
**Act of Toleration,** 83
**Adams, Abigail,** 147, *p*166, 244, 254
**Adams, Henry,** 316
**Adams, John,** 147, 160, *p*161, 173, 242, 249; construction of the White House, 244; forms Federalist party, 248; as Federalist candidate, 252; XYZ affair, 252–253; Convention of 1800, 254; portrait, *p*254; Supreme Court appointments, 262
**Adams, John Quincy,** portrait, *p*291; election of 1824, 292
**Adams, Samuel,** 143, 144, 148, 151
**Adams-Onís Treaty,** 289
**Addams, Jane,** 532, 533, *p*533, 537, 573, 607
**advertising,** 489, 627
**affirmative action,** 725
**Afghanistan,** 746, *m*753
**AFL.** *See* American Federation of Labor.
**Africa,** *m*H9, 18, 75, 350, 743, 755; slave trade from, 19, 75–76, *p*76; triangular trade routes, *m*129; immigration from, 620
**African Baptist Church,** 335
**Agnew, Spiro,** 731, 735–736
**Agricultural Adjustment Administration (AAA),** 646, *c*651
**Agricultural Marketing Act,** 634
**agriculture,** 451; Indian, 4–10; in Spanish colonies, 51; in New England Colonies, 97–98; in Southern Colonies, 103–105; in Middle Colonies, 107; sectionalism and, 285–286. *See also* farming; *particular farm products.*
**Aguinaldo, Emilio,** 558
**Aiken, George,** 339

**Air Force, U.S.,** 671, 672
**aircraft,** in World War I, *p*600, 603; Lindbergh's flight, 630; in World War II, 668, 670–672, 676; in Vietnam War, *p*727
**Alabama,** 8, 42, 288; gains statehood, 287; cotton in, 328–330; slavery in, *m*339; secedes from the Union, 405; in Civil War, 420, *m*426; in Reconstruction, 452; civil rights movement in, 706–707, 720
**Alamo,** Battle of the, 375–376, *p*376, *m*379
**Alaska,** 4; Russian claim to, 290; U.S. purchases, 552–553, *p*552; parks, *m*581; gains statehood, 704; pipeline, 733
**Albany, New York,** 168, *m*171, 188
**Albany Plan of Union,** 188
**Alcott, Louisa May,** 540
**Alger, Horatio,** 540
**Algeria,** 261, *m*768
**Algonquins,** *m*5, 7, *p*8, 90, 113
**Alien and Sedition Acts,** 254–255
**Allegheny Mountains,** 139, 140
**Allen, Ethan,** 158, *m*159, 165
**Alliance for Progress,** 716
**Allied Powers (Allies),** in World War I, 594–598, 600–603, *m*602, 605–606, *m*606; in World War II, 667–670, *m*668, 675–681, *m*676, *p*677, *m*679
**amendments,** 239–241. *See also* Bill of Rights; *individual amendments by number.*
**American Anti-Slavery Society,** 351, 352, 353–354
**American Colonization Society,** 350–351
**American Federation of Labor (AFL),** 496–498, 527–528, 654
**American Indian Movement (AIM),** 734
**American Independence party,** *m*730
**American Red Cross,** 537
**American System** (economics), 286
**American Temperance Union,** 358
**"American's Creed,"** 598
**Amherst College,** 348
**Amnesty Act,** 449
**Amundsen, Roald,** 31
**anaconda plan,** 415
**anarchists,** 620
**Anasazi Indians,** 6
**Anderson, Robert,** 407
**André, John,** 170
**Anglican Church.** *See* Church of England.
**Annapolis, Maryland,** 195
**Anthony, Susan B.,** 358, 538
**Antietam, Battle of,** 421, *m*421

**antiexpansionists,** 557
**Antifederalists,** 201, *c*201, 202
**Apaches,** *m*5, 7, 374, 468
**apartheid,** 756
*Apollo 11,* 733
**Appalachian Mountains,** 111, *m*112, 139, 189, 193, 263, 337
**Appomattox, Virginia,** 426, 437
**Aquino, Corazon,** 756
**Arafat, Yasir,** 757
**architecture,** 55, *p*55; 332, *p*333; 476, *p*477
**Argentina,** 40, 751, *m*768
**Argonne Forest,** Battle of the, 603
**Arizona,** 41, 45, 761; missions in, 52, 55; gold in, 471; gains statehood, 478; farming in, *m*463, 508–509; parks, *m*581
**Arkansas,** 42; gains statehood, *m*268, 269; in Great Depression, 643; civil rights movement in, 705–706
**Arkwright, Richard,** 308–309
**Armenian immigrants,** 525
**arms race,** 707–708, 745
**Armstrong, Neil,** 733
**Army, U.S.,** 237; in World War I, 599; in World War II, 671, 672
**Arnold, Benedict,** *m*159, 170
**arts,** development of American style, 348, 474, 541, *p*541; Hudson River school, 348; Western, *p*371, *p*386, *p*467, *p*470, 474, *p*474, 541; Ashcan school, 574, *p*574; Depression Era, *p*635, *p*642, 648, 658, *p*658
**Arthur, Chester A.,** 532, 534; portrait, *p*534
**Articles of Confederation,** 189–191, *c*200; achievements under, 193–195; weaknesses of, 192–193; foreign affairs and, 193, 195
**Ashcan school of art,** 574
**Asia,** *m*H9, 3–4; trade routes to, *m*15, 17–19, *m*18; immigration from, 525, 620, 755, *g*758; American policy in, 557–558, 560–563, 695, 698, 717–718, 727–729, 755; in World War II, 665, 666, 669–670, *m*670, 675; in cold war, 693. *See also particular countries.*
**Asian Americans,** 758. *See also particular countries of origin.*
**assembly line,** 488–489, *p*625, 626
**Astor, John Jacob,** 369
**Atahualpa,** 38
**Atlanta, Georgia,** in Civil War, *m*404, 425, *m*426, 450
**Atlantic and Pacific Tea Company,** 489
**Atlantic Ocean,** *m*H9, 20–23, 630; in World War II, 675

INDEX

# XYZ